1001 SONGS

THE GREAT SONGS OF ALL TIME
and the artists, stories and secrets behind them

Toby Creswell

THUNDER'S
MOUTH
PRESS

This one goes out to
Samantha and Alice

Published in the US in 2006
by Thunder's Mouth Press
An Imprint of Avalon Publishing Group, Inc.
245 West 17th Street, 11th floor
New York, New York 10011

First published in 2005
by Hardie Grant Books
85 High Street
Prahran, Victoria 3181, Australia
www.hardiegrant.com.au

ISBN-10: 1-56025-915-9
ISBN-13: 978-1-56025-915-2

Edited by Martine Lleonart
Cover and text design by
   Gayna Murphy, Greendot Design
Typeset by Pauline Haas, bluerinse setting
Printed and bound in Thailand by Imago Productions

10 9 8 7 6 5 4 3 2 1

Acknowledgements

This book would not have been
possible without Foong Ling Kong who
commissioned it, Julie Pinkham who ran
with it, and mostly Mary Small who has
done a magnificent job of wrestling it into
shape. Martine Lleonart did a robust
copyedit. Gayna Murphy designed with her
usual elegance. Rachel Pitts and Pauline
Haas worked tirelessly to the end. Hardie
Grant is an author's delight.

My appreciation goes to Rose Creswell,
Lesley McFadzean, Jane Cameron and the
staff of Cameron's Management.

I am grateful to Ed Kuepper, Brad
Lonard, Murray Power, Tom Kristensen and
David Messer for their suggestions on
selections.

Chris Moss, Ed St John and Nadya
Balzarolo very kindly sent me albums.

For assistance of all kinds I would like to
thank Martin Fabinyi, Alex Cameron, Jackie
Dennis, Catherine Courtenay, Ross
Brookes, Jolyon Burnett and Anne Briggs,
Bruce Daly, Margaret Merten, Geoffrey
Datson and Annette Hughes, Paul and
Anne Trenoweth, Kate Butchart and Martin
Pedersen.

This would not have been possible
without Tim Singleton and Gwen Creswell.

I also cannot thank John O'Donnell,
John Bush, Tara Anderson and Clinton
Walker enough.

Introduction

'A song is like a dream, and you try and make it come true.'
Bob Dylan, *Chronicles Volume One*

In 1975 I learnt an important lesson about popular music.

For seven hours and twenty-one minutes each day I was a Class One clerk in the Repatriation Department in Sydney. My responsibility was to authorise chiropody for war widows and returned servicemen. In my lunch hour I would sneak off to a record bar called Ripple in the Angel Arcade that sold import LPs. In those days less than half of the releases in the UK or the US were available in Australia. The import stores were like Alladin's caves.

Ripple's chief asset was Jules Normington, the assistant manager. If you can imagine Championship Vinyl, the shop fictionalised in Nick Hornby's *Hi-Fidelity* – but without the sarcasm, irony or one-upmanship – then you have some sense of what Jules was like. Often I'd wander in and he would exclaim, "Listen to this. This is the best record ever made!" It might be Robert Palmer's 'Sneaking Sally Through the Alley' or Rick Danko's first solo album or Lou Reed's 'Coney Island Baby', or later it might be Television's 'Little Johnny Jewel' or Leonard Cohen. At the time I aspired to the great calling vocation of rock criticism and Jules' wayward enthusiasm was heresy. I thought that rock & roll was an art form, and if it was an art form, then it must have a canon as painting and poetry and literature and the cinema did. There must be some hierarchy. If rock & roll is a real art form, then Disco Tex & the Sex-O-Lettes' 'Get Dancing' certainly can't be "the best record ever".

Of course I was wrong. What Jules meant was that right here and right now, Disco Tex was in the pocket. It hit the sweet spot. It made its own kind of logic. It didn't matter whether people would be listening to Disco Tex in thirty years time or not (and they're not).

There is no greatest song of all time. And if there is no greatest song and no canon, then in those three minutes when Disco Tex & the Sex-O-Lettes are taking you higher, 'Get Dancing' might as well be the greatest. This is music – the food of love, not the cure for cancer.

So the lesson I learnt was to evaluate music first with my heart. With that in mind, you find that some songs and some artists come back again and again; they become part of the fabric of your life. For a moment, 'Get Dancing' will be up there, but over time, '(I Can't Get No) Satisfaction' by the Rolling Stones may hit the sweet spot more times than most others. It's true that some records are indeed timeless, but other records are beautiful because they're transient.

The next question is, "does it shake your hips?" and from there we move on to the other issues – is it adventurous, amusing, provocative and lastly, do the lyrics say something interesting?

Popular music has been the guiding influence in my life. It has informed me, stimulated me, led me into the world and told me about myself. It has made me glad to be alive but has also broken my spirit. It's real and true, but ephemeral and capricious and sometimes prone to fantasy.

So, this is a book about 1001 songs. There is no #1. There is no canon. Some of the songs are better than others. Each has its own qualities.

These are 1001 songs that will enrich your life and broaden your palette. Some of these songs are terrible. John Lennon's 'Imagine' is, in my opinion, pretentious and insincere. But I know I'm in a minority there. On the other hand, some songs I believe to be the apotheosis of western art – like, say, Tommy James & the Shondells' 'Hanky Panky', you may think to be rubbish. But beyond opinions, this book will, I hope, provide some background about the tunes and a point of view from which you can hear things differently; perhaps discover gems and re-discover classics.

The choices, of course, reflect my experience. As I was being born in North Sydney, Chuck Berry was on the South Side in Chicago laying down 'Maybelline', and so post-war popular music features heavily. Mostly all of this music derives from the blues and has branched out into many and varied forms from there. There's an obvious bias towards the giants of the rock & roll era.

However, the selection is not entirely subjective. I have tried to give an overview of popular music and a sense of its shape. To that end we have John Cage's piece '4' 33"', commonly known as 'Silence', and then at the other end of the spectrum is the industrial white-noise overload of Lou Reed's 'Metal Machine Music Part 1'. Everything else is light and shade between these two poles.

My editors have made many jokes about there being too many Bob Dylan entries. I thought quite the reverse. Dylan is in a class of his own, far out front of any other figure in 20th-century popular music – not so much as a lyricist but for the courage of his talent and the sheer musicality of his songs, and the way they embody and transform the traditions of pop.

It's true to say that there are probably too many songs by Neil Young and the Velvet Underground in here. And there are definitely artists that I have missed.

These are not all necessarily my favourites. While I do think that each of these songs should be heard at least once, I would rather gnaw my own arm off than listen to Supertramp again. I feel much the same about Pink Floyd and the Soft Machine, yet their influence is as undeniable as it is maligned.

The selection also reflects the fact that it was made in Australia. A similar collection compiled in the US or the UK would not include Dragon or X or Stephen Cummings, but that's an accident of history and geography. I think we've all gone past the cultural cringe.

The first thing I personally pay attention to in a song is the rhythm section – the bass and drums. For me that's the meat of the matter; without it you ain't got a thing. On top of that comes the melody, the lyric and the performance.

Looking back over the songs I've noticed that very large proportions of these tracks were recorded live or almost live. For me, the art of popular music is capturing the moment. It's the serendipity of performance that usually exposes the truth. Popular music is not like poetry or literature where revision and craftsmanship is an essential part of the process. I don't rate artists who spend years perfecting a song; I think that bleeds the life out of it, but having said that, I'll acknowledge that others do.

When we first talked about this book, my publisher Julie Pinkham suggested that there was no need to have an overarching rationale; rather to let the chips fall where they may. So I did. In looking back however, the book feels like a jigsaw. Each selection leads to at least one other selection. Somehow each of these songs is connected to another. It's in part because so many of them came from a common root – the songs sung on plantations in the Mississippi Delta one hundred years ago.

I think a lot about Charley Patton, a man a generation out of slavery, maybe two generations out of Africa, scuffling around Mississippi with a guitar. He was just a guy with a song to sing for a few bucks on a Saturday night, playing in a bar to people whom the world never gave much thought to. Here was a guy who probably never read many books and never met men of wealth and power, but his songs touched on the eternal and the ineffable. They resonated through the whole world.

There is another, more ill-defined connection here. Popular music doesn't have a hierarchy or even the shape of one. If popular music had a third dimension it would look like a Mobius strip. It's a continuum with a twist in it.

The oldest song in this book is 'The St James Infirmary', which dates back to 1790 when it was called 'The Unfortunate Rake'. It has been through a hundred permutations, turned into country and jazz and blues and folk songs. But every time the core of the song remains the same – it's about toting up the ledger before the final reckoning. That process hasn't changed since 1790 and it isn't going to. That's what songs do – they carry the message. Songs have been doing that since David was a boy. Although it was first noted in 1790, I'll bet they were singing it a thousand years before.

Songs have been with us always. We all sing them to each other and ourselves. They recognise no boundaries. Songs have no empirical effect on us, but neither you nor I have gone a day without singing at least in our heads a song or two.

NOTE: These songs have many and varied provenances. The year generally refers to the first recording or publishing of the song. The album cited is the preferred album on which the track can be found.

Remember that up until about 1966 albums were often cobbled together from singles and other tracks. Many of the selections even pre-date the long-playing record. Also, record companies change over time and according to the country, so the record company listed is mostly there as a guide.

The main research source for *1001 Songs* was the All Music Guide (www.allmusic.com). When in doubt, this has been consulted for release dates, songwriting credits and album listings.

The other invaluable resource was the website Rock's Backpages (www.rocksbackpages.com), a repository for some of the world's best writing on popular music.

Bird on a Wire Leonard Cohen

(Leonard Cohen) ❄ Columbia ❄ 1969 ❄ Appears on: *Songs from a Room*

"I remember sitting beside a window in my house in Greece years ago and I think they just put up the telephone wires," Cohen recalled. "There hadn't been any telephone wires or electric wires and no electricity, and I just noticed the bird on the wire there.

"And the next image comes from there – from that little village where I used to live. Other late night drinkers would come home maybe two three in the morning, and they'd stumble through the streets with their arms around each other's shoulders singing these just perfect three-part harmonies. And nobody ever minded because even if you woke up to those strains you didn't mind."

In 1960, Cohen bought a small house on the Greek island of Hydra. The cottage had no telephones, electricity or running water but the island offered him the opportunity to write and to mingle in the small expatriate community there (which included Australian writers George Johnston and Charmian Clift). The introduction of the telephone signified the arrival of the 20th century to Hydra, to Cohen's disappointment.

Cohen cut a version with David Crosby producing but the project was scrapped. It was then recorded for Cohen's second album, which was produced in Nashville by Bob Johnson who was also Bob Dylan's producer. This may explain the slight country lilt that the song has and why it has been popular with country stars.

Kris Kristofferson, who oddly recurs in Leonard Cohen stories (see 'Chelsea Hotel #2') said that the first lines of this song would be his epitaph: "Like a bird on a wire/Like a drunk in a midnight choir/I have tried, in my way, to be free".

Johnny Cash did an extraordinary reading of the song in his Rick Rubin period, bringing that ancient voice to the song and giving it a mythic weight.

Joe Cocker recorded the song with an R&B arrangement on *Mad Dogs and Englishmen* and brought out the gospel overtones that are implied in many of Cohen's best songs.

"This is a song that is really good to sing because it has a confession in it. It has a line: Like a baby stillborn/like a beast with his horn/I have torn everyone/who reached out for me," he said in 1968 on the BBC. "But I swear by this song/and by all that I have done wrong/that I will make it all up to thee."

Tales of Brave Ulysses Cream

(Eric Clapton/Martin Sharp) ❋ Polydor ❋ 1967 ❋ Appears on: *Disraeli Gears*

The Speakeasy was the hang-out for the new aristocracy of Swinging London. The tiny club catered for the ultra-hip. It was in the Speakeasy that Australian artist Martin Sharp, then in London working on the controversial *Oz* magazine, was introduced to Eric Clapton. When Sharp was told that Clapton was a musician he offered him a set of lyrics to be put to music. Clapton did not know then that Sharp was the great pop artist of the era. Sharp didn't know that Clapton was the great instrumentalist of the day with the group Cream. The two became friends and later flatmates. Cream became the biggest thing in the world and Sharp designed their best LP sleeves.

The first Cream album was mostly obscure old blues songs. On the second, *Disraeli Gears*, they were making a statement, and it is an album quite unlike any other. It was a new pop sound and 'Tales of Brave Ulysses' captured some of the whimsy and trippiness of the time.

The song is a psychedelic masterpiece. Clapton made extensive use of his new wah-wah pedal – one of its first appearances on record. The guitar line Clapton later realised was taken from the Lovin' Spoonful's 'Summer in the City'.

"Ahmet told me he wanted me to record this English group, who were arriving that afternoon, over the next three days because they had to be on a plane at seven o'clock on Sunday evening, which was when their visa would expire," said engineer Tom Dowd. "All of a sudden, these tons of equipment start coming into the studio, and I'm wondering how big this group can possibly be, but it was just Eric, Jack and Ginger. They had just finished a short tour, and it had been decided to record them before they left for the second album, *Disraeli Gears*. We started on the Friday morning and got into their limousine at five o'clock on the Sunday with the album done.

"It was the first contact I had had with a group of that nature," said Dowd. "And I was just absolutely carried away with their musicianship and precision. They were incredible – I never saw anything so powerful in my life, and it was just frightening."

Sharp designed the sleeve of *Disraeli Gears* and it is one of the most iconic covers of the period.

365 is My Number/The Message King Sunny Ade

(King Sunny Ade) ✳ Mango ✳ 1982 ✳ Appears on: *Juju Music*

Juju music sprang up in Nigeria in the '20s and soon spread through West Africa as the main form of pop music. King Sunny Ade, who was related to Nigerian royalty, moved to Lagos and by the '70s was Nigeria's biggest star. In the early '80s he began recording for Mango, an offshoot of Island, and he took juju to the west. It was very much a two-way street. Ade was keen to incorporate western instruments and technology into the juju groove.

"I always wanted to introduce the pedal steel," he said. "Then I introduced the keyboard. My ancestors had already introduced the accordion but the people who played the accordion used to stand still at a microphone. With my kind of music, you have to dance around; you have to jump up. You can't jump up with an accordion on your chest! So I introduced a DX-7 synthesiser to it and, within a DX-7, you can find so many sounds."

His aim, he said, was to "fuse it with western instruments, but play it in an African way."

Juju music evolved from the Nigerian talking drums, so the groove was the fundamental element and in '365 is My Number/The Message', the twenty-piece combo added soul and dub flavours.

"We don't want to go along with any other music in the world. We want to differentiate our own kind of music," said Ade, explaining that his pedal steel player didn't play country music. "He has to play his own kind of solo on a danceable step, according to African music."

Down by the River Neil Young & Crazy Horse

(Neil Young) ✳ Reprise ✳ 1969 ✳ Appears on: *Everybody Knows This is Nowhere*

'Down by the River' is the signature tune for Neil Young and Crazy Horse. The original recording runs to nine minutes – and that was edited down.

Neil Young confessed to *Spin* magazine that he had no idea why the character in this song shot his baby down by the river. It matters little. What does matter is the autistic, spastic groove that Crazy Horse get on this song and the space that allows Neil Young and his black $50 Gibson Les Paul to wrestle with the tune. 'Old Black' is part of Young's legend – it's a guitar whose tendency is to distortion and feedback and Young wrestles the instrument, trying to control its manic spirit.

Crazy Horse is the best worst bar band in the world. Young met them in 1968, and he has worked with them on and off ever since. For that entire time Young has been advised to get rid of the Horse on the grounds that they can't play to a standard to match the singer/songwriter. That's sort of true. Crazy Horse don't play well. Ralph Molina sounds like a one-idea drummer and the others (Frank Sampedro, who replaced Danny Whitten, and Billy Talbot) are much the same. But their limitations make them perfect. They have a particular groove and they can hang in there no matter how crazy anything gets or how long it takes. If Young wants to go on a feedback jag for fifteen minutes, Crazy Horse will be there. They also have solidity. They sound like a concrete pour – unruffled, inexorable, not too much colour and really heavy.

"We got the vibe, but it was just too long and sometimes it fell apart, so we just took the shitty parts out," said Young of this track. "Made some radical cuts in there – I mean you can hear 'em. Danny played so cool on that. He made the whole band sound so good."

Ain't Wastin' Time No More   The Allman Brothers Band

(Gregg Allman) ✳ Capricorn ✳ 1972 ✳ Appears on: *Eat a Peach*

In October 1971 the Allman Brothers' double live album *At Fillmore East* was in the Top 10 in the charts. Duane Allman, then regarded as the hottest guitarist in the US, had taken a well-deserved rest to detox from heroin – a habit he picked up when adding the immortal riff to Eric Clapton's 'Layla'. One autumn day he told his roadies and friend Red Dog, "We got it made now. We're on our way. Ain't gonna be no more beans for breakfast." Before the month was out, Allman would die in a motorcycle accident at the age of 24.

When Duane Allman came off his bike, the Allman Brothers Band went into shock. In early 1972 they began to pick up the pieces of the album that Allman had already titled *Eat a Peach*. There's some suggestion that the title refers to the Allmans' response to the Vietnam War; however, it's more likely that the Georgia-based group is referring to young women who were affectionately known as Georgia peaches.

Two sides of the LP were taken with a half-hour-plus version of Donovan's 'There is a Mountain' and sundry other live cuts plus a few studio tracks that had been worked on for the project.

'Ain't Wastin' Time No More' is one of Gregg Allman's best blues. Guitarist Dickey Betts plays molten blues lines in tribute to his dead friend and Allman sings the hell out of the lyric.

"Playing the blues is an outlet for the real blues itself," said Gregg. "Playing in general is an outlet, an escape, to vent your problems. It's a shame everyone doesn't have an art form or something you can turn to when all else fails."

Karma Chameleon   Culture Club

(Mikey Craig/Roy Hay/Jon Moss/George O'Dowd/Phil Pickett) ❋ Virgin ❋ 1982 ❋

Appears on: *Colour by Numbers*

Boy George was more than just a singer. In fact, he wasn't much of a singer. He wasn't good-looking in the usual way and he was on the verge of coming out. All of these factors made Boy George one of the most interesting pop phenomena of the century. The fact that he made killer soul/pop records helped.

"Today, people forget that it isn't just music and it isn't just 'being weird'. You have to find a correct balance," George told *Creem* in 1985. "And also (more seriously) you have to have a good explanation. If you intend to confront the world with your extravagances, you have to have a good reason; it's OK to be a clown in the circus but not in the supermarket. And – there are certain serious implications with doing certain things. Like you don't call yourself Scarlett O'Hara if you want to be a serious musician.

"I just hate those compliments you get like 'Oh, he's a freak but I love the music'. I mean, have you heard about that guy in Detroit who's started a fan club for people

who can't stand to look at me? That's . . . it's sad in a way. Because that sort of thinking just misses the point of Culture Club. We really are trying to educate people towards some sort of tolerance on a moral basis. And also in regards to humanity.

"It's obvious that those people don't listen to the lyrics, that they hear no politics inside the music. Which is – very depressing. And dumb. It's as dumb as anyone who can look at me and go 'Oh God, this guy's just an image,' and that's the end of it."

Culture Club grew out of the New Romantic scene in early-'80s London. What distinguished Culture Club from Duran Duran and Spandau Ballet – aside from George, of course – was their embrace of soul and R&B. They sounded less European and more American.

Culture Club were affectionate. They felt in love and there was a sweetness and inclusiveness to their work rather than the ironic distance of much pop of the era.

Producer Stewart Levine gave this second Culture Club album a warmth and a summer feeling. Where the first album, *Kissing to be Clever*, had been full of wistful, angsty ballads, this second record was optimistic and full of romance. The addition of second vocalist Helen Terry pumped up the vocal parts so that the songs had the range demanded of soul music.

In the final analysis, though, it was George and his unique persona that sold the hits: 'Karma Chameleon', 'It's a Miracle', 'Church of the Poison Mind', 'Miss Me Blind'. George couldn't have been more wrong than when he sang on 'Karma Chameleon': "I'm a man who doesn't know/How to sell a contradiction".

E-Bow the Letter R.E.M.

(Michael Stipe/Bill Berry/Mike Mills/Peter Buck) ❊ Warner Bros. ❊ 1998 ❊

Appears on: *New Adventures in Hi-Fi*

"I think it's one of the best things I've ever written," is Michael Stipe's summation of the song. "I feel it plumbs something inside of me that I wish I could ... I wanted this record to have heart. And that song maybe comes as close as anything on the record to being really real."

The E-Bow is an electromagnetic device that, when held over the strings of an electric guitar, creates a sustained note.

"I've had one for a while now and I've used it on a couple of things just as background," said Buck. "It's really nice ... If you're looking for a cello-type sound, you can get a really nice sustain out of it. And it's really nice for background stuff. When I first wrote the thing and we demoed it, I just did that as an overdub. And it was really cool. It was totally chaotic and noisy. And the demo is really pretty amazing. It's totally fucked up and out of time because we'd only really played it once but it sounds really neat. I always kind of thought, well E-Bow, I'll keep using it on that song."

The track for the song had been around for two years and was recorded for the sessions of the *Monster* album but was put on ice. Then Stipe came up with an appropriate lyric.

"Michael basically had a rough draft of a letter," Buck recalled. "It was kind of stream of consciousness communication. Instead of sending the letter, he started singing it to the song and it fit in perfectly. It just had the rhythm. And it was like some words he had and he actually just did them in one pass in sound check one day and it sounded great."

Patti Smith was invited to duet with Stipe on the song. The singer credits Smith's *Horses* as one of the defining moments of his life, "I bought it the day it came out," he said. "I went home and listened to it all night on headphones. I didn't take them off till the morning, when I had to go to school. It was one of the single most cathartic moments of my life. It just felt right. It felt like: this is music, this is what I'm going to do." He laughs. "I was really naïve; I mean, I was fifteen. I was simple-headed, but it was a defining moment for me. Remember the whole punk aesthetic was that anybody could do it. You didn't have to be special or talented. Or beautiful or rich or whatever. I just decided that I knew I'd be a singer. That was that."

Smith had only recently returned to the public eye following the death of her husband Fred Sonic Smith. Her presence on this song is haunting. "You've got this one monochromatic musical element going through the verses and the chorus seemed to be somehow really different in texture," Buck told Michael Goldberg of Addicted to Noise. "We're friends with Patti. He brought it up and we just went, 'Yeah. Let's see if Patti would want to sing it.' I was thrilled with the idea that she would even consider it. She came in and it worked out perfectly. It was moving to see someone whom I've admired for so long come in and sing a song that I wrote."

Stipe's typically allusive lyric is built around the mantra, "aluminium tastes like fear".

"Have you ever really been afraid? You get a taste in your mouth – it tastes like chewing on aluminium foil," said Stipe. "Adrenaline tastes like aluminium, and when you're really afraid, you taste it in your mouth. It's when the creature part of us completely takes over human, rational everything. Your eyes dilate. Your nuts creep up inside you. You start breathing through your mouth. Your mouth tastes like aluminium. That's what fear tastes like."

The image is Stipe at his best – particular detail with a truth that makes an emotional connection unattached to any literal meaning.

"And there was a time in the mid-'80s when I was not in a good head. I was just stretched too tight. I wasn't sure if I wanted to be in a band or anything. And if someone slammed a door or if a car blew a horn, or someone came up behind me and touched me on the shoulder, it would alarm me, and I would taste it. I can kind of taste it now, but it's coffee and bad dental work. It's not fear.

"You get it when you drink mineral water in Mexico. All the *agua mineral* in Mexico tastes like fear. It's because they recycle the bottles and put the caps on."

Beachy Head Throbbing Gristle

(Throbbing Gristle) ✳ Industrial ✳ 1979 ✳ Appears on: *20 Jazz Funk Greats*

The brainchild of Genesis P-Orridge and Cosey Fan Tutti, Throbbing Gristle is better described as performance art than rock music. Their early work was confronting and brutal and mostly existed in the context of the London avant-garde art scene (or as George Harrison once said, "avant-garde a clue"). Combining pornographic images and the Royal Family, as they once did, is a very English art statement – like gratuitous nudity, every aspiring performance artist has to say something shocking about Her Majesty – and an easy way to get notoriety.

When punk arrived in the late '70s, Throbbing Gristle fitted right in with the shock tactics of the time.

Jon Savage, a writer and fan, put it well in his sleeve notes to their *Greatest Hits*, "However, the noise, while important, was ancillary: I see Throbbing Gristle as being very absolute seekers after a particular truth and set of truths. Truths about the limits of human behaviour that we are encouraged to ignore – love, despair, coercion, bestiality, repose, intense sexuality, frustration and incredible violence."

So, by accident and design, Throbbing Gristle found themselves as pioneers in what was known as industrial music – confronting, hard and uncompromising. On the album *20 Jazz Funk Greats* they have moments such as 'Beachy Head' where the insistent, industrial noise of the early sequencer pounds out the blueprint for Nine Inch Nails and Marilyn Manson.

Are You Gonna Go My Way? Lenny Kravitz

(Lenny Kravitz/Craig Ross) ✳ Virgin ✳ 1993 ✳ Appears on: *Are You Gonna Go My Way?*

"The people I gravitate to are the older ones – Jagger and Bowie, whoever," Lenny Kravitz told Mat Snow shortly after the release of *Are You Gonna Go My Way?* "I was raised on good music," he continued, "and I haven't met a lot of musicians from this time period that inspire me. I listen out for good new music, but the recording fucks me off right from the beginning. People accuse me of being Mr Romantic for the old stuff – I'm sorry, but I hear better melodies, better musicianship, better music. Maybe I'm just stuck, but I think the whole thing was better. I'm a snob."

Unashamedly retro in its sound and approach 'Are You Gonna Go My Way?' was a song completely out of time. It had huge drum patterns like souped up soul music and layers of guitars pulsing forward.

Kravitz could get away with it because he exudes pure sex appeal and the song had an immense sense of humour about it. The early '90s were caught up in the style wars – Generation X, grunge and club culture – whereas Kravitz was having none of it. Going his way meant letting the freak flag fly and having a great time. Who can argue with that?

Everybody Wants to Rule the World Tears For Fears

(Chris Hughes/Roland Orzabal/Ian Stanley) ✳ Mercury ✳ 1985 ✳

Appears on: *Songs from the Big Chair*

The English have perfected the irritating anthem that purports to be good for you. They write these saccharine hooks that are so tightly on the money and then they wrap them in layers of serious and sensitive male vocals. The lyric is pretty much fatuous nonsense but the riff is a killer. The companion piece to this track on the album is a football terrace anthem called 'Shout', disguised as a tune about primal scream therapy. 'Rule the World' could be a nice tune with which to advertise chardonnay.

After some success, 'Rule the World' put Tears For Fears over the top and number one on the American charts.

Tears For Fears were like Wham! without the wham part. Roland Orzabal who writes the material for Curt Smith to sing is perpetually whingeing about something. Often the subject of complaint was not readily discernible and perhaps irrelevant – simply a general sense of ill ease. Without wishing to be flippant, it's hard to understand what the problem is in as much as Orzabal is big on platitudes but short on specifics. He grew up on a council estate in Bath, a provincial English city where he was picked on at school and his dad founded the Portsmouth Philosophical Society. From there things were relatively simple – a deal with Mercury based on a demo of two songs – 'Suffer the Children' and 'Pale Shelter'. You could tell right there that they weren't gonna be a lot of fun. Half a decade later and they sold nine million albums. Largely thanks to this single. No wonder then it took three years to feel bad enough to make a follow-up.

My Prerogative Bobby Brown

(Bobby Brown/Gene Griffin/Teddy Riley) ✳ MCA ✳ 1988 ✳ Appears on: *Don't Be Cruel*

Bobby Brown had been a teen star in the group New Edition but he found lasting fame as the voice of New Jack Swing. The style of hip-hop devised by Terry Riley had a huge, syncopated beat that swung the melody widely, anchored by the kick drum. Brown was young, sexy and energetic.

Brown was born 5 February 1969 in Boston. At the age of ten he was singing with friends Michael Bivins and Ricky Bell and they were turned into child stars by svengali producer Maurice Starr as New Edition. A deal with MCA followed. After a few years of teen stardom, Brown was the first to break out into a solo carer. His first album (*King of Stage*, 1987) showed promise but it was producers LA Reid and Babyface who had invented New Jack Swing and found in Brown a perfect vehicle. 'My Prerogative' is perhaps the best example of the partnership. It's boastful and confidant without being confronting. There's some humour over a great R&B joint. The self-assertion of the title could refer to his coming of age in leaving New Edition and could equally be asserting his independent spirit – the downside of that being his decade long battle with drugs and the police.

America Simon & Garfunkel

(Paul Simon) ❋ Columbia ❋ 1968 ❋ Appears on: *Bookends*

This is such a cinematic song – two young lovers riding Greyhound buses looking for the spirit of America. It's a song full of small detail and the big picture ("So we bought a pack of cigarettes and Mrs Wagner pies/And we walked off to look for America"). It's full of romance – the troubled young man watching the moon rise over an open field with his girlfriend asleep, her head on his shoulder. It's sung in a beautiful six/two time, lilting and dancing forward. The Kathy in the song refers to Simon's ex-girlfriend Kathy Chitty. Simon here has distilled much of Kerouac's *On the Road*. But the times were different. Simon's rending of the romance of youth and the hollowness of the American Dream have never been better expressed.

"I don't really know what was in my mind when I wrote this," he said to Q in 1993. "I think it's very 1968, kind of about a generation of kids who have just started to travel the country. But it doesn't much take me back when I listen to it, but then I'm not very nostalgic except for some pockets of arcane rock & roll of the '50s. I'm a much more future-orientated person than I am reflective. I'm not sure I could even tell where the images came from – the riding on the bus. The girl is Kathy, my girlfriend in England. She was the model for the girl, but we never actually took a trip like that. None of those events actually occurred to me in my life. In many ways, this is a song with no physical roots."

Fade into You Mazzy Star

(David Roback/Hope Sandoval) ❊ 4AD ❊ 1993 ❊ Appears on: *So Tonight that I Might See*

It was said of Mazzy Star guitarist/songwriter David Roback that he had three tempos – slow, slower and slowest. His somnolent psychedelic atmospheres were a comfortable environment for the waifish whisperings of singer Hope Sandoval. One writer described their creative relationship as, "She's moody and he's withdrawn". There is something of a narcotic magic to their occasional recordings. They're a little bit country and a little bit Velvet Underground but their songs are enduring in the sense that they are spectral in substance but they haunt the imagination long after the record has finished spinning.

Roback had been around the Los Angeles alternative rock scene since the early '80s. Even then he was playing moody, slow country music. Sandoval had been a fan of his group the Rain Parade and they eventually began an affair – since ended – and a writing partnership. Mazzy Star are steadfast in their introverted dreamscapes, each song being an exquisite small world of gently sliding guitar notes as perfectly expressed on their most well-known song.

"I don't often hear how people interpret our music," said Roback. "But it wouldn't really surprise me if people interpreted it in a very personal way, because I think that that's the way that people react to music. If you took a well-known song and asked ten people to write down what the lyrics are, you'd find surprisingly different interpretations of what the lyrics are because people hear what's in their own imagination."

Let's Get Lost Chet Baker

(Frank Loesser/Jimmy McHugh) ❊ Pacific Jazz ❊ 1955 ❊
Appears on: *The Pacific Jazz Years*

Chet Baker took this nice, witty Loesser and McHugh song and made it his own. Then Bruce Weber in his 1988 documentary melded the two together forever. Baker, a leader of the West Coast cool school in the '50s had a powerful personality as a trumpeter and vocalist. Written for the 1943 film *Youth on Parade*, this is a cute love song with a neat metaphor. Chet Baker's arid vocal tone milks the conceit for all it's worth.

Baker was a hipster – a trumpet playing, acting and singing artist who threw himself completely into the jazz world. Not for him the powerful spiritual and emotional storms of Coltrane or Mingus. Baker was laid-back and emotionally cavalier. Although capable of great elegance and beauty, he was also wayward. He was, for most of his life, addicted to heroin with a side interest in beautiful women. 'Let's Get Lost', then, is a hipsters anthem. Baker sings the lyrics with ambiguity – is it to a woman or to narcotics? Is he after privacy or oblivion? The song, as sung by someone as flawlessly handsome and as dangerous as Chet Baker, reeks of romance.

Pale Blue Eyes The Velvet Underground

(Lou Reed) ❉ Verve ❉ 1969 ❉ Appears on: *The Velvet Underground*

This recording of this song is amongst the most sublime love ballads in all of popular music.

"That's a song about Lou's old girlfriend in Syracuse, by the way," said Sterling Morrison, whose guitar lines are integral to the rich atmosphere of the track. "I said, 'Lou, if I wrote a song like that I wouldn't make you play it'. We did the third album deliberately as anti-production. It sounds like it was done in a closet – it's flat, and that's the way we wanted it. The songs are all very quiet and it's kind of insane. I like the album."

The song has been covered many times (though very rarely by Reed) and never bettered than on this take on the third Velvet Underground album.

Fear is a Man's Best Friend John Cale

(John Cale) ❉ Island ❉ 1974 ❉ Appears on: *Fear*

Having made his pop album *Paris 1919* in Los Angeles, John Cale went to London to make a rock album. His credibility as a former member of the Velvet Underground stood the Welsh singer/songwriter in good stead. Roxy Music's Brian Eno, guitarist Phil Manzenera and saxophonist Andy McKay came on board, as did session guitarist Chris Spedding. The sound they made with Cale was the dark side of glam rock.

Soft Machine's Kevin Ayres had recently staged the super-art rock concert featuring Eno, Cale, himself and Nico that is captured on the album *June 1, 1974*. That concert shows some of the level of paranoia and violence that was part of Cale's repertoire at the time. He was doing "a lot of dope and drinking".

The first track on the *Fear* album shows the shape of things to come. "'Fear is a Man's Best Friend' is an idea," Cale wrote in his autobiography. "It's about paranoia. It's not the sort of thing where you can say it's true or false. It's more a dialectic – a position which you can or you can't take." The song swings between high and low like a lurching, bouncing ball of angst. Gentle piano riffs gradually become more and more intense and erratic and the song builds into a frenzy of paranoia and aggression. 'Fear is a Man's Best Friend' wasn't going to be a pop single but it set the agenda for the next decade of Cale's work and for much of the British art-music establishment.

Fight for Your Right Beastie Boys

(Beastie Boys/Rick Rubin) ✳ Def Jam ✳ 1986 ✳ Appears on: *Licensed to Ill*

"As for us, when we were thirteen and fourteen and went to clubs and heard the DJ mix Big Youth and Treacherous Three with James White or Delta 5, it wasn't, 'Hey, now we're finding out about what people from another culture are about.' It was

just great music," said Beastie Boy Mike D. "All the kids at my school were into Led Zeppelin and the Eagles and that was what I defined myself against. So it was more a case of cool music versus uncool music."

In fact Mike Diamond, Ad-Rock and MCA put the cool and uncool music together, aided by producer Rick Rubin, and the result changed music.

The Beastie Boys were just three kids from rich New York families who liked black culture. When they cut 'Fight for Your Right' they had little understanding of rap or black culture. They just liked the idea. Rick Rubin who had produced most of the old school rap on the New York Def Jam label was one of the few producers who understood metal crunching guitars and drums – especially John Bonham's drum sound from *Led Zeppelin IV* – and he also understood the rhythms of rap rhyme. Plus they were funny. What started as a lark turned into a revolution in sound.

Spicks & Specks The Bee Gees

(Barry Gibb) ✳ Spin ✳ 1966 ✳ Appears on: *Monday's Rain*

The Gibb family migrated from Manchester to Australia in 1958, settling in Brisbane. Hughie Gibb was a sometime musician. His three sons took to performing and were discovered singing at a local Brisbane car racing event. They were soon in Sydney appearing on TV. While still a teenager, Barry Gibb was writing songs for other singers and the Bee Gees were themselves recording artists, although not making much headway in the charts.

Nat Kipner is an American record producer and songwriter who worked with the Bee Gees in a shed-cum-studio in the Sydney suburb of Hurstville. The studio was owned by Ossie Byrne and the Bee Gees spent a lot of time there working on material.

While cutting a track for another singer, Maurice Gibb started vamping out a chord progression that caught Barry Gibb's ear and in less than twenty minutes he had written a song based on it.

'Spicks & Specks' is a monumental ballad. The Gibb voices climb above a menacing, dramatic piano figure that is coloured by a simple horn line. It was here that Gibb had found the Bee Gees' forte – the desperate love song with heartbreaking male harmonies. 'Spicks & Specks' has a piano part that is so rigid in its insistent rhythm that you can't help but feel the force of desire and then the vocals on top bring home the turmoil.

With 'Spicks & Specks' finally breaking the Australian charts, the Bee Gees were ready to board the *Fairsky* and return to England and thence conquer the world.

Angie The Rolling Stones

(Mick Jagger/Keith Richards) ✳ Rolling Stones Records ✳ 1973 ✳
Appears on: *Goat's Head Soup*

Despite years of speculation on the matter, it's unlikely that the song 'Angie' is evidence that Mick Jagger was having an affair with David Bowie's wife Angela, or indeed David Bowie. Keith Richards suggested the title because it came to him with the tune. Richards' second child, Dandelion, who was born around this time, was later called Angie and if there is a personal connection for the title, this would seem to be the more likely source. 'Angie' is one of the better Rolling Stones' ballads with a lush melody and a very vulnerable Mick Jagger singing.

This entire album was written and recorded in two months in between tours. While there might not have been a close relationship between the principals, the group itself was in sharp form. *Goat's Head Soup* was the beginning of a new era. The Stones were now more complex and less sure of themselves. The centre was lost but there were still flashes of brilliance such as on *Goat's Head Soup*, a record that has improved with age like fine cheese.

"I sort of remember the album *Exile on Main Street* being done in France and also the United States, and after that going on tour and becoming complacent and thinking, 'It's '72. Fuck it. We've done it'," Mick Jagger once confessed. "We still tried after that, but I don't think the results were ever that wonderful. Maybe some people liked *Goat's Head Soup*, *It's Only Rock & Roll* and *Black and Blue*, but basically those albums do not represent the best of the Rolling Stones."

Killing in the Name Rage Against the Machine

(Rage Against the Machine) ✳ Epic ✳ 1992 ✳ Appears on: *Rage Against the Machine*

Wow, these guys were angry. The cover of the eponymous first album pictured a Buddhist monk on fire, but Rage didn't go in for that kind of passive aggression. Guitarist and Harvard graduate Tom Morello and singer Zack De La Rocha were both second-generation militant leftists who saw Rage as a vehicle for insurgency as well as entertainment. Morello, drummer Brad Wilk, bass player Tim Commerford and De La Rocha were familiar with rap, hip-hop and heavy rock and fused the styles with the solder of righteous indignation. But they could also play. Morello, especially, found a new language for the electric guitar – capricious and vengeful and just plain gobsmacking in his virtuosity.

"Throughout the course of my guitar playing in a lot of the bands I've been in," he said, "much of it was a search for my voice on the instrument to find a unique way to express the anxiety of suburbia through six strings and a piece of wood. I began to really find that in Rage Against the Machine."

'Killing in the Name' was the centrepiece of the debut album and a rallying call for millions of angry young men and women with its chorus of, "Fuck you, I won't do what you tell me!"

Rage Against the Machine only made two proper albums in six years, in most part due to internal conflicts. After them, however, came the deluge of rap rockers such as Linkin Park, Limp Bizkit and Korn. None of them had the depth or the wit of Rage Against the Machine although there is now a tradition of political hardcore in groups such as System of a Down that is Rage's legacy. Neither hip-hop nor hardcore nor heavy metal, Rage Against the Machine were completely uncompromising in their politics and their music.

Levi Stubbs' Tears Billy Bragg

(Billy Bragg) ✳ Go! Discs ✳ 1986 ✳ Appears on: *Talking with the Taxman about Poetry*

The Levi Stubbs of the title is the singer in the Four Tops. This oddly affecting song tells the story of a working-class woman who marries too young to the wrong man and finds herself desperate, alone and miserable with only the sound of Motown to comfort her.

"When the world falls apart some things stay in place/Levi Stubbs' tears run down his face." Bragg sings the song accompanied only by his electric guitar and that too adds to the oddness. It's like something very crucial is missing (beyond tunefulness), Bragg just has the emotion of the song. "Yes, I listen to tapes and I'm sure I'm singing flat on all the songs," he said. "I want to sing like I talk so I'm never going to be a great singer. I don't think I have to sing in tune all the time for the lyrics to come across. It would be nice but it becomes behind a few other priorities. It's like what you wear onstage, what does it matter?"

Bragg made his name as a radical left-wing songwriter, a pamphleteer, so 'Levi Stubbs' Tears', which drips with sentimentality, sounds out of place alongside the workers' marching anthems. Its context on this album raises questions about how art, especially escapist art, functions and the song is decidedly and correctly ambiguous.

On the face of it, 'Levi Stubbs' Tears' should be a forgotten novelty but it remains a powerful and disturbing song.

Music Madonna

(Mirwais Ahmadzaï/Madonna) ✳ Maverick ✳ 2000 ✳ Appears on: *Music*

On 1998's *Ray of Light* Madonna embraced techno. On *Music* two years later she pushed that button harder. She enlisted French producer Mirwais Ahmadzaï who introduced other tones and flavours – a tougher edge to the grooves and more hip-hop feels.

Madonna was on a voyage of discovery that ran through her entire career, so it's misleading to see her changes in terms of a reinvention. *Music* was a delight – sparkling, witty and more carefree than she had been since her downtown days of the mid-'80s.

"I feel like . . . an animal that's, like, ready to be sprung from a cage," she told *The Face* at the time this LP was released. "I've been living a pretty low-key domestic existence . . . and I miss things. Like, I miss performing, and dancing, and being on the road, that kind of energy. So part of the record is about that. And then the other part is about love. So there's the frivolous side of my life and then there's the – hopefully – non-frivolous side of my life. I usually make a record that's one or the other, and I feel I did both on this one."

Merry Go Round The Replacements

(Paul Westerberg) ✳ Sire ✳ 1990 ✳ Appears on: *All Shook Down*

The Replacements were known as a hard-drinking band. That was part of their shambolic charm. Then Paul Westerberg, the singer, songwriter and guitarist, resolved to get himself sober and move on from the group. For contractual and personal reasons, however, *All Shook Down*, which is effectively a Westerberg solo album, became the Replacements' swan song.

It had been a long decade for Westerberg. The group was lauded around the globe as one of the great rock & roll bands of all time. Success, however, eluded them. By 1990 Westerberg was tired and burnt out. His personal life was in upheaval. He was tired of the responsibility of leading a band. He was also moving away from the Replacements sound in search of something more personal and intimate.

'Merry Go Round' was Westerberg's farewell to the past. A song that celebrates the abandon, the wildness of life. "Yeah, 'Merry Go Round' is really 'Achin' To Be' in a different key," he said. "It's the kind of character I tend to be interested in. The winners in life don't attract me.

"I've never been able to get a handle on that, I've tried to write 'em [songs about winners], but they always ring false. It's like someone else's words coming out my mouth, just a slogan to pat yourself on the back and kid yourself that it's all gonna be all right. 'We're gonna make it.' That emotion has never been strong with me. I've always been kinda defeatist! A lot of it does come from drink. I didn't stop drinking in the hope that now I'd have a positive outlook on life. But at least maybe I'll be able to see some glimmers of the other side of life."

The *All Shook Down* sessions were still ragged – emotionally raw – but musically more sophisticated. This is one of those songs where the artist is standing naked, for better or worse. As it happens, this was one of Westerberg's best moments.

"I sound very tired and weak on it, and I was," he said. "I was not healthy, not caring much. I sort of erased all the real angst, the pissed-off and the humour and took only the elements that were a little deranged, a little sad and a little pathetic and put them together. I was pretty fucking desperate there, and it shows.

"I'm glad we captured it."

Goodbye Astrid Cold Chisel

(Don Walker/Jimmy Barnes) ❋ WEA ❋ 1978 ❋
Appears on: *You're 13, You're Beautiful and You're Mine*

Jimmy Barnes wrote all three chords and Don Walker the lyrics to this classic small piece of misogyny. At the time of first writing, Cold Chisel was to all intents and purposes, five Adelaide boys going nowhere fast and loudly so. Living in dive hotel rooms and playing three sets a night in any bar that would have them, Chisel lived the rock & roll dream. What set them apart, however, was impeccable taste in dirty rock & roll.

'Astrid' was a twelve-bar thrash in the style of the Troggs, although even with a tune as rudimentary as this, Chisel brought a unique touch. Foremost is Ian Moss' sandpaper guitar lines.

Don Walker's tale of marriage break-up is full of wit and attitude. There's no melancholic, wistful sense of lost possibility; just "seven long years of give a little, take a little, put a little money away". This is the Australian version of *Men are from Mars, Women are from Venus*. The narrator lets fly his scorn for the woman's lifestyle. All the bottled-up anger spews out, all the feelings he has suppressed are vomited up. "Turn up the tears/And make sure you let the neighbours see/What a lowdown deal you got/When you married me".

'Astrid' lent itself to the full force of Chisel on stage – Ian Moss' breakneck guitar leading the way for a tightly swinging rhythm section of Steve Prestwich's versatile drumming and Phil Small's solid bass with Walker's Jerry Lee Lewis piano playing. Then there was Jimmy Barnes who let fly on this song like his life depended on it. His vocal here was a tsunami of emotion way beyond the usual scope of rock & roll and completely his own. Cold Chisel wrote more literate songs and more sophisticated tunes but taking three chords and a simple story and transforming them into a unique and confronting piece like this takes real genius.

Unfinished Sympathy Massive Attack

(Robert '3D' del Naja/Grantley 'Daddy G' Marshall/Shara Nelson/J Sharp/Andrew 'Mushroom' Vowles) ❋ Virgin ❋ 1990 ❋ Appears on: *Blue Lines*

The Wild Bunch were a group of DJs in Bristol, a provincial British town. Gradually the members of the Bunch and their friends seeped into recording and have been some of the most potent figures in British music since 1990: producer Nellee Hooper, Tricky, Goldie, Portishead, Neneh Cherry and the three DJs behind Massive Attack – Andrew 'Mushroom' Vowles, Grant 'Daddy G' Marshall and Robert '3D' del Naja.

"When we were the Wild Bunch," said Daddy G, "we got our reputation as a sound system from the fact that we played all kinds of music – punk, funk, reggae. For us to try and make an album that's all one sound just wouldn't be natural."

Instead *Blue Lines* is a sublime melding of soul, R&B, rare groove, hip-hop, reggae and dub.

The music was made organically with the players improvising with samples and grooves in the studio, gradually assembling the tracks. The songs have the ambience and the energy of a group of people who know that they're on the verge of making something entirely new. Indeed the sound of *Blue Lines* has spawned thousands of imitators.

Much of it is due to the phenomenally soulful voice of Shara Nelson. But the songs are also mesmerising. 'Unfinished Sympathy' has an incredible groove that just grabs you along like the Nile in flood – big and deep and wide. It's a song that resonates through your consciousness; it taps into the eternal where only the best music can go.

'Unfinished Sympathy' began as a jam with just Nelson and a drum machine and a keyboard and it gradually built up the groove with strings and layers of keyboards.

"Right from the start, we never made music in line with the tempos that were required in clubs," said Daddy G. "It's made for after clubs, when you want to chill out, learn how to breathe again."

1/1 Brian Eno

(Rhett Davies/Brian Eno/Robert Wyatt) ✳ EG ✳ 1978 ✳
Appears on: *Ambient 1: Music for Airports*

The opening track on *Ambient 1: Music for Airports* heralded a whole new phase for popular music – music without tunes. Eno recognised the existence of tuneless music and then gave it a name. From there followed all kinds of permutations from the New Age noodling of hippies wanting meditation soundtracks to ambient house music and all kinds of dynamics in between.

Perhaps then, it's not surprising that the idea came while Eno was recovering from a head injury after being knocked over by a taxi.

"A friend came to visit and, as she was leaving, I asked her to put a record of harp music on the stereo," he recalled. "Well, one channel wasn't working. It was very quiet, pouring with rain outside and I thought, 'Oh shit, I'll have to wait for the next visitor to turn it up.' Then I started to listen to it . . ."

Eno had achieved his ambition of taking the musician out of the music-making process and he was "very, very pleased" with the result.

"It was done," he admitted, "with a minimum of good intentions. I didn't go into it thinking, 'I'm going to make a very interesting piece of music here'. I went into it thinking I just wanted to make something that would work in an airport, that would actually make you think that flying was a pleasant thing to do instead of an unbearably uncomfortable thing, as I think it generally is."

Eno's instruments were a series of very long tape loops – some as long as 20 minutes.

"There were twenty-two loops," he explained. "One loop had just one piano note on it. Another one would have two piano notes. Another one would have a group of girls singing one note, sustaining it for ten seconds. There were eight loops of girls' voices and about fourteen loops of piano. I just set all these loops running and let them configure in whichever way they wanted to, and in fact the result is very, very nice."

In fact, for a piece of music composed by machines, the effect is surprisingly organic.

"The interesting thing," Eno noted, "is that it doesn't sound at all mechanical or mathematical. It sounds like some guy is sitting there playing the piano with quite intense feeling. The spacing and dynamics of 'his' playing sound very well organised. That was an example of hardly interfering at all. When the piece was finished I listened to it and there was just one piano note I didn't like. It seemed to appear in the wrong place, so I simply edited it out. A lot of the so-called systems composers have this thing that the system is always right. You don't fiddle with it at all. Well, I don't think like that. I think that the system is as right as you judge it to be. If, for some reason, you don't like a bit of it, you must trust your intuition on that. I don't take a doctrinaire approach to systems."

Johnny B Goode Chuck Berry

(Chuck Berry) ※ Chess ※ 1958 ※ Appears on: *The Anthology*

Chuck Berry wrote the template for the rock star with 'Johnny B Goode'.

First there's the story – the young man who dreams of playing his guitar all the way to stardom. That was certainly the case with Berry (although he changed the lyric from "coloured boy" to "country boy" "or else it wouldn't get on the radio," he recalled).

Berry was a hairdresser who wanted to play the blues. Then, in 1955, 'Maybelline' was his ticket into show business. 'Johnny B Goode' was Berry's story in part –

although all the details had been changed – but it became more the template for white guitar heroes. It's a song that has less wit than most Berry tracks, perhaps because it was so literal. Part of its attraction for young white boys was the ease with which it could be mastered – simple changes over a boogie tempo.

The song was produced by Leonard and Phil Chess at their Chicago studio with a crack blues band – Fred Below on drums, Willie Dixon on bass and the incomparable Lafayette Leake on piano. The piano is the key to this ode to the guitar. Berry developed his signature phrasing by transposing the stride piano style of his accompanist Johnnie Johnson – whose name inspired the title – to the guitar, thereby inventing rock & roll guitar playing.

West End Girls Pet Shop Boys

(Chris Lowe/Neil Tennant) ❊ Parlophone ❊ 1985 ❊ Appears on: *Please*

A pop journalist (Neil Tennant) and a synthesiser geek (Chris Lowe) were an unlikely pair. Not particularly photogenic, quite camp and possessed of a wry wit to compensate for dry vocals, the Pet Shop Boys nonetheless had a massive impact on the music scene in the '80s. They helped to make club music accessible for the mainstream white audience and they were so odd that they invited the suburban straight audience to check out hip-hop and dance music, which was confined to gay clubs outside the US.

"Slightly to the left of Stock, Aitken and Waterman," quipped Tennant shortly after their second album had sold over a million copies, surpassing the first. "And then we often get accused, particularly in Europe, of being a yuppie group, and that our LPs are bought on CD for people to listen to on their car stereos. To be honest, it's true to an extent. And when we did record signings in America, in Dallas a whole family came to see us: the mother, her daughter and the grandmother were all Pet Shop Boys fans. We do get a lot of letters from mothers. Mothers like me! And also I get the fans that write poetry: I have a slight David Sylvian crossover audience, whereas Chris gets the sex audience, the ones who write obscene letters! It's quite thrilling, actually!"

Their first single 'West End Girls' sold a million right out of the box. The track is sexy and dangerous. Lowe laid down a widescreen background for Tennant's story about class and seduction and the meeting of money and violence. 'West End Girls'

has a haunting quality – recreating the late night streets, the possibility of getting into something one shouldn't. Tennant said that he was inspired by Grandmaster Flash's 'The Message' and transferred it to London. Which may be true but he has touched the subconscious, the pleasure zone. While it may be creepy, courtesy of Chris Lowe we have white suburban Englishmen laying out hip-hop beats and hypnotic melody lines.

As they often pointed out, the pair were not pin-ups. They made no pretence to be straight. Neither of these things were in the end obstacles that a great pop song couldn't overcome.

Idiot Wind Bob Dylan

(Bob Dylan) ❋ Columbia ❋ 1975 ❋ Appears on: *Blood on the Tracks*

Dylan's mid-'70s resurgence hit its high point with the album *Blood on the Tracks*. As has been extensively reported, the album coincided with the break-up of Dylan's marriage to Sara Lowndes.

Most of the songs on the record are love songs of one sort or another. The exception is 'Idiot Wind', a seven-minute epic of elegantly phrased bile. Line readings of the lyrics tend to fall short. This is not a song based on logical exposition. Rather, here Dylan piles up a list of frustrations, public and private. It's a song that expresses a man's disgust as to where his life has lead and he lashes out at the barking dogs of gossip that have bedevilled the protagonist. No-one is excused "from the Grand Coolle Dam to the Capitol". The idiot wind would seem to be the words that come from people's mouths.

"That was a song I wanted to make as a painting," said Dylan of 'Idiot Wind'. "A lot of people thought that song, that album *Blood on the Tracks*, pertained to me. Because it seemed to at the time. It didn't pertain to me. It was just a concept of putting in images that defy time – yesterday, today, and tomorrow. I wanted to make them all connect in some kind of a strange way. I've read that that album had to do with my divorce. Well, I didn't get divorced till four years after that.

"I thought I might have gone a little bit too far with 'Idiot Wind'. I might have changed some of it. I didn't really think I was giving away too much; I thought that it seemed so personal that people would think it was about so-and-so who was close to me. It wasn't. But you can put all these words together and that's where it falls. You can't help where it falls.

"I didn't feel that one was too personal, but I felt it 'seemed' too personal. Which might be the same thing, I don't know. But it never was 'painful'. 'Cause usually with those kinds of things, if you think you're too close to something, you're giving away too much of your feelings, well, your feelings are going to change a month later and you're going to look back and say, 'What did I do that for?'"

'Idiot Wind' is an older and wiser companion piece to 'Like a Rolling Stone'. It's a song that contains much of Dylan's most scathing and acute observations fractured through a crumbling consciousness.

Dylan recorded 'Idiot Wind' with steel guitar, organ, and bass on 12 September 1974. A week later he redid the song without pedal steel. He then returned to the song in December in Minnesota when he recut the song and each time he changed the lyrics. It's a song about a state of mind rather than a specific incident.

"Yeah, you know, obviously, if you've heard both versions you realise, of course, that there could be a myriad of verses for the thing. It doesn't stop," Dylan told writer Bill Flanagan. "It wouldn't stop. Where do you end? You could still be writing it, really. It's something that could be a work continually in progress. Although, on saying that, let me say that my lyrics, to my way of thinking, are better for my songs than anybody else's. People have felt about my songs sometimes the same way as me. And they say to me, your songs are so opaque that, people tell me, they have feelings they'd like to express within the same framework. My response, always, is go ahead, do it, if you feel like it. But it never comes off. They're not as good as my lyrics. There's just something about my lyrics that just have a gallantry to them. And that might be all they have going for them. However, it's no small thing."

Freedom Run Kyuss

(Brant Bjork/Josh Homme) ✻ Dali ✻ 1992 ✻ Appears on: *Blues for the Red Sun*

To the initiated, there was something almost messianic about Kyuss, coming as they did from the wilds of the California desert. They were so isolated they had to use a generator to power their instruments. There were also no guitar tuners so Josh

Homme tuned his guitar down to C and played through a bass amp. The beauty of the desert is that no-one can hear you scream and ask you to turn it down.

Kyuss (vocalist John Garcia, guitarist Josh Homme, bassist Nick Oliveri, and drummer Brant Bjork) were four hardcore fans who spent their days jamming in what has wishfully been compared to John Coltrane and a hardcore band. "You had to play just for the sake of playing and you had to go a little farther than just playing what was hip," said Homme. "Sometimes we get to a point where we feel we've gone far enough and we decide to add a little structure. It doesn't matter what it is, but eventually you feel like you've been doing something too much. You know that philosophy that says anything that's worth doing is worth overdoing? I don't subscribe to that. The goal isn't to be the heaviest band in the world."

But they were.

Their first album showed a lot of promise. But it was the second, *Blues for the Red Sun*, that knocked the heavy rock world for six. Suddenly Kyuss were the kings of stoner rock – perhaps in part the reputation came from the fact that they took their name from a *Dungeons & Dragons* character.

There was also the fact that they were not afraid to take on an epic like 'Freedom Run', which had the slow, inexorable build of a '70s progressive rock track before just collapsing under its own supreme heaviness.

Kyuss soon collapsed too and Homme and Oliveri formed Queens of the Stone Age, who are one of the most significant current rock & roll bands.

"We realised early on that it's not so much 'we are the desert' or some corny shit like that," said Homme. "It's more a case of we were dealt the desert because of where we grew up. We were dealt some beautiful scenery, some of the best places to try and cultivate ideas."

Can't Hardly Wait The Replacements

(Paul Westerberg) ❄ Sire ❄ 1987 ❄ Appears on: *Pleased to Meet Me*

"Around the time of the fourth album, *Let it Be*, things were really rolling," said Replacements leader Paul Westerberg. "Everyone was saying we were headed for the top. For a while we were the coolest band in America. We thought, 'We're going to be rich in a couple of years', and then two years later the crowds are thinning out and you suddenly realise that that was your heyday."

This sense of disappointment that came over the Replacements, and also a desire to break away from the hardcore tag, led Westerberg further in the direction of pop. Producer Jim Dickinson was enlisted in the cause. Dickinson was part of the Memphis country soul scene and worked with Alex Chilton at Ardent. He worked with the Byrds (he played them the demo of 'Mr Tambourine Man') and the Rolling Stones.

'Can't Hardly Wait' is on its way to being radio-friendly – the rawness of the early Replacements had been polished into hook-laden choruses as on 'Can't Hardly Wait' with the addition of strings. This is an '80s version of pure pop. It's ironic and knowing but still with a genuine affection for rock & roll music.

"I think the marriage of honesty and melody are my two main things," said Westerberg. "If I'm short in one suit, then I try to overcompensate with the other. It has to be one of those two for me to be truly interesting."

In the Midnight Hour Wilson Pickett

(Wilson Pickett/Steve Cropper) ❋ Atlantic ❋ 1965 ❋ Appears on: *In the Midnight Hour*

Wilson Pickett wrote 'In the Midnight Hour' with Booker T and the MGs' guitarist Steve Cropper in an afternoon while the pair of them were holed up in a hotel room in Memphis. It was the first in a series of cooperative arrangements Atlantic would strike for its soul singers with the Memphis label, Stax.

A band of Stax regulars put the track down in the studio the next day. Atlantic president, Jerry Wexler, was in town for the session and offered advice on the rhythm – kids on the street, he said, were doing this dance called "the jerk" – so Cropper and MGs drummer, Al Jackson, gave the song its distinctive back beat.

Cropper considers he was doubly blessed that afternoon in the Memphis hotel because the following year, he was asked to pen something for another soul singer, Eddie Floyd. The song he came up with was 'Knock on Wood' which, he once confessed to *Rolling Stone*, "was 'In the Midnight Hour' played backwards."

Fuck tha Police NWA

(Ice Cube/MC Ren) ❋ Priority ❋ 1989 ❋ Appears on: *Straight Outta Compton*

Niggaz With Attitude (NWA) were the most important rap group on the US West Coast. Where Public Enemy had pioneered political hip-hop on the East Coast and saw their work as part of a struggle for emancipation, NWA on their second album, *Straight Outta Compton*, were more anarchic. This was ghetto life of bangin – sex and drugs and fighting cops.

NWA was the home of some heavyweight talent, not least of which was Eazy-E (Eric Wright), Dr Dre (Andre Young) and Ice Cube (O'Shea Jackson). Easy was more your traditional rap producer big on the blackface style of rap. Ice Cube and MC Ren, however, upped the ante in glamorising ghetto life. In their view, rap music was the story of the streets but it needed to be told in full Panavision. It was exciting – the idea of running with guns and women.

Straight Outta Compton was the real beginning of gangsta rap. Where Ice T had recorded his life on the street, NWA made it seem heroic. The crucial tracks on this album are Ice Cube's 'Express Yourself' and its following joint: 'Fuck tha Police'. This latter track drew the line. It justified outlaw behaviour and drew a line around the Compton ghetto defining who was in and who out; it was, at base, a call to anarchy. It was uncompromising. The strength of the hip-hop on the track, its muscularity and its undeniable invention made the record an underground hit. It couldn't be a mainstream hit because the FBI and law enforcement agencies the world over tried hard to suppress the violently anti-police message.

This was virtually the end of NWA though. Ice Cube went solo and became a big star. Dr Dre became the most important single producer in hip-hop. They left a legacy in NWA that would last for ten or more years.

All I Wanna Do Sheryl Crow

(David Baerwald/Bill Bottrell/Wyn Cooper/Sheryl Crow/Kevin Gilbert) ❋ A&M ❋ 1993 ❋ Appears on: *Tuesday Night Music Club*

Sheryl Crow had a Cinderella story to tell. A music teacher in a small Missouri town ups and leaves for Los Angeles to get into the music business. Bingo. Within months she's singing back-up for Michael Jackson and then a variety of A-list rock gods. In the meantime she's having these Tuesday night jam sessions with musicians in various stages of success and ends up with an album she calls the *Tuesday Night Music Club* and sells ten million of the suckers.

"But that's exactly how it was," she said. "It was a result of us all being sort of disgruntled about being in Los Angeles, and we wound up just falling into it one night a week. It was kind of a joke at first. But after we'd been together a few weeks it seemed like a really fun way to make a record without being really corporate. So we just went ahead and got on with it. Everyone made themselves at home. They'd come in and out and suggest and collaborate and all that. But at the end of the day it was my record, I had the final call on everything."

'All I Wanna Do' captures the craftsmanship of Gilbert, Baerwald and Bottrell, and Crow sings it with an ingénue's charm. Of all the songs on the album, the pop purity of this track holds up the best.

Things did not end well for the Club. Gilbert, who had been Crow's lover, died in an autoerotic accident. Crow and Bottrell fell out. One song, 'Leaving Las Vegas' (later to be a movie), was based on a book by John O'Brien, a friend of Baerwald's. O'Brien committed suicide after the album's release in part, according to Baerwald, because he was unacknowledged on the album's sleeve. It's such a Los Angeles story. And so far from the sunshine of 'All I Wanna Do'. "You can hear we were enjoying ourselves," Crow said at the time of the song's release.

Mrs Robinson Simon & Garfunkel

(Paul Simon) ❋ Columbia ❋ 1968 ❋ Appears on: *The Graduate*

Although 'Mrs Robinson' is the name of the heroine in *The Graduate* for which this song is the main theme, the narratives in the song don't have any common ground really. This is possibly one of the most public examples of passive aggression in popular music.

Simon and Garfunkel were both interested in working on a film project and Simon liked Mike Nichols, a former comedian who was making his directorial debut with *The Graduate*. The duo was under pressure to finish their album *Bookends* and Simon didn't much like Charles Webb's book on which the film was based. Simon wrote two tracks, 'Overs' and 'Punky's Dilemma', but they were rejected. Nichols chose some old Simon & Garfunkel songs but was stumped for a theme until Art Garfunkel had an idea.

"Paul was writing a song called 'Mrs Roosevelt' and he was going nowhere and he was going to chuck it," Garfunkel recalled. "Paul and I were in Hollywood working with Nichols on the soundtrack. We still needed one up-tempo tune that Paul hadn't written and Mike was struggling. And I said, 'There is an up-tempo song that Paul is despairing of, but it is very commercial. It's called 'Mrs Roosevelt' but we could change 'Mrs Roosevelt' to 'Mrs Robinson''. And Mike loved that thought. So we sang it against the screen. And all that existed of the song was the chorus. That's why the verses are 'Doo doo doo doo . . .' There are no lyrics there. And it worked."

Now with the song in a film, Simon had to write the verses and the fate of his Mrs Robinson doesn't relate to that of the woman in *The Graduate*. It does contain the memorable lines: "Where have you gone Joe DiMaggio?/A nation turns its lonely eyes to you" and is also the first use of the word "Jesus" in a non-religious pop song.

"Nobody had said 'Jesus' before," said Simon. "People thought it was a word you couldn't say in pop music."

Gimme Some Lovin' The Spencer Davis Group

(Spencer Davis/Muff Winwood/Steve Winwood) ✳ Fontana ✳ 1966 ✳

Appears on: *The Best of the Spencer Davis Group*

Although named after the guitarist, this was always the Steve Winwood Group. Blessed with an other-worldly soul voice and a natural gift with the Hammond B3, Steve Winwood was only fifteen when he recorded the Spencer David Group's first hit, 'Keep on Running'. The following year they topped the charts with Winwood's composition 'Gimme Some Lovin''.

According to Davis, a former professor of German from the University of Birmingham, the song grew out of a jam session. "Muff had a bass riff from an old Homer Banks record, 'Whole Lotta Lovin''. I added a G-, A- and C-minor to it, Steve played a Ravel's 'Bolero' kind of thing and said to me to play minors, not majors." According to bass player and Winwood's brother Muff: "Steve had been singing 'gimme some lovin'', just yelling anything, so that became the title. It took about an hour to write, then down to the pub for lunch."

American Jimmy Miller – who was imported to London for the Spencer Davis Group, and who later worked with the Rolling Stones, Traffic and many of the key artists of the period – produced the recording.

'Gimme Some Lovin'' is mostly based around Winwood's rave up style where the fat organ sound and his keening beautiful voice accelerate on an adrenaline rush through the changes.

Winwood himself was in a hurry. The record topped the charts in the UK and the US but within a few months of its release he had quit the Spencer Davis Group to form Traffic.

Are You Lonesome Tonight? Elvis Presley

(Lou Handman/Roy Turk) ☀ RCA ☀ 1961 ☀ Appears on: *Elvis 30 #1 Hits*

Elvis biographer Peter Guralnik said, "I came to see the songs he recorded after his return from the army as an expansion of his ambition, a very conscious attempt to broaden his musical talent. To a lesser extent, I came to see the Las Vegas years in the same way."

This song dates back to 1926 when Roy Turk and Lou Handman added it to their already extensive songbook of music hall hits. Prior to his stewardship of Elvis Presley, Colonel Tom Parker had managed crooner Gene Austin. 'Are You Lonesome Tonight?' was one of Austin's best numbers and a favourite of the Colonel's wife Marie. It's generally believed that Parker asked Elvis to record this song as a favour and moreover that it is the first time the Colonel had ever requested Presley cut a particular song.

Presley had just returned from army service in Germany and had grown up considerably since his hard rockin' days. It was a new Elvis Presley in 1960.

The song was cut at four o'clock in the morning at RCA's Nashville studios. Presley runs through the song backed with brushed drums, acoustic guitar, bass and the vocals of the Jordanaires. The session has the intimacy of a man singing close to the microphone in the wee small hours and then when Presley's magnificent baritone drops into a spoken word section the song becomes a lover's conversation. Producer Steve Shoals always puts Presley's vocal to the fore. Here it's like Cinerama, and the King is whispering in your very ear.

Presley was unhappy with the take — some equipment was knocked over and he felt that his singing failed to do the song justice. He was prevailed to do another take. However, it's the first take that was issued as a single and went to number one, becoming one of Presley's signature tunes.

It's said that Presley's friend Lamar Fike heard the song and exclaimed, "It'll sell five million! Play it again. It'll sell seven million. It'll be the biggest goddamn record you ever made!"

I Just Want to Make Love to You Muddy Waters

(Willie Dixon) ❋ Chess ❋ 1954 ❋ Appears on: *Muddy Waters – the Chess Box*

Big Willie Dixon played the bass in Chess studios like Vulcan worked the immortal forge. Not only was he masterful as a bandleader and producer, Dixon was one of Chess' best songwriters. His songs were full-bodied, romantic and lustful, expressing the huge masculine power of these blues giants.

'I Just Want to Make Love to You' is pretty clear right there in the title. The song was originally titled 'Just Make Love to Me' and the switch in emphasis is significant. Muddy Waters here is the hunter, not the game. It's partly rampant ego but it's also a song of pride and self-confidence that will not be mitigated by desire.

The original version of the song featured the perfect Chess band – Otis Spann on piano, Jimmy Rogers on guitar, Little Walter on harp, Fred Below on drums and Dixon himself on bass. 'I Just Want to Make Love to You' is one long tease, the musicians find themselves a groove and move it steadily forward, bringing it to false climaxes and then falling back and starting again. There's a touch of the gospel in the way Muddy seduces his prey; there's the promise of epic lovemaking in the gradual build. There's the pressure of desire that can barely be contained by the band. It's perhaps the closest that Chicago blues gets to soul music.

'I Just Want to Make Love to You' is a classic of its type that has been extensively covered, notably by the Rolling Stones, Van Morrison and Etta James. Live, of course, Muddy took the song to even greater heights. As bluesologist Paul Oliver wrote in 1958, "He sang unhampered, stamping, hollering, his whole body jerking in sheer physical expression of his blues. He would double up, clench his fists, straighten with a spring like a flick-knife, leap in the air, arch his back and literally punch out his words . . ."

Stone on the Water Badly Drawn Boy

(Badly Drawn Boy) ❊ Twisted Nerve/XL ❊ 2000 ❊ Appears on: *The Hour of Bewilderbeast*

Badly Drawn Boy's debut album, *The Hour of Bewilderbeast*, won the 2000 Mercury Prize, Britain's most coveted music award. It seemed a bit much to be giving such a big prize to a small man in a woollen beanie. Damon Gough, who is Badly Drawn Boy, wrote the material himself and played almost all the instruments on the LP . . . and he made a virtue out of being beneath the underdog.

"The word bewilderbeast came from this guy who was in the band when we were playing in Japan," Damon told Ben Thompson of the *Telegraph*. "He was a bit the worse for wear – a bit bewildered, the way you get. He said, 'I feel like a bewilderbeast,' and that name just stuck in my head as a picture of what I wanted the album to be about. I wanted this to be our hour: not just mine, but everyone who's ever had that underdoggy feeling which anyone who's got a bit of humility feels sometimes, even if they're an achiever."

The Hour of Bewilderbeast is a delightful feast of melody. Snatches of ditties come and go. Tunes spring out of the patchwork of melody that sews this album together. The songs are generally reflective pieces, very much in the style of the late Nick Drake.

Gough can be full of himself: "The only thing you need to know is I'm the figurehead and culmination of Manchester music since the year dot. And I am the god that has been sent to save the music scene – to start with, Manchester, and then the rest of the world," he told one reporter. You can tell, though, that he is more humble and serious in the creation of his own record.

'Stone on the Water' starts with an extended instrumental intro and Gough is very much in the service of the song. There are hints of jazz chording and a folk cast to the tune but it's very much novel 21st century rock & roll. Like the mythic bewilderbeast of the title, 'Stone on the Water' doesn't have the answers but is in rapture at the questions.

Mystery Train Elvis Presley

(Little Junior Parker/Sam Phillips) ✳ Sun ✳ 1955 ✳ Appears on: *For LP Fans Only*

The farewell to Sun, 'Mystery Train' was the last A-side Elvis recorded for Sam Phillips' label. The session took place in July 1955 with Presley's usual sidemen Scotty Moore on guitar and Bill Black on bass with drummer Johnny Bernero. The song was written by Little Junior Parker, a southern blues singer who recorded for Sun as Little Junior Parker and his Blue Flames in 1953.

Writer and academic Greil Marcus has written extensively about this song and the link that it provides, running through American music like the mighty Mississippi. His book *Mystery Train* is great, though it's unlikely anything as profound was running through the minds of the half-dozen people in that small Memphis studio on that hot evening. The mystery train is perhaps the doom that awaits us all across the dark prairie night, or it may just be the promise of adventure.

"It was the greatest thing I ever did on Elvis," Phillips has said. "It was a feeling song. I mean, it was a big thing, to put a loved one on a train: are they leavin' forever? Maybe they'll never be back. It was pure rhythm. And at the end he was laughing, because he thought he's screwed it up."

Far from it, 'Mystery Train' was Elvis' first number one country hit. Phillips, facing bankruptcy, now had an asset he could sell and RCA paid him $35,000 for the last year and half on Elvis' contract.

According to New York songwriter Doc Pomus, "The first time that I heard Elvis Presley, it was 1955, and I was singing in this joint on 70th St called the Musicale when I heard this record on the jukebox called 'Mystery Train' – and I just couldn't believe it. It sounded like somebody just came out of the swamp. It was just the most fascinating record to me."

Lola The Kinks

(Ray Davies) ✳ Reprise ✳ 1970 ✳

Appears on: *Lola Versus Powerman and the Moneygoround*

One of the most controversial songs of its time, 'Lola' was the first pop hit about transexuality. Ray Davies tells the tale of a man in a nightclub that goes home with a woman who may well be a man; not surprising now, perhaps, but in 1970 this was certainly new territory for pop.

Lola has the ring of documentary to it, and it's been reliably reported that Davies did date Candy Darling, one of Andy Warhol's superstars at the Factory. Darling was one of the first famous transvestites and was soon made even more widely known by Lou Reed's 'Walk on the Wild Side' ("Candy never once gave it away ..."). Davies commented on the relationship: "It was the stubble that gave it away."

The Kinks turned in an amazing take on the single, their best riff since 'You Really Got Me' and one equally steamy. It was so good that radio had to play the 45 despite the subject matter. Only the BBC got their back up about the lyric – they insisted that "Coca Cola" be changed to "Cherry Cola" because they couldn't be seen to be advertising a soft drink.

Tower of Song Leonard Cohen

(Leonard Cohen) ❈ Columbia ❈ 1988 ❈ Appears on: *I'm Your Man*

Emerging from four years of silence, Leonard Cohen's *I'm Your Man* album was full of dry humour at his own expense, lustful songs about women and a new keyboard-based sound that was part chanson and part Kraftwerk. The gem of that album was the immensely witty 'Tower of Song', which placed the singer in the delightful imprisonment of his muse.

"This is my story," he told an audience at the time. "It's a dismal story. It's a shabby story. It's a funny story. But it's my story."

Increasingly Cohen devoted himself to the service of his life as a whisky-drinking Zen monk and related his writing to his religious practice and vice versa.

"If you're going to think of yourself in this game, or in this tradition, and you start getting a swelled head about it, then you've really got to think about who you're talking about," he said in 1994. "You're not just talking about Randy Newman, who's fine, or Bob Dylan, who's sublime, you're talking about King David, Homer, Dante, Milton, Wordsworth, you're talking about the embodiment of our highest possibility.

"So I don't think it's particularly modest or virtuous to think of oneself as a minor poet. I really do feel the enormous luck I've had in being able to make a living, and to never have had to have written one word that I didn't want to write.

"But I don't fool myself, I know the game I'm in. When I wrote about Hank Williams 'A hundred floors above me in the tower of song', it's not some kind of inverse modesty. I know where Hank Williams stands in the history of popular song. 'Your Cheatin' Heart', songs like that, are sublime, in his own tradition, and I feel myself a very minor writer. I've taken a certain territory, and I've tried to maintain it and administrate it with the very best of my capacities. And I will continue to administrate this tiny territory until I'm too weak to do it. But I understand where this territory is."

'Tower of Song' became the title for the second tribute album devoted to the songs of Leonard Cohen. Unlike its predecessor, this project featured middle-of-the-road artists covering Cohen classics. The record label promoted the album by sending sample copies to cafés across America judged to have "the Leonard Cohen vibe". "I'd like to go to some of those," Cohen said. "I can rarely locate my own vibe."

Car Wheels on a Gravel Road Lucinda Williams

(Lucinda Williams) ❋ Mercury ❋ 1998 ❋ Appears on: *Car Wheels on a Gravel Road*

"I moved around a lot as a kid because my dad was teaching in different places," said Lucinda Williams. "But I also think it's part of the American folklore tradition. I have a sense of some places I'd like to be, but I don't know if I'd ever settle down that long in one place. I'll probably always be kind of movin' around."

On this her fifth proper studio album, Williams uses the landscape, especially the American south, as a canvas for a long emotional journey. The roadside is littered with lost loves and death. The final result, though, is greatly uplifting.

Williams recorded this album three times. One of the producers, Steve Earle, described it as "the least amount of fun I've had working on a record". The end result is both strong and sublime. Long-time producer Gurf Morlix had a go and finally ex-E Street Band keyboardist Roy Bittan polished the record into a classic.

There's a restless hungry feeling to Williams' work. She throws herself into situations feet first and then clambers out of there, wipes off the scars and moves on. 'Car Wheels on a Gravel Road' is told from the perspective of the young girl in the backseat watching her parents' relationship disintegrate and it's not too much of a leap to suggest that the lessons learnt at the knee were carried through into her work. Rarely do songwriters get this close to the bone without self-pity and with compassion.

'Car Wheels' delivered – with help from friends like Earle and the great Buddy Miller – on Williams' promise. The album won a Grammy, topped the prestigious Village Voice Poll and took Williams out of the shadows. Clearly it was worth the wait.

Grace Kelly Blues Eels

(Mark Oliver Everett) ❊ Dreamworks ❊ 2000 ❊ Appears on: *Daisies of the Galaxy*

Tom Waits described the Eels as "Electric Jungian therapy on vintage pawn shop instruments. Tribal grooves and garage energy. The Eels are outsider-like folks that paint with fingernail polish. I eagerly await each new release. What's not to like about cheap microphones, distortion melody and great songs?" The accolade made Mark Oliver Everett happy for three days. Everett (aka E), who is for all intents and purposes the whole band, is not always a happy guy. Both his parents died early and his sister committed suicide. E is accustomed to depression and grief. But 'Grace Kelly Blues', which opens the album *Daisies of the Galaxy* is a wonderful song about acceptance. The new folk tag is not far off – he sounds like Beck with an R&B groove and there is a sweet and positive tune to go with the spirit of the lyric.

"To me, these are happy records," he told the *LA Weekly*, "the most positive records I could have made. And I think *Electro-shock Blues* [largely about his sister's suicide and his mother's impending demise] is even more positive than *Daisies*. It's a hard-won victory, but it's a victory, you know? You have to think about how much trouble it is to get up every day and make a record like that. If you're passionate about something, you're doing pretty good."

E wound up in Los Angeles where he met Lenny Waronker, producer and patron of Randy Newman. Waronker no doubt recognised in E the same acerbic wit and dark humour that had been Newman's stock-in-trade. While E's records are obviously personal, they're not specifically confessional and therein lies their longevity.

"When you wear the mask of another's point of view, you get more daring and end up revealing more," he said. "Often people thought it was me whining about my life for twelve songs, but it's really different people whining about their lives."

Everybody's Talkin' Harry Nilsson

(Fred Neil) ✳ RCA ✳ 1968 ✳ Appears on: *Aerial Ballet*

Derek Taylor, the legendary Beatles' publicist, sang Harry Nilsson's praises to director John Schlesinger who was looking for songs for his upcoming film, *Midnight Cowboy*. The track he picked from Nilsson's second album *Aerial Ballet* was a version of Fred Neil's 'Everybody's Talkin''. Nilsson's sweet, perfect, pained voice improves on Neil's world-weary original. The song fitted so neatly into the film that it's now impossible to imagine one without the other.

Neil's story mirrors that of the hero, Joe Buck – a southern boy who comes to New York looking for fame to match his talents, discovers that success in his profession isn't all it's cracked up to be and then flees back to Florida and the ocean.

If the million sales of the single 'Everybody's Talkin'', the Grammy and countless cover versions did little to improve Fred Neil's mood, it made Nilsson a superstar.

Nilsson came across the song through his producer. "I happened to be at RCA one day and my producer, Rick Jarrard, was listening to a Fred Neil album," Nilsson recalled. "He played me a cut which he had intended to use with a group called Stone Country. I liked it a lot and we decided to record it."

Nilsson brought a purity and innocence to the vocal part that was augmented by strings and bittersweet arrangement by George Tipton.

'Everybody's Talkin'' launched Nilsson – his fan base to that point was confined to the LA hipsters and cognoscenti. He was better known as a songwriter for *Three Dog Night* than as a vocalist. Following this hit, his biggest success was as an interpretative singer.

"I mean it sold a million copies and it will make a lot of money. But I just don't feel that it has made me successful. It hasn't fulfilled any of my goals," Nilsson said. "I don't know what those goals are, but 'Everybody's Talkin'' wasn't one of them. I guess I'll only find out when I get there. All this hit has given me is a little more confidence."

"'Everybody's Talkin'' … I find that a very strange and beautiful song," said master songsmith Jerry Leiber. "I didn't like much of the material that came out in the hippie period, I didn't like the psychedelic frame of reference, but Fred Neil wrote some things that were surreal, and they were truly beautiful melodically and lyrically."

Let's Stay Together   Al Green

(Al Green/Al Jackson Jr/Willie Mitchell) ✳ HI ✳ 1972 ✳ Appears on: *Let's Stay Together*

'Let's Stay Together' was Al Green's second number one hit. It was a softer vocal from the Sam Cooke devotee but the groove was more complex.

"All my life I have tampered in jazz chords," said producer Willie Mitchell. "One Saturday afternoon I was tampering around on the piano and I came up with this melody of 'Let's Stay Together'. I played it for Al on the piano. Al Jackson was playing drums with his hands, creating the rhythm. So Al said, 'Give me five minutes and I'll write some words to it.' About fifteen minutes later he came back with some words and we started messing with the song. About a week later we put the track down."

Mitchell's approach to recording Green was to "keep it funky and keep it simple."

Lyrically the song is not simple – it has a prismatic view of relationships – is it over and he wants it back? Is it a song of devotion? Mostly the answer is in the groove. It's a very pure love song that is as multifaceted as love itself. The song has been widely covered but never with the style and the smoothness of Green's original.

"Once after a performance," Green recalled, "this couple walks up to me, about forty-seven years old, and they're holding hands, smiling, and they say, 'You know, we're newlyweds and the reason for us getting married was that song you done, 'Let's Stay Together'.' Now, that's what I call getting through!"

Summertime   Big Brother & the Holding Company

(D Hayward/G Gershwin) ✳ Columbia ✳ 1968 ✳ Appears on: *Cheap Thrills*

George Gershwin's exquisite ballad from *Porgy and Bess* has been rendered by so many great artists that it stands as one of the true highpoints of 20th-century song. Janis Joplin understood exactly that when she included it in the Big Brother set.

The recording of *Cheap Thills*, the second Big Brother album, was fraught with tension. Producer John Simon was an exacting perfectionist with a background in classical music and was blessed with perfect pitch. Big Brother on the other hand could barely and rarely tune their instruments. In between the two was Janis Joplin – full of ambition for the recording and loyalty to her band.

Much of the album has the soulful, bluesy feel that made Joplin's reputation. Then there is this psychedelic reading of Gershwin's sublime melody.

Sam Andrew introduces the song with his own arrangement of Bach's 'Prelude in C Minor' played at half tempo. According to Simon, "the band seemed to think you could simulate Bach when each musician played a stream of steady eighth notes.

They hadn't paid much attention to the fact that eighth notes always had to create harmony between them. As a result the Bach they made was much more dissonant than I suspect even they had hoped."

Once Joplin's voice comes in she transforms the track, tripping through the jazz and blues and pop inflections of the melody and confidently claiming this song of hope for her own. Even Simon, who hated the album so much he took his name off the credits, called the song "exquisitely beautiful".

Walking on Thin Ice Yoko Ono

(Yoko Ono) ✳ Geffen ✳ 1981 ✳ Appears on: *Season of Glass*

Yoko probably did break up the Beatles. John Lennon frequently said that Ono saved him and certainly she rescued him as an artist. Almost everything that Lennon did after first meeting Ono was directly influenced by her, and the material he wrote without her was the poorer for it. His final sessions, the *Double Fantasy* album, were a joint effort but the best elements were clearly Ono's simple but strong ideas compared with Lennon's silly love songs.

Ono came from an avant-garde background working with musicians and composers like LaMonte Young, John Cage and Ornette Coleman. Lennon taught her about pop music and her best work melds the two worlds.

Lennon and Ono were mixing 'Walking on Thin Ice' on the evening that he was shot. That context reshapes this song into a chilling widow's lament. A tough, unsentimental dance beat forms the background over which Ono wails the dirge of a widow whose husband is shot in front of her eyes. It's one of the most powerful pieces of pop music. The lyrics are spare and very pregnant without platitudes. It's closer to haiku than the Beatles. The music acknowledges the hard edges that were coming out of the post-punk scene. It's visceral and bitter and brutal in ways that most music only pretends to be. You can't take too much of this reality.

Babylon New York Dolls

(David Johansen/Johnny Thunders) ✳ Mercury ✳ 1974 ✳

Appears on: *Too Much Too Soon*

Elegantly wasted. The New York Dolls took the Rolling Stones blueprint – obsessive love of R&B and pop music plus great style in clothes – and gave it a downtown New York context. The New York Dolls were so far over the top of what was thought

to be acceptable in the early '70s that they stood no chance of being understood once they left the island of Manhattan. Of course history has given them their due as complete originals.

As devotees of '60s pop, it made sense for the Dolls to enlist Shangri-Las producer Shadow Morton to help with their second album, *Too Much Too Soon*.

"The Dolls had energy, sort of a disciplined weirdness," said Morton. "I took them into the room as a challenge. I was bored with the music and the business. The Dolls can certainly snap you out of boredom. We were pushing it. We were running twenty-six hours each day. They had an incredible amount of energy. God, I remember the scenes in the studio . . . the word intense is not intense enough! I let them do what they naturally did and merely tried to catch some of it on tape."

The Dolls had great ideas. They couldn't play that well. They had terrible problems with drugs. In the studio they dressed up the R&B songs and then pulled them apart with a trashy nonchalance. 'Babylon', which opened the album, is a tribute to what downtown New York was like at the time – junkies, strippers and guys going nowhere fast. It was not a long stretch from here to the Ramones and Television and Blondie.

The Dolls tottered through the song like a tipsy drag queen negotiating the street on platform shoes. All dressed up to go out in style.

I Want You to Want Me Cheap Trick

(Rick Nielsen) ✳ Epic ✳ 1979 ✳ Appears on: *At Budokan*

In one of those ironies of pop, Cheap Trick had dumped 'I Want You to Want Me' from their set before their first Japanese tour in April 1978. The group had two unsuccessful albums out in the US but were superstars in Japan. They were overwhelmed. They went from playing bars in the US to the Budokan, Japan's major stadium. "The first night we almost dropped our gear," said drummer Bun E Carlos. "We didn't know it was coming; it freaked us out."

They were short of material on tour and put 'I Want You to Want Me' back in the set. The group had been working with producer Tom Werman, who had smoothed some of the rough edges from Cheap Trick's bar-band sound. 'I Want You to Want Me' had been written years earlier as an ironic pop song but now the wit went into the musical phrases and harmonies, and allowed the song to be a magnificent anthem of teen love.

At Budokan, originally recorded as a Japan-only release, became a massive hit in the US.

"It's hard when you don't really know what made you famous," said Carlos. "We didn't know why people liked the live versions and not the studio versions. We didn't know what to do next."

Just a Little Lovin' Dusty Springfield

(Barry Mann/Cynthia Weil) ✳ Atlantic/Philips ✳ 1968 ✳ Appears on: *Dusty in Memphis*

The opening track to *Dusty in Memphis* is pop music at its most sensual. You can hear the mussed bed-hair in her playful voice and the warm, dreamy sexuality of its come-on. The track has delightful jazz chords from Eddie Hinton's guitar and a smooth southern groove that plays off against Dusty's Englishness.

Dusty in Memphis is the masterpiece from England's greatest pop vocalist of all time and this track is the irresistible come-on that the next ten deliver on.

Now recognised as a pivotal moment in pop music, the Memphis sessions were not as easy as the grooves suggest. Springfield was an established artist; the first British singer to invade the US in the wake of the Beatles. She signed to Atlantic specifically for the opportunity to work with producer Jerry Wexler, the undisputed master of soul music. Wexler then called on the crack team of co-producer Tom Dowd, arranger Arif Mardin and the cream of Memphis players. However, as she recalled to the *Oxford American*, Springfield was deeply unhappy and unsure for the entire project.

"It was a difficult situation," she told Ben Fong Torres in 1973. "The only person who knows what to do with me is me. I wasn't given very much chance to say what I wanted to say. Also, I lost a lot of confidence because I was basically still a foreigner. I'm working here at a hit machine, and who am I to argue with them? So I backed down.

"I just didn't like the mix. The songs, I liked. I had lots to do with choosing them. I don't know what went wrong. They just couldn't find more material for me; they didn't know what to do with me."

Things went so poorly in the studio that Dusty didn't sing anything in Memphis – the vocals were done later in New York.

In the liner notes to the 2002 reissue of *Dusty in Memphis*, Elvis Costello said, "Dusty Springfield's singing on this album is among the very best ever put on record by anyone. It is overwhelmingly sensual and self-possessed but it is never self-regarding. The delivery might be confident, intimate or vulnerable in the opening lines of a song only to explode in the chorus with unknowable emotion. Every crescendo is well judged ..." Nowhere is this more evident than on the opening track.

Four singles – 'Son of a Preacher Man', 'Forget about Me', 'Breakfast in Bed' and 'Windmills of Your Mind' – were pulled from the album, but 'Just a Little Lovin'' was overlooked.

"I didn't like 'Son of a Preacher Man'," Springfield said in 1973. "I knew it was a hit song, but I didn't like the record; I liked the other side ['Just a Little Lovin'']." Me too.

A Message to You Rudy The Specials

(Lee 'Scratch' Perry/Lee Thompson) ✲ 2 Tone ✲ 1979 ✲ Appears on: *The Specials*

With punk rock in full flight in the UK, reviving the past glories of the early rock & roll years, it was only a matter of time before the mods and their musical accessory, ska, returned also. Ska (with its variations of blue beat and rock-steady) is a limited style of Jamaican music, which was popular for a couple of years before it evolved into reggae. It fell to keyboardist Jerry Dammers to start the ska revival with his outfit, the Specials. They came properly accessorised with the tight suits and the small hats, the scooters and the attitude. Their sworn enemies were the skinheads who similarly recreated the look and racist ideology of the original skins ten years earlier. Unfortunately the skins too had loved ska so, right from the start, the music came with its own tension.

England has always been a land of subcultures. Tribes of skinheads, mods, teddy boys and rastas had existed since the '60s. After punk rock and its new tribes arrived under a media spotlight, culture wars erupted, sometimes violently. Jerry Dammers well understood British pop culture. He created a new tribe – the modern rude boy – and the Specials came not just with a sound but an ideology. Dammers also formed his own label, 2 Tone, and developed logos and design ideas to brand both band and label. Other groups – notably Madness and The Beat – sprung up in The Specials' wake. Both went on to significant success over the next decade.

Ska drew out the pus on the simpering wound of racism that existed in the UK at the time. The Specials were proudly multi-racial and they talked it like they walked it. They were a ferocious live band with two singers and a horn section; the insistent beat of ska hopped up a few notches in honour of the punk years. Their music was less laid-back, more passionate and darker than classic ska.

There was a real intensity to the Specials that matched the agit-rock of the Clash and Elvis Costello. 'A Message to You Rudy' was their second single and, produced by Elvis Costello, it had a raw power missing from Dandy Livingstone's rock-steady original.

Opus 40 Mercury Rev

(Jonathan Donahue/Mercury Rev) ❋ V2 ❋ 1998 ❋ Appears on: *Deserter's Songs*

Mercury Rev is one of those few groups who can overcome their own hype. The Rev – Jonathan Donahue and Sean 'Grasshopper' Mackiowiak – came in on the same dispassionate slacker horse as Dinosaur Jnr. Based in upstate New York, however, they gradually became less slacker and with that commitment came some of the most passionate American music of recent years. Their breakthrough was *Deserter's Songs* and the key track 'Opus 40'. Donahue has a vaporous singing style that blows around the melody. On *Deserter's Songs* they teamed up with a couple of locals – drummer Levon Helm and organist Garth Hudson of the Band. Not only does their presence put Mercury Rev into a definite tradition, but it also gives the record an earthy grounding. Donahue in particular has a great ear for texture and for experiment but the end result on 'Opus 40' is the synthesis of the avant-garde and roots music. The music, too, matches the lyric, which dives into existential pain. "*Deserter's Songs* is more internalised," Donahue told *MOJO*'s Andy Gill. "I think the lyrics are a lot deeper embedded emotionally. The record has to do with feeling deserted and at the same time deserting someone. It's like love: sometimes you're leaving and sometimes she's leaving – it's never easy to quite say which."

Cold Turkey Plastic Ono Band

(John Lennon) ❋ Apple ❋ 1970 ❋ Appears on: *Live Peace in Toronto*

On a whim John Lennon agreed to play at a festival in Toronto to aid world peace. Lennon's real motivations are unclear still but it seemed like a good idea at the time.

The Plastic Ono Band was hastily assembled – Eric Clapton on guitar, session drummer Alan White, bass player Klaus Voorman and John Lennon and Yoko Ono. Rehearsals took place on the aeroplane flight between London and Toronto. It had been four years since Lennon had last played to a large audience at Candlestick Park in San Francisco. The ex-Beatle was in a difficult place creatively. He was keen to make music with Yoko but felt constrained to remain with the Fab Four. His tastes in music were right out on left-field or back in the '50s, so that's what the Plastic Ono Band did – a series of rock & roll covers and some long improvisations for Yoko's avant-garde workouts.

Lennon was ill before going on stage, vomiting with stage fright. Then he came out and tore through a quick set.

'Cold Turkey' is a song about heroin withdrawal – something that he and Yoko and Clapton were all familiar with. This live version of the song, which had recently been a single, is raw and naked and on the edge, full of fear and pain and much more intense than the studio version. Clapton tears apart the guitar lines at the top of his game and with an aggression not usually found in his playing. Lennon just lets it all out and Yoko's vocals in support add to the drama. On this song Lennon achieves what he had struggled to do on the last Beatles' sessions and his own solo singles – express a modern sensibility with the crude power of '50s rock & roll.

Heartbreak Hotel Elvis Presley

(Mae Boren Axton/Tommy Durden/Elvis Presley) ✳ RCA ✳ 1956 ✳
Appears on: *Elvis Presley*

Elvis Presley was still a rockabilly singer in Memphis when he discovered the 'Heartbreak Hotel'. Jacksonville schoolteacher and mother of two Mae Boren Axton had written the song with Tommy Durden, inspired by a suicide victim who'd left a note that read "I walk a lonely street". Axton was moved to pick up a pen. "I said to Tommy, 'Everybody in the world has somebody who cares. Let's put a Heartbreak Hotel at the end of this lonely street.'"

Axton was writing for the teen press and had done some publicity for Presley's manager Colonel Tom Parker and through him reached the singer. Elvis liked the song enough to not only record it but to take a third of the publishing credit and income.

'Heartbreak Hotel' was to be his first national number one hit.

Elvis recorded the song at RCA's Nashville studio on 10 January 1956 with Scotty Moore on electric guitar, Bill Black on bass, DJ Fontana on drums and Floyd Cramer on piano. The reverb that dominates the sound of the track was created by putting a speaker at the end of a hallway. It was the second song recorded at the session, only two days past Presley's twenty-first birthday.

'Heartbreak Hotel' is a kind of ghoulish song. It was not the usual Top 40 fare. It was released as a single on 17 January 1956 and went on to sell two million copies. Mae Axton's son became a major country star and the writer of many hit records himself.

Dancing Queen ABBA

(Benny Andersson/Stig Anderson/Björn Ulvaeus) ✳ Polygram ✳ 1977 ✳
Appears on: *Arrival*

Like any mega pop group, ABBA was not going to buck a trend. So when disco ruled the American airwaves, ABBA went disco. 'Dancing Queen' was ABBA's only number one record in the US.

According to the *All Music Guide*, 'Dancing Queen' was originally called 'Boogaloo' and was based on George McCrae's 1974 disco single 'Rock Your Baby'. Over the course of some months, 'Dancing Queen' evolved with lyrics, partly contributed by ABBA manager Stig Anderson. Benny Andersson and Björn Ulvaeus gradually developed the rhythm track, which is a Euro pop version of American disco – supposedly with a New Orleans influence care of Dr John. Essentially ABBA was replicating the "wall of sound". The major difference between ABBA and Spector is the grandeur of the vision. Where Spector built a monument to passion and romance, 'Dancing Queen' was more filigree and immediate. Where Spector created a mansion, ABBA had a nightclub. Which is not to take anything from 'Dancing Queen'.

The vocals were layered so that Frida Lyngstad and Agnetha Faltskog were entwined in the mystery of the dancing queen. The dynamism of the vocal track is enhanced by the fact that the vocal is brought in halfway through a chorus. 'Dancing Queen' was the ultimate in Euro pop; seductive but not sexy. Like all good pop it was filled with the promise of a Saturday night in your best dress.

Heroin The Velvet Underground

(Lou Reed) ❋ Verve ❋ 1967 ❋ Appears on: *The Velvet Underground & Nico*

This was not the first song about hard drugs in the canon of popular music. It was the first song that told it like it was. The innovation of Lou Reed's writing in this song was the dispassion; there are no moral judgements, simply a statement of the experience.

After leaving college, Lou Reed worked for a music publisher, Pickwick, turning out anonymous would-be Top 40 tunes. It was here that he wrote 'Heroin'. Unsurprisingly, Pickwick thought there was little commercial potential. The Velvet Underground, though, was ideal for this literary material because they mixed in art circles (the group comprised a couple of English graduates and a fine music graduate in John Cale). The song is worked up in an organic warm style that belies the subject matter.

The group had also found it difficult to get a recording deal. According to guitarist Dr Sterling Morrison, "Ahmet Ertegun liked it, but said, 'No, no, no, none of this – no drug songs.' Then we took it over to Elektra, who said some of the content was unacceptable and the whole sound was unacceptable. 'This viola – can't Cale play anything else?'

"So then we talked to Tom Wilson, who was still at Columbia. He told us to wait and come and sign with him when he moved to Verve because he swore that at Verve we could do anything we wanted. And he was right. We gave something up of course because there was no effective marketing on Verve; we were stuck there with the Mothers of Invention and Richie Havens."

Artist Andy Warhol financed the making of the album at a reported cost of $2500. The recording conditions were difficult in that one studio was barely finished and didn't work properly.

Tom Wilson, one of the great producers of the '60s, signed the group to Verve largely because he was romantically interested in singer Nico but played very little part in the recording of the record.

According to drummer Mo Tucker, "'Heroin' is such a good song but it's a pile of garbage on the record. The guys couldn't have their amps up loud in the studio so I couldn't hear anything. When we got to the part where you speed up it became this mountain of drum noise. I couldn't hear shit. So I just stopped and, being a little wacky, they just kept going. And that's the one we took."

Frank Zappa delayed the release of the Velvet's album to avoid the release of the Mothers of Invention. No radio stations would touch it and according to Morrison, "They wouldn't even accept advertising for the album, because it was about drugs and sex and perversion."

So what? 'Heroin' changed the way rock & roll songs were written ever after.

Hope R.E.M.

(Leonard Cohen/Michael Stipe/Peter Buck/Mike Mills) ❋ Warner Bros. ❋ 1998 ❋
Appears on: *Up*

Having just lost drummer and founding member Bill Berry, the chemistry of R.E.M. was profoundly changed and the group was in crisis during the sessions for this LP. They have subsequently disowned the album; however, I personally think it's one of their best. It's electronic and computerised and muddy all at once. 'Hope' has not only the slightly futuristic sound of the turn-of-the-century R.E.M. but in a slightly psychotic arrangement.

"All our previous road maps were destroyed," said Mills. "We were given this opportunity to totally do anything we wanted to."

"We managed to take all the '70s technology and tie in the '90s technology and we ended up with kind of real modern psychedelic record," said Buck. "I don't think psychedelia ended in the '60s. DJ Shadow or the Chemical Brothers sound really psychedelic to me. The first day we got in the studio they were doing drum sounds and I was bored and I walked down the street to this shop that sells '60s poster art, Fillmore stuff. I went in and brought twenty of them. It was great; we had Moby Grape, Jefferson Airplane, Lenny Bruce and all those people looking down at us, which was nice.

"Michael had writer's block. He was like, 'Oh jeez, this is so much stuff. I'm completely staggered by what you've done', and so little of it sounded like R.E.M. He had to really challenge himself. Later he said, 'You did a good job, I was just overwhelmed by it all.' He's happy with it now."

'Hope' deals with the dialectic struggle between religion and science while using some melody and lyric from Leonard Cohen's 'Suzanne'.

"I was real excited about exploring the place where the two big bullies in the opposite corners, religion/spirituality and science/technology, come clashing together," Stipe explained. "That was something I'd been thinking about a lot. That's pretty evident in several of the songs. The song 'Hope' is the most obvious place. And then the usual R.E.M. territory of identity and memory and dreams and where the real world and the fantastic world come together and overlap."

Sunday Bloody Sunday U2

(Bono/Adam Clayton/The Edge/Larry Mullen Jr) ✳ Island ✳ 1983 ✳ Appears on: *War*

On Sunday 30 January 1972 soldiers from the British Army's 1st Parachute Regiment opened fire on unarmed civilian demonstrators in the Bogside, Londonderry, in Northern Ireland. Thirteen demonstrators were killed protesting the British policy of internment without trial. Bloody Sunday highlighted the butchery and uselessness of the British occupation of Northern Island in the public consciousness. It was a turning point in the struggle for a republic. The first Bloody Sunday was 21 November 1920. Republican activist Michael Collins assassinated fourteen British intelligence officers known as "the Cairo Gang". In response the British army descended on a football game at Croke Park in Dublin, slaughtering hundreds of spectators, some as young as eleven years old.

In 1983 U2, who were Protestants from Eire (the south), put their views on the issue into this song.

The Edge began writing the lyric while Bono was away on his honeymoon. The initial take on the song was stridently anti-violence. The original first line was, "Don't talk to me about the rights of the IRA". Together they made the lyrics more general and concentrated on the central existential question, "How long must I sing this song".

"It means so much to me, that song, because . . . I'm not sure I got it right," Bono told the late Timothy White. "I mighta got it wrong, I'm not sure. I originally wanted to contrast the day, Sunday Bloody Sunday, when thirteen innocent people were shot dead in 'Derry by the British army, with Easter Sunday. I wanted to make this contrast because I thought that it pointed out the awful irony of the fact that these two warring faiths share the same belief in the one God. And I thought how . . . it's so absurd, really, this Catholic and Protestant rivalry. So that's what I wanted to do. In the end, I'm not sure I did that successfully with the words. But we certainly did it with the music. The spirit of the song speaks louder than the flesh of it."

Maybelline Chuck Berry

(Chuck Berry) ✳ Chess ✳ 1955 ✳ Appears on: *The Anthology*

Chuck Berry was born 18 October 1926 in St Louis, Missouri. His father, Henry, was a deacon in the local church and his mother, Martha, a schoolteacher. After an early run-in with the law over joyriding in a car, Berry tried a number of professions including hairdressing and photography, while keeping up his guitar playing. On New Year's Eve 1952, he joined the Sir John Trio, led by stride piano player Johnnie Johnson. The Sir John Trio played the Cosmopolitan Club in St Louis and it was here that Berry played around with the country song 'Ida Red'. In 1955 while in Chicago, Berry met Muddy Waters, who introduced Berry to Chess Records.

When Berry arrived at Chess studios on 21 May 1955 he was hoping to start a career as a blues musician in the style of Muddy Waters. Producer and proprietor Leonard Chess had other ideas.

Berry had a song called 'Ida Red' about a duel between a Ford and a Cadillac, Chess changed the name of the song to 'Maybelline', which was the name on a cosmetics packet on the studio floor, and recorded this hillbilly blues number.

Four songs were recorded in the session: 'Maybelline', 'Wee Wee Hours', 'Thirty Days' and 'Together We Will Always Be'. Backing Berry's guitar and vocal were Johnny Johnson on piano, the legendary Willie Dixon on bass, Jerome Green on the maracas and Jasper Thomas on drums. The combination of hillbilly and blues with the driving drums was a unique sound.

"The body of the story of 'Maybelline' was composed from memories of high school and trying to get girls to ride in my 1934 V-8 Ford," wrote Berry in his autobiography. There is another subtext to this battle between a Cadillac and a Ford that is class warfare.

Chess knew they had a hit. To ensure its success, Leonard Chess gave influential disc jockey Alan Freed and his associate Russ Fratto two-thirds of the writing credits and publishing income. The song was released in July 1955 and was the most important single track in the development of rock & roll, introducing the pivotal role of the guitar and of the singer/songwriter. Berry was rewarded by being hounded by the police and put in jail.

Black & White The dBs

(Peter Holsapple) ✳ ✳ IRS ✳ 1981 ✳ Appears on: *Stands for Decibels*

"If we are seen as a revivalist group then it's melody and memory we're reviving," said Peter Holsapple, guitarist/founder of the dBs. He and Chris Stamey were pop nerds, forever entranced by the spell of sweet pop melodies especially coming from the like of Big Star, the Raspberries, the Beach Boys and other '60s artists. Like rock critics, they were attuned to pop music that was never actually really popular in the chart sense. Certainly by the early '80s when the dBs were issuing records it was not popular at all. This was a time of big drum sounds and simplistic songs. The dBs were too clever to have hits. They were art pop.

Stamey and Holsapple had worked together with Alex Chilton before making a debut album as the dBs. Their songs were filled with cute ideas – snatches of guitar melody, innovative production sounds and clever lyrics. They didn't have strong vocals, however, and the songs were probably too clever for their own good. 'Black & White', which kicks off the first album, *Stands for Decibels*, is a perfect example of the dBs at their best – the instruments play off each other with a vicious, almost sarcastic irony. Will Rigby's drums bounce around the track adding depth and colour. This was not the '60s pastiche of so many groups in the day, but genuinely adventurous '80s music with fresh ideas and joy and excitement in its execution.

On 'Black & White' Holsapple takes the perennial battle of the sexes and skews it enough so that it's a completely fresh look at the conflict while still sounding familiar. This kind of art pop was an influence on R.E.M. and the better alternative unpop pop of the '90s. But the original is still classic.

Suspicious Minds Elvis Presley

(Mark James) ✳ RCA ✳ 1969 ✳ Appears on: *From Memphis to Vegas*

Elvis Presley's self-reinvention in the late '60s was an extraordinary achievement. The greatest rock & roll star, the King was in decline as a consequence of ten years of song choices and increasingly poor films. Elvis was pretty much finished as a recording artist until he returned to Memphis for the 1968 *From Elvis in Memphis* album and a subsequent TV special.

By the late '60s, Memphis was a music capital with its writers turning out country-soul hits. The field was there for Presley to claim. What he needed, though, was the right material.

Lincoln 'Chips' Moman, an esteemed songwriter and producer, was one of the fathers of country soul. He had made a record with singer/songwriter Mark James that had flopped but did have a song for Presley, 'Suspicious Minds'. Usually the singer demanded a cut of the songwriting royalties but, whether out of perversity or cunning, Moman refused to split the track with Presley and finally the King conceded.

The song was cut at Moman's American studios. The sessions, over two days, yielded thirty-five songs. Somewhere between four and seven in the morning of the first session Presley captured 'Suspicious Minds' on the fourth take. The song is full of speedy paranoid energy. The band is well oiled and Presley sings as if everything depends on it. He allows his vulnerability to come through as well; it's a remarkably open performance. The success of 'Suspicious Minds' sealed the King's comeback and it remained a centrepiece of his repertoire until his final concert.

Before Today Everything But The Girl

(Ben Watt) ❋ Atlantic ❋ 1996 ❋ Appears on: *Walking Wounded*

Ben Watt of Everything But The Girl was laid up for a year with a terrible and rare disease. In the meantime, Todd Terry remixed Tracey Thorn's vocal and Massive Attack asked her to sing on their second album and Watt began DJing in clubs. The straight-laced, nice middle-class pair with a solid line in sophisticated jazz/folk were suddenly the doyens of the club scene. On the *Walking Wounded* album they forsook guitars for trip hop beats.

"It's mostly through the DJing lately that this nocturnal existence has opened up to me," said Watt. "I used to drive up to my DJ gigs and drive home and would therefore have to remain fairly sober, and the activities of most people on the streets at night are almost cartoon-like in their extremity.

"I became more and more intrigued with the way we go out to dance and drink with each other, and yet so many of us end up going home alone. There seemed to be a really interesting tension between the community spirit of the night, and the way the city can be quite an alienating place. Simple lines like 'Are you on your own?' are pregnant with meaning. On the one hand you're asking, 'Are you lonely?' and on the other hand it's just a straightforward pickup line. All that seemed to appeal to the Everything But The Girl frame of mind."

Watt embraced the underground culture of clubs in the way that he had enjoyed punk a decade-and-a-half earlier. Electronic music also offered new colours of melancholy for both Watt and Thorn. 'Before Today' may have its share of electronic beats and samples but the sentiments are timeless. It's writing of this order that helps to move a style such as trip hop from being a gimmick into an expressive palette. The alienation and warmth that go with the sound adds to the desperate and direct message of the lyric.

"I like being the human voice in that context," said Thorn. "When you've done acoustic music for a long time, you reach a point where you feel everything's coming from the same place. It's more interesting to set up this tension between the music that's being generated electronically and a voice like mine, which is almost completely without any kind of artifice. It's a very simple voice, and I think if it works then that's perhaps why."

Since I Left You The Avalanches

(R Chater/A Diblasi/E Drennen/G McQuilten/J Salo/D Seltmann/J Webb) ❋ Modular ❋ 2000 ❋ Appears on: *Since I Left You*

Melbourne collective the Avalanches had a haunting quality to their collage of samples and sounds. While the first major track from them, 'Frontier Psychiatrist', was quirky and fun in the way that cut-and-paste records can be; with 'Since I Left You' there was something more haunting. The snatches of melodies, the rhythm of repetition and the underlying groove all hang together in a way that is unsettling. There is a gorgeous elegance to the track and a deep sadness. The song was originally written around the tragic story of Daryl Buggins, Australia's Evil Knievel, who committed suicide.

"Musically that song hung around for about three years," Avalanche Robbie Chater told *Juice* magazine. "We used to do a silly song over the instrumental break about Daryl Buggins. That bit about Daryl had to go, unsurprisingly, but we kept the loop and then used it when we found the vocal sample."

The Avalanches' secret was their ability to shop – specifically for old vinyl. "We scoured every charity shop in Melbourne," said Darren Seltmann. "We divided the city into a grid and went through every one. We'd buy up loads wholesale and listen to them for possible lifts and then sell of all the ones we'd rejected by putting an ad in the local paper. We'd get rid of a thousand at a time occasionally."

"We knew what we were looking for," said Chater. "We'd go for that era at the beginning of stereo recording and labels that were well recorded. There's signposts."

(Your Love Keeps Lifting Me) Higher and Higher
Jackie Wilson

(Gary Jackson/Raynard Miner/Carl Smith) ✳ Brunswick ✳ 1967 ✳

Appears on: *Mr Excitement*

Jackie Wilson needed to be lifted up in 1967. The soul singer was one of the leaders in his field, having sung his way off the Detroit assembly lines and into the charts, first with the Dominoes vocal group and then as a star in his own right.

Then, on the evening of 15 February 1961, he was on his way back to his New York apartment. A fan he passed in the lobby followed him upstairs. When he opened the door to her knock, Juanita Jones shot him in the torso and the lower back with a .38 calibre revolver. Wilson survived the assault but his career was severely curtailed and then further damaged by the arrival of the Beatles and the sea change that followed.

In 1967 he teamed with Chicago producer Carl Smith. The best of their efforts was 'Higher and Higher', which drew on a gospel arrangement as played by the legendary Motown ensemble the Funk Brothers (bassist James Jamerson, drummer Richard 'Pistol' Allen, guitarist Robert White and keyboardist Johnny Griffith) and Wilson's delicate soul singing to create a classic. The track was cut on 7 July 1967, and Wilson was back at the top of the charts for one last go round.

"My luck really changed because Carl came up with some good stuff," said Wilson. "I always wanted to try things like that and to me 'Higher' was more gospel than R&B, nearer to what I'd sung as a kid. I felt more at home."

Lowdown Boz Scaggs

(David Paich/Boz Scaggs) ❊ Columbia ❊ 1976 ❊ Appears on: *Silk Degrees*

After six or seven years of trying different approaches, Boz Scaggs hit on his most commercial album and what became the gold standard for blue-eyed soul in the late '70s. Scaggs teamed up with a crew of new session players – Jeff Porcaro, David Paich and David Hungay – who became Toto. He wrote with Paich and developed melodic ideas beyond his capacity as a guitarist. He hung up his instrument in favour of concentrating on the vocals, which were perfectly slick to the last note and coloured by tasteful horn arrangements. This was adult contemporary music before there was such a category. Scaggs' singing had a certain soulfulness and integrity that warmed these tracks and lifted them out of the blandness of most soft rock music. The grooves were light but catchy and the backing tasteful. It was hard to be offended and the 'Lowdown' single is also hard to shake.

The record was not an instant hit, but radio play on a soul station spread the word across the world and the album sold four million copies and won a Grammy for 'Lowdown'.

Madame George Van Morrison

(Van Morrison) ❊ Warner Bros. ❊ 1968 ❊ Appears on: *Astral Weeks*

'Madame George' is a whirlpool of emotion and remembrance, of melancholy, joy and empathy. It's like a beautiful dream that takes you back to a place of innocence and freedom and purity and possibility. Listening to 'Madame George' you can hear, you can even smell, those vast blue-sky days of your childhood. 'Madame George' is potent music. It's the eye of *Astral Weeks*, an album that has been equalled but never bettered.

'Madame George' ostensibly takes place in the Belfast of Morrison's boyhood and he recalls events of his childhood and a character, Madam George, about whom young boys would gather. The identity of Madame George has been the subject of much speculation but there's been no illumination from the writer himself. Fellow Woodstock musician Happy Traum suggested to Morrison that Madame George was a drag queen. "Whatever gave you that impression?"

Morrison replied. "It all depends on what you want, that's all, how you want to go. If you see it as a male or as female or whatever, it's your trip. How do I see it? I see it as a . . . a Swiss cheese sandwich. Something like that."

Morrison isn't, I think, being disingenuous. Looking for a literal narrative here is missing the point. The song mixes up snatches of remembered moments but, essentially, Morrison is getting in touch with the ineffable.

"Sometimes you *do* know where the ideas are coming from and sometimes you don't," he said ten years later. "You might get a song coming through that you just don't know about. I didn't know what some of the stuff on *Astral Weeks* was about until years later. There's a lot of sub-conscious stuff you may write but you don't then suddenly sit down and take out your analytical books and say: I'm determined to find out where this came from. You'd probably be wrong anyway.

"If the spirit comes through in a 'Madame George'-type of song, that's what the spirit says. You have very little to do with it. You're like an instrument for what's coming through. It's the same thing as a primitive tribe of Africans, Indians, nomads or whatever – when they start getting up and doing their ritual and doing the dance, it's just what's coming through. It's the spirit. Rock & roll is still primitive. We might think that we're really intellectual and we're going to check out the library to research the meaning every time somebody puts out a new record. It's still primitive stuff. It's the same now as it was at the beginning. It's no different now. Rock & roll is spirit music – it's just coming through people. When you start to analyse it, it's only because you don't understand it. You're just not connecting with it once you have to start analysing it."

The *Astral Weeks* album was cut in three sessions in 1968. Producer Lewis Merenstein hired jazz players – Richard Davis on bass, guitarist Jay Berliner and Modern Jazz Quartet drummer Connie Kay were the core. The musicians were not chosen by Morrison and barely spoke with him during the sessions. They had his vocal and acoustic guitar part around which they improvised.

The first *Astral Weeks* session was booked for 7 p.m. 25 September at Century Sound studios in New York. 'Madame George' was the second song attempted.

"I can't remember ever really paying attention to the lyrics," said Davis. "We listened to him because you have to play along with the singer, but mostly we were playing with each other. We were into what we were doing, and he was into what he was doing and it just congealed.

"You know how it is at dusk, when the day has ended but it hasn't. There's a certain feeling about the seven-to-ten session. You've just come back from a dinner break, some guys have had a drink or two, it's this dusky part of the day, and everybody's relaxed. Sometimes that can be a problem – but with this record, I remember that the ambience of that time of day was all through everything we played."

'Madame George' is thick with atmosphere. The claustrophobia of Madame George's house, the free air of the kids skipping stones and then it leads up to the coda where Morrison goes into a trance scatting "the love that loves to love" and he's completely lost into that place beyond words, floating on Davis' liquid bass lines. Neither Van Morrison nor anyone else has found their way back there.

I Can't Get Next to You Al Green

(Barrett Strong/Norman Whitfield) ❋ Hi ❋ 1971 ❋ Appears on: *Gets Next to You*

Al Green was a struggling soul singer on the Chitlin Circuit when he met Willie Mitchell in 1969. Mitchell, then a trumpeter and bandleader, found Green at a gig in Texas and when the show was over he offered the singer the chance to record. "I suggested he come back to Memphis with me and cut a record," Mitchell recalled. "He said, 'How long will it take before I become a star?' I told him about eighteen months. He said, 'I don't have that long.'"

It was in fact 1970 when Green and Mitchell hit on their perfect sound and put Al Green on the charts with a remake of the Temptations hit, 'I Can't Get Next to You'.

Where there were five parts, Green pulled them all into one. Where the song was forceful and pushing, Green held it all back into a love groove. The Hi Records band that consisted of Al Jackson on drums and the Hodges brothers on everything else had the perfect light touch for Green's airy voice.

Al Green and Willie Mitchell found another way to make soul records and Green stepped into the space left vacant with the death of Otis Redding.

"To me," Green said, "Otis was like GATTA-GATTA-GATTA, you know, very choppy, which was very effective but a little rougher than me. I'm usually tinkling with the high notes and floating between the chords . . . trying to create some, uh, colour."

Mr Tambourine Man The Byrds

(Bob Dylan) ✳ Columbia ✳ 1965 ✳ Appears on: *Mr Tambourine Man*

"What we have here is a conscious effort to blend the sound of Dylan and John Lennon's voice. It was my purpose to do that, trying to aim right between them, to aim right between folk and rock, a place where nothing had been done and I was shooting for that," Byrds singer Roger McGuinn told Sid Griffin. "I just rearranged it into a Beatles song – as opposed to a two-four Dylan song, made it four-four and cut it down to one verse as radio wouldn't play anything over two and a half minutes back then."

The Byrds were folk musicians who had flipped out over the Beatles only months before this. It was a transition that Dylan was keen to make himself and McGuinn showed him the door.

Memphis legend and pianist Jim Dickson had heard an acoustic version of the song that had been cut for *Another Side of Bob Dylan* but left off the album. He played it for the Byrds, who were initially underwhelmed. Nonetheless they agreed to try it at a session for CBS on 20 January 1965 with Doris Day's son, Terry Melcher, producing. He was a friend of the Beach Boys and had already had success with hot-rod songs.

Hal Blaine's Wrecking Crew – Leon Russell, Larry Knetchel, Blaine and Jerry Cole – did the backing track. Byrds David Crosby and Gene Clark added harmonies. McGuinn copped a riff from Bach to introduce the song and also added his twelve-string guitar that gave rise to the jangly sound that has permeated American rock since.

Apparently, a lyric about drugs wasn't a problem and 'Tambourine Man' flew up the charts and pretty much started folk rock and the whole singer/songwriter tradition. Prior to the release of the Byrds' single Bob Dylan was highly regarded by beatniks and college protest kids but was not played on commercial radio.

"We weren't really thinking about the folk background," McGuinn said. "In fact, we were trying to subdue it and become legitimate rock & roll people. Fortunately, we weren't able to shake it, and the residue is what made us sound interesting."

Can't Buy Me Love The Beatles

(John Lennon/Paul McCartney) ✳ Parlophone ✳ 1964 ✳ Appears on: *A Hard Day's Night*

'Can't Buy Me Love' was the first truly perfect marriage of rock music and celluloid. The song features in Richard Lester's film *A Hard Day's Night* as the Fab Four, having been cooped up with the straight world, suddenly burst out of the fire escape door and down the metal staircase with the sound of this tough guitar riff ringing in their ears. Nothing before or since has expressed so well the liberating feeling of rock & roll.

Paul McCartney wrote 'Can't Buy Me Love' while on tour in France in January 1964 and it was cut in Paris – the only Beatles session to happen outside London. Lester included it in the film after rejecting the first song written for the sequence. George Martin also played a big role in the song by suggesting that it begin with its chorus, giving it not only a hook but also extra momentum. The driving rock of the verses and then the major key changes into the chorus are typical of how strong the Beatles were getting with composition. The guitar solo by Harrison is as unbridled as the sequence to which it was synced. *A Hard Day's Night* was the first all-Beatles written album and that reflected their independence and the pace at which they were growing. You can hear it all on this track.

Circle Game Joni Mitchell

(Joni Mitchell) ✳ Reprise ✳ 1970 ✳ Appears on: *Ladies of the Canyon*

Joni Mitchell was born Roberta Joan Anderson on 7 November 1943 in the province of Alberta, Canada. She aspired to be a graphic artist and painter but was drawn into the Canadian folk scene. It was in this milieu that she met another Canadian singer/songwriter Neil Young. They met in 1964 at the Fourth Dimension folk club at the University of Manitoba, and she encountered him again in the Yorkville district of Toronto in 1965. It was likely at the latter venue that Mitchell first heard Neil Young's 'Sugar Mountain', which he had written on his nineteenth birthday, regretting the loss of his youth.

Mitchell wrote 'Circle Game' in response: "So the years spin by and now the boy is twenty/Though his dreams have lost some grandeur coming true/There'll be new dreams, maybe better dreams and plenty/Before the last revolving year is through".

The song, full of compassion and wisdom and generosity, is remarkable for a twenty-one year, old as Mitchell then was.

In reply Neil Young wrote 'Sweet Joni from Saskatoon' for her. When she moved to Los Angeles, Young introduced her to his circle of friends, the leading tastemakers and powerbrokers in music at the time.

'Circle Game' was first recorded by folk duo Ian and Sylvia in 1966 and with 'Clouds' was one of her first hit songs.

"What I realise now is that songs like 'Circle Game' and 'Big Yellow Taxi' have almost become nursery rhymes, they've become part of the culture," Mitchell said recently. "I didn't write 'Circle Game' as a children's song, but I'm very pleased to see it go into the culture in that way."

Mack the Knife Bobby Darin

(Kurt Weill/Bertolt Brecht/Marc Blitzen [translation]) ✳ Atlantic ✳ 1959 ✳
Appears on: *That's All*

Another murder ballad that topped the charts. 'Mack the Knife' introduces the character of Macheath in Brecht and Weill's *The Threepenny Opera*. Given that Brecht was an outspoken Communist, it's somewhat surprising that *The Threepenny Opera* should have met with such a warm reception on Broadway. Even more surprising was that in the '50s the sound would be revived with a swing arrangement by Louis Armstrong and shortly thereafter by Bobby Darin.

Walden Robert Cassotto, aka Bobby Darin, was an accomplished and sophisticated songwriter who had been successful as a teen idol. Ahmet Ertegun, the urbane co-president of Atlantic, had an instinctive touch and teamed Darin up with 'Mack the Knife', taking him out of the pop world and into a more adult sphere.

"Jazz and blues records wasn't going to pay the rent," said engineer/producer Tom Dowd. "So they wanted to find something that was in that tradition that they enjoyed doing, that used the people that they had revered and idolised for so long,

and that they could exploit because it had some value. In the early days in New York City, nobody went out looking for Atlantic Records as a label they wanted to be on; they'd rather go to RCA or Columbia. So Atlantic was always on the look-out for new and innovative artists who could preserve the blues or jazz tradition, but the company was concerned that songs should be timely and would cater to the root of the artist, and at the same time would be merchandisable."

'Mack the Knife' made number one. It was the first non-R&B pop hit for Atlantic and helped establish the label's future.

Brecht would have appreciated the irony of his bloodthirsty song being sung by so many sophisticated bourgeois bachelors.

Come On The Rolling Stones

(Chuck Berry) ❊ Decca ❊ 1963 ❊ Appears on: *The Rolling Stones*

The Rolling Stones were the second cab off the rank. Once the Beatles had broken through it was apparent that there was a surge of interest in this beat music. The Beatles were essentially a pop band from the north. The Rolling Stones were a blues band from London and clearly cooler as a proposition. The Rolling Stones' manager Andrew Loog Oldham was a wonderful marketeer who understood sex appeal and the attraction of a dark side.

Unlike the Beatles, the Rolling Stones did not write their own material; rather, they refashioned American blues and R&B. For their first single Oldham chose 'Come On', an obscure Chuck Berry song. "It was middle ground," guitarist Keith Richards recalled. "It was also very pop. We threw it in with a couple of Bo Diddley's songs and I think it was chosen because it was so obviously more chart orientated."

Recorded in one take, 'Come On' has the urgency of the best Stones material. There's a frustration and a speedy anxiety as though life is passing by at breakneck pace.

"That one track did it," Richards recalled. "And then suddenly you're sitting there in that terrible jacket on *Top of the Pops* and going, 'This isn't the vision I had.'"

Like a Virgin Madonna

(Tom Kelly/Billy Steinberg) ※ Sire ※ 1984 ※ Appears on: *Like a Virgin*

This track told the world that Madonna was not here to mince words. It's about sex. The startling thing was how untroubled Madonna seemed to be about the whole affair. She took what could have been a torch song and just played with it. The production and the beats are light and airy and tossed off in a flirting style. Working with Chic producer Nile Rodgers the record had a masterful pop sheen and an innate sense of where the beat lay.

Mostly it's attitude that put Madonna into a class of her own. She was an icon to a generation of emancipated women. She sexualised everything. That "Boy Toy" buckle was pure irony and in taking control of her sexuality, Madonna was a leader in the next wave of emancipation.

'Like a Virgin' was controversial, with the Christian Right trying to keep it from the airwaves. Nonetheless it was Madonna's first number one single.

"I mean … there's a lot of really narrow-minded people," Madonna told MTV Europe, "I really can't predict how far-reaching that can be and how many people I can change and how much tolerance will grow of the messages I put in my music."

River Song Dennis Wilson

(Dennis Wilson/Steve Kalinich) ※ Caribou ※ 1977 ※ Appears on: *Pacific Ocean Blue*

"Dennis Wilson passed through New York last week to spread the word that the Beach Boys are no longer going to rely on their golden oldies to maintain their current status as a major concert attraction in the US," said a newspaper report from 1976.

Dennis Wilson, youngest Beach Boy, drummer, heartthrob and the only surfer in the group, may have wanted to move on but rock & roll's favourite dysfunctional family were never going to get past their mini epics of the beach. Wilson, however, was already writing the last great album of Beach Boys-related songs.

Despite having named the Beach Boys fifteen or so years before, Dennis was the least respected musician in the group. The lead vocals usually went to Mike Love or Carl Wilson and, of course, brother Brian was the resident genius who was as likely to make their album doing all the parts himself.

In the mid-'70s the Beach Boys were a nostalgia act, unable to make a listenable record. Factions in the group were satisfied with the money from the road and they still saw themselves as a pop band. Dennis Wilson's solo work was somewhat more sophisticated and album-orientated.

In desperation the group nestled under the wing of James William Guerico, the man behind the pop-jazz phenomenon Chicago. Meanwhile, with co-writer Steve Kalinich and co-producer Gregg Jakobson, Wilson put together his first solo album.

Pacific Ocean Blue begins with 'River Song', a magnificent piece of pop gospel that features the Double Rock Baptist Choir. On 'River Song' Wilson approaches the watery spirituality of the Beach Boys but in a context that could be made sense of.

Wilson binged his way through these sessions, as he did his life. For all that though, there is a sense of raw talent breaking through.

As it turns out with the Beach Boys, everything always goes back to the summer fun hits and Dennis Wilson, like his brother Brian, never did realise his full potential, although there's certainly a great record here.

Dirge Bob Dylan

(Bob Dylan) ✳ Columbia ✳ 1974 ✳ Appears on: *Planet Waves*

The lyric starts off with the lines "I hate myself for loving you and the weakness that it showed" and they just get less compassionate after that. With just Dylan playing piano and Robbie Robertson on guitar, 'Dirge' is a searing, vitriolic missive – as self-loathing, fear and hatred and shame all come to the fore by turns.

For the past three years Dylan had written love songs to his wife – indeed on the same sessions that he cut 'Dirge' there was 'Wedding Song' that was as clear a statement of devotion as you could find. 'Dirge' seems to come from some other place. The way the perspective moves around and the bitterness in the lyric is a pointer to the songs on *Blood on the Tracks*.

The turmoil that descended on Dylan in the '70s was just

beginning when he entered the studio to record *Planet Waves*. Dylan had agreed to his first major concert tour in almost eight years, going out with the Band as backing group and support act. It was the biggest rock & roll tour undertaken up to that time. Dylan's contract with Columbia Records had expired after a decade and he signed instead with David Geffen's Asylum. Things were not as smooth as they seemed.

'Dirge' was the shape of things to come.

Producer Rob Fraboni recalled that a version of the song had been cut early in the sessions for the album and they were mixing the record.

"All of a sudden, he came in and said, 'I'd like to try 'Dirge' on the piano'," Fraboni recalled. "We had recorded a version with only an acoustic guitar and a vocal a few days earlier ... we put up a tape and he said to Robbie, 'Maybe you could play guitar on this.' They did it once, Bob playing piano and singing and Robbie playing acoustic guitar. The second time was the take."

I Am Woman Helen Reddy

(Helen Reddy/Ray Burton) ✳ Capitol ✳ 1972 ✳ Appears on: *I Am Woman*

Australian singer Helen Reddy had one hit in the US with 'I Don't Know How to Love Him' but was struggling to establish herself there when she came up with an anthem for the burgeoning women's movement. The phrase 'I am woman, hear me roar' has since become part of common parlance.

"I wanted songs that reflected the very positive sense of self that I had gotten from the women's movement," she said. "I thought about the women in my family, how strong they all were, how, during the world wars and the depressions and the pretty-much-useless husbands, they had been the glue that held the family together.

"I wanted a song that reflected that, that was my idea of womanhood. I realised I was going to have to write it myself. I'd never thought about being a songwriter. I was lying in bed one night and the phrase, 'I am strong, I'm invincible, I am woman', kept going over and over in my head. I wasn't even sure what 'invincible' meant, but it sounded like the beginning of something.

"I had the lyrics and I was trying to write music to go with them, but I needed somebody to come in. The Executives was an Australian group I used to hang out with, we used to play water polo and stuff. I asked one of the guys in the band, Ray Burton, would he take a shot at it. So he wrote the music for the song.

"It was on my first album and it was mentioned in reviews but it never got any airplay. Then, as the women's movement became more and more popular, a producer at Columbia decided to make a film to exploit what they thought was a hula-hoop fad, this fad of women's lib. They put a script together out of Robyn Morgan's book *Sisterhood is Powerful*, which was a series of anecdotes. They wanted to use 'I Am Woman' under the opening credits. That version was on my third album and that was the version that became the hit."

It is somewhat ironic that Reddy enlisted a man to co-write the song.

"Helen used to have a dozen of her girlfriends sometimes come up on a Sunday and no guys allowed," Burton recalled. "I was allowed up there a couple of times. But there I was – one guy with a dozen girls and they're all whingeing about their husbands and their boyfriends. They went home and I'm still there with Helen having a wine and I said, 'look, if you're really serious about this why don't you write some words down and I'll take it away and make a song out of it?' That's basically what happened. She wrote it out on a piece of paper. The next day I took them home and worked on it and then 'I Am Woman' evolved from it.

"I find it very disheartening that Helen never mentioned my name in any interviews."

"'I Am Woman' is my legacy," said Reddy. "I have so many women, to this day, who will come up to me in public and say, your song gave me the courage to get out of an abusive relationship, or it was because of your song I went to law school or things like that."

I-94 Radio Birdman

(Deniz Tek/Chris Jones) ✳ Trafalgar ✳ 1977 ✳ Appears on: *Burn My Eye*

Guitarist and songwriter Deniz Tek was raised in Michigan but moved to Sydney, Australia, with a white Epiphone guitar that had once belonged to Fred Sonic Smith of the MC5. The sound of the MC5 permeated Radio Birdman, the group Tek formed in 1974. There were plenty of other styles in there too – the New York Dolls, the Stooges, Jan and Dean, the Velvet Underground, Alice Cooper, the

Blue Oyster Cult, the Missing Links and the Rolling Stones, but pretty soon they had a sound and style all their own. In 1977 Radio Birdman was shaking Sydney apart just as the Clash was doing in London and the Ramones did in New York.

'I-94' was Tek's homesick note, name checking the interstate highway between Chicago and Detroit. It also contained the line "I got Garland Jeffreys on the car radio/You know I don't need you," which is among my very favourite couplets in rock & roll – especially when spat out by Birdman's singer Rob Younger. (The reference is to Jeffreys' single 'Wild in the Streets', which had been a regional hit in the early '70s.)

Financed by Anthony O'Grady, the editor of *RAM* magazine, Radio Birdman's first recording was an EP cut live just as the group was beginning to hit its straps. Teenage guitarist Chris Masuak added a melodic touch that complemented Tek's fierce, intense guitar playing and Ron Keeley's swinging drums while bass player Warwick Gilbert held the fire fight together and Younger seethed.

Tek told Birdman biographer Vivien Johnson, "I remember one day in Detroit, it was winter time and so many clouds and so much mist, you could look at the sun and all you could see was great distant sky behind the clouds. It was cold and bitter. It was like all snow and ice, grey streets and grey sun. I remember just looking at that and thinking it was a really powerful image and it came out in that song. I find those kind of days and those kind of landscapes moving. They make me feel kind off sad and kind of happy at the same time and I guess they show in my songs quite a bit. I actually wrote this song 'cause I was really homesick. I'd been in Australia about a year-and-a-half and I really wanted to go home bad, and I wrote some songs that are just full of Michigan references – this is one of them."

Dear Mr Fantasy Traffic

(Jim Capaldi/Steve Winwood/Chris Wood) ❋ Island ❋ 1967 ❋ Appears on: *Dear Mr Fantasy*

Traffic singer Steve Winwood had one of the most soulful voices in British pop as demonstrated by his work in the Spencer Davis Group. He abandoned that outfit and with three novices – drummer Jim Capaldi, saxophonist Chris Wood and guitar roadie Dave Mason – set out on a whimsical path.

"I was playing with this band, Deep Feeling, at the Elbow Room in Birmingham," said Capaldi. "Having dropped a large capsule of stuff courtesy of this rich kid from Bromsgrove, we were starting to do acid rock. Steve started to come and jam with us. He was attracted by this weird new energy that was coming out of our group."

Rather than stay in the centre of the action, Traffic moved to the countryside, to Sheepcott Farm, a former gatekeeper's cottage at Aston Tirrold, Berkshire. Tucked away in a copse of hazelnut and pine trees, the slate-roofed two-storey white stucco-fronted building had no electricity.

"We were living in a basement in London, and couldn't play because people would complain," said Winwood. "So we moved about an hour out of London to this cottage in Berkshire where we could play all the time. It was doomed to fail: four blokes not even out of their teens shoved together, living in squalor.

"As a marketing angle, somebody decided this was 'getting it together in the country'. At the time, I didn't know about that; I didn't really care either."

Winwood had his own vision of the future of British music. "The original line-up of Junior Walker and the All-Stars was sax, organ, guitar and drums with no bass," he said. "That was the Traffic concept. We were determined to make a uniquely British form of rock & roll that incorporated or evoked traditional music."

Traffic's first singles and EPs evidenced a very fresh and novel sound. They were clearly influenced by British folk music, jazz and pop music. Early hits were coy and cute drug songs 'Paper Sun' and 'Hole in My Shoe'. The track that put them on the map as serious contenders was the ten-minute jam, 'Dear Mr Fantasy', which did for pop jazz what Cream had done for blues.

'Dear Mr Fantasy' was a drawing that Capaldi had done and became the title for a tune worked up by Winwood and Wood, culminating in an extraordinary guitar part by Winwood.

"Of course those jams had nothing to do with folk or classical, and we didn't really know what was going to happen," said Winwood. "Although we thought we did."

One Step Beyond Madness

(Cecil Campbell) ✳ Stiff ✳ 1979 ✳ Appears on: *One Step Beyond*

"Hey You! Don't watch that! Watch this!" exclaimed Chas Smash as he introduced the "heavy, heavy monster sound of Madness". The seven-piece ska band were the ideal antidote for the often self-righteousness of punk rock in Britain. When the pop world was locked into a battle for the soul of the nation, then came Madness. They had pork pie hats and mod suits and they kicked up a real storm. Like an Ealing comedy with a Jamaican soundtrack, Madness was unafraid to look stupid in their vaudeville poses and crazy dances. This was entertainment. The nutty boys were a breath of fresh air and they had more than a dozen chart-topping hits in four years.

Madness evolved from a ska party band into writing their own material, which turned out to be celebrations of suburban England, in the manner of Ray Davies but lower-brow. They were gentle celebrations of ordinariness. When asked to define the Madness credo, backup singer Smash said, "It's alright to be ordinary. Everything around you is beautiful". The sound gradually developed too as Mark Bedford added Motown influences and traditional British pop arrangements to the pumping ska beat in his tunes.

'One Step Beyond' was a ska classic as recorded by Prince Buster. Madness play the track like it was a party – pounding out the sax and pumping up the tempo. Here was where the blueprint for the nutty, nutty sound of Madness started.

Kite U2

(Bono/U2) ✳ Interscope ✳ 2000 ✳ Appears on: *All that You Can't Leave Behind*

This most magnificent of Bono's lyrics was also the most intimate. 'Kite' was written around the time that the singer's father died. Theirs was a complex relationship that was only being resolved in the last few years.

The kite in the song belonged to Bono's children. "It's a reference," he said, "to an absurd moment of parenting, where I took a kite up on Killiney Hill with Jordan and Eve – I'd been away, and wanted to do the dad thing. The kite blew off the line and smashed to smithereens on the first flight, and Evie just asked if they could go home and play with their Tamagotchis. Then I realised, I went back in my head, and I remembered being in Rush or Skerries, one incident where exactly the same thing happened. We used to have a caravan, and I sort of felt the goodbye aspect of the song was not from me to him, but from him to me. That's the thing about songwriting – you're the last to know what you're on about."

It's a song about letting go – of fathers of children and perhaps of yourself. It's a song about identifying with the wind and recognising the role of fate. U2 bring all of their talents to bear on the backing – huge swooping guitar breaks from the Edge counterpoint to a soaring string section.

Then when things get too heavy, Bono brings the song back to the real world "when hip-hop drove the big cars and new media was the big idea". He's dating the song but also mocking our temporal vanities.

Addicted to Love Robert Palmer

(Robert Palmer) ✳ Island ✳ 1985 ✳ Appears on: *Riptide*

After years exploring funk, calypso, reggae, soul and electronica, Robert Palmer suddenly became a star. The Power Station, a "super group" helmed by Chic's Bernard Edwards and featuring Palmer as well as Tony Thompson and Duran Duran's Andy Taylor, was suddenly a pop phenomenon. The slightly disco feel and hard rock crunch, pumped up by Edwards' production, was crass but diverting pop.

Palmer brought it home alone with 'Addicted to Love'. The song is funky and bluesy but very modern in its production – massive gated drums and a thunderous, if simple, hook line.

"It's not like I was looking for hits," said Palmer. "I don't know why one takes off, and the other doesn't. Maybe it's the weather.

"Even though you get famous for one peak or kind of thing, it doesn't delineate everything you've done."

'Addicted to Love' was accompanied by an incredible video clip. There was Palmer, always comfortable in a suit, fronting an all girl band in little black dresses and classic cocktail styling. The clip may have been a self-parody but its images were so arresting that it has become one of the most famous video clips ever made.

"I think it was a package rolled into one that had to do with the timing, the sounds . . . everything fell into place. It struck a fashion note in all directions. And I don't think any one aspect was more important than the other," Palmer recalled. "The director said, 'You stand there and mime'. I know it's become an icon but it's nothing to do with me. I don't regret it. It had an extremely fun and humorous tongue-in-cheek elegant humour about it. And as the French say, 'What is the use of audacity without grace?'"

I Don't Believe in the Sun The Magnetic Fields

(Stephin Merritt) ✻ Merge ✻ 1999 ✻ Appears on: *69 Love Songs*

Stephin Merritt, the singer, songwriter and philosopher behind the Magnetic Fields is on a quest to discover a new pop aesthetic. It's part camp – the line-up consisted of one gay man, one straight man, one gay woman and one straight woman – and part bubblegum, part rock and some pop. Merritt had a fantasy of himself as the Brill Building hack toiling away at his desk while his friends presented the songs to an eager, or at least interested, public. After a couple of albums it became apparent that Merritt would have to get out front.

For the Magnetic Fields' breakthrough album, *69 Love Songs*, Merritt pulled out all the stops and wrote sixty-nine love songs. By and large as on 'I Don't Believe in the Sun' they are ironic but engaging and sort of powerful romances.

"While writing *69 Love Songs* I had a three-songs-a-day quota, which I always filled successfully," he said. "Most of the songs came out well, a few of them didn't, and I had to throw them away. Generally I edit them a little bit later, and if the music isn't quite up to snuff, I might keep the lyric and change the music or the other way around. My main activity is sitting alone and writing songs, so it's easy for me to be prolific. I don't like quiet when I'm writing songs. I like to be in a bar or café. There has to be music on – a jukebox playing."

Merritt is a refreshing change for the usual 21st century New York songwriter. "Rock should have consisted of only the Paul McCartney branch," he told Simon Reynolds. "Not the Lennon/Jagger/Richards one."

The Boys of Summer Don Henley

(Mike Campbell/Don Henley) ✻ Geffen ✻ 1984 ✻ Appears on: *Building the Perfect Beast*

As the singing drummer for the Eagles, Don Henley saw the liberal possibilities of the '70s dissolve into consumerist apathy. 'The Boys of Summer' from Henley's solo album is a companion piece to 'Hotel California'. However, where in the latter the characters sink into decadence and lethargy, in 'Summer' the symbols and icons and ideas of a progressive generation are transformed into cheap baubles and knick-knacks. The art that helped to change the world was now little more than a bumper sticker. Henley got all that information into a pop song of under four minutes.

"I was driving down the San Diego freeway," he told the *NME* of the genesis of the song. "I got passed by a $21,000 Cadillac Seville, the status symbol of the right-wing upper-middle-class American bourgeoisie – all the guys with the blue blazers with the crests and the grey pants – and there was this Grateful Dead 'Deadhead' bumper sticker on it."

Henley didn't look back when recording the track. Rather than replicate the country-rock style of the Eagles, Henley embraced synthesisers and drum machines to get a modern sound to the record.

"'Boys of Summer' was one of those great, rare moments where I got so inspired by the track that Mike Campbell had given me that it just sort of wrote itself," he told Bud Scoppa. "It came just screamin' out of me. And I was jumping up and down in the car 'cause I knew I had something there."

The song was a massive hit, though it perhaps didn't do much to stop the commodification of revolution. Henley's despair just became more name-checking of consumer brands.

"I wonder what happened to my generation," Henley mused. "All those great liberal ideas we had. Now everything's swung back to the right, the TV preachers with their own networks . . . it's pretty scary."

John the Revelator Blind Willie Johnson

(Traditional) ✻ Smithsonian Folkways ✻ 1927 ✻

Appears on: *Anthology of American Folk Music, Vol. 1–3*

Willie Johnson had a hard life. Born in Texas in 1902, he was, according to legend, blinded at age seven when his mother threw lye in his face in a jealous rage at her husband. Less than forty years later Johnson died when his house burnt down. As a child he sang in churches or on the streets with a tin cup around his neck. It was here that he developed his distinctive vocal style, switching from a bass to a tenor for a dynamic range that would work in the streets of Texas. His guitar style was similarly idiosyncratic; using a pocket-knife as a slide on a guitar made from a cigar box. Despite these handicaps, or perhaps because of them, Johnson is regarded as one of the most influential guitar players by modern musicians such as Eric Clapton, Ry Cooder, Bob Dylan and Jack White.

At age five, Johnson announced he intended to be a preacher. All his songs are religious rather than profane blues. His songs include: 'Nobody's Fault but Mine' (covered by Led Zeppelin), 'Motherless Children' (covered by Eric Clapton), 'In My Time of Dying' (covered by Bob Dylan), 'Jesus Make Up My Dying Bed' and 'If I Had My Way I'd Tear the Building Down'. Ry Cooder based his soundtrack of the film *Paris, Texas* on Johnson's 'Dark Was the Night Cold Was the Ground', which he described as "The most soulful, transcendent piece in all American music".

Johnson is best known for 'John the Revelator', which Harry Smith incorporated on his *Anthology of American Folk Music* (1952). Johnson's guitar is spare but driving and very powerful as he growls praise to the author of the Book of Revelations.

'John the Revelator' is the song for which Johnson will be forever known – it was covered broadly by the Blues Brothers and sublimely by Gillian Welch. Carl Sagan had the song put on a disc aboard the *Voyager 1* spacecraft for the listening pleasure of alien life forms. It's likely that they will be downloading 'John the Revelator' into their interstellar iPods.

Come Out and Play The Offspring

(The Offspring) ❋ Epitaph ❋ 1994 ❋ Appears on: *Smash*

The Offspring were arguably the best of the So Cal punks in the '90s because they at least had a sense of humour. They also had some lyrically interesting takes on alienation, teenage wasteland and the state of the nation. If their sound wasn't as dark as many other punks, they still put out convincing riffs as on this track from their breakthrough *Smash* album. 'Come Out and Play' has an absolutely killer guitar riff backing up the vocal hook – "You gotta keep 'em separated!" The song is a satiric take on teenage gun violence that doesn't evade the issue but doesn't get bogged down in self-pity.

Although not as cool as most punks, the Offspring were considerably more hardcore, releasing their albums on an indie label and offering their music on the Internet free. Singer Dexter Holland, guitarist Kevin 'Noodles' Wasserman, bassist Greg Kriesel and drummer Ron Welty maintained a consistent dedication to rock, despite six years of indifference from the business and the fans. The group had a strong DIY ethic that stood them in good stead after 'Come Out and Play' made them stars.

"I remember reading articles on bands," said Holland, "and they'd say, 'For the first year there were only twenty-five people at our shows'. Now that sounds funny to me, because for the first ten years there were only twenty-five people at our shows. Literally, it was that long. Even just before *Smash* came out we played our hometown and drew a hundred people. We were actually pretty stoked about that."

The satiric style continued through to mega hits like 'Pretty Fly for a White Guy'. "I'm really glad we did it that way," said Holland. "Because it really was an adventure and it was a lot more real. It wasn't like we got together and tried to find a fancy lawyer and sign to a big label. We were just doing what was natural to us, making music. So doing our own tours and making our own shirts was simply an extension of that."

The pop element of their power pop – especially in the guitar riff – will keep the Offspring on the radio forever, when so many of the cool school have vanished.

All Shook Up Elvis Presley

(Otis Blackwell/Elvis Presley) ✳ RCA ✳ 1957 ✳ Appears on: *Elvis 30 #1 Hits*

Otis Blackwell was inspired to pen this lyric by an excited bottle of carbonated soft drink. According to legend, Blackwell's publisher came into his Brill Building office shaking a can of soft drink and said, "You can write about anything. Now write about this!" The song was initially recorded by the now long-forgotten David Hill. After the success of 'Don't Be Cruel' all of Blackwell's output, including the slightly second hand, went to Presley who gave this a hillbilly hiccupping treatment. The percussion sound is said to be Elvis slapping the back of his acoustic guitar. Recorded in Hollywood on 12 January 1957, Elvis was at the peak of his powers. He was running from TV appearances with Ed Sullivan to recording sessions for film soundtracks and his own sides as well.

In the years 1956–57 he recorded ten number one singles. 'All Shook Up' was the number one song of 1957. The song was his biggest hit to that point and is possibly his most raw and rock & roll performance ever.

Frozen Warnings Nico

(Nico) ✳ Elektra ✳ 1969 ✳ Appears on: *The Marble Index*

It was here on her second album, *The Marble Index*, that Nico found her voice. She had attempted to be a girl singer in the waifish style of Marianne Faithfull but with little commercial success. Two years later she was teamed with John Cale and for the first time produced an album's worth of her own songs. Often described as "European," Nico's work was sparse, minimal, elegantly Gothic and haunting. If some of those qualities are contradictory, so be it.

Nico found herself a record deal with Elektra. The title for the sophomore album came from a poem by Wordsworth and it was appropriate for a record that was definitely poetic in every sense.

Nico wrote her tunes on the harmonium, a less than colourful instrument that doesn't lend itself to group playing. According to John Cale, "It was not exactly in tune with itself, or with anything else; its notes were 'in the cracks'". Nonetheless, Cale recorded and mixed the album in four days. Cale's viola on this track is some of his best work. "We had only four days to make it, but luckily Jack Holzman at Elektra really understood that there was a very powerful sense of style involved here," said Cale. "It wasn't just throwing notes around."

"The songs just spoke for themselves," said Danny Fields, who was briefly Nico's manager. "You didn't have to know that they came from this heavenly creature."

Just as she had done on *The Velvet Underground and Nico*, the singer put a new tone into music.

I Don't Want to Talk About It Everything But The Girl

(Danny Whitten) ✳ Blanco y Negro/Sire ✳ 1988 ✳ Appears on: *Idlewild*

Tracey Thorn and Ben Watt have had an odd career, negotiating the demands of the marketplace with their wandering muse. They started out as a folk duo playing in colleges, went rock for awhile and moved into a laid-back jazz tip like a literate Sade. Thorn has a intimate, plaintive voice and Ben Watt plays delicate, sophisticated melodies. Their admirers include Bono and Prince. They're not quite folk and not quite rock but with a bit of both and some jazz thrown in there as well.

The songs have ranged from generalised romance to strict politics and the documenting of the dissolution of their own romantic relationship.

On *Idlewild* they absorb the lessons of the past and move on. While their own songs are intriguing and warrant close attention, their remake of Danny Whitten's ballad is breathtaking. Originally written for his band Crazy Horse's debut LP, Rod Stewart also did a great version of the song. But Everything But The Girl strips this song right back to its elements. Thorn's vocal is dry and exhausted but the purity of her tone and phrasing give the track an emotional nett. Watt's jazz-tinged backing is similarly minimal. But it's the spaces and the pieces left out that really anchor the emotional message.

Beth KISS

(Peter Criss/Bob Ezrin/Stan Penridge) ❋ Casablanca ❋ 1976 ❋ Appears on: *Destroyer*

One of the first power ballads, 'Beth' is the story of the eternal struggle between a man's band and his girlfriend. Drummer Peter Criss wrote the song in 1971 when he was in a band called Chelsea with Stan Penridge. The inspiration being a mate's nagging girlfriend interrupting their rehearsals.

"She was the world's greatest hypochondriac," said Criss in a 1994 interview recalling the woman in question. "She was always sick. And she was continually calling up and interrupting our rehearsals. So after a month, six weeks, of this going on, we'd know it had to be her when the phone rang. So I would start writing down what Michael was saying back to Beck. He would literally say, 'Beck, I heard you calling but I can't come home right now'. He'd be pissed off, you know. 'Me and the boys are playing here and we've got to get the sound together. Give me another hour and I'll be there'".

The song lay dormant until the sessions for *Destroyer*. Initially titled 'Beck', Gene Simmons suggested a change in title to avoid confusion with guitarist Jeff Beck and he suggested that Criss submit the song for the next album. Producer Bob Ezrin made some minor changes and orchestrated the song with monumental string arrangements performed by the New York Philharmonic Orchestra. Originally the flipside to 'Detroit Rock City', a radio station started playing the track and it was eventually issued as a single in its own right and became KISS' first Top 10 single.

Good Thing Fine Young Cannibals

(Roland Gift/David Steele) ✳ London ✳ 1989 ✳ Appears on: *The Raw and the Cooked*

In a drunken moment, guitarist Andy Cox described the Fine Young Cannibals' second album as "thirty years worth of pop music in thirty minutes". He wasn't, however, too far off the mark. There are all kinds of influences bubbling under the Fine Young Cannibals – reggae, ska, dance music, R&B and even sometimes rock. 'Good Thing' is the perfect Fine Young Cannibals track – just built around a riff and groove which the three Cannibals – Cox, bassist Dave Steele, and singer Roland Gift – ride for
all its worth. Everything is here New Orleans piano that resolves into a '60s garage band sound, '50s rock & roll doo-wop harmonies, gospel handclaps, twangy surf guitar and the futuristic metronome drum machine. Gift had an extraordinary voice – like a souped up Nat King Cole that complemented the spiky ideas of his ex-Beat colleagues with a Tamla Motown Marvin Gaye tone.

"We don't need anything other than a good song and a good beat," said Steele.

Mr Soul Buffalo Springfield

(Neil Young) ✳ Atco ✳ 1968 ✳ Appears on: *Buffalo Springfield Again*

For the first time Neil Young borrows a Rolling Stones tune to write one of his own. While recovering in hospital following an epileptic attack, Young adapts the riff of '(I Can't Get No) Satisfaction' for a cynical and weary look at the music business. Young was just starting his career as guitarist in Buffalo Springfield and already he was worried about selling out. As it turns out, the pressure to perform 'Mr Soul' on a variety TV show caused a major rift in the tempestuous five-piece outfit.

'Mr Soul' was first recorded while the group was on tour in New York. Otis Redding came to the session with a view to cutting the track himself but Young was reluctant to part with the song and refused permission. The song was eventually recut and included on the second Springfield album. Its toughness is symptomatic of one of the directions that Young was heading in as the group fell apart.

"There were a lot of problems happening with the Springfield," he told journalist Nick Kent. "There were a lot of distractions too. Groupies. Drugs. Then there were all these other people . . . They were always around, giving you grass, trying to sell you hippy clothes . . . I never knew what these people really wanted. And there were so many of 'em! Not to mention all the women . . . all the clubs, places to go, things to do. I remember being haunted suddenly by this whole obsession with 'How do I fit in here? Do I like this?'"

Grazing in the Grass Hugh Masekela

(Harry Elston/Philemon Hou) ✳ UNI ✳ 1968 ✳ Appears on: *The Promise of a Future*

Hugh Masekela is one of the leading lights for South African music. He took up trumpet and flugelhorn at the age of fourteen, mastering bebop, cool jazz and pop styles. Being black in the apartheid era meant that opportunities in South Africa were limited and the climate of oppression didn't lend itself to jazz. In the late '50s he was at the centre of South African music. In 1961 he fled to Europe with his wife, singer Miriam Makeba. Masekela was soon at the centre of European and American jazz, mixing with the likes of Harry Belafonte, Dizzy Gillespie and John Dankworth. Masekela continued to move through a range of genres bringing his particular rhythmic style and warm, emotive tones.

In 1968, he had a major pop hit with 'Grazing in the Grass' and his fusion ensembles were much in demand especially with rock audiences. Masekela has continued to play jazz and world music, including a time with Fela Kuti. He also assisted Paul Simon on the *Graceland* project.

'Grazing in the Grass' began as 'Mr Bull, no. 5' when recorded by Masekela in Zambia during the early '60s – hence the 'Grazing'. The mood suggests a deeper version of the light jazz of Herb Alpert and Herbie Mann. Masekela, however, brought a more soulful and complex ambience to the record. According to legend, Masekela had finished his session and was just filling in time and tape with 'Grazing'. It was knocked off in one take. Executive producer Russ Regan heard the potential in the song and issued it as a single. His instincts were right and the song crossed over from the jazz to the pop charts and sold four million copies.

Close to Me The Cure

(Robert Smith) ✳ Fiction ✳ 1985 ✳ Appears on: *Head on the Door*

Robert Smith had been through the wringer a couple of times by the mid-'80s. His group the Cure started out as moody existentialist art rockers who were immediately successful, despite their limited musical talents. Smith struggled with his success through career defeating albums and years of drug and alcohol abuse. However, the pop songs kept creeping out. In an attempt to demystify the Cure he had penned 'Let's Go to Bed' and inexplicably the track was a hit in the US.

In early 1985, Smith resolved to get happy. In two weeks he wrote a new album, *Head on the Door*. It was recorded with an unashamed delight for hooks and catchy melodies. Smith and the group's video director Tim Pope cut some of the group's most whimsical film clips.

"I think the Cure really started again at this point," said Smith. "It felt like being in the Beatles – and I wanted to make substantial 'Strawberry Fields'-style pop music. I wanted everything to be really catchy.

"We're in a very strange position in that we're able to play really crass pop songs and yet people still accept that I can sing about issues with far greater emotional depth and take it seriously."

I Still Carry You Around Steve Earle

(Steve Earle) ✳ Warner Bros. ✳ 1997 ✳ Appears on: *El Corazón*

Steve Earle took the bad boy image a little too far. A heroin addiction that lasted more than twenty years and five marriages followed by a crack habit finally landed the Texan singer/songwriter in jail. Prior to his sentence he had been in a revolving door of arrests and court appearances that was crippling his career and, between the lawyer and the drug dealers, sucking away his time and creativity.

Suddenly, in 1995, after the jail sentence looked too real, Earle quit drugs. He returned to performing and writing; first solo then with various outfits.

El Corazón (the heart) was his third post-rehab album. It crossed the entire spectrum of Earle's work. "Well, you understand where my writer's block came from," he said. "From about $750–$800 a day's worth of writer's block. My drug habit reached a point where there wasn't any time or energy to do anything else. So now that I don't have to find hundreds of dollars worth of drugs just to get up in the morning, it's amazing – I feel like I have all the time and energy in the world. I write something every day. The only thing that scares writers worse than ex-wives is a blank piece of paper.

"With *El Corazón* I finally managed to write an entire album without the devil in one song. I'm proud of that. I just wanted to see if I could do it."

Earle re-embraced country music styles, especially bluegrass. For one song he teams up with Del McCoury, a bluegrass bandleader well into his seventies at the time. As he wrote in his notes for the album, "I wrote this song specifically to have something to play with the Del McCoury Band. They are just the best bluegrass outfit in the business right now. Del is the best tenor, Ronnie is the best mandolin player, and Rob plays banjo like no-one else.

"Bluegrass is the original alternative country music. After I retire, I'm gonna buy a bus and play bluegrass festivals."

The Rockafeller Skank Fatboy Slim

(John Barry/Fatboy Slim/Winford Terry) ✳ Skint ✳ 1998 ✳
Appears on: *You've Come a Long Way, Baby*

This track was the beginning of the end of club culture. Fatboy Slim's 'The Rockafeller Skank' was a monster that went beyond its genre (big beat). Recorded at home, 'The Rockafeller Skank' has a touch of the novelty record about it. It is kind of funny but mostly it has a huge fat vocal hook in the sample "Check it out now, the funk soul brother". It has big dirty guitar lines in its eclectic selection of samples from the John Barry Seven's score for the movie *Beat Girl* and the Just Brothers' *Sliced Tomatoes*. The record sold five million copies and at that point, dance culture, which required an alternative self-image, was blown wide open. It's still a great track and the break beats are still compelling. Most of all, Norman Cook (aka Fatboy Slim) mixes the track like he's DJing at a great party and having a wonderful time doing it. "I think what separates me from other DJs is the vaudeville element of it," he said.

Setting Sun The Chemical Brothers

(Noel Gallagher/Tom Rowlands/Ed Simons) ✻ Heavenly ✻ 1996 ✻

Appears on: *Dig Your Own Hole*

The Chemical Brothers described their second album, *Dig Your Own Hole*, as "the best breaks they've ever broken. A bloody good soundtrack for people living today." The Chemical Brothers (Tom Rowlands and Ed Simons) were the most fashionable DJs in Britain and Noel Gallagher was the biggest rock star when they put rock and big beat together on this single. The Chemical Brothers had a spot at the ultra-hip Heavenly Social – a club night in London. The pair looked the part – like Chaucer-reading nerds with turntables. They were photogenic and visible and they toured, and thus they were important in making DJs a significant part of the music landscape as artists. On 'Setting Sun' Oasis' Noel Gallagher added his vocal and guitar to the mix of white noise paranoia and artillery-like break beats.

"We had this idea to do something like that for quite a while," said Rowlands, "the past couple of years or whatever. It was good that we managed to get Noel – he offered to do something with us back in '95 when we saw him at this festival. He was saying 'On the next album you should get me in'. That was kinda nice really, it was just cool that he was up for doing it and he liked the track. It was a painless procedure."

The Chemical Brothers were always eclectic both in their DJ sets and on record. From straight-ahead techno to rock party chemical beats to 'Setting Sun', to low looping weird tracks with Beth Orton singing on them. Where many techno/dance artists were regarded as faceless, the Chemical Brothers exuded personality.

"We've always based what we do on a wide appreciation of music, and we aren't frightened to show it," said Rowlands. "Dance music is made to play in clubs, even if it's nosebleed techno, it's still for a certain section of the population to enjoy this music … There's not a lot of intellectualising that has to go on if you dance a lot. Dance is the pivotal thing."

Runaround Sue Dion and the Belmonts

(Dion DiMucci/Ernie Maresca) ✳ Laurie ✳ 1961 ✳ Appears on: *Runaround Sue*

When Dion DiMucci puts on a rare show in Manhattan, the guest list includes Paul Simon, Billy Joel, Lou Reed and Bruce Springsteen. All these artists were inspired by Dion's late '50s and early '60s hits. With his Italian tough-guy attitude and a magnificently expressive voice, Dion was New York's first white rock & roll star. His background was in street-corner doo-wop, but with 'Runaround Sue' he created a crossover hit that prefigured rock & roll writing. Most of all, though, there are incredible rhythms in the vocal parts. The song bounces around like a pinball, the Belmonts providing support and encouragement. Sue may be running around with other guys, but Dion isn't wasting tears over her.

"It was primitive," Dion told biographer Gene Sculatti. "It had a rhythm, a back beat and nothing else. The problem was in trying to record it. Drummers, I don't know what it is, but they hear a certain tempo and they want to play what they know. I said, 'No, it goes like this', and we simplified it back to what it was when it was created – spontaneously, with people clapping and banging on things."

'Runaround Sue' was one of the last great New York songs before the Beatles came and changed everything three years later.

Rag Mama Rag The Band

(Jaime Robbie Robertson) ✳ Capitol ✳ 1969 ✳ Appears on: *The Band*

For the recording of their second album, the Band moved to Los Angeles with their families to escape the harsh Woodstock winter. They rented Sammy Davis Jr's mansion and turned the pool house into a studio. The five players set up their equipment much as it had been in Big Pink with the musicians together in a large room, generally playing at the same time.

"Everything in rock was kind of going in that high-end direction," said Robbie Robertson. "We wanted something different, a kind of woody, thuddy sound." Robertson played guitar and engineered while producer John Simon also played on some tracks. All the other musicians played multiple instruments. This swapping of instruments gave *The Band* a distinctive sound. It was particularly important for

Levon Helm, who had to phrase his vocals around his drumming, giving many of the songs a country funk feel.

"I started thinking that the music was finally taking shape with the second album," said Helm. "We had actually figured out some methods of how to really turn the heat up and get the music to cook: how to blend our voices three different ways, how to get the track together and not make it so complicated. We'd sit and talk about medicine shows and, shit, the tune would just come to us. A lot of those good lessons Dylan had given us started to manifest themselves."

The Band's imagery suggested a 19th century ambience of pre-Civil War backwoodsmen and God-fearing patriarchs. In fact, the Band was anything but that. They were a group who had been playing tough rock & roll for a decade in bars and clubs across America. They were not familiar with folk music and not much accomplished with country. The group's bass player, Rick Danko, for instance, took his style from jazz virtuoso Ron Carter and the Motown sound of Chuck Rainey and James Jamerson.

However, Robertson's myth was the context for everything. Part of that myth relied on the voice and the personality of Levon Helm, who was at least from the backwoods of Arkansas and gave a veracity to songs like 'Up on Cripple Creek', 'The Night They Drove Old Dixie Down' and 'Rag Mama Rag'.

The latter song was a perfect example of the Band's modus operandi. Helm moved to mandolin. Richard Manuel played the drums in his own loping, behind-the-beat style, Danko moved to fiddle and John Simon played the bass part on tuba even though he hadn't previously played the instrument.

"'Rag Mama Rag' was like, 'Well, this is an extra one and if we don't have anything better to do we might as well cut this one'," said Robertson. "It didn't have very much importance to it until after we recorded it. It showed something else that we could do: Richard plays the drums, Rick played violin – we got to show something else that we do in a style that doesn't exist. You know – 'Name this music!'"

The song had the appearance of an old folk song but it is, in fact, pure funk.

"Me and a bunch of guys from New Orleans would listen to *The Band* all the time," said Mac 'Dr John' Rebennack. "The music sounded to me like a cross between Memphis and New Orleans. It was really in the pockets of those places without ever copying the original stuff."

Solsbury Hill Peter Gabriel

(Peter Gabriel) ✳ Charisma ✳ 1977 ✳ Appears on: *Peter Gabriel*

Peter Gabriel quit the progressive rock band Genesis for a career as an art rock star. At the time of his departure, Genesis was poised to become one of the most popular groups in the world. England had been conquered and the US beckoned. Much of their success came from the theatrical and confronting live show that Gabriel had developed. Then Gabriel jumped ship. Genesis continued and became huge in America and indeed one of the most successful groups of the '80s.

'Solsbury Hill' was Gabriel's statement of intent, his explanation for leaving Genesis. Allegedly the inspiration was a Bruce Springsteen concert. Be that as it may, he needed the excitement of a solo life. He also, one suspects, needed to start again. 'Solsbury Hill' is that place.

Producer Bob Ezrin brought a Detroit rock connection – Steve Hunter, Dick Wagner – and Gabriel brought along the best of British boffins – Kate Bush, Robert Fripp, Peter Hammill and Paul Weller. The record sounded quite unlike anything else in its time. 'Solsbury Hill' also featured a peerless vocal from Gabriel – he sounds like a man with the wind in his hair. He knows that "open doors will be shut" but seems not to care.

(I Wish It Could Be) 1965 Again The Barracudas

(Jeremy Gluck/Robin Wills) ✳ Zonophone ✳ 1980 ✳
Appears on: *Drop Out with the Barracudas*

No group ever wore its nostalgia so proudly on its sleeve than the Barracudas, a surf music band formed in London in 1978 by a couple of guys who couldn't surf. Singer Jeremy Gluck and guitarist Robin Wills were punk rock fans who wanted a band. The music they cherished was mostly '60s pop and the act they were probably closest to was the Flamin' Groovies. In lieu of musical strength, Gluck and Wills had great ideas.

"Well, being quite bright, Robin and I decided that, to make any impression, we had to actually choose one genre of all those we loved (punk, surf or pop) and make of it a Grail," said Gluck. "We chose surf, simply because it was chronologically correct and the least likely to invite competition." Most of the early Barracudas material was based around a surf theme. However, the centrepiece of their debut album was '(I Wish It Could Be) 1965 Again', which was a history of popular culture through the '60s, name checking the great records and artists of the period. It's funny and its accurate and it had a massive Flamin' Groovies sound. Of course it's too obscure to have been the hit they hoped for but it remains a classic of its type.

"So we hit on the surf thing with a vengeance, and reaped rich dividends," said Gluck. "We soon had many mods into us ... if only because we favoured white Levi's ... and many others, all the fringe weirdos, and others who just liked a laugh, because we were as silly as we were unprofessional! And in fact critics adored us ... because we were different and not drab. It got better ... I recall boarding a tube train one evening carrying a genuine surfboard to go to a gig at the Music Machine. It was like that ... a movie we lived ... we all went to see *Big Wednesday*, we all hung out ... we became gossip-worthy ... Oh, it's the Barracudas, they are the surf band ... as an exercise in naïve marketing, it was genius!"

Wake Up, Niggers The Last Poets

(Jalal Mansur Nuriddin) ❋ Douglas ❋ 1970 ❋ Appears on: *The Last Poets*

Before there was rap there was poetry and jazz and rhythm. The Last Poets were poets operating in the African-American traditions of poetry and jazz like Amiri Baraka (Le Roi Jones). Their verses were revolutionary, in the spirit of the times, and not adverse to a violent revolution to overthrow the racist ruling paradigm. The most significant difference between the Last Poets and Public Enemy was the accent had moved from the four-beat to the one-beat. Otherwise it's a pretty clear lineage.

Jalal Mansur Nuriddin met Omar Ben Hassan and Abiodun Oyewole while in jail for refusing to serve in Vietnam. They grew to a larger ensemble including Gylan Kain, Felipe Luciano and Suliamn El Hadi and called themselves the Last Poets after a poem by South African Little Willie Kgositsile. "When the moment hatches in time's womb there will be no art talk," Kgositsile wrote.

"The only poem you will hear will be the spearpoint pivoted in the punctured marrow of the villain . . . Therefore we are the last poets of the world." The ranks of the Last Poets swelled and their style of performance poetry gained a lot of attention. One person who took notice was Jack Douglas, producer of jazz records, another was Jimi Hendrix, who saw the Poets doing a TV spot.

"I called the station immediately and got a number for them," Douglas told writer David Dalton. "There was a lot of distrust between blacks and whites at that time, a lot of tension. Going up to Harlem was intense. Around two the next afternoon I drove up there in my silver Jaguar. The address turned out to be a basketball court: there were about twenty black guys standing around. As I walked across the court they parted until there were only four guys left, the three poets and the conga player. Jalal was standing under the hoop – no net – and when I came close he said, 'Stand there, on the foul line'. And then for the next forty minutes they played their repertoire. When they were done I asked them if they wanted to make a record. They said they would and we all piled into the Jaguar and went down to a little studio on 77th and recorded the whole album then and there in four hours."

While the Last Poets were ready for war with white society, they weren't letting blacks off the hook either. Tracks on the first album like 'Wake Up Niggers' are critical of black apathy. The song broke into the hip white arena with its appearance in the film *Performance*.

"But with the Poets, we were angry and we had something to say," explained Abiodun Oyewole. "We addressed the language. We just put it right in front of your face. We parented to the hip-hop generation. I can't deny that. I worked with a lot of them and they have the same rage and I understand that. There was a movement back then with the Panthers and other organizations, trying to secure human rights for the community. We had these guidelines and guard rails. These kids don't have these guard rails. The rage is going every which way. It's self-destructive."

Just Like Honey The Jesus and Mary Chain

(William Reid/Jim Reid) ✳ Blanco y Negro ✳ 1985 ✳ Appears on: *Psychocandy*

'Just Like Honey' starts off with Phil Spector's drum phrase from 'Be My Baby' immersed in even more echo than the original and then followed by a guitar riff that is mostly echo and feedback in a majestic wall of '80s sound. The Reid brothers, who are the Jesus and Mary Chain, knew what they were quoting and what they were doing with it. This was a meeting of British punk rock attitude with classic rock.

"With *Psychocandy*, we never arrived drunk in the studio and went wild with guitars," said William Reid. "We sat for months making sure. We had white noise sampled on an AMS machine, punching it in at certain places. It wasn't as spontaneous as everybody would like it to be. A lot of people seem to think you turned up, you were on speed, you fucked around with guitars and that record magically happened. It's magic and it did happen, but not the way people wanted it to. It took time and a lot of effort."

The record inspired hundreds of imitators and prefigured the shoe-gazer fad that took over British rock for a couple of years in the '80s. 'Just Like Honey' is a record of terrible beauty. It's dark and obsessive but also strangely awe-inspiring. Unlike so many post-punks, the Jesus and Mary Chain weren't deconstructing rock but, rather, assembling it again from its decayed parts. The song is viscerally exciting and emotionally moving in a way that so few rock tracks from that period are.

Mad World Tears For Fears

(Roland Orzabal) ❊ Mercury ❊ 1983 ❊ Appears on: *The Hurting*

Psychologist Arthur Janov had his primal scream therapy placed on the pop map by John Lennon who claimed that Janov's techniques had enabled him to be brutally honest with himself and as a consequence he wrote his purgative eponymous solo album. Ten years later, out of the town of Bath comes Roland Orzabal, fired up on Janov, and produces the primal whispering album of sensitive pop all about unnameable suffering. The key track here being the melodically rich 'Mad World'.

Take for instance the lyric from 'Mad World' – "the dreams in which I'm dying are the best I've ever had". Orzabal claimed this means that if dreams release tension, then the ones in which you have an intensely emotional experience, like dreaming of death, will release the most tension. Heavy.

Orzabal was happy to drop names like Sartre and Freud in interviews with the pop press and engage in deep philosophical discussions about the meaning of it all. "What Freud says is it's not so much what happened to you during childhood that's important, it's more how you experienced it," he told *Melody Maker*. "But where Janov comes from is, you were a victim, you were born innocent and they did this to you. I suppose the truth is somewhere in between. What I believe is that at some point you have to take account of your own actions. We can't keep on saying the problem is capitalism or communism or poverty or the ecology. Of course, these things have to be dealt with, but we have to stop blaming the Other and look inside."

Gorgeous, complex melodies and Curt Smith's sweet vocals ameliorated the pain of it all. "Primal therapy isn't a religion, a cult, a sect, a mythology," Orzabal explained to the readers of teenybopper mag *Smash Hits*. "It isn't anything weird at all, just a theory about the importance of relationships between children and their parents. We're not into primal therapy. We're just into living life to the full."

I'm Waiting for the Man The Velvet Underground

(Lou Reed) ✲ Verve ✲ 1967 ✲ Appears on: *The Velvet Underground & Nico*

If 'Heroin' on the first Velvets album told you of the experience of taking the drug, 'I'm Waiting for the Man' told you where to get it – the corner of Lexington Avenue and 125th Street. Also the price – $26. It also told you that while waiting you would experience withdrawal and the Velvet Underground made a sound like that.

The churning rhythm guitar on 'I'm Waiting for the Man' is the prototype for what became punk rock. They grind through the changes – where there are changes – oblivious to the demands of R&B, just straight chording and overtones. It's extraordinary playing and was hugely influential on the development of heavy rock as it occurred in the '70s, particularly with David Bowie. Where 'Heroin' was an epic poem, this is more urgent and minimal. It remains one of the great rock & roll songs.

The critic Lester Bangs said in the late '70s, "modern music starts with the Velvet Underground". In fact, it starts with this track.

Little Girl Blue Janis Joplin

(Lorenz Hart/Richard Rodgers) ❄ Columbia ❄ 1969 ❄
Appears on: *I Got Dem Ol' Kozmic Blues Again Mama*

Joplin takes her cues on this from Nina Simone's arrangement of the song from the musical *Jumbo*. The song was written for a middle-aged character reflecting on her life but Joplin, barely in her mid-twenties, sings the song with a lifetime of experience in her voice.

Sam Andrew's guitar has a beautiful counterpoint to Janis' melody line and producer Gabriel Mekler dresses the song with gorgeous strings and organ parts, but everybody keeps their distance from Janis' vocal. Joplin was a singer that usually went for the epic emotion and the big note, but here she hangs back in total control.

Joplin not only discards Lorenz Hart's first verse, but many of the other lines as well and twists the syntax to make this song an autobiography. Even though the delivery is measured, there's a raw quality here – Joplin's opening up her heart – and the disappointment and pain and rejection and confusion which was so much a part of her short life is there for all to see.

Frankie Teardrop Suicide

(Alan Vega/Martin Rev) ❄ Red Star ❄ 1977 ❄ Appears on: *Suicide*

Alan Vega and Martin Rev started Suicide in 1971 in New York playing the downtown circuit with just Vega singing and Rev playing primitive synthesisers and drum machines. Suicide took the Stooges and the Velvet Underground and some Elvis Presley and Otis Redding and then reinterpreted it as if they were Kraftwerk. They were rightly regarded as true pioneers and when punk rock moved above ground in 1976 and 1977, Suicide surfaced with it. The Clash and Elvis Costello both added Suicide to their tours and caused riots at their concerts. The world was not yet ready for industrial techno. Suicide's heirs – Devo, Ultravox, Depeche Mode, Jesus and Mary Chain, Sisters of Mercy, Daft Punk, Air, Chemical, Nick Cave to name but a few – benefited from their pioneering sheets of industrial music.

The '70s certainly weren't ready for 'Frankie Teardrop' – a ten-minute epic about a man trapped in a factory. Rev's keyboards are angry and agitated and frustrated and desperate. Vega's singing walks the line between despair and madness until the song ends in violent tragedy.

"That's what's happening all over the place," said Vega. "Everybody's blowin' everybody else away, and who are these people? They're not maniacs. They're just ordinary people gone a little berserk because life just got too hard for them."

'Frankie Teardrop' is hard in the way that the Velvets' 'Sister Ray' is hard. The key to it is that amongst Vega's screams and crooning pain is a pumping heart. It's not a song you're going to want to hear a lot, but it will stay with you.

Just Like a Woman Bob Dylan

(Bob Dylan) ❊ Columbia ❊ 1966 ❊ Appears on: *Blonde on Blonde*

Dylan claims the he wrote this song in Kansas City one Thanksgiving. The *Blonde on Blonde* album was a cycle of songs mostly about the changes that were happening in Dylan's life. He was cleaning house – saying farewell to old lovers and celebrating his new marriage. 'Just like a Woman' falls into the former category. There has been much speculation about which ex-lover Dylan addressed with this song – Joan Baez perhaps, although its been suggested that Warhol starlet Edie Sedgwick can be seen here (the line "With her Fog, her amphetamine, and her pearls" – the Fog being a London Fog raincoat).

Melodically, 'Just Like a Woman' is one of Dylan's finest – the arrangement of the musicians playing against Dylan's syncopated vocal is exceptional. It was on this album that Dylan claimed he reached his ideal sound. "It's that thin, that wild mercury sound. It's metallic and bright and gold, with whatever that conjures up. That's my particular sound," he said in 1978. As with the rest of the album, the musicians are Nashville studio cats plus New Yorker Al Kooper and the songs are cut pretty much live.

'Just like a Woman' caused some controversy on its release. It was attacked as being misogynist, although it's hard to see how. Dylan relished 'Just Like a Woman', especially the way he could play with the words. The version on *The Concert for Bangladesh* is a particularly good example of the elastic phrasing of the words and the way the tune can be teased – the song can be spiteful or compassionate depending on the circumstances of the night.

Is This It The Strokes

(Julian Casablancas) ❉ RCA ❉ 2001 ❉ Appears on: *Is This It*

The best thing about the Strokes' debut album is that it comes in at under 40 minutes. It runs at the same length as an LP. There was so much retro about the Strokes that they make it all sound new again. Of course, they were criticised for imitating the Velvet Underground, Television and the Stooges. They were doing to downtown Manhattan what the Rolling Stones had done to southside Chicago thirty years previously.

'Is This It' opened the account for the Strokes with a defiant blast of New York rock. It's all weary singing from Julian Casablancas, ruthless guitar from Albert Hammond Jr and Nick Valensi and sharp drums from Fabrizio Moretti. "Even from the beginning, when people saw us live it was like they so badly wanted us to bring back something from the past," said bass player Nikolai Fraiture. "They laid every name on us from back then and a lot of the time it has nothing to do with us. People liked that music and for good reason, and they see us and they hope that it still exists."

The frame of reference couldn't be more different. The Strokes are rich kids – one's dad owns a model agency and another's writes hits for Julio Iglesias – whereas the founders of the sounds were struggling on the breadline. That said, the Strokes understand what cool is all about. 'Is This It' stood out at the beginning of the 21st century because almost no-one else did.

Karmacoma Massive Attack

(Robert '3D' del Naja/Robert Locke/Grant 'Daddy G' Marshall/Tim Norfolk/A Thaws/
Andrew 'Mushroom' Vowles) ❉ Virgin ❉ 1994 ❉ Appears on: *Protection*

Massive Attack came straight out of Bristol with the hip-hop reggaeish *Blue Lines* – melancholy and spiritually uplifting. Then came the second effort, *Protection*, much more downbeat and disturbed as on the key track, 'Karmacoma'.

It has a chill-out groove but the ambience of 'Karmacoma' is dark and sinister. The presence of Tricky as a rapper adds to the dope-filled atmosphere of the track. "We just write as we think, which is with fragments of ideas and the images they conjure up," said 3D, who also raps on the track. "You end up with raps that are almost like streams of consciousness – cut up and put back together like William

Burroughs or something – it doesn't have to have a point, so long as there's information in there which people can retrieve if they want to."

'Karmacoma' is built on a sly, almost comatose beat and the track is once again brilliantly embellished by Massive's hip-hop ornamentation as the song testily critiques the slacker attitude of the blunted youth. Unsettling but seductive.

Hey Porter Ry Cooder

(Johnny Cash) ✳ Reprise ✳ 1972 ✳ Appears on: *Into the Purple Valley*

Ry Cooder's guitar sound is one of the most distinctive of the last forty years, whether that be with the Rolling Stones, Little Feat or dozens of soundtracks. It was based around his inventive tunings and his distorted tone combined with a sly and witty use of bottleneck guitar.

Born a white middle-class baby boomer to bohemian parents, Cooder developed an obsession with folk blues in the early '60s. What set him apart from the hundreds of other white kids learning blues from the old masters was that Cooder didn't try replicating the old songs and style but adapted them into something entirely particular.

Cooder did his time at the arthritic knees of the greats. At times he was paying for lessons from artists such as Gary Davis.

"You absorb by watching a guy and you learn where it's coming from. Not so much how it's played, because who knows how anybody plays anything, but you get a feeling of what kind of energy's in it, and what the people look like and how they move around, which was very illuminating. People like Gary Davis were fantastic . . .

"You give the guy some money – what are you going to do, not give him money? It comes down to a question of what the rewards are for folks like that, who have been poor beyond your wildest imagination for their whole life, and still were that poor, except that they happened to be playing for middle-class white kids like me. Which doesn't change the fact that they're still poor beyond your wildest imagination. So you just say, 'Here's five bucks – how do you play that song?', and it seems like the right thing to do, money being about the only way you can show any kind of appreciation to such people. One by one, these guys died poor – John Estes, they had to borrow dirt to bury him, and Gary Davis and everyone died so destitute . . . But it had never changed. On one side, you've got a group of people indulging their sensibilities in the warm bath of ethnic purity, and on the other, you've got the guys who actually do it, but who can't afford firewood, and that creates a certain kind of ambivalence that you can never resolve."

Cooder's bottleneck style was learnt from another white blues fan, John Fahey, who had actually been south and seen many of the Delta players using the necks of wine bottles.

Cooder also adapted the attitude, the funky slapping drum sound and the loose swinging rhythm of folk blues. His mandolin playing, which adds even more sweet, high vibrato to the tunes, generally complements the vibrato in his slide playing.

Cooder's second solo album, *Into the Purple Valley*, was designed loosely around the concept of the Great Depression and the journey that the Okies made from the dustbowl of the Midwest to the promised land of California. Many of the tunes were from that era, augmented by other travelling songs such as 'Hey Porter'. The irony of the similarity between being poor in the Depression and being part of the underclass in modern California was pretty much lost on the public who regarded Cooper as some kind of musicologist.

"A fair amount of money was spent on that album in terms of promotion, which resulted in a lot more visibility," said Cooder. "But that presented certain problems, because you can't forge a career based on social-type music in an era when that music is becoming less and less current, and less interesting to people. But I still thought it was the sort of stuff I should do, and I still think it's good."

'Hey Porter', although not from the '30s, is a masterful compilation of Cooder's talents. With Jim Dickinson's tack piano grounding the track, Cooder's mandolin dances around the melody solo and partners with the guitar and piano.

'Hey Porter' has a brief acoustic postscript to 'Great Dream from Heaven' by Joseph Spence. "There's a handful of guys that have something to do with the way I play now, in particular Joseph Spence, the Bahamian guitarist," said Cooder who in describing Spence pretty much explained his own style. "He always played in a melodic and rhythmic way that I found exotic, intricate and fascinating, with bass, melody, chord and this interior syncopation all going on at the same time, like juggling. He played mostly church music, old Protestant hymns. But he'd sit down with a hymn that everybody knew and twist it up so even his own wife can't sing along with him. He could play 'Jingle Bells' and make it sound unrecognisable, but it's how he likes to hear it. As far as he's concerned, everyone else is wrong."

Spoonful Cream

(Willie Dixon) ✳ Polydor ✳ 1968 ✳ Appears on: *Wheels of Fire*

Cream introduced the extended improvisation into mainstream rock & roll. Prior to Cream's 1967 tours, extended improvisation was not an element in rock & roll music that was built around concise songs with a carefully defined structure. Extended instrumental workouts were not part of the blues lexicon either. Improvisation was a jazz concept that required musicianship way beyond the capacity of most rock & roll bands. Once jamming became fashionable, everyone did it whether they had the ability or not. On *Wheels of Fire*, Cream also introduced the drum solo – something that Cream drummer Ginger Baker and perhaps a dozen others have been able to carry out but which plagued concerts for the next fifteen years.

"The Windsor Jazz and Blues Festival 1966, which was almost our first gig, we found that we ran out of numbers so quickly that we just had to improvise," said guitarist Eric Clapton. "So we just made up twelve-bar blues and that became Cream. That became what we were known for. I liked it up to a point, but it wasn't what I wanted."

Cream's most successful recorded jam is this version of Howlin' Wolf's 'Spoonful', which goes for about seventeen minutes. The three virtuosos in Cream all battle it out over the riff without disappearing. This is close to a jazz logic but with a very, very heavy arrangement.

Clapton found that the live shows were losing their charm when he noticed that the individuals were soloing without reference to the others.

"I just experimented one night," he said. "I stopped playing halfway through a number and the other two didn't notice, you know! I just stood there and watched and they carried on playing 'til the end of the number. I thought, well fuck that! You see, Cream was originally meant to be blues trio, like Buddy Guy with a rhythm section. I wanted to be Buddy Guy, the guitarist with a good rhythm section.

"With Cream we had our ups and downs. We had good gigs and bad gigs. We had gigs when you could have mistaken us for Hendrix, it was that good, and other times we were like the worst band in the world. It was this kind of inconsistency that relied upon the improvisation factor. All our songs had a starting theme, a finishing theme, and a middle that was up to us. On a good night it was great and on a bad night it was awful. I couldn't take this kind of up and down."

'Spoonful' was recorded on a good night.

Wendy Jesse Malin

(Jesse Malin) ❋ One Little Indian ❋ 2002 ❋ Appears on: *The Fine Art of Self Destruction*

Jesse Malin grew up playing New York rock & roll. His group, D Generation, were somewhere between Johnny Thunders and Tom Petty in style and substance. In 1999, D Generation disbanded. Malin, back to playing his own songs, built up a reputation as a songwriter to watch. Ryan Adams produced his first proper solo album, which features 'Wendy', cutting the record in just six days. "It gives it a real vibe, a snap shot of what was happening, an urgency, a rawness," said Malin of the pressurised sessions. "The lo-fi recording adds to the sincerity somehow. You don't have to order in the sushi and the dancing poodles; you can actually bang it out if you have only a certain budget and a certain amount of time. At the time we were doing it I thought it was rubbish, but the way Ryan [Adams] had me work has really brought something up that has given it a uniqueness."

   'Wendy' is an exemplary rock & roll track full of massive guitars, and a song about a girl and dreams and all the touchstones of the cool life. Malin's voice is gutsy and impassioned and sounds a little ragged and dangerous as well.

   "I just think that every day we walk through life doing things that aren't always the best for us," said Malin. "When I grew up watching my parent's marriage fall apart, if someone gave me a real nice gift, guitar or toy, I'd just want to smash it. You have something really good and you have the urge to kind of mess your life up. I don't know where that really comes from. The record deals with a lot of that kind of conflict, but in the end despite all the sad songs and dark stuff I like to think of it as a soulful record."

Please, Please, Please James Brown

(James Brown/Johnny Terry) ❋ King ❋ 1956 ❋ Appears on: *Star Time*

"I was working ten hours a day for less than $100 a month," said James Brown of his first hit 'Please, Please, Please'. "I love that song like I love one of my relatives. You know, if it wasn't for that song, I'd still be a janitor."

Recorded in Cincinnati, Ohio, in February 1956, 'Please, Please, Please' took the gospel background and the adept vocal backing of the Famous Flames doo-wop group and put that with the titanic force of James Brown's personality. It was this combination of the blues (the chorus is based on the blues standard 'Baby Please Don't Go'), doo-wop and gospel that sent 'Please, Please, Please' to the top of the charts. Like a penitent at a Pentecostal church, James chants over and over again going from the seductive to the desperate and then moving into some other place as he prostrates himself before the salvation of a woman's love. James is supported by the Flames and a killer rhythm section as produced by Ralph Bass.

It was this song that convinced Bass to sign Brown. "I didn't know James Brown from a hole in the ground," the producer said. "I went to the club that night and saw him do his show, crawling on his stomach and saying 'Please, Please, Please' – he must have said please for about ten minutes."

God Only Knows The Beach Boys

(Brian Wilson/Tony Asher) ❊ Capitol ❊ 1966 ❊ Appears on: *Pet Sounds*

"There's something about the simplicity that people respond to," said lyricist Tony Asher. "And it's such a compelling thing to say to someone – the phrase that implies 'I am who I am because of you.'" Asher was a jingle writer and advertising copywriter when he was introduced to Beach Boy Brian Wilson. Asher's job was to provide lyrics to *Pet Sounds*, an intensely personal piece of work by a man whom he barely knew. Surprisingly, the partnership proved perfect – there is an honesty to the album that is sometimes almost too candid.

Brian Wilson was a troubled man. The demons of his life have been documented to death elsewhere; suffice to say that at the time of making *Pet Sounds* Wilson was feeling conflicted about his role within the Beach Boys and as an artist. He was also feeling conflicted in his relationships with his family and especially with his wife Marilyn. 'God Only Knows' is a song of complete devotion to Marilyn that also suggests Wilson's apparent helplessness in dealing with the other forces in his life. It's the song of a man barely hanging on, and in a few years he would be over the edge.

Carl Wilson takes the lead vocal covered in heavenly sounds of sleigh bells, harp, violins, cellos, flutes and French horns. The vocal melody appears to drift off into the ether like a Tiepolo ceiling – a thing of high, proud, delicate beauty.

On hearing the song Paul McCartney instantly felt competitive and rushed off and wrote 'Here, There and Everywhere' but, for once, failed to match Wilson's stunning achievement.

"I wanted to write a song that would last forever," said Wilson.

The Mercy Seat Nick Cave & the Bad Seeds

(Nick Cave) ❄ Mute ❄ 1988 ❄ Appears on: *Tender Prey*

"My death it almost bored me/So often was it told" sang Nick Cave on *Tender Prey*. He had only himself to blame. His heroin habit was world-famous. The six months it took to record the album was interrupted by Cave dealing with his addiction. As usual, most of his songs had a morbid cast. If it wasn't his death he was writing about then it was somebody else's damnation.

It had been ten years before the mike when Cave began this album. He'd come a long way from bands the Boys Next Door and the Birthday Party. Cave had recently completed his novel *. . . And the Ass Saw the Angel*, his first serious prose, and was finally getting close to a mature voice. The southern Gothic – Flannery O'Connor meets Johnny Cash – was beginning to become more than fevered opiate dreams. The Bad Seeds, too, found their voice on *Tender Prey*. This was the first record where they sounded like a rock band and not an anti-rock band.

'The Mercy Seat' – Cave's ode to the electric chair – had all the dark grandeur that musical director Mick Harvey was capable of. It had a cinematic quality – a dark, noir-ish B-movie cinema (one thinks of *Shock Corridor*). The galloping rhythms of the Bad Seeds here matched the waves of fear that came with execution. Cave sings without irony in the bravado of someone who has faced death.

As to Cave's summation of *Tender Prey*: "It's patchy," he said.

Crosstown Traffic The Jimi Hendrix Experience

(Jimi Hendrix) ✳ Track Record ✳ 1968 ✳ Appears on: *Electric Ladyland*

Jimi Hendrix's third studio album began regularly enough on 20 October 1967. 'Crosstown Traffic' was in the first bunch of songs for this album, recorded at Olympic in London. The Experience was primed from two years of solid playing on stage and occasionally in the studio. 'Crosstown Traffic' is a straightforward

blues given a very tough twist by Hendrix. The speed of the song as it rips through riffs shows not only Hendrix's confidence but also the way his life was getting wilder and wilder. 'Crosstown Traffic' is jagged and speedy and a little crazy, like trying to juggle priorities and keep everything moving.

"People who put down our performance, they're people who can't use their eyes and ears at the same time," Hendrix said. "They've got a button on their shoulder blades that keeps only one working at a time. Look, man, we might play sometimes just standing there; sometimes we do the whole diabolical bit when we're in the studio and there's nobody to watch. It's how we feel. How we feel and getting the music out, that's all. As soon as people understand that, the better."

Electric Ladyland would take another year to finish and on the way Hendrix would go on one of the most incredible journeys in music.

Tecumseh Valley Townes Van Zandt

(Townes Van Zandt) ❋ Tomato ❋ 1969 ❋ Appears on: *For the Sake of the Song*

"I think of Townes as the greatest folk songwriter that my native state of Texas ever gave birth to," said Nanci Griffith. "Some of us songwriters are just lyricists, but he was definitely a poet."

In the mid-'60s, Van Zandt, born into a wealthy Texas oil family, forsook the family business to become a singer and songwriter. His was the world of the road and the American archetypes to be found there. He transformed these stories with an eye for detail and a poetic sense that owed a debt to both Bob Dylan and Elvis Presley. Johnny Cash's producer Jack Clement recorded his first album, *For the Sake of the Song*.

Van Zandt's influence was to transform Texas songwriting for Guy Clark, Lyle Lovett, Steve Earle, Joe Ely, Jimmie Dale Gilmore and others. His influence can also be heard in Rosanne Cash, Paul Kelly, Emmylou Harris and countless more who are better known than Townes will ever be.

'Tecumseh', on his first album, is a perfect example of a Townes song – full of tragedy and pain, a kind of wilfulness to live and a story line that is saved from cliché by the rhythm of its telling.

It Could Have Been a Brilliant Career Belle & Sebastian

(Stuart Murdoch) ❋ Matador ❋ 1998 ❋ Appears on: *The Boy with the Arab Strap*

Belle & Sebastian was the band that Britain had to have. The Scottish combo, which took its name from a kids TV show, started with just two – Stuart Murdoch and Stuart David. They put themselves in that English tradition going back to Nick Drake and Ray Davies and Morrissey – all bedsits and wet weekends and weak tea leavened with sarcasm and irony. Belle & Sebastian weren't afraid to build delicate melodic arrangements, but they also weren't afraid to be playful with them either. While there is a sense of melancholy through their work, there's little of Nick Drake's self pity.

Belle & Sebastian's version of kitchen sink folk rock arrived just as Brit-pop priapism had reached its peak. Their first LP was a critical triumph, though, most of the public never heard it. A second LP was better realised. By this third album, Belle & Sebastian were finding their feet.

'It Could Have Been a Brilliant Career' opens *The Boy with the Arab Strap* with Belle & Sebastian's beautiful sense of melody and Murdoch's wry take on the possibilities of youth.

"What really excites me is bands prepared to borrow from absolutely everything but come up with something their own," said bass player Stuart David. "And we're becoming a wee bit more willing to do that."

Janie's Got a Gun Aerosmith

(Tom Hamilton/Steven Tyler) ✳ Geffen ✳ 1989 ✳ Appears on: *Pump*

Aerosmith staged one of the great comebacks in rock & roll – a cruel business not known for giving second chances. They were superstars in the '70s with record-breaking drug habits. By the early '80s they were broke and unemployable. Then with the help of manager Lou Cox and Narcotics Anonymous they joined the recovery nation, reformed and went back on the road accompanied by their own drug police. The surprise to everyone, however, was that they resumed recording and writing at least as well as when they had fallen apart a decade previously. Aerosmith 1 had been sleazy rock & roll. Aerosmith 2 was '80s stadium rock.

"What scared the shit out of us was that, although we had the band back together, we weren't able to write a song to save our lives. So we were already primed for a change," said singer Steven Tyler. "It was just such a simple idea, but it wasn't within our grasp to think of it like that, because we were always such a party band with a tear-down-the-walls attitude, so for all of us to all do it at once, I don't know if it could have happened."

'Janie's Got a Gun', on their second sober album, *Pump*, was the best of their reformed singles. No longer the sloppy junkies, everything on this track is tight and beautifully balanced. The orchestration and arrangement is steady. The use of oriental flavours at the intro adds some mystery and drama. This is clean-cut rock. What gives the song an edge is its stark tale of child abuse, incest and murder. Tyler delivers the song without resorting to metal melodrama and makes the tale that much more real.

Sleep to Dream Fiona Apple

(Fiona Apple) ✳ Clean Slate/Epic ✳ 1996 ✳ Appears on: *Tidal*

Fiona Apple was a star at nineteen. Her debut album, *Tidal*, featuring 'Criminal' and 'Sleep to Dream', was a major hit even though her singer/songwriter style – she jokingly referred to her image as "tragic waif ethereal victim" – came with a jazzy piano colouring and confronting lyrics. But then, Apple had much to get off her chest. Not least of her issues was the anger that followed being raped at twelve years old.

"I have problems," she said, "but everybody's got problems, and I sometimes honestly have felt in my life that people have used me as a way to make themselves feel better, because I'm a very good subject to save. And sometimes I think, 'I'm not that bad off; it's really you that's making me feel like shit'".

Apple certainly fitted into the category Alanis Morissette created with 'Ironic' in 1995, but Apple is more complex than just pop psychiatry. Her influences are rich and her style is idiosyncratic. Producer Andy Slater encountered a young woman with a piano and he encouraged her to draw on all her influences rather than just fit her into the singer/songwriter box. They went record shopping and she stocked up on the Roots, the Pharcyde, Miles Davis, Ella Fitzgerald and Marvin Gaye.

'Sleep to Dream' is a defiant break-up song, written for her ex-boyfriend Tyson. "I'm very thrilled that other people can get something out of my songs," she said. "But I write them for myself."

It's Oh So Quiet (Blow a Fuse) Björk

(Hans Lang/Bert Reisfeld) ✳ Elektra ✳ 1995 ✳ Appears on: *Post*

In a career full of surprises, Björk's oddball version of big band jazz with this cover of Betty Hutton's 1948 hit 'Blow a Fuse' ranks near the top. It was a song she learnt on the tour bus and it became her biggest hit.

"Isn't that the best song you've heard for five years?" asked Björk rhetorically. "In a way it was against my principles to do an old cover version because I'm so anti-retro. But it has this story, this narrative: there's a beginning and something happens in the middle and the ending is different. So many pop songs, especially with

English lyrics, are just 900 different ways of saying 'she left me!' Which I actually love because it's pop, just one idea, very simple, but it doesn't mean it's cheap. I can relate to it, but I belong to the storytelling group."

The song has a bi-polar arrangement that Björk amplifies with her dramatic vocal and her propensity to cause trouble.

Ghost Town The Specials

(Jerry Dammers) ✳ 2 Tone/Chrysalis ✳ 1981 ✳ Appears on: *The Singles Collection*

Having started a ska revival, the Specials keyboardist Jerry Dammers pushed the genre into a new shape. Using the bouncing, slightly spastic ska rhythm and drenching it in lashings of dub echo, Dammers made a requiem with what was essentially party music.

'Ghost Town' was written in the wake of the massive riots in the Jamaican ghetto of Brixton and in the context of the rampantly conservative Thatcher government, the rising unemployment and the climate of racism that engulfed Britain at the time. The Specials' gigs had been targeted as recruiting sites for right-wing groups such as the National Front, which led to confrontations between mods and skinheads. Their shows were regularly stopped because of violence on the dance floor. 'Ghost Town' became an urban anthem in Britain in the summer of 1981.

The paranoia that positively seeps out of 'Ghost Town' was also a consequence of the deteriorating relationships in the band. Shortly after the song's release singer Terry Hall, Neville Staple and Lynval Golding jumped ship for the less dictatorial collective Fun Boy Three. 'Ghost Town' sounds like its name – it's spare and haunted and frightening.

Moonlight Mile The Rolling Stones

(Mick Jagger/Keith Richards) ✳ Rolling Stones Records ✳ 1971 ✳
Appears on: *Sticky Fingers*

Drugs began to take over Keith Richards' life in 1970, to the point where he started missing sessions or was too stoned to play. 'Moonlight Mile', the final track on *Sticky Fingers*, sounds like the closing song for an era; the culmination of the

Rolling Stones' life from an arty blues band in London through the chaos of the early stardom and then to their status as the coolest group of their era. In a sense, 'Moonlight Mile' is an answer to 'Satisfaction', which came only five years earlier.

This song captures the atmosphere of the dawn breaking on the third day without sleep. The gentle acoustic guitar and its lilting melody introduces the mood and then Charlie Watts' cymbals and little picks of sharp notes add to the cocaine references. Jagger sings this song as though he is stuck on the road and has no expectation of ever getting off. Paul Buckmaster's elegant string arrangement is strung on nervous tension. Mostly, though, it's Mick Taylor's guitar that makes this song work. He has a fluid, eloquent style that expands the melodic possibilities in the Rolling Stones more than any other player ever has, and with Richards missing in action the stage was all his.

This was, in fact, the end of an era. With *Sticky Fingers*, the Rolling Stones started to drift apart and the drugs began to take over.

Pills and Soap The Imposter

(Elvis Costello) ✳ Imp/Demon ✳ 1983 ✳ Appears on: *The Very Best of Elvis Costello*

Elvis Costello is generally in danger of entangling his work in his own puns and the sheer weight of his record collection. One album followed the next with stylistic twists, but by the mid-'80s the world was suffering Elvis Costello overdose.

Then he rose again. The occasion was the 1982 Falklands War; a military adventure, the sole purpose of which was increasing support for Margaret Thatcher. Costello penned 'Shipbuilding' about the effect of the war on the average English person and how the dockyards would come back to life on the blood of soldiers and sailors in the southern Atlantic. Sung by Robert Wyatt, it was a deeply affecting song.

The following year, he followed it up with 'Pills and Soap'.

"Lyrically speaking, it carried on in a sense from 'Shipbuilding'," he said. "The intention behind releasing it at such a time was that some people might sympathise with it. That's all."

Costello's panoramas of modern Britain under Thatcher were stark and spare, filled mostly with Steve Naive's funereal organ and piano against the lament of Costello's voice:

The king is in his counting house, some folks have all the luck
And all we get is pictures of Lord and Lady Muck
They come from lovely people with a hard line in hypocrisy
There are ashtrays of emotion for the fag ends of aristocracy . . .
Give us our daily bread in individual slices
And something in the daily rag to cancel all the crises . . .

Costello wanted the record out quickly and his deal with Warner Bros. was not concluded so he released the track himself, as the Imposter. The disguise was somewhat blown though when Costello personally delivered the record to radio and the press.

"I wanted the song to be heard at this particular time," he said. "It couldn't wait the month or two that it will take to finalise legal matters."

It was further asserted that the single would only be pressed in a limited edition of 15,000 copies.

"'Pills and Soap' had already been a hit," said Costello. "Albeit with a bit of a con trick on the retailers and the BBC, when we threatened to delete it in a week, which helped catapult it into the charts. But in effect it was a broadside, a protest song."

Deep River Blues Doc Watson

(Traditional/Doc Watson) ✳ Vanguard ✳ 1964 ✳ Appears on: *Doc Watson*

Born in 1923, Arthel 'Doc' Watson was already middle aged when he made his first major concert and subsequent recording date. Doc Watson was born in Deep Gap, North Carolina. Blinded by childhood illness, he took to music learning hillbilly, bluegrass and western tunes and the pop music of the '40s. He played banjo and guitar around the Carolinas in a variety of bands all the while devising a unique flat-picking guitar style. By the time he made his New York debut with the Clarence Ashley String Band he was an undisputed master.

Watson was one of the unqualified discoveries of the '60s folk boom. He sang with a mellifluous, sometimes broken and forlorn voice but his guitar playing absolutely shone. Watson's fingers moved around a melody with a sureness and logic that was simply breathtaking. In part, Watson's style comes from his diverse range of influences, such as the gypsy jazz player Django Reinhardt, the dark minimalism of Furry Lewis, and the fact that he tried to adapt fiddle playing to the flat-picked guitar. More than technique though, there is always a sense of grace in his fingerpicking.

'Deep River Blues' is the standout track from Watson's first album. The playing has a warm, deep tone that flows like the great rush of black water and as Watson picks his way through the tune and sings the mantra-like blues he comes as close as possible to rendering the divine.

My Favourite Things John Coltrane

(Richard Rodgers/Oscar Hammerstein II) ✳ Atlantic ✳ 1960 ✳
Appears on: *My Favourite Things*

The Sound of Music opened on Broadway in 1959. By 1965 it would be the biggest movie of its era and its songs – 'Do-re-mi', 'Edelweiss', 'The Sound of Music' and 'My Favourite Things' – part of the fabric of society. Fortunately, by then John Coltrane had been able to interpret 'My Favourite Things'.

The thirty-four-year-old saxophonist had recently left Miles Davis and made his own very impressive statement with his 1959 album *Giant Steps*. He had assembled his classic quartet (McCoy Tyner on piano, Jimmy Garrison on bass, and Elvin Jones on drums). Coltrane's agenda involved the modal style developed with Miles and his own spiritual journey, which included an interest in Asian scales and influences. Coltrane had studied Indian music through his friend Ravi Shankar and that's part of the mix of 'My Favourite Things'.

"I knew it was going to be an experience because John had composed *Giant Steps* and some other great tunes," McCoy Tyner said of joining Coltrane's quartet. "I was aware of it because he did some of the composing in his mother's home in Philadelphia, and it was during that period that I really got close to him. It was an amazing challenge for me. I knew that that's where I belonged, and that was the next step for me. We got along very well. We had a good feeling for each other, similar conceptually as far as music was concerned. I knew that is where I needed to be. I was really anxious and excited about it.

"I think with that band, the form wasn't set. We had a tonality that was set, we had a key we were in, of course, but we had the freedom to do what we wanted. One thing about John, and I think Miles Davis had this as well, is that he knew how to pick people to play with. That is very important. If it didn't work, you don't force it, and I think that happens a lot of times. Communication is very important, and I think the Quartet is a testament to that, because we were able to do things like make up a song around a scale, and that was it! It wasn't in your typical form. It wasn't completely 'out there', it had some form, but it wasn't limiting."

'My Favourite Things' was a popular success. Casual jazz fans easily understood it. It's a piece of rare beauty with exceptional nuances from Coltrane, Jones and Tyner that keep the piece timeless.

It's Only Rock & Roll The Rolling Stones

(Mick Jagger/Keith Richards) ❋ Rolling Stones Records ❋ 1974 ❋
Appears on: It's Only Rock & Roll

Ron Wood's sessions for his first solo album were a house party. At one session Mick Jagger offered to help Wood with his track 'I Can Feel the Fire' in return for Wood's assistance on 'It's Only Rock & Roll', which he cut at Wood's home studio with David Bowie on backing vocals, Andy Newmark on bass and Kenny Jones of the Faces on drums. It's symptomatic of the state of the Rolling Stones at this point – Mick Taylor was hardly present and about to quit, Richards was mostly stoned and producer Jimmy Miller was cracking up.

But then, rock & roll in general was in pretty bad shape in 1974. All of the first wave of rock stars from the '60s were well past their prime – all the groups were disbanded or should have been and not one of the '60s stars was making records even close to their past form. The new generation were mostly caught up in glam rock and metal – David Bowie and Elton John and Alice Cooper dominated the era. Mostly, though, the excitement and the sense of being on the edge of a social change had all but completely dissipated by the early '70s. The revolution was over and in place of zeal there was irony and cynicism. 'It's Only Rock & Roll' was Jagger's most cynical song – denying any response to his work other than the most superficial. Jagger was fortunate that such a fickle lyric was matched with a killer riff that made him a liar.

I'd Rather Be the Devil John Martyn

(Skip James) ✳ Island ✳ 1973 ✳ Appears on: *Solid Air*

The Glasgow-raised Martyn went to London at age seventeen and was quickly recognised as a prodigy on the London folk scene of the mid-'60s. He was welcomed as a guitar virtuoso – in a town that was full of highly original stylists. Martyn's temperament kept him a little aside from John Renbourn, Bert Jansch, Richard Thompson and others but he was widely respected and on this 1973 album is backed by Fairport Convention.

Martyn's technique is derived from the blues but interpreted through jazz and traditional English folk music to have a sound entirely his. 'I'd Rather Be the Devil' was written by American blues artist Skip James with an obvious gospel overtone. In Martyn's hands it's completely transformed. Using the echo effects and his manic, highly stylised picking style the song is stripped of its American roots and becomes decidedly English. It's as though the tune has been taken out of the southern Baptist church and translated into the Presbyterian. What is left is Martyn's feverish personality creating great walls of guitar harmonics that rise and clash against each other and his frantic vocal, which struggles against the tune as though wresting the Devil inside.

Common People Pulp

(Nick Banks/Jarvis Cocker/Patrick Doyle/Steve Mackey/Russell Senior) ✳ Island ✳ 1995 ✳ Appears on: *Different Class*

At the height of Brit pop in the mid-'90s when Oasis were tipped to take over the world and Blur were to redefine Englishness for the new millennium, Pulp came out with a classic British pop tune that was a state of the nation. Essentially, as singer/lyricist Jarvis Cocker observes on this track, Britain is now and ever will be a land of small people living small lives.

The pop rock band Pulp came out of the impoverished and provincial city Sheffield in the early '90s. Early on it became clear that Cocker had all the makings of Ray Davies when it came to observing his fellow English. This was not a band given to grand statements but rather to acute, witty sketches accompanied by delightful, naïve tunes.

'Common People' is ostensibly about young rich girls wanting to slum it with proletarian chic. Jarvis certainly makes fun of both sides of that bargain, but there is a dark and angry strain of class contempt in his lyric, the acknowledgment that art students can slum it with the working class but they always have an escape. This was not a popular view in the gung-ho new Britain.

"'Common People' was written in about June of '94 and the first time we played it, it became clear to me it was a significant song," Cocker told Q in 1996. "It seemed to be in the air, that kind of patronising social voyeurism, slumming it, the idea that there's a glamour about low-rent, low-life. I felt that of [Blur's album] *Parklife*, for example, or [Oliver Stone's film] *Natural Born Killers* – there is that noble savage notion. But if you walk round a council estate, there's plenty of savagery and not much nobility going on. In Sheffield, if you say someone's common, then you're saying they're vulgar, coarse, rough-arsed. The kind of person who has corned-beef legs from being too close to the gas fire. So that's what attracted me to calling it 'Common People', the double meaning, 'Oh, you're common as muck' and then Emerson, Lake & Palmer's 'Fanfare for the Common Man'."

John Coltrane Stereo Blues Dream Syndicate

(D Mehaffey/Karl Precoda/David Provost/Kendra Smith/Steve Wynn) ❊ A&M ❊ 1984 ❊
Appears on: *The Medicine Show*

Dream Syndicate had the misfortune to be labelled the leaders of a movement. The term Paisley Underground loosely grouped cutting edge guitar bands together. Their common influence was nothing paisley but, rather, the Velvet Underground, the Byrds and early Neil Young. Dream Syndicate leader Steve Wynn acknowledged those influences but added some more – specifically free jazz.

'John Coltrane Stereo Blues' was a free-form improvisation. Intense, sprawling, reckless, hypnotic and cathartic. 'John Coltrane' took a gutsy rock and blues riff and just went with it. It wasn't jazz but experimental rock & roll that paid off.

"It's a free for all," said Wynn of the song. "But it isn't just an obligatory measure of wildness, it's for a band that knows it well enough to jam on. It's probably my favourite song on the album, but it's got to be right."

'Coltrane' appears on the group's second album. They had moved from the indie Slash to the more corporate A&M and had hard rock producer Sandy Pearlman (Blue Oyster Cult, the Clash) at the helm to make an album that was harder and slicker. 'Coltrane' was the moment when it all came together for them.

"When we formed we went out there playing whatever you'd call it – psychedelic garage or indie/underground noise – and we weren't seeing it anywhere," said Wynn. "I think it just opened a lot of people's ears to some alternatives at the time – to Duran Duran or Haircut 100 or whatever people thought was hip and groovy at the time. We just say, 'Nahh. There's another darker, weirder, deeper, creepier side of underground music. Check this out!' We were advocates for this music that excited us. And I think we had something to do with bridging the gap with what came before – the Stooges, the Velvets, the Modern Lovers, Big Star – and all the things that came afterwards – Yo La Tengo, Nirvana, and bands like that."

Rollin' Stone Muddy Waters

(McKinley Morganfield) ✳ Chess ✳ 1948 ✳ Appears on: *The Chess Box*

Muddy Waters (aka McKinley Morganfield) learnt the blues when he lived in the Mississippi Delta. The blues is a fluid medium where songs are passed around and evolve very quickly. It was in the Delta that Muddy learnt 'Catfish Blues' and from that song created his own 'Rollin' Stone'.

Little did he know when he wrote the lyric to describe his rambling lifestyle that his phrase would be taken by a group of young white English men. In no way could he have imagined that they would become the world's greatest rock & roll band – given that the form had not yet been invented – or that they would make his name immortal all over the world in nations that he had never heard of. Nor could he have imagined that Bob Dylan would use his phrase for one of the greatest songs of the 20th century. None of these things could have existed in anybody's wildest dreams in 1948 when Muddy Waters cut 'Rollin Stone' as the flip side to Robert Johnson's 'Walking Blues'.

Muddy had the good fortune to cross paths with Johnson about the time he was driving tractors on Stovall's plantation for 22 cents an hour. Muddy ran an illegal juke joint on the plantation and played a little blues himself, although he could neither read nor write. Having made some field recordings for a musicologist, Muddy knew he could sing. When his request for a 3-cent raise was declined, Muddy Waters left the plantation and went to Chicago to make his name in show business.

'Rollin' Stone' has a driving electric guitar riff and a tough-as-nails attitude that transcended its roots. This was a new music for the modern age: not particularly rooted to the cultural traditions of the rural south, the Chicago Blues could be transplanted. It carried the heft of thousands of years of tradition. But mostly it had the noise and the power of the electric guitar in the key of E. Coming out of the juke joints of the south and the Chicago Southside, it also had a sleazy propulsion – there could be no mistake what was on the singer's mind.

From this little thing, great wonders grew.

O Superman (for Massenet) Laurie Anderson

(Laurie Anderson) ❋ 110 ❋ 1981 ❋ Appears on: *Big Science*

Laurie Anderson is referred to as a performance artist, which means that her work usually appears in serious art contexts such as galleries, museums and festivals. Which is where it would have stayed except that legendary BBC DJ John Peel began playing an excerpt of one piece on the radio and put 'O Superman (for Massenet)' at the top of the charts.

An eight-minute poem set to electronic loops plus abstracted voice and minimal instruments, it was actually a very catchy version of the kinds of things that Eno and Talking Heads had been doing. For this reason, Anderson wasn't thought of as art by the pop audience and was still taken as art by the art audience. Incidentally, the 'for Massenet' refers to Jules Massenet, the French operatic composer whose 'O Souverain' influenced this track.

'O Superman (for Massenet)' is about paranoia and communication and technology and it's put into a sound-scape that is both deliciously inviting and slightly unnerving. She has taken the self-consciousness of Brian Eno and made it warm and melodic. She used voice as both abstract and percussive and treated it with electronics – the heavy breathing underneath the poem pushed the boundaries of popular recording. Robert Christgau called 'O Superman (for Massenet)' "the pop event of the year".

Loaded Primal Scream

(Bobby Gillespie/Andrew Innes/Robert Young) ❊ Creation ❊ 1991 ❊

Appears on: *Screamadelica*

Primal Scream spanned so many moments in British rock. Bobby Gillespie got his start in the pop scene as the drummer of the Jesus & Mary Chain. Gillespie's friendship with Creation Records supremo Alan McGhee placed him in the midst of the Manchester scene. In 1986 Primal Scream's debut was a return to the eternal rock values. All these elements and the club and rave culture of the late '80s came together on Primal Scream's classic album *Screamadelica*. This was rock music with a new flavour.

'Loaded' is based on Andy Weatherall's remix of Primal Scream's 1989 track 'I'm Losing More than I'll Ever Have', updating the rock & roll song with the ambience of acid and club land. Most of all, 'Loaded' accentuates a groove. Described by one critic as "a bizarre cross between the Rolling Stones' 'Sympathy for the Devil' and Soul II Soul".

"All the great white rock of the past has been influenced by black music, but post-punk music lost touch with that influence," Gillespie said. "'Loaded' taught us about rhythm and space. We've always been good at harmony, but learning how to use a sampler gave us a new palette of colours. The sampler opens up a whole new world of psychedelic possibilities."

The *Screamadelica* album is full of humour and sensuality. It's joyful in the way that so much rock of the '90s wasn't and it bridged the gap between rock and dance music.

'Loaded' pretty much explains itself in the title. Gillespie was allegedly taking drugs for England. The chemicals brought a spiritual or at least spacey aspect to *Screamadelica*.

"When I was younger, I really thought that by 1991 we'd all be living in outer space and wearing cool silver space suits," he said. "I thought that automation would have taken over all manual labour so that people could be free to express themselves. All those moon shots in the late '60s and early '70s, I think they affected me and lot of my generation. I was really bummed out when I found out that NASA

have wound down the whole space program. See, I have this romantic image of the early explorers like Vasco Da Gama or Columbus, who were going into the beyond despite the fear that the world was flat and they'd disappear into oblivion. I think there should be a space program for spiritual reasons, as a leap into the unknown.

"I keep thinking about all these astronauts. Surely they must have been drastically altered by going up there? What did they think about while looking down at the world? I'm sure they must discover a lot about themselves, during the training and while they were in space looking at the Earth. I'd still love to go up there. But I've got to get an album out! But one of the ideas behind 'Higher than the Sun' is this really crazy thought I had that, because the prospect of people going into outer space has disappeared, we've got to explore inner space."

Killing an Arab The Cure

(Michael Dempsey/Robert Smith/Lol Tolhurst) ❋ Fiction ❋ 1978 ❋
Appears on: *Standing at the Sea: the Singles*

Robert Smith started the Cure like many other young Englishmen as a kind of art school statement. Encouraged by punk rock, which was then the rage, the Cure was gloomy, dark, perverse and funny. Smith's vocals were fey and his tunes were obtuse to disguise their early amateurishness. But clearly early on he had a gift. The first two songs, '10:15 Saturday Night' and 'Killing an Arab', displayed a unique talent for songwriting, which was literate and whimsical.

The Cure's early sessions were conducted in the Jam's studio downtime, using their instruments.

They were sufficiently striking to make it to the head of the post-punk pack. "People picked up on it, because it sounded very different from anything else at the time," said Smith in retrospect. "The whole LP did. Because Lol couldn't drum very well, we had to keep everything very, very simple. Our sound was forced on us to a certain extent."

Albert Camus' novel *L'Étranger* inspired the single 'Killing an Arab'.

"When I wrote the song I realised it was a very inflammatory title taken out of context," said Smith. "But I never imagined that the two could be divorced. 'Killing an Arab' is a title of a song which is about a certain prescient event which happened in a book written by Albert Camus. Otherwise, you might as well give titles purely for shock value like heavy metal bands do. I found it absurd that a group like the Cure should be singled out for that kind of attack."

The title created a significant controversy in the US where the group had hitherto been largely ignored.

"For a couple of days we made the national news in America," said Smith. "And it was the last thing in the world I wanted to get caught up in. Debating Camus on American cable TV was totally surreal."

Smells like Booty Freelance Hellraiser

(Rob Fusari/Beyoncé/Falonte Moore/Stevie Nicks/Kurt Cobain/Dave Grohl/Krist Novoselic)
❋ no label ❋ 2001 ❋ Appears on: *The Best Bootlegs in the World Ever*

The mash-up phenomenon swept clubs at then turn of the century. DJs and geeks used turntables and computer programs like Acid to mash together tracks from entirely different sources. Fatboy Slim was mashed onto the Rolling Stones, Herb Alpert jammed with Public Enemy. This was the logical extension of the sampling fever of the '80s taken to its dumbest extreme. Whereas Public Enemy and the Beastie Boys had carefully chosen samples for effect, mash-ups tended to go for the massive sugar hit of recognisable tunes distorted with a big beat. Lawyers and artists who attributed a fee to their music closed down the sampling era. The mash-ups, however, are right outside the music industry. They have no interest in "clearing" or getting permission to use the samples. But then, they're not planning to launch careers on the backs of their mash-ups. There's a real punk rock attitude attached to the movement. The tracks are either made live or made available over the Internet with some compilations being sold generally at fleamarkets or specialist record stores below the radar of the major labels.

Tracks like 'Smells like Booty' crunch big riffs. The track also carries a cultural message with the last rebel rock anthem ('Smells like Teen Spirit') and Destiny's Child's massive hip-hop hit ('Bootylicius') contrasting with each other and playing off the cultural baggage each has. It's the ultimate post-modern pop song. Or as DJ Bobby Carlton put it, "This is culture jamming in its purest form".

I've Got My Mojo Working Muddy Waters

(Preston Foster) ✳ Chess ✳ 1960 ✳ Appears on: *At Newport*

Mojos were common throughout the Mississippi Delta right up until the second world war. "We all believed in mojo hands," Muddy Waters told Robert Palmer. "You get you a mojo, and if you're gamblin', it'll take care of that; you win. If you're after the girls, you can work that on the woman you want and win. Black people really believed in this hoodoo." The culture of West Africa came to America on the slave ships less than a full generation before. Those beliefs and religions relating to curses and potions like black cat bones or the St John the Conqueror root were still very much alive.

Muddy Waters was born in 1915 in the Delta to a poor rural family. He grew up on and around Stovall's plantation where Charlie Patton had set the fire that would become the blues. Muddy was a gifted guitar player who learnt first- and second-hand from the greats. The music of the blues was just another cultural tradition imported from Africa like mojos.

In 1943 Muddy joined the exodus from the Delta north to Chicago where his sister told him, "They don't listen to that kind of old blues you're doin' now, don't nobody listen to that, not in Chicago".

Muddy adapted to the electric blues. He kept the openness and the swing of the Delta but his new sound was tough as steel, his slide playing sharp and piercing. In conjunction with harmonica player Little Walter Jacobs, Muddy Waters drew the blue print for the Chicago blues sound.

'I Got My Mojo Working' was like a reference to how far they had come from the plantations of the Delta to the modern city. Having once spent his hard won money on a worthless piece of superstition, he could now laugh about the quaint country ways.

'I Got My Mojo Working' was written by songwriter Preston Foster and first appeared around 1957. Waters put it into his act. While he no longer believed in the voodoo alchemy, 'I Got My Mojo Working' has its own magic. It's a song of lust and in his performance at the Newport Folk Festival he piles on the power, pounding out the riff and pumping the anticipation to the point where you think its going to explode.

This song put "mojo" into everyday speech providing the name for an estimable music magazine and giving Austin Powers his catchphrase.

Dixie Chicken Little Feat

(Lowell George/Martin Kibbee) ❋ Warner Bros. ❋ 1973 ❋ Appears on: *Dixie Chicken*

"Lowell had the 'Dixie Chicken' music," lyricist Martin Kibbee recalls. "Little Feat used to rent a rehearsal space. We had been going all night, dying. At two in the morning, I decided to go home, and I drove past this place with a sign that says 'Dixie chicken'. This riff was running through my head, and by the time I got home, I'd written the lyric. I showed up the next day. Lowell read it and said, 'You fuckin' nut. No way.'" The track shortly thereafter became a signature tune.

On their third album the members of Little Feat changed and the band went immediately funky. The record is steeped in New Orleans grooves and a heavy, foggy texture. 'Dixie Chicken' is vintage Little Feat – an oddball, cockneyed version of the traditional temptress song. This one is played out among the indoor palms and fibreglass flamingoes of a mythical motel.

What's So Funny about Peace, Love and Understanding Nick Lowe

(Nick Lowe) ❋ Demon ❋ 1999 ❋ Appears on: *The Doings*

Nick Lowe is one of the great characters of British rock. He was the bass player in Brinsley Schwartz, the group generally regarded as the forerunners of the pub rock movement. Certainly Lowe saw the shift in the wind in the mid-'70s. He produced Dr Feelgood and Graham Parker and helped establish the Stiff label with its witty slogans and irreverent take on rock & roll. Lowe was a major supporter of Elvis Costello and the producer of the Damned, and somewhere found time to make his own records and to record and tour with Dave Edmunds under the name Rockpile. Lowe himself was known as 'Basher', for his production technique, which was to bash it down in the studio as near to live as possible.

"Apart from the fact that he's a drunkard, he's a good guy . . . a madman . . . that's why we got on with him," said Feelgood's singer Lee Brilleaux.

"He was a real one-take merchant like they say. Just bash it down and tart it up later. That really is his motto. Like when we did '60 Minutes' for *Be Seeing You*. We

just couldn't get it right. So he suggested we went round the boozer and have a pint then when we went back, we'd do one take and that'd be the one, whatever it was like. And it all worked."

Lowe's songwriting generally reflects his sense of humour. His classic, though almost devoid of humour, is 'What's So Funny about Peace, Love and Understanding'. At least it appears to be without humour. The song has been attempted creditably by both Elvis Costello and Midnight Oil. The question it asks is reasonable enough and the fast and furious tune is wonderfully uplifting. There's a real pathos in this commonsense proposition. The sadness in the melody carries the despair the singer feels at man's inhumanity. The furious tempo counterbalances the melody with its sense of vast human spirit.

Damned drummer Rat Scabies summed Nick Lowe up: "I have yet to meet another musician who can write songs with such deep, meaningful lyrics and . . . a complete surrender to sincerity and true art."

I Want Your Sex George Michael

(George Michael) ✳ Columbia ✳ 1987 ✳ Appears on: *Faith*

It was a big leap from the squeaky clean Wham! to the sleazy insistence of 'I Want Your Sex'. But the potential was always there. Michael had composed and played all of Wham!'s hits from the early age of nineteen and on 'I Want Your Sex' he grew up. In Wham! he was the sort of boy you could bring home, but 'I Want Your Sex' was immediately banned (briefly) by the BBC and many American radio stations. The video was similarly restricted and started numerous rumours about Michael's sexuality. There was something in the groove to the track that suggested primal and anonymous and unrestricted coupling. It was hardcore dance-floor rebrushed as commercial pop. The subject matter of the *Faith* album, when attention was paid, showed Michael in mature territory – AIDS, drug addiction and his personal confusion were to the fore.

Faith sold over fourteen million copies and made Michael a superstar. He crossed so many styles and his talent was so extensive that he made his own genre. But he has never seemed comfortable in the role he worked so hard to make for himself. His songs are personal and impersonal in the same way. He's hiding in plain sight. This ambivalence gives Michael's work a unique depth, nowhere better than in 'I Want Your Sex'.

Eight Miles High The Byrds

(Gene Clarke/David Crosby/Roger McGuinn) ✳ Columbia ✳ 1966 ✳

Appears on: *5th Dimension*

The Byrds were on a steep learning curve in 1965. On the one hand they were part of the new aristocracy – Bob Dylan, the Beatles (now on acid) and the Rolling Stones. On the other hand they were still folkies and they toured with John Coltrane and Ravi Shankar. All of these elements came together in the influential 'Eight Miles High'.

Spending an evening with Brian Jones of the Rolling Stones inspired Gene Clarke. McGuinn added his version of the organ break from the Zombies' 'She's Not There'. He also borrowed a lick from Coltrane's 'India', which he transposed to twelve-string Rickenbacker. McGuinn's Coltrane-inspired guitar runs all the way through the song in a counter melody reinforced by the harmony singing from the band. This was a completely new conception for pop music.

Given the times and the radical, edgy and clearly psychedelic aspects to the song, 'Eight Miles High' was branded a drug song – despite McGuinn's denials (although singer David Crosby has admitted to the drug implications). This meant that many radio stations who had previously seen the Byrds as America's Beatles dropped the group from their playlists. Whatever its intentions, 'Eight Miles High' remains one of the masterpieces of the psychedelic era.

Sunday Morning Coming Down Kris Kristofferson

(Kris Kristofferson) ❋ Monument ❋ 1970 ❋ Appears on: *Kristofferson*

Kris Kristofferson turned thirty working as a janitor in Columbia Studios in Nashville. He had been a Rhodes scholar, reading poetry at Oxford University, and had also been a pilot in the American military. He had a wife and family. But he wanted

to be a janitor because that got him close to musicians. One of them was Columbia recording artist Johnny Cash who championed Kristofferson as a songwriter and gave him a hit with 'Sunday Morning Coming Down' (awarded the Country Music Association's Song of the Year for 1970).

It's an outsider's song – waking up on Sunday morning with a hangover and a mouth like an ashtray and wondering where the next slice of oblivion will come from whilst all around there are normal people living normal lives with well-adjusted families.

Cash made it a hit, but Kristofferson's own version on his first solo album has a dark beauty, in part due to his dry, flat singing.

Kristofferson's songs were one of the first steps towards the new country music that moved beyond the caricatures of Nashville pop and opened the way for country music to be a medium for self confession as well as entertainment.

Kristofferson said, "That song was literally what I was living at the time, and it just expressed itself. Aw, Christ, with that song in particular, in that song, there's a guy swinging this laughing little girl as I walked past him. Shit, I'm the guy who's swinging the little girl now. And, man, for that, you've gotta feel gratitude."

Highway 61 Revisited Bob Dylan

(Bob Dylan) ❋ Columbia ❋ 1965 ❋ Appears on: *Highway 61 Revisited*

Bob Dylan grew up on Highway 61. This interstate highway runs north/south parallel to the Mississippi River. It passes Duluth, Minnesota, just before hitting the Canadian border, near where Dylan spent his early childhood years. Highway 61 was the road travelled by many of the blues artists heading out of the cotton fields of the Mississippi Delta and up to the industrialised cities of Chicago and Detroit. 'Highway 61' was also the title of a blues song by Mississippi Fred McDowell. Dylan's version is therefore revisiting it. His *Highway 61 Revisited* album was a bold beginning to a new chapter in what was essentially a blues tradition.

'Highway 61 Revisited' was recorded on 2 August 1965. Mike Bloomfield, then the pre-eminent white blues guitarist, provided searing guitar lines. Al Kooper backed Dylan with a warm and animated organ sound that glued the music together. Dylan ranted through this song with a series of vignettes satirising the state of the world. In those mid-'60s records Dylan just piled on the imagery, lashing out at the hypocrisy he saw around him in the world of politics and show business.

While the song is full of dark imagery, essentially it's a black comedy. The words are very much in the style of Dylan's talking blues – comic narratives such as 'Talking Bear Mountain Picnic' or 'Motorpsycho Nightmare' rather than being a specific commentary. It's likely also that Dylan loved the way that Bloomfield mimicked the sound of a police siren in his guitar licks. Al Kooper had brought the whistle to the sessions and used to blow it when someone was using drugs. Dylan fixed the toy whistle into his harmonica rack and blew so hard producer Bob Johnston thought his head was coming off.

I Could Hurt You Now Aimee Mann

(Aimee Mann) ❋ Geffen ❋ 1993 ❋ Appears on: *Whatever*

'I Could Hurt You Now' was the coming of age for singer Aimee Mann. The Boston-born singer/songwriter had seen some success with her band Til Tuesday and one mid-'80s hit. On *Whatever* she emerged as one of the most astute lyricists of her generation and a very able tunesmith.

"We've had a joke going recently that the new album has three themes: despair, defeat and revenge," Aimee Mann once said, and those themes are apparent in all her solo work.

"Maybe those clichés about things happening in your childhood affecting you later are true after all," said Mann, who is the daughter of a psychiatrist. "But what are you supposed to do about it? Bringing it out into the open robs it of its power, while the process of creating a song transcends the mood you're examining."

She had been bedevilled by bad luck with record labels. This album was recorded labelless, with ex-boyfriend Jon Brion as multi-instrumentalist and producer and guests such as drummer Jim Keltner and former Byrd Roger McGuinn. Not surprisingly, career issues appear in many of her songs. The best tracks, though, are where she takes on the conflicts she has in her emotional life. 'I Could Hurt You Now' certainly covers revenge pretty well, but even in triumph there's more than a touch of lament.

"For me, songwriting is a way to figure it out, whatever it happens to be," she told *Details*. "That's why songs usually are about problems. Because when you can define a problem clearly, it relieves you of the burden of having to go on feeling it. Once you say, 'Yes, I feel completely like giving up, there's no point', suddenly that becomes the point. And then you can continue."

That's Entertainment The Jam

(Paul Weller) ❋ Polydor ❋ 1980 ❋ Appears on: *Sound Affects*

Paul Weller was never bashful about his reverence for the Kinks' Ray Davies. According to the Jam's singer/songwriter, "He was the only person writing in that way at the time – writing about basic, ordinary life. And it's very pure English language that he uses – there are never any Americanisms in it." Weller achieved his own 'Waterloo Sunset' with a song that he claims he knocked off in just ten minutes after returning from the pub.

'That's Entertainment' has the wonderful, rich and dreamy melody of classic Kinks. However, where Davies saw an urban pastorale of the working classes going about their daily business in a divine and sunny Britannia, untroubled about the future or the world, Weller's London was entirely different. It starts with "A police car and a screaming siren/A pneumatic drill and ripped up concrete/A baby waiting and stray dog howling" and gets more bleak from there. The refrain "That's entertainment" is the key to the track, prefiguring the media overload that was to come in the next decade, the pornography of misery churned out on cable news channels so that the audience is eventually immune to the pain on the screen. Weller and the Jam captured the darkness, paranoia and disappointment of the modern city.

The singer and songwriter based the lyric on a poem, 'Entertainment', which he had previously published. The music was a step forward for the group, which three years earlier had pounded out lightning fast punk rock. 'That's Entertainment' was built around a wall of acoustic guitar that allowed the melody room to flow. The *Sound Affects* album took all of three months in the studio – about three times the length of any previous albums – and it shows. Reportedly the Jam's inspirations for these sessions were the Beatles' *Revolver* and Michael Jackson's *Off the Wall*.

'That's Entertainment' is Paul Weller's masterpiece, as powerful today as when it was recorded in the summer of 1980.

Pink Moon Nick Drake

(Nick Drake) ❋ Hannibal ❋ 1972 ❋ Appears on: *Pink Moon*

This is Drake's finest moment. The singer/songwriter had been through hell and his sensitive mental health had declined steadily over the three years he had been recording. Then there was the frustration of not selling records. Drake was too sophisticated for the folk and the middle-of-the-road crowd and not in tune with the rock audience. The fact that he was a recluse and barely played in public didn't help.

"The most startling conversation I ever had with him was when we were making *Pink Moon*," said John Wood, who produced the album. "As you've probably read we made the record in, I think, two evenings. Nick was determined to make a record that was very stark, that would have all the texture and cotton wool and sort of tinsel, that had been on the other two, pulled away. So it was only just him. And he would sit in the control room and sort of blankly look on the wall, and say: 'Well, i really don't want to hear anything else, I really think people should only just be aware of me and how I am. And the record shouldn't have any sort of tinsel.' That wasn't the word he used, I can't remember exactly how he described it. He was very determined to make this a very stark, bare record and he definitely wanted it to be him more than anything. And I think, in some ways, *Pink Moon* is probably more like Nick is than the other two records."

It's a singular season in hell, which has out-lasted so many pretenders. Drake brought the tapes in unannounced to Island. He stayed for a cup of tea and left the tapes with the receptionist on his way out.

Shortly afterwards, at the age of twenty-six, Nick Drake died of an overdose.

He's on the Beach Kirsty MacColl

(Kirsty MacColl/Gavin Povey) ❋ Polydor ❋ 1985 ❋ Appears on: *Galore*

It's extraordinary that an artist of MacColl's abilities slipped through the cracks, relatively unknown at the time of her accidental death in 2000. The daughter of folk singer and songwriter Ewan MacColl and the wife of producer Steve Lillywhite, Kirsty MacColl was a songwriter with unique gifts and a singer with a voice that was by turns heartbreaking and uplifting.

MacColl led, by all accounts, a very full life. Much of it happy and some of it depressed. The spectre of her father who left the family before she was born cast an unfortunate shadow.

"It's misleading to say I had no contact with him or I didn't love him," MacColl said. "I didn't grow up in the same household but people assume that because my dad was into music and I've got two half-brothers who are performers that it was like the Waltons, all sitting around playing acoustics. It wasn't like that at all. I grew up with my mum. I felt really excluded from that lifestyle.

"Children are happy if their parents are happy. They shouldn't have to feel responsible for the cock-ups of grown-ups. I felt guilty about a lot of things that were nothing to do with me. Loving is not saying, 'I love you' to someone, it's giving them what they need. I'm not sure what I needed but I don't think I got it.

"I don't want to make my mum unhappy. She wanted it all to be all right. She didn't turn against my father, she loved him and she never loved anyone else. I wish I'd been closer to him, but he was a sad man and it made him close up. Childhood was just something I had to get over in order to get on with my life."

MacColl started in pop music when still a teenager. Her first song 'They Don't Know' was a minor hit for her and later a smash hit for Tracey Ullman. Her first real action came in 1981 at age nineteen with 'There's a Guy Works Down the Chip Shop Swears He's Elvis', which was both funny and an accurate portrait of male narcissism. MacColl's next hit was a version of Billy Bragg's 'A New England', that she made tuneful and meaningful in ways that Bragg never quite could.

Her follow-up to the Billy Bragg hit was 'He's on the Beach'. Like 'Elvis' this was a carefully rendered character study of a person who had escaped the dreariness of England for a free life. MacColl imbued the song with a wonderful sense of promise and sunshine and a taste of victory while on the same tune capturing the other character's feeling of loneliness and entrapment.

"If you live in England you do get depressed," she said in an interview some time after the release of 'He's on the Beach'. "You are surrounded by apathy all the time. It's dark half the winter. It has that effect on me. I feel rooted here but I spend a lot of time travelling and that's quite a relief. I can't imagine not going away from time to time, just to get things in perspective. There's something about England ... we just [exasperated sigh] ... I think you need to go abroad to realise how insignificant we are."

'He's on the Beach' is a perfect piece of pop that sounds like Beach Boys records and blue skies and the endless expanse of new possibilities.

Lady Marmalade Labelle

(Bob Crewe/Kenny Nolan) ❋ Epic ❋ 1974 ❋ Appears on: *Nightbirds*

A meeting of exceptional talents made 'Lady Marmalade' the best single of the '70s. Although it has been tarnished of late through overuse and poor cover versions, 'Lady Marmalade' exploded on the airwaves in 1974 with funk and disco and pop all burning through the track and the scorching vocals of Labelle over the top. Producer Allen Toussaint brought New Orleans music into the space age.

Labelle – Patti Labelle, Nona Hendryx and Sarah Dash – had been Patti Labelle and the Bluebelles doing the R&B circuit since 1962 when they had their first hit 'I Sold My Heart to the Junkman'. By the early '70s they had moved to New York and were working with the likes of Laura Nyro. They started to do more music by contemporary artists and Nona Hendryx began writing. In the early '70s, they took over Bette Midler's residency at the Continental Baths in New York and suddenly had a gay following. Then someone suggested they record with Allen Toussaint in New Orleans.

The *Nightbirds* album is pure sex on wax. Labelle channelled the era – gay lib, women's lib, hedonism. They were all for liberation. "I don't wear tampons [on stage] because if it run down my leg, that's what you see and that's what you git," said Dash. "We told our band, 'We like to reach orgasms on stage' . . . I really came in Philadelphia."

New York notwithstanding, Labelle decided to record with Allen Toussaint in the Crescent City (New Orleans). Toussaint was the John the Baptist of the New Orleans sound since the days of Fats Domino right through to Dr John.

"What a record is all about is the singer – a showcase for the voice," he said when quizzed about his production style. "Whatever else goes on in a track, is *for* the voice. We build all the other instruments with the singer in mind. I prefer the highlights of a voice. Most singers have particular highlights and the way to record them is to move towards the highlights, bringing them out."

To bring out Labelle's highlights, Toussaint assembled a cast of the best New Orleans musicians, including local legends the Meters. Among the songs chosen was this story of a prostitute and voodoo queen, Lady Marmalade. The backing track was built out of a deep, funky bass, piano and percussion and the whole thing was syncopated within an inch of its life. The rhythm tracks are deeply in the groove but playing with verve and spontaneity.

This is as good as pop gets – dirty and sleazy and funny and impossible to avoid. Over the top of that Labelle wail the lyric, reaching choruses like they're about to explode with pleasure.

'Lady Marmalade' broke out first in the discos and amongst the gay community. It soon transferred to pop radio – despite efforts by church groups to have the track black-listed.

"I like appealing to both men and women. I have no preferences," said Nona Hendryx. "I don't limit myself. I'm all sexes, I don't know what a heterosexual or a bisexual or a homosexual or a monosexual is. I don't understand the differences."

These were strong words in 1974.

But then, as Hendryx said, "Labelle was ahead of our time because we did something opposite from what was happening for a black girl group."

Rock & Roll All Nite KISS

(Gene Simmons/Paul Stanley) ✳ Casablanca ✳ 1975 ✳ Appears on: *Alive!*

'Rock & Roll All Nite' had lain dormant on KISS' third album. Indeed, in 1975 KISS were going nowhere fast. To stimulate his label's cash flow, Neil Bogart of Casablanca records enlisted producer Eddie Kramer to record a KISS live album. Imaginatively titled *Alive!*, KISS couldn't sell the records but they knew how to stage a show. Their music benefited from the exchange of a great live room. 'Rock & Roll All Nite', like most anthems, was dumb and it too benefited from the energy of a concert audience.

Simmons and Stanley had cobbled the song together from an old tune ('Drive Me Wild') and a general desire to reproduce the dynamics of a rave-up like Sly Stone's 'I Want to Take You Higher'.

KISS' audience was out in the suburban wasteland, the kids who were alienated from the arty superstar rockers and really just wanted colour and movement and drama. The credo "I want to rock & roll all nite and party everyday" was a spot-on description of their wildest dreams. It fulfilled KISS' dreams too – the album went Top 10 and sold over five million copies.

Greetings to the New Brunette Billy Bragg

(Billy Bragg) ✳ Go! Discs ✳ 1986 ✳ Appears on: *Talking with the Taxman about Poetry*

Billy Bragg was a middle-class boy writing about the working classes with a touch of BBC affectation – but beneath it all he had a fundamental belief that really the yobbos are missing the point. The characters in 'Greetings to the New Brunette' are well drawn (if a little brutally) in the manner of Ray Davies, although Davies I think isn't overly harsh in his criticism. Bragg's enduring political statement would be his assertion of Englishness, the common or garden lifestyle that exists outside of global capitalism. "I'm not an angst depresso person, I try to be positive," he said. "But this is Britain and I'm afraid it isn't all 'Karma Chameleon' and happy happy. I don't think people need reality slammed down their throats but it doesn't hurt to remind people who, for whatever reasons, are not aware we're living in a country where we're not looking after everybody. We all say our priority is the welfare state but it doesn't even work anymore and the government is trying to pull it apart."

Bragg's mission, as was Woody Guthrie's, was to keep the forgotten and the dispossessed in the culture and the landscape. He does that with 'New Brunette' and he's funny as well: "How can you lie there and think of England/When you don't even know who's in the team" and "Your sexual politics have left me all of a muddle/We are joined in the ideological cuddle," which is British college humour.

With some help from Smiths' guitarist Johnny Marr and singer Kirsty MacColl, 'New Brunette' was a new level of sophistication for Billy Bragg as a writer and the song is still strangely affecting.

I Can't Make You Love Me Bonnie Raitt

(Mike Reid/Allen Shamblin) ✳ Capitol ✳ 1991 ✳ Appears on: *Luck of the Draw*

At home in Nashville one day, former football star Mike Reid read a story in the morning paper. A local man had been arrested for getting drunk and shooting his girlfriend's car. When asked what he had learnt from his experience he replied, "I learned, your Honour, that you can't make a woman love you if she don't". The irrefutable wisdom of that and the poetic way in which it was revealed stayed with the songwriter when his partner Allen Shambin arrived for a writing session.

The song was tried a number of ways before Reid stripped it right back to the melody and lyric and let the pathos out. The pair decided that the song belonged to either Bonnie Raitt or Linda Ronstadt. The former was looking for tracks for her post-comeback album. Raitt started recording in the early '70s as a hardcore blues singer who drifted into rock before her life and career hit the skids of alcoholism. Then, in one of the most startling resurrections in 1989, her *Nick of Time* album turned her into a superstar. A rollercoaster life such as this allowed Raitt to inhabit a song as deep as 'I Can't Make You Love Me'.

"I was astounded the first time I heard it," said the singer. "And I knew I had to record it. I'm a big fan of Mike's voice, and the two of them together wrote probably one off the most exquisite songs I've ever heard. I think it stands among the best songs ever written."

That's a sentiment that's widely shared. Both Prince and George Michael have recorded the song. Carole King recently told *MOJO* magazine, "It's torn from the depths of feeling, from that really horrible place where your love is unrequited".

Sin City Emmylou Harris

(Chris Hillman/Gram Parsons) ❊ Reprise ❊ 1975 ❊ Appears on: *Elite Hotel*

Emmylou Harris was content being a folksinger until one day Chris Hillman of the Flying Burrito Brothers saw her sing in a club and suggested to his partner Gram Parsons that they hire her. Parsons caught her act the next night in Baltimore. Harris became Parson's muse and after his death in 1973, picked up the torch he had lit. Parsons was a gifted songwriter who was refashioning country music away from the hayseed Nashville archetype. His lyrics were more sophisticated, his moods more complex.

"It's hard to pinpoint any one quality about Gram," said Harris at the time. "It was a collective talent – the vision, the songs, the voice and the feel. Most people have one or two of those things but there is always something lacking. He really had everything. Someone needed to take country music and not change it but lift it up and over and say kind of 'look at this'. He brought it to a new audience and to a completely new level."

Having the torch, Harris had little choice other than to run with it. She engaged the Hot Band – including James Burton on guitar and Rodney Crowell on keyboards – and proceeded to put some of her own style into country.

Elite Hotel captures Harris and the Hot Band in concert at their peak. 'Sin City' was a signature tune for the Burrito Brothers but, here, Harris is clear about the dark goings on in Sin City and she takes it all in with equanimity. She is sexy and strong and her voice is a pure wonder.

Iron Man Black Sabbath

(Geezer Butler/Tony Iommi/Ozzy Osbourne/Bill Ward) ❊ Vertigo ❊ 1971 ❊
Appears on: *Paranoid*

Heavy metal starts here. The big, dumb riff under big, dumb lyrics and a monster beat delivered at a funereal pace. 'Iron Man' is one of the cornerstones of '70s rock.

Is the Iron Man of the song just the Marvel cartoon character or does it represent the real feelings of male teenagers who need to build the psychological defences that they will need in adulthood? Isn't there an Iron Man inside every boy?

"When we started writing things we didn't want to present bullshit like 'I'm gonna see my chick and we're gonna get it on.' It's all hypocritical," said Ozzy Osbourne. "This love trip is so grossly distorted. One week you fall in love, the next week you fall out and start doing dope and blow your mind out. I don't believe there's anyone in this world that is one hundred per cent in love. I don't think anyone is totally happy; you can't really wake up in the morning free of hassles and do what you want as long as you don't harm anybody else. If you wanna stick needles into your arm it's your own life. Like, I'm not into taking heavy dope although I have taken dope. People who take it just have hang-ups that they can't deal with.

"If you haven't got your own mind and can't do what you want, you're not an individual, just part of a mass. The society trip in England is that you go to school, then get a job, and at the age of twenty-one you get married. You work the rest of your life in a factory and when you retire at the age of sixty-five you get a gold watch; forty-five years in a factory with stinking oil, polluting the land. I used to work in a factory and I used to see these blokes dying on their machines. That just blew my mind.

"They're saying you should cut your hair and get a good job – for what? So people can suck off you? They're picking your bones, getting all that energy out of you, when it could be put to so much better use."

By the time Sabbath cut this, their second album, they had devised a sound that was simplistic and direct. The tempo of 'Iron Man' was set not for dancing but for banging one's head, especially when imbibing the downer drugs that were plentiful in the '70s or, indeed, marijuana and cheap wine.

Black Sabbath were initially not taken seriously by the rock critics, but young boys understood and from this small acorn grew the first wave of British heavy metal and, later, Nirvana and grunge rock.

Sad Eyed Lady of the Lowlands Bob Dylan

(Bob Dylan) ✳ Columbia ✳ 1966 ✳ Appears on: *Blonde on Blonde*

Well, this is a track that blew everyone's minds. Dylan's double album *Blonde on Blonde* was a big gambit. He had changed the course of music less than two years earlier with *Bringing It All Back Home*, then gone on a blistering world tour and delivered another masterpiece in *Highway 61 Revisited*. The two-record set of which the last entire side was one song of hallucinatory imagery.

We now know, courtesy of Dylan's own pen, that 'Sad Eyed Lady of the Lowlands' was written late at night in the Chelsea Hotel. Its subject is Sara Lowndes, Dylan's future wife. The title suggested as much.

The studio band was called for two in the afternoon on one day but Dylan kept them waiting into the night as he polished the words. By the time he was ready, most of the players were falling asleep. Kooper was on organ, the guitarists were Jerry Kennedy, Charlie McCoy, Wayne Moss and Joe South, the pianist was Hargus 'Pig' Robbins, Henry Strzelecki was on bass and Kenny Buttrey on drums. Dylan began the country waltz in 6/8 time, strumming his acoustic guitar. The verses just kept coming. According to Buttrey, "I was playing left-handed, looking at my watch and it kept on and kept on". There's a halting, lurching quality to the song which may be in part because the band were expecting to reach a crescendo at each verse not realising that there was more to come.

The sheer size of the song (eleven minutes) and the potency of its images piled on each other, images that owed more to Rimbaud than rock & roll, put Dylan in an entirely new class of his own. This was a piece of rock & roll that had never been attempted before or probably since. When finally completed, 'Sad Eyed Lady of the Lowlands' took up one entire side of the album – the longest song yet recorded in popular music.

Take It Personal Gang Starr

(Keith Elam/Christopher Martin) ❋ Chrysalis ❋ 1992 ❋ Appears on: *Daily Operation*

Guru (Keith Elam) and DJ Premier (Christopher Martin) made Gang Starr one of the more influential rap duos of the early '90s by melding jazz and rap traditions using soul jazz performers and inventive beats. Guru also recorded a couple of estimable albums under the brand Jazzmatazz with Roy Ayers, Donald Byrd and N'Dea Davenport. Premier produced joints for Notorious B.I.G., Nas and Jay-Z. Jazz has been an important ingredient of hip-hop. The jazz tradition lends authenticity and a melodic vocabulary to the best hip-hop. In the early '90s this honeyed soul jazz was a critical element in the hip-hop vocab, in large part thanks to Gang Starr.

According to saxophonist Branford Marsalis, "Gang Starr looked up and said, 'We see what they're doing on the radio and on the videos, and we don't care. It's not that we won't try to make radio songs or to make videos, but we will make the songs as they are true to us. Not as it is defined by some faceless pencil pusher or program director.'"

"The whole gimmick is that there is no gimmick," said Guru. "It's just an MC and a DJ. The original elements that the art form was based upon when it started."

Listen to the Lion Van Morrison

(Van Morrison) ✳ Warner Bros. ✳ 1972 ✳ Appears on: *St Dominic's Preview*

"I've been a student for a long time," Van Morrison told Happy Traum back in 1970. "There's this one cat, John Lee Hooker, who plays guitar . . . I mean he can play that thing until it talks. And when it talks, he doesn't have to speak . . ." John Lee Hooker could just play one chord over and over like a mantra, Van Morrison learnt that lesson well and applied it to his instrument – his voice.

"My bag is approaching something and taking it to another place," he told Ritchie Yorke. "Like words – you take a word and by the time you've finished with it, you milk it and you go through the emotion of what it is, what it means there and then. It's the emotion . . . each word has got a connotation and symbolism and the thing is finding what's behind the word – what meaning it has and what emotion. I'm really into vocal repetition as a definite art form."

'Listen to the Lion' has almost no words, just the phrase "Listen to the lion inside of me," which Morrison returns to again and again as the music ebbs and flows. Acoustic guitar and synthesiser dominate the song with its leonine rumblings. Against that spare backing he jams on the vocals, playing wildly with the phrasing to show subtle shifts of emotional content. He sings the phrases like an incantation, sometimes desperate and longing for love and at other times boasting of the power of his passion; and then at other times he sings in despair that these emotions have brought him nothing but ruin. He doesn't need to speak, there's nothing more to be said, but to let yourself drift off beyond the words and the narratives and just feel the rush and the pause and savour those moments.

Excursion A Tribe Called Quest

(Jonathan Davis) ✳ xJive ✳ 1991 ✳ Appears on: *The Low End Theory*

Yet another outfit from the Native Tongues Posse alongside De La Soul and the Jungle Brothers, A Tribe Called Quest were into conscious hip-hop that combines sharp rapping with jazz and bass-heavy grooves. 'Excursion' opens the rap quartet's second album – one that is widely considered to be a milestone in rap music. *The Low End Theory* carries the Afrocentrism of the Tribe one step further with the engagement of master bass player Ron Carter, one of Miles Davis' great sidemen.

Q-Tip kicks off *The Low End Theory* with the 'Excursion' manifesto:

Back in the days when I was a teenager
Before I had status and before I had a pager
You could find the Abstract listening to hip-hop
My pops used to say, it reminded him of bebop
I said, well daddy don't you know that things go in cycles
The way that Bobby Brown is just ampin like Michael

The rhymes and beats here are perfectly in sync, bouncing around and making a point without preaching. Q-Tip and Phife Dawg swap rhymes effortlessly. They roll with the beat rather than attack it and they allow their words to sit with groove rather than fight it. So while their message is by no means weak, their style is less macho and confronting than the gangstas.

Christian's Automobile The Dixie Hummingbirds

(Archie) ✳ MCA ✳ 1998 ✳ Appears on: *Thank You for One More Day*

Perhaps the best known and longest surviving gospel group, the Dixie Hummingbirds had a direct link to the beginning of the African-American tradition where the slaves reinterpreted their music through the prism of the southern churches.

James Davis formed the choir in 1928 as an itinerant vocal group travelling through South Carolina. Davis was a congregant of the Church of God Holiness where he learnt shape singing.

The Dixie Hummingbirds cut their first sides for Decca in 1939 by which time teenage singing sensation Ira Tucker and bass singer Willie Bobo made up the classic line-up. In that same year John Hammond staged From Spirituals to Swing at Carnegie Hall, which for the first time brought the full range of African-American music to middle-class New York. The Dixie Hummingbirds' place on the bill elevated them to a pre-eminent position amongst gospel groups of the era.

Unlike many of their contemporaries, the Hummingbirds threw everything into a performance – holy rolling and dancing to their spectacular vocal improvisations. They were a major inspiration to soul singers such as Hank Ballard, Jackie Wilson and later groups like the Temptations and the Four Tops.

Although the Hummingbirds stayed close to the church they moved with the times. In the '60s they were involved in the civil rights movement and their material became decidedly political.

In 1973 the Dixie Hummingbirds made the pop charts as the backing on Paul Simon's hit 'She Loves Me like a Rock'. 'Christian's Automobile' with its rollicking churchy feel is a perfect example of the Hummingbirds at their best. Using the metaphor of the automobile in the context of salvation is both pretty funny and is typical of the Hummingbirds' capacity to swap between the sacred and profane.

Black Steel in the Hour of Chaos Public Enemy

(Public Enemy) ❋ Def Jam ❋ 1988 ❋

Appears on: *It Takes a Nation of Millions to Hold Us Back*

Public Enemy's 1988 album, *It Takes a Nation of Millions to Hold Us Back*, was one of the most powerful albums ever made and they expressed the issue of race in the US as concisely and clearly as it had ever been stated. Chuck D drew on the tradition of African-American poets and intellectuals – the Last Poets, Rap Brown, Eldridge Cleaver, the nation of Islam, Gil Scott-Heron and others – and he opened a new chapter in that tradition. 'Black Steel in the Hour of Chaos' is one of his most acutely argued early songs.

As powerful a rapper as Chuck D clearly is, Public Enemy's real weapon is the Bomb Squad, their production team who mixed samples with sound effects to create a sound-scape like an aural battleground.

"The first thing we would do is the beat, the skeleton of the track," explained Hank Shocklee, head of the Bomb Squad. "The beat would actually have bits and pieces of samples already in it, but it would only be rhythm sections. Chuck would start writing and trying different ideas to see what worked. Once he got an idea, we would look at it and see where the track was going. Then we would just start adding on whatever it needed, depending on the lyrics. I kind of architect the whole idea. The sound has a look to me, and Public Enemy was all about having a sound that had its own distinct vision. We didn't want to use anything we considered traditional R&B stuff – bass lines and melodies and chord structures and things of that nature.

"Back in the day, things was different. The copyright laws didn't really extend into sampling until the hip-hop artists started getting sued. As a matter of fact, copyright didn't start catching up with us until *Fear of a Black Planet*."

In the late '80s when 'Black Steel in the Hour of Chaos' was made there was no regulation of sampling. Hence the entire record is made up of bits and pieces of other discs. Public Enemy was not the first to use samples to make songs. They were the first to do it with such violence though. The record's success meant, ironically, few more records could be constructed in this way – although Tricky used 'Black Steel' as a basis of a track of his own on *Maxinquaye*.

"The first thing that was starting to happen by the late '80s was that the people were doing buyouts," said Shocklee. "You could have a buyout – meaning you could purchase the rights to sample a sound – for around $1500. Then it started creeping up to $3000, $3500, $5000, $7500. Then they threw in this thing called rollover rates. If your rollover rate is every 100,000 units, then for every 100,000 units you sell, you have to pay an additional $7500. A record that sells two million copies would kick that cost up twenty times. Now you're looking at one song costing you more than half of what you would make on your album. It would be impossible to do *It Takes a Nation of Millions to Hold Us Back* now."

21st Century Schizoid Man (Including Mirrors)

King Crimson

(Robert Fripp/Michael Giles/Greg Lake/Ian McDonald/Peter Sinfield) ❋ Island ❋ 1969 ❋

Appears on: *In the Court of the Crimson King*

Possibly the best progressive rock band (if that isn't an oxymoron) opened their account with '21st Century Schizoid Man', the first track from their 1969 debut album, *In the Court of the Crimson King*. Crimson was the brainchild of guitarist Robert Fripp with Ian McDonald on the reeds, woodwinds and Mellotron, bassist Greg Lake, drummer Michael Giles and lyricist Peter Sinfield. Together they created a sludgy portentous music that aspired to be Wagnerian. "At the time," Sinfield recalled, "the music was very weighty and red. It was very majestic."

'21st Century Schizoid Man' was a kind of Orwellian sci-fi epic. Sinfield foresaw the rape and pillage of families, death and destruction and prophets ignored. It was a world described by a freak-out Mellotron played backwards with phasing effects. Progressive rock acts could typically never settle on a time signature and that is certainly the case with Crimson. This leads into a passage of angular and nasty guitar work from Fripp before the apocalypse descends on the whole thing.

"I find it easier to write when I'm angry, sad or depressed," said the lyricist/poet Sinfield. "When I'm happy the things I write are banal and trite. I've nothing to say. It's the state of mind I want to be in so I just enjoy it."

Six years later when Fripp disbanded Crimson to better prepare himself for the collapse of the West he predicted, "The transition will reach its most marked point in the years 1990 to 1999. Within that period, there will be the greatest friction and, unless there are people with a certain education, we could see the complete collapse of civilisation as we know it and a period of devastation that could last, maybe, 300 years. It will be comparable, perhaps, to the collapse of the Minoan civilisation."

'21st Century Schizoid Man (Including Mirrors)' is the apex of British progressive rock, it certainly didn't get any better – especially with bassist Greg Lake's next project Emerson, Lake and Palmer. The best thing about the group was Barry Godber's painting on the front cover of *In the Court of the Crimson King* – one of the best covers of the LP era.

Parchman Farm Mose Allison

(Mose Allison) ✳ Prestige ✳ 1957 ✳ Appears on: *Greatest Hits*

Born in Tippo, Mississippi, in 1927, Luther Mose Allison is as much a blues player as a jazz pianist. His hard driving tempos come from the juke joints of the south but his tonal vocabulary goes beyond what is generally described as blues. There are touches of the bebop of Charles Ives and Louis Jordan. Allison's piano is very forthright. He backs that with a singing voice that is also tough but very articulate. In the tradition of the players from the juke joints and bars, Allison sounds like he's enjoying himself.

'Parchman Farm' is like many of Allison's tunes, a story of the south and of hard times. His original version is positively pneumatic with the force he puts into the piano line. Bobbie Gentry, Alex Harvey, Hot Tuna, the La De Das, Manfred Mann and Chris Spedding have subsequently covered the song, to name just a few.

"It's not anything I have studied to attain, it's just a matter of doing it, listening to people you like and trying to sing the best you can," he told *MOJO*. "I heard a lot of country blues as a kid, in Mississippi, Tampa Red, Memphis Minnie. Then Lightning Hopkins, Charles Brown, Percy Mayfield, Muddy Waters, all of 'em, you know. Louis Jordan and Nat Cole were big influences."

Be My Baby The Ronettes

(Jeff Barry/Ellie Greenwich/Phil Spector) ✳ Phillies ✳ 1963 ✳

Appears on: *Presenting the Fabulous Ronettes featuring Veronica*

In the beginning there is the drum pattern. Four beats. Coming out of eternity with a thump that breathes on the void. Then there are the handclaps and the strings, the percussion and the pianos all heralding the arrival of Ronnie, whose voice sounds like pure honey. 'Be My Baby' is breathtaking.

Phil Spector was twenty-two years old when he cut this track, still building his ' 'wall of sound'. Spector was the first record producer who stamped his personality

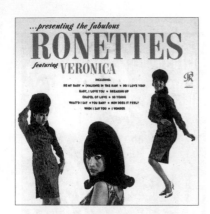

on a record to the point where the vocalist was of secondary importance. The vocalists and groups were almost interchangeable. Indeed, Spector had put the Crystals on the road but kept Darlene Love in Los Angeles to keep cutting Crystals records.

Spector wasn't the first great record producer but his spectacular vision was to utilise the recording studio as a dream factory. He transformed popular music in the way that Hollywood had transformed the cinema.

"I don't know who coined the term [wall of sound]," said Jack Nitzsche, who was one of Spector's chief arrangers and pianists. "The sound just got bigger and bigger. If you notice, there's more echo on each song we cut. It really hadn't been done like this before. People on the business side, the promotional side of the record industry, felt it was different. He didn't listen to them.

"The musicians played at once. This was groundbreaking for me. During the Spector sessions, a lot of the time we had two and three piano players going at once. I played piano as well. Phil knew the way he wanted the keyboards played. It wasn't much of a problem who played. The pianos would interlock and things would sound cohesive.

"Vocalists. It would last all night. Background groups doubling and tripling so it would sound like two or three dozen voices. Phil would spend a lot of the time with the singers. I would split and he'd still be working on lines with the singers. The rhythm section and the horns were done together. Vocals and string parts were overdubbed later.

"We did most of the sessions at Gold Star Studios in Hollywood. There were four echo chambers, and I remember Stan Ross, who was a co-owner, telling us many times that the echo chambers were acoustically and geometrically designed to get the right amount of balance and reverb. That added to the impact of Phil's recordings. I loved the echo. It's like garlic. You can't get too much."

Although Spector used many musicians on his sessions, the records were sparse. 'Be My Baby', for instance, has wonderful moments of perfectly judged silence.

In this mythical world, Spector had to have his Pygmalion, his Fair Lady. Her name was Veronica 'Ronnie' Bennett and she sang with her sister Estelle and cousin Nedra Talley (although Veronica is the only Ronette on this track). Ronnie couldn't match the vocal dexterity and range of Darlene Love but she had a quality – a tough/vulnerable quality that gave the Ronettes sides a personality. Certainly she cast a spell over Spector.

Love was in the air.

"We were very big into the boy/girl, 'I love you and you love me and I hope it works out' kind of mentality," said writer Greenwich. "We were young and falling in love and we would talk like that. We'd go on a date, go to the beach, and say, 'Won't you be my baby?' I mean, you could gag hearing it, but that's how romantic we were."

"Ronnie's voice," said Nitzsche. "Wow! I was amazed at her vibrato. It got bigger and bigger with each record. That was her strong point. When that tune was finished, the speakers were turned up so high in the booth that people had to leave the room."

Following the success of 'Be My Baby' the Ronettes found themselves touring the UK with the Beatles, and Ronnie was reported to be romantically involved with both John Lennon and Keith Richards. It was too much for Spector, who shortly thereafter married her himself and locked her in his mansion, allowing her out once a year to see Elvis Presley perform in Las Vegas. The marriage failed and Phil lost his mind, and Elvis died melodramatically. The opening bars of 'Be My Baby', however, remain pure and majestic. It's the sound of rapture.

When I Get to the Border Richard & Linda Thompson

(Richard Thompson) ❋ Hannibal ❋ 1974 ❋ Appears on: *I Want to See the Bright Lights Tonight*

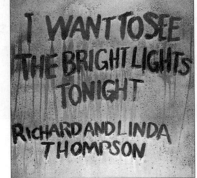

Having recently left Fairport Convention in 1971, Richard Thompson was feeling unconstrained. "Bands do just disintegrate, it's the general rule, because people want to do different things. You need freedom to make mistakes and flex your muscles," he said. "I was writing all this stuff, and I couldn't see how Fairport would do it, it was so self-indulgent."

Meeting singer Linda Peters, who was to become his partner in crime and his wife, also buoyed Thompson. *I Want*

to See the Bright Lights Tonight, their first album together, is full of the first blush of love, the excitement of being young and at the crest of their powers and musicianship. "We made that record in three days and it cost £2500," said Thompson. "And Island [Records] hated it – it didn't come out for a year. It was only acclaimed in retrospect. When you make records you don't think, 'Gosh, we're making history here, a classic.' If you've got any sense anyway."

The album opens with 'When I Get to the Border' – a glorious romp throwing off the straight life for serendipity and the open road. Like many of Thompson's songs there is a cosmic aspect to the lyric. The modal guitar playing, with its short burst of excitement that rips into the tune, reinforces it all. Dulcimers and mandolins intensify the joy and openness of the track. On this open road, Thompson was opening a new chapter in British folk rock. This was his first solo masterpiece.

Fool's Gold The Stone Roses

(Ian Brown/John Squire) ❋ Silvertone ❋ 1989 ❋ Appears on: The Stone Roses

The Stone Roses' eponymous debut album was a watershed in British pop in the '80s. It came out in May 1989, when the ecstasy-fuelled club scene was at its height.

The Roses were a rock band that had successfully incorporated club textures and grooves.

The album closes with a nine-minute epic, 'Fools Gold', which seamlessly put together the Manchester sound. It was a record unlike any other – seductive, lyrical and psychedelic. It was a joyful sound. The Stone Roses were the inspiration for the massive upsurge in the Manchester music scene that peaked with professional Mancunians Oasis.

"When we'd finished recording, [producer John] Leckie comes up to us and says 'Listen, this is really good. You're going to make it.' And I remember thinking 'I know.' It could've been even better," said singer Ian Brown. "A big thing was happening in England at that time with ecstasy, and we arrived at exactly that time. I felt great, righteous. I felt we were pure, that we weren't conning anyone. We were real and beautiful."

Chuck E's in Love Rickie Lee Jones

(Rickie Lee Jones) ❄ Warner Bros. ❄ 1979 ❄ Appears on: *Rickie Lee Jones*

Discovered by Little Feat's Lowell George, Rickie Lee Jones was not much more than a kid when she wrote 'Chuck E's in Love' for the bass player Chuck E Weiss. The song had a smoky, swinging jazz feel with a touch of R&B. Rickie Lee Jones sounded like a beatnik waif. "I was pretty much just winging it," she told Andy Gill. "Looking to the next day to see if you would have money for gas, looking to the next week to see if you would get a job; always thinking about what you have to do to escape poverty, to create art that is going to catch the world on fire. You have to live in the moment totally to create a moment that is compelling, and though it may be kind of bohemian, it does make the earth of your soul richer."

Jones was then a little under the wing of Los Angeles hipsters such as her ex-boyfriend Tom Waits. Her songs, like his, were populated by the characters of the American underbelly, and Jones had seen plenty of that in her time. Her mother was a waitress, her father a waiter and her grandfather a vaudevillian. They had moved a lot through her childhood and this transitory lifestyle had made Jones both strong and a little lonely. There's an affection in Jones' singing – celebrating a friend's romance, rather than writing about her own love life. That vulnerability comes through on this track but it's subsumed by the playfulness of the lyric – and Chuck E's warm, rich bass playing.

Gotta Serve Somebody Bob Dylan

(Bob Dylan) ❄ Columbia ❄ 1979 ❄ Appears on: *Slow Train Coming*

"Jesus put his hand on me. It was a physical thing," Bob Dylan told Karen Hughes in 1980, shortly after his conversion to Christianity. "I felt it. I felt it all over me. I felt my whole body tremble. The glory of the Lord knocked me down and picked me up. Being born again is a hard thing."

At least Dylan chose an easy selection of people to lead him into his next life. If you're going to make a gospel record you could choose a lot worse producers than Atlantic's Jerry Wexler and Muscle Shoals keyboard player Barry Beckett. Dylan augmented them with Mark Knopfler and Dire Straits drummer Pick Withers. On

'Gotta Serve Somebody' they find themselves a nice groove and then lay back in it as the singer/songwriter rains down the fire and brimstone. It's a long walk from "Don't follow leaders/Watch the parking meters" to "It may be the Devil or/It may be the Lord/But you're gonna have to serve somebody".

Although this song would win Dylan his first Grammy and top the charts, it was the beginning of Dylan's most wretched decade as he sought answers artistic and spiritual. It was the path that almost killed him.

"At every point in my life I've had to make decisions for what I believed in," he said. "Sometimes I've ended up hurting people that I've loved. Other times I've ended up loving people that I never thought I would.

"It's Him through you. 'He's alive', Paul said. 'I've been crucified with Christ, nevertheless I live. Yet not I but Christ who liveth in me.' See Christ is not some kind of figure down the road. We serve the living God."

Jive Talkin' The Bee Gees

(Barry Gibb/Maurice Gibb/Robin Gibb) ✳ Polydor ✳ 1975 ✳ Appears on: *Main Course*

The Bee Gees were going nowhere fast in the mid-'70s. Their heyday as pop balladeers was pretty much over. The siblings had already been through tumultuous years of bickering and drug and alcohol problems. Their ace in the hole was working with Arif Mardin, an arranger/producer who had worked on many of the classic R&B sides from Atlantic right through the '60s. Mardin was also hip to the groove-based flavour that was changing R&B and he introduced the Bee Gees to that style. The *Mr Natural* album had been a step in the right direction. Things started to come together with their next project, which was recorded at Criteria studios in Miami. The rhythm of tyres on a bridge gave the brothers Gibb a new groove.

"Arif was an R&B man; the Bee Gees were balladeers. They were writing but they still hadn't quite come up with that new formula," said David English, who worked with the group at the time. "We were going home to [the house at] 461 Ocean Boulevard. Fanny got the meal ready already and we're in the station wagon. We went over the Sunny Isles Bridge and all three of them looked at each other, this is the important thing. It was always a three thing. They saw something. Barry said, 'Let's go back'. They went back to the studio and said, 'Arif, we've got an idea'.

They got the guitar and they wrote 'Jive Talkin'' and that was the riff and that's how it all came about and that drive back in the station wagon changed their whole career."

On that bridge the Bee Gees discovered blue-eyed soul for the '70s.

Beat Dis Bomb the Bass

(C Black/E Pasquez) ❉ Rhythm King ❉ 1987 ❉ Appears on: *Into the Dragon*

DJ Tim Simenon, aka Bomb the Bass, broke out of the London clubs with a house 12 inch that was heavy on the samples, very hard on the beats and hard edged in its attitude. 'Beat Dis' with its samples from Public Enemy, Ennio Morricone and the *Thunderbirds* is one of the defining tracks in house music. Most house music had come out of the US into the underground of clubs in the UK. Simenon and some of his colleagues heard a uniquely British style of house that was to develop over the next decade. 'Beat Dis' eventually crossed over into the mainstream charts and out into the suburbs. Simenon's gift was to translate the excitement of a live DJ and his feel for the listener into a track that worked outside the club as well as in. The club culture and the arrival of ecstasy made house and acid house the dominant styles in British pop culture in the late '80s with the combination of hip-hop attitude and swing with a rock & roll energy.

Simenon went on to produce more records than he cut, working notably with Michael Hutchence and Neneh Cherry. 'Beat Dis' will transport you back to the speedy hot nights of 1987.

Arcadian Driftwood The Band

(J Robbie Robertson) ❉ Capitol ❉ 1975 ❉ Appears on: *Northern Lights/Southern Cross*

After a brilliant start with two albums, the Band buckled under the weight of their own reputation and, of course, drugs and money. Ill feeling in the group started when the other players felt that Robbie Robertson was getting an unfair share of the credit and the revenue. *Northern Lights* was to be their last album (not counting the contractual obligation of *Islands*) of new material. It has two real gems, 'It Makes No Difference' and 'Arcadian Driftwood', another historical epic that bookends 'The Night They Drove Old Dixie Down'.

'Arcadian Driftwood' is the story of a group of Canadians who fled the British and moved south, settling in Louisiana where they became known as Cajun. It's a story that roughly follows Robertson's own biography and certainly fits in with his affinity for the music of New Orleans.

"After the war between Montcalm and Wolfe [1759]," Robertson explained, "there was a question whether Canada was going to belong to France or Britain. After Britain finally won, it was put to the people living there that they had to swear allegiance or give up their land. So some of them went to the old country, some of them went to the French islands, the Caribbean, and some across the border down the Mississippi to Louisiana. This took place over some three years and what happened out of this was the birth of the Cajun population.

"I've always found it a fascinating story and anyone I've spoken to about it has said, 'No kidding. I didn't know that.' It's kind of an untold story. I was overwhelmed when I found out very few people knew where the Cajuns came from."

With fiddle accompaniment from Bryon Berline and accordion from Garth Hudson, it was the ideal swansong for the Band.

The Horses Rickie Lee Jones

(Walter Becker/Rickie Lee Jones) ❋ Geffen ❋ 1989 ❋ Appears on: *Flying Cowboys*

Rickie Lee Jones sold two million albums on her 1979 debut and like many of her fellow singer/songwriters she probably wasn't ready for it. Over the next ten years she struggled with her work and her personal life. Like many of her colleagues, that involved slinging into a dark period of drugs and creative struggle. The 1989 album *Flying Cowboys* was the light at the end of that tunnel.

Having sung pop and R&B and jazz, Jones developed a new style on this album (co-produced with Steely Dan's Walter Becker).

Born on the same day as Bonnie Raitt and a day after Joni Mitchell, Jones found herself a place somewhere between those two divas.

"It was just part of that girl singer thing," she said. "It was just so competitive. It seemed like there was just one chair at this men's club and they'd only let one girl in at a time.

"Joni and I did have a kind of war going on, just a quiet war – she called it the War of the Berets. I worked with Julie Last, Joni's engineer, and I was a bit nervous about hiring her because I'd heard from mutual acquaintances that she, Joni, was not that fond of me because of things I'd said about her earlier in my career. I don't remember it but it was detrimental, the kinda thing people say when they've just come out and they try to discredit everyone who came before them.

"During recording earlier this year, Joni sent me a gift, through Julie, of a hat, and inside the hat she wrote 'Peace – Joni Mitchell'. I was so touched."

'The Horses' is a song that sounds like it's addressed to her daughter. It's a song of freedom and possibilities and a tranquil kind of love that had been missing from earlier records.

"Records are little diaries of how you are and what you are," she said. "Weakness and power."

Losing My Religion R.E.M.

(Michael Stipe/Mike Mills/Peter Buck/Bill Berry) ✳ Warner Bros. ✳ 1991 ✳

Appears on: *Out of Time*

This was the song that would make R.E.M. household names in 1991. Stipe's beautiful, yearning voice sings about indecision and regret and fear in an abstract lyric that sits atop their most beguiling tune. The melody was written by Peter Buck in 1990, shortly after he bought his first mandolin – an instrument he barely uses other than for this song.

The group thought that the song would keep them out of the charts and maintain their cult status. "There's no chorus, there's no guitar, it's five minutes long, it's a fucking mandolin song. What kind of a pop song is that?" asked Stipe.

"Musically it's very straightforward," said bass player Mike Mills. "There's something satisfying about that song, in the sense of the way the sound of the mandolin combines with the chords, the appealing, evocative nature of the lyrics – and a fabulous video. And you put that together and it's kind of a fluke, but thank goodness. I'm not even sure if that song could be a single now but it came out in the right time at the right place."

Lonely Teardrops Jackie Wilson

(Tyran Carlo/Gwen Fuqua/Berry Gordy Jr) ✳ Brunswick ✳ 1959 ✳

Appears on: *Mr Excitement*

Jack Leroy Wilson was initially a boxer before he, like his local buddies Levi Stubbs, Hank Ballard and Little Willie John, took up singing. He was profoundly influenced by Al Jolson – a Jewish man who sang in blackface. Wilson sang gospel and pop and came to the attention of Billy Ward, leader of the first popular R&B group the Dominoes. In 1953, Wilson replaced lead singer Clyde McPhatter in the Dominoes. By 1956 he had made his own name – Elvis Presley was heard to praise him – and gone out on his own.

Wilson's friends from Detroit were an important part of his success, notably the songwriting team of his cousin Roquel Davis (aka Tyran Carlo) and Berry Gordy Jr, who later started Motown records. In 1959, Wilson cut their epic 'Lonely Teardrops'. The song's spare backing allowed Wilson's voice the space to perform its magic.

'Lonely Teardrops' was a seminal soul single and a profoundly influential vocal from Wilson. In 1975, while singing the song at a casino in New Jersey, Wilson suffered a heart attack that put him in a coma and left him paralysed until his death in 1984.

Heart Shaped Box Nirvana

(Kurt Cobain) ✳ DGC ✳ 1993 ✳ Appears on: *In Utero*

Courtney Love gave her husband a heart-shaped box. Then followed a tempestuous romance of drugs and fame and power and children all conducted under the perpetual gaze of the tabloid media.

Cobain was a star and Courtney wanted to be. There's no doubt that he loved her and that she gave him something he needed. But it's also clear that he regarded the volatile relationship as a co-dependency. After police were called to his house following a particularly loud argument, Cobain was accused of choking his wife, something both parties denied.

"Sure. Courtney and I fight. We argue a lot," he told Jon Savage. "But I've never choked my wife. It's an awful fucking thing to be printed, to be thought of you. You know, we haven't had any problems, any bad reports, any negative articles written about us in a long time. We thought we were finally over it – that our curse had worn itself out". When Savage suggested that "people have perceived you as a threat," Cobain replied, "I think Courtney is more of a threat than I am".

As usual, Cobain hedges his bets. Perhaps he never really knew himself. The arrival of his daughter Frances Bean complicated matters further. There's a feeling of entrapment in 'Heart Shaped Box'. Kurt Cobain was indeed trapped at the time by his addiction, his fame, his desire for fame and his marriage. It's surprising that he made such a pretty song out of it all.

Kick out the Jams MC5

(Michael Davis/Wayne Kramer/Fred 'Sonic' Smith/Dennis Thompson/Rob Tyner) ✳ Elektra ✳ 1969 ✳ Appears on: *Kick out the Jams*

'Kick out the Jams' is the absolute pinnacle of high-energy rock & roll. The Detroit-based MC5 slammed their way through their first album. Very few groups start out with a live album, but the MC5 were totally correct here. They had done a few lame studio singles for independent labels but when they signed to Elektra they intended to blow the lid off the music business.

The MC5 – the name stands for Motor City 5 – were managed by John Sinclair, a local Detroit activist who formed the White Panther Party to get in on some of the revolutionary action that the Black Panthers were stirring up. He declared MC5 the cultural arm of the White Panther Party. Not only did they bankroll the White Panthers but also they gave a national spotlight to a local revolution. But then it would be hard for young men to resist a revolutionary front whose manifesto was "dope, guns and fucking in the streets".

"The phones were always tapped – you could hear them clicking and popping – the police would come by our house and run their siren at night while we were sleeping, flash their spotlights on the windows," guitarist Wayne Kramer recalled. "And anytime we stepped out, we were subject to search and the vans were always pulled over. The police would come up onstage and tell us we couldn't play that song. It was really out of control. And that was only the tip of the iceberg, we found out later that clearly there was a plan in place, coming from the highest offices of power, to destroy us."

The main venue in Detroit in 1968 was the Grande Ballroom and this is where the MC5 took the stand for their first album. The energy in the Grande Ballroom was everywhere in the air, bouncing around off the walls. The guitars of Wayne Kramer and 'Sonic' Smith crunched against each other in wild squalls of electric noise while the bass and drums pounded out a Motown-meets-metal beat.

But all that White Panther rhetoric has been lost in the winds of history. There was a lot of hype that the group were trying to emulate free jazz but they are nowhere near that. What we have here is absolute high energy rock & roll, which has seldom been matched and never bettered.

"We were struggling how to learn our instruments and play songs to be able to perform for people," Wayne Kramer told *Perfect Sound Forever*. "We gravitated to a certain kind of material, like the music of Chuck Berry and instrumental records and certain records that had a . . . what we'd call . . . 'high energy'. We later became articulate enough to define it as music that was real visceral. It was about a lot of heat and energy, like the music of James Brown, black gospel music."

Their fervour was aided by the fact that they were on a cosmic mission.

"Pure sound energises," the late Rob Tyner told a magazine at the time. "The more energy in the sound, the bigger the sound that gets to you, and the more intense the experience is, the more intense reality is – your metabolic reality at that moment, you know, an intensive feeling of your metabolism – that's where you find your reality. And music is equated on that level too, because it does make metabolic changes. Like on the stage, I notice metabolic changes at every instant. So fast – your heartbeat and your respiration and everything, because you're using your body one hundred per cent – that's what music is supposed to make you do. It's supposed to use your body one hundred per cent, so that you can force yourself out, put out as much energy as possible and make a perfect circuit so that there's an energy flow between the music and the audience, it all becomes one big thing, and it reinforces itself and everybody feels pure and clean. We send it out, and they send it back to you, and we send it out harder and it culminates in a reaction – things happen in the room.

"It's necessary, it's the killer experience and the purge: purification and a resensification on all levels. Resensify you back to your meat, because that's the way you take it in. Your meat is your senses, because your senses are made out of meat. And if you don't keep into contact with your meat . . . that's why all these straight people are so fucked up, man, 'cause they let their meat loaf – and it just rots, it rots."

'Kick out the Jams' by contrast is still as fresh as the day it was performed.

"The MC5 always played with reckless abandon and I think we were probably the first band that did that," said bassist Michael Davis. "We were always reaching into the unknown and I think that's it. No-one else played that way before and that's really what hardcore punk was all about – playing with reckless abandon with no regard for the safe things that you know about. And that's it. We were bad."

Novocaine for the Soul Eels

(DJ Paul Edge/Mark Goldenberg) ❉ Dreamworks ❉ 1996 ❉
Appears on: *Beautiful Freak*

Eels frontman Mark Oliver Everett, who goes by the name of E, was perfectly placed for the era of complaint rock in the mid-'90s. He was troubled. He was alienated. He was also talented and his songs transcended self-pity, and it would be unfair to lumber him in with most of those now-forgotten whingers. 'Novocaine for the Soul' has a beguiling new folk arrangement and production help from Michael Simpson – one half of the Dust Brothers. It's a beautiful song of alienation and sorrow that is also uplifting. The strings and the gentle backing recall the classic Los Angeles productions by Lenny Waronker.

"I was always aware of this immense sense of loneliness, that I now recognise as being a fish out of water," he said of his life as a teenager growing up in Virginia before he moved to Los Angeles. "The upbringing was what I thought of as typical suburban. But of course there is no 'typical'. It was lonely, I didn't get what I needed as a child, emotionally, and that created a lot of problems for me. But I've been working hard as an adult to even things out and for a long time music has saved me, and been my way to deal with it.

"Someone that's wallowing in sadness and has given up doesn't write these songs," said E. "The act of writing these songs is hopeful, there's a life-affirming quality to the music, and there's almost always a positive punch line. It does have something in common with angst-rock, but then it departs from it at a certain point. I'm surprised that people have noticed that it is different."

The Loco-Motion Little Eva

(Gerry Goffin/Carole King) ✳ Dimension ✳ 1962 ✳ Appears on: *The Loco-Motion*

The tale behind this song is a true Cinderella story. Eva Narcissus Boyd came up from Bellhaven, North Carolina, to New York where she babysat the two daughters of Gerry Goffin and Carole King.

By day, the husband and wife team worked for Don Kirshner's Aldon Music in an office at 1650 Broadway, described as an annex to the Brill Building. "We were part of the thing that involved Donny Kirshner saying 'So-and-so is *up* and needs a *follow-up!*' and all the writers would go into their cubicles and work away," King told Barry Miles, describing the Brill Building scene. "We would just simply go home because we happened to be married, but it was the same idea. You would come in the next day and everyone would play their song, hoping that *they* would be the one to get the follow-up, *knowing* that the others were also doing the same thing."

Goffin and King came up with a dance-craze song, 'The Loco-Motion', and used their babysitter to do a guide vocal on the demo. Kirshner liked it so much he put the demo out as the first release on his Dimension label and the first Gerry Goffin production, and the song shot to number one. It was also a big hit for Grand Funk Railroad in the '70s and for Kylie Minogue in the '80s.

According to Carole King, "There never was a dance called the loco-motion until after it was a hit. Everyone said, 'How does this dance go?', so Little Eva had to make up a dance."

It's a Long Way to the Top (If You Wanna Rock & Roll) AC/DC

(Bon Scott/Angus Young/Malcolm Young) ✳ Alberts ✳ 1975 ✳ Appears on: *TNT*

This was Bon Scott's life story. He had been a singer with pop group the Valentines in the '60s, topping the Australian charts, then a member of bluesy progressive rock collective Fraternity on the hippie trail in London. Bon had tasted success and failure. Mostly the latter. When he joined AC/DC they were punk kids playing a circuit of suburban dances, high schools, rough pubs and the like for no money and less glory. Although the group were related to Australian rock royalty (Angus and

Malcolm were brothers of George Young, member of the Easy Beats), their early years were a tough grind of loud music, abuse and poverty. As Scott wrote to his wife around this time, "I just wanna be famous I guess. Just so when people talk about you it's good things they say."

Things changed in 1975 when the group began recording and having some radio play. Quite clearly the Young brothers had a unique chemistry as guitar players and through the months of solid touring had developed their own style. With the first album getting some serious attention, perhaps Scott felt there was some hope.

Produced by Harry Vanda and George Young, 'Long Way' was recorded at Alberts Studio One in King Street, Sydney. "It was very small," said bass player Dave Evans. "We used to record in the side room, had two Marshall stacks and bass rig pointing towards the wall and miked up, and in what used to be the kitchen, drums in there – everything put down at once, generally the fire was in the first couple of takes."

'It's a Long Way to the Top' had the addition of Bon Scott playing a bagpipe solo – the first one on a rock & roll record. The track captures a particular battler spirit that reflects the Australian roots of the song and is one of the reasons why it has become an iconic number in Australia. When they wrote the song, AC/DC could have no idea how close to the top they would get. It's unfortunate Scott wasn't with them when it happened.

Stoned Soul Picnic Laura Nyro

(Laura Nyro) ✳ Columbia ✳ 1968 ✳ Appears on: *Eli and the Thirteenth Confession*

Laura Nyro was only nineteen when Blood, Sweat and Tear's version of her song 'When I Die' became a number one hit record. The daughter of a piano tuner and sometime trumpet player, Laura Nyro had a delicate gift for pop songs. The early success and the fragility of her temperament contributed to her early retirement. Within three years of her second album, she was already withdrawing from show business. But it was precisely this delicacy that comes through on her own records and has made her a legend. She was David Geffen's first client. He arranged for her to audition for Clive Davis at Columbia and she insisted that all the lights be turned off as she played by the light of a TV set. Davis then advanced her $3 million to record at Columbia.

Nyro's is a particularly New York sensibility. Doo-wop, the girl groups of the early '60s and R&B all informed her pop sensibility, while there was a strong dose of jazz in her elegantly romantic harmonies and melodies.

"From the time I could read, from six years old, I always loved poetry," she told Bill Flanagan in the '80s. "I would find these little books of the poets of different countries. I just always loved it, I trusted it, and I found it to be a pure expression of something that was going on. And all the music that was happening when I was a kid was, I think, *luscious* music. John Coltrane was really happening, and very late-'50s rock & roll, very romantic, melodic stuff. I loved the guys' voices then – the street singers – they had beautiful voices. Then the very early-'60s R&B – there was a lot of music and poetry in life. And I think it influenced me."

'Stoned Soul Picnic' from her second album became a smash hit for the Fifth Dimension and was covered by Sinatra and Aretha Franklin amongst many others. Her own version, though, is more fragile. The joy of getting a little high on wine on a sunny afternoon has a delicious quality when she sings of it and a sense of how fleeting joy can be. Floating on the breeze of this melody we can faintly hear the Shangri-Las and the soulfulness of Nina Simone. Mostly what you hear in this track is the sound of a perfect moment.

Autobahn Kraftwerk

(Ralf Hütter/Florian Schneider/Emil Schult) ✳ Elektra ✳ 1974 ✳ Appears on: *Autobahn*

Florian Schneider and Ralf Hütter first met as classical music students at the Dusseldorf Conservatory. They joined the experimental music community in Berlin and in 1970 adopted the name Kraftwerk (Powerplant). The pair early on embraced the advantages of a mechanised future – "our drummers don't sweat!" they proudly exclaimed.

After three albums Kraftwerk hit on the idea of recording the street. They drove around Berlin and recorded the sounds of traffic and ambient noise and then constructed music from their experiments. "What we are doing is making sound-pictures of real environments, what we call tone-films. We strive for clarity, not nebulosity; we are trying to recreate realism, not vague images. In our music we make the machines sing: in 'Autobahn' the cars hum a melody."

The song was, to everyone's surprise, a massive global hit. Certainly there was a novelty factor to the song's success. Essentially no-one had conceived of using the synthesiser and drum machine to create songs in this way. The instruments were no filler or ersatz versions of other instruments, but exploring their own melodic and harmonic possibilities.

'Autobahn' was a new palette for popular music.

The Big Country Talking Heads

(David Byrne) ✴ Sire ✴ 1978 ✴ Appears on: *More Songs about Buildings and Food*

Talking Heads may have been able to claim the prize for best album title but that would have meant little had not the music been right. The previous year they were awkward art-school geeks. On *More Songs* they were confident arty rock musicians.

They give some credit to Brian Eno, who is the most artful of record producers. "Eno taught us to relax in the studio," said bass player Tina Weymouth. "Which I think was his intention all along. He found that we were very willing to be experimental, as he was, and he was delighted with that ... to find a band that would allow him to race everybody's track and not get artistically sensitive and precious about it.

"What makes Eno a great leader is that he's willing to share everything he knows. Eno thinks our albums are hoovering music, which was suggested by David's manner of moving around in the studio," Weymouth said. "David moves around the studio as if he were a janitor cleaning up and vacuuming while whistling an idiotic tune. His second description of our music is 'music to do your housework by'."

This contrast between normalcy and the avant-garde is the crux of the album's best song, 'The Big Country'. Bryne sings a beautiful songlike poem to suburbia and its geometric harmonies and the glories of the economic and social forces that have created it. Then he undercuts it with the line "I wouldn't live there if you paid me".

There's a tension in Talking Heads' music, a twitch in the grooves between Byrne's affection for the button-down world and his need to escape from it. So much of rock & roll, and especially punk rock, is about breaking free into unbridled self-expression, but so much of that is really a cartoon pastiche in which neither the artist nor the listener really understand what is being said. That wasn't the case with Byrne in this song or many others where he floats dispassionately above the shopping malls of the world observing the straight people in their cages.

"I think people confuse coldness and unfeelingness with the fact that we're aware of what we're doing," said Byrne. "I know that may suggest arrogance or awkwardness, but I mean it in just the literal sense of being aware of what you're doing, like: 'Look at the funny place we're in, we're in front of people doing this'. That might seem cold to some; to me, it just seems realistic."

Round Midnight Thelonious Monk

(Bernie Hanighen/Thelonious Monk/Cootie Williams) ✳ Blue Note ✳ 1947 ✳
Appears on: *Genius of Modern Music, Vol. 1*

Thelonious Monk's longevity as a composer would have surprised most of the jazz buffs who saw him perform from the '40s through the '60s. Monk was a stalwart at Minton's Playhouse at 208 W. 118th St in New York where bebop was distilled by Charlie Parker, Dizzy Gillespie, Coleman Hawkins and the pantheon of post-war jazz geniuses. Monk played the piano in a style that was learnt from James P Johnson but interpreted by Monk's singular genius. Monk found new intervals in the music, he found new compositions and harmonies where no-one had heard them before. Monk had a logic as though he could hear an entirely new music.

"Thelonious was never like ordinary people, not even as a child," said Nellie Monk, his wife who seemed to be his connection with the world in which the rest of us live. "He always knew who he was. Sometimes when he plays the blues, he goes back to the real old-time pianists, like Jelly-Roll Morton and James P Johnson. I'm always amazed, because I know he hasn't spent a lot of time listening to these pianists – yet it's there in his music.

"He has smaller hands than most pianists, so he had to develop a different style of playing to fully express himself."

Monk disappeared into his own world when he was playing. In concert he would often stand up and wander around the stage during the course of a tune. Monk's eccentricities were eventually diagnosed as a mental illness and he suffered for many of his later years.

'Round Midnight' was one of Monk's first compositions when he was playing with the Cootie Williams Orchestra in 1944. The blues heritage is apparent in the underlying foundations of the tune and may explain part of its popularity. However, it's the colour Monk brings to the changes and the melody that make the song the most popular jazz tune of the last century.

Hey Joe The Jimi Hendrix Experience

(Billy Roberts) ❋ Track ❋ 1967 ❋ Appears on: *Smash Hits*

Billy Roberts remains an obscure figure in the California music scene. However, in 1962 he copyrighted a song 'Hey Joe', which has been covered some 800 times. David Crosby of the Byrds claims that he was taught it by Dino Valente of Quicksilver and the Youngbloods in 1965 before Valente went to jail on a drug bust. The song is attributed to Billy Roberts who has never been heard of or from apparently. In any case, 'Hey Joe' was a big hit on the folk scene and amongst garage rock bands in the mid-'60s. Between 1965 and 1968 it was recorded by Love, the Byrds, Tim Rose, Leaves, Shadows of Knight, Mothers of Invention, Wilson Pickett, Deep Purple, King Curtis, Cher and the Music Machine.

Chas Chandler, who was in the Animals and also a manager, liked the song, as did his client, Jimi Hendrix. According to legend, Chandler heard Hendrix doing the song at the Café Wha? in New York and that's what convinced him to take on the guitarist. Hendrix played the Tim Rose arrangement from the folkie's 1967 debut LP.

In any case, on 23 October 1966 the Jimi Hendrix Experience recorded 'Hey Joe'. At that moment the song became his. The Experience was three weeks old. Chandler had brought Hendrix back to London where they had found drummer Mitch Mitchell and bass player Noel Redding.

'Hey Joe' is a murder ballad – a man resolves to shoot his unfaithful lover. The lyric here is full of suppressed rage and Hendrix's guitar is similarly holding back, but you can feel the pressure. There's a heavy, almost ponderous feel at work, a sense of doom.

The version that became the Experience's debut was the first take of the first song attempted by the group in the studio. "I'm sure not a lot of time was spent on 'Hey Joe'," Mitch Mitchell recalled. "Studio time was expensive and there simply wasn't the budget for endless recording."

Hallelujah   Rufus Wainwright

(Leonard Cohen) ✳ Dreamworks ✳ 2002 ✳ Appears on: *Shrek*

There are many hallelujahs in a life, even in a day. Some of them are religious, many are not, but this song touches both the sacred and the profane.

Of all Leonard Cohen's songs, this has most lent itself to other voices and interpretations. John Cale's readings, live and in the studio, have been confronting. He brings out the robust sexual urge in the song. Jeff Buckley again both live and in the studio makes the song more ethereal and accentuates the spirituality of the lyric and the intent. Rufus Wainwright treads a middle path, acknowledging both, being tender and agnostic.

"I wanted to get into this tradition of the composers who said 'Hallelujah', but with no precisely religious point of view," said Cohen. "And then I realise there is a 'Hallelujah' more general that we speak to the world, to life … It's a rather joyous song. I remember singin' it to Bob Dylan after his last concert in Paris. The morning after, I was having coffee with him and we traded lyrics. Dylan especially liked this last verse, 'And even though it all went wrong/I stand before the Lord of song/With nothing on my lips but "Hallelujah".'

"He said, 'I want to do the song 'Hallelujah'. How long did it take you to write that?' I said, 'I'm really embarrassed to tell you, it took me at least two years'. And then the conversation went on, and I praised one of his songs, 'I and I', and I said, 'How long did it take you to write this?' And he said, 'Fifteen minutes'. And it's true, and they're both really good songs."

A Love Supreme   John Coltrane

(John Coltrane) ✳ Impulse! ✳ 1964 ✳ Appears on: *A Love Supreme*

John Coltrane's masterpiece was comprised of four suites over two sides of an LP. Recorded with his quartet (McCoy Tyner, Elvin Jones and Jimmy Garrison), the piece was a musical interpretation of a spiritual journey. Coltrane's mother was a church pianist and his father played violin. Both his grandfathers were ordained ministers in the African Methodist Episcopal Zion Church. Music and God were entwined for Coltrane. 'A Love Supreme' is a sublime piece of sacred music. The slowly revealing theme and its embellishments culminate in the hypnotic chanting of the title at the climax of the piece. Coltrane composed the song while reading one of his poems, 'A Psalm', on the music stand.

"I remember that Rudy Van Gelder, who was a premier jazz recording engineer at the time, cut the lights down, which made it more like a club atmosphere," pianist McCoy Tyner recalled of the *A Love Supreme* session. "I don't think we even rehearsed that music. Usually John would play the music and then we would record it and see what could happen, because it usually developed. Once we started playing it, new ideas would form . . .

"Many of the arrangements were head arrangements. There was only one horn so we were able to do that easily, and he just had things sketched out that he would want – nothing in detail. We had reached a point where we had that kind of high level communication between us."

Esteemed jazz writer Gary Giddins regards *A Love Supreme* as one of the pinnacles of jazz. "Coltrane," he said, "was a great jazz composer who created original and unforgettable melodic ideas, which is something you can say about relatively few jazz musicians. *A Love Supreme* was just filled with them. It had vocals; it had the group chanting 'A love supreme', which was completely novel at the time. Everything about the record lets you know that this was an important event."

Girls & Boys Blur

(Damon Albarn/Graham Coxon/Alex James/Dave Rowntree) ❋ Food ❋ 1994 ❋
Appears on: *Parklife*

Singer Damon Albarn was inspired to write Blur's real breakthrough single while on holiday in the Mediterranean. "It's about those sorts of holidays," he told the *NME*. "I went on holiday with Justine last summer to Magaluf and the place was just equally divided between cafés serving up full English breakfasts and really tacky Essex nightclubs. There's a very strong sexuality about it. I just love the whole idea of it, to be honest. I love herds. All these blokes and all these girls meeting at the watering hole and then just . . . copulating. There's no morality involved, I'm not saying it should or shouldn't happen. My mind's just getting more dirty. I can't help it.

"The Pet Shop Boys have agreed to do a mix of it for us, and that should be brilliant. What I'm hoping for is that they can come up with a version that becomes the big summer hit in all those nightclubs in Spain and Majorca. That's exactly what we want. I'd love those people to be into Blur . . ."

The *Parklife* album from which 'Girls & Boys' came has a very Kinks-y view of modern Britain where after Margaret Thatcher's innovations brought middle-class prosperity to middle Britain so much of the national character became simply consumerist and bland.

'Girls & Boys' is cheeky and trashy and vaguely sexual in the way that David Bowie once was. It also has a Benny Hill/seaside postcard feel to the jaunty chorus: "Looking for girls who are boys/Who like boys to be girls/Who do boys like they're girls/Who do girls like they're boys/Always should be someone you really love".

"For me the album is like a loosely linked concept involving all these different stories. It's the travels of the mystical lager-eater, seeing what's going on in the world and commenting on it," said Albarn. "Everyone goes on about the idea of the sensitive artist, but for me that's all bollocks. I can't stand the idea of being a sad, lonely bedsit poet. I'd much rather be perceived as loud and arrogant, because all our sensitivity's in our records."

Mr Jones Counting Crows

(David Bryson/Adam Duritz) ✳ Geffen ✳ 1993 ✳
Appears on: *August and Everything After*

Counting Crows always did have high-profile fans. No less than the Band's Robbie Robertson encouraged his daughter to see their show with the advice: "They're a really good band, a little derivative perhaps, but worth seeing".

Duritz is a songwriter who sees himself very clearly in the American tradition of Robertson and the Band, Tom Petty and Bob Dylan. His breakthrough song, in fact, takes its title from Bob Dylan's hapless reporter in 'Ballad of a Thin Man'.

"I really wanted to be a rock star – since I was five years old doing 'Can't Buy Me Love' in front of the mirror with a tennis racquet," Duritz confessed. "But I also thought that it was a really crazy thing to want, that there was a disaster in there that I wasn't seeing clearly. That's what 'Mr Jones' is actually about – a rather sad but tongue-in-cheek song about daydreaming of being famous. Now it's happened, the tongue-in-cheek part's gone and all that's left is bitterness."

The Counting Crows debut album sold about five million copies worldwide, in part due to 'Mr Jones'. It was a time when angst was very popular and Duritz was angsty but knew how to give his pain the sweetest possible context.

"People say to me it should be fun, but I don't agree," Duritz told *MOJO*. "I don't care about fun. Not in music. It's not fun. I don't enjoy it. I feel it though. It moves me deeply; I have a deep satisfaction. But fun? Fuck fun. Go have fun somewhere else. I do it so I can be who I am in my life. But fun? Go have fun later. But right now, I want your soul and I want it on tape . . ."

Christine Siouxsie & the Banshees

(Steve Severin/Siouxsie Sioux) ✻ Polydor ✻ 1980 ✻ Appears on: *Kaleidoscope*

"I like to think the vocals rely a lot on sound rather than tune. Nobody in the band's into melody, thank God," said Siouxsie Sioux. Having started out proudly incompetent, by their third album *Kaleidoscope*, the Banshees had found their stride. John McGeoch of Magazine was playing an inventive role as guitarist and Budgie was one of the more interesting London drummers.

Kaleidoscope is a vaguely psychedelic album in as much as it's heavily textured in ways by both design and accident. Siouxsie was by this time a role model for legions of young women who dressed in black. She was iconoclastic. She was rude. She was glamorous but also strangely down to earth. 'Christine' is a young woman's song, full of the fears and the excitement of finding identity in the England of tepid tea and tabloid papers. "That wonderful land of manicured lies and stifling conformity," as Siouxsie put it. "Where do you find such fertile breeding grounds for disparate malcontents." The Banshees were just that and in their incoherence they made a particular sense. 'Christine' may have been the anthem for post-feminist goths but its angular melodies have a truth.

Little Red Corvette Prince

(Prince) ✳ Warner Bros. ✳ 1983 ✳ Appears on: *1999*

Like Chuck Berry thirty years before, it was a car song that crossed Prince's funk/soul and rock style over to a mainstream audience. The song was written in a pink Ford Edsel belonging to Lisa Coleman from Prince's backing band, the Revolution. The *1999* album accelerated the momentum that Prince had begun only three years before. He installed a state-of-the-art studio in his house and the next day cut 'Little Red Corvette'.

At the time Prince was putting together careers for Vanity 6 and the Time as well as his own full touring and recording schedule. Perhaps in the spirit of time management, Prince also bought an early drum machine. "I felt like an auto assembly worker looking at a robot for the first time, wondering if I still had a job," said drummer Bobby Z. "Prince said, 'Here it is, figure out what you're going to do with it'".

'Little Red Corvette' like Berry's 'Maybelline' eroticised the automobile, taking the metaphor one step further. Prince's presentation, both vocally and in the video clip, was pure sex. "He was trying to become as mainstream as possible," said the Revolution's Matt Fink, "without compromising".

A Woman's Worth Alicia Keys

(Alicia Keys/EJ Rose) ✳ J-Records ✳ 2001 ✳ Appears on: *Songs in A Minor*

Alicia Keys' triumph is also Clive Davis' triumph. Davis had been dumped by the BMG label, the implication being that as he neared seventy years of age he had lost his touch. Then he went out and signed an eighteen-year-old girl from Harlem and sold ten million albums. Keys has the killer combination of R&B and cool jazz smarts, and is a prodigious writer. She is often and fairly compared with that early '70s diva Roberta Flack. Keys had already had a record deal at age sixteen, and walked away from it to preserve her artistic integrity. She found her partner in Davis and the *Songs in A Minor* LP is that rare meeting of artist and development.

'A Woman's Worth' showed a depth to Keys beyond her instrumental skill. Here was a wisdom that came from growing up with a single mother. "When I had nothing else," she said, "I had my mother and the piano. And you know what? They were all I needed."

Keys' roots are in classical music and jazz but she has also had an ear for the street. "I like to draw from a broad palette," she told the *Guardian*. "When I was a kid I'd practise Chopin on piano – and I love Chopin! He's my dawg! Then I'd go out on the stoop and blast the radio. I'm from New York, the concrete jungle. Hip-hop influenced me from day one." She cites her influences as the Notorious B.I.G., Tupac Shakur, U2, Nirvana and Mary J Bilge alongside the masters – Marvin Gaye, Curtis Mayfield and Donny Hathaway. It was the latter soul singer whom she said gave her the inspiration for her writing. "That's when I was like, 'Oh my gosh, I don't have to use somebody else's blueprint. I can use my own life and the things I've seen and be truthful about it.'"

(You Make Me Feel Like) A Natural Woman

Aretha Franklin

(Gerry Goffin/Carole King/Jerry Wexler) ❋ Atlantic ❋ 1968 ❋ Appears on: *Lady Soul*

"There was a sadness, and you couldn't define it. It was ungraspable, like quicksilver. But it was my job to furnish the most nurturing context for the music, to get the kind of players who were alert to the little changes or improvisations that Aretha might throw in there," said Jerry Wexler.

Wexler had been in love with Franklin's voice ever since he first heard her sing gospel on a Chess record in the '50s. The producer waited out her contract with Columbia where she was cutting polite jazz. As soon as it expired, Wexler signed Aretha Franklin to Atlantic, a label he co-owned, and he "took her back to church". This was one of the stellar partnerships in pop music. With Wexler at the board, she cut 'I Never Loved a Man the Way I Loved You' then 'Respect' and suddenly Aretha Franklin was the Queen of Soul.

Franklin had grown up in church – her father was a preacher. By the time Wexler found her, she had lived a little as well. On the sides they cut together at Atlantic, Aretha married the sacred and the profane.

'(You Make Me Feel Like) A Natural Woman' was written for Franklin by Gerry Goffin and Carole King – the greatest husband and wife writing partnership in pop.

Wexler suggested the title as a brief for Goffin and King. Where 'Respect' is a song that asserts and demands, 'Natural Woman' is more sensual. It's not any less powerful or feminine than 'Respect' but certainly it's a softer lyric.

Wexler enlisted Wilson Pickett's band for the backing. 'Natural Woman' has an organic build to it, and that's the key. Franklin allows the song to swell and evolve and she goes with it, rising to the occasion rather than pushing the arrangement. Many have tried this song but only Franklin and Carole King have done it justice. They're the only singers who have allowed the song to make its 'natural' way.

Surf City Jan & Dean

(Jan Berry/Brian Wilson) ❋ Liberty ❋ 1963 ❋
Appears on: *Surf City and Other Swingin' Cities*

Jan Berry and Dean Torrence were a singing duo who were swept up in the wave of the California surf sound. Berry, the creative force in the pair, befriended the Beach Boys' Brian Wilson to crank out anthems for an idealised Californian summer. 'Surf City' is the greatest teen anthem of the '60s. The song is set in an adventure – young kids going into the new paradise of the beach where there was "Two girls for every boy".

Berry was by all accounts a creditable producer, but nothing compared with Wilson. Jan & Dean were destined to be also rans to the Beach Boys. If Berry, who sings the lead on this track, had been any better the record would lose much of its garage charm.

Berry did most of his recording at Western Recorders on Sunset Boulevard with the same team of A-class players as Phil Spector, the Beach Boys and the Byrds used. Wilson was at this date too and sang the falsetto part, somewhat edging out Torrence. According to Wilson, "Jan asked me. He said, 'Will you sing with me on the lead part?' So I doubled with him, but he was louder than I was. Ya know, he didn't wanna make me louder than him on a Jan & Dean record." Wilson's participation was uncredited, as he was then contracted to a rival label, but the sound was so much of a piece with the early Beach Boys that it was all just part of one long beach party.

The song hit number one in July 1963. California surf music was an extraordinary phenomenon. On the basis of a couple of records, a fantasy world of unblemished teenagers having innocent, wacky hijinks while engaging in water sports was sold to teenagers the world over. It was more popular in the Midwest of the US and in the UK than it was in California. Surf music and 'Surf City', in particular, was the last innocent utopia on the airwaves.

Mais Que Nada Sergio Mendes & Brasil '66

(Jorge Ben) ✳ A&M ✳ 1966 ✳ Appears on: *Sergio Mendes & Brasil '66*

Sergio Mendes cut his teeth as a jazz pianist in Brasil working with Antonio Carlos Jobim and João Gilberto pioneering the bossa nova. Mendes was certainly well regarded as an instrumentalist and arranger playing with visiting American jazz masters such as Stan Getz, Dizzy Gillespie, Charlie Byrd and Roy Eldridge. While visiting New York in 1962 he cut an album with Cannonball Adderley. Mendes was astute enough to balance his more adventurous playing with commercial sessions and recordings.

In 1964 he moved to the US and a year later formed his own combo – Brasil '65 which, a year later, became Brasil '66 and came to the attention of trumpeter and impresario Herb Alpert who signed Mendes to his A&M label. Brasil '66 had a string of easy-listening hits, regularly charting in the Top 10 pop charts of the time. Often their hits were bossa nova versions of Beatles' songs and the like but equally they had Latin tunes that found an audience. Mendes ran a tight band of three instrumentalists and two very winsome female vocalists. 'Mais Que Nada' is typical of the supple, swinging ensemble playing with Mendes' witty piano and the breathless voice of Lani Hall bringing the romance of South America into the suburban living room.

"It's good that Brasil '66 has succeeded, because it confirms one's belief that, musically, these are fluid times, with more openings than ever before for contemporary creative endeavour," wrote Derek Taylor in his liner notes to the album. "I cannot see how substantial international achievement can elude this group who have marketed, with considerable taste, a delicately-mixed blend of pianistic jazz, subtle Latin nuances, Lennon-McCartneyisms, some Mancini, here and there a touch of Bacharach, cool, minor chords, danceable up-beat, gentle laughter and a little sex."

Don't Be Cruel Elvis Presley

(Otis Blackwell/Elvis Presley) ❋ RCA ❋ 1956 ❋ Appears on: *Elvis*

The flip side to 'Hound Dog' became a hit in its own right. Otis Blackwell, a New York-based songwriter, wrote the song and Presley was keen to record it. By this time he was getting submissions from songwriters like Blackwell who had previously only worked with black artists. Presley crossed their work over to a pop audience.

'Don't Be Cruel' was cut during Presley's first New York sessions on 2 July 1956. The song was begun in late afternoon, after lunch and took some thirty takes to get right – a stupendous effort in those days.

'Don't Be Cruel' shows Presley's vulnerable side in a terrific vocal performance. The rest of the band remains completely understated. His presence really swings the song with a touch of what his manager called "western bop". Sam Phillips, his old producer, was flabbergasted, so much so that he had to pull the car over to the side of the road when the song first played on his car radio.

Phillips said later, "I thought, 'They have finally found this man's ability'. The rhythm was right, and it was moving along just right, it had that absolute spontaneity, and yet Elvis still had command."

Across 110th Street Bobby Womack

(JJ Johnson/Bobby Womack) ❋ United Artists ❋ 1972 ❋
Appears on: *Across 110th Street*

One of the first and seminal blaxploitation films features an incredible score by jazz composer JJ Johnson and songs by Bobby Womack. The title track is a beautiful deep soul tune with as funky a groove as is possible.

The film has all the qualities of great blaxploitation plots – drugs, sleaze, sex, ghetto life and rough justice. 110th Street is the border of Harlem. Womack, who grew up there, instinctively knew how to marry the content and the music.

"I lived there all my life," he said. "When you talk about the ghetto, I can write that blindfolded. I knew what that was about. I started writing my life story. It's about what you do when you're put under pressure.

"I was always fighting with my record company [United Artists, which was also a film studio]. I said, 'I can't understand why you all would go outside of the company and let other artists score movies. Curtis Mayfield, Isaac Hayes. I mean they're good, but I got the same talent, why don't ya'll do it here?' 'Bobby', they said, 'You never scored a movie before'. I said, 'Right, and I never had a hit record before I had one'.

"I told 'em, 'You know what, if you don't let me have the score this time, every time I cut an album, I'm just gonna cut somethin' real silly. 'Jingle Bells', anything.' And I was serious. I said I'd burn the tapes. They said, 'OK, you start on tour in a week. You gonna come by today and look at the movie.' There was no music there, so I looked at the music and I taped the dialogue. Every night after the show I would write. When I got a break, I ran down to Muscle Shoals and in four days, we had the whole album cut."

In the space of two weeks Womack had the thing wrapped up and the soundtrack remains a deep soul classic.

Deathly Aimee Mann

(Aimee Mann) ✳ Superego ✳ 2000 ✳ Appears on: *Bachelor No. 2*

Director Paul Thomas Anderson wrote his exceptional film *Magnolia*, he claims, while listening to Aimee Mann songs. The film is about misfits lost in the Los Angeles night trying to deal with the connections between each other and the deep sorrow they each carry. *Magnolia* is a film about fathers, but Mann's songs are about us all.

'Deathly', which appears in the *Magnolia* soundtrack, is a song about low self-esteem. Anderson based the character of Claudia the cocktail waitress on the song. "Everything Aimee seemed to be thinking were things that I was thinking," he wrote. It's a song about how someone can be afraid to live and perhaps it's better to die than suffer the indignity of hope. Mann sings the song with her usual beguiling voice that sounds so sweet but creeps up on you with the bitter part. The backing, too, is inventive and seductive. Mann, a former pop star in her twenties, has a mature approach to her song craft – these are not tunes with easy answers, but they are gorgeous in their complexity.

All Apologies Nirvana

(Kurt Cobain) ✳ DGC ✳ 1993 ✳ Appears on: *In Utero*

The last song on the last studio album from Kurt Cobain is a song of regret and "apology". As usual he seems lost in a fog of other people's expectations and his own low self-esteem.

He was sorry to his fans that he had abandoned them by being successful, he was sorry to his family, but mostly he was sorry for himself.

In Utero was the follow-up to *Nevermind*. Naturally Nirvana rejected the pop sound of that breakthrough album and went for the most hardcore producer they could find – the notoriously hardline Steve Albini.

"The main reason we recorded the new album *In Utero* with Steve Albini is he is able to get a sound that sounds like the band is in a room no bigger than the one we're in now," said Cobain. "*In Utero* doesn't sound like it was recorded in a hall, or that it's trying to sound larger than life. It's very in-your-face and real."

Like most of Cobain's lyrics, 'All Apologies' is based around a number of images that are strung together with a solid emotional through line in the melody. "For the most part, I write songs from pieces of poetry thrown together," he told Jon Savage. "When I write poetry it's not usually thematic at all. I have plenty of notebooks, and when it comes to a time to write lyrics, I just steal from my poems. Sometimes, I finish the lyrics months before we go into the studio, but for the most part, ninety per cent of them are done at the last minute."

'All Apologies' is right up close and perfectly in the minute.

Long Black Veil The Band

(Marijohn Wilkin/Danny Dill) ✳ Capitol ✳ 1968 ✳ Appears on: *Music from Big Pink*

Perhaps the most famous "murder ballad," this song has been extensively covered by country, folk and rock artists including Lefty Frizzell (from whom the Band learnt it), Johnny Cash, Joan Baez, Nick Cave and the Bad Seeds, Marianne Faithful, Jerry Garcia, Burl Ives, Jason & the Scorchers, the Kingston Trio, Bill Monroe, the Move,

Fred Neil, the New Riders of the Purple Sage, the Proclaimers, the Seldom Scene, the Sir Douglas Quintet, the Stranglers, Barry White and many others. As you can see from the diversity of artists who have covered the song, it has a universal quality.

The simple waltz here carries a powerful story told from beyond the grave. The narrator was unable to use the alibi that would have saved him from the gallows – he was in the arms of his best friend's wife. Now six feet under he watches as his lover tends his grave. 'Long Black Veil' is romantic and Gothic and stark. It suited Rick Danko's plaintive voice and the style to which the Band aspired on their first album. As Jaime Robbie Robertson said, "I thought it was a great song. It was in the tradition that I wanted to begin writing in."

According to producer John Simon, "It's much more of a country wail or moan. [This] was more of a wail from the heart or gut."

Fever Peggy Lee

(Eddie Cooley/John Davenport) ✳ Capitol ✳ 1958 ✳

Appears on: *The Best of Miss Peggy Lee*

Naked but for bass, drums, voice and seductively clicking fingers, Peggy Lee whispered her way into history. Lee developed her style singing in a nightclub called the Doll House in Palm Springs. Unable to be heard above the noise in the room, Lee dropped her voice to a whisper and the audience, intrigued, suddenly quietened themselves.

At age twenty-one, Lee became bandleader Benny Goodman's singer in his heyday. Later she went solo as an actress and singer. Her full figure and come-hither singing style made her a massive star and one of the first great sex symbols of the '50s.

Lee was a talented actress, nominated for an Academy Award for *Pete Kelly's Blues*. She acted in Disney's *The Lady and the Tramp* and wrote much of the score. Nonetheless she is best remembered for 'Fever'.

The song was written by Otis Blackwell ('Don't Be Cruel', 'Great Balls of Fire', and 'All Shook Up') under the name John Davenport with his friend Eddie Cooley. The song was given to R&B singer Little Willie John who initially rejected it, but was persuaded to record the track. It was an R&B chart-topper for him in 1956. Peggy Lee brought an entirely different attitude to the song when she recorded her version a year or so later. *The New Yorker*'s music critic Whitney Balliett put his finger on it when he wrote, "Peggy Lee sends her feelings down the quiet centre of her notes. She is not a melody singer. She does not carry a tune; she elegantly follows it. She is a rhythm singer who moves all around the beat, who swings as intensely and eccentrically as Billie Holiday."

Fire The Crazy World of Arthur Brown

(Arthur Brown/Vincent Crane/Mike Finesilver/Peter Ker) ✳ Track ✳ 1968 ✳

Appears on: *The Crazy World of Arthur Brown*

"I am the god of hell fire!" declared Arthur Brown dressed in phosphorescent robes, black and white face paint and with flames shooting from his hat. He was British psychedelia at its best. Lillian Roxon notes, "a voice that shifted from gentle softness to raving maniac screeching, all in a manner of seconds. Probably the only voice like it in rock music. Finally, a strange spastic dancing like some sort of space-age ritual ..."

The Crazy World were popular at the Speakeasy, London's hippest club in 1968, which is where the Who's Pete Townshend and manager Kit Lambert caught the act. Townshend was sufficiently impressed to produce them and the single 'Fire', powered by the freak-out organ sound of Vincent Crane, made the top of the British charts.

The highly theatrical show presented by the Crazy World of Arthur Brown made the group a very popular attraction at underground happenings and festivals for quite a few years but, unfortunately, there was no second hit single. Organist Vincent Crane went on to other things including the bands Atomic Rooster and Dexy's Midnight Runners before his untimely death. Arthur Brown eventually returned to being Arthur Wilton of Whitby, East Riding. He resumed teaching, moving for a time to Burundi, West Africa. More recently he is reported to have been running a painting and decorating business with Jimmy Carl Black of the Mothers of Invention. But there is a part of him that will always be the god of hell fire.

Gangsta's Paradise Coolio

(Coolio/Doug Rasheed/Larry Sanders/Stevie Wonder) ✳ Tommy Boy ✳ 1995 ✳
Appears on: *Gangsta's Paradise*

Coolio (born Artis Leon Ivey Jr) grew up in Compton, South Central Los Angeles. Like many rappers he did his time with drug addiction, running with gangs and some jail time, but when he went straight Coolio stayed away from the thug life. His first hit, 'Fantastic Voyage', was more about booty than violence.

However, Coolio's biggest hit was the ballad 'Gangsta's Paradise', which crossed over from the R&B chart into the pop list, and then topped that. The record company had so little faith in the song that rather than put it out as a single they gave it to the soundtrack of the film *Dangerous Minds* and from there it went ballistic.

Based on a riff from Stevie Wonder's 'Pastime Paradise', Coolio is reflecting on the consequences of gang life and why he escaped it. Coolio's version of life in Compton was more compassionate and more realistic than the music that had come from NWA or Dr Dre. Coolio's manner, too, was agreeable rather than abrasive.

"You see, I don't think I'm the best or the baddest," he told *Q*. "I know I'm not the greatest rapper in the world. I'm just one of many. In order for people to know what my full self is, I show all sides of my personality and all sides of my life. I don't always win, I lose sometimes, and you gotta talk about those times too. I want people to know that I'm genuine, I'm not fake, I'm not phoney, I'm not an egomaniac."

I Can't Explain The Who

(Pete Townshend) ✳ Brunswick ✳ 1965 ✳
Appears on: *Meaty, Beaty, Big and Bouncy*

When the Who went into the studio to cut this track in late 1964 they were a mod R&B combo from Shepherd's Bush with one failed single under their belt. There was so little expected from the group that producer Shel Talmy had booked guitarist Jimmy Page for the session to cover for Pete Townshend, and girl group the Ivy League to cover

difficulties with the vocals. At the end of the two hours it took to cut two sides, the Who emerged with a unique, explosive sound and a songwriter who would change the course of rock & roll a few times.

Talmy had produced the Kinks, London's other major group, and aspired, as did the Who, to make a record that sounded like the Kinks.

"Well, Shel Talmy didn't think that Pete's lead guitar playing was up to it and he didn't think our backing vocals were up to it," recalled singer Roger Daltrey. "He was right about the backing vocals. And obviously in those days you weren't in overdub facilities. You made the record and that was it. So if you wanted to put a solo on you had to do it when you were doing the record." (Page plays rhythm guitar on the track and lead on the flipside, Talmy's tune 'Bald-Headed Woman'.)

"There is little to say about how I wrote this," Townshend wrote in 1971. "It came out of the top of my head when I was eighteen-and-a-half. It seems to be about the frustrations of a young person who is so incoherent and uneducated that he can't state his case to the bourgeoisie intellectual blah blah blah. Or, of course, it might be about drugs."

Aneurysm Nirvana

(Kurt Cobain/Dave Grohl/Krist Novoselic) ✳ DGC ✳ 1992 ✳ Appears on: *Hormoaning*

According to Nirvana this was "a recent attempt at getting back to our New Wave roots". 'Aneurysm' definitely rocks. It's more of a pop song than almost everything else on the *Nevermind* album. 'Aneurysm' has a gigantic, crunching two-chord chorus and a massive descending riff that is just perfect for arenas and blows the walls out of the small theatres in which Nirvana mostly played.

The rush of the tune and the lyrics suggest that the inspiration for the song was Kurt's affection for heroin. The drug was readily available in his teens and indeed it swept through the Seattle music scene like a plague. Cobain had been a long-term junkie. He claimed the heroin was mostly for the analgesic benefits it gave him as relief from his chronic stomach pain.

"I'd taken heroin for a year-and-a-half," Cobain told Jon Savage, "but the addiction didn't get in the way until the band stopped touring about a year and a half ago. But now things have got better. Ever since I've been married and had a child, within the last year, my whole mental and physical state has improved almost one hundred per cent. I'm really excited about touring again. I'm totally optimistic: I haven't felt this optimistic since my parents got divorced, you know."

Like most junkies, Cobain was not being honest about his drug use, which was chronic. It had been bad before the group started and it just got worse as Cobain's responsibilities increased. A year after this track was released, Cobain's drug habits had torn the band asunder and made recording nigh impossible.

But on 'Aneurysm' he's full of life. Everything is possible and nothing matters except riding this firestorm of a track.

Down in the Tube Station at Midnight The Jam

(Paul Weller) ✳ Polydor ✳ 1978 ✳ Appears on: All Mod Cons

The third Jam album in less than two years started inauspiciously. The initial demo tapes presented to Polydor were rejected and singer Paul Weller was persuaded to record a Kinks song ('David Watts') as filler. Then Weller found himself as a writer; firstly with 'A Bomb in Wardour Street', which captured the paranoia, violence, anger and the siege mentality of London then undergoing an IRA bombing campaign.

Weller's first single with the Jam was 'In the City' and he made London a core part of his writing. It was the landscape on which he projected his emotional life. While contemporaries the Clash and the Sex Pistols drew their inspiration exclusively from across the Atlantic, Weller was steeped in British sounds and rhythm and the lyrics were too particular in their detail to come from anywhere else.

'Down in the Tube Station at Midnight' is a complex narrative telling the story of a man on his way home to suburbia with a takeaway curry who gets mugged in the train station. The detail is so acute you can picture the thugs and feel his humiliation as he hits the concrete. Weller turns the perfectly ordinary location of a train station into a horror show. So much of it is in the carefully chosen detail – the Queen on the coin, the graffiti "from some atheist nutter," the toffee wrappers, "wormwood scrubs/And too many right wing meetings". These are the details that make up a life. The telling of them here speaks of both the hopelessness of daily life and the black futility of taking it.

Then there's the chilling coda "They took the keys/She'll think it's me" and with just that couplet you can picture the whole *Clockwork Orange* scenario. 'Tube Station' is powered by the Jam hitting their straps and moving out of the punk thrash of their first two albums. Here there's light and shade and a steadily increasing tension. 'Tube Station' marked the point where the Jam and Paul Weller came out of the shadows of their '60s forefathers and laid the ground for a new era of British rock that carried right though to the Brit pop of the '90s and beyond.

Everybody Hurts R.E.M.

(Michael Stipe/Peter Buck/Bill Berry/Mike Mills) ✳ Warner Bros. ✳ 1992 ✳
Appears on: *Automatic for the People*

You'd think they'd be happy. R.E.M. were kings of the world in 1992 after the commercial breakthrough of the *Out of Time* album. Their next record, though, was sorrowful and brooding. The album took a relatively long time to record, cut in studios in three cities. The songs were superficially simple but were made up of complex layers of atmospherics and subtle touches.

"The stuff we were turning out was pretty dark," guitarist Peter Buck told John O'Donnell. "It wasn't as if we gave him a bunch of pop songs and he wrote down these lyrics. And overall I think the record is pretty positive, but there are certain songs about death. It's kind of inward looking more than anything.

"Sometimes you've got to let the music direct you and this time it just felt that everything we wrote that was really quality, musically and lyrically, tended to be more reflective and slower."

'Everybody Hurts' is a painful ballad with a straightforward melody line – courtesy of drummer Bill Berry – and an almost prosaic lyric from Stipe that is sung with heartbreaking directness. "The subject of 'Everybody Hurts' is exactly what it sounds like," said Mills. The song became the group's biggest hit, as was the album *Automatic for the People*.

"I bought this awful $20 Univox drum machine," said Buck. "But it made sense, because the song had a metronome-ish feel. Mike and I cut it live with this dumb drum machine which is just as wooden as you can get. We wanted to get this flow around that: human and non-human at the same time."

Reckless Australian Crawl

(James Reyne) ❋ EMI ❋ 1984 ❋ Appears on: *Semantics*

Melbourne singer/songwriter James Reyne was an acute lyricist who frequently allowed the bombast of his band Australian Crawl to obscure the simple elegance and wit of his verses. 'Reckless', as produced by Mark Opitz, came out unadorned and has become a classic Australian pop ballad.

The song is a reverie juxtaposing images of solitude and loneliness – Burke and Wills' tragic desert expedition on which they died of starvation, or Scott abandoned in the Antarctic, or a Russian submarine trapped under the Arctic ice. Then there is the chorus: "Throw down your guns, don't be so reckless."

"The mood of 'Reckless' was not at all conscious," said Reyne. "It fell out ... There was no conscious decision to make the mood this, or it should be about this and I'll have these images. The way I sat and played my guitar on that day is how it came out.

"I wrote 'Reckless' when I did this mini-series called *Return to Eden*. I was amusing myself, by myself with my guitar. I watched a ferry go by and honestly – it sounds pretentious – but the song took about as long to write as it does to play it. I never thought it was any good.

"I was going out with this girl and I'd been away, and then she got a job on a film that was being shot in the South Pacific so we didn't see each other for about nine months for one particular year.

"It doesn't really hang together for me, all the imagery. It's about being alone or lonely or something. The lyrics are a series of images but honestly, from memory, they pretty much fell off the top of my head trying to think of people alone or [of] aloneness.

"Recently there'd been one of those Russian submarines that got stuck under the ice and they couldn't find it, and the old Burke and Wills story, of course, and Scott of the Antarctic. It really came out.

"And then 'She don't like that kind of behaviour', what does that mean? No idea. Then, 'Throw down your guns, don't be so reckless.' What the hell does that mean? I've had people say, 'Oh, it's an anti-war song.' OK. If you like.

"I honestly don't know the reason a lot of people think that 'Reckless' has some resonance. I don't want to play it down because I honestly don't know."

Let's Have a Party Wanda Jackson

(Jessie Mae Robinson) ❋ 1958 ❋ Capitol ❋ Appears on: *Best of Wanda Jackson*

Wanda Lavonne Jackson turned professional about as soon as she finished high school in 1955. She had already cut some country sides while still at school at the

urging of Hank Thompson and his Brazos Valley Boys.

While on the road through the south with the Ozark Jubilee she met a young singer named Elvis Presley. Before the romance petered out, he suggested that the next big thing would be rock & roll music. In Los Angeles in June 1956 Wanda recorded 'I Gotta Know' for Capitol. The country tune lets rip in the middle into a hillbilly rock & roll track before regaining its composure. The message was clear, however, and Wanda Jackson became the first woman to cut rock & roll records.

Jackson was a hellcat in red lipstick, tight dresses and high heels and she went wild on her monogrammed guitar. Jackson's best songs weren't romantic weepies but were about getting in on the action. She was the prototype for Quatro and Hynde and the 'rriot grrls' of grunge.

In 1958 she recorded her signature tune, 'Let's Have a Party', a wild-ass rockabilly knockdown that featured Jackson's Oklahoma twang being belted out in complete abandon. The lyrics were classic rockabilly/country nonsense: "I never kissed a bear, I never kissed a goon/But I can shake a chicken in the middle of the room."

Was this lascivious? It was certainly as nuts as Jerry Lee Lewis could get and better than Presley's version. She was the First Lady of Rockabilly.

Get on Top of Me Woman   Tim Buckley

(Tim Buckley) ❄ Bizarre ❄ 1972 ❄ Appears on: *Greetings from LA*

Too much hanging around with the Frank Zappa crowd got Tim Buckley thinking that he should reinvent the jazz-rock that he did with Starsailor. The album bombed and although in all his interviews he said he didn't care about money and fame, he apparently went into a deep depression from which he emerged with an album that was enjoyable, innovative and spurred a thousand one-night stands among its listeners.

"After Starsailor, I took about a year off and started a book – movie scripts which will be turned into books – and I'm told, 'Well, you better make another album'," Buckley said by way of explaining his new direction. "And I said OK and I was just sitting there ... I hadn't touched the guitar in a long time and I thought, well, I have to get up-to-date. I saw nine blaxploitation movies, read four black 'sock-it-to-me-mama' books, and read all the rock criticisms. I took a week off, and finally realised that all of the sex idols in rock & roll weren't saying anything sexy.

"Or had I learned anything sexually from a rock song? Or for that matter [anything] pornographic? So I decided to make it human and not so mysterious, and to deal with the problems as they really are, so I guess that's where the innocence went."

Buckley now fronted a muscular, funky band that fired up grooves that suited a title like 'Get on Top of Me Woman'. *Greetings from LA* is a record that is so upfront as to be anathema to the commercial radio that Buckley was aiming at, yet the grooves were undeniable and the song became a cult hit, especially for some reason in Australia.

Perhaps, too, his new relationship with his last wife, Judy, was a positive influence on his writing about sex. Certainly the usually troubled troubadour sounds happy.

"Ball and chain on the old brain," he said of the need to write a hit record. "I don't see it as a compromise though. It's just part of my life having to do something like that and doing it the best that I could. When you run out of ideas for a particular type of song you have to move on. In my early career it was the semi-rock folk ballad which was a pretty creative form of song, because it got you to stretch out and enabled you to say a lot. It was almost like an art song. But then when I started playing more gigs and going out on stage just before the psychedelic people it was fruitless to do an art song, so I stretched out by experimenting with rhythms and time signatures."

Or as he later put it, "I listened to the radio a lot before writing the songs for this album. There's a lot of radio music in it. It's full-out blues-type barrelhouse rock. The album really rocks, and I'm very pleased with it."

I'm So Lonesome I Could Cry Cassandra Wilson

(Hank Williams) ✳ Blue Note ✳ 1995 ✳ Appears on: *New Moon Daughter*

Cassandra Wilson calls herself a jazz vocalist. With inspiration not only from Miles Davis and the immortal divas of the '50s, Wilson also brings a modern sensibility to jazz.

Wilson was raised in Jackson, Mississippi, and her father was a jazz guitarist of some note. She began performing as a teenager accompanied only by her acoustic guitar, very much in the thrall of Joni Mitchell. She found her way to New York where she joined the Black Rock Coalition, but drifted into experimental jazz before finding a home with more acoustic flavours. "It's a very organic music, and it's very open, it's very spacious. I don't know where it's heading, but I'm following it," she said.

Her material is not only her own compositions and standards, but also country, pop, rock & roll and blues. On her breakthrough *New Moon Daughter* LP she took Hank Williams' honky tonk classic and squeezed all the moonshine out, leaving a gorgeous, haunting and soulful ballad full of elegant pauses.

"Well, the south is a wonderful place for music," she said. "It's got all of it. It's got country music, it's got R&B, it's got blues, it's jazz – it's all of these musics. These kinds of music actually emanate from the south. So it's really natural for me to do this kind of music because it's a music that I heard growing up. I always loved Hank Williams. And I never drew the line between what Hank Williams does, you know, his artistry, and what BB King does."

Love to Love You Baby Donna Summer

(Pete Bellotte/Giorgio Moroder/Donna Summer) ❋ Casablanca ❋ 1975 ❋
Appears on: *Love to Love You Baby*

Boston-born LaDonna Adrian Gaines wound up in Germany in the early '70s in the cast of *Hair*. She married, took an Anglicised version of her husband's name and met Giorgio Moroder, an Italian-born producer. With co-writer Pete Bellotte, Moroder and Summer created the absolute disco epic 'Love to Love You Baby'. Moroder structured the song as a DJ would play the track in a club – all seventeen minutes of it. Summer provided the moaning and groaning of simulated sex over the Eurodisco beat and the record notched the disco phenomenon up a little.

Moroder's production of 'Love to Love You' brought Eurodisco to the US in a big way and radically altered the way records sounded for the next ten years right up through techno and house music. It's a masterpiece.

'Love to Love You' with its unabridged sexuality (she has said that she was inspired by Marilyn Monroe) was a hit in gay clubs and brought straight white people into discos as never before. The song captured the hedonism of the time.

"You were coming out of the Vietnam War, the '60s, the protest era, and I was coming out of it as well," she said recently. "I think people were just in a different mind set. When dance music came out, with that beat and that movement, it was a switch. In that period, people were in a dance mood. They wanted to be lifted up, they wanted to have fun, they didn't want to think."

... Baby One More Time Britney Spears

(Max Martin) ❋ Jive ❋ 1998 ❋ Appears on: *... Baby One More Time*

Britney Spears was the turn-of-the-century ingénue. Her story was loaded with contradictions. Here she was a fresh-faced teen from the Mickey Mouse show who acted like a porn star and claimed, against commonsense, that her virtue was still intact. Britney Spears was the embodiment of the decline of America in as much as she sold highly sexualised chastity and Baptist Christianity in the one, bare-midriff package.

Spears' '... Baby One More Time' was a massive global hit for the sixteen-year-old. Swedish hit maker Max Martin who had also given careers to the Backstreet Boys wrote the song. It was controversial to start off with. The hook line "Hit me baby, one more time," has sadomasochistic overtones and an odd acceptance of domestic violence. "It doesn't mean physically hit me," said Spears in a vain attempt at rationalisation. "It means just give me a sign basically. I think it's kind of funny that people would actually think that's what it meant." This begs the question of whether a sheltered Baptist child star understands the implications of her lyrics. However, in the same *Rolling Stone* interview she does go on to discuss the marketing trajectory of her sexuality.

"It was a sexual song. This may be a little old for me. Because of my image thing. I don't want to go over the top. If I come out being Miss Prima Donna, that wouldn't be smart. I want a place to grow," said Spears.

All of this is only an issue because '. . . Baby One More Time' is a fantastic piece of pop. The beat, a loping R&B groove bounces around Spears' vocal giving her just enough lift and never losing sight of the dance floor.

"Pop music is popular music," said the Lolita diva. "I'm just bringing pop music to a different level. It's always going to be pop music. That's what I love to do. I love to dance, and pop music incorporates that. I'm just bringing it to the next level."

Ghosts Japan

(David Sylvian) ✳ Virgin ✳ 1981 ✳ Appears on: *Tin Drum*

Starting out as a glam rock band, Japan rode the New Wave, becoming more arty and esoteric with each release. Manager Simon Napier-Bell, one of Britain's legendary impresarios, persuaded the group that their only chance of success was with Motown covers. Singer David Sylvian gave breathless, introspective and mono-chromatic readings of Smokey Robinson songs while dressed in heavy make-up.

The styling paid off, however, and the group attracted a loyal fan base at home and in Japan. By their fifth album, *Tin Drum*, they had developed a sound of heavily orchestrated and dreamy synthesiser melodies that betrayed oriental and Middle Eastern influences behind Sylvian's weary, whispering vocal.

The group essentially ground to a halt by the time the album was released. Then one track, 'Ghosts', took off and became a Top 5 hit in the UK.

According to Simon Napier-Bell, "[Sylvian] was determined to make amends to the God of creativity by dressing in horse hair and taking a shot at the charts with the most uncommercial track he could find. It was 'Ghosts', a torrid, dark-sounding moan above an atonal track lifted from Erik Satie's music; probably the least commercial single ever to enter the British Top 10. But by now Japan's fashionability overcame all commercial obstacles."

Help Me Make it Through the Night Kris Kristofferson

(Kris Kristofferson) ✻ Monument ✻ 1970 ✻ Appears on: *Kristofferson*

"He brought country music songwriting into its own. Before Kris, most of the songs didn't have that much depth to them," said the late Waylon Jennings. "His songs were about sex, but the undercurrent all the way through was love."

'Help Me Make it Through the Night' became a major hit for Sammi Smith in 1971, and following Janis Joplin's cover of 'Me and Bobby McGee', assured Kristofferson's reputation as a songwriter. This version on his first solo album had none of that triumph in his voice. At the time he was a scuffling singer/janitor/helicopter pilot and his life was in desperate straits. Kristofferson brings that history to bear on the tune.

"I fell in love with the whole life, of songwriters hanging out writing songs to each other, and seeing people that I had heard of on the Grand Ole Opry since I was a little kid," said Kristofferson. "I decided to get out of the army and go back there. To the horror of my parents, my wife, my peers. For about four years they thought I had lost my mind."

Kristofferson eventually came to the attention of Johnny Cash who could relate to the songwriter's hell-raising lifestyle and the deep poetic sensibility behind the lyrics. Kristofferson has a deep empathy for the struggle in life, the temptations and pain.

"I think so far what I've had to contribute has been a certain way to look at things, at emotions," Kristofferson said of his work. "And I think in general my work has been human and made people respond to the things I like to respond to. That's the way my brain responds to my experience. It works it out in lines when it's working the best. It doesn't always work it out like that, but it works it out in lines that make sense. It makes more sense than you think it would. But I do think you can wear your heart on your sleeve, and mistakes I've made in that direction have usually been when I was under the influence of something that made me more confident of my surroundings than I deserved.

"But when I decided I was going to write songs, I decided I was gonna do it right – be true to the best of it – and I think I was pretty idealistic. I thought I would show, in the best way I could, all the emotions I could."

Driva Man Max Roach

(Oscar Brown Jr/Max Roach) ✳ Candid ✳ 1960 ✳

Appears on: *We Insist! Max Roach's Freedom Now Suite*

Max Roach came of age as a drummer in the bebop era and was one of the two pre-eminent percussionists of the time. His patterns were as complex as the bebop horn players and very emotional as well as structured. Roach continued through the post bop years of cool jazz, often playing with Ellington, Dizzy Gillespie, Charlie Parker and Miles Davis, and co-led a legendary quartet with the trumpeter Clifford Brown. In 1960, on the occasion of the 100th anniversary of the Emancipation Proclamation, the National Association for the Advancement of Coloured People commissioned Roach to write a song. The result was a seven-part suite, *We Insist! Max Roach's Freedom Now Suite*. The poetry of Oscar Brown Jr was sung by Abbey Lincoln with the backing of Coleman Hawkins.

'Driva Man', which kicks off the suite in a typically uncompromising way, sees Hawkins let free with some of his most impassioned horn work. Lincoln, a former nightclub chanteuse is similarly liberated in being able to bring her soulful voice to something as clear and as hard as this song. Roach swings the track so that you can hear the deep blues clearly in the militant tune. The result was sufficiently controversial to be banned in South Africa.

"I always resented the role of a drummer as nothing more than a subservient figure," said Roach. "The people who really got me off were dealing with the musical potential of the instrument."

Loser Beck

(Beck/Karl Stephenson) ❈ Bongload ❈ 1994 ❈ Appears on: *Mellow Gold*

The other slacker anthem, 'Loser' was more humorous than Nirvana's 'Smells like Teen Spirit'. Beck Hansen had twenty-something world-weariness, a disdain for slickness, a homemade, lo-fi sound and the general fuck-you attitude – but it was also kind of funny. It was an instant anthem for Generation X. There was a hip-hop groove and bashed-up acoustic guitar line and the whole thing sounded like it had come out of a trash can and been dusted off.

"The first time I heard it on KCRW, they said it was a slacker anthem, but it was a completely silly song, just a takeoff on rap," said Beck. "It was very braggadocios [sic], like you hear in rap songs, but it was so not the mack. It was the opposite of mack.

"It's pretty jarring to be thrown in the air in plain view and be scrutinized and sized up and chopped up and sewn back together. You just have to have a sense of humour about it. You know, somebody saying you're great. Somebody saying you should be exterminated. I saw a lot of negative stuff out there."

Beck and his friend Karl Stephenson recorded 'Loser' in January 1992 on a home eight-track recorder. The following year it came out on the indie label Bongload and came to the attention of Geffen records. Beck was signed and the single was released followed by the cathartic *Mellow Gold* album, which had a similarly psychedelic hillbilly sound.

"It's a tribute in a way to those Greatest Hits packaged records of the '70s, the 'freedom rock' records," said Beck of his sound. "The easy-goin' rockin' order-it-over-the-mail C.O.D. for $19.95, or $6.66 C.O.D. – 'Care of the Devil'. It's sort of taking those songs, peeling the surface off and checking out the mixture of sausage and fibreglass."

'Loser' made Beck a star overnight. "I was the überslacker, which was always kind of ridiculous to me. I don't even know what slacker means," he said. "I wore clothes from thrift stores because I was poor."

That made his next step harder than the first. "Truly cool people aren't afraid of making an ass of themselves, not at the expense of others at least," Beck told *Dazed and Confused*. "The same thing applies with irony. It's a good device, a humorous device, and in such a straight, unimaginative time it's sometimes the only way to get some oxygen, y'know, but it can be over-indulged. It can be another mask, it's very easy to latch onto that, it's much harder to break through the stifling normalcy that's around. But y'know, there's a real American spirit still alive, where people really communicate, that's a real old school thing. But a lot of the time all people can do is look at a screen ...

"The nihilism of the whole grunge thing in America was just a purge. A purging of the materialism and elitism that was the '80s. But ultimately there's a place to go after that. Trouble is, people have got stuck in that. A lot of people are still there, y'know? It's very easy for people to uprise and rebel against something, but it's harder once you've done that to come up with something better. To get a functioning state of things back ..."

Back to Life Soul II Soul

(Paul Hooper/Simon 'The Funky Ginger' Law/Beresford Romeo/Caron Wheeler) ❋ Virgin ❋ 1989 ❋ Appears on: *Club Classics, Vol. 1*

Throughout the '80s the warehouse party scene in Britain was where the true underground music was being made. Much of it came from the sound system DJs – a Jamaican tradition of DJs who set up their own mobile discotheques for parties. That tradition was co-opted into warehouse parties and a new type of music began to develop – heavy on the reggae and dub but with soul music, rare groove and R&B in the mix.

The most popular of these outfit was the Soul II Soul sound system, run by Beresford Romeo aka Jazzie B and childhood friend Philip 'Daddae' Harvey. Jazzie's family had operated sound systems so there was already a record collection of reggae discs. To this they added some hip-hop. "It's a love train, a family," Jazzie told *The Observer*'s Cynthia Rose. "Many an early occasion we would put up the money to play. Then came hip-hop, warehouse parties and the pirate radio explosion. Those things changed British music and helped shape Soul II Soul."

The collective grew to incorporate singers Caron Wheeler, Rose Windross and Do'reen Waddell to augment the dance floor beats.

Soul II Soul moved into recording and enlisted Bristol producer Paul Nellee Hooper who understood the bass-heavy grooves and sweet melodies they wanted.

'Back to Life' featuring Caron Wheeler was the sound of the summer of 1989. It blasted from radios and in every club on the planet that year, a unique, sublime blend of Jamaica, Africa and Europe.

"When you nurture a sound and build the system yourself, like Soul II Soul, you know your speakers very well," said Jazzie. "But then you need to know your studio monitors and every separate stage of record production. And, more important than all of this, is giving it that emotion."

Loan Me a Dime Boz Scaggs

(Fenton Robinson) ✳ Atlantic ✳ 1969 ✳ Appears on: *Boz Scaggs*

Texan-born Scaggs moved to San Francisco – "after the summer of love, In the winter of mild discontent" – to play with the Steve Miller Band where he had a reputation as a hot shot blues guitarist. *Rolling Stone* editor Jann Wenner produced his first solo album.

"At that time he [Wenner] was being courted by a lot of key people in the industry who saw the emergence of *Rolling Stone* as very important," said Scaggs. "He was meeting the likes of Jerry Wexler and Ahmet Ertegun and Clive Davis – and at some point he took a tape of my work to Jerry, and Jerry liked it. We decided to do the album at Muscle Shoals, with Barry Beckett, Roger Hawkins, David Hood, Eddie Hinton, Pete Carr and Duane Allman."

With those people involved the record was going to be very strong on R&B and soul grooves. Allman was only then getting a reputation as a guitar virtuoso. His work on the thirteen-minute 'Loan Me a Dime', where he duets with Scaggs, is one of his finest pieces. Unlike many blues improvisations, the song never gets indulgent and never loses its groove.

"He was a powerful guy in a low-key way, and he added a real spark to everything we did – on 'Loan Me a Dime' his solo was a real catalyst," said Scaggs. "There's real magic in those guys, a chemistry to the way they play. They leave room for just that one quality of the other player that fits, and they take that space knowing that the other guy's going to give way. Jann just directed traffic and called the big shots."

The record was not a hit of any magnitude, but it has stood the test of time.

I'm Eighteen Alice Cooper

(Michael Bruce/Glen Buxton/Alice Cooper/Dennis Dunaway/Neal Smith) ☀ Warner Bros. ☀ 1971 ☀ Appears on: *Love it to Death*

It's hard now, after all we've been through, to understand what Alice Cooper really meant in 1971 when 'I'm Eighteen' put him under the noses of nice middle-class people. Here was this greasy guy from Detroit with a girl's name, women's clothes and a snake for a pet. That was all shocking enough – in the '70s the conservative parties in the federal parliament tried to have Alice Cooper kept out of Australia. But the question on the minds of right-thinking people everywhere was: what was his agenda? And the answer was disturbing – he didn't have one. He just wanted to turn civilisation on its head for the hell of it. Alice Cooper was all that trash coming right out of the TV set, right back at ya!

"People that haven't seen us yet are shocked because they think that Alice Cooper must be a female folksinger," said Alice. "They don't expect the whole thing. And the whole thing is a direct product of TV and movies and America, 'cause that's where America's based. That's where their heart is from – the sex and violence of TV and the movies, and that was our influence.

"We weren't brought up under a blues influence. We were brought up under an electronics influence – the bomb (I'm not knocking the bomb, I think the bomb's a gas), but TV has been the main influence for this generation, and that's why this whole thing is happening.

"You just let your lower self go, and then it takes on all these aspects of the society – the city with horns blowing, the people yelling things at each other, and the all-in-all violence and chaos of the city. Put that on stage with music, and that's what this is.

"It's like this – these five members have been influenced of course by other groups, because that's where this generation's groups came from – an environment like the Beatles, the Rolling Stones, the Yardbirds, and the Who. People like that. They were five years ago, and when they first came out, we were influenced by them – Zappa and people like that.

"So now we've taken that influence – we've done that whole trip, the sounding-like-other-people trip – and now we're applying it to a theatrics basis, to a statement and what the statement is, is nothing."

There had been teen anthems before. 'I'm Eighteen' was the teen anthem for the kids in the 'burbs loaded on TV and mandrax.

"I got a baby's brain and an old man's heart/Took eighteen years to get this far/Don't always know what I'm talkin' about/Feels like I'm livin' in the middle of doubt/'Cause I'm eighteen."

Tiny Dancer   Elton John

(Elton John/Bernie Taupin) ❄ DJM ❄ 1971 ❄ Appears on: *Madman across the Water*

One of Bernie Taupin's best songs, 'Tiny Dancer' was written on John and Taupin's first American tour. The tiny dancer in question is Maxine Feibelmann, Bernie Taupin's future wife and a sometime "seamstress for the band".

Taupin evokes that early '70s mythology of life on the road, which in those days was more along the lines of a travelling gypsy caravan than the well-oiled machine that it has become. Cameron Crowe obviously picked up on this and used the song for that purpose in his film *Almost Famous*.

Until that point, most of Taupin's lyrics had been fantasies based on his tales of the old West or ephemeral pop confections. On this fifth Elton John album, Taupin is taking greater risks. So did Elton. The production and Paul Buckmaster's string arrangements are lavish and ornate but not overbearing. Within this luxury, 'Tiny Dancer' is a beautifully crafted gem.

Coming Down Again   The Rolling Stones

(Mick Jagger/Keith Richards) ❄ Rolling Stones Records ❄ 1973 ❄
Appears on: *Goat's Head Soup*

By late 1972, following their enormously successful US tour, the rift between Jagger and Richards widened – Jagger with his new wife and jet-set life and Richards with a raging heroin habit. Richards was truly an exile at this point with drug arrests and tax problems keeping him out of the UK and France. The Rolling Stones moved to Jamaica to record at Dynamic Sound in Kingston. Richards was not the only one with drug problems – producer Jimmy Miller and engineer Andy Johns were both also falling apart.

Melody Maker's Michael Watts who was in Jamaica for the *Goat's Head Soup* sessions noted: "He [Richards] looked very wasted, very frail. You expected this tough guy and he looked as if you could blow him over, which, of course emphasised his myth and made him seem all the more interesting. I think it became a terrific strain for Jagger to hold this guy up."

'Coming Down Again' is Keith Richards at his best – the song has the ambience of a dream, so laid-back it could fall over at any moment. The texture is dense and smoky and the playing all subsumed into the lotus-eating mood. It's clear from this song that these are people going nowhere fast, but it is the musical embodiment of the phrase "elegantly wasted".

Here Comes the Rain Again Eurythmics

(Annie Lennox/Dave Stewart) ✳ RCA ✳ 1983 ✳ Appears on: *Touch*

"Dave and I wrote 'Here Comes the Rain Again' one afternoon in a room in the Mayflower Hotel in New York," said Annie Lennox of the writing session that involved a wrestling match on the hotel room floor. The phenomenal success of the Eurythmics was due to Stewart's innovative approach to pop songs and Lennox's soul-bearing singing.

'Here Comes the Rain' moves on from the synth-pop of earlier records with the addition of a string section. But you still have the quirky arrangement with its absence of a chorus. You have a melody that borrows from torch songs but doesn't quite go to the same places.

Lennox is at her finest here. Most of her best work deals with her struggle with anxiety and depression. "I lived like that for years, sort of verging on suicide," she said. "I certainly don't mean I'd ever do away with myself, but it's as if I did toy with the idea for a long time. And now, I feel I'm coming out of it.

"No matter how much you want to get out of that sort of thing, or how much help you get, it's a very hard thing to crack. And, in the end, it has to come entirely from within yourself.

"But, although these bad experiences can be horrific, with a bit of luck and a *lot* of grit, you can also turn them into something creative. I do believe in self-improvement and I don't think one is always a victim, not at all."

Carrie Anne The Hollies

(Allan Clarke/Tony Hicks/Graham Nash) ❋ EMI ❋ 1967 ❋
Appears on: *The Hollies' Greatest Hits*

The Hollies first claim to fame was that they took over the Beatles' gig at the Cavern Club when the moptops moved on to bigger and better things. The Hollies, who named themselves in honour of Texan singer/songwriter Buddy Holly, were one of the better groups of the British beat boom. History has passed them by, largely because they were so nice. The Hollies' sound was based on harmony singing and especially the beautifully blended voices of Allan Clarke and Graham Nash. Their sweetness was no match for the Rolling Stones or other more colourful artists. The Hollies, however, could really sing and at their best they were amongst the leaders of their field. Their best-known song is the Graham Gouldman penned 'Bus Stop'. But it was on 'Carrie Anne' that the voices really flew.

'Carrie Anne' was one of their first compositions to become a hit in the US and the UK. It is squeaky clean but it's also built on amazing vocal dynamics over a three-chord melody. In its way it's at least as clever as anything the Byrds were doing. Indeed, guitarist Tony Hicks was listening to the Byrds on the Hollies' 1965 tour of Norway when he got the idea for this masterpiece. The song was finally cut on 3 May 1967 in two takes.

Essence Lucinda Williams

(Lucinda Williams) ❋ Lost Highway ❋ 2001 ❋ Appears on: *Essence*

"Lucinda Williams should be at the very centre of country music. She is an example of the best of what country at least says it is," said Emmylou Harris back in 1995. The songs on the *Essence* album are slightly darker, more seductive and more elusive than on her breakthrough *Car Wheels on a Gravel Road*. *Essence* is mostly sadder than its predecessor, no doubt assisted by the eloquent, mournful guitars of Ryan Adams and Charlie Sexton, and David Mansfield's plaintive violin.

'Essence', the title track, is playful in a narcotic sort of way. Williams is no stranger to the wilder side of life, having spent many years on the road doing damage to herself. In this song she uses heroin as a metaphor for a lover. Or vice versa. It's sometimes hard to tell. For example: "I am waiting here for more/I am waiting by your door/I am waiting on your back steps/I am waiting in my car/I am waiting at this bar/I am waiting for your essence."

The song is a shimmering piece of modern country with production from Sexton and treated guitar from Ryan Adams. There's a come-hither quality and a weariness at the same time. The ambiguity and the rich production make this quite uncountry while still relying on the conventions of a country song.

Without labouring the point too much, this is an album about dangers – low esteem, lost love – and solutions – drugs, passion, God. The title track is the abridged version. Taken as a whole, it's an expedition to the end and back in under six minutes.

Bessie Smith   Bob Dylan & The Band

(Rick Danko/Jaime Robbie Robertson) ✳ Columbia ✳ 1975 ✳
Appears on: *The Basement Tapes*

Before they signed on to be Bob Dylan's backing band, Levon and the Hawks were a bar band. They were ill educated in anything other than rock & roll, plain and simple. They didn't read novels or poetry or go to art movies or the theatre. They didn't know about much more than the next gig. Suddenly they were in the forefront of a cultural revolution, getting booed every night from New York to London to Sydney. It was an eye-opening experience, especially for Jaime Robbie Robertson.

"I got this hunger for education and knowledge because I hadn't gone to school [since] I started with Ronnie Hawkins when I was sixteen," said Robertson. "So I started to read a whole lot and I started to see these kind of films. I got into all kinds of mythologies – European, Nordic . . . it influenced me in a style of storytelling. It influenced me in covering something."

An early attempt at this storytelling was this song, apparently sung by the ex-boyfriend of blues singer Bessie Smith. 'Bessie Smith' has the gently rolling bar room atmosphere of the Band with a very poetic, wistful ambience in the playing.

The song was demoed for the Band's first album and not recorded in the basement at Big Pink although it did surface on *The Basement Tapes*.

"What it meant for me was a sense of relief in a way, because he wrote more poetry-oriented things than I did," said Robertson about Dylan's influence. "But that just made me think I could write these stories and not feel like that every song I'm writing is, 'There was a tall oak tree and a bad one broke ...', and that everything was like, 'Once upon a time ...' I was inclined to write songs like that and it didn't make me feel as self-conscious about writing them, after he [Dylan] had already disrupted the whole thing in the way that he did. When I was writing, I thought, this is only going to work if Jimmy Rodgers was singing it. I would have songs I'd be embarrassed to tell people. It broke down that barrier, and I wasn't embarrassed after that because [Dylan] just kind of opened up the door."

Like a Prayer Madonna

(Patrick Leonard/Madonna) ❋ Sire ❋ 1989 ❋ Appears on: *Like a Prayer*

Madonna took the manipulation of media and PR to a new level in the '80s and right into the '90s. Her shows were outrageous. If there was a holy cow she ran into it. It came to a head with 'Like a Prayer'. Having accepted a massive sponsorship deal from Pepsi, Madonna then released her first Pepsi-sponsored video and caused a massive storm. The song had its spiritual overtones. The video took scandal to a new level with Madonna not only eroticising Christ but a black Christ at that. Pepsi immediately cancelled their sponsorship. Madonna had found the limits and the reality of corporate sponsorship of the arts.

The religious overtones of 'Like a Prayer' were apparently not motivated especially by a desire to cause controversy.

"Spirituality is still really important to me," Madonna told *The Face*. "But I don't feel so inspired to write songs about it. I mean, I go to church: I go to Church of England, I go to Catholic churches, I go to synagogues, I partake in all religions. In my bones, I'm Catholic, because that's how I was raised, but I am just as intrigued by Judaism as I am by Catholicism."

'Like a Prayer' is a beautifully crafted devotional song in the guise of perfect pop. God is in the drum machine.

I Heard It Through the Grapevine Marvin Gaye

(Barrett Strong/Norman Whitfield) ❈ Tamla ❈ 1968 ❈ Appears on: *In the Groove*

Motown put the factory in 'hit factory'. Songwriter/producers cut tracks with the house band and then allocated the house stars to the particular tunes. No song illustrates the process better than 'I Heard It Through the Grapevine', which Barrett Strong initially gave to Gladys Knight and the Pips. Fellow inmates the Isley Brothers and the Miracles also cut the song.

A month after the Pips had recorded 'Grapevine', producer/writer Norman Whitfield recut the track for Marvin Gaye, accenting a more churchy, Ray Charles feel. Whitfield replaced the acoustic piano with an electric Wurlitzer. For the drums he wanted an 'Indian' sound with the accent on the toms. He slowed the track down to a voodoo chant pace and built a powerful groove.

"I came up with a little idea on the piano, the bass-line figure," said Barrett Strong. "We thought it was great, and I thought of this title, 'I Heard It Through the Grapevine', because I'd heard people saying it so much but nobody had ever written a song about it. We just went from there."

With Gladys Knight's version reaching number two on the charts, the Gaye version was shelved and it took a year of insistence before Motown supremo Berry Gordy agreed to release the track. He's reported to have said to Whitfield, "Mention that fucking record again and you're fired".

The song stayed in the vaults until uncovered by archivist/quality control manager Billie Jean Brown who needed a filler for a Gaye album. A Chicago radio station began playing the album track and it took off. 'I Heard It Through the Grapevine' became Motown's biggest hit of the label's first twenty years. The song was also reinterpreted by Creedence Clearwater Revival into a swamp rock jam.

Even Marvin himself was apparently ambivalent about the song at first. "I was being a good artist at the time," he said in 1972. "They tell you, 'Marvin, you gotta come in and do this tune, because this song is a good song for you and it was written by so and so, and so come right in there and be a good guy and cut it, OK?' And that always bugged me. Generally I say go take your song and stuff it. But this particular time I said, 'Oh. Hell, I'll be a good artist'. But it was the Lord who was working and He knew I should have gotten to do it so I did. And that's why it became a big hit."

The James Bond Theme John Barry Orchestra

(Monty Norman) ❋ EMI ❋ 1962 ❋ Appears on: *The Best of James Bond: 30th Anniversary*

The producers of *Dr No*, the second James Bond film (but the first with Sean Connery), engaged London songwriter Monty Norman to score the film. He began the job but, apparently due to time pressure, the producers thought he needed some assistance. John Barry, the leader of John Barry and the Seven, was brought it. Norman and Barry finished the 'Theme' and Barry went on to score the film.

Relying on an inventive horn arrangement and swinging but quite tough percussion, 'The James Bond Theme' evokes danger, exotica and sex appeal. Mostly, though, it is modern in its sound. A touch of R&B rhythm with jazz phrasing makes it swing like the '60s were just about to. Barry's father had operated a cinema and he had run a jazz band for many years and understood the marriage of the two so well.

"John Barry came into our lives when we were making *Dr No*," recalled director Terence Young. "We had someone else doing the music and although the score was all right, we didn't have anything exciting for the title music. I think it was someone at Chappell who said you must listen to him. He had a little band called the John Barry Seven [sic] and he came in and wrote this Bond theme."

The theme, especially when accompanied by the silhouette animation in the original title sequence, says everything you need to know about James Bond. And no character, before or since, has been so tied to a piece of music.

Blind Willie McTell Bob Dylan

(Bob Dylan) ❋ Columbia ❋ 1991 ❋

Appears on: *The Bootleg Series Vol. 1–3 (Rare & Unreleased) 1961–1991*

Blind Willie McTell was born in 1901. Like many blind black men of the time, unable to perform manual labour, he became an entertainer and later a preacher. McTell's compositions were amongst the most popular folk blues of the time, including classics 'Statesboro Blues' and 'Delia'. He died in 1959 at the height of the folk renaissance, just as his music was reaching a white college audience. One college student at the University of Minnesota picked up on McTell's songs and sang some of them in 1960 in coffeehouses. Later in life, when he was the greatest songwriter of his generation, he would return to Willie McTell's 'Broke Down Engine' for one of his albums.

'Blind Willie McTell', regarded as one of the finest of Bob Dylan's recordings, was cut for the *Infidels* album in 1983 and lay unnoticed even by Dylanologists for eight years until uncovered for *The Bootleg Series Volumes 1–3*.

The tune is based on the traditional 'St James Infirmary'. Dylan refers in the song to "... staring out the window/of the old St James Hotel" and from that window he looks across the world and sees only "power and greed and corruptible seed". 'Blind Willie McTell' comes at the end of Dylan's preaching period. No longer writing evangelical songs, he returns to writing apocalyptic ones. He sees the corruption of the modern world and hears in Blind Willie's music the sound of history – which is more of the same.

Caldonia   Louis Jordan

(Fleecie Moore) ❋ Decca ❋ 1945 ❋ Appears on: *No Moe! – Greatest Hits*

Born in 1908, Louis Jordan was a pivotal figure in American popular music. He learnt his trade in the blackface minstrel shows and with some of the seminal blues singers such as Ma Rainey. Jordan's tastes tended towards jazz with his group the Tympany 5. In the immediate post-war era Jordan refined his jump blues style, added a bit of jazz and created R&B. The jazz scene at the time was dominated by bebop, which appealed almost exclusively to intellectuals and beatniks. Jordan, with his crazy dancing and his pumping bands and comical songs, led the way into a new style of African-American music: "I wanted to play for the people, for millions, not just a few hep cats," he said. Indeed, five of Jordan's early singles sold over a million copies.

Although credited to his wife Fleecie Moore, 'Caldonia' is one of Jordan's most popular songs. When his wife left him she also took the publishing income from songs such as this hit. Some credit for the Jordan sound here should go to Milt Gabler. After Decca and Jordan parted ways in 1965, Gabler produced the groundbreaking sides for Bill Haley and the Comets and the similarities are there to be heard. Gabler even admitted the Comets' sessions were based around the feel of the Tympany 5 "We'd begin with Jordan's shuffle rhythm ... you know, dotted eighth notes and sixteenths," he told the *NME*. "We'd build on it. I'd sing Jordan's riffs to the group that would be picked up by the electric guitars and tenor sax. They got a sound that had the drive of the Tympany 5 and the colour of country and western."

Although he predates most rock & roll, Louis Jordan's jive blues have lasted considerably better than most other records of the period.

"We did original tunes, we did every song that came out," said Jordan. "See, before I got a band, I knew what I wanted to do with it. I wanted to give my whole life to making people enjoy my music, make you laugh and smile, so I didn't stick to what you'd call jazz, to instrumentals. Songwriters would bring me songs with jokes to them. I have always stuck to that, entertainment."

Do You Realise?? The Flaming Lips

(The Flaming Lips) ❋ Gravity ❋ 2002 ❋ Appears on: *Yoshimi Battles the Pink Robots*

As their name suggests, the Flaming Lips were a punk band. That was back in the mid-'80s. With only meagre success to encourage them, the Lips (especially Wayne Coyne and Michael Irvins), remained steadfast. They survived college rock and grunge, coasting along on a quirky angst vibe. Then when the new rock started, the Flaming Lips just blossomed off into another direction of quirky pop.

"We were such amateurs we were laughable, but we had enthusiasm," said singer Wayne Coyne. "In the beginning it was just the mess. We did want to be beautiful but – no way. I was singing! Come on! It's just by sheer accident that it seemed charming rather than just stupid. There's a fine line there."

The Flaming Lips are known for having one of the truly great multi-media shows of their time. There's no shortage of other pop ideas either, including an album that could only be listened to with four synchronised CD players going at once.

Pursuing their own star they arrived at their super pop sound on *The Soft Bulletin* in 1999. The next album – *Yoshimi Battles the Pink Robots* – featured 'Do You Realise??', which is a gorgeously baroque and gentle song about the inevitability of death. Oddly, the song and the band featured in a Hewlett-Packard commercial.

"People treat music like it's their football team: 'Our music's great and yours sucks'. But we'd be listening to the Bee Gees and Barry Manilow in the car as we pulled up to a show," said Coyne. "We never looked at music like it was 'us against them'. Our best moments are an accumulation of the Bee Gees and the Butthole Surfers. To us that's what music was about, living at both extremes."

Goodbye Girl Squeeze

(Chris Difford/Glenn Tillbrook) ✳ A&M ✳ 1979 ✳ Appears on: *Cool for Cats*

Chris Difford and Glenn Tillbrook, the songwriting team behind Squeeze, are regularly compared with Lennon and McCartney, Leiber and Stoller and any manner of songwriting couples. The comparisons are more relevant to the structure of the partnership than to its output. Difford wrote the lyric and Tillbrook the music and together, at their best, they captured that whimsical Bristishness – their songs were often populated by recognisable everyday English people just trying to make the best of things. In short, Squeeze was perfect at kitchen-sink drama.

Difford claimed Bob Dylan as a formative influence. "I just loved the way he could create an imaginary story that would be right there in your mind as you're listening to the song," he said. "'Lily, Rosemary and the Jack of Hearts' for me, is the most fantastic lyric for that particular scene within your mind. Where you can play the track and you can see the film running by. And I thought I'd like to be able to do that sort of thing, to be able to create a mini film in someone's head."

His writing blossomed on *Cool for Cats*, Squeeze's second album. So many of the songs had beautiful vignettes. The best of them is 'Goodbye Girl', a story of a bloke who scores a one-night stand and wakes up with his wallet gone and some apologising to do.

Difford captures so many shades and particulars in the space of this short narrative – the excitement of picking up a girl, the abandon of a night on the turps, the terrible consequences for his relationship when he returns home, the betrayals. It's all there in that moment of waking and realising the terrible truth of the daylight. There's a bittersweet quality to the song too, as the narrator distills the pureness of the passion in a one-night stand.

Squeeze have many such moments, including 'Black Coffee in Bed', 'Up the Junction' and 'Tempted', but none has quite the quality of this track.

Children of the Revolution T. Rex

(Marc Bolan) ✻ EMI ✻ 1972 ✻ Appears on: *Tanx*

'Children of the Revolution' broke T. Rex's stride as a hit machine in 1972. Like all the T. Rex songs, this was a twelve-bar boogie tune that updated the classic '50s styles into something more appropriate to the '70s. Marc Bolan was T. Rex (the drummer and bass player notwithstanding). The whole enterprise had one purpose, which was to turn Marc Bolan into a true star. Like a true star, the message was peripheral. If he was required to be a hippie mystic, then he was. If it was required that he be a retro rocker then he was that and if he had been required to be a protest singer, he would have been that too. The excitement that he felt as a pop star was infectious, and we felt it too.

Perhaps it signified the beginning of apathy amongst the hippie movement, perhaps the song wasn't sexy enough – it was slightly more '50s and a little less taut than previous T. Rex songs. Its faltering in the charts didn't of course deter Bolan who just went back to the well for another series of hits. Ironically though, 'Children of the Revolution' is probably Bolan's best-remembered song, having been revived well by the Violent Femmes and less well by others, and having been used in TV commercials.

"But it's not all just fun, there's substance as well," said Bolan of his lyrics. "It really makes me cry to know that I can't explain the stuff to people who purchased the LP. I don't write nonsense as some of the English papers have inferred."

'Children of the Revolution' is thus a heavy song, its final verse declaring, "Well you can bump and grind/And it's good for your mind/I drive a Rolls Royce/'cause it's good for my voice/But you won't fool the children of the revolution". Whether this is meant as a critique of the aristocracy of rock or simply a boast is not clear. It probably wasn't for Bolan either.

Clint Eastwood Gorillaz

(Gorillaz) ✻ Virgin ✻ 2001 ✻ Appears on: *Gorillaz*

"I think for all the people behind it, it's a lab where all the things they really like can be put together and mutated. You can get away with anything as long as you do it well. That's the idea – freedom," said Blur singer Damon Albarn of his side project

Gorillaz. "It's a liberating experience. There are no human beings involved, so they don't get caught up with that crap about personalities and stuff. And you just listen to the music. And if you like the idea of where the band is coming from and the comic thing, then that's great as well."

Gorillaz was a meeting of Brit rock in Albarn, hip-hop from Del the Funkee Homosapein, and hip-hop and techno from producer Dan the Automator with graphics from *Tank Girl* creator and comic book artist Jamie Hewlett.

Like most projects of this kind, much hype followed the release of the eponymous debut album but what's left is a killer single, 'Clint Eastwood', which updates the Specials' 'Ghost Town' with both reverence and cheek.

Miss Misery Elliott Smith

(Elliott Smith) ❋ Capitol ❋ 1997 ❋ Appears on: *Good Will Hunting*

Singer/songwriter Elliott Smith seemed to come from nowhere and suddenly he was singing 'Miss Misery' at the Academy Awards. Smith, then 28, from Portland Oregon, had been making alternative rock records for some time when he was discovered by filmmaker Gus Van Sant who used his music in the film *Good Will Hunting*.

Smith was ideal for the job. His songs have an intimacy and candour – a powerful combination. His vocals were almost whispered, muffled like the child who is afraid to speak out. There was a haunting quality to Elliott Smith even then.

Smith joined the pantheon of doomed singer/songwriters in October 2003 when he stabbed himself twice in the heart. For many years, Smith had battled with drug addictions – alcohol, heroin and, reputedly, crack cocaine. There were rumours and suggestions – not least in his lyrics – that his childhood had been so unhappy that he had never really recovered from it. That haunting quality is there in all of Smith's work including 'Miss Misery'. It's a song that works on a number of levels – he allows us to become intimate by degree.

"I just sorta do my thing, and I don't even really know what it is," he told Barney Hoskyns. "I do know that if you're not in a band and you play acoustic guitar, there's even more of an inclination to box you into a corner than if you are in a band. Playing acoustic definitely makes it possible to be more sensitive, but it doesn't mean that it's any more sentimental."

Firestarter The Prodigy

(Kim Deal/Anne Dudley/Keith Flint/Trevor Horn/Liam Howlett/Johnathon J Jeczalik/
Gary Langan/Paul Morley) ❄ Mute ❄ 1996 ❄ Appears on: *The Fat of the Land*

Somewhere in the mid-'90s the next big thing was going to be called electronica. Rock was dead again, caught in its own morbidity following the grunge years. As interest in rock declined, thousands of young people were putting on raves – immense parties with large sound systems, often in the country. A platoon of DJs and a seamless fabric of repetitive beats to accompany ecstasy trips. Songs were no use. The beat was everything. The buzzards of music industry descended on rave culture and within a few years it was, of course, gone. Given the heat it generated, rave music produced few artists of any substance. One of the half-dozen was the Prodigy.

Liam Howlett is the brain behind the Prodigy. His singular gift is to use electronic music to express emotion – in his case a passionate misanthropy. Howlett had a chip on his shoulder and he made angry techno. He used hip-hop and rock sounds. It wasn't just about the beat any more. The rest of the Prodigy was dancer/vocalists Keith Flint, Leeroy Thornhill and Maxim Reality. The former's spiky hair and copious facial piercings made him look genuinely menacing.

The Fat of the Land was one of the high points of electronica (the Chemical Brothers had the other) and its signature tune was 'Firestarter', which featured Flint on vocals. The song had the relentless, mind-numbing techno beat, amped up a notch. With Flint's vocals it also moved further towards rock and it was nasty. The music track was built around the rocking Breeders' song 'SOS' and the Art of Noise's dark electronic mood, 'Moments in Love'.

Howlett told Ben Thompson in his book *Seven Years of Plenty*, "He [Flint] expresses himself onstage dancing, but I guess he felt like he'd done as much as he could do in that area, and he just needed something else to let himself go with. When he first said he wanted to have a go at doing some vocals, I didn't realise how serious he was, but then he came round to my house and we both sat down and wrote the lyrics. Basically, they're just a description of Keith: what happens with him onstage, the way he is – his headstrong personality. That record sums him up.

"We didn't go out to write a song you could play on the piano. The records I've always liked are the ones you can't sing along to."

Big Time Sensuality Björk

(Björk/Nellee Hooper) ✳ Elektra ✳ 1993 ✳ Appears on: *Debut*

"A lot of my songs – including 'Big Time Sensuality' – are about my friends, not my lovers," said Björk to *Record Collector* magazine. "It's not erotic or sensual even if it may sound like that. As you know, you create pretty deep, full-on love relationships with friends. A lot of it is also about myself. I can be a coward a lot of the time and there comes a moment when I write a song when I get quite brave. It's a lot about me dealing with myself rather than attacking other people. Would I like to know the future? No. There's a side to me that likes to plan a little bit ahead and there's a side that just needs to be free. I've got problems with booking airline tickets – I always change them. Sometimes I wonder if it's just for me to feel free. To kind of not be nailed in is really important to me."

It was a time of courage for the Icelandic singer: after arriving on the world stage five years earlier with the Sugarcubes, Björk set out on her own. She had initially been a solo artist, cutting her first album at the age of eleven. This time she opted to work with Soul II Soul svengali Nellee Hooper and together they crafted a pop record unlike any heard before.

Brassy with jazz and R&B flavours inside an avant-rock framework, *Debut* is haunting and beguiling.

"In my head there were all these little ideas that had to be completed, or I would go mad," said the singer. "I was always very happy singing with the Sugarcubes, being a housewife in Iceland and making film music. But slowly I began to feel that I had to do this thing, get my songs out, otherwise I would feel guilty for the rest of my life. And to do this properly, I had to move to London. It's very precious to me, this album. It may be the only album I ever make, so I wanted to do it right.

"I met this guy in LA and fell in love with him, and he turned out to be Nellee's best friend. So when he brought me back to London, he introduced us. I would probably never have thought of Nellee, because what he has done in the past has been too sophisticated, too tasteful compared to what I was thinking. I was bored to death with current pop music. But when I got to know Nellee, I felt that he was the person who could do the whole thing with me, so I ended up dropping everybody else. I'll work with them later, but it became a bit of a Björk/Nellee affair. I start the songs, and he finishes them."

I Think It's Going to Rain Today   Randy Newman

(Randy Newman) ✳ Reprise ✳ 1971 ✳ Appears on: *Randy Newman Live*

This emotionally charged track was a little out of place in Randy Newman's songbook. It was a song worthy of Bacharach or Gershwin – it's the introspection and melancholy that jars with the rest of Newman's songwriting. Judy Collins had a hit with the track in 1966 bringing a folky wistfulness and poignancy to the piece. It was also a minor hit for Barbra Streisand and was well interpreted by Dusty Springfield and Nina Simone.

On his live set, Randy Newman achieves that time-stopping moment. The appreciative audience who had been talking throughout the set fall completely silent. Newman's piano is so spare that he seems to be sketching the melody with Zen brushstrokes.

While the humour in many of Newman's songs has worn thin through familiarity, 'I Think It's Going to Rain Today' remains as poignant and powerful as ever.

"I used to think that it was just sophomore, college-boy romantic misery somehow," Newman said recently of the tune. "But it's not bad. You know, 'Scarecrows dressed in the latest style . . .' Just the fact that the song uses the word 'implore', it's almost outside the vocabulary you use for pop music nowadays."

Peggy Sue   Buddy Holly & The Crickets

(Jerry Allison/Buddy Holly/Norman Petty) ✳ Coral ✳ 1957 ✳ Appears on: *The Complete Buddy Holly*

Buddy Holly stands apart from the pack of '50s rock & roll stars. Only Chuck Berry wrote as well and as prolifically as Holly. Holly was not a hell raiser, at least not in public. Indeed, his death happened in part because he wanted to catch a plane to the next concert date so that he could do his laundry. Holly was, however, spectacular in his own right. He was the prototype for the rock & roll bands of the future. The Beatles were strongly influenced by him as were most UK artists of the time, not least the Hollies who borrowed his name.

'Peggy Sue' is one of Holly's signature tunes. The country influence is strong in the hiccupping vocal that echoes the rockabilly drumming from Jerry Allison. The playing from Holly, Allison and bassist Joe B Mauldin was a grungy Tex Mex sound that is resolved in the chorus into pure pop.

It was originally titled 'Cindy Lou' after Holly's baby niece, however, the song was renamed in honour of Allison's girlfriend (and future wife) Peggy Sue Gerron. An almost throwaway quality lifts the song and makes it irresistible. The track was cut as part of a three-day session at Norman Petty's studio in Clovis, New Mexico. The spare, dry sound that Petty engineered was critical to Buddy Holly – the Crickets had a tight, country sound that included using cardboard boxes for drum kits. Allison's distinctive beats were a major part of Holly's distinctive style.

'Peggy Sue' became an icon; the song put a name to the bobby soxer and certainly its innocent beginnings support that. Peggy Sue got married – as we know – but then got divorced. She's now a motivational speaker, has a website and appears at auto shows.

Hey Ladies Beastie Boys

(Beastie Boys/The Dust Brothers) ❋ Capitol ❋ 1989 ❋ Appears on: *Paul's Boutique*

"Most people viewed *Paul's Boutique* as a total commercial failure," Mike D told *iD* magazine, "but it was necessary to get us to where we are now." Mike Diamond is talking from the perspective of the Beastie Boys being the hippest white group on the planet in the '90s. Their debut, *Licensed to Ill* was a teenage dream – crunching rap music with heavy metal and mocking anything that moved. Three years later they showed, with *Paul's Boutique*, that white, middle-class kids could understand rap music.

'Hey Ladies' has that Beastie Boys irreverence and the video is loaded with '70s iconography. It's like a dream set in a second-hand store. But so is the music. Of course many of the group's fans couldn't understand the dense mix of sounds without the crunch. On the first record the Beastie Boys were obnoxious kids fighting for the right to party. On 'Hey Ladies' they're still sort of obnoxious, but also very, very smart with the samples.

But the Beastie Boys were ahead of the curve here. In partnership with the Dust Brothers, the New York trio constructed an album of samples from all over the place but with a unique sensibility. *Paul's Boutique* didn't have any hits and it didn't sell, but it demonstrated that the Beastie Boys had a talent beyond being obnoxious.

All Along the Watchtower Bob Dylan

(Bob Dylan) ✳ Columbia ✳ 1967 ✳ Appears on: *John Wesley Harding*

At a time when the Beatles were at their most baroque and the world was going psychedelic with the opportunities offered by new recording studios, Bob Dylan recorded his album *John Wesley Harding* accompanied only by a bass player and drummer with pedal steel on two other tracks. It was a complete about-face. For some months Dylan had been recording demo tapes with the Hawks. Over a hundred songs had been written. Dylan went to Nashville, however, to cut his new album and used none of them.

John Wesley Harding is full of ancient images from the Wild West and the Bible. The characters in these songs deal with eternal truths, in oblique ways.

'All Along the Watchtower' is an apocalyptic song set in a mythical landscape of castles and horsemen and strange portents. It's a song with images that don't lend themselves to a literal reading. The vampiric businessmen probably refers to manager Albert Grossman whom Dylan felt was exploiting him. The sense of paranoia probably comes from the hordes of hippies who besieged Dylan's property at this time. There was a sense that this generation of freaks and hippies and dropouts was leading somewhere and the most prescient commentators such as Joan Didion had started to speculate about the dark side of the social anarchy of the '60s.

Despite its obscure imagery, 'All Along the Watchtower' was a song that spoke to its time. The song's biggest fan was guitarist Jimi Hendrix who, upon hearing it, booked a studio with his band the Experience and guitarist Dave Mason and cut a version on the spot. Hendrix rearranged the tune and added his own tempestuous guitar lines – swirling around like the gathering storm. Hendrix had a major hit with the song. Dylan, too, preferred the cover version over the original and when playing live he uses the Hendrix arrangement rather than his own.

Lithium Nirvana

(Kurt Cobain) ✷ DGC ✷ 1991 ✷ Appears on: *Nevermind*

Kurt Cobain was the leader not of the alternative nation but of the Ritalin Generation. The singer had a troubled childhood, growing up poor in a fractured family. "It was when I was seven," he told Jon Savage. "I had a really good childhood and then all of a sudden my whole world changed, I remember feeling ashamed. I became antisocial and I started to understand the reality of my surroundings, which didn't have a lot to offer. It's such a small town that I couldn't find any friends who were compatible. I like to do artistic things; I like to listen to music. I could never find any friends like that.

"I felt so different and so crazy that people just left me alone. They were afraid. I always felt that they would vote me 'Most Likely to Kill Everyone' at a high school dance. I could definitely see how a person's mental state could deteriorate to the point where they could do that. I've got to the point where I've fantasised about it, but I'd have always opted for killing myself first."

Cobain's family suffered through the great changes that happened in society in the '60s and '70s with prescription drugs and blurred notions of family. These kids were the victims of massive social change. Cobain clearly went through the eye of that storm medicated with Ritalin and other drugs, both from the pharmacy and the street corner. He was a junkie primed to happen.

'Lithium' reflects the intense emotional confusion that was Cobain's short life. The phrases "I love you," "I miss you," "I killed you" are contrasted with the cry "I'm not gonna crack!" On this track you can hear Cobain holding it all inside and, in hindsight, that last cry was actually bravado.

Shakin' Street MC5

(Michael Davis/Wayne Kramer/Fred 'Sonic' Smith/Dennis Tomich/Rob Tyner) ✷ Atlantic ✷ 1970 ✷ Appears on: *Back in the USA*

The MC5's debut album was neither revolutionary nor commercial enough. The label Elektra dropped the group and MC5 began to distance themselves from the White Panthers. They signed with Atlantic records and hired rock critic Jon Landau to helm the recording for the next album. Landau would soon become manager and producer of Bruce Springsteen and other platinum records. However, the MC5 sessions were his first.

Landau thought that the MC5's high energy needed to be contained and cleaned up. He had no time for the revolutionary politics but wanted to bring out the group's musical qualities.

"We met up with Jon Landau and he was good for us in a couple of ways," said guitarist Wayne Kramer. "He was trying to stress discipline, trying to get us back to where we were about a year-and-a-half before when we made our first record – just being a solid, tight, aggressive rock & roll band. He tried to clean us up but he went overboard with it. He wasn't the right producer to be doing the MC5's second record."

If the sessions for the second album didn't have the fury and the capricious crunch of the live album, the songwriting had come along. 'Shakin' Street', written by guitarist Fred 'Sonic' Smith, is a wonderful pop song based on the insistent tempo of hard-strummed acoustic guitars embellished by a motorvatin' electric guitar riff. Despite complaints about the production, 'Shakin' Street' is a great pop song that established a sound that would be mimicked at the end of the decade by groups such as the Flamin Groovies and the Dictators and their followers in the American New Wave. Smith's vocal also lifted the track. While not a strong singer, he had more control and more character than Rob Tyner who usually warbled for the 5.

"We really wanted to prove we were a great rock & roll band," said Kramer of the second album. "And, you know, when you're young and you've put your first album out and you've opened your heart and soul for the whole world to see, and you get criticized the way we got criticised. And they came down on us with a sledge-hammer, not only were we too revolutionary for the straight world we weren't revolutionary enough for the revolutionary world. So we got it from both sides. That we could handle, but when we were criticized for our musicianship that really hurt us; that got us where we lived and damaged our little egos. So we really wanted to prove ourselves – because we knew we could play and that we were a great rock & roll band – so the second album was designed to win over all those people that said that we were the revolutionary hype or that we couldn't tune our guitars. The funny thing is that we put out an album of two-and-a-half-minute, highly focused, content-heavy political rock songs in a day when they were featuring fifteen minute guitar solos."

I Cover the Waterfront Frank Sinatra

(Johnny Green/Eddie Heyman) ✳ Capitol ✳ 1957 ✳ Appears on: *The Capitol Years*

Max Miller had a column in *The New Yorker* that reported on the maritime stories around New York, its docks and waterways. In 1933 United Artists wanted to make a film starring Claudette Colbert and Ben Lyon based on Miller's work. They enlisted Eddie Heyman and Johnny Green to write the theme song.

"I didn't want to do it," Green recalled. "I said 'what kind of a title is that for a love song?' But my beloved Eddie Heyman, he said 'I think I can lick it'. And did he ever. I mean you only have to think of the first couple of lines of that verse that Eddie wrote: 'Away from the city that hurts and mocks/I'm standing alone by the desolate docks/In the still and the chill of the night'. Do I have to go any further? It's one of the great song poems ever written. In the refrain, the chorus: 'I cover the waterfront/I'm watching the sea/Will the one I love be coming back to me?' That's it!"

With the lyrics half-written, Green was able to match the forlornness of Heyman's poetry with a melody that is equally melancholy.

Frank Sinatra is one of many singers who have attempted the song. He brings to it that melancholia that he has – the existential quality of Sinatra's best work. This is a song that in a few bars paints an entire cityscape, the void of an ocean and the lonesomeness of both in the absence of love.

Few titles have entered the vernacular as this one has. The film is long forgotten but the tune and its lyrics remain.

Last Goodbye Jeff Buckley

(Jeff Buckley) ✳ Columbia ✳ 1994 ✳ Appears on: *Grace*

Ethereal, intangible, otherworldly – these are the kinds of words brought to mind by Jeff Buckley's short career. Buckley seemed fragile – abandoned by his rock star father, he was a songwriter with a tremulous voice, a beautiful face and a clear picture of the dark side of life.

Buckley was also out of sync with the times. His songs didn't fit with alternative rock, which was the prevailing style of 1994. Buckley's music was literate – understanding jazz and blues and ethnic styles as well as rock.

'Last Goodbye' was as close to a conventional pop song as Buckley would write. In it he absorbs influences from Pakistan to Memphis and turns them into something resembling rock music.

The sessions for *Grace* where 'Last Goodbye' was cut took place at Bearsville, outside New York, with producer Andy Wallace, who had mixed Nirvana's *Nevermind* and was therefore hot.

Buckley had made a name for himself as a singer/songwriter playing small clubs in New York and it was expected that the debut album would reflect that. However, over the five weeks spent at Bearsville, the chemistry in the group – guitarist Michael Tighe, bass player Mike Grondahl and drummer Matt Johnson – brought these songs to new and better lives.

"'Last Goodbye' means a lot to me because at the time that I wrote it, a long time ago, I was around an environment that thought that [my songs] were completely loser songs," Buckley told me in 1996. "I put them on the album to prove at least to the songs that they weren't losers. They were worth recording. Sort of like finding kids that have been told all their lives that they're pieces of shit, and finally you have to go around proving to them, by putting them in a completely other setting, that no, they are worth knowing and loving."

'Last Goodbye' covers that sense of loss that stalks so much of Buckley's work. So many of his inspirations – Edith Piaf, Miles Davis, Judy Garland and Nina Simone – were artists who had trouble living. Buckley's music is haunted by them. The muscular guitar and bass riffs that drive this song play off against the raga-like second guitar and the spectral atmosphere of the tune.

"Some people are just born into bodies, born into lifespans that just don't fit anywhere else and they have very little to hang onto to validate and also it's a very lonely thing to notice a certain sense of life and be able to relate that to anyone," he told me. "It's probably the onset of madness, or it must seem so to the person who sees the world in a certain way. Maybe they see spirits everywhere or maybe they divine information from certain happenings and certain peoples that are invisible to most of us, and as a result people deem those experiences not valid and not important, and crazy too, and that can damage a person ... There's a lot of strength to the self-destructive soul."

Most of the Time Bob Dylan

(Bob Dylan) ❋ Columbia ❋ 1989 ❋ Appears on: *Oh Mercy*

Bob Dylan thought Bob Dylan was pretty much finished in 1989. He was even knocked back from joining the Grateful Dead. At the suggestion of Bono from U2, Dylan teamed up with producer Daniel Lanois and quickly cut an album at his Kingsway Studios in New Orleans.

Lanois was a hard taskmaster for Dylan, who was often uncomfortable working in studios. Indeed, he hadn't made a record that sounded any good for fifteen years. Lanois gave Dylan a new sound.

'Most of the Time' is a song about time. It's about recalling a lover from the past and carrying that memory. It's in that sense a rewrite of 'Girl from the North Country'. What distinguished the song, however, was the beautiful bass guitar figure that booms through the canyons of loneliness. Then there's Dylan's voice, which plays with the idea of a man in denial about his own regret.

Cornbread Moon Joe Ely

(Joe Ely) ❋ MCA ❋ 1978 ❋ Appears on: *Honky Tonk Masquerade*

One third of the famous Austin songwriters' triumvirate, Joe Ely recovered from the disappointment of the Flatlanders project with a startling solo career. Ely had a straight-up style, a cowboy stoicism but with a rock & roll attitude. His grasp of country music was broad enough to encompass the honky tonking and poetic narratives of Texas songwriting. Ely hailed from Lubbock and he has much in common with its other charming native son, Buddy Holly.

Ely's second solo album, *Honky Tonk Masquerade* is the pick of his early recordings. Produced by Chip Taylor, it presents the big picture – some tunes from the Flatlanders and some of his own. The integrity of the record is the key to its modernism. This also helped Ely to be adopted by the Clash and introduced to a rock audience (paving the way for Steve Earle and the other new traditionalists). 'Cornbread Moon' is a perfect statement of intent from a man who sees himself in the Hank Williams honky tonk tradition.

"Being a live musician is what I've always done; I've always played on the road, played in bands since I was a kid," he said. "I kinda take in my environment everywhere, and with the demise of the Texas honky tonks, the band evolved, the clubs changed, the music changed, different musicians – I find when I write, I write around the instruments that I'm working with. On the first album, I think I wrote more around the steel guitar in the melodies, and with later albums, I've written more around maybe blues guitar or saxophone. I play a lot, and I try to keep my eyes and ears open to take in wherever I'm at and I feel a little bit like the environment that I'm in. Honky tonks is a nice myth that Nashville tries to carry on, but they just don't exist – country places today are discos."

Teardrop Massive Attack

(Robert 'ʒL' del Naja/Elizabeth Fraser/Grantley 'Daddy G' Marshall/Mushroom Massive Attack) ✳ Virgin ✳ 1998 ✳ Appears on: *Mezzanine*

The latest in a long line of sublime singers, Cocteau Twins' vocalist Elizabeth Fraser contributed to four tracks on Massive Attack's *Mezzanine* and gave them their first hit single with 'Teardrop'. Fraser's voice itself was epic. Here it slowly unfolds against the dreamy Massive Attack tunes. One critic said of the song, "Hearing it for the first time is like holding a fine piece of filigree glasswork on the tip of your tongue and then recklessly biting into it, only to find out that it is actually made of sugar."

Massive Attack made the record as the trio was splitting apart. Their debut album, *Blue Lines* (1991), was one of the defining moments of popular music – deep bass and soul grooves met reggae and hip-hop. There was pressure on the group to keep pushing boundaries and that led to dissent.

"The problems within the group are nothing to do with cultural differences, they're to do with the fact that we don't necessarily get on as people," said Daddy G (aka Grantley Marshall). "Things are never really disposed of," said Marshall, "because you're at such close quarters all the time. The same stuff crops up over and over again and you think 'Shouldn't we have got that out in the open a long time ago?'"

The tension amongst the parties led to a tension in the music, over which Fraser's voice could skate.

"She's very excitable and quite mad in the best way," said Robert '3D' del Naja of the singer. "She threw a million words into the air and we tried to grab a few and work out what she meant. Me and Mush met her in Sainsbury's and invited her up to the studio. There was this nerve-wracking moment before she arrived and I said, 'It's really sterile in here, let's light some candles in here and make it funky for her'. She loved our Siouxsie and the Banshees sample off 'Metal Postcard' – she'd just had this Siouxsie and the Banshees tattoo removed from her arm. We didn't use that track but she's really cool. Her voice is so immense and ethereal."

Waterfalls TLC

(Marqueze Etheridge/Lisa 'Left Eye' Lopes/Organized Noize) ❋ La Face ❋ 1994 ❋
Appears on: *Crazy Sexy Cool*

In their short and volatile career, TLC made some of the best R&B of the '90s. Starting out pretty rough with raps and attitude, by the time they made *Crazy Sexy Cool* they had incorporated Prince's erotic moves, LA Reid and Babyface's no-nonsense new jack production, and their own street smarts. They made the tabloids with fights with lovers and hard partying. In the meantime they sold a lot of records.

"What I really loved about TLC when I first met them was that they had a definite opinion of what kind of group they wanted to be," said LA Reid. "TLC won't sing songs that don't represent their points of view – I don't care who wrote it or how big a hit it could be."

The group started as part of Organized Noize in Atlanta where the hip-hop scene thrived around writer/producers such as Dallas Austin (Boyz II Men) and Rico Wade, who co-wrote 'Waterfalls'.

Lisa 'Left Eye' Lopes tended to supply the attitude while Tionne Watkins and Rozonda Thomas brought the vocals, which were both sexy and inviting while also being strong and conscious. TLC might go out with you but they weren't going to leave the attitude behind. TLC were emancipated women and modern women responded.

'Waterfalls' was TLC at their most Princely and seductive.

"See, we came pretty much as is," said Watkins. "We knew how we were going to sing, dress and everything. All you had to do was the paperwork."

Whip It Devo

(Gerald V Casale/Mark Mothersbaugh) ✳ Warner Bros. ✳ 1980 ✳

Appears on: *Freedom of Choice*

Two years after they first appeared with their controversial 'Jocko Homo' 45 (the flipside was 'Mongoloid') and then their stripped-down version of the Stones' 'Satisfaction', Devo were no longer weirdo outsiders in the rock & roll world. They were spearheading the New Wave with their doctrine of Devolution.

"Devolution was a combination of a Wonder Woman comic book and the movie *Island of Lost Souls*, the original, with Bela Lugosi, Lon Chaney, Charles Laughton," said Casale. "That was various things I'd been thinking about Devolution, of going ahead to go back, things falling apart, entropy. It grabbed every piece of information and gave it some kind of cohesive presence – it was a package. Just as our music and our identity exist as technique rather than a style."

They were lauded by Bowie and Neil Young. They were cute and funny, and kind of slick. They were one of the first groups to make complete use of drum machines as rock instruments in their own right. On 'Whip It' the ascending and descending runs of the song in a slightly obscure time signature and with heavy emphasis on the synthesiser made the song both familiar and novel at the same time.

The tortured tunes of early Devo gave way to a dense synthesiser sound over the robotic, automated beats. This sound fitted with the group's belief that society was becoming increasingly contrived and standardised. Ironically, this attack on mass consumerism was embraced by the masses and Devo became major rock stars.

'Whip It' works on a number of levels. There are the S&M connotations, of course, and the fact that the video was shot in the style of a low-budget porn movie. The lyric is also clearly a satire on the self-help jargon and New Ageish affirmations that were starting to creep in to regular discourse. It's unlikely, however, that much of the satiric content registered with the million Americans who bought this track and the album *Freedom of Choice*.

Devo, said Jerry Casale in 1978, "is just the enema bag … the clean-up squad. We're getting the broom out to make way for the '80s." And they did.

Bohemian Rhapsody Queen

(Freddie Mercury) ✲ EMI ✲ 1975 ✲ Appears on: *A Night at the Opera*

Queen were the little hard-rock band that could. They had seen some success with their first three albums but not much more was expected and the group seemed to lack direction. Then, when recording their fourth album, *A Night at the Opera*, singer Freddie Mercury turned up with a six-minute song in four parts that included a light operetta section. The whole thing was set in medieval Italy.

'Bohemian Rhapsody' is one of the dumbest ideas in the colourful tradition of pop. So much so that it is a masterpiece in a class all its own. It has been reliably voted Britain's favourite-ever single and has become one of the best known pop songs of the 20th century. It was a major hit when first released and enjoyed a whole new lease of life courtesy of the film *Wayne's World*.

Producer Roy Thomas Baker recorded the song in six studios over three weeks. The various parts, once committed to tape separately, were stuck together with sticky tape. The most difficult section was the 'opera' portion, with as many as 120 vocal parts bounced down to twenty-four tracks over the course of a week's continuous rerecording by the quartet. Equally well known is Brian May's grandiose guitar solo, so beloved of air guitarists.

"Freddie came in pretty well armed for that song," said Brian May. "He had these little pieces of company paper from his dad with the notes of the chords. As I remember, I don't think he had a guitar solo as such planned. I guess I steamed in and said, 'This is the point where you need your solo. And these are the chords I'd like to use.' Because it's like a piece of the verse, but with a slight foray into some different chords at the end to make a transition into the next piece that he had. I'd heard the track so many times that, when it came time to play the solo, I knew what I wanted to play, in my head. And I wanted the melody of the solo to be something extra, not just an echo of the vocal melody. I wanted it to be an extra colour. So I just had this little tune in my head to play. It didn't take very long to do. The heavy part was really part of Freddie's plan. I didn't change what he had very much. Those riff things that everybody bangs their heads to are really more Freddie than me.

"If I were to do it now, however, I would adjust the tuning. It's not quite right. Things like that bother me a lot these days. Because, if you get overexcited, the guitars really go sharp. And that's what happened there. I'm giving away precious secrets. You can tell, because the piano sounds a little flat in the end. And that's because I was a little over the top in vibrating there. These days I would probably harmonise it down to make it in tune. And that probably would have ruined it."

'Bohemian Rhapsody' is a triumph of kitsch. Clichés are strung together in a rococo structure and piled on top of each other. If the Beatles' 'A Day in the Life' were a meal, 'Bohemian Rhapsody' would be an all-you-can-eat buffet in a food court.

Just as Mercury had piled odd tunings and keys together over the basic pop structure, the lyrics of the song are full of exotica – characters from Italian opera and theatre, Islamic phrases and names, and some archaic English words combine around an obtuse narrative.

"We didn't speak to each other about lyrics," said May. "We were just too embarrassed to talk about the words. When we were recording 'Bohemian Rhapsody', it was a nerve-racking time. We were all very competitive and we knew there was a lot at stake."

"A lot of my songs are fantasy," said Mercury in 1974, prior to the *Opera* sessions. "I can dream up all kinds of things. That's the kind of world I live in. It's very sort of flamboyant, and that's the kind of way I write."

Clearly it paid off. British radio DJ Kenny Everett was so enamoured of the track that he played an advance of the disc fourteen times in one weekend. The song went to number one on release and transformed Queen from contenders to champions.

Sweet Jane The Velvet Underground

(Lou Reed) ❊ Mercury ❊ 1974 ❊ Appears on: *1969 Live*

'Sweet Jane' is Lou Reed's most enduring song. A simple riff given Reed's idiosyncratic timing. It's not surprising then that the song has been covered so often by so many different artists. The Velvet Underground themselves never came to a definitive version in the studio – a verse was chopped out without Reed's permission.

'Sweet Jane' is a song about bohemia. It's about the choices we make. This was a subject dear to Reed's heart. He had a difficult relationship with his parents, who committed him to mental institutions and signed off on electric shock treatment. He understood the attractions of suburbia but he also knew that it was not a possibility for him. It's a song about the gulf between his life as an artist and the parallel universe of people "who've got to work".

It's a song without bitterness. It's an elegy.

The best version of the song is on the Velvet Underground's *1969 Live* album. The Velvets were a formidable force live; they opened songs up and never played them the same way twice. On this laid-back version the group relaxed into its groove and let the song speak for itself.

Bring the Noise Public Enemy

(Anthrax/Chuck D/Eric 'Vietnam' Sadler/Hank Shocklee) ❋ Def Jam ❋ 1991 ❋
Appears on: *Apocalypse 91 … The Enemy Strikes Black*

On their 1987 album *It Takes a Nation of Millions to Hold Us Back*, Public Enemy's first version of 'Bring the Noise' sampled thrash metal band Anthrax, suggesting a meeting of two musics and fan bases that shared little more than attitude. However, the cross fertilisation of ultra-white thrash metal and ultra-black hardcore rap has been a major dynamic in music through the '90s and beyond.

Much of the audience for hardcore rap and for Public Enemy in particular came from white male teenagers who identified with the aggression in the music, although it's unlikely that many of the audience went along with Chuck D's politics.

"Metal has attitude and it has speed, and that's two things that I like," said Chuck D, Public Enemy's leader. "In rap, groups are treated like they're disposable, and so they become disposable. Heavy metal groups are involved in how their music is presented, packaged, marketed. They have control of the merchandising and their logos, whereas the vast majority of rap groups have no control at all."

On *Apocalypse 91* Public Enemy reprised 'Bring the Noise' with Anthrax duetting with the rappers. This is about as angry a sound as you can get.

Over the Rainbow Judy Garland

(Harold Arlen/EY Harburg) ✳ Premier/Rhino ✳ 1939 ✳ Appears on: *The Wizard of Oz*

At its inception, 'Over the Rainbow' was neither a gay anthem nor a little girl's plea for silver lining. It was penned by a pair of unabashed lefties as an expression of hope for America under Roosevelt's 'New Deal'. Arlen had made his name at Harlem's Cotton Club and Harburg had written the depression-era protest hit, 'Brother Can You Spare a Dime?'

Yet from these earthbound beginnings, the song's soaring melody carried generations from Dorothy's monochromatic Kansas home to the bright dreamscape of Oz and elevated Judy Garland to the status of icon. She didn't shake her association with the song to her dying day. Indeed, she claimed she had no desire to.

"I've sung it time and time again and it's still the song that's closest to my heart," Garland said.

Harburg, who was haunted by the song, went on to write lyrics for the musical, *Finian's Rainbow*, after which his career plummeted when he became a victim of the '50s McCarthy-era witch hunts.

Sexy Boy Air

(Jean-Benoît Dunckel/Nicolas Godin) ✳ Astralwerks ✳ 1998 ✳ Appears on: *Moon Safari*

Air – a French electronica duo – are a 21st century version of Bert Bacharach or Sergio Mendes. The music is appealing, relaxing, intelligent, witty and sophisticated. Jean-Benoît Dunckel and Nicolas Godin have a warm, laid-back sound, slightly jazzy and slightly spacey. Their affection for old-school electronics like the Moog synthesiser has a strange nostalgic quality – who thought space age instruments could one day sound nostalgic? – and that adds to the relaxing quality of their soundscapes.

'Sexy Boy' is the track that launched Air across the Channel and the Atlantic. Obviously there is some frisson to the lyric that is sung by Dunckel and Godin in campy falsetto. It's a track that has their light touch in the melody lines while the bass is grounding and grooving. Air mostly provides sophisticated chill-out ambience but this is laid-back music that can get you on the dance floor. More Campari than Red Bull.

Baba O'Riley The Who

(Pete Townshend) ❈ Track ❈ 1971 ❈ Appears on: *Who's Next*

Peter Townshend crammed multiple obsessions into this track. The title is an amalgam of the names of his guru Meher Baba and avant-garde composer Terry Riley. Then at the end Townshend returns to his perennial theme of youth culture, in this case a "teenage wasteland".

Having had massive success with his first rock opera *Tommy*, Townshend turned his attention to a more complex concept album based on the teaching of Meher Baba. The project, Lifehouse, was never finished but fragments of the work turned up in a number of places. 'Baba O'Riley' was originally a nine-minute track recorded for Lifehouse. This truncated version recorded by the Who opens *Who's Next* with a dramatic flurry of notes from the ARP synthesiser, then a very new instrument that Riley was teaching the Who guitarist to play. The cascaded riff is one of the more dramatic moments in '70s rock. The Who then come in behind with a massive, muscular sound and singer Roger Daltrey at the absolute top of his form. In a song about spiritual poverty, the music has a very different message.

Cry Me a River Julie London

(Arthur Hamilton) ❈ Liberty ❈ 1955 ❈ Appears on: *Julie Is Her Name*

Actress Julie London took this torch song and made it completely her own. She sings this song as though her heart is breaking.

London was married to actor Jack Webb, best known for his leading role in the TV police series *Dragnet*. He was also a producer and director. 'Cry Me a River' was written for Ella Fitzgerald to sing in Webb's film *Pete Kelly's Blues*. When Webb declined the track, London picked it up and sang it in the musical comedy, *The Girl Can't Help It*. Jazz bandleader Bobby Troup (who wrote 'Route 66') was the producer on the song and used minimal backing – guitarist Barney Kessel and Tommy Dorsey's bassist Ray Leatherwood. London's vocal is halting and timorous as she eases her way through the song. There is clearly a huge well of emotion just waiting to burst forth in the song.

London and Troup later married and in the '70s they both appeared in the TV series *Emergency*, which was produced by Webb. London became an overnight star on the back of this song and thanks to the visibility of the film. The song was an instant classic and has been covered by almost every serious singer in the past fifty years.

Da Doo Ron Ron (When He Walked Me Home)
The Crystals
(Jeff Barry/Ellie Greenwich/Phil Spector) ❊ Phillies ❊ 1963 ❊ Appears on: *Back to Mono*

The title of this song is one of those perfect pop abstractions, an onomatopoeia for the sound of a crush. "We'd gotten stuck and didn't know what to say there," said songwriter Ellie Greenwich. "So it was like, 'Why don't we just keep "da doo ron ron"? It sounds right, it feels like fun, so let's just leave it.'"

According to Sonny Bono, a Spector protégé, "It took me some time to understand that when Phil asked, 'Is it dumb enough?' what he really meant was, 'Is everybody going to get the simplicity of this?' Will the simplicity of the hook cut through everything and grab them? I was standing beside him as the final playback of 'Da Doo Ron Ron' finished. Phil pointed to the speakers and flashed me a sneaky smile. Trying to impress him, I said, 'Man, that sure is dumb enough.' 'No Sonny', he said. 'That's gold. That's gold coming out of that speaker.'"

"I met him on a Monday and my heart stood still/Somebody told me that his name was Bill" is pretty much "dumb" but Spector turned this commonplace into a masterpiece for the ages. Part of it was the casting – getting the personality of the vocalist to fit the lyric. Much of the rest was orchestration – the loading up of percussion and the arrangements of the parts – a bit of R&B, a touch of Latin and a slice of jazz in the phrasing and then getting the whole thing to sit in a majestic sea of echo.

Although credited to the Crystals, 'Da Doo Ron Ron' was first cut with Darlene Love doing the vocals in Los Angeles. The Crystals were in Washington DC. Unhappy with the results, Spector flew the group to New York to cut the backgrounds. They caught a flight in the morning, did the session and were back in Washington for that night's show. The youngest Crystal, LaLa Brooks, was shuttled to Los Angeles to sing the lead part the next day.

"A Phil Spector session was a party session," said drummer Hal Blaine. "There'd sometimes be more percussionists than orchestra. I used to call it the Phil-harmonic. It was an absolute ball."

"Those records, when I was making them," said Spector, "they were the greatest love of my life."

Happy The Rolling Stones

(Mick Jagger/Keith Richards) ✳ Rolling Stones Records ✳ 1972 ✳

Appears on: *Exile on Main Street*

"*Exile on Main Street* is not one of my favourite albums, although I think the record does have a particular feeling," Mick Jagger said. "I'm not too sure how great the songs are, but put together it's a nice piece. However, when I listen to *Exile* it has some of the worst mixes I've ever heard. At the time Jimmy Miller was not functioning properly. I had to finish the whole record myself, because otherwise there were just drunks and junkies. I was in Los Angeles trying to finish the record, up against a deadline. It was a joke."

Exile on Main Street is the apotheosis of the rock & roll album. It is perfect in its imperfections. Jagger is right in observing that the mix is dirty and there are no hits, but it does have a particular quality all of its own.

In 1971 the Rolling Stones moved to France to avoid the punitive British tax rates. Keith Richards set up a base in Nellcote on the Mediterranean. A studio was set up in his wine cellar and much of *Exile* was recorded there. There's a myth the album reflects life in Richards' house but most of the tracks had been sitting in the vaults, some going back to the *Beggars Banquet* sessions of 1968. What *Exile* really represented was the culmination of their golden era: *Beggars Banquet*, *Let it Bleed* and *Sticky Fingers*.

'Happy', recorded almost entirely by Keith Richards and sung by him with some gusto, is autobiographical: "Well I never kept a dollar past sunset/It always burned a hole in my pants/Never made a school mama happy/Never blew a second chance". It is a true outlaw song that just bristles with the simple joys of defiance and indifference, and captures the ragged dirty feel of *Exile* so perfectly.

"The basic track was Bobby Keyes on baritone sax, myself on guitar and Jimmy Miller on drums. 'Happy' was cut in one afternoon," Richards explained. "We were basically doing the sound check and the track just popped out. I had this idea for a song, but it really was like a warm up."

Rocket 88 Jackie Brenston & The Delta Cats

(Ike Turner – credited to Jackie Brenston) ❋ Chess ❋ 1951 ❋
Appears on: *I Like Ike! The Best of Ike Turner*

Ike Turner doesn't believe his song 'Rocket 88' was, as the Rock & Roll Hall of Fame would have it, the first rock & roll record. "Let me say this; I don't think that there's a characterising," he explained. "Rock & roll is nothing but boogie-woogie with paint on it. And if you're black, they name it R&B and if you're white, they name it rock & roll. To me it was just another song I was doing. When I was doing 'Rocket 88', I was just doing what Pinetop Perkins taught me to play on the piano. I added what he taught me to what I felt I had in myself. And so, they called it rock & roll."

In the late '40s and early '50s Ike Turner and his Kings of Rhythm were a hot jump blues band rolling around the south. Turner was a student of the great blues pianist Pinetop Perkins, but in the juke joints of Mississippi he perfected a lean, aggressive style all of his own.

In April 1951, radio DJ and guitarist BB King arranged for Turner and his band to go to Memphis and cut some sides at Sam Phillips' studio. According to Turner, he wrote 'Rocket 88' in the car (a Chrysler) on the seventy-mile drive from Clarksdale, Mississippi, to Memphis.

The subject of the song is a 1950 Oldsmobile V8, then one of the sharpest cars around – offering a rocket engine and all the futuristic fantasies that implies.

The drive was eventful in as much as there was an accident with one of the amplifiers and a speaker was damaged. When the group arrived at Sun Studios, Turner elected to leave the speaker slashed and distorting.

At Sam Phillips' suggestion, saxophonist Jackie Brenston took the lead vocal on 'Rocket 88', largely so that other songs could come out under Ike's name simultaneously. Led by Turner's frantic piano playing, the Kings of Rhythm rocked into 'Rocket 88' with a vengeance and had the whole thing turned around in under three minutes.

Phillips licensed the four songs done at the session to Chess records in Chicago – without telling Turner, or informing him that 'Rocket 88' would be credited to Jackie Brenston & the Delta Cats. The band was paid in cash for the recording and publishing rights.

Within four months of recording, the song was at the top of the national R&B charts. Unlike most "race" records, this track had caught the ear of white radio DJs and they crossed it over to a new suburban audience. Brenston believed his own hype and embarked on a solo career that ended with him back in the Kings of Rhythm a few years later. Ike Turner was off and running though. Within two years he had established himself as a producer, talent scout and writer and one of the seminal characters in the history of the blues. Sam Phillips used the money from the hit track to finance his own record label, Sun, which first recorded Elvis Presley, Johnny Cash and many others.

"Back in the days I cut 'Rocket 88', the white radio stations in the south didn't play black music, but white stations played 'Rocket 88' on the radio," said Turner. "And then they found that all the white kids were going to the record shops to buy it. So rather than the white man keep calling it whatever they were calling it – 'race music' – at the time they got a white boy to sound like a black boy and changed the name to rock & roll".

Just Like Tom Thumb's Blues Bob Dylan

(Bob Dylan) ✳ Columbia ✳ 1965 ✳ Appears on: *Highway 61 Revisited*

This extensive, elegiac ballad owes more to Rimbaud and the Symbolist poets than to the blues tradition. Ostensibly set in Juarez, Mexico, 'Just Like Tom Thumb's Blues' is a song about drugs. Writer Robert Shelton noted that Rimbaud referred to himself as "Tom Thumb in a daze", and that may be the case. Dylan in this period was certainly taking his poetry seriously and was hanging with Allen Ginsberg and the other Beat generation poets.

The lyrics, though, are more clear than that: "I started out on burgundy/But soon hit the harder stuff".

'Tom Thumb's Blues' has some of Dylan's most adept lines as he describes the attraction of oblivion. It's a night-time world of temptations that may be better than the daytime world of compromise. Like many writers of the period, Dylan notes that the underworld is more honest than the straight one. It's certainly an attractive place, Juarez, but in the final lines Dylan rejects it and goes back to New York City.

Dylan cut the track on 4 August 1965, immediately before going into the epic 'Desolation Row'. It's tempting to be blinded by the richness of the language in these songs. There is a considerable amount of humour, including in 'Tom Thumb's Blues'. He is serious about not becoming a junkie but the experience has clearly not been without its charms.

Too Much Monkey Business Chuck Berry

(Chuck Berry) ❋ Chess ❋ 1957 ❋ Appears on: *After School Session*

After Bob Dylan, Chuck Berry is the most significant lyricist and songwriter of the rock era. Berry was not the first singer and songwriter, nor was he the only one to marry country and R&B. But he did these things arguably better than anyone else. Berry's great achievement was that he established the lyric vernacular of rock & roll. His guitar style was the bedrock on which rock & roll guitar playing was built.

Berry was a genius with words. He wrote about the real world and included the product names. He even gave them prominence, acknowledging the importance of status objects – what would later become known as brands.

Berry was the first writer to address so many teenage concerns, especially in terms of their self-image and activities. If you play Chuck Berry's recorded works from the '50s you get a pretty strong idea of what life was like in contemporary America. Berry had the pulse of the time. Not only did he celebrate being young but he also expressed their frustration. The world of Chuck Berry songs is peppered with the fears of young people – their fights with parents, their struggle to find love.

Berry was the first protest singer, or at least the first to use music to fight the generational battle. 'Roll over Beethoven' is a pretty strident assertion of teen pop culture over the Establishment. 'School Days' is quite obvious but is still a protest song.

Berry's most significant song, though, is 'Too Much Monkey Business'. This is the song of a man who is stuck in the rat race and doesn't want any part of it. In three verses he rejects the straight world:

Salesman talkin' to me – tryin' to run me up a creek
Says you can buy it, go on try it – you can pay me next week,
Blond haired, good lookin' – tryin' to get me hooked.
Want me to marry – settle down – get a home – write a book!
Same thing every day – gettin' up, goin' to school.
No need for me complainin' – my objection's overruled, ahh!

This was a song that rejected everything in the button-down world of the '50s and '60s and prefigured the rage that was to come. The staccato delivery of the song and its tight rhymes anticipated rap while the sentiments have simply been regurgitated by angry young men in songs such as '(I Can't Get No) Satisfaction', 'Like a Rolling Stone' and 'Smells Like Teen Spirit'.

I Try Macy Gray

(Macy Gray/Jinsoo Lim/Jeremy Ruzumna/David Wilder) ✳ Epic ✳ 1999 ✳
Appears on: *On How Life Is*

The first thing you notice about Macy Gray is her voice. Warm, powerful, shredded. Like all divas, Gray brings her biography to the session – single mother, poor background, strong will. This makes the single 'I Try' all the more potent. It has the hallmarks of a conscious hip-hop artist but there's also a vulnerability front and centre and she talks about the conflicting emotions of leaving a dysfunctional relationship.

Gray grew up in the Midwest and found her speaking voice was an embarrassment, but when she sang there was no shortage of approval. A failed relationship with Atlantic Records led her to Andrew Slater, a producer/manager (also of Fiona Apple) who found her a berth at Epic and produced her first album, bringing his sophistication to her raw power. The kicker, though, is Gray's forthrightness.

"I don't know – all I can say is that's just the way I write," she told *MOJO*. "There's a lot of different styles of writing – a lot of people use, like, symbolism, everything kinda poetic, y'know? I don't really know how to do that, rather than just to say it. I don't know whether that's good or bad, but it's the only way I know to write."

Psychokiller Talking Heads

(David Byrne/Tina Weymouth/Chris Franz) ❉ Sire ❉ 1977 ❉

Appears on: *Talking Heads '77*

The most frightening song of the punk rock era came from a quartet who tried their hardest to look normal. In 1977, when most would-be rock & roll stars had leather jackets and clothes designed for shock and awe, Talking Heads had slacks and nice, pressed shirts as if playing rock & roll was another day at the office. Their signature tune, however, was a chilling monologue from a psychopath.

'Psychokiller', with its minimal chord changes and swinging, minimal groove, was a very spooky song.

"When that was the song that drew all the attention, it used to bother us," said singer David Byrne. "But we rationalised it by telling ourselves that it was that driving meter of the bass line and chord changes that had the appeal.

"I realise now, that the idea of a personality close to the edge has something to do with the song's attraction. I don't mean that in a sensational way – it's just a normal human attraction for something a little out of the ordinary."

Byrne wrote 'Psychokiller' while still at the Rhode Island School of Design and it was in the group's repertoire while they were still a trio (Tina Weymouth on bass and drummer Chris Franz) playing at CBGB in New York, alongside Television and the Ramones.

"That was the first song that actually got performed," said Byrne. "I attempted, when I was much younger, to write some songs. Gosh, they were really terrible! They were like fake Bob Dylan songs. And I never finished them. That one was the first one that got finished. It was a way to see if I could do it. And we all worked together on it."

"David came in and said, 'I've got this song, it's like an Alice Cooper song – sort of'", Franz recalled. "He started to play it, saying, 'This is as much as I've got'. Between the three of us, we managed to make it complete."

The hook line is the refrain sung in French, as translated by Weymouth.

"David had asked somebody else to do it in another language because he wanted to create a split personality," said Weymouth. "He was trying to recreate a person who has a criminal mind. The people who he originally approached to do it said, 'It's about a psycho killer? No, we won't contribute to that song'. They were socially minded. So he came to our studio where we were painting, because I knew French. So I put in the stuff that sounds like a Napoleonic complex. Then David said, 'OK, we've got this French. So what would a French band do with this rock & roll song?' I said, 'Well, the French right now are really into what they call "Yeah Yeah" music, because of the Beatles.' So he put in all those 'Fa fa fa's' instead of 'Yeah yeah'."

Another One Bites the Dust Queen

(John Deacon) ✳ EMI ✳ 1980 ✳ Appears on: *The Game*

"We did hate each other too for a while," said Queen guitarist Brian May. "Recording *Jazz* and those albums we did in Munich, *The Game* and *The Works*, we got very angry with each other. I left the group a couple of times, just for the day, you know. I'm off and I'm not coming back! We've all done that. You end up quibbling over one note." Apparently one major bone of contention between bassist John Deacon and drummer Roger Taylor was a tune based around a very simple funk bass line. According again to May, "Roger, at the time, certainly felt that it wasn't rock & roll and was quite angry at the way it was going. And Freddie said, 'Darling, leave it to me. I believe in this'. John had written the song. But it took Freddie's support to make it happen."

Mercury clearly understood that Queen's horizons could extend beyond operatic pop and hard rock. 'Another One Bites the Dust' took them into funk and gave them a crossover hit on all radio formats in America. The track sold three million copies.

The funk/hard-rock crossover was an important step in building the bridge between rock and R&B – swinging rock songs and toughening up R&B. The 'Dust' riff was picked up by Grandmaster Flash for his 'Adventures on the Wheels of Steel' and became one of the first and most recognisable break beats in rap.

Deportee (Plane Wreck at Los Gatos) Judy Collins

(Woody Guthrie/Martin Hoffman) ✳ Warner Bros. ✳ 1968 ✳
Appears on: *A Tribute to Woody Guthrie*

Woody Guthrie wrote songs about those whose own voices could not be heard. Guthrie frequently took stories from the newspapers and turned them into ballads, immortalising folk heroes and events. One of his last great songs was inspired by a plane crash over Los Gatos Canyon in California where a plane, packed with poor, illegal immigrant workers, crashed, killing all on board. The twenty-eight Mexican farm workers were on their way back to Mexico. It's likely that they would be processed through the red tape and then make their way back to California to do it all again. The fruit industry exploited the law as a mechanism to keep labour costs low. The practice continued into the '60s when Ceasar Chavez finally brought union power into the industry. The practice of exploiting and endangering the poor for the benefit of the wealthy continues, though.

Guthrie penned a poem after reading reports in the newspaper on 29 January 1948. In 'Deportee' he simply chronicles the tragedy of the plane crash and highlights the anonymity of the victims ("You won't have your names when you ride the big airplane/All they will call you will be deportees"). Guthrie's lyric is both universal and particular.

A schoolteacher, Martin Hoffman, wrote a melody to Guthrie's words and Pete Seeger added it to his set in 1959. It has since become one of Guthrie's most performed works – in no small part due to Hoffman's contribution, which is more tuneful than most of Guthrie's own compositions.

When You Sleep My Bloody Valentine

(Kevin Shields) ✳ Creation ✳ 1991 ✳ Appears on: *Loveless*

Kevin Shields, for all intents and purposes, is My Bloody Valentine, and is as difficult and conflicted as his music. Shields was born in New York but grew up in Dublin before moving to the UK where he became a demi-god. The British love their rock stars half-mad. This is partly why Shields and My Bloody Valentine are regarded with such reverence in the UK. With only two albums and a handful of other songs to their credit, My Bloody Valentine are said to have saved British rock, first in the late '80s by inventing the shoe-gazer sound and then in 1991 with the *Loveless* album, which put British rock back on its feet.

My Bloody Valentine doesn't deal in songs so much as soundscapes, huge shards of guitar noise from which melody appears. Shields piles up the guitars in magnificent, flowing arrangements.

Loveless is the soundtrack to a mind in glorious meltdown.

After the success of *Is It Anything* in 1988, Shields retreated to his house and became almost a recluse for much of the three years it took to finish *Loveless*.

"I'm crazy, but I'm not mentally ill. There's a difference. I was pretty crazy, for sure," he said, "and it was a very manic, overdrive kind of state, but it never got out of control. I can look after myself better than most people; I'm self-contained. I just didn't do what I didn't want to do. And I got away with it. When you keep on getting away with it year after year, you think you can just live like that. And you can. I wouldn't work. I wouldn't get up till late afternoon. I watched a lot of shit films."

It was worth it. Shields had a singular vision for his guitar rock & roll, which was somewhere between Paul McCartney and Sonic Youth. The voices too – Shields and girlfriend Bilinda Butcher – were all worked into the densely mixed texture of a volatile emotional landscape. It was a record of breathtaking courage.

"I've never been normal and I never will be," said Shields. "The world will change before I will."

Caught Out There Kelis

(Chad Hugo/Pharrell Williams) ✳ Virgin ✳ 1999 ✳ Appears on: *Kaleidoscope*

The debut single from Kelis, 'Caught Out There', was a one-two combination punch. The track announced the arrival of a woman with attitude and also the production team of Chad Hugo/Pharrell Williams who, as the Neptunes, became the hottest thing in hip-hop production over the next few years.

Kelis was the daughter of a pastor and had his evangelical fire, but she was secular enough to be thrown out of home at age sixteen. "I could've gone back if I'd humbled myself," she said, "but that's not what I'm good at." 'Caught Out There' is far from humble. The subject of the song is a woman who has been wronged and the force and passion of her retribution is matched by the savagery of the Neptunes' sonic attack. "I hate you so much right now!" she screams in the refrain.

"*Kaleidoscope* was an experiment," she said. "I got into the studio, eighteen years old. I was angry, I was anxious and waaaaahhhhh! Whatever came out, came out."

Gimme Shelter The Rolling Stones

(Mick Jagger/Keith Richards) ✳ Decca ✳ 1969 ✳ Appears on: *Let It Bleed*

According to writer and sometime confidante Stanley Booth, Keith Richards wrote the words and music to 'Gimme Shelter' while alone in Robert Fraser's London flat. Mick Jagger was nearby, shooting the film *Performance* with Richards' girlfriend Anita Pallenberg as his co-star. The love scenes were all too actual for Richards' taste and he refused to go anywhere near the set or contribute to the soundtrack. But Richards was not only consumed by jealousy. He faced a prison sentence for drug possession. No wonder the song sounds paranoid.

"It was a grey afternoon," Richards recalled. "It was basically just like a chord structure at first. It just keeps going up and down. It's a strange sort of scale."

The song is about a coming storm; an apocalypse. To add to the mood, producer Jimmy Miller added an incredible vocal from session singer Merry Clayton as a banshee howl on top of Richards' layers of guitar. Musically it was a progression from 'Jumping Jack Flash' and 'Sympathy for the Devil'. However, the song soon acquired a tragic and even darker context.

'Gimme Shelter' was the lead track for the last Stones album of the '60s. The Woodstock Nation was born in August of 1969, the same summer that Charles Manson ordered his homicidal rampage and less than five months before the Rolling Stones concert at Altamont where the Hells Angels fatally knifed a crazed fan. The Beatles sang 'All You Need Is Love', the Rolling Stones responded with, "Storm is threatenin'/My very life today/If I don't get some shelter/Oh, I'm gonna fade away". It's obvious now who was the most prescient.

The Rolling Stones 1969 tour on the back of *Let It Bleed* finished at Altamont and the film of that tour, made by the Maysles Brothers, was titled *Gimme Shelter*. It set the tone for the coming decades.

Be-Bop-a-Lula Gene Vincent

(Tex Davis/Gene Vincent) ❋ Capitol ❋ 1956 ❋

Appears on: *The Screaming End: the Best of Gene Vincent*

Mick Farren, a writer and sometime rocker, put it best when he said, "Gene Vincent was a drunk, a pill-head and, at times, a dangerous and creatively erratic asshole, but that may have been the true power of the man. If rock was literature, he'd probably have been Jean Genet. He was the true pioneer of rock & roll self-destruction in the grand manner. He made it clear, from first to last, that rock was about the dark side and the underbelly, and he conducted his career as though the music he played was some kind of mortal combat with destiny. His leather clothes have been copied so many times down the generations that they have become one of rock's visual clichés. His attitude has been borrowed in some part by most of rock's wannabe philosopher desperadoes and pretend warrior poets."

Vincent had a doomed aura about him. A motorcycle accident left him partially lame and hungry for painkillers. Legend has it that while laid up in Portsmouth Naval Hospital he composed 'Be-Bop-a-Lula', inspired by the cartoon character Little Lulu. This is disputed by Dickie Harrell, drummer in his band the Blue Caps, who claimed that Vincent and his manager Bill 'Sheriff Tex' Davis bought the song outright from its writer for $25 cash. Whatever its provenance, Vincent made it his own.

Capitol Records, who were on a quest to find their own Elvis, had discovered Vincent. It's unlikely this Virginia boy would have had the broad appeal of Presley though. He was too troubled and too dark.

Vincent was a hillbilly singer, steeped in country and rockabilly. He had the hiccup in his voice, a slapping bass happening and a killer guitarist in Cliff Gallup. The slowish, bluesy pace of the song and the big echo gave it lustful intent, but mostly it was Vincent's surly manner that marked this track as a rock & roll classic. Gallup's sharp guitar lines cut massive swathes through the song, inspiring imitators such as George Harrison and especially Jeff Beck and Jimmy Page.

It was in England that Vincent really made his mark. His early tour with Eddie Cochran became legendary and he somehow appealed to the English, especially in his somewhat tougher and beaten-down aspect. The British could identify with the lingering tragedy of a career cut short and with the pain that he suffered until his death in 1971.

Ball and Chain   Big Brother & The Holding Company

(Willie Mae Thornton) ❊ Columbia ❊ 1968 ❊ Appears on: *Janis*

In DA Pennebaker's film of the concert, Janis Joplin takes the stage on the Sunday night of the Monterey Pop Festival in her nicest evening wear – slingback shoes and a gold lame pantsuit and she looks a little try-hard, like a girl on her best behaviour for a cocktail party. Then she took it all off. Joplin sang naked emotion.

Big Brother, a rough garage blues band, starts the song with rudimentary bass, drums and guitar slipping and sliding through the blues changes. Then Joplin comes in with a smooth reading of the verses ratcheting up the emotional content. As she reaches the chorus suddenly the floodgates open and the pain and the hope and joy just come screaming out. The song goes from a blues into a soul arrangement with its stop-start dynamics and Joplin gets higher and higher every time and crashes further down in the breaks. The esteemed jazz writer Nat Hentoff said he had been in contact with "an overwhelming life force". Joplin told writer Michael Lydon, "When I sing I feel like when you're first in love ... I feel chills, weird feelings, slipping all over my body, it's a supreme emotional and physical experience." Big Mama Thornton may have written the song, but Janis Joplin made it her own – in eight minutes she has the highs and the lows; the joy and the pain and the need and desire and shame. Entertainment is about simulated emotion. Janis Joplin can get so far into a song that artifice evaporates. This is real.

'Ball and Chain' was a favourite blues of Joplin's even as a teenager. She identified with the great women blues singers such as Big Mama Thornton and Bessie Smith and brought that sensibility to Big Brother & the Holding Company's psychedelic rock. The band was on the lowest rung of the burgeoning San Francisco scene, regarded, with some truth, as dopers with a thin grasp of tunefulness. With Joplin, however, they had a natural resource.

According to drummer Peter Albin, "We changed Big Mama Thornton's 'Ball and Chain' to a minor-key blues. We used the slash-and-burn method of arranging. The chainsaw method." This was necessity rather than invention. Nonetheless there is a raw charm and excitement to the Big Brother recordings that is true to the blues, and which has definitely lasted beyond the '60s. At the end of the day, though, it was only ever the Janis Joplin show.

This version of 'Ball and Chain' was recorded on the Saturday night at Monterey and they were given a second spot the following night so that Pennebaker could include them in his film. Big Brother was a largely unknown band that had nothing to lose and everything to gain from the showcase at Monterey. Everything depended on a great set. At the end of it, as the crowds went wild, so did Clive Davis, the head of Columbia, who signed them on the spot, and Albert Grossman, manager of the Band and Bob Dylan, who then took on Janis Joplin.

Monterey introduced Janis to the world. There has never been a singer who has even come close.

Happy Man Sunnyboys

(Jeremy Oxley) ❋ Mushroom ❋ 1981 ❋ Appears on: *This Is Real*

It was early in the spring of 1979 at the Rock Garden on William Street. The room was called the Whisky Au Go Go when it opened for R&R Americans in the '60s, but by the late '70s it was home to punk rock and power pop and whatever else was going. It was the room du jour. My band was supposed to be second on the bill to INXS but we pulled out because they were too naff for our righteous support. So the Sunnyboys stepped in. They weren't on a crusade like us. I went along and got way too drunk and ended up in a car somewhere in the early dawn hours with Richard Burgman and some girl called Jane. Then it was just me and Jane and Richard slunk off on the road to fame. That's the way it was then: nobody knew where anything would lead, everyone was feeling their own way in the dark, knowing only that there would be adventures and girls and VB and rocking guitars.

I'd like to say that they blew INXS away, but frankly I'm not sure that they did. I know, though, that they did rock hard and furious and solid and they were dependably powerful.

Few rock groups have been better named than the Sunnyboys. They were pretty much happy guys from the country just delighted to be playing rock & roll in Sydney. You couldn't meet guys who were more easygoing than Richard (guitar), Bil Bilson (drums) and Peter Oxley (bass). In fact, in my whole life I don't think I've met a better character than Pete. The singer Jeremy, though, gave the name an ironic twist . . . But let's go back a bit.

This was a very fertile time for Sydney with many great bands: the Lipstick Killers, the Passengers, the Professors, Flaming Hands, Kamikaze Kids, Laughing Clowns, the Riptides, the Hoodoo Gurus, Minuteman, Mental As Anything and X blazed away. The town was abuzz with a do-it-yourself ethic, which meant that you didn't go cap in hand to some man with a cigar and booking agency but just found yourself a pub, stuck up some posters, hired a double four-way PA and let it rock. Almost all of these bands had contact with one another somehow and the whole thing fed off itself.

So into this melting pot comes Jeremy Oxley, barely nineteen, and Bil Bilson. They'd been playing with Pete since they were kids in Kingscliff, near Byron. They didn't care about cool; they just liked what they heard. Jeremy picked up on what was happening – particularly rediscovering the garage punk thing and the Boston group the Remains, who were, in their 1966 day, dubbed America's answer to the Fabs.

Jeremy had been writing songs and now he got a really strong batch. Pete, Richard, Bil and Jeremy found themselves in the Day Street rehearsal space in an old warehouse on the western edge of Sydney.

Then suddenly in August 1979 the Sunnyboys were born.

Great name – courtesy of artist Liz Croll. All of the best bands in history have two essential qualities – a great name and a great rhythm section. Bil Bilson's style was to hit them hard and take no prisoners. He swung the beat like a gladiator swings those chains with the spiky balls on the end. Pete pulled the bass down to a volcanic rumble and both of them paid respect to the discipline of the pop song. On top of that, the guitars of Richard and Jeremy slashed away, the sound glinting in the mix like rays off a chainsaw.

On arrival, the Sunnyboys were the toast of the town. Hottest live band, first EP on Phantom sold out twice, they got signed to Mushroom. In only a few short months, the Sunnyboys were stars.

That first Sunnyboys album is a complete gem. It's hard as a diamond but it's got a great spirit and is complete and pure in the way that too few albums ever are. The single 'Happy Man' is the distillation of the Sunnyboys – bright but filled with the confusion of being a teenager. The trials of adolescence writ into an epic frame.

The thing that you notice is Jeremy's lyrics, which are generally first person, the stories of an "I" struggling with the existential confusion posed by relating to other people.

Jeremy was prone to mental illness. At a very tender age he had his ego blown. He went from shy art student surfer to the spokesman for a generation and sex god in no time flat. And, of course, there were temptations and who wouldn't ... the options for self-medication probably didn't help things and they probably masked deeper problems. But you only have to listen to the lyrics to know that Jeremy was a complex guy crying out for some understanding.

This is still one of the best rock & roll tracks of that era. It's bound so tight that you can't see the seams and sounds so fresh you'd think it was plucked just as it flowered.

Spin the Black Circle Pearl Jam

(Pearl Jam) ❋ Epic ❋ 1994 ❋ Appears on: *Vitalogy*

By the time they recorded this third album, Pearl Jam were in the ambiguous position of reluctant superstars. They had far surpassed the fame of the other grunge generation – even that of Nirvana – but it didn't make them happy. Pearl Jam craved privacy and despised the trappings of rock stardom, but the more they turned their back, the bigger they became.

Vitalogy is their toughest album, with the hardest edge and rawest of the band's writing. It's as though they stepped back from the brink in order to embrace life rather than showbiz. The first single from the album, however, showed another side to Pearl Jam. It's a hymn to the long-gone 7 inch single. It's unlikely that many of their fans had ever encountered such a thing in 1994, but singer Eddie Vedder was a nut. This song, then, is something of a touchstone to a more pure version of rock & roll. Pearl Jam takes the tune at a punk pace in homage to the music and no doubt to alienate radio stations that would soon jump on the power ballad 'Better Man'.

She Thinks I Still Care George Jones

(Steve Duffy/Dickey Lee Lipscomb) ❋ Musicor ❋ 1962 ❋
Appears on: *The New Favourites of George Jones*

Having started out as a rockabilly singer with 'Why Baby Why', George Jones really found his stride on country ballads. His voice is rich and expressive and he brings to it the baggage of a life lived hard. Sometimes he's dealing with the consequences of his actions and other times he's dealing out tough lessons. This track falls into the latter category.

The song's main writer, Dickey Lee Lipscomb, was like Jones – a journeyman singer doing a bit of rock and bit of country as the market demanded. This song is a small masterpiece. It's been covered extensively by artists including Elvis Presley. Jones, however, has the definitive reading. Spare, with lots of room for the vocal, this song is sung by Jones with an ambiguity that is beguiling.

"I don't think there's anyone in the business that can touch George," said his ex-wife Tammy Wynette. "There never has been, never will be. I've always said that, regardless of marriage, divorce, whatever. He isn't part of country music, he is country music."

Chameleon Herbie Hancock

(Herbie Hancock) ❋ Columbia ❋ 1974 ❋ Appears on: *Headhunters*

Having spearheaded fusion in Miles Davis' Quintet, Hancock went off on his own tangent in the early '70s. He embraced the possibilities of the synthesiser and electronic keys. The albums *Mwandishi* and *Sextant* were well regarded in jazz circles, but his next major release broke new ground again.

James Brown, Sly Stone and George Clinton refined R&B music into a new style of funk. Hancock was listening. "I knew that I never heard any jazz players really play funk like the funk I had been listening to. Instead of getting jazz cats who knew how to play funk," he said, "I got funk cats who knew how to play jazz."

Headhunters was a crossover smash, due in part to an edited single from the lead track 'Chameleon'. As if to underline his new direction, Hancock revisits 'Watermelon Man' – the first cut on his debut a dozen years before. That song then leads into 'Sly', a tribute to Sly Stone.

Headhunters was a massive success on the charts, it was a true crossover hit in the sense that very few jazz albums have ever been. If not exactly what the jazz community wanted, it confirmed Hancock's position as an architect of American pop. The influence of this album and Hancock's later LPs were to be heard in hip-hop and electronica a decade on.

Ray of Light Madonna

(Dave Curtis/Christine Leach/Madonna/Clive Muldoon/William Orbit) ❋ Maverick ❋
1998 ❋ Appears on: *Ray of Light*

In the perpetual evolution of her life and work, Madonna went to Europe and picked up William Orbit, the producer du jour, known for his ambient techno mixes. Orbit gave Madonna a new tonal palette – electronica as put through Madonna's pop sensibility.

Before getting to London, Madonna had worked on songs with Babyface and Rick Nowels and Pat Leonard. She then spent four and a half months in the studio with Orbit developing her new sound. "In the studio she's totally sleeves-rolled-up," said Orbit. "You think of her as a performer, a pop icon, this force of entertainment. You don't perceive Madonna as a great producer, but that's exactly what she is. Madonna's on this journey, and if you're smart you'll get on board for the ride. But it doesn't matter if you do or you don't, because she's going to get there anyway."

"I always go for the cook in the kitchen," said Madonna of her choice of Orbit. "I like to work with people who take chances. Usually they're undiscovered, because once people are successful they don't like taking risks.

"I let William play mad professor. He comes from a very experimental, cutting-edge sort of place – he's not a trained musician, and I'm used to working with classically trained musicians. But I knew that's where I wanted to go, so I took a lot more risks. Often times the creative process was frustrating because I wasn't used to it; it took longer than usual to make this record. But I realise now that I needed that time to get where I was going."

The album has a freshness that recent releases had been short of. It was also a hit in the clubs – Madonna claimed that it would sound great while on ecstasy but it didn't turn off her initial audience either who were now heading for early nights. The textures are lush and romantic and sensual rather than erotic and pulsing. There is a strong sense of spirituality that runs through this album and the title track, in particular. A search for enlightenment.

"I left off partying on 'Ray of Light'," she said. "But I'd just had a baby, so my mood was complete, like wonderment of life, and I was incredibly thoughtful and retrospective and intrigued by the mystical aspects of life ..."

Please Please Me The Beatles

(John Lennon/Paul McCartney) ✳ EMI ✳ 1963 ✳ Appears on: *Please Please Me*

The Beatles' second single, 'Please Please Me', was written largely by John Lennon, inspired by Bing Crosby's 1932 hit 'Please', which Lennon claimed had been a favourite of his late mother. The other influence was Roy Orbison's 'Only the Lonely', which was then a hit on the radio.

The Beatles cut the track in their second session with Parlophone and needed to rearrange the song significantly to avoid comparisons with Roy Orbison's sound. Indeed, this is the Beatles' trademarked Merseybeat sound – the hyped-up energy from years of playing clubs, the harmony vocals and the neat sharp licks from George Harrison's guitar. 'Please Please Me' confirmed that the Beatles were not a quick fad and also confirmed that their unique ability came from being able to meld rhythm and blues with the traditional popular song.

Bonde Ali Farka Toure with Ry Cooder

(Ali Farka Toure) ✳ Hannibal ✳ 1994 ✳ Appears on: *Talking Timbuktu*

Most of Mali is the Sahara Desert. Timbuktu was a once great trading city and is now a shadow of its former self. Mali is one of the poorest countries in Western Africa and blighted by poverty and AIDS. The music of Mali is rich with French, Arab, Moorish and African influences. Into this mix comes the particular talent of Ali Farka Toure.

He began playing the guitar in 1956 at age seven and developed a style of his own that sounds, to western ears, not too far removed from the rural blues of Lightnin' Hopkins and John Lee Hooker. Essentially his tunes set up a drone and a groove that he embellishes on the guitar or with other instruments.

American guitarist Ry Cooder made the trip to Timbuktu with bassist John Patitucci, drummer Jim Keltner and blues guitarist Gatemouth Brown to play with Toure, who brought along his cousin Hamma Sankare on calabash and his brother Oumar Toure on congas. Over the course of the album *Talking Timbuktu*, Toure sings in a number of languages (none of them English) with a warm, expressive style and lets the groove do the talking. Absolutely sublime music that transcends time and space and nationality.

A Sailor's Life Fairport Convention

(Traditional) ✳ Hannibal ✳ 1969 ✳ Appears on: *Unhalfbricking*

In America the rock groups were taking traditional music – blues and country – and exploding it. In that spirit, singer Sandy Denny, drummer Martin Lamble, bass player Ashley Hutchings, and guitarists Richard Thompson and Simon Nicol formed Fairport Convention to do the same thing with English folk.

"The climate in Britain at that time was bad music *à la* Geno Washington, and blues bands – and a sheen of psychedelia was creeping in over the top," said Thompson. "By the time we turned professional we had what might be called a 'psychedelic' audience. You'd have a light show, an attempt to recreate the kind of environment that was being so successful in America with the Fillmores and the Avalon Ballroom. The audiences were basically fashion-conscious.

"Probably since about '65 we'd been playing the odd British traditional tune, and when Sandy joined she brought with her a fairly good traditional repertoire that she'd been singing around the folk clubs, and we started to incorporate that into what we were doing.

"There was a certain amount of scholarship in it. We thought because we were British we should be playing the indigenous music. This was something at which we could excel, whereas we may never excel at being second-rate BB Kings or third-rate Waylon Jenningses. We also saw that there was a need for the traditional music in this country to be revived. It was unpopular with British people, so we wanted to bring it up to date. We were white liberal intellectuals, I suppose."

Vocalist Sandy Denny was already a veteran of the English folk scene when she joined Fairport Convention. One of the songs she brought was a very old tune full of moral complexity.

'A Sailor's Life' is a love story in which the sailor is the romantic figure who loves and travels on. One woman, however, follows him to her own doom.

Denny learnt the song from Martin Carthy and taught it to the band backstage at Southampton University. Fairport Convention took to the song and ran with it; Richard Thompson and Simon Nicol stretched out the guitar parts, competing with Dave Swarbrick's violin. A sea shanty became an epic voyage and a grand passion. The tune runs for over eleven minutes. It completely refashioned Fairport Convention and the sound of British music.

When the Levee Breaks Led Zeppelin

(Jimmy Page/John Paul Jones/Robert Plant/John Bonham/Memphis Minnie) ※ Atlantic ※ 1971 ※ Appears on: untitled fourth LP

On their fourth album, Zeppelin created their masterpiece, one of the highpoints of rock music. Having spawned heavy metal and then gone bucolic the year previously, on this untitled album they pulled all their influences together in an entirely new way.

The album was recorded at Hedley Grange, a three-storey Victorian workhouse. Its large stairwell became the drum booth with a microphone two storeys up.

John Bonham, particularly, shines here. The closing track, 'When the Levee Breaks', is the biggest and heaviest drum part in all of rock. It's a twisted blues-like Howlin' Wolf on steroids.

"I recall Page and I listening to Electric Mud at the time by Muddy Waters," said bass player John Paul Jones. "One track is a long rambling riff and I really liked the idea of writing something like that – a riff that would be like a linear journey. The idea came on a train coming back from Page's Pangbourne house. From the first run-through at the Grange we knew it was a good one." Bonham's slow, insistent groove is unique and was one of the most popular drum samples in the early days of hip-hop.

Don't Bring Me Down The Pretty Things

(Johnny Dee) ※ Fontana ※ 1965 ※ Appears on: *The Pretty Things*

They were not pretty. The group led by singer Phil May and Dick Taylor was the dirtiest R&B group in London in the early '60s. Taylor's claim to fame was that he was almost in the Rolling Stones. Having gone to school with Mick Jagger and sharing his love for blues, Taylor was rehearsing with him when Jagger started playing with Keith Richard as Little Boy Blue and the Blue Boys. Shortly afterwards Brian Jones came on the scene and they became the Rolling Stones while Taylor drifted into the Pretty Things with May. From early on they prided themselves on their raw interpretations of blues.

The Pretty Things found themselves on Fontana where producer Bobby Graham helped them translate their urgent and rough sound to record. Songwriter Johnny Dee gave them a straight pop song, 'Don't Bring Me Down'. Taylor wrote a nasty blues guitar part and the rhythm section gave the track pumping beat with a funky swing to it. May's vocals were appropriately robust – enough to get the song banned by US radio.

Although the song was a huge hit in the UK, success elsewhere eluded them. They were, however, a major cult band in America and Australia. David Bowie covered 'Don't Bring Me Down' and another Pretty Things song, 'Rosalyn', on his LP *Pin Ups* and has always cited them as a major influence. By and large, though, the Pretty Things were too far out.

"The thing about the Pretty Things was, we found, in people like Jimmy Reed and Howlin' Wolf and Muddy Waters, a kind of kindred music that we could identify with," May told Ritchie Unterberger. "But we weren't respectful in the fact we didn't copy it. We played it fast because we were seventeen, eighteen years old. So the urgency where we were standing was overlaid on basically songs about being marginalised and being fucked up by society. And that's what was happening to us.

"It was just, where we were, where we stood, in society, which being art students, was right on the fringe. We were outside of society. So this music – we just added some kind of thrash metal to it. We put some urgency into it. And we played it at a speed, which early godfathers of British R&B said, 'ah, disgraceful!'"

Beck's Bolero   The Jeff Beck Group

(Jimmy Page) ✳ Epic ✳ 1968 ✳ Appears on: *Truth*

Track eight of *Truth*, 'Beck's Bolero', is a seminal moment in British rock. It was worked up in Jimmy Page's living room with the Led Zeppelin guitarist and his future bassist, John Paul Jones, Keith Moon (who named Zeppelin) on drums, Nicky Hopkins on piano and Rod Stewart singing. These were the characters who would shape British music for the next decade and this notion of improvised progressive rock was the sound of the future. But this particular supergroup didn't last beyond that session.

Unbelievably loud and hostile, the arrogance and ambition that runs through 'Beck's Bolero' announced that a new style of British rock was being born.

Unfortunately, Beck's difficult personality meant that he was unable to keep this group together long enough to fulfil its promise.

Beck then put together his first Jeff Beck Group (Rod Stewart, Ron Wood, Mickey Waller) and cut an album in four days. Producer Mickie Most was the master of British pop and steered the sessions away from Beck's more progressive interests. Hence you have a remake of Beck's hit with the Yardbirds ('Shapes of Things') and some naff standards ('Ol Man River', 'Greensleeves').

"There was so little money available that I don't think Mickie Most even wanted to bother, but we had this act, so all we had to do was go in there, get a decent sound and play it," the guitarist explained. "Rod just had to open his mouth around a mic and you had a song. It was a shame we didn't follow through."

Stealin' Stealin' Memphis Jug Band

(Gus Cannon) ❊ Yazoo ❊ 1927 ❊ Appears on: *Memphis Jug Band*

Generally just called 'Stealin'', this song was part of the lingua franca of the folk and blues scene in the early '60s. It was recorded by every singer with an acoustic guitar – Bob Dylan, the Grateful Dead, John Sebastian and literally all of their contemporaries.

The jug bands were one of the first versions of a blues combo. They started in Louisville, Kentucky, around 1900. Jug music was so called because there was generally someone keeping time by blowing across the opening of a liquor jar. Early jug bands included a mixture of fiddle, banjo, mandolin or guitar.

The most well known of the jug bands was Gus Cannon's Jug Stompers. Cannon was born the son of a slave on Henderson Newell's plantation in Marshall County Mississippi in 1883. He made his first banjo from a guitar neck and a bread pan and played in dances and juke joints around the Mississippi Delta at the turn of the century.

By the time the armistice had been signed after the Great War, Cannon was plying his trade in the travelling medicine shows or playing in Beale Street Memphis. Beale Street, the birthplace of jazz, was also populated by whorehouses with names like The Castle of Missing Men where cocaine, reefer and easy virtue could be obtained at reasonable prices.

Cannon's Jug Stompers – with Noah Lewis on harp – began recording in 1928 with a Noah Lewis song called 'Minglewood Blues', which was covered by the Grateful Dead some fifty years later. Cannon continued recording and playing until his death in 1966, by which time one of his songs ('Walk Right In') was a hit on the pop charts.

One of Cannon's chief rivals was the Memphis Jug Band led by Will Shade. The Memphis Jug Band was the most recorded group of its era. They cut 'Stealin' Stealin'' on 15 September 1928, crediting the song to Gus Cannon although he never recorded the song himself. It remains a fine piece of stompin' blues around the hook: "Put your arms around me like a circle round the sun". The rawness of the jug band and their rhythmic strength had a natural affinity with rock & roll and nowhere better perhaps than on 'Stealin''.

Suffragette City David Bowie

(David Bowie) ❋ RCA ❋ 1972 ❋

Appears on: *The Rise and Fall of Ziggy Stardust and the Spiders from Mars*

David Bowie raised the stakes in 1972 by declaring to the *NME*, "I'm gay". He has subsequently remarked it was the best thing he ever said. There is an irony in a heterosexual man claiming to be queer, but it was a great publicity stunt. Bowie then invented himself a character complete with a concept album. While other rock stars of the era were struggling to get out a dozen songs, Bowie was playing on a whole new field.

"It's one of those instantaneous vision things you get," said Bowie of his inspiration for the concept album. "It all came to me in a daydream about what this whole thing was about." The character Ziggy Stardust was loosely based on an American rock & roll singer, Vince Taylor, who had moved to Paris and become something of a cult figure. That was added to the Legendary Stardust Cowboy, the singer of 'Paralysed', often thought to be the worst single ever recorded. There was possibly also a nod to Iggy Pop, who was one of Bowie's idols at the time. This pastiche of rock iconography was tied into a science fiction storyline. What mattered in the end was the playing on the *Spiders from Mars*.

'Suffragette City' was a homage to the Velvet Underground. Lou Reed's driving guitar was mimicked and embellished by the more adroit Mick Ronson, who added sweetness and light to the mix. "He provided this strong, earthy, simply-focussed idea of what a song was all about. And I would flutter around on the edges and decorate," said Bowie.

'Suffragette City' rocked. It was pure energy. At an early performance Bowie dropped to his knees and gave Ronson's guitar oral pleasure, which not only looked exciting and dangerous but added to the already loud furore over Bowie's sexuality.

Ziggy Stardust made Bowie a superstar. "I packaged a totally credible plastic rock star," said Bowie. "Much better than any sort of Monkees fabrication. My plastic rocker was much more plastic than anybody's."

Song for Europe Roxy Music

(Bryan Ferry/Andy Mackay) ❋ Island ❋ 1973 ❋ Appears on: *Stranded*

Bryan Ferry recorded three albums in 1973 and reconstituted Roxy Music without Brian Eno. "The reason it fell apart, I think, is that Bryan was doing all the work and Eno getting all the glory," a friend was quoted as saying. "It was Eno who got to shag all the girls, and I think that drove Bryan completely bonkers. I mean, Eno was literally shagging non-stop; he was on for it all the time, like a fucking rabbit."

"There was that aspect of typical young male competitiveness about it," agreed Eno. "But I really wanted to do something else. And the band wanted to do something else, too, and they did it really well. My favourite Roxy album, actually, is the third one. I love that record, and it might also be because, since I wasn't involved in making it, it just comes together as a single finished thing."

With the addition of Eddie Jobson and Johnny Gustafson, Roxy more closely resembled a rock band.

The new sound was used to best effect on 'Song for Europe' – a dark and magnificently brooding piece. It's overblown and the tense and slightly obtuse saxophone from Andy Mackay undercuts the elegiac mood. This song prefigured Bowie's European years and later the post-punk intent of Ultravox and their ilk.

"*Stranded* was done in the same year as *For Your Pleasure*," said Ferry, "but not having Eno on that album meant that it suffered a bit, it lost a bit of edge. But it gained other, more musical things."

The Power and the Passion Midnight Oil

(Rob Hirst/Jim Moginie/Peter Garrett) ✳ CBS ✳ 1982 ✳
Appears on: *10, 9, 8, 7, 6, 5, 4, 3, 2, 1*

No-one, not even Midnight Oil, saw *10–1* coming. The group had made three albums of blistering agit rock. Angry, straight ahead, drums and guitars to the floor, pub rock. Then they took it all apart and started from scratch.

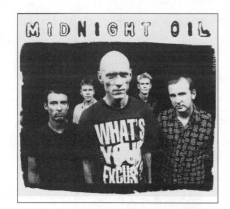

In 1981 Midnight Oil were one of the most popular bands in Australia, having dominated the pub rock scene with their massive rock & roll sound and their strident, individualistic attitude. Then just as it was about to pay off, they moved to London to work with a new producer and a whole new sound. The risks were substantial. Everything that the group had was reinvested into the project and they were living on subsistence wages, barely enough to eat. Drummer Rob Hirst recalled the reaction to his fear, "I'd come into the studio and just bash out my aggression."

Hirst and the rest of the band were also responding to the global paranoia that then engulfed the world. At the height of the Cold War, nuclear missiles were being deployed in Britain. A holocaust appeared not just possible but likely. The album took its title from such apocalyptic times.

Producer Nick Launay had come to the Oils' attention through his work with Killing Joke, Public Image and the Birthday Party, although this was his first solo production job.

Having been liberated from the live sound, as Hirst put it, the acoustic guitars came to the fore on songs like 'The Power and the Passion' and 'US Forces'. Elsewhere a breakneck rock track, 'Read about It', slammed biased media with their most short, sharp lyric, and the atmospheric keyboards of Jim Moginie established moods that were quietly doom-laden and at other times sensual.

'The Power and the Passion' is a song about apathy. The lyric points to the urgency of the time with growing US militancy and the decline of the left while the singer laments the 'I'm all right Jack' indolence of the Australian public. It's a call to arms in a nation put to sleep in a sunburnt complacency.

Hey Jude The Beatles

(John Lennon/Paul McCartney) ❋ Apple ❋ 1968 ❋ Appears on: *Hey Jude*

Paul McCartney's consolation note to John Lennon's son Julian evolved into an epic that transcended the specifics of the Lennon family.

The lyric and tune came to McCartney on a trip to visit the estranged family after Lennon had set up house with Yoko Ono. "I originally thought of it whilst driving my car out to visit Cynthia and Julian after John's divorce from them," McCartney said in *Many Years from Now*. "We'd been very good friends for millions of years and I thought it was a bit much for them to suddenly be persona non grata and out of my life, so I decided to pay them a visit and say, 'How are you doing? What's happening?' . . . I always feel sorry for kids in divorce. The adults may be fine but the kids . . . I had the idea by the time I got there. I knew it was not going to be easy for him. I started with the idea 'Hey Jules', which was Julian, don't make it bad, take a sad song and make it better. Hey, try and deal with this terrible thing, you know."

Being egocentric, Lennon heard the lyric as a message to him. "I heard it as a song to me," he said. "If you think about it . . . Yoko's just come into the picture, and Paul's saying, 'Hey Jude – hey, John'. I know I'm sounding like one of those fans who reads things into it, but you can hear it as a song to me. The words 'go out and get her' – subconsciously he was saying, 'Go ahead, leave me'. On a conscious level he didn't want me to go ahead. The angel in him was saying, 'Bless you'. The devil in him didn't like it at all, because he didn't want to lose his partner."

This seems unlikely given the many times McCartney has talked about the beginnings of the song. It is perhaps typical, though, of Lennon's distant parenting of his first child.

"I've never really wanted to know the truth about how dad was with me," Julian said. "There was some very negative stuff talked about me – like when he said I'd come out of a whisky bottle on a Saturday night. Stuff like that. You think, where's the love in that? Paul and I used to hang about quite a bit – more than Dad and I did. We had a great friendship going and there seems to be far more pictures of me and Paul playing together at that age than there are pictures of me and my dad."

McCartney felt proud of the song and was very strict about its arrangement. The bulk of the tune is straightforward – although Lennon misses a backing vocal and can be faintly heard to exclaim "Fuckin' hell!" – and then at the end comes a repeating phrase with a massed choir made up of Beatles and the orchestra providing hand claps and vocals. The mantra-like vocals are set against McCartney's scat singing, which owes more than a little to James Brown and Little Richard. The tension here between the melody and the beat is wound as tight as any soul session. The vamp at the end builds over four minutes – more than the length of time a radio station would ordinarily allow for one song. Despite its modal nature, there's such spirit in the tune and the performance that it's hard to cut.

As the first release on the Beatles' custom imprint Apple (with 'Revolution' on the flip side) it was decided to promote the single with a TV performance on which they were introduced as "the greatest tea-room orchestra in the world".

Will the Wolf Survive? Los Lobos

(David Hidalgo/Louie Pérez) ✹ Slash ✹ 1984 ✹ Appears on: *How Will the Wolf Survive?*

Los Lobos, the world's greatest bar band, made their start playing Latino music in the East Los Angeles barrio. Their first recording, ... *And a Time to Dance*, was pureish Mexican music played like there was no tomorrow. The group – David Hidalgo, Louie Pérez, Cesar Rosas, Conrad Lozano and Steve Berlin – were adopted into the Los Angeles punk scene in the early '80s in part because of their exotic authenticity. At the same time, Los Lobos began writing rock & roll songs. As their first album began to take shape, so the rock & roll increased.

The title track was almost the last to be written. Pérez saw an article in *National Geographic* about the extinction of the wolf and he related (especially given the band's name translates as: the Wolves). "It was like our group, our story," he said. "What is this animal that the record companies can't figure out? Will we be given the opportunity to make it or not?"

The metaphor is broader than just Los Lobos. The song of a working man trying to survive is one of the most heartfelt, honest and open songs of its type especially coming from a rock group in the '80s. The rich, warm vocals from Rosas and Hidalgo have a soulfulness that is at the heart of Los Lobos.

Sneakin' Sally Through the Alley Robert Palmer

(Allen Toussaint) ✳ Island ✳ 1974 ✳ Appears on: *Sneakin' Sally Through the Alley*

The elegantly tailored suits and beautiful grooming obscured Robert Palmer's love for dirty R&B and sleazy funk. Palmer will forever be remembered for the iconic video 'Addicted to Love' and for the relatively bland pop tunes of his '80s heyday.

Palmer was, at his best, an interpreter of songs and grooves. His first album, *Sneakin' Sally Through the Alley*, was recorded with the Meters and it remains the best hybrid of Crescent City funk and white rock. The grooves are deep and long and Palmer knows how to make the best out of them. The title track is an Allen Toussaint number and Palmer brings a witty but sensual vocal to the steamy groove.

Most of the material is by Palmer and it's short on lyrics but deep on feel. He glides along with the rhythm section, allowing his voice to be buffed by the keys and guitar. It all sounds effortless, like a breeze, but the mastery of his instrument and the discretion with which he uses it are impeccable.

Although his upbringing was strictly working class, Palmer assumed the couture of a gentleman and that characterised his career – discreet, appropriate and tasteful. But under the Armani was a heart of funk.

Bitter Sweet Symphony The Verve

(Richard Ashcroft/Mick Jagger/Keith Richards) ✳ Hut ✳ 1997 ✳ Appears on: *Urban Hymns*

"When you live in a place like Wigan, your senses aren't exactly bombarded with stimuli," said Richard Ashcroft, lead singer of the Verve, on the occasion of the release of the group's first album, *A Storm in Heaven*. "So, when you make music, you don't want to reflect your environment, you want to create something bigger than what you see around you. That's what we want our music to do – transport the audience beyond the everyday. I've had enough of Billy Bragg and that brand of social-realist pop. I've got enough shit going on in my life; I don't want to be reminded of how dismal everything is. I want to be elevated, not dragged down."

Ashcroft was one of the last true romantics of British rock. The Verve was about big soundscapes and often dark lyric themes. Ashcroft, however, had the skeletal demeanour and sunken cheeks to pull it off. Despite a loyal following – which included Noel Gallagher of Oasis, who wrote a song about Ashcroft – the Verve seemed unlikely to see out the decade. Ashcroft and guitarist Nick McCabe fought vigorously and Ashcroft had a reputation as a heavy drug consumer.

Things were not looking up until Ashcroft brought the song 'Bitter Sweet Symphony' along to the sessions for the group's third album, *Urban Hymns.*

Here was an urban hymn. It had the majestic sweep of a conversation with the eternal and almighty. It was lush and lonely and troubled and elegant, expressing some of Ashcroft's alienation.

"All I can think of is that music gives you an excuse to go on stage and be something else, do something else and get something out," Ashcroft told Sascha Stojanovic. "I think we are all a million different people every day. I think we all play games with each other, mind games to protect ourselves. When I write lyrics I mean it. I've got nothing to hide from."

The track as produced by Youth is a magnificent epic with grand string arrangements and the group's impassioned backing of Ashcroft's soulful vocal. The song recalled the '60s British pop in that it criticised the wage slavery and at the same time recognised the redeeming power of music. Certainly it worked and 'Bitter Sweet Symphony' was a massive global hit. Unfortunately, Ashcroft lost all the publishing royalties on the song in a dispute over an uncleared sample.

Every Breath You Take The Police

(Sting) ✳ A&M ✳ 1983 ✳ Appears on: *Synchronicity*

Sting famously announced, "I do my best work when I'm in pain and turmoil." This was his best work and he did it sitting at the desk on which Ian Fleming wrote the James Bond books. If one is in pain and turmoil, it's nice to be in the Bahamas.

Sting had come to the end of a seven-year marriage to Frances Tomelty and his even longer relationship with Andy Summers and Stuart Copeland was over for all but the shouting. The sessions for the *Synchronicity* album were, according to the players, fraught with conflict. Perhaps that's why the songs were so dark.

'Every Breath You Take' is Sting's finest moment, if only because he's not trying to be clever. A simple R&B chord progression, played with finesse but always understated, seduces the audience into a sense of wellbeing. The lyrics come up. A desperate tale told by a paranoiac stalker, this is more malevolent than mellow. Yet this song has launched a thousand weddings. Finally Sting has some irony.

Into the Groove Madonna

(Stephen Bray/Madonna) ❋ Sire ❋ 1984 ❋ Appears on: *The Immaculate Collection*

'Into the Groove' appeared in Madonna's film *Desperately Seeking Susan*. Madonna is in a downtown club dancing to this magical tune floating above the sound system. It's a black groove with a sweet, limited white tune on the top, and there's Madonna – all thrift-shop chic – dragging the straight world into this subterranean paradise. All the magic of the '80s is right here.

The film was a crucial step in Madonna's career – not least because it gave the diva the idea she could act well. More importantly it was a film about the gap between downtown and the suburbs. Madonna's character was an update of Holly Golightly. But the difference between Madonna and Truman Capote's heroine is that Madonna had no guilt. She was slumming – this was reality and it was more attractive than the astroturf-baracalounge New Jersey world. In a way, though, *Susan* destroyed the downtown by exposing it to the mass culture.

The mystery and the delight of the nightclub is all there in the slight air of this song. "The dance floor was quite a magical place for me," Madonna told *Q* magazine. "I started off wanting to be a dancer, so that had a lot to do with it. The freedom that I always feel when I'm dancing, that feeling of inhabiting your body, letting yourself go, expressing yourself through music. I always thought of it as a magical place ... even if you're not taking ecstasy."

Goin' Down The Monkees

(Diane Hildebrand/Peter Tork/Michael Nesmith/Micky Dolenz/David Jones) ❋ Colgems ❋ 1967 ❋ Appears on: *Pisces, Aquarius, Capricorn & Jones, LTD*

The Monkees suffered from accusations that they couldn't play their instruments and therefore were not a legitimate rock & roll band. That they were created specifically for a TV program didn't help their cause in this matter. However, many of the most credible artists of the period such as Them and the Byrds didn't play on their records either. It matters little now except to marvel at 'Goin' Down', on which the Monkees wrote an extremely complex arrangement.

Composed by the Monkees and lyricist Diane Hildebrand, who was bassist Peter Tork's girlfriend at the time, the lyrics are a freeform jazz riff that Mickey Dolenz charges into, capturing the intricate cross rhythms of the words. Mike Nesmith plays guitar and Peter Tork bass, with Davy Jones on percussion. The legendary jazz arranger Shorty Rogers back him with jazzy, bright horn charts. The tune is based on Mose Allison's jazz/blues standard 'Parchman Farm', but the Monkees just tear it apart.

Whatever their shortcomings in the beginning, by the time they cut 'Goin' Down' the Monkees were as sophisticated as any of their hipster friends. 'Goin' Down' has a sublime mix of metaphors and sly wit, and Dolenz just explodes with his delivery.

He Stopped Loving Her Today George Jones

(Bobby Braddock/Curly Putman) ✳ Epic ✳ 1980 ✳ Appears on: *I Am What I Am*

George Jones' solution to his alcoholism was to start using cocaine. By 1980 he was as much of a wreck as his career. One man who stood by him was producer Billy Sherrill, who found this song and produced the session that put Jones back on the top of the charts.

According to Jones in his autobiography: "The song is about a man who loved a woman so much, it killed him when she left. He said he would love her until he died, and only on his deathbed did he stop ... Billy loved 'He Stopped Loving Her Today'. He said he was unable to sleep the night after first hearing the song. But he thought it was incomplete ... Putnam and Braddock killed the song's main character too soon in their early versions. Billy kept telling them to kill the guy at a different time and then have the woman come to his funeral. The writers thought that might be too sad, and Billy did, too. But he knew the song, on a scale of one to ten, was about an eight. He saw it as a potential eleven."

Sherrill cut the track at Columbia's Nashville studio, laying down the basic track live. The vocals and especially the spoken word section took quite a while to get right. Jones said that while he had no problem singing while drunk, he couldn't speak without slurring. Such was his drinking that the four lines took months to record.

"It took them a while, but they were striving for something a bit out of the normal," said engineer Ron 'Snake' Reynolds. "They knew they had something special, especially Billy, I think. One thing kind of funny about it was that the melody was so close to 'Help Me Make it Through the Night' that George kept singing the melody to 'Help Me Make it Through the Night'. He couldn't get that out of his head. That gave him a bit of a problem early on, and they took their time to get the narration just right."

It was worth it. As Jones writes in his autobiography, the song saved his career. "I went from a $2500 act who promoters feared wouldn't show up, to an act who earned $25,000 plus a percentage of the gate receipts. That was big money for a country artist sixteen years ago ... To put it simply, I was back on top. Just that quickly. I don't want to belabour this comparison, but a four-decade career had been salvaged by a three-minute song."

Radio Radio Elvis Costello & the Attractions

(Elvis Costello) ❋ 1978 ❋ Radar ❋ Appears on: *This Year's Model*

On the cusp of global stardom, Elvis Costello wrote a song attacking mainstream radio, announcing, "I want to bite the hand that feeds me." It was possibly his finest moment, and he just kept spewing out the bile. The Attractions, newly in place in the Costello show, were also hitting strides with Steve Naive's squeaking Vox Continental organ. Although the song is an attack on the parlous state of the radio waves, Costello's lyrics really nail everybody in the supposedly activist late '70s: "Some of my friends sit around in the evening/And they worry about the times ahead/Everybody else is overwhelmed by indifference and the promise of an early bed/You either shut up or get cut out. They don't want to talk about it/It's only inches on the reel-to-reel."

Costello was on a roll. It had only been a couple of months since his first album,

My Aim is True, and he was anointed the premier lyricist of whatever-the-hell-was-happening-these-days. He appeared to be a punk rocker the music Establishment could understand.

Costello, though, was nothing of the kind. He was cranky and he was enjoying it.

"My next album on the one hand will sound harder and harsher, while on the other hand it will be less about me. It will sound somewhat more arrogant too, because I want to get people off the notion that I'm a kind of super loser. I don't feel like wearing that tag for the rest of my life," he said shortly after the release of the debut LP.

Music and the radio were subjects dear to his heart. "People used to live their lives by songs," he said in 1978. "They were like calendars or diaries. And they were pop songs. Not elaborate fucking pieces of music. You wouldn't say, like, 'Yeah, that's the time I went out with Janet, we went to see the LSO playing Mozart.' You'd remember you went out with Janet because they were playing 'Summer in the City' on the radio.

"That's why I like and write short songs. It's a discipline. There's no disguise. You can't cover up songs like that by dragging banks of fucking synthesisers and choirs of angels. They have to stand up on their own. With none of that nonsense. Songs are just so fucking effective. People seem to have forgotten that."

Before his second album was released, Costello made a four-track demo with an early version of 'Radio Radio' titled 'Radio Soul'. Then, it was a sentimental celebration of late-night broadcasts; in two years things changed.

The response to 'Radio Radio' was not uniformly positive.

Tony Blackburn, Britain's most popular DJ, called Costello "a silly little man" and commented, "I wonder what radio would be like in the hands of people like Elvis Costello."

Unfortunately, twenty-six years on, Costello's words still stand true – the radio is still "in the hands of such a lot of fools trying to anaesthetise the way that you feel."

Young Americans David Bowie

(David Bowie) ❋ RCA ❋ 1975 ❋ Appears on: *Young Americans*

According to Tony Visconti, Bowie's third reinvention of the decade came to him in a phone call out of the blue. "David said, 'I've got the most fantastic band lined up for this next album, and I'm really into black music.' This was by trans-Atlantic phone call, and I said, 'Great, who have you got?' and he said, 'Willie Weeks on bass, Andy Newmark on drums, and this new guy from New York called Carlos Alomar', and I said, 'Say no more, I'll be on the next plane'."

Bowie was sitting on a string of three hit albums in the US, each bigger than the last. His stage show was state of the art. His band had reinvented rock. Then Bowie discovered disco.

The *Young Americans* album picked up on the sounds of Philadelphia; the funky but chic new style of R&B was pretty much off the radar for most rock fans but Bowie embraced it fully. His cocaine addiction might also have helped the taste for fast and choppy guitar.

Essentially, though, Bowie was simply doing what all good mods do and picked up on what American R&B artists were doing.

The first song recorded was 'Young Americans'.

"However, despite the fact that I was so tired, there was an electrifying atmosphere that night, and we recorded the 'Young Americans' track, and the next week or two went down like a breeze. But towards the end, that album did get very strange because we didn't know what we were doing – David did mostly live vocals, and although all the songs were written, they were being heavily rearranged as time went on, but nothing was organised, and it turned out to be one enormous jam," said Tony Visconti.

During his stay in New York, Bowie befriended John Lennon and they recorded a new version of the Beatles' 'Across the Universe' and a collaboration, 'Fame', which was Bowie's first number one US single. 'Young Americans', however, topped the R&B charts. The song gave a whole new lease of life to an artist who was beginning to burn out.

"'Young Americans'," said Bowie, "is about a newly-wed couple who don't know if they really like each other. Well, they do, but they don't know if they do or don't. It's a bit of a predicament."

Bowie's departure from dress-up annoyed his fans but showed his sense of the winds of change. In the next two years disco would change the face of popular music. But by then Bowie would have gone from disco too.

House of the Rising Sun The Animals

(Traditional/arrangement Alan Price) ❉ Track ❉ 1964 ❉ Appears on: *The Animals*

"We had a three-hour session booked, did two takes of 'House of the Rising Sun' in fifteen minutes, completely live, in mono, kept take two and made the rest of the album in the remaining two-and-three quarters hours," recalled producer Mickie Most of the session that gave him a career. "It's one of the greatest keyboard solos

of all time – if not the best. Alan wrote it. Beautiful soul/jazz feel on that little Vox organ. I can remember putting 'two minutes sixty-eight seconds' on one single. As long as they saw the two it was OK, a three and they got worried."

The song was a traditional folk song about a brothel and the lyric caused some radio stations to stay away from the track. However, the performance was so strong that most stations turned a blind ear and the track became an international number one hit.

Success was not for everyone. The Animals were known for their internal volatility and keyboard player Alan Price in particular was unhappy with topping the charts.

"Essentially, all of the product was the result of a conflict of interest," he told *Goldmine* magazine. "We had a missionary zeal about blues music, and I felt, particularly, that Mickie Most was attempting to homogenise, sweeten, and make it accessible for the mass market. Which is understandable if you're the producer, but aggravating if you're the artist.

"As I say, the Animals had a particular concept of themselves as a band. There was an anarchic spirit in it, which was being flattened by commercial designs, attitudes, and needs."

Price left the band shortly after.

Sledgehammer Peter Gabriel

(Peter Gabriel) ✳ Charisma ✳ 1986 ✳ Appears on: *So*

Peter Gabriel's most light-hearted album was written during some of his darkest days – the collapse of his first marriage. As Gabriel navigated a jungle of analysts, self-help gurus and therapists, his ear was turned to Africa. He had already started recording African artists, especially Senegal's superstar Youssou N'Dour. Gabriel was also keenly interested in electronic music and American R&B. The *So* sessions were notable if only because they featured the coolest musicians from three continents: Laurie Anderson, Wayne Jackson, Nile Rodgers, Larry Klein, Bill Laswell, Tony Levin, Richard Tee and Jerry Marotta from America; PP Arnold, Jim Kerr, Kate Bush and Stewart Copeland from Europe; and Djalma Corrèa, Manu Katché and Youssou N'Dour from Africa.

'Sledgehammer' is the most fun Gabriel has ever had on a record. The lyric is a slightly quirky take on an R&B song. From that premise Gabriel and co-producer Daniel Lanois loaded up layers of sound and meaning to create a new type of blue-eyed soul. Accompanied by a groundbreaking video, 'Sledgehammer' was a massive hit single and gave Gabriel a whole new audience. The sound and the groove became industry standard for some time to come. It seemed as though it would be possible to make music that had the joy of '60s soul and the depth and experimentation that would keep musicians going into their middle age. For a moment, *So* looked like the future.

"We had mutually decided on a philosophy for the record," said Lanois. "We would incorporate a playfulness and a humanness. I thought it was important for Peter to be very clear with some of these songs."

Live Forever Oasis

(Noel Gallagher) ✳ Creation ✳ 1994 ✳ Appears on: *Definitely Maybe*

Oasis charged out of Manchester full of attitude. They harked back to the glory days of the empire when the Englishness of the Faces and the Kinks was forgiven because they represented the true spirit of the English. Oasis were the prophets of Cool Britannia – proud to be English and not terribly educated. The Gallagher brothers were naturals – they loved being in the tabloids, Noel could write a classic song just like ringing a bell and Liam could sing with wounded passion. 'Live Forever' was their anthem, a manifesto of the promise of good times.

"If you're on the dole and writing songs, you're not going to write about how crap your life is, 'cause you already live that life. You want to write about how great life could be if you were a rock & roll star," said Noel. "Damon Albarn [Blur] and Brett Anderson [Suede] write songs about going to the dogs and being pantomime horses, which is all very well but it doesn't mean fuck-all to me, it means nothing to 99% of the population, it's too self-centred, too me-me-me. It's why those bands never make it in America, 'cause it's just not universal enough.

"I'm not mithered about this or that, or being a sex symbol or the voice of a generation. All I'm arse about is getting down alongside Ray Davies, Morrissey and Marr, Jagger and Richards, Lennon and McCartney, Pete Townshend, Paul Weller and Burt Bacharach."

Say Goodbye   Hunters & Collectors

(Hunters & Collectors) ❋ Mushroom ❋ 1986 ❋ Appears on: *Human Frailty*

Perhaps the most direct song about the sexual revolution, 'Say Goodbye' is powered by the magnificent rumble of John Archer's bass guitar and Mark Seymour's refrain: "You don't make me feel like I'm a woman anymore!"

"People have run out of things to say about the power struggle between men and women," Seymour told me in 1986. "I wanted to write a lyric that expressed having gone through this whole process of negotiation, organising the relationship so it was all running smoothly, and suddenly one day the man looks up from his newspaper and realises he hasn't been giving her what she needs and she's pissed off about it. The most basic, fundamental thing you've forgotten about because you've been setting up your domestic environment."

The song became an instant classic; especially as a climax in the Hunters incendiary live performances. The group by this stage was just coming into its own, having flung off the pretensions of their early years in search of a sound that reflected their largely male Australian audiences. Although they set their sights on talking to the common punter, the Hunters were too eclectic a bunch to ever really cut straight rock songs, and that tension between ambition and their musical limitations is what made them exceptional. That and the notion that you could write a pub rock song with a feminist perspective.

"The whole song is a mixture of images," said Seymour. "One is a conversation I heard through a wall and another is having my girlfriend jump on top of me and grind her finger into my breastbone. It's pretty funny. It's ironic. It's even more ironic when you get a thousand blokes screaming it at the top of their voices."

Blitzkrieg Bop The Ramones

(Joey Ramone/Johnny Ramone/Tommy Ramone/Dee Dee Ramone) ✳ Sire ✳ 1976 ✳
Appears on: *The Ramones*

"What they want I don't know/All revved up and ready to go."

Straight out of CBGB in New York, the Ramones set the template for punk rock. They had the look – torn jeans, motorcycle jackets, bangs and sneakers. They had the sound – stripped back rock & roll that was big and dumb. They had the good fortune to stumble on the downtown New York scene of Max's Kansas City and CBGB where their primitive rock could be recast into a movement complete with an aesthetic and a momentum.

"We came first," said Johnny. "We did what came naturally to us."

The four Ramones had met in the suburbs. They liked the Spector sound and they liked bubblegum and big rock, the Bay City Rollers and '60s garage band rock. What they didn't like was the limpness that had overcome most of the superstars of rock and the fact that it had become so removed from the audience.

"We were having fun," Joey Ramone said shortly before his death in 2001. "The Ramones were always about having fun. Fun disappeared in 1974, there were too many serious people out there at the time.

"I always felt like I was a rock fan first, because I am. So I just remembered what

I loved about rock & roll and put that into the Ramones. When the Ramones got together that was pretty much all gone from music. I just loved the excitement, the dare, the challenge, the passion, and the sincerity. Having a point of view on things. Nobody cares about that any more, it's all about business today."

The Ramones took to writing songs about dumb things mostly – sniffing glue, cartoon ideas, violence. There were also some heavy subjects such as Dee Dee's years as a prostitute and junkie. By and large the Ramones were ground zero.

'Blitzkrieg Bop' was the opening salvo from the first Ramones album and it is the perfect call to arms. It was such a good song that the Ramones kept on recording it. As have a million groups ever since.

"The first time we went to CBGB to audition, Hilly [Kristal, proprietor] said, 'Nobody's going to like you guys but I'll have you back'," Joey recalled. "He knew we had something. Our first show was just the bartender and his dog, but then we got the Warhol, arty crowd. It always seems to be gays who pick up on things first."

I Am the Walrus The Beatles

(John Lennon/Paul McCartney) ❊ Apple ❊ 1967 ❊ Appears on: *Magical Mystery Tour*

The fact that most of 'I Am the Walrus' was written while John Lennon was on acid should come as no surprise. The fact that it is utter nonsense enhances rather than detracts from it as one of the Beatles' more interesting songs.

"The first line was written on one acid trip one weekend. The second line was written on the next acid trip the next weekend, and it was filled in after I met Yoko," Lennon said in 1980. "Part of it was putting down Hare Krishna. All these people were going on about Hare Krishna, Allen Ginsberg in particular. The reference to 'Element'ry penguin' is the elementary, naïve attitude of going around chanting, 'Hare Krishna', or putting all your faith in any one idol. I was writing obscurely, a la Dylan, in those days."

According to Lennon's school friend Pete Shotton, much of the more nonsensical lyrics were prompted by a fan letter.

"I just dipped into a sack," Shotton said, "and pulled out a letter that happened to be from our old school, from a pupil at Quarry Bank. He said his English teacher was getting them to read and analyse Beatles lyrics, find out hidden meanings, what they were really all about. This got John off remembering lines we used to recite when we were at school."

This was the poem – "Yellow matter custard, green slop pie/All mixed together with a dead dog's eye/Slap it on a butty, 10 ft thick/Then wash it all down with a cup of cold sick."

Lennon riffed on those ideas and some other free association. The walrus section simply came from the Lewis Carroll verse 'The Walrus and the Carpenter'. Lennon later noted that on rereading the poem it occurred to him that, in fact, it was the Carpenter who was the hero but it was too late for him to change it.

The first fragment of the tune comes from a police siren that passed his window. The second fragment relates to "sitting in a country garden", and the third is more offbeat to match the surreal lyric. George Martin welded these ideas together masterfully, adding a cheesy singing group and allowing the sound of a BBC production of *King Lear* to bleed into it.

The free associations of lyric, tune and sound effects work together to make their own kind of logic. Then there is the finale where Lennon declares himself "the eggman, coo coo ca choo". It's worth remembering that Martin's claim to fame before he produced the Beatles was as producer of the Goons and Peter Sellers. This piece of English absurdism fits into that tradition. It's also worth noting that for all the nonsense, 'I Am the Walrus' became one of the Beatles' most popular songs and has well outlasted the putative A-side 'Hello Goodbye'.

"It actually was fantastic in stereo," said Lennon. "But you never hear it all."

Hindu Gods of Love Lipstick Killers

(Lipstick Killers) ❉ Lost In Space ❉ 1979 ❉

Appears on: *Do the Pop: the Australian Garage-Rock Sound 1976–87*

Let's face it, most of what passes for rock & roll these days is rubbish. On the one hand you've got the emaciated bleating of fey little alternative rock boys whining in their bedsits about fuck knows what because they're not honest enough to say that they just can't get laid. On the other hand you've got the noise boys also full of self-important self-flagellation, but they're doing it "because it's the genre, man" and they've studied the form, and they can make the same cardboard cut-out records that the other guys make, their heads full of marketing plans, their best friends their lawyers. It's all so dull and self-serving. Where's the excitement, the flash, the dumb moves that haven't been suggested by their publicist? And the fake rebellion, the tatts and the piercings as badges of outsiderness? Please give us a break. Where's the spontaneity? When was the last time that you played a record and were *surprised*? Who was the last act that blew your mind wide open? Which was the last act whose sound didn't match their trousers? And don't start talking about punk rock. Jesus Christ, I'm glad the last punk revival is over now. That was the worst of it. People are still carrying on about the Sex Pistols and the wretched-looking Johnny Rotten as though they had anything to do with punk rock – of course, all the '90s punks picked up on the hair style and didn't get the point of punk at all. The Lipstick Killers' 'Hindu Gods of Love' may be the best Australian rock & roll single ever.

Get It On T. Rex

(Marc Bolan) ✳ Fly/EMI ✳ 1972 ✳ Appears on: *Electric Warrior*

Like Chuck Berry and most of the '50s rockers on whom he styled himself, Marc Bolan really only had one song. The trick is to have that one song versatile enough for lots of re-renderings and Bolan had a number of hits with his. Sometimes they were called 'Telegram Sam', sometimes 'Jeepster' – all very much the same, but the details made them soar to the heavens.

Bolan's boogie was a cornerstone of glam rock. Bolan and producer Tony Visconti made the blues changes even more simple, riding along on a light-footed boogie style and guitars that sounded like they were distorted by fairy dust.

Like all of Bolan's best work, the lyric was less than minimalist. A phrase, preferably nonsensical, but one which could, with a teenage imagination, be salacious, would suffice. Bolan's vocal was sly and sexy without ever being threatening. The music was all about the groove, and for that reason it is as glorious now as ever.

Visconti, who produced this and most of Bolan's work, recalled the session as being easy. "Bolan was very much a feel person," he said. "If the feel was there, we'd get it down in two or three takes."

Police and Thieves The Clash

(Junior Murvin/Lee Perry) ✴ Epic ✴ 1977 ✴ Appears on: *The Clash*

The Sex Pistols may have started punk rock but the Clash made it mean something. Their songs of dispossessed youth forgotten in the shadows of capitalism were better said and better played than any of their comrades down at the 100 Club.

The Clash's first album is a stone classic. The song 'White Riot' is a perfect teenage anthem. It also suggests that the Clash, and singer Joe Strummer in particular, had a wider view of the social and political hierarchy than most rock singers. 'White Riot' is a song about identifying with the underclass, especially the non-whites.

The album included a track lasting longer than three minutes and with a non-rock rhythm, which announced that the Clash were not going to be confined to any category – not even a punk one.But the key track on *The Clash* is their blistering cover of Junior Murvin's Jamaican hit 'Police and Thieves'.

"The poor blacks and the poor whites are in the same boat," said Strummer at the time. "They don't want us in their culture, but we just happen to dig Tapper Zukie and Big Youth, Dillinger and Aswad and Delroy Washington. We dig them and we ain't scared of going into heavy black record shops and getting their gear. We even go to heavy black gigs where we're the only white people there.

"We'd just like to bridge the gap between the two things, I'd like to have black people coming to hear us, right, but primarily we gotta be concerned with young white kids because that's what we are. But we ain't nothing like racist, *no way*."

The Clash was recorded over three weekends by their live soundman, who had never made an album before. The essence of the record was the group's live sound – the fiercely slashing guitars over Strummer's screams and the deep dub bass from Paul Simonon. The song's simple message of paranoia about police fitted perfectly with the rest of the album. Mostly, though, it's a great groove – not so much reggae as a hybrid that sounds complete and confident and undeniable. "It was just a wild idea I had one night. I wanted to play reggae when the band first started but I was talked out of it. Rightly so," said Strummer. "And we can't really play reggae. Who the hell could play them reggae drums apart from a black man? We just did it within our limitations. If it had sounded shitty we'd have dropped it. But it sounded great. There's hardly any reggae in it at all – just a few offbeat guitars thrown in for a laugh – it's all rock & roll. I think it's an incredible track."

Anthrax Gang of Four

(Dave Allen/Hugo Burnham/Andrew Gill/Jon King) ❋ EMI ❋ 1979 ❋ Appears on: *Entertainment!*

Michael Hutchence described the Gang of Four as "art meets the devil via James Brown". The Gang of Four pretty much rewrote the book of rock with their debut album. It had the strident leftist politics of the best punk, but then deconstructed rock music to its core and added some funk. The album closed with 'Anthrax', a perfect example of a song that had a hook that was profoundly disturbing.

Andy Gill used his guitar like a machete, taking to the beat and slashing it to pieces. The music was best described as "itchy": scratching guitar over beats that came and went. There were ominous hollow spaces in the music and shouted epigrams. It was clearly a balancing act of startling proportions.

The funk and rock four-piece was the brainchild of singer Jon King and guitarist Gill, who saw the group as a vehicle for leftist political agitation. The title of this album suggests that entertainment was a tool of the ruling class but that it could also be used to subvert the dominant paradigm (as one said in those days).

"If you think of the first crop of punk stuff, it was all just tedious guitars cranked up through Marshalls," Andy Gill said recently. "In the wake of the Damned and the Sex Pistols, it was heavy metal but faster and not as well played.

"Gang of Four was radically different from that. The guitar was very staccato, very stripped down, very repetitive, loop-based. The drumming was basically funky but not through copying various icons of black music, more through simply deconstructing the nature of drumming and where you place the beats. It was like starting from ground zero with the drumming. Anything that sounded like rock drumming, I would change . . .

"The same thing happened with the melodies. The tunes had vocals to it but it was very rhythm- and phrase-related. You could tell by listening to Gang of Four music that punk had happened. But it definitely wasn't punk music."

Gang of Four saw the construction of rock music in political terms.

Having had some success with an indie single, Gang of Four signed with EMI, a political contradiction perhaps. The upshot was that it gave them the opportunity to have free rein in the studio to develop the masterpiece that is *Entertainment*.

"It's a very accurate representation of where the band was at," said Gill. "You pretty much get the whole picture there. It's not all one thing. There's a variety of things going on. 'Anthrax' is a cool track. It was just this idea to have these very simple elements, like the guitar is just going to do feedback and the drums are going to play this weird pattern and they're just going to stop and they're just going to start. That's really its strength – to take the idea to a logical point and not get distracted and to avoid the frills and really just take it to its conclusion.

"I love its directness, simplicity, the minimalism of it, the powerfulness of it. The guitar is so simple and spare through the whole track and it rocks."

As Bono put it, "Andy Gill's chin is the very black hole of '90s music we should have all disappeared into ... if we had sense ... a dimple atop the body politic, a pimple on the arse of pop. A Gang of Four metal guru, a corporation of common sense, a smart bomb of text that had me 'at home feeling like a typist'."

White Honey Graham Parker & the Rumour

(Graham Parker) ✳ Mercury ✳ 1976 ✳ Appears on: *Howlin' Wind*

Parker was a little ball of energy, spewing forth great rock & roll songs like there was no tomorrow – he released a second, equally good album (*Heat Treatment*) within months of this release. Parker was wordy like a new Dylan with a new urgency. There was a huge well of spite and anger just under the surface of songs like 'Don't Ask Me Questions' and the title track that was ameliorated by naïve pop on 'Hotel Chambermaid' and the deliciously viscous 'White Honey'. Parker came screaming out of the blocks like somebody with something to say, even if he couldn't sing it all that well.

The singer was greatly aided by producer Nick Lowe, who was known to record quickly, with maximum ambience and minimum fuss. He also had the services of the Rumour – a band made up of pieces of the best London pub bands. They were versatile, tackling blues, R&B, reggae and straight rock (all the records he made after parting ways were distinctly one-dimensional). Basically the whole thing sounded like they were on the same urgent mission as the singer. Together they cooked beautifully. The colours that they brought to 'White Honey' and 'Gypsy Blood' gave the songs a warmth and passion that transcended simple rock & roll.

Parker was an instant critic's darling – any vaguely literate songwriter in the arid mid-'70s was hailed as the new Springsteen. Parker was never that. His songs rarely moved from the personal and immediate. But for a while Parker believed the hype too, and his albums became increasingly grandiose and career-orientated.

It was here on the first album that you got the raw, confused, randy, sceptical and vaguely bitter Parker performing with musicians of impeccable taste and smarts. Perhaps not since Robbie Robertson joined the Band have talents melded so well and the results been as enduring.

Suzie Q Creedence Clearwater Revival

(Dale Hawkins) ☀ Fantasy ☀ 1968 ☀ Appears on: *Creedence Clearwater Revival*

"I wanted the band to sound mysterious, to have its own definition," said John Fogerty, Creedence Clearwater Revival's singer, songwriter, guitarist and producer. "So I decided to mess around with 'Suzie Q', which was a cool rock & roll song by Dale Hawkins. I kind of did the same thing with 'I Put a Spell on You'. Those songs took us to another place than where we'd been for ten years."

The group started around 1960, when Fogerty was just thirteen years old, first as the Blue Velvets playing the jukebox hits at high school dances. Rhythm guitarist Tom Fogerty got a job in the warehouse of jazz label Fantasy and they began cutting records as the Golliwogs in 1963, having respectable regional success in northern California around San Francisco. John Fogerty started getting more interested in blues and southern music – the Golliwogs' 'Walk on the Water' was an amazing R&B jam. Gradually the group took on a heavier sound, exemplified by a demo version of an extended jam on the song 'Suzie Q'. The tape was picked up by underground radio and was eventually released as the first Creedence Clearwater Revival 45.

'Suzie Q' is based around a standard twelve-bar but it has a slow, insistent rhythm that is more rock than blues and Fogerty's lengthy guitar solos are quite extraordinary. The term "swamp" was often bandied about to describe the Creedence sound – luscious, thick, dangerous and festering jams.

Fogerty went on to write his own southern boogies – 'Lodi', 'Proud Mary', 'Bad Moon Rising' – and contribute to this mythic bayou country that was soon adopted by others such as Robbie Robertson. The "swamp" feel that Creedence established on this record was to be consistently regenerated, especially in the early '80s.

Creedence did more than anyone other than the Rolling Stones to put the blues back into rock & roll.

"I think about what Muddy Waters really did and he's every bit as seminal, as ground-breaking, as epochal, as Elvis Presley. It's funny that they're both from Mississippi. It's kind of the same journey, just some years apart. Initially, they went to different parts of our culture, but they ended up in the same place."

Sympathy for the Devil   The Rolling Stones

(Mick Jagger/Keith Richards) ❋ Decca ❋ 1968 ❋ Appears on: *Beggars Banquet*

"'Sympathy' was one of those sort of songs where we tried everything," drummer Charlie Watts said. "The first time I ever heard the song was when Mick was playing it at the front door of a house where I lived in Sussex. It was at dinner. He played it entirely on his own, the sun was going down – and it was fantastic. We had a go at loads of different ways of playing it; in the end I just played a jazz Latin feel in the style Kenny Clarke would have played on 'A Night in Tunisia' – not the actual rhythm he played, but the same styling. Fortunately it worked, because it was a sod to get together."

The recording of 'Sympathy for the Devil' at Olympic studios in London was documented by the French director Jean Luc Godard in his film *One Plus One*. Godard captured the laborious process the group went through – trying different arrangements – to get the song to work. Godard cut this footage with storylines about the coming revolution, and the whole makes some kind of sense. Keith Richards plays the guitars and bass, Brian Jones is sidelined in a corner with his guitar disconnected from the recording machines, Nicky Hopkins plays piano and Rocky Dijon plays congas while everybody is finally drafted into singing the haunting backing vocals.

Jagger's lyric came from the Mikhail Bulgakov novel *The Master and Margarita*. It reflected the singer's growing interest in the occult. The book is about Satan's visit to Russia after the Bolshevik revolution. In a time of optimism about a future of peace and love, Jagger was pointing out the evil that lurks in the hearts of men.

I Me Mine The Beatles

(George Harrison) ✻ Apple ✻ 1970 ✻ Appears on: *Let It Be*

The last song recorded on the final Beatles recording session (although John Lennon wasn't there) is George Harrison's critique of ego. An Austrian marching band he saw on TV inspired the melody. The words were inspired by his interest in Indian mysticism. As the Beatles were in turmoil about each other's egos and battles over money, it's likely that this impacted on the lyric as well.

The song, as finished in the studio, was only a ninety-second riff that Phil Spector edited into double that length. The tune's saving grace is the melancholic guitar lines from Harrison in the chorus, which work against the pushy and testy mood of the verses. The quiet Beatle, it appears, had the best perspective on what was tearing apart the Fab Four.

I Feel the Earth Move Carole King

(Carole King) ✻ Ode ✻ 1971 ✻ Appears on: *Tapestry*

In the late '50s, while studying to become a teacher, Carole Klein was drawn into the Brill Building scene where she met her future husband, Gerry Goffin. Goffin/King were a hit-making machine from the bobbysoxing '50s through to the hippie era of the mid-'60s: 'Will You Love Me Tomorrow', 'The Locomotion', 'Up on the Roof', 'Chains', 'I'm into Something Good', 'Don't Bring Me Down', 'Wasn't Born to Follow', 'Pleasant Valley Sunday' and '(You Make Me Feel Like a) Natural Woman'. The hits kept coming until the couple divorced in 1967.

It was a feminist fairytale when the newly unshackled King recorded her own songs. Recorded in 1970, *Tapestry* was the female equivalent of her friend James Taylor's *Sweet Baby James*. It was like a calming coda to the turbulent '60s. The cover photo says it all – hair long and natural, blue jeans, casual shirt, bare feet and tabby cat. Here was a genuinely natural woman for the post-Woodstock era. Casual, sexy and real. King reworked two of her Brill Building hits: 'Will You Love Me Tomorrow' and '(You Make Me Feel Like a) Natural Woman', which laid a bridge between the songcraft of the pre-Beatles era and the cynical Nixon years. Her mellifluous piano matched her singing voice, which was sensual and mature.

'I Feel the Earth Move' is a mature version of the breathless love songs of her youth, powered by a very funky band and King's joyous vocal. The song was perfect for the liberated woman.

Her first solo album shifted five thousand copies. *Tapestry*, her third, moved over ten million, making it the largest selling album by a female artist until Alanis Morissette's *Jagged Little Pill*. King also spearheaded a movement towards the confessional singer/songwriter that was to dominate rock & roll for decades. King once said, "Until I met Gerry, I was just a musician who wrote bad lyrics." *Tapestry* proved otherwise.

Born Slippy Underworld

(Darren Emerson/Karl Hyde/Rick Smith) ✳ Junior Boys Own ✳ 1995 ✳
Appears on: *Trainspotting*

The hook line "lager, lager, lager" ensured that Underworld's breakthrough techno hit would reach beyond clubland to the furthest regions of the suburbs and the heights of the football terraces. The song's appearance in Danny Boyle's film *Trainspotting* put it right over the edge – an overdose of drugs and adrenalin. The song is a relentless, intoxicating electronic track of keyboards and drum machine driven by a rhythmic vocal chant. *Trainspotting* was a key moment in the '90s; an underground film full of moral complexity and great music. It had a definite '90s atmosphere; the '80s were like ancient history, and Underworld had gone through that same transformation. They were an '80s pop rock band with one small hit ('Underneath the Radar'). Then singer Karl Hyde and his long-time collaborator Rick Smith enlisted DJ Darren Emerson and refashioned their sound.

'Born Slippy', which takes its name from a greyhound, was a song that Hyde wrote about his personal battle with alcoholism. "It was all about the horrors I'd experienced whilst being over-medicated on alcohol for a lot of years," he explained. "And I kind of thought if I just write out this autobiographical piece that's horrific, you know, people will go 'Oh, my God, Jesus, what's that about? That's horrible, what's that about?' And I'd be able to say 'That's about me, how's about a bit of help?' But we came out and explained it and then Danny did what he did with the film, and I think that the whole balance was redressed and it's fine if people want to use it as a drinking anthem, I really don't have any problem with that now."

Keep Your Lamps Trimmed and Burning Hot Tuna

(Rev Gary Davis) ❊ Grunt/RCA ❊ 1971 ❊ Appears on: *First Pull Up, Then Pull Down*

When life in the Jefferson Airplane got too weird, guitarist Jorma Kaukonen and bass player Jack Casady started a side project playing ragtime blues. Their first album, recorded live with only the addition of harp player Will Scarlet, was a low-key gem of mostly old time blues. As the Airplane further splintered, Hot Tuna kept getting better. By their second album they had added fifty-something fiddle player Papa John Creach and drummer Sammy Piazza and they were overtaking the Airplane. Indeed, when the Airplane reconvened for two albums, Creach and Piazza were in the line-up.

There was no shortage of white boys playing old time blues in the '60s. Hot Tuna was something else, however. Kaukonen's principle influence was Rev Gary Davis, who had a distinctive ragtime technique. Kaukonen upped the dynamics of Davis' style with an explosive, almost violent fingerpicking style of his own. Casady, one of the best bass players of the time, brought a swing to the rhythm section and a rare melodic invention. In short, he was funky. Davis' songs tended towards the fire and brimstone, which suited the dark psychedelic side of Hot Tuna to a tee.

Unfortunately, Kaukonen was not much of a writer. The best Tuna original ('Third Week in the Chelsea') was co-opted for an Airplane album. Hot Tuna's albums became increasingly weak the further they got from their roots and from the audience.

This second album, however, recorded live, bursts with dark molten energy. The key song, 'Keep Your Lamps Trimmed and Burning', sounds nothing like a traditional blues but is a gutsy, ominous improvisation. Even the more traditional blues numbers like 'Candy Man' jump and rock with a hopped-up energy. Kaukonen and Casady were perfect at riding the tiger. They fed off the audience and each other in splendid combustion and few LPs burned so bright.

The End The Beatles

(John Lennon/Paul McCartney) ❊ Apple ❊ 1969 ❊ Appears on: *Abbey Road*

The Beatles assembled *Abbey Road* as a farewell (*Let It Be*, the final album, was already recorded and at this point discarded) so it's an entirely appropriate note on which to end. Most of the second side of the album was an extended medley of half-formed songs patched together by Paul McCartney that rises up to 'Carry That Weight' – one of the many songs the Beatles wrote about the trials of being in the Beatles. Then comes Ringo Starr's only recorded drum solo followed by a farewell guitar solo taken by the other three Beatles in turn. As John Lennon said, "There's a nice little bit I played on *Abbey Road* . . . Paul gave us each a piece, a little break where Paul plays, George plays and I play. It stops, on 'Carry That Weight', then suddenly it goes boom-boom-boom on the drums and we all take it in turns to play. I'm the third one on it. I have a definite style of playing, always had. But I was overshadowed. They call George the invisible singer, I'm the invisible guitarist."

Finally there's a brief lyric – "The love you take is equal to the love you make" – which even had the approval of Lennon himself. Not a big hit, 'The End' has a delicate, concise sweetness and is a fitting farewell. Lest anyone get too serious, the song is undercut by the twee 'Her Majesty'. The perfect ending to a perfect career.

Want Rufus Wainwright

(Rufus Wainwright) ❋ Dreamworks ❋ 2003 ❋ Appears on: *Want One*

"I'm a big fan of the Pre-Raphaelites," Rufus Wainwright once explained. "Millais, Edward Burne-Jones, and I realised recently that my music is Pre-Raphaelite in a certain way, in that it reinvents an older era and romanticises it, puts it in this gilded frame."

Unlike the Pre-Raphaelites, however, Wainwright looks dead in the face of the modern world. On *Want One* he describes, with sumptuous orchestrations, a season in gay hell.

Wainwright was an instant cult hero on the release of his 1998 eponymous debut. His lineage – the son of Loudon Wainwright III and Kate McGarrigle, friend to Lorca Cohen, Sean Lennon, Jenny Muldaur, et al – helped but it was really his strikingly original songwriting that made the album one of the year's best. Wainwright then shot up his celebrity and dived into a binge of anonymous sex and hardcore drugs, culminating in a night on "a combination of crystal meth and ecstasy and special K [ketamine] and cocaine, and God knows what." Wainwright went temporarily blind. Time for rehab and a new album.

Like his father, Rufus writes about himself, his family and, with a fairly sardonic wit, the times in which he lives. He is not a folksinger like his dad but rather more sophisticated in both his lyrics and instrumentation. The phrases "theatrical" and "operatic" are bandied about but it's the plush sound of his piano and the dexterity of his voice that recall the Depression-era writers.

His lyrics display an enormous self-absorption but, then, it's quite a story to tell. He documents the ambivalence and anger between absent father and son, his depression and the traumas of a unique life (including his rape at age fourteen) and his inability to find love and sex in the same place at the same time.

This third album, produced by Marius deVries (Björk), is seductive and immensely powerful. Wainwright will be one of the most memorable songwriters of the new century. On the title track he pulls it all together with a rambling cry, "I don't want, no I really don't want/To be John Lennon or Leonard Cohen/I just want to be my dad/With a slight sprinkling of my mother/And work at the family store."

Love Unlimited Fun Lovin' Criminals

(Fun Lovin' Criminals) ❋ Capitol ❋ 1998 ❋ Appears on: *100% Columbian*

They came to prominence with the novelty hit 'Scooby Snacks', which mixed pot cravings with dialogue sampled from Quentin Tarantino's *Pulp Fiction*. However, there's much more to this trio. They are to rap what Martin Scorsese is to gangsters, which is to say somewhere between an affectionate tribute and a parody. The Fun Lovin' Criminals inhabit an imaginary Brooklyn of small-time action and big-time romance but there is great distance between their cartoon gun totin' fantasies and the real life on the streets.

But the essential factor here – even greater than the apparent wit of the lyric – is the classic melodies that they have appropriated. Much of the music goes back to the Delta Blues and the Chicago Chess records of Bo Diddley and Chuck Berry. The Fun Lovin' Criminals have recontextualised the staples of R&B, filtered it through a Lou Reed blender to get a touch of deadpan poignancy, and then added a pop melody that just won't quit.

"One of the reasons I liked the Stones is because they could play country and western, rock or blues and still be the Stones," said Huey, who writes, sings and plays the guitar. "Their energy transcended style. Bands now are 'alternative grunge' or 'alternative hip-hop'; they can't just be a band. Van Gogh painted other shit other than *Starry Night*. He painted flowers and all types of shit. He painted himself with the ear gone." On this track they get busy with the super strings of Barry White and the deeply sexual moods of the Love Unlimited Orchestra reduced to a trio. It's both funny and sexy.

"The lyric thing? I never really did that before this band. I'm like Tom Waits with a lobotomy!" Huey said. "Some people say to me: 'Talk to us about rapping,' and I'm like, 'Maybe you should talk to somebody else, like a rapper.' You know what I'm saying?"

Don't Dream It's Over Crowded House

(Neil Finn) ✳ Capitol ✳ 1986 ✳ Appears on: *Crowded House*

"We didn't know when we finished the first album that 'Don't Dream It's Over' was going to be a big hit at all," Neil Finn admitted. The track, accompanied by a magnificent video by director Alex Proyas and non-stop touring by Crowded House, eventually topped the US charts and was the cornerstone of their brilliant career.

The medium-tempo ethereal ballad owed a small debt to the Beatles' 'Across the Universe' and had a similar dreamlike quality.

"I'm never conscious when I'm writing of any kind of intellectual requirement for the song," said Finn. "It's a case of being able to drift off and dream away in the right manner, and then falling upon something that seems to bring an emotion out within you. At that point you try and get as much of that feeling down on paper as you can and resist the urge to go off and make a cup of tea as a reward. 'Don't Dream It's Over' I wrote in one go on my brother's piano in his house in Melbourne. There were people around visiting at the time and I shut myself away in a room and that was the reason I wrote 'They come, they come to build a wall between us.'"

Recording the first album in Los Angeles was a difficult process. At one point producer Mitchell Froom brought in session supremos Jerry Scheff and Jim Keltner to replace House members Nick Seymour and Paul Hester. The next day they recorded 'Don't Dream' and the new trio clicked. "It had a particularly sad groove to it," said Finn. "I think because Paul and Nick had faced their own mortality."

The song brought a new beginning to the group, away from straight guitar pop and into a more sophisticated territory.

"Mitchell was very influential on certain things about that first record and the feel in particular," said Finn. "Having come from a pretty white anglophile pop band with Split Enz, Mitchell played these very out of the way keyboards that just suspended the chords in a very dreamy and appealing way and that again was different."

The song was later covered by Paul Young and that version kicked off the House's career in Britain, and has been covered numerous times since.

Like most songwriters, Neil Finn remains uncertain why this particular song became a classic. "It has a certain universalness about it," he offered. "There's a hopeful, positive sentiment to it, but it's turned into melancholy and that's real life too. And I think in America if you put the word 'freedom' in the first line it really helps. Beyond that I have no idea, the way the chords and the melody work together is always a deep mystery and it just seems to work."

Caught Up in the Rapture Anita Baker

(Glenn Garry/Dianne Quander) ✳ Elektra ✳ 1986 ✳ Appears on: *Rapture*

The queen of quiet storm, Anita Baker's second album drew comparisons with jazz greats Sarah Vaughan and Ella Fitzgerald although there was a strong strain of R&B and soul in her tracks and a strong groove as befits a Detroit girl. Baker had made one acclaimed album, *The Songstress*, before she signed with Elektra and cut an album that influenced the shape of R&B in the mid-'80s.

"I didn't know I had that in me," she said later. "I wanted a smooth product with energy and heart, but I surprised myself. There's passion there. I knew I could pop a note, but the nuances I think are what's important."

Baker executive-produced the album, choosing old friend Michael J Powell as producer for most of it. She fought a difficult legal battle to get out of her previous contract because she wanted creative freedom and she wasn't going to give it up. Elektra, she said, "left me the hell alone. I knew what I wanted to sing, and I knew what kind of production I wanted, which was the minimalist approach."

As the title suggests, *Rapture* is an album of sensual joy and spiritual peace. The combination of jazz, gospel, soul and R&B flavours was unique. It was music for adults as well as the pop charts.

The key track is the intense and intimate 'Caught Up in the Rapture'. Part of the charm of the record was that it was made without any expectations of major success and its unadorned romanticism made the grooves that much more sensual. From a virtual unknown, *Rapture* made Baker an instant superstar, no-one being more surprised than the singer herself. "I didn't think anybody was gonna hear it," she said.

Cinnamon Girl   Neil Young & Crazy Horse

(Neil Young) ❋ Reprise ❋ 1969 ❋ Appears on: *Everybody Knows This Is Nowhere*

"*Everybody Knows This Is Nowhere* is probably my best," Neil Young said in the early '70s. "It's my favourite one. I've always loved Crazy Horse from the first time I heard the Rockets album on White Whale. The original band we had in '69 and '70 – Molina, Talbot, Whitten and me. That was wonderful. Everything I've ever done with Crazy Horse has been incredible. Just for the feeling, if nothing else."

'Cinnamon Girl' opens *Everybody* with its cryptic love-song lyrics over the crunching power of Crazy Horse. The music was largely improvised. "We suck at rehearsals. We just don't have any attention span," said Sampedro of the group's attitude.

In 1969 Neil Young was still finding his feet, having tasted success with the Buffalo Springfield and failure with his first solo album. All the tracks on this record have the tentative sense of a songwriter struggling to find his muse. The lyrics are feverish, as is the tune – based on an open tuning he learnt with the Byrds that enabled him to attain a raga-like groove that mirrored the 103°F fever from which he had recently recovered. A single edit and mix was done of the track and that started Young's solo career. It's the cinnamon taste of the song – spicy, tart and sweet – that makes the track interesting still.

As the most eloquent rock critic John Mendelssohn put it: "In his best work, as in *Everybody Knows*, wherein Crazy Horse's heavy, sinister accompaniment made unmistakable the message (of desperation begetting brutal vindictiveness), which the almost impenetrably subjective words hinted at only broadly, the basic sound of a song further vivified what lyric fragments suggested."

In a Big Country   Big Country

(Stuart Adamson) ✳ Mercury ✳ 1982 ✳ Appears on: *The Crossing*

For a moment there it looked like Big Country might save rock & roll. Things were looking dire. America was full of corporate rock bands. Britain had gone New Romantic. Then out of the Scottish heather, with their guitars ringing like bagpipes, came the entertaining Big Country, sporting anthems that sounded like they had something to say.

Adamson's first band, the Skids, had a creditable punk career in the late '70s after which the guitarist and singer found himself back in Scotland. Taking inspiration from the Celtic influences around him, he became fired up with the notion of creating "positive" music with broad soundscapes in the style of U2, Simple Minds and the Bunnymen. "If there are any kindred bands," Adamson said of those comparisons, "it is those who are presenting music as something to be shared. I think we should be wary of making an antifashion into a fashion. One of the reasons certain groups are being lumped together, ourselves included, is that there is still a certain innocence about what they do. A lot of people still feel very deeply about music and that's a good way to be.

"But I think it's great that a lot of kids in their early teens are buying records like ours as well as buying the Duran Duran and Kajagoogoo, because there's nothing lightweight about our songs. If there's any future for music, it has got to come through young people being shown that you can express yourself honestly through music."

Recorded in May 1983 with U2's producer Steve Lilywhite at the helm, *The Crossing* delivered on Adamson's grand design. The bottom end came from Joy Division but the layers of chiming guitars were unique. The epic scale of songs like 'In a Big Country', 'Fields of Fire' and 'The Storm' didn't dilute the passion or the bite delivered by Adamson and Stuart Watson's guitar duets.

Big Country never again matched the glory of their debut hit single and Adamson struggled for many years with his career and his alcohol problems until his untimely death in 2001.

"I still believe music has a very important part to play in people's lives," Adamson said in 1983. "If we ever do anything that helps to give people an idea of self, then we'll have done something worth doing."

Beware of Darkness Leon Russell & the Shelter People

(George Harrison) ✳ Shelter ✳ 1971 ✳ Appears on: *Leon Russell and the Shelter People*

Leon Russell was the pivotal figure in rock & roll between 1969 and 1971. He brought together the discipline of a studio musician and his raw southern rock and soul music. He was the bandleader extraordinaire. For those few years, the south infatuated the superstar elite – especially Brits like Eric Clapton – and a new generation of southerners came through. Russell moved effortlessly between the parties. He was a catalyst for some of the best records of the period.

He was raised in Tulsa, Oklahoma, and in his teens Russell's band backed Jerry Lee Lewis as the Killer barnstormed across the south. He wound up in Los Angeles playing piano and bass in Hal Blaine's Wrecking Crew – the session men for Phil Spector, Terry Melcher and other producers. He appeared on thousands of hits by the likes of Frank Sinatra, Ike and Tina Turner ('River Deep, Mountain High'), the Rolling Stones, the Byrds ('Mr Tambourine Man'), Bobby Darin, Sam Cooke, the Beach Boys ('California Girls' and the album *Pet Sounds*) and Herb Albert and Tijuana Brass to name just a few. Russell never lost his sense of southern-fried soul and gospel music. In the late '60s he hung out with Delaney Bramlett, another southerner in a similar position.

"I think the first record experience where I really did just what came off the top of my head was the Bonnie and Delaney album [*Accept No Substitute*]," he said. "We just all got around and had a party. That's what it sounds like."

The party continued a few months later when Joe Cocker landed in Los Angeles looking for a band. Having just recorded a Russell song, 'Delta Lady', the connection was easily made and Russell assembled the Mad Dogs and Englishmen, which in turn made him famous as indeed it did almost every player on the tour. Over the next year he made his own records, produced Bob Dylan's single 'Watching the River Flow' and featured heavily in the Concert for Bangladesh.

The Shelter People suggested a return to the holy rolling anarchy of the Mad Dogs. Russell was at the prime of his career, fired up on gospel and soul, and the Shelter People were in fact made up of players from either the Mad Dogs or the Muscle Shoals, aided by incredible soul backing singers and a few guests.

"We mainly went down to Muscle Shoals to record the new Shelter People album because that's where everybody goes for a certain type of music that we like," Russell said in one of his rare interviews. "It's mainly the musicians. They have that unique experience of playing together for quite some different artists, and they really are easy to work with. I also cut a George Harrison song in London with the Dominos over there, which is nice, and there was one that I just kind of wrote on the spot, so there'll be two songs with the Dominos on the album.

"I did one session with George and Ringo in London, but I haven't gotten around to writing the words for it. The music on the album is considerably more laid-back than in the first album. The songs are just a diary of what I was into at the time."

The album starts with 'Stranger in a Strange Land', adapted from Robert Heinlein's sci-fi novel which had been co-opted by the counterculture as a metaphor for themselves. There's 'Crystal Closet Queen', an ode to Little Richard. There are the semi-autobiographical 'Ballad of the Mad Dogs and Englishmen', which is curiously poignant, 'Home Sweet Oklahoma' and one of Russell's better songs, 'Of Thee I Sing'. Three Dylan songs include a soulful 'Hard Rain'. The album's best moment comes at the end with the definitive reading of George Harrison's 'Beware of Darkness'. Gospel and southern Gothic were never far from the surface, or each other, and he brings chiaroscuro to this song about Eastern mysticism.

Rockit   Herbie Hancock

(Michael Beinhorn/Herbie Hancock/Bill Laswell) ❋ Columbia ❋ 1983 ❋
Appears on: *Future Shock*

"The last few records I don't consider jazz at all," Herbie Hancock said in relation to his groundbreaking 1983 album. After a long journey from bop to fusion and funk, Hancock enlisted Bill Laswell to help him find a relationship with hip-hop.

Laswell was an important player in the art rock scene of New York with his own group, Material. Laswell's tastes went from classic jazz and fusion though to European art rock, disco and hip-hop. *Future Shock* embraces all of these styles in a completely original sound.

Laswell enlisted his Material partner Michael Beinhorn and a group of downtown art rock stars including Anton Fier, Bernard Fowler, Nicky Skopelitis, plus Fred Frith and drummer du jour Sly Dunbar. He then added DJ Grandmixer D.ST on turntables. This crew, plus Hancock's particular sense of funk and jazz vocabulary, created a techno/electro/hip-hop crossover. The song 'Rockit', with its MTV-friendly video, became a smash hit.

"I had just finished doing a series of hip-hop records and I was very tired," Laswell recalled in Stuart Nicholson's *Jazz Rock: A History*. "I wanted to do something crazy and experimental." Laswell cut a track, 'Rockit', with Grandmixer D.ST and took it to Hancock, who wasn't certain how to react. Laswell directed Hancock's parts and in less than three hours had finished the track. He took it to an audio shop to test out some speakers and after a few moments of play, "for a few weird seconds there was a feeling in the room like something was happening. I turned around and there was literally like a hundred kids going, 'What was that.' At that moment we realised what we had done. And then it blew up."

The Nips Are Getting Bigger Mental As Anything

(Martin Plaza) ❋ Regular ❋ 1979 ❋ Appears on: *Get Wet*

In the '60s, art schools were the crucibles of blues bands. Mental As Anything were the epitome of an art school band, given that they met at Alexander Mackie, Sydney's leading art school in the mid-'70s. Reg Mombassa (Chris O'Doherty), his brother Pete, Martin Plaza (nee Murphy), Wayne 'Bird' Delisle (David Twohill) and Andrew 'Greedy' Smith had the most humble of intentions – drinking beer

pretty much – behind forming the group. Their Monday night stand at the Unicorn Hotel, however, soon became a hive of hipsters paying $0.80 to hear versions of Roy Orbison, the Monkees or Michael and the Messengers' 'Just Like Romeo and Juliet'. Gradually original songs began to appear in the set.

The Mentals' signature tune, 'The Nips Are Getting Bigger', was an ode to alcohol and heartbreak coloured by a primitive, cheesy organ sound and the Zen bass of Peter O'Doherty. The song is witty and true. A perfect power pop anthem and possibly the best 45 to come out of Australia in the entire decade.

The fledgling Regular Records hastily put the Mentals into the studio for their debut album, produced by regular co-supremo Cameron Allen. "The first two records that we made were Darlinghurst records," Martin Plaza said. "They were badly executed and not that well considered but with a naïve charm." He is being typically and unnecessarily modest.

Mental As Anything celebrated laziness and dissolute behaviour with songs like 'The Nips' and 'Business and Pleasure Don't Mix'. They had their finger on the pulse of the modern world as only a bunch of slack art students could.

Interstellar Overdrive Pink Floyd

(Syd Barrett/Nick Mason/Roger Waters/Richard Wright) ❋ Harvest ❋ 1967 ❋
Appears on: *Piper at the Gates of Dawn*

Dubbed "space rock," this instrumental was recorded at the Floyd's sessions for their debut single, 'Arnold Layne', and then revisited on their debut album, *Piper at the Gates of Dawn*. The song marked the transition from psychedelic pop group to something else – an English jamming band heading off into their own universe. At this stage, Syd Barrett was still at the helm, having not yet disappeared into his own psychotic cosmos.

According to legend the song started from manager Peter Jenner humming Love's 'Little Red Book' at Barrett, who picked the melody out on his guitar and brought it to the Floyd, who improvised the rest.

Barrett named the group after two obscure blues musicians and their initial interest was in emulating American records. However, as Nick Mason has observed, they weren't particularly accomplished musicians. Nonetheless, they were lauded by the London underground scene of the late '60s, with newspapers like the *International Times* and venues like UFO London emulating the hip scene of San Francisco. Pink Floyd became the house act. This freeform environment and accessible LSD encouraged the group to stretch out and play to their strengths – no matter how long it took (in the case of this track, 9:41). Richard Wright's keyboards laid epic textures for Barrett's idiosyncratic guitar, and Mason's steady hand on the tempos allowed for the Floyd to create free-flowing, elegant and sometimes unsettling pieces. This might have been the beginning of British psychedelia but it was also the inspiration for a million insufferable ambient tapes.

'Interstellar Overdrive' was, then, the template for the Floyd's first golden era and it was followed by similar favourites – 'Saucerful of Secrets' and 'Set the Controls for the Heart of the Sun'. Syd Barrett was soon gone, replaced by David Gilmore, who encouraged a more sober approach.

"Syd was fantastic, a great guy, but the Pink Floyd he was in was a completely different band to the one that came afterwards," said Gilmore. "If people say we weren't the same after Syd left, fair enough. The first album was English whimsy at its best, with large slices of psychedelia thrown in, but it bears very little resemblance to anything we've tried to do since." 'Interstellar Overdrive' was the bridge to that gap.

I Want You (She's So Heavy) The Beatles

(John Lennon/Paul McCartney) ✳ Apple ✳ 1969 ✳ Appears on: *Abbey Road*

In the '60s, rock & roll music created pop culture. Essentially unschooled musicians and lyricists were taken seriously as artists for the first time in history and this upward cultural mobility meant that rock musicians rubbed shoulders with, and were influenced by, more serious and academic artists and they started to incorporate those ideas into pop. When one of the Beatles was involved in that exchange then the result immediately went out into the culture at large.

Yoko Ono's influence on John Lennon was significant – her minimalist theory and practice in the visual arts and the avant-garde milieu from which she came reinvigorated Lennon's work. Often the results were unimpressive, but 'I Want You (She's So Heavy)' is a masterstroke. The minimalist lyrics are sung almost as a mantra over swirling layers of noise.

Lennon's guitar and the bluesy melody build up, improvising and adding as they go, then moving into a jazzy section and finally into the ascending guitar riffs at the end of the song with the Beatles' voices blending and spiralling upwards. The Beatles also used an early Moog synthesiser on the track and brought in Billy Preston to add organ licks.

Lennon plays against the lack of lyric by using his voice to run through a whole gamut of emotions from petulance to pleading to screaming. The band, too, mirrors these emotional shifts. Then the song just ends.

Hotel California The Eagles

(Don Felder/Glen Frey/Don Henley) ❋ Asylum ❋ 1977 ❋ Appears on: *Hotel California*

The Eagles started as a humble country-rock outfit riding the coat-tails of Jackson Browne. By 1976 when they recorded 'Hotel California' they had become, mostly, a drug dependent parody of decadent rock stars. Camaraderie had become open hostility yet the high, keening vocals and the gnarly, meshing guitars were the sound of modern America.

'Hotel California' was their finest moment, in part for the extended Joe Walsh and Don Felder guitar tussle, but also for its self-loathing and its unsentimental appraisal of what was happening to America and to the Eagles.

The starting point of the song was drummer Don Henley's break-up with girlfriend Loree Rodkin. From there it got more universal. Henley told *Uncut* recently, "It's about loss of innocence, fading glory and decadence. I was trying to use California as a microcosm for the rest of the nation . . . I think it was about the dark underbelly of America at large." There's also a dig at Steely Dan: "They stab it with their steely knives but they just can't kill the beast."

No-one could. The chugging groove with a touch of reggae was largely from Felder.

The process of recording this album took seven months in between touring and commuting to the studio in Miami where it was recorded. The song itself is weighted down by the excess – too many drugs, too much money, too many concerts and too much pressure. By the end of the process the Eagles were over their peak and on the way out.

Sign o' the Times Prince

(Prince) ❋ Paisley Park ❋ 1987 ❋ Appears on: *Sign o' the Times*

By 1987, Prince was the gold standard by which almost every other artist was measured. His drive to keep pumping out new and provocative material, his changes of direction, of style, sound and groove set a cracking pace that few were able to match. In the '80s, marketing had overtaken the creative departments and careers were scheduled in the record label's financial forecasts. Artists were encouraged to be true to their branding. Prince, however, released records as he pleased and in whatever form he chose.

Sign o' the Times was originally intended to be a three-album set with a jazz tip but Warner Bros. baulked and it was cut down to a double. This was the first step in Prince's argument that Warner Bros. was stifling his creativity and that he was enslaved to the label.

In the end Prince wrote, recorded and performed almost the entire album and he took it off from his flower power period into a deeper soul-funk direction.

While still focused on being busy in the bedroom, *Sign o' the Times* also deals with wider social issues such as AIDS, gangs and racism.

The album was conceived and executed swiftly, marking the transition from the end of the *Revolution* period and the end of his relationship with Susannah Melvoin. The song 'If I Was Your Girlfriend' was, according to engineer Susan Rogers, a plea for Melvoin to have him back. Other people in Prince's circle identified 'Forever in My Life' as about her.

The icing on the cake was the title track – minimalist Curtis Mayfield's soul backing over a very direct lyric about AIDS and drugs. The song was written, recorded and mixed in a single day.

Saxophonist Eric Leeds said of the album, "There was a refreshing feeling about making his own music unencumbered again."

John Walker Blues Steve Earle

(Steve Earle) ✳ Artemis ✳ 2002 ✳ Appears on: *Jerusalem*

In reaching down to the personal, Steve Earle came close to finding the reasons behind this unreasonable situation in which we find ourselves.

Earle called his post-9/11 album *Jerusalem*. It's in that city that this holy war is going on and it's precisely in that part of the world, that symbolic sacred site, that the answer is also contained.

The most controversial track on the album is 'John Walker Blues'. Told from the viewpoint of John Walker Lindh, the Californian kid who joined the Taliban, it's the story of an American who wanted something to believe in: "Just an American boy, raised on MTV ... I seen all the boys in the soda pop bands and none of them looked like me." From that clearly follows the unsurprising acknowledgment that US consumer culture doesn't necessarily meet spiritual needs. Earle's John Walker isn't a warmonger, he's just following a calling from above.

Earle began his career as an outlaw Texan singer/songwriter in the mid-'70s although his career didn't really begin until a decade later and then was quickly brought to a halt by drug addiction and jail. Having straightened himself out, Earle has subsequently produced a series of classic albums, of which *Jerusalem* is up there with the best.

Certainly Earle retains his outlaw roots in as much as he refuses to settle on a particular style, and his albums flit from rock to acoustic country blues, bluegrass and indeed any place else he chooses. *Jerusalem* is musically somewhat outside the country styles; there are beds of keyboards and modal structures, especially in 'John Walker Blues', which ends with a chant from the Koran. It's not the most profound song, but it is rock & roll music doing what it's supposed to do.

It's All Too Much The Beatles

(George Harrison) ✳ Apple ✳ 1969 ✳ Appears on: *Yellow Submarine*

Written while on acid in 1967, George Harrison's feedback freak-out is one of the great Beatles tracks. While they had experimented with John Lennon's trippy dreamscapes and with McCartney's riffing rock, 'It's All Too Much' put both those things together and rocked the hell out of them. One session player noted, "George Harrison was in charge of the session. I don't think he knew what he wanted." It sounds like he wanted more. Harrison plays a fierce Hammond organ and then plugs in for a lead guitar battle with John Lennon, full of feedback and howling notes. McCartney just hangs on the one droning bass note. When things get dull he riffs on a recent hot single with a line from 'Sorrow'. Then there are the horns, the backing vocals and the handclaps. Harrison is also adapting the drones of Indian music to a full-on rock band. It's as though he's embracing the post-LSD enlightenment and he does it with an abandon that's not generally found on Beatles records.

Clearly the quiet Beatle was enjoying being noisy, but he had just found LSD and Ravi Shankar and was beginning his spiritual quest. As he sings here: "Show me that I'm everywhere/And get me home for tea."

In the Street Big Star

(Chris Bell/Alex Chilton) ※ Ardent ※ 1972 ※ Appears on: *#1 Record*

Alex Chilton was on the run from pop stardom when he formed the band that for so many rock critics defined pure pop for now people. Chilton had been the singer for the Box Tops and had a number of hits while still a teenager. By 1971 he had dropped out, been to New York and returned to Memphis looking to record. Through Ardent studios Chilton met songwriter Chris Bell and, with Jody Stephens and Andy Hummel, Big Star was born.

They took their name from the supermarket across the road from the studio and they took their sound from the Kinks, the Beatles and the Velvet Underground, with some soul and country. Mostly though it was jangly guitars. At the time the radio was dominated by southern boogie, Led Zeppelin or progressive rock, and Big Star wrote concise pop songs with innovative guitar textures. Nowhere was this better caught than on 'In the Street'. The riff for the song was copped from Blind Willie McTell and the recording sounds like Paul McCartney backed by the Rolling Stones.

The sound of the first Big Star album was the template for R.E.M. and the Replacements and indeed most of the first wave of college rock artists. According to Robert Gordon's *It Came From Memphis*, "Though they are ostensibly a pop band, there's an underlying menace to Big Star's work. They meld the winsome with the twisted."

This Charming Man The Smiths

(Johnny Marr/Morrissey) ※ Rough Trade ※ 1983 ※ Appears on: *The Smiths*

"Many people who go into this business think that they have to have a very aggressive machismo or a very aggressive stage image," singer Morrissey told Jon Savage in January 1984. "It's time for a different version: not everybody is like Ozzy Osbourne. The normal rock & roll terminology sounds like a chant of agony. I think we need more brains in popular music."

'This Charming Man' was a manifesto of the fey, the twee, the alternative bookish types of the '80s versus the bombastic rock stars. Kicking off with the spiky, spine-tingling guitar of Johnny Marr against the cartoonishly wimpy voice of Morrissey, the Smiths' second single was a war cry for passive aggressives. Morrissey's vocal and his word play emboldened thousands of fans who later became the alternative nation.

"Up until then, either you were a chart group with no substance or you were an indie group no-one got to hear," said Johnny Marr. "'This Charming Man' found a happy compromise. It brought a real commercial sound together with interesting lyrics and a good groove.'

You Really Got a Hold on Me The Beatles

(William 'Smokey' Robinson) ✳ Parlophone ✳ 1963 ✳ Appears on: *With the Beatles*

"The Beatles became quite experts on obscure records we'd never heard of, and they were mostly Motown or black rock & roll, the early Goffin and King numbers," said producer George Martin. "Those kinds of things. The real building stuff and of course, it was very, very good stuff."

The second Beatles album was recorded in five frantic months as the group rapidly ascended to being the toppermost of the poppermost. It was the first pop album to sell a million copies (the first album to do so was the *South Pacific* soundtrack). Most of the songs were cover versions and the best of them were the rereadings of Motown tracks.

"When they started out, back in the 'Love Me Do' days, they weren't good writers," Martin said. "They were a raw group whose main repertoire was other people's stuff. They stole unashamedly from existing records. It wasn't until they tasted blood that they realised they could actually do this, and that set them on the road to writing better songs."

John Lennon dominated this reading of the Miracles hit. He has an earthy insistence in his voice that matches the driving beat from Ringo Starr. Where the Motown original was a supplication, Lennon sings the song like he's half out of his mind with lust. The refrain becomes a chant or an incantation. The band's arrangement has a James Brown dynamic. While Motown tried to smooth the rough edges of R&B with sophistication, the Beatles' lack of sophistication really brought the song home. The track is best heard in mono as it appeared on *With the Beatles*.

Falling at Your Feet Bono & Daniel Lanois

(Bono/Daniel Lanois) ❋ Interscope ❋ 2000 ❋ Appears on: *The Million Dollar Hotel*

"We wrote it for *The Million Dollar Hotel* and I guess the lyrics could have made their way onto a U2 record," said Daniel Lanois. "I thought I wanted to give the song a bigger life. Bono started the lyrics with the 'falling at your feet' idea. The idea that no matter what bags you might be carrying, at some time in life you'll end up at a crossing point. It's a spiritual song. We share a fascination with old Simon & Garfunkel songs, so I put on the Afro and he put on the bangs."

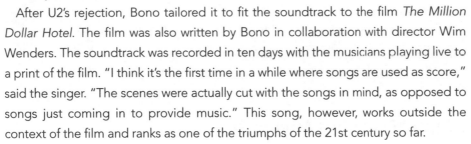

Lanois and Bono wrote the song together after the lyric had been rejected by U2. It's another one of Bono's list songs. A litany of humiliations and of moments of pride, the lyric resolves itself into a song of devotion – a hymn, in fact.

Although the song has another version on a Lanois record, this is the definitive moment where the backing is dark and delicate and the vocals carefully snake around each other.

After U2's rejection, Bono tailored it to fit the soundtrack to the film *The Million Dollar Hotel*. The film was also written by Bono in collaboration with director Wim Wenders. The soundtrack was recorded in ten days with the musicians playing live to a print of the film. "I think it's the first time in a while where songs are used as score," said the singer. "The scenes were actually cut with the songs in mind, as opposed to songs just coming in to provide music." This song, however, works outside the context of the film and ranks as one of the triumphs of the 21st century so far.

Overcome Tricky

(Marcella Detroit/Siobhan Fahey/Tricky) ❋ Island ❋ 1995 ❋ Appears on: *Maxinquaye*

The opening track of Tricky's first solo effort, *Maxinquaye*, is claustrophobic, paranoid and sensual all at the same time, like making love during an anxiety attack.

Maxinquaye was clearly an intense experience. The album was named after Tricky's mother, who died when he was four years old. The songs are sung by

Martina Topley-Bird, whom he met when she was a schoolgirl and who became the mother of his child. In this emotionally charged environment, the writer/producer smoked a huge amount of marijuana and tried to push the boundaries of trip hop and reggae.

"I'm always in a melancholy mood," he said. "When I was young my nan would have me sit in the middle of the floor listening to Billie Holiday and Nina Simone and stuff like that. She used to keep me up late at night and keep me home from school for company."

With that jazzy sensibility in the background, Tricky took his cues from the great Jamaican dub producers who build a groove and then bring elements to the fore and mix others in the background.

"Dub's an influence in that it isn't perfectionist. Dub, it's just bottom-end heavy with loads of noises, and it's not musically correct," he said. Tricky takes it to a new level on *Maxinquaye* – the structure is forever fluid, the elements are by turns paranoid, beautiful, delicate and abrasive, but somehow there is a logic here. On 'Overcome' the bass keeps a heartbeat pulse and the sound of breath is all promise and defeat and expectation.

It's at once dangerous and sexy. "I get beautiful girls in Italy come up to me and say, 'I have sex with my boyfriend to your album'," he said. "I really don't need to know that. I say, 'Why don't you have sex with me listening to my album?'"

I Ain't Marching Anymore Phil Ochs

(Phil Ochs) ✳ Elektra ✳ 1965 ✳ Appears on: *I Ain't Marching Anymore*

Phil Ochs had the misfortune to arrive on the Greenwich Village folk scene at the same time as Bob Dylan. Ochs was a folkie in the Guthrie tradition of broadsheet protest songs. Of a similar age to Dylan, Ochs wasn't in his class and, even after his suicide in 1976, was always discussed in comparison with his friend. He was partly known for Dylan's outburst: "Get out of the car, Ochs! You're not a folk singer; you're a journalist!"

The strident anti-war song 'I Ain't Marching Anymore' remains his best known work. Like so many folk songs it draws on history – the battles that made the Republic, and their human cost.

In the context of Vietnam in 1965 it was a powerful song that picked up the standard that Dylan had abandoned. Ochs remained politically active, although manic depression and alcoholism took their toll.

"For me songwriting was easy from 1961 to 1966 and then it got more and more difficult," Ochs told Bruce Pollack. "It could be alcohol; it could be the deterioration of the politics I was involved in. It could be a general deterioration of the country. Basically, the country and me were deteriorating simultaneously and that's probably why it stopped coming. Part of the problem was that there was never any pattern to my writing. The point of discipline is to create your own pattern so you can write, and I haven't done that. I always make plans to do that – I'm now thirty-three and I may or may not succeed. But ever since the late '60s that's constantly on my mind – discipline, training, get it together, clean up your act. I haven't been able to do it yet, but the impulse is as strong as ever. To my dying day I'll always think about the next possible song, even if it's twenty years from now. I'll never make the conscious decision to stop writing."

Some Velvet Morning Nancy Sinatra & Lee Hazlewood

(Lee Hazlewood) ❊ 1968 ❊ Reprise ❊ Appears on: *Nancy & Lee*

Lee Hazlewood was a radio DJ, producer and songwriter (he launched the career of superstar instrumentalist Duane Eddy). In the mid-'60s he was hanging around Reprise records when he was invited to help out the boss' daughter, Nancy Sinatra. She had been through a failed marriage and her career too was on the rocks when Hazlewood gave her 'These Boots Are Made for Walking', which, Hazlewood told Barney Hoskyns, he instructed her to sing "like you're a sixteen-year-old girl who goes out with forty-five year old truck drivers."

'These Boots' was a massive hit and has become a standard. It also set Sinatra's image as a girl with long legs, short skirts and a tough attitude. She was luscious sex kitten with attitude.

The Sinatra/Hazlewood team spun out a series of hits (including the Frank/Nancy duet 'Something Stupid'). Hazlewood was not your average songsmith. His own material tended towards the surreal. He understood the heightened romanticism of orchestral pop while developing his own southern Gothic stories. And he drank a lot.

Hazlewood's part-Indian ancestry made him darkly handsome, his face shaped around a handlebar moustache. He began recording with Sinatra, most notably on the album *Nancy & Lee*, where her blonde playfulness played against his brooding, troubled masculinity.

Sinatra told Hoskyns that "Lee always had some kind of underlying message in

his songs. I guess it's partly what he used to call 'beauty and the beast', the young girl and the older guy – that fantasy. We didn't have an affair, we didn't have a physical relationship and yet we created something that indicated that we did and I guess people thought that was interesting because we were so different in age."

"When Nancy did her songs she was a ballsy, shit-kickin' broad. When we did our songs together, we were some space-o unit, or an old man foolin' with a young girl, or whatever it was," said Hazlewood. "Most of our duets are not double meaning, they're kinda triple meaning. If you're some Santa Monica doper sitting on the street, then it's a

dope song. If you're just some little innocent girl sitting in Nebraska, it's just a song. And then if you're really a Nancy and Lee fan, it means a lot of other things too. It's everything combined."

This is nowhere more evident than on the gorgeous 'Some Velvet Morning' with its lush strings and psychedelic melody. It's a lyric that alternates spacey lines about flowers with a straightforward promise of lovemaking. It's a schizophrenic song that is the more alluring for its mystery.

"He was an amazing writer," said ex-girlfriend Suzi Jane Hokom. "He'd sit there with his Scotch and these things would just come out of him. He was a very complex guy, a dichotomy unto himself. There's a part of Lee that's just out there, but there's still the guy from Oklahoma, the wildcatter's son … there's a real dark side to Lee, and you can hear that in some of his music."

Locomotive Breath Jethro Tull

(Ian Anderson) ※ Chrysalis ※ 1971 ※ Appears on: *Aqualung*

Another perfectly good British band ruined by the concept album. Tull was the brainchild of Ian Anderson, who played the flute and sang while standing on one leg. When the group formed in 1967 they had the folk thing, some jazz, the blues and a certain Englishness all going for them. 'Cat's Squirrel' from the first album (*This Was*) is an excellent example of their revved-up blues style.

There were, even from the beginning, signs that Anderson was too big for his thigh-high boots. There's a Rashaan Roland Kirk number on the first album and the co-write with JS Bach on the second is the giveaway. Anderson, with his unkempt long hair, raincoat and tweeds (or worse still, tights and codpiece), was an amazing front man whose manic energy on stage matched the pumping and spiralling heavy bluesy bottom end. Each of their records has its charms and at least one or two timeless cuts.

Rock & roll wasn't ever going to be big enough for Anderson, though. Like Peter Townshend, he yearned to make some "statements". The first of these was *Aqualung*. A song cycle involving a derelict and God and organised religion, Anderson's writing was increasingly constrained by his pretensions. Those moments where the group was able to fly, such as 'Locomotive Breath', 'My God', 'Cross-Eyed Mary' and 'Wind Up' were gems despite themselves. The band cooks even when the singer is overdone.

Anderson followed this album with *Thick as a Brick*, which was one dodgy narrative song extended over three-quarters of an hour. The sheer nerve of Tull to make such an album made them heroes, beloved of heavy metal fans across the USA.

Aqualung is a stepping stone to progressive rock and remains Tull's finest moment.

Remember (Walkin' in the Sand) The Shangri-Las

(Shadow Morton) ※ Redbird ※ 1964 ※ Appears on: *Golden Hits of the Shangri-Las*

The Shangri-Las had a sexuality that would steal the breath right out of your body. They were cute and pure but you could tell that they knew what was really going on and that, given the right boy, they would go there. Mary Weiss whispered stories of suburban romance. The most epic of their songs is 'Leader of the Pack' – a song that was revolutionary when it came out and has now entered the vernacular. But the Shangri-Las were never better than on their first disc.

Shadow Morton was a childhood acquaintance of Ellie Greenwich, who, by 1963, had become a very successful songwriter in the Brill Building factory. Greenwich's partner, Jeff Barry, dared Morton to make a record in four days.

Morton rounded up musicians and a local girl group, the Shangri-Las – sisters Mary and Betty Weiss, and twins Mary Ann and Marge Gander. Although there were officially four, generally the twins rotated according to other commitments.

According to his own legend, Shadow Morton was on his way to the studio to cut his first record when he discovered that he didn't have a song so he pulled over to the side of the road and wrote 'Remember', complete with a four-minute spoken introduction. It's the tale of a girl who has just been dumped by her boyfriend and her world has ended.

The song is magnificent in its simplicity. Mary's vocal lags just behind the beat from a vamping piano (played by Billy Joel). Everything is compressed and disciplined as though her chest is barely able to contain the devastation and the tragedy. Then comes the chorus with the girls – release! Reminiscence of the good times. Although even there, the relationship is muted and constrained.

Rock & roll music just doesn't get more passionate than this.

Morton found them nice cinematic pop tunes about the lives of girls who do. The Shangri-Las had other hits – notably 'Out in the Streets' and 'Give Him a Great Big Kiss'. But we always remember the first time.

LA Blues The Stooges

(Iggy Pop/Dave Alexander/Ron Asheton/Scott Asheton) ✳ Elektra ✳ 1970 ✳
Appears on: *Fun House*

The closing track of the second Stooges album is sleazy, sweaty, honking, squalling and as out of control as rock music gets.

Where the Who and Jimi Hendrix used auto-destruction in their finale, anti-destruction was the Stooges' act. Off stage as well as on. Their first album was nihilistic and apathetic but the second was hyper-charged and purposeful and epic.

"We said, right, what you're doing is trying to get intoxicated, trying to get sexually gratified, trying to get out there. We stepped into that vortex and showed them the vulgarity, the base side that they pretended didn't exist," said Iggy Pop of the Stooges. "And the other thing that would feed my fire was the way that audiences would fail to receive what we gave them. They'd look at us like this music was bullshit. People would shake their fists and give me the finger, which gave me an easy confrontation. That was very juvenile of me, very jive, but it was really good entertainment, I tell ya!"

Having signed the Stooges and after little success with the first album, Elektra assigned Don Galluci to produce the second LP. His claim to fame was as a member of the Kingsmen, who had had a hit with 'Louie Louie'. The Stooges took that piece of dumb rock and disassembled it, and turned the three chords into a whole new style of music.

Gallucci's approach to the album was to get the band to run down their set in the studio as close to the live experience as they could get. The Stooges came off tour in Los Angeles with their confidence primed from playing live and went straight into the studio to up the ante.

'LA Blues' is the sound of a garage band attempting free jazz mixed with rock. The track on *Fun House* comes in at just under five minutes; the original on the *Fun House* sessions was an eighteen-minute jam.

"That was our tribute to ourselves, our original roots," said Ron Asheton. "I was deeply into John Coltrane and Pharaoh Sanders. Our whole set was a freak-out. We'd say, 'Now it's time to freak out.' So we'd end the set, we'd be playing a tune and it just like ... Unlike the record, where they made it a separate thing, it would just digress or progress into the total free form. I thought, 'Let one go and go wherever you wanna go until you're totally peaked out and then just leave the stage.' I'd have blood all over my guitar and strings; I'd loose my pick.

"But they wanted to make 'LA Blues' separate and it was way sterile compared to how we usually do it. It's way sterile compared to how we really did it. I got a couple of good things in there. But it was much more violent in person because it was the culmination of the show."

It was almost the end of the Stooges too. Shortly afterwards they became junkies and the original band fell apart. 'LA Blues' is rock at its most intense and abstract; its sound wouldn't return for fifteen years, until Sonic Youth and Nirvana broke through.

Within You Without You The Beatles

(George Harrison) ✳ Parlophone ✳ 1967 ✳

Appears on: *Sgt Pepper's Lonely Hearts Club Band*

The Beatles' concept album has attracted way more attention and been given far more artistic baggage than the disc can carry. The Beatles were obviously taking their work to a new level. Hailed as a concept record, there is no discernible theme – musical or lyrical – through the songs. By Beatles' standards they're not particularly good songs at that. The production techniques were interesting. The artwork was unusual and the album was a phenomenon. It's now almost fifty years since Sgt Pepper taught the band to play and pretty much only three of the tunes have lasted, Harrison's 'Within You Without You' being one. Where 'A Day in the Life' deconstructed pop, 'Within You Without You' really opened pop up to ethnic influence in a whole new way. Not only were the Beatles using non-Western instruments, they were doing it in conjunction with non-Western spirituality.

The impact of George Harrison's interest in the East cannot be overstated. When he became interested in the Maharishi and then Hindu mysticism, the world followed. After George the world suddenly had heard of Krishna. The influence in the West of transcendental meditation and meditation in general, the Hare Krishnas, the Orange People, the gurus Muktananda and Maharaji is a direct result of Harrison. India suddenly became hip. The hippy highway from London to Kathmandu was open for business and all things Indian were popular.

Harrison came to mysticism by way of music. In August 1965, David Crosby, then with the Byrds, introduced Harrison to the music of sitar virtuoso Ravi Shankar. He was immediately intrigued and by December that year was adding sitar licks to the *Rubber Soul* album. Six months later he met Shankar and went to India for six weeks of intensive study.

This song was written early the following year. According to writer David Fricke, Harrison was at Klaus Voorman's house for dinner when the first line came to him: "We were talking – about the space between us all." Voorman, a friend of the Beatles since the Hamburg days, had a new harmonium and Harrison was "doodling on it, playing to amuse myself when 'Within You' started to come."

The lyric reads on the one hand as an interpretation of Hindu notions of being and nothingness, but on the other it also sounds like a song about estrangement from the Beatles. None of the other Beatles appear on the track — an Indian ensemble, an orchestra and Beatles' confidant Neil Aspinall accompany Harrison.

'Within You Without You' stuck out amongst the novelty tracks but it was also the first time that what would be called world music was thrust into the mainstream. It has lasted much better than 'Being for the Benefit of Mr Kite'.

"It was an interesting song," said George Martin. "I find it more interesting now than I did then."

Let's Get Funky Hound Dog Taylor & the Houserockers

(Hound Dog Taylor) ❋ Alligator ❋ 1975 ❋ Appears on: *Beware of the Dog*

"Hound Dog was sort of a throw back," said Bruce Iglauer, who started Alligator Records specifically to release the Hound. "He didn't use a bass because bass players couldn't keep up with him. Like what had happened before in other blues bands, he used a second guitar for bass lines. There was a drive that you couldn't get out of a Fender bass. The sounds were so raw and distorted — Hound Dog played on $50 Japanese guitars through Sears amplifiers and cracked speakers. The whole attitude was 'Who gives a damn? We're just playin' for fun.' The music basically could have been played at a juke joint in Mississippi next door to where Muddy Waters was playing in 1949. It was totally unvarnished by virtue of the energy level and the distortion."

In my opinion, 'Let's Get Funky' as recorded here is the absolute apotheosis of rock & roll. It doesn't get more joyful, more raw, more Zen than this. Taylor sets up an insistent riff and then just rides it for absolutely all its worth. This is music that is pointless to intellectualise about and impossible to deny. It's sexy and dirty and irresponsible and pure.

Theodore Roosevelt 'Hound Dog' Taylor was fifty-five when Bruce Iglauer discovered him playing reckless slide guitar in clubs with Brewer Phillips hanging on to the bass lines on guitar and Ted Harvey pounding out a houserocking beat for $15 a night.

Iglauer set up Alligator for a first eponymous album, which was an enormous hit, and then followed it with *Natural Boogie*. The songs are perfect, snappy vehicles for lewd lyrics and incredible slide guitar.

Compositionally, *Natural Boogie* has the best tracks: 'Hawaiian Boogie', 'Roll Your Moneymaker', 'See Me in the Evening' and 'Sadie', but it's this live album, released shortly after his death in 1975, that captures the sheer insanity (and does include the classic 'Give Me Back My Wig').

It's worth noting that Hound Dog's two guitars and no bass have become a template for alternative blues acts in the '90s such as the Jon Spencer Blues Explosion and more famously the White Stripes.

"They didn't rehearse," said Iglauer. "That was sort of a rule. They followed that rule very closely. They also followed the rule that you *really* shouldn't perform unless you'd had a reasonable amount of alcohol. He set an example for that. In that regard, he was sort of an exemplary bandleader."

Bridge over Troubled Water Simon & Garfunkel

(Paul Simon) ❋ Columbia ❋ 1970 ❋ Appears on: *Bridge over Troubled Water*

Bridge over Troubled Water is one of the great statements about modern relationships. The friendship between Simon and Garfunkel – ripped apart by ego and competing careers – and Simon's relationship with his wife, with his audience and with music are laid out in perfectly measured melodies, decorated by massed voices over the course of an LP.

The album as a whole is a masterpiece of pop, its production (by Simon, Garfunkel and Roy Halee) is flawless, and the lyrics are multi-dimensional, wry and often heartbreaking.

'Bridge over Troubled Water' was written in Los Angeles, in the same house George Harrison immortalised in 'Blue Jay Way'. Simon was listening to a Swan Silvertones' recording of 'O Mary Don't You Weep' and thinking about his wife Peggy.

Two verses came quickly and he presented the song to Garfunkel, who initially declined the lead vocal.

"We were all renting this house. Me and Artie and Peggy were living in this house with a bunch of other people throughout the summer," Simon recalled. "I said, 'Here's a song; it's in G, but I want it in E flat. I want it to have a gospel piano.' Each night we'd work on the piano part until Larry Knechtel really honed it into a good part. Now, the song was originally two verses, and in the studio, as Larry was playing it, we decided – I believe it was Artie's idea – to add another verse. I always felt that you could clearly see that it was written afterwards. It just doesn't sound like the first two verses.

"Then the piano part was finished. Then we added bass – two basses, one way up high, the high bass notes. Then we added vibes in the second verse just to make the thing ring a bit. Then we recorded the drum with a tape-reverb that made the drum part sound different, because of that after-beat effect. Then we gave it out to have a string part written. This was all in Los Angeles and then we came back to New York and did the vocals. Artie spent several days on the vocals.

"I didn't think it was a hit, because I didn't think they'd play a five-minute song on the radio. Actually, I just wrote it to be two verses done on the piano. But when we got into the studio, Artie and Roy wanted to add a third verse and drums to make it huge. Their tendency was to make things bigger and lusher and sweeter. Mine was to keep things more raw. And that mixture, I think, is what produced a lot of the hits. It probably would have been a hit with two verses on the piano, but it wouldn't have been the monster hit that it became. I think a lot of what people were responding to was that soaring melody at the end.

"Funny, I'm reminded of the last verse. It was about Peggy, whom I was living with at the time: 'Sail on, silver girl … Your time has come to shine' was half a joke, because she was upset one day when she had found two or three grey hairs on her head."

The song was the crowning glory on an album about mixed feelings. Two of the best tracks were about the separation of Simon & Garfunkel ('The Only Living Boy in New York' and 'So Long Frank Lloyd Wright'). 'The Boxer' was a harrowing piece of self-laceration but elsewhere Simon affirmed his passion for music of all kinds.

'Bridge' was to be their biggest hit. But for many years it was a sore point with Simon, in part because of its ubiquity.

"When I wrote and first sang the line 'Like a bridge over troubled water, I will lay me down,' I burst into tears," Simon revealed in an interview some ten years after the fact. "I was thinking of Peggy. That I would lie down and be a bridge for her. It was an overwhelming feeling coupled with that melody. Now it's been sung so many times by so many people that I have no feeling whatsoever for it. But at the moment of creation, it was huge."

Walk on the Wild Side Lou Reed

(Lou Reed) ❄ RCA ❄ 1972 ❄ Appears on: *Transformer*

The cultural impact of this song is only matched by its perfection as a pop track. Lou Reed put the downtown Manhattan scene – the hustlers, whores, transvestites and desperates – into the mass media and he did it without romanticising them.

The best description of the inspiration for this track is from Reed himself on the *Take No Prisoners* live album. He describes, with many asides, how he ran away

from the imminent success of the Velvet Underground and while unemployed and with no prospects was commissioned to write songs for a stage musical version of Nelson Algren's novel *Walk on the Wild Side*. The project faded but Reed kept the title and wrote a talking blues about the people who hung around Andy Warhol's Factory – stud actor Joe Dallesandro, the transvestite/transsexual superstars Holly Woodlawn, Candy Darling and Jackie Curtis. Warhol's enduring creation was to take these flowers in the dustbin and call them superstars – he glamorised outsiders and turned the notion of status on its head. Warhol's view of what was glamorous or cool eventually became everybody's. Of course, one of his first makeovers was the Velvet Underground and Reed remained forever (mostly) grateful.

When he made the *Transformer* album Reed was pretty much nobody. The Velvets were never popular. Reed's first solo album was a flop. The fact that David Bowie agreed to produce was a key factor in this record being made at all. Bowie's production is masterful. The sweet touches in the vocal harmonies, and the quick and deceptively simple arrangements are in large part due to Bowie.

The hook in 'Walk on the Wild Side', though, belongs to Herbie Flowers. It's the most famous bass line in pop music. Flowers, an old session hand, played a simple, stripped-back double bass. He claims that he suggested adding an electric bass part so he could double his fee. With the electric bass counterpointing the acoustic part and this wonderful fairy story lyric, the whole song is virtually there.

Now with the Top 40 audience he had so long claimed he craved, Reed followed the sexy and witty *Transformer* with a concept album about junkies dying. So much for success. "It was a fluke anyway," he deadpanned.

The Captain Kasey Chambers

(Kasey Chambers) ✳ EMI ✳ 1999 ✳ Appears on: *The Captain*

Ostensibly country music, Kasey Chambers' solo debut defied many categories. She had played in the family business, the Dead Ringer Band; however, on her own she fits better with alternative rock girl Jill Sobule or alternative country star Lucinda Williams. These songs evoke real life as country music is supposed to, but they also have the kinds of quirks to mark the arrival of a truly gifted songsmith.

Songs like 'You Got the Car', 'We're All Gonna Die' and 'Last Hard Bible' have the resonance of great blues while 'These Pines' is wonderfully emotive and oddly personal. Similarly, 'Southern Kinda Life' is so caught up in the Nashville tradition that it sounds stupid coming from an Australian.

Speaking of odd, however, the title track is the most un-PC song ever sung by a woman. One hopes that this extreme offer of subjugation is addressed to a deity rather than a lover, but the melody is so infectious that you really want to forget the sentiment. But that's the mark of Chambers as a writer. She had no barriers and simply let the words come unfiltered. Her voice, too, reflected the honesty. Fortunately perhaps, Chambers forgot the Captain and went on to marry someone else.

Brass in Pocket The Pretenders

(James Honeyman-Scott/Chrissie Hynde) ✳ Real/Sire ✳ 1980 ✳
Appears on: *The Pretenders*

"I have no illusions," Chrissie Hynde told the NME's Chris Salewicz shortly after the release of The Pretenders' eponymous debut. "I know how low the standards are. I'm aware of why things happen in the music business. I know why the album did so well; we got our timing right.

"The market was wide open for a band like ours with a girl vocalist and solid, simple, straight ahead rock songs. It sounds perfect on the radio, too, which is a large reason why it happened in America. And that is the exact reason why it sold 300,000 copies in California alone. I mean, why should we sell records there? Because, quite simply, it doesn't jar when it's played next to Foreigner or Styx.

"That said, though, I hated 'Brass in Pocket' with a vengeance. Fuckin' Ada. I hated it so much that if I was in Woolworth's and they started playing it I'd have to run out of the store."

The Pretenders were absolutely the right band at the right time. Their rightness was largely due to Hynde, whose concise songcraft came out of a tomboy persona with a sultry chanteuse voice.

Hynde, originally from Akron, Ohio, was in London for the birth of British punk – she worked at Malcolm McLaren's Sex Shop, taught guitar to Johnny Rotten, palled around with the Clash's Mick Jones and the superstar rock journalist Nick Kent.

"I'd arrived in England naïvely thinking that I'd bump into Marc Bolan or Jeff Beck on every street corner," she said. "All I had was a coupla hundred dollars and three albums by Iggy and Lou Reed, and of course it was instant disillusion – I was living in these really cheap, skuzzy hotels, having to sell leather handbags in one of those sucker tourist markets on Oxford Street and modelling at St Martin's School of Art. And, like, no-one knew what the hell I was talking about when I mentioned the Stooges or Lou Reed."

Once Hynde had her band together – James Honeyman-Scott on guitar, Pete Farndon on bass and drummer Martin Chambers – Nick Lowe spent a day in the studio recording a single. The A-side, a cover of an obscure Kinks song, 'Stop Your Sobbing', was an instant hit.

Hynde's songs were carefully observed vignettes of life made spectacular by Honeyman-Scott's guitars and Hynde's elegantly detached delivery. Hynde, sometimes bitchy, erotic or wistful, told it like it was in the spirit of punk but without the alienated trappings.

The album cruised from one hook to another. Producer Chris Thomas specialised in taking melodic garage bands (including the Sex Pistols) and casting their vignettes as epics. Under pressure to follow up the hits – each of the first three Pretenders 45s was a smash hit – Hynde's entire repertoire went onto the record. Meanwhile the group was finding its feet after fewer than a dozen shows. All these elements cooked *The Pretenders* into one of the best pop albums of all time.

The Pretenders had the perfect sound – they had the '60s pop moves and the punk rock credibility but unlike most other punk groups they could play. Honeyman-Scott's guitar parts bristled with ideas – sparkling melodic touches that complemented Hynde's prickly lyrics. Chambers and Farndon put a soulful bedrock under Hynde whether she was bitter or wistful – as is the case with 'Brass in Pocket', which secured their place at the top of the tree.

"We're all on £50 a week," she said when quizzed about her instant stardom. "I've got to leave my flat tomorrow and move in with a friend, I've got no bank account, no publisher and no management – at least nothing signed, it's all on a trust basis. I'm not really that concerned with whether I'm being ripped off. I'm in too much of a fizzy, I'm too busy writing songs."

Highway Patrolman   Bruce Springsteen
(Bruce Springsteen) ✳ Columbia ✳ 1982 ✳ Appears on: *Nebraska*

No-one in 1982 is reported to have heard *Nebraska* and announced: "I have heard the future of folk music!" No-one, it has to be said, was looking for the future of folk music. Certainly not from Bruce Springsteen. Viewed by the industry as career suicide and shunned by most of his fans, *Nebraska* is a high point in Bruce Springsteen's career. It has inspired one classic film (*The Indian Runner*) and a sublime cover version by Johnny Cash ('Johnny 99') amongst many other tributes. *Nebraska* has survived the slings and arrows of fashion. It has been consistently magnificent.

Although the '80s album *The River* had been Springsteen's strongest work to date, his personal life was a mess. He was depressed and isolated. He was also picking up on the pall that had fallen over America as a consequence of the recession and Reaganomics. Springsteen was reading Flannery O'Connor and watching films about the American soul – Louis Malle's *Atlantic City*, Terence Mallick's *Badlands*, John Huston's *Wise Blood*, and *True Confessions*, written by Joan Didion and John Gregory Dunne.

In January 1982, at home alone with his tape recorder, he recorded *Nebraska* in less than three hours (the same sessions also produced the songs 'Born in the USA' and 'Pink Cadillac'). With minimal backing over a spare vocal and guitar, this was a bleak album with none of the redemptive moments Springsteen had previously supplied. Moreover, the songs failed to respond to the band and in the end it was the home recordings that became *Nebraska*. Fifty years previously, Alan Lomax had taken primitive tape recorders into the depths of America and returned with songs that became the billion-dollar rock & roll business and superstar brands of which

Bruce Springsteen was the apotheosis. Now, in his bedroom, Springsteen reversed the journey.

Springsteen was looking at the core of his own beliefs and family. There are tales like 'Used Cars' and especially 'My Father's House' which come literally from that experience. From there he was able to extrapolate more generally; the moral dilemma of family has rarely been as well expressed as on 'Highway Patrolman'. Nihilism has rarely been better expressed as on the album's final cut, 'Reason to Believe', which opens with a vignette of a man poking a dog's carcass by the side of the highway hoping that the animal will come back to life.

"When I wrote *Nebraska* . . . I'd found the record's centre. The songs tapped into white gospel and early Appalachian music, as well as the blues. In small detail – the slow twirling of a baton, the twisting of a ring on a finger – they had found their character," Springsteen wrote in his book, *Songs*.

"If there's a theme that runs through the record, it's the thin line between stability and that moment when time stops and everything goes black, when the things that connect you to your world – your job, your family, friends, your faith, the love and grace in your heart – fail you. I wanted the music to feel like a waking dream and the record to move like poetry. I wanted the blood on it to feel destined and fateful."

Comfortably Numb Pink Floyd

(David Gilmore/Roger Waters) ✳ EMI ✳ 1979 ✳ Appears on: *The Wall*

Pretty much the last significant gasp from Pink Floyd, *The Wall* was, like so much of Floyd's work, on the brink of insanity. Roger Waters conceived the album in an epiphany of self-hatred and contempt for his audience while on stage. He spat on a fan. Then this huge double album was gradually vomited out. The tale of a rock star whose fame had sent him mad is also an essay on alienation.

Waters had his demons – troubled childhood, father who died in WWII – and he thought the rest of the group were not much better. He fired keyboard player Rick Wright during the sessions for this album and producer Bob Ezrin owed his job to an ability to keep some peace between Waters and guitarist Dave Gilmore.

Insanity had dogged the band since it lost its founder, Syd Barrett, but Waters also empathised. "On the couple of occasions in my life where I have felt myself approaching mental breakdown it has felt like delirium," he said.

As the group was facing bankruptcy at the time, there was a pressing need for a new album, so whoever had the idea was bound to get a green light.

"But there were things about it where I thought, 'Oh no, here we go again – it's all about the war, about his mother, about his father being lost.' I'd hoped he could get through all this and eventually he could deal with other stuff, but he had a fixation," keyboard player Rick Wright told *MOJO*. "Every song was written in the same tempo, same key, same everything. Possibly if we were not in this financial situation we might have said, 'We don't like these songs,' and things might have been different. But Roger has this material, Dave and I didn't have any, so we'll do it."

"Initially I had two images – of building a wall across the stage, and of the sadomasochistic relationship between audience and band, the idea of an audience being bombed and the ones being blown to pieces applauding the loudest because they're the centre of action, even as victims," said Waters. "There is something macabre and a bit worrying about that relationship – that we will provide a PA system so loud that it can damage you and that you will fight to sit right in front of it so you can be damaged as much as possible – which is where the idea of Pink metamorphosed into a Nazi demagogue began to generate from."

Ezrin constructed a scenario from the songs at the beginning of the project around which the album could be built. As part of the process Gilmore also contributed ideas while the others sat on the sidelines.

The album's centrepiece is the last real collaboration between Gilmore and Waters: 'Comfortably Numb'.

"Things like 'Comfortably Numb' are really the last embers of Roger and my ability to work collaboratively together – my music, his words," Gilmore told *MOJO*. "I had the basic part of the music done. I gave Roger the bits of music, he wrote some words, he came in and said, 'I want to sing this line here, can we extend this by so many bars so I can do that,' so I said, 'OK, I'll put something in there.'"

"'Comfortably Numb' started off as a demo of Dave's – a piece in D with a lovely, soaring chorus and a very moody verse," said Ezrin. "At first Roger had not planned to include any of Dave's material but we had things that needed filling in. I fought for this song and insisted that Roger work on it. My recollection is that he did so grudgingly, but he did it. He came back with this spoken-word verse and a lyric in the chorus that to me still stands out as one of the greatest ever written. The marriage of that lyric and Dave's melodies and emotionally spectacular solo – every time I hear that song I get goosebumps."

I Can Feel the Fire Ron Wood

(Ron Wood) ✳ Warner Bros. ✳ 1974 ✳ Appears on: *I've Got My Own Album to Do*

The real title of this album should be *I've Got My Own Album to Do and It's Better than What My Superstar Mates are Doing*. Ron Wood is the most gregarious man in British rock and his first solo album features Rolling Stones, George Harrison, David Bowie (uncredited), Rod Stewart and the Faces, aided by some of the best sidemen of the era. Unlike so many similar albums, Wood's solo venture sounds like a house party. The groove, mostly from Andy Newmark and Willie Weeks, is pretty much unstoppable, especially on tracks like the opener 'I Can Feel the Fire' with Jagger and Richards helping out. This is arguably the last great Rolling Stones cut. And on top of that is layered the work of the cream of British rock. These sessions in the early spring of 1974 at Wood's Richmond house occurred just as the British invasion artists ran out of steam, and the album sounds like the going away party. The egos, including George Harrison, Rod Stewart and Paul McCartney, had been checked at the door and the rhythm section is left to shine. If Wood had more than a thin and rasping voice, perhaps this track might have been a hit, but that would have destroyed the bonhomie.

What Are Their Names? David Crosby

(David Crosby/Jerry Garcia/Phil Lesh/Michael Shrieve/Neil Young) ✳ Atlantic ✳ 1971 ✳ Appears on: *If I Could Only Remember My Name*

David Crosby's talent is so fleeting that its moments in full flight are absolute treasures. Crosby had been a founding Byrd and later of Crosby, Stills, Nash and Young, where his harmonic sense was so subtle it has rarely been given its due, but it has lifted both these enterprises to a higher level. Crosby's songs tend to be the weird, political and edgy ones that put the backbone onto the platitudes of his comrades.

Crosby's other talent is his affability. His friends were legion and many of them dropped by the sessions for this first solo album. Jefferson Airplane's Jack Casady, Grace Slick, David Freiberg, Paul Kantner, Jorma Kaukonen, the Grateful Dead's Jerry Garcia, Mickey Hart, Bill Kreutzmann, Phil Lesh and Santana's Gregg Rolie,

Michael Shrieve along with Joni Mitchell, Graham Nash and Neil Young all appear on these songs, which are about as free form as American rock has ever been. These are mysterious tracks unlike anything else before or since.

At the time of recording Crosby was accelerating the drug binge that dominated the first half of his life. His girlfriend, Christine Hinton, had been killed in a car crash. Crosby, Stills, Nash and Young were imploding under their own egos.

"The studio was almost the only place I felt I could function," Crosby told *MOJO*. "So I would go there every night and my friends would come. A lot of really wonderful people would just show up and I would start a song and whoever had come that night would join in. Sometimes it made magic and sometimes it made mud."

'What Are Their Names' starts out very clearly as a guitar duel between Jerry Garcia and Neil Young – both at the height of their powers and feeding off each other until the vocal comes in with an acidic taunt to the Establishment (with help from Grace Slick).

On this record, Crosby fulfilled the hippie dream of musicians getting together. But only Crosby could pull it off.

Taxman The Beatles

(George Harrison) ❊ Parlophone ❊ 1966 ❊ Appears on: *Revolver*

Harrison wrote in his autobiography, "'Taxman' was when I realised that even though we had started earning money, we were actually giving most of it away in taxes." The song is not entirely serious, with delightful backing vocals name-checking Mr Wilson and Mr Heath (the leaders of the Labour and Tory parties at the time). It was clearly a subject dear to the Beatles' hearts given that they were paying up to 90 per cent of their earnings to the internal revenue.

'Taxman' opens *Revolver*, the Beatles' most mature and complex to date, and arguably their best overall disc. (Starr suggested the album be titled *After Geography* because the latest Rolling Stones album was called *Aftermath*.) Harrison has a killer riff here – played by Paul McCartney – over a tough soul rhythm pattern, and the record has a live feel that would soon disappear from the Beatles. Perhaps not Harrison's most enduring lyric, but the riff certainly is durable – the Jam copped it wholesale fifteen years later.

Willie the Pimp   Frank Zappa

(Frank Zappa) ✳ Bizarre/Reprise✳ 1970 ✳ Appears on: *Hot Rats*

By the late '60s, Frank Zappa realised that he wasn't going to be taken seriously by the art Establishment. So he sought refuge in that other academy for rockers – jazz. Having outgrown the Mothers of Invention, Zappa called in some top-line studio players plus multi-instrumentalist Mother of Invention Ian Underwood, two violinists (Don Sugarcane Harris and Jean-Luc Ponty) and John Guerin on drums.

   The sessions in the autumn of 1969 were remarkably free. Zappa relaxed into his guitar playing – his chief talent – and apologetic jokes or scatology do not undercut the songs. The album's highpoint is the reunification of Zappa and his school chum Captain Beefheart on 'Willie the Pimp' and its stinging solo from Zappa where the jazz meets the blues.

The Needle and the Damage Done   Neil Young

(Neil Young) ✳ Reprise ✳ 1972 ✳ Appears on: *Harvest*

Neil Young once tellingly introduced the song on stage with this speech: "This is a serious song I'd like to do about some people you know, some people I know and some people that neither one of us knows. It's about heroin addiction. Somewhere in the universe there's probably a place where all the great art is that didn't get out. A museum of incredible lost art that didn't get out because of heroin."

   Neil Young is rarely this blunt. The song is one of the most famous anti-heroin songs because it is so simple and so direct. It was written for Crazy Horse guitarist Danny Whitten, who was then a heroin addict and would soon be dead. With the escalation of the Vietnam War in the late '60s and into the early '70s, when GIs returned from South-East Asia, heroin became increasingly commonplace in American cities. Shortly before this song went into Young's live repertoire Janis Joplin, Jim Morrison and guitarist Al Wilson died from heroin overdoses. Then Jimi Hendrix died from an overdose of drugs – the number of junkies around the music business was increasing rapidly.

   This track was recorded live and has that stark beauty. Young was not used to being so prosaic in his lyrics, but when he does he's very forceful.

People Who Died The Jim Carroll Band

(Jim Carroll) ✳ 1980 ✳ Rolling Stones Records/Atco ✳ Appears on: *Catholic Boy*

Carroll was a downtown hipster poet in the late '60s and early '70s, living for a time with fellow poet Patti Smith. His first recorded performance is on the Velvet Underground's *Max's Kansas City*, where he is overheard asking Lou Reed for drugs. Carroll's poetry – his memories of a Catholic boyhood – brought him into contact with Allen Ginsberg and the Beat poets as well as Andy Warhol's Factory scene. He left New York in the mid-'70s to kick his heroin habit and in the meantime, his first novel, *The Basketball Diaries*, was a hit. At Patti Smith's urging Carroll turned his hand at music. His one classic track was 'People Who Died' – it was, in fact, *The Basketball Diaries* set to music.

"I probably wouldn't have become involved with rock & roll if it hadn't have been for my friend Earl McGrath, who at the time was the president of Rolling Stones Records," Carroll recalled. "He was the one who played this $100 demo tape I had made to Keith Richards of the Stones. Earl understood things in literary terms, and obviously most people in the record business didn't.

"Originally when I signed, it was with the Stones' label, and the idea was for Keith to produce that first album *Catholic Boy*. It was totally, like, strangeness to me 'cause I had just come back to New York to make the paperback deal for *The Basketball Diaries*, and I'd been in this long recluse period in California where the highlight of my day was walking my dog down to the post office."

'People Who Died' featured Lenny Kaye from the Patti Smith Group on what is a genuinely great piece of power pop. It's funny in a black way, like a Ramones song only sweeter.

"A lot of the kids I graduated with from Catholic grammar school went to Vietnam," Carroll told *Interview* magazine. "Forty kids graduated with me and eleven of them died there. It's an incredible percentage. Also, a lot of my friends from when I was young died or went to jail or got into drugs and died. I got into drugs at the same time and fortunately … This song is about that. It's like an elegy but it's not sentimental. It just lists the people who died, how they died, how old they were and that's all.

"It's really up."

You Can't Put Your Arms Around a Memory
Johnny Thunders

(Johnny Thunders) ✳ Real ✳ 1978 ✳ Appears on: *So Alone*

Johnny Thunders, former guitarist of the New York Dolls and the Heartbreakers, found himself living the life of a slightly shop-worn Messiah in punk rock London. The new generation of punks worshipped the Dolls and the Heartbreakers. The pint-sized New Yorker had credibility, charisma and a world-beating heroin habit. Thunders' life had two poles – getting stoned and playing guitar. Usually he combined them.

Following the demise of the Heartbreakers, Thunders found himself in the studio with no shortage of collaborators – the Only Ones, Steve Marriott, Phil Lynott, Chrissie Hynde and a couple of Sex Pistols. Over three weeks he bashed out the best record of his life and certainly the best sounding record he ever made.

Producer Steve Lilywhite captured sessions that were clearly loose and spontaneous but he recorded them beautifully and unobtrusively. "My biggest problem was keeping him awake," said the producer. "But just when you'd think he was dead, he'd get up like a shot and do a blinding solo."

So Alone is a perfect rock & roll album. Serendipities, great, loose playing and a Zen feel. The key song, however, is Thunders' lament for his life as a junkie. 'You Can't' is a wonderful, tough song about the bittersweetness of acceptance. Listening to the song you can hear Thunders drift perfectly into the moment, just allowing himself to be honest. It's a small moment but a perfect one.

I Threw It All Away Bob Dylan

(Bob Dylan) ✳ Columbia ✳ 1969 ✳ Appears on: *Nashville Skyline*

In 1969 Dennis Hopper and Peter Fonda made *Easy Rider*, a film about two young freaks riding through the American south on motorcycles. The film ends when rednecks shoot Hopper as he's riding down the highway letting his freak flag fly.

Easy Rider was not far off the mark in the way the northern longhairs were looked upon by the good ol' boys. In that same atmosphere, Bob Dylan's *Nashville Skyline* album – where the leader of the '60s freak show went to Nashville to make a country album – left many perplexed, on both sides of the generation gap.

Nashville Skyline was yet another side of Dylan. No longer obscure in the lyrics, neither protesting nor howling, but writing straightforward, classic country and western songs. The first song was a duet with Johnny Cash saying so much for the generation gap. There was another clue on the cover where Dylan posed in parody to a Rambling Jack Elliott album cover. Dylan's voice too was different. The raspy, sometimes whining voice he had made famous was replaced with a croon. According to old friends, this was Dylan's real voice before he had started mimicking Woody Guthrie. Dylan, too, said of *Nashville Skyline*, "The songs reflect more of the inner me than the songs of the past. They're more to my taste than, say, John Wesley Harding."

'I Threw It All Away' is the most elegant of the songs on *Nashville Skyline*. Given that this was one of the happiest periods of Dylan's life, this desolate regret for lost love is unlikely to be particularly autobiographical. Understated, gentle and forlorn, the song is pure craftsmanship.

Baby's on Fire   Brian Eno

(Brian Eno) ❊ Island ❊ 1974 ❊ Appears on: *Here Come the Warm Jets*

Brian Eno was well on the way to becoming an art teacher when he was sidelined into making music by saxophonist Andy Mackay. Shortly thereafter he found himself on the cutting edge of British art pop with Roxy Music and became a star in his own right. "The only thing I could actually play when I first started doing records was a tape recorder," he said. "It was the only thing I felt any understanding and control over. Synthesisers ran a distant second, and other instruments nowhere."

After two albums with Roxy Music, he was out on his own with a solo album, *Here Come the Warm Jets*, written, according to producer Chris Thomas, in ten days.

"What I wanted to do was focus on this new way of making music in the studio, so I started making my own records, which in retrospect sound pretty weird as well," he told *MOJO*. "I saw the studio as a place to study sound, invent sound, craft it in ways you couldn't do with live instruments. The main thing on 'Needle in the Camel's Eye', for instance, is Phil Manzanera playing a riff on rhythm guitar;

meanwhile, I'm banging his whammy-bar, beating it in rhythm. We did three of four tracks of him and I doing exactly the same thing, so you're getting four rippling guitars pulsing against one another.

"The title *Warm Jets* came from the guitar sound on the track of that name, which I described on the track-sheet as 'warm jet guitar' because it sounded like a tuned jet. Then I had the pack of playing cards with the picture of that woman in there, and they sort of connected. That was one of the other things that was going on at the time: this idea that music was still tied to some idea of revolution, and that one of the revolutions was a sexual revolution. I wasn't making a big political point; I just liked having fun with those things. Most people didn't realise for a long time – it was rather deeply concealed!"

For someone so avant-garde, the album was a pop success, not least of all for the track 'Baby's on Fire', which was somehow just too outrageous in sound and lyric to be ignored.

The song is about a woman catching on fire. It's a nice play on the sexual clichés of popular song but it's also darker and more brutal than that, especially with Eno's flat vocal delivery. The stark, mannered lyric is almost chanted over two chords and a kind of spastic rhythm pattern that is embellished by guitar playing from Paul Rudolph and King Crimson's Robert Fripp. 'Baby's on Fire' has become an oft-covered, art-rock classic.

"My first album, *Here Come the Warm Jets*, is my least favourite," said Eno many years later. "It sold best of all. But a lot of people genuinely prefer it; another instance of mystique at work. They heard that under the condition of wanting to like it a lot, and that makes a difference."

You're Gonna Miss Me The 13th Floor Elevators

(Roky Erickson) ✳ International Artists ✳ 1966 ✳

Appears on: *The Psychedelic Sounds of the 13th Floor Elevators*

Of all the groups of the garage punk era, the Elevators were the most timeless. They matched the Rolling Stones for inventive, hard, guitar-based R&B. Their songs such as 'You're Gonna Miss Me' and 'Fire Engine' prefigured the New Wave by more than a decade. Driving, angry and impassioned, the Elevators had an attitude and a sophistication that put them way ahead of their contemporaries. This wasn't long, meandering improvisation, nor was it filled with the wonder of the universe. The Elevators had a different acid rock trip – it was hypnotic and deranged and dirty. It was the other side of acid – when your mind is blown and the wind whistles through the haunted corridors between your ears. Stacey Sutherland's guitar was nasty and often brutal in its riffs while Tommy Hall's electric jug added a particular weirdness. The key was Roky Erickson's vocals – big and rich and theatrical.

What cut the Elevators' career short was the same thing that lengthened their legend. Roky was known as a man who took the acid in acid rock seriously – at every level. According to the legend he took hundreds of psychedelic trips and eventually fried his brains. When he was arrested for marijuana possession in 1969, he pleaded insanity and spent three years in a mental hospital. Some say that it was the acid, some say it was the incarceration but, whatever the cause, Roky never made much sense again.

Be all that as it may, this debut from the Elevators lives up to its title and may be the definitive garage punk album of all time. 'You're Gonna Miss Me' was the enduring punk pop classic where the three-chord pyramid of rock & roll met the third eye in the centre of Roky's troubled head.

Whole Lotta Love Led Zeppelin

(John Bonham/Willie Dixon/John Paul Jones/Jimmy Page/Robert Plant) ✳ Atlantic ✳

1969 ✳ Appears on: *Led Zeppelin II*

"From the release of the first album, and our first tour in the States when we supported Vanilla Fudge, all of a sudden the name of the band travelled like wildfire," Jimmy Page recalled in *MOJO*. "We were supporting bands and they weren't turning up, because we were really quite an intimidating force.

"We toured on the strength of the first album, and we just toured and toured and toured. In between times, we fitted in a small amount of recording at Olympic, where we did part of 'Ramble On' and 'Whole Lotta Love' and a couple of others, and the rest of the album was recorded at various times, and finally I mixed it with Eddie Kramer in New York. And then we were touring on the strength of the second album. And it wasn't until we had a real break, and that break was probably only a couple of months, but to us it seemed an eternity."

Everything about Zeppelin was bigger than life. They looked like they didn't give a fuck about anyone. As soon as they started headlining they dispensed with support acts and took to the stage with three hours of loud rock. Plus they had the charisma between Plant and Page at the front of the stage radiating cool.

The second album, called, of course, *II*, didn't break new ground but it did take them up a notch from the first.

Robert Plant comes more to the fore with his immense voice. By this time he was more comfortable in the role of sex god, enjoying the sleaze and the double entendres of the blues idiom.

Most of all, however, the album is known for its opening track. 'Whole Lotta Love', based on Muddy Waters' 'You Need Love', is pretty much five minutes and thirty-five seconds of the sound of a man having sex. It was recorded in an afternoon.

"It came from, if memory serves, it came just from just having a perfect symmetry of musicianship, where we could just go off on a tangent, just go off here, there and everywhere, and come back together again," Plant explained. "Jimmy had just discovered the theremin, that sort of 'whoop-whoop-whoop', and it just got into the groove. And it worked perfectly. But that was the way we played. That was how we felt we expressed ourselves best, with all the emphasis, and then having the abstraction in the middle of it. It broke it up in order to turn people's heads."

Against the band's initial wishes, 'Whole Lotta Love' was edited and released as a single, which simply increased their audience.

Led Zeppelin were the prototype of the third generation of rock & roll bands. They were apolitical, and boasted of huge appetites for sex, drugs and money. They were removed by their management and their wealth from their fans. They were the first band to become gods.

I Feel Fine The Beatles

(John Lennon/Paul McCartney) ❋ Parlophone ❋ 1964 ❋ Appears on: *The Beatles 1962–1966*

John Lennon proudly claimed the distinction of being the first guitarist to use guitar feedback on a pop record with this single. "That's me, including the guitar lick with the first feedback ever recorded," he said in 1980. "I defy anybody to find an earlier record – unless it is some old blues record from the twenties – with feedback on it."

Lennon started writing the song at the beginning of October 1964 while trying to figure out his part for 'Eight Days a Week'. "Anyway, going into the studio one morning, I said to Ringo, 'I've written this song but it's lousy.' We tried it, complete with riff and it sounded like an A-side, so we decided to release it just like that."

One of Lennon's few optimistic songs, possibly because he didn't think too much about the lyrics, its super-charged riff and sense of abandon took the Beatles one step further into their own. Coming on the back of *A Hard Day's Night*, which was their first all-original long player, the Beatles were further emboldened to find their own style. Backed with 'She's a Woman', the 45 was yet another number one hit. The track wasn't included on *Beatles for Sale*, the album they compiled for Christmas 1964, but the liner notes of that disc from Derek Taylor could easily apply here. He wrote, "There's priceless history between these covers. When, in a generation or so, a radioactive, cigar-smoking child, picnicking on Saturn, asks you what the Beatle affair was all about, don't try to explain all about the long hair and the screams! Just play them a few tracks from this album and he'll probably understand. The kids of AD 2000 will draw from the music much the same sense of well being and warmth as we do today."

Love is in the Air John Paul Young

(Harry Vanda/George Young) ❋ Alberts ❋ 1978 ❋ Appears on: *Love is in the Air*

Harry Vanda and George Young had their own hit factory in the '70s, churning out tunes for a selection of singers. One of them was the reluctant pop star John Paul Young, who had had a part in *Jesus Christ Superstar*. As soon as Vanda and Young had 'Love is in the Air' down they knew the man to sell it.

"They had exactly what they wanted to hear in mind," said Young. "Other people attack the song. When you hear the original it's almost as if a guy's getting out of bed as he's singing it. It's such a throwaway thing and that's part of the magic of the song and that's part of the magic of George and Harry too. It's not just the song, it's not just the musos, it's not just the words, it's just this whole attitude that a song has to have and it's very important to them."

Vanda and Young, when not producing AC/DC and other hard rock acts, played around with their version of heavily synthetic Euro pop. It was a unique formula at the time.

"It's almost a little bit French cabaret when you think about it with a Latin beat," said Vanda. "You can hear all that and so it can only be treated in a certain way really. All these ingredients dictate what the song is going to be all about. John was the obvious guy to sing it. He put it down live and it all fitted beautifully."

Not only was the song a hit, but Baz Luhrmann gave it a new lease of life with the film *Strictly Ballroom* and the song has become a classic.

"I suppose it pushes the right buttons," said Young. "The casual delivery of it, the title itself – 'Love is in the Air' – it has a devil-may-care attitude about it. There's so many little bits you could dissect it all day and say well gee that's good, the run up is fantastic; that really sets it up for the chorus. But you try sitting down and writing another one and that gives you an idea as to how bloody hard it must be. You can't order them up."

Like a Hurricane Neil Young & Crazy Horse

(Neil Young) ✳ Reprise ✳ 1977 ✳ Appears on: *American Stars and Bars*

'Like a Hurricane' is one of Young's guitar epics where the basic riff as carried by Crazy Horse (Frank Pancho Sampedro, Billy Talbot and Ralph Molina) is a jumping-off point for any manner of guitar playing from pure noise to sublime lyricism.

"We were all really high, fucked up. Been out partying. Wrote it sitting up at Vista Point on Skyline," Young said of the genesis of the song. "Supposed to be the highest point in San Mateo County, which was appropriate. I wrote it when I couldn't sing. I was on voice rest. It was nuts – I was whistling it. I wrote a lot of songs when I couldn't talk."

The tune was in the live set for some time before the group tried it in the studio. Like the best Crazy Horse material, the tune was captured live in all its tempestuous glory.

"Well, we learn the songs, and sometimes the songs have parts where it's extended solos, where it's a matter of us playing together improvising," said bassist Billy Talbot. "We're not jazz musicians, and we don't play jazz, we play rock & roll, but at the same time it's an improvisational thing, and that takes us to other places that you could never rehearse."

"Even when we learn the songs, it doesn't guarantee that we're going to remember them," said guitarist Sampedro, "or that Neil's going to remember the lyrics, or we're going to sing the chorus or anything. Once we get going, anything can change at any time, and you just have to keep your head up rather than down. That just all adds to being a band. You just have to be really there with each other. It's not like every night we're going to play the same arrangement – that never happens, never."

Neil once said about bass player Talbot specifically, though it could apply to Crazy Horse in general, "Billy is a massive player who only plays two or three notes. People are still trying to figure out whether it's because he only knows two or three notes, or whether those are the only notes he wants to play."

Good question. But tracks like this make the point moot.

Box of Rain The Grateful Dead

(Phil Lesh/Robert Hunter) ✳ Warner Bros. ✳ 1970 ✳ Appears on: *American Beauty*

The Grateful Dead recorded *American Beauty* within months of their country-style *Workingman's Dead*. This second acoustic-flavoured album is like a baroque country album – the textures of guitars, pedal steel and mandolin are bright and open and welcoming in ways that most of the Grateful Dead's music isn't. On 'Box of Rain' lyricist Robert Hunter is both cosmic and reasonable. Hunter's lyrics in this period reflect his reading of Buddhism, and Zen Buddhism in particular.

"Phil Lesh wanted a song to sing to his dying father and had composed a piece complete with every vocal nuance but the words," said Hunter. "If ever a lyric 'wrote itself', this did – as fast as the pen would pull. He'd just written these lovely changes and put 'em on a tape for me. And he sang along so the phrasing was all there. I think I went through it two or three times, writing as fast as I could, and that song was written. I guess it was written for a young man whose father was dying."

"My dad was dying of cancer, and I would drive out to visit with him, in the hospital, and also at the nursing home he spent his final days in, and after Bob gave me the lyrics, on the way out there I would practise singing the song," Lesh recalled. "I identified that song with my dad and his approaching death. The lyrics that he produced were so apt, so perfect. It was very moving, very moving for me to experience that during the period of my dad's passing. I felt like singing it in other situations similar to that since then."

The box of rain in the title refers to the planet, and it's a gentle song of acceptance. More sophisticated than the average pop song, even for the Dead. It's also more sophisticated musically, even for the Dead.

"I meant the world we live on," said Hunter. "But 'ball' of rain didn't have the right ring to my ear, so box it became, and I don't know who put it there."

When You Were Mine Prince

(Prince) ❋ Warner Bros. ❋ 1980 ❋ Appears on: *Dirty Mind*

"Prince's third album for Warner Bros. continues his safari through the jungle of teenage lust and heavy breathing." (*Minneapolis Tribune*, 7 November 1980.)

Prince's second album had sold over a million copies, mostly to a black audience. For his third, *Dirty Mind*, Prince was determined to cross over. He was seen as an oversexed junior Rick James who couldn't keep his clothes on. Few pundits could see the influence that Prince would have on music after this.

There was some curiosity value in the fact that this man with only one name wrote, recorded and produced almost every note on his records, and had been doing so since his teens. Beyond the curiosity value though, Prince was clearly imparting a singular vision more strongly than most.

Sure Prince wrote about sex – oral pleasure, incest, multiple partners. Prince pushed the boundaries. According to keyboard player Matt Fink, "That really was him at the time. He was rejoicing in his own sexuality. He was saying 'Sex is a reality. Don't be afraid of it.'"

Songs like 'When You Were Mine', however, were not only sexually adventurous, but also sonically so. The production borrowed from Curtis Mayfield and New Wave pop but had, at its core, a hook that couldn't be beat.

"He knew he was entering some hot soup. Anytime you do when you're pushing the envelope, you know?" said drummer Bobby Z. "He really found himself with that album. I think he wrote better songs. And the roughness of it gave it an edge – it was a little more garage sounding."

The cover – a stark black-and-white photo of Prince against bed springs, wearing a military outfit over nothing more than his underwear – is a statement of intent.

"Of course it was a risky record," co-manager Bob Cavallo said. "Some thought we were losing our minds."

Love My Way The Psychedelic Furs

(John Ashton/Richard Butler/Tim Butler/Vince Ely) ✳ Columbia ✳ 1982 ✳
Appears on: *Forever Now*

This is a song about what to do when your girlfriend is bisexual. The Psychedelic Furs, according to singer and writer Richard Butler, spearheaded the second wave of the New Wave in the early '80s. Butler's influences were primarily the Velvet Underground, Bob Dylan and David Bowie.

The sound and atmosphere of their early records – energetic, slightly speedy and dreamy – had been established with the help of producer Steve Lillywhite. For their third, they moved to Bearsville to work with the auteur of art rock, Todd Rundgren.

"I was supposed to have been working on a song which I hadn't done," Butler said. "I had one of those stylophone things and I had this 'dadadadadada nanananananana' – just those two changes. I'd been listening to [David Bowie's] *Scary Monsters*, that must have informed it a bit, and came up with this vocal melody and all the words within the space of about an hour. We put it down, and then Ed Bueller, a friend of ours, came round with his keyboard and put the marimba part on. We sent it off to Todd who said, 'Well, the vocals sound a little bit angry, why don't you try singing a little bit more,' and I was like, 'Yeah, OK.'"

Unlike the Bunnymen and their other British contemporaries, the Furs were more intimate, more flesh and blood and more sexy. There is an effeteness to Butler's singing that betrays a degree of honesty. As the name implies, they're looking for heightened experience and not simply art for art's sake.

"The sound of the band really came together completely by accident," said Butler. "We weren't very good musicians. We still aren't, it's an ideas thing."

Will the Circle Be Unbroken The Nitty Gritty Dirt Band

(AP Carter) ❊ EMI ❊ 1972 ❊ Appears on: *Will the Circle Be Unbroken*

In the '20s, AP Carter, one of the first and most prolific country songwriters, took 19th-century Scottish and English ballads and the folk music of his time, spiced them with some jazz and blues and pushed them through a string band arrangement. This formula has remained true to this day. As country music evolved and grew in popularity, hillbilly music remained a backwater, notable mostly for giving us the theme for *The Beverly Hillbillies*. Perhaps then it's fitting that the film *O Brother, Where Art Thou?* spurred the most recent bluegrass revival. In amongst the hokey settings and the clichés there are timeless truths to be discovered.

Which is exactly what the Nitty Gritty Dirt Band (John McEuen, Jeff Hanna, Jimmie Fadden, Les Thompson, and Jim Ibbotson) were searching for six days in August of 1971 when they assembled the living legends of country for what became a three-album disc appropriately titled *Will the Circle Be Unbroken*.

You have to cast your mind back to a time when guys like the Dirt Band, with hair down their backs, stood across a chasm of the ages from rednecks. *Easy Rider* was only two years in the can and the sentiments in that film's finale as the rednecks murdered the longhairs were not far from anyone's mind.

By the time tape rolled, the players on this album included Roy Acuff, Earl Scruggs, Randy Scruggs, Merle Travis, Doc Watson and Mother Maybelle Carter, three generations of country royalty, to which they added some newcomers: Norman Blake and fiddler Vassar Clements. Of these characters, Earl Scruggs invented bluegrass banjo when he was with Bill Monroe, while Mother Maybelle Carter made her first record in 1928 with the Carter Family. Her daughter June was to marry Johnny Cash and their children Carlene Carter and Roseanne Cash continued the family business. Doc Watson, a blind guitarist from North Carolina, was one of the three most influential guitar pickers of the last century. The other one, Merle Travis (after whom Watson named his son), was also at these sessions (it was the first time the two had met). Family, the real rock of ages, runs through every moment of this album. There's a palpable sense of time being conquered, of the thickness of both music and blood.

The tracks here are often familiar: 'Keep on the Sunny Side', 'Tennessee Stud', 'Wreck on the Highway', 'I Saw the Light', 'Nine Pound Hammer', 'Honky Tonkin', 'Orange Blossom Special', 'Wabash Cannonball', 'Lost Highway', 'I'm Thinking Tonight of My Blue Eyes', 'I Am a Pilgrim', 'Wildwood Flower' and 'Soldier's Joy'. These renditions have the freshness of truly sublime art. The album's penultimate song is, appropriately, the Carter Family's hymn, 'Will the Circle Be Unbroken', performed with three generations of musicians who loved their country music pure.

I Walk on Gilded Splinters Dr John the Night Tripper

(Dr John) ☀ Atco ☀ 1968 ☀ Appears on: *Gris Gris*

Mac Rebennack literally grew up in the New Orleans music scene alongside Fats Domino and Dave Bartholemew and the blues and R&B artists who played the New Orleans clubs and bordellos. In the mid-'60s he moved to Los Angeles, where he teamed up with another Crescent City native, Harold Battiste, who was working with Sonny Bono. Using some Sonny and Cher downtime, Battiste and Rebennack collected other New Orleans émigrés and cut the *Gris Gris* album – a deep, swampy and funkified version of New Orleans music that was way further out than the acid rock on FM airwaves.

For the album Rebennack assumed the persona of Dr John the Night Tripper – a characterisation of a voodoo priest.

"I had been working on some kind of voodoo idea for a couple of years," said Rebennack. The album closed with the epic 'I Walk on Gilded Splinters', which bubbles along on a sly funk bass and deep, ghostly, echoed percussion hanging back way behind the beat while Dr John mumbles his incantations. This is a very spooky and beautiful record.

"Atlantic reacted to it like, 'What the fuck is this? What are we gonna tell our promotions people'," said Harold Battiste. "None of us thought of a name for what we were doing but I knew the press would do that, call it Voodoo Rock or Swamp Rock or whatever. It was a tongue-in-cheek thing for me. It was the psychedelic period out in California and I said, 'Well, we're gonna give 'em some new shit to go underground with!'

"I had always wanted to do that sort of Afro-centric stuff. Really it was just a gathering of things that went with our heritage: the Indians, the Africans, the Cajuns, everybody that was making up our culture."

On 'Splinters' Dr John incants his voodoo lyrics and the mysterious sensuality of the song's groove is as strong as ever.

Time Tom Waits

(Tom Waits) ✳ Island ✳ 1985 ✳ Appears on: *Rain Dogs*

Tom Waits said he wrote the *Rain Dogs* album "thinking of the guy going back to Philadelphia from Manhattan on the Metroliner with the *New York Times*, looking out the window in New York as he pulls out of the station, imagining all the terrible things he doesn't have to be a part of."

This is a deeply melancholy album. Waits' jazz blues muse is orchestrated by Marc Ribot's tense, staccato guitar, which squeaks and squawks the most precise and elliptical lines against the funereal march bass of Larry Taylor and Waits' eccentric percussion – bits of drums and glass and metal.

All that cacophony is boiled down to just Waits on guitar, Taylor on double bass and William Shimmel on accordion for the drunken waltz at the heart of the album. 'Time' is that perfect moment between waking and sleep, between life and death – a still point where time itself stops and everything that you can see is simultaneously uplifting and sad and going neither up nor down: you're suspended out of time. "And the things you can't remember/Tell the things you can't forget that/History puts a saint in every dream," Waits sings.

The LP's title refers to the condition of dogs after a rainstorm when all their markings have been washed away: "They go to sleep thinking the world is one way and they wake up and somebody moved the furniture." As he sings the refrain, "It's time, time, time/That you love" you have the sense of drifting off into the unknown.

Helpless Crosby, Stills, Nash & Young

(Neil Young) ❋ Atlantic ❋ 1970 ❋ Appears on: *Déjà Vu*

"There is a town in North Ontario/With dream comfort memory to spare/And in my mind/I still need a place to go/All my changes were there." This, the first verse of 'Helpless', makes it explicit that this is about as explicit as the north Canadian singer/songwriter is going to get. "Well, it's not so much a specific town as a feeling," Young said to Nick Kent on the occasion of the former's fiftieth birthday. "Actually it's a couple of towns. Omemee, Ontario, is one of them. It's where I first went to school and spent my formative years. Actually I was born in Toronto. 'I was born in Toronto' . . . God, that sounds like a Bruce Springsteen song. But Toronto is only seven miles from Omemee."

'Helpless' was Young's first contribution to Crosby, Stills, Nash & Young. It was one of only four songs the group ever recorded together – the other tracks were done individually due to competing personalities. The track has a certain cohesion and warmth that's lacking from much of Crosby, Stills, Nash & Young.

'Helpless' is a delicate ballad that Young sings up in his top register where he can get the maximum ache to a lyric about lost innocence. The modal arrangement recalls Joni Mitchell's 'The Circle Game', which was a song written for Neil Young on the occasion of his nineteenth birthday. 'Helpless' is simple, beautifully melancholic and one of Young's finest moments.

They Took the Children Away Archie Roach

(Archie Roach) ❋ Aurora ❋ 1989 ❋ Appears on: *Charcoal Lane*

Few songs have so clearly, concisely and emotionally covered the issue of the Stolen Generation as this. Archie Roach himself was stolen from his parents as a child and he lived in the halfway hell of many Aboriginals. Roach did it tough, at one point hitting bottom with the bottle. His salvation came through writing poetry and music and also through his relationship with fellow singer and songwriter Ruby Hunter.

"I wrote for myself and friends and family," he said. "Writing for me, at first, was cathartic. I was happy working during the day and singing when I felt like it, but I wouldn't change anything. I love this work."

Roach's song is emotive without sentimentality. His delivery is spare and considered but the song packs a terrific punch. Part of its success is that Roach expresses the universality of this matter within the specifics of the case.

"You start to get away from this tag of Aboriginal singer/songwriter," he said. "What does it mean? Does it mean I just write songs dealing with Aboriginal people? Of course not. Does Paul Kelly just write music on Irish/Italian themes? Music transcends barriers. I feel obliged, when things are going wrong, to get up, maybe not so much on behalf of my people but on behalf of every decent, intelligent, caring person in Australia."

Poptones Public Image Ltd

(Public Image Limited) ✳ Virgin ✳ 1979 ✳ Appears on: *Metal Box* (second edition)

If Johnny Rotten (nee Lydon) sounded angry when he fronted the Sex Pistols, that was nothing compared to the bile and spite that spewed forth from Public Image Ltd. Already an alienated teen, by the end of the Sex Pistols he was full of disgust at manager Malcolm McLaren, his fellow Pistols, full of sorrow over the fate of Sid Vicious, and generally annoyed. He had rushed to form PiL and whipped out a first album that was little more than a new version of the Pistols' punk sound. For the second album, the band had free rein.

Lydon's chief collaborators were guitarist Keith Levine and bass player Jah Wobble. The former had a very nasty attack with a spiky guitar while the latter had no experience whatever.

With those ingredients, a brace of dub albums, some Kraut rock and too much cheap speed, cough medicine and marijuana, PiL set out to make a grand statement. The record grew organically and it has the nasty edge of cheap drugs, which is amplified by the huge slabs of dub bass from Wobble punctuated by Levine's noise. This is the sound of chalk being dragged over the blackboard – very slowly. There are long, improvised tunes that are perverse in their refusal to resolve themselves. Lydon, sticking to his anti-rock stance, falls back into the mix, a ghost of his former self. Frankly, Lydon's lyrics have rarely been strong and he was wise to let the soundscape take the spotlight. 'Poptones' is a harrowing example of Levine's misanthropic guitar going out of control in a vortex of spindly notes.

This was pretty much as anti show-business as it was possible to be – the original album didn't have song titles and the whole thing was released as three 12-inch singles in a film canister.

Despite the best efforts of PiL, the record became something of an icon against which the post-punk bands measured themselves. Shortly afterwards the band fell apart, to be resuscitated by Lydon with new players. To his dismay, PiL didn't bring down rock & roll.

Buffalo Stance   Neneh Cherry

(Booga Bear/Neneh Cherry/Jamie J Morgan/Phillip Ramacon) ❋ Circa/Virgin ❋ 1989 ❋
Appears on: *Raw Like Sushi*

Neneh Cherry is as eclectic as her heritage – her mother is Swedish, her father is West African and her stepfather is the great jazz trumpeter Don Cherry. Neneh started her music career as a teenager with the jazz/post-punk combo Rip Rig and Panic and then in the late '80s dropped one of the great club hits of the era.

'Buffalo Stance' is an eclectic track referencing Malcolm McLaren, the Wild Bunch and Bomb the Bass. It is one of the masterpieces of the late '80s club era.

The lyric is directed specifically at a gigolo attempting to corrupt young women, but it is more generally applicable to the macho sensibility. This is an empowerment anthem that seduces with its grooves and melodic hooks. Cherry's rap is right on the money – conscious, tuneful and masterfully syncopated with the music.

Production on the track is by Tim Simenon (aka Bomb the Bass) but the sound is strongly influenced by the Bristol style of the Wild Bunch and Massive Attack, with whom Cherry and her husband Cameron 'Booga Bear' McVey often recorded. There are touches of reggae and dub in this dense hip-hop mix.

"It really encompassed a vibe that was around at that time," said Cherry of 'Buffalo Stance'. "The whole club thing had started to happen, like hip-hop – still more underground than, say, now. But it was definitely something that people could identify with. And 'Buffalo Stance' was like a song that bridged over that, while at the same time it was a pop record. It also shed a lot of stereotypes that people were bored with – it seemed to make them happy or relieved."

I Got You Split Enz

(Neil Finn) ✳ 1980 ✳ Mushroom ✳ Appears on: *True Colours*

Tim Finn had led Split Enz through five years of the storm and tempest of art rock and pop music. Things were looking grim until his little brother Neil popped out with a very simple pop song that had a slightly menacing melody.

"Tim and I were living in a house in Sydney, in Rose Bay, and we were throwing titles at each other every day, in readiness for recording *True Colours*," said Neil. "He gave me 'I Got You'. I think he did anyway. I wrote the verse and the chorus actually as it is, but in my mind the chorus was always too corny and I'd have to come back and try and change it and fix it up. Which is probably one of the reasons why it's a smash hit single, it was because it was corny. I felt intimidated by its directness, but as soon as the band played it, I realised it had something very strong about it. But on the day, I remember liking the verse but thinking the chorus sucked."

Split Enz had twisted time signatures into pretzels for some years. Faced with this naïve tune they arranged it as plainly as possible yet still there's a sense of dark tension in the verses, which is released with the impossibly catchy hook. On the back of this track Split Enz became a pop band with a twist and went on to sell over a million albums. This song remains one of the enduring pop songs of the decade.

As for the perfectly paced guitar riff that opens the track? "That was the only one I knew how to play at the time," Neil admitted. "That was me learning how to play electric guitar."

Modern Love David Bowie

(David Bowie) ✳ EMI ✳ 1983 ✳ Appears on: *Let's Dance*

David Bowie had, at last, tasted real success with the unlikely R&B hit 'Young Americans', which bled the Philly soul sound. His reaction to pop success had been to retreat to a cocaine haze in Berlin and make a series of groundbreaking avant-rock albums with Brian Eno and Iggy Pop. Bowie was more active as an actor in the early '80s. His musical career seemed if not stagnant, then going nowhere fast.

The thin white Englishman had an innate sense of R&B. His intention was to make a hit album, perhaps out of gratitude for the $20 million EMI had just advanced. Bowie chose Nile Rodgers of Chic as co-producer and, at Mick Jagger's suggestion, Texan guitarist Stevie Ray Vaughan as principal instrumentalist. The combination of Vaughan's aggressive blues style and the heavy, deep funk from Rodgers gave *Let's Dance* a unique style.

Bowie also had a couple of classic songs up his sleeve. The cynical 'Modern Love', perhaps inspired by the disaster and fallout from his marriage to Angela, had his best hook since 'Young Americans'. The arrangement had a swing to it, made more powerful by the massive drum sound.

"It's more Nile's album than mine," Bowie has said of *Let's Dance*. While that may be true, the decision to use the Power Station rhythm section and the rock styling of Vaughan were directed by Bowie and the material was very much his. The album is global in the best sense. The videos for two tracks were shot in Australia, where Bowie's son went to school, and they reflected the political hue, albeit slight, on the album. Rodgers put together the musicians and the album was cut in three short weeks.

Bowie briefed the producer saying, "Nile, I want you to do what you do best – make great commercial records." And he did.

Cortez the Killer Neil Young & Crazy Horse

(Neil Young) ❋ Reprise ❋ 1975 ❋ Appears on: *Zuma*

'Cortez the Killer' makes little or no sense as a lyric. A meeting between the explorer and the doomed king – Montezuma may be a metaphor for the '70s superstars living like kings in southern California, sacrificing virgins to their godlike egos and not knowing what is about to hit them. Perhaps this is a prefiguring of punk or perhaps it's all another fever dream from Neil Young. It matters little. The song is a three-chord template for some of his most incendiary guitar playing.

A power failure during the recording cut into the song. "They missed a whole verse, a whole section," said Young. "You can hear the splice on the recording where we stop and start again. It's a messy edit. But yeah that's true . . . it was a total accident. But that's how I see my best art, as one magical accident after another.

"My guitar improvisations with Crazy Horse are very, very Coltrane-influenced," he said to Nick Kent. "I'm particularly taken by work like 'Equinox' and 'My Favourite Things'. Miles I love just because of his overall attitude towards the concept of creation, which is one of constant change. There's no reason to stay there once you've done it. You could stay for the rest of your life and it would become like a regular job."

The *Zuma* album came as the sky was breaking in Young's life – he had left his second wife and had finished mourning the loss of his friends. He was back with Crazy Horse making a huge sound. *Zuma* was his release and a return to form. As Lou Reed said, summing up Young's career, "He's done it once – 'Cortez the Killer'."

"It was a combination of imagination and knowledge," said Young. "What Cortez represented to me is the explorer with two sides, one benevolent, the other utterly ruthless. I mean, look at Columbus! Everyone now knows he was less than great and he wasn't even there first. It always makes me question all these other so-called 'icons'."

Rain The Beatles

(John Lennon/Paul McCartney) ❄ Parlophone ❄ 1966 ❄ Appears on: *Hey Jude*

Decidedly psychedelic, 'Rain' is a gentle, lazy observation of the outside world that is one of John Lennon's most interesting songs. The track has entered history as the first use of backward tape. Lennon claimed that he discovered the technique while fooling around at home, although Beatles' producer George Martin also takes credit. In those days music was recorded onto magnetic tape, which ran through "heads" on the console. Obviously, spooling the tape in reverse gives a completely different sound. It was a popular technique as the Beatles continued to use it up until the *White* album. Ringo was particularly happy with his drum part. Lennon's vocals were recorded slow and then speeded up to give the melody an extra trippy feel. Backward vocals tagged onto the back of tracks eventually became de rigueur with death metal bands.

'Rain' and the *Revolver* album, which followed, were high points for the Beatles' sonic experiments. Twisting sounds soon became pretentious, gimmicky and meaningless. However, here they are at the top of their form.

Lust for Life   Iggy Pop

(Iggy Pop/David Bowie) ✳ RCA ✳ 1977 ✳ Appears on: *Lust for Life*

David Bowie brought Iggy Pop to Berlin to rescue both of them. Iggy was a chronic drug addict who had been in and out of mental hospitals for some years. David Bowie was a superstar in need of a new direction.

At Hansa studios in the shadow of the Berlin Wall, Bowie, who also had his share of drug problems, left behind his cocaine addiction, his wife and his previous persona. With a variety of collaborators, including Tony Visconti and Brian Eno, he whipped through some seminal albums of his own as well as two for Iggy. The sound of Berlin was hard, metallic and compressed. Iggy's first album there, *The Idiot*, which shows the influence of Bowie most, was not the sequel to *Raw Power* for which the punk crowd waited. It was dark and obsessional and passionate.

The second Iggy Pop album was done very quickly, in the same year as *The Idiot*. Inspiration was running low and Bowie would ask Iggy for his favourite Rolling Stones song. Iggy would pick one, which Bowie then rearranged and created a new tune for, and Iggy added lyrics. They went through a dozen classic artists and styles.

Iggy's best known song is the title track. Bowie wrote the riff, which is carried by the drums and bass, on the ukulele. It was based on the theme tune for American Armed Forces Radio in Germany. Iggy added lyrics that were essentially a happier update from the world's most forgotten boy. 'Lust for Life' was a statement of purpose.

"There's two ways with David," Iggy told Barney Hoskyns. "One contribution he makes is sort of conceptual and even gets to the point where he writes some of the lyrics himself. He collaborates on the lyrics with me, not on all tracks but on some of 'em, or he'll give me a concept or a title ... 'Lust for Life', for example. For that he had a chord progression which was written on a ukulele in the TV room, and I've always been in the habit of watching my instrumentalists and seeing if they get that gleam in their eye, and if they do I'm off like a shot to get the tape recorder. It wasn't even supposed to be a song, but he saw me there with my eyes on him like, come on, come on, fucker, pull it out."

The song was not popular when it appeared and didn't really break through until the '90s, when it was used magnificently in the opening sequence of the film *Trainspotting*. An update of the Bo Diddley beat, it's got a sprung energy and it really just sits with the beat and a voice. Pop's lyric appears to refer to himself and it's both cocky and amusing and confident in ways that his band the Stooges never were.

Eagle Rock Daddy Cool

(Ross Wilson) ✳ Sparmac ✳ 1971 ✳ Appears on: *Daddy Who? Daddy Cool*

"Now listen!" Ross Wilson exclaims at the beginning of the track, and then the guitar riff comes in and you know you've got to take notice. One track, 'Eagle Rock', was so powerful it kicked off a whole generation of Australian musicians. The sound was so catchy and so unique it was, in the true sense of the word, inspiring.

"I was trying to teach myself a bit of finger-picky guitar," said Wilson. "I was playing that riff, 'der-na-lang-dan-dan-da-na', over and over and over and over. I'd go around to people in the house in this place we were staying in England, going, 'you heard this riff before?' cause I thought I must've pinched it from someone. It seemed really, really good. I started to think, this is going to be called 'Eagle Rock'."

Wilson's career started as a high school kid recording 'Louie Louie' with the band the Pink Finks. After school he formed the Zappa-inspired Sons of the Vegetal Mother. By the beginning of the '70s, though, people craved simplicity and good-time music.

Daddy Cool was that. There was a solid rhythm section and the genius guitar of Ross Hannaford, who picked Wilson's lick as though Bach was whispering in his ear.

"In two nights we cut the entire album," recalled producer Robbie Porter. "Every song is either first or second take. The band is so together I remember we started in the afternoon and finished like 3 or 4 in the morning."

'Eagle Rock' had an influence that was subtle and benefited another artist: Elton John. Elton heard Daddy Cool while on his first Australian tour.

"So then the next thing happens is, [Elton] goes off and he makes another album and he brings out a song called 'Crocodile Rock'," said Wilson. "He's totally changed his look to zany, and he's gone back to playing this happy, happy stuff instead of this sombre stuff. And Bernie Taupin's on the back of the album with a *Daddy Who?* badge. So, like, I think we had a bit of an impact there."

Good Lovin' The Young Rascals

(Rudy Clark/Arthur Resnick) ❊ Atlantic ❊ 1968 ❊ Appears on: *The Young Rascals*

The guitarist and critic Lenny Kaye once said, "I know this may sound a little overboard, but there once was a time when the Young Rascals were the greatest rock & roll band in the world. I say this without flinching, and in full realisation that such combinations as the Rolling Stones and the Beatles were in the process of turning out their finest work. I say it in spite of the fact that there are those who would much rather see the Remains, ? and the Mysterians, the Daily Flash, or some other heart-felt favourite stand in the top spot. And I say it knowing far too well that if you never had a bit of the Long Island psyche to guide you on your way, the chances are quite good that the group never made much of an impact on you, one way or another."

This one track proves it all. This is white-hot, blue-eyed soul and though there have been many versions, none has come close to this. The Rascals were a New York band of Italian Americans. The tradition of Italian R&B is a long and venerable one stretching back to Dion. If they lacked the cultural traditions of black Americans they had an equal intensity and theatricality. Unlike most groups in that tradition, however, the Rascals rocked.

The track jumps to the finely tuned rhythm section that powers like something out of Memphis – stopping on a dime and then bursting out again with wailing vocals and Felix Cavaliere's tempestuous Hammond organ.

The song was originally recorded by the Olympics. The Rascals were unsure whether their take would be a hit; however, Atlantic – the premier R&B label of the '60s – persuaded them otherwise.

"I immediately heard how hot the song could be," Cavaliere said. "But we were dissatisfied with our version too and didn't want to put it out. It wasn't as vital as in our live act." That would have been something to see.

I'd Rather Go Blind Etta James

(Bill Foster/Ellington Jordan) ❋ Chess ❋ 1968 ❋ Appears on: *Tell Mama*

Jamesetta Hawkins' mother was only fourteen years old when she had her. Jamesetta was only fifteen herself when she became Etta James and went on the road with Johnny Otis. She had her first hit record with 'Dance With Me Henry' – the answer to 'Work With Me Annie'. Of course, James never got paid much and her story is all too familiar – drug addiction, wrecked career and no management. Along the way down, however, James signed to Chess, where she made some of the best female blues and early soul sides of the '60s.

James' crowning achievement – and there were many highpoints – was recorded at Muscle Shoals with Rick Hall producing the classic Memphis soul ensemble. "Well, Rick Hall was a kind of cat . . . I had never been down to that part of the south, and it was really a relaxed atmosphere. He was cool, a southern cat," James told

writer Barney Hoskyns. "He didn't tell you what to do exactly, he'd just stop you if you overdid something or just give you an idea or two. He was one of the producers I really enjoyed working with. 'I'd Rather Go Blind' would have never sounded like that if Rick Hall hadn't-a produced it, 'cause he was one of those ex-alcoholic cats who was on the brink of losing his wife; there was just something I liked about him, he had that survivor kind of thing."

At Muscle Shoals James cut 'Tell Mama', which was a Top 10 hit for her in 1968. The flipside was 'I'd Rather Go Blind', an extraordinary, heartbreaking blues song. While the backing with Barry Beckett and Spooner Oldham on keys is as flawless as could be expected, it's James' reading of the song that is so breathtaking. The intervals at which she phrases this song of obsessive love and jealousy are completely inspired. Her singing throughout is controlled but you can tell the enormous power that she holds in reserve. The song has been often covered but never equalled.

Qhwayilahle (Leave Him Alone) Moses McHunu

(Moses McHunu) ✳ Shanachie ✳ 1986 ✳ Appears on: *The Indestructible Beat of Soweto*

In 1986 everything was about Africa. If it wasn't the famine up top it was apartheid in the south. Interestingly, the most potent messages about the fate of Africa came through music. Partly it was Peter Gabriel, but mostly it was the music that spoke for itself and there is no better indication of the power of the human spirit than the sound of "township jive".

Soweto was the largest "township" outside Johannesburg where the black workers lived in dormitory suburbs. The existence of Soweto itself was a monument to oppression that was compounded by chronic poverty. Yet the music which came from there, known as mbaqanga or "township jive", was glorious in its chiming guitars and flavours of jazz and reggae and African folk styles. This is music that is full of celebration, more so even than reggae or blues. It's music for dancing.

The Indestructible Beat anthology album put a whole new range of sounds into the western vocabulary. Its most significant influence was felt the following year when Paul Simon recorded a couple of tracks with South African musicians led by Ray Phiri. This album, however, contains the full spirit of the music and artists like Ladysmith Black Mambazo, Mahlathini, and Moses McHunu in full flight.

According to Trevor Herman, who assembled this album, "In most parts of Africa, music is more than entertainment – it's part of life. Everything is celebrated in song, in the rhythm of living."

Thunder Road Bruce Springsteen & the E Street Band

(Bruce Springsteen) ✳ Columbia ✳ 1975 ✳ Appears on: *Born to Run*

Bruce Springsteen wrote his first masterpiece, *Born to Run*, as the post-war boom faded. As he wrote in *Songs*, "There was a continuing gas crisis ... no gas ... no cars. People were contemplating a country that was finite, where resources and life had limits." The characters on the *Born to Run* album defied those limits. Gas crisis or no, they took to the road in a sometimes desperate crusade for deliverance.

The song that was to open this new volume was originally called 'Wings for Wheels' until it was rightly renamed after a New Jersey drag strip. According to

Springsteen, "'Thunder Road' opens the album, introducing its characters and its central proposition: Do you want to take a chance? On us? On life?"

This album was a make-or-break for Springsteen. His first two had established a cult audience, but Columbia was not satisfied with the level of sales. Springsteen was not satisfied with his recorded sound. He spent five months in the studio reworking and layering parts. He was also not satisfied with his producer/manager Mike Appel and they fought frequently. Eventually Springsteen brought in his friend, the rock critic Jon Landau, to co-produce. It was on 'Thunder Road' that Landau showed he had a vision and aptitude to match the singer/songwriter's own. This was a transitional song – an epic like he used to do, but it's stripped back, less jazzy and more forceful. Unlike the title anthem, 'Thunder Road' is very much of its time – two people acknowledging their imperfections, abandoning romance and also looking back to the '50s. Springsteen builds the lyric with small details into a very full character sketch and then, in impatience, demands that Mary get in the car because: "It's a town full of losers and I'm pulling out of here to win!"

According to keyboard player Roy Brittan, "He wanted a record where the singing sounded like Roy Orbison and the music sounded like Phil Spector."

King Ink The Birthday Party

(Nick Cave) ✳ Missing Link ✳ 1981 ✳ Appears on: *Prayers on Fire*

The Birthday Party pulled down the house of rock & roll, made a pyre and watched it burn. Their sound was huge and dark with the spastic beats of Mick Harvey counterpointing the massive bass rumble from Tracey Pew and the elliptical, electrical fragments from Rowland Howard's earring scratching guitar. Over which Nick Cave declaimed rather than sang tales of fire and brimstone as if his guts were burning.

It reflected on the one hand their love of aggressive anarchic music from the likes of the Pop Group and Suicide, while reacting against the self-importance of the likes of Echo and the Bunnymen.

The Birthday Party had grown up playing the Australian pub scene in the wake of the Saints and Radio Birdman. By contrast they found the British music scene to be too genteel.

"Compared to the gigs in Australia, especially in Sydney, they're nothing," Cave told the *NME*. "In Australia, you really feel you're turning decent people into monsters. But look, we're not setting ourselves up as some kind of demonic force, it's just that things are generally more successful when they become blind and unconscious, when you feel anything could happen.

"Coming to London has been one of the most disillusioning experiences of my life, partly for a lot of obvious reasons, like everything closing down at eleven o'clock, but more important, because when we came here we thought here at least people were doing more than standing around twanging their guitars. I was really shocked. When we arrived, we saw this package show at the Lyceum, with Echo and The Bunnymen, A Certain Ratio, Teardrop Explodes and so forth and . . . Well, I've never been able to take English music seriously since. It was horrible."

But then the Birthday Party were never a happy bunch. "*Prayers on Fire* stinks, quite honestly," Pew told the *NME*. "The engineer slept through the entire session for a start."

"*Prayers on Fire* was a kind of reaction to the major disappointments we felt when we went to England," Cave said in retrospect. "I think the members of the Birthday Party began to see a vision and I don't think we were really that positively influenced by things, more negatively influenced. There were a lot of things we didn't want to be like, we didn't want to be like the English New Wave pop groups of the time."

The album was recorded in Melbourne with engineer Tony Cohen also producing. As the group struggled with creating their own identity some of them also began indulging an appetite for alcohol and heroin.

"I think with this particular record we were digging for something and we kind of just found it with certain songs," Cave said. "Some of the songs on that record are quite horrible. 'Zoo Music Girl' is a massively embarrassing song. But it also has a song like 'King Ink' on it and I think we knew by the end of *Prayers on Fire* that we'd discovered a certain kind of sound that we wanted to work with on records after that."

Critic Ed St John summed *Prayers on Fire* up best: "It's well played, but that's hardly the point, for this is an expression which ebbs out beyond the confines of proficiently played music. Listening to this album is akin to watching a film of Jackson Pollock painting or listening to Dylan Thomas in full alcoholic flight."

Quasimodo's Dream The Reels

(Dave Mason/Craig Hooper) ❋ Polygram ❋ 1981 ❋ Appears on: *Quasimodo's Dream*

"I suppose it was original and it was ahead of its time for Australia," said singer and songwriter Dave Mason. "We were pretty free in those times to do what we wanted, and we did. So it was like an adventure."

Having arrived in Sydney as a jumpy, quirky New Wave act, on their second album the Reels revealed a much darker sensibility. There were plenty of pop songs: 'After the News', 'Stand and Deliver' and 'According to My Heart'. The sequined synth melodies from Polly Newham and Craig Hooper shone brightly against the prevailing winds of Oz rock. Beneath that was an itchy, unhappy mood.

Between squabbles amongst the band and the record company, it took almost a year for the record to be released and the conflicts pretty much finished the group thereafter.

However, the real gems on the album were the deeply melancholy 'Kitchen Man' and the title track. The former captures the existential dread of suburban loneliness over a sweet and seductive keyboard line. The latter, which has often been covered and is greatly admired by other songwriters, is a grim but beautiful tale of alienation and self-hatred.

Or is it? "I don't consider it to be my best song," said Mason. "The whole lyric just doesn't make sense. But that's what I'm like in the studio. I never finish my lyrics until the last minute. It's just annoying. I think it was one of those things that people took to their hearts."

Rid of Me PJ Harvey

(PJ Harvey) ❋ Island ❋ 1992 ❋ Appears on: *Rid of Me*

"There's nothing wrong with provocative art. I hope to do something that shocks even myself," PJ Harvey told Phil Sutcliffe from the *Melody Maker* prior to the release of her second album. "In fact, I've done it. It's a song called 'Rid of Me'." Having come from the west country wilds of Dorset only a year or so earlier, PJ Harvey burst onto the British music scene with a fierce and confronting take on the relations between men and women.

Harvey's music was spare and dry and uncompromising, to match her lyrics. For her second album, *Rid of Me*, she enlisted the production support of hardcore guru Steve Albini, who made her sound even more brittle.

This title track with its masochistic refrain is blanching in its candour – the sublimation of everything including sex just to keep a wayward lover. Harvey said that, at the time, she was listing to Chess blues artists Howlin' Wolf and Willie Dixon and was impressed by their raw sexuality and dispassion.

"What I listen to mostly now is Howlin' Wolf and every single song is about sex," she said. "Well, I think that is the most invigorating, exciting and extreme subject I can write about.

"Love? Mm. Sex and love, they don't always go together, do they? I like the darker shades, like in 'Wang Dang Doodle'. I admire Willie Dixon's lyrics so much. There's a party going on in that song, but what kind of party? All the people he describes: Butcher-Knife-Totin' Annie, Razor-Totin' Jim, Fast-Talkin' Fanny. Then there's that line, 'Now when fish scent fills the air/There'll be snuff juice everywhere'. Fish scent must be female genitalia, 'my little oyster' and all that, but 'snuff juice'? I'm not sure."

The sound she aimed for on the album is a mixture of that spare, dark Chess sound and the size and heft of Led Zeppelin. And she and Albini did achieve something of that.

"If I play *Rid of Me* at home I get to the end of the first side and I can't breathe. Can't handle it. I'm taking it apart all the time. Analysing. I certainly wouldn't put it on for an enjoyable evening. It's uncomfortable."

That's not a bad thing.

Sultans of Swing   Dire Straits

(Mark Knopfler) ❊ Vertigo ❊ 1978 ❊ Appears on: *Dire Straits*

It's indeed fortunate that Mark Knopfler is such an erudite guitar player because he has to be the most inexpressive singer in the history of rock. My friend Amanda who worked on the Straits' multi-month Australian tour remembered that the same notes were played in the same place every single night. If Mark Knopfler ever had a bad day, you wouldn't know it from the concert.

Dire Straits were initially regarded as a New Wave band. They landed in this company having come up through the London pub scene with a vaguely gloomy name. But you can't imagine them getting so worked up that they slashed into a power chord in sheer frustration at the blandness of the straight world or whatever it was that got New Wavers going.

Dire Straits were, in fact, the perfect representation of the '80s – an era of post-modernism. They played long songs that appeared to have flights of improvisation but were tightly scripted. The lyrics had a Dylanesque obscurity but lacked poetry or much meaning.

Dire Straits, however, did have their moments. The first of them is 'Sultans of Swing' on the debut album. The lyric is about some long-lost band and is inconsequential. The thing here is the hook that Knopfler lays down with fluid and inventive guitar runs while the rhythm section maintains a gentle funk undertow. Knopfler's voice is ethereal and laid back, as befits the lyric. He's not upset that the Sultans are no longer here, just passing the information on.

Ultimately, if he doesn't care, why should we?

I've Seen All Good People Yes

(Jon Anderson/Chris Squire) ❊ Atlantic ❊ 1971 ❊ Appears on: *The Yes Album*

"Three-quarters of the way through we realised that for the first time we were making something that might possibly last," is how Jon Anderson described the making of *The Yes Album* to journalist Penny Valentine. "I'm never sure that the things I've written are going to last any kind of time, so much music seems a momentary thing. We were only talking the other day about the possibility of rock music – in the next ten years – really developing into a higher art form. Building up the same way classical music did into huge works that last and stand the test of time. Rock musicians will make music that will last a hell of a lot longer in the future."

Which explains why this album is about half good and what happened to make a perfectly fine little progressive rock outfit into the most faintly ridiculous behemoth that it became.

Classical-rock fusion was at best a daft idea.

It had been a promising beginning back in 1968 when singer Jon Anderson and bass player Chris Squire bonded over Simon & Garfunkel and determined to form a group modelled on the 5th Dimension. Their pop sensibility was augmented by drummer Bill Bruford, Tony Kay on organ and Peter Banks playing guitar. By this, their third album, Steve Howe had replaced Banks.

No doubt in a desire to emulate classical music Yes began to forsake songs for suites. They abandoned love songs for space operas and heavy themes (and generally impenetrable ones at that).

What Yes had on *The Yes Album* was chemistry and discipline. Bruford is one of the finest drummers – subtle and fluid to match Squire's bass lines. Steve Howe's complex and elegant guitar, however, makes the record spark.

The album's best cut is the single 'I've Seen All Good People'. The track sparkles with the light from Anderson's voice. 'Good People' was their first hit, and it was downhill ever after. Kaye was replaced by the classically trained, unspeakably pretentious keyboardist Rick Wakeman. In their search for the kudos of art, Yes honed their technique and lost their soul.

I Can't Live Without My Radio LL Cool J

(LL Cool J/Rick Rubin) ✳ Def Jam ✳ 1984 ✳ Appears on: *Radio*

On 'I Can't Live Without My Radio' LL Cool J showed himself to be a lover, not a fighter. Indeed he was a gawky, geeky teenager when *Radio* became a landmark hip-hop album. The album's opening salvo and key track, 'I Can't Live Without My Radio', was a perfect summer anthem – strong beats with resprung hooks and a dexterous rhyme jumped LL to the front of the queue. 'Radio' was a major step in recasting the vocabulary of rap music away from toasting and boasting over extended jams to being something else again.

Elsewhere on the album LL professes his love and pretty much nails the claim to be the first rap heartthrob. Working with producer Rick Rubin, LL Cool J shows the range and diversity that a rap artist could explore. Until this point most rappers had developed a single persona and rarely strayed from it. With *Radio* stretching the boundaries, Rubin and LL Cool J showed that rap was going to develop into a multifaceted musical form just as profound as jazz or rock.

(I Can't Get No) Satisfaction The Rolling Stones

(Mick Jagger/Keith Richards) ❋ Decca ❋ 1965 ❋ Appears on: *Out of Our Heads*

The perfect rock & roll record. The riff. The lyric. The delivery. Perfect.

The song began in guitarist Keith Richards' fitful sleep on 9 May 1965 in a Clearwater, Florida, motel. He woke and bashed the blues figure and the title out on an acoustic guitar into his cassette recorder and then fell back asleep. The next morning, as they sat by the motel pool, Jagger added a lyric. "It was my view of the world. My frustration with everything. Simple teenage aggression," said Jagger. "It was about America, its advertising syndrome, the constant barrage."

A few days later they began to record the song in the Chess studios in Chicago. These studios had been the home of Muddy Waters, Howlin' Wolf, Willie Dixon and Chuck Berry. For the Stones to record there was akin to a pilgrimage. However, the song wasn't finished until a marathon session at RCA studios in Los Angeles. As Charlie Watts noted, the same studio in which Duke Ellington cut 'Take the "A" Train'.

The song as Richards imagined it had a soul feel with a horn section carrying the riff, which he had sketched using fuzz tone guitar. "When it was by the pool it was a rather lilting acoustic melody," said Jagger. "It only got to the snarl when we got this fuzz box in the studio, which was the first time we'd used one." Producer/manager Andrew Loog Oldham, however, understood the power of the track.

"To my mind," said Richards, "the fuzz tone was really there to denote what the horns would be doing. But Andrew spotted the spirit of the track and we were already back on the road before we heard that they'd decided that 'Satisfaction' was going to be the single. We had thought we were going to cut a better version."

The song is grounded in Chicago blues; the guitar feel is not a million miles from Hubert Sumlin or Jimmy Reed.

Jagger's lyric pulls it all together – sexual frustration, contempt for consumer culture, alienation. He's witty but he also means it. He sings with the beat, improvising lyrics to match Watts' feel, and the staccato lyrics impress the point of the song. The lyric, no matter how appropriate and witty, is just dressing the anti-social attitude. Everything is in the nuance of Jagger's vocal. He sings the song like he really doesn't care about the nine-to-five world that is being marketed to him. That indifference made this the most revolutionary record of the '60s. Their pop comrades the Beatles were part of the machine, manufacturing Beatles wigs and Beatles cartoon shows and Beatles lunchboxes and adding to extraneous crap.

Bob Dylan wasn't really on the mainstream radar. Out in the suburbs he was regarded as a poet who couldn't sing. The Rolling Stones, however, couldn't be denied and they didn't give a fuck. The straight world could deal with rock & roll until the Stones announced with this single that they wouldn't be coming to the negotiation table. While all that has changed, the song remains relevant today.

"We were just saying what anybody would say among their own generation," said Richards. "It was the reaction that was interesting: we were shocked to find out they were shocked."

Rufus is a Tit Man   Loudon Wainwright III

(Loudon Wainwright) ❊ Columbia ❊ 1975 ❊ Appears on: *Unrequited*

A few years ago, Loudon Wainwright III addressed a college audience on the subject of writing. "By 1973, despite, or possibly due to, having made it big, I was miserable," he said. "Married and the father of two small children, I was never home, drunk a good deal of the time, and apparently felt it necessary to sleep with every waitress in North America and the British Isles. But guess what? All these beans have also been spilt in song."

The most eloquent beans are to be found on Wainwright's fifth album. By this stage, the songwriter was comfortable with his role as a humorist, having had chart success with the novelty song 'Dead Skunk'. Here he comes into his own as the sardonic chronicler of a relationship break-up. The songs are witty in a Cole Porter kind of way. It's a remarkably even-handed look at the dissolution of his marriage to Canadian folk singer Kate McGarrigle.

This was Wainwright's big shot at the charts. The production is clean and features some of the best players of the era, including bass players Harvey Brooks, Freebo and Klaus Voorman and a pre-Spinal Tap Christopher Guest. Jim Keltner on drums and David Sanborn on saxophone add their usual classy touches. These songs of emotional breakdown rollick along, especially when buoyed by Richard Greene's violin. Even classier are the backing vocals from Kate and Anna McGarrigle. The family touch is most gentle here in 'Rufus is a Tit Man', dedicated to his heir by that name. Wainwright's problem was that the lyrics are too sophisticated for a pop audience and the record never did sell much. Rufus went on to spill his own beans.

Theme from an Imaginary Western Jack Bruce

(Jack Bruce/Pete Brown) ❋ Polydor ❋ 1971 ❋ Appears on: *Songs for a Tailor*

The final notes of Cream's farewell concert were still reverberating around the Royal Albert Hall a year later when the bass player dropped this elegant, masterfully constructed piece of jazz-rock.

Although Bruce had written and sung the lion's share of Cream's songs, he was overshadowed by the myths of guitarist Eric Clapton and drummer Ginger Baker. The unassuming nature of this project and its lack of pop sheen consigned it and Bruce to obscurity.

The power trio recipe in Cream was two jazz players (Bruce and Baker) and a blues guitarist. Bruce had played the bass for bandleaders Alexis Korner and Manfred Mann and notably the jazzy Graham Bond Organisation. Then he joined Cream. What the rhythm section brought to the deal was an understanding of extended improvisation – a jazz concept that had no relation to R&B or blues music. However, after two years of jamming, Bruce returned to the song format.

Bruce kept it close to home with his first solo LP. Cream producer Felix Pappalardi was back behind the boards. Poet Pete Brown, who had written lyrics for most of Bruce's tunes with Cream, was also back. George Harrison played on one track, but mostly it was Bruce's old pals Dick Heckstall-Smith on saxophone and drummer Jon Hiseman.

Cream was a band that dripped with brutal music. The competitiveness between the players pushed the music forward. Left to his own devices, Bruce allows the songs to shine. Brown's lyrics are opaque at best, but the song 'Theme for an Imaginary Western' is beautifully constructed jazz pop. The problem really is Brown's. His pretentious lyrics fail to connect and without the instrumental fireworks of Cream, the record wasn't well received by the public. Had the songs been more accessible, this could have been the British equivalent of the first Blood, Sweat and Tears album. The musicianship – especially Bruce's soulful vocals – remains timeless.

The album title refers to American clothes designer Jeannie Franklin, who made clothes for Cream. She was the girlfriend of Fairport Convention's Richard Thompson and died in a car accident while on tour with him. On the day she died, Bruce received a letter that said, "Sing some high notes for me."

Watermelon Man   Herbie Hancock

(Herbie Hancock) ❋ Blue Note ❋ 1962 ❋ Appears on: *Takin' Off*

Despite his contribution to Miles Davis' legendary mid-'60s Quintet, the successes of his own projects and a continuing influence on R&B, jazz purists regard Herbie Hancock with suspicion. A child prodigy on the piano, Hancock moved from classical studies to jazz. He came to the attention of Coleman Hawkins and Donald Byrd – the latter bringing him to New York and the attention of the Blue Note label. At twenty-two he recorded this, his first solo album. The opening cut, 'Watermelon Man', is a joyous, bluesy piano riff that drew from R&B, soul-jazz and bebop and put it all into a pop hook. 'Watermelon Man' became a hit for Mongo Santamaria and for Hancock, and was to return when he moved to jazz-fusion a decade later. Hancock's style was to form a bridge in sensitivity to acid jazz in the early '90s.

Here on *Takin' Off* he's joined by horn players Dexter Gordon and Freddie Hubbard and the immensely funky rhythm section of bassist Butch Warren and drummer Billy Higgins. The key here is always the groove. Hancock loved to swing and if his changes were less hard-edged they were audacious and colourful. It was his sense of adventure that led him into Davis' group shortly after this album was recorded and from there onto fusion and beyond.

Space Oddity   David Bowie

(David Bowie) ❋ RCA ❋ 1969 ❋ Appears on: *Space Oddity*

He had been a mod and then an acoustic troubadour with a Bob Dylan fixation. Then Stanley Kubrick's space epic *2001* gave David Bowie the idea of a lifetime. It was the year of the moonwalk and space definitely seemed the place. 'Space Oddity', in its production, its lyric and in David Bowie, signalled the end of one decade of rock and the beginning of a new mannerist period. Bowie's song, rather than celebrating the conquest of the void, is a haunting ballad about alienation.

Inspired by *2001* and a "flirtation with smack," 'Space Oddity' has the now-immortal line "Ground control to Major Tom". The astronaut is trapped in his spacecraft with no hope of returning to Earth. Essentially it's a folk song strummed on acoustic guitar. Bowie took the performance to another level – his deadpan, world-weary singing was quite unlike anything that had come before. There was a whole new slant on ambivalence here.

George Martin and Tony Visconti turned down the opportunity to produce this track. Visconti thought it an attempt to cash in on the Apollo mission. Gus Dudgeon was enlisted and brought along string arranger Paul Buckmaster and Rick Wakeman on the Mellotron. Dudgeon's use of strings and keyboards made the record sound slightly futuristic and trippy without losing its sense of the narrative.

The song was recorded in one day – 20 June. It was played to the public at the Rolling Stones' free concert in Hyde Park on 5 July and released as a 45 a week later. The BBC adopted 'Space Oddity' as its theme for its coverage of the first moonwalk that summer and the song became a hit.

Search and Destroy Iggy & the Stooges
(Iggy Pop/James Williamson) ✳ Columbia ✳ 1973 ✳ Appears on: *Raw Power*

Hard to believe, but Elektra dropped the Stooges after two albums. Admittedly the Stooges were considered something of a joke by the music business and most critics ... and somewhat less than that by the public. Their pure, desperate noise was ten years ahead of its time. In hindsight we can see that a handful of rock critics and musicians were right and the Stooges were one of the most exciting and revolutionary rock & roll bands of all time. The only influential fan they had was David Bowie, who took the Stooges under his wing. He persuaded Columbia to commission this album and persuaded singer Iggy Pop to reform the band that was then in tatters.

Raw Power delivers exactly what the title promises, right from its opening cut, 'Search and Destroy' – from the open shards of screeching torn notes from James Williamson's guitar and Iggy singing, "I'm a street walking cheetah with a heart full of napalm/I'm a runaway child with a nuclear A bomb/I am the world's most forgotten boy/The one who searches to destroy."

Iggy teamed up with old pal James Williamson and then sent for the other Stooges, Ron and Scott Asheton. Ron was moved to bass and Scott provided his usual monolithic beat.

Once in London the Stooges rehearsed six hours a day and then went into the studio for two months in the height of the 1972 summer. Iggy, who claims he was on serious drugs (the others claim the band was mostly clean at the time), produced the album and it sounds like semi-structured chaos.

"At the time when we were over in England, we had just gotten off of drugs," Williamson said. "We were actually pretty good almost the entire time, at least through most of *Raw Power* there was very little drugs involved. A lot of drinking and just the regular dope scene but by the end of the album we'd met a few people and sort of slid back . . . by the end we were playing around with that, but I wouldn't say that was our heavy period of drug abuse."

The songwriting was the sharpest the Stooges had ever done. Sheer, cold aggression and bitterness had replaced the unformed improvisations of their early albums. Williamson's guitar playing on 'Search and Destroy' is like being attacked by a switchblade. It tears through the rhythm section like it's carving live flesh. Iggy's lyrics are funny and also poetic and focused. This is a song not just of an alienated white trash junkie; these are the words of a man who has crossed the line, and they would come to bear on the cultural nemeses of the next twenty years; whether they be named Travis Bickle or Mark Chapman or Osama Bin Laden.

The album was, by the end of the sessions, a mess, and Bowie took the tapes and mixed them for release. Much criticism has come subsequently for the mix and its treble sound (Iggy remixed it himself a couple of years ago) but that high, thin, rapier sound is part of its intensity.

'Search and Destroy' was an anthem of the punks some years later but they never captured its elemental force.

"This new album by the Stooges – aptly titled *Raw Power* – had the very same effect on me the first time I heard it," critic Ben Edmonds wrote in 1973. "It's like your first hard-on or the first time you got really high: an experience so over-powering that it forces new definitions for even the most familiar things."

When Your Lonely Heart Breaks Neil Young & Crazy Horse

(Neil Young) ✳ Geffen ✳ 1987 ✳ Appears on: *Life*

An extraordinary minimalist ballad from Neil Young. The melody is trained and stretched out over impossibly long, sustained chords and Young chants the lyrics (which don't amount to much more than the title). Then there is the drum beat – the occasional single beat of the snare crashing into the melody like metal punctuation. This is Neil Young in a trance. In getting beyond the words, Young lets the sound of the voice and the melancholy, far-away guitar do all the talking that's needed. "Sometimes we just play one chord for a long time. D or B or one of those G things," said bassist Billy Talbot. "I figure if I'm going to play a note I'm going to play it with everything I have, whether it's two or three or fifteen or twenty. I like that. Whatever is appropriate, I like to make the thing feel good to me, so I do what I can do the best."

Sweet Child o' Mine Guns N' Roses

(Guns N' Roses) ✳ Geffen ✳ 1987 ✳ Appears on: *Appetite for Destruction*

"Metal stems from sexual frustration," said Guns N' Roses guitarist Slash. "We come from an amazing background of repression, stifled childhoods ..."

Although they crawled out of the gutter, and perhaps because of that, Guns N' Roses had no interest in staying there. They were an outlaw group who grabbed for the gold with both hands. Their opportunity came with their second album, *Appetite for Destruction*. It was at a time when rock, especially hard rock, had become a parody of itself: a blow-dried big hair joke. A damp squib. Then out of the Los Angeles metal scene came Guns – junkies with a killer guitar player in Slash and a singer who wore his damaged psyche on his heavily tattooed arms. Guns N' Roses were the main event of the turn of the decade. Singer Axl Rose was totally plugged into the Zeitgeist – the '80s obsessions with self-psychobabble and money.

Although they looked and originally sounded like the love child of the Rolling Stones and the New York Dolls, Axl Rose's inspirations were closer to Queen and Elton John.

"I thought about trying to sell more records than Boston's first album," said Rose. "I always thought that and never let up. Everything was directed at trying to achieve the sales without sacrificing the credibility of our music. We worked real hard to sell this many records. Maybe *Appetite* will be the only good album we make, but it wasn't just a fluke."

Appetite for Destruction covered all the usual sociopathic bases, but the real classic was their epic 'Sweet Child o' Mine'. The delicate melancholy ballad written by Rose about an ex-girlfriend is his best vocal. It's perfectly in counterpoint to Slash's extensive, eloquent guitar melody. Spikey. Tough. Sad but brilliantly played. According to Rose, "My favourite part of the song is Slash's slow solo; it's the heaviest part for me."

"Most of the songs on *Appetite* are first, second, or third takes," said drummer Steven Adler. "'Sweet Child o' Mine' we only played once. I think that's why the record did so well – it was real."

I Got Rhythm Ethel Merman

(George Gershwin/Ira Gershwin) ❋ Smithsonian ❋ 1930 ❋

Appears on: *American Musical Theatre: Shows, Songs and Stars, Vol. 1*

This variation of the twelve-bar blues has been one of the bedrock tunes in 20th-century music. George Gershwin wrote the tune first and his brother Ira struggled to find words to fit. Starting out with nonsense rhymes, Ira moved to a less rigid lyric, which he anchored to the hard beats in the song. The tune comes straight out of the blues and ragtime but is given an extra-fast tempo and Gershwin's elegant swing.

According to radio station NPR's 'The 100 Most Important American Musical Works of the 20th Century', 'I Got Rhythm' was a key moment in the Broadway musical *Girl Crazy*, which featured a young singer with a big voice. George Gershwin said of Ethel Merman that "she could hold a note longer than the Chase Bank." They were aided by the orchestra on that show, which included Glenn Miller, Benny Goodman and drummer Gene Krupa – all of whom became giants of jazz.

The tune was indestructible. It has been rearranged by every major jazz artist either as itself or given a new title, and it featured in the 1943 film version of *Girl Crazy* with Judy Garland singing. Gene Kelly had a shot at it in *An American in Paris* and even Madonna had her turn in conjunction with Stephen Sondheim in *Dick Tracey*. The rapid changes and the blues roots in the song have meant that its DNA can be found in many parts of popular song.

She Does It Right Dr Feelgood

(Wilco Johnson) ✳ United Artists ✳ 1975 ✳ Appears on: *Down by the Jetty*

"How can anyone be so basic in 1975? Are they really four zombies who fell asleep in the early '60s and snored happily through the 'progressive' rock era? After ten years of remorseless rock progress from psychedelia to sophistication to decadence to degeneracy, until every other band is carting around its very own oratorio about the downfall of civilisation, Dr Feelgood turn up looking like hoodlums from some long forgotten B picture, and sounding as though the idea of musical progress had quite simply never occurred to them," wrote Mick Gold in *Let It Rock*.

Dr Feelgood were ahead of their time. That description of the skanky R&B quartet could be read as a manifesto of the punk tsunami that overtook London a year and half later. In 1975 the Feelgoods were the cure for what was rotten in British rock. Formed in Canvey Island, in London's industrial wasteland, Dr Feelgood were one step better than a bar band due to the riffs, hooks and songs that spewed from Wilco Johnson's guitar.

On stage, Wilco played like a zombie strutting back and forth, zigzagging, twirling around with his eyes permanently fixed in a thousand-yard stare. Lee Brilleaux's vocals had that alcohol-soaked heft of early Van Morrison as he lurched around like a deranged bank clerk (his description).

This first album sounded like John Lee Hooker on an amphetamine bender. The opening cut is the deepest: 'She Does It Right' has a blistering riff that just bounces out. To honour the creative debt to both Hooker and the Animals, the Feelgoods rip into 'Boom Boom' before taking off into another eight Johnson originals before closing with a slamming version of 'Tequila'. Like the Ramones, Dr Feelgood's monochrome cover with the industrial end of the Thames in the background is a statement of intent – stripped back, no nonsense, go for the throat, classic R&B. Only the Rolling Stones' first album matches this for lean, mean rocking blues.

The beauty of Dr Feelgood was their singularity. They reeked of the time and place of their birth. As their pal Nick Lowe said, "They're the greatest local band in the world." *Down by the Jetty* is so redolent of its time and place that you can positively smell the pollution. It's one of the classics of British rock & roll.

Sleeps with Angels Neil Young & Crazy Horse

(Neil Young) ❋ Reprise ❋ 1994 ❋ Appears on: *Sleeps with Angels*

Many people were shocked by the 1994 suicide of Nirvana singer Kurt Cobain, but only Neil Young was quoted in his suicide note. Although they had never met, there was a mutual admiration. "I really could hear his music," said Young. "There's not that many absolutely real performers. In that sense, he was a gem. He was bothered by the fact that he would end up following schedules, have to go on when he didn't feel like it, and be faking, and that would be very hard for him because of his commitment."

The *Sleeps with Angels* LP was hastily assembled following Cobain's death. Young corralled Crazy Horse up at his ranch and together they made the best album they'd done since *On the Beach* twenty years earlier. On the title track Young marshals the awesome power of Crazy Horse in full cry and then subsumes it in murky production, buries it in a fog of sound so that it's full of ethereal menace.

Although the album is one of Young's masterpieces, he refused to promote the record or discuss it, in deference to Cobain's memory.

As he said to Nick Kent in *MOJO*: "*Sleeps with Angels* has a lot of overtones to it, from different situations that were described in it. A lot of sad scenes. I've never really spoken about why I made that album. I don't want to start now."

He doesn't have to; the title track says it all.

Waves of Fear Lou Reed

(Lou Reed) ❋ RCA ❋ 1982 ❋ Appears on: *The Blue Mask*

Lou Reed confessed that the title track of this album was too much even for him to listen to, a tale of sexual adventure turned holocaust. Of course, Lou was the man who put sadomasochism into the rock vernacular back in 1968. A decade and a half on he had witnessed what it was like to walk on the wild side. It's one thing to talk about polymorphous perversity and quite another to experience it and see how people can destroy themselves through hedonism.

Given the darkness of this album – and 'Waves of Fear' is one of the most physical and searing pieces of music he has ever made – Lou was living the suburban dream. He was happily settled with Sylvia Morales and his career was chugging along –

hence his domestic ode 'My House'. It's only from the safety of that vantage point could he look at the demons and see the shadow.

Lou was also in the middle of another supportive relationship – with Fernando Saunders and Robert Quine. Saunders is one of the most soulful bass players and his sparse, beautifully rounded low notes are as eloquent as Reed's words. They carry the weight of the world. Quine was an absolute devotee of Reed, understanding both the avant-garde and the trashy sides of Lou's personality, which he conveyed in elliptical, stabbing guitar lines. As Robert Christgau noted in his review, "Never has Lou sounded more Ginsbergian, more let-it-all-hang-out than on this, his most controlled, plain spoken, deeply felt, and uninhibited album. Even his unnecessarily ideological heterosexuality is more an expression of mood than a statement of policy; he sounds glad to be alive, so that horror and pain become occasions for courage and eloquence as well as bitterness and sarcasm. Every song comes at the world from a slightly different angle, and every one makes the others stronger."

The Blue Mask was recorded live in the studio (except for vocals) doing a song a day in one or two takes with no rehearsals. Reed has continued to make the rock quartet go places it has never been before and this is one of them.

Visions of Johanna Bob Dylan

(Bob Dylan) ✳ Columbia ✳ 1966 ✳ Appears on: *Blonde on Blonde*

'Visions of Johanna' is one of Bob Dylan's masterpieces. It's mysterious, brimfull of vivid images and ultimately inscrutable. Set in the Chelsea Hotel, it's the late-night musings of a man with one woman in his arms and another on his mind. The song veers from the prosaic ("In this room the heat pipes just cough/The country music station plays soft") to the surreal ("On the back of the fish truck that loads/While my conscience explodes"). All kinds of meaning have been attributed to these abstruse lines – is it about ex-girlfriend Joan Baez, his wife Sara? Is it about God or the Devil? It's unlikely that we will ever know. Trying to decipher the literal meaning of 'Visions of Johanna' is a fruitless task. The meaning is there in the narcotic mood of the music, which is dense and opaque and drifting like smoke. The clanging of the plumbing, the faint hum of the radio and the reflections of the world of straight people going about their lives go on whilst in the night Dylan goes through his sweet turmoil.

Originally titled 'Seems Like a Freeze Out', 'Visions of Johanna' was one of the few songs that had been in Dylan's repertoire before he went to Nashville for the *Blonde on Blonde* sessions. Keyboard player Al Kooper and guitarist Robbie Robertson accompanied Dylan; the other players were all country music sessioneers. It was the highpoint of an amazingly fertile period in Dylan's work, where he refashioned the shape of rock music.

Most of the songs on the album were written in Dylan's Chelsea Hotel period, where he ended his relationship with Joan Baez, hung around the fringes of Warhol's Factory crowd, possibly had a romance with starlet Edie Sedgwick and fell in love with Sara Lowndes, whom he married shortly after. It was also the culmination of a creative surge that took Dylan from the folk scene to the centre of rock & roll music.

The answer to the riddle of Johanna's visions isn't to be found in anything beyond itself.

Return to Forever Chick Corea & Return to Forever

(Chick Corea) ❋ ECM ❋ 1972 ❋ Appears on: *Return to Forever*

Chick Corea, yet another alumnus of Miles Davis' Bitches Brew sessions, took fusion into his own direction. With bassist Stanley Clarke, Joe Farell on flute and sax, percussionist Airto Moreira and Airto's wife, Flora Purim, singing, Corea knew he had something unique.

The pianist was particularly interested in putting a strong rhythmic Latin colour to his music. Stan Getz offered the opportunity to keep the band together as his backing, while in downtime Corea recorded this album. The group Return to Forever was to be one of the most enduring fusion or jazz-rock groups of the early '70s.

Like many of his contemporaries, Corea saw his future not in terms of the increasingly esoteric world of jazz but in crossing over into rock. It was not to be.

"I have a very clear intention now, which is shared by the others: to present very high quality music and to communicate to a lot of people," he said at the time.

"Right now we've been working the standard jazz circuit, because that's what we're mainly known as. But more and more, as we play this music, we're getting opportunities to play to the audiences that we feel would like what we do more – colleges, concert dates, and pop audiences also."

Corea's problem was that he was too intellectual a composer and his music too sophisticated for even the progressive rock market of the time.

"Forever is a word which means a duration of time without ending, you see, and it implies a place where people are when they're not thinking about time, not embroiled in the world, and they're very much themselves," he said of the title song. "Where time just passes without being noticed. And it's a very beautiful place to be; it's a very light, happy place, where a lot of production and creativity happens. It's not really a place or a time – it's just a way of being; and it's a return to that, you see.

"Returning to it is necessary because I think this is a basic goal that all people share – just to be happy, to be very creative, and to communicate with one another very freely. Such a way of existence smacks of truth. But people have moved away from the awareness of this. All you have to do is take a look around you, and inside you, to observe how far we've travelled from it."

Corea was an inspired pianist and composer but he lacked the aggression of John McLaughlin or the spacey styling of Weather Report, and so somehow fell between the cracks. His solo piano work would ultimately last longer. But on this first album the fluid, innovative bass playing of Clarke, Corea's own work and the Latin colours of Airto make it a classic.

Is This Pop? XTC

(Andy Partridge) ✳ Virgin ✳ 1977 ✳ Appears on: *White Music*

"I'd like to think we're the Vasco de Gamas of popular music," said XTC bass player Colin Moulding. The five-piece from the provincial English town of Swindon had formed in 1973 as the Helium Kids in a pathetic attempt to be a glam rock band from the suburbs. Then punk rock hit. Although guitarist Andy Partridge claimed to be underwhelmed by first exposure to the Sex Pistols, punk rock opened doors for their high-energy, eccentric pop music.

Recorded in a week, *White Music* deconstructs pop music. It's angry and angular, zigzagging across the stereo with half-formed ideas. The album credits three producers, including three British superstars of the desk, Robert John 'Mutt' Lange, Steve Lillywhite and John Leckie, who more than compensate for the group's furious youth.

It's a much better record than Partridge, who was the main composer, recalls. "The first album, *White Music*, was just snotty, naked baby photos," he said in the early '80s. "I don't know if I'd want to see them now. Don't get them out, Mother, I'm not like that any more. I get embarrassed by *White Music* now because I was really trying too hard to find a style in which to say these things. But the paradox was, at that point in time I had nothing to say. I was just writing lyrics and they never gave me any pictures other than the total thing of that sort of modern, loud, noisy guitar, bass, drums, organ mess.

"The chords were picked because they upset more than they were musically well crafted. After *White Music* I started to feel like I really wanted to get out cohesive ideas."

Its lack of cohesion is its strength. He was more accurate when he described it as "Captain Beefheart meets the Archies . . . I can see now it's just everything we'd ever listened to. The Beatles are in there, Sun Ra, Atomic Rooster in there, anybody who'd done anything we liked in the previous lifetime. We just thought it was real, dead original."

The single 'Is This Pop?' was, in its own way, a manifesto on the state of the art. Their confusion about the nature of pop was an important step, spearheading a movement that, for want of any better phrase, was called power pop and later, of course, New Wave.

Partridge's vision has always guided the group and he saw himself in the eccentric tradition of Ray Davies and Syd Barrett. As time went on, he became better at the craft and the singles were better, but the weirdness developed into self-consciousness and was less and less powerful.

XTC probably made better records as time went on, but this first one – right down to the pop art style of the cover, the typeface, and the clothes they wore – had a unique bravery. The kind of blind nerve that it takes to explore the ends of the Earth. Moulding was right when he said, "The most impressive thing about it is the energy."

She Said She Said The Beatles

(John Lennon/Paul McCartney) ❋ Parlophone ❋ 1966 ❋ Appears on: *Revolver*

If ever there was acid rock this is it. The song was inspired by Lennon and Harrison tripping on LSD with actor Peter Fonda and the Byrds in Los Angeles in 1965. "I remember sitting on the deck of the house with George, who was telling me that he thought he was dying," Fonda recalled. "I told him there was nothing to be afraid of and that all he needed to do was to relax. I said that I knew what it was like to be dead because when I was ten years old, I'd accidentally shot myself in the stomach and my heart stopped beating three times because I lost so much blood. John was passing at the time and heard me say 'I know what it's like to be dead.' He looked at me and said, 'You're making me feel like I've never been born. Who put all that shit in your head?'"

Fonda actually reprised the scene and some of the dialogue for the acid sequence in his film *Easy Rider*.

When it came to recording the track, the Beatles, George Martin and engineer Geoff Emerick threw all their ingenuity into it to capture the spacey, brittle and a touch nasty edge of the song.

"John brought it into the studio pretty much finished," McCartney said. "I'm not sure, but I think it's one of the only Beatles records that I never played on. I think we'd had a barney, or something, and I said, 'Oh, fuck you!' and they said, 'We'll do it.' I think George played bass."

One of the earliest takes has the lines: "Who put all that crap in your head?/You know what it's like to be dead/And it's making me feel like my trousers are torn."

Bo Diddley Bo Diddley

(Ellas McDaniel) ❋ Checker ❋ 1957 ❋ Appears on: *Bo Diddley*

The 'Bo Diddley' beat is one of the essential parts of the vocabulary of rock & roll. Its basic syncopation is a jazzed-up blues with a heavy accent on the drums and it's been at the core of every rock & roll band's repertoire from Buddy Holly to U2. The Bo Diddley beat sounds so natural that it has been assumed that Ellas McDaniel (aka Bo Diddley) is part of an African tradition, but McDaniel disputed this. "The name and the beat go together," he said. "I had the name, and then I made the beat with it. I came up with that beat. They tried to say it's actually a jungle beat, and so it may be. It may be connected somewhere, but I ain't heard no jungle cats playin' it, you know? People should ask Bo Diddley if they wanna know the story. When you go to the dentist, you go to the dentist to get a tooth pulled. Don't go round the corner to the mechanic. All these people try to tell you what you sound like, and that sucks."

Diddley/McDaniel was a Chicago street corner musician when he went down to Chess studios to see about recording. His repertoire was mostly R&B covers. Diddley had studied the violin and shifted to guitar almost accidentally. His big hands didn't lend themselves to chording so Diddley used an open E major tuning, which is suited to rhythmic work. The other part of his sound was Jerome Green's maracas as percussion.

On 2 March 1955 Bo Diddley and his band, featuring Jerome Green, Billy Boy Arnold on harmonica and Clifton James on drums, cut their first tracks for Chess. It was to be one of the most incredible double A-sides, with Diddley's powerful, stirring blues: 'I'm a Man' on one side and 'Bo Diddley' on the other.

Bo Diddley recalled the recording of his namesake song: "When I started playin' Phil [Chess] called his brother Leonard in . . . they told me to rewrite it. The words was a little tough. It had lyrics like, 'Bowlegged rooster told a cross-legged duck, Say you ain't good lookin' but you sure can . . . crow.' It took me about seven days to rewrite it and that song became 'Bo Diddley'."

Tonight's the Night Neil Young & Crazy Horse

(Neil Young) ❊ Reprise ❊ 1975 ❊ Appears on: *Tonight's the Night*

The *Harvest* album put Neil Young in the middle of the road and as he famously sang, he "headed for the ditch". Young and his friends were indulging and two of those close to him – guitarist Danny Whitten and roadie Bruce Berry – died as a result of drugs.

"'Tonight's the Night' is like an OD letter," Young said around the time of the album's release. "The whole thing is about life, dope and death. When we [Nils Lofgren, Talbot, Molina and Young] played that music we were all thinking of Danny Whitten and Bruce Berry, two close members of our unit lost to junk overdoses.

"The *Tonight's the Night* sessions were the first time what was left of Crazy Horse had gotten together since Danny died. It was up to us to get the strength together among us to fill the hole he left. The other OD, Bruce Berry, was CSNY's roadie for a long time. His brother Ken runs Studio Instrument Rentals, where we recorded the album. So we had a lot of vibes going for us. There was a lot of spirit in the music we made.

"It's funny, I remember the whole experience in black and white. We'd go down to SIR about five in the afternoon and start getting high, drinking tequila and playing pool. About midnight, we'd start playing. And we played Bruce and Danny on their way all through the night. I'm not a junkie and I won't even try it out to check out what it's like ... but we all got high enough, right out there on the edge where we felt wide-open to the whole mood. It was spooky. I probably feel this album more than anything else I've ever done."

The album was shelved for more than a year until manager Elliot Roberts added some live tracks and other songs from the vault. It still lay dormant until Young was about to release another country-style album, *Homegrown*, and played the two albums back to back. He then shelved the country record for the less commercial *Tonight's the Night*. A wise move, as it's one of his greatest moments. The loping title song captures the essence of the album – collapsing and getting up again.

"I know the first time I listened back on *Tonight's the Night* it was the most out-of-tune thing I'd ever heard," he said. "Everyone's off-key. I couldn't hack it. I took *Tonight's the Night* because of its overall strength in performance and feeling.

"I fully expect some of the most determinedly worst reviews I've ever had. I mean if anybody really wanted to let go, they could do it on this one. And undoubtedly a few people will. That's good for them, though. I like to see people make giant breakthroughs for themselves. It's good for their psyche to get it all off their chests.

"I've seen *Tonight's the Night* draw a line everywhere it's been played. People who thought they would never dislike anything I did fall on the other side of the line. Others who thought 'I can't listen to that cat. He's just too sad,' or whatever ... They listen another way now."

Graceland Paul Simon

(Paul Simon) ✳ Warner Bros. ✳ 1986 ✳ Appears on: *Graceland*

"After everything was finished, I had no title for the album. In the chorus where it says 'Graceland', I fought for a long time to get rid of it. I didn't like it," said Paul Simon. "I thought it was distracting. I figured people would think I'm writing about Elvis Presley, and this is a South African record and I'm now writing a song about Mississippi and Graceland . . .

"I took a long time before it settled and I got comfortable with it and said, 'Oh that's fine. You're not writing about Elvis Presley and it doesn't matter if they think you are. Those that get it will know that you're not, and those that don't get it won't care, they'll be just as happy that you're writing about Elvis Presley. It's not going to do any harm and in fact, it's kind of fun in a way.'"

The title track of *Graceland* tells the story of three journeys. Ostensibly Simon is recalling a trip to Memphis, Tennessee, that he took with his son Harper after the break-up of his marriage. The township jive of his African band and Simon's melodic precision melding together is another journey whereby the New York superstar threw off his status and went to Africa to learn about music. That was an act of grace that led to Simon's redemption and his resurrection as an artist after a decade in the doldrums.

"Losing love is like a window in your heart," he sings. In opening the window, Simon found humility and grace.

The sanctity, too, is in the music, and there lies the third journey – from Africa to Memphis.

The *Graceland* album was surrounded by idiot politicians and activists charging that Simon had endorsed apartheid by using South African musicians. As Simon said, the project was akin to going to Nazi Germany and playing for the Jews. The message of this song is in the higher, redemptive power of music: that it can overcome the feeble hearts of men.

"The thing about it is, you don't even know if you're right," he said. "I tried for months to try to dislodge the idea that I was writing a song about Graceland. I mean, really, I just spent months and months thinking, 'When is this going to go away?' And I ended up calling the album that. So I don't think that I know either. I don't really know."

Love Me Do The Beatles

(John Lennon/Paul McCartney) ✳ Parlophone ✳ 1962 ✳ Appears on: *Please Please Me*

EMI's house producer George Martin had liked the Beatles at their audition but was not happy with the drummer. Between the audition and the Beatles' first proper session Ringo Starr replaced Pete Best. The first time they cut 'Love Me Do' Ringo's drumming was judged poor and session player Alan White was behind the kit for the second try. Martin eventually gave Ringo the OK and the song was recut, but the White version appeared on the album.

George Martin recalls, "In about January '62, I met Brian Epstein and he was tryin' to get the Beatles off the ground and get some record label together. Anyways, to cut a long story short, when I heard what Brian had to offer on tape, it wasn't very good. In fact, it was awful. But I said, I really wanted to find out more about them . . . there was something about them that I wanted to investigate. So, they came down a couple of months later, and I spent an evening, afternoon, and evening with them in Abbey Roads Studios. I fell in love with them. I thought they were wonderful people. I mean, they showed no signs of being great songwriters. The best they could offer me were pretty ordinary songs. I thought 'Love Me Do' was the best. 'PS I Love You' was another one and 'One after 909'. They weren't great songs, but they had tremendous charisma."

'Love Me Do' has a tough R&B feel with a delicious pop melody and the incredible close harmony singing of Lennon and McCartney. Lennon's harmonica riff, inspired by American Delbert McClinton, with whom the Beatles had toured, lifted the song and added to its blues edge.

If the song seemed slight, it cut through the pop charts of the day with a new sound that would, as you know, change everything.

Changes David Bowie

(David Bowie) ✳ RCA ✳ 1971 ✳ Appears on: *Hunky Dory*

Starting out with a stutter like the mod anthem 'My Generation', 'Changes' was Bowie's first manifesto. Rock songwriters to that point had been at pains to place themselves in some tradition or other, whether it was blues or folk music or

Modernist poetry. With 'Changes', Bowie announced that his artistic personality was in flux; its future shape would be mercurial and respect no rules. This was image-making like nothing before.

Bowie – half the time dressed as a woman and half as an alien – also announced that his identity would be in flux. In many ways the '70s were far more revolutionary than the '60s, particularly in the area of personal liberation, and Bowie was right on the barricades.

Bowie had recently signed a deal with RCA and visited New York. While in Manhattan he met Andy Warhol and Lou Reed and visited the Factory, but these influences were already apparent in his work. It was decadent, arty, playful and ironic. Bowie put those attitudes on the charts.

'Changes' shows Bowie's relationship with guitarist Mick Ronson starting to blossom, with the furious tempo changes in the song coloured by Bowie's subtle shifts in vocal layers.

The music was new and shiny. Rick Wakeman's piano glistened through the bass-dominated glam-sounding bottom end. The lyrics on the *Hunky Dory* album reflected extreme states of madness, drugs and the state of the human race. 'Changes' was the perfect introduction to that album, but on its own it was an introduction to the decade to come.

Song of Being a Child Van Morrison

(Van Morrison/Peter Handke) ❋ Polydor ❋ 1998 ❋ Appears on: *The Philosopher's Stone*

The sheer transcendental spirit that Van Morrison achieved between *Moondance* (1970) and *A Period of Transition* (1977) reached its peak with *St Dominic's Preview* (1972) and *Veedon Fleece* (1974) when the self-proclaimed Belfast cowboy combined soul music, rock and mysticism in an intense potion that is some of the finest rock & roll music ever made. Although his record sales increased in the '80s when he moved from the US back to Europe and embraced Celtic music even more closely, for my money Morrison almost never again reached the heights of his American years. There's a smoothness to his '80s recordings and a desire to work within the rules and redefine his own vocabulary. It's excellent music but not life-changing. But then, as Lester Bangs once observed, if one has looked into the abyss of existence as Van

Morrison did in his twenties and come back from there, who can begrudge him a little comfort in maturity. Occasionally he touched the sublime again. 'Song of Being a Child' is one of them. The lyric comes from German poet/playwright Peter Handke and is recited by Morrison and June Boyce over the top of a meditative keyboard part. Whether it was Morrison's study of jazz or spiritual texts, it's through modal arrangements like these and his rhythmic phrasing that he can touch the ineffable. Morrison's best subject, too, is the loss of innocence, which naturally chimes with the subject matter here: "When the child was a child ... It couldn't imagine nothingness/And today shudders in the face of it." The sound of shuddering in the face of the abyss and never giving in is where Van Morrison's true voice lies.

Sweet Fire of Love Robbie Robertson

(Robbie Robertson) ✳ Geffen ✳ 1987 ✳ Appears on: *Robbie Robertson*

A decade went by between the Band's *Last Waltz* and singer/songwriter/guitarist Robbie Robertson's first solo album. But then Robertson's myth has always been greater than his output. The Band made only two great albums and a smattering of classic songs in their illustrious career. There's a sense of stage fright all through *Robbie Robertson*.

Robertson enlisted fellow Canadian Daniel Lanois as co-producer. Lanois had only just become known through his work with U2 and Peter Gabriel, but it was an inspired choice. Lanois brought atmosphere to a project that otherwise could have been clinical. He also brought his friends – there was U2, who performed 'Sweet Fire of Love', Peter Gabriel, Gil Evans, and some lesser known up and comers including Lone Justice singer Maria McKee, plus the members of the Band. The consequent album sounds like a John Ford movie – huge landscapes of sound reproducing something that was supposed to be organic and primitive. At times, his collaborators swamp Robertson – especially U2, who were on the ascendant and whose sound is so distinctive. Robertson often seems content to hang back and let others do the talking.

"When I was younger, I thought I was too young to be really personal," Robertson said. "I thought that what I was feeling and thinking might be half-baked." He really faced the problem that it could be overcooked.

Way Over Yonder in the Minor Key   Billy Bragg & Wilco

(Woody Guthrie) ❊ Elektra ❊ 1998 ❊ Appears on: *Mermaid Avenue*

Bob Dylan wrote in his memoir, *Chronicles Volume 1*, that Woody Guthrie, then hospitalised and on his death bed, sent the young Dylan over to his house in New Jersey to recover a box of unrecorded songs the Dustbowl balladeer would be happy for Dylan to record. On the day, there was some confusion and Dylan went home empty-handed. The songs lay in a box for the next thirty-five years until Guthrie's daughter Nora gave the box to English protest singer Billy Bragg, who teamed up with new country's current young thing, Wilco, for an amazing album.

These songs from Guthrie's later life in New York show a very different side to his work. They are more about entertaining word-play than class warfare. Wilco brings a melodic complexity to the folk songs that had never been apparent in Guthrie's work nor his followers'. Bragg, too, finds a harmonious and somewhat less strident tone that had previously escaped him.

"That's something I learned from Woody," said Bragg. "There's no cynicism in his songs. He always said, 'I never want to write songs that put people down.'

"For those of us who want to build a better world, cynicism may be a worse enemy than capitalism. People who just sit on their butt, saying everything would be fine if it were done just the way they want, are as much a problem as the Tories. It's easy to sit back and criticise, but that doesn't change anything."

Bragg also benefited from the extraordinary versatility of Wilco. "Before," he admitted to *Harp* magazine, "I had had to come up with all the ideas, and if anything went wrong, everyone looked to me. It was me pulling from the front and me pushing from the back. It wasn't like that with Wilco. We sat down and learned the songs together, and each person's idea had as much weight as the next person's. With them I could go back to the hotel and trust them to carry on with another song."

'Way Over Yonder in the Minor Key' shines through its ensemble performance and is a mark of what needs to happen if the folk tradition is to get out of the museum.

"Come back Woody Guthrie," sang Steve Earle as an opening line to his album *El Corazon*. Bragg and Wilco achieved that.

Blue Monday New Order

(Gilbert/Hook/Morris/Sumner) ✳ Factory ✳ 1983 ✳ Appears on: *Power, Corruption & Lies*

The reverberations from this song were still being felt in popular music twenty years later.

New Order, born from the ashes of Joy Division, developed their distinctive, gloomy Manchester rock on their debut, *Movement*. This was the sound of the industrial wasteland of Britain's north country viewed through the prism of Bowie's Berlin recordings. The songs were humourless, relentless and thick with guitar and keyboards. There was a singularity to New Order's vision that made it compelling, especially to troubled teens.

The key to New Order wasn't, however, their sombre lyrics but rather the erupting rhythm section of Peter Hook on bass and drummer Stephen Morris. The monochromatic Joy Division groove – part Kraut Rock, part industrial and part metal – was an entirely new approach to rock and became the industry standard for post-punk rock. There were thick slabs of synthesiser propelled by the molten bass lines from Hook and coloured by the keyboards of Gillian Gilbert, who replaced the late Ian Curtis. The ghost of Curtis hung around the early years of New Order giving a gravitas to their monotonous, bleak songs. Paul Rambali put it well in *Face*: "Their music has reached deep into the sensitive isolation of nineteen-year-old male bedrooms. Playing a kind of refined, high-tech heavy metal, stripped of all the stucco frills but not lacking in melodrama ..."

The change in the group's sound came with Peter Hook and Stephen Morris investing in computers and sequencers.

"With guitar, bass and drums you've got limited horizons," said Hook. "We'd like to increase our range of sounds and rhythms. If you come up with an idea for a song, you know exactly what you want the machine to do. You want a machine that can do everything! But that hasn't been built yet. We thought the Emulator was going to be it – but you get one and you soon find it has its limits."

So with their new toys and an appreciation of nightclubs, the song 'Blue Monday' gave New Order its first hit single, a dance floor anthem and a new purpose in life. The 12-inch is a perfect synthesis of German and industrial music with a pop melody. This is one of those moments where the shape of popular music was altered forever.

New Order then teamed up with New York remixer Arthur Baker, who had fused hip-hop and Kraftwerk so seamlessly with Afrika Bambaataa. Baker and New Order remixed this rock/dance music fusion so well that 'Blue Monday' became the template for dance music to come.

New Order was very much a live rock & roll band with a "heavy" sound. Their live shows brought a rock credibility to dance music. The sales of over 250,000 12-inch singles of 'Blue Monday' were evidence of the change in audience tastes. They retained a simplistic, punk attitude to their progressive rock styling and that simplicity was crucial to their popularity. "There's not one of our songs that uses a black note on the keyboard," said Hook. "That's true!"

Street Fighting Man The Rolling Stones

(Mick Jagger/Keith Richards) ✵ Decca ✵ 1968 ✵ Appears on: *Beggars Banquet*

'Street Fighting Man' is an ambivalent call to arms recorded while students in Paris, London and across the US were literally building the barricades for a revolution.

The song began life as 'Did Everybody Pay Your Dues'. Keith Richards had cut a cassette demo with Charlie Watts playing a '30s toy drum kit and Richards on acoustic guitar. That set up, complete with cassette player, was replicated at Olympic studios, where the track was redone. The song has a massive drum sound that sits just behind the beat, layers of churning and ringing acoustic guitars all piled up by Richards, and bass, also from Richards.

These were the first sessions with American producer Jimmy Miller. It was a relationship that produced their golden run of classic Rolling Stones albums.

Richards and Jagger both felt they were in the eye of the storm of history. They were being persecuted by the British police and for a time locked in Wormwood Scrubs prison. Meanwhile the aristocracy invited them to the best parties. At the same time, intellectuals and radicals around the world saw the Rolling Stones as the spearhead of a revolution. It's not surprising that the sentiments in the song are somewhat confused.

'Pay Your Dues' was scrapped as a single release, replaced by 'Jumping Jack Flash'. The lyrics were rewritten and vocal redone by Jagger to emerge as 'Street Fighting Man'.

"'Street Fighting Man' is a funny song to play on stage in an era when you don't fight in the street any more," said Charlie Watts. "To play the song is fantastic, but the lyrics are very much about the events of 1968 in Paris, which is when Mick wrote it. It was political; not that it was going to change the world, but it was extremely influenced by what was going on – a very strong song about what was happening at the time."

Sun City Artists Against Apartheid

(Little Steven & the Disciples of Soul) ✳ EMI ✳ 1985 ✳ Appears on: *Sun City*

In the mid-'80s rock stars were expected to save the world. The Live Aid, Amnesty tours and the like were everywhere. The most interesting of these projects, however, was *Sun City*, an album that focused on the issue of apartheid. Sun City resort paid huge sums to induce artists to break the UN cultural boycott of the South African regime and play their showrooms – hence the mantra in the song, "I ain't gonna play Sun City."

Bruce Springsteen guitarist Steve Van Zandt conceived the project and it's his hardcore leftist politics and impeccable taste in musicians that gave the album a bite other benefit projects didn't have.

While other cause albums had simply culled artists from the hit parade, Van Zandt's guests were generally politicised. They came from the entire spectrum of music – rap, R&B, downtown avant-garde artists, punk rockers, superstars and jazz players. There were Pat Benatar, Jackson Browne, Bob Dylan, Peter Gabriel, Bob Geldof, Ringo Starr, Afrika Bambaataa, Stiv Bators, Big Youth, Rubén Blades, Kurtis Blow, Ron Carter, Clarence Clemons, Jimmy Cliff, George Clinton, Peter Garrett, Robert Gordon, Grandmaster Melle Mel, Daryl Hall, Nona Hendryx, Linton Kwesi Johnson, Stanley Jordan, Eddie Kendricks, Darlene Love, John Oates, Bonnie Raitt, Joey Ramone, Lou Reed, David Ruffin, Run-DMC, Scorpio, Gil Scott-Heron, Shankar, Bruce Springsteen, Zak Starkey, Pete Townshend, Doug Wimbish, Peter Wolf and Bobby Womack.

Miles Davis contributed a track for which Van Zandt added Ron Carter, Herbie Hancock and Tony Williams. Peter Gabriel contributed his own piece. At the last moment Bono arrived with 'Silver and Gold', which had been cooked up in a hotel room with Keith Richards and Ron Wood.

This was the last time so many artists were united on an album.

Dream Baby Dream Suicide

(Martin Rev/Alan Vega) ✳ Ze Records ✳ 1980 ✳

Appears on: 'Dream Baby Dream' (12 inch single)

Roy Trakin is a rock writer and friend of the duo called Suicide. They were among the first synthesiser groups and came under a great deal of flak for their live performances. Trakin put it perfectly when he wrote, "Suicide is NOT about alienation, but about hope; NOT about perfection, but rather about the inevitability of human error. Suicide telescopes their frailties, their inadequacies, their mistakes, like some improvising jazz band, into a unified whole whose theme is simple: 'To err is human, to forgive divine.' Suicide's message is not anti-life, as so many have assumed, but a plea to grasp life by the lapels. It is a paean to the common man as it is an ode to New York City, the place without which the act is inconceivable. Alan Vega is Suicide's heart and soul and mind; Martin Rev is the body in which all those parts are housed."

In 1980 Ze Records put Suicide in the studio with their friend and admirer, and leader of the Cars, Ric Ocasek. Their second album, called *Suicide* (like their first one) was a gentler affair. Rev's keyboards carried more melody and Alan Vega went positively Frank Sinatra. 'Dream Baby Dream' is a song that forever pops up on Suicide records, starting out as 'Keep Your Dreams' on the first LP. It's the warm and gentle side of the group where Vega encourages us to let go of the conscious; like a hypnotist he invites us to float away. It's the most gentle lyric and tune imaginable. They finally perfected it on the 12-inch version, where the delicate balance of words and music is at its most acute.

Even in 1980 in a New York club where Alan Vega put on the most mesmerising and intimate show I have ever seen, Suicide were having bottles thrown at them and demands of "Where's the drummer?" It would take a few years before this music was widely appreciated. But it's never been better than on 'Dream Baby Dream'.

"I guess we were further ahead of our time than we thought," said Vega recently. "I mean, I never thought so at the time, I just thought everyone else was behind the times. It's funny that people are reacting to it now as if it is something that's brand new. All these young kids – kids that weren't even born when I first started doing Suicide – come to me to produce them."

New Jack Hustler Ice-T

(Tracy Marrow) ❋ Sire ❋ 1991 ❋ Appears on: *OG Original Gangster*

Ice-T was indeed an original gangsta. Tracy Marrow (aka Ice-T) did have personal experience with the streets, drugs and the police and this was the initial meat for his material. His first records were hard-hitting and literate portrayals of the life of many black Americans. The legacy of his early work, though, was to be the cartoonish gangsta rap – misogynistic and violent, and generally a pose put on for white middle-class boys.

On 'New Jack Hustler' Ice-T refines the sound of rap with a particularly tough and inventive use of the beat and his own powers of observation. This is a piece about exploiting women and abusing drugs but you don't get the sense that it's a celebration of the gangsta life – rather, a documentary. He poses the question: "Is this a nightmare? Or the American dream?"

The political, moral and racial questions that are raised by 'New Jack Hustler' – the cost of drugs on the black community, the price paid by the hustlers for whom every other person on the street is a potential assassin, and the meritocracy of America – were soon forgotten in the wake of gangsta rap that turned what was a poetry and a dialogue into a Jerry Bruckheimer film.

Sugar Man Rodriguez

(Sixto Rodriguez) ❋ Sussex ❋ 1970 ❋ Appears on: *Cold Fact*

Sixto Rodriguez was a folksinger in Detroit in the late '60s. Born and raised in Michigan in a working-class family of Mexican descent, Rodriguez had a warm, expressive voice with strong folk-rock tunes and very confronting lyrics. Signed to Buddah offshoot, Sussex Records, he went into the studio in August and September 1970 to cut his debut album *Cold Fact*. Producer Mike Theodore enlisted local session players, including Motown alumni, and cast Rodriguez's songs in a jazzy rock setting. The album and its sequel two years later both failed to garner any action in the US. Rodriguez retired from music and went into education and local politics.

Then out of the blue, in the mid-'70s, Double J began playing Rodriguez, specifically the tracks 'I Wonder' and 'Sugar Man'. The public responded instantly. Rodriguez had a hit. Although he had never played a gig in the US, in Australia he headlined rock festivals and sold out a theatre tour. Rodriguez was particularly popular amongst surfers and they took his records to Brazil and South Africa, where he likewise had platinum sales.

'Sugar Man' – originally titled 'Sugar Man on Prentis' after a Detroit street – is a song about drugs, an ode to a pusher. Rodriguez's delivery is guileless, somewhat hard, but his voice is intoxicating. The backing is a deep groove with jazzy flavours that make it quite distinct. Rodriguez shared a label with Bill Withers and there is a similar ambience to the material, but Rodriguez has a harder, more authentic feel.

More recently, rapper Nas sampled the track on his *Stillmatic* album. Rodriguez's cult status is starting to spread to the UK. Perhaps he will finally come out of those Michigan shadows.

For What It's Worth Buffalo Springfield

(Stephen Stills) ❋ Atco ❋ 1967 ❋ Appears on: *Buffalo Springfield*

In August 1966, Pandora's Box was a small nightclub on the Sunset Strip – at the intersection of Crescent Heights and Sunset Boulevard – frequented by longhairs. The Strip was seething with possibilities on those warm nights, but the authorities had decided to close it down. The kids were having a wake when the LAPD arrived, and a riot erupted. Stephen Stills, a twenty-two-year-old guitar player, saw the melee and was shocked by the violence. Having just returned from Latin America he made the connection between what was happening in Los Angeles and the behaviour of the juntas south of the border.

"The LAPD decided to run a line-up across the street, like there was some kind of a revolution going on or something," said Stills. "It's a bunch of kids having a funeral for a bar. There was no big political point to it. There was no nothing to it. It was just a bunch of kids having a party."

'For What It's Worth' had a beautiful ringing guitar part – basically one note – from Neil Young that sounded like heaven opening. The entire apocalypse was in that one note. Then there was Stills' acoustic guitar riff to complement the message. The song had a motion and an urgency to it that made it sound like the barricades were being erected on Sunset the next afternoon.

"'For What It's Worth' was one of our best, early records," said Young. "It just happened real easy and it was real natural. You had the acoustic thing happening on it, which was really cool."

The song first appeared as a stand-alone single. When it reached number seven in the charts it was added to the first Buffalo Springfield album, which was then reissued. 'For What It's Worth' established the careers of the Springfield – one of the most influential combos of the mid-'60s – and the subsequent adventures of Neil Young, Stephen Stills, Richie Furay, and the bands Crosby, Stills, Nash & Young and Poco.

Where Did You Sleep Last Night? Nirvana

(Leadbelly) ✻ DGC ✻ 1994 ✻ Appears on: *MTV Unplugged in New York*

It was a mark of their superiority as a band that Nirvana first turned the volume of music up and started the grunge revolution; then, while it was in full swing, they rejected volume and brought in cellos.

On the back of *In Utero*, their third studio album, which was even more caustic than the other two, Nirvana agreed to an *MTV Unplugged* session. Rather than just running through their material, leader Kurt Cobain chose an eclectic selection of tracks such as David Bowie's 'The Man Who Sold the World' and this ancient song from Leadbelly.

'Where Did You Sleep Last Night?' is a murder ballad. Leadbelly's tune is as dark as a lake and Cobain carries that same weight into his reading of the track. He had first recorded it in a jam with Mark Lanegan of the Screaming Trees back in Seattle, with Lanegan singing. This time Cobain is an accomplished musician and a master of irony and understatement. He goes with the flow of the song, putting himself "In the pines, in the pines/Where the sun don't ever shine/ I would shiver the whole night through." He had grasped the haunted, hundred-year tradition of this song and gave it a new life.

Suzanne Leonard Cohen

(Leonard Cohen) ❊ 1967 ❊ Columbia ❊ Appears on: *The Songs of Leonard Cohen*

Leonard Cohen is a Canadian poet and novelist who in the mid-'60s fell into the folk scene. His is a singular style of songwriting – his voice almost monotonous and his tunes reeking of flamenco dancers and cantors.

'Suzanne' was his first hit. It's startling in its accurate rendition of places like the sailor's church – Notre-Dame-de-Bon-Secours – by the harbour and poetic in ways that not even Bob Dylan had approached – sensual and sacred all at once.

"Suzanne Vaillancourt was the wife of a friend of mine. They were a stunning couple around Montreal at the time," Cohen told the BBC. "But there was no … well, there was thought, but there was no possibility, one would not allow oneself to think of toiling at the seduction of Armand Vaillancourt's wife.

"I bumped into her one evening, and she invited me down to her place near the river. She had a loft, at a time when lofts were … the word wasn't used. She invited me down, and I went with her, and she served me Constant Comment tea, which has little bits of oranges in it. And the boats were going by, and I touched her perfect body with my mind, because there was no other opportunity. There was no other way that you could touch her perfect body under those circumstances."

"He got such a kick out of seeing me emerge as a young schoolgirl I suppose, and a young artist, into becoming Armand's lover and then wife," Suzanne recalled some thirty years after the first meeting with Cohen. "So, he was more or less chronicling the times.

"With Leonard, it happened more in the beginning of the '60s. I was very much interested in the waterfront. The St Lawrence River held a particular poetry and beauty to me and [I] decided to live there with our daughter, Julie. Leonard heard about this place I was living, with crooked floors and a poetic view of the river, and he came to visit me many times. We had tea together many times and mandarin oranges.

"I would always light a candle and serve tea and it would be quiet for several minutes, then we would speak. And I would speak about life and poetry and we'd share ideas.

"He became a big star after the song was launched and he became a songwriter. Our relationship did change with time. I travelled, went to the US, and we'd see him and bump into him. In Minneapolis for instance, he did a concert there and he saw me back stage and received me very beautifully, 'Oh Suzanne, you gave me a beautiful song.'"

In 1966, folk singer Judy Collins was looking for material and Cohen offered her some of his songs, including 'Suzanne', which he sang to her over the telephone. Word spread of Cohen's abilities and he was invited to New York to audition for Columbia's legendary talent scout John Hammond (who signed Billie Holiday, Bob Dylan and many of the other key jazz, folk and blues artists from the '30s to the '60s).

Hammond recalled discovering Cohen: "A friend of mine said, 'John, there's this poet from Canada, who I think you'd be interested in. He plays pretty good guitar, and he's a wonderful songwriter, but he doesn't read music, and he's sort of very strange. I don't think Columbia would be at all interested in him, but you might be.'

"So, I listened to this guy, and he's got a hypnotic effect. I thought he was enchanting ... because that's the only word you can use. He was not like anything I'd ever heard before. I just feel that I always want a true original, if I can find one, because there are not many in the world; and the young man set his own rules. They all looked at me at Columbia and said, 'What, are you ... A forty-year-old Canadian poet? How are we going to sell him?' I said, 'Listen to him ...' and, lo and behold, Columbia signed him."

Within two weeks, Cohen (who was thirty-two at the time) was in the studio recording his first album. Cohen's one request was for a mirror to be set up in front of his microphone so that he could serenade himself. At one point in the sessions, Hammond shouted out, "Watch out Dylan!"

"It was a small studio we had at 49 East 52nd Street," Hammond recalled. "He was alone, in the studio, and it used to be lit with incense and candles; and we had no lights on in the studio, and it had a very exotic effect. He had a hypnotising effect on everybody. And he felt comfortable with the mirror.

"So, the record came out, and it sold remarkably well. And I had a lot of fun with him. He was a completely weird guy, who liked to go around the streets of Montreal and play pinball. And I liked to play pinball, too, so that was a great bond that we had. The only thing I could do was to stay out of his way, and give him whatever reassurance he needed, and I could do that pretty well."

'Suzanne' sparked Cohen's career and a thousand imitators. Randy Newman wrote a parody but the song itself defies the ravages of imitation and time.

Suzanne Vaillancourt became a masseuse and New Age therapist in Los Angeles, near the Mt Baldy monastery where Cohen lived for a time. Although their paths crossed, he never did touch her perfect body.

"Once when he was visiting Montreal, I saw him briefly in a hotel and it was a very, very wonderful, happy moment because he was on his way to becoming the great success he is," she recalled. "And the moment arose that we could have a moment together intimately, and I declined. I forget that Leonard is more than just an amazing poet and philosopher. He's also a human being who happens to be a man.

"I'm flattered somewhat. But I was depicted, I think, in sad terms too in a sense, and that's a little unfortunate. You know I don't think I was quite as sad as that, albeit maybe I was and he perceived that and I didn't."

In the City The Jam

(Paul Weller) ✳ Polydor ✳ 1977 ✳ Appears on: *The Jam*

They were the junior partners in the British punk invasion. Where the Sex Pistols and the Clash demanded the abolition of the class system and the destruction of the rock superstars, Paul Weller's band the Jam were more nostalgic. They wore mod suits and aped the sounds of Swinging London albeit with a tough punk attitude.

Like all bands of the era, the Jam started out with a manifesto. Because Weller, then still a teenager, was the sole composing force in the Jam, their songs right from the start tended towards the personal.

This first single was really about shaking off their lower-middle class suburbia and getting amongst the action. It was originally titled 'In the City There's a Thousand Things I Want to Say to You'. "London was where it all seemed to be happening," said Weller. "Life there seemed so removed from sleepy Woking ... and that was the feeling that we were trying to capture."

The song is fast and furious, based as it is on the Who-ish bass line from Bruce Foxton and the explosive drums from Rick Buckler. This had the amphetamine energy of the mod era. The whole first album was made in one hundred hours. Like most of Weller's material at the time, it was tied into this notion of a dynamic youth wanting to grasp the future with both hands and shake it.

Love Goes On! The Go-Betweens

(Grant McLennan/Robert Forster) ✳ Capitol/Mushroom/Beggars Banquet ✳ 1988 ✳
Appears on: *16 Lovers Lane*

16 Lovers Lane was the Go-Betweens' finest hour and remains one of the finest albums of all time. It's the perfect sound of being in love. The opening salvo 'Love Goes On!' (note the exclamation mark) is a defiant statement of rebirth ("I know a thing about darkness/Darkness ain't my friend"). The group had returned to Australia in the summer of 1987. After half a decade of struggle they had found a level of acceptance around the world that coincided with their personal maturity.

"Without being too pretentious, the summer was very important to the record. It was a brilliant summer," singer Grant McLennan told journalist John O'Donnell. "After years of gloom, which is what it seems like when you live in England, to come back to brilliance, to shadow and contrast, that really helped us. It helped me very much spiritually and creatively."

The group's acoustic guitars and violin beamed with sunshine. This track gallops along, powering the radiant melody.

Wide Open Road The Triffids

(David McComb) ✳ White Hot ✳ 1986 ✳ Appears on: *Born Sandy Devotional*

The Triffids were already old hands by the time they cut *Born Sandy Devotional* in London in 1985. The group had begun as teenagers in Perth, high on New York punk rock and Perth's own Victims. Principal songwriter David McComb was kind of literary with a knack for writing sublime pop tunes but he also liked dirty rock & roll. McComb was a fervent admirer of Nick Cave; his modesty wouldn't permit him the realisation that he ploughed the same field as Cave but with far greater gifts.

Perhaps coming from Perth it's not surprising that distance and deserts, both physical and emotional, played a big part in McComb's writing. Their first album, *Treeless Plain*, is a magnificent, muscular piece of work that pounds out simple, powerful rock songs – one of the best indie rock albums of its day. *Born Sandy Devotional* is a leap ahead of that album.

The Triffids left Australia behind for a life on the breadline in London squats. This album reeks of that sense of distance.

"How much longer will we be leaving friends behind in Australia?" McComb said to me once. "There's such a polarity in my personal and professional lives. It all gets very Faustian."

Nowhere is this more apparent than in the song 'Tender is the Night', which tells the story of a man who is emotionally torn apart to his core by ambition, and which also touches on what is lost when you travel across the planet. It's a chilling waltz.

The album is full of places. The grit of the Nullarbor desert sand gets in your eyes and you can almost taste the Indian Ocean.

These songs exist in their little hermetically sealed world. McComb's fables are wrapped in the heavenly melodic support of Graham Lee (pedal Steel), Rob McComb (violin) and, especially, the delicate bass lines of Martyn Casey.

The axel of the album is 'Wide Open Road'. It's an angry song that finds the cost of freedom is aloneness:

The sky was big and empty
My chest filled to explode
I yelled my insides out at the sun
At the wide open road
Then it's a wide open road
It's a wide open road
And now you can go any place
That you ever wanted to go

After some months the Triffids established themselves in London and made the cover of the *NME*. There were great expectations for this album. Young producer Gil Norton, who shortly afterwards recorded the Pixies, brought a lush sound to the group without losing their idiosyncratic dynamic. The sessions were jeopardised when the money ran out and the album was finished by maxing out a credit card. You can feel the urgency – lack of cash meets vaulting ambition.

As critic Clinton Walker said, "The Triffids brought a new bent – a dry indigenous light and air – to rock & roll."

Wild in the Streets Garland Jeffries

(Garland Jeffries) ✲ A&M ✲ 1977 ✲ Appears on: *Ghost Writer*

Garland Jeffries' first notable contact with the world of rock was the friendship he struck up with Lou Reed while they were both at Syracuse University in the '60s. He appeared on John Cale's first solo album, *Vintage Violence*, but made little impact until one single, 'Wild in the Streets', was a minor radio hit in 1973. The song has a beautiful slashing Stones feel with big open chords set against an insistent drum beat. A massive back beat that pulses behind a song about social breakdown and the abandonment of kids by a cold-hearted society. The song appears to reference the '60s exploitation movie of the same name where goofy college kids take over America – only in Jeffries' version it's not the idle rich but the kids in the ghettos who are breaking out. Mostly, though, the song resides in the vitriol of the riff that drives it like a battle anthem.

La Grange ZZ Top

(Frank Beard/Billy Gibbons/Dusty Hill) ✲ Warner Bros. ✲ 1973 ✲
Appears on: *Tres Hombres*

Billy Gibbons grew up the son of an orchestra conductor in Houston, Texas. His first band, the Moving Sidewalks, were a psychedelic garage band in the footsteps of the 13th Floor Elevators. His big teenage moment came when the Sidewalks opened for Jimi Hendrix, who praised his playing, gave him a guitar and advised him, "The best thing you can do is turn it up as loud as it will go."

This he did in February 1970 when he, Dusty Hill and Frank Beard formed ZZ Top, a blues rock bar band. They play twelve-bar boogie with a dynamic rhythm section on top of which Gibbons lays witty, sharp guitar lines that sound deceptively simple.

Mostly, though, it was the attitude that broke ZZ Top out of Texas – mindless, sexual, irreverent beer-drinking music is what they specialised in. That style met its pinnacle with 'La Grange' from *Tres Hombres*. The track became a teenage boy classic and its riff is as powerful as a Chuck Berry hook. The album features other classics such as 'Waitin' for the Bus', 'Jesus Just Left Chicago', 'Beer Drinkers & Hell Raisers' and 'Hot, Blue and Righteous'.

"We're still attempting to qualify as interpreters," said Gibbons of the band's blues roots. "Which is a posture I can rest comfortably within because, fortunately, there are still plenty of living exponents who qualify as originators. We're at a place in time – it shouldn't even be called history – where we can still expose ourselves to those kinds of resources, and if one is really willing to understand it, then maybe the original attitude – the original intention – can be embraced. And I think, without meaning to sound too I-know-it-all, that so far we've been pretty successful."

London Calling The Clash

(Mick Jones/Joe Strummer) ❋ Epic ❋ 1979 ❋ Appears on: *London Calling*

You couldn't have a better war cry. Or a more accurate one. On this magnificent double album, the Clash landed the third Great British invasion. There was subterfuge – the album's cover rips off Elvis Presley's first LP – but mostly it was sheer force. And nowhere was that more evident than on the opening track.

'London Calling' is a call to arms – to resist oppression, to resist drugs and to confront the apathy and materialism and mostly the nostalgic state of pop culture. The riff is taken from the BBC World Service call sign. It's a song that takes on the terror of nuclear war (then a possibility) and thumbs its nose. For the past four years the punk rockers in London had been saying the same thing, preaching loudly to the converted. 'London Calling' reached out beyond that ghetto.

'London Calling' had none of the amateurish noise of punk rock. Strummer was here shaking off the pretensions of London at the time and acknowledging the fact that the music of his heart was part Woody Guthrie and part pub rock. His lyrics and vocals then came into sharper focus. Fortunately he had Mick Jones and Paul Simonon to lift the music out of his limitations.

The sound is a hybrid of roots rock and dub but there is nothing here to get in the way of the message. Simonon's deep, rich bass punctuates the marching beat – kept by Jones' and Strummer's guitars, which sound like weapons rather than instruments. By the third verse, 'London Calling' is a firefight.

Jones said of the sessions that producer Guy Stevens was "exhorting us to make it more, to increase the intensity, to lay the energy on." They succeeded in that.

Boogie Chillun   John Lee Hooker

(John Lee Hooker) ✵ Modern ✵ 1948 ✵

Appears on: *John Lee Hooker: The Ultimate Collection*

Like the Zen monks who comb their pebble gardens the same way day after day, John Lee Hooker combs his blues groove, getting ever so slightly closer to the ineffable each time. His signature line was the growling, mystical phrase, "How? How? How? How?"

He said it best on the talking blues track, 'Teaching the Blues': "There's not a whole lot of chords in it. Just a big beat. Your fancy chords don't mean nothin' if you ain't got that beat. Throw those fancy chords away and just get this slow beat."

John Lee Hooker was born in 1917 at ground zero of the blues, Clarksdale, Mississippi. His stepfather, Wil Moore, was by some accounts one of the pioneering blues players in the Delta at that time. "I was living with my mother and her husband," Hooker told Judah Bauer of the Jon Spencer Blues Explosion. "He was a guitar player. What I'm playing now, that's what he taught me to play, his style. I played a guitar like his – a Stella. I always watched his tunings – open A, regular tunings, and I played them in all keys. When I'm playin' 'Boogie Chillun', that's in open A. I heard my stepdaddy doin' something like that, but he didn't call it 'Boogie Chillun'. He just played it."

With John Lee Hooker there is only one song, which goes either slow or really slow. He is the Zen master.

Hooker left the Delta for Detroit, where he became a janitor. He was eventually discovered playing house parties and given a recording deal with Modern. Hooker hit one out of the park with his first track, 'Boogie Chillun', and that set the template – heavily syncopated guitar that just sits in a groove while John Lee growls over the top. This boogie music was closer to rock & roll than blues; it had the pronounced beat of the hormonally pumped white music. It's impossible to hear Hooker and not move your hips.'Boogie Chillun' could even be an anthem for the '60s youth-quake with its lyrics about doing what "mama don't allow".

For precisely that reason, John Lee Hooker was a particular favourite with the young British bands of the early '60s, notably the Animals who had a hit with 'Boom Boom', but he was an inspiration to all the British R&B players. White American kids caught on to his style as well and both Canned Heat and ZZ Top made careers out of essentially recycling Hooker's boogie.

Shine on You Crazy Diamond Pink Floyd

(David Gilmour/Roger Waters/Richard Wright) ❋ EMI ❋ 1975 ❋

Appears on: *Wish You Were Here*

Pink Floyd's best track was an elegy to founder Syd Barrett, who went insane shortly after the release of their first album in 1968.

"I think the whole album sprang from that one four-note guitar phrase of Dave's in 'Shine On'," keyboard player Rick Wright told *MOJO*. "We heard it and went, 'That's a really nice phrase.' The wine came out, and that led to what I think is our best album, the most colourful, the most feelingful."

Wright recalled being in the studio as the track was being finished and meeting a disassociated Syd, now a shadow of his former self.

Dave Gilmour's melancholy guitar part was developed into a lengthy portrait of Syd – the manic and the tragic sides of his personality. The song also reflected the mixed feeling of Waters about having continued so long in his shadow.

The song had been worked up in concert and, at Waters' suggestion, the final twenty-five minute studio version is split into two parts, opening and closing Floyd's only listenable album of the '70s.

The Inner Mounting Flame The Mahavishnu Orchestra

(John McLaughlin) ❋ Columbia ❋ 1971 ❋ Appears on: *The Inner Mounting Flame*

John McLaughlin revolutionised the guitar in jazz. Not only did he have a ferocious melodic dexterity and gift for improvisation, but he also brought incredible volume into play.

McLaughlin got his break in the London jazz/blues boom, playing on Top 40 hits for Georgie Fame and with Jack Bruce and Ginger Baker in the Graham Bond Organisation. The guitarist was besotted with the hard bop of Miles Davis and John Coltrane. The former gave him his major break. The latter steered him into the mystic. "Coltrane became a dominating influence on my life, spiritually as well as musically," he told *Guitar Player* magazine.

McLaughlin became interested in the philosophy and the music of the sub-continent. He acquired a guru, Sri Chinmoy, and his harmonic palette expanded. In the late '60s he joined former Miles Davis protégé drummer Tony Williams in the group Lifetime. He also came to Davis' attention and played on the seminal album *In a Silent Way*. He continued to record with both Lifetime and Davis and played a major role in Miles' *Bitches Brew*, the sessions that became the cornerstone of jazz-rock fusion.

In 1971, McLaughlin went out on his own with the Mahavishnu Orchestra. The ensemble comprised Billy Cobham on drums, Rick Laird on bass, Jan Hammer playing keyboards and violinist Jerry Goodman. Each of the players has subsequently had esteemed careers in jazz. But Mahavishnu Orchestra was not honourable so much as visceral.

The Inner Mounting Flame, inspired by the teaching of Sri Chinmoy, was the psychedelic fusion of jazz and rock. McLaughlin's flights on his double-necked guitar drew on the aggression and urgency of rock while still using an expanded jazz vocabulary. At a time when guitar virtuosos were everywhere, McLaughlin was not only eloquent on his double-necked instrument but unbelievably fast. *The Inner Mounting Flame* was a cult hit amongst rock fans and put the group on the rock circuit. It was a major hit by jazz standards. However, the incendiary music was a reflection of volatile, large personalities – not the least of which was the guitarist himself – and the group imploded under the pressure.

"I wanted to play loud," said McLaughlin. "I was conscious of what I wanted to do, the way I wanted to play nobody was doing. But it took the years I spent with Tony and Miles to give me the possibility of giving birth to the form that I wanted to use, which was primarily expressed in the first Mahavishnu Orchestra."

Red Red Wine UB40

(Neil Diamond) ✳ Virgin ✳ 1985 ✳ Appears on: *Labour of Love*

UB40 made their name as a politically inspired reggae band, but it was an album of covers and love songs that broke them. The eight-piece group took its name from the stationary serial number on the dole form. In the '80s, chronic unemployment, especially in the northern cities of Britain such as UB40's Birmingham, was a disastrous by-product of class war.

Their first album, *Signing Off*, was a mostly bitter diatribe at the state of Thatcher's Britain. Unfortunately, songwriting was never a particular strength. The band built a large following mostly on the back of Ali Campbell's vocals and the ferocious groove they presented live. With solid R&B chops and a reggae backbone with touches of pop, UB40 were kings of the road.

For their fifth album they selected a bunch of classic and not-so-classic reggae and pop tunes. One of the most obscure, an old Neil Diamond composition 'Red Red Wine', became an international smash hit.

"*Labour of Love* is a non-political album, a pet project that we've been nursing for five years," Ali Campbell told the *Los Angeles Times*. "It sums UB40 up, really. They're the songs we grew up on. The originals were what got us into reggae in the first place."

You Better Move On Arthur Alexander

(Arthur Alexander) ✳ Dot ✳ 1962 ✳ Appears on: *The Muscle Shoals Sound*

Paul McCartney is reported to have said, "If the Beatles ever wanted a sound, it was R&B. That was what we listened to, what we wanted to be like – Arthur Alexander." One of the first soul singers, Alexander grew up in Alabama and was an integral part of the group of songwriters and players who founded southern soul in the '60s and established Muscle Shoals as a music capital.

Alexander had seen some minor success when he was working in a Muscle Shoals hotel and wrote 'You Better Move On', inspired by his future wife, who already had a boyfriend.

"When I met her out of high school, he was still hanging in there," he recalled. "His family was pretty well off. I didn't have no money, but I knew she liked me. It was a small town and people would be talking. That's where I got the idea for the song. I didn't talk to him personally. I said it in song."

The track was recorded in an abandoned tobacco warehouse. It found a home at Dot and was the beginning of a string of hits such as 'Anna', 'Every Day I Have to Cry' and 'Sally Sue Brown', which were covered widely by the Beatles, Dusty Springfield and the Rolling Stones (who cut 'You Better Move On'). Like almost all his colleagues, Alexander saw none of the royalties and his career was dogged by disappointment, although he staged a few comebacks before his death in 1993.

One O'Clock Jump Count Basie & His Orchestra

(W Basie) ❋ Decca ❋ 1937 ❋ Appears on: *Ken Burns Jazz*

The Count Basie Orchestra was a dance band. The group came out of Kansas City, Missouri, where songs were known, for good reason, as "stomps" and "shouts". This track is called a "jump" and the physicality of the music is integral to it. The Basie Orchestra were hot. As horn player Earl Warren told NPR of their New York debut in 1936, "We had acclaimed ourself as the finest swing band in the land. When we went into the Savoy you couldn't get in there. I used to come off there wringing wet. When we got on that bandstand, we blew."

Part of the group's strength was their closeness to the blues. In fact, the Basie Orchestra had worked up a song called 'Blue Ball'. When they were scheduled to perform the track live on a midnight radio broadcast, the announcer demurred at the name and so Basie suggested 'One O'Clock Jump'.

Although the song is credited to Basie, it was written by Buster Smith and Eddie Durham. They began with a rearrangement of Fats Waller's 'Six or Seven Times' and then they preceded this theme with a series of twelve-bar phrases that steadily built in intensity and rhythmic power. The simplicity of the blues was a perfect forum for the likes of the legendary saxophonist Lester Young, who just soars through these choruses, flying on his tenor.

The sixteen-piece Basie Orchestra recorded the song on 7 July 1937 and it remained his closing tune for the remainder of his working life.

LA Woman The Doors

(Robbie Kreiger/John Densmore/Ray Manzarek/Jim Morrison) ❋ Elektra ❋ 1971 ❋
Appears on: *LA Woman*

Over three years, the Doors recorded five albums, became one of the hottest groups in the world and then after Jim Morrison exposed himself to an audience in Miami, a target for police everywhere. Drugs and alcohol fuelled the already unstable Morrison. He thought himself a poet but was regarded as a teenage girl's pin-up idol.

For their sixth album, producer Paul Rothchild walked away from the group, promoting engineer Bruce Botnick to co-producer. Then they built a studio in their rehearsal space to make what Morrison promised the *LA Free Press* would be a blues album. "That's what we do best. Just your basic blues."

When Morrison wasn't in a fog of drugs he was dealing with police charges relating to the Miami incident. The rest of the Doors carried on. Within three months of the album's release, Morrison was dead.

"At the time of *LA Woman* the Doors were looking like a doomed thing and I felt like Paul was a rat deserting a sinking ship," said guitarist Robbie Krieger. "We couldn't play anywhere, *Morrison Hotel* didn't do that well, Jim looked bad and was getting fat. And I think we came up with something so loose exactly because there was no pressure. We figured we were already screwed, so we were having fun again."

"As his self destruction, alcoholism and drug abuse increased, it became more and more obvious just how crazy he was," said Densmore. "Unfortunately, we had to pull away, and it became three and one instead of four great friends in a great band. But that was personal. Musically, I think we had a sweet democracy that somehow survived all the madness. It's really odd, but there was some wonderful kind of thing that happened when we were together writing and rehearsing."

This was the last album under the Doors' contract and Morrison contemplated leaving rock & roll to be a full-time poet. Perhaps that sense of freedom was part of the special kick of *LA Woman*.

The title track is the crowning glory in the Doors' career – an ode to Los Angeles, the city that had nurtured them. The song began life as a slow blues but the tempo picked up, reflecting the images of cars on an endless night-time freeway.

"'LA Woman' was completely live, and I think that could be the quintessential Doors song," said Krieger. "The way we came up with it was amazing. We just started playing and it came together as if by magic. Jim made a lot of it up as he went along, and I think it's one of his most poetic songs."

Keyboard player Ray Manzarek also cites 'LA Woman' as a career peak. "It represents to me a drive across the great American South West," he said. "Driving on the freeways and highways through the desert – Arizona or New Mexico – or driving up the coast of California on Highway 1, from Los Angeles to San Francisco. It's alive, it's free, it's young and it's wild."

Cowgirl in the Sand   Neil Young & Crazy Horse

(Neil Young) ✳ Reprise ✳ 1969 ✳ Appears on: *Everybody Knows This Is Nowhere*

There is a story of a monk going to monastery in search of enlightenment and being given a broom and told to sweep. After a year of sweeping he asks the master what is the secret of enlightenment and he's told not to ask but to go back and sweep and ask again in five years. Five years later the same thing happens and he goes back to sweeping and then one day he understands enlightenment.

Young said of Crazy Horse, "A lot of people think we play simple and there is no finesse. But we're not trying to impress anybody; we just want to play with the feeling. It's like a trance we get into."

Supposedly Neil Young had a fever while he was writing his second solo album and three songs came to him then – 'Down by the River', 'Cowgirl' and 'Cinnamon Girl'. The former two are showcases for Young's particular guitar architecture – long and drawn-out lines that play with distortion and chaos. What he's doing in these songs is mining the four-chord rock song for its last possible nuance. He finds a groove and then mines it back and forth like the proverbial Zen monk and the broom.

The River   Bruce Springsteen & the E Street Band

(Bruce Springsteen) ✳ Columbia ✳ 1980 ✳ Appears on: *The River*

Plenty of songwriters have invented characters and narratives and spun those out over a concept album. Bruce Springsteen upped the ante by running that story over decades. It's not a story with a happy ending either. The kids who slammed the screen door shut and took to Thunder Road with such abandon on *Born to Run* in 1975 had lost all their dreams by 1980. Their adolescence had ended just as a worldwide recession gripped working-class America and this is a glorious album about diminished expectations. Things had got serious on *Darkness on the Edge of Town*, but they went positively gloomy on *The River*. The characters all had their Chevys up on blocks while they pulled the nightshift down at the plant. The possibility of escape, of feeling their own machismo, had faded not only in the face of a global recession but also because they were trapped by women. All the women on this album are jailers. There are no happy families and the only possibility of romance is on the weirdly jaunty hit single 'Hungry Heart' – with someone else's wife.

The title track is the story of a young couple who fall in love, she falls pregnant and the singer gets "a union card and wedding coat". Marriage and children is not a wonderful new adventure but a drift into alienation; passion disappears from the singer's life along with hope. On his 22nd birthday his life is over.

"I was trying to answer 'Where are these people going now'," Springsteen told *Rolling Stone*. "I had an idea but I wasn't really sure. I guess I didn't know where I was going."

Springsteen's E Street Band rose to the challenge of this album, bringing Roy Brittan's keyboards to the fore over the sax-based R&B of their earlier albums. The songs were more complex and diverse while also less pompous and grandiose.

'The River' is one of Springsteen's least popular singles, probably because it's one of his most direct. He'd become the future of rock & roll with albums full of teenage fantasy, but 'The River' carries a truth that all of us experience but none of us likes to swim in.

Sharp Dressed Man ZZ Top

(Billy Gibbons/Dusty Hill/Frank Beard) ✳ Warner Bros. ✳ 1983 ✳ Appears on: *Eliminator*

"I hate to draw dividing lines," Billy Gibbons once mused, "but where does Muddy Waters meet Brian Eno?" The answer is *Eliminator*. After fifteen years and eight albums playing variations of John Lee Hooker's 'Boogie Chillun' as a blues trio, ZZ Top (Billy Gibbons on guitar, Dusty Hill on bass and Frank Beard on drums) went into Ardent studios, fired up the drum machines and the synthesisers and came up with a whole new synthetic boogie. It looked to all intents and purposes like a real rock band but it was in fact an entirely new sound. One that vaulted ZZ Top to the first rank of rock bands. The metal fans who had always supported the group couldn't tell the difference. The mid-'80s pop market, listening to the Human League, loved the pop pastiches of it.

A tour of Britain attuned the band to the possibilities electronics offered. Although he appears to be the Texan parody he plays in public, guitarist Billy Gibbons is also a very complex artist. It was Gibbons who steered ZZ Top into a new age.

"When we really did return from England to get our work done, I think curiosity was a real magnet to turning on those things," he said. "What you got was a bunch of cowpoles on blues twisting knobs from outer space."

The songs were the traditional lowbrow ZZ Top fare – cartoon stories about women mostly. To this they added the real cartoons. It was the beginning days of MTV and ZZ Top illustrated their songs with corny videos featuring blondes and cars while forever in the background were the two guys with surreal beards and the guy called Beard without one. The hits just kept coming: 'Gimme All Your Lovin'', 'Legs', 'Sharp Dressed Man' and 'TV Dinners'.

As Gibbons once said of 'Sharp Dressed Man', "That solo was truly the successful marriage of a techno beat with bar band blues style overtones from the guitar department, and that certainly includes a wide range of southern inspiration. We were becoming increasingly attracted to the beats, you see, and yet the Allman Brothers remain some of our biggest heroes. On 'Sharp Dressed Man', we brought those two worlds together. It remains a performance favourite and a really raucous ignition point, whether one is on stage or sitting on the tailgate out in the middle of nowhere sipping a cold beverage."

Eliminator was perfect pop art in every sense. As Gibbons told the *NME*'s Barney Hoskyns, "I don't think we've ever set out to present ourselves as the Talking Heads or anything, and yet there are so few bands who are aware of what American culture is about."

Trouble Comin' Every Day

Frank Zappa & the Mothers of Invention

(Frank Zappa) ✳ MGM/Verve ✳ 1966 ✳ Appears on: *Freak Out!*

Freak Out! is significant as the second rock-era double album and as the only interesting album Frank Zappa ever made.

Zappa grew up in the suburbs of Los Angeles entranced by R&B and doo-wop music, which he understood perfectly. However, Zappa could never trust his love. He also had a hankering for "real" art as expressed by modern classical composers, in particular, Edward Varese. Although he fronted a number of garage bands in the very early '60s, Zappa was never satisfied. He wanted to be taken seriously according to his square definition of what a real composer did. So he tried to marry the two. One can't help suspect that perhaps he wasn't really up to serious composition and that passing ineptitude off as satire was his best option.

Zappa had a gift for controversy. His target was hypocrisy, always an easy mark. His barbs were aimed not only at the Establishment but also at the counter culture – his audience. Zappa's tirades were full of self-righteousness and overbearing egomania. No-one but Zappa followed the one true path.

The cover of *We're Only In It for the Money*, the third Mothers of Invention album, was a grotesque parody of the Beatles, implying that they had sold out and that Zappa (who was much more financially savvy than any of the Fabs) was in it for the art.

Zappa's occasional glimpses of astute satire were outweighed by his lumbering caricatures of social types and an increasing tendency towards scatology.

Over time Zappa's attacks on the hippies smacked of self-loathing and fear. Although he had a curious moustache, Zappa led a very moralistic and straight life. More disturbing, however, was the misogyny that ran through all his work. He was obsessed with ridiculing sexually independent women. The modern composer had the perspective of a redneck who repressed himself because he had to live in the rock & roll world.

Tom Wilson, the producer of Bob Dylan and the Velvet Underground, signed Frank Zappa and the Mothers of Invention to Verve/MGM. (It's notable that the Velvets elegantly played avant-garde rock & roll without having to bang on endlessly about their credentials. Basically, Frank Zappa never did get the point.)

In early 1966 Zappa made *Freak Out!* as an extension of the Mothers' live act – some R&B mixed with dadaist noise experiments that were given obtuse names. Wilson was apparently delighted with the exuberance of it all and blew the budget out to a whopping (in those days) $21,000.

The saving grace of the disc is the dirty garage R&B track 'Trouble Comin' Every Day'. Written in response to the Watts riots that set the Los Angeles ghetto on fire, this is Zappa at his most unselfconscious. The song ranks with 'Satisfaction' as a description of the turmoil of the times and it still resonates now.

In the long run Zappa is known by his disciples – a bunch of nerds, generally without girlfriends, who can spout Zappa lyrics as easily as they recite the scripts of early Monty Python. Zappa will be remembered for discovering Alice Cooper and

Captain Beefheart. The former he championed because he thought Alice epitomised all that was terrible with rock & roll – childishness, theatricality and amateurism. Little did Zappa know how great his protégés were. Beefheart, aka Don Van Vliet was a school friend who had a unique take on the blues. He was what Zappa aspired to be – except that Zappa died a very wealthy control freak and Van Vliet lives in a trailer in the desert. Who was only in it for the money?

Ticket to Ride The Beatles

(John Lennon/Paul McCartney) ※ Parlophone ※ 1964 ※ Appears on: *Help!*

Lennon claimed that 'Ticket to Ride' was the first "heavy metal" song. While that is clearly nonsense, it is the heaviest song the Beatles had recorded until then. Harrison's twelve-string riffs give a touch of folk rock, McCartney adds a bluesy lead guitar and Lennon a driving rhythm. The real star of the track is Ringo, whose tempestuous drum patterns really push the urgency and anger in the song. The Beatles were starting to master the studio in 1964 and do more than just replicate their live show – something which is evidenced by the multi-tracking guitars and the recording of the drums here.

Lennon's penchant for puns sparked the title although he had used it before. Steve Turner in his book *A Hard Day's Write* quotes a story that Lennon devised the phrase back in Hamburg: "The girls who worked the streets in Hamburg had to have a clean bill of health and so the medical authorities would give them a card saying that they didn't have a dose of anything … John told me that he had coined the phrase 'a ticket to ride' to describe these cards. He could have been joking – you had to be careful with John like that – but I certainly remember him telling me that."

The song was reportedly cut in two takes on the same day that Lennon passed his driving test.

In *Many Years from Now*, McCartney is quoted as saying, "I think the interesting thing about it was the crazy ending: instead of ending like the previous verse, we changed the tempo. We picked up one of the lines, 'My baby don't care', but completely altered the melody. We almost invented the idea of a new bit of a song in the fade-out; it was something specially written for the fade-out, which was quite cheeky. It was quite radical at the time."

Leaps and Bounds Paul Kelly

(Paul Kelly/Chris Langman) ✴ Mushroom ✴ 1986 ✴ Appears on: *Gossip*

The grand themes of Paul Kelly's work are all here – Melbourne, football, transcendence and memory. Paul Kelly went through a transformation in the mid-'80s. He was a washed up singer/songwriter with two brilliant albums that no-one cared about. Many parts of his life were a mess.

Things really started to turn when he formed the Coloured Girls – Michael Barclay (drums), John Schofield (bass), Peter Bull (keyboards) and Steve Connolly (guitar). This was a versatile outfit that turned its mind to country, rock and reggae with equal alacrity. Then, with the *Gossip* album, a sprawling two dozen tunes, Kelly found his feet. Much credit goes to guitarist, the late Steve Connolly, whose apeggiated lines lifted Kelly's tunes two feet off the ground. This track had been written six years previously with his band the Dots, assisted by guitarist Chris Langman (who became a filmmaker).

'Leaps and Bounds' is a small moment – a remembrance of an autumn day in May that sends the singer's heart soaring. Paul Kelly is a detail man – the temperature, the location, the foliage – and through the particulars he captures the invisible, the intangible. The last verse here is about acceptance and the strength to start over.

"Gossip," said Kelly at the time, "is like that. It deals with really trivial things and also life and death issues, gossip reduces it all."

That being said, the Coloured Girls, and especially Connolly, built it all up again.

Zoo Station U2

(U2) ✴ Island ✴ 1991 ✴ Appears on: *Achtung Baby*

In November 1989 in a Sydney pub, Bono Vox, the most potent rock star of that decade, declared, "The '80s was just a rehearsal. I mean that." Two years later U2 fulfilled their promise with a radical reinvention of everything they stood for and sounded like with the album *Achtung Baby*.

Co-producer Brian Eno wrote of the year-long sessions that went into making the record, "Buzz words on this record were trashy, throwaway, dark, sexy and industrial (all good) and earnest, polite, sweet, righteous, rockist and linear (all bad). It was good if a song took you on a journey or made you think your hi-fi was broken, bad if it reminded you of recording studios or U2. Sly Stone, T. Rex, Scott Walker, My Bloody Valentine, KMFDM, the Young Gods, Alan Vega, Al Green and Insekt were all in favour. And Berlin itself, where much of the recording was done, became a conceptual background for the record . . .

"U2's state of mind was similar to that before *The Unforgettable Fire*: ready for something bigger, rebelling against its own stereotypes . . . you might be forgiven for thinking that the band knew just what they wanted before they went in, but I don't think that's true."

Beginning in January 1989 with the team of co-producer Daniel Lanois and engineer Flood, with Eno overseeing, U2 turned itself on its head, absorbing the energy of the still nascent hardcore and grunge scene with European techno and dance. While the Edge searched out the angular and the extreme, Larry Mullins and Adam Clayton kept the big picture in sight.

The furious industrial noise of 'Zoo Station' opened the record like a futuristic poem to the new, chaotic and free Europe. The record was also more highly sexed than their anthemic '80s albums. As Bono said, "Rhythm. That is the sex of music . . . That's what was missing in the puzzle for U2."

In changing direction so radically with *Achtung Baby*, U2 avoided becoming parodies of themselves and being swept aside by the grunge and techno revolutions. *Achtung Baby* prefigured the even more experimental direction they pursued for the next ten years. They may have lost their old fans but they maintained the rage.

Hey Hey, My My (into the Black) Neil Young & Crazy Horse

(Neil Young/Jeff Blackburn) ✳ Reprise ✳ 1979 ✳ Appears on: *Rust Never Sleeps*

Punk rock really took the rock royalty by surprise. The '70s superstars were mostly dismissive of the snotty new generation, failing to recognise their younger selves or understand the attraction of feeling over technique. Neil Young was one of the few among his generation who embraced punk rock, because he'd been feeling that way himself.

He appreciated the attitude of the Sex Pistols and the wacky theories of Devo, from whom he took the concept of rust as it relates to cultural icons as well as the phrase "rust never sleeps".

"When you look back at the old bands, they're just not that funny," he said. "People want to have a good time. That's why the punk thing is so good and healthy. People who make fun of the established rock scene, like Devo and the Ramones, are much more vital to my ears than what's been happening in the last four or five years."

He said as much in 'Hey Hey, My My (into the Black)', where he had the temerity to compare Johnny Rotten with Elvis Presley: "The King is gone but he's not forgotten/This is a story about Johnny Rotten/It's better to burn out/'Cause rust never sleeps/The King is gone but he's not forgotten."

The companion song 'My My, Hey Hey' contains the line, "It's better to burn out than to fade away." Tragically Kurt Cobain used the phrase in his suicide note fifteen years later.

Young recorded the song once as an acoustic ballad and then a second time with the full-on attack of Crazy Horse. Everything here is subsumed by a massive drum beat from Ralph Molina (who claims he was imitating Queen). This is truly a great monument to the enduring power of rock.

Blue Suede Shoes Carl Perkins

(Carl Perkins) ❋ Sun ❋ 1956 ❋ Appears on: *Dance Album*

Johnny Cash heard one of his army buddies admonish another saying, "Don't step on my blue suede shoes." The line stuck with him. One night in 1955 the rockabilly singer, as he then was, played on the same bill as country guitarist Carl Perkins and he passed the phrase on. When Perkins heard someone in the crowd at a dance in Jackson, Tennessee, come up with the same line he knew he had something. The rest of the lyrics came to him in a dream that he copied out on a potato bag, spelling "suede" as "swaed".

America was abuzz in 1955. The baby boom was coming on stream, on the back of unprecedented economic growth. The kids were taking over. With them came a new style of casual fashion that celebrated their youth. It was all about status and style.

In December that year, a few months after penning the track, Perkins and his band – featuring his two brothers – were ready to record. Perkins grew up the son of one of the few white sharecroppers and his first music was the blues, taught to him by his black neighbours. He also loved country, so when the new 'hillbilly bop' took the world by storm, championed by Elvis Presley, the sound was not so foreign.

Perkins, like Cash, Presley, Jerry Lee Lewis and others, found his way to Sun Studios in Memphis, where producer Sam Phillips changed the song. After the first run through, Phillips suggested the line, "Now go boy go!" change to "Go cat go!" and he had a song that expressed everything that needed to be said about the fashion wars of the '50s. With a touch of country in the delivery, the hard-edged rockabilly track was an instant classic. *Billboard* wrote of 'Blue Suede Shoes' in their country music review section: "Perkins contributes a lively reading on a gay rhythm ditty with a strong R&B styled backing. Fine for the jukes."

'Blue Suede Shoes' was released on 1 January 1956 and was an immediate regional hit throughout the south. It entered the *Billboard* Hot 100 in the same week as 'Heartbreak Hotel' and, although Presley denied him the number one spot on the Hot 100, Perkins' tune was the first track to top both country and R&B charts. By mid-March Elvis was singing 'Blue Suede Shoes' in his set and was among the dozen performers to have already recorded the track.

Then tragedy struck. While driving to New York, Perkins' car hit a poultry truck, killing the driver. Perkins suffered a broken shoulder, cracked skull and lacerations. He was laid up in hospital and his career never regained momentum.

Carl Perkins continued to write and record in the rockabilly vein. He was a particular influence on George Harrison of the Beatles, who cut a number of his songs. Inevitably, Perkins was overshadowed by Presley, who eventually made the shoe song his own.

Superstar The Carpenters

(Leon Russell/Bonnie Bramlett) ✳ A&M ✳ 1971 ✳ Appears on: *The Carpenters*

Tragedy and darkness haunted the Carpenters. The brother and sister act with the perfect hair and shiny teeth looked like they were cast by David Lynch. Richard Carpenter's spare, gentle, middle-of-the-road arrangements, which featured his piano and generally a mournful saxophone, sounded positively haunted. In the light of Karen Carpenter's 1982 death by anorexia it just seems all too sad.

Growing up in the white-bread middle class suburbs on both coasts, Richard Carpenter was a piano-bar jazz player, eventually bringing his sister in to sing and play drums. Their second single for A&M, the Bacharach/David song 'Close to You', was a massive global hit. Richard Nixon's Silent Majority now had a voice. The Carpenters, with their apple-pie grins and Karen's neck-to-knee gowns, were the antidotes to a decade of free love, sexual revolution, flower power, civil rights and student power.

"The thing is, it had to do with what we represented, Middle America and all. We weren't trying to stamp down rock. I like rock. We just made the records we wanted to make, and it so happened that radio was ready for it and it clicked," Richard Carpenter said. "But they would throw these barbs at us, clawing at us. I'm not saying everyone should like it, but no-one can ever tell me those records weren't well made."

They were exquisite in their pain. Carpenter was meticulous in a kitsch way. All the parts fitted so smoothly together there was a soft-focus sentimentality to each bar. Karen was perpetually wistful and discreet. Her songs were sung like a girl alone in her bedroom imagining the prince that would one day come to rescue her from the soft toys. There was not a touch of lust or passion on a Carpenters' track. Dionne Warwick, that other Bacharach medium, brought desire and pain to his torch songs; the Carpenters channelled sentimentality.

Their third album is much like its predecessors; tributes to Bacharach and Henry Mancini give a sense of its direction. The album's chocolate box hits, 'Rainy Days and Mondays' and 'For All We Know', are Karen at her most passive and warm. There is one out-of-character song here – Leon Russell and Bonnie Bramlett's 'Superstar'. Richard Carpenter heard Bette Midler perform the song and persuaded Karen to cut a version. Legend has it that it was done in one take to protect Karen's sensibilities. It's the story of a groupie waiting for her rock star boyfriend to return – a modern take on *Sleeping Beauty*.

Richard Carpenter is right when he points to the singularity of the Carpenters. Although it was probably their other-worldliness and the sense of panic in Karen's voice rather than the bulk of the songs. "I really think we were unique," he told Joe Smith. "I really do. We made good records, the songs were great, and Karen was a fabulous singer. The public knew. Maybe they couldn't articulate it, but they knew." Of course they couldn't articulate it; they were the Silent Majority.

Midnight Train to Georgia   Gladys Knight & the Pips

(Jim Weatherly) ✳ Buddah ✳ 1973 ✳ Appears on: *Imagination*

One of the soul classics of the '70s was inspired by *Charlies' Angels* star Farrah Fawcett Majors going home to see her family.

"The original title of 'Midnight Train to Georgia' was 'Midnight Plane to Houston'," said songwriter and long-time Pips collaborator Jim Weatherly. "I was good friends with Lee Majors who played the *Six Million Dollar Man* on television. One day I called up to Lee's house and it was right when he was dating Farrah Fawcett. Farrah answered the phone and we were talking. She said she was packing because she was going to take the midnight plane to Houston to visit her folks. When I got off the phone the title stayed with me. I wrote the song based around Lee and Farrah's relationship. Not that it was them – it was about a girl that comes to LA to be successful but maybe she's not successful but the guy loves her and goes home with her."

Gladys Knight snapped up the song. But she had a problem with the lyrics. Being from Atlanta, Georgia, herself she suggested a change in destination and transportation.

"I've gotta believe it before I can make you believe it, so how about we do 'Midnight Train to Georgia'. I love that train," she said. "I was so glad we got to do a song about it."

The track was cut in one evening at the end of a long day's sessions. The Pips were on form, especially in the extended vamping vocals at the close of the song. It became the group's biggest hit.

Up Around the Bend   Creedence Clearwater Revival

(John Fogerty) ✳ Fantasy ✳ 1970 ✳ Appears on: *Cosmos Factory*

If you want to hear what match fitness sounds like, Creedence's *Cosmos Factory* is it. Recorded in ten days, it was their fifth album in two and a half years. When not in the studio they were on the road. Every single they made in those years went to the top of the charts, as did the albums. *Cosmos Factory* also saw the group shift gear, away from the swampy feel of previous records into a muscular, versatile and hyped-up quartet, paying tribute to Little Richard, Marvin Gaye and Roy Orbison, but with a rust-proof edge. By the time they recorded *Cosmos Factory* there was no question but that Creedence were immortals and that Fogerty had the other great white rock & roll voice (alongside John Lennon).

"*Cosmos Factory* may actually be our best record," said Fogerty. "I always thought it was the culmination. By that time, Creedence had all these records and we looked back and put everything on it. It was almost redemptive, you might say. We'd done all these things and it was like 'Boom! There, I said it again.'"

Cosmos touches on the blues workouts and anti-war songs of previous albums but on this LP they let their hair down more. 'Up Around the Bend' is a furious slide guitar boogie pursued at breakneck pace. It was like taking on Little Richard at his own game.

Serious rock groups in 1970 rarely released singles that were viewed as a teeny-bopper medium. Creedence blew that right out the window with their often biting songs and their superb musicianship. This song celebrates the joys of rock & roll and its simplicity remains as thrilling now as it did a generation ago.

Way of the World Max Q

(Ollie Olsen) ✳ CBS/Atlantic ✳ 1989 ✳ Appears on: *Max Q*

Michael Hutchence was a man of many sides. Having shown the world that he could be a sex god and superstar, he took a holiday from his group INXS to explore the darker side of music. Hutchence had always loved the post-punk noise that came out of Melbourne in the early '80s. He came into close contact with it when he starred in the film *Dogs in Space* and befriended musical director Ollie Olsen.

Olsen is a pure beatnik. His musical career with Whirlywirld, No and Orchestra of Skin and Bone was, to put it mildly, extreme. Hutchence and Olsen put their heads together and produced one of the most innovative dance music albums of the decade. Critic David Fricke called it "compelling in its desperation, irresistible in its attack." Olsen as the musical director threw everything – hard rock, string sections, house beats and pop melodies – at these apocalyptic tales of global warfare and emotional violence. Hutchence, who wrote much of the music, put in an extraordinary performance and had the time of his life.

Although the record failed to sell in large quantities, it was one of the most significant statements Hutchence was to make. "A matter of whims and calculated guesses," he said.

Cold Cold Heart Hank Williams

(Hank Williams) ✳ MGM ✳ 1950 ✳ Appears on: *40 Greatest Hits*

It's impossible to overstate the importance of Hank Williams to 20th-century songwriting. Born in Alabama in 1923, Williams became a working musician in his teens, playing honky tonks and state fairs and the like backed by the Drifting Cowboys. His music drew on blues, spirituals and Appalachian folk stylings. His particular talent was to put the emotional details of his difficult life into his songs in such a way that they reached a wide audience. In that sense Williams began a tradition of the confessional singer/songwriter.

Williams' life was troubled, first by his tempestuous marriage to Audrey Sheppard Guy, and then by his own demons. He suffered from a spinal disorder that caused chronic pain, which he self-medicated. By the time he died in the back seat of his sky-blue Cadillac at the Skyline Drive-In in Oakhill, West Virginia, on New Year's Day 1953, Williams had been to the top and back. He had been fired from the Grand Ol' Opry for being drunk and belligerent on stage. Off stage he was addicted to alcohol, amphetamines and Demerol and that was what finally killed him.

In 1947 Williams signed with the music publishing company Acuff-Rose. It was their guidance that helped Williams define his style. "He was a plain country boy writing songs and playing honky tonks," Acuff recalled. "I introduced him to Fred Rose and I believe that's one of the greatest moments in country music, when I introduced those two gentlemen together. Fred was the writer of a whole lot of songs that Hank gets credit for. I don't say nothin' about that because Hank was due that. Hank had ideas and Fred just carried 'em out."

'Cold Cold Heart' was adapted from the 1945 country song 'You'll Still Be in My Heart' with lyrics penned after yet another fight with Audrey. According to legend he learned that she had aborted another man's child that she had been carrying.

Williams told his friend Merle Kilgore, "Boy, if you want to make it, you can't fake it. You got to live it. You've got to love somebody and have them break your heart into a million pieces."

Southern Man Crosby, Stills, Nash & Young

(Neil Young) ✳ Atlantic ✳ 1971 ✳ Appears on: *Four-Way Street*

Neil Young's take on racial issues in the south is one of the highlights of his end-of-the-world album *After the Goldrush*. As with many of his apocalyptic tales, this is filled with images of burning estates and a society in flames. Its Crazy Horse-style loping tempo and Young's burning guitar lines made 'Southern Man' an instant live favourite. It also alienated southerners like Lynard Skynard, who penned the anti-Young song 'Sweet Home Alabama'.

'Southern Man' had its best reading, though, on *Four-Way Street*, the live double album from Crosby, Stills, Nash & Young. Over thirteen minutes the song evolves into a ferocious guitar duel between the ragged, spastic guitar lines from Young and the more considered but no less violent solos coming from Stephen Stills. Despite its length, not a note is superfluous.

Four-Way Street encapsulates the excess that was beginning to overtake rock during this period. The audience had grown exponentially in only a couple of years and the pockets and the egos of the arts had swelled accordingly. Plus, in the wake of Cream, extensive improvisation was regarded as an essential part of the concert experience. This lasted only a couple of years before improvisation was beyond the capacities of artists and the concert experience became too large to effectively accommodate such an intimate discourse. On 'Southern Man', however, Young and Stills go over the top together. The volatile relationship between the two friends becomes an on-stage competition full of surprising thrusts and unexpected parries, veering off into new directions never touched again.

Debris The Faces

(Ronnie Lane) ✳ Warner Bros. ✳ 1972 ✳

Appears on: *A Nod is as Good as a Wink ... to a Blind Horse*

They saw themselves as the wild cards of the second division although they put most of the premier league teams to shame. Few groups have had so much promise and then been too lazy to fulfil it. Few groups have understood and communicated the joy of playing rock & roll quite as well as the Faces did.

The problem was Rod Stewart. The singer joined the former Small Faces while maintaining his solo career and when that took off, in no small part because of the Faces, Stewart kept his best stuff for himself and hamstrung the group.

A Nod is as Good as a Wink, the third Faces studio album, is as perfect as Stewart's albums of the time – boozily sentimental, socially gormless, laddishly sexist but enormously charming – with a recurring theme of missing the late night bus. The Faces sounded like they really didn't care.

The Faces may have been loose but they were one of the most powerful live acts of the time; Wood's fuzzed-out guitar and buzzing slide-work against Kenny Jones' massive drumming made them the equal of any of their contemporaries. The Faces were much maligned in their time as sloppy and ill-focused but they were also the template for Squeeze, the Black Crowes, Oasis and, more recently, Jet. Interestingly, the back-to-basics movements tend to draw on the Faces more than any others.

While the Rolling Stones and the Who grappled with metaphysics and jet set models, the Faces lived in the suburbs trying to make a go of it – even for a night – with plain birds. On 'Too Bad' they crash a trendy party but are shown the door "before we could shake a leg". "Well let me please explain/'Cause we're not to blame/We just don't have the right accent," sang Stewart.

The soul of this album is bass player Ronnie Lane though. His kitchen-sink stories of couples married too young and now failed ran through the album. The best of them is the magnificent 'Debris', which flows along as two lovers drift apart. It's a concise portrait of stagnation in an affair, using once again buses as a metaphor for passion:

> There's more trouble at the depot,
> With the general workers union
> And you said, "They'll never change a thing."
> Well, they won't fight and they're not working.

Sung in Lane's small, cracking voice, the melody is overpowering.

By the time *A Nod* came out Stewart was ready with *Never a Dull Moment* to make him a superstar and then it became Rod Stewart and the Faces and it was pretty much last orders please. But this remains a classic.

Stand by Me Ben E King

(Ben E King) ✳ Atlantic ✳ 1961 ✳ Appears on: *Stand by Me: The Best of Ben E King*

Ben E King joined the Drifters and brought a tougher edge to their R&B sound. Most of their material was supplied by the extraordinary production/songwriting duo of Jerry Leiber and Mike Stoller, but King also penned hits. In the late '50s, R&B was still finding its comfortable blend of gospel, blues and pop music. Most of the singers came from a church background and that sense of the divine opened up their melodies.

"I took 'Stand by Me' from an old gospel song recorded by Sam Cooke and the Soul Stirrers called 'Lord I'm Standing By' or something," King recalled. "The song more or less wrote itself. I rehearsed it with the Drifters and they liked it very much. We went downtown to the Drifters' manager and he liked it but he looked at me and said, 'It's not a bad song but we're not looking for material at the moment.'"

King left the Drifters soon after. When cutting some tracks with Leiber and Stoller they asked if he had anything. He presented 'Stand by Me' and they wrote an arrangement on the spot. Up-ending a snare drum and stroking the springs against the drum skin created the distinctive percussive noise that flows through the song.

'Stand by Me' was a moderate hit on its release. It had a second lease of life in the mid-'70s when John Lennon recorded a particularly moving version for his *Rock & Roll* album. Then in the '80s the song appeared in a Levis ad and its title was used for a Rob Reiner/Stephen King film and it all started again, turning King's version into a classic.

The mixture of a rich deep vocal and a spare gospel arrangement is timeless.

Killing Me Softly with His Song Roberta Flack

(Norman Gimbel/Charles Fox) ✳ Atlantic ✳ 1973 ✳ Appears on: *Killing Me Softly*

Surprisingly, this song is a true story. Well, not literally the killing bit. The songwriter/protagonist is Don McLean and the song in question is neither of his hits ('American Pie' and 'Vincent') but an album track, 'Empty Chairs'.

"I was going through some difficult things at the time, and what he was singing about made me think, 'Whoa! This person knows me! How could he know me so well?'" poet Lori Lieberman told journalist Johnny Black. "I went home and wrote a poem and showed it to the two men I was working with at the time. Never having written a song, I didn't know how to put my poem into lyric form. Norman was able to do that. The finished lyrics are Norman's, but he was very careful to make sure that all of the feelings were coming from me."

Gimbel changed the last word in the title from 'Blues' to 'Song' and helped Lieberman record the track. Her original version was not a hit. However, singer Roberta Flack heard the song on an in-flight program.

"I was flying from Los Angeles to New York," Flack said. "Looking at the in-flight magazine, I saw the picture of this little girl, Lori Lieberman, and the title of the song. Before I heard the song, I thought it had an awfully good title, and when I heard it, I loved it. By the time I got to New York I knew I had to do that song and I knew I'd be able to add something to it.

"My classical background made it possible for me to try a number of things with it. I changed parts of the chord structure and chose to end on a major chord. It wasn't written that way."

Flack's producer Quincy Jones worked with the singer and the writers to develop a lushly romantic and forlorn atmosphere. The track shot to the top of the charts in February 1973, which is when McLean heard about his fan's obsession.

When Roberta's version came out, McLean told *Blender*, "Somebody called me and said, 'Do you know there's a song about you that's number one?' I said, 'What – are you kidding?' And they said, 'The girl who originally recorded it had it written for her after she saw you at the Troubadour in Los Angeles. She went on TV and talked about it.'"

'Killing Me Softly' was rearranged yet again in 1996 when the Fugees gave it a hip-hop treatment, and it surfaced again in 2002 when it featured in the film *About a Boy*. According to *Blender* magazine, 'Killing Me Softly' is the eleventh most performed song of all time.

Wichita Lineman Glen Campbell

(Jimmy Webb) ✳ Capitol ✳ 1968 ✳ Appears on: *Wichita Lineman*

"Jimmy Webb is my favourite songwriter," Glen Campbell said. "I think Jimmy's the best musical poet to come out of America."

Webb was the master of sad. His songs were complex, erudite pop masterpieces. Webb was lavishly melancholic with a sort of existential Americana – loners out in the vast American night.

'Wichita Lineman' is his most concise and powerful lyric – the telephone guy out in Kansas, isolated by the immenseness of the Great Plains but still connecting lovers across the country. The imagery here is so clear and simple that it only takes two verses to break your heart.

In 1968 Glen Campbell was an in-demand session guitarist around Los Angeles. He had worked with the legendary studio players of the '60s, and for a time joined the Beach Boys as a vocalist. His solo career really took off with his version of a Jimmy Webb song, 'By the Time I Get to Phoenix'. He turned to Webb again. The songwriter had been driving through the mid-west when he saw a man repairing telephone wires.

"I had been driving around northern Oklahoma, an area that's real flat and remote – almost surreal in its boundless horizons and infinite distances," he told *Blender*'s Johnny Black. "I'd seen a lineman up on a telephone pole, talking on the phone. It was such a curiosity to see a human being perched up there in those surroundings."

The song took approximately two hours to write, but was still unfinished – hence its brevity – when Campbell called for a track. Using his friends from the LA session pool, Campbell cut the track in ninety minutes. Carol Kaye provided the distinctive bass notes that open proceedings and Campbell played the guitar solo on her bass. Producer Al De Lory did the string arrangement that gently mimics the morse code signals down the wire.

The most difficult part of the production was Campbell's attempts to reproduce the sparse lonesomeness of Webb's demo recording. The songwriter had a large electronic organ that was brought into the studio to add ambience. "I had a Gilbranson," said Webb, "which had a humming, resonating, reverberating electronic sound with a tremolo quality, but also an echo, so there was a lot of sustain. Kind of a bubbling noise. Just three notes, but it produced a kind of electronic chiming – which might be a telecommunications sound, a satellite sound or something of that nature."

Campbell gave a flawless reading of the track, his voice quivering and cracking with sadness and resignation and desire.

My Funny Valentine   Frank Sinatra

(Lorenz Hart/Richard Rogers) ✳ Capitol ✳ 1955 ✳ Appears on: *Songs for Young Lovers*

Rogers and Hart were the odd couple. Rogers was patrician, disciplined, methodical, temperamental, inventive and almost scholarly. Hart was the opposite – dissolute, forever troubled about his almost dwarf stature, his homosexuality, drinking and gambling. At times he had to be locked in a room to finish the lyrics for a show. Rogers recalled their first meeting as, "Larry came to the door wearing house slippers, tuxedo trousers and some kind of a shirt. Larry was twenty-three years old. I was sixteen. I knew I was in the presence of talent. What he had to say about lyrics was tremendously stimulating."

Together they composed some 650 songs for musicals, many of which have become standards. Rogers wrote the music to order and Hart wrote the lyrics to a deadline.

'My Funny Valentine' was composed first and then proposed for a Broadway show, *Babes in Arms*. The two were so proud of the song they had the name of the hero changed to Valentine so that his love interest could sing the lyric as written.

"He wrote about himself all the time," said the journalist Max Welk. "You listen to the lyric and there you are in a little short man who smoked big cigars and scribbled lyrics on the back of anything that was around."

The song has a deep, deep longing in it. Yet there's also a crucial resolution in that after the woman has listed her lover's many and varied faults she says, "Don't change a hair for me/Not if you care for me."

'My Funny Valentine' is one of the standards of 20th-century music. Rogers' languid, rich melody is the very essence of melancholy. It is a profound test for any vocalist and many have found glory in its folds. Curiously, male vocalists have excelled here following in the footsteps of Frank Sinatra. The Chairman of the Board cut this track as part of his mid-'50s comeback. The *Songs for Young Lovers* was one of the first concept records. The concept is simple enough – romance. Sinatra puts everything into the ballad. Elvis Costello recently observed, "'My Funny Valentine' is a woman's song but I always associate it with male vocalists. When a man sings it, it has a strange dreamlike quality."

Take the "A" Train   Duke Ellington & His Orchestra

(Billy Strayhorn) ✳ Columbia ✳ 1941 ✳ Appears on: *Ken Burns Jazz Vol. 1*

The "A" Train goes up Manhattan to the Sugar Hill section of Harlem. We know this because 'Take the "A" Train' is one of the classic jazz songs.

Billy Strayhorn was a poor black pianist in Pittsburgh in 1938 when he scored an audience with Duke Ellington. The meeting took place after Ellington had given a show and the great bandleader was obliged rather than eager to hear from this kid. Strayhorn got behind the piano and played 'Sophisticated Lady', one of Ellington's hits, perfectly in the Duke's style. Then he said, "This is how I would do it ..." and rearranged the track. Ellington was stunned.

In part it was the kid's piano playing but mostly his gift for arrangement that prompted Ellington to give Strayhorn his address and ask him to come to New York.

Strayhorn, of course, jumped at the chance. To impress Ellington, on the way to New York he took the directions and wrote a song out of them.

'Take the "A" Train' bristles with its own urbanity. The horns swing and swoop with an excited nervousness that prefigures Charlie Parker and bebop. The pianos have an insistent percussive vamping. At the same time there is a majestic quality to the song. It bustles. It's modern. Ellington added the sense of subway motion to the piece and you have an anthem of 20th-century city life.

This became Ellington's theme song and the beginning of a productive friendship with Strayhorn. 'Take the "A" Train' was one of the most popular songs of its time and is still the theme that conjures up the excitement of the American century. Both Ellington and Strayhorn were buried to the tune.

"The steady hand of his good judgement pointed the way that was fitting for both of us," said Ellington of his "right arm."

The Message   Grandmaster Flash & the Furious Five

(Duke Bootee) ✳ Sugarhill ✳ 1982 ✳ Appears on: *Louder than a Bomb*

Block parties where a DJ set up a sound system and played records were a feature of life in the Bronx in the mid-'70s. A group of DJs began beat matching – extending the music by mixing two songs together on the beat. MCs improvised verse over the top – and there you have the beginnings of rap. By the turn of the decade DJs were becoming stars – Cool Herc, Afrika Bambaataa and Grandmaster Flash were the three innovators leading the charge.

Joseph Saddler (aka Flash) was a master of the break. He collected a group of MCs – the Furious Five (Melle Mel, Kid Creole, Cowboy, Scorpio and Raheim) – and invented much of the hip-hop style right there.

Sugarhill Records put Flash in the studio to make 'Adventures on the Wheels of Steel', which was the first record made solely from mixing other records.

"It took three turntables, two mixers and between ten and fifteen takes to get it right," he recalled. "It took me three hours. I had to do it live. And whenever I'd mess up I would just refuse to punch. I would just go back to the beginning."

Sylvia Robinson, co-owner of Sugarhill, then pressed a tune written by the house band percussionist Ed 'Duke Bootee' Fletcher. Flash and the Five were unconvinced by the political message and just plain didn't like the song. Robinson insisted and the record was cut with Melle Mel on the lead vocal.

The rest is history. 'The Message', with its stark images of ghetto life, also has the killer hook, "Don't push me 'cause I'm close to the edge," which had universal appeal. The record was a Top 10 smash around the globe and sold over half a million 12-inch singles. So much broke out with that one record – scratching, angry political rap lyrics and the nascent hip-hop style were all introduced on that single. What had once been a party trick became the most significant cultural movement of the next three decades. 'Adventures on the Wheels of Steel' opened the way; 'The Message' brought rap to the world.

"I was first," Flash told the *Guardian* newspaper. "I don't care who's better, who's worse. My contribution is first. Because first is forever."

Statesboro Blues/Church Bell Blues David Bromberg

(Luke Jordan/Blind Willie McTell) ❋ Columbia ❋ 1974 ❋ Appears on: *Wanted Dead or Alive*

David Bromberg is a virtuoso guitar player with a seamless facility in blues, folk, bluegrass and R&B. Unfortunately, having neither a particularly tuneful voice nor a pin-up's looks, Bromberg's career has mostly been in traditional music. His brief stint at Columbia, however, bore three interesting albums of which the third was best.

Bob Dylan contributed one track, 'Wallflower', George Harrison a co-write, and the Grateful Dead did most of the backing alongside some sublime players, but *Wanted Dead or Alive* was not much wanted.

Bromberg's oddball humour is well represented with 'Someone Else's Blues', 'Danger Man' and 'Send Me to the 'Lectric Chair'. His hangdog personality was honed through years of coffee houses and playing support to Jerry Jeff 'Bojangles' Walker. The humour never gets in the way of incredible timing and feel, however. Elsewhere Bromberg stretches out with his own 'New Lee Highway Blues', a wonderful song about road fatigue and the break-up of a relationship. The centrepiece of the album, however, is a version of 'Statesboro Blues', which has the nuance and the deftness of Blind Willie McTell and the same plaintive mood. The segue into 'Church Bell Blues' is seamless. It's here that Bromberg loses his self-consciousness and touches the sublime.

I'm a Believer The Monkees

(Neil Diamond) ✳ Colgems ✳ 1966 ✳ Appears on: *More of the Monkees*

'I'm a Believer' was the third most popular song of the '60s. It was recorded in October 1966 and a month later was the number one single in the US and became the biggest selling single of 1967.

The key to the Monkees was their connection, through executive producer Don Kirshner, to the Brill Building. This songwriting factory based in New York was under siege once the Beatles broke. Almost overnight the fashion changed towards groups who wrote their own material. The Monkees were a group through whom the Brill Building writers could fight back.

Neil Diamond left school to become a songwriter in the Brill Building tradition. He came under the wing of producer Bert Berns and the production/songwriting duo of Ellie Greenwich and Jeff Barry. His first session with Barry yielded three hit songs, one of which was 'I'm a Believer'. Barry produced the track in New York and then Monkey Mickey Dolenz added his vocal. The song has an amazing garage-rock energy, a touch of the Beatles in the long guitar runs and a touch of the Phil Spector sound in the percussion, the backing vocals and the harmonies. Pop doesn't get any more perfect.

Rhapsody in Blue   George Gershwin

(George Gershwin) ❋ Victor ❋ 1924 ❋ Appears on: *Rhapsody in Blue/American in Paris*

George Gershwin, born into a Russian Jewish immigrant family on New York's Lower East Side in 1898, was twenty-five when he wrote 'Rhapsody in Blue'. It's one of the first multi-cultural works of the 20th century. The sprawling fifteen-minute tune pulls together classical music and jazz, the music hall songs and Gershwin's Jewish cultural heritage. When it was performed on 12 February 1924 to an audience that included Rachmaninoff amongst other musical heavyweights, 'Rhapsody in Blue' left most of them bewildered.

Gershwin left school at sixteen to work for a music publisher. Five years later he had the biggest hit in the world with 'Swanee', as sung by Al Jolson in the world's first musical film.

Gershwin wanted to take his work out of Tin Pan Alley and onto a concert stage. He discussed this ambition with bandleader Paul Whiteman, who had similar ideas.

According to NPR's *All Things Considered*, Gershwin and Whiteman went their separate ways. Then Ira Gershwin saw an ad in the paper. "One day in January 1924 I called George's attention to an item in the music column of the morning paper," Ira said in a radio interview. "To the effect that Whiteman was going ahead with the idea of doing a concert that would feature a suite by Victor Herbert and something by George Gershwin."

With less than four weeks until the concert, Gershwin immediately contacted Whiteman and agreed to write a rhapsody because it was a more free-form piece that would allow improvisation.

Gershwin composed the basis of his rhapsody on a brown paper bag on the way to Boston, where he was working on his latest Broadway show. The writing took three weeks to complete after which the musicians rehearsed and it was in the rehearsals that Gershwin changed the tempo from a speedy jazz to the more stately and epic arrangement we have. The genius of the piece was, however, the diversity of the stylings which were woven into one piece of music. It reflected the multicultural aspect of New York – something that was further confirmed by the irregularity of the song's structure. This was highbrow pop music that became an instant popular standard.

Totally Wired The Fall

(Marc Riley/Craig Scanlon/Mark E Smith) ❋ Factory ❋ 1980 ❋
Appears on: *Grotesque (after the Gramme)*

If chemical compounds could make a noise, this is what amphetamine sulphate would sound like. Taut, twitchy, dissonant music and Mark E Smith tunelessly screaming, "I'm totally wired. I'm totally wired!" Well, yes. Who wouldn't be? Here's this northern English guy who founded the first punk fanzine (*Sniffin' Glue*) and, inspired by the spirit of DIY, starts his own band. Having done it, of course, he realises that, yes, everyone can start a punk band. But it takes something else to start a good punk band. But here he is with the Fall and nobody but himself to blame. Wouldn't that drive you to sniffing speed?

'Totally Wired' mostly resembles the Legendary Stardust Cowboy's 'Paralysed' for its live feel and sense of abandon. The Fall took it one step beyond and it sounded like a New Wave record played badly rather than a punk record played well. Whether by accident or design, though, 'Totally Wired' is primal and angsty, desperate and stupid music, and perfect for letting your hair down.

If I Had a Boat Lyle Lovett

(Lyle Lovett) ❋ Curb ❋ 1987 ❋ Appears on: *Pontiac*

Lyle Lovett is not your ordinary country singer. While his music is steeped in that tradition, Lovett stands a little outside and to the left of it. "There's something gratifying, I think, about not fitting in exactly," he told Barney Hoskyns. "Some of the songs are pretty silly – at least, they're supposed to be humorous – but then there are some that aren't silly. I don't know enough about music to come up with my own musical language, but I feel like I'm on a more singular path than most country artists. I'm not upholding any sort of tradition, and I'm not part of a larger country music picture."

Born and raised in Texas, Lovett grew up listening to the new country of Guy Clarke and Townes Van Zandt. These were lyricists in a folk and rock tradition rather than a Nashville one, and although their tunes could usually accommodate a pedal steel guitar they were deeply soulful and literate.

Lovett was even further out than his heroes, particularly on his stark and confronting debut album, *Pontiac*. He opened that account with the whimsical 'If I Had a Boat', ostensibly the story of a man who wishes to ferry his horse on his dinghy. There is, in the conjunction of melody and words, a whole universe of longing, a sense of loneliness and sadness that is to be escaped.

Lovett, however, claimed it was mere autobiography. He said he tried to ride a pony across a pond and then wished he had a boat.

Mama Weer All Crazee Now   Slade

(Noddy Holder/Jim Lea) ❋ Polydor ❋ 1972 ❋ Appears on: *Slayed?*

"The beat is the main thing with us. We like to hit their guts with the beat and get some feeling going through their bloodstream into their hands," Slade singer Noddy Holder told *Melody Maker*. "If you want to come and sit down and delve into the music, it's no good coming to see us. I think we could play like that if we wanted to, but we don't want to. We get our kicks from pulsating music."

Coming out of Birmingham and the industrial midlands of Britain at the turn of the decade as Ambrose Slade, the shortened Slade were unashamedly a people's band. Not for them the arty sounds of progressive rock or the charms of Ancient Albion. Slade – guitarist Dave Hill, bassist Jimmy Lea and drummer Don Powell – were here to rock. Initially a skinhead group, Slade distanced themselves from the violence associated with skinheads and they started dressing in glam outfits with nose-bleed platform shoes and silver jumpsuits.

"Basically we're known in England as the people's group," Dave Hill said, "being as we've worked with the working class people – they're the ones who're with us now that actually made us in England. It seems to me they go for our kind of music 'cuz it's mixed. We're not puttin' out the same kind of thing every record. We've got a style, a sound and we're in with 'em. And we don't mind mixin' with our fans whereas most groups usually get to the stage where they don't even talk to 'em."

Slade's sound – which barely varied from one hit to the next – was typical of the English glam sound, which was big on simple, massive beats designed for clubfooted dancers wearing boots. The drums fought their way through a heavy sludge of guitar, piano and bass. It was simple and powerful. It grew from ham-fisted versions of '50s rock & roll and developed into a style all Slade's own. Their songs were misspelt anthems to a good time – 'Get Down and Get with It', 'Cos I Luv You', 'Look Wot You Dun', 'Take Me Bak 'Ome.'

Holder was inspired to write 'Mama Weer All Crazee Now' when he contemplated a typical Slade rave up. "I thought, 'Christ, everyone must have been crazy tonight'," he said.

"You see, everyone was so hip and cool in England that when anything would come out big, it was a hype or something," Hill said. "A section of the population was hairies, you know, who didn't want to know any kids comin' out that way. To them, any group with short hair … you couldn't play guitar or couldn't play this. You know what I mean? That's the way they thought, which was ridiculous really. You're still a bloke. Hair's got nothing at all to do with it."

Lovers in a Dangerous Time Bruce Cockburn

(Bruce Cockburn) ❊ Columbia ❊ 1984 ❊ Appears on: *Stealing Fire*

Canadian singer/songwriter Bruce Cockburn has been releasing albums since 1970. As a left-wing Christian he tackles the big subjects of life, death and politics often observed in the small details. In the early '80s, Cockburn visited Central America. The results can be heard on *Stealing Fire*, where Latin and African influences can be discerned on songs of outrage.

The opening track, 'Lovers in a Dangerous Time', sets up the album's descent into insanity. The song, which contains the great couplet, "But nothing worth having comes without some kind of fight/Got to kick at the darkness 'til it bleeds daylight," was inspired by contemplating his own children.

"I was thinking of kids in a schoolyard," said Cockburn. "I was thinking of my daughter. Sitting there wanting to hold hands with some little boy and looking at a future, looking at the world around them. How different that was when I was a kid when, even though we had air-raid drills, nobody took that seriously that the world would end. You could have hope when I was a kid. And now I think that's very difficult. I think a lot of that is evident from the actions and the ethos of a lot of kids. It was kind of an attempt to offer a hopeful message to them. You still have to live and you have to give it your best shot."

Hound Dog Elvis Presley

(Jerry Leiber/Mike Stoller) ❋ RCA Victor ❋ 1962 ❋ Appears on: *Elvis' Golden Records*

The song forever associated with Elvis Presley was originally written for bandleader Johnny Otis, who was recording Willie Mae 'Big Mama' Thornton.

"The day we brought in 'Hound Dog' on a piece of paper, Johnny Otis had a bunch of his acts auditioning songs in his garage," said writer Jerry Leiber. "And Willie Mae sang 'Ball and Chain' and she knocked us out. We'd actually written 'Hound Dog' ninety per cent on the way over in the car. I was beating out a rhythm we called the buck dance on the roof of the car. So we got to Johnny's house and Mike went right to the piano … didn't even bother to sit down. He had a cigarette in his mouth that was burning his left eye, and he started to play the song.

"And to make a long story short, we took the song back to Big Mama and she snatched the paper out of my hand and said, 'Is this my big hit?' And I said, 'I hope so.' Next thing I know, she starts crooning 'Hound Dog' like Frank Sinatra would sing 'In the Wee Small Hours of the Morning'. And I'm looking at her, and I'm a little intimidated by the razor scars on her face, and she's about 280 to 320 pounds and I said, 'It don't go that way.' And she looked at me like looks could kill and said, 'White boy, don't you be tellin' me how to sing the blues.'

"We finally got through it. Johnny brought Mike back in the room and asked him to sit down at the piano, which was not easy because Johnny had this female piano player who was built like Arnold Schwarzenegger. They finally exchanged seats and did the song the way it was supposed to sound. And that was one of those where we said, 'That's a hit.' And I thought immediately: we both said it, it's gonna put a hex on it!"

Presley heard the song not from Big Mama's recording but in Las Vegas where it was part of Freddie Bell and the Bellboys' act. Presley sexed the song up considerably and made it the finale to his own show before cutting it in New York on 2 July 1956. They did thirty-one takes before Presley was content.

The hex was clearly off as the Presley version shot to number one, which is how the writers first heard it.

"I heard the record and I was disappointed," said Mike Stoller. "It just sounded terribly nervous, too fast, too white. But you know, after it sold seven or eight million records it started to sound better."

Song 2 Blur

(Damon Albarn/Graham Coxon/Alex James/Dave Rowntree) ❊ Food/Virgin ❊ 1996 ❊

Appears on: *Blur*

Blur are a British band in the tradition of the Kinks and the Jam, which means that their best work passeth the understanding of Americans. With a view to crossing the great water, Blur's self-titled album embraced rock and grunge. Albarn told me at the time that the group's new sound was due to his friendship with Pavement's Steve Malkmus and that may be a part of the story. In any case, the coy humour was dropped for something louder and subtler.

"Our choice of singles has been spectacularly inept for the American market, really," said Albarn at the time. "With 'Song 2', we've released something that is at least tangible. Whether it'll do business, I don't know. But it's the first thing I think we've done since 'Boys and Girls' that is tangible. It feels right in America."

'Song 2' is a parody of Nirvana. The lyric mocks the self-loathing of Kurt Cobain while the music is a better produced and louder version of the soft/loud arrangements that Nirvana based their work on. In essence the big guitar riff is matched with Albarn's "Woo hoo!" shout as if he melded Homer Simpson and Kurt into one.

Albarn claimed that the whole album was a portrait of the band. "The songs are entirely about a band, about being in a band, about this band," he said to Erik Himmelsbach. "It's been really interesting to start thinking like that when I'm writing a song. I've always found songs to be magic things, and that by playing them they can somehow become guardians of your future in the sense that you can sing about things and make them come true.

"So once you start singing about yourself, it's a precarious thing. Because if you're honest about how you feel, you can sing really quite dark things, which are then a source of somehow obsessive stories of possibilities of your own demise."

'Song 2' was hardly their demise, even if it didn't break them in America. In fact it has become even more ubiquitous than 'Teen Spirit'. In the US the National Hockey League used the song. It is heard in ads for Paul Verohoven's *Starship Troopers* and has appeared on many soundtracks and, most memorably, as a car commercial around the world. It's fitting that 'Song 2' even got an airing in *The Simpsons*.

Forever Young   Bob Dylan

(Bob Dylan) ✳ Asylum ✳ 1974 ✳ Appears on: *Planet Waves*

In his notes for the *Biograph* album, Dylan said, "'Forever Young' I wrote in Tuscon. I wrote it thinking about one of my boys and not wanting to be too sentimental. The lines came to me; they were done in a minute. I don't know. Sometimes that's what you're given. You're given something like that. You don't know what it is exactly that you want but this is what comes. That's how that song came out. I certainly didn't intend to write it – I was going for something else, the song wrote itself …"

Dylan's son Jakob was about to reach his fourth birthday at the time. Howard Sounes in his book *Down the Highway* also notes that Keats used the phrases "For ever painting and for ever young" in his 'Ode to a Grecian Urn'. That sentiment would accord with this extraordinary blessing.

The *Planet Waves* album, on which the song appears in two versions, was recorded in three days with the Band. Much of the record appears to be about the commitments of family. On this track the skipping reels of Robbie Roberston's guitar sit like jewels in the song.

'Forever Young' is remarkable amongst Dylan's songs in as much as it is so naked. The imagery is simple and spare and touched with a little of the Divine. It's a beatitude.

Chelsea Hotel #2   Leonard Cohen

(Leonard Cohen) ✳ Columbia ✳ 1974 ✳ Appears on: *New Skin for the Old Ceremony*

Leonard Cohen introduced this song at a concert in San Francisco in 1993 with this anecdote: "I was in the manager's office downstairs and on the wall I saw a picture of a woman. It remembered to me the time that I left Montreal for New York City. My mother said to me, even though I was a grown man, 'Watch out for those people, Leonard, they aren't like we are.' I was deeply offended by her presumption of giving a man of such years this advice but after I'd lost the copyright to 'Suzanne' and 'The Stranger Song' and 'Dress Rehearsal Rag', I think I knew what she was talking about.

"There were, however, some compensations, some consolations, a sophisticated hotel on 23rd Street. You could enter with a pygmy and a polar bear and not an eyebrow was raised, the key was just shoved across the counter. I used to ride the elevator late at night, up and down. I noticed that there was a young woman in that elevator. I did not know the great fame, the renown she had attained. All I knew was that she was a nightrider like myself, trying to pass the hours of the early morning. I gathered my courage and I summoned the most razor-like approach that I could carve for her presence and I said, 'Are you looking for someone?' She said, 'Yes I'm looking for Kris Kristofferson.' I said, 'Lady, you're in luck tonight. I'm Kris Kristofferson.'

"Well, such was the generosity of those times that she never called me on it. A couple of years later after she passed over to the other side, I found myself at this bar in a Polynesian restaurant in Miami Beach. Life leads the thoughtful man on a path of many windings. I was drinking a cocktail out of a ceramic coconut.

"This was an imponderable mystery because the entire place was frothing with actual, authentic coconuts. I hold these mysteries on the level of the Trinity. Not only can they not be penetrated but there is no need to penetrate them. They are comforting in their obscurity. The very obscurity is what offers such solace.

"I think we can take a lesson from this. Many of the mysteries that seem to beset us, just lie back on them and relax. The thought of the young woman came to me very strongly as I sat at that bar and I wrote this song for Janis Joplin."

'Chelsea Hotel #2' documents the evening and includes the immortal lines: "You were giving me head/On an unmade bed/While the limousine waits in the street."

Janis Joplin was the most fragile of performers with a deep pool of loneliness. The performances she gave were of extraordinary power and beauty and selflessness for which she received less love in return than she needed.

"Janis Joplin would sing to twenty or thirty thousand people who were drooling at her feet and I'd see her wandering around the Chelsea Hotel at three in the morning trying to find somebody to have a cup of coffee with," Cohen said in an interview. "So how do you reconcile those things? I don't know. She stood for something beautiful and nervous and high, and surrendered completely, and yet she couldn't have those things, she couldn't manifest simple things, simple beautiful things in her own life, that's really what I mean."

So What Miles Davis

(Miles Davis) ✳ Columbia ✳ 1959 ✳ Appears on: *A Kind of Blue*

In the spring of 1959, seven musicians got together in a converted church on 30th Street in Manhattan and made jazz history. Over forty years have passed since Miles Davis assembled his famed sextet to record *A Kind of Blue*, and in that time the album has risen to the level of masterpiece.

Davis' sextet was widely and rightly regarded as one of the first rate jazz ensembles of the period – John Coltrane on tenor sax and Cannonball Adderley on alto, Bill Chambers playing bass, drummer Jimmy Cobb and Bill Evans playing piano (except for one track where Winton Kelly sat in). Davis developed these players into a combo that could play as one. He walked into the 30th Street studio with ideas and then encouraged the players to embellish them.

The results in *A Kind of Blue* were so breathtaking that these sessions are spoken of as a revolutionary moment. That's not quite the case. Davis had become interested in modal jazz – where musicians improvised on a scale and melody rather than pushing through changes – as an antidote to the increasingly excessive bebop style. Miles was going this way already with *Porgy and Bess* and 'Milestones' and he certainly didn't invent modal jazz.

In his liner notes to the reissue of *A Kind of Blue*, Robert Palmer quotes an interview Miles gave a year before these sessions in which he said, "The music has gotten thick. Guys give me tunes and they're full of chords. I can't play them … I think a movement in jazz is beginning away from the conventional string of chords and a return to emphasis on melodic rather than harmonic variation. There will be fewer chords but infinite possibilities as to what to do with them."

The massive success of *A Kind of Blue* changed jazz and opened it up to new directions. Davis developed the modal line through the '60s and into fusion while Coltrane took another direction into his own spiritual quest and then into the free jazz of his later period.

If the specifics of these tunes were new to the Miles Davis sextet when they arrived at the sessions, the ideas and direction were not. Miles worked very hard to craft the performances out of the sextet. He carefully set up the arrangements and then, once the tune was established, he let the players have their heads. Four of the five songs on the album were cut in one take.

"I … planned that album around the piano playing of Bill Evans," Miles wrote in his autobiography. He also planned it around the blues, using the African-American tradition as the bedrock for a number of the tunes. The title is a clear play on words suggesting both the melancholy atmosphere of the album and the quiet strength of the blues.

A Kind of Blue opens with its best known song, 'So What'. "'So What' is a simple figure based on sixteen measures of one scale, 8 of another and 8 more of the first, following a piano and bass introduction in free rhythmic style," wrote Bill Evans in his sleeve notes.

Chambers brings in the rhythm and the themes and then hands it over to Miles, whose trumpet is so graceful and elegant and sad. The track is minimal and spare but full of life in its details.

'So What' is the most recognised jazz song of its era, the signature tune for cool jazz. Davis' reflection twenty-five years later was equally cool. "*A Kind of Blue* – those things are there. They were done in that era, the right hour, the right day, and it happened. It's over, it's on the record." That's true, but it is one of those tunes that has become woven into our collective subconscious.

I Shot the Sheriff The Wailers

(Bob Marley) ❋ Tuff Gong ❋ 1973 ❋ Appears on: *Burnin'*

This was the song that introduced reggae to the west via Eric Clapton's version on his *461 Ocean Boulevard* album. After Clapton's hit in 1974, the rock audience started to take notice of what was happening in the Caribbean. Clapton's rock arrangement, of course, lacked the steaming Jamaican groove and the ambience of Harry J's ganja-filled studio. This comic tale of a battle with the police had a strong narrative but lacked the rebel fire of the best Wailers music. The fact that it was slightly rebellious and the stoned ambience in the lyric and tempo were obviously appealing to teenagers. This was a pop song for the Wailers, picking up on the theme of *The Harder They Come*, the tune had sprightly groove.

Burnin' was a difficult album to make in as much as the Wailers were falling apart. Marley was clearly the dominant force in the group and his rapid ascendancy alienated his former friends Peter Tosh and Bunny Livingston. After *Burnin'* the releases became Bob Marley and the Wailers.

Move on Up Curtis Mayfield

(Curtis Mayfield) ❋ Curtom ❋ 1970 ❋ Appears on: *Curtis*

Mayfield's first solo album away from the Impressions is sublime soul funk and, on this track, a hint of gospel. Mayfield's grandmother was a minister and he grew up in a church environment while also listening to the blues that was so much a part of his hometown Chicago. The positive message that ran through the Impressions' work continued on *Curtis*.

"I came up in the church, and heard her words of inspiration and her ability to speak to the people of matters that would make them think and inspire or motivate them. Living with a grandmother who is trying to earn her ministry, you certainly stay in church," he said. "Anyway, a combination of common sense and growing up in that area with those women probably helped to mould what I'm about lyrically."

The soulful, feel-good funk of 'Move on Up' shows off Mayfield's guitar playing. He finds here a sublime little groove to match the lyrical message and he inflects with an individuality that few soul singer/songwriters had, other than Hendrix and Marvin Gaye, at that time. Mayfield's guitar playing was a significant inspiration to both Hendrix and Robbie Robertson of the Band and influenced scores of players in between.

'Move on Up' is a defiant song without militancy. Like Dr King, the lyric doesn't guild the lily or make light of the task, but stresses a positive outlook and faith as the solution to the problems of black people in America. Of course, the song can have wider implications and it has been greatly covered.

The Jam covered 'Move on Up' and then Paul Weller jazzed it a bit with the Style Council and put Mayfield on the map for a later generation who came up through acid jazz and new soul groups. Primal Scream's 'Movin' on Up' shows a clear influence. American singer and songwriter Mark Eitzel has also done an interesting '90s version. 'Move on Up' has also been sampled to the point of ubiquity.

"I was observing things, what happened politically, what was in the paper, what was on TV," Mayfield said of his influences in the early '70s. "Asking what things were wrong that oughta be right. It was just straight from the heart and I didn't have answers all the time. The songs were food for thought, I hoped my music was inspirational in manner. It could speak in a dialogue that makes you think for yourself. What would I do if I seriously gave this some thought?"

Strange Fruit Billie Holiday

(Lewis Allan) ✳ Commodore ✳ 1939 ✳

Appears on: *Billie Holiday – The Complete Commodore Recordings, 1934–44*

Abel Meeropol, who wrote under the name Lewis Allan, showed the lyric for his song 'Strange Fruit' to Billie Holiday one night during her season at the New York Café Society club. "Some guy's brought me a hell of a damn song," she told bandleader and trumpeter Frankie Newton.

On the first night she performed it, the room was plunged into darkness but for a tiny spot that lit her face. The bar was closed and waiters were ordered to remain still while Holiday pulled from her soul her interpretation of Allan's dark lyric about southern trees whose leaves and roots were dipped in the blood of lynching. The audience was divided between those who were moved beyond words and those who were moved to complain.

Holiday wanted to record it, which, in 1939, was an act of enormous courage, but her label, Columbia, refused. She approached a small, independent jazz label, Commodore, and she recorded the song with Frankie Newton and his band. The result was an instant hit, in spite of a ban by much of commercial radio.

After Holiday performed 'Strange Fruit' at the Harlem Apollo, Jack Schiffman from the venue told *MOJO* that he remembered "a moment of oppressively heavy silence and then a kind of rustling sound I had never heard before. It was the sound of almost 2000 people sighing." The song has been covered by artists as diverse as Nina Simone, Cassandra Wilson, Tony Bennett, Sting and UB40, and has resonated deeply in successive generations, well beyond the African American community.

My Generation The Who

(Pete Townshend) ✳ Brunswick ✳ 1965 ✳ Appears on: *The Who Sings My Generation*

The demo tape of 'My Generation' sounded like "Jimmy Reed at ten years old suffering from nervous indigestion," according to Pete Townshend, its author.

The song has since become an anthem for several generations. Nothing expresses the urgency and passion of youth better than the line "Hope I die before I get old". Townshend recalls the song's beginnings as being somewhat more prosaic. It was, he has written, a slow blues that appeared when he mucked around with his new tape machines.

In 1971 he wrote, "I had written the lines of 'Generation' without thinking, hurrying them, scribbling on a piece of paper in the back of a car. For years I've had to live by them, waiting for the day someone says, 'I thought you said you hoped you'd die when you got old in that song. Well, you are old. What now?' Of course most people are too polite to say that sort of thing to a dying pop star. I say it often to myself."

The Who's managers Chris Stamp and Kit Lambert immediately recognised the brilliance of this song, which so perfectly captured the generation gap. In the hands of a group with the anarchic mindset of the Who, 'My Generation' was a monster.

Having penned the anthem, Townshend had made himself the spokesman for his generation. He needed to articulate the meaning of the song. It has variously been described as representing the mods in particular and the hippies in general; sometimes he talks about how the song relates to his relationship with Roger Daltrey. The reality is that Townshend tapped into the Zeitgeist and his interpretation of the song (and, indeed, the public's) represents his position at any particular point in time. In 1977 when punk rock was sweeping the Who's generation from history, the song was without irony adopted by the punk rockers. If the '60s generation wish to remember the joys of their youth, 'My Generation' is a touchstone for them.

Like most Who sessions, this one with producer Shel Talmy was quick. "Well, for the *My Generation* album, there was nothing to be nervous about in them days," Daltrey told *Goldmine* magazine. "We used to take every day as it came. Every day was just a gig and I think we did the recording between gigs literally. We did the whole album in two afternoons and by the end of the week we were playing the stuff on stage."

Talmy, who also produced the Kinks, was not averse to keeping some of the Who's rough edges. He cut the song in two takes on 13 October 1965. It was on the street three weeks later. Townshend's guitar feeds back and becomes a feature of the song. Roger Daltrey famously sings with a speech impediment and that too becomes a feature. "Kit Lambert [manager] came up to me and said, 'Stutter the words – it makes it sound like you're pilled.'"

Then there is the group's ensemble playing – Keith Moon ignites the session with a frenetic figure on the drums that the rest of the group race to catch. This is not a groove song; it's like the rush of history and you're swept up in its wake. The feedback, the fumbling for words (which promise they're going to be obscene), the manic rhythm section, the ascending key changes, create an atmosphere of chaos and disorder and that's the revolutionary meaning behind the song.

"It's a fucking great record," said Daltrey. "It really is."

Copperhead Road Steve Earle

(Steve Earle) ❋ MCA ❋ 1988 ❋ Appears on: *Copperhead Road*

In 1986, Steve Earle was the poster boy for the new Nashville. He'd paid his dues for twelve years since he first arrived as a folk singer. The capital of country music was hoping that it wouldn't be too different from the old Nashville, with handsome young guys in cowboy hats singin' about lost love and the like. Pretty soon though Steve Earle wasn't so welcome. He had a string of bad marriages and a raging and very public drug habit.

By 1987–88, when he made his third album, *Copperhead Road*, Steve Earle was out of control. The album he made with its mixed-up confusion he dubbed "heavy-metal bluegrass," and he welcomed the rock audience, 'cause Nashville wasn't too keen. Earle had crossed the line from favourite son to prodigal son.

The album deals with the screwed-up world as Earle sees America, and his own life. The title track however is based on a real incident, going to a baseball game with a friend who was a Vietnam Vet.

"I asked him if he thought the fireworks were going to bother him, 'cause if they were, we'd leave," Earle said. "But he said this was something he really needed to get through. And he tried his best, bless his heart, but after about thirty seconds, he stuck his head down between his knees.

"It wasn't the sound that got to him; it was the light. He was on one of those river patrol boats in the war, and they used to keep the rivers lit up at night with parachute flares. Explosions didn't bother him at all. He said they used to welcome the explosions; it was the quiet that drove everybody nuts, going up those rivers under those lights waiting for something to happen.

"So that's how I started to write 'Copperhead Road'. It's part of what's going on in the whole country: people who were in Vietnam have suddenly started talking about it. It's time; it's the only way a lot of those men are ever going to get well. That's why I wrote 'Copperhead Road'."

Earle's character in the song is an American stereotype – the country boy whose granddaddy made moonshine and who now grows marijuana. He nurses the scars of Vietnam and chooses to live outside the law.

This record is part of an outlaw tradition going back to Johnny Cash and Waylon Jennings and beyond, and forward into rock & roll. "I don't see that much difference, attitude-wise, between real rock & roll and real country," he said at the time. "It's really about your life and the way you live – which isn't about living up to the stereotypes and having to be fucked up. It's a matter of how committed you are to what you're doing. I'm a rock act because I'm being played on rock radio right now."

Copperhead Road was recorded in Memphis, some 320 kilometres from Nashville. "With 'Copperhead' some big steps were made socially," he said. "Some envelopes we'd been pushing at all along finally broke."

Manic Monday The Bangles

(Prince) ✳ Columbia ✳ 1986 ✳ Appears on: *Different Light*

Prince wrote 'Manic Monday' in 1984 under the name Jamie Starr. It was for his protégé Apollonia, but was eventually given to the Bangles with the writing credit changed to Christopher. Clearly, The Artist Now Known As Prince has always had a thing with names. It was rumoured that he also had a thing for Bangles guitarist Susanna Hoffs, being seen on what looked like dates and sending her guitar-shaped birthday cakes. Prince joined the group on stage on a couple of occasions.

The Bangles were the all-girl heirs to the Go-Go's – cute and New Wave. They were more accomplished musicians than the Go-Go's and had a better sense of pop music. Their choices of covers were impeccable – Alex Chilton, Liam Sternberg and Prince – and their own compositions were none too shabby. The second Bangles album, *Different Light*, is a magnificent pop album with just one hit after another.

'Manic Monday', which was the Bangles' first US number one, was also Prince at his most disciplined. It is glistening pop: its straightforward lyrics deal with everyday people in their everyday worlds, but it gives these lives – and by extension our own – a beautiful glow.

Nighttrain Public Enemy

(Chuck D/Cerwin Depper/Gary G-Wiz/JBL/Stuart Robertz) ✳ Def Jam ✳ 1991 ✳
Appears on: *Apocalypse 91 ... The Enemy Strikes Black*

Chuck D, Public Enemy's mouth-in-chief, described rap music as the black CNN. Their music certainly sounded like it was coming from the front with its aural gunfire and bomb bursts.

Most of Chuck D's vitriol was directed at the white Establishment, but he was not above sending a message to the ghetto. 'Nighttrain' on *Apocalypse 91* is a terrifying missive about the drug epidemic affecting black America. In this context he describes drug dealers as agents of white capitalism.

"Of course," he said, "they're victims too, but they're conscious. They know what they're doing. And when they're doing the wrong thing, they've got to suffer severe penalties. No more time for the psychoanalytical approach. We can't feel sorry, we can't even get emotional. It's damn near prophesied that the motherfuckers will be slain outright, by the doers of good over the doers of evil.

"What's going to happen is the same thing that developed in South Africa, where the only way to develop unity and organisation is to eliminate the agents. In South Africa, they put 'rubber neckties' on them. Here in America, you're soon gonna see brothers who want to get paid saying to themselves: 'Why bother to sell drugs, why don't I just stick up and kill drug dealers?' You already got groups coming up who say, 'We love to rob the dope man.' We're gonna see an apocalyptic situation with the rise of black vigilantism."

'Nighttrain' is a scarifying ride with sounds from the Bomb Squad that match the ferocity of the great free jazz players. The extremity of Public Enemy's position is somewhat undercut by the drug use of one of its own – Flavor Flav – and by the outrageousness of Chuck D's solution. But it is one hell of a piece of rap music.

Tainted Love Soft Cell

(Ed Cobb) ※ Phonogram ※ 1981 ※ Appears on: *Non-Stop Erotic Cabaret*

"I've always loved the idea of glamour in squalor – filth and squalor and sleaziness and seediness – there's always something really glamorous and sort of really sparkling," Marc Almond told *Face*. "That's what I … I find it curious, I have a fetish about those places. It's a bit like … I always feel like a spectator, which is wrong but, I like it anyway." Almond should know: as the singer for the duo Soft Cell he mixed both glamour and sleaze together and topped the charts with a cover of 'Tainted Love'.

Almond and keyboard player David Ball were familiar with northern soul, a strand of R&B popular in the north of England in the early '70s. Marc Bolan's wife Gloria Jones had a northern soul hit with 'Tainted Love', which Soft Cell covered in their electronic style. Most synthesiser artists of the time were making clinical, clever and sweet tunes with the new technology. Soft Cell made the keyboard as dirty and sexual an instrument as any other. The computerised rhythm track didn't have the supple play of a live band but the pressing, uncompromising, insistent beat had an emotional message of its own.

Almond brought a sleazy sexiness to the song. His camp reading also intimated other kinds of polymorphous perversity – the listener was invited to let their imagination wander in the knowledge that everyone dreams of the forbidden. There was something in the way that Almond's seduction played against the synthesiser – and of course the strength of the song – that made this track irresistible.

Pump Up the Volume M/A/R/R/S

(Martyn Young/Steve Young) ※ 4th & Broadway ※ 1987 ※
Appears on: *Pump Up the Volume*

"This is a journey into sound" – that sample was indeed a journey into a whole new way of making records out of samples. Certainly tracks had been made with samples before 1987, but 'Pump Up the Volume' was the Rosetta Stone of the form with its bits of hip-hop, soul and rock and found sounds.

M/A/R/R/S was put together by Ivo Watts Russell, the proprietor of 4AD records, using members of Colourbox and AR Kane, mixer CJ Mackintosh and London DJ Dave Dorrell. The samples came from hip-hop artists Eric B & Rakim (the line "Pump up the volume" and various other samples and bass lines), Public Enemy, Fab Five Freddy, Trouble Funk, the films *Wattstax* and *Mars Needs Women*, the sound effects demonstration record *Journey into Stereo Sound*, and various other sources. Most troublesome was the sample from Stock, Aitken and Waterman's 'Roadblock' on the 12 inch mix. Stock et al sued and effectively ended the M/A/R/R/S project, but not before the stable door was opened.

Naked Eye Luscious Jackson

(Jill Cunniff) ❋ Grand Royal ❋ 1996 ❋ Appears on: *Fever In Fever Out*

Luscious Jackson was a Beastie Boys spin-off. As friends of the rap trio, the four women in Luscious Jackson – Jill Cunniff, Gabrielle Glaser, Kate Schellenbach and Vivian Trimble – couldn't really play that well. They took their name from a Philadelphia basketball player back in the '60s, so they had the right attitude. "We'd known Jill and Gabby since our early teens, when we were New York club brats going to see bands like the Slits and Gang of Four," said Beastie Boy Mike D. "That late '70s–early '80s phase, when post-punk bands were turning to funk and reggae, is one of the great lost periods of music and it was when music had its greatest impact on us. It was also the beginning of rap, with Sugarhill Gang, Fearless Four, Treacherous Three, Funky Four Plus One. Anyway, Luscious gave us their demo and we were all set to make up some excuse, but it turned out to be our favourite thing to listen to on the tour bus." By the end of that tour the Beastie Boys had determined to start their own label – Grand Royal – and to sign Luscious Jackson.

A first EP, *In Search of Manny*, and an album, *Natural High*, were creditable if unexciting discs. For their second album Luscious Jackson teamed up with Daniel Lanois. Both group and producer were out of their comfort zone for the album, which was mostly recorded in a New York apartment. The ambience on the tracks is warm and inviting, with gently layered textures. On the opening track, 'Naked Eye', there's a very powerful sensuality and playfulness, appropriate for a song about the joys of nudity.

River Deep, Mountain High Ike & Tina Turner

(Jeff Barry/Ellie Greenwich/Phil Spector) ✳ Phillies/A&M ✳ 1966 ✳

Appears on: *River Deep, Mountain High*

Phil Spector was in a slump when he signed up Ike and Tina. Ike Turner – one of the most innovative producer/songwriters of the '50s – was in a slump too, and agreed to sit out the sessions which Spector assured him would put Ike and Tina Turner back on top.

The track was from the recently divorced team of Jeff Barry and Ellie Greenwich. "Phil wanted to make this definitive rock & roll anthem symphony," said Greenwich. "What happened was that all of us had individually started different songs. We sat down at the piano and it was, 'What about this? What about that?' And you can hear the different versions."

"I went over to Phil's house," string arranger Jack Nitzsche recalled. "And we went over the arrangement note by note. Phil said, 'I've got a song for Tina.' I knew who she was. I had seen them perform at the California Club. When he played me 'River Deep, Mountain High' on the piano I knew it was great song. We did the rhythm track in two different three-hour sessions."

Spector had worked with the Ike and Tina Turner Revue on a special he produced (the *Big TNT Show*) and had subsequently bought them out of their old recording deal. Spector's vision was to utilise Tina Turner's explosive sexuality and the power of her delivery in the way that he made ingénues of the Ronettes and the Crystals some years earlier.

The recording took place in Spector's favourite studio, Gold Star. Nitzsche brought Mick Jagger along to watch the proceedings.

Spector built one of his typically epic arrangements for the song: massive walls of pianos and strings and percussion. The song was triumphant in the way that it contrasted the tender verses with the faux naïveté of a girl's rag doll or puppy, with the monumental chorus that featured the full-bodied sensuousness of Turner's vocals.

"I must have sung that 500,000 times," Turner said. "I was drenched with sweat. I had to take my shirt off and stand there in my bra to sing."

"It was amazing to watch 'River Deep' grow," said Nitzsche. "Even during the cutting of the track, when she was putting on a scratch, Tina was singing along as we cut it and was so into it she was holding her crotch on the high notes. Oh, man, she was great, doing a rough, scratch vocal as the musicians really kicked the rhythm section in the ass. Once in a while a vocalist would run through a song, but this time Tina made everybody play better."

Surprisingly, the song was Spector's first real flop, failing to even crack the Top 40 in the US, although it was a hit in Europe and Australia. As a consequence of the record's failure, Spector announced his retirement – from which he was soon coaxed by John Lennon.

"Phil antagonised some people," opined Nitzsche. "He had thirteen hits in a row without a miss. Around 'River Deep, Mountain High', people started to want him to fail. That's how it is with sports and everything. You get too good and people don't like it, too successful and people don't like it."

"I thought 'River Deep, Mountain High' would be the biggest record Phil ever made. I thought it was an obvious number one. I couldn't believe it didn't happen here. I was happy it charted in England. But even before 'River Deep', Phil felt that it was starting to come to a close. The enthusiasm was gone. We had done it so many times. The musicians were changing. It was a combination of things, and it just stopped being so much fun. The Beatles were coming."

"I think when it came out, it was like my farewell," said Spector. "I was just sayin' goodbye, and I just wanted to go crazy for … four minutes on wax."

The Lonesome Death of Hattie Carroll Bob Dylan

(Bob Dylan) ✳ Columbia ✳ 1975 ✳ Appears on: *The Bootleg Series: 1975 Live*

Hattie Carroll, fifty-one, was a maid at a charity ball in Baltimore, Maryland, on the night of 8 February 1963. William Zantzinger, then twenty-four, was a guest at the ball. Annoyed at the service he was getting, Zantzinger struck Hattie Carroll with his cane, killing the mother of eleven children. Zantzinger, a local landowner and tobacco farmer, was charged with her manslaughter and received six months' jail. Zantzinger was, of course, wealthy and white and Hattie Carroll, the opposite.

Dylan's retelling of the events is remarkable for its detail – the behaviour of the participants, the atmosphere of the Baltimore Hotel and later the courtroom. Dylan has a keen eye for the issues here, which are class and justice.

Many of Dylan's songs of this period were ripped from the news. Dylan learnt of this case from newspaper reports – Zantzinger was jailed on 15 September, and Dylan recorded the song on 23 October 1963. He wrote the song while staying with Joan Baez at her house in California. 'Hattie Carroll', however, is most notable for the economy of its writing.

The song first appeared on Dylan's third album, *The Times They Are A-Changin'*, with just Bob on guitar and harmonica. He reprised the track for the Rolling Thunder tour where the starkness of the original was replaced by the fire and the passion of the Rolling Thunder ensemble. This is a song where righteousness surges up with each chorus to be defeated by the dismay at the injustice of Hattie Carroll's life. It was twelve years between versions, but the tragedy had not diminished. (Zantzinger eventually went into real estate. He was charged with fraudulently collecting rents from poor black tenants but was acquitted.)

Memory Motel The Rolling Stones

(Mick Jagger/Keith Richards) ❋ Rolling Stones Records ❋ 1976 ❋
Appears on: *Black and Blue*

Black and Blue is the least rock & roll album the Rolling Stones ever recorded. Most of the songs tend towards funk, reggae and R&B with none of the linear, knockdown rock tracks or pop tunes. With three new guitarists – Harvey Mandel, Wayne Perkins and Ron Wood – plus Billy Preston's keyboards, the Rolling Stones here stretch their boundaries. Much derided on its release, *Black and Blue* holds up remarkably well.

The rehearsals and recording took place in Munich so that Richards could be close to his girlfriend Uschi Obermeier, with whom he was besotted. The songs were only half formed, mostly just funk jams or obscure covers. The outstanding cut on the album is 'Memory Motel', with Richards on electric piano and Jagger on acoustic piano, and both Perkins and Mandel playing guitar. It is one of the Stones' last epics.

'Memory Motel' was very likely inspired by Obermeier, although Jagger told Jonathan Cott, "The girl in 'Memory Motel' is a real, independent American girl. Actually, the girl in 'Memory Motel' is a combination. Nearly all the girls in my songs are combinations."

Fu-gee-la The Fugees

(Lauryn Hill/Natalie Jean/Teena Marie/Allen McGrier/S Michel/Salaam Remi) ✳ Ruffhouse
✳ 1996 ✳ Appears on: *The Score*

Refugee Camp, which became the Fugees, brought a whole new style to hip-hop in the mid-'90s. Prakazrel Michel ('Pras') and his cousin Wyclef Jean ('Clef') were of Haitian descent, which may have added some exotica to an already diverse mix of sounds and styles – reggae, soul, R&B, rap and jazz all found their place on the Fugees' second album, *The Score*. And let's not forget Lauryn Hill, one of the great voices of her time.

The Score reinvented black American pop music. It featured a couple of interesting covers, including Roberta Flack's 'Killing Me Softly with His Song' and Bob Marley's 'No Woman, No Cry', which were reinterpreted with a hip-hop frame of mind. 'Fu-gee-la' was their statement of purpose, though. It was a song of strength and struggle but freed of the violent hype of so much revolutionary rap music. The reggae beats and the eloquent bass rumbles powered the song as the three MCs stood their ground.

With this manifesto the Fugees sold more than seventeen million albums of literate, intelligent and non-violent hip-hop.

One U2

(Bono/Adam Clayton/The Edge/Larry Mullen Jr) ✳ Island ✳ 1991 ✳
Appears on: *Achtung Baby*

'One' is one of the best pop songs of the '90s. Its surly momentum owes more to German industrial music than to rock. There's a darkness to the song – it's not about harmony, but acknowledging differences and the fact that we are stuck with each other. Like the best U2 songs, it's a record that is both intensely personal and universal as well.

Over the twelve months that U2 spent working on *Achtung Baby* there was slow progress made through the compiling of ideas. Both singer Bono and guitarist the Edge were trawling through fragments of work and 'One' came about from the melding of ideas. The Edge's marriage was finishing and that inspired the beginning of it. According to Bono, "There were a couple of things going on, and as usual I meant to resolve them, but the best U2 songs seem to occupy this place of contradictions. I had a lot of things going on in my head at the time, about forgiveness, about father and son angst. I was trying to write a story song I think, and I'm just not good at that. The lyrics came really quickly. The humbling bit about songwriting is that anything above good usually feels like an accident. A lot of U2 songs are first drafts."

The group was recording at Hansa Studios in Berlin, where Bowie and Iggy Pop had made their Kraut-rock albums.

"It wasn't going well," the Edge told Q magazine. "Adam and Larry's rather jaundiced view of Bono's and my songwriting ability was becoming more and more evident as our various experiments went nowhere. We were listening to a lot of industrial music, and the sounds we were making were quite intense.

"In the midst of all this I go off into another room to put together some ideas for 'The Fly'. I came back with two, neither of which worked where they were meant to, but on Daniel Lanois' suggestion we put them together and Bono was really taken with it. So we all went out into the big recording room – a huge, eerie ballroom full of ghosts of the war – and everything fell into place. Bono's melodies and phrases were following, and by the end of the day we basically had everything, the whole form of the song.

"Everyone recognized it was a crucial moment in the development of what became *Achtung Baby* – ironically it went in a totally different direction from everything we'd been working on. But everyone recognized it was a special piece. It was like we'd caught a glimpse of what the song could be. Then it was about capturing its essence, but also trying to keep our hands off it. Those songs that seem to arrive perfectly formed – you don't want to mess with them too much.

"The lyric was the first in a new, more intimate style. It's two ideas, essentially. On one level it's a bitter, twisted, vitriolic conversation between two people who've been through some nasty, heavy stuff: 'We hurt each other/Then we do it again.' But on another level there's the idea that 'we get to carry each other.' 'Get to' is the key. The original lyric was 'we have to carry each other' and it was never quite right – it was too fuckin' obvious and platitudinous. But 'get to'? – it's like our privilege to carry one another. It puts everything in a different perspective, introduces that idea of grace.

"Still, it blows me away when it's played at weddings. I wouldn't have played it at any wedding of mine. But I suppose it's because, despite all the other stuff in there, the power of 'we get to carry each other' overwhelms everything. And the honesty of it helps – the bare-knuckle telling-it-like-it-is-ness."

Poor Boy   John Fahey

(John Fahey/Bukka White) ✳ Takoma ✳ 1965 ✳

Appears on: *The Transfiguration of Blind Joe Death*

By all accounts, John Fahey was a complex and troubled man who brought considerable intellectual and artistic skills to his guitar playing. He was passionate about rediscovering and preserving old blues artists and songs but was determined to move music forward.

Born in 1939 in Maryland he became fascinated by the blues and began to search out the original singers and writers. He tracked down Skip James, Robert Pete Williams and Bukka White and reissued many of their sides on his Takoma label. His championing of Delta blues had a strong effect on other white guitarists, especially his friends Ry Cooder and Canned Heat's Al Wilson.

Fahey travelled through the south, door-knocking on houses to buy old 78rpm discs. His knowledge of the blues and bluegrass was complemented by his appreciation for modern composers such as Charles Ives. His own compositions started with the blues but went places previously uncharted.

Fahey was troubled by depression, which contributed to his alcoholism and drug abuse. This was no doubt tied to sexual abuse by his father. Part of what he identified in the blues was anger.

"The reason I liked Charley Patton and those other Delta singers so much was because they were angry," he told the *Wire*. "Their music is ominous. Patton had a rheumatic heart and he knew that he was going to die young, which he did. In Son House you hear a lot of fear, in Skip James you hear a lot of sorrow, but also a lot of anger. When I first heard these guys I couldn't identify the emotions because I didn't acknowledge that I had them myself. I didn't learn the names of these emotions until I was under psychoanalysis. I played some of the records to the doctor and he said, 'These guys are as angry as hell.'"

Fahey's fingerpicking guitar style was completely original. The harmonics and phrasing he employed were more modern than ancient. His dexterity was unparalleled as he worked the melodic implications of a tune backwards and forwards.

"When he took a basic theme, like 'Poor Boy', you'd have to listen hard to hear the melody of the original [Bukka White] recording," said former Captain Beefheart guitarist Gary Lucas. "He liberated these forms."

Why Does My Heart Feel So Bad? Moby

(Moby) ✳ V2 ✳ 1999 ✳ Appears on: *Play*

Moby had been there at the start of the dance music movement back in the mid-'80s, before it was fashionable. That credibility allowed him to bring home an album like *Play* that put techno at every dinner party in the bourgeois world. Having done techno and experimental electronica and hard rock, Moby (aka Richard Hall) made an album around the idea of mixing Negro spirituals and field recordings as the vocals over an electronic tune.

"I'm a white guy who doesn't really understand African-American culture," he said. "But if you look at contemporary black music, they borrow heavily from soul, disco, jazz, R&B, and funk, but they don't borrow from the blues tradition. The only conclusion I can come to is that the blues and traditional Negro spirituals, music from the fields, is poverty music. Hip-hop is about money, cash, respect. So maybe the blues represent a part of the tradition they're not comfortable with any more. I love contemporary black music but I also love Negro spirituals. I see it as part of a great continuum that the African-American community doesn't seem to reflect."

Moby was no doubt excited by *Sound of the South* some forty years after Alan Lomax lugged his Nagra tape recorder through the cotton fields. But it wasn't the ethnomusicologist in Moby that assembled 'Why Does My Heart Feel So Bad?'. He recognised the deep and vigorous sound of the spiritual singers and how that would contrast to the thin, blanched electronica.

"I was responding to the music genuinely with a love of the source material," he said. "I didn't hear it and think to myself that I could use it and make a lot of money off of it. I just thought, what wonderful performances."

I Can't Stand Up for Falling Down

Elvis Costello & the Attractions

(H Banks/A Jones) ❃ 1980 ❃ Radar ❃ Appears on: *Get Happy!!*

Elvis Costello's fourth album featured a frantic, almost berserk embrace of soul music. The centrepiece is this cover of a Sam & Dave track that positively sweats cocaine.

"Speaking quite frankly, I'm amazed that no-one at the time exposed the fact that I was into almost totally wrecking myself on drink and chemicals for … well, three years virtually non-stop," Costello told journalist Nick Kent. "I was into a daily thing of artificial stimulation – drinking myself into a stupor, fuelling myself on cocaine, but no-one suspected a thing.

"But it got carried away and in the process I became falsely 'enigmatic', if you like, and very contrary. At the same time I don't want this to sound schizophrenic because I'm not, and the person who wrote those songs has always been me. Plus I was very, very bitter and angry and … well, the first year I played with the Attractions I was performing live almost exclusively on this level of anger and just incredible nervous energy. And then it got to that stage where I would be functioning on mental or, y'know, 'artificial' energy. But I found that as I continued, it became automatically a thing of me never letting my guard down."

Costello reaped the whirlwind. Phenomenal success in the press and in the charts, at least in the UK, played significantly with his head – the former geek with poor social skills and low self-esteem was overnight the voice of a generation. As well as the drugs, Costello attracted some of the world's most beautiful women. Not surprisingly, his marriage collapsed.

When he sang 'I Can't Stand Up for Falling Down' it was pretty much the simple truth.

"*Get Happy!!* was made under extreme self-inflicted emotional stress," he said. "It was a very extreme record from the point of view of the condition that I and the rest of the band were in. The aftermath of what happened in America and just generally very emotional, you know, shattered nerves. Too much drinking. That's why it sounds unfinished – because it's about all we were capable of doing."

The Loved One The Loved Ones

(Ian Clyne/Gerry Humphreys/Rob Lovett) ❊ In ❊ 1966 ❊ Appears on: *Magic Box*

Gerry Humphreys was a true star. His eccentric stage manner and his gorgeous blues voice was the perfect instrument to front a band like the Loved Ones. Half of the group came from the Red Onions Jazz Band and the other half from the R&B garage outfit the Wild Cherries. This supergroup – by the standards of backwater Australian rock in the mid-'60s – played mostly covers until their first recording session, where they worked up a riff by guitarist Rob Lovett that has become one of the few Australian classics from the period. 'The Loved One' has a chord progression that moves inexorably through a simple cycle while Humphries wails over the top in an orgiastic fury supported by a rising intensity in the guitar and organ lines.

Red Onions organist Ian Clyne had a relationship with W&G records that scored him three hours in the studio. The group decided they needed an original song in a hurry and, according to Lovett, he offered a chord progression he had lying around. "Well, I had been playing these three chords, so when Gerry asked if anyone had anything I nervously mentioned it and Ian said, 'Well, how does it go?'" Lovett told journalist Christopher Hollow. "So I played it. I had been interested in the big chord music by the Who's Pete Townshend and when Gerry asked, 'What's the melody?' I mumbled that the idea was that it had 'sort of – you know, no melody …' To my relief he took this on board, but said he'd need another sequence because there wasn't enough in this one. I think, 'It's a bit boring' was how he, tactfully, put it. So I came up with the second one. 'That's more like it, I can work with that.' Ian came up with the bass line and the lead guitar line. He played guitar as well as piano, in fact he played guitar far better than I did.

"Then Gerry said that it was going along OK but it needed a chorus, a real sing-along, and just wrote down the most obvious lines he could think of. Ian asked how it would go and he sang it while Ian worked out the chords. It still didn't have enough for Ian, and on the night before recording he went to the Winston Charles nightclub and had a long talk to the organist.

"Yeah, the organist said he liked it but he thought we should put some handclaps in so the audience didn't get lost. In those days most people were brought up with 'easy listenin'' music – country and western, very straightforward. In the end, the handclaps were more dominant than the two-beat pattern so the whole thing sounded a bit like a crazy waltz. As it turned out the organist was absolutely right. It would never have made it without his suggestion and the way he played. He really gave it some atmosphere and suspenseful excitement – building up on the first chord sequence till it burst out into the second and Gerry screamed out his, 'Yonder she's walking'.

"It's so crazy. I mean, who says 'yonder' any more? But Gerry was good like that. He didn't give a shit if it made sense as long as it was easy to sing and with his rough voice it didn't sound dorky."

'The Loved One' is one of the few Australian records of the era to remain continuously in print and was recorded by INXS on their second album. English producer Chris Thomas liked the song so much he suggested it be re-recorded for the *Kick* album.

The title of the song was pretty much serendipity, based on the brief fashion for appropriating the titles of classic novels. According to Lovett, "When Lindsay, the engineer, asked what he should write on the tape, we didn't have a title, so he simply wrote on it 'The Loved One', which is the actual name of the Evelyn Waugh book. No-one ever thought to change it."

Paralyzed The Legendary Stardust Cowboy

(Norman Carl Odam) ❋ Mercury ❋ 1968 ❋ Appears on: *Texas Music, Vol. 3: Garage Bands and Psychedelia*

Norman Carl Odam was born in Lubbock, Texas, where he was a schoolmate of Joe Ely. While the latter became one of the most respected songwriters of his generation, Odam combined his two interests – the Wild West and space exploration – into the persona of the Legendary Stardust Cowboy.

"When I was fourteen," he wrote in 1969, "I started doing Rebel yells and Indian whoops because I am part Shawnee. I taught myself to do birdcalls and jungle sounds. I figured that by singing I was able to attract all the girls."

Music, in the conventional sense, was not his forte, but he did record one timeless single. 'Paralyzed' is a demented yowl of Indian war whoops, cat calls, yelps and chanted lyrics recorded at a breakneck pace. Suddenly the guitar stops and he picks up a bugle and blows a free jazz solo. "The band was just me on drums, and he had a Dobro with a broken neck, so he could only play on the first fret," said T-Bone Burnett who, as a trainee engineer at the studio, was assigned the session. "We just set up two microphones. Norman gave me some instructions – 'Play drums in the same tempo I'm singing in' – and I said, 'I could do that.' Maybe probably. Then he said he was going to take a bugle solo, and he wanted me to take a drum solo, and I found that all agreeable. It was explosive, to say the least."

'Paralyzed' became a hit single, and Odam appeared on national TV. Three more songs were recorded but real stardom proved elusive.

The Ledge, as he is known, has had many influential admirers, but none so public as David Bowie, who heard 'Paralyzed', 'Down in the Wrecking Yard' and 'I Took a Trip on a Gemini Spaceship' in 1971. "The integrity, honesty and innocent, brutal focus entranced me," he wrote in *MOJO*. In admiration, Bowie took the surname for his alter ego, Ziggy Stardust, and eventually recorded 'I Took a Trip on a Gemini Spaceship' for his *Heathen* album.

"For me, he's up there with people like Wild Man Fisher – it's the original outsider music," said Bowie in 1996. "Music by people probably not playing with a full deck. He played guitar, and he had a drummer and a one-legged trumpet player. They assembled their music without any awareness that there are supposed to be rules to follow. And so they go in directions that wouldn't occur to even a semi-trained musician. And it's such a freeing exercise, listening to them commit to those performances with full integrity – knowing that they are not joking."

God's Song (That's Why I Love Mankind)
Randy Newman

(Randy Newman) ❊ Warner Bros. ❊ 1972 ❊ Appears on: *Sail Away*

The notoriously self-deprecating Randy Newman recently said, "'God's Song' is a really good song, in all modesty."

Raised a non-practising Jew in Los Angeles, Newman's satirical songs are not afraid to tackle sacred cows, even religious ones. 'God's Song' looks at the world from the deity's point of view. It's fairly clear-cut existentialism expressed beautifully, with more than a little debt to Brecht and Weill:

Man means nothing, he means less to me
Than the lowliest cactus flower
Or the humblest Yucca tree
He chases round this desert
'Cause he thinks that's where I'll be
That's why I love mankind
I recoil in horror from the foulness of thee
From the squalor and the filth and the misery
How we laugh up here in heaven at the prayers you offer me
That's why I love mankind

Passionate Kisses Lucinda Williams

(Lucinda Williams) ✳ Rough Trade ✳ 1988 ✳ Appears on: *Passionate Kisses*

"My vocal style is kind of a culmination of the old country style and the old blues style coming together," said Lucinda Williams in an interview with Barney Hoskyns. "I was influenced by singers like Hank Williams and Loretta Lynn from an early age, and then later by a lot of the Delta country blues singers like Robert Johnson and Skip James. Just that real haunting kind of rougher edged style." She may as well have been talking about her songwriting as well. Williams confidently walked the road between country and blues.

The daughter of an English professor and poet, Miller Williams, Lucinda has a spare use of words. "He's been my mentor," she said. "Instead of going to college and taking creative writing, I learned by writing, by trial and error, and by showing [my father] what I was working on and listening to his criticism." Miller was a Hank Williams fan and Lucinda's mother liked Joan Baez. But for young Lucinda the whole thing came together when she heard Bob Dylan's *Highway 61*.

"That was it for me," she said. "I had somehow found the combination, the link of heavy, intense, brave lyrics – he'd obviously listened to a lot of blues – great melodies, and a voice that wasn't perfect."

Two of Williams' albums in the early '80s were promising, and then she came out with 'Passionate Kisses' and the album of the same name in 1988. Unusually for an American country singer, it was on Rough Trade, an independent English label.

'Passionate Kisses' is a post-feminist lyric, a reasonable demand for a woman to have it all – a full house, a rock & roll band and passionate kisses. The song is brimful of joyous energy. While the delivery may sound flippant, you get the feeling that there is a serious message underneath.

Mary Chapin Carpenter picked up on it and had a major hit and a Grammy with it in 1994.

Killing Floor Howlin' Wolf

(Chester Arthur Burnett) ❋ Chess ❋ 1964 ❋ Appears on: *The Chess Box*

"If I had to pick one person who does everything I loved about the blues, it would be Howlin' Wolf," Bonnie Raitt once said. "It would be the size of his voice, or just the size of *him*. When you're a little pre-teenage girl and you imagine what a naked man in full arousal is like, it's Howlin' Wolf. That's how I feel when I hear Howlin' Wolf – and when I met him it was the same thing. He was the scariest, most deliciously frightening bit of male testosterone I've ever experienced in my life."

Chester Burnett was forty-one years old when he made his recording debut for Sam Phillips' Sun label in Memphis in 1951. He had a lifetime of the blues already in his voice. He stood 6' 3" and weighed over 300 pounds. He had a voice to match – strong and versatile and expressive, capable of carrying heavy loads.

Wolf was inspired to become a blues singer after a meeting with Delta legend Charley Patton. His sister married Sonny Boy Williamson and that relationship encouraged his harmonica playing. Through it all Wolf had a sense of a hard driving beat and his growling voice.

Wolf specialised in songs that were at best morally ambiguous. He wasn't a hearts and flowers kind of guy; instead, his songs were mostly about lust and evil. His own guitar style tended towards sharp slide playing and aggressive riffs.

After moving to Chicago, Wolf teamed up with guitarist Hubert Sumlin, who would prove to be his consummate foil. Sumlin didn't play chords so much as little jabs of guitar spiking out of the melody. He was one of the most distinctive electric blues guitarists. The combination of the two made for a series of hits unmatched in the Chess catalogue.

'Killing Floor' is the perfect tag team of Wolf and Sumlin. It was first recorded in August 1964 with the great Sam Lay on drums, Lafayette Leake on piano and Buddy

Guy playing acoustic guitar. Sumlin's slide tears off shards and shards of vicious melody. Howlin' Wolf broods and smoulders in his anger and disgust at the relationship he's comparing to the killing floor of an abattoir. 'Killing Floor', especially Sumlin's guitar, inspired the next generation of blues players – Jimi Hendrix, Mike Bloomfield and Jimmy Page all covered the song (the latter retitled it as 'The Lemon Song'). This was perhaps the bridge between the real blues and the blues-rock that dominated the late '60s.

King Harvest (Will Surely Come) The Band

(Jaime Robbie Robertson) ✳ Capitol ✳ 1969 ✳ Appears on: *The Band*

"'King Harvest' was part of the theme of that album," said guitarist Robbie Robertson. "When I was writing most of the songs for that album it was that time of year, and at that time of year Woodstock was very impressive. Everything turned red and orange and it just made you think this breeze was coming in – it was quite noticeable. It made me think of how this was the culmination of the year for so many people. And then the history in the background, our forefathers – that's when it all came down, whether the year worked out or not. So, thematically, in that record, I kept coming back to that, and 'King Harvest' was the most focused of any of the material as far as coming right out and saying it.

"We were trying to do a type of timeless music. We were thinking, hopefully, you could listen to this in twenty years or fifty years; we'd admired so many people whose music had lived on, regardless.

"With *The Band* album, that's when I really knew who we were. This is when I said, 'This is what we sound like, this is what we do.' You can go on and make other records and do this and do that. You can change your clothes, you can change your hat. It doesn't matter. That is who it is!"

'King Harvest' was the most complex and subtle of the songs on *The Band*. It was epic in scope with an incredible attention to detail. Much of that was in Robertson's guitar parts.

"This was the new way of dealing with the guitar," said Robertson. "This was very subtle playing, leaving out a lot of stuff and just waiting till the last second and then playing the thing in just the nick of time. It was an approach to playing where it's so delicate. It's the opposite of the 'in your face' guitar playing that I used to do. This was the kind of thing that was slippery. It was like you have to hold your breath while playing these kinds of solos. You can't breathe or you'll throw yourself off. I felt emotionally completely different about the instrument."

'King Harvest' is an epic in microcosm and a completely unique piece of rock & roll.

The Boxer Simon & Garfunkel

(Paul Simon) ✳ Columbia ✳ 1969 ✳ Appears on: *Bridge Over Troubled Water*

Paul Simon uses the story of a boxer who comes to the big time and is beaten down as a metaphor for his own struggle as a songwriter and artist.

"I knew 'The Boxer' was great," said singer Art Garfunkel. "For one thing, it's a style that is our strong suit. Whenever we did those folky, running things, the syllabication is ideal for what we had learned. We were tapping into something that went way back for us, and something we could get a blend on. So I knew, I had a particular feel that I could do really well, and match Paul and make the whole thing ripple and articulate it just right. And the lyric is real nice. And the amount of labour in the studio was just unbelievable. That one took so many days."

Simon recalled that the song started on an aeroplane as he was thumbing through a Bible and came across the phrase "workman's wages". The rest of it was gradually pieced together. There are personal references: "the whores on Seventh Avenue" are possibly Columbia Records, whose offices were on Seventh. It's a small story given an epic frame by the massed synthesisers and sound effects from co-producer Roy Hallee and the huge, surging harmonies. The "lie la lie" vocal section was recorded in a church for the acoustic value of the high stone ceilings.

"In fact, for me," said Simon, "I thought that 'lie la lie' part was a failure of songwriting. I didn't have any words! But, it's not a failure of songwriting, because people like that and they put enough meaning into it, and the rest of the song has enough power and emotion, I guess, to make it go, so it's all right. But for me, every time I sing that part … I'm a little embarrassed."

I Thought I Was A Child   Bonnie Raitt

(Jackson Browne) ✳ Warner Bros. ✳ 1973 ✳ Appears on: *Taking My Time*

Raitt began as a blues player following the likes of Mississippi John Hurt and perfecting her slide guitar technique. After signing with Warner Bros. in 1970, however, her recordings drifted further from the blues and closer to mainstream pop and rock music. Not always with the best results.

Raitt was a natural outsider, which was what attracted her to the blues. "I ran away from a normal life and it's real easy to let that take over and be your life," she said.

Her third album, *Taking My Time*, has her with the crack Warner Bros. team of the era – Van Dyke Parks, Little Feat and Jim Keltner. Mostly the blues have gone, distilled just to a ghost, albeit a strong one, in her voice and delivery. "I had started doing *Taking My Time* with Lowell George," she said, "when he and I were real close, but we were like locking horns, just too strong personally. We waited six months to get in the studio together, and when we finally got in there, he wanted to play slide guitar, and so did I, so we were just fighting."

Jackson Browne's song from his second album has that strange quality of being both youthful and bearing the wisdom of the ages. It's a dichotomy that Raitt understands and one that allows her voice to range widely.

Viva Las Vegas   Elvis Presley

(Doc Pomus/Mort Shuman) ✳ RCA ✳ 1964 ✳ Appears on: *2nd to None*

The title track to Elvis Presley's fourteenth film was relegated to the B-side of his version of 'What'd I Say'. Nonetheless, 'Viva Las Vegas' has become one of Presley's most loved tunes. It was one of the few records he made after returning from the army where he still had the vigour of the '50s. The track had an energy plus a crack session band that brought a jazzy feel to the R&B tune.

It was written by the team of Doc Pomus and Mort Shuman specifically for the film in which Elvis' character, Lucky Jackson, dives into the world of fast money, fast women and faster cars in Las Vegas. The song took on an ironic context late in Elvis' career when he accepted a long-standing residency in a Vegas casino and his creativity was sapped away.

"The Vegas crowd is also different," said guitarist James Burton, who was Presley's musical director for most of the Vegas years. "You're dealing with people who come to see a show, a public which has seen almost every type of show you could imagine. Vegas is a part of the entertainment scene, and people go there to see good shows and good talent, and it's basically critics you're dealing with in a Vegas-type audience. I think Elvis didn't necessarily want to change his basic format, but what we did was a little more of an updated thing with an orchestra as well. I think it's probably one of the greatest feelings an artist can have to be able to walk out on stage to sing with a thirty-piece orchestra behind him, although Elvis didn't really need a thirty-piece orchestra, he could walk out there by himself and do what he was there to do. It was like he felt that the six guys behind him represented the real Elvis."

I Will Follow U2

(Bono/Adam Clayton/The Edge/Larry Mullen Jr) ❋ Island ❋ 1980 ❋ Appears on: *Boy*

On U2's first American tour they played 'I Will Follow' twice in their set because they didn't have enough songs. The Irish group's first single and the opening track of *Boy*, their first album, was a strong if inchoate debut. What is immediately apparent is the way that drummer Larry Mullen Jr and bass player Adam Clayton have essentially taken their patterns from the Factory sound of Joy Division and given them a sense of uplift rather than doom. The Edge's spiky guitar owes a direct lineage to Tom Verlaine of Television. U2 adopted the innovations of the first wave of punk rock and adapted them. Bearing in mind that their level of musicianship wasn't of the highest order.

Bono said that the song was a response to his childhood – his lack of contact with his father and his mother's death, which occurred when he was fourteen.

"To be honest, I don't remember that much about my mother," he told *Rolling Stone*'s David Breskin in 1987. "I forget what she looks like. I was fourteen or fifteen when she died, but I don't remember. I wasn't close to my mother or father. And that's why, when it all went wrong – when my mother died – I felt a real resentment, because I actually had never got a chance … to feel that unconditional love a mother has for a child. There was a feeling of that house pulled down on top of me, because after the death of my mother that house was no longer a home – it was just a house. That's what 'I Will Follow' is about. It's a little sketch about that unconditional love a mother has for a child: 'If you walk away, walk away I will follow', and 'I was on the outside when you said you needed me/I was looking at myself I was blind I could not see'. It's a really chronic lyric."

Turning that pain into an epic is what made U2 great.

Night and Day Ella Fitzgerald

(Cole Porter) ✳ Polygram ✳ 1956 ✳

Appears on: *Ella Fitzgerald Sings the Cole Porter Songbook, Vol. 2*

More than one hundred singers have recorded 'Night and Day'. The tune requires its vocalists to bring themselves to its nuances in ways that other songs don't. Ella Fitzgerald was a supreme interpreter of Porter's ballads and her reading of this one is sublime if not definitive.

New Yorker writer Margaret Case Harriman in her 1940 profile of Cole Porter records the comment of an oboe player critiquing 'Night and Day': "Wouldn't you think that guy Porter would have the initiative to get off that one goddam note?" he said. The grumpy woodwind man was referring to the opening of the song in which one note is repeated thirty-five times before the tune moves up a reluctant half-tone and then a half-tone more before sliding back down the scale. It was a touch that Porter had picked up from sacred Arab music he heard on the rooftops of Morocco. The tension in the song as a consequence of this motif is quite excruciating. The tune here imitates the delicious intoxication of infatuation.

Porter wrote 'Night and Day' for the 1932 Broadway musical *Gay Divorce*. He said that he began the tune one Saturday night in the Ritz Carlton and finished the lyric the next morning on the beach at Newport. Harriman, however, reports that Porter tended to have almost completed the words and music in his head before he put pen to paper:

"In contrast to lyric writers and composers who sweat in lonely toil over a pad and pencil or a piano, Porter relaxes at a party, drinks champagne, and gets home at dawn with a fairly complete outline of a new song, suggested, perhaps, by something someone else has said." Certainly Porter's songs reflected the breezy urbane world in which he lived. They also captured his sense of romance in its many guises, including the sad undertow of heartbreak.

Gay Divorce was to star Fred Astaire and Porter composed with that singer's limited range in mind. Nonetheless, 'Night and Day' is full of drama. Pianist Bobby Short has noted a debt to Beethoven's 'Moonlight Sonata' and Ravel's 'Bolero'. It had both the obsessive qualities of one and the light touch of the other.

Irving Berlin wrote to Porter, "I am mad about 'Night and Day'. All the orchestra leaders think it is the song of the year and I agree with them. I think it is your high spot."

Surfin' Bird The Trashmen

(Al Frazier/Robert Harris/Carl White/Brian Wilson) ❋ Garrett ❋ 1963 ❋
Appears on: *Surfin' Bird*

The esteemed rock critic R Meltzer claimed in his definitive, if indecipherable, *The Aesthetics of Rock* that 'Surfin' Bird' was the apotheosis of rock & roll songs. Not quite, but close.

The Trashmen (originally Jim Thaxter & the Travelers) were a surf band from the landlocked state of Minnesota who had come to surf music after following the crazes that had preceded it. 'Surfin' Bird' is a medley of the Rivingtons' 'Pa Pa Ooh Mow Mow' and 'The Bird's the Word'. With the lyrics thus pasted together, the Trashmen added a psychotic and generic surf instrumental that rocked into overdrive and pushed the pulsing vocal and ratcheted up the echo on the whole thing so it sounded like it came straight from hell. And the entire song is just three minutes (or less) of glorious insanity. The track was rightly a hit and was resurrected in the '70s by the Ramones and became a classic covered notably by the Cramps and Silverchair. Stanley Kubrick used the Trashmen's single in *Full Metal Jacket* to capture the insanity of the Vietnam War and it worked a treat.

Sister Anne MC5

(Fred 'Sonic' Smith) ※ Atlantic ※ 1971 ※ Appears on: *High Time*

By the time they recorded their third album, *High Time*, the MC5 had finally worked out their sound. Unfortunately, it was too late – Atlantic records was no longer interested and the drugs were starting to take hold. It remained for another generation of tough punk rockers to pick up where 'Sister Anne' left off. In the three years since their first record, *Kick Out the Jams*, the group had been lauded and derided. Manager John Sinclair (leader of the militant revolutionary White Panther Party) had been jailed on spurious drug charges. They had been kicked off one label and were about to be kicked off another. Nonetheless, the record sounds joyful.

The hallmarks of the first LP are here in the high-energy, dual guitar attack of Wayne Kramer and Fred Sonic Smith. The sense of structure and dynamics that they learnt on *Back in the USA* are here marshalling all that high-energy music.

Produced by Geoff Haslam and the band, *High Time* sees some of the best playing the 5 was capable of. For all their talk of being influenced by free jazz, the group was best when playing revved up boogie music over which the guitarists jammed. They had a better grasp on Motown than Sun Ra's Arkestra.

'Sister Anne' is fun, slinky, impassioned and a little bit psychedelic. "It's just good," said drummer Dennis Thompson. "It's loose and it's strong and it's powerful. It sounds good for those days. There's a quality to it, timelessness to it, a classic feel to it that you don't have on the second record. To me, it's not just the material, 'Skunk' and 'Sister Anne' and 'Over and Over', the production's correct and the attitude's correct. First record's live – oops, that's us. Second record has a Nazi producer. The third record is us producing ourselves after we sort of gained some experience. So that's the best record. Flat out."

"So if you look at our situation again in the context of having lost the support of a label and having lost our manager and ultimately, lost the connection with each other," said Kramer. "Because once we lost the spiritual connection, and once we lost the principles that were bigger than us as people, then we were no more than just another creepy rock band. And we were a creepy rock band with a big attitude and I, myself, had started to develop a pain-relieving campaign of serious drug and alcohol use and that is the kiss of death for a band."

Pinball Wizard The Who

(Pete Townshend) ❋ Track ❋ 1969 ❋ Appears on: *Tommy*

Kit Lambert, co-manager of the Who, was the son of composer and conductor Constance Lambert, one of the leading lights of the British cultural Establishment. Almost from the start of the Who's career, Kit urged Pete Townshend to write something grander than a pop song. It was largely his influence behind the mini-opera *A Quick One*. Finally in 1968 Townshend wrote *Tommy*, the first rock opera. It's not an opera in the formal sense but closer to a sacred cantata.

"It was Kit Lambert's idea to do the full rock opera," said Daltrey. "Basically the story line of *Tommy*, the holiday camp, was Keith's idea. The actual story line is more Kit Lambert than Pete Townshend. You don't very often hear Kit Lambert's name mentioned when it comes to *Tommy* these days but I haven't forgotten."

The *Tommy* book is completely preposterous. A young boy sees a murder; goes deaf, dumb and blind; is molested by an uncle; given LSD by a witch; becomes a pinball champion and is elevated to god-like status; recovers his senses; and eventually, after various spiritual realisations, the idol falls.

"It's about life," said Townshend.

Operas are frequently preposterous, as are pop songs. This one is particularly so, especially when surrounded by so many philosophical allusions. It would have been much better if it didn't take itself so seriously.

At the time, Townshend was deeply involved in the teachings of Indian guru Meher Baba. He struggled with his fame and with the demands the Who placed on him as writer and leader. He was a man who had always struggled with himself. His friend Nik Cohn, one of the best commentators on rock & roll, was a pinball fanatic. All of these factors plus the suggestions of the band (Entwistle contributed the child molesting, Moon the holiday camp) went into writing *Tommy*. At the end of the day they had a double album of mostly extraordinary songs, beautifully recorded and strung together with a flimsy scenario. Townshend's extensive analysis mostly just gets in the way of the record.

This might have been an opera but the Who were a rock & roll band and they needed singles. The obvious choice on *Tommy* was 'Pinball Wizard'.

"The whole point of 'Pinball Wizard' was to let the boy have some sort of colourful event and excitement," Townshend explained. "'Pinball Wizard' is about life's games, playing the machine – the boy and his machine, the disciples with theirs, the scores, results, colours, vibration and action.

"People play their own pinball in other ways, like I muck around with tape recorders all the time. Most people's pinball machines are their cars. The car obsession is overwhelming, but it's there and I imagine it can only increase. I think it's groovy – why not? I thrive on modern things – good hi-fi, amplifiers, tape recorders, colour TV. A lot of them look like they're all padding, but there's far less than you'd imagine."

Whatever the context, 'Pinball Wizard' is an extraordinary piece. Townshend uses a wall of acoustic guitars in an almost flamenco style of lightning-fast strumming to set the atmosphere, which is then pierced with fat chords of electric guitar peeled off and then allowed to float through the air. (The arrangement bears a similarity to the Pretty Things' 'Old Man Going'.) Townshend plays his guitars off against each other like an argument with himself that can never be resolved. Daltrey is at the top of his form, for once not fighting with the others but allowed get inside the melody.

When performing *Tommy* live, Keith Moon would on occasion wave his drum sticks like a conductor and was known to yell, "Stop laughing! This is serious. It's a fucking opera."

Life During Wartime Talking Heads

(David Byrne) ✳ Sire ✳ 1979 ✳ Appears on: *Fear of Music*

"We were under a lot of stress and pressure so [the title] *Fear of Music* seemed perfect," said bass player Tina Weymouth of the Talking Heads' third album. The group developed very fast from its minimalist garage folk beginnings at CBGB. Within two years they had moved on from itchy rock to a new kind of funk. Producer Brian Eno had encouraged the group to experiment more and so for the third album they began with a blank slate.

The first two albums were written before the group had a recording deal. For the third they started with bass and drum grooves that were worked into songs and then recorded over two days, after which Byrne added his lyrics and the songs were polished.

'Life During Wartime' is a particularly disturbing song, sung from the point of view of a character trying to survive in the middle of a war zone. The singer is saying that "this ain't no party/this ain't no disco" as he sorts through the rubble. It's a song that mocks the nightclub lifestyle and the political grandstanding of rock stars who sing about wars and foreign affairs; it's also a perspective that's probably true for thousands of people all over the Third World.

The legacy of Talking Heads will be the way that they brought a particular style of funk to white rock and no-one has dug that groove better.

"I think Jerry puts it best," said Weymouth. "When we were discussing this record … Brian wanted to say it was his record, David wanted to say it was his record. They both thought it was the greatest venture of their lives. But Jerry said, 'No, we didn't all have the same idea. We all came in with different ideas of what we were going to do. It was the collective influences that created the result.' No-one could put an individual claim to it.

"Plus, Eno had always said that he wanted to go into the studio cold with us, without any material, so that we could learn the way he makes albums, simple things layer upon layer. It's really not novel at all, it's just the old idea of jamming, one key, no chord changes … and everybody played and everybody produced. The songs were written by the five of us."

Many of the phrases from 'Life During Wartime' have entered the vernacular and the song is still as fresh as its scenario is perennial.

Pink Turns to Blue Hüsker Dü

(Grant Hart) ❋ SST ❋ 1984 ❋ Appears on: *Zen Arcade*

Hüsker Dü's music has lasted better than the vogue for umlauts in band names. The Minneapolis power trio were leaders of the early '80s hardcore scene. Like many of those groups they had a righteous attitude – no fills, no show biz, just angst and loud guitars taken straight with no chaser. So it was surprising that their fourth album, *Zen Arcade*, was a double – a sprawling twenty-three songs including meandering jams. This would have been a heresy had they not delivered what was effectively the hardcore *Exile on Main Street*. Recorded in eighty-five hours, most of the songs are first takes, and that blunt energy carries through whether they are thrashing, going pop, freaking out or, as is the case with 'Pink Turns to Blue', making a solid point with a minor key ballad.

Grant Hart's haunting song about drug addiction and its cost demonstrated that hardcore could be flexible and that the chief architects of the form weren't going to be constrained by it. 'Pink Turns to Blue' has moments of poignant, specific observation and is more powerful for that shift.

"There's politics in the sense of people trying to gain control of their own destiny," said Hart. "Life is too short to worry about who's on top at any given time – politics is like advertising, the basic products beneath the different wrappers are much the same – it's more important to avoid being stepped on, to find a life that doesn't involve a giant foot hovering over your head perpetually. The golden rule is: be neither a foot over someone's head, nor a head under someone's foot."

Koyaanisqatsi Philip Glass

(Philip Glass) ❊ Nonesuch ❊ 1998 ❊ Appears on: *Koyaanisqatsi*

Avant-garde composer Philip Glass operates in the twilight world between high art and popular taste. His music, which borrows from Indian traditions as well as the West, relies on repetition and minimalism and electronics. Somewhere in the middle he meets up with the art side of rock & roll. There's a common language here. Glass' most successful popular work is the soundtrack to Godfrey Reggio's 1982 film *Koyaanisqatsi*. The original release of the music on the soundtrack album was edited for time considerations. In 1998 Glass re-recorded the score.

The film's title is a Hopi Indian phrase meaning "life out of balance". The eighty-seven minute film is a selection of images from around the globe – from deserts to cities and all manner of life situations. Although there are no words, Reggio's intent was clear: nature=good; urbanisation=bad.

Central to the film and somewhat more ambiguous is Glass' music. Without any other narrative, the score certainly gives a particular take on the images. It's rare for a composer to be given this sort of opportunity and Glass made the most of it.

"We didn't mean to spend that much time on it, but it took three years to get the money to finish the film," said Glass. "Godfrey and I would work on a few things, then he'd get more money and go out and shoot some more. He'd come back five months later and we'd work on a few more things. It gave us a long gestation period with a lot of time to think about it, to look at and reflect on it.

"Godfrey came in with a very strong, almost political, social, and ideological construction. He had a film language he wanted to work with. He had a concept of the piece. And he even had a whole ideological background that he could supply me with – books, articles and lectures. He's sort of a full-service intellectual. So we had an opportunity to wed the parts of the film together very organically. In a sense you could say the text … although the text never appears … the text, the image, and the music become very organically intertwined."

Writers have called it a "tone poem" but it's really just the longest art music video ever made. The film was a success and introduced post-modern minimalist composition to a mass audience. Glass' hypnotic keyboard passages entered the vocabulary of popular instrumental music, especially techno and ambient in the '80s and beyond.

"The piece kind of became a classic without our realising it," said Glass.

Wild Thing   Tone Loc

(Matt Dike/Michael Ross/Anthony Smith/Marvin Young) ❋ Delicious Vinyl ❋ 1988 ❋
Appears on: *Loc-Ed After Dark*

One of the most delightful tracks from rap's first golden era, 'Wild Thing' gave the world a new phrase for love making. The song was funny and Loc's steel-wool vocal was, well, sexy. And the beats were just perfect.

Written by Loc, the Delicious Vinyl team and Young MC, 'Wild Thing' also launched producers the Dust Brothers and their witty use of beats and samples. 'Wild Thing' kicks courtesy of a sample from Van Halen's 'Jamie's Crying'. There was a great video that parodied 'Addicted to Love' and was shot for $350. Mostly though, it's the charm of Tone (Anthony Smith) Loc.

"When Matt and Mike started the label," said Loc, "they were really bored with East Coast rappers, they were looking for a West Coast rapper with a certain kind of voice or style. They spoke to me on the phone, fell in love with my voice and knew they had to make some kind of record with me.

"About nine years ago I had a stripped throat, you know when your throat kills you, it hurts to talk, you can't swallow. To soothe the soreness I drank some hot tea with brandy in it, and it scorched the shit out of my throat, it's been like that ever since."

Pride (In the Name of Love) U2

(U2) ✳ Island ✳ 1984 ✳ Appears on: *The Unforgettable Fire*

The sessions for U2's *Unforgettable Fire* were as fraught as any for the group. It was here that producers Daniel Lanois and Brian Eno helped U2 to find their mature voice. The textures between bass and guitar are more complex and Lanois' ambient atmospheres start to creep in. But that aside, it's here that U2 really start to swing. The group still had those ringing guitar tunes over a throbbing beat but they were starting to stretch.

'Pride' was inspired by the life and work of Martin Luther King, who combined political activism with his Christian beliefs in a way that the Irish could understand. According to the Edge, "Because of the situation in our country, non-violent struggle was such an inspiring concept."

"I originally wrote 'Pride' about Ronald Reagan and the ambivalent attitude in America," Bono told the *NME.* "It was originally meant as the sort of pride that won't back down, that wants to build nuclear arsenals. But that wasn't working. I remember a wise old man who said to me, don't try to fight darkness with light, just make the light shine brighter. I was giving Reagan too much importance, then I thought Martin Luther King, there's a man. We build the positive rather than fighting with the finger."

The track was U2's first Top 40 hit in the US and has been one of their most enduring songs.

Song to the Siren Tim Buckley

(Tim Buckley/Larry Beckett) ❊ Bizarre/Straight ❊ 1971 ❊ Appears on: *Starsailor*

Tim Buckley was a restless soul and equally itinerant with his music. Starting out in the mid-'60s as a folkie, he embraced rock and R&B but increasingly wandered towards jazz. He was gifted with an extraordinary voice – a six-octave range that in its baritone registers could sound like pure sex.

At the time Buckley was making the *Starsailor* album he had just started a romance with his last wife and was living happily in California, while spinning, according to friends, sides by Olivier Messiaen, Satie and Penderecki.

"I even started singing in different languages – Swahili, for instance – just because it sounded better," Buckley later wrote. "An instrumentalist can be understood doing just about anything, but people are really geared for hearing only words come out of the mouth … The most shocking thing I've ever seen people come up against – besides a performer taking off his clothes – is dealing with someone who doesn't sing words. I get off on great-sounding words. If I had my way, words wouldn't mean a thing. It shocked the hell out of the people. It was refreshing."

The *Starsailor* album, produced by the Lovin' Spoonful's Jerry Yester, was expected to be the breakthrough album for Buckley after a couple of promising LPs and a solid cult following. Instead it was jammed with experimental epics and jazz flavours and judged by the public and his own fans to be unlistenable. All except 'Song to the Siren', which has an appropriately haunting atmosphere to it. It was the song that most resembled Buckley's early work: ephemeral and moody and full of melodic texture. Buckley agreed that it was one of his best tracks.

In 1983, the song became a major cult hit in Britain when Liz Fraser of This Mortal Coil reinterpreted it and, of course, a terrible Brit rock band called themselves *Starsailor*. Nonetheless 'Song to the Siren' remains enchanting four decades on.

"Sometimes you're writing and you know that you're not going to fit," Buckley said at the time. "But you do it because it's your heart and soul and you gotta say it. When you play a chord, you're dating yourself … the fewer chords you play, the less likely you are to get conditioned, and the more you can reveal of what you are."

Sam Stone John Prine

(John Prine) ✳ Atlantic ✳ 1971 ✳ Appears on: *John Prine*

John Prine's first album on Atlantic announced the arrival of a bold voice. Certainly this ex-Army, former postal worker was sitting in the singer/songwriter tradition and had an uncanny eye for detail. Prine was almost Nashville with his raspy voice, laid back well behind the beat. However, the subject matter was a little too literate for all but the new Texan school, which was starting to bubble through in the early '70s. Prine was thus tagged the new Dylan, a label he deserved no better than any of the others.

"Usually the best thing is a real, real strong line that's a strong image," he said to Bruce Pollack. "Sometimes an entire song will pour right out after it, if it's real strong. In most of the ballad stuff I do I try to use a chorus like a needle and thread, to pull the song together. A lot of times I've written just with the idea of experimenting. 'Donald and Lydia' – I had no idea what I was going to write about, but I knew how I was going to set the song up. I was going to set it up character by character."

The most striking song on his debut album is 'Sam Stone', the story of a soldier who returns from Indochina with a raging heroin habit. There is the memorable chorus: "There's a hole in daddy's arm where all the money goes/And Jesus Christ died for nothing, I suppose." That's strong.

Lazy Sunday The Small Faces

(Ronnie Lane/Steve Marriott) ✳ Immediate ✳ 1968 ✳ Appears on: *Ogden's Nut Gone Flake*

Right at the top of their form, the release of 'Lazy Sunday' brought the Small Faces to a crashing end. The song was part of the song-cycle *Ogden's Nut Gone Flake*, which was the Small Faces' masterpiece. Andrew Loog Oldham, who owned the Immediate label, thought the song would be a hit and released it as a single. The group was livid, no-one more so than singer/guitarist Steve Marriott. In the middle of a concert at the Alexandra Palace, as the group were playing what had become a number three single, Marriott put down his guitar, walked off stage and out of the band.

'Lazy Sunday' is a beautiful, small piece of whimsical psychedelia. The group had been a popular mod band, rushing out 45s in between hectic touring schedules. *Ogden's Nut Gone Flake* – which appeared on a circular cover – was conceived as a song cycle with state-of-the-art production. As the album sleeve and, indeed, most of the songs made clear, there was a considerable amount of cannabis being

consumed. The group had already had a hit with the acid ditty 'Itchycoo Park', and 'Lazy Sunday', with its jokey asides in the lyrics, was the perfect stoner's song to be a sequel.

"It was a year, actually, on and off," said McLagen of the recording process. "And 'Lazy Sunday', we didn't want to do that in the first place. Andrew put that out without our permission. He saw it as a potential hit single, which it was. It's like telling a joke: you don't want to tell the same joke three times over. 'Here we all are, sitting in a rainbow.' It's funny and then it becomes tedious. And we were stuck with doing that every night."

Pressure Drop Toots & the Maytals

(Toots Hibbert) ✳ Island ✳ 1973 ✳ Appears on: *Funky Kingston*

The vocal trio of Toots and the Maytals – Toots Hibbert, Jerry Matthias and Henry

'Raleigh' Gordon – was one of Jamaica's finest vocal groups. They found considerable success through the '60s. In 1966 Hibbert was jailed for eighteen months on a ganja smoking charge. He emerged from jail an even more committed Rasta and a more popular artist. The Toots and the Maytals' records took on a harder edge.

With 'Pressure Drop' they combine close singing with a very deep and insistent reggae backing as provided by Leslie Kong's production. 'Pressure Drop' is the single best track from reggae's golden era perhaps because it transcends so many styles of music, from gospel to reggae via R&B. It's a track that sounds deceptively simple but is, in fact, a highly complicated mixture of rhythm and vocal melody. It's a track that has more hooks than a tuna fleet and coming out of that is Hibbert's song of defiance. 'Pressure Drop' has a universality. It's built on the particular experience of Jamaicans and Rastas but can equally appeal to everyone everywhere.

The track was used to great effect in the film *The Harder They Come* and then on the album *Funky Kingston*, which launched Toots and the Maytals in the west. Consequently, 'Pressure Drop' has been covered widely – notably by Robert Palmer and the Clash – but never to match the original.

Andalucia John Cale
(John Cale) ❄ Reprise ❄ 1973 ❄ Appears On: *Paris 1919*

In his autobiography, John Cale wrote, "*Paris 1919* was an example of the nicest ways of saying something ugly." Nicest in the sense that he enlisted a great producer (Chris Thomas) and talented musicians (Little Feat) and wrote gorgeous melodies. Thankfully he buried the meaning of most of these songs deep enough that you aren't much troubled by the ugly things.

The album is deeply romantic. The title, one assumes, alludes to the Versailles Peace Conference after the Great War – a moment of reason and optimism and, of course, being Paris, romance. Other songs on the album are called 'Graham Greene', 'Child's Christmas in Wales', 'Hanky Panky Nohow' and 'The Endless Plain of Fortune'. It's all a bit whimsical for the usually dark and intoxicated viola player.

'Andalucia' is evocative of the pastoral, rocky land between Spain and France which its title refers to, and it's also about a love affair. Cale's viola has never sounded so sweet and his deep Welsh voice is warm and wistful. It's a gentle and haunting song.

"It really shows the value of writing all of the songs before going into the studio, that's for sure," said Cale of *Paris 1919*. "And I really learnt a lot from Chris Thomas, who produced that record. His kind of caution and scrutiny paid off in the overall quality of the record."

Welcome to the Terrordome Public Enemy

(Chuck D/Eric 'Vietnam' Sadler/Keith Shocklee) ☀ DEF JAM ☀ 1990 ☀

Appears on: *Fear of a Black Planet*

Chuck D announced, "I got so much trouble on my mind," and then the Bomb Squad (Eric 'Vietnam' Sadler/Keith Shocklee) and DJ Terminator X opened Pandora's box. A snatch of the Temptations' 'Psychedelic Shack', a dose of James Brown, some Instant Funk. 'Terrordome' lived up to its name.

"We were taking thousands of sounds," said the rapper. "If you separated the sounds, they wouldn't have been anything – they were unrecognisable. The sounds were all collaged together to make a sonic wall."

"A guitar sampled off a record is going to hit differently than a guitar sampled in the studio," Shocklee explained. "The guitar that's sampled off a record is going to have all the compression that they put on the recording, the equalisation. It's going to hit the tape harder. It's going to slap at you. Something that's organic is almost going to have a powder effect. It hits more like a pillow than a piece of wood. So those things change your mood, the feeling you can get off of a record. If you notice that by the early '90s, the sound has gotten a lot softer."

The use of sampling here added to the sense of anarchy and urgency in Chuck D's vision of modern America. After three albums, too, the Bomb Squad had perfected their work to the point where it almost went beyond rap and into the area of jazz, mirroring the later work of John Coltrane. At the time of the album Public Enemy were under attack for many of their views and their relationship with the Nation of Islam. Their militancy was bringing a lot of heat on the group and this song screams paranoia.

"Number one, we set out to make this a trend, and make it hip," said Chuck D. "And you know that the down side is that it cycles out into something. But for the people who pick it up, and learn about themselves, it will always be with them. You can't revert to going back to stupid. You know that. You get smart and it sticks with you. So yeah, that movement, understand, it was meant to be a seed that sprouted a tree."

Undecided Masters Apprentices

(Bower/Harrison) ✳ Astor ✳ 1967 ✳ Appears on: *Hands of Time*

"Our songs were a mishmash of styles," said Masters Apprentices singer Jim Keays. Mishmash or not, they got off to a very good start with their first single, 'Undecided'. The flip side ('Wars and Hands of Time') was a psychedelic anti-war masterpiece but the A-side was a burning, rocking garage classic straight out of Adelaide, Australia, sounding like the Rolling Stones in a bad mood. Snarly, crunching guitar riffs over Keays' sex-starved vocals brought a unique urgency to 'Undecided'. The song is still fresh and it was most recently covered – faithfully – by Silverchair jamming with Radio Birdman guitarist Deniz Tek.

"So we got a letter from Astor Records saying, can you put down some demos and send them to us," said Keays. "So we went into a little studio in Adelaide. In fact I put the vocals down in a warehouse across the lane because the echo in there was monstrous. Anyway we did the songs and sent them over to them and basically forgot about it. I was at the drive-in with my girlfriend one night and in between the two movies I put on the car radio and 'Undecided' came on, one of the songs we'd recorded as a demo. And I couldn't believe it; it was just a shock. And it was a monstrous hit for us, it thrust us from the garage band virtually straight into a national band, virtually overnight."

The track was written in the studio by guitarists Mick Bower and Rick Harrison in less than fifteen minutes. In his memoir *His Master's Voice*, Keays notes, "It had no real chorus line and no lyric that seemed to jump out as a title. 'What shall I write on the tape box?' inquired Max Pepper, studio proprietor. 'I don't know I'm undecided', I said. That was it. 'Undecided' was boldly printed on the tape box as song number four."

Le Freak Chic

(Bernard Edwards/Nile Rodgers) ✳ Atlantic ✳ 1978 ✳ Appears on: *C'est Chic*

The biggest selling single in Atlantic's history came about after Chic was refused entry to the chic Studio 54. The pair – Bernard Edwards and Nile Rodgers – left their date Grace Jones and walked down the street chanting "Aw, fuck off," which evolved into the hook "Freak out!" Once in the studio Rodgers and Edwards jammed the rest of the song into place with the help of drummer Tony Thompson.

The Chic style started when Rodgers was in London at a Roxy Music concert.

"I went to see Roxy. I thought this shit is happening," said the guitarist. "If we could take this sophisticated, cerebral stuff, put a beat to it, make it black and our own thing, we could really be happening, too.

"We also idolised KISS. When KISS were on stage, they had a certain vibe and image, and once they left that stage, you had absolutely no idea who they are. That's what Chic was like. Our costumes made us look like bankers and business people. To us, it was just as over-the-top and flamboyant as KISS."

Chic had the songs too – whether for Chic records or for artists such as Sister Sledge ('We are Family'). They weren't the first disco band but they took disco from being a dance craze into a lasting musical style. Their influence is still heard on the radio.

"It was a three-piece band playing all the rhythm tracks and then we started overdubbing," said Edwards, who played the bass. "When you're first laying down the rhythm track, you want it to be tight and the less people playing, the tighter. If it's just me and Nile and the drummer, we know the rhythm track's going to be solid.

"My main role is to keep the bottom there, keep the groove solid and steady. I play a lot on the E and A strings and I play down in the first five frets mainly to keep a really fat, chunky sound. I usually start more basic – I don't like to get too note-y and it's usually a reaction to some rhythm that Nile's playing. He'll start playing a chord and I'll pick up on it and put notes to the rhythm.

"A lot of times there's no melody so I have total freedom as to what I'm going to play – just knowing whether it's a major or minor mode and then I can go with it. I'll come up with a line and maybe we'll write around that line."

Of course, the irony is that no group defined the disco era so well as Chic. Rodgers and Edwards had a groove that was both rock and R&B, that was light and heavy. This was disco. Dance music with wit. Rodgers' snappy, rhythmic guitar style perfectly complemented Edwards' heavy bass lines. "Our philosophies defined our personalities. I had my bohemian lifestyle and Bernard was the family man," said Rodgers. "Everything that was systematic about Bernard was exactly what my anarchy needed."

Psychotic Reaction The Count Five

(Craig Atkinson/Sean Byrne/Byron Atkinson/Roy Chaney/Kenn Ellner/John Byrne/John
Michalski) ❋ Double Shot ❋ 1966 ❋ Appears on: *Nuggets: Original Artyfacts from the
First Psychedelic Era, 1965–1968*

Storming out of San Jose, California, in Dracula capes, brandishing guitars that may
have been tuned by the devil himself, the Count Five's 'Psychotic Reaction' is a
definite classic. Formed in 1964, like just about everyone else on the planet, the
Five (or the V, as they liked to be known) were high on the sounds of the British
invasion. They had a raw edge that bore not a little resemblance to the Rolling
Stones and the Yardbirds, especially the fuzz guitar freak-out that gives this song
its title.

'Psychotic Reaction' is a naïve song about teen heartbreak but there is the hint of
the lysergic in the title and the guitar and harp rave-ups gave the song its pizzazz
and sent it briefly to the Top 5. The rhythm section was a little lacking in swing but
that only gave heart to teenagers in garages everywhere. Perhaps rightly, the Five
considered themselves avatars of a new tradition rather than just rehashing the
British invasion.

"If you look at the records, the Yardbirds never came close to the popularity of
'Psychotic Reaction'," said John Byrne. "I like the Yardbirds, but they did not
influence 'Psychotic Reaction'."

Psycho Elvis Costello

(Leon Payne) ❋ Radar ❋ 1981 ❋ Appears on: *Almost Blue* (reissue)

Leon Payne was one of the most esteemed Texan songwriters, if only on account of
'Lost Highway', which was made eternal by Hank Williams. Blind almost from birth,
Payne joined Bob Wills' Texas Playboys in 1938 but shortly thereafter went freelance
as a writer and performer. His own biggest hit was 'I Love You Because' and his work
was in demand by George Jones, Ernest Tubb, Hank Snow, Don Gibson and Elvis
Presley.

In 1955 Payne wrote a novelty song, 'Psycho', which tells the story of a maniac
who is confessing to the murders of at least his ex-wife and her lover to his mother,

whom he realises finally is also dead. It's perversely funny in that B-movie style but it's also strangely moving and sympathetic. The narrative cleverly jumps back and forth from pathos to slapstick and the switching subjectivity of a deranged mind. For instance this verse:

Oh you recall that little girl mama
I believe her name was Betty Clark
Oh don't tell me that she's dead mama
'Cause I just saw her in the park
We were sitting on a bench mama
Thinking of a game to play
Seems I was holding a wrench mama
Then my mind just walked away

It's not hard to see a similarity with Talking Heads' 'Psycho Killer', and the line "Then my mind just walked away" was borrowed by Paul Kelly.

'Psycho' was first a hit for the forgotten Jack Kittel in 1974 but has subsequently been revised a number of times, most famously by Elvis Costello in 1981 and very creditably by the Beasts of Bourbon in 1984.

Miss You The Rolling Stones

(Mick Jagger/Keith Richards) ✳ Rolling Stones Records ✳ 1978 ✳ Appears on: *Some Girls*

"A lot of these songs like 'Miss You' were heavily influenced by going to the discos," said Charlie Watts. "Mick and I used to go to discos a lot. A great way to hear a dance record was by listening to it in a dance hall or disco. In the '70s there were some fantastic dance records out. As dopey as their clothes might have looked, the actual records that Earth, Wind & Fire released, for example, were fabulous."

Jagger was clearly plugged into the changes that were overtaking the charts. Meanwhile, Keith Richards was fighting legal battles and perpetually detoxing from heroin. After three less than stellar albums, the Rolling Stones put themselves under pressure. The *Some Girls* album was hailed as a return to form.

'Miss You' is one of their more enduring tracks. It has the four-on-the-floor of the Philadelphia sound but still maintains a rock & roll feel. Along with Blondie's 'Heart of Glass', it was an important step in breaking down the the rock audience's antipathy towards dance music.

While Richards struggled to get his life back together, Jagger took control of the Rolling Stones and *Some Girls* is very much his album. The record both satirises and applauds the decadent New York of the late '70s with its disco and champagne and trash aristocracy. The lyrics mock not only Andy Warhol but also Jagger's wife ("You're the easiest lay on the White House lawn"), and the record acknowledged New York as the new centre of the universe.

On 'Miss You' the Rolling Stones reconnected with the people. The groove is driven by Jagger's guitar style, and his playful vocals, especially in the upper register, are some of his best. 'Miss You' is a modest proposal, not to be the greatest band in the world, but just to be on the dance floor once more.

Dirty Old Town   The Pogues

(Ewan MacColl) ❋ Stiff ❋ 1985 ❋ Appears on: *Rum, Sodomy, and the Lash*

It's unlikely that Ewan MacColl would have approved of the Pogues' version of 'Dirty Old Town'. MacColl saw himself as a socialist revolutionary, using folk music to celebrate the working classes, and as a medium for information and encouragement in the struggle against capitalism. When not penning songs or reviving old folk songs, MacColl wrote and acted in plays for the glories of the workers. An awkward scene change in 1949's *Landscape with Chimneys* called for a song and 'Dirty Old Town' was born.

'Dirty Old Town' is a waltz set allegedly in the northern industrial town Salford, Lancashire, where MacColl was born. It's a love–hate story – the sentimental memories of a first kiss by the factory wall and the dreams by the old canal lead into a reverie about the industrial landscape and finally the vow to destroy the poverty and despair of the place.

The Pogues' version floats on the ambiguous affection for the past and it's more maudlin than versions by Rod Stewart, Richard Thompson or Townes Van Zandt. Produced by Elvis Costello, it's one of their finest and roughest moments.

Easy to Slip Little Feat

(Lowell George/Martin Kibbee) ❋ Warner Bros. ❋ 1972 ❋ Appears on: *Sailin' Shoes*

Intended originally for the Doobie Brothers, 'Easy to Slip' opened Little Feat's second album with their trademarks – elliptical lyrics, bittersweet slide guitar and funky rhythm patterns. 'Easy to Slip' was begun by Martin Kibbee, whose wife had recently left him. It's a gorgeous song of bereavement, of bad things happening just because that's the tragedy of life. It's a sensibility that George got from the blues. The other thing he got was a slide guitar technique. George could make his guitar shine and cry at will. Using a socket wrench rather than a thinner bottleneck produced his distinctive tone.

Nothing with Little Feat was quite what you expected. The musical parts were syncopated in ways that no-one else could do. The lyrics were always a little oblique but the emotional content was always straight and true.

"I think he had the audacity of a schizophrenic, which I associate with great work, whether it's Van Gogh or Ravel," said Van Dyke Parks, who frequently worked with George in the early '70s. "Lowell had a madness in his work that he wanted to explore, and he had the integrity to do it. That is what makes him an artist. I see the physical comedy in Lowell George that you get out of Buster Keaton. It's the tragicomedy of man in crisis – that's what Lowell did for me. He filled a void, because it takes a lot of intelligence to get away with that."

The Dark End of the Street James Carr

(Dan Penn/Chips Moman) ❋ Vivid Sound ❋ 1967 ❋ Appears on: *The Essential James Carr*

Dan Penn is one of the most gifted southern songwriters. Growing up as a white kid in segregated Alabama, his only contact with black music – R&B, rock & roll and jazz – was from the radio. Nonetheless, once he heard Ray Charles, his course was set. He made his way to Memphis, where he started writing country songs for Conway Twitty, and befriended Spooner Oldham and Arthur Alexander and was seminal in establishing the Muscle Shoals Sound. In bridging country and R&B, Penn was instrumental in founding the southern soul sound.

"We were only in there for about thirty minutes," Dan Penn told Barney Hoskyns when recalling the writing of the song. It was specifically penned for James Carr to sing. "I guess 'Dark End of the Street' was the culmination of two or three years of thinkin' about cheatin'," he said.

'The Dark End of the Street' is an aching ballad about forbidden love – perhaps the definitive word on adultery. The song has a touch of country and a big dollop of soul and there's also a hint of gospel that only adds to the plaintive nature of the tune. The singer laments being forced to meet up in the shadows and to hide his feelings. It's a record that drips with guilt and with dark passion and the song has proved durable enough to be covered by men and women across the disciplines.

Good Times Chic

(Bernard Edwards/Nile Rodgers) ❋ Atlantic ❋ 1979 ❋ Appears on: *Risqué*

"During the late '70s we were going through the greatest recession since the depression," said Chic guitarist Nile Rodgers. "During the Great Depression they wrote 'Happy Days are Here Again', because they could drink booze again. Every lyric in the song was a throwback to depression-era songs. I even ripped off 'Happy days are here again/The time is right for making friends' (the opening verse of 'Good Times'). Then I took an Al Jolson song that said 'The stars are going to twinkle and shine this evening, 'bout a quarter to nine' – so I went 'let's get together, about a quarter to ten.'"

It's unlikely that the millions around the world who did the Bump and the Hustle to 'Good Times' in the late '70s in their white suits picked up on Rodgers' commentary. Rodgers grew up in a semi-bohemian atmosphere in New York. As a youth he hung with R&B combos and the Black Panther party. His songs may have been disco but they were informed by cultural politics.

"It was all about authenticity," the guitarist explained. "Being African Americans, because our skin is black, we've never been able to assimilate into culture the way other races have. During the Harlem Renaissance, people who were descendants of slaves came up with their own class system and royalty to beat this: 'Duke' Ellington, 'Count' Basie, 'King' Pleasure.

"We were paying tribute on *Risqué* to people who were oppressed and not having any voice apart from their music and their art. Everything had to fit the vibe. We got the Nicholas Brothers to dance on 'My Feet Keep Dancing'. We were saying 'thank you' to the aristocrats in the ghetto, and their form of dancing was tapping. We thought no-one would know why we did it, but we didn't care."

Chic's third album, *Risqué*, was one of the highpoints of 20th-century pop. Its lead single, 'Good Times', provided the bass line for the seminal rap track 'Rapper's Delight' by the Sugarhill Gang and was also appropriated for Queen's 'Another One Bites the Dust'. It was the riff that kept on giving.

'Good Times' was the sound of the era though, with its minimal, precise bass riff and its showy lyrics celebrating the superficial, kitschy wealth of the era. It was a fantasy as big as the groove.

Rock & Roll Lou Reed

(Lou Reed) ✻ RCA ✻ 1974 ✻ Appears on: *Rock & Roll Animal*

This anthem first appeared on *Loaded*, the fourth Velvet Underground LP. In the booklet accompanying the Velvets' box set, *Peel Slowly*, Lou Reed wrote, "'Rock & roll' is about me. If I hadn't heard rock & roll on the radio, I would have had no idea there was life on this planet. Which would have been devastating – to think that everything, everywhere was like it was where I come from. That would have been profoundly discouraging. Movies didn't do it for me. TV didn't do it for me. It was the radio that did it."

The definitive version, however, exists on Reed's solo *Rock & Roll Animal* album. That tour followed Lou's hit single 'Walk on the Wild Side' and his *Berlin* album, which was recorded by Alice Cooper and KISS producer Bob Ezrin. For the tour Reed retained the *Berlin* musicians – especially the guitarists Steve Hunter and Dick Wagner. Their sound was hard, shiny and impenetrable, and that fitted Lou Reed's style at the time.

"*Rock & Roll Animal* is still one of the best live recordings ever done," said Lou Reed, and it's impossible to dispute him. "I've got enough distance on it now that I can hear it today. Those songs were made for that. And there's also a vibe on there that's – phew! I can't listen to any of it, it's just too difficult to relate to."

Purple Haze   The Jimi Hendrix Experience

(Jimi Hendrix) ✳ Track ✳ 1967 ✳ Appears on: *Smash Hits*

"I had these dreams that something was gonna happen, seeing the numbers 1966 in my sleep, so I was just passing time till then," Hendrix said. "I wanted my own scene, making my music, not playing the same riffs."

Legend has it that 'Purple Haze' started out as a poem, 'Purple haze – Jesus saves', to which Hendrix added this incredible riff and finished the song backstage in a club on Boxing Day 1966 just as their first single, 'Stone Free' (backed with 'Hey Joe'), was crawling up the charts.

It's clear that 'Purple Haze' is a homage to LSD. The song kicks off with a fuzzed-out two-note riff and then the guitar goes crazy and the lyrics follow – with the immortal line, "'Scuze me while I kiss the sky". On this track Hendrix was doing things with his upside-down guitar that nobody had ever dreamed of. He was inventing a new vocabulary for the guitar in the same way that Charlie Parker had done for the saxophone. According to engineer Eddie Kramer, Hendrix was so much in command of his own instrument that he could literally create those sounds without the use of a studio. He could make himself sound backwards even though he wasn't.

'Purple Haze' was recorded on 11 January 1967. "Hendrix came in and kind of hummed us the riff and showed Noel the chords and the changes," said drummer Mitch Mitchell. "I listened to it and we went, 'OK, let's do it.' We got it on the third take as I recall."

Released on 17 March that year, 'Purple Haze' became Hendrix's signature tune.

I Will Dare   The Replacements

(Paul Westerberg) ✳ Twin Tone ✳ 1984 ✳ Appears on: *Let It Be*

"We were five years ahead of our time, ten years behind," Replacements lead singer and songwriter Paul Westerberg recalled, more in sorrow than in anger. The subject of his regret is the fact that the grunge revolution that made Pearl Jam and Nirvana millionaires was in part constructed on the sound and the audience that was built up by the Replacements. This Minneapolis quartet was known for its ragged glory – proudly drunk but rarely tight, they put a spirit into '80s rock that wasn't found on MTV. But the spirits that made them do it also spelt their doom before it was time to cash in. Westerberg, however, is philosophical. "When you see guys come out and sell three million right out of the garage, you wonder, what are we doing wrong?" But his hindsight is realistic. "If we'd have sold three million *Let It Be*s when it came out we would have been dead in a month. We couldn't have handled it."

Let It Be was the group's fourth album and their masterpiece. 'I Will Dare' was a statement of intent – a song with mandolin and country-rock flavour partly due to R.E.M.'s Peter Buck guesting on guitar. The song was a classic rock & roll love song – the Everly Brothers meets the Velvet Underground – but unfortunately it didn't cross over from the group's college rock fan base, despite great reviews.

"I think we happened to like all of the funky quirks of the classic rock bands – the Who, the Rolling Stones – that critics found endearing. We didn't have the things that made those bands huge, we had the thing that made them infamous and decadent and, perhaps, great.

"When it came to writing the songs, I was never as fucked-up and dumb as people assumed," he said. "There was always a method to the madness. The songs were about what we were. It was never a pose. It may have come suspiciously close when we got attention for being fuck-ups. We accentuated it, and maybe even stretched the limits of what we actually were. Essentially, when we started we were mixed-up kids and we wrote about it.

"It's funny that the people who related to it the most weren't fucked-up kids. Our fans have always been, dare I say, a little more intelligent than the band was labelled as. I always thought that ironic."

In the Ghetto Elvis Presley

(Mac Davis) ❋ RCA ❋ 1969 ❋ Appears on: *From Elvis in Memphis*

In 1969 Elvis Presley made a dramatic career turnaround. For the past decade he had appeared in a series of increasingly silly films and his recordings were limited to inane soundtrack songs. Even Elvis Presley could see that he was no longer King and was in danger of being the court jester. His solution was to get back to his roots. Having grown up in Memphis, steeped in southern music, Presley felt like going home.

Everything about *From Elvis in Memphis* was surprising. But Presley kept the best for last. The final track was a soulful ballad about poverty and struggle.

'In the Ghetto' is almost political. It's an empathic story of hardship and honest toil. While Presley was now wealthy, his family had been dirt poor and it didn't take much for him to reach back and pull out the memory of those hard times. There was no question that Presley could call on the emotions. It was surprising that after so long he did.

Mac Davis, then a promising young singer/songwriter who had contributed to songs for Presley's film soundtracks, had written the ballad not intending it for Elvis. However, the singer insisted.

"With 'In the Ghetto', he was just really into it," said guitarist Reggie Young. "I remember it being stopped a few times – he just wanted to do it better. It was like he was finally doing a song with some meaning to it, with some soul – it would have to turn him on. By this time he was really enthused about what he was doing, he really cared … Instead of it just being a party, you know, go to the studio and have a party, he was really trying."

Respect Aretha Franklin

(Otis Redding) ❋ Atlantic ❋ 1967 ❋ Appears on: *I Never Loved a Man the Way I Love You*

On Valentine's Day 1967 Aretha Franklin walked into Atlantic Studios in New York City as a promising singer with six years of unfulfilled promise on her back. She left the room Lady Soul – the absolute queen of pop, the greatest female R&B singer in the history of the world. Her crowning glory was 'Respect'.

Franklin had been signed to Columbia for six years, where she made respectable jazz and R&B sides but failed to set anyone's inspiration alight. Jerry Wexler, house producer at Atlantic, heard the gospel power in Franklin's voice and brought her to Atlantic, where he matched her abilities with the southern sensibility of the Muscle Shoals sidemen – organist Spooner Oldham, guitarist Jimmy Johnson, bass player Tommy Coghill and drummer Roger Hawkins. Wexler and his team of engineer Tom Dowd and arranger/engineer Arif Mardin had created a particular brand of soul music that was harmonically sophisticated, rhythmically completely perfect and dripping with the sensuousness of R&B and the grandeur of southern gospel.

Franklin's first Atlantic side, 'I Never Loved a Man the Way I Love You', was released in February 1967 and was already on the radio. Wexler knew he was on to something. He had two other singles in hand and towards the end of the 14 February date, they turned their attention to a version of a song that had already been a hit for Otis Redding. "The song lines are great," said Redding of his version. "The band track is beautiful. It took me a whole day to write it and about twenty minutes to arrange it. We cut it once and that was it. Everybody wants respect, you know."

Everybody understood the implication of a black person demanding R-E-S-P-E-C-T in the racially charged climate of the mid-'60s. Aretha understood the repercussions of switching gender on the song. "It could be a racial situation," said Tom Dowd. "It could be a political situation, it could be just the man–woman situation. Anybody could identify with it. It cut a lot of ground. If the issue was universal, it was the particular talent that Franklin brought to the tune."

First of all Aretha sings the hell out of the tune. She's supported by her sisters Carolyn and Erma on those incredible backing vocals that just burn off the track, particularly the "sock-it-to-me" breakdown and the spelling of the title, which lifts the track into a revivalist meeting. The vocal arrangement came from Franklin herself.

According to Wexler, "She had a piano at home and she would sit there with her sisters. I put the song together with the rhythm section, but it wound up being a realisation of an arrangement that already existed in her mind.

"Aretha added another dimension to the song. This was almost a feminist clarion – whenever women heard the record, it was like a tidal wave of unity. 'A little respect when you come home' doesn't only connote respect in the sense of having concern for another's position; there's also a little lubricity in there – respect acquires the notion of being able to perform conjugally in optimum fashion. It was just a very interesting mix: an intuitive feminist outcry. A sexual statement and an announcement of dignity. And a minority person making a statement of pride without sloganeering."

The production and the playing on the track is perfect, from the opening sound of the call and response between King Curtis' sax and Johnny Johnson's guitar with the drum beat skipping across the top like a stone on a pond. The track jumps from the start and just builds from there with Aretha's piano and the backing voices. Wexler added an instrumental bridge by using a riff from 'When Something is Wrong with My Baby' and inserting it. Everything is perfectly judged. But nothing sounds laboured or sterile.

Wexler played the finished track to Otis Redding. "He looked at me with a big grin and said, 'That girl done stole my song.'"

Weather With You Crowded House

(Tim Finn/Neil Finn) ❋ Capitol ❋ 1991 ❋ Appears on: *Woodface*

The brothers Finn write sweet songs that generally disguise enormous turmoil. Both Neil and Tim Finn have demons lurking not far beneath the surface. In 1990, Neil had experienced success in America with Crowded House's debut album but the second one had failed to fire. He'd also had chronic writer's block and he turned to his brother Tim to help with inspiration. The result was a magnificent pop album. *Woodface* was a series of dark and deeply personal songs like 'Weather With You'.

"I had the opening chords E minor 7th to A7, to A9th," Tim recalled. "I had that as a strum going on the guitar and I had, [lyric] 'Walking round the room singing 'Stormy Weather''. That's all I had and I played that to Neil.

"He liked it; he came back with 'At 57 Mount Pleasant Street'. We had this place and we had this feeling of some guy walking around singing 'Stormy Weather' so things weren't that great. We had a mood and then Neil came up with, 'Things ain't cookin' in my kitchen', and that sounded like it could've almost been a chorus for a while. For a day or so that was what we had and then I'd remembered this other part, which I wrote backstage when I was doing a TV show in Portugal.

"I'd never been to Portugal before, never been since, but I loved it and I was feeling very buoyant and they made me feel like a star. I was feeling pretty wacky and pretty loved and I started singing, so I had that and then after a day or so I suddenly realised that 'always take the weather with you' would fit perfectly as a chorus. So I played it to Neil and he agreed and it all came together. You've got the verse part, and then the middle part, then the chorus. But the guitar figure is extremely hooky and it's one of the most memorable parts of the song obviously. That was Neil just jamming over those first two chords, the E minor and the A."

Relax Frankie Goes to Hollywood

(Peter Gill/Holly Johnson/Mark O'Toole) ✳ ZTT ✳ 1984 ✳ Appears on: *Hollywood's Welcome to the Pleasuredome*

Trevor Horn's father was a professional musician who played in show bands. Horn followed in his father's footsteps, spending the '70s performing in ballrooms around Britain. In the '80s he moved behind the desk and became an über producer who embraced the innovations computers offered to recording. His first hit, with the Buggles' 'Video Killed the Radio Star', was a smash. Then, Phil Spector-like, he manipulated or created a number of entities including the Art of Noise. Perhaps his most famous work, however, was with a Liverpool band called Frankie Goes to Hollywood, whom he completely reshaped in the studio.

"I saw how people reacted to songs that made them dance, because of my big band job, so I made 'Video Killed the Radio Star', a single that you could dance to," Horn said. "'Relax' was the same. It has exactly the same beat as *Saturday Night Fever* because that's what I was playing with my band every Saturday night at the Hammersmith Palais."

Frankie was mostly singer Holly Johnson, who was the only member of the group to make a significant contribution to the first Frankie album. Johnson was openly gay, which make the highly sexual 'Relax' all the more controversial.

Horn used members of Ian Dury's Blockheads and Steve Howe of Yes (of which he was a sometime member) for the instrumental work. Johnson provided the personality. The end result was a massive hit. The heavy breathing and the stuttering musical passages owed a debt to Giorgio Moroder's singles with Donna Summer.

"When I used to go to the dances in Durham with my dad in the early '60s the beat groups were appearing and everyone was afraid," said Horn. "On the one hand you had men who could read music and knew what they were playing, and on the other you had guys banging a guitar around. When we started making electronic music I imagined that the reaction we got from the rock musicians must have been similar to the one the beat groups got from people like my dad."

'Relax', with its Hi-NRG (a genre that was very popular in clubs in the mid-'80s) feel and its joyful, tongue-in-cheek lasciviousness, was indeed the shape of things to come – and it still sounds great.

Days The Kinks

(Ray Davies) ✳ PYE ✳ 1968 ✳ Appears on: *The Kink Kronikles*

By 1968, when he penned 'Days', Ray Davies was beyond the point of exhaustion. In four years he had taken the always-volatile Kinks to the top of the charts in Britain and the US, invented hard rock (or at least its prototype) and changed the way that British popsters wrote lyrics. However, by the end of the '60s the Kinks' run of hits was starting to slow. In America they were no longer as fashionable as they had been. Davies' writing was becoming more personal and eccentric.

'Days' is not another slice-of-life drama for which he had become famous, but really a gentle love song that reveals his fragile emotional state.

"I remember when I heard Ray start playing 'Days' round the piano," his brother and guitarist Dave recalled. "I was really full of emotion. It made me feel like it didn't matter if anybody didn't like it, because we were together."

"The Swingin' '60s were over," said Ray Davies. "[the] *Top of the Pops* producer put us on the last show of that decade and insisted that we sing 'Days', because he felt it was an anthem for the end of an era. That wonderful period of fertility from '63 with the Beatles emerging to '66 when we had 'Sunny Afternoon' was coming to an end – the great pop golden era. As a movement, as a period, that was the magic time."

Lay My Love Brian Eno & John Cale

(Brian Eno/John Cale) ✳ Opal ✳ 1990 ✳ Appears on: *Wrong Way Up*

Brian Eno and John Cale were the princes of avant-garde rock. Eno was a conceptualist in Roxy Music, a solo artist of great ingenuity and a producer for Ultravox, David Bowie and U2. Cale started out as a student of art music then formed the Velvet Underground, made a number of challenging solo records and produced the Stooges, Patti Smith and others. Eno and Cale had worked together, notably on the live album *June 1, 1974*. Although they had launched many pop careers, they had never themselves had a pop hit. Finally, in 1989 they attempted to make a "commercial" album.

"I thought *Wrong Way Up* was more commercial than it actually turned out to be," said Eno in retrospect. The album should have been a massive hit. 'Lay My

Love' shimmers in its keyboard melodies all piled up against sparkling rhythm tracks. In the hands of a more marketable unit the album would have been a platinum smash.

"Cale is sort of a genius," said Eno to *MOJO*. "My image of working with him is of him playing a part on the keyboard whilst talking on the phone to somebody and reading a newspaper at the same time. And he'll play great parts that way, too – music comes very easily to him, and he has to take up the rest of his intelligence by doing other things at the same time. It was nice, but very fractious at times – since we didn't use an engineer, we didn't have anyone else to blame: it was just two producers, two songwriters, and two singers, both in the same room. Two chiefs, and absolutely no Indians!"

Why Do Fools Fall in Love? Frankie Lymon & the Teenagers
(Frankie Lymon/Morris Levy) ❋ Gee ❋ 1956 ❋
Appears on: *The Very Best of Frankie Lymon and the Teenagers*

Frankie Lymon was only thirteen when he wrote a song for his girlfriend. Lymon and his similarly aged friends had a doo-wop group, the Teenagers, and the song started to get a reaction around Harlem, where they lived. The act came to the attention of George Goldner and Joe Kilskey, who recognised a hit when they heard one.

'Why Do Fools Fall in Love?' went to number one and was one of the biggest records of the doo-wop era. The song was melodically so strong that it also translated into the mainstream pop repertoire and in time became a standard.

Frankie Lymon & the Teenagers were overnight sensations. Alan Freed, rock & roll's chief impresario, had them co-headline "The Biggest Rock & Roll Show of 1956" with Bill Haley. He also cast them in the film *Rock Rock Rock*. They appeared on Ed Sullivan. They toured Europe. They turned over a lot of money. Lymon was an incredible singer and a talented writer. His melodic sensibility was way beyond most of the other doo-wop singers of the time.

Unfortunately, as for many black artists of the period, success was a double-edged sword. Lymon developed a heroin dependence and was dead before he was twenty-six.

No Surprises Radiohead

(Colin Greenwood/Jonny Greenwood/Ed O'Brien/Phil Selway/Thom Yorke) ❋
Capitol ❋ 1997 ❋ Appears on: *OK Computer*

After their first two albums, Radiohead became the saviours of British rock; they were a muscular, sometimes caustic rock & roll band with something to say. So much else was style and beats without substance.

OK Computer was to be their masterwork. Dense layers of sound mostly from the electronics kit of Jonny Greenwood, and Thom Yorke's haunting lyrics. Together with the rest of this tight-knit combo they created rock & roll like it had never been heard before.

What was it all about? Not always easy to say but it was meaningful nonetheless. The complexity of the music gave sense to the words. 'No Surprises', for instance, is about a man who feels trapped, perhaps to the point of suicide, by the mundanity of his life. In Radiohead's hands that hoary old chestnut comes alive with swelling waves of emotion – even if the emotion is regret or resignation. Ultimately there's potency in the music, which really elevates it beyond its own mundanity.

The group first wrote the song when on tour with R.E.M. in 1995 and they recorded it pretty much straight, before adding that layer of Radiohead texture. 'No Surprises' was a surprise hit of sorts, paving the way for *OK Computer*, one of the best albums of the '90s.

Jump Van Halen

(Eddie Van Halen) ❋ Warner Bros. ❋ 1984 ❋ Appears on: *1984*

"Why should rock & roll be meaningful?" Alex Van Halen asked Mikal Gilmore once. "Is sex . . . I was going to say meaningful but I guess that's the whole point. If something feels good, then it's meaningful. And since our music is designed to make people feel good, it's meaningful."

The other question, of course, is, does it matter? On *1984*, Van Halen, the biggest of the big hair groups, made something that mattered. Seven years earlier, at the height of the punk rock hysteria, Warner producer Teed Templeman discovered Van Halen playing in a suburban Los Angeles dive. Based on an appreciation for Eddie Van Halen's virtuoso guitar work and David Lee Roth's over-the-top persona, he signed the band.

Van Halen caught the next wave of heavy metal. Their first two albums sold seven million copies. Roth was a natural for MTV, which was then just breaking. They were a light version of Led Zeppelin. Flashy. Loud. Larger than life but with no evil purpose beyond pulling blonde chicks. Roth, with his long hair, his body always on

show and his ability to make fun of absolutely anything, especially himself, was a major star. Eddie was the other side of the teenage boy's dream – a genuine guitar hero who had the kung fu wisdom to shut up and let the instrument do the talking. In the back there were Alex and Michael Anthony, not saying much either.

Things changed with *1984*. Basically this was an album where Van Halen dropped the guitar for a synthesiser. The single 'Jump' was a glorious, subtle piece of pop written on keyboard. Roth wrote the lyric in a taxi on the way to the studio, and the song took metal to a new place. It was to be followed by Bon Jovi and the further legion of hair bands.

'Jump' upped everyone in the band's egos and soon Roth bailed for his solo career. But in the wake of the track heavy metal had got softer and began to dominate the charts.

The subtleties of 'Jump' mixed both art and heavy metal – David Lee Roth's thoughts about art notwithstanding. "I mean," he told Gilmore, "people might like to talk about art, but look where art is: it's in the fucking gutter, starving. Van Halen likes to keep things simple; none of this vague, symbolic shit. All we're doing is giving our daily lives melodies, beats and titles – what we sing about is what we live."

If You Leave The Hummingbirds

(Hummingbirds) ❋ RooART ❋ 1989 ❋ Appears on: *loveBUZZ*

Had the Hummingbirds come from Seattle or South Carolina rather than Canberra they would have been superstars amongst the college rock/alternative rock set.

They had all the right ingredients – cute, alternative-looking girls, goofy drummer, heart-on-sleeve-but-slightly-abstract lyrics, untogether stage act – and they had fuzz boxes and they knew how to use them. But it was not to be. It was the Hummingbirds' fate to be glorious in their obscurity.

Right from their early single on Phantom Records, the Hummingbirds had something. There was fragility, a defencelessness, that marked them from other fuzzy pop bands of the time. Robyn St Clair and Allanah Russak had both a come-hither tweeness and street smarts. They were sexy as hell. Less so were Mark Temple and guitarist/songwriter Simon Holmes, but they had other qualities. It was Holmes' determination that drove the band to the heights they reached on this debut album.

Produced by Mitch Easter, the album is a battle of guitars worthy of Dire Straits but soaked in distortion so that the sweet vocals seep through.

The songwriting here is peerless. Distance from the orthodoxy of alternative rock allowed the Hummingbirds to develop their own voice – one much more fragile than their colleagues across the Pacific. It was clean fun too, free from the maudlin Generation X despair of, say, Nirvana (although the album gets its title from a track on Nirvana's *Bleach*).

Every moment of *loveBUZZ* is a gem. 'If You Leave' is a Zen-simple lyric over a candy-coloured Sonic Youth-scape, a glorious mess of meshing guitar parts and echo chamber effects that packs a devastating emotional punch.

"The whole thing with making a record," Holmes said, "is that you can't afford to be unambitious."

Beyond the Sea Bobby Darin

(Jack Lawrence/Charles Trenet) ✳ Atco ✳ 1959 ✳ Appears on: *That's All*

Bobby Darin was targeted to be a teen heartthrob but the mantle never fitted well. In 1959 Atlantic Records president Ahmet Ertegun produced a sophisticated pop album for Darin and a star was reborn. Interestingly, the two hits from the record were both adaptations of European songs – the first being 'Mack the Knife' from

The Threepenny Opera and the other being the gorgeous 'Beyond the Sea' (or as it was known in its native France, 'La Mer').

Charles Trenet was one of France's leading singer/songwriters in the '30s and '40s. Jack Lawrence was an American lyricist who regularly contributed English lyrics to Trenet's French hits.

According to *Vanity Fair* magazine, Trenet wrote 'La Mer' shortly after the end of the war in 1945 while riding on a train. The composition borrows its title from Debussy's tone poem and also attempts to convey the changing moods of the ocean.

The song was a major hit in France and in 1946 Lawrence had a crack at the lyric. He never felt bound to merely translate. Instead he conceived the tune as a vehicle for a love song.

According to Lawrence, "I was brought in and given the song. He had written a kind of mood poem about the different moods of the sea, and how the sea affected him – the tides reflecting the skies, sometimes the clouds – and how the sea could be happy or sad. That was the thrust of the whole lyric, and I said, 'Well, I don't want to do that. I'm not going to write a poetic-type thing. I don't think that would mean anything as an American pop song.'

"I made it into a love song. There's somebody standing on the shore waiting for their lover to come back, never to sail again, so they can be together." Lawrence added the word 'beyond' and gave the song an epic quality with just that gesture.

New lyrics notwithstanding, the song didn't find an audience in America until one day in 1958 when Lawrence met Bobby Darin, who had a hit with the novelty bathing song 'Splish Splash'.

Lawrence told *Vanity Fair*, "He was just on his way up. He was very brash and arrogant, but a great talent. I gave him a copy of the song and I said, 'You might be able to do something with this'. It wasn't until maybe a year later that he called me and said, 'I'm gonna do it, but I don't like what they've done with it so far. I don't wanna do a long, drawn-out, mournful song. To me it needs a beat.' He started snapping his fingers and he said, 'I can do it that way.' I said, 'Listen, you're a very talented guy – do it your way.'"

Putting some rock & roll juice into the swing jazz was a masterful stroke that greatly benefited the song – and Darin.

Shake Some Action   The Flamin' Groovies

(Cyril Jordan/Chris Wilson) ❋ Sire ❋ 1976 ❋ Appears on: *Shake Some Action*

The Flamin' Groovies were from San Francisco but sounded like a British Invasion band direct from Carnaby Street. They were formed partly from the ashes of the Charlatans – the original San Francisco ballroom group – the scene that would later produce the Grateful Dead and the Jefferson Airplane. The Flamin' Groovies were a reaction against the long jamming of the late '60s, preferring tight pop songs in the manner of the Beatles. The group struggled through the late '60s and early '70s with projects like the *Teenage Head* album – beloved of rock critics, ignored by the public. A single, 'Slow Death', was one of the all-time great rave-up guitar records with an incredible dynamic, but it failed to chart.

In the early '70s they found themselves in the UK and wound up at Rockfield Studios, working with guitarist/producer Dave Edmunds. The group had changed somewhat since its early days but still revolved around the partnership of guitarist/singers Chris Wilson and Cyril Jordan. Still enamoured by '60s pop, on 'Shake Some Action' they took that template and made something completely new. This is a guitar duet with carefully placed vocal harmonies, but it has a particular gloss and warmth in its bottom end that makes the song immediately individual. 'Shake Some Action' is a kind of manifesto in the way of these songs – it's a rallying cry for rock & roll, which in 1976 was looking pretty light on. It failed to ignite the charts at the time but was an enormous inspiration for groups over the next few years and is the prototype for what was to be called power pop. It remains one of the all-time greatest rock & roll singles.

Ruler of My Heart   Irma Thomas

(Naomi Neville) ❋ Minit ❋ 1962 ❋ Appears on: *Ruler of Hearts*

By the age of seventeen, Irma Thomas had three children and a second husband. She had also made a hit record, the belting '(You Can Have My Husband, But Please) Don't Mess with My Man'. She moved to New Orleans producer Allen Toussaint's care at Minit records and began cutting sides with him. Toussaint wrote 'Ruler of My Heart' under his mother's maiden name (Naomi Neville) and although it didn't make the charts, it remains one of the most elegant and powerful soul tracks of the '60s. Thomas keeps her cool the whole way. Toussaint keeps the backing understated but insistent, slowly drawing closer to climaxes on the chorus but never going right over the top. Thomas' strong and warm voice is sensual and generous. There's something quite hypnotic about 'Ruler of My Heart'.

Although never a big star, Thomas had her fans: Otis Redding's version of 'Ruler' became 'Pain in My Heart' and Keith Richards encouraged the Rolling Stones to cover this tune and another Thomas song, 'Time is on My Side'.

Ramblin' Man The Allman Brothers Band

(Dickey Betts) ✷ Capricorn ✷ 1973 ✷ Appears on: *Brothers and Sisters*

The Allman Brothers Band really took off once its founder Duane Allman died. Allman was considered to be one of the supreme guitar players of the day. The group's dual guitar/dual drum sound had been their calling card and yet with Duane gone they blossomed. Second guitarist Dickey Betts stepped up to the plate, writing an album's worth of tunes, and they shifted the group from blues jams into a country tempo that eventually became known as southern rock.

"Duane was a very strong leader," said the manager and proprietor of Capricorn records Phil Walden. "After he died there was a real struggle between Dickey Betts, who leaned very strongly towards country, and Gregg, who probably found country music offensive."

The Allman Brothers were mostly an electric guitar rock band although Betts and Allman were leaning towards acoustic music when Duane died. Betts had played Allman his song 'Ramblin' Man' as early as 1971.

"You get a hint of 'Ramblin' Man' on *Eat a Peach* with 'Blue Sky'," said producer Johnny Sandlin. "Generally their harmonies had been very pentatonic and blues-based, and when Dickey wrote 'Ramblin' Man' it was very major, very up-sounding, and it took a while to enjoy that."

It didn't take the public long. The song was a smash. The *Brothers and Sisters* album had a positive message – right from the picture of a blonde hippie child on the cover through to the country-style photography. The sounds of the record were strong on traditional values – lots of dobro and slide guitar and warm piano. 'Ramblin' Man' was a country lyric – the notion of the hobo on the road was a southern stereotype and the world was ready for the rise of the south. More than any of the other Allman records this sets the template for the success of Lynard Skynard, the Charlie Daniels Band and a resurgence of interest in bluegrass and country.

But 'Ramblin' Man' was to prove the end of the Allman Brothers. Almost immediately after its release they vaulted into the top echelon of American groups and one of the most popular live acts. But the Olympic-level drug taking continued, as did the personal squabbles. Their subsequent records were just a pale imitation of past glories.

"I remember certain high spots, but what I really remember is bein' afraid a lot," said Gregg Allman. "I don't know, when my brother went … you never know how much you're leanin' on somebody 'til they die. And that pissed me off with myself, and pissed me off with him for dyin'. It was just a whole circus of changes, man."

When the group's roadie and drug courier Scooter Herring was busted for drugs, Gregg Allman testified against him. The rest of the group fired the last Allman brother from the Allman Brothers Band.

My Ever Changing Moods   The Style Council

(Paul Weller) ❋ Polydor ❋ 1984 ❋ Appears on: *Cafe Bleu*

Paul Weller's changing moods played a significant part in changing a nation. In 1977 the Jam arrived as the third part of the punk triumvirate. They represented youth (Weller was only seventeen) and Englishness – a tradition going back to the Who and the Kinks. While others conquered America, the Jam had a three-year lock on the UK singles' charts and Weller became a national hero. So, when he broke up the Jam in 1982 for a new direction in music, he took a large section of Britain on the journey.

The other half of the Style Council was organist Mick Talbot; a soul-jazz feel replaced the Motown rave-ups of the Jam. 'My Ever Changing Moods' is a good example of the Style Council's debt to Curtis Mayfield with its discreet but intoxicating groove.

Weller hung up his Rickenbacker guitar in favour of Talbot's keyboards. This was indicative of a shift away from rock music and into the more sophisticated realm of club music. In Britain pop music is an important medium to express changes in the culture. The Style Council did exactly that. The sweaty authenticity of punk rock was junked in favour of a middle-class aspirational lifestyle where fashion and design and modernism existed in a disciplined, engaged and thoughtful lifestyle. Punk symbolised catharsis and abandon. The Style Council stood for improvement and change and reason and control. Punks wore rags held together by safety pins; the Style Council were casual but neat with jumpers tied around their shoulders in case the weather should become inclement. This shift of values has been a part of British popular culture ever since. 'My Ever Changing Moods' is a manifesto for a lifestyle unencumbered by ideology. And it has a nice tune.

Oscillations Silver Apples

(Simeon/Warren Stanley) ✻ Kapp ✻ 1968 ✻ Appears on: *Silver Apples*

For a moment in 1968, Silver Apples looked like the future of music. The duo of Dan Taylor and Simeon played (respectively) tuned drums and the Simeon, which was an assemblage of oscillators and other electronic junk wired together to make music. This was a garage version of what serious music composers had been doing since Percy Grainger left his country garden. But Silver Apples lived in a rock & roll context. They took their name from a Yeats poem. And as Simeon noted, "The silver part reminded us of the solder that held all the junk together, and the apples we felt linked us to New York."

The Simeon was made of at least nine oscillators, each tuned differently, making rhythmic noise and rough melodies accompanied by the drums, and sometimes poetry. For a time the Silver Apples toured widely and held down a residency at the ultra-hip Max's Kansas City. The Mayor of New York commissioned them to write and perform a piece celebrating the first moonwalk in 1969. The Apples were briefly the toast of the underground, performing the scores to off-off-Broadway theatre. "Theatre producer and director John Vacarro had a reputation for putting on the most outrageous theatrical experiences in New York. He was producing a musical called *Cockstrong* and wanted Silver Apples to create the music for it," Simeon recalled. The star of the show was to be one of New York's most famous transvestites named Jackie Curtis. There was one dance number called 'The Kama Sutra' where we were allowed to improvise for ten minutes while the players, in their clothes, tried to accomplish all the sexual positions, both couples and groups. One night the audience seemed to be very into it and Danny and I decided to keep it going a while longer. I didn't realise how physically demanding it was for the actors and after a while they started screaming for mercy. I thought they were just acting and kept going. Soon there was open rebellion on the stage and the actors, while still in their contorted Kama Sutra positions, were shaking their fists at me and giving the 'cut' sign with their fingers across the throat. They were really glaring at me and the audience was roaring with delight. I finally gave in, and Jackie Curtis went into her final number, 'Cockstrong', during which this enormous, erect, papier-mâché penis slowly expanded out over the stage pointing at the audience."

Surprisingly, commercial success never came their way after that. Instead they have gone into history as the precursors of Suicide, Orchestral Manoeuvres in the Dark, the Human League, Brian Eno, Kraftwerk, the Prodigy and electronica acts everywhere.

Stuck in a Moment You Can't Get Out Of U2

(Bono/U2) ✳ Island ✳ 2001 ✳ Appears on: *All That You Can't Leave Behind*

Michael Hutchence, the lead singer of INXS, hung himself in a hotel room in 1997, apparently a suicide. Hutchence's life had been difficult in the previous few years. His relationship with TV personality Paula Yates was volatile and she was the mother of his child. INXS had not been going well, nor his singing career. He had developed a heroin habit. He was also being treated for depression. It was all too much. Yates, who was in the UK at the time, claimed that Hutchence's death was from sexual misadventure. The facts of the night could never be proven one way or the other but suicide seems the likely outcome.

There seems to be a moment with many suicides where the world closes in so tight that there is no way out and this song goes right into the moment.

U2 and INXS were of the same era. Moreover, a personal friendship had developed between Hutchence and Bono that went beyond the professional. Hutchence's death had a profound effect on him.

"I think other people who have lost a mate to suicide will all tell you the same thing – just the overpowering guilt that you weren't there for that person," he told Chris Heath. "As anyone around here will tell you, friendship is a thing that I hold very sacred. So it really threw me. Can you really be that busy that you don't notice your mate on the slide, as it were? I am the most loyal, and the most unreliable, friend. It's the way I am. So I just remember feeling this overpowering sense of guilt. And then anger. And annoyance. That song is an argument. It's a row between mates. You're kind of trying to slap somebody around the face, trying to wake them up out of an idea. In my case it's a row. Although, oddly enough, we discussed suicide a few times. And we both agreed how pathetic it was.

"So in the song, I'm right there – it's like, just wanting to be in that half an hour. I wanted to have that argument in that half an hour. But I didn't put down that it was about Michael Hutchence because, for me, songs, I never make things specific to anything. And I didn't feel comfortable saying it while Paula was alive, because I knew it was important to her that he didn't commit suicide. But he did, and we have to say that. And I know the people that he called that night, and I know.

"I felt the biggest respect I could pay him was not to write some stupid soppy fucking song, so I wrote a really tough, nasty little number. Sort of, you know, slapping him around the head. And I'm sorry, but that's how it came out for me."

Surrender Cheap Trick

(Rick Nielsen) ✳ Epic ✳ 1978 ✳ Appears on: *Heaven Tonight*

Cheap Trick was like a fifth column in the British Invasions, a group from America's mid-west who loved British pop. Guitarist Rick Nielsen was an Anglophile with a deep understanding of the quirky British bands such as the Move with their musical witticisms. They also envied the British ability to frock up and present a visual as well as musical package. For all of that, though, Cheap Trick was from the Midwest and on 'Surrender' they recorded the first 'dysfunctional family' hit.

"Mommy's all right, Daddy's all right/They just seem a little weird," sang Robin Zander in a beautifully high voice. He posed the question of what to do when your parents are smoking pot and making out on the couch. The answer – get out the KISS records. Cheap Trick outlined the slacker manifesto.

'Surrender', a song that had been around since the group's first album (*Cheap Trick*, 1977), was on their third. It was given the power pop treatment by producer Tom Werman. The combination of big power chords and repetitive sixteenth-note passages recalled the Who's 'Baba O'Riley'. This was indeed a teen anthem. Cheap Trick put the power back into pop.

Tangled Up in Blue Bob Dylan

(Bob Dylan) ✳ Columbia ✳ 1975 ✳ Appears on: *Blood on the Tracks*

Bob Dylan often refers to 'Tangled Up in Blue' in terms of it being a painting. Part of the mystery in the song is the shifts in perspective as though the narrator is sometimes a protagonist and sometimes an observer, and the action takes place in the present and the past simultaneously. It's an ambitious lyric to say the least.

Dylan recorded the seven-minute epic twice in September 1974, and then re-recorded it in late December 1974 in Minnesota. Each time there were subtle changes in the lyric. Dylan, who claims the version on 1984's *Real Live* is the best, has frequently altered the song's words. The details in the song are flexible. It's the emotional core that's constant.

Whether the song somehow documents the writer's relationship with his wife is impossible to know. His son Jakob has said that the *Blood on the Tracks* album is like listening to his parents arguing. In any case, Dylan has certainly disguised the characters enough to remove it from the historical to the metaphysical. Dylan here again refers to getting a woman out of a jam as he has referred to Sara ten years previously. The scenes down on Montague Street, however, recall his years in the Village before he became famous.

The gist of 'Tangled Up in Blue' is that we live lives governed by the winds of fate. Change is constant – who we are and where we are and what happens to us is in the lap of the gods.

"That was another one of those things where I was trying to do something that I didn't think had ever been done before in terms of trying to tell a story and be a present character in it without it being some kind of fake, sappy attempted tear jerker," said Dylan. "I was trying to be somebody in the present time while conjuring up a lot of past images. I was trying to do it in a conscious way. I used to be able to do it in an unconscious way, but I wasn't into it that way any more. That particular song was built like that, and it was always open to be cut better. But I had no particular reason to do it because I'd already made the record.

"See, what I was trying to do had nothing to do with the characters or what was going on. I was trying to do something that I don't know if I was prepared to do. I wanted to defy time, so that the story took place in the present and past at the same time. When you look at a painting, you can see any part of it or see all of it together. I wanted that song to be like a painting."

Oye Como Va Santana

(Tito Puente) ✻ Columbia ✻ 1970 ✻ Appears on: *Abraxas*

When Michael Goldberg asked Mexican guitarist Carlos Santana for the secret to his two-decade career, he answered, "They say it's the merging of the congas and timbales with the electric guitar. But I feel the main reason, the prime motivation that gets people out of their houses to see us and buy our albums, is the cry." The cry is Santana's unique guitar style – part blues, part fusion and a lot of Latin.

Carlos Santana lived in San Francisco in the Summer of Love and started playing his Latin blues at the same time as the Jefferson Airplane and the Grateful Dead were doling psychedelic rock. Unlike the white groups, Santana's mostly Hispanic band relished intricate melody lines and polyrhythms.

The group appeared at Woodstock and their eight-minute workout of 'Soul Sacrifice' was a highlight of the subsequent film. On the back of that promotion Santana became a massive hit. A self-titled first album was a smash and its sequel, *Abraxas*, spent a year in the charts. On *Abraxas*, Santana perfected the merging of Latin, jazz and blues styles together, bringing songs such as Tito Puente's 'Oye Como Va' to a rock audience.

"*Abraxas* was the peak of that band on that level I would say," said Santana. "When I hear the word 'Abraxas', it brings to mind Miles Davis – he was hanging around a lot and calling us up, and he liked the direction of the band. And Jimi did too – a lot of people were becoming aware that this bunch of guys had something to say that musically was made in Chicago … and the Rolling Stones got congas and cowbells and all kinds of things. So that album is very significant, mainly because of the colours and the instruments that it brought to rock & roll. It injected a whole lot of stuff – Bo Diddley led to that beat, which comes from Latin music to the blues, and I feel we did it again to rock & roll, to a certain extent. Not that we were the first, but we were just there in a way that nobody was doing it – Motown already had congas, but they didn't have them upfront, or timbales, and they didn't have a guitar upfront. That's what *Abraxas* reminds me of – a group of people who became significant, if you will."

When Doves Cry Prince & the Revolution

(Prince) ❋ Warner Bros. ❋ 1984 ❋ Appears on: *Purple Rain*

Surreal, psychedelic and sexy, 'When Doves Cry' was Prince reaching a new level of maturity as a writer and performer.

The song bears the influence of his band at the time, the Revolution. Its arrangement is somewhat more pop and sophisticated than the funk of the previous album.

According to engineer Peggy McCreary, Prince "came in, cut it and mixed it in a day. He was listening to it playing back and just popped the bass out." It was unheard of for any major album to go without a bass part, especially one in the R&B field, but Prince insisted. His whole process in recording the song was to pile up a complete and conventional arrangement of the song and then to nip and tuck so that the spaces created tensions and made the single sound unsettling.

Unlike so much of Prince's previous work, 'When Doves Cry' is almost baroque in its romanticism. It was the peak of his Purple period – characterised, of course, by the film *Purple Rain*, which Prince was conceiving as he wrote the music to the album of the same name. The music is closer to traditional R&B and jazz than funk and initially caused some fear in the Warner Bros. ranks. "They were a little afraid," said engineer David Z. "They didn't know what to do with it because it was drastically different."

The public did though. It was the biggest selling single of 1984 ahead of Springsteen and Jackson.

Born in the USA Bruce Springsteen

(Bruce Springsteen) ❋ Columbia ❋ 1984 ❋ Appears on: *Born in the USA*

'Born in the USA' was written as an acoustic protest song for his earlier album, *Nebraska*, but Springsteen "electrified" it with the E Street Band and created one of the great (if often misunderstood) anthemic moments in rock.

"The sound of 'Born in the USA' was martial, modal and straight ahead," said Springsteen of the song's central contradiction. "The lyrics dealt with the problems Vietnam vets faced when they came back home after fighting 'the only war that America had ever lost'. In order to understand the song's intent, you needed to invest a certain amount of time and effort to absorb both the music and the words . . .

"The first guy I played the finished version for was a Vietnam veteran . . . He came into the studio and sat between two large speakers at the front of the console. I turned up the volume. He sat there for a moment listening to the first couple of verses, and then a big smile crossed his face.

"On the other hand, for years after the release of the album, I had little kids in red bandannas knocking on my door with their trick-or-treat bags, singing, 'I was born in the USA . . .' They were not particularly well versed in the 'had a brother at Khe Sahn' lyric but they all had plenty of lung power when the chorus rolled around. I guess the same fate awaited Woody Guthrie's 'This Land is Your Land' around the campfire. But that didn't make me feel any better."

The song became the title track to Springsteen's follow up to *Nebraska*. The album was two years in the making and dominated the charts for more than a year after release. It was on this album that Springsteen translated his skill with personal, raw, folk-inspired material into full-tilt, electric rock & roll.

Bye Bye Love   The Everly Brothers

(Felice Bryant/Boudleaux Bryant) ✳ Cadence ✳ 1957 ✳ Appears on: *The Everly Brothers*

Husband and wife team Felice and Boudleaux Bryant were struggling songwriters in the late '50s. Boudleaux had been a working country musician and their songs were mostly in that vein. With the arrival of rock & roll and Elvis Presley, though, country music changed and the Bryants easily adapted to the tougher, more urgent sound. One of their early songs, 'Bye Bye Love', had been rejected almost thirty times when it came to the attention of producer Archie Bleyer, who had signed Don and Phil Everly to his Cadence label.

According to legend, the brothers were nonplussed about the song but were appreciative of the fee of $64 each that they received for the session.

The Everly Brothers were a little bit country and a little bit hillbilly. Their close harmony singing was sunny and warm and it suited the pace of rockabilly – although they were not strictly a rockabilly act. 'Bye Bye Love' bounces along with an enthusiasm and joy that runs counter to the dark heartbreak sentiments, but it hardly matters. This is pure teenage joy.

Love in Vain The Rolling Stones

(Robert Johnson) ✻ Decca ✻ 1970 ✻ Appears on: *Get Yer Ya Yas Out*

Robert Johnson's 'Love in Vain' was cut for the *Let It Bleed* album, but this version recorded on the 1969 tour – probably at Baltimore Civic Centre – is the best blues recording the Rolling Stones ever made. The Taylor and Richards team that was first tested on this tour was the most fertile period for the Rolling Stones. Taylor was a very talented player, particularly with fluid and inventive melodic lines to counterpoint Richards, and they bring a completely new life to Robert Johnson's delicate blues song.

The rest of the album sounds like a hurricane of slashing guitars and horns. Then, on this song, they pull it right back to a funeral march pace, Charlie Watts keeping time like the clock of doom. Mick Jagger's vocal is full of dragged out, vulnerable, yearning syllables working against the beat. As he draws the note, Watts' kick drum thumps in punctuation. Then the guitars slowly come up behind with gorgeous notes left to float in the ether or to slide against each other. There's a wonderful to-and-fro effect, a tension and release that transcends the song itself.

Sweet Dreams (Are Made of This) Eurythmics

(Annie Lennox/Dave Stewart) ✻ RCA ✻ 1982 ✻
Appears on: *Sweet Dreams (Are Made of This)*

It wasn't singer Annie Lennox's sexual ambiguity that made 'Sweet Dreams (Are Made of This)' the most controversial single of 1982. It was the fact that the song, which topped charts all around the world, was made, effectively, in a home studio. Forget the gigantism that had taken over show business. This was do-it-yourself delivering on its promise.

Then there were the sounds – all electronic drums and layers of synthesiser – that for once didn't sound cold and synthetic. With one single, guitarist Dave Stewart created a new direction for pop to go in.

Stewart and Lennox had been in New Wave band the Tourists. When that combo split they began working with friends from the German electronic scene – Conny Plank, members of Deutsche Amerikanische Freundschaft, Can drummer Jackie Liebezeit and Holger Czukay all contributed to the first Eurythmics album. Stewart quickly moved on, however, creating a new style of synth-pop that owed a debt to Kraut rock but was more in the style of British pop.

"People think that album is so high tech," said Stewart. "But we couldn't even afford a claptrap – the classic disco thing, you know, that goes ckkk-ckkk-ckkk! It's just me and Annie, banging on the wall with a handful of picture-frames. If we'd had the money, of course, we would have used a claptrap. But not having it made us a lot more inventive.

"That was basically Conny and Holger's influence. They'd always say, 'If there's no fun involved, if you just press a button and *that* does that, then you tend to just say, oh, we'll use that button to do that and this one to do this.' And your music just goes further and further away from you."

For the second album, Stewart and Lennox extracted themselves from their management and incurred a huge burden of debt. 'Sweet Dreams' was their DIY manifesto.

"We had been so stitched up when we started out as the Tourists in '78, and even as Eurythmics at the beginning, we just had to take things into our own hands," recalled Annie. "That line in 'Sweet Dreams' about being 'used and abused' refers directly to my own experiences. Not just in love, but in this business too. Right at the beginning Dave said to me, 'Annie we must have a manifesto', so we wrote down all the things we liked to do on a big sheet of paper."

The Eurythmics also understood how to present themselves through video. MTV was then still a novelty and Stewart and Lennox were among the first to use videos to break records internationally.

"We discovered that America was very reactionary about how somebody looked. I suddenly became this threatening entity, which I quite liked but I'd never intended it to be that controversial," said Lennox. "I thought the ambiguity gave me a degree of power, because up to that point women had been portraying – and betraying – themselves in an overtly sexual way, which is fine, but it didn't suit me. We also felt there should be something different about Eurythmics' presentation. We weren't too sure if we were a group or not and at one point said categorically we weren't. We wanted to wear the same sorts of clothes so we could say that, at least visually, there was no difference between us.

"'Sweet Dreams' kicked things off in a big way. It was a definite hit, and a hit everywhere. You no longer had to prove yourself to anybody. All of a sudden it felt like a lot of doors were flung open, like the world wanted to know you, and I got a bit scared. It really was like going on a roller coaster. Our tour seemed to go on forever, and though I could have chosen not to, I wanted to see how far the thing could go."

Hurricane Bob Dylan

(Bob Dylan/Jacques Levy) ❋ Columbia ❋ 1976 ❋ Appears on: *Desire*

The sound of Dylan's *Desire* album, of which 'Hurricane' is the best song, was a consequence of the way the album was made. Dylan was separated from his wife and children and revisiting the haunts of his youth, writing songs with another lyricist and recording with pick-up bands. The violin that dominates the sound of the album was played by Scarlett Riviera whom Dylan had seen walking down the street and then asked along to the sessions. This was the first time Riviera had been in a recording studio but her playing gives a gypsy wind to the album.

'Hurricane' is based on the experiences of Ruben 'Hurricane' Carter, a boxer. In 1966 he and another person were convicted of the triple murder of three people in a bar. Carter was sentenced to life in prison for the crimes. While incarcerated he wrote a book, *The 16th Round*, which Dylan read and responded to.

"I think I ran into Jacques [Levy] downtown and we went off and just wrote some songs," said Dylan. "The people from the Hurricane Carter movement kept calling me and writing me. And Hurricane sent me his book, which I read and which really touched me. I felt that the man was just innocent, from his writings and knowing that part of the country. So I went to visit him and was really behind him, trying to get a new trial. So that was one of the things I brought to Jacques, too. I said, 'Why don't you help me write this song and see if we can do something?' So we wrote 'Hurricane', and then we just wrote a bunch of others. An album came out of it."

The Hurricane Carter story had so many of Dylan's themes already – racism and unfair imprisonment had been subjects of his songs going back to his early folk days.

Dylan and Levy, a playwright, recast the story and trial of Hurricane. It's an amazing piece of songwriting with a multitude of characters and action. Clearly it's part of a tradition going back to Guthrie and the old folk ballads. However, Dylan and Levy provide so many layers to the narrative that the song is completely unlike any other.

The extensive narrative flows on the violin line. The melody rushes forward, maintaining the tension and the sense of frantic activity.

'Hurricane' was a major hit single for Dylan in November 1975. As a result of the publicity from Dylan's crusade, Carter was freed in March 1976. In November 1976 Carter was retried and found guilty. In 1985 Carter's appeal against his sentence was upheld on procedural grounds and he was released from prison after nineteen years. The story was recently made into a feature film with Denzel Washington in the lead.

Mongoloid Devo

(Gerald V Casale) ✳ Stiff ✳ 1977 ✳ Appears on: *Hardcore Devo*

Devo started out angry. Based in the industrial city of Akron, Ohio, Devo was a bunch of art students (or should have been) who developed a group that satirised the straight world of Middle America. They did it with primitive guitars and synthesisers and a few riffs. Their first sessions took place in December 1976 with a four-track Revox tape recorder in the garage. It was so cold that Mark Mothersbaugh played guitar with his gloves on.

Mittens notwithstanding, Devo's sound on their first release was jerky and angular and squeaking. The beats were speeded up and the time signatures suggested a sort of spastic rock sound. It fitted perfectly with the deconstructed fashion of punk rock. Nonetheless, Devo got their first single, 'Jocko Homo', and 'Mongoloid' out of it.

When asked by Jon Savage to describe the smell of the song 'Mongoloid', writer Jerry Casale replied, "Pabulum and bacon frying. Hospitals."

Devo – Jerry Casale, Mark Mothersbaugh, Jim Mothersbaugh, Bob Casale and Alan Myers – were very big with the concepts. The idea of Devolution suggested that the human race was getting more stupid or de-evolving. 'Mongoloid' is about a man with an extra gene who just fits right into the button-down-world of the modern post-industrial society.

"Devolution's a big idea about the way things are," said writer and bass player Gerald Casale. "Everyone has a big idea about the way things are. Whether they admit it or not, a lot of people's ideas masquerade themselves as non-ideas, which we find the most dishonest.

"Devo just has the biggest, best and most interesting idea about reality that allows people to discover things, which is exactly what other ideas don't allow. Other ideas begin by ignoring what's there so their idea doesn't account for the whole picture. It's like when people thought that the earth was at the centre of the universe but the movement of certain planets didn't really match up to that idea – they couldn't make it match because their idea of what was happening was at basis wrong. And when the premise is wrong, everything else that follows is sick."

Our Lips are Sealed The Go-Go's

(Terry Hall/Jane Wiedlin) ❋ IRS ❋ 1981 ❋ Appears on: Beauty and the Beat

"I get really annoyed when I see these periodic women-in-rock articles, and the Go-Go's are not even mentioned," said bass player Kathy Valentine. "I don't see how you can omit a band that was the first female band to play all their instruments, write their own songs – and we were on a little label ..." In fact the first all-girl rock & roll band was Fanny some ten years earlier than when the Go-Go's hit the charts, but no previous group had made such a spectacular impact on the music scene as this punk rock band from Los Angeles.

Original bass player Margot, singer Belinda Carlisle and guitarist Jane Wiedlin were all part of the formative Los Angeles punk scene, living with the other scenesters/dropouts at the Canterbury apartment house in Hollywood, determined to get a band together.

By all accounts their first two years showed enthusiasm rather than talent but by 1980 the group had started to find its voice.

"When I joined the band, they had a lot of songs that were politically oriented," said guitarist Charlotte Caffey. "I can remember asking them why not take advantage of the word Go-Go? You don't have to do sweet, power-pop stuff. We started writing songs using the idea of the name of the band rather than the hard-core punk we played in the beginning because, I imagine, it was the easiest to play."

Just the existence of an all-girl band without a male svengali was a political statement. Like other punk groups of the period, they knew their '60s pop and for their first album enlisted producer Richard Gottehrer, whose credits went back to the Angels' 'My Boyfriend's Back' and the Strangeloves' 'I Want Candy' and forward to the first Blondie and Richard Hell albums.

The Go-Go's stayed true to punk rock even as they improved their playing and writing. Their songs had the energy and excitement of punk rock – they were still far from slick. The album *Beauty and the Beat* featured great tunes, especially 'Our Lips are Sealed', written by Wieldin and Specials singer Terry Hall after the two groups had toured together and a romance ensued. 'Our Lips' had the hallmarks of classic girl group pop updated to the '80s.

The Go-Go's announced girl power before it was fashionable. "The first reviews we got that really made me feel that this band was going to work said, 'The Go-Go's are to punk rock what botulism is to tuna'," said Caffey. "Stuff like that really inspired me. We wrote our best songs after we heard that."

She Sells Sanctuary The Cult

(Ian Astbury/Billy Duffy) ✳ Beggars Banquet ✳ 1985 ✳ Appears on: *Love*

Guitarist Billy Duffy recalled that his idea of a good night out was to see Uriah Heep and then cross the road to catch Johnny Thunders. That was pretty much the Cult – heavy metal crunch and punk style.

Originally a quartet called Southern Death Cult, they shrunk to being just the Cult with Duffy and singer Ian Astbury. Their look was part-glam and part-goth. Astbury was a devotee of the American Indians and their mystical beliefs.

Duffy's huge guitar sound was a distinctive feature as was Astbury's oft-ghoulish howl. Their sound was big and dumb but occasionally irresistible as on this, their first real hit. "I took a perverse pride from writing as many Top 20 singles as I did using the same three chords," said Duffy. "AC/DC did it, Metallica did it." 'Sanctuary' was more stripped back though with an incredible force and the slightest touch of Astbury's mysticism. Duffy lets fly with his guitar zooming off on sparkling lead runs and riding feedback swells like a pro surfer. He has the epic quality of the Edge while keeping the dirtiness of Johnny Thunders. It's one of the great metal guitar breaks. The song is their highpoint and a key track for suburban goths everywhere.

Gloria Them

(Van Morrison) ✳ Decca ✳ 1965 ✳ Appears on: *Them*

"I was sitting in my room one day, and I picked up my guitar and I played these chords, exactly this . . ." Van Morrison told an audience before plucking out the stuttering riff of 'Gloria'. In 1964 when he wrote the song, Morrison was the singer in the blues band Them which held down a residency at Belfast's Maritime Hotel playing stormy versions of Leadbelly and Bo Diddley, Sonny Boy Williamson and the like.

'Gloria' was cut at Them's first Decca recording session on 5 July 1964. Morrison, volatile at the best of times, was extremely nervous at this first session. According to Clinton Heylin's biography, manager Mervyn Solomon recalled, "Van worked very hard on those sessions. When we did the rehearsing in the studio Van was not too bad, but by the time they came in for the session, all he kept doing was shaking. He was really nervous."

Producer Dick Rowe pushed Morrison hard, particularly on 'Gloria'. He wanted the singer to "really shout – make it aggressive". That's exactly what Morrison did.

In the end 'Gloria' became the flip side to Them's forgettable first single 'Don't Start Me Crying Now'. A year later Chicago garage band the Shadows of Knight covered 'Gloria' and turned it into a smash hit. Consequently, Them was born.

'Gloria' became a perennial with '60s garage bands and was later transformed by Patti Smith on her debut album. In the meantime the original was re-released and gave Them their start.

It's the song of a stalker. It's a hard-blues feeling worthy of Howlin' Wolf but ragged as well, with its trademark door-knock drum break and the spelling G-L-O-R-I-A. Mostly though, Morrison summons up a steamy, confused lust. You can feel his nervousness as he sings as though his life depended on it.

Lonely Avenue Ray Charles

(Doc Pomus) ✳ Atlantic ✳ 1955 ✳ Appears on: *Atlantic Rhythm & Blues 1947–1974*

Ray Charles takes this Doc Pomus blues and squeezes every bit of gospel from it. A Memphis writer once asked Charles about reconciling the blues and gospel, but

the genius saw no difference: "I was raised in a Baptist church. What you talking about?" he said. "I went to revival meetings; I went to BYPU [Baptist Young People's Union] meetings on Sunday as a kid. And on Sunday you went to church in the morning, you stayed there all day, you went to church on Sunday night, and if there was a revival you went to all those things. I was around religious music, just like I was around the blues. Both had an effect on me."

'Lonely Avenue' showcases Charles' magnificent, powerful command of the piano and his unique sense of tempo. The slow blues has the sense of space and isolation the title suggests. Charles brings the force of his personality and his beautiful, expressive voice to bear on the session so that a song about forlorn love becomes positively existential.

"We were more or less monitors. We provided a soundboard," said Jerry Wexler who, with Ahmet Ertegun, co-produced most of Charles' Atlantic sides. "He'd call me up while he was on the road and say he had this tune worked out and ask us to set up a studio for such and such a time. He'd tell me he needed some girl singers to back him up or a country type of guitar player. Then, in the studio, Ray would listen to our opinions regarding tempo and balance. As for changing an arrangement, this very, very rarely happened. It was almost unthinkable; the issue never came up.

"Ray's genius is never more apparent than in the recording studio, where his best efforts go into every record he makes, no matter how long it takes or how difficult the job. You can be sure that when you hear a Ray Charles record, whether or not you happen to like the song, you will never hear a record made with more enthusiasm or devotion – because Ray is like that."

I Knew These People Ry Cooder

(Ry Cooder) ✳ Warner Bros. ✳ 1989 ✳ Appears on: *Paris, Texas*

Paris, Texas, directed by Wim Wenders and written by Sam Shepard, is an abstract film on god knows what – fathers, America, whatever. German director Wenders is especially attuned to the power of music and he found an ideal collaborator in

Ry Cooder. Much of the film is simply long stretches of lonely desert, which is made into a poetic meditation by Cooder's spare, precise and emotive guitar playing. Wenders cast Harry Dean Stanton in the lead role of Travis. Stanton was not only a gifted character actor but also a sometime country and western singer. Nastassja Kinski plays Jane, the wife who abandoned Travis to work in a peep show.

"*Paris, Texas* is a film that if you push it the wrong way, you blow it out of the water," said Cooder. "If you breathe on it wrong, it's gone. Wim Wenders took this spooky bottleneck piece I'd recorded years ago ['Dark is the Night' by Blind Willie Johnson] and put it in what they call a temp track to show me the kind of thing he was thinking about. Once I saw the film, it was easy for me to place that musical thought here and there like glue. That's like a perfect career job. I don't expect too many jobs like that because there aren't too many films like *Paris, Texas*."

After wandering a deep, vast desert, Travis and Jane meet across one-way glass in the peep show. 'I knew these people' is the dialogue between them. There's a cracked sadness in Harry Dean's voice as he delivers his largely improvised words, full of romance and love and madness. You can tell he used to be a singer by the rhythm in his delivery. Then Cooder's guitar and Jim Dickinson's piano start up in the background with a lonesome Mexicali tune. It is so terribly heartbreaking. It could only be delivered by an actor with Stanton's background, who can make the mythical appear in the flesh.

Ode to Billie Joe Bobbie Gentry

(Bobbie Gentry) ❋ Capitol ❋ 1967 ❋ Appears on: *Ode to Billie Joe*

Perhaps the greatest mystery of the '60s was what Billie Joe MacAllister had thrown off the Tallahatchie Bridge and what he had done with a girl up on Choctaw Ridge. This question is the basis of Bobbie Gentry's 'Ode to Billie Joe', which topped the charts in 1967. The narrator is at the family dinner table as Billie Joe MacAllister's suicide – he eventually jumped off the Tallahatchie Bridge – is told amongst the news of the day. A year passes and the family survives tragedy and good fortune, but the dark mystery of Billie Joe hangs over the singer's life.

Set against a spare acoustic backing and strings, the song is a haunting southern Gothic drama, uncannily haunting. Gentry, then twenty-three, wrote the song (and initially produced it as well).

Originally seven minutes long, it's said that Capitol shortened the song to four minutes and pressed it as the flip side to Gentry's debut single, 'Mississippi Delta'. There has been speculation that the mystery of Billie Joe lies in the lost verses, but

that seems unlikely. If a longer version existed it would have appeared on an album by now. A 1976 movie, which suggested that Billie Joe was a closeted gay man and he was throwing a rag doll off the bridge, is also unconvincing. The fact that the drop from the bridge in Greenwood, Mississippi, is only 20 feet and unlikely to kill anyone is also irrelevant.

"Those questions are of secondary importance in my mind," said Gentry. "The story of Billie Joe has two more interesting underlying themes," she said. "First, the illustration of a group of people's reactions to the life and death of Billie Joe, and its subsequent effect on their lives, is made. Second, the obvious gap between the [narrator] and her mother is shown when both women experience a common loss (first Billie Joe, and later, Papa), and yet Mama and the girl are unable to recognise their mutual loss or share their grief."

Quite clearly 'Billie Joe' signalled the arrival of a major talent. Gentry's smoky tenor voice was pure southern sexuality – which the large brunette 'do and the beautiful dark eyes confirmed. Gentry had a rare talent for telling southern Gothic stories. 'Billie Joe' was influential in starting a torrent of 'behind closed doors' country songs.

Gentry, though, was a real original and no pop country singer has come close to replicating her dark majesty. "I'm completely responsible for it. It's totally my own from inception to performance," she said. "I originally produced 'Ode to Billie Joe' and most of my other records, but a woman doesn't stand much chance in a recording studio. A staff producer's name was nearly always put on the records."

Running Up That Hill (A Deal With God) Kate Bush

(Kate Bush) ✳ EMI ✳ 1985 ✳ Appears on: *Hounds of Love*

This duet between Peter Gabriel and Kate Bush was initially titled 'Deal with God'. "For me, that is the title," said Bush, "but I was told that if I insisted the radio stations in at least ten countries would refuse to play it because it had 'God' in the title – Spain, Italy, America, lots of them. I thought it was ridiculous. Still, especially after *The Dreaming*, I decided I couldn't be bloody-minded. You have to weigh up the priorities. Not creatively compromise, but not be so obsessive that ... I had to give the album a chance."

This song and its album represented a more mature phase for the idiosyncratic British singer/songwriter. She had steadfastly avoided getting her private life into the tabloids; however, her music was clearly personal and the specifics changed only slightly. Whether this song was part of an affair with Peter Gabriel or what the specifics of her marital difficulties were is not spelt out, but *Hounds of Love* is an album about coming to terms with the onset of mid-life. Much of the artifice of Bush's early hits was gone and what remained was infinitely more interesting.

Layla Derek & the Dominos

(Eric Clapton/Jim Gordon) ✳ Atco ✳ 1970 ✳ Appears on: *Layla and Other Love Songs*

"I'm terribly proud of that song," said Eric Clapton of 'Layla'.

"To have ownership of something that powerful is something I'll never be able to get used to. I've tried to recapture the sense of that again and again. And it cannot be done. I've realised it's pointless. Just leave it be."

In the summer of 1970 Eric Clapton had a new band, dubbed the Dominos. They were the cream of young American players – Carl Radle on bass, drummer Jim Gordon and keyboard player Bobby Whitlock were veterans of Leon Russell's Mad Dogs and Englishmen project and Delaney and Bonnie. They found themselves in the UK hanging out with Eric Clapton and working on George Harrison's *All Things Must Pass*.

At the time Clapton was obsessively in love with his close friend Harrison's wife, Patti Boyd. All of the songs he would write in this period were songs of unrequited love and most of the cover versions he played were on this topic. "Well, it was the heaviest thing going on at the time so, yeah, I suppose it came about like that," said Clapton. "I didn't consciously do it, though, it just happened that way. That was what I wanted to write about most of all."

In August 1970 Clapton and the Dominos moved to Criteria Studios in Florida, where producer Tom Dowd worked. Dowd was then producing the Allman Brothers Band and had a history going back to the great Atlantic R&B sides of the '50s.

At Criteria the group just jammed. Then Dowd introduced Duane Allman to the mix. Allman had been doing sessions for Wilson Pickett and Aretha Franklin on the side and his band had a reputation for their extended improvisations on stage. At the time Allman was just becoming recognised as one of the great innovative guitarists of his generation.

Dowd took Clapton to an Allman Brothers Show and introduced them. "It was love at first sight," the producer recalled. "And that's how the whole *Layla* thing got to be, because they just sat at the back of the studio and traded instruments and licks for the next five days, and that made an album."

"I went down there to watch them make that record because I was interested in it," said Allman. "I've been an admirer of Eric Clapton for a long, long time; he inspired me a lot and I always just personally dug his playing. Figured I'd get a chance to meet him and watch this thing go down, y'know. So when I saw him he acted like he knew me, like I was an old friend. And he said, 'As long as you're here we want you to get on this record and make it with us, we need more guitar players anyway,' so I did. I was real flattered and glad to be able to do it."

"He took it from being an all-right record to being something completely extraordinary," said Clapton. The key song was recorded almost last. The lyric came from a Persian story of the tragic love affair between Layla and Mahoun. "I had no idea what 'Layla' was going to be," said Clapton. "It was just a ditty."

Duane Allman opened the proceedings with a riff adapted from Albert King's 'The Years Go Passing By' and speeded up into a torrent of guitar. From there the guitars are layered up with acoustic and electric lines crammed on top of each other. The track is as close to perfect as a rock & roll song can be.

Two months after the recording had finished, the Dominos told Dowd they wanted to add a coda to 'Layla'. Jim Gordon had a piano instrumental that he had been jamming on for some years.

Although primarily a drummer, Gordon was an accomplished multi-instrumentalist much in demand. Gordon recorded his instrumental at some point during the *Layla* sessions and they asked Dowd to mix it into the end of the song. "And that's how it went on," said Dowd. "The piano portion at the back of it was added months after the initial composition, but the rest of it was the way it was done in initial concept and pursuit. The last part came in during a playback session, when the album was all mixed, so we had to remix 'Layla', but that was no problem, it was a pleasure."

'Layla' clocked in at seven minutes – too long for a single, so an edited version eventually went to radio. The record was not well received. The general public weren't aware that this was a Clapton project and the double album was long and intense. It took two years before the record finally started selling and the song 'Layla' became Clapton's signature tune.

The Dominos were a group beset by tragedy. By all accounts except Dowd's, there was a massive consumption of drugs at Criteria – especially cocaine and heroin. Clapton became a junkie and a semi-hermit. His wife, Alice Ormsby-Gore, also became an addict. Eventually their marriage broke down and Clapton married Patti Boyd. Carl Radle became a heroin addict and died in 1980 of heroin-related illness. Worst of all, however, was Jim Gordon, whose mental illness became progressively worse and one day in 1983 he stabbed his mother to death.

Just Be Good to Me The SOS Band

(James Harris/Terry Lewis) ❋ Tabu ❋ 1983 ❋ Appears on: *Rise*

Jimmy Jam and Terry Lewis were members of the Time, one of Prince's subgroups and doing production work on the side for the SOS Band. They had slipped off tour to make a recording date in Los Angeles and their flight to Texas was waylaid by a freak snowstorm causing them to miss a date. Prince suggested that it was time they were encouraged to move on. As it turns out, they would have been happy to go; the SOS Band hit number two with 'Just Be Good to Me' and Jam and Lewis became one of the most successful production teams of the '80s and '90s.

Led by Mary Davis' measured but sweet vocal, 'Just Be Good to Me' has a glorious deep groove lined with layers of sweet synthesiser pads. A gently funky drum track and a melodic, honeyed bass line complement the ambiguous situation of the singer ("I don't care about your other girls/Just be good to me"). She's in some pain but stoic and desperate. Jam and Lewis defined their own style, which owed something to Prince's funk but with the warmer feel of the Philly sound of Gamble and Huff. They went on to produce Janet Jackson and many other platinum artists while 'Just Be Good to Me' was revived by Fatboy Slim's Beats International as 'Dub Be Good to Me'. It remains one of the defining grooves of the '80s.

(What's the Story) Morning Glory? Oasis

(Noel Gallagher) ✳ Epic ✳ 1995 ✳ Appears on: *(What's The Story) Morning Glory?*

The title track of Oasis' second album is a state-of-the-nation message. Oasis came flying out of the New Britain. Specifically the New North. For decades poverty and indifference of the south had cowed the industrial north of England. Northern culture had just gotten stronger, especially in music and football. As Britain crawled its way back to the first world there was resurgence in national pride and a confident pop culture. Oasis' big guitar sound announced that attitude.

'(What's the Story) Morning Glory?' is a masterpiece of production. It opens with the sound of choppers as if we're back in *Apocalypse Now!* The adrenaline is pumped further by the guitar squalls and then Noel Gallagher crashes in with a massive wall of guitar noise (and later, with a chorus riff that sounds almost identical to the one in R.E.M.'s 'The One I Love'). Then Liam Gallagher chimes in with his song about modern life and being chained to the razor and the spoon.

"I put drug references in Oasis' songs because I take them and I write about what I know," said Noel Gallagher. "Me and my mates have been doing drugs since we were fourteen and, personally, I can't help it.

"The number of times I've sat round this flat off my tits and sorted out what's wrong with everything in the world and the next morning I can't remember a thing. It gets so that you can only operate when you're out of it – while you're chained to the drugs, sure, your life is a bowl of cherries. But it's exactly that, you're chained to it. And I do know a lot of people will take that lyric in 'Morning Glory' straight, which is a shame."

'Morning Glory' is, however, one of the best pieces of rock & roll music recorded in the '90s. If you want to know what it was like to be up for it in 1996, this is it.

Set Adrift on Memory Bliss PM Dawn

(Attrell Cordes/Gary Kemp) ✻ Gee Street ✻ 1991 ✻
Appears on: *Of the Heart, Of the Soul and Of the Cross: The Utopian Experience*

The first spiritual hip-hop crew, PM Dawn's name, according to leader Prince B, is "an abbreviation of the idea that in the darkest hour comes the light." In the '80s, rap and hip-hop were the sounds of the street. Then came PM Dawn (vocalist Attrell Cordes aka Prince B and Jarrett Cordes aka DJ Minute Mix). They came from a musical family – their stepfather played in Kool and the Gang – and their quest was mostly internal.

'Set Adrift on Memory Bliss' heralded their debut album, *Of the Heart, Of the Soul and Of the Cross: The Utopian Experience*. Based around a sample from Spandau Ballet's lush pop ballad 'True', the track piled up hip-hop grooves and soulful, gospel vocals. The end result, though, was reflective and enchanting rather than confrontational. The song itself was a vaguely religious discussion about the abandonment of the material world. It's a genre-busting track that opened up immense new possibilities for hip-hop and dance music in coming years. Both the album and single made number one in the pop charts and it was an important record in the process of extending the hip-hop audience beyond the black community.

Trampoline Joe Henry

(Joe Henry) ✻ Mammoth ✻ 1996 ✻ Appears on: *Trampoline*

Joe Henry had almost exhausted his acoustic junior Gram Parsons phase. On 'Trampoline' you can hear some touches of jazz, some beats and synthesisers, but you never lose the sense of Henry's roots. This was one of the most intriguing songs of the mid-'90s; understated and confused, 'Trampoline' is a beguiling portrait of a man contemplating his life. There's a strong defiance in the refrain, "this time I'm not coming down," but it's tempered with knowledge of gravity. A perfect song to also reflect Henry's transitional position as a songwriter.

"When I started making *Trampoline*, I was determined to learn a new way to work," Henry told David Byrne in an interview. "Usually because I didn't have enough money and I didn't know how to work any other way. Just live in the studio.

Get a band, circle the wagons, and then just kind of hack at it. And it's more like making a documentary film; you get what you get, problems and all. More like live theatre. That's what it is. And I wanted to think more like a filmmaker, I wanted to be able to manipulate things more. And work on it in bits and pieces and I started by setting up a little studio at home and exactly that.

"I came up with a drum loop first, and thought, 'Jeez, I've never written, here's a rhythm, I've never operated under this umbrella. Let's do this one', and then made myself write to that. And, I just learned to work backwards. I think it's good to be disoriented to a certain degree."

Crush With Eyeliner R.E.M.

(Michael Stipe/Bill Berry/Mike Mills/Peter Buck) ✳ Warner Bros. ✳ 1995 ✳
Appears on: *Monster*

After hitting the mainstream charts in a big way with cheesy pop tunes and then the lush ballads 'Drive' and 'Everybody Hurts', R.E.M. wanted to make a tough rock & roll record that they could take on tour. The sessions for the album became overshadowed by Kurt Cobain's suicide and his wife Courtney Love's public meltdown. Stipe was a close friend of both the Cobains and so every track on this album appeared to have something to do with the doomed couple.

Is 'Crush With Eyeliner' about Courtney Love? Who knows? It is a great rock & roll song though.

According to Stipe, "'Crush With Eyeliner' is completely, to me, a paean to the New York Dolls, with reference to 'Frankenstein', which of course is one of their songs, and a lot of this album is referring back to Iggy and the Stooges and Patti Smith and Television, and stuff like that. I went back and listened to *Marquee Moon* while we were making this record, and to this day I have no idea what those songs are about, but I can sing each one from beginning to end. There are unbelievable analogies and images: 'The Cadillac pulled out of the graveyard' and 'Dressing up like cops'. So cool, all that stuff."

The song came out of a distorted tremolo guitar riff from Peter Buck. "They knew it had to sound sonically very different," producer Scott Litt told writer Michael Goldberg. "The pulsing guitars and pulsing bass would usually start with that effect. They'd find a tremolo effect box and plug it in and say, 'Wow, this is a neat sound.' They'd build stuff from that. And that really goes with Michael's philosophy of having a little bit of a sound-scape from which to work, and some space. And tremolo pulses give you that space."

The glam-meets-grunge sense of the song was aided by the guest appearance by Sonic Youth's Thurston Moore.

"Michael had always heard Thurston doing that part, 'I'm the real thing', in the way that only Thurston can do it. Michael wanted to work with those guys. He really admires them. Thurston is a friend. He was out in LA for maybe some MTV thing and came by and did that part in like twenty minutes. Just came to the studio and sang it."

The beauty of 'Crush With Eyeliner' is the glam rock groove over the grunge sounds – the distorted guitar and the loping bass and Stipe's lyrics. Mostly, after all those serious ballads, it sounds like R.E.M. being a rock & roll band. As Litt said, "They wanted to turn up and play loud and add some guitars. So there was a concept there."

Copper Kettle Bob Dylan

(Albert F Beddoe) ❋ Columbia ❋ 1970 ❋ Appears on: *Self-Portrait*

Dylan's *Self-Portrait* album is one of his most perplexing releases. A double album with such a title, it contained mostly cover versions of folk and country songs, sometimes in multiple versions, plus four live Dylan tracks recorded on the Isle of Wight and a couple of originals without significant lyrics. Dylanophiles were flabbergasted – was he cracking up? Was it a joke? Who knew?

In 1985 Dylan told journalist Kurt Loder that the intention with *Self-Portrait* was all along to commit career suicide to put off the hordes of hippies who were making his life hell. "I wish these people would just *forget* about me. I wanna do something they *can't* possibly like, they *can't* relate to. They'll see it, and they'll listen, and they'll say, 'Well, let's get on to the next person. He ain't sayin' it no more. He ain't given' us what we want', you know? They'll go on to somebody else. But the whole idea backfired. Because the album went out there, and the people said, '*This* ain't what we want', and they got *more* resentful. And then I did this portrait for the cover. I mean, there was no *title* for that album. I knew somebody who had some paints and a square canvas, and I did the cover up in about five minutes. And I said, 'Well, I'm gonna call this album *Self-Portrait*.'

"And to me it was a *joke*.

"Well, it wouldn't have held up as a single album – then it *really* would've been bad, you know. I mean, if you're gonna put a lot of crap on it, you might as well load it up!"

The fact of the matter is that *Self-Portrait* is a charming record, a hodgepodge of brilliance and rubbish. 'Copper Kettle' for instance is one of Dylan's most sublime moments. It was a moonshiner's song written by Texan singer/songwriter Albert Beddoe. Dylan is completely laid-back into the tune – the tale of generations of moonshiners hanging around the still. This is the kind of music on which Dylan grew up and he has a sense for the timelessness of the situation. Timelessness was soon to become the dominant theme of his world.

Dylan recorded it along with a dozen other songs in a day in New York. Al Kooper played keyboards, David Bromberg played guitars and Emanuel Green added violin. The raw tracks were sent to Nashville where other instruments were added.

'Copper Kettle' is a song for the ages and Dylan's reading of it here is as emotional and as true as any of his best work.

White Rabbit Jefferson Airplane

(Grace Slick) ❋ RCA ❋ 1967 ❋ Appears on: *Surrealistic Pillow*

Singer Grace Slick retold Lewis Carroll's Alice stories as a metaphor for the hypocrisy of the straight world in the mid-'60s. The comparisons were all there and the connection between Alice's eat-me cake and the new drug LSD was too rich to ignore.

The key line in the song is "feed your head," which not only implied taking mind-expanding drugs but also finding a new awareness whether that be spiritual, political or sexual.

"It also means you gotta feed your brains," said the now-retired Slick recently. "Our parents wanted us to get educated, and we did. We found that you could either get married and live in a suburb with a station wagon and two bratty kids, or you could live like Alice B Toklas, Picasso or Diaghilev. We chose the latter, to live a relatively free and artistic life. The phrase is: 'Fuck you, we do what we want.'"

Slick wrote the song when in her first band, the Great Society. When she joined the Airplane for their second album, *Surrealistic Pillow*, the Airplane adapted it. Jorma Kaukonen brought his acidic, sharp guitar tones to the tune and Spencer Dryden's staccato drumming made it a very unsettling. Most of all, though, there was Slick's caustic, banshee voice that just tore down the melody. To hear Slick scream "feed your head" is to have a psychedelic experience.

You Shook Me All Night Long AC/DC

(Brian Johnson/Malcolm Young/Angus Young) ❋ Alberts ❋ 1980 ❋

Appears on: *Back in Black*

When Bon Scott died of misadventure in February 1980, the Young brothers, Malcolm and Angus, resolved that AC/DC wasn't going to stop there. The group was by then a success in Europe and Australia and poised to crack the American market. Perhaps a fresh start was required anyway. Bon Scott was possibly too raunchy and wild for the United States. New singer Brian Johnson had the voice to carry the music but no discernible personality. Let alone an attitude.

'You Shook Me All Night Long' was in many ways a classic AC/DC sound – big solid riffing guitars without too much subtlety. The group was now working with Robert 'Mutt' Lange, the most polished and powerful metal producer in the history of rock. He took the rough diamond band and buffed them to perfection. There's still enough grunt in the tune to satisfy the black-shirted heavy metal kids, there's enough swing to know that the Youngs have heard their share of Chess blues, but it's also clean and large enough to fit into commercial radio.

The lyrics, like classic AC/DC, were naughty and sexual. However, 'You Shook Me' has none of the sleaze of earlier AC/DC. It's not overly sexist, it's not demeaning to anyone and there's nothing really R-rated.

This was the new AC/DC and *Back in Black* became one of the biggest selling records of all time, and one of the most loved.

This Land is Your Land Woody Guthrie

(Woody Guthrie) ✳ Smithsonian Folkways ✳ 1967 ✳ Appears on: *This Land is Your Land*

This version of Woody Guthrie's alternative American anthem comes from his last commercial session, made for Decca on 7 January 1952. Although he lived another fifteen years, his body and motor skills steadily degenerated due to Huntington's Chorea, a genetic wasting disease.

No-one can do jingoism better than the Yanks. Woody Guthrie, the Left's best and most prolific songwriter, wrote 'This Land is Your Land' in February 1940 as a response to Irving Berlin's 'God Bless America'. It is now sung as a triumphant anthem for the march of Anglo-American progress and the doctrine of Manifest Destiny. Without much effort, the US presidency under George W Bush could use the lyric as its rallying cry across the globe.

Guthrie objected to involving God in the matter. He claimed the country "From the redwood forest, to the gulf stream waters" for the people and the natural world. It's a bucolic view of American wonder as represented by Walt Disney. It's how Americans like to see themselves.

There is a kicker, though, in the verses (left out of popular songbooks that carry the title). The verses go:

Was a high wall there that tried to stop me
A sign was painted said: private property,
But on the back side it didn't say nothing –
That side was made for you and me.
One bright sunny morning in the shadow of the steeple
By the relief office I saw my people –
As they stood hungry, I stood there wondering if
God blessed America for me

'This Land' is a defiantly political song that celebrates the romantic, rebel tradition that Guthrie saw as the best tool the rugged individual had in the struggle not to be defeated by the capitalist bosses.

The sentiment, especially in the 'lost' verses, remains strong, especially when accompanied by a guitar ringing like a freedom bell.

Silver Dagger Joan Baez

(Traditional) ❋ Vanguard ❋ 1960 ❋ Appears on: *Joan Baez*

The folk boom had been going for some time when the nineteen-year-old Joan Baez appeared on the scene and immediately became its queen. The part Hispanic Baez was breathtakingly beautiful and also a little sombre. She looked like she had recently stepped out of some medieval English world and her voice was as pure as an angel's. The folk artists to this point had mostly been political activists or would-be beatniks. They had about them a faux nostalgia for these old songs that they attempted to render faithfully. While many good records were made in this period it was a little – certainly with the commercial end of it – like going to school and being lectured by the nerds. Joan Baez, by virtue of her beauty, made folk music cool and sexy. Baez sang these songs of ancient sorrows like she knew them in her heart. Her first record was an instant smash in folk circles.

"I recorded my first album in a hotel ballroom in New York City," she wrote in the liner notes to the box set *Rare, Live and Classic*. "We could use that room every day except Wednesday when it was used for a bingo game.

"There were two microphones, one for voice and one for guitar, and two wires which ran upstairs to a little room which had a tape recorder in it.

"Back then I trotted into the studio with the latest fifteen songs I had learned, put them all down on tape and that was the record. I could make a record with just ballads."

Political Science Randy Newman

(Randy Newman) ❋ Warner Bros. ❋ 1972 ❋ Appears on: *Sail Away*

In an unfortunate foresight, Randy Newman put George W Bush's foreign policy to music back when W was still organising keg parties and reputedly avoiding military service.

Newman could be Texas' favourite son when he sings over a jaunty piano figure: "No-one likes us, I don't know why/We may not be perfect, but heaven knows we try/But all around, even our old friends put us down/Let's drop the big one and see what happens."

You can hear Donald Rumsfeld chiming in: "Asia's crowded and Europe's too old."

The premise of the song is that the rest of the world doesn't understand America, so America might as well stop apologising for itself and realise its Manifest Destiny.

Boom goes London and boom Paree
More room for you and more room for me
And every city the whole world round
Will just be another American town
Oh, how peaceful it will be
We'll set everybody free

"When I wrote it, I thought, 'Well, all that is a joke.' But that kind of ignorance and arrogance and jingoism is actually out there, to some extent," the songwriter said recently. "Saying 'old Europe'. Who would have ever dreamed that anyone would say that in public? God knows what they've said in private, or what was done, like with Allende. Secret stuff that you find out twenty years later. But they're keeping it right out in front now. Since we became one world power, we've been acting like Rome."

As a songwriter and satirist, Newman is notoriously unpopular although his soundtrack work for Pixar is massively commercial. Perhaps he's too close to the bone.

"I don't have any great hopes that any one song will change anything, but it's intended to get people to feel superior to the jingoistic sentiments expressed in the song," he said. "With a lot of my songs you can certainly feel better about yourself, because you're definitely better than the people in them."

It's not just the crisp production with Newman's ragtimey piano to the fore that has kept 'Political Science' so fresh. Unfortunately.

Knockin' on Heaven's Door Bob Dylan

(Bob Dylan) ❋ Columbia ❋ 1973 ❋ Appears on: *Pat Garrett & Billy the Kid*

Sam Peckinpah's film *Pat Garrett & Billy the Kid* was a retelling of the Wild West story in which Billy the Kid is hunted down and killed by his old friend Garrett. Bob

Dylan had a small role in the picture and was asked to write the soundtrack. A song was called for in the scene where the old sheriff, played by Slim Pickens, dies in his wife's arms. Dylan came up with a masterpiece that outshone the rest of the film. In a movie that is largely about doom and fate, Dylan, then in his early thirties, expresses it all in a few spare lines. Dylan's melody moves at a funereal pace and the lyrics are spare, but the song says it all.

This is one of Dylan's most covered songs. In 2003 Warren Zevon did perhaps the most emotional reading for his album *The Wind*. Diagnosed with lung cancer and with only weeks to live, Zevon recorded the song, finding in it not only an acceptance of death but also a resolution of life.

In the outtakes from the *Pat Garrett* sessions you can hear Dylan light-heartedly call for another run through of the track. "OK, let's do it without the vocal," he says. "It's the last time I work for anybody though, on a movie. With music."

Alive Pearl Jam

(Stone Gossard/Eddie Vedder) ❋ Epic ❋ 1991 ❋ Appears on: *Ten*

"It's about incest; and it's about murder; and you know all those good things," said Pearl Jam singer Eddie Vedder. "And if you can picture it in your mind, the third song takes place in a jail cell. So this is our own little mini-opera here."

The first part of the mini-opera is 'Alive', the first song on Pearl Jam's debut album, *Ten*.

Vedder explained the lyrics to filmmaker Cameron Crowe. "Everybody writes about it like it's a life-affirmation thing – I'm really glad about that. It's a great interpretation. But 'Alive' is … it's torture. Which is why it's fucked up for me. Why I should probably learn how to sing another way. It would be easier. It's … it's too much.

"The story of the song is that a mother is with a father and the father dies. It's an intense thing because the son looks just like the father. The son grows up to be the father, the person that she lost. His father's dead, and now this confusion, his mother, his love, how does he love her, how does she love him? In fact, the mother, even though she marries somebody else, there's no-one she's ever loved more than the father. You know how it is, first loves and stuff. And the guy dies. How could you ever get him back? But the son. He looks exactly like him. It's uncanny. So she wants him. The son is oblivious to it all. He doesn't know what the fuck is going on. He's still dealing, he's still growing up. He's still dealing with love, he's still dealing with the death of his father. All he knows is 'I'm still alive' – those three words, that's totally out of burden.

"Now the second verse is 'Oh she walks slowly into a young man's room … I can remember to this very day … the look … the look.' And I don't say anything else. And because I'm saying, 'The look, the look' everyone thinks it goes with 'on her face'. It's not on her face. The look is between her legs. Where do you go with that? That's where you came from.

"But I'm still alive. I'm the lover that's still alive. And the whole conversation about 'You're still alive, she said. And his doubts: 'Do I deserve to be? Is that the question?' Because he's fucked up forever! So now he doesn't know how to deal with it. So what does he do, he goes out killing people – that was [the song] 'Once'. He becomes a serial killer. And 'Footsteps', the final song of the trilogy, that's when he gets executed. That's what happens. The Green River killer … and in San Diego, there was another prostitute killer down there. Somehow I related to that. I think that happens more than we know. It's a modern way of dealing with a bad life.

"I'm just glad I became a songwriter."

Vedder had a serious Who habit, which may explain his desire to write rock operas. In any case it's sufficiently impenetrable for most Pearl Jam fans that simply adopted the song as an anthem.

The music for the song comes from 'Dollar Short', a tune that guitarist Stone Gossard had worked up some months earlier and was one of the songs he played to prospective band members. "I knew we had a band," guitarist Mike McCready said, "when we started playing that song 'Dollar Short'."

The tape with 'Dollar Short' and some other tracks was posted to Eddie Vedder to add lyrics and as a result, Vedder came to Seattle and joined Pearl Jam. The first song they played together was 'Alive'.

On 11 March 1991 Pearl Jam embarked on a month in the studio where they cut *Ten*, which was released the following September. It took five months to make the charts but once there, Pearl Jam went on to dominate the rock scene for the next three years.

Wonderwall Oasis

(Noel Gallagher) ❋ Epic ❋ 1995 ❋ Appears on: *(What's the Story) Morning Glory?*

Noel Gallagher, not known for wearing his heart on his sleeve, wrote this song for his then girlfriend Meg Matthews. There are the obvious Beatle references – *Wonderwall* was a film for which George Harrison wrote the music. Mostly though, Gallagher nailed the chord progression and crafted a ballad that had instant classic written all over it. Just as it seemed rock & roll had used up its vocabulary, Oasis came up with the song.

Gallagher felt sufficiently strongly about the melody to want to sing it himself, but brother Liam insisted on taking the lead vocal.

"But I don't need no pat on the back," said Liam. "I know how good I am and how shit everyone else is, I just get in there and do it. Noel writes his words down, does me a guide vocal. I have a read, have a little sing in my head and that's it, I'm done. I had a bad throat halfway through recording the album, and when it came time to do 'Wonderwall' our kid was wanting to do the vocal, saying, 'You can't even speak.' But I did it, and it worked straight off. Big time. It didn't matter to me that Noel had written that song as a personal love song about his girlfriend Meg. It doesn't matter if it's about President Clinton or whatever, because if a song needs to be sung about that kind of feeling then I'm the man to do it.

"When I sing a song like 'Wonderwall', I'm not thinking about one person. Not ever. I just think about love in general. Love's just mood isn't it? It's a solid, positive thing, it's about everything."

Tears of Rage The Band

(Richard Manuel/Bob Dylan) ❋ Capitol ❋ 1968 ❋ Appears on: *Music from Big Pink*

'Tears of Rage' opened an album that changed music. Bootleg copies of the song had circulated on *The Basement Tapes* – the rehearsal tapes of Bob Dylan and the Band in their basement at the Big Pink House. *The Basement Tapes* made George Harrison want to split the Beatles and Eric Clapton to split Cream. "I got hold of a bootleg tape of *Big Pink* at the end of the last Cream tour," recalled Eric Clapton. "I used to put it on as soon as I checked into my hotel room, do the gig and be utterly miserable, then rush back and put the tape on and go to sleep fairly contented until I woke up the next morning and remembered who I was and what I was doing. It was that potent!" For Clapton, "the sound of music changed drastically after that first album."

Rather than competing over solos and threatening to burn down the world, the Band proposed a return to family values and togetherness. 'Tears of Rage' was a song about a relationship between a father and daughter.

"It's from a parent's side of view," said Robertson. "So what if your parents did you wrong? Maybe they did, but so what? Everybody's just doing what they can do, right or wrong. I'm just tired of hearing all of this – that little girl Janis Ian. You know, Jim Morrison and those people. I just think they're a drag. Even if that is their situation, who cares? That's got nothing to do with music."

Dylan arrived at Big Pink with the lyric and gave it to Manuel, who swiftly added a piano melody. "I had a couple of movements that seemed to fit, so I just elaborated a little," said Manuel.

It's really Manuel's soaring and desperately sad vocal that makes this track work, however. The languid pace of the arrangement gives enormous space to what is an extraordinary vocal.

The song was cut live on A&R's four-track studio in New York. The majestic sound of Garth Hudson's organ and Robertson's guitar, fed through a Leslie speaker, and Helm's muffled drums all serve Manuel's voice. It's something not completely rock & roll nor country but ancient and dark and sad.

As Robbie Robertson put it, "It's the most heartbreaking performance he ever sung in his life."

It's All Over Now   The Rolling Stones

(Bobby Womack/Shirley Jean Womack) ✳ Decca ✳ 1964 ✳
Appears on: *The Rolling Stones*

Bobby Womack and his brother Curtis were discovered by soul stirrer Sam Cooke and put to work recording gospel songs as the Valentinos in Los Angeles.

"He said, 'Get on Route 66 and stay on it all the way.' I talked my oldest brother into buying a Cadillac, because that's what I saw all the pimps in the neighbourhood driving," Womack recalled of his invitation to join the music business. "Of course, we get on the freeway and it starts to rain, the windshield wipers won't turn on, and the car's running out of gas every fifteen seconds because the tank's got a hole in it. We wound up in the hospital for a week, because we were overcome by gas fumes. And then the headlights came off!

"Two weeks later, we show up in LA, pushin' the car down Hollywood Boulevard, all of us with our do-rags on. We called Sam, and he said, 'Man, where the hell are y'all?' 'We on Sunset. The car ain't got no more gas.'"

They didn't do well with gospel either and switched to R&B, where they had a major hit in 1962 with 'Lookin' for a Love' and a minor hit with 'It's All Over Now'.

"The Stones was over here at Chess Records looking for songs," said Womack. "Our record had just come out and it was very big. The Stones heard it and said, 'Man, we got to cut that song.' Sam came to me and said 'Bobby, I got some good news and bad. The Rolling Stones want to cover your song.' And I said, 'Man, when these Pat Boones gonna stop?'

"Sam said, 'Bobby, they'll do more for your career than you'll ever believe. This group is gonna be huge and the longer they live, the bigger they're gonna get. It's a new thing happening, man, and I can see it already.' So I just said, 'I don't want them to sing the song. Tell 'em to get their own song.' Sam says, 'Bobby, they sell tons of records. This is gonna be the first record that breaks for them in the States. You know what that means? You introduced 'em.'"

The strong beat in the track and its eclectic melody made the track perfect for a crossover to pop radio – a little blacker than most white pop bands of the time. It was ideal for the Rolling Stones' image and it certainly launched Womack's name as a writer. He has since become firm friends, to the point of writing and producing Ron Wood's brilliant album *Now Look*. At the time, though, the track was an important bridge across the genres.

"They came out with 'It's All Over Now' so quick and I was laughin' because some of the words they thought we said, we didn't say. Mick said something totally different. I said, 'This is how a black person talk, the English sound different.' We were laughing, but I was still furious. They took our song and everybody thinks it's their song, never mind Sam talking about it's gonna make me a legend and all that. But I remember the first cheque I received, it was about $400,000. I been chasing 'em ever since tryin' to get 'em to do one of my songs."

God, Part II U2

(Bono/U2) ✳ Island ✳ 1988 ✳ Appears on: *Rattle and Hum*

Following the supernova success of *The Joshua Tree* album, U2 went on a search through their roots. *Rattle and Hum* mapped the band's journey back through rock & roll music and the blues. BB King joins them, one track is recorded with a gospel choir, they cover a Bob Dylan song, a Beatles track, and Hendrix's 'Star Spangled Banner'.

Perhaps the most powerful track, though, is the revision of John Lennon's song 'God' from his first solo album. In that lyric, Lennon lets fly with a list of illusions in the world and comes to the conclusion that the only things he believes in are his wife and himself.

'God, Part II' starts out with the same structure, perhaps inspired by the Lennon biography by Albert Goldman that had recently been published and which cast the ex-Beatle in a particularly harsh light.

Bono was not in a mood to tear down his heroes; however, he does point to the hypocrisy of rich artists writing about the poor and he doesn't attempt to canonise Lennon. "This band is full of contradictions," said the Edge in 1988. "The song 'God, Part II' is really Bono trying to express his own internal feelings of conflict. I have doubts, but I don't feel guilty."

'God, Part II' is a manifesto. The verse "Don't believe in the '60s/The golden age of pop/You glorify the past/When the future dries up" is a manifesto to which U2 have adhered when their contemporaries have generally become nostalgia acts.

The arrangement of the song is brutal and angry and bitter. It's much more strident than other U2 tracks and its emphasis on the bass and drums reflects the fact that U2 finally learned how to play the blues.

"John Lennon is somebody that I really respected, not necessarily looked up to … or looked down, or even looked sideways at, he's just a great songwriter that inspired me," said Bono. "I despise Albert Golddigger's attempt to pick a fight with a dead man.

"And I attempted to point out that the contradictions of John Lennon's life and times … You know, the fact that he was crippled inside, as he said himself, does not negate his brilliance as a musician. We're all full of contradictions; he was just brave enough to own up to them in his songs and we certainly didn't need to read a book to find out about them. But the more dangerous thing about Albert Goldman's books – on Lenny Bruce, on Elvis Presley, and on John Lennon – is he is really attempting to write off the culture from which they came. He is a New York intellectual who is attempting to write off Elvis Presley as the idiot, the idiot-savant actually, and John Lennon as just a very screwed-up guy – we knew these things.

"You know, he attempted to write off a culture that is rock & roll, and rock & roll is an expression for people like myself who aren't university educated and the like and I really objected to it. And 'God, Part II' is my statement on that."

Spill the Wine Eric Burdon & War

(Papa Dee Allen/Harold Brown/BB Dickerson/Lonnie Jordan/Charles Miller/Lee Oskar/Howard Scott) ❋ Polydor ❋ 1970 ❋ Appears on: *Eric Burdon Declares "War"*

In 1969 Eric Burdon had abandoned the Animals, the group he had led through half a tempestuous decade. The man with the richest voice in Britain was looking for something more funky than a bunch of white English boys. He found a soul-funk outfit called the Night Shift and renamed them War. "I once had a dream of finding the finest black musicians in America and putting them into a band who'd become world-beaters," he said. "War are a realisation of that dream now."

In January 1970 they entered the studio to record the album *Eric Burdon Declares "War"*. Burdon was an artist in search of a form and he was enthusiastic about War's jazz funk.

The highpoint is 'Spill the Wine'. The session is a light-hearted jam where War lay down their groove and Burdon free associates across the top of it. The song is exotic – sexy girls coming to him in a dream. There's a tropical, Latin groove here and Burdon speaks most of the track with that deep honey voice before letting go in the final verses for a very soulful crescendo.

'Spill the Wine' made it to number three in the charts. In September 1970 the group played London and were joined on one night by Jimi Hendrix. It was to be his last live show.

Smells Like Teen Spirit Nirvana

(Kurt Cobain/Dave Grohl/Krist Novoselic) ✳ DGC ✳ 1991 ✳ Appears on: *Nevermind*

The crowd at the OK Hotel in Seattle on the night of 17 April 1991 heard history being made. It was the public debut of 'Smells Like Teen Spirit', a new song that the group Nirvana had worked up in preparation for the major label recording sessions that summer. Cobain introduced the band by proclaiming, "Hello, we're major label corporate rock sell-outs." Although the lyric and the arrangement would change, 'Teen Spirit' was a song that sounded like a hit.

That January, Nirvana, a promising punk rock band from Olympia, Washington,

via Seattle had moved from the local independent label Sub Pop to DGC, a subsidiary of Geffen Records. They had a solid first album out in the underground scene with its hardcore and Black Sabbath riffs. Nirvana and Geffen decided on Butch Vig to produce and sent him some indecipherable demo tapes. Rehearsals began in May at Sound City Studios in Van Nuys, California. In the '70s and the '80s it had been home to Tom Petty, the Jacksons, Rick Springfield and Fleetwood Mac. The group liked the room's "live" sound and the ancient equipment. The album was cut there in June on a budget of $130,000.

Teen Spirit was a cheap fragrance for teenage kids. Fellow punk rocker Kathleen Hanna of Bikini Kill graffitied the phrase "Kurt smells like Teen Spirit" on Cobain's bedroom wall after a party one night and the phrase stuck. Cobain turned it into an attack on consumerist society. He was also venting his own self-loathing. Signing to Geffen was, he believed, selling out his indie-rock principles.

"The songs were basically in really good shape, but I did do more arranging with them," said Vig. "'Teen Spirit' was longer and the little ad-libs after the chorus were actually at the end of the song. I suggested putting those in at the end of each chorus as a bridge into the next verse. And I remember Kurt sitting down with the acoustic and he had a couple of variations of the melody and the verse he was singing and we picked the one that was best. But most of the songs were fairly finished. I don't know whether they played them live a lot, but I know that they did practise a lot. It wasn't like, 'What are you playing here?' They knew. Chris had figured out his bass lines, and the drum patterns for the most part were worked out, and Kurt had a pretty good idea of what he wanted to do. But he had a couple lines in some songs that he was still working on. I was so into the song I had them play it as much as possible! The song was amazing."

For the most part, Vig says the sessions were fairly relaxed. "The band was really loose. They were going out all night and partying. I think that they had a certain sense of 'We can do whatever we want.' Typically, I would go in before them, like around noon or one, and they would get in mid-afternoon, 3 or 4 o'clock and we'd work until 11 o'clock or midnight. And they'd leave and I'd usually work a little longer."

"Kurt had the chorus of the song – that four-chord riff and the vocal melody," said Novoselic. "We jammed on that riff, broke it down into a groove, and that turned out to be the verse of the song. There's that little bridge. And that's the song. The recording was just as brisk. Nirvana cut the basic track for 'Teen Spirit' live in three takes; the second was the keeper."

'Teen Spirit' is a strange combination of garage rock and the big chording of FM rock bands like Boston. Cobain claimed that his inspiration was the Pixies, who pioneered the loud/soft dynamic.

"He squashed his pop sensibility," said Vig. "He had that dichotomy of punk rage and alienation but also this vulnerable pop sensibility. In 'Teen Spirit', a lot of that vulnerability is in his singing, in the tone of his voice."

The song recorded, Andy Wallace mixed it into an epic.

'Teen Spirit' was accompanied by a video directed by Samuel Bayer. The group here played in a basketball court from hell with a pack of screaming fans and a line of cheerleaders played by strippers recruited at the last minute. Dressed in their usual thrift shop clothes and flannelette shirts, Nirvana suddenly put the working-class underground onto MTV. It was clear that a whole subculture existed that was just full of energy in a way that hadn't been seen in rock & roll for decades.

'Smells Like Teen Spirit' was released on 10 September 1991. By the end of the year Nirvana was the hottest band in the world. The grunge revolution had started.

"The song was a call to consciousness," Novoselic said. "There was this conservative government. Culture was stagnant. The song was this sledgehammer that came along and bonged it all."

Sister Ray The Velvet Underground

(John Cale/Sterling Morrison/Lou Reed/Maureen Tucker) ❉ Verve ❉ 1967 ❉

Appears on: *White Light/White Heat*

They say that heavy metal starts here. Certainly it's a metallic, hard, dark song about sex, drugs, violence and murder. The guitars of Lou Reed and Sterling Morrison battle John Cale's organ while Maureen Tucker thumps relentlessly on her kettle drum. While other groups in 1967 indulged in long free form improvisations, the Velvet Underground had no peace and love behind their world view.

"No producer could override our taste," said Morrison. "We'd do a whole lot of takes, and then there would be a big brawl over which one to use. Of course everyone would opt for the take where they sounded best. It was a tremendous hassle, so on 'Sister Ray', which we knew was going to be a major effort, we stared at each other and said, 'This is going to be one take. So whatever you want to do, you better do it now.'

"And that explains what is going on in the mix. There is a musical struggle – everyone's trying to do what he wants to do every second, and nobody's backing off. I think it's great the way the organ comes in. Cale starts to try and play a solo. He's totally buried and there's a sort of surge and then he's pulling out all the stops until he just rises out of the pack. He was able to get louder than Lou and I were. The drums are almost totally drowned out.

"John and I were very happy with 'Sister Ray' type music. Although I'm teaching English now, I don't really care about lyrics in music. I like energy and emotion, yelling and grunting. Snarls and hisses like in 'The Black Angel's Death Song' – that's Cale hissing. Lou placed heavy emphasis on lyrics, while Cale and I were more interested in blasting the house down."

Train Kept A-Rollin' Johnny Burnette

(Tiny Bradshaw/Howard Kay/Lois Mann) ❉ Coral ❉ 1957 ❉

Appears on: *Johnny Burnette and the Rock & Roll Trio*

The Rock & Roll Trio was made up of boxers Johnny and Dorsey Burnette and their friend Paul Burlinson. They tore around the streets of Memphis with a hotted-up country and hillbilly sound. They, like Elvis Presley in another part of town, were developing what would become rockabilly. The Rock & Roll Trio had the energy and the smarts to make it outside a regional audience but they lacked the sex appeal of the great '50s stars. It's appropriate that Johnny Burnette would find most success as a writer for Ricky Nelson.

'Train Kept A-Rollin'' was a jump blues song that Tiny Bradshaw had written for his orchestra in 1951 and it had made the charts in that year. On 2 July 1956 Johnny Burnette and the Rock & Roll Trio were booked for a session with Nashville producer Owen Bradley. On the way to the studio, a valve in guitarist Paul Burlinson's amplifier came loose. The amplifier gave off a distorted sound and Bradley left it that way. The Trio jump into this song with the usual locomotive metaphor but they cut so loose and wild that it goes beyond simple rockabilly and into the stratosphere. Dorsey Burnette's bass sounds like its on the run from hell and Johnny Burnette's vocals go crazy to match Burlinson's riotous guitar lines.

The song was not a hit but it was a major inspiration for the next generation of rock & roll guitarists. Aerosmith covered it. Jeff Beck, in particular, recorded the tune a number of times with the Yardbirds and solo. When director Michelangelo Antonioni wanted the Yardbirds to perform a song in his classic film *Blow Up* that symbolised the convulsion of the swinging '60s, they chose ' Train Kept A-Rollin''.

Stir It Up Bob Marley

(Bob Marley) ✳ Tuff Gong ✳ 1973 ✳ Appears on: *Catch a Fire*

The *Catch a Fire* album was the beginning of Bob Marley's infiltration of the West. With the help of Island's Chris Blackwell, he took the long and rambling Trenchtown jams and crafted them into an album that would be intelligible to rock & roll fans.

In 1971, Bob Marley and the Wailers met with Chris Blackwell who owned Island and he advanced them £8000 to make an album in Jamaica. Blackwell saw in Marley an artist whom he could market to a rock audience; Marley too was ready to cross over. For Vivien Goldman, who joined Island as a press officer in 1974, *Catch a Fire* "altered the landscape of reggae completely and irrevocably". "We're talking about an era in which the notions of the singer/songwriter and the album were paramount in the critical hierarchy," she told *MOJO*. "Chris knew this and knew

Bob was capable of extended work rather than just singles, so the two of them made it happen. There was a great mutual respect and trust there: they were in it together."

Back in Jamaica the Wailers jammed out the songs. Many of them lasted up to twenty minutes. The tracks went back to London, where Blackwell supervised their editing, in consultation with the Wailers. American keyboard player John 'Rabbit' Bundrick and guitarist Wayne Perkins were brought in to sweeten the tracks a little for rock fans.

'Stir It Up' was one of the hits from the record, in as much as there were hits. It's close to an R&B groove with a rock-steady feel. It's long, slow burn makes it one of the most seductive reggae tracks, using all the usual blues and R&B motifs for the same end.

Henry New Riders of the Purple Sage

(John Dawson) ✳ Columbia ✳ 1971 ✳ Appears on: *New Riders of the Purple Sage*

The New Riders of the Purple Sage started in the summer of 1969 as a country band fronted by guitarists John Dawson and David Nelson, who were friends with Grateful Dead guitarist Jerry Garcia. The New Riders was a Grateful Dead side project that evolved its own identity. The name was adapted, at the suggestion of Robert Hunter, from Zane Grey's pot boiling western novels.

Dawson's country-rock tunes were modified for the Dead audience. 'Henry', for example, is more dope seed than hayseed.

The New Riders had a readymade audience amongst the Deadheads. In 1971, Clive Davis signed the band to Columbia and they began recording. Less authentic and less serious than the Flying Burrito Brothers or Gram Parsons, the New Riders were a honky tonk version of cosmic country rock. Their idea of farming extended as far as cultivating a marijuana crop.

"I do remember the evening that everybody was passing around the Acapulco Gold [a type of marijuana] and the joint was just about finished," recalled Dawson. "Everybody was sitting there and Garcia said, 'I want to make enough money to stay high like this forever.' And he did, even if it killed him."

Morning Dew The Grateful Dead

(Bonnie Dobson/Tim Rose) ✳ Warner Bros. ✳ 1972 ✳ Appears on: *Europe '72*

'Morning Dew' is one of the most durable of folk songs. It was written by a Canadian folksinger, Bonnie Dobson, who sang it on the coffeehouse circuit in the early '60s. The song came to the attention of Elektra recording artist Fred Neil, who was an estimable songwriter himself. Folksinger Tim Rose also recorded the song and incidentally added his name to the songwriting credits without ever meeting Dobson or talking to her. From there came the Jeff Beck Group's cover of the song with Rod Stewart singing.

Dobson wrote the words after seeing the film *On the Beach*, which is set after a nuclear holocaust.

"It made a tremendous impression on me, that film," said Dobson. "Particularly at that time because everybody was very worried about the bomb and whether we were going to get through the next ten years.

"I remember I was singing in Los Angeles at the Ashe Grove. I was staying with a girl named Joyce. She went to bed and I just started writing this song. I had never written anything in my life. I'd written some poetry as a kid. I'd never written songs and this song just came out. Really it was a kind of re-enactment of that film where at the end there is nobody left and it was a conversation between these two people trying to explain what's happening.

"The first time that I know that I performed it where it actually made an impact was at the first Mariposa festival in Toronto. I remember vividly the review in the *Globe & Mail*, they said some things about me and a mournful dirge called 'Morning Dew'. That's what it was really about, it was really about that film and the feelings, the fearful feelings we had at that time. And then things got better and then they got worse and we are where we are now. Actually I think that the song, if anything, is more of this time, of the present than it ever was then."

The Grateful Dead recorded the song on their first album with a lacklustre reading. It entered their set, however, generally as the closing number. 'Morning Dew' became one of their great jam songs. *Europe '72* closes with a twenty-minute free form improvisation that slowly resolves itself into the blues changes of 'Morning Dew' and it becomes a beautiful showcase for the lyrical guitar playing of

Jerry Garcia. The guitar weaves its way through the melody until the final verse where Garcia's guitar explodes with a glissando of high chords and then the song crashes to an end. The end of the world could not be as sweet as these transcendental few moments.

The Tracks of My Tears Smokey Robinson & the Miracles

(Smokey Robinson/Pete Moore/Marv Tarplin) ❊ Tamla ❊ 1965 ❊
Appears on: *Going to a Go Go*

The creation of the Smokey Robinson and the Miracles classic was a long and complex process in which many people – sometimes unwittingly – played a part. The first artist in the chain was Harry Belafonte, whose calypso hit 'The Banana Boat Song' gave Miracle guitarist Marv Tarplin the inspiration for the melody. "It's basically the same changes," said Tarplin, "but at another tempo with another type of feeling."

"Marvin used to come up with lots of licks and melodies and when Smokey and I heard one we liked, we would write a song to it," recalled Pete Moore. "This was a little more difficult than most. We wanted to make sure that the lyrics were real meaningful."

According to Robinson, he had a flash of inspiration one Friday afternoon. "No-one had ever said 'tracks of my tears'. The whole thought of tears was that you could wipe them away so no-one could tell you'd been crying," he told Motown historian Nelson George. "To say that I can't even wipe them away because they've left these tracks, y'know? I thought that was a good idea."

Most of the lyric came from Robinson with some key couplets from Moore. Then Motown managing director Berry Gordy added his view on extending the refrain at the end to create maximum intensity.

The recording went smoothly once the basic issues had been sorted out. Most of all there is the gossamer sweet vocal from Smokey Robinson that floats above the groove.

"There was just something about it that people loved," said Moore. "It had some underlying feel which really tapped into the depth of their emotions. Every time we sang that song people in the audience would cry."

Is It My Body? Alice Cooper

(Michael Bruce/Glen Buxton/Alice Cooper/Dennis Dunaway/Neal Smith) ✳ Warner Bros. ✳ 1971 ✳ Appears on: *Love It To Death*

Once Alice Cooper dumped his first mentor Frank Zappa and moved to Detroit in 1970 things started to get interesting. With the help of producer Bob Ezrin, Alice's sound became a stripped back, lean and shining metal machine with beautiful gleaming guitar riffs and solid, muscular rhythms. He picked up on the Motor City madness of the MC5 and the Stooges, but they could play real well.

'Is It My Body?' is a beautiful, slinky mess of power chords and snappy time changes. The song is kind of complex for Alice – it's a rock star wondering about the interests of a groupie and it plays on the identity issues involved: "What have I got/That makes you want to love me/Is it my body?/Someone I might be?"

In calling himself Alice Cooper, the one hundred per cent straight Vincent Furnier raised gender issues that had long been taboo – especially in the US. He was the first man to adopt a woman's name and to publicly wear drag while doing so. Because he wasn't gay or a transvestite, and indeed because he had nothing to lose, Alice pulled sexual fetishes and lifestyles out of the closet and put them on *American Bandstand*.

Alice didn't care about the politics of sex. He just wanted to shake things up.

"Like, we're taking sex, which is probably another half of American entertainment, sex and violence, and we're projecting it, and we're saying this is the way everything is right now," he said in 1969. "Biologically, everyone is male and female, so many male genes and so many female. And so what it is we're saying is 'OK, what's the big deal.' Why is everybody so up tight about sex? About faggots, queers, things like that. That's the way they are. That's like making fun of a maniac because his brain isn't completely right, because he isn't in the norm.

"People don't accept that they are both male and female, and people are afraid to break out of their sex thing because that's a big insecurity that's doing that. Consequently, people will make fun of us. We don't mind that, that's making them accept more, making fun that we accept that. The thing is this is the way we are. We think it's a gas."

Don't Renege on Our Love   Richard & Linda Thompson

(Richard Thompson) ✳ Hannibal ✳ 1982 ✳ Appears on: *Shoot Out the Lights*

Break-up records are rarely pretty affairs. After ten years and three children, the Thompson's marriage was cracking and shortly after this album's completion, Richard left Linda for another woman. Their union was announced by the album *I Want to See the Bright Lights Tonight* and it's impossible to hear the opening song of *Shoot Out the Lights* other than in the context of their marital lives. It's an approach that Richard is wary of, but not dismissive. "Songs are very much a product of imagination," he said. "They may be founded in reality; they're certainly founded in experience. But they're an imaginative projection beyond that. It devalues the songs to say that they're just soap opera. I think the songs have a broader meaning than that."

The album was recorded quickly by producer Joe Boyd and the austerity of the sound complements the hard edge of the sentiment in most of these relationship songs. Thompson's guitar brings that home. His jazz inflected folk style is pitiless, wiry and taut with tension, anger and shame. There's a bitterness to his playing that is breathtaking. Linda Thompson was later to describe their marriage as "abject misery". 'Don't Renege on Our Love', however, is the complete antithesis of that.

Runaway   Del Shannon

(Max Crook/Del Shannon) ✳ Mercury ✳ 1961 ✳ Appears on: *Greatest Hits*

Del Shannon knew about heartbreak. "There was once a girl I really thought was in love with me," he said frequently in interviews. "I mean, my heart would pound when she came around. She gave me her bracelet to wear, or, well, more likely I pestered her till she let me wear it. And the next day I saw her out with this other guy.

"I took that bracelet off and laid it out on a railroad track. I mean – I was that person. I couldn't get songs which expressed that from anybody else, they just didn't write what I felt. So I had to write. Sure I wanted someone to give me hits, but they all just wrote stuff that sounded like the last song I'd written myself."

The song he wrote called 'Runaway' made him a pop star.

He was Charles Westover playing the Hi-Lo Club in Battle Creek Michigan, backed by an ensemble with Max Crook playing an organ called a Musitron.

"I was tired of doing the same old C, A minor, F and G sounds, which was like 'Blue Moon' a hundred times over with different words," Shannon recalled. "One night, Max Crook, at the Hi-Lo Club in Battle Creek, played an A minor and G, and I said, 'I never heard such a great change.' I said, 'Follow me!' So I went right down the scale. Then I remembered a Hank Williams song called 'Kaw-Liga' where it went from minor to major, and I said, 'Kick into A major! I'm a walkin' in …'"

So began 'Runaway' – one of the most aching songs: "I'm a-walkin' in the rain/Tears are fallin' and I feel the pain". With its galloping tempo and the weird organ, Shannon had one of the most distinctive sounds – the Musitron plus Shannon's lonesome countryish voice – in pop.

"I remember calling up the record company from the Hi-Lo to see how 'Runaway' was doin' and they said, 'The record's sellin' 80,000 a day; you open at the Brooklyn Paramount next week.'"

European Son   The Velvet Underground

(John Cale/Sterling Morrison/Lou Reed/Maureen Tucker) ❊ Verve ❊ 1967 ❊

Appears on: *The Velvet Underground & Nico*

This and the track before it, 'Black Angel's Death Song', were the point where John Cale's classical/avant-garde interests intersected with Lou Reed and Sterling Morrison's literary rock & roll.

Morrison recalled the group's early residency at the Café Bizarre in Greenwich Village: "One night we played 'The Black Angel's Death Song' and the owner came up and said 'If you play that song one more time you're fired!' So we started the next set with it – the all-time version – and got fired."

The Velvets were then an intersection of avant-garde art and rock & roll, just as Dylan had done with literature. In fact, Reed and Morrison had both read English under the poet and academic Delmore Schwartz (best known for his story 'In Dreams Begin Responsibilities'), to whom 'European Son' is dedicated.

"No-one knows why that is," Morrison told Mary Harron. "Everyone thinks it's because the song is thematically appropriate: 'You killed your European son/You split on those under twenty-one'. Incidentally that may be true, because Delmore was the son of Jewish émigrés and a great poet who was never accepted.

"But the real reason is that it has only two stanzas of lyrics and a long instrumental break. Delmore thought rock & roll lyrics were the worst things he'd ever heard in his life; he despised songs with words. As this was our big instrumental outing on the album we dedicated it to him."

Where It's At Beck

(Beck Hansen/John King/Michael Simpson) ✳ DGC ✳ 1996 ✳ Appears on: *Odelay*

Beck Hansen's mother was a former acolyte at Andy Warhol's Factory, his grandfather was an avant-garde artist and his father a bohemian musician. Beck grew up poor and white in black and Hispanic neighbourhoods. He was a true child of alternative culture. It's impossible to speculate on how his background – the nature and/or nurture of it – created his artistic vision, but we can say that Beck understood the fundamentals of folk art in the most profound ways and reinterpreted those folk arts in an entirely fascinating series of records. By the time he released the *Odelay* album he was light years ahead of the pack. That album's lead single, 'Where It's At', was indeed where it was at.

The first thing is the blues. Beck cites Woody Guthrie and Mississippi John Hurt as primary influences. "It was just a guitar, and I liked the sound of it," he said. "It was really simple, the antithesis of the '80s. Once I discovered this traditional folk music, country music, Delta blues, I had a whole world to get lost in."

Beck understood the connection between Mississippi John Hurt and hip-hop. He recognised the hip-hop groove that was implied in the Delta blues and having identified the groove, he made it explicit.

"The interchange between black and white music doesn't seem to have continued," he told *Dazed and Confused* back in 1996. "It has in hip-hop, and in the dance world, but as for alternative bands there doesn't seem much of an understanding left. I recognize that things are headed in a certain direction: I just hope to attempt to preserve some things that are lost, some of the old sensibilities. Like the way we looked at the world before machines ran our lives …

"I walk a fine line because I don't want to surrender to the '90s, I just feel that a lot of the '90s is incredibly fad-based and already dated, even like this new U2 thing. I look at a lot of the alternative bands and it's already so played out, it's already been done over and over. The silver pants and that sexy-but-not-sexy attitude. That sort of phoney ambivalence. It's the whole attitude of angst and cynicism."

As an artist working in pop culture, Beck trawled through the recent pop past, the discards of yesterday's fashions, and he refashioned them into something new. The arrival of the sampler was a key tool. On *Odelay* he had the assistance of the Dust Brothers (John King and Michael Simpson), who had been so pivotal to the Beastie Boys' *Paul's Boutique*.

'Where It's At' was a homage to hip-hop constructed mostly out of acoustic moods and sounds. The refrain "two turntables and a microphone" recalled the punk simplicity of the seminal Bronx parties where hip-hop started in the '70s. The samples of found sounds were playful; the rock & roll flavours brought it together.

"I draw on the past because there's so many things there that were really great, that we undervalue and scoff at," he said. "We're so led by this idea of laughing at the past. We're driven by this consumer need to have the newest thing all the time, so we tend to dispose of what was good. But at the same time I'm against that one-dimensional nostalgia, just doing a retro thing. I think it negates the past, it just makes it one-dimensional. I try to be subtle."

Take Me to the River Al Green

(Al Green/Mabon 'Teenie' Hodges) ✳ HI ✳ 1974 ✳

Appears on: *Al Green Explores Your Mind*

Success wasn't enough for Al Green. Raised in the church, as his secular success increased so too did the spiritual need. In 1973, Al Green was saved.

"I was 'born again'," he said. "I had flown my girlfriend to Los Angeles, done a show in San Francisco in the evening, then another at midnight at Disneyland. So when she got there, I says, 'Man, I am pooped. I am tired. So good night, right? In the other side of the suite, right? 'Cause I am gonna hit it, right?' Man I went in there, and I got in bed and I went to sleep, simple, like the rest of the twenty years I'd went through. About 4:30 that morning, man I woke up praising and rejoicing.

And I had never felt like that before, and I have never felt like that again. So many things were changing so fast, and I had this input, like a charge of electricity. To create a new 'person-all' and I do mean all. To come in and just change your whole personality. I said, 'Man I don't understand.' So I ran into the bathroom. My girlfriend is knocking on the door wondering what's happening. I'm saying, 'Thank you Jesus, hallelujah, praise God.' I says, 'Huh? I never said that before.' I tried to cover my mouth, to keep from saying this stuff, because she's going to hear me. And I heard a voice saying, 'Are you ashamed of me?' And man, I had to come out of there. I came out of there saying, 'No, I am not ashamed. I am not ashamed and I never will be ashamed.' And I kept that. I was feeling so good, I've tried to keep that feeling for as long as I could.

"I'm trying to do my best to be a rock & roll, R&B artist, and I had no control over what was happening. We were all kind of dumbfounded. So I told my mom and I told my dad, 'I don't know what to do, I'm totally confused.' My dad said, 'What's the problem?' I said, 'I've been born again.' He said, 'Well, thank God.' So he went into tears. My mother says, 'Oh Hallelujah', so she went into tears. I said, 'Y'all are not much help, I gotta figure out what to do!' I've got a million dollar career going here, and I'm telling folks they need to be born again. I mean this is tripping me out. On stage, I'd be doing great. I'd be singing 'Love and Happiness', 'I'm Still in Love', all that stuff, then something starts happening, I'd get this impulse – vroom vroom – all of a sudden: scriptures."

The 1974 sessions were a transitional time for Green as he shed the secular songs. 'Take Me to the River' is obviously a baptism song – John the Baptist rebirthing his flock in the holy waters.

Green drew on his gospel roots here and his past as an R&B singer. The song has one of the most powerful and memorable grooves in pop music. Mabon 'Teenie' Hodges rightly gets credit for the tune. It's a harder edged song that reflects Green's turmoil and need for salvation. But there's also strength in the bottom and a sensuality that was so much a part of Green's best work.

"I'm good and bad. I'm right, I'm wrong. I'm light and I'm darkness, I am spiritual and I love to hold my old lady's hand and walk on the beach," said Green. "God made us like that to love. I had to build on 'Take Me to the River'. People see me and say, 'He sure did seem a little rock & roll.' I can't help being like I am. That's the way I am."

Jump in the Fire Metallica

(James Hetfield/Dave Mustaine/Lars Ulrich) ❋ Megaforce ❋ 1983 ❋ Appears on: *Kill 'em All*

"Anger and aggression are just part of our personalities," said Metallica guitarist Kirk Hammett. "It's deep rooted, and that's why it was there in the first place."

It was the blue fire of their anger that set Metallica apart from other heavy metal bands in the early '80s. While death and despair and alienation were the stock-in-trade of every big-riffing hard-rock band, Metallica meant it, man.

Metallica started out as the classic metal outfit. Drummer Lars Ulrich was a Danish-born junior tennis prodigy who teamed up with James Hetfield, a working-class kid from suburban Los Angeles, in 1981. They were thrashing out metal riffs with future Megadeath guitarist Dave Mustaine, as shown perfectly on 'Jump in the Fire'.

A 1982 demo tape, *No Life 'til Leather*, made Metallica's reputation in the underground metal scene. Conflicts – personal and musical – led to Mustaine being fired and replaced by Hammett. By the time *Kill 'em All* was released on the indie label Megaforce, Metallica was the metal band most likely.

Kill 'em All (original title '*Metal Up Your Ass*') was an album of blind fury that went by at such a pace they called it speed metal. There was a dash of punk attitude as well as tempo behind the monumental bottom end from Ulrich and Burton. Then there were the thrash riffs from Kirk Hammett and James Hetfield.

Kill 'em All is the prototype thrash-metal album. After it, the deluge: Slayer, Anthrax and Megadeath.

The speed of execution was one thing, but Metallica's secret weapon was their anger, which was so deeply entrenched in their personalities (especially James Hetfield's) that it resonated beyond the clichés of big hair and hard rock.

"I mean, let's face it, the world is not a pretty place," said Hammett. "The world is pretty sick. There's a lot of ugly things out there and no matter how much you try and escape you always have to wake up and face the fact that the world is fucked-up and ugly."

Me, Myself & I De La Soul

(Pasemaster Mase/Posdnuos/Prince Paul/Trugoy the Dove) ✳ Tommy Boy ✳ 1989 ✳
Appears on: *3 Feet High and Rising*

'Me, Myself & I' has the De La Soul stamp of joy – some jazz and funk, some beautiful guitar samples and some perfect break beats. It's a song that is filled with the positive energy that made De La Soul rap revolutionaries and the album *3 Feet High* a watershed.

De La Soul was a trio of teenagers – Pasemaster Mase, Posdnuos, Trugoy the Dove – with a sampler. Their eclectic choice of samples – Sly Stone, Johnny Cash (whose sampled phrase gave the LP its title), Yma Sumac, Steely Dan, Public Enemy, Hall & Oates, Otis Redding and hundreds of obscure albums – created an entirely new sound when combined with the languid De La Soul grooves. "I consider it a

crime if you're not going to make it sound better or different than it originally was," Posdnuos told Michael Azzerad. "A lot of new R&B music consists of old ideas from other singers anyway, so you could also say that was stealing. Sampling is borrowing ideas too – it's just easier to see where they're coming from."

When rap was 'jacked by the gangstas and the excessive macho posturing of many rap stars, De La Soul went the other way with humour and a more down-to-earth attitude – they avoided, for instance, wearing designer logos and the like. Unfortunately, they made history when one sample by the Turtles incurred a lawsuit and a large payment – that was the last time a label allowed samples to go uncleared.

Stairway to Heaven Led Zeppelin

(Jimmy Page/Robert Plant) ✳ Atlantic ✳ 1971 ✳ Appears on: Untitled fourth LP

Jimmy Page had begun work on the tune at Bron-Yr-Aur before taking it to Plant, who almost instantly came out with the lyric.

"I was holding a pencil and paper," he said. "All of a sudden my hand was writing out the words, 'There's a lady is sure, all that glitters is gold, and she's buying a stairway to heaven.' I just sat there and looked at them and almost leapt out of my seat."

The impenetrable, quasi-medieval story is, according to Plant, about a woman who gets everything she wants without reciprocating.

It's unlikely that there is a literal reading of the lyrics for 'Stairway'. It's full of allusions that go nowhere and yet it's couched in such a stately tune and performance that it appears to have some meaning. The song's enigma is part of its charm and made the track a staple of rock radio for two decades. Aside from the lyrics, however, it's Page's guitar work that is simply breathtaking in its lyricism. His dynamic arrangements of the parts for drummer Bonham and bassist Jones are also quite extraordinary. 'Stairway' was again a case of Zeppelin upping the ante in terms of making pop songs into epics.

The track was finished in London with engineer Richard Digby Smith. He recalled, "[Page] did three takes. He didn't use headphones, he monitored the backing tracks through speakers, which was how the classical soloists who used that studio did it."

In just three years Zeppelin had redefined electric blues rock, dabbled in British esoteric, emulated the greats of the '50s. Here everything came together.

(We're Gonna) Rock Around the Clock
Bill Haley & the Comets

(Jimmy DeKnight/Max Freedman) ✳ Decca ✳ 1954 ✳ Appears on: *Bill Haley & His Comets – From the Original Master Tapes*

"We premiered this music," said Bill Haley. "We put country and western together with rhythm and blues, and that was rock. The first three years were all ours, until Presley came along." It was Bill Haley's fate, like Robespierre, to start a revolution but be overtaken by the force of history.

On 12 April 1954 Bill Haley went into the studio and recorded 'Thirteen Women' and another song, '(We're Gonna) Rock Around the Clock', as the flipside. Haley was born in Detroit and was basically a country player. Yet he was hip to the new sound, cutting a cover of 'Rocket 88' as early as 1951 and 'Rock the Joint' in 1952, which shifted a very respectable 75,000 copies.

Haley's agent, James E Myers (using the nom de plume Jimmy DeKnight), had co-written 'Rock Around the Clock' with Max Freedman, a sixty-year-old composer. The song was a regional hit for Sonny Dae & His Knights in 1954, but Haley thought the track had more promise. He brought a country and western swing flavour to the R&B changes so that it sounded like sophisticated hillbilly music (admittedly an oxymoron). The Comets rocked the track, which was dominated by the double bass and Haley's spirited performance.

'Rock Around the Clock' went onto the B-side and little more was said. However, MGM had a teenage delinquent movie called *Blackboard Jungle* and they needed a song to signify teenage rebellion. Myers placed the Haley version of his own song with the film's producers. Despite its relatively dour denouement, teenage rebellion was the thing of the moment and 'Rock Around the Clock' hit the spot. *Blackboard Jungle* was a hit but the song was bigger. Teenagers went to screenings of the film and tore the cinemas apart.

Where rock & roll had bubbled along on the radio, it was mostly confined to black or regional stations and specialist DJs. *Blackboard Jungle* wised-up teenagers all across America and around the world to the new sound.

Haley truly opened the door. Within months of the film's release, rock & roll was a major craze. More than Elvis Presley, Haley was the white guy who played the black music. He was soon a film star in his own right and headlining concerts around the world.

Bill Haley was all of thirty when 'Rock Around the Clock' hit. He was genial and portly with open, round features. He was never going to be a sex symbol. Elvis Presley and Ricky Nelson and others more handsome soon overtook him. But for a moment he was the King of Rock & Roll.

You've Lost that Lovin' Feelin' The Righteous Brothers

(Phil Spector/Barry Mann/Cynthia Weill) ✳ Phillies/A&M ✳ 1964 ✳

Appears on: *You've Lost that Lovin' Feelin'*

There is an often-told story that when Phil Spector first laid out the arrangement of this song he gave the lion's share to tenor Bill Medley. Bass singer Bobby Hatfield then sarcastically enquired what was he supposed to do: "What do I do when he's singing the whole first verse." Spector quipped, "You can go directly to the bank."

"That's true," Spector told Mick Brown of the *Saturday Telegraph* in 2003. "It's also true that they didn't want to do 'Lovin' Feelin''. They wanted to do rock & roll, ooh-bop-a-doo stuff.

"I worked six months on that fucking record, overdubbing and re-overdubbing, and finally I had it down right where I thought it was pretty good, but I was worried that nobody would get it. I played it for a few people and nobody had heard anything like it. I didn't know whether we'd changed the world or done something completely catastrophic. So I had to go back to New York.

"I played it for Barry Mann and Cynthia Weill. I put it on, the record goes, 'You never close your eyes', and Barry says, 'Whoah, whoah, wait. Wrong speed.' I said, 'What?' He goes, 'Wrong speed, Phil.' That's the first comment I hear.

"So I immediately called Dr Kaplan, my psychiatrist, and I said, 'Doc, I have to see you right away. I just worked six months on this record; it cost me $35,000 and the fucking co-writer thinks it's on the wrong fucking speed.' I called Larry Levine, my engineer, and said, 'You given me the right pressing?' I'm fucking paranoid. I didn't know what to do. So I called Donnie Kirshner, the co-publisher, and said, 'Donnie, I got to play you this record.' He said, 'I hear it's a monster.' I said, 'You've got the best ears in the business.' So I bring it over and put it on. He goes, 'Boops, it's great, it's great, it's great; what do you call it?' I said, 'You've Lost that Lovin' Feelin''. He said, 'How many you got pressed up?' I said, 'Half a million.' He said, 'Bring Back that Lovin' Feelin'' – that's your title.'

"That's the second opinion. So I call Dr Kaplan again.

"Then I call Murray the K, the biggest DJ in New York City. I said, 'Murray, I have this new Righteous Brothers record. I need you to play it on the show, because it's a four minute and five second record; there's never been a record this long before.'

And I'm lying on the label; I put three minutes five seconds – I got in a lot of fucking trouble for that. So he comes over and he listens to the record. This is the last opinion of the day – five o'clock in the afternoon. And he's listening and listening, and it gets to the middle section, and he says, 'That bass line, that 'La Bamba' thing, what's that?' I said, 'That's part of the song.' He said, 'That's fucking sensational.' I said, 'Well, yeah.' He said, 'That's how it should begin.' I said, 'It can't begin that way, Murray.' He said, 'Make that the beginning.'

"And those are my three experts: the co-writer, the co-publisher and the number one disc-jockey in America all killed me. I didn't sleep for a week when that record came out. I was so sick, I got a spastic colon; I had an ulcer."

He needn't have worried. 'You've Lost that Lovin' Feelin'' topped the charts around the world – twice – and has been successfully covered many times. For Spector though it was his most adventurous production to date.

The husband and wife team of Mann and Weill wrote the bulk of the song in their room at the Chateau Marmont; Spector helped them finish the tune and then began assembling the track. Jazz guitar legend Barney Kessel, who played on the song, described Spector's sessions "like he was going to invade Moscow".

Spector discovered the Righteous Brothers at San Francisco's Cow Palace in 1964 and took over their contract from Moonglow Records. They proved to be argumentative, not especially cooperative with each other or Spector and a far cry from the more pliable girl groups he had worked with. Medley and Hatfield were clearly nervous doing a blue-eyed-soul aria that seethed sexuality.

"We knew it was a phenomenal production and a great record," said Medley. "But you have to remember that kind of record was not topping the charts in those days. It was a real adult song. Compared to what was going on."

You Oughta Know Alanis Morissette

(Glen Ballard/Alanis Morissette) ✳ Maverick ✳ 1995 ✳ Appears on: *Jagged Little Pill*

Alanis Morissette was like a fantasy – the teen singer disappears and then comes back looking beautiful and talking dirty. The Canadian teen queen emancipated herself by moving to Los Angeles at age nineteen, found a producer in Glen Ballard and then let it all out on the album *Jagged Little Pill*. Then there was the single 'You Oughta Know' with its hook lines, "Are you thinking of me when you fuck her?" and "Would she go down on you in a theatre?"

"'You Oughta Know' was written from a desperate, dark almost pathetically sad place within my subconscious," she said.

Alanis was a person in the right place at the right time with the right record. The anger that filled the airwaves with grunge was mostly male. Morissette tapped into a female energy with its own issues. It was a time when candour was the coin of the realm.

"This record came from a place in me I had to release," she told Mat Snow at the time. "A lot of the anger comes from the fact that I didn't face it, out of fear, the whole Pollyanna approach I had when I was younger. I denied myself any revelling in my darker side. But as soon as I started writing, I came to terms with it."

Ballard was a professional songwriter/producer, mostly for middle-of-the-road acts, when he met Morissette in 1994. Rather than turn her pop, Ballard encouraged her instincts and helped to arrange them on record. No matter where they went.

"A few lines in 'You Oughta Know' had me thinking, 'God, this is exactly how I feel, but I don't want to hurt anybody.' For years I had been a little guarded, but that was horribly unfulfilling," the singer recalled. "Glen said to me, 'Just remember how bad you felt when you did censor yourself. You have to do this.'

"So, 'Are you thinking of me when you fuck her?' was one hundred per cent honest. For me to take that back would be telling a half-truth and I didn't want to do that ever again. It took me about a day to get over it, to let go of the fear of how it was going to be responded to."

My Boy Lollipop Millie

(Johnny Roberts/Morris Levy) ✳ Fontana ✳ 1964 ✳ Appears on: *Tougher than Tough*

Little Millie Small was a popular Jamaican singer. The English producer Chris Blackwell, who spent a lot of time in Jamaica and is largely responsible for introducing Jamaican music to the west, brought her to London to cover this old R&B song.

'My Boy Lollipop' was recorded by Barbie Gaye in 1956 and was a regional hit. Millicent Small had been singing in ska (also then known as blue beat) bands for

some time and was generally regarded as one of the few solid female artists in the genre.

Blackwell took her to London and brought in a Birmingham band, the Five Dimensions, who at one point had featured a young Rod Stewart. Contrary to myth, Stewart doesn't play the distinctive harmonica part. Jamaican guitar legend Ernest Raglin, however, does feature on the track.

Recorded at Olympic in London, Blackwell was keen to get close to the reverb and rangy sound of Kingston studios. "On that record, the reverb came from a sort of cupboard in the back of the studio that we used as a live chamber," Blackwell recalled. "It was a mono record, and we fed the sound in, adding a bit more of the reverb on Millie's voice."

It was partly the exotic blue beat sound and Millie's cute demeanour that made the record an instant hit on its release in November 1964. "The record worked well for radio," said Blackwell. "Partly because it was a minute and fifty-one seconds. That was important for people at radio who were putting playlists together. Also, Millie's voice was irresistible – for a certain length of time, anyway. So a short record worked well for her."

The song was the first commercial ska/blue beat record and went on to make number two in the US and sell seven million copies. Later it had a new (and less naïve) lease of life as a track for the Spice Girls.

Berlin Chair You Am I

(Tim Rogers) ✳ RooART ✳ 1993 ✳ Appears on: *Sound As Ever*

The Berlin Chair is a sculpture in Canberra that singer/songwriter Tim Rogers thought symbolised his relationship with his girlfriend Tracey Forrester. She provided the strength Rogers needed to stay upright. As he told Craig Mathieson in *Juice* magazine, "I was feeling that at the time with Trace that I had a typical male ego that couldn't be honest or express the way I felt. It's like, 'I should support you, but I'm not going to be that supporting. I'm this cold but frail thing.'"

Rogers' lyric wears his heart and his insecurities strongly on his sleeve. It's hard not to be charmed by the song, however. You Am I make the most of it with their explosive mod sound. Recorded in America with Sonic Youth's Lee Ranaldo producing, the group sidestepped being caught up in grunge whilst having sufficient attitude and taste to stay current with the early '90s hit parade. The track just bursts out of the radio. The song was their biggest hit as a single and propelled the album to number one on release.

"But y'know, making records and travelling is the greatest thing," said Rogers. "We had some big laughs, discovered Maker's Mark Bourbon, cheap Milwaukee beer, and I got to say I never, never thought 'Berlin Chair' was ever going to be a single!"

Sweet Thing Rufus & Chaka Khan

(Chaka Khan/Tony Maiden) ❄ MCA ❄ 1975 ❄ Appears on: *Rufus Featuring Chaka Khan*

"I've always thought of songs in terms of the sexual act – first comes the foreplay, then the climax. Everything I do is sexual. I need a lot of physical love. It's the energy behind everything I do," Chaka Khan told the *Face*. "Singing is the closest thing to making love or what I imagine it would be like to be able to fly. It's a kind of euphoria. Sometimes, when my voice is playing up, then it doesn't happen and I'm mad as hell. But when it's been good, it gives you that same high as good sex. It's a unique experience, and I feel sorry for those who can't go through it. It's like coming and having people applaud too …"

Chaka Khan, especially when backed in the '70s by Rufus, was about the closest thing to sex on vinyl that it was possible to get. Rufus helped. The racially integrated Chicago band was adept with jazz-fusion and funk. Their riffs were exotic and danceable and sensual. Over which came Chaka Khan's jazzy wailing.

Yvette Mane Stevens was thirteen when she became Chaka Khan – the Woman of Fire. "My dad was a beatnik who played congas and sang," she said. "He would play Max Roach and Miles Davis records all day, and when my mother got the chance she'd listen to opera and stuff like Sarah Vaughan. We'd all go about the house singing." That came with a political interest in the Black Panthers and the development of Afro-American culture.

In the smouldering funk of Rufus you can hear Chaka Khan's sexuality just boiling over.

"But it has to be that way," she told the *Face*. "If it's not sexual, then it's not real. You can usually tell if people are giving everything by looking at their faces when they sing. They should be in a state of total abandon, total openness. The best singers always look like gorillas on heat."

Take Five Dave Brubeck Quartet

(Paul Desmond) ✳ Columbia ✳ 1959 ✳ Appears on: *Time Out*

In the late '50s, the Dave Brubeck Quartet (pianist Brubeck, alto saxophonist Paul Desmond, drummer Joe Morello and bass player Eugene Wright) was one of the most popular jazz outfits in the US. Their clean-cut cool jazz was a little bit cerebral and a little bit physical and nicely colourful with the tuneful musing from Brubeck's piano and Paul Desmond's saxophone. Brubeck's quest was to explore new areas in polytonality and in rhythm, bearing in mind oriental and Middle-Eastern ideas. When planning the album that would become *Time Out*, he asked the group to think about playing in different time signatures and getting away from four/four.

"What I was putting together for that session – without Columbia's knowledge – was doing an experimental album using different time signatures," said Brubeck. "They tried to stop the album because it broke some unwritten laws of the label. First, they thought people couldn't dance to it because of the odd time signatures. And it was all original compositions on an LP, which was against their rules as well. They wanted you to have a standard tune between originals. I had to argue with everybody. Luckily, the president of Columbia loved it. But the sales department was against it. They said, 'It'll never sell. Don't waste your money on it.'

"Joe Morello was playing and then improvising off of that beat backstage and Paul would pick up his horn and start playing against it. And I said, 'There's a tune I want to get into this album because it's in five/four time. So Paul, write down some of these things that you're playing against Joe's beat.' So he came to rehearsal and the first thing he said was, 'I can't write a tune in five/four time.' And I said, 'Well did you put anything down?' And he said, 'Yeah, I put a couple of themes down.' I said, 'Let me see 'em.' So he played one of 'em, then he played the other. And I said,

'Look, if you repeat this one and then use that second theme as a bridge and then go back, you have the typical jazz form or the thirty-two bar form that Broadway shows use so much, which is A section, repeat A section, B section – which you call the bridge – and go back to A.' So that's what we did."

'Take Five' was a massive hit single and *Time Out* was one of the first jazz albums to sell a million copies. The breezy, confident playing of the Dave Brubeck Quartet adds to Desmond's fresh-sounding theme. 'Take Five' is probably the most played jazz theme; it's used in hundreds of situations where the sound of modernity is called for.

Al Capone   Prince Buster

(Cecil Campbell) ✳ Melodisc ✳ 1965 ✳
Appears on: *The Story of Jamaican Music: Tougher Than Tough*

Prince Buster (aka Cecil Campbell) was one of the first Jamaican record producers. He ran a sound system in the early '60s for which he produced his own records. According to writer Steve Barrows, Buster wanted to create a distinctive sound so he had his guitarist Jah Jerry play on the after-beat thus creating the stop start rhythm of reggae music. Prince Buster was popular with mods and his records, especially 'Madness', were seized upon by the Two-Tone movement in the UK in the early '80s – not least by the group Madness.

The Jamaican sound system producers were churning out discs to satisfy their dance club audiences, many of them instrumental. The MCs started talking over the top of the grooves in what was called toasting. Eventually this influenced the start of rap in the US.

Like the rappers, the early reggae and ska musicians identified with outlaws. There was a massive gun culture in Jamaica and a large drug industry.

'Al Capone' was homage to the Chicago gangster. Buster's track is mostly instrumental with some toasting. The sound is huge – courtesy of the Skalights' backing. The track is a classic ska cut with the rhythm section right on top of every beat, the sound effects of police and the attitude. This same blueprint would be followed twenty years later by Ice-T and the gangsta rappers. Buster's song, however, is both lighter and more intense.

Bennie and the Jets Elton John

(Elton John/Bernie Taupin) ❋ Rocket ❋ 1973 ❋

Appears on: *Goodbye Yellow Brick Road*

Elton John and glam rock were made for each other. "She's got electric boots a mohair suit" is a line that Elton understood in his bones. "Pop music is fun, and there's only one way to keep your sanity in it. Don't take yourself seriously," he said. "I love pop music. It's my whole life. I love it because it *is* fun. I really have a ball dressing up, wearing the crazy clothes. But there's one thing I do take seriously, and that's the quality of the music. The music has to be there."

Glam was a mixture of the simplistic values of '50s rock & roll with a touch of futurism. 'Bennie and the Jets' obviously hailed back to the idea of the street gangs of the '50s but the post-modern production was actually ahead of its time – the processed drum and bass sounds and John's syncopated piano were an entirely different spin on R&B. The vocal arrangement was also quite challenging. The singer described the track as "One big hook. The strangest cut on the album *Goodbye Yellow Brick Road* – I think I sound like Frankie Valli on the song."

WJLB, a black station in Detroit, picked the track as an album cut and its popularity spread to R&B stations across the country. It was a new audience for Elton John and eventually 'Bennie' made it to number one in the R&B charts.

Fairytale of New York The Pogues

(Shane MacGowan/Jem Finer) ❋ Island ❋ 1987 ❋

Appears on: *If I Should Fall from Grace with God*

Drunken sentimentality came easily to singer Shane MacGowan, so perhaps it's not surprising that one of the Pogues' best known songs is a Christmas tune about being drunk and dreaming of Christmas in Manhattan.

The Irish acoustic band with a reckless and ribald approach to pop music was a delightful anomaly in the over-produced '80s. They built their reputation on white-knuckle breakdowns of folk tunes but their best work was the ballads. Their 1987 album *If I Should Fall from Grace with God* was recorded by producer Steve

Lillywhite and sees the group sounding better than previously. Lillywhite also encouraged his wife Kirsty MacColl to duet with MacGowan on this track and her voice brings a bittersweet tang to MacGowan's tobacco rasp.

The title for this song comes from JP Donleavy's novel *A Fairytale of New York* but the subject matter has little in common. MacGowan mixes the caricatures of New York cops with name checks of traditional Irish songs in that Irish/American tradition. Were it not for the playing of the Pogues and their guest, the song would have been a parody of itself. 'Fairytale', like all good fairytales, is in the telling.

Little Wing The Jimi Hendrix Experience

(Jimi Hendrix) ❊ Track ❊ 1967 ❊ Appears on: *Axis: Bold as Love*

The sessions for the Jimi Hendrix Experience's second album were rushed. His whole life was going at break-neck speed. 'Little Wing' was an idea begun in 1966 when Hendrix was still playing Greenwich Village haunts and the song has that floating quality. Its sound is gently enhanced by putting the guitar through a Leslie speaker, which gives a floppy distortion, and also by the use of glockenspiel. The song is full of beautiful bits of filigree that are simply delightful.

Only two verses long with no chorus, Hendrix described the song as "like one of those beautiful girls that come around sometimes."

We Can Be Together Jefferson Airplane

(Paul Kantner) ❊ RCA ❊ 1969 ❊ Appears on: *Volunteers*

The combination of LSD and cultural revolution reached its apex in the Jefferson Airplane. President Nixon's daughter Tricia invited singer Grace Slick to a class reunion. Slick intended to take Abbie Hoffman, then wanted by the FBI as a subversive, and she threatened to dose the White House punch with LSD. Guitarist Kantner was forever devising crackpot scenarios about outer space or the military industrial complex or avoiding it all and floating off to live on nuts and berries with his daughter, called god (with a modest, lower-case g). It was at least very entertaining, sometimes provocative, and the music was exceptional.

'We Can Be Together' is the romantic anarchist love song of the era; outlaws as lovers and cultural terrorists.

> We can be together
> Ah you and me
> We should be together
> We are all outlaws in the eyes of America
> In order to survive we steal cheat lie forge hide and deal
> We are obscene lawless hideous dangerous dirty violent and young

Kantner was picking up the dissent that was everywhere in those later years of the '60s. "Much of the lyric content of the first verse was inspired by and amplified upon, or came directly from, graffiti on various walls around town and country, much of it from Berkeley, politically angry, yet in an adolescent fashion," he wrote. Other key lines came from the ether or in the case of the final cry "tear down the walls" from fellow folksinger Fred Neil.

The music for Kantner's revolution was inspired by David Crosby, who suggested an old folk banjo line. Kantner wrote using a modal scale of firsts and fifths and using archaic guitar tunings that gave the songs a slightly tart sound. 'We Can Be Together' was the perfect soundtrack to an anarchist revolution. It's worth hearing just for the way that Grace Slick enunciates the hook "Up against the wall motherfucker."

Fell in Love with a Girl The White Stripes

(Jack White) ❋ Sympathy For the Record Industry ❋ 2001 ❋
Appears on: *White Blood Cells*

Jack and Meg White – brother and sister, or husband and wife (depending on who you believe), but certainly guitar and drums and that's it – just the bare facts. Given the baroque state that rock had got itself into, the return to fellow Detroit native John Lee Hooker and Chicago's Hound Dog Taylor's basic recipe was nothing but a good thing. The White Stripes had a sense of humour with their deconstructed rock, which is always welcome. To the basic blues they added some of that other Detroit band the MC5. Being white kids from Detroit the whole thing was highly stylised, of course, and given a kind of art framework. The White Stripes were full of sharp angles and controlled and messy swathes of sound, but sticking to a basic blues framework they couldn't go too far wrong. Good thing too on this, their third outing.

'Fell in Love with a Girl' is a perfect piece of pop that's more than a bit fractured – as modern love tends to be – but beautiful nonetheless.

The Ballad of Lucy Jordan Marianne Faithfull

(Shel Silverstein) ✳ Island ✳ 1979 ✳ Appears on: *Broken English*

In the '60s, Shel Silverstein was what was termed "a humorist". He drew amusing illustrations for *Playboy* magazine, wrote humorous poetry and sold folk and country songs. Silverstein's best known number was 'A Boy Named Sue', made famous by Johnny Cash. In the early '70s he was associated with the band Dr Hook for whom he penned a number of ribald lyrics and some hits ('Sylvia's Mother'). Silverstein gave them the out-of-character 'The Ballad of Lucy Jordan' for their 1973 album *Belly Up!*. Marianne Faithfull, who was a hopeless junkie at the time, liked the track enough to commit it to record herself.

In one of those strange show business coincidences, Silverstein contributed to the soundtrack on Tony Richardson's film *Ned Kelly*, in which Marianne Faithfull was cast. Upon arriving in Sydney to begin shooting, Faithfull took an overdose of drugs. This precipitated the end of her relationship with Mick Jagger and her quick descent into drug addiction. Faithfull had been a very delicate beauty with a similarly fragile voice and as her habit worsened (and the smoking and drinking) she tore her instrument apart.

By the time she returned to singing she was a very different kind of artist. The *Broken English* album actually sounds more German than British with the brooding synthesiser textures and dark atmospheres. The songs too have that cast – they possess little hope and they're big on coming to terms with the existential questions.

'The Ballad of Lucy Jordan' is about a housewife who realises at the age of thirty-seven that she will not have romance or excitement or exhilaration and so jumps off the roof of her house. Marianne Faithfull sings the song with the parched passion of someone who has stood on that roof and looked over the edge. However, there is the redemptive tone in her voice – she didn't do it and in that knowledge we can feel the warm wind in her hair.

Love is All Around The Troggs

(Reg Presley) ❋ Fontana ❋ 1968 ❋ Appears on: *Love Is All Around*

After pumping out some of the best pop in Britain in the '60s, the Troggs came out with this massive ballad. Its modal guitar riff has a faintly Elizabethan feel to it against the inexorable rhythm. Singer Reg Presley, although trying to be sweet, still has that deeply sexual undercurrent in his vocal. The Troggs had followed 'Wild Thing' with their own 'I Can't Control Myself', which was even more wild than the first track. 'Love is All Around' puts that brutish past behind the Troggs. This is a real chocolate box ballad. There's so much personality here, especially in the ham-fisted but well-meaning backing vocals.

'Love is All Around' was yet another hit in Britain and their second smash in the US, although none of this transferred into long-term success for the band. 'Love Is All Around' has lived on through cover versions by R.E.M., Everything But the Girl and the bloodless but popular version by Wet Wet Wet on the soundtrack for the film *Four Weddings and a Funeral*.

Blue Moon of Kentucky Bill Monroe

(Bill Monroe) ❋ Harmony ❋ 1946 ❋ Appears on: *Blue Moon of Kentucky*

The father of bluegrass, Bill Monroe, grew up in Kentucky playing the mandolin and guitar. In 1938 at age twenty-seven he formed his Blue Grass Boys and synthesised gospel, country and string band music by playing the tunes really fast. This style of music came to be known as bluegrass in honour of the band and the fact that it came from the bluegrass state of Kentucky.

Monroe was a songwriter of no mean ability. 'Blue Moon of Kentucky' is the state song and was an inspiration to the young Elvis Presley, who made it the flipside of his first single, amping up the ballad into one of the first rock & roll songs. "We thought it was exciting," said Presley guitarist Scotty Moore. "We just sort of shook our heads and said, 'Well, that's fine, but good God, they'll run us out of town.'"

Monroe then went into the studio and recorded a new version that was even faster than Presley's.

"Back in those days, it seems every trip we made was from Kentucky to Florida driving back and forth," Monroe said of the inspiration for the song. "I always thought about Kentucky, and I wanted to write a song about the moon we could always see over it. The best way to do this was to bring a girl into the song. I wanted words to this, because most of my songs were instrumentals. 'Kentucky Waltz' had come earlier and I knew I could write both words and music, so I wrote it in the car on the way home from one of those Florida trips."

Who Knows Where the Time Goes?
Fairport Convention
(Sandy Denny) ✳ Hannibal ✳ 1969 ✳ Appears on: *Unhalfbricking*

Sandy Denny was the unquestioned queen of British folk music. Her clear soprano voice rang like a bell through tunes already centuries old. Denny also turned her hand to songwriting.

Fellow singer Linda Thompson recalls that in the '60s, women didn't write. That was a man's work. Nonetheless, Denny persevered. "'I'm going to write some songs', she said to me," Linda Thompson recalled to Jim Irvin. "I said, 'What do you mean write songs?' It's hard to believe, but it never occurred to us to write back then. The next thing I knew we were watching the TV in her attic in Gloucester Road and a butter ad came on, this voice singing, 'We're all a lot better for butter.' And it was Sandy! She said, 'Promise me you won't tell Richard [Thompson] I did this, he'd kill me! But I got £40!' Then she played me 'Who Knows Where the Time Goes?' and I was stunned."

Her second attempt, 'Who Knows Where the Time Goes?', made at the age of nineteen, was placed with traditional act the Strawbs and also quickly covered by Judy Collins before finding its definitive home on this 1969 recording by Fairport Convention.

This is a song about the big issues – mortality, the worth of a life – but Denny sounds neither naïve nor twee. The metre is often eccentric and the melody wanders into difficult areas that only Richard Thompson's guitar can navigate to support her, but that only serves to make this one of the most captivating tracks of its era.

Everyday People Sly & the Family Stone

(Sylvester 'Sly Stone' Stewart) ✳ Epic ✳ 1969 ✳ Appears on: *Stand!*

Sly Stone walked it like he talked it. Sly & the Family Stone was a group that was black and white and male and female. Forty years later how many American groups have there been with that kind of diversity? Really only Prince has found multi-cultural groups and he was a Sly Stone devotee.

'Everyday People' is one of the most beguiling and literate songs about racial harmony. The light funk groove underneath the track is irresistible and the melodies that play on top are delightful. However simplistic the sentiments may seem, one only has to consider how little distance has been travelled since 1969 to see that they're not easy to maintain.

This has been the most enduring of Sly Stone's songs; it lends itself to both rock and hip-hop treatments.

Are You Gonna Be My Girl Jet

(Nic Cester/Cam Muncey) ✳ EMI ✳ 2003 ✳ Appears on: *Get Born*

Taking their name from Paul McCartney's 1974 song, Jet are a band on the run. They translate the ragged, loose sound of the mid-'70s into the sober and punctual 21st century. Jet come from Melbourne. They are influenced by old records and new music from the likes of You Am I. They have, in a charming rock & roll way, appropriated much of the sentiment of the Faces. The songs are about trendy nightclub disc jockeys who look down their nose at these suburban kids or the middle-class housewives in off-road vehicles. They're essentially unpretentious young people singing their way in a world of phonies and straights. Most important of all, though, is that they're trying to get laid.

'Are You Gonna Be My Girl' will go down in history as one of the signature guitar riffs. It's a line that could have been on a record by Iggy Pop or the Stooges or the Kinks or indeed the Beatles. It sounds familiar yet is quite new and unique.

If Jet's music seems retro, the marketing isn't. 'Are You Gonna Be My Girl' was adopted as the theme for the first advertisements for the Apple i-Pod. The perfect synthesis of maximum rock & roll and new technology.

Stay Free The Clash

(Mick Jones) ❋ Epic ❋ 1978 ❋ Appears on: *Give 'Em Enough Rope*

"It wasn't the easiest thing I've ever I done, that's for sure," said Sandy Pearlman, producer of the Clash's second album, *Give 'Em Enough Rope*. The album took six months to finish in between illness and a dispute with their svengali manager, Bernard Rhodes. Its clear brilliance notwithstanding, CBS declined to release the first Clash album in America because they didn't believe the sound quality was up to standard. Sandy Pearlman, the producer of Blue Oyster Cult, signed on to make the Clash sound respectable. With mixed results. "The object was to make them sound as fiery and spirited as they do live, only better," said Pearlman. He didn't quite get there though.

Give 'Em Enough Rope doesn't have the brimstone of its predecessor. Nor does it have the songs. The Clash sound like they're in some mid-Atlantic limbo. In trying to make them sound like a hard rock band they risked losing their identity completely.

'Stay Free', however, is a key moment. A Mick Jones vocal, it is a highly personal song about leaving behind the childhood gang. Jones outlines the choices for kids in the slums – get out or go to jail. He does it with a tough but wistful tune that shows, for the first time, the sentimental side of the Clash. This was a step out of the punk ghetto for the band as well, proving they were able to go beyond the slogans and the headlines and write from the heart.

Like a Rolling Stone Bob Dylan

(Bob Dylan) ❋ Columbia ❋ 1965 ❋ Appears on: *Highway 61 Revisited*

Al Kooper, who played the distinctive organ on the track, recalled that he snuck into Columbia Studios in the hope of playing on a Dylan date. He was a session guitarist and songwriter looking for a chance. As he waited for Dylan to arrive, Michael Bloomfield arrived with his Fender Telecaster. Bloomfield had no case for the instrument so he just brushed the snow off and began tuning up. Kooper realised that he couldn't compete so he stood behind the Hammond organ – an instrument he had not played before. Dylan arrived and ran 'Rolling Stone' down, Kooper busking his part. When it came to the playback, producer Tom Wilson tried to keep

Kooper's organ in the background but Dylan told him to turn it up. These few minutes would influence the rest of Al Kooper's life.

'Like a Rolling Stone' was so different, so sophisticated, that it shaped the future of rock & roll.

"My wife and I lived in a little cabin in Woodstock, which we rented from Peter Yarrow's mother," said Dylan. "I wrote the song there in this cabin. We had come up from New York and I had about three days off up there to get some stuff together. It just came you know. It started with that 'La Bamba' riff."

It's likely that at least one character in the song was Edie Sedgwick, an aristocratic waif who had come to New York and fallen in with Andy Warhol's Factory crowd. Dylan spent some time with her and Warhol – whom he seemed not to like much – around this time. Sedgwick was a doomed beauty who may have been romantically involved with Dylan and was certainly involved with his friend Bob Neuwirth.

The last session that Dylan would have with producer Tom Wilson included pianist Paul Griffin, bassist Russ Savakus and Bobby Gregg, whose sharp crack on the snare drum announces the start of the song. While Dylan had taught Bloomfield the chord changes most of the musicians were improvising from beginning to end.

Bob Dylan wrote in *Rolling Stone* magazine, "The song was written on an old upright piano in the key of G sharp, then later at Columbia recording studios transferred to the key of C on the guitar. The chorus part came to me first and I'd sorta hum that over and over, then later figured out that the verses would start low and move on up. The first two lines which rhymed 'kiddin' you' with 'didn't you' just about knocked me out; and later on, when I got to the jugglers and the chrome horse and the princess on the steeple, it all just about got to be too much."

Blue Sky Mine Midnight Oil

(Midnight Oil) ✳ Sony ✳ 1990 ✳ Appears on: *Blue Sky Mining*

Having refashioned their sound on the *Diesel and Dust* album, Midnight Oil's next project was more forceful.

The opening track on the album begins with a harmonica riff from singer Peter Garrett that signals the fact that the group is back on the barricades.

The target this time are the corporate giants who continued to mine asbestos even after they knew that they were sending the workers to certain, protracted and painful death from mesothelioma. Not only that – once the death toll started to mount, the mining and sugar cane companies adopted delaying tactics through the courts so that the workers died and their compensation claims expired with them. It remains one of the great acts of capitalist bastardry of the 20th century. 'Blue Sky Mine' pulls no punches in bringing the matter to the fore. The fact that the story is set against a backing track that is full of as much melody as righteous indignation only ensured that the song would be a hit.

No Matter What Badfinger

(Pete Ham) ✳ Apple ✳ 1970 ✳ Appears on: *No Dice*

Badfinger were Britain's first '70s power pop act. Originally called the Iveys, they were one of the first acts signed to the Beatles' Apple label and their first single, 'Come and Get It', was written and produced by Paul McCartney. It was a national smash but placed Badfinger forever in McCartney's shadow. It was a pity given that Pete Ham and Tom Evans were accomplished songwriters themselves.

The Badfinger quartet – Pete Ham, Tom Evans, Mike Gibbins and Joey Molland – lacked a clear frontman. Ham was an exceptional guitarist and both he and Evans wrote catchy, intricate pop songs. As well as working with McCartney, Badfinger were used by George Harrison on *All Things Must Pass* and they appeared in the Concert For Bangladesh.

'No Matter What', from their second album, *No Dice*, was a muscular piece of pop music with elegant harmony vocals filling out the sound. The melodies were sophisticated and the harmonies delightful. "A lot of it is a load of rubbish," said bassist Molland in 1970 of the contemporary pop scene. "They play a guitar riff and write a number round it. They should try writing a number and finding a guitar riff to fit it. That's much harder. I think people will get back to more melodic things soon. They have all learned to improvise now and they will use this in writing good songs. That is what we are trying to do."

The record was a major hit and the album did well. However, music in the early '70s was moving into a heavier phase and Badfinger seemed a little twee. The group struggled along until 1975 when leader Pete Ham committed suicide.

The Boys are Back in Town Thin Lizzy

(Phil Lynott) ❋ Mercury ❋ 1976 ❋ Appears on: *Jailbreak*

Phil Lynott wanted to be a rock & roll star. He just never really knew what kind. He guided Thin Lizzy through hard rock and revamped Irish folk songs and finally found his biggest hit by imitating Bruce Springsteen. Lynott was charisma in search of a muse. By dint of his personality and the band's strong live shows, Lizzy had a following. Then Lynott took the riff from Springsteen's 'Kitty's Back' and adapted it to a lyric about a returning Vietnam veteran. The subject matter had no resonance and the verses evolved into a song about male bonding and camaraderie – a subject to which the Irish Lynott could relate. This was a great working-class anthem. The rousing sentiments and the massed harmonies and guitars made 'The Boys are Back in Town' a perfect rock song for its day. The year 1976 was a notoriously soft time for rock & roll – the calm before the storm of the New Wave – and Thin Lizzy were one of the few rocking voices standing out against the mellowness.

   "I just like blood and guts," said Lynott. "I've seen every Clint Eastwood movie goin'. I get off on aggression. One of the main reasons I get up on a stage is to let the aggression out, to put the aggression to a good purpose like rock & roll. I'm sure I'd be fookin' locked up now if I didn't play in a group. I'd be in this jail I'm always singin' about."

Death Don't Have No Mercy Rev Gary Davis

(Rev Gary Davis) ❋ Vanguard ❋ 1959 ❋ Appears on: *Rev Gary Davis at Newport*

The Rev Gary Davis played the guitar with a distinctive fingerpicking and bottleneck style. His songs never lost sight of Judgement Day. In the '20s Davis broke his left wrist after slipping on the snow. The bones were set improperly and the deformity affected the way he held his instrument.

   Born in 1896 in South Carolina, he was raised in the Piedmont area and his rapid fingerpicking and ragtime tunes fits with the style of Piedmont blues. Davis was blind from shortly after birth. Like many handicapped African Americans he turned to music and/or the Church for employment. His fame as a guitarist spread far and wide although he recorded occasionally until the '50s when he moved to New York. Davis preached on the streets of Harlem between gigs. He was discovered by a white audience in the folk revival of the late '50s and early '60s, by which time his repertoire consisted of spirituals and gospel blues accompanied by a ferocious, lyrical guitar style. Davis also made a living teaching. His pupils included folk legend Dave Van Ronk, guitar virtuoso Stefan Grossman, Taj Mahal, the Grateful Dead's Bob Weir and Jefferson Airplane's Jorma Kaukonen. The latter guitarist developed an explosive fingerpicking style directly updated from Davis and recorded a number of Davis' songs.

It's doom alone that counts with 'Death Don't Have No Mercy'. Interestingly for a spiritual, God doesn't have any mercy here either. This dark song is set against a ragtime blues track that's simple and blunt but incredibly elegant for all of that.

Shakin' All Over The Who

(Johnny Kidd) ❋ Track ❋ 1970 ❋ Appears on: *Live at Leeds*

'Shakin' All Over' was the first British rock & roll hit as such. Johnny Kidd wrote and sang the song with his group the Pirates and topped the UK charts in 1960. It was a big deal for Roger Daltrey and his mates. Ten years later it was in their set when they made the greatest live album of the rock era. It's big and loud and incredibly exciting.

"*Live at Leeds* is my favourite album by the Who and it's the only Who album I still play," said John Entwistle shortly before his death.

It's hard to explain just why *Live at Leeds* is such a perfect record. The Who are down to the basic quartet. Listening to it you can feel the room. Townshend rips big chords from his guitar and then lets them boom around the walls. You can feel the energy coming off Keith Moon as he flails around the kit not keeping the beat so much as pushing the song forward. Then there's Entwistle carrying the melody on his bass guitar.

The Who were not a band so much as four soloists who agreed on a tune, each retaining the right to do it their way. On *Live at Leeds* you can hear the interplay as Townshend calls the shots and you can feel, almost touch, the empathy between the players.

'Shakin' All Over' kicks off like a taut boogie carried by Entwistle's bass riff. But Kidd's song is just a jumping-off point and the Who explode the tune with flashes of brilliance coming from all quarters.

"*Live at Leeds* is the best and most exciting Who live stuff I've heard," said Townshend. "It may be a bit of a head-banging album. It's not pretty or brilliantly performed or anything, it's just energy."

Would I Lie to You? Eurythmics

(Annie Lennox/Dave Stewart) ✳ RCA ✳ 1985 ✳ Appears on: *Be Yourself Tonight*

Having invented electro pop, Eurythmics guitarist/producer Dave Stewart then developed a number of other production styles, the most powerful of which was his soul period.

In the mid-'80s he applied the clean lines and discreet sound of electronic music to the beat and feel of classic soul. As he said in response to a review in the British music press, "That was one thing I couldn't understand in the review of the single in the *Melody Maker*. The guy was saying 'Stewart who fancies himself as the svengali producer' and all this, and he said it was like a kind of watery sound, where to me 'Would I Lie' is the most powerful, up, intense Stax sound of anything I've heard on the radio lately. When I watched *Top of the Pops* it all seemed like watery kind of discoey … the whole thing was ploddy-ploop, y'know? And then suddenly our single comes on the radio and it's …"

Everything is built around the massive drum sound that pushes right up against the beat. It's a tsunami of energy coloured by Lennox's impassioned vocals and Stewart's bluesy guitar lines.

"I was always looking for a good relationship, and you can see it in the songs, all this unrequited love," said Lennox. "I was never in one spot, so my emotions were in turmoil. I never really enjoyed it – I should have settled down. Eurythmics was the mainstay of my existence and yet it was hollow. The irony was that though I was lonely, miserable and unsatisfied, it's a fantastic source for songs. The more hurt I'd get, the more intense the songs. 'Would I Lie to You?' and 'Thorn in My Side' I'm afraid are honed from the same tree. It wouldn't take much of an IQ to figure out they came out of the break-up with my first husband."

The Revolution Will Not Be Televised Gil Scott-Heron

(Gil Scott-Heron) ✳ Flying Dutchman ✳ 1970 ✳

Appears on: *Small Talk at 125th and Lenox*

Gil Scott-Heron was a prodigy, publishing poetry and prose while still a teenager. He identified with the Harlem Renaissance movement and was influenced by the writers Langston Hughes and LeRoi Jones. While at university in 1968, he met jazz musician Brian Jackson. They started putting the words and music together and formed the Midnight band. Producer Bob Thiele recorded Scott-Heron's work using some of the finest jazz and funk musicians for his Flying Dutchman label.

'The Revolution Will Not Be Televised' is his best known work. It's very funny as a satire on mass media and white-dominated culture, but it is also a very angry call to arms for African Americans. No-one is spared.

"We as black people haven't had the proper forums to display our art," said Scott-Heron of his role in showbusiness. "We've had to be dependent on society at large to provide these forums and they're often more interested to show Elvis Presley than Little Richard, or the Osmonds than the Jacksons.

"It's consistently been an issue. And going back, the Tommy Dorseys and the Benny Goodmans and the Stan Kentons were hailed as innovators when in actuality you have to look at Count Basie and Duke Ellington as the springboards for that whole feeling that swept America and continues to sweep the world."

Brian Jackson provided the funk but it was Scott-Heron's adept way with words that made 'The Revolution' a classic. The mixture of funk and rhymes – especially in militant verse like this – was the prototype for rap that was to come fifteen years later.

"You know the consciousness is first. In any movement for change," Scott-Heron said, "education comes before organization and action, so you would like to see a continuing period of enlightenment and awareness going around so people know exactly where they are and what they're dealing with. We live in a world now where communication and information and stuff is readily accessible for people who have their antenna up trying to pick up on those types of vibes, the information is there. Those are the people who inevitably relate ideas that bring change about, people who are conscious initially are springboards for other periods of consciousness."

I Shall Be Released The Band

(Bob Dylan/Richard Manuel) ✳ Capitol ✳ 1968 ✳ Appears on: *Music From Big Pink*

The Basement Tapes were the most famous bootleg in rock history. Dylan and the Band were living in upstate New York playing songs together and recording them on a reel-to-reel tape recorder. There was no agenda or deadline. Possibly the songs would be used in the future. Possibly they would be shopped to other performers or none of the above. Such was Dylan's stature, however, that once the rumour mill started, the "Basement Tapes" soon became indistinguishable from the Holy Grail. Copies of the tapes began to circulate and were among the first bootleg albums.

"Maybe 150 songs were recorded in a seven or eight month period," said bassist Rick Danko referring to the Basement Tapes. "Bob would come and bang the songs out on his typewriter and we'd go down into the basement and make some music up for them. The tapes were part of Bob's rehabilitation – he was getting stronger and feeling better. And from that we started getting our writing chops together a little bit."

Although the Basement Tapes are discussed in terms of Bob Dylan's work, the transformation in the Band was way more profound. Over those months, the Band went from being a singer's backing group to a complete ensemble with its own sound.

"Bob helped us more than anybody ever did," said drummer Levon Helm. "What Bob was doing, it's easy to see now, was showing us how to construct songs, how to put songs together, and he was doing it right there with us, in front of us. He and Rick were writing 'This Wheel's on Fire', and he and Richard had written 'I Shall Be Released'. Bob had set the Band on fire, and everybody was starting to write, Richard and Robbie especially."

'I Shall Be Released' is one of the gems to emerge from those sessions. This was one of the few songs to be rerecorded for the Band's first album. It's a disconsolate cry for redemption – spiritual or physical.

The troubled Richard Manuel with his plaintive falsetto was the ideal singer to take the lead on this track with Danko and Helm backing up the lower registers.

"Up to this point I've been harping on Bob Dylan, on everybody, about this sound, and I don't mean electronic trick sounds," said Robertson. "All of that plays a part, but there's a vibe to certain records, a quality, whether it's a Motown thing or a Sun Records thing or a Phil Spector thing. [Bob] was saying, 'Who cares about that? I'm only interested in the lyrics.' Well, that's not the way I felt about it all.

"I wanted to discover the sound of the Band. So I thought, I'm gonna do this record and I'm not gonna play a guitar solo on the whole record. I'm only going to play riffs, Curtis Mayfield kind of riffs. I wanted the drums to have their own character, I wanted the piano not to sound like a big Yamaha grand. I wanted it to sound like an upright piano. I wanted these pictures in your mind, I wanted this flavour.

"I didn't want screaming vocals. I wanted sensitive vocals where you can hear the breathing and the voices coming in. This whole thing of discovering the voices – don't everybody come in together. Everybody in records is working on getting all the voices together until it neutralises itself. I like voices coming in one at a time, in a chain reaction kind of thing like the Staple Singers did. But, because we are all men it will have another effect.

"All of these ideas come to the surface and what becomes the clear picture is that this isn't just clever. This is emotional and this is storytelling. You can see this mythology."

Dance to the Music Sly & the Family Stone

(Sylvester 'Sly Stone' Stewart) ❊ EPIC ❊ 1968 ❊ Appears on: *Dance to the Music*

The first Sly & the Family Stone record had not done well. The pressure from the record company had got to the point where Epic was trying to tell Sly Stone what to record. According to sax player Jerry Martini, this got Sly's back up.

"I remember Sly and I going over to CBS Records," Martini recalled. "They gave us some shit and Sly threw it down and he looked at me and said, 'OK, I'll give them something.' And that is when he took off with his formula style. He hated it. He just did it to sell records. The whole album was called *Dance to the Music*, dance to the medley, dance to the shmedley. It was so unhip to us. The beats were glorified Motown beats. We had been doing something different, but these beats weren't going over. So we did the formula thing. The rest is history and he continued his formula style.

"On 'Dance to the Music', one of the sub-hooks was my clarinet. We used it on the medley. It was snowing in New York and if we wanted to get paid by the union, which was so strong, you had to bring an instrument to the session. If a union guy came in, you better have your horn. I was freezing and just wanted to carry my small clarinet. I had already done my horn parts. I was in the back room, just fucking around with the tune. Sly walked by the studio and called me over. So then, on a lot of things, I used clarinet. That is how hits happen. He was smart. He heard something unique and it was the sound of a clarinet. When is the last time you heard of somebody in rock using a clarinet? I used to take my clarinet on the road for a long time until we got too fucked up, then I just played the lick on my sax. A lot of people thought that it was a soprano sax on that, but it was B flat clarinet."

'Dance to the Music' built on the soul plus gospel that the group had developed in its years in Vegas and on the road. Sly & the Family Stone were one of the greatest live acts in the country and with material like 'Dance to the Music' they conquered every venue they played. One of the crucial dates was Woodstock, where the medley that starts with 'Dance to the Music' completely stole the show and the Woodstock film.

"Our songs would segue one into the other and many times there wasn't a place where you could get a big audience response," said bass player Larry Graham recalling the Woodstock gig. "When we did stop playing, there was this tremendous roar unlike anything we had ever heard. It was dark and you couldn't see all those people, but to hear that was like, wow. To go back out and play the encore after hearing that, it made us rise to a level we had never been musically. There was so much energy; everybody reached deep down inside and pulled out some stuff we didn't know was there. From that point on, once you tap into a certain zone, you know you can go back there because you have now tasted that. The audience might not be as big as Woodstock, but to play anything after that, you know you have capabilities beyond. So that took our concerts up to a whole other giant notch, to where the concerts became an experience, for the audience and for us. We started playing in this new zone we had never played in before and it was some of heaviest stuff I had ever been involved in."

American Idiot Green Day

(Billie Joe Armstrong/Green Day) ❋ Reprise ❋ 2004 ❋ Appears on: *American Idiot*

In the madness that has gripped America since 2001, Green Day is the only group that has raised a voice of protest loud enough to be registered in the charts. You pretty much have to go back two decades to the Clash to see this kind of clear political stance from a band. Of course, that's not where the Clash comparison ends – the churning guitars are not too far removed from 'White Riot'.

In 1994 Green Day were one of the best So-Cal punk bands, but that's not saying too much. Their songs were snotty and adolescent and they sold ten million copies of their *Dookie* album. Seven albums later, though, they were married and millionaires and no longer snotty with anything but each other. They resolved to write an album that would take the group to another level.

Having sorted their differences, singer and lyricist Billie Joe Armstrong looked at the world at large. After four and a half months of assembling twenty songs the tapes were stolen and they started again from scratch.

American Idiot was released in September 2004 and Green Day went on the road opposing President Bush and the Iraq war.

"I felt like I was too old to be angry anymore," he said. "I didn't want to come across as the angry older guy. It's sexy to be an angry young man, but to be a bitter old bastard is another thing altogether."

But righteous indignation is still cool. 'American Idiot' is a song that will forever characterise the Bush era.

Stayin' Alive The Bee Gees

(Barry Gibb/Robin Gibb/Maurice Gibb) ❋ Polydor ❋ 1977 ❋
Appears on: *Saturday Night Fever*

Robert Stigwood moved into film production in the '70s sensing not only the excitement of Hollywood but the opportunities for film and music tie-ins. He got involved with the production of a film based on a magazine article by journalist Nik Cohn called 'Tribal Rites of a New Saturday Night'. Cohn's story was set in the world of the 2001 Disco in Bay Ridge, just across the bridge from Manhattan. Although Cohn made up most of the details, he described a vigorous subculture of working-class kids, mostly from European immigrant backgrounds, who loved to dance. These were people whose cultural life was not represented in film and TV. Their preferred style of music – disco – was regarded as somewhat low-rent and gimmicky.

Stigwood read the article in *New York* magazine, called Cohn and within twenty-four hours had made a deal for the movie rights for $10,000.

While Stigwood put the film together, the Bee Gees were in France making their next album. Stigwood picked 'Stayin' Alive', 'Night Fever', 'How Deep is Your Love', 'More than a Woman' and 'If I Can't Have You' for the soundtrack.

This was not a musical in the traditional sense of the term – none of the cast broke into song – but music was central to the film in a way that it had never been expressed before.

Saturday Night Fever was a low-budget film with a gritty, not particularly romantic story. It was Stigwood's genius that put John Travolta with the Bee Gees and caused a massive ruction in the otherwise smooth, and then colourless, worlds of music and film. To see Travolta as Tony Manero striding down the Bay Ridge street to the beat of 'Stayin' Alive' is to get that astonishing rush when you see the collision of a groove and an attitude.

Stigwood had given the Bee Gees an outline of the film, but essentially the Bee Gees were just getting on with it.

"We never really knew what was going on," said Robin Gibb. "It just so happened that the songs worked, especially 'Stayin' Alive'. It's a very straightforward song about survival in the city. That's what it was and that's the statement."

Saturday Night Fever was a massive phenomenon that broke disco wide open. It became the biggest selling soundtrack in history with over thirty million copies sold. It was a true cultural milestone and no-one will ever think of the '70s without an image of Travolta in a white suit with one hand in the air and one on his hip.

The Times They are A-Changin' Bob Dylan

(Bob Dylan) ✳ Columbia ✳ 1964 ✳ Appears on: *The Times They are A-Changin'*

Quoting the Bible and referencing Irish and Scottish balladry, Bob Dylan's 'The Times' was a manifesto that implicated his elders in slowing the progress of the world. Although he had a reputation in folk circles, Dylan's name at this point was based on his "protest" songs as popularised by Peter, Paul and Mary. In 1964 the times were indeed a-changin' fast, even though the issues of Vietnam, sexual liberation, women's liberation and the race riots of the '60s were yet to come.

Not only is Dylan anticipating the coming troubles, he lays the blame on the shoulders of the older generation. "Your sons and your daughters are beyond your command," he said somewhat pretentiously and indeed they soon would be.

In December 1963 Dylan had given a speech to the Emergency Civil Liberties Committee where he said, "I only wish that all you people who are sitting out here tonight weren't here and I could see all kinds of faces with hair on their head … because you people should be at the beach.

"Old people when their hair grows out, they should go out. And I look down to see the people who are governing me and making my rules and they haven't got any hair on their head. I get very uptight about it."

Clearly Dylan's battle wasn't just with conservatives but was more with conservative ways of doing things – whether that be running Civil Rights marches or traditional politics. This is the song of a young man in a hurry. It's full of the arrogance of youth. While it clearly refers to the changes in American society at the time – the civil rights movement, which was gathering apace, the spirit of liberalism that was then ascendant, the changing values in post-war society and the nuclear age – the song also reflects Dylan's personal struggle. It's not just Roosevelt and Goldwater that are in the way but jazz tragics like Mitch Miller and the ossified New York folk scene that were just as conservative.

The effect of 'The Times' was shocking. The song instantly polarised Dylan's audience. The album of that name was a stark, black-and-white affair with an unsmiling, unaccompanied Dylan with verse and polemics coming straight from the cold heart of America. There were none of the love songs to ameliorate the powerful tales of racial violence and political hypocrisy. "I knew exactly what I wanted to say and who I wanted to say it to," he said.

The phrase "the times they are a-changin'" went quickly into the vernacular as one of the catch-phrases of that decade.

Of course, within six months of the album's release, Dylan stopped writing his overtly political songs.

"I wanted to write a big song, some kind of theme song, with short, concise verses that piled up on each other in a hypnotic way. This is definitely a song with a purpose."

(Sittin' On) The Dock of the Bay Otis Redding

(Otis Redding/Steve Cropper) ✵ Stax ✵ 1968 ✵ Appears on: *Dock of the Bay*

"Elvis was the king of rock & roll and Otis was the king of soul," said Steve Cropper. "Had he lived, I think he would have been king of them all."

With the backing of Booker T and the MGs, Redding was the most versatile singer in the Stax stable and a performer of immense charisma. His show-stopping set at the 1967 Monterey Pop Festival had poised him to step out from a strictly soul and R&B market into the pop charts. 'Dock of the Bay' was the song that could do it.

Redding began the song in August 1967 while living on a houseboat in Sausalito, outside San Francisco. Back in Memphis in December, MGs' guitarist Steve Cropper helped him to finish it. "I'm not sure he knew, but my trick was always to write about Otis. So I came up with the lines 'I left my home in Georgia/Headed for the 'Frisco Bay.' It was so easy," said Cropper.

"When he came in with it, he played me the melody and he had almost one whole verse completed. We sat down in the studio by ourselves and within two hours we had the completed song. I helped him with part of the second verse and the bridge and the changes. Then I did the arrangement.

"Right before the accident, he came into the studio for one whole week and then off and on for another two weeks," Cropper told *Hit Parade* magazine. "We cut a lot of stuff on him then. At the time, he was going out on weekend dates. He'd come back and cut from Monday to Thursday. This time we cut some final horn lines of a Friday morning. He said, "I'll see ya'all." He went off to Nashville to do *Up Beat* and then the next night he left for Wisconsin. He was due back here Monday to cut more songs."

The track was recorded in one day including an improvised whistling part at the end and Redding's vocal. The MGs were in perfect form. The song is ostensibly a homesick ballad but there's a deep forlornness there that is mirrored by Cropper's guitar line, which weaves a majestic melody underneath Redding's wistfulness.

Redding never finished the track. Four days later while on tour, his plane crashed into a lake killing everyone on board.

Cropper spent three weeks mixing the song and it did give Otis Redding his number one in the pop charts.

Sister Morphine The Rolling Stones

(Mick Jagger/Keith Richards/Marianne Faithfull) ❋ Rolling Stones Records ❋ 1971 ❋

Appears on: *Sticky Fingers*

'Sister Morphine' was begun in May 1968 during the sessions for *Beggars Banquet* and Marianne Faithfull released her own version in January 1969. By the time the song appeared on *Sticky Fingers*, Faithfull had broken up with Jagger and had a heroin habit, and Keith Richards was well on the way down that track.

The song is literally about the victim of an accident hanging out for painkillers. However, in the context of this album and the Rolling Stones at this point in time, 'Sister Morphine' is one of the most harrowing and powerful drug songs.

It starts with an unsettling dream against an acoustic guitar and then the other instruments slowly come in, as the lyric becomes more deranged. Ry Cooder's jagged, bluesy guitar answers the vocal with a continuous melody line. Jack Nitzsche's piano turns the dream into a nightmare with sheets of treated sound playing off against Charlie Watts' delightfully sloppy but hard drums. Rather than playing as an ensemble, each of the notes here accentuates the lyric and builds into the most sophisticated arrangement the Rolling Stones had yet tried.

While drugs had long been a part of the rock & roll scene, 'Sister Morphine' made it clear, in no uncertain terms, what was going on.

Bullet with Butterfly Wings The Smashing Pumpkins

(Billy Corgan) ❋ Virgin ❋ 1995 ❋ Appears on: *Mellon Collie and the Infinite Sadness*

The most ambitious record of the alternative rock era, at least in scope, *Mellon Collie and the Infinite Sadness* placed Billy Corgan's intimate pain on a large stage, inviting influences from progressive rockers such as Queen and early Elton John.

'Bullet with Butterfly Wings' is vicious in its majestic attack. It's a song where Corgan opens up and the pain just screams out. Corgan is lashing out at the world at large and internally at himself. This is a song about a struggle to overcome self-hatred. Corgan, though, transcends himself with the track and makes one of the most complex pieces of music of the era.

"You're talking about a bunch of people who can't understand why they feel so empty and jaded and apathetic," said Corgan shortly before the release of the *Mellon Collie* album. "I mean, people who feel hateful. People used to take their hate out on black people and minorities. In some parts of Europe, they're starting to do that again. But in America, I don't feel that our generation feels those feelings. They're not taking them out on anybody. They're taking it out on themselves. They don't even know why they feel this hatred, why they feel such apathy. I don't know if this will make any sense to you, but to play a concert and to stand before your generation and the one that's about to follow us, ages fourteen through twenty-eight, and just see how jaded people are. A good song, a smiling face, a true feeling, doesn't do it. People want to see things smashed to bits. They want to see you rip your heart out. Then you start to wonder, you start to question what is this. It's not a feeling. It's a lack of it.

"And I do really identify with that. It's built into our psyche to feel this. Even if you didn't come from a broken home, you grew up around people who did. Call it what you will, Generation X or whatever. We're it."

Corgan was abandoned by his mother and then shortly afterwards by his father and left to be raised by his stepmother. The emotional scarring was deep and informed everything that Corgan did as a composer. He chose to channel the anger into the music.

"The classic story is that after eighteen months on the road behind *Siamese Dream*, we came off [concert tour] Lollapalooza and three days later I started writing *Mellon Collie*," he said. "There is no break for me. I'm twenty-nine years old, and every year that goes by I lose some of that chip-on-the-shoulder energy of youth."

Tipitina Professor Longhair

(Henry Roeland Byrd) ❋ Atlantic ❋ 1972 ❋ Appears on: *New Orleans Piano*

"Professor" was a New Orleans honorarium for a piano player. Henry Roeland Byrd (aka Professor Longhair) was the most respected of New Orleans pianists. In the '30s and '40s he developed a style of playing – a boogie-woogie meets rumba with some Calypso and Latin spice – that was the recipe for New Orleans R&B. From

New Orleans this style spread and became one of the cornerstones of rock, R&B, funk and soul.

Longhair (born in 1918 and died in 1980) worked as a boxer, street dancer and professional card shark before turning his attention to music in the late '30s. He claimed that he was taught piano by his mother using an instrument rescued from the trash heap. "My mother started teaching me what few keys they had left on it," he said. "I guess that's why I learned the style that I learned. When I was playing, I had to remember what keys were good and what was bad and skip them and jump 'em. Some of the guys said I was cross chording but, whatever it was, I was getting to the right keys. With these good pianos, it's simple for me to do what I was doing then."

In 1949 he was playing regularly around New Orleans as Professor Longhair and his Shuffling Hungarians. The following year he cut his first record, 'Bald Head'. The track was not a hit. It set the standard though. It had a characteristic syncopation in the bass part played against drums, then there was a heavy right hand sticking with a four/four attack and, then, touches of colour.

In 1953 he cut 'Tipitina', his signature tune. 'Tipitina' marshalled New Orleans rhythm into a sparkling package. Longhair's style had a profound influence on Fats Domino and his producer Dave Bartholomew, as well as Allen Toussaint and Dr John. "I was teachin' all the guys in New Orleans. Practically all of them. I helped Toussaint, Sugar Boy, Guitar Slim, Fats, any of them that come to me for help. It looked as though Fats was gonna make some money, an' I thought if he had some of my musicians, I would've been the first friend he would've thought of," said Byrd. "I thought that. But I been thinkin' wrong over a lotta things, looks like everythin' I was thinking was wrong, so I just quit."

The song was not a hit and Longhair gradually faded from the music scene. He retired in 1964. In 1971 the New Orleans Heritage Festival found Byrd working as a manual labourer and put him on the bill. He was quickly embraced by a new generation of white rock stars – Paul McCartney was a high profile supporter of Fess (as he was known), among many others. A large and popular bar in New Orleans was named Tipitina's after the Longhair tune.

"Fess wanted the band to rawmp and frolic," said Dr John of working with Longhair. "Just to get what he meant by rawmp and frolic was the whole thing."

Friday On My Mind The Easybeats

(Harry Vanda/George Young) ✳ Alberts ✳ 1967 ✳

Appears on: *Nuggets, Vol. 2: Original Artyfacts From the British Empire & Beyond*

Easyfever swept through Australia in the mid-'60s. With the screaming, kinetic hobbit Stevie Wright out front of a pile-driving mod sound, the Easybeats were the real deal at the wrong end of the world. Five British and Dutch expatriates who met around the Villawood Hostel, the Easybeats not only mastered the sound from Swinging London but had their own spin on it courtesy of guitarist George Young and his partners Wright and fellow guitarist Harry Vanda. By the time they moved to the UK, Wright was so overcome with fame that he had stopped writing, so it fell to the others to sit in the bedroom and come up with the hits.

They hooked up with the producer of the day, Shel Talmy, who had made hits for the Kinks and the Who amongst many others. Having presented him with a hundred ideas, he thought there might be some promise with one, 'Friday On My Mind'.

"We actually got stuck on that song. It almost didn't make the grade," Vanda said in the documentary *A Long Way to the Top*. "There was a devil of a part to get to the chorus 'cause there was a key change problem that finally fell into place. We played it to Shel and he said, 'That's the one.' We said, 'OK Mr God, Sir.'

"So he took us in the studio and said, 'Play big guys, run through it.' Then he said, 'Thanks'. We were thinking of going through this long drawn-out creative process where the skies would open and revelations would come and that was it, one take."

'Friday On My Mind' has a raga-like ascending guitar riff that appears effortless over the top of a rhythm section that plays like their life depends on it. The mastery of the song though is in its lyrics – the working man's daydream of the delights of the weekend. It's a perennial theme that goes back to the roots of rock & roll, but the Easybeats give it a new cast that is a little bit psychedelic but mostly just urgent.

The song was not only an inspiration to working-class kids but also to David Bowie, who covered the track on *Pin Ups*, and Bruce Springsteen, who performed it live.

"I guess it was a good omen," said Vanda, "that when we left the studio a guy was walking through the hall humming it. It was just one of those songs, it took off with a vengeance."

I Want You Back   The Jackson 5

(Freddie Perren/Fonce Mizell/Deke Richards/Berry Gordy Jr) ✳ Motown ✳ 1969 ✳

Appears on: *Diana Ross Presents The Jackson 5*

Joe and Katherine Jackson's boys had been signed to Motown for a year when 'I Want You Back' was released. It became the first of their four consecutive number one hits and seven Top 10 hits in the two years that followed.

The song had originally been penned for Gladys Knight as 'I Want To Be Free'. Motown executive Berry Gordy Jr heard it and suggested a rewrite, as he was interested in hearing what the five brothers he'd just signed from Indiana could do with it. Gordy had input on the rewrite and was a perfectionist in the studio, sending the boys back time and again until every vocal line hummed with pure soul energy.

Michael Jackson credits those sessions as a major influence on his future recording career. "I observed every moment of the sessions where Berry was present," he said in his book *Moonwalk*, "and never forgot what I learned ... His persistence was his genius."

Diana Ross (whose Supremes had recently split) was enlisted as industry godmother to the boys. The invitation to the record launch was a telegram signed by the Motown diva herself. She was soon to be eclipsed by Michael, the squeaky little singer who brings bouncing passion to this track.

Pancho and Lefty   Townes Van Zandt

(Townes Van Zandt) ✳ Tomato ✳ 1977 ✳

Appears on: *Live at the Old Quarter (Houston, Texas)*

Although revered by other country singers and songwriters, Townes Van Zandt was pretty much unheard of. As a teenager he was diagnosed as a manic depressive with schizophrenic tendencies, and spent time in institutions. Throughout his life he rambled, gambled, drank and fought off depression. As critic Robert Gordon put it, "To hear Townes' songs was to face desperation and beauty."

'Pancho and Lefty' was one of his first and most popular songs. A rambling tale of friendship, rivalry and death, it has been widely covered, most notably by duo Willie Nelson and Merle Haggard, whose version topped the country charts in 1983.

In 1973, Van Zandt had been recording for some time with little success and was preparing to leave Houston, which had been his home. Four nights were recorded at the one hundred-capacity nightspot the Old Quarter, from which a double album was distilled. Steve Earle called Van Zandt, "the most riveting solo performer I've ever seen – just closed his eyes and played and sang and you couldn't take your eyes off him." The tapes of the show were regarded as being among the best versions of these songs, but the album languished without a label to back it for some four years. It's now regarded as a definitive collection of live Van Zandt and the breadth of his writing, including, of course, Willie's future hit.

Refried Boogie   Canned Heat

(Canned Heat) ✳ Liberty ✳ 1968 ✳ Appears on: *Living the Blues*

Canned Heat were John Lee Hooker's real 'boogie chillun'. Led by blues nuts Bob 'The Bear' Hite on vocal and harmonica and guitarist Al 'Blind Owl' Wilson, the Heat took the essence of Hooker's boogie blues style and modernised it dramatically. Wilson had played with Son House and they took their name from a blues metaphor for homemade alcohol dating back to the '20s.

On their third album, Canned Heat came into their own with their biggest pop single, 'Goin' up the Country', while also stretching out for jams lasting three-quarters of an hour. There's also the brilliant anti-drug anthem 'Amphetamine Annie'. Hite and Wilson were sufficiently deep into the blues tradition to pull off what would otherwise be self-indulgence. Indeed, the success of the Heat led to the formation of thousands of boogie bands all over the world and effectively put an end to the blues revival.

The key to the Heat was Wilson, whose playing was always tasty and economical and kept in service of the pulsing rhythm section. They were also pretty funny, sending themselves up as well as the police force and the drug culture.

All forty minutes of 'Refried Boogie' are the beginning and the end of the genre right there.

Wilson died in 1970 from a heroin overdose and the group never really recovered, although they did an excellent project, *Hooker 'n' Heat*, with their spiritual guru John Lee. The Heat's vein was fundamentally a thin one, which they thoroughly mined, and after the death of Wilson it was inevitably thinner and of interest only to biker gangs. But in their heyday, hanging around Topanga Canyon, with their laid-back, heavily bearded sense of the righteous groove, Canned Heat were the epitomy of cool.

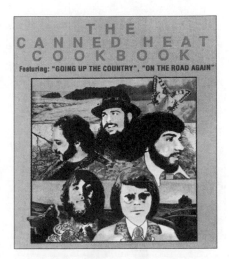

I'm Not Angry Elvis Costello

(Elvis Costello) ❋ 1977 ❋ Stiff ❋ Appears on: *My Aim is True*

Elvis Costello was vital to British rock in the late '70s. Punk rock was a revolution in a teacup, not a bad thing at all, but Costello's lyric gift and his sound, which was both angry and melodic, gave a weight to what would otherwise have been not much more than a fashion statement.

The genius of *My Aim is True* is how nasty it is about romance. 'I'm Not Angry' lets fly at the unfaithful lover while having a swipe at the cosmetics industry on the way through.

"I'm an extraordinarily bitter person," he said. "I don't like to sound as if I'm too obsessed and can't feel any other way, but it just happens that those songs evince that kind of feeling and, therefore, the album is like that. The next one could be very, very different, although I don't think it's necessarily going to be any kinder. In fact, if anything, the way I feel at the moment, it's going to be a lot crueller.

"People have noticed that a lot of the album is about being rejected, but I don't like the idea of getting too analytical about it. Just like everyone else I have good days and bad days. The things that mean the most to you or affect you most, you write songs about."

Costello worked for Elizabeth Arden cosmetics to support his wife and child. He had been trying to break into show business for some years until he found the newly formed Stiff and became their first recording artist.

"I didn't go in and say, 'Look, I've got these songs and, well, with a bit of patching up and a good producer I might make a good record'," Costello recalled. "I went in and said, 'I've got some great fucking songs, record them and release them.' Stiff were the only ones that showed that kind of faith in me."

"I happened to be in Stiff's office when Elvis Costello came in with his tapes all those years ago," BP Fallon wrote some years later. "I came to know him as brittle, tense, nervous, agitated. Paranoid would not have been too strong a word. Today, Elvis Costello sleeps less often with clenched fists. His talent as a writer and singer doesn't seem to hurt so much. And he laughs a lot."

A single, 'Less Than Zero', was followed shortly thereafter by an album. The LP was recorded on sick days Costello took off from work. House producer Nick Lowe enlisted California country rock band Clover (later, as the News, they backed Huey Lewis).

"I wasn't stupid," Costello said. "When I wrote the first album, I saw that the most direct and most aggressive songs seemed to hit home. The rhythm of the times was like that. I seemed to get across to people with those ones, both when I played in clubs and when I was sending the demos in.

"I was writing songs very fast, and one day I went to Pathway Studios where Nick Lowe was producing a Wreckless Eric record. Wreckless was very nervous, so Nick took him for a drink to loosen him up a little bit, and I recorded eight songs while they were gone, just guitar and voice. That was the bulk of the demos for *My Aim is True*."

'I'm Not Angry' is strong in its groove and in Costello's delivery. It has none of the gimmicks of other tracks on the album, but has a veracity and immediacy that has rarely been matched in rock. 'I'm Not Angry' seethes with rage, distrust, disgust, repulsion and black humour. This is the sound of adolescent misanthropy at its very best.

Hey Ya! OutKast

(Andre Benjamin) ❋ La Face ❋ 2003 ❋ Appears on: *Speakerboxxx/The Love Below*

For his *The Love Below* section of OutKast's 2003 double album, Andre Benjamin did his best to shift hip-hop perceptions. He has placed himself in a lineage of Sly Stone, George Clinton and Prince, which means not only dressing up but also playing on the edges of rock and hip-hop. For 'Hey Ya!', which is kind of a throwback to '60s pop rock and an immensely witty R&B flavoured tune, Benjamin played all the instruments himself.

The Love Below is a complex, if often humorous, exploration of modern mores and the quest for love and happiness. "In hip-hop, people don't talk about their vulnerable or sensitive side a lot because they're trying to keep it real or be tough," Benjamin told the *Guardian*. "They think it makes them look weak. That's what *The Love Below* means, that bubbling-under feeling that people don't like to talk about, that dudes try to cover up with machismo." It shows a rapid maturation in Benjamin's writing on every level.

"'Hey Ya!' is an upbeat, breakneck jam about the state of relationships today," he told VH1. "A lot of people stay together for tradition. All I'm saying is I think it's more important to be happy than to meet up to somebody else's expectations or the world's expectations of what a relationship should be. So this is a celebration of how men and women relate to each other in the 2000s. But you wouldn't know that if you were just dancing all night. You really have to sit down and listen to it."

Tonight I Think I'm Gonna Go Downtown

The Flatlanders

(Jimmie Dale Gilmore/John Reed) ❋ Rounder ❋ 1990 ❋

Appears on: *More a Legend Than a Band*

In 1970 when they found themselves living together on 14th Street in Lubbock, Texas, they were just three young songwriters who would call themselves the Flatlanders. Butch Hancock, Joe Ely and Jimmie Dale Gilmore were to have an immeasurable effect on country music – even though it took twenty years before their record was released.

"We just coincidentally moved back to Lubbock at the same time and started playing together," said Gilmore. "There was no design to put a band together as such but the chemistry was so great that it just took on a life of its own. We all had a common love of folk music, country and country blues – but then we also loved the Beatles. We had very eclectic taste. There was great radio in Lubbock at that time, especially the border stations at night. We listened to it all."

As a school kid Gilmore had recorded with Ely back in Lubbock at the behest of Buddy Holly's father. Hancock and Gilmore had known each other since they were teens. The songs they wrote together were informed by the influence of rock & roll and the subject matter and tone more clearly represented their generation than what was perceived as country at the time. They plugged into the roots of Hank Williams and the Stanley Brothers and Jimmie Rogers with a touch of Robert Johnson and the real folk blues.

The best Flatlanders song is the plaintive 'Tonight I Think I'm Gonna Go Downtown'. Gilmore, as a student of Eastern mysticism, is perhaps singing about the nature of existence. As someone who has had his share of problems with drugs, he may also be singing about that or it may be that the song is just the lament for a lost love. In any case the melody aches so hard you think your heart will break.

"It's pretty crude but there's a certain flavour about the record," said Joe Ely. "It had an eerie, lonesome sound which reflected our roots in Lubbock and the wind, the dust and the environment."

You Don't Have to Say You Love Me Dusty Springfield

(Giuseppe Donaggio/Simon Napier-Bell/Vito Pallavicini/Vicki Wickham) ❊ Philips ❊ 1966 ❊ Appears on: *Golden Hits*

Dusty Springfield discovered 'Io Che Non Vivo (Senza Te)' at the San Remo Festival. On returning to England she asked Vicki Wickham to write an English lyric. According to Simon Napier-Bell, Wickham and he penned a lyric one evening after dinner. Springfield and her producer Johnny Franz were both a little unsure of the quality of the words but had a shot nevertheless.

"Dusty was insecure about her singing ability," Napier-Bell writes in his memoir *Black Vinyl White Powder*. "When it came to recording she would accept nothing less than perfection and always presumed she could come nowhere near it. The night she recorded our song she complained that the echo on her voice wasn't right. The engineer ran downstairs to the basement to adjust the inputs to the echo chamber. As he did, he noticed how good the echo sounded in the stairwell of the seven-storey circular staircase. Five minutes later, Dusty was halfway up it, singing into a mike hanging in space in front of her. What she sang was one of the great pop performances of all time. Sheer perfection from the first breath to the last."

Springfield's insecurity probably had much to do with the power of this recording. It's a song that carries the entire yearning drama of a person bereft of self-esteem. It's a song of enormous emotional truth just laid bare. Songs like this tend to disappear in their own pathos and kitsch dramatics but Dusty Springfield sings it like a confession and it's impossible to look away from his honesty.

Girls on Film Duran Duran

(Simon Le Bon/Nick Rhodes/Andy Taylor/John Taylor/Roger Taylor) ❋ EMI ❋ 1981 ❋
Appears on: *Duran Duran*

After all those depressing years of dressing in black and worrying about the government, the British working classes rebelled. Throughout the provinces the boys got out the grease paint and the sewing machines and descended on London for a good time. In London the clubs were playing European disco and hip-hop and soul music. Roxy Music and David Bowie were the new role models.

It was colourful. It was exciting. The synthesiser replaced the guitar as the instrument of the day.

Duran Duran, a quintet from Birmingham, was very much of the moment. "The whole London scene seems very superficial," said keyboard player Nick Rhodes. "In Birmingham, people really look forward to the weekends when they can get dressed up and go to somewhere like the Rumrunner, which is the hip club there. And it's all sorts of people – office workers, factory workers, students. The London lot seem very tense."

"What we're doing is European white disco," said bassist John Taylor.

"What we wanted to do," added Rhodes, "was just pick out all the elements of various musics. Disco's pretty good on its own, but a lot of the vocals wreck it.

We've got really strong melody lines. I think that's something that disco's lacking. In general, melodies have been missing over the past couple of years."

Whatever their intention at the time may have been, Duran Duran were an instant sensation amongst teenage girls. They were pop gold. Amid all the hype, though, are some excellent grooves and tunes, perhaps the best of them being 'Girls on Film', which just oozed shop-assistant sexuality. It combined the notion of illicit sex with the erotically charged medium of the day – photography.

The fact that a risqué film clip accompanied the song only added to the excitement.

From there it was a steep ride to the top and then a steep ride down.

"We had been forced by our own desire for success into a stereotype of a teen-idol group. We were spending far more time worrying about clothes, make-up and photo sessions than we were about writing songs," said Simon Le Bon recently. He is, however, relaxed about the whole ride. "Many of my friends from school now spend a lot of their time in pubs swilling down beer and getting big bellies. They go home at night to watch TV and are hassled with mortgage payments."

Toys in the Attic   Aerosmith

(Joe Perry/Steven Tyler) ❊ Columbia ❊ 1975 ❊ Appears on: *Toys in the Attic*

Aerosmith's Stephen Tyler didn't always respond well to criticism. When a reviewer in *Creem* magazine suggested that the group's album *Toys in the Attic* lacked "class," Tyler was not happy. "Class. I'll give him some fuckin' class. Obviously, anyone who writes about class is looking for a rock & roll band with class, right? So he's got the wrong group. Our music is rock & roll, and rock & roll is rock & roll. Some people would never admit they still masturbate. I think class is puttin' something over really well. That's what class is."

"We were drug addicts dabbling in music, rather than musicians dabbling with drugs," said singer Joe Perry by way of explaining his singer's behaviour.

'Toys in the Attic' is classy. In a trashy classy way.

This was the opener for Aerosmith's second album. It was a rock & roll track that was raw and dirty and ragged. The track sounds strung out on speed, like it was made in cheap hotels. At the time Aerosmith aspired to be the Yardbirds but sounded more like the New York Dolls. They were living the rock & roll dream – all of it. Aerosmith in 1975 were determined to be the next Led Zeppelin or die trying. They almost accomplished both those things and this is what it sounds like.

Wild Thing The Troggs

(Chip Taylor) ❋ Fontana ❋ 1966 ❋ Appears on: *From Nowhere*

Chip Taylor was a professional songwriter and record producer (and brother to actor Jon Voight) when he knocked off 'Wild Thing' in a 1965 afternoon on assignment for a group named Jordan Christopher and the Wild Ones. He improvised the song and engineer Ron Johnson added the whistling solo. "I was on the floor laughing when I was through," he said. "As soon as I did it I said 'What is this monster?' Because, basically, it was just a guttural expression, some kind of sexual thought."

'Wild Thing' is the foundation stone, the Rosetta Stone and the Magna Carta of rock & roll.

The original recording stiffed, as did a version by British studio outfit Hedgehoppers Anonymous. Then manager/producer Larry Page thought it might be good for the Troggs. Fronted by Reg Presley, the Troggs were considered to be not very bright. However, Presley's limited but powerful voice was perfect for the simple yet powerful song.

"We recorded 'Wild Thing' and 'With a Girl Like You' at the same sessions," said Presley. "And they were recorded really fast because we only had about three-quarters of an hour to get our gear set up, get a balance, do the record and then move out."

Instead of whistling, the Troggs supplemented an ocarina solo. The ocarina is a musical toy mostly used by children and this is its first and only appearance on a number one record. Not only did 'Wild Thing' top the charts, it set the benchmark for perfect raw rock & roll and has never been bettered. In 1966, pop music ventured off into the world of concept albums and art. The Troggs were the conscience of rock & roll. 'Wild Thing' remains a stellar classic now that the Moody Blues and their ilk have, thankfully, vanished.

"It's not like the chords don't sound like a thousand other songs," said Taylor. "But there's something within the simple structure that's magical. It's still inspired, even in its dumbness."

With or Without You U2

(U2) ✳ Island ✳ 1987 ✳ Appears on: *The Joshua Tree*

U2 started out as teenagers full of vigour and spit and attitude. By 1987 they had learnt the power of understatement and on 'With or Without You' they hit on the perfect balance.

It can be read as a song about either marital romance or spiritual need but singer Bono made it clear where the song came from. He told Timothy White when quizzed about it, "I've said it before, but to me there's nothing more radical, there's nothing more revolutionary than two people loving each other. One, 'cause it's so uncommon these days, and two, 'cause it's so difficult to do."

U2 were aware of their status as the band who were about to become superstars and the cost weighed heavily on Bono's head in the years leading up to and just beyond *The Joshua Tree*.

"In 'With or Without You' when it says 'and you give yourself away and you give yourself away' – everybody else in the group knows what that means," he told Niall Stokes. "It's about how I feel in U2 at times – exposed. I know the group think I'm exposed and the group feel that I give myself away. And funny enough, Lou Reed said to me, 'What you've got is a real gift: don't give it away because people might not place upon it the right value.' And I think that if I do any damage to the group, it's that I'm too open. Because there's a cost to my personal life and a cost to the group as well."

La Bamba Ritchie Valens

(Ritchie Valens) ✳ Del-Fi ✳ 1958 ✳ Appears on: *The Best of Ritchie Valens*

A plane crash made Ritchie Valens immortal – the fateful trip with Buddy Holly that ended in a cold January morning on Clearwater Lake. Valens earned another place in the history books as the first Hispanic rock & roll star.

Richard Steve Valenzuela grew up in Los Angeles and was enamoured of rockabilly and rock & roll. Local producer Bob Keane signed Valens to his independent label Del-Fi where he cut a minor hit, 'Come On Let's Go'. Despite being a small label, Keane used the very best session players of the time – Earl Palmer (drums), Carol Kaye (guitar), Red Collendar (stand-up bass), Ernie Freeman (piano) and Rene Hall (guitar). They also cut a second single, 'Donna', written for Ritchie's girlfriend Donna Ludwig, that made number two in the national charts after the plane crash. On the flipside of that track was the first Spanish language rock & roll song, 'La Bamba'.

Valens was an aficionado of traditional Spanish music. 'La Bamba' was a rock & roll adaptation of a traditional style of song – a *huapango* – from the Vera Cruz region of eastern Mexico, generally composed of nonsense lyrics and designed for dancing at parties. Valens adapted the time signature and added electric bass and guitar to the sound.

'Donna' was a hit in early 1959 but 'La Bamba' also charted. In the '80s Richie Valens was the subject of a biopic called *La Bamba* and the song was revived by Los Lobos, who took it all the way to number one – the first Hispanic number one hit in the US charts.

Uncle John's Band The Grateful Dead

(Jerry Garcia/Robert Hunter) ❄ Warner Bros. ❄ 1970 ❄ Appears on: *Workingman's Dead*

The Grateful Dead were an electric blues band given to jamming for up to six hours at a time. Their music was often formless, closer to jazz than to rock & roll and decidedly uncommercial. Despite a devoted live following, the group's albums were epic financial disasters. In 1969 the group's leader, guitarist Jerry Garcia, junked the formless rock. He picked up on a trend towards country that was happening at the time and drew on his own roots as a bluegrass banjo player. Garcia wanted to make an album of songs and to cut it quickly so as to have some chance of paying off the group's debts.

Workingman's Dead was sort of country although the songs by Garcia and lyricist Robert Hunter tackled themes close to them. Hunter's lyrics were uncharacteristically direct while Garcia's tune respected the conventions of pop music.

The first track, 'Uncle John's Band', was almost a statement of purpose. It was inspired by the folk music that Hunter and Garcia loved as teenagers, especially the bluegrass and folk of the New Lost City Ramblers.

Hunter assembled the lyrics from old folk and bluegrass tunes: 'Buckdancer's Choice', 'Stories the Crow Told Me' and others. Hunter references the 1776 Revolutionary War and the tradition of baptism. Like so many artists of the late '60s – Dylan, the Byrds, the Band – the Dead were hoping to get in touch with traditional American values.

'Uncle John's Band' had its debut at the Fillmore Auditorium on 4 December 1969, two days before the Dead played the fateful Altamont Concert at which their friends the Hell's Angels stabbed a man to death in the crowd and brought the hippie dream crashing down. The Dead recorded 'Uncle John's Band' shortly thereafter. It remains one of their most tuneful and positive songs.

Cold Water Tom Waits

(Tom Waits/Kathleen Brennan-Waits) ✳ Epitaph ✳ 1999 ✳ Appears on: *Mule Variations*

'Cold Water' is another low-life song from Tom Waits on the *Mule Variations* album. It's a hardcore blues that is both tragic and funny and always beautifully observed and sung.

"I marvel at [Huddie] Leadbelly, who just seems to be a fountain of music," he said in 1999. "When he started working with Mose Ash, he told Huddie he wanted to record anything – nursery rhymes you remember, whatever. He said, get up and tapdance, and we'll put a microphone on the floor, and we'll put that on the record. And play a squeezebox, or tell a story about your grandmother. They were like concept albums. They're kind of like photo albums, with pictures of you when you're a kid. I love the way the songs unfolded, the way he would go from telling a story about the song right into the song, and there wasn't even a bump in the road when he started singing. He could have just talked for another three minutes, and that would have been fine, too. A lot of the litany in his songs were – well, he'd have a lot of repeats. 'Woke up this morning with cold water, woke up this morning with cold water …' It's a form. They're like jump-rope songs, or field hollers. The stuff he did with John Lomax is out on Rounder right now. It's like a history of the country at that time."

Tutti Frutti Little Richard

(Robert 'Bumps' Blackwell/Dorothy LaBostrie/Little Richard) ❉ Specialty ❉ 1956 ❉
Appears on: *Here's Little Richard*

When Andy Gill of *MOJO* asked Little Richard to name his greatest achievement, he replied, "To me, in my life, 'cause I came from a poor black family of twelve in a little country town, my greatest achievement would have to be 'Tutti Frutti'. It took me out of the kitchen – I was a dishwasher at the Greyhound bus station, makin' $10 a week workin' twelve hours a day, and 'Tutti Frutti' was a blessin' and a lesson. I thank God for 'Tutti Frutti'." So do we all.

Little Richard is a stone genius. He only did one thing, which was to pound out a gospel-flavoured three chords at either fast or breakneck pace, but Richard is truly one of the great artists of the 20th century.

"Awopbopaloobopalopbamboom!" That was his opening phrase to the world. As Nik Cohn pointed out in his book of that name – that's pretty much rock & roll from genesis to revelation right there. The piano is supercharged and manic and the band, a crack New Orleans session crew under the direction of 'Bumps' Blackwell, just rides the tiger. Blackwell discovered Richard playing 'Tutti Frutti' at the Dewdrop Inn in New Orleans and put him in the studio with Fats Domino's band.

Richard, a young gay black entertainer brought all of those issues to bear on the scream that starts the record off. Richard is going crazy in the button-down '50s and he's screaming to be let out.

Most of all it was pure sexual energy.

"When I came out, there wasn't no-one singing rock & roll," he told *MOJO*. "There was country and there was a bandleader called Swingin' Sammy Kaye, singing a song called 'Pennies from Heaven', but they wasn't fallin' over in my neighbourhood, so I had to get out and create somethin'.

"So I took rhythm and blues and boogie-woogie, put it together and came up with rock & roll. But I was only able to use my own singing style when I went to Specialty. I had that style all the time, but the other companies wouldn't accept it! They wanted me to sound like other people, to be a blues singer. I had this other thing, they'd never heard nothin' like it, so they was afraid of it. But when I went to Specialty with Awopbopaloobopalopbamboom! they said, 'OK!'"

To hear Little Richard is to experience art at its most sublime.

Everything I've Got Belongs to You Ed Kuepper

(Ed Kuepper) ❋ Hot ❋ 1990 ❋ Appears on: *Today Wonder*

This song was recorded in two days with just Ed Kuepper playing guitar and Mark Dawson playing drums and cardboard box. After the incendiary years of the Saints – which were a roller coaster from hard rock through R&B to jazz – and then his years with the jazzy rock of the Laughing Clowns, Kuepper had begun to simplify his work.

The most striking thing about Kuepper at this time is his openness. He had been a master of the poetic dissemble through a dozen records. Whether it was midlife crisis or something else, Kuepper is sufficiently liberated to pen songs that are as simple and direct as his instrumentation.

"I think where I made the first tentative step was with *Today Wonder*," Kuepper told *Juice* magazine. "That's where I first thought: 'I can do this ...' I get self-conscious about being on stage and singing and I get self-conscious about writing personal lyrics."

Taking the title from a jazz standard, Kuepper puts on his best Mel Torme voice. There are the classic lines, "Time has proved I'm churlish and I'm rude/And I find a real contentment in bad moods." It's a complex self-portrait from a guarded man and it's also a beautifully rendered portrait of a marriage. Plus he deserves extra credit for getting the word "churlish" into a song.

Voodoo Chile The Jimi Hendrix Experience

(Jimi Hendrix) ✳ Track Record ✳ 1968 ✳ Appears on: *Electric Ladyland*

This fifteen-minute epic blues track had a very simple start. Hendrix had fought with his bass player Noel Redding while recording the *Electric Ladyland* album. At Steve Paul's the Scene nightclub, where Traffic was playing, Hendrix ran into Jefferson Airplane bassist Jack Casady. Hendrix invited Casady and Traffic's Steve Winwood and Chris Wood to come to the studio and cut a tune along with regular Experience drummer Mitch Mitchell.

Hendrix had block booked New York studio the Record Plant – an unheard of concept in those days – and simply recorded as much as possible. Hendrix's explorations led to tensions with his manager Chas Chandler, who had to bail out halfway through the project because he couldn't stand the wasted studio time. Nonetheless, *Electric Ladyland* is a landmark recording – indulgent, sprawling and innovative at every turn.

There were three versions of 'Voodoo Chile': the first run-through; the second, on which Hendrix broke a string; and the third, which was a charm.

"'Voodoo Chile' is really a straight improv in a blues format," said Casady. "Jimi sketched out the chords, everybody got it, and counted it off. And we didn't stop 'til 7.30 a.m. There was no sign of how monumental it was after we'd finished. It was just, 'Hey, that was fun to do. See you later, I got to catch a plane.'"

Sunshine of Your Love Cream

(Pete Brown/Jack Bruce/Eric Clapton) ✳ Polydor ✳ 1967 ✳ Appears on: *Disraeli Gears*

'Sunshine of Your Love' launched the era of the heavy riff in rock & roll. This is all about the riff zigzagging up and down the fret-board. Jack Bruce screams the lyrics as though he's chained to this guitar sequence.

'Sunshine of Your Love' was a perfect title for 1967 – meaningless but with the right catchphrases. According to journalist Ritchie Unterberger, lyricist Pete Brown came up with the line "It's getting near dawn" because while Jack Bruce was playing his bass part he looked out the window and it *was* getting near dawn. But the whole track has that explosive serendipity. Clapton's guitar sounds like it's on fire. Most important, however, was Ginger Baker's wild syncopation. The difference between Cream and their heavy metal imitators was Ginger Baker's drumming and his capacity to move around the kit with the dexterity of a crazed jazz player (which he was) and that kept the song buoyant. 'Sunshine of Your Love' influenced every rock band of the day and every blues-based band since.

"I'm very fond of this simply because it's a riff that has entered the consciousness," said Bruce. "It's very nice if you can write something that gets across to everyone. It was, I suppose, a kind of synthesis of things that were around at the time – there's a bit of 'You Really Got Me' in there – but the unusual thing about it was the way it syncopates towards the end of the riff, which is more of a Latin thing, a very un-British, un-pop thing to do.

"I just got a thing commemorating a million plays of it in America. It has been covered by many people. A lot of Latin bands like Tito Puente have done it and there's a really good version by Ella Fitzgerald, sung live with a trio. The song gets used in films a lot. My favourite is *GoodFellas* where Robert De Niro slices a guy up to it. You can't get any better recognition than that."

The Weight The Band

(Jaime Robbie Robertson) ✳ Capitol ✳ 1968 ✳ Appears on: *Music from Big Pink*

'The Weight' became a signature song for the Band, although no-one much thought it would be at the time. "'The Weight' was another one that after we recorded it, it became what it was," Robertson told *Musician* magazine. "It was like, 'OK, this doesn't have a very complicated chord progression, it's just kind of traditional, so we'll cut that when we get stuck for a song.' And then we cut it and we thought, 'Gee, it's kind of effective when you hear if back at you like that.' It happens sometimes. A song takes on a character after you've done it."

This song was loaded up with characters and semi-religious allegories that went nowhere much in an opaque story. Over time, and as a result of its powerful melody, the song has accumulated a sense of profundity. If you break it down, however, it sounds like Robertson was copying Bob Dylan's style in search of his own voice.

Later in interviews, Robertson would ascribe more meaning to its lyric, likening it to the films of Spanish anarchist filmmaker Luis Buñuel.

"He did so many films on the impossibility of sainthood," said Robertson. "People trying to be good in *Viridiana* and *Nazarin*, people trying to do this thing. In 'The Weight' it's the same thing. People like Buñuel would make films that had these religious connotations to them but it wasn't necessarily a religious meaning. In Buñuel there were these people trying to be good and it's impossible to be good.

"In 'The Weight', it was this very simple thing. Someone says, 'Listen, will you do me this favour? When you get there will you say 'Hello' to somebody or will you pick up one of these for me? Oh, you're going to Nazareth, that's where the Martin guitar factory is. Do me a favour when you're there.' This is what it's all about. So the guy goes and one thing leads to another and it's like, 'Holy shit, what has this turned into? I've only come here to say "Hello" for somebody and I've got myself in this incredible predicament.' It was very Buñuelish to me at the time."

The literal meaning of the song is elusive, however. Levon Helm's vocal and the ensemble playing is completely in the pocket with Robertson's avowed inspiration from Curtis Mayfield on the guitar and the steady rambling arrangement.

"You pick things that come to mind and [they] sometimes have to do with personal experiences and people that you have known. But, they are not 'specific' stories," said Robertson. "It was North American folklore in the making."

Cypress Avenue Van Morrison

(Van Morrison) ✳ Warner Bros. ✳ 1974 ✳ Appears on: *It's Too Late to Stop Now*

It's Too Late to Stop Now is one of the few indispensable live rock & roll albums. Morrison's live band, the Caledonia Soul Orchestra, had the classical sensibilities of violinist Nathan Rubin and the jazzy edginess of guitarist John Platania, pianist Jeff Labes and the seamless rhythm section of David Hayes on bass and Dahaud Shaar on drums. This was Morrison's most consumate ensemble. They could cover all of his moods with ease and the instrumental flourishes brought these songs alive in ways that the studio versions never did.

Mostly Morrison here was on an R&B trip. He sounds like he's enjoying himself and he's recasting the folk and soul jazz of his early '70s work in the style of Ray Charles. It's invigorating to hear the eleven-piece band go through the paces of

'Cypress Avenue'. In its original form on *Astral Weeks* it's full of suppressed emotion and pain. It was a song about a desire that could never be consummated. With the Soul Orchestra it's a triumph of love and passion. Morrison puts the group through all the changes – the false stops, the wild flights of melody. Morrison sings the hell out of it, competing again and again with the strings and horn section with a James Brown dramatic line. Unlike so many live albums, where the material is made simpler and more bombastic, Morrison opens up 'Cypress Avenue' and lets new things into the arrangement. What had seemed morbid in 1968 was by 1974 transformed into a breathtaking combination of rock, pop and soul.

Walking Down Madison Kirsty MacColl

(Kirsty MacColl/Johnny Marr) ❊ Virgin ❊ 1991 ❊ Appears on: *Electric Landlady*

Best known for her wistful, wry pop songs and her work with the Pogues, Kirsty MacColl's 'Walking Down Madison' was something of a surprise. Written with the Smiths' guitarist Johnny Marr, it had a dance groove underpinning an acute observation of the dichotomy between wealth and poverty – the Madison obviously being Madison Avenue in Manhattan.

"I wrote the lyrics when I was working in New York, when I was actually walking. I couldn't find the right musical approach for ages, I tried writing stuff and asked some other people to try, but it never worked until I got a tape through the post with some ideas from Johnny Marr. The minute I heard his guitar I dug out the lyrics and sussed out a melody.

"It was quite an observational song, I really did see a beaming boy from Harlem, even if it wasn't on Madison. It's a nod to Bob Marley, it's 'I Shot the Sheriff', really isn't it! That idea of being killed for something you may or may not have done, and that you're more likely to get killed if you look a certain way."

The beats and samples perfectly complemented MacColl's sweet, dry vocal and gave MacColl her last hit single.

"I don't think I should define myself by other people's narrow-mindedness," MacColl said. "I do a lot of different things, not because I'm a dilettante, but because I really love lots of different kinds of music."

Way to Blue Nick Drake

(Nick Drake) ❋ Hannibal ❋ 1969 ❋ Appears on: *Five Leaves Left*

Nick Drake was still a student at Cambridge when Fairport Convention's bass player Tyger Hutchings came across the singer/songwriter at a twelve-day festival at London's Roundhouse. Hutchings alerted producer Joe Boyd, who asked to hear some tapes.

"I've always had a very strong taste for melody and it has obviously been reflected in the people I have worked with," said Boyd. "It was Nick's melodies that really impressed me. There was also a considerable feeling of sophistication and maturity about his songs and the way they were delivered. While the tapes were in the office, I was playing them to someone who came in, and he made a remark to the effect that they sounded like Donovan, and although a lot of people went on to echo that sentiment it was one that had never occurred to me. I really did feel that I was listening to a remarkably original singer. And from the point of view of a producer, I felt that they lent themselves perfectly to good arrangements. So when he came into the office we decided to do an album."

Boyd signed Drake to Witchseason, his production company. They spent an entire year developing Drake's first album, *Five Leaves Left*, with enthusiastic help from Fairport guitarist Richard Thompson and Journeyman bassist Danny Thompson.

Still only twenty years of age, Drake had strong ideas about how to develop his melancholy folk songs. He insisted his friend Robert Kirby work on the strings, which are central to the gorgeous 'Way to Blue'. The song has the sense of theatre and drama that is central to Drake's songs and lifts them from a mire of self-pity. There are also touches of jazz and blues here. Unfathomably, *Five Leaves Left* was a commercial disaster and may well have cast a pall over Drake's brief life.

Forgetting Philip Glass

(Laurie Anderson/Philip Glass) ❋ CBS ❋ 1986 ❋ Appears on: *Songs from Liquid Days*

High art meets pop. Phillip Glass broke down the distinction between minimal art music and pop songs with his album *Songs from Liquid Days*. He invited singer/songwriters Paul Simon, David Byrne, Suzanne Vega and Laurie Anderson to submit lyrics, to which Glass put his own music and then recorded using both pop singers and his own Ensemble and the Kronos Quartet. The result is intriguing and often haunting.

"I began by asking David Byrne to write words that I could then set to music," Glass wrote. "We had worked together once before, and I found it such an easy and natural collaboration that I thought of extending the process with an entire record of songs.

"The words come first. From these I fashioned a set of six songs which, together, form a cycle of themes ranging from reflections on nature to classic romantic settings."

The best of them is Laurie Anderson's 'Forgetting', which closes the record. The song starts with the image of a man waking from a dream of old lovers. Once awake he thinks of the qualities that go to making up a righteous man. It's an abstract piece that becomes more so as Linda Ronstadt and the Roches move from singing words to just singing the notes. It's a deeply haunting and beautiful song.

"Songs are perhaps our most basic musical expression," wrote Glass. "Though I have worked widely in the fields of opera and music theatre, I had not until this last year worked with the song form as such. Writing the song cycle *Songs from Liquid Days* became for me truly a voyage of discovery."

Stop in the Name of Love The Supremes

(Brian Holland/Lamont Dozier/Eddie Holland) ❋ Motown ❋ 1965 ❋

Appears on: *More Hits by the Supremes*

For three years in the mid-'60s, the Supremes defined the evolving face of American womanhood, from doe-eyed innocent to streetwise sister. They did it with fifteen sweet, sassy soul singles of which ten reached number one.

This song was inspired by a disagreement between one of the songwriters, Lamont Dozier, and his girlfriend. The argument reached fever pitch when one of them shouted, "Stop, in the name of love!," and they both dissolved in laughter at the absurdity of the line.

On first listening, Diana Ross and her soul sisters, Mary Wilson and Florence Ballard, thought the song insufficiently feminine, too forthright. Once in the studio, however, they had a lot of fun with it and later developed the song's trademark choreography with the help of the Temptations on the Motown Revue British tour of 1965.

The record's rich, dynamic sound was created by producers Brian Holland and Lamont Dozier and the incomparable Motown session band. Three guitars (played by Robert White, Eddie Willis and Joe Messina) were layered to fatten the rhythm, whose foundation was laid by James Jamerson on bass and Benny Benjamin on drums. Two keyboardists (Earl Van Dyke and Johnny Griffith) were enlisted, while James Gittens' vibes and Mike Terry's bold baritone sax set the song apart.

When the record was finished, the producers called a bunch of other acts into the studio to hear it. "Motown was like a small community," Mary Wilson told *Rolling Stone.* "You'd have Marvin Gaye, the Temps, the Supremes, the Marvelettes, all in the studio listening. Then we'd take the records home and pass them out around the projects."

Black Magic Woman   Fleetwood Mac

(Peter Green) ❋ Epic ❋ 1969 ❋ Appears on: *Pious Bird of Good Omen*

Guitarist Peter Green and drummer Mick Fleetwood were fired from John Mayall's Bluesbreakers in 1967. With second guitarist Jeremy Spencer and bass player John McVie, Fleetwood Mac was born as a backing group for Green's erudite blues playing. Green was one of the early guitar heroes, guaranteed to pull a crowd. Fleetwood was a distinctive showman drummer, so the enterprise got off to a flying start.

The combination of blues guitar and percussion was no doubt attractive to Santana, who covered 'Black Magic Woman' and had a hit with it in 1970.

"I actually wrote 'Black Magic Woman' when I was with John Mayall," Green recalled in a 1983 interview. "I was living in John Mayall's house when I started to write that. John Mayall started me writing the blues things; he said that I could do what he did sometimes. If you're singing or playing someone else's song and you really, really like it, if you're bubbling over with it, then you should take the first line and write another song. I took something out of Otis Rush's 'All Your Love'. It wasn't really like 'All Your Love' in the end, it was more like BB King's 'Help the Poor'."

Tell Me When It's Over Dream Syndicate

(Steve Wynn) ❋ Slash ❋ 1982 ❋ Appears on: *The Days of Wine & Roses*

According to the Dream Syndicate's main man Steve Wynn, "The greatest thing that happened to music and the worst thing that happened to music, happened first from punk rock and mostly from the era of R.E.M., Replacements, Dream Syndicate. It was the era when people said, 'If you're fan, you can have a band.' With punk rock you still had to be the cool outcast, you didn't have to be a good musician, the first step was you had to be charismatic and weird and the guy with the wildest haircut. Then all of the sudden, in the early '80s, if you just had the right record collection, you could form a band." Which is what Wynn did. Only Dream Syndicate became not only a band but also avatars of a new wave of guitar bands dubbed the Paisley Underground.

The Dream Syndicate was the name avant-garde artist La Monte Young called his ensemble of experimental musicians in the early '60s, which included future Velvet Underground founder John Cale. Right there you know that Wynn is up on his rock history and he prefers his music extreme.

The Dream Syndicate were known for complex layers of guitar feedback and dissonance creating odd harmonics like Crazy Horse times two.

The album *The Days of Wine & Roses* was recorded in one session from midnight to 6 a.m. (with vocals added the next day). 'Tell Me When It's Over', which opens the record, has a spirit of live performance. It's a cocktail of exhaustion and adrenalin.

"I can never imagine doing an album like *The Days of Wine & Roses* again – that's the type of thing you do when you've never done a record before. It's naïve, it's all guts, no tampering with the mind. There are people who say, and I used to say it, that's the way to record – all guts, all sex and passion and no mind. It's the mind that fucks you up. That's kind of true, it's great when you do things through passion."

'Tell Me When It's Over' was the manifesto that kicked it off.

"That's the most optimistic endemic thing we've ever done," said Wynn of the track. "In short it's the whole attitude of you wanting to do something and somebody is telling you that it won't work."

The Dream Syndicate never did reach the mainstream like R.E.M., but their influence was present in literally hundreds of alternative rockers for the next two decades.

What Time is Love? The KLF

(Isaac Bello/Jimmy Cauty/Bill Drummond/L McFarland) ✻ Rough Trade ✻ 1990 ✻

Appears on: *The White Room*

The KLF – Bill Drummond and Jimmy Cauty – were probably better known for banal stunts mocking the music and fine arts industries than for their music. Which is unfortunate given that their stunts – mocking the Turner Prize, burning £1,000,000, retiring from the music industry – were neither particularly novel nor interesting. Their music, even the crass 'Doctoring the Tardis' (as the Timelords), was better. 'What Time is Love?' was an early acid-house anthem. Drummond and Cauty were pioneers in the use of samples and beats and the mixture of the two. They understood what it was to be in the middle of a rave and they translated that feeling – wasted emotion – into a pop format. In doing so they helped to expand the vocabulary of pop music and influence its direction for the next fifteen years. Mostly there's a great sense of a beat here and the timing with which it is interjected. The record pumps in the manner of the best pop music and its textures are spooky and exciting at the same time.

Goodnight Irene Leadbelly

(Leadbelly/John A Lomax) ✻ Smithsonian ✻ 1934 ✻ Appears on: *Death Letter Blues*

John Lomax and his son Alan travelled through the US making recordings of regional folk music for the Library of Congress. They brought to light some of the greatest folk and blues artists of the 20th century. The most famous song recorded on their travels was 'Goodnight Irene', which they heard in July 1933 performed by Huddie Ledbetter, aka Leadbelly, then an inmate of the Louisiana State Penitentiary.

"My father and I met Leadbelly in the Angola Penitentiary in 1933," Alan Lomax recalled. "We came there looking for the roots of American black song, and we certainly found them with Leadbelly.

"He approached us all the way from the building where he worked, with his big twelve-string guitar in his hand. He sat down in front of us and proceeded to sing everything that we could think of in this beautiful, clear, trumpet-like voice that he had, with his hand simply flying on the strings. His hands were like a whirlwind, and his voice was like a great clear trumpet. You could hear him, literally, half a mile away when he opened up. He was at his peak then."

Lomax quickly saw the power of this dark waltz – it had a touch of blues but was not particularly idiomatic. In 1935, after Leadbelly's release, Lomax took the Texan singer north, where he had a career singing this and other popular songs such as 'The Midnight Special', 'Cotton Fields' and 'Rock Island Line'.

According to John Reynolds, an adviser to the Lead Belly Society, the song first appeared in Cincinnati, Ohio, and he further states that a song with this title and in three/four time may have been performed for a few years in the late 1800s. Leadbelly claimed he learnt it from his uncle Tyrell Ledbetter. That doesn't discount the beauty and originality that Leadbelly brought to the song.

'Goodnight Irene' is a very complex piece. The narrator is a troubled man who needs love and stability but doesn't have the constitution for them. It's a song that is so troubled that the singer calls for morphine and contemplates suicide. Yet the love that he feels for Irene is transcendent and gentle and life-giving. The tune is simply magnificent and in that flowing waltz we have a sense of the love that he craves.

Pete Seeger and his vocal group the Weavers cut a definitive version in 1950 that went to number one on the hit parade, six weeks after Leadbelly died in New York City on 6 December 1949 of amyotrophic lateral sclerosis. As a result of the Weavers' version the song became ubiquitous – part of the standard repertoire of dance groups throughout the west. Ken Kesey also borrowed a line for the title of his second novel, *Sometimes a Great Notion*. While it's not true that 'Goodnight Irene' softened the governor's heart and ensured Leadbelly's release from prison, after hearing the song you know it's not beyond the bounds of possibility.

I'll Fly Away Carolyn Hester

(Albert E Brumley) ✳ Columbia ✳ 1962 ✳ Appears on: *Carolyn Hester*

Known as the Texas Songbird for her pure soprano tone, Carolyn Hester was the queen of the coffeehouse circuit during the folk boom of the early '60s. Extremely beautiful with long dark hair, Hester was a commanding figure on the Greenwich Village and Boston folk scenes. She also carried some of the twang and the openness of her Texan background – Buddy Holly helped her get started. Hester married Richard Farina, who hoped to be a beatnik author and folksinger (he died days before publication of his first novel, *Been Down So Long*). The marriage broke down; Farina eventually married Joan Baez's sister Mimi.

The eponymous Columbia debut by Hester is notable for its eclectic range of folk songs and it's elegantly produced by the legendary John Hammond. Bruce Langhorne provided gorgeous accompaniment on guitar with Bill Lee (film director Spike's father) on bass. This opening cut, 'I'll Fly Away', also features Bob Dylan on harmonica – his first recording session and his introduction to Hammond, who signed him to Columbia shortly thereafter.

'I'll Fly Away' was an old spiritual, written in 1932. "I was picking cotton on my father's farm," its author Albert Brumley said. "I was humming the old ballad that went like this: 'If I had the wings of an angel, over these prison walls I would fly' and suddenly it dawned on me that I could use this plot for a gospel-type song. About three years later, I finally developed the plot, titled it 'I'll Fly Away', and it was published in 1932."

Hester stayed a folkie while Dylan, Baez and the others chased a rock & roll audience. She has remained modest and true to that calling. She recently told Hugh Blumenfeld, "What I was in it for was the music, the melodies, the haunting melodies and the poetry of the lyrics."

A Case of You Joni Mitchell

(Joni Mitchell) ❋ Reprise ❋ 1971 ❋ Appears on: *Blue*

Few records in popular music are as intimate as Joni Mitchell's *Blue* album. Mostly the record documents the end of her relationship with singer/songwriter Graham Nash. Mitchell, at age twenty-seven, was also coming to terms with the rest of her life – the success and fame and the loss of the daughter she gave up for adoption.

"By the time of my fourth album, I came to another turning point – the terrible opportunity that people are given in their lives. The day that they discover to the tips of their toes that they're assholes," she said. "And you have to work on from there. And decide what your values are. Which parts of you are no longer really necessary? They belong to childhood's end. *Blue* really was a turning point in a lot of ways."

'A Case of You' is the album's finest moment. Spare and delicately drawn, this song spells out absolute devotion while the singer knows full well that the love she needs will never come.

Mitchell's language is carefully balanced in the rhythm of the song. When asked once who she considered to be her peers she replied, "Dylan, Leonard Cohen ... that's about it as far as lyricists go. I'm influenced by Shakespeare, not so much by the reading of him as by the idea that the language should be trippingly on the tongue, and also by the concept of the dark soliloquy, with a lot of human meat in it." This is her best and darkest soliloquy. It's also a song that has enormous resonance to anyone that has lost love or found it unrequited.

"I was beginning an emotional descent at the time of *Blue*," said Mitchell. "They'd call it a nervous breakdown in this country – and when you're depressed, everything is up for question. You see how unbelievably phoney the world is and most of your survival mechanisms fall away. So that album was made at a time when I had no defences at all. As many a person has pointed out, *Blue* works really good if you're really low. These five girls came up to me once in a bar and said, 'Joni, before there was Prozac, there was you.'"

Time is Tight   Booker T & the MGs

(Booker T Jones/Steve Cropper/Al Jackson/Donald Duck Dunn) ❊ Stax ❊ 1969 ❊
Appears on: *Booker T and the MGs Greatest Hits*

The funkiest and best known instrumental of the '60s grew out of a jam amongst the session players in the Stax studio. "We were trying to think of something as funky as possible," said Steve Cropper of the song 'Green Onions'. And they did. The song went Top 5 and suddenly the session cats needed an identity – hence the MGs (Memphis Group). Now not only were they the most in demand session team for soul tracks but they had their own career.

The MGs' funkiness drips out of all the classic sides by Eddie Floyd, Aretha Franklin, Otis Redding and Wilson Pickett to name but a few. In 1964 the tougher Duck Dunn replaced Lewis Shinberg and the MGs continued to have hits like the spectacular, sexy and slightly jazzy 'Hip Hug Her'.

Their final hit, 'Time is Tight' reflected the jazz touch but was still with the funky, bluesy sound. The key to the record is its simplicity – not a move is in haste or misjudged. Everything sits perfectly in the pocket.

By 1969 they were still powering but the mood at Stax and amongst the group had changed. The one constant, however, and the secret to their success was drummer Al Jackson.

"Al was just the cleanest drummer in the world," Dunn told Barney Hoskyns. "The pocket where Al put everything was the real secret of Stax. Every time we recorded, he was ninety-eight per cent correct on just about everything we did. And even today, every drummer I play with asks me, 'What was it like to play with Al Jackson?'"

"I can't really define it as a secret formula, but we did make a concerted effort to keep things simple through the years," Booker T Jones told Hoskyns. "That was the one kind of unspoken and sometimes spoken agreement among the Stax producers. It just happened to be the chemistry of the time and the players."

Sound and Vision David Bowie

(David Bowie) ❄ RCA ❄ 1977 ❄ Appears on: *Low*

In 1977, David Bowie moved to Berlin to save his life. Bowie had changed his identity so many times in seven years that he no longer knew exactly who he was. Taking cocaine didn't help. In Berlin, near the Wall, Bowie found Hansa studios. There, he strained the pop out of his music with the help of Brain Eno.

Bowie and Eno created songs out of small riffs and ambient moods, unafraid to be self-consciously arty.

"We both work in very different ways," said Eno. "David works very fast. He's very impulsive and he works like crazy for about two hours or sometimes three-quarters of an hour – and then he takes the rest of the day off. And in that time, he does an incredible amount, very well, very quickly and faultlessly. He just puts on track after track and they're all just right and then he goes away, and that's it for the day. Quite often that's how it works.

"Whereas what I do is to – quite slowly – build things up over a period, you know. Since I'm using a monophonic synthesiser, it's incredibly tedious putting on one line at a time, 'da-da-da-da ...' like that. Very slow. So I get terribly nervous about working with other people around because so little seems to be happening."

Bowie and Eno played with the texture of contemporary music and on 'Sound and Vision' gave the rock world the opportunity to hear the mixture of ambience, melody, voice and machine in new ways. While 'Sound and Vision' was not a hit, this track and the album *Low* deeply affected the direction music would take in the '80s.

"I don't think people realise how finely he can tune his singing, in terms of picking a particular emotional pitch," said Eno. "It's really scientific the way he does it, very interesting. He'll say, 'I think that's slightly too theatrical there, it should be more withdrawn and introspective' – and he'll go in and sing it again, and you'll hear this point-four of a degree shift which makes all the difference. It's one of the very few times you get to see real craftsmanship, where someone will tell you about what they're going to do, then do it. He picks up the mood of a musical landscape, such as the type I might make, and he can really bring it to a sharp focus, both with the words he uses and the style of singing he chooses."

Motel Blues Loudon Wainwright III

(Loudon Wainwright III) ❋ Atlantic ❋ 1971 ❋ Appears on: *Album II*

The *New York Times* put it so well: "Over thirty-one years on twenty-two albums, Mr Wainwright has built a much-admired, moderately remunerative, undeservedly obscure career out of an unlikely mix of offbeat humour and confessional angst." The starting point is on his second release. Here he is the angst-ridden son of the moderately famous journalist. This album has a sheer darkness that Wainwright would in future gild with jokes. It has its humour ('Samson and the Warden', 'Plane Too') but it's mostly dark. Most compelling is 'Motel Blues', which is a devastating song of isolation and loneliness and truly empty sex. 'Old Friend' is a scathing departure note to the past. Even his spare reading of the folk song 'Old Paint' is full of seething anger. Wainwright, then dubbed a new Dylan, had been encouraged to record with a band but his instincts told him to stick to the bleakness of his acoustic guitar and voice. He was right. 'Motel Blues', for instance, still chills the blood.

Doll Parts Hole

(Hole) ❅ DGC ❅ 1994 ❅ Appears on: *Live Through This*

"I wrote this in Boston," Courtney Love told the TV show *Rage*. "I wrote this song in Joyce Linehan's apartment. I was really impressed. She was a lower level music executive and she had lots of matching Body Shop shampoo and I'd never seen that before. And I thought one day I'll have enough money and all my cosmetics are gonna match. I also thought that the guy I was going out with – who I later married . . . and that wasn't the transvestite in Las Vegas the other time . . . I thought that he didn't like me and that he liked this total poser idiot girl, so I wrote this song about him and it's called 'Doll Parts'."

Courtney Love will be forever bound to the memory of her husband Kurt Cobain. Their love affair was as epic as his short life was tragic. He was the singer and songwriter of the disaffected youth of the '90s. Courtney Love tried on his role and made herself a feminist warrior. However, where Cobain had a natural gift for rock & roll, Love had merely the determination to be a rock & roll star. To watch her struggle with her career as a musician was to see a struggle of pure will. Then, of course, Cobain committed suicide on the eve of the Hole's album release, leaving a note wishing Love all the best with album sales. (The saddest part of Cobain's saga is his obsession with the mythology of rock.)

'Doll Parts' could be Courtney's anthem, but then it is a song that perfectly expresses the fears that are common to so many women. Love turns those fears into a revenge story: "I want to be the girl with the most cake/I love him so much it just turns to hate/I fake it so real, I am beyond fake/And someday, you will ache like I ache." It's a powerful lyric, perhaps more so as she did get the most cake.

The backing by Hole is the group at its pop best, with textured production from Paul Kolderie that smooths Hole's rough edges without losing their raw power.

Dream a Little Dream of Me The Mamas & the Papas

(Gus Kahn/Wilbur Schwandt/Fabian Andre) ✳ Dunhill ✳ 1968 ✳

Appears on: *The Papas and the Mamas*

Gus Kahn was a songwriting machine. With his wife Grace at the piano playing the tune, Kahn added words to suit. In 1931, a tune came to him from journeymen musicians Wilbur Schwandt and Fabian Andre, who reckoned they knocked up the melody in a ten-minute break between sets at a date in Paw Paw, Michigan. With the addition of Kahn's lyric, the song attracted many covers from Frankie Laine, Kate Smith, Nat King Cole and Frank Sinatra.

"My dad always tried to keep his lyrics simple," his son Donald Kahn told NPR. "But he also said that young men and women do not know how to say 'I love you' to one another so we say it for them in thirty-two bars."

In 1950 a six-year-old girl called Michelle was introduced to Fabian Andre, then playing piano in Mexico City. Eighteen years later she was one of the Mamas and Papas, one of the most successful recording groups of its time. They were in the studio when they heard the news that Andre had fallen down a mine shaft in Mexico City and died. The childhood incident was recalled and there was nothing for it but to run through the song, with Cass Elliott singing lead. According to Michelle Phillips, Cass Elliott always envied Barbra Streisand but, Phillips told NPR, "Streisand could never match the sweetness and love in Cass' voice."

Mississippi Goddam Nina Simone

(Nina Simone) ✳ Philips ✳ 1964 ✳ Appears on: *Nina Simone in Concert*

Nina Simone intended to be a classical pianist. To put herself through study in the '50s she worked in Atlantic City bars playing jazz. Gradually her eclectic tastes, which ranged from pop hits to Kurt Weill, traditional blues and jazz, extended. Simone was always politically militant and she kept step with the civil rights movement in the '60s.

In June 1963, Byron Beckwith, who was twice acquitted by all-white juries, gunned down civil rights activist Medgar Evers outside his house in Jackson, Mississippi. In September a group of white supremacists bombed a church in

Birmingham, Alabama, killing four black children. Simone's response was the searing 'Mississippi Goddam', the most strident song of its era.

"This is a show tune, but the show hasn't been written for it yet," Simone told her Carnegie Hall audience in 1964. She was treading the same territory as Bertolt Brecht and Bob Dylan but with less compromise in her music. Simone was rare amongst protest singers because she underpinned her message with a soulful alto voice and a rare musicality.

Her uncompromising nature and radical politics didn't help her career much. Through the early '70s she became disillusioned with the black struggle and contemptuous of America – eventually moving first to Africa and then to France.

"After Martin Luther King and Malcom X got killed, after Lorraine Hansberry and Langston Hughes and Medgar Evers died, and after Stokley Carmichael and Miriam Makeba went to Africa, yes, I felt the movement died," she said. "I left because I didn't feel that black people were going to get their due, and I still don't.

"There's no other purpose, so far as I am concerned, for us except to reflect the times. The situations around us, and the things we're able to say through our art, the things that millions of people can't say." Very few said it all so well.

Fake Plastic Trees Radiohead

(Colin Greenwood/Jonny Greenwood/Ed O'Brien/Phil Selway/Thom Yorke) ❈ Capitol ❈ 1995 ❈ Appears on: *The Bends*

Radiohead supremo Thom Yorke has said that 'Fake Plastic Trees' was the first song of which he was not embarrassed. The first single, 'Creep', from their debut album was a kind of grunge novelty hit which nonetheless shot Radiohead to success, selling a million copies of the LP *Pablo Honey*. A second album, *The Bends*, appeared to be titled in response to their new circumstances. The bends is a life-threatening condition suffered by divers who surface too quickly.

Radiohead are generally miserabilists and 'Fake Plastic Trees' appears to be a whinge about the superficiality of the modern world. The lyrics are possibly the least interesting aspect of the song. "When we did demos, words would be made up on the spot," said Yorke. "You throw it away or it sticks because it sounds amazing and you find the significance in it when you read it afterwards."

The real guts of it are in the atmosphere created by the band, and Jonny Greenwood's guitars and electronics in particular. This dense wall of musical texture is an environment that well suits Yorke's voice. There's a general malaise in the air but a beautiful one – a technicolour melancholy that is so rich the group became popular despite itself. This is not a pop song but it has the majesty of the best pop.

"I'm not sure what we all thought would happen when we started doing this," said Yorke. "But definitely not what actually happened. It's been a very strange experience."

Will You Love Me Tomorrow? The Shirelles

(Gerry Goffin/Carole King) ✳ Scepter ✳ 1960 ✳ Appears on: *Girl Group Greats*

Carole King first made the charts as the subject of a song. Her school friend Neil Sedaka had a major hit with his song 'Oh! Carol'. Carole King tried her hand at being a performer with little success. Then she met Gerry Goffin, a pharmacist who aspired to write.

"When I met Gerry he had a play that he had written, complete with lyrics, but he wanted music," she told the journalist known as Miles. "He was interested in the theatre and Broadway and jazz at that time. Didn't think much of rock – rock & roll, that's what it was then. It was just before people in the Village, the intellectuals, the neo-Beats, got turned on to it. And we began to write rock & roll. I wrote music for his play, which never went anywhere, and he wrote lyrics for my rock & roll songs, which did go somewhere! And so we stayed with that because it was financially lucrative, which was, at the beginning, our main concern. We were either about to or were getting married and I was also pregnant so money was definitely an issue."

At first Goffin and King held down day jobs (as a chemist and secretary respectively) and worked for Don Kirshner's Aldon music on the side, until Kirshner heard 'Will You Love Me Tomorrow', at which point he advanced them $10,000 and they never looked back.

Florence Greenberg of Scepter Records gave Goffin/King their first hit, 'Will You Love Me Tomorrow?'

"I remember giving her baby a bottle while Carole was writing the song," said Greenberg.

"I came up with the basic melody one day and Gerry came home from work, he was a chemist at the time … he came home from work and I played him the melody and he wrote the lyric," said King. "It was as if he'd been thinking of the lyric all day at work and I'd been writing the melody and, you know . . . 'Tonight you're mine . . .' That's really how it happened."

In the late '60s the lyrics were obviously risqué – the implication being a girl wondering whether she should spend the night with a man clearly not her husband. Shirelles' lead singer Shirley Owens brings a full, woman-like sensuality to the song. Nonetheless, the song was a number one hit in November 1960, heralding the permissive society and the era of girl groups.

As a consequence of this hit Goffin and King were able to get an office in the Brill Building and become the most popular songwriting team of the decade and Carole King the most successful woman songwriter of the century.

Trans-Europe Express Kraftwerk

(Ralf Hütter/Florian Schneider/Emil Schult) ❋ Capitol ❋ 1977 ❋

Appears on: *Trans-Europe Express*

Having had a massive success in 1974 with a piece of music based on the sounds of cars on the autobahn, Kraftwerk turned their attention to rail transportation and 1977's 'Trans-Europe Express' was another popular work for them. Kraftwerk were popular with the punk and New Wave crowds because the music was anti-emotional and intellectually progressive. Bowie's German period and the Kraut-rock movement (especially the groups Can and Neu!) had softened the otherwise tough rock fans.

In 1982, rap artist Afrika Bambaataa lifted a piece of 'Trans-Europe Express' for his seminal 'Planet Rock' 12 inch. The hard German industrial noise fitted perfectly. New York hip-hop producer Arthur Baker was also a Kraftwerk devotee and he used their metronomic style in hip-hop remixes. Baker also re-introduced Kraftwerk to Manchester band New Order when he worked on the mix for their single 'Blue Monday'. The dispassionate, mechanical sound of Kraftwerk was then put back into the mainstream as part of one of the most impassioned and angsty groups of the era. Meanwhile in Detroit, black kids like Derrick May were using Kraftwerk beats to create a new style of dance music, to be dubbed techno.

According to Ralf Hütter, "Our music has been called industrial folk music. That's the way we see it."

Who Do You Love? Bo Diddley

(Ellas McDaniel) ✳ Checker ✳ 1957 ✳ Appears on: *Bo Diddley*

Just total genius. The images – forty-seven miles of barbed wire, a cobra snake necktie, a brand new house made from rattlesnake hide, a chimney out of a human skull, a tombstone hand and a graveyard mind – are so rich. To hear them chanted over the big beat and bone-rattling maracas you know that voodoo has arrived in popular music. Then there's the kicker: "Just twenty-two and I don't mind dying." This is a very heavy song, especially for its time. Diddley ramps up the blues vamp in the song aided by the bursts of Jody Williams' guitar that come out of the mix like assassin's bullets while the beat goes ever on, again embellished by the percussion from Jerome Green.

This song, recorded at Chess in May 1956, is just groove and mood. It's lent itself to many interpretations – notably by the Doors, who brought an appropriate sense of dread and despair and sexual energy, and Ronnie Hawkins, who had the backwoods voodoo down pat, and the garage-rocking Hoodoo Gurus.

"I don't like a lot of keenin' screamin' guitars," Diddley said. "If the bottom is right, crazy."

King of the Road Roger Miller

(Roger Miller) ✳ Smash ✳ 1965 ✳ Appears on: *Golden Hits*

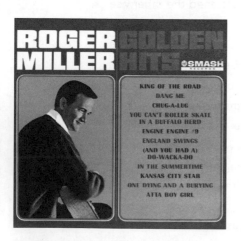

When he was a scuffling songwriter in the early '60s, Roger Miller used to say, "Boys, one day I'm gonna write a song so big they'll play it at ball games." It was a common refrain doing the rounds of Nashville publishers but, damn, if Roger Miller didn't do it. 'King of the Road', the layabouts' national song, is one of the most quoted and well known songs of the century.

'King of the Road' is a good-natured update of Huckleberry Finn – a world of no phone, no booze, no pets, where two hours of pushing broom will provide enough cash for another day.

"I start with a catch phrase," said Miller. "I'll take the first line and I'll sing it, like running up to a wall, and just before I hit that wall the second line will come to me, by forcing myself to sing it. Eventually I find I've gotten the wall to move enough to show me the whole song."

According to family friend Glenda West, 'King of the Road' was written on the back of a credit card application form. "He only got one verse and got stuck," she said. "So he was in an airport and saw a picture of a hobo and that gave him the inspiration for the rest of the song."

Miller was more than just a writer of novelty songs – although he had a number of them amongst his eleven Grammys. He had a gift for the rhythms of speech and the musicality of the southern tongue. Miller was held in the highest esteem by Nashville until his death in 1992.

As Joe Allison said when inducting Miller into the Country Music Hall of Fame, he was "a creature whose vocabulary has a built-in jazz syncopation that flows with such delightful cadence – that one hardly needs a melody to sing his songs."

You only need to read this to hear the melody:

Third boxcar, midnight train
Destination . . . Bangor, Maine.
Old worn out clothes and shoes,
I don't pay no union dues,
I smoke old stogies I have found
Short, but not too big around
I'm a man of means by no means
King of the road.

Building Steam with a Grain of Salt DJ Shadow

(Jeremy Storch/DJ Shadow) ✳ Mo' Wax ✳ 1996 ✳ Appears on: *Endtroducing ...*

Josh Davis (aka DJ Shadow) elevated record collecting to an art form. His collage songs made entirely of samples from obscure and not-so-obscure vinyl stretched the boundaries of music in the '90s.

His first album, *Endtroducing . . .*, is one of the seminal records of the century. The powerful 'Building Steam with a Grain of Salt' is built from a sample from a 1970 song by Jeremy Storch titled 'I Feel a New Shadow'.

"I called [the album] *Endtroducing* because to me it's an introduction," he said. "On the other hand, this is a sound I've been developing for four years, and I don't intend to be doing this next year or the year after. In a lot of ways it represents not just the nine months of work that it took to make it, but like what we are up to now. So the next album is going to be a lot different, 'cause I will be inspired by different things. And so the album is an end to that sound."

He told *Salon* magazine, "What I've noticed more and more is that what I do appeals mostly to people who are older and have been listening to hip-hop. All the people that I respect and that I credit for giving me my inspiration – because everything I do is based on something else – those people understand what I do and are not threatened by it."

Where's Your Head At? Basement Jaxx

(Felix Buxton/Simon Ratcliffe) ✳ Astralwerks ✳ 2001 ✳ Appears on: *Rooty*

In the generally faceless world of house music producers and DJs, Basement Jaxx burst out of London with a debut album (*Remedy*, 1999) that was often banging not just with techno but with touches of punk, reggae and jazz. Mostly, though, Jaxx had a sense of humour. Unlike most house artists, too, Basement Jaxx – Felix Buxton and Simon Ratcliffe – had a second album in them. *Rooty* is also witty, at times soulful and generally danceable. 'Where's Your Head At?' is classic Jaxx. It's magnificently constructed although it sounds random, and there's a wit behind the samples.

"When we were making *Rooty*, we definitely felt more freedom, because we had confidence in what we had done before," Buxton told *Juice* magazine. "It doesn't need to be classic songwriting. The main thing is you're putting across a certain vibe, a certain personality in your music." There wasn't a lot of personality in most house music, but Basement Jaxx were like the guy on everybody's party list – full of energy and fun and games. A real mixer. 'Where's Your Head At?' pounds along and then suddenly veers in another direction and then pounds along some more. Unpredictable and delightful.

Heart of Glass Blondie

(Debbie Harry/Chris Stein) ✳ Chrysalis ✳ 1978 ✳ Appears on: *Parallel Lines*

It's hard to believe that in 1978 rock fans were up in arms about disco music. There were events where disco records were destroyed and punks proudly pronounced "Death to disco!" Rock fans regarded this syncopated soul music as a form of cultural leprosy. Thus it fell to Blondie to unite the warring parties and join disco and rock on the most important single of the decade – 'Heart of Glass'.

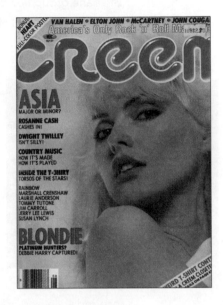

In fact, the song had been kicking around for some years: it was one of their first demos. It wasn't until producer Mike Chapman came on board for their third album, *Parallel Lines*, that they found a way to put it together.

"I wanted to produce Blondie because I loved them. I'd seen them live and couldn't wait to get into a studio with them," said Chapman. "Anyway, after that first day of rehearsal, we were walking down the street, Debbie and Chris and myself, and Debbie looked at me and said, 'Mike, I really like what you did with our songs today.' Suddenly I felt relieved and I said, 'Thank you, Debbie.' She said, 'Yeah, as a matter of fact, what you did to 'Heart of Glass' sounds really good,' because I had completely rearranged the song – it was nothing like that, it was a reggae song, or something. So I thanked her and told her it would probably come off very well in the studio, and she said, 'Well, why don't we talk about some of the other songs?' Debbie Harry, I must say, has become the most important artist I've ever worked with in my life, both as a friend and as an artist."

'Heart of Glass' has it all. It's kind of camp, and sly in its humour, and it has a rock backbone and touches on disco. There was no surprise that the song was an international smash hit. Blondie was not only the first punk group to break out of downtown New York but they changed the entire rulebook.

"*Parallel Lines* is good tight listening," Chapman said. "That's what Blondie's all about . . . I didn't make a punk album or a New Wave album with Blondie. I made a pop album."

Like a Dog Powderfinger

(Powderfinger) ❋ Universal ❋ 2000 ❋ Appears on: *Odyssey Number Five*

Brisbane group Powderfinger started out inauspiciously enough in the late '80s. By sticking to their beliefs and sticking together they grew into a strong songwriting

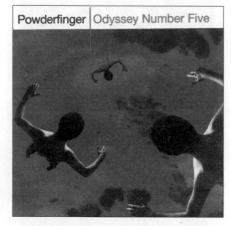

Powderfinger | Odyssey Number Five

ensemble. There's something fundamentally conservative about Powderfinger – they don't go in for costumes or gimmicks or the latest in production styles. On their own terms they have become a fine group.

They were not conservative politically, however. In the '90s, when few musicians were brave enough to speak out against the madness, Powderfinger whipped out the vitriolic and immensely powerful 'Like a Dog', a song aimed directly at Prime Minister John Howard and the racist agenda pursued by the Australian government against both refugees and indigenous Australians, and the general mean-spiritedness of the government policy.

The song begins with a riff from guitarist Ian Haug that inspired vocalist Bernard Fanning to some pointed lyrics.

"That song ['Like a Dog'] has an overt political message," Fanning told *Juice* magazine. "I probably just went home after a band session and read the paper and they denied the existence of the Stolen Generation. It was just the snowball effect of what arseholes they are, this government. I'm just saying what I think. It's just a point of view like all the other songs are. It's just a bit sad for Australia, the opportunity we missed by getting rid of [Paul] Keating, and we could've made Australia one of the most tolerant and best places to live for everybody. It's going to be another fifteen years at least before that can even begin."

Rock Lobster The B-52's

(Fred Schneider/Ricky Wilson) ❋ Reprise ❋ 1979 ❋ Appears on: *The B-52's*

The B-52's' independent single 'Rock Lobster' got them from Athens, Georgia, to New York City. Then everything went crazy. "Chris Frantz and Tina Weymouth of

Talking Heads came to our shows, and we were invited to Debbie Harry and Chris Stein of Blondie's house – we were so excited being over for cocktails and celery dip!" said singer Kate Pierson. "Just to be in the scene! When we first performed at the Mudd Club, we played this thing called the Nova Convention. It was a benefit for *Semiotext(e)*, which was a constructivist magazine. None of us knew what the hell a constructivist was, but we met David Bowie and Frank Zappa backstage, and a man in a giant lobster suit that was so heavy the stage collapsed. Cindy and I were in the basement, changing and half undressed, and in walks this man in a lobster suit, Frank Zappa and William Burroughs. They were very nice and enthusiastic. Burroughs came to the sound check and he had two people with him wearing trench coats, and he pulled out a piece of paper and started writing, and so did these two guys. They sat through the sound check, writing ..."

'Rock Lobster' became a cult hit. It took off first in Australia thanks to the TV show *Countdown*. The group quickly attracted other fans as well.

"At the end of 'Rock Lobster', Cindy does this scream that was inspired by Yoko Ono," said drummer/guitarist Keith Strickland. "John heard it in some club in the Bahamas, and the story goes that he calls up Yoko and says, 'Get the axe out – they're ready for us again!' Yoko has said that she and John were listening to us in the weeks before he died."

The first B-52's' album was a raw affair that captured the spirit of their party, the tinny instruments and the oddball ideas. Which is not to say that there wasn't a political undertone to their good times.

"Keith thought of the name," said Kate Pierson. "He had a dream, like a vision of a little lounge band and they all played organs and had bouffant hairdos, and someone said, 'Look, it's the B-52's.' B-52 was slang for a nosecone-shaped hairdo, named after the bomber. We thought, this is a great name: it's a number and a letter, it's really different and snappy. But now, there's this plan to prolong the life of the B-52 bomber, and we're lending our name to a campaign to stop it."

I Can See for Miles The Who

(Pete Townshend) ❋ Track ❋ 1967 ❋ Appears on: *The Who Sell Out*

Townshend claims that this song is not about drugs but the story of a jealous man with exceptionally good eyesight. In the context of 1967, no-one bought that explanation. 'I Can See for Miles' was seen as the Who going psychedelic. Ideas of seeing truth and reality – whether in a personal or spiritual sense – is at the heart of all Pete Townshend songs and this one is no different.

Townshend was very proud of the song. "'I Can See for Miles' was just released after 'Happy Jack': I'd written it in 1966 but had kept it in the can for ages because it was going to be the Who's ace-in-the-hole," he said.

Having made a big splash at the Monterey Pop Festival in June, the Who thought that it was time to take their career up a notch. Manager/producer Kit Lambert allocated three whole days for the recording in three different studios. The last one was Gold Star in Los Angeles, where Phil Spector had made most of his classic

tracks. The Who intended to use the famous echo chamber for the layers of vocals on the choruses.

"The actual track and the lead vocal was done literally in a couple of hours and then we spent eight hours overlaying harmony after harmony after harmony," said Daltrey.

While it was a commercial flop, 'I Can See for Miles' is the most dynamic track the Who had yet recorded, reining in the chaos of Keith Moon's drums and the brutality of Townshend's guitar in the service of the song. Most of the best Who tracks are an argument between the guitar and the drums. On 'Miles', Townshend opens the discussion with sustaining guitar and gets a fierce response from Moon. The song continues with that push and pull, with the verses and choruses changing tempo. This and the echo chamber of the vocals and the massed harmonies keep you guessing – reflecting the confusion of the song.

It's a track where the energy starts high and keeps on building. That the track was a Top 10 hit in the US, but didn't work in the UK, still bothers Townshend. Townshend still considers it a masterpiece (with a preference for the mono mix).

Monkey Gone to Heaven Pixies

(Black Francis) ✳ 4AD ✳ 1989 ✳ Appears on: *Doolittle*

Black Francis started the Pixies in 1986 with more enthusiasm than know-how and aimed for a sound somewhere between Hüsker Dü and Peter, Paul and Mary. That's just about what he got.

When all is said and done, however, it was the songs by Black Francis (who later changed his stage name to Frank Black), and especially his unique imagery, that made the Pixies the seminal alternative rock band. Bass player Kim Deal would go on to lead the Breeders, one of the best alternative bands of the '90s, while the flatish drumming of David Lovering and the bristling guitars of Joey Santiago played their part in establishing the alternative rock blueprint. "We tend to get along just fine," said the singer. "We're all sort of pleasantly mismatched. And it's kind of nice."

'Monkey Gone to Heaven' is one of the Pixies' best songs, with the group providing a backing as quirky as the lyrics and somehow piling in the hooks to a song that sounds like it will fall apart at any moment. Meanwhile Black Francis ponders the animalism of mankind and our simian nature – though not quite so specifically of course. "We're not trying to be wacky or kitsch like the Cramps or the B-52's," said Black Francis. "I'm trying to romanticise sci-fi and treat it like it's reality at the same time. It's not a pastiche."

Translucent Carriages Pearls Before Swine

(Wayne Harley/Herodotus/Tom Rapp) ✳ ESP ✳ 1968 ✳ Appears on: *Balaklava*

Well, you've got to credit a song that was co-written with Herodotus, the father of history. But then Rapp was elsewhere quoting from lines written on Roman walls. He had made his stage debut in a Minnesota talent quest where he placed third behind a young Bob Dylan. Eventually he drifted to Florida, where he assembled the Pearls – the pearls represented likeminded hippies and the swine were the Pentagon and the Establishment. History was much on Tom Rapp's mind in 1968, at the height of the Vietnam War. The singer/songwriter and leader of Pearls Before Swine wrote this idiosyncratic folk-rock album about the horrific idiocy of war. Instead of Vietnam, however, he used the Crimean War as a metaphor, especially the 1854 Battle of Balaklava, where the Light Brigade senselessly charged to their slaughter. The album begins with an 1886 recording of one of the survivors, Trumpeter Landfrey, who sounded the charge.

Rapp called his particular style of psychedelic folk – with big strings and marimbas, clavinets and horns – "constructive melancholy". Unfortunately, although Rapp and Pearls had a sizeable cult following, his recording career came to an early end and he went on to practise as a civil rights lawyer.

Woman's Gotta Have It Bobby Womack

(Darryl Carter/Bobby Womack/Linda Womack) ✳ United Artists ✳ 1972 ✳
Appears on: *Understanding*

Bobby Womack was never much of a joiner. His initial training was in gospel. He played guitar for the Five Blind Boys of Jackson, Mississippi, before working with Sam Cooke. Through the '60s he was mostly a session guitarist and songwriter based out of Memphis and Muscle Schools. Those two towns had particular house bands and particular "sounds". Womack developed his own brand of funky soul music, which came to the fore on a number of records he made under his own name for United Artists.

"I'm bridging the gap, if you like," he said. "R&B is one thing, but I also believe in rock, using electronics, but in good taste, not to the point where it distorts what you're tryin' to say. A lot of blacks tell me that I'm a strange cat; that I sing funky but hang out with some of the differentest cats, one minute with Donald Byrd, the next minute with Segovia. But to me all music makes sense. I can't stand to hear no one thing constantly."

'A Woman's Gotta Have It' was a wonderful deep soul track that chimed perfectly with the era of women's emancipation.

The inspiration for the song came from Darryl Carter, an engineer at Chips Moman's American Sound Studios in Memphis. It was based on a real couple's marital difficulties, and he and the Womacks intended the track for Jackie Wilson. It was Bobby Womack's version that went to number one in the R&B chart though. The track has since been covered by a number of artists including Wendy Matthews, the Neville Brothers, James Taylor and Prince.

To Love Somebody The Bee Gees

(Barry Gibb/Robin Gibb) ✽ NEMS/Atco ✽ 1967 ✽ Appears on: *Bee Gees 1st*

By the time the Bee Gees arrived in London in 1967, they had been professional entertainers for almost ten years – and none of them had reached twenty-one. The Bee Gees had the good fortune to have Australian expatriate impresario Robert Stigwood as their major fan. Stigwood had taken over Brian Epstein's empire (except for the Beatles) and saw limitless potential in the three Gibb Brothers. Stigwood signed them to NEMS and Atlantic.

The Bee Gees recorded their first album between 7 March and 21 April 1967. Their first single was the unlikely named 'New York Mining Disaster 1941 (Have You Seen My Wife Mr Jones?)', which was a sizeable hit in the US and the UK.

The next single from the album was not a hit. 'To Love Somebody' was written that March, not for the Bee Gees but for Otis Redding.

"Robert Stigwood had brought me to New York," Barry Gibb recalled. "I'd never been to New York before so it was a great thrill for me. I met Otis Redding early in the evening and Robert Stigwood had sort of suggested I write a song for Otis Redding, and I said I would try. I was inspired because I had just met him. That first flash you get – you meet somebody like that who you really admire and something happens. The rest of the evening I was alone and I sort of concocted most of it in that time. But the song was finished with Robin and Maurice."

Despite its unexpected failure as a single for the Bee Gees, 'To Love Somebody' has been wonderfully covered by the Flying Burrito Brothers, Janis Joplin and best of all by Nina Simone, who smoulders through a soul reading of the tune.

YMCA Village People

(Henri Belolo/Jacques Morali/Victor Willis) ✽ Casablanca ✽ 1978 ✽
Appears on: *Can't Stop the Music*

It is still hard to believe that a song about promiscuous sodomy has become a popular dance anthem sung by school children and adults in all walks of life.

Henri Belolo and Jacques Morali were two French songwriters and record producers attempting to crack America. They worked with Casablanca Records, the home of mainstream disco in the mid-'70s, where they hit upon the idea of writing disco songs for the gay community. A first try, 'Macho Man' was a hit. To promote the record they cast straight singer Victor Willis and a group of actors and singers, each of whom was costumed according to the then current gay 'clones': the mechanic, the GI, the construction worker, the cowboy, the leather man, the cop, the Indian.

The gay bar scene was at the time taking off in New York and San Francisco and much of the good time was fuelled by disco music. A perfect marriage. Disco music and clubbing presented a wide-open field.

Then one day the pair – Morali was gay and Belolo just a fellow traveller – walked past the 23rd Street YMCA, then a popular beat for cruising. "Jacques asked what they did in there," said Belolo. "We went inside, saw what was happening and started humming the song." Willis helped with the lyrics. Belolo and Morali recorded the track mostly in Philadelphia. "So much fun," Belolo told *MOJO* magazine in 1998. "We knew it was a hit straightaway. We had those goose bumps. We tested it at Studio 54 and it killed the room. Killed it."

The song was an instant smash hit. Most of the public didn't understand the gay imagery of the Village People, let alone the culture stereotypes of cruising, and those that did simply thought the joke too delicious to pass up. The characters of the Village People, as much as they represented gay culture, did so in a non-threatening way.

However, the outfits, the jokes – all would have meant nothing had the record itself not had a perfect groove.

"I've been a DJ for more than ten years and I can't remember not playing it," Broadway Disco's Darren Reuben told *MOJO*. "Nor can I remember having to teach anyone the actions."

Debaser Pixies

(Black Francis) ✳ 4AD ✳ 1989 ✳ Appears on: *Doolittle*

"The closest I get to a manifesto is that I like the Surrealists. I agree with their idea that reason is overrated," said Black Francis. "Rock & roll has been a pose from the beginning. There are those who still hail rock as being a force for radicalism, but it's not any more, it's a force on the stock market. The Pixies are just a tiny hiccup in a huge industry. Our records are in the racks next to all the others. It's only our content that isn't quite as stale or stiff as the other groups. You don't have to hike into the desert to see us. We're a part of mass culture."

The Pixies were, in the end, more than just a hiccup. Black Francis' quirky, surreal songs with their stop/start tempos and quiet/loud arrangements were the prototype for the alternative rock revolution of the '90s – especially the work of Kurt Cobain. The Nirvana leader wrote 'Smells Like Teen Spirit' in what he thought was the style of the Pixies.

'Debaser' is a classic hook-laden track from the Pixies' breakthrough album. The song is about the joys of watching the Luis Buñuel film *Un Chien Andalou*, a surrealist classic, and is the most perfect 'stream of unconsciousness' ever made.

God John Lennon
(John Lennon) ❋ Apple ❋ 1970 ❋ Appears on: *John Lennon/Plastic Ono Band*

At the end of the '60s John Lennon should have been a happy man. He was one of the most esteemed artists of his time, wealthy, powerful and respected, and married to the woman he loved. Lennon, however, seemed at a loss. He and Yoko Ono had been in and out of heroin addiction, he was confused and tormented by the success of the Beatles, and he had issues with his parents that were still unresolved. As part of his search for happiness, he tried therapy, including primal scream – a technique developed by Arthur Janov for letting pent-up feelings out. So Lennon's first real solo album, written while using Janov's techniques, is known as the primal scream record.

'God' is one of the album's cornerstones. It's a litany of the things that Lennon once held dear but now has seen through. These include the Beatles and Bob Dylan and, of course, God in all his incarnations. Lennon finally concludes with the phrase "the dream is over," meaning the Beatles. The phrase has gone into the popular vernacular as a summation of the idealism of the '60s.

Although 'God' is not a pop song or even an easy song to listen to, it is, as Yoko Ono has said, "as important as Sgt Pepper". Mostly for the daring arrangement and the strength and minimalism involved.

Clocks Coldplay

(Guy Berryman/Jon Buckland/Will Champion/Chris Martin) ✻ Parlophone ✻ 2002 ✻
Appears on: *A Rush of Blood to the Head*

The follow-up to Coldplay's five million-selling debut album, *Parachutes*, was always going to be a more considered affair. Recorded in London and Liverpool over nine months, *A Rush of Blood to the Head* affirms Coldplay's position as band of the first water. "I'm incredibly excited by what we've done," said singer Chris Martin. "The danger was we'd make a half-arsed, shitty, bargain bin, average follow-up record with songs not half as good as 'Yellow'. I'm not interested in, 'Here are some off-cuts of the first album and I've got loads of money and coke and I'm in *OK!* magazine.' That's bullshit."

Betraying some influence to Echo and the Bunnymen and the atmospheric English rock of the early '80s, 'Clocks', the second single from the second album, is a masterful piece. Martin's piano propels the song with its powerful, dark melodies against the soaring strings.

Coldplay continue painting the big picture here with this elegant song about doom. "Let's see ... what's the new album about?" Martin joked. "What every album's about: your fear of death, your love of girls and your anger at the shit that politicians talk. Mainly about girls, though."

My Name Is Eminem

(Dr Dre/Eminem) ✻ Interscope ✻ 1999 ✻ Appears on: *The Slim Shady LP*

Marshall Mathers has an identity crisis. First up there's Marshall Mathers, then there's his homicidal, misogynistic alter ego, Slim Shady, and finally there's Eminem – the white rap superstar. His breakthrough single, 'My Name Is', as its title suggests, is a meditation on identity. To that end, Eminem relates the trash existence that is the lot of the America underclass and then he lights a fuse on the garbage heap introducing the contentious subject of race and sex.

Part of Eminem's success is due to the hip-hop smarts of producer Dr Dre who helped Eminem cut 'My Name Is' in about an hour. The connection with Dre also allowed Eminem to get past the "can a white boy rap" issue.

"My whole market, my whole steez, is through the underground; if those hip-hop heads love it, I'll rise above," he told *Spin* shortly after 'My Name Is' topped the charts. "It's like, you hardly ever hear a Wu-Tang song on the radio, but they rose from the underground on word of mouth.

"In the beginning, the majority of my shows were for all-black crowds, and people would always say, 'You're dope for a white boy', and I'd take it as a compliment. Then, as I got older, I started to think, nobody asks to be born, nobody has a choice of what colour they'll be, or whether they'll be fat, skinny, anything. I had to work up to a certain level before people would even look past my colour; a lot of motherfuckers would just sit with their arms folded and be like, 'All right, what is this?' But as time went on, I started to get respect. The best thing a motherfucker ever said about me was after an open mic in Detroit about five years ago. He was like, 'I don't give a fuck if he's green, I don't give a fuck if he's orange, this motherfucker is dope!' Nobody has the right to tell me what kind of music to listen to or how to dress or how to act or how to talk; if people want to make jokes, well fuck 'em. I lived this shit, you know what I'm sayin'? And if you hear an Eminem record, you're gonna know the minute that it comes on that this ain't no fluke."

"If he remains the same person that walked into the studio with me that first day, he will be fucking larger than Michael Jackson," said Dre. "There are a lot of ifs and buts, but my man, he's dope and very humble."

Wuthering Heights   Kate Bush

(Kate Bush) ✳ EMI ✳ 1978 ✳ Appears on: *The Kick Inside*

"I was brought up on movies: love, revenge and death," said Kate Bush. It's all there in her first single, a retelling of Emily Brontë's Gothic epic in four and a half minutes. Bush was then only eighteen years old and had lived a comfortable middle-class English life. The doomed, passionate romance of *Wuthering Heights* appealed to her, as to so many teenage girls, and she adapted it to song, partly no doubt because she had not yet experienced that level of romantic passion herself. Sharing the same name as the heroine of the book probably increased her identification.

"I felt that to actually get your name anywhere, you've got to do something that is unusual, because there's so much good music around and it's all in a similar vein," she said after the release of 'Wuthering Heights'. "It was, musically, for me, one of my strongest songs. It had the high pitch and it also had a very English story-line, which everyone would know because it was a classic book."

'Wuthering Heights' is a magnificent artifice of trembling vocals and breathless choruses. The entire track overflows with nervous energy. There is a Gothic sexuality that comes panting out of 'Wuthering Heights'. "Don't you think art is a tremendous sensual-sexual expression? I feel that energy is often ... the driving force is probably not the right way to put it," she said, more than a little disingenuously. "I felt very flattered that those people should think of me in those sex symbol terms. That was my first reaction, but it can be very destructive. For a start, there are so many incredibly good looking women around, and their craft is in that. They're either models or acting, so their physical image is important. What I really want to come across as is as a musician, and I think that sort of thing can distract, because people will only see you on a superficial level."

'Wuthering Heights' was an instant hit, which Bush backed up with the equally idiosyncratic 'The Man with the Child in His Eyes' and she has continued to follow her own star since.

Town Without Pity Gene Pitney

(Dimitri Tiomkin/Ned Washington) ❋ Musicor ❋ 1961 ❋ Appears on: *The Anthology*

Gene Pitney's voice was the sound of heartbreak itself. He had a jazz tone and a country singer's twang and the whole effect was dramatic, lending itself to narrative songs such as this, which dealt with the difficulty of modern relationships. His songs were also very adult in their lyrics although Pitney appealed to teens as well. 'Town Without Pity' is an epic tale of two young people whose love is thwarted by the town in which they live and its constrictive morals. This is a theme that would run through pop music for the rest of the '60s.

Pitney started playing music in high school with his band the Genials in Connecticut, just outside New York. By the time he had finished high school he was recording his own material and playing all the instruments. He started writing songs and in a brief career wrote 'He's a Rebel' for the Crystals and 'Hello Mary Lou' for Rick Nelson. However, Pitney was best known as a vocalist. 'Town Without Pity' was his first major hit record. Film composer Dimitri Tiomkin wrote the tune for the film of the same name, hence the melodramatic exposition. The song was nominated for an Academy Award and won a Golden Globe. It's a song with portentous strings and female vocals that are more than a little camp as Pitney pines for the freedom to express his love.

Your Love is King Sade

(Sade Adu/Stuart Matthewman/Gordon Matthewman) ✳ Epic ✳ 1984 ✳

Appears on: *Diamond Life*

Everything about Sade is exotic. Her looks. Her birthplace – a village outside Lagos, Nigeria's capital. Her name – Helen Folasade Adu. Most of all, though, her music oozes exotic, languid Latin motifs and jazz stylings. Sade's first album, *Diamond Life*, swept through the airwaves of 1984 like a sublime perfume on a quiet night's breeze.

Sade had been the singer for the eight-piece soul and jazz band Pride, which included Stuart Matthewman, Paul Denman and Andrew Hale for some three years before signing with Epic records. Sade's obvious influences – Donny Hathaway, Billie Holliday, Curtis Mayfield and Marvin Gaye – were subsumed by the jazz influences in the band, especially Matthewman's playing and the demands of the London clubs. "What nobody in England has really understood," said bass player Denman, "is that it's a live thing and not a style thing. We have never been influenced by what's going on. Before we recorded *Diamond Life* we'd been going around playing those songs for years. We still record a lot of our best stuff just how we perform it, live in the studio."

'Your Love is King' was the standout track that established Sade's style – erotic and gentle, humorous and languid in the tradition of the best pop jazz. Mostly, though, it had a melodic line that just wouldn't quit. Where her bigger hit 'Smooth Operator' seemed bound up in the ambitions of the '80s, 'Your Love is King' is as inviting as ever.

"We were picked up on because we were different from anything else that was going on at that time," said the singer. "I am much more myself and less committed to promoting an image than, say, Morrissey or Bruce Springsteen or Mick Jagger."

How Do You Sleep? John Lennon

(John Lennon) ✳ Apple ✳ 1971 ✳ Appears on: *Imagine*

'How Do You Sleep?' is one of the most direct and most vitriolic personal attacks ever put on record. John Lennon accuses his former partner Paul McCartney of being boring as a person and a pretender as a songwriter. In fact, Lennon was venting his feelings about himself and about the Beatles phenomenon as much as he was attacking McCartney.

"I used my resentment against Paul that I have as a kind of sibling rivalry resentment from youth to create a song ... not a terrible vicious horrible vendetta ..." Lennon said shortly before his death in 1980. "I used my resentment and with-drawing from Paul and the Beatles, and the relationship with Paul, to write 'How Do You Sleep?'. I don't really go round with those thoughts in my head all the time."

"'How do you sleep?' I think it's silly," McCartney told the *Melody Maker* at the time. "So what if I live with straights? I like straights. I have straight babies. It doesn't affect him. He says the only thing I did was 'Yesterday'. He knows that's wrong. He knows and I know it's not true."

"It's not about Paul, it's about me," Lennon later admitted. "I'm really attacking myself. But I regret the association ... well ... what's to regret? He lived through it. The only thing that matters is how he and I feel about these things and not what the writer or commentator thinks about it. Him and me are OK."

Interestingly, Lennon created a backing track that was as nasty and mean-spirited as the lyric. Much of the credit here should go to George Harrison, who played the caustic guitar part and who did have an abiding resentment towards McCartney that apparently hadn't lifted by the time of Harrison's death.

In Dreams Roy Orbison

(Roy Orbison) ✳ Monument ✳ 1962 ✳ Appears on: *In Dreams*

"I wasn't trying to be weird, you know? I didn't have a manager who told me how to dress or how to present myself or anything," said Orbison twenty-five years later. "But the image developed of a man of mystery and a quiet man in black and somewhat of a recluse, although I never was, really."

'In Dreams' was an extraordinary record. A soulful country ballad with surreal lyrics that fit with the singer drifting off to sleep. He seems liberated from the usual conventions of popular music. The arrangement that starts off simply enough gradually builds through the introduction of the rhythm section and an orchestra. The lonely reality of the day to day is transformed into a dream world where the boy can get the girl.

While Fred Foster's production is masterful, the song depends entirely on the versatility of Roy Orbison's voice.

"Once I started singing, it was sort of a wonder," Orbison said. "I've always been in love with my voice. It was it. It's a gift, and a blessing, just to have a voice. And I'm proud that people do appreciate it, you know? It's a long way from being overwhelmed because you don't know whether you are worthy, to realising that if you have a gift, it should be precious to you and you should look after it and respect it."

A quarter of a century after its first release, David Lynch made 'In Dreams' the centrepiece of his film *Blue Velvet* and the eerie song came alive in that grotesque context. 'In Dreams' is a song outside its time and space.

You Keep Me Hangin' On Vanilla Fudge

(Lamont Dozier/Eddie Holland/Brian Holland) ✲ Atco ✲ 1967 ✲ Appears on: *Vanilla Fudge*

Vanilla Fudge took a complex and bright Motown melody and beat it to a pulp.

The Electric Pigeons, led by organist Mark Stein, were a blue-eyed soul cover band playing Top 40 songs in bars around Long Island, New York. In 1966 they started to improvise, utilising the prodigious talents of bass player Tim Bogart and drummer Carmine Appice. Their agent badgered legendary producer Shadow Morton, who was then contemplating retirement, to catch their act, and a seven-minute heavy version of the Supremes classic blew his mind.

"I wasn't about to take on anything," Morton told *Goldmine*. "As I walked out of the Action House, Mark Stein began to play and I stopped. I stopped at the door. I was out the door and I turned around to listen to Mark Stein. I was mesmerised.

"When Mark played that organ on 'You Keep Me Hangin' On', it impressed the hell out of me. I don't remember whether he told me or if I came to the conclusion myself, but the reason he played it that way ... slow and soulful ... was that was the way he had been listening to the Supremes doing 'You Keep Me Hangin' On' on a 45 record going at 33 to learn the song! I was so taken by the feeling of that, he was just so into it ... I turned around at the door and I walked back into the room."

Stein's massive organ sound laid down a huge theatrical basis for this seven-minute reworking of the Supremes hit. Where Diana Ross was full of fire and life, the Fudge's version was dark and desperate. Dramatic in an entirely different way.

Morton recorded the band that same week, cutting the track in one take. He signed the group to Atlantic imprint Atco, who suggested they change their name and issue a first jam-based album. The record didn't take off immediately. But some months later, after an appearance on the *Ed Sullivan Show*, the song went ballistic. In that time the fashion had turned, following Hendrix and Cream, to long instrumental epics and Vanilla Fudge were a somewhat dumbed down version of that.

The group became quite popular and the rhythm section of Bogart and Appice were much in demand in the '70s, notably in their group Cactus and with Jeff Beck. The latter however opined on Bogart and Appice, "They thrived on excess and overplaying. If you could zero in on the energy, you got the goods, otherwise it was a cacophonous, horrible noise."

16 Shells From a Thirty-Ought Six Tom Waits

(Tom Waits) ❋ Island ❋ 1983 ❋ Appears on: *Swordfishtrombones*

Having started out as a wordsmith who produced metaphors to order by the tonne, Waits learnt the value of brevity. Capable of sentimental heart tug and wistful melody, in the '80s Waits transformed his sound yet again.

'16 Shells From a Thirty-Ought Six' is Waits' attempt to write a chain gang song. It's full of old time imagery – a thirty-ought six is a shotgun made in 1906, a Washburn is an old make of guitar – and the percussion includes a locomotive's brake pad.

"I tried to get a chain gang/work song/field holler," Waits told an interviewer in 1983. "Get a low trombone to give a feeling of a freight train going by. It's Stephen Hodges on drums, Larry Taylor on acoustic bass, Fred Tackett on electric guitar,

Victor Feldman on brake drum and bell plate and Joe Romano on trombone. So, I wanted to have that kind of a sledgehammer coming down on an anvil.

"Originally I saw the story as a guy and a mule going off looking for this crow. He has a Washburn guitar strapped on the side of his mule and when he gets the crow he pulls the strings back and shoves this bird inside the guitar and then the strings make like a jail. Then he bangs on the strings and the bird goes out of his mind as he is riding off over the hill. So I tried to make the story a bit impressionistic but at the same time adding some very specific images in there.

"I worked a long time on this. The feel of it was really critical. I added snare and we pulled the snare off 'cause it made it shuffle too much. I liked the holes in it as much as I liked what was in them. It was a matter of trying to get that feeling of a train going. Originally I tried it just with organ and bass. Then I was afraid to add too much to it 'cause sometimes you get a feel that's appropriate. If you try to heap too much on it then it crumbles into the strain."

The Sound of Silence Simon & Garfunkel

(Paul Simon) ❊ Columbia ❊ 1964 ❊ Appears on: *The Sound of Silence*

No-one was more surprised at the success of 'The Sound of Silence' than Paul Simon. He and Art Garfunkel had cut the track with just Simon's acoustic guitar as backing for their album *Wednesday, 3 AM*. That LP was a flop and Simon & Garfunkel disbanded. Garfunkel went back to university to study maths and architecture and Simon went to Europe to be a solo troubadour around the folk clubs. Meanwhile, folk rock took off. Columbia, which represented the Byrds and Bob Dylan, enlisted Dylan's producer Tom Wilson to add an electric backing to the song with the same session players Dylan used. As they didn't bother to inform Simon of this, the first he knew of it was picking up a copy of *Billboard* while in Denmark and seeing his song racing up the charts.

"We were in my kitchen in my apartment on Amsterdam Avenue, uptown in Manhattan, when I was a student at Columbia College," Garfunkel recalled. "Paul would drive in from Queens, showing me these new songs. And that was the sixth song he had written, 'The Sound of Silence'. And he showed it to me in my kitchen and I went crazy for how cool it was."

Simon & Garfunkel began their career as a rock & roll vocal group in the '50s when they were still at school. Things changed quickly for Simon after he heard Bob Dylan and he began to write material that was more personal. The potent opening line, "Hello darkness my old friend," was inspired by his habit of playing his guitar in a darkened bathroom for the echo effect. From there the song ranges across many personal and general themes.

"'The Sound of Silence', which I wrote when I was twenty-one, I never would have wrote it were it not for Bob Dylan," said Simon. "Never. He was the first guy to come along in a serious way that wasn't writing a teen language song. I saw him as a major guy whose work I didn't want to imitate in the least. Not because I didn't admire it but because I didn't see any way out of being in his shadow if I was going to be anything like that. And I looked at him and said that's really fabulous and the Beatles are really fabulous and the Rolling Stones are really fabulous and it's going to be really hard for my little group – me and my friend, Art Garfunkel – to even find a slice of this pie that is original. And it was so hard because those guys were so great at what they did it was like, 'Well, what can you be?'"

His first song released, however, went to number one in the charts. Simon & Garfunkel hastily reformed and cut a folk rock album.

"I had just come back from England, and Art was still living at home," said Simon. "He was still at college and we were sitting in my car . . . smoking. And 'The Sound of Silence' came on and they said: 'Number one record 'The Sound of Silence' by Simon & Garfunkel.' We were just sitting there at night, we hadn't anything to do, and Artie turned to me and he said: 'Those guys must be having so much fun!'"

A Good Year for the Roses George Jones

(Jerry Chesnut) ✳ Musicor ✳ 1971 ✳ Appears on: *George Jones with Love*

George Jones is generally regarded as the best balladeer in country music. Heartbreak was his stock-in-trade and 'A Good Year for the Roses' is a classic of Jones' middle period.

By 1971 he had met Tammy Wynette and they were being marketed as the King and Queen of Country. Jones' more longstanding romance with the bottle was also in full swing at this point.

"In the '70s, I was drunk the majority of the time," Jones wrote in his autobiography. "I had drunk heavily for years and had pitched benders that might last two or three days, but in the '70s, I was drunk the majority of the time for half a decade. If you saw me sober, chances are you saw me asleep. It was a five-year binge laced with occasional sickness from sobriety … Some folks think they're in pain if they've had one too many cocktails the night before. They have no idea how it feels to have one too many pints. It's like going through a violent food poisoning with an axe in your skull."

'A Good Year for the Roses' then is a song of great regret. It's a song about losing it all and the narrator is prepared to shoulder the blame. Produced by Pappy Daily, who had given Jones all his hits to this point, the song's lyric is economical and the sadness, because it's understated, is eternal: "When you turn to walk away, as the door behind you closes/The only thing I know to say, It's been a good year for the roses."

From Little Things Big Things Grow
Paul Kelly & the Messengers
(Paul Kelly/Kev Carmody) ❊ Mushroom ❊ 1990 ❊ Appears on: *Comedy*

In the '60s the Gurindji people on Wave Hill Station in the Northern Territory made a claim to the land on the grounds that it was sacred to them. The land was owned by Vestey's, a British corporation, then one of the largest landholders in Australia. Vincent Lingiarri led the Gurindji protest for eight long years, quietly demanding justice and refusing to be bought off.

The matter was eventually settled in favour of the Gurindji. In 1975, the prime minister Gough Whitlam flew to Wave Hill to formally acknowledge the handover. At the suggestion of his adviser Nugget Coombes, Whitlam bent down and picked up a handful of dirt that he ran through his fingers into the hands of Lingiarri.

The Wave Hill dispute was a significant step towards acknowledging the rights of Aboriginal people in Australia.

Carmody and Kelly tell the story of Vincent Lingiarri with careful detail and a strong sense of character. They are as understated in their language as Lingiarri was with his.

Surf's Up The Beach Boys

(Van Dyke Parks/Brian Wilson) ✳ Caribou ✳ 1971 ✳ Appears on: *Surf's Up*

As if being beaten and betrayed by his father and losing his hearing and then going insane wasn't enough, Brian Wilson has been subjected to more ridiculous journalism than any musician deserves. Much of the verbiage revolves around the lost album *Smile*.

The legend goes like this: Wilson, the pop genius of the Beach Boys, creates the masterpiece song cycle in *Pet Sounds* in 1966. He then embarks on his masterwork, *Smile*, which he refers to as a symphony to God. The lyrics, by Van Dyke Parks, are an extended meditation on the birth of the United States. In any case, things get too weird. The other Beach Boys, especially cousin Mike Love, hate the project and want the songs to get back to the beach.

The *Smile* album was eventually abandoned. Bits of it surfaced, notably the singles 'Good Vibrations' and 'Heroes and Villains' and also this song, 'Surf's Up', which was rerecorded and appears on the *Surf's Up* album.

In 2004 *Smile* was reconstructed and it's easy to see why the project was abandoned – it's completely uncommercial. Wilson and Parks weren't just trying to outdo the Beatles and Phil Spector now; they took on Aaron Copeland and Leonard Bernstein and the real heavyweights.

So, 'Surf's Up' is magnificent, but let's not attribute to it qualities it doesn't have. The melody is a gorgeous nocturne. Its notes soar off into the darkened sky, and the vocal melody, sung with exquisite grace by Carl Wilson, flits through this dreamscape. The lyrics are nonsense, but that doesn't matter, they add to the dreamlike mood.

"We were taking LSD and marijuana and amphetamines," said Brian Wilson. "So our heads were, like, spaced, and we got into some very advanced, avant-garde music. And we started creating some of the songs for *Smile*, and we got about two movements done, and then we decided to junk it, because we thought it was too advanced for people."

So he clearly wasn't that stoned. *Smile was* too advanced. Wilson, in his quest to compete with some of the greatest musicians of the time, had pushed the possibilities of pop beyond their envelope. *Smile* remains a glorious folly with some moments of near perfection, and 'Surf's Up' is one of them.

Hazey Jane II Nick Drake

(Nick Drake) ✳ Hannibal ✳ 1970 ✳ Appears on: *Bryter Layter*

In 1970 Nick Drake moved from Cambridge to London. He had one critically acclaimed but poor-selling album under his belt and was coming to terms with his folk-jazz muse. On 'Hazey Jane II', perhaps he was also coming to terms with himself.

Drake was plagued by depression that alienated him from most other people. As he sang on 'Hazey Jane II': "If songs were lines/In a conversation/The situation would be fine." Richard Thompson, who played guitar on the record, remembered, "He is a very elusive character. It was at Trident I think, and I asked him what he wanted, but he didn't say much, so I just did it and he seemed fairly happy. People say that I'm quiet, but Nick's ridiculous. I really like his music; he's extremely talented, and if he wanted to be, he could be very successful."

'Hazey Jane II' is a song that accepts doom but sees its funny side.

"*Bryter Layter*, for me, is the most satisfactory record I've ever worked on," said producer Joe Boyd. "Usually when you make a record there's something you think: Well, I'd like to go back, I'd like to re-mix that or it is a shame we didn't use such and such a musician or ... it's a shame this wasn't better or ... and there's nothing on Bryter Layter that I'll ever want to do again or replace, and that is the only record I think I've ever worked on that I feel like that about.

"Most people, to have the recognition that he has, would have to go out and work day after day, week after week, go on the road, and he never did any of that. So I think he's had more than his fair share of recognition, really. I think basically, he just was shy ..."

Whatever the reason, around the time of the album being finished, Drake started to hit bottom and moved home.

"He said to me once: 'I have failed in everything I have tried to do.' I said, 'Oh Nick, how can you' ... and then I listed all the things that he had so plainly done," said his mother, Molly. "It didn't make a difference. He had failed to get through to the people that he wanted to talk to. I think he had rejected the world. Nothing made him happy."

According to Boyd, "... you can't explain the kind of songs he wrote. His unique introspection, his candour about himself and his surroundings, his extraordinary ever-present awareness of his destiny. The world he created in his songs completely transcends sources and he's someone whose story really is in the songs. He could talk through his songs but he had a very great difficulty in talking to people. The songs in a way became less about other people and more about himself as time went on."

In-a-Gadda-da-Vida Iron Butterfly

(Doug Ingle) ✳ Atco ✳ 1968 ✳ Appears on: *In-a-Gadda-da-Vida Iron Butterfly*

One of the great novelty records of the '60s turned the music business on its head. Iron Butterfly were a mid-range band playing the fertile Sunset Strip scene in the late '60s. They'd had a little success with a first album, *Heavy*, when they entered the studio to cut a second.

According to legend the group was warming up in the studio with a jam. Seventeen minutes later they were told it's a take and the result is 'In-a-Gadda-da-Vida', which became a massive hit despite its length. Of course the scope of the piece was everything. There was time for a lengthy drum solo, a ponderous organ solo, and a bass work-out as well as some guitar histrionics. The core riff was simple and strong enough to hold the whole thing together, and so you had this massive work of counter-cultural kitsch. The lyric, or at least that part of it that's discernible,

like the title, offers a glimpse of utopianism (it translates as 'In the Garden of Eden').

In short, this was heavy stuff for the kids in the suburbs and they bought four million copies – the biggest selling rock album of the time. They were one of the first bands to be labelled heavy metal. To the world's dismay, hundreds of kids assumed that if the Butterfly could jam and people would take it, then they should too.

Ahmet Ertegun, the founder of Atlantic records and considered by many to have the best tastebuds in the business, claimed in *Rolling Stone* to be bewildered by the Butterfly: "They ran through the songs, and I said, 'This is terrible, I mean the new guitarist.' And Doug said to me, 'Well, of course, he's only been playing three months.' I said, 'You mean he's been with the band for three months?' He said, 'No, he's only been playing the guitar for three months.' And I thought, 'Jesus!' ... But I tell you, this record came out, and, man, it seemed like every college student, like the whole country went out and bought it. It became the biggest record that we'd ever had up to that time – with a band that was just learning their instruments."

Lost Someone   James Brown

(James Brown/Bobby Byrd/Lloyd Stallworth) ❊ King ❊
1963 ❊ Appears on: *Live at The Apollo*

James Brown's records have changed the course of popular music. But live he was a force of nature. No-one knew this better than James Brown, of course. By 1962 he had some success on the charts and his live concerts were well attended, so Brown resolved to put his magnificence on wax. Sid Nathan, the proprietor of King records, was not convinced. Concert records rarely do well. They are generally stopgaps in an artist's career.

Unable to get Nathan's support, Brown booked the Apollo theatre in Harlem and brought in the recording equipment. It was Wednesday 24 October 1962, after the notorious amateur night, where the crowd would generally be at their most rowdy.

Lucas 'Fats' Gonder gave his famous introduction – "Thank you and thank you very kindly. It's indeed a great pleasure to present to you at this particular time the performer nationally and internationally known as the Hardest Working Man In Show Business, Mr Dynamite, the amazing Mr Please Please Himself, the star of the show, James Brown and the Famous Flames!"

Brown then came out and launched into the most powerful soul show ever captured for posterity. All those thousands of nights travelling through the south, all those thousands of hours in church. All that plus the fact that James had all his money riding on this show.

Brown didn't just reproduce concert versions of his recordings, he brought them alive. He animated them. None more so that 'Lost Someone', which was stretched into ten minutes of abject despair, out of which the singer fights through sheer will. No-one has been more alone than James Brown in the middle of 'Lost Someone'. No song has been more existential, no act of will more triumphant, than James Brown fighting back from the abyss of loneliness. James took the 1500 fans in the Apollo that night through a dark night of the soul and led them into the promised land.

These Days Nico

(Jackson Browne) ✳ Verve ✳ 1967 ✳ Appears on: *Chelsea Girl*

Starlet in Fellini's *La Dolce Vita*, siren in the early Velvet Underground, Nico eventually struck out on her own with *Chelsea Girl*. Both of the leading lights in the

Velvet Underground – Lou Reed and John Cale – had fallen for her, as did many other singer/songwriters (although Nico took up with an eighteen-year-old boy from California who was like her – handsome and troubled). Jackson Browne wrote some of his best early work for Nico, including 'These Days', which he would later record himself.

Nico's style was a weary monotone and it suited Browne's fatalistic melody and lyrics.

Tom Wilson, who had worked with the Velvet Underground, produced the *Chelsea Girl* album. Indeed, this record with backing from Reed, Cale and Sterling Morrison is almost a de facto Velvets' album. She brought to these songs a deadpan, emotionless reading. However, for all the arid delivery, Nico also presented a very fragile, delicate and beautiful persona. It's this paradox that makes the song and its album so compelling.

What's Going On Marvin Gaye

(Renaldo Benson/Marvin Gaye/Al Cleveland) ✳ Tamla ✳ 1971 ✳
Appears on: *What's Going On*

"Something happened to me in that period. I felt the strong urge to write music and to write lyrics that would touch the souls of men," said Marvin Gaye. "In that way I thought I could help."

His brother, Frankie, had recently returned from Vietnam with tales of horror, and his good friend and Motown label-mate Tammi Terrell had been slain by a brain tumour. When Obie Benson of the Four Tops showed him a song he'd written with Al Cleveland it reflected like a slow, shiny river Gaye's feelings of quiet despair. He tinkered with the lyrics, adjusted the melody, enlisted a session band of Motown's finest and insisted on producing the song himself, which was unheard of at the hit factory. The result was also revolutionary: powerful, pure-hearted protest with a mournful, mellow jazz-inspired groove. Bass player James Jamerson went home from the studio and told his wife that he'd just cut a classic.

The label refused to release it. Gaye (the 'Prince of Motown') dug in his heels and refused to record anything else until they did. His stubbornness paid off. 'What's Going On' shipped 700,000 units in its first week and was one of the label's fastest selling records. Its stay in the charts exceeded even that of 'Grapevine', Gaye's giant hit of 1968, and no record company suit attempted to mess with Gaye's creative process thereafter.

Innocent When You Dream (78) Tom Waits

(Tom Waits) ✳ Island ✳ 1987 ✳ Appears on: *Frank's Wild Years*

Frank O'Brien, the protagonist of *Frank's Wild Years*, was an entertainer who left his home to become a big star and in the usual trajectory of these things has come down the other side and landed in suburbia and regret.

"It actually starts out with Frank at the end of his rope, despondent, penniless, on a park bench in East St Louis in a snowstorm, having a going-out-of-business sale on the whole last ten years of his life," Waits told Glenn O'Brien. "Like the guys around here on Houston Street with a little towel on the sidewalk, some books, some silverware, a radio that doesn't work, maybe a Julie London album. Then he falls asleep and dreams his way back home. I've been saying that it's a cross between *Eraserhead* and *It's a Wonderful Life*.

"Well, it's a story about a guy [Frank] who went out to be an entertainer, left a small town, went to Vegas, had this song 'Innocent When You Dream'. And a year later, he had taken the same song and turned it into 'You're in a Suit of Your Dreams' to advertise suits in an all-night clothing store. And that is the type of thing that happens."

It's a disturbing song with the line about stealing memories and the title 'Innocent When You Dream', which implies guilt through all the waking hours.

The 'Innocent When You Dream (78)' version is made from the original treated by Waits to reproduce the sonic quality of a 78rpm recording.

"The 78 version of that was originally recorded at home on a little cassette player. I sang into a $7 microphone and saved the tape. Then I transferred that to twenty-four track and overdubbed Larry Taylor on upright bass, and then we mastered that. Texture is real important to me; it's like attaining grain or putting it a little out of focus. I don't like cleanliness. I like surface noise. It kind of becomes the glue of what you're doing sometimes."

The Lamb Lies Down on Broadway Genesis

(Tony Banks/Phil Collins/Peter Gabriel/Steve Hackett/Mike Rutherford) ❋ Charisma ❋ 1974 ❋ Appears on: *The Lamb Lies Down on Broadway*

The concept album, or rock operetta, was an almost exclusively British quirk. It's an odd form, suited best to the British because they care about artistic respectability. Thus you have concertos for groups and orchestras and grandiose statements like this two-album set from Genesis. Being private school boys, Genesis had something to prove.

'The Lamb Lies Down on Broadway' opens proceedings in the operetta of the same name. The story unfolds with homeless urchin Rael emerging from the subway into the light of New York accompanied by the cascading tinkling of Tony Banks' piano. Then Genesis pounds into a rock track that simulates the excitement of Gotham.

Gabriel here is picking up on a change in mood in the music audience, looking for something more visceral than the overblown art rock of the mid-'70s. However, guitarist Steve Hackett opined at the time, "We tend to keep away from the present. We're very hesitant to make any commitment to how we feel about what's happening now." That would soon be their undoing. Gabriel meanwhile was hoping that "spending time in America might well change our music for the better by making us seem less isolated in our opinions. Soul music excites me more than rock & roll. There's more emotion and I like the rhythm better. A lot of rock & roll seems to be working at a high speed, but not a high intensity."

'The Lamb Lies Down on Broadway' starts out with the best of intentions and contains the most intensity that Genesis would manage for some time. But it was downhill from there.

Coal Miner's Daughter Loretta Lynn

(Loretta Lynn) ❋ MCA ❋ 1971 ❋ Appears on: *Coal Miner's Daughter*

Born a coal miner's daughter in Butcher Hollow, Kentucky, Lynn Webb married Doolittle Lynn at fourteen. A grandmother at age twenty-nine, their daughter Loretta Lynn embodied all the clichés of country – teenage marriage to a philandering drunkard. Lynn was able to write and to sing evocatively of her struggle and that struck a real chord amongst American women who had the same problems, though perhaps somewhat less intensely. Lynn was one of the early women country singers who wrote her own material. She started out in 1959 with 'I'm a Honky Tonk Girl' and by 1962 was appearing at the Grand Ole Opry and had a song in the country Top 10.

Country singer Tanya Tucker said Lynn "was one of the first to tell it like it is." Tammy Wynette also said, "Loretta definitely paved the way for me, I was always so proud of Loretta, she was so honest, she was so sincere."

Lynn was never afraid to tackle the difficult subjects: 'Don't Come Home A-Drinkin' (with Lovin' on Your Mind)', 'Fist City', 'Your Squaw is on the Warpath' and, later, 'Rated X' about divorce, and 'The Pill', which was denounced from pulpits around the US.

So much of Lynn's work comes from her own experience as summed up in 'Coal Miner's Daughter' and she never forgot her dirt-poor upbringing.

"My early childhood memories probably are some of my best," she said. "They stuck with me more, and if they didn't I probably wouldn't be who I am today. If you don't remember who you are or where you come from, you get lost in the shuffle as you get older.

"Back in the mountains they wrote about everything that happened. If anybody got killed they wrote about that, if anybody died they wrote about that, if anything happy happened or if there was a day that was a good day, like Christmas, they wrote about that. There was always mountain music."

There She Goes The Las

(Lee Mavers) ❊ Go! Discs ❊ 1988 ❊ Appears on: *The Las*

This was the blueprint for '90s Brit pop, the template from which the Gallagher Brothers fashioned their tabloid fame. The Las were from Liverpool and played beautiful guitar melodies, hence inviting irrelevant comparisons with the Beatles. The Las were a live band with a solid repertoire at the centre of which was this pop diamond, a perfectly formed gem with an '80s edge.

Lee Mavers, who played guitar, sang and wrote the group's material, was steadfast in his pursuit of pop essence. Having toiled for some years to get the group off the ground, they made one album and were not heard from again.

When asked to describe the difference between the Las' sound and their contemporaries', he simply replied, "Ours is soul, theirs is fashion. The Las are the only ones who are making music; the others are just manners and things. Keep music alive, you know. Other music is nothing but sampled beats so everything feels and sounds the same."

Mavers was unhappy with the sound of the group's first album and made no bones about telling the public. Producer Steve Lillywhite had given the group's sound a modern treatment while hanging onto the integrity of their '60s style. But perhaps it wasn't authentic enough for Mavers.

"Can't you hear the church bells?" he said when queried about the group's jangling guitar sound. "That's what that sound means to me. I grew up listening to that sound and it fascinates me and never fails to move me. It has fuck all to do with the Byrds or any of this indie shit."

Tennessee Arrested Development

(Speech) ✳ Chrysalis ✳ 1992 ✳
Appears on: *3 Years, 5 Months & 2 Days in the Life Of ...*

When the imagery around rap artists was hardcore urban landscapes – it still mostly is – the Atlanta-based Arrested Development were out hanging in the countryside. When the rap stars like Dr Dre and Ice-T and Ice Cube looked like hard-bitten warriors, Arrested Development's main mouth, Speech, looked like a hippie. Actually, he mostly resembled Bob Marley with his warm, loping beats, a touch of reggae and a belief in family values.

The standout track, 'Tennessee', from the debut album, *3 Years, 5 Months & 2 Days in the Life of ...*, is both an admission of a non-urban heritage and an attempt to come to terms with that past. 'Tennessee' wraps up the spirituality and the positivism of Arrested Development without ignoring the darker realities of the '90s – in much the same way as Marley did in Jamaica. Arrested Development expanded the vocabulary of rap as well as its visual scope. Their shows in particular were more along the lines of a soul revue than the turntableist hardcore rap. 'Tennessee' is by any measure a great song.

"We try to make sure our minds are clear so that we can address the issues as opposed to let them totally engulf us," Speech told Barney Hoskyns. "We have a mission in mind, but I'm leaving the direction up to the Creator."

Albatross Fleetwood Mac

(Peter Green) ✳ Epic ✳ 1969 ✳ Appears on: *Pious Bird of Good Omen*

This beautiful and beguiling instrumental built around the languid guitar of Peter Green was Fleetwood Mac's first hit.

Green wrote the song while playing in John Mayall's Bluesbreakers – filling the vacancy left by Eric Clapton's departure. The initial guitar part came, he said, "from a phrase that Eric Clapton played when he was with John Mayall, one of the groups of notes."

"When 'Albatross' came out, we were still very much a blues band," said drummer Mick Fleetwood. "It was an extension of 'The Supernatural', an instrumental Peter wrote when he was with John Mayall. Obviously it was influenced by Santo & Johnny's lap steel hit 'Sleep Walk'. It went to number one during our first tour of the States, and when we came back it was all over the music papers: 'They've sold out.' It signposted what was going to happen; *Then Play On* epitomised that vision Peter had of going forward. We just didn't want to keep treading water, and that album was the real start of Fleetwood Mac."

'Albatross' floats through the airwaves, picking up touches of blues and jazz and calypso. It has an ethereal quality, too, that transcends any particular style.

"We had four or five hit records," Green said in 1983, "so I know the audience received us. They knew us from 'Albatross'. 'Albatross' is a kind of symbol for a hit record."

Kool Thing Sonic Youth

(Kim Gordon/Thurston Moore/Lee Ranaldo/Steve Shelley) ✳ DGC ✳ 1990 ✳
Appears on: *Goo*

Sonic Youth opted to leave their downtown loft and suck on the corporate teat for the album *Goo*. That means that they wrote some songs with standard verse and chorus arrangements that come in at around four minutes. However that doesn't mean they would be any less radical.

'Kool Thing', for instance, gets right into the middle of the culture wars. Using satire as a weapon, Kim Gordon takes on the MTV world and the sexual politics involved in the images that come through popular culture. She also takes aim at the sexual politics of most militant male rap, posing the question "Fear of a female planet?" Or even better, the line "Something I gotta ask ya. I just wanna know, what are you gonna do for me? I mean, are you gonna liberate us girls from male white corporate oppression?" When LL Cool J was unavailable to spar with Gordon, Public Enemy's Chuck D stepped into the breach.

The polemics of the song would be meaningless without the support of a great, kicking groove from Sonic Youth. The Youth at their best sound like the Rolling Stones meets Marc Bolan and the Velvet Underground.

'Kool Thing' is one of the most potent feminist statements of '90s music and it lives up to its title.

When Love Breaks Down Prefab Sprout

(Paddy McAloon) ✳ CBS ✳ 1985 ✳ Appears on: *Steve McQueen*

Paddy McAloon, who is for all intents and purposes Prefab Sprout, was one of Britain's more interesting songsmiths in the early '80s. He was a lyricist of considerable wit and his melodies were lush and full and complex. McAloon's first album was beloved of rock critics and English literature students. In an attempt to get more modern and perhaps more commercial, synthesiser expert Thomas Dolby was invited to produce the album *Steve McQueen* and the result is regarded as a masterpiece.

McAloon has a good line in tongue-in-cheek braggadocio, claiming at one point to be the best writer in the world, but also acknowledging that Dolby's production made the songs shine.

Prefab Sprout's highpoint for the non-anorak wearing public was 'When Love Breaks Down'. "It is a very personal song," McAloon told the *Melody Maker*. "It's not that far removed from personal experience. I've worked so hard, it's been to the detriment of other things. Relationships have suffered, I don't mind saying that. But I know if I don't work hard I won't get that golden moment. I know I can go even further but to do that I have to narrow down my interests."

'When Love Breaks Down' is one of the more remarkable moments in '80s pop. Acknowledging the singer/songwriter tradition, Dolby and McAloon created a pop symphony quite unlike anything else.

Band on the Run Paul McCartney & Wings

(Paul McCartney/Linda McCartney) ✳ Capitol ✳ 1973 ✳ Appears on: *Band on the Run*

As Beatle fans will know, McCartney treasured the idea of being in a band more than any of the other Beatles. He believed that the way forward for that group was to behave like a band and get in front of people with pop and rock songs. On the demise of the Beatles, McCartney formed his own group, Wings, and tried to approximate the chemistry of the Fab Four.

It came together for a few brief years. The best of the work was *Band on the Run*, which appeared to be a loosely themed album. 'Band on the Run' itself is a wonderful homage to the idea of the rock band as travelling gang. McCartney here finds the balance in the group – the song has a more steady and propulsive theme than much of his work and it is, in short, a delight.

Cabaret Liza Minnelli

(Fred Ebb/John Kander) ✳ MCA ✳ 1972 ✳ Appears on: *Cabaret*

The writing team of Fred Ebb and John Kander was described as "a little sassy and with mustard". Their work was often political, sexually ambiguous and morally complicated and some of the most vigorous material to come out of Broadway. In 1966 they were contracted to write songs for a musical based on the unlikely topic of Christopher Isherwood's memoirs of Weimar Berlin. Isherwood lived in the demimonde of whores, entertainers and poets. One of his characters, Sally Bowles – a nightclub singer and goodtime girl – became the centre of a story about Berlin, libertarians and the Nazi storm that was brewing.

Isherwood's stories are not overly sentimental, nor is the play, nor its songs. The screen adaptation was in the inspired but troubled hands of director Bob Fosse and starred the brilliant but troubled Liza Minnelli.

The result was a masterpiece. Not least of all due to Kander and Ebb's songs.

The title song is a triumph of ambiguity and will. When she sings it, Sally has had an abortion and she knows that the life she leads is quite probably killing her. She belts out "Life is a cabaret" full of irony. It's a song that Liza Minnelli owns in every way. She is full of regret and fear and yet she gets up and pounds out this belief that:

> What good is sitting alone in your room?
> Come hear the music play
> Life is a cabaret, old chum
> Come to the cabaret

It's an extraordinary moment and one of the few times in a Broadway song when the real ambiguities of life at its most raw all come together. "'Cabaret' is one of the happiest memories I have," said Ebb. "Because it was mostly what I had in mind, and I think mostly is the best you can do."

Bloody Well Right Supertramp

(Rick Davies/Roger Hodgson) ✳ A&M ✳ 1974 ✳ Appears on: *Crime of the Century*

At the risk of being accused of hyperbole, it should be said that Supertramp were probably the worst rock & roll group, and at the very least the embodiment of everything that threatened to destroy the genre in the '70s. They were a progressive rock band with duelling keyboards that played complex melodies underneath banal lyrics.

Supertramp – essentially a vehicle for Rick Davies and Roger Hodgson – had pretensions to reshape music and the world at large. Their vaguely conceptual albums like *Crime of the Century* looked at the "big picture" in a not very amusing manner. They suffered from schoolboy lyrics in tricked-up pop songs.

They reached their nadir with 'Bloody Well Right' simply because the hook to the song was so indelible, stupid and charmless. Supertramp could claim a series of equally irritating and infectious songs that sold millions of copies. Thank Christ it's over.

Winona Matthew Sweet

(Matthew Sweet) ✳ Zoo ✳ 1991 ✳ Appears on: *Girlfriend*

Matthew Sweet's album *Girlfriend* has one of the best covers of the '90s. It's a photo of young Tuesday Weld caught up in a rapture of infatuation and fur. Sweet's album is like that – all style, a little bit retro and a little bit ironic. 'Winona' on that album is all of those things too – a great little pop song about the actress Winona Ryder.

Sweet's record was a supersession of New York hipness – drummer Fred Maher (Scritti Politti, Lou Reed, Bill Laswell), guitarists Robert Quine (the Voidoids, Lou Reed), Richard Lloyd (Television) and Lloyd Cole, and the twenty-six year old Sweet himself producing and playing bass. He attracted musicians of this calibre on the basis of his pop songcraft.

Sweet was like Alex Chilton without the drug problems. He was like the pop Messiah, here to deliver on the promise of the Raspberries or Todd Rundgren. "It's funny, the first time I ever heard of those people was when the critics used to say to me, 'You're Powerpop, like the Raspberries'," he said. "The stuff I listened to as a teenager was mostly British: the Beatles, of course, then Nick Lowe, Elvis Costello, the Buzzcocks, XTC. I was always into the more melodic stuff that was going on at the time – New Wave rather than punk.

"When I first started out as a musician, I was a bass player. I was way too shy to sing for anybody, let alone be ready to deal with the idea of being the lead guy. But I guess it was people like Nick Lowe or Elvis Costello that made me want to write songs."

'Winona' is on the surface a gentle and kind of goofy love song to a star, but Sweet and his sidemen make it a well-crafted piece of pop with a tougher edge. In his worship of the screen legend you can hear the absence of a real woman in his life. Perhaps that reflects Sweet's then-broken heart.

"I don't try to capitalise on my or anybody else's pain for my music but people don't always believe me," he said. "I spend too much time debunking the idea so maybe they're more autobiographical than I think . . ."

Cherry Bomb The Runaways

(Kim Fowley/Joan Jett) ❋ Mercury ❋ 1976 ❋ Appears on: *The Runaways*

That they couldn't play very well at all is incidental to the significance of the Runaways. They were the second all-women rock & roll outfit but the first to break through to the public. Five very suburban girls with bad attitudes, or rather good/bad but not evil, the Runaways were a great rock & roll band.

Kim Fowley, a Los Angeles scenester, was the music business equivalent of Roger Corman. He made B-records and exploitation records that were trashy and low rent and he excelled himself with the Runaways.

Fowley and his coterie of Anglophiles like DJ Rodney Bigenheimer and journalist/record maker Greg Shaw had an acute appreciation for the glam-metal pop that had come out of England with the Sweet, Mud, Slade and the like, which was right off the radar of the serious rock fan but dear to the hearts of the kids in the vast suburban teenage wasteland.

"They're young, white, suburban American girls, a segment of society that hasn't had anyone to identify with," said Fowley, describing the Runaways in 1976. "When a boy takes his girl to a Black Sabbath concert, the girl has to keep quiet because it's his show really. And what do the girls have to relate to? Joni Mitchell singing about Laurel Canyon? Now the guys can drool over the girls and enjoy the music, and the girls can identify with the young white chicks on stage."

The group was assembled around guitarist Joan Jett, a Suzi Quatro neophyte. They were not intimidated by their limitations but, rather, rushed headlong into a fantasy world. To quote from *Bomp* magazine, "The Runaways are the quintessence of everything that's great about teenage girls – not the giggly demure saps, but the aggro ones who never came to school because they were out too late at Rodney's the night before. And they're living it right now; they don't write songs from idyllic memories that gain romantic scope over the years.

"The Runaways are as real as getting beat up after school. Their songs are about juvenile delinquent wrecks, sex, pressure, and anything incidental like drugs and parties. Sometimes the reflections on these are good, often bad, but there's always the underlying, understood agreement that the state of Teenage is what it's all about. They take all the elements of their lives, punch 'em up into catchy anthems set to the beat of the street, plug it into their amps and sing it all out loud to your crotch or your feet or your head; whichever they hit first."

The Runaways' first single, 'Cherry Bomb', was written on the spot by Fowley and Jett in imitation of Suzi Quatro. The song exploded with the suggestion of illicit sex and the loss of virginity while also referring to the homemade explosives favoured by American teenage boys. The sound was pure third-generation Chinnichap – big unison voices and a British beat. With it, the Runaways kicked down the door and a generation of women have followed.

True Love Ways Buddy Holly

(Buddy Holly/Norman Petty) ※ Coral ※ 1960 ※ Appears on: *The Complete Buddy Holly*

Although best known for his geeky look and spectacles, Buddy Holly's influence spread profoundly through popular music following his death in January 1959. Holly had a gift for melody whether in R&B or country, rockabilly or pop. He also encouraged the songcraft of others – he helped Waylon Jennings and others get started. Where most '50s rockers were either bland or mad, Holly trod a neat line.

He came out of Texas a hayseed country boy. But soon after moving to New York in 1958 he expanded his horizons.

'True Love Ways' is a gorgeous ballad with a touch of western swing in its arrangement, but mostly it's a sophisticated pop song of its era. Holly expanded his backing from the rockabilly trio to include jazzy horns and piano.

'True Love Ways' didn't appear until after Holly's death at age twenty-two. Author Jonathon Cott dug up a high-school essay Holly had written shortly before rock & roll took off. "My life has been what you might call an uneventful one, and it seems there is not much of interest to tell," he wrote. "I have many hobbies. Some of them are hunting, fishing, leatherwork, reading, painting and playing western music. I have thought about making a career out of western music if I am good enough but I will just have to wait and see how that turns out . . ."

Awaiting on You All George Harrison

(George Harrison) ✳ Apple ✳ 1970 ✳ Appears on: *All Things Must Pass*

George Harrison burst out of the Beatles like a man who had been cooped up for too long.

Like his friend Eric Clapton, Harrison had played with Delaney and Bonnie. That backing band was now Derek and the Dominos and was preparing to record the *Layla* double album. Meanwhile Derek and the Dominos were at Harrison's service. His other group assembled around Ringo Starr, Billy Preston and Klaus Voorman.

Harrison had for the past three years been on a spiritual journey that took him through Krishna consciousness in India and back through Christianity. The other guru in the mix was producer Phil Spector, who had come into the Beatles' orbit remixing *Let It Be* and was now working with George and John Lennon.

"Some of the sessions were very long in the preparation of the sound and the arrangements," Harrison wrote in his notes. "The songs were played over and over until the arrangements were sorted out. Many of the tracks were virtually live."

There's an exuberance to 'Awaiting on You All' where the performance of the musicians mirrors the sense of revelation and salvation in the lyric. The galloping rhythm section and the always-tasteful guitar parts are sublime and divine. 'Awaiting on You All' is gospel and rock & roll finding common ground.

Come Away with Me Norah Jones

(Norah Jones) ❊ Blue Note ❊ 2002 ❊ Appears on: *Come Away with Me*

New York pianist Norah Jones was the most unassuming star of 2002. Her light soulful jazz tunes based around her small combo and her own piano playing sold ten million albums that year.

Jones was the chilled-out queen – a return to the basics of songcraft and performance. She was aided in this by Arif Mardin, a producer who cut his teeth on the legendary Atlantic sessions of the '60s and his work with the Bee Gees. Jones was signed to the legendary jazz label Blue Note. Comparisons with jazz singers are often trotted out but she has never aimed for that tortured intensity. She is closer to a modern jazz singer like Cassandra Wilson

"I don't think anyone would even use the word jazz [to describe 'Come Away with Me'] except that it's on Blue Note," she said on *Austin City Limits*. "Maybe you can tell I come from that background, so maybe there are traces in there. You could probably guess I like that, but I wonder if it would be brought up as much if it wasn't on a jazz label. I don't care, if you think it's jazz than that's fine – it's jazz – but I don't think it is.

"I don't think what I do is pop music in today's sense of the word. See us live – we interact with each other, we're a small group so we're like a jazz group but we're playing country songs too, so I don't really know who they are. I have a problem naming names. Who am I to say who I sound like? It's happened so quickly, you don't know any of my contemporaries.

"The songs are pretty simple songs, they're love songs, they're not about anything modern. It's human things, I think, so in that sense it's a timeless record."

Oh Well Fleetwood Mac

(Peter Green) ❊ Reprise ❊ 1969 ❊ Appears on: *Then Play On*

Initially a purist blues group, Fleetwood Mac followed the eccentricities of guitarist Peter Green and drummer Mick Fleetwood into uncharted territory. This almost nine-minute song was a stretch into what would become heavy metal. Green leads the band through a series of moods from the violent to the serene. While building on blues, the guitarist allows in a number of flavours from Africa, Spain and the Caribbean. Green's inspiration for the song was in part Muddy Waters who, according to Green, frequently used the phrase, "Oh well, oh well".

"The following that Peter had was a very strong movement," said Fleetwood. "These people in the clubs and ballrooms would travel all over the place. Fleetwood Mac was their band. Then other bands got drawn into it; even Jethro Tull were categorised as a blues band, but with all due respect they were never a blues band. Peter was, in the nicest possible sense, very ambitious. He knew what was right, which is why his legacy, even in the short amount of time he made it, is still very much alive."

Daughter   Pearl Jam

(Dave Abbruzzese/Jeff Ament/Stone Gossard/Mike McCready/Eddie Vedder) ❋ Epic ❋ 1993 ❋ Appears on: Vs

Nirvana may have kicked off the grunge thing but it was Pearl Jam, the other Seattle band, that made it into a movement. Eddie Vedder had the sense of a troubled child about him; self-conscious, like the character in a Pete Townshend song, he had been so bruised in his childhood that he retreated into a world of rock & roll.

'Daughter', on their second album, Vs, was yet another song about a troubled teen. "The child in that song obviously has a learning difficulty," Vedder told the Melody Maker's Allan Jones. "And it's only in the last few years that they've actually been able to diagnose these learning disabilities that before were looked at as misbehaviour, as just outright fucking rebelliousness. But no-one knew what it was. And these kids, because they seemed unable or reluctant to learn, they'd end up getting the shit beaten outta them.

"The songs ends, you know, with this idea of the shades going down – so that the neighbours can't see what happens next. What hurts about shit like that is that it ends up defining people's lives. They have to live with that abuse for the rest of their lives. Good, creative people are just fucking destroyed."

Vedder's mumbling vocals suggested confusion while the boiling sound of Pearl Jam's guitar-powered rock suggested rage. It was a combination that was hard to beat and rarely matched by the legions of Alternative Nation.

Cornflake Girl Tori Amos

(Tori Amos) ❋ Atlantic ❋ 1994 ❋ Appears on: *Under the Pink*

Although Tori Amos fitted neatly into the tradition of piano-playing singer/ songwriters that goes back to Carole King and Laura Nyro and forward to Norah Jones, Amos was strikingly original. She had been a prodigy, an accomplished musician of sorts by the time she started school. Amos rebelled against the strictures – mostly artistic – imposed by her father, an Episcopalian minister, and her mother.

By the time she was ready for her first album, *Little Earthquakes*, she had much to get off her chest. While her sound may not have fitted with the loudness of the early '90s, her therapy songs certainly did.

One of Amos' most beguiling songs was 'Cornflake Girl' from her second album. Playful but dark, Amos wrote the lyric as a unique call on the mother–daughter relationship.

"I read the Alice Walker book *Possessing the Secret of Joy* and there's umm, in that book, the mothers take the daughters to the butchers to have their, let's say their genitalia removed," she said in a 1994 interview. "And even though it's a patriarchal culture that she's talking about, and that this custom was put into practice a long, long time ago by the patriarchy, it's the mothers that take their daughters.

"And what I was singing about was, it's funny how from generation to generation women really betray each other in the ladies' room. There is a whole secret society that happens, and a lot of times a mother will say 'I'm doing this for your good' whether it was binding the feet in the Eastern cultures or whether it's marrying your daughter to this gangrene, smelly-breathed, old, decrepit, rotting scumbag that's eighty years old with dough. 'You know, this is really the best for you,' when the truth is, it's the best for everybody else.

"And that's an extreme of women's relationships ... but betrayal is betrayal, and I was thrown into many situations as I was reading that book where girls, my girls, we were just dissin' each other. The things that we were doing, umm, it's like I would have never imagined that we could be so unsupportive of each other, and it was just happening while I was reading this book, and 'Cornflake Girl' is the betrayal really of girls."

I Walk the Line Johnny Cash

(Johnny Cash) ❋ Sun ❋ 1956 ❋ Appears on: *Johnny Cash and His Hot and Blue Guitar*

While serving in the Air Force, Johnny Cash had taken to writing songs with the aid of a tape machine. One night he turned the machine on and discovered a mysterious tune that he couldn't get out of his head. The tune was unlike anything he was used to.

"I never got that chord progression out of my mind – from E to A to D back to A to E to B seventh back to E. It broke all the musical laws in history, but I couldn't forget it," Cash recalled. "After I got back home and was already touring, there was Carl Perkins and myself playing Gladewater, Texas, one night at a high school auditorium. This was mid-1955. I just had my first record out and those chords kept goin' through my mind – that chord progression. And Carl Perkins asked me, 'So what are you doing?' We were backstage and I was fooling around with those chords and I said, 'I don't know. It's just something that I had on my tape recorder in Germany that has really bugged me all these years and I was just going over it again.' And he said, 'Well you don't go from E to A to D and back to A to E and B seventh and then back to E to start a song' and I said, 'Yea, you do, you know – it's like it's carved in stone in my mind.' And he said, 'That's really different.'

"He said, 'Sam Phillips is looking for something different. Why don't you write a song and use that progression?' and I said, 'I don't know what it would be' and we dropped the subject.

"Then a little bit later on we got to talking about our wives and about the guys running around on the road and so forth. I had a brand new baby and I said, 'Not me buddy, I walk the line' and he said, 'There's your song title.'

"I had given Carl the title for 'Blue Suede Shoes' from a friend of mine in the air force who kept saying, 'Don't step on my blue suede shoes man' when he'd get spiffy and go out, you know. And Carl gave me the title for 'I Walk the Line' and I used that chord progression. And I wrote it all that night in just fifteen or twenty minutes."

Johnny Cash cut 'I Walk the Line' on 2 April 1956 with the Tennessee Two – guitarist Luther Perkins and bass player Marshall Grant – plus Carl Perkins and Cash accompanying himself on guitar with a piece of paper wedged in the strings to give a percussive sound. The chord progression that had so intrigued Cash helped him to cross over to a pop audience with this song.

Don't You Want Me The Human League

(Phil Oakey) ❋ Virgin ❋ 1981 ❋ Appears on: *Dare*

It seems morbidly poetic that the last music the superstar rock critic Lester Bangs would hear was the Human League. Not the angsty, angular 'Being Boiled' but the saccharine strains of *Dare*. Lester would've died happy. *Dare*, pretty much universally panned by the serious rock critics of the day, was big and dumb. It's three chords and a platitude, sung flat by a man in make-up.

The Human League came out of Sheffield on the back of punk in 1977 and they were dark, angsty and difficult. Then, in 1980, the brains in the group – Martyn Ware and Ian Marsh – quit for the post-modern BEF and Heaven 17, leaving just Phil Oakey and the guy who did the slides (Adrian Wright). Oakey met schoolgirls Joanne Catherall and Susan Sulley in a bar and formed the next Human League. The fact that neither Jo nor Susan could sing or dance was not a barrier to employment.

And so *Dare* was born.

Perfectly styled with a smart/casual elegance plus the aforementioned lippy, the Human League, as *Smash Hits* noted, were "striking just the right balance between glamour and ordinariness; they look good, but it could just as easily be you up there." The songs too were prosaic – tales of ordinary boys and girls working in offices. The synthesisers gave it all a nice futuristic aspect. Where visions of the just-dawning computer age tended towards the dystopic, the Human League were all nice and pastel, clean and polite. It was a comforting thought.

The message of *Dare* is "don't be afraid".

Then there were the riffs – solid, beautiful, dumb hooks based around the synthesiser. Martin Rushent from Manchester (where he produced Joy Division et al) gave the album his characteristic layers of melody and some gravitas at the same time. It was as old as rock & roll but sounded different somehow. 'Don't You Want Me' was a hymn about a waitress in a cocktail bar turned into an overnight star, and the consequent drama that unfolded. Here was *Pygmalion* rewritten for checkout chicks in bobs and bubble skirts. Rarely has pop so shamelessly mimicked life.

My Sharona The Knack

(Berton Averre/Doug Fieger) ❋ Capitol ❋ 1979 ❋ Appears on: *Get The Knack*

"The Knack approached me to produce them, and the first song they played me was 'My Sharona', so how could I not go into the studio with that song?" said producer Mike Chapman. "I knew it was a number one two bars into the song. 'My Sharona' was one of those records that was just different from everything else, and it captured the imagination of the whole country. It was played so much that I even got sick of it myself after about two weeks. You didn't hear anything but 'My Sharona' on the radio, and it was the talk of the industry to the exclusion of every other topic."

The Knack (Doug Fieger, Berton Averre, Bruce Gary and Prescott Niles) were waiting to happen. Capitol immediately saw the potential of a fresh-faced power pop group who dressed in the black-and-white style of the early Beatles. They put a massive push behind the launch of the Knack and the album became the fastest selling debut in history. The album was recorded in eleven days for a budget of $18,000. While critics and the cognoscenti regarded the group with suspicion, their clean, big pop was impossible to deny. Chapman simply boosted the drums and simplified the hooks, and it is, at the end of the day, a really great pop song.

"Sharona was a girl that worked in a children's clothing store across from where my girlfriend cut hair," singer Doug Fieger revealed in a 1998 interview. "She was still in high school. I was visiting my girlfriend, and we bumped into Sharona in front of the shop that she was working in. It literally was love at first sight for me, or at least lust. Later, when the band was rehearsing, we came up with that opening drumbeat and bass line. Our drummer didn't like it. In fact, he almost refused to play it, but the rest of us thought it was really catchy.

"Nothing lyrically really came to mind at first, but after working on it a little bit, I came up with 'Ma-ma-ma-my Sharona', and the guys said, 'You can't sing that. Are you crazy? Your girlfriend will kill you!' Once I had the direction, it didn't take long to finish the record.

"[It's] actually Sharona on the cover of the jacket for the single. She's also on the cover of our second album. We ended up living together for four years. She's now a very successful real estate agent in California."

Sail Away Randy Newman

(Randy Newman) ❋ Warner Bros. ❋ 1972 ❋ Appears on: *Sail Away*

This song has been widely covered, yet its lyric is incredibly bleak and mean. In a 1972 interview Newman outlined the song's narrator – a 19th-century trader recruiting slaves from Africa. Newman imagined a band playing 'Take Me Out to the Ballgame' and then 'Campdown Races' and an old Irish ballad and then, finally, the trader sings a song about America, which is 'Sail Away':

> In America you'll get food to eat
> Won't have to run through the jungle
> And scuff up your feet
> You'll just sing about Jesus and drink wine all day
> It's great to be an American
>
> Ain't no lions or tigers
> Ain't no mamba snake
> Just the sweet watermelon and the buckwheat cake
> Ev'rybody is as happy as a man can be
> Climb aboard, little wog
> Sail away with me

Of course the lyric is a satire on racism and the stain of slavery. However, it equally applies to the lie of modern America as well. It undercuts the whole jolliness of the songs we sing to make ourselves feel better.

'Sail Away' took six months to arrange. Newman's uncles were amongst Hollywood's most esteemed conductors, composers and arrangers, so Randy knew how to put an emotional narrative into the fabric of a melody. This is the key to the power of 'Sail Away': the music tells us that we've bought the con.

This was Newman's biggest production to date. At the end of the session, he declared "I think it's the greatest thing I ever heard."

Us and Them   Pink Floyd

(Roger Waters/Richard Wright) ❋ Harvest ❋ 1973 ❋ Appears on: *Dark Side of the Moon*

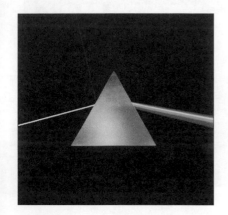

Pink Floyd's concept album, *Dark Side of the Moon*, appeared to be a carefully constructed cycle of songs with deep meaning. In fact, it was constructed on the run amidst a hectic touring schedule. Bits and pieces were worked up on the road before bass player Roger Waters announced he had an overarching theme.

"When we started on a new album, we'd always dredge through old tapes to see if there was anything left over we could make use of," said guitarist David Gilmour. "When Roger walked into Broadhurst Gardens [rehearsal space] with the idea of putting it all together as one piece with this linking theme he'd devised, that was a moment."

"The concept was originally about the pressures of modern life – travel, money and so on," drummer Nick Mason said. "But then Roger turned it into a meditation on insanity."

With the entire band producing and engineering, the studio was turned into an instrument of its own. Waters and Gilmour were at creative loggerheads through the sessions and producer Chris Thomas had to be brought in as a referee. Waters in particular wanted to stretch his muscle in the group and insisted on writing all the lyrics. This was really the moment when Floyd started saying serious things rather than psychedelic space waffle. Whether the lyrics and the album live up to its pretence is open to question.

Floyd embraced all that technology had to offer, especially the recently devised synthesisers and their general 'space' vibe. For all of its state-of-the-art sheen, *Dark Side* is very human in its songs, in the vocals and guitars, and in the addition of a saxophone and wailing female vocals.

The album's most human track is 'Us and Them'. The core of the song is a piece written by keyboard player Richard Wright for Michelangelo Antonioni, for a scene in the film *Zabriskie Point*. Waters added a lyric to the piece and Gilmour did the vocals.

"We were underground until *Dark Side of the Moon*," said Mason. "Before, we were seen as some form of intellectual rock & roll. But its success was our defining moment."

The Low Spark of High Heeled Boys Traffic

(Jim Capaldi/Steve Winwood) ❈ Island ❈ 1971 ❈

Appears on: *The Low Spark of High Heeled Boys*

Actor Michael J Pollard (cult star of *Bonnie & Clyde*) came up with the phrase "the low spark of high heeled boys," which the Traffic lyricist used as the title of one of his best songs.

Lyrically the song seems to be about the commodification of youth culture. However, the key here is the twelve-minute exposition by Winwood and Chris Wood, and borrowing a little from later Miles Davis. There are plenty of other flavours in this stew, including some African percussion, some blues and always Winwood's expressive soulful voice.

The song develops in a very organic manner from a bass, sax and piano figure. The jamming is getting very jazzy when suddenly the group crunches into rock & roll and finally finds its way back, guided by Winwood's piano.

"We were testing the boundaries of musical reality like the Doors were testing the boundaries of reality, period," Capaldi told *MOJO*.

"I mean, such little preparation before the recording, but capturing such a great spontaneity, yet not overly investigating a song to a point where the song ain't fresh any more either."

"Of everything Steve's done, that title track always seems to me to be the song that's most like him – bizarre, clever, complex, loose, not well formulated, but with a great groove," said Muff Winwood, his brother and sometime record producer. "Depending on my mood, it's my favourite and least favourite track. It kind of sums him up for me."

Big Yellow Taxi Joni Mitchell

(Joni Mitchell) ❈ Reprise ❈ 1970 ❈ Appears on: *Ladies of the Canyon*

One of Joni Mitchell's most well known songs, 'Big Yellow Taxi' combines the global and the personal in a playful, jaunty song that nonetheless makes its point.

· Mitchell told journalist Alan McDougall that the song was inspired by waking up in the Royal Hawaiian Hotel on Waikiki Beach.

"Living in Los Angeles, smog-choked LA, is bad enough but the last straw came when I visited Hawaii for the first time," she said. "It was night-time when we got there, so I didn't get my first view of the scenery until I got up the next morning. The hotel room was quite high up so in the distance I could see the blue Pacific Ocean. I walked over to the balcony and there was the picturebook scenery, palm tree swaying in the breeze and all. Then I looked down and there was this ugly concrete car park in the hotel grounds. I thought, 'They paved paradise and put up a parking lot' and that's how the song 'Big Yellow Taxi' was born."

The world was only starting to recognise the threats to the ecology in 1970 when the song was written. Fears about pollution and industrialisation were regarded as part of the hippie fringe. Over the ensuing thirty years Mitchell's song has, of course, become prescient.

Mitchell was a folk singer in the early '60s and the melody and arrangement reflect that light folk pop feel, although Mitchell has said, "The first music that I made that was my own, when I stopped singing folk songs, was rooted in Chuck Berry. 'Big Yellow Taxi' is rooted in Chuck Berry."

The final verse of the song brings the problem back to the personal and if you treat your lover as we treat the planet they will leave in a big yellow taxi.

While Mitchell's versions are hard to beat, the song has been a hit for a number of other artists, including the Counting Crows, who recently put it back into the charts.

The Other Side of This Life Fred Neil

(Fred Neil) ❋ Elektra ❋ 1965 ❋ Appears on: *Bleeker & McDougall*

As the talent manager at the Café Wha in Greenwich Village in 1960, Fred Neil knew everybody. Everybody apparently looked up to Neil as one of the pre-eminent folk writers of the time. He and partner Vince Martin were a dynamic live act with a wide range of blues and folk standards to augment Neil's original material. On the cover of his first solo album he's pictured on the corner of Bleeker and McDougall streets – ground zero for Greenwich Village at the time.

While Neil may have been a great companion to his fellow folksingers – the list of his friends includes Bob Dylan, Al Kooper, Felix Pappalardi, John Sebastian, Dino Valente, Karen Dalton, Al Wilson, Bruce Langhorn, Gram Parsons, Buzzy Linhart,

David Crosby and Stephen Stills – he was reclusive by nature. He only gave one interview in his career. After he left New York in the late '60s he rarely performed and stopped recording.

While Neil's reclusiveness may simply have been a personal preference, his songs suggest that he was not a happy man and that he struggled with alcohol and drugs. Neil retired from music to Florida, where he worked with dolphins, and died in 2001.

He will be remembered as a songwriter for Roy Orbison ('Candy Man') and Nilsson ('Everybody's Talkin'') but perhaps his best and most autobiographical number is 'The Other Side of This Life' (which was covered by the Jefferson Airplane).

"The kids today are more hip than ever and they want to hear some honest songs for a change," Neil said in his 1966 interview with *Hit Parader*. "They're tired of all the baloney and they're saying just that. Much of this is responsible for the new interest in folk music. The lyrics are saying something. I still don't know exactly where I'm going myself. I'm following the music, trying to write it as I see it, I'll even say that. Someone once said that in 'Other Side of This Life' I got away with saying, 'Would you like to know a secret . . . I don't know what the heck I'm doing.' But at least I wasn't copping out."

'The Other Side of This Life', recorded with Felix Pappalardi and John Sebastian, was folk-rock with a jazzy feel behind Neil's honey baritone. While clearly in a folk tradition, Neil had a very modern sensibility.

"I can tell you that, as a songwriter, the natural way that he could combine these various styles was just by being who he was. It wasn't any kind of an alchemy thing of 'We're gonna pour a little of this, and a little of that.' It was just who he was. That was very inspiring," said John Sebastian. "And it also was a real lesson in how to let a lyric sound like it just fell out of your mouth, like you hadn't really laboured over it. Fred always had that quality about his songs."

I Fought the Law The Bobby Fuller Four

(Sonny Curtis) ✳ Mustang ✳ 1965 ✳ Appears on: *The Best of the Bobby Fuller Four*

Sonny Curtis of Buddy Holly's band the Crickets recorded this song in 1959. It was another Texan, Bobby Fuller, who made the song a major hit.

Fuller was a native of El Paso, Texas, and a devotee of Buddy Holly. In 1964 he and his band moved to Los Angeles. Fuller was making some headway with his own brand of Texas rockabilly. In October 1965, Fuller cut 'I Fought the Law' and in February 1966 the song peaked in the Top 10.

Then, in the morning of 18 July 1966, Fuller's corpse was discovered on the front seat of his mother's 1962 Oldsmobile, which was parked outside his Hollywood apartment. The body was covered in gasoline. The coroner ruled the death a suicide but many of Fuller's friends suggested that he had become involved in the drug scene and that he was murdered by organised crime figures.

The ultimate rebel anthem, 'I Fought the Law' tells the tragic story of a man seduced into a life of crime but who gets his comeuppance. However, the song has become a rebel anthem for groups from the Clash to Green Day. The galloping tempo of the song and the powerful six shots from the drums at the finale just add to the exuberance of the outlaw hymn.

Crazy in Love Beyoncé

(Shawn Carter/Rich Harrison/Beyoncé/Eugene Record) ✳ Columbia ✳ 2003 ✳

Appears on: *Dangerously in Love*

If Destiny's Child were the heirs to the Supremes' mantle, and it's arguable that they were, then Beyoncé Knowles was the Diana Ross. The group came out of the south in the late '90s with a fresh approach to the girl group sound – conscious but sexy. This was a theme pursued by Knowles on her first solo effort, *Dangerously in Love* and its lead single, 'Crazy in Love'.

The groove on 'Crazy in Love' was not quite like anything else on the charts – tougher than pop but too smooth for the average R&B hit. The extra element would seem to be the singer herself.

"I actually produced 'Independent Woman' and 'Jumpin, Jumpin', and the record label sent me to the studio to write another song, and it was 'Survivor'," said Knowles. "After that they sent me to the studio to write still another song and it was 'Bootylicious'. They continued to send me back to the studio and, before I realised it, I had written and produced an entire album."

'Crazy in Love' is one of the best pop songs of the early 21st century.

Super Freak Rick James

(Rick James/Alonzo Miller) ❋ Motown ❋ 1981 ❋ Appears on: *Street Songs*

The late Rick James achieved immortality with a bass line. James conceived the riff as a humorous parody of a dance beat, then he added some fat synthesiser sounds, the Temptations on backing vocals, and salacious lyrics. The result was debauched and playful at the same time.

James had a truly tragic life – he was destroyed by an addiction to crack cocaine and involved in sadomasochistic sex, which eventuated in kidnapping and assault charges and jail time. However, 'Super Freak' is a classic. The bass line was revisited by MC Hammer on his global number one hit 'U Can't Touch This'.

"I am trying to make multi, multi-millions of dollars, I am trying to make Paul McCartney white boy money, so I can sit back and have a big house in Spain and not ever work again," said James. "Right now I got a few million dollars and I'm doing all right; I hope to have twenty million soon, so I can sit back real fat like Mick Jagger and Rod Stewart and all them other assholes who sit out there and talk shit and procrastinate and talk that hypocritical ass bullshit about their 'art' …"

The Mad Daddy The Cramps

(Lux Interior/Ivy Rorschach) ❋ IRS ❋ 1980 ❋ Appears on: *Songs the Lord Taught Us*

"First of all it's not music," said singer Lux Interior of the sound of his band the Cramps. "It's misdirected noise." According to one journalist, "they make a noise that's 20% Johnny Burnette's Rock & Roll Trio, 6% Screamin' Jay Hawkins, 16% Iggy, 3% Aleister Crowley, 1% 'Repulsion', 8% Lenny Kaye's *Nuggets*, 5% Rolling Stones, 15% Billy Lee Riley's 'Flying saucers rock & roll', 9% Loony Tunes, 4% Ramones, 1% Clairol, 5% *Night of the Living Dead*, and 6% Herbie Duncan's 'Hot Lips Baby', Lux's all-time favourite piece of rockabilly dementia." They say the same thing on 'The Mad Daddy', which could well be an autobiography for Lux.

Interior and his girlfriend guitarist Ivy Rorschach started the Cramps out of a love of trash Americana and outsider art – the world of Russ Meyer films, Elvis Presley, serial killers, B-movies and old blues. Surprisingly, they were really good at it. They had great lyrics like the line in 'Human Fly': "I cry ninety-six tears with my ninety-six eyes". Most of all the Cramps had a particular understanding of a part of the rock & roll psyche, which was to just do it. Faced with the inevitable problem for any garage band – who has to play the bass? – they simply dispensed with the instrument and still worked up a throbbing, swampy sound.

The Cramps' first album, *Songs the Lord Taught Us*, was produced in Memphis by the legendary alcoholic Alex Chilton, and it has a particular raw glory. "The mixing was a problem," said Lux, "because we couldn't get any engineers that could stand to listen to this music. They'd sit there and say "How can you listen to this distortion all day?" And any time Alex wanted to put his hands on the board to move the faders, it was 'How dare you?'"

"For us, we've loved rock & roll all our lives, and this band is the end of it," said Ivy. "We're not using the band to get into galleries or become mime dancers or anything. We want to be a rock & roll band, and I'll do it till past when I'm dead."

D-I-V-O-R-C-E Tammy Wynette

(Bobby Braddock/Curly Putman) ✳ Epic ✳ 1967 ✳
Appears on: *The Essential Tammy Wynette*

One of Tammy Wynette's early hits, 'D-I-V-O-R-C-E' was a subject with which she was familiar. She was at the time parting from her second husband and about to

enter a tumultuous marriage with country star George Jones. She would eventually divorce him too.

'D-I-V-O-R-C-E' was one of the songs that really reflected the way that country music was picking up on the changes that were happening in society. It was a 'countrypolitan' style song, in tune with the '60s. Wynette brought the soap opera of her life to the song and to her career. That adds to the camp quality of 'D-I-V-O-R-C-E' and the image that country had – trailer trash white people with big hair and drunken husbands – through the '70s.

"I just don't understand how a young person of twenty-one or twenty-two can sing about walking out and hearing the baby cry," Wynette told *MOJO*. "I just don't understand how they can put their heart and soul into it because it's never happened to them. It happened to us."

You Don't Pull No Punches But You Don't Push the River Van Morrison

(Van Morrison) ❋ Warner Bros. ❋ 1974 ❋ Appears on: *Veedon Fleece*

Van Morrison has enjoyed an eclectic spiritual journey. In the early '70s he lived in America but became increasingly interested in the cultural, spiritual, mystical traditions of his native Ireland and Britain – in particular the mystic poetry of William Blake, John Donne and WB Yeats. At the same time he became interested in Gestalt therapy. All these ideas collided on the epic 'You Don't Pull No Punches But You Don't Push the River'.

The phrase "Don't push the river" is the title of a book by therapist Barry Stevens, but it also occurs frequently in Taoist and Zen Buddhist stories.

In this song Morrison is as usual going back to a time of innocence but this time it's to meet William Blake, the Sisters of Mercy and other mystic poets. As in his best work, on this eight-minute epic he worries at the theme until such time as he gets to the bottom of it.

All Van Morrison's work comes back to four themes. There are the workmanlike R&B love songs, there are songs about how he was cheated by the music business, there are songs about his longing for his Irish childhood and there are songs about his spiritual quest. Occasionally these intersect. Due to the fact that he was a singer with an acoustic guitar at the end of the '70s, he was typecast as a singer/songwriter, but in fact his muse has never swung that way. Morrison has more of a jazz singer's sensibility, where the emotion dictates the meaning of a song and the melody dictates the words.

"A lot of times people say, 'What does this mean?' A lot of times I have no idea what I mean," he told journalist Ritchie Yorke. "If you can't figure out what it means, or it's troubling you, it's not for you. It means what it means. That's what I like about rock & roll – the concept – like Little Richard. What does he mean? You can't take him apart; that's rock & roll to me."

"People were intellectualising their own interpretations on top of the trip. Labelling me a song poet and all that. I'm not saying that I can't do that and that I'm not a song poet. I've been as influenced by Jack Kerouac as the next person. But who the fuck hasn't been? Everybody has been influenced by Kerouac. What I don't like is taking it to extremes and making all these intellectualisations about what basically is simple music. It's simple stream-of-consciousness stuff in my songs. What I'm trying to get across is misinterpreted."

On 'You Don't Pull No Punches' you can just drift along the river of the song, catching the glimpses of the mystics.

Whipping Post The Allman Brothers Band

(Gregg Allman) ✳ Mercury ✳ 1971 ✳ Appears on: *At Fillmore East*

'Whipping Post', from their first album, was a live favourite of the Allman Brothers. "I had this girlfriend in LA," said Gregg Allman about the song's inspiration. "She was using this pseudo love on me like an M16. She kept putting me through all kinds of tricks."

The Allman Brothers Band put this song through all kinds of tricks. To its blues-based structure they added the jazz inflections of their two guitars/dual drum attack.

"The stage is really our natural element," said guitarist Duane Allman. "We kind of get frustrated doing the records, so consequently our next album will be for the most part a live recording to get some of that natural fire on it. We have rough arrangements, layouts of the songs, and then the solos are entirely up to each member of the band."

To that end, producer Tom Dowd recorded the group's two dates (12 and 13 March 1971) at the Fillmore East in New York. "My favourite album of theirs," said Dowd, "is when I did them at the Fillmore. They were at their absolute peak, the playing just flowed. It's the greatest fusion album I've ever heard."

The album closes with a twenty-two-minute version of 'Whipping Post'. The song is in six/eight time, led by Berry Oakley's firm but fluid bass attack and then follows the swelling, surging organ against the firestorm of guitars. Dickey Betts pulls out a hint of his 'Les Bres in A Minor', which was inspired by John Coltrane, and Duane Allman answers. This was the closest that rock got to jazz in the '70s and it's unlikely that many of the fans who sent the record into the Top 10 realised it.

Jim Marshall's cover photo of a long-haired group of southerners surrounded by road cases was an iconic image of the sublime beauty of rock music in the early '70s. 'Whipping Post' is its aural equivalent.

Twenty-Four Hours from Tulsa Gene Pitney

(Burt Bacharach/Hal David) ❋ Musicor ❋ 1964 ❋ Appears on: *Blue Gene*

Gene Pitney's almost cracking upper register and his histrionic delivery lent itself to narrative songs such as this and Bacharach and David's 'The Man who Shot Liberty Vallence'. 'Tulsa' has since become a classic although a feud with his label Musicor and Bacharach and David meant that the song was never supported in the US.

The origin of the lyric is a mystery to Hal David. It just sounded like it was going to be a good story. From there he constructed a narrative of a travelling man on his way home and "only one day away from your arms" when his heart is taken by another woman. There is so much drama in this song – the sense of motion and the advancing time – as David sketches out the landscape of the interstate and the motels and truck stops. The tempo of Bacharach's tune propels the melody. There's the kind of jittery feeling that comes from driving too long on too little sleep and too much bad food. There's a sense of being in limbo and of the salvation that is offered by the singer's home. A salvation that he will never reach. This is one of the most inventive break-up songs, but really only works because of Gene Pitney's delivery of Bacharach's very complex melody. It's a song of mystery and romance, of a life changed in a moment.

Willin' Little Feat

(Lowell George) ❋ Warner Bros. ❋ 1972 ❋ Appears on: *Sailin' Shoes*

The story of a lonely truck driver kicked off the career of one of America's most interesting, if short-lived, writers. 'Willin'' is sung from the perspective of a truck driver trapped on the perpetual highway of life. Superficially it's a country song but George makes this scenario into an existential condition. George's command of the language lifted the song from the typical truckdriver lament into something that was more gorgeous, more poetic.

"The whole West Coast of the United States is going to look like the whole East Coast – one hamburger stand right after another," George said. "I admit I have a thing about truck drivers. After all, they're stuck like the rest of us. He might enjoy himself, the freedom of the road, but he's been through hell too."

George, a native of Los Angeles, wrote the song during his tenure as singer in Frank Zappa's Mothers of Invention. Keyboardist Bill Payne believes that the drug references in the song got him fired because of Zappa's notorious paranoia about drugs.

Everyone else who heard it loved it. Clarence White heard a version and took it to the Byrds, who cut it. Linda Ronstadt did a version. As a result of this interest, in 1971 Lenny Waronker at Warner Bros. signed the group and made three of the best albums of the decade.

George may never have driven a rig himself but he was behind the wheel in 'Willin''. Most of his life he battled demons. He was famously overweight with a healthy appetite for drugs. By the mid-'70s he was withdrawing from the group unable to write any longer. He was eventually fired from his own band and shortly after completing a solo album, weighing 300 pounds, he died of a heart attack.

Midnight Special Leadbelly

(Leadbelly) ❋ Smithsonian ❋ 1934 ❋ Appears on: *Death Letter Blues*

Leadbelly was born Huddie Ledbetter in Louisiana in the 1885. By the turn of the century he was an itinerant musician, cotton picker and railroad gang labourer. He was also a repository of hundreds of songs – dance tunes, prison songs and blues. In 1933 he was incarcerated at Angola, the Louisiana State Penitentiary, where he met John Lomax and his son Alan who were travelling through the south recording folk songs for the Library of Congress.

According to legend, Leadbelly was serving a murder sentence and sang his way out of jail twice. The truth is a little more prosaic.

Leadbelly was in jail in Texas on assault charges. He escaped but two years later was convicted of murder following a fatal argument over a woman. Leadbelly claimed self-defence. He received seven to thirty years and was released in 1925 after serving the minimum.

In January 1930 he was again convicted, this time of assault with intent to murder Dick Ellet of Mooringsport, Louisiana, whom the sheriff described as a "splendid white citizen". The details of the matter are obscure, but again Leadbelly claimed, with some support, self-defence. Leadbelly's jail tenure suggests that he was a man with a violent temper. However, jail and police harassment were an everyday part of life for southern blacks until the late '60s.

The Lomaxes were public advocates for Leadbelly and tried to promote his release. According to unreliable legend again, his songs secured clemency from the governor. Alan Lomax is reported to have said, "We agreed to make a record of his petition on the other side of one of his favourite ballads, 'Goodnight Irene'. I took the record to Governor Allen on 1 July. On 1 August Leadbelly got his pardon. On 1 September I was sitting in a hotel in Texas when I felt a tap on my shoulder. I looked up and there was Leadbelly with his guitar, his knife, and a sugar bag packed with all his earthly belongings. He said, 'Boss, you got me out of jail and now I've come to be your man.'"

However, Warden LA Jones wrote to a New York probation officer in 1939: "This man has been the recipient of wide publicity in various magazines of national circulation, the story usually being that he sang or wrote such moving appeals to the governor that he was pardoned. Such statements have no foundation in fact. He received no clemency, and his discharge was a routine matter under the good time law which applies to all first and second offenders."

By then, Leadbelly was in showbusiness and a colourful history is never bad for the box office. The *Herald Tribune* announced his arrival in New York on 3 January 1935 with the line, "Lomax arrives with Leadbelly, Negro minstrel/sweet singer of the swamplands here to do a few tunes between homicides."

As a folk singer, Leadbelly was portrayed as a kind of primal Negro capable of great violence – he pulled a knife on Lomax once, cooling their relationship – and passion, but also with a natural gift for song.

'The Midnight Special', one of Leadbelly's best known numbers, draws on his prison experiences. He took a traditional jail song – there are extant versions dating from as early as 1925 – and adapted it to his particular experiences, recording conditions in particular prisons and with particular personalities.

Leadbelly found universality in the song: the sense of being imprisoned as an emotional state rather than only a physical one. 'Midnight Special' with its inexorable tempo set against an uplifting melody has been a standard, especially amongst white rock performers. It's not quite a blues but it is a link right back to the oral traditions of the work and prison songs of the 19th century that still finds a place in the popular repertoire.

My Drug Buddy   The Lemonheads

(Evan Dando) ❋ Atlantic ❋ 1992 ❋ Appears on: *It's a Shame About Ray*

Well, the title is self-explanatory. It's a story of a couple of slackers who spend their days scoring drugs and then doing it again. Not the most interesting of stories but Dando makes the scenario something more profound than just the routine of addiction. The melody here is wistful and dreamy. He creates a relationship between the two characters that is more than just getting out of it. Part of it is the matter-of-fact tone with which he delivers the song. Without either moral judgement or a description of the excitement of getting high, Dando here is describing a bond between two people. Maybe it's romance, maybe it's friendship. There's a dreamy quality that really makes it irrelevant. The melody on the song is just sublime.

"*Ray* is all about this girl from the Hummingbirds, Alannah, who suggested that the Lemonheads should come out to Australia," said Dando, describing the classic *Shame about Ray* album. "I'm proud of that record! It's glowy, bright and shiny."

Gloria   Patti Smith

(Van Morrison/Patti Smith) ❋ Arista ❋ 1975 ❋ Appears on: *Horses*

Writing about the conception of the Patti Smith Group in 1974, the singer said 'Gloria' was bred of this time, crossing the poem 'Oath', written in 1970, with the Van Morrison classic. It was to be the first Patti Smith Group single and in the words of writer Paul Williams, "a declaration of existence. 'Gloria' gave me the opportunity to acknowledge and disclaim our musical and spiritual heritage. It personifies for me, within its adolescent conceit, what I hold sacred as an artist. The right to create, without apology, from a stance beyond gender or social definition, but not beyond the responsibility to create something of worth."

'Gloria' opens with the unforgettable statement, "Jesus died for somebody's sins but not mine", which is pure teen arrogance in the style of the most surly of French teens, Arthur Rimbaud. 'Gloria' is a play on the Latin use of the name in worship and in Van Morrison's hymn to desire, 'Gloria', which also has a lineage through its many reinterpretations by '60s garage bands.

"A lot of songs started off as jams and soon we found that things would organically come together," said guitarist Lenny Kaye. "'Gloria' started as a jam. We'd do chordal riffs over which Patti would chant, poeticize, and tell stories. We never thought about it becoming as big as it did. We were satisfied playing for local art audiences. We just liked doing what we were doing. It didn't have a category. It was an attitude."

It's all here – God, sex and great rock & roll 45s. There's no coincidence in the fact that the flipside was a reworking of the Who's 'My Generation'. *Horses* was one of the first albums in what was to be called punk rock, not only because there was an outsider attitude and a penchant for black and white photography, but because it placed a new sensibility and rawness into the context of the classic, stripped back '60s music. Not only did Patti Smith help to build (literally) the stage at CBGB, with 'Gloria' she gave an intellectual backbone to the music that was to come out of there.

Try a Little Tenderness Otis Redding

(Jimmy Campbell/Reginald Connelly/Harry Woods) ❋ Stax ❋ 1966 ❋

Appears on: *The Very Best of Otis Redding*

"Otis made a better musician out of you," bass player Donald 'Duck' Dunn told Barney Hoskyns. "He just brought out things you didn't know you had in you. You got happier, you felt better, and your hands and fingers moved better. He was a star. He wore the halo. Elvis, Sinatra, the Beatles ... Otis was one of 'em."

Redding was a big man whose voice matched his size. 'Try a Little Tenderness' is his most complex song – emotionally and musically. It goes through a number of changes from supplication to intense passion in about three minutes. Part of the dynamic structure of the song came from drummer Al Jackson switching around the beat. "We didn't know he was gonna do that," said Dunn. "It was amazing."

Where Redding's songs had been powerful soul grooves, 'Tenderness' itches. It's tense and nervous and uncomfortable, starting out as a whisper that's desperate to become a scream. It was originally a hit for Bing Crosby and later for Sam Cooke, but Redding fills up the song and then moves around in there until it's ready to burst at the seams.

'Try a Little Tenderness' was a very mature song for the period and it reflected Redding's own personality.

"His love for people showed up in his songs," guitarist Steve Cropper told *Hit Parader* magazine. "He was always trying to get back to his baby or he missed her – she was the greatest thing in the world. He always had a positive approach. It's hard to convince the public with a negative song, 'You did me wrong.' Otis showed me the best way is to write positive. Otis didn't get to be with his wife and three children as much as he wanted. He had a definite thing for them. Whenever he had time, he'd think about them. He brought his wife and kids to recording sessions quite often."

My Ride's Here Warren Zevon

(Warren Zevon/Paul Muldoon) ✳ Artemis ✳ 2002 ✳ Appears on: *My Ride's Here*

Death and Warren Zevon were never far apart. For much of his life he indulged in self-destructive behaviour. He survived as long as he did as much through good luck as good management. Tragically, he died too young in 2003 at fifty-six of lung cancer.

Zevon was not only an atheist and cynic but a pragmatist as well. While his songs often showed up sides of human nature beyond the ken of other songwriters, Zevon deplored the idea that he was some kind of visionary.

"I think you have to say, and I've *always* said this, 'Perry Farrell, Perry Como: same job, same guy.' Same fuckin' guy. I don't care if he rubs broken glass on his chest, or if he wears a white dinner jacket. It's the same fucking job! Don't be a hypocrite. If you can say something serious and important and moving, and something about your feelings and/or humankind, that's great. But as soon as it gets stupid, you better get 'em laughing. Because otherwise, it'll be horrible. Hypocrisy and pompousness, which go hand-in-hand – that shit'll make your *skin* crawl.

"The purpose of art is *not* to educate. The purpose of art is not to proselytise or sway the vote. There's something else for that, and that's fine, but it's not art. Not fine art. The purpose of fine art is to say, 'Gee, this planet's not so bad.' ... 'You know, 'I'm just a person, like this Paul Simon fellow. *That* makes me feel better.' That's what art is supposed to do. One of the things my ex-girlfriend used to say is the thing she hated more than anything, about any kind of art or any kind of show, was being *told* how to feel. So, if you find yourself *telling* people how to feel, then you're straining for effect, and you're better off trying to make people laugh. It's fine to tell 'em how *you* feel. Not to tell *them* how to feel. Thanks for the thought, my dear."

With that in mind, few people have written their own obituaries with such wit and dignity. This song is set amongst the mythical corpses of Milton and John Wayne, Keats and Jesus and Charlton Heston.

I was staying at the Marriott
With Jesus and John Wayne
I was waiting for a chariot
They were waiting for a train
The sky was full of carrion
'I'll take the mazuma'
Said Jesus to Marion
'That's the 3:10 to Yuma
My ride's here . . .'

Money for Nothing Dire Straits

(Mark Knopfler) ❋ Vertigo ❋ 1985 ❋ Appears on: *Brothers in Arms*

The '80s are remembered as a time of excess and extreme behaviour, but a look at the pop charts tells a different story. No-one exemplified the beige-ness of the decade more than Dire Straits. Mark Knopfler's endless instrumental passages had the patina of jazz and rock improvisation but were cold and detached; bourgeois muzak to relax with after a day on the money markets. Finally, on the fifth album, they broke a smile, cut back on the solos and made one of the blockbuster albums of all time.

'Walk of Life' was a delightful, jaunty single with a touch of rockabilly. Then came the knockout punch – 'Money for Nothing' – which satirised MTV and rock stardom while getting high rotation MTV exposure and making Mark Knopfler a rock star. Of course, there was irony here (finally). No-one could imagine Knopfler – the man who made a fashion statement of headbands – getting chicks. MTV notwithstanding.

Family Affair Sly & the Family Stone

(Sylvester Stewart) ✳ Epic ✳ 1971 ✳ Appears on: *There's a Riot Goin' On*

Apparently there was a riot goin' on in Sly Stone's mind during the making of this album. In previous years Sylvester Stewart (aka Sly Stone) had revolutionised soul with his rainbow coalition bands and his futuristic gospel sound. This was fresh and powerful music.

Unfortunately, Sly developed a taste for the drug angel dust, also known as PCP, and his life went off the rails. He stopped turning up for concerts and his behaviour became increasingly erratic.

The recording of *Riot* went months over time. Bobby Womack, Miles Davis and Billy Preston all showed up for sessions but there is no evidence that their parts were kept or any proof of their visits. Sly Stone was endlessly recording and rerecording tracks.

The album budget blew out to a massive $1,000,000 – unheard of in those days. The party atmosphere of previous records was played down in a fog of paranoia.

Through it all came 'Family Affair' – a beautiful piece of funk and one of the first hits to feature electronic drums. The song was elastic enough to be shaped by the listener into a song of paranoia or a song of love. Depending on where your head is.

The First Time Ever I Saw Your Face Roberta Flack

(Ewan MacColl) ✳ Atlantic ✳ 1969 ✳ Appears on: *First Take*

Ewan MacColl was a Communist folk singer who deplored pop music. He led the ridiculous British protest against Bob Dylan's electric music and publicly campaigned against the hit parade. Ironically, his enduring legacy is firmly in pop. His daughter, Kirsty MacColl, was a talented writer and singer of pop songs and MacColl himself will be forever remembered for 'The First Time Ever I Saw Your Face'.

'The First Time' was penned on the spot at the request of MacColl's second wife, Peggy Seeger, in 1957. It entered the folk songbook and was covered by Peter, Paul & Mary, Marianne Faithfull, Gordon Lightfoot and Bert Jansch before Roberta Flack gave it the definitive reading on her debut album, *First Take*, in 1969. Every major interpretive singer has covered it since that time, never as well as Roberta Flack (although Peter Blakeley did a sublime version on *Harry's Café De Wheels*).

Flack was a jazz and soul singer who brought her classical training to her piano and vocals. *First Take* is a masterpiece of controlled emotion. Flack makes much use of the spaces and silences to give the emotions a genuine space to play on. Her reading of 'The First Time' is devastating in its architecture. She sings as though she is in a rapture, floating above the real world. The first time to which she refers in the song is a moment outside of time, as we know it. It's Flack's phrasing that brings the lyrics to life and transforms a prosaic folk melody into something timeless and full of flesh and blood. It's one of the glorious monuments of pop. Clint Eastwood recognised the power of the song and included it in his 1972 film *Play Misty for Me*. Consequently the song was released as a single and spent six weeks at the top of the charts.

Flash Light Parliament

(George Clinton/Bootsy Collins/Bernie Worrell) ❈ Casablanca ❈ 1977 ❈

Appears on: *Funkentelechy vs the Placebo Syndrome*

'Flash Light' was one of the funkiest tracks of the '70s. George Clinton's Parliament – one version of his umbrella for musicians – was looking for something that could be both political and danceable. This track is powered by the synth bass lines of Bernie Worrell working off a Bootsy Collins groove in the belief that after freeing the ass the mind would follow.

"As far as Parliament was going, we wanted to be saying something to black people," said Clinton. "I figured all I had to do was give black people something to be proud of, and as long as the music's slick and funky then it'll start working on its own. We got a momentum going that don't logically hold up, but once that momentum steps in you ain't got to explain shit.

"Parliament is more vocal, more disco with horns, and a bit more conservative. Funkadelic is more guitars, no horns, more free-form feelings, and more wild. Sometimes there's a criss-cross, but generally Funkadelic gets more pussy than Parliament.

"We made it cool to be funky again, like James Brown had done."

Senorita   Justin Timberlake

(Chad Hugo/Justin Timberlake/Pharrell Williams) ❉ Jive ❉ 2002 ❉ Appears on: *Justified*

Free of the boy band *NSYNC, Justin Timberlake, former Mousketeer and heartthrob, remade himself as a serious artist. His *Justified* album was a superior pop confection. Timberlake was significantly aided by the Neptunes – production duo Chad Hugo and Pharrell Williams. The light-funk-meets-soul-and-Latin stew that is 'Senorita' is a welcome advance on Timberlake's earlier work. 'Senorita' is a joyful piece of pop that allows Timberlake to grow up a little while also moving forward.

   "I take my hat off to Pharrell too, because socially, they did something that was advanced from everything they've done," Timberlake told MTV. "I think that when people hear what they've done, with the bridges that they wrote, the actual songs that we did – it's not just a beat.

   "Pharrell's a friend. And we're constantly talking about how music's changing and needs to change. And when you hear some of the songs that he's done for the next NERD album, you're gonna be blown away again."

Hello It's Me   Todd Rundgren

(Todd Rundgren) ❉ Bearsville ❉ 1972 ❉ Appears on: *Something/Anything*

Todd Rundren is one of the anomalies of American music. His work as a songwriter and singer has been a little too arty for mainstream taste. As a producer he has been consistently eclectic – sometimes commercial and other times obtuse. 'Hello It's Me' is the closest he came to bringing his diverse range of tricks together on one piece of wax.

   The song originally appeared in 1969 on the first album by Rundgren's garage band, the Nazz. He went on to form another band and make two critically acclaimed but poor-selling albums before he came to 1972's *Something/Anything*. This was a four-sided set and on three of the sides, Rundgren produced and played everything.

   "I only once did an album by myself [*Something/Anything*], or at least a major part of it was myself," Rundgren wrote back in the mid-'70s. "It was the only album where I had the attitude that I had to do it all. It was only because I was experimenting, not because I was establishing myself as a solo virtuoso artist. On this new album, it was just a case of hearing certain things, and if I couldn't perform it, I'd get someone else to do it. You can only have so much technique, and I always hear things that exceed my technique.

"The success of 'Hello It's Me' doesn't bother me, but having to perform the song does bother me. Having to do anything bothers me when it's not something I feel naturally inspired to do. I'm not really into singles; I don't record records specifically to be singles. I may do it for somebody else, but I don't do it for myself. If I do things that sound like singles, it's just that that's the way I think it should sound."

Rundgren had an art rock approach to American music. In the context of the early '70s that meant removing any irony and constructing a song around hooks. To the public it sounds like a hit record. To the cognoscenti it sounds like a clever pose.

"I wrote 'Hello It's Me' that way. I analysed a lot of successful popular songs and figured out what it was that made them successful, the emotional ingredients, you might say," he said. "I was writing a song that I knew would have a certain success because I was composing according to a proven formula. I don't think that writing that way means that I have to compromise my intentions, because my intentions are to write successful songs."

Disarm The Smashing Pumpkins

(Billy Corgan) ❊ Virgin ❊ 1993 ❊ Appears on: *Siamese Dream*

Chicago's Smashing Pumpkins released a single on Seattle's Sub Pop label and issued their first album, *Gish*, on the same day as Nirvana's *Nevermind*. Consequently they were lumped in with the grunge sound of the early '90s, despite the fact that musically they were worlds apart. If *Gish* was raw, though, the second album, *Siamese Dream*, demonstrated that head Pumpkin Billy Corgan had a unique sense of arrangement and a revolutionary vision for rock & roll songs.

"The whole idea behind the band is not at all to go backwards," said Corgan. "It's all about going forwards. But there are intangible elements to rock & roll that you cannot get around. Loudness. Powerful grooves. And you look at any music – an industrial band uses a drum machine, but they're doing the exact same things. They still have loudness and they're still playing with heavy rhythms.

"Here's the thing: if you grew up in America, whether you like it or not you heard Aerosmith, you heard Black Sabbath, you heard Led Zeppelin. It's just part of the culture. Even our manager had a hard time understanding why we played loud, hard music. Because he just didn't understand it. He said, 'You play such beautiful music, why are you playing this ugly rock music?' But it's part of what we are."

'Disarm' from *Siamese Dream* has the heavy atmosphere of a Black Sabbath song but presented with an angular guitar figure and Corgan's pleading vocal. Even though the song was lighter than much of their rock fare it was equally disturbing.

Smoke on the Water Deep Purple

(Ritchie Blackmore/Ian Gillan/Roger Glover/Jon Lord/Ian Paice) ✳ Harvest ✳ 1972 ✳
Appears on: *Machine Head*

This is the classic air guitar song and for over thirty years the epic three-chord riff has blown the minds of millions of teenage boys in black T-shirts.

Guitarist Ritchie Blackmore, a refugee from Screaming Lord Sutch's band, formed Deep Purple in the mid-'60s. A short jab at the pop charts with 'Hush' led to a fascination with progressive rock. The arrival of Hammond organist Jon Lord brought some pretensions towards classical music while singer Ian Gillan had a banshee's range. In one of the dumbest conceits by a rock band, Deep Purple booked the London Philharmonic for the *Concerto For Group and Orchestra*. Fortunately they quickly abandoned such affectation for savage, hard-edged rock on their excellent *Deep Purple in Rock* (1970). Within two years they were Led Zeppelin's poor cousins and doing well enough to make a record in Switzerland.

The *Machine Head* sessions in December of 1971 were scheduled to take place in the Casino at Montreux. On the night they were to start, a fan at a Frank Zappa gig in the venue ignited a flare, burning the Casino to the ground. The occasion was quickly committed to song: 'Smoke on the Water'.

"Everybody was running out of the place, but I didn't know why," Blackmore recalled. "I thought it was an intermission or something, because I had got tired of Frank Zappa within the first ten minutes, and I was more interested in this girl who was quite well endowed. I took her outside and was talking to her, and all these people were running past me with white faces, and I presumed it must be an intermission and that they were going to get ice creams until I saw the smoke coming out and realised something was wrong.

"It's a good job I realised it, because otherwise I'd have been with this certain young lady somewhere, in some kind of cupboard, up to some sort of mischief, and I would have been burnt down with the place, because it was a habit of mine to disappear into cellars and places . . .

"We had already recorded the backing track before the fire, and we did it in about four takes because we had to – the police were banging on the door, and we knew it was the police, but we had such a good sound in this hall that we were waking up the neighbours about five miles away because the sound was echoing through the mountains. We had just finished it when the police burst in and said we had to stop, and since we'd finished it, we did. Then Ian wrote the words after the fire."

Dancing Barefoot   Patti Smith Group

(Ivan Kral/Patti Smith) ❋ Arista ❋ 1979 ❋ Appears on: *Wave*

The fourth album from the Patti Smith Group marked the end of a journey. In 1975, high on Symbolist poetry and the Rolling Stones, she had kicked off her *Horses* album with a defiant challenge to Christ. She embraced her own theology of mystical rock & roll like Joan Of Arc with a Fender Duo-Sonic. By 1979, when she wrote most of the fourth album, Smith was devoting her life and beliefs to her husband-to-be Fred and to Jesus Christ.

'Dancing Barefoot' is a song that brings together mysticism and her subservient love for Fred together. It's a song about submission in the same way that the Sufis regard their twirling dance as a submission to the Divine.

The melody of 'Dancing Barefoot' (which seems to owe a debt to the Go-Betweens' 'Karen') has a vertiginous quality; a modal meditation on love in all its forms.

Todd Rundgren (whose early work Patti Smith had reviewed in the pages of *Rolling Stone*) produced the album. It's probably the best recording the group made.

"I thought it might be the last album I did," she said. "I felt it was time for me to evolve as a human being. I hadn't ever really planned to make records. I came to that organically, and I felt that I had really expressed everything that I knew how to express. So I had a lot of thoughts doing that record: both joyful thoughts and . . .

"Todd's an old friend of mine, I thought that it would be nice to work with a friend and also he's a great musician and I knew that he would contribute to the musical sense of the record. He was very good with using keyboards, he was a pianist himself and a lot of those songs evolved around that. It was not an easy record to make and Todd works very quickly – I work quickly too but not as quickly as Todd, but I think the sound of that record is beautiful."

Get Ur Freak On Missy Elliott

(Missy Elliott/Tim Mosley) ❊ Goldmind/Elektra ❊ 2001 ❊
Appears on: *Miss E ... So Addictive*

Missy Elliott and Timbaland are the hip-hop producers to call if you want to cross over into pop megastardom. Not only did they engineer the supernova explosion of Destiny's Child, but Missy Elliott's records were themselves state-of-the-art records. Timbaland (Tim Mosley) had a spare style of smooth beats that owed something to drum 'n' bass and even to Eastern flavours. Mostly though, Missy never lost sight of the fact that hip-hop is about dancing and booty.

"This record is your backyard dance the whole time," she said. "It's futuristic as far as being on another level but that's not the direction I wanna go. You see, I change my music and I change my image at the same time. I felt like as long as me and Hype continued to work together we would probably keep it going in the same kind of direction."

Elliott didn't fit into the waif stereotype of singer and was proud of it. Her approach to love and romance was similarly realistic. She "doesn't make music for sad little men hiding under the covers with their flashlight and their Barbie doll". 'Get Ur Freak On' is the real deal.

To Zion Lauryn Hill

(Lauryn Hill) ❊ Ruffhouse ❊ 1998 ❊ Appears on: *The Miseducation of Lauryn Hill*

The Fugees singer didn't take long to break out on her own with *The Miseducation of Lauryn Hill*. "I think the piece as a whole communicates my personality; it is the culmination of my experiences, the sum total of what I had gone through at a certain point in my life," she said to the *Times*.

One of the key factors in cutting her first solo album was the birth of her child Zion David to boyfriend Rohan Marley – son of the late reggae legend. Her pregnancy effectively put a hold on the Fugees and she clearly felt some pressure to make compromises about competing loyalties. It's most clearly spelt out in the song 'To Zion'.

"That song," she said, "is about the revelation that my son was to me. I had always made decisions for other people, making everybody else happy, and once I had him that was really the first decision that was unpopular for me. It was one that was based on my happiness and not what other people wanted for me or for themselves. And it was the best decision that I could have ever made, because I'm the happiest and healthiest that I have ever been. It also revealed to me which relationships were right, which ones were sincere, and which ones were based on exploiting and hurting me. It was a godsend all the way round – 360 degrees of that whole situation were nothing but a blessing. And I'm so happy that I made the choice that I did."

Hill enlisted the help of Carlos Santana for the guitar part.

"That totally came from my parents' record collection," she said. "I remember finding *Abraxas* in the basement, and looking at the cover going, 'Wow! This is real. What's this?' It had all this stuff going on, all this beautiful artwork on the cover. And then I remember putting on the record and wanting to cry. I put on this one song, 'Samba Pa Ti', and it just gave me chills. I used to write my first songs to other people's music, and this particular album had this beautiful, soulful guitar, and it was instrumental, so I was in heaven.

'To Zion' is a song about a future, specifically the future of her son, but it also spelt out Lauryn Hill's future as a major hip-hop writer.

Jealous Guy John Lennon

(John Lennon) ❊ Apple ❊ 1971 ❊ Appears on: *Imagine*

John Lennon was not a particularly easy person to get along with. He admitted to being violent and to being insanely jealous. Just on the basis of its remarkable candour, Lennon's 'Jealous Guy' would have to rank with one of his finest songs.

The song had been begun for the *White Album* sessions and was originally titled 'Child of Nature'. Lennon revisited the tune for the *Imagine* album and recast the lyric.

Over the top of a beautiful and beguiling melody, Lennon admits to his feelings of jealousy and the violence that wells up within him. He sings with such an openness that one can't help but marvel at his passion – of which the jealousy simply seem to be the reverse of his real feelings. It's the most tender of nasty songs.

Waterloo ABBA

(Benny Andersson/Stig Anderson/Björn Ulvaeus) ❋ Polygram ❋ 1974 ❋
Appears on: *Waterloo*

The Battle of Waterloo was a defining moment in the relations between England and wider Europe, with England reigning victorious. ABBA reversed the result with this piece of corny pop. First they conquered that bastion of naff music TV, the Eurovision Song Contest, and then marched on to the British charts and from there to world domination.

The song's title was changed from 'Honey-pie' to the sexier 'Waterloo' by manager Stig Anderson, himself a songwriter. Already occupying the Euro charts, ABBA developed a long-term invasion strategy with 'Waterloo', spending the winter of 1973–74 working on the arrangement. The challenge for ABBA was no mean one. Sweden had a minor pop industry; mostly, the radio broadcast politically correct symphonic music. They also battled against history – traditionally the Europeans can do everything well except rock and pop music. "You have to realise that, in Sweden, we don't have the rock & roll background that there is in Britain or America," said Benny Andersson. "We listened to Chuck Berry and the Rolling Stones, of course, but we didn't quite grow up with them in the same way that you did."

ABBA's rhythmic and melodic sensibility was based on different parameters to most pop – something more aligned with the traditional music of Northern Europe. "Our folk songs sound like that," Andersson said. "The first instrument I ever had was an accordion. My parents bought it for me when I was about ten."

But years poring over the Beatles and Phil Spector showed through.

Whole Lotta Shakin' Goin' On Jerry Lee Lewis

(Dave Williams/Roy Hall) ✳ Sun ✳ 1957 ✳ Appears on: *Jerry Lee Lewis*

Jerry Lee Lewis is more like a force of nature than a piano player. He wandered into Memphis' Sun studios where producer Jack Clement thought he might have a future as a wild country & western singer. Clement had previously done sessions with Lewis and was familiar with his go-for-broke, maniacal approach.

As has been noted, especially by Nick Tosches in his book *Hellfire*, Jerry Lee had that Baptist Holy Roller in him but he also had the Devil there as well. When Lewis let fly, his piano became Pandora's box and everything came out.

Lewis' first record session with Clement was winding down when Jerry Lee suggested they try a song called 'Crazy Arms', which had been a pop hit for the Andrews Sisters. "At the time the bass player had wandered out somewhere. The guitar player was in the bathroom. So really all it was on the record was piano and drums. And right at the end the bass player walked in and thought we were just clowning around, which we kinda were. So he picked up the guitar and hit this little chord and that was the record." The song was a regional hit.

For his next record Clement had set up a song of his own, 'It'll Be Me'. At the end of the session, Jerry Lee suggested they run through a song he had been playing for some time and so the band fired up for one take of 'Whole Lotta Shakin' Goin' On'. According to Clement, "I just simply turned on the machine, mixed it on the fly." On this one shot, Lewis gave everything. The result is a barnstorming orgy of innuendo and passion that sold six million records within a year.

(Ghost) Riders in the Sky Marty Robbins

(Stan Jones) ✳ Columbia/Legacy ✳ 1978 ✳

Appears on: *The Essential Marty Robbins: 1951–1982*

Stan Jones was employed by the National Park Service and stationed in Death Valley. According to his wife Olive, in the evenings he sat on the porch with his Martin guitar and played western songs.

Jones was fascinated by tales of the old west and by ghost stories. At age twelve while still living in Arizona he had watched a storm come across the horizon and heard the story of how the clouds contained the Devil's herd – all red flashing eyes, being rounded up by a posse of phantasmal cowboys condemned to ride across the skies for eternity.

One evening he put it all together in a song. '(Ghost) Riders in the Sky' is a wonderful western epic and a marvellous piece of storytelling that also has one hell of a tune. The song has been covered over a thousand times and many of the versions are instrumental.

One of Jones' jobs for the Parks service was to look after crews from Hollywood filming in Death Valley. The Hollywood people encouraged him in his songwriting. Eventually '(Ghost) Riders in the Sky' came to the notice of Burl Ives and another western singer, Vaughn Monroe. The song became a massive hit in 1949 and quickly from there a standard covered by Bing Crosby, Peggy Lee and countless others.

Jones came to the attention of John Ford, the great director of westerns. He engaged Jones to write music for the films *Wagonmaster*, *Rio Grande* and *The Searchers*. Jones became a small player in Hollywood until his death in 1963.

Of the many classic versions of '(Ghost) Riders in the Sky', Marty Robbins' is one of the very best. Robbins was a pop singer who also strayed into western territory and he treads a nice balance between the various styles that this strange song sits astride.

Move It Cliff Richard

(Ian Samwell) ❋ EMI ❋ 1958 ❋ Appears on: *Cliff*

British rock & roll was born somewhere around 8 p.m. on the night of Thursday 24 July 1958. A seventeen-year-old singer, Cliff Richard, was there to cut a single in the style of this American rock & roll that was sweeping the pop charts. He had two songs. One was a cover of an American track and the other was 'Move It'. Ian Samwell played guitar in Richards' band the Drifters (later the Shadows) and he had written the song while riding on the bus. It was on the rockabilly side with a driving guitar riff which, in the hands of Ernie Shears, marked the track as a hit.

Veteran EMI producer Norrie Paramor was not particularly impressed with this rock & roll fad. "Norrie Paramor thought that 'Move It' was rubbish," said engineer Malcolm Addey. "At that point, none of us knew one end of a rock & roll record from the other. On that first session with Cliff, Norrie loved the sound that was coming out of the speaker, and that was good enough for him. For his part, Cliff was a nice kid. The record simply consisted of whatever was on the tape.

"Ernie played an absolutely wonderful introduction. He was one of those guys who would play whatever was required without getting uptight, and so he just let it rip. It came out really great, and that's what got everybody's attention. For his part, Cliff liked to play while he was singing, so Norrie allowed him to hold onto his guitar, and after a false start we completed the song in a couple of takes. There were no edits whatsoever – we did very few edits in the pop field, and those were usually only on an LP, which might be a little more complex."

Television producer Jack Good loved the song and promoted it heavily on his TV show all the way to number two on the British hit parade. Cliff Richard soon became the British equivalent of Elvis Presley. He opened the door not only to his own career but also to the Beatles and everything after.

Wrecking Ball Emmylou Harris

(Neil Young) ❊ Elektra ❊ 1995 ❊ Appears on: *Wrecking Ball*

"On every Neil Young album, there is an undiscovered Neil Young masterpiece – the forgotten song – that was the Neil Young masterpiece – forgotten song – off of *Freedom*," said Emmylou Harris of the title track of her 1995 album. "Really, in its own way it is kind of like a country song. It's pretty straightforward but it's got that wonderful kind of ambiguity about it. It sort of tells a story but it's more an impressionistic fill in the blanks kind of thing."

Harris recorded the album in New Orleans with producer Daniel Lanois, who had put his distinctive stamp on recordings for U2, Bob Dylan and Luscious Jackson. Lanois is a producer who is known for his perspective and his productions generally are a turning point in an artist's career. Harris has described working with Lanois as 'turbulent'. *Wrecking Ball* is a new direction for her. It's not by any means country, nor is it particularly rock. It's an opportunity for her to radically interpret the songs of her generation.

Lanois brings a particular ambience to his mostly live recordings, steeped in reverb and antique instruments. There is an otherworldly quality to many of his sessions and this is no exception.

'Wrecking Ball' – with vocal backing from Neil Young – sounds like a forlorn love affair, a tender hope for connection from someone who has been beaten so many times in the past. There's also the spirit of hope here for Harris, after three marriages and children and twenty years in a career, she can start off in a new direction.

"He pretty much gave me my homework assignment," she said of the Lanois experience. "He told me, 'It's time now for you to write.' I knew he was right. I felt with *Wrecking Ball*, I had almost reached my peak as an interpreter. Songwriter was the only option besides waiting tables, which I wasn't very good at either."

Hanky Panky Tommy James & the Shondells
(Jeff Barry/Elle Greenwich) ✳ Snap ✳ 1964 ✳ Appears on: *Anthology*

Tommy James was only twelve years old when he cut the original version of 'Hanky Panky' at the studios of radio station WNIL in Niles, Michigan. Written by the songwriting duo of Barry and Greenwich and recorded by them as the Raindrops, Tommy James had seen a local band play it in their set, so he included it in his.

Ostensibly, the hanky panky was a dance, but even a twelve-year-old boy knew better than that.

Tommy James and the Shondells rearranged the song, stripping it right back to its elemental three chords and the progression that pulses forward until it climaxes in a "Ohhhhhh!". The guitar solo is a wild freak-out, as orgasmic as the singing. James' vocal is perfect. He has a sweetness to his tone but there's also a part of the song where he gets very guttural and primitive. There's no doubt that it is a song of desire.

'Hanky Panky' was recorded live to two-track and pressed up on local indie Snap, where it gathered dust for two years. Then in 1965, out of the blue, a disc jockey in Pittsburgh started playing the track and it became a regional hit and then, with a label change, a national hit.

'Hanky Panky' is pop music at its most simple and innocent. It's three great chords and a cute lyric conceit cut live and in its moment. There are more sophisticated records, better produced, more intelligent, and there are many moments that equal the pure perfection of 'Hanky Panky', but it never ever gets better than this.

Groove is in the Heart Deee-Lite

(Deee-Lite) ❋ Elektra ❋ 1990 ❋ Appears on: *Groove is in the Heart*

The ultimate New York club outfit of 1990, Deee-Lite was multi-racial and multi-gendered. Lady Muss Keir made an impressive and charismatic vocalist while DJ Dmitry and DJ Towa Towa just looked cool. Deee-Lite was playing all styles – hip-hop, pop, jazz and funk. But they did it with incredible verve. Their finest moment was 'Groove is in the Heart', which featured Bootsy Collins on bass and the saxophone of Maceo Parker.

'Groove' is one of the best hooks of the decade – light and bouncy but irresistible as well. If nothing else, they had good taste, sampling the likes of Herbie Hancock. Hancock said, "Deee-Lite, that's the group. I was told that somebody had sampled something from the *Blow-Up* soundtrack that I had done. I had never heard it. And then one day, my daughter and I were getting in my car and the radio was on and she said, 'Dad, that's that song.' She pointed it out because I didn't even remember the song. I had to go and get the record to remember what the thing was."

Tired of Being Alone Al Green

(Al Green) ❋ Hi ❋ 1971 ❋ Appears on: *Gets Next To You*

"I wrote 'Tired of Being Alone' about 5 o'clock one morning," Al Green recalled. "I was dreaming about me singing this weird song and I'd never heard that song before. I woke up and it kind of frightened me. I was singing these lyrics, "I'm so tired of being alone," and wondering, where did that come from? So I took a pen and paper and my guitar, and wrote it. I guess I got done about 7:30 that morning and I went back to sleep."

Flush with the success of 'I Can't Get Next to You', Green lobbied hard for this track as his next hit. When Hi Records finally did put the song out and it wasn't getting airplay, Green took matters into his own hands. "Three months passed. Nothing happened. Four months. Five months," Green said. "I said, 'Look, I need to go to New York – tonight!' So I went to London Records. I says, 'I gotta call a general house meeting of everybody in here!' I was nuts. I don't see how I did that.

This big, huge company, these people looking at this kid. I says, 'I want this record 'Tired of Being Alone'. You've just gotta hear it.' So they played it and they really liked it."

Green's charisma overpowered the staff and they got behind the single, pushing it to radio stations. Once people heard Al Green's distinctive style, they were converted. It was to be his first million-seller.

The band is in wonderful form. Drummer Al Jackson, one of the greatest soul timekeepers, sits the tune right in the pocket. Teeny Hodges' guitar is ultra smooth and also just colouring the groove. It's here too that Al Green finds his real voice, taking producer Willie Mitchell's advice. "Al always sang really hard," said Mitchell. "And I used to tell Al, 'You've got a good falsetto, you need to soften up some.' I said, 'You need to settle this music down.'"

You Can Call Me Al Paul Simon

(Paul Simon) ❈ Warner Bros. ❈ 1986 ❈ Appears on: *Graceland*

"The songs starts almost like a joke. Like the structure of a joke cliché: 'There's a rabbi, a minister and a priest.' 'Two Jews walk into a bar . . .' 'A man walks down the street.' That's what I was doing there," Paul Simon told Paul Zollo. From there the song goes into a shaggy dog story, part based on his ideas about African stories, part based on his life and the collapse of his marriage to Carrie Fisher – he used to call her Betty and she used to call him Al.

This is the song of a fat man, full of self-pity and confusion, thinking about his life and drifting off into a surreal world where he finds himself contemplating angels in the architecture.

"'You Can Call Me Al' starts off very easily with sort of a joke: 'Why am I soft in the middle when the rest of my life is so hard?' Very easy words," Simon told Zollo. "Then it has a chorus that you can't understand. What is he talking about? 'You can call me Betty, and Betty, you can call me Al?' You don't know what I'm talking about. But I don't think it's bothersome. You don't know what I'm talking about but neither do I. At that point.

"And by the time you get to the third verse, and people have been into the song long enough, now you can start to throw abstract images. Because there's been a structure, and those abstract images, they will come down and fall into one of the slots that the mind has already made up about the structure of the song.

"So now you have this guy who's no longer thinking about the mundane thoughts, about whether he's getting too fat, whether he needs a photo opportunity, or whether he's afraid of the dogs in the moonlight and the graveyard, and he's off in, listen to the sound, look what's going on, there's cattle and . . ."

'You Can Call Me Al' opened up *Graceland*, a series of trips into mythical and real places. It shifts back and forth from the spirit world to this one.

"It starts with that synthesiser, which is playing what was really a Ray Phiri guitar lick," said Simon. "I tried like hell to get that synthesiser sounding better, but I couldn't. But the lick is immediately recognisable as 'You Can Call Me Al'. It has such a light happy feel to it that I think people tend to think of it as a funny song where in fact it has an interesting development."

I Love Rock & Roll Joan Jett

(Alan Merrill/Jake Hooker) ❋ Boardwalk ❋ 1981 ❋ Appears on: *I Love Rock & Roll*

As a teenage Suzi Quatro wannabe, Joan Jett formed the Runaways on Los Angeles' Sunset Strip. On New Year's Day 1980, she was a solo artist. With one solo album under her belt, Jett teamed up with producers Kenny Laguna and Richie Cordell. The latter had been a major force in British music at the end of the '60s, producing Joe Cocker and then teaming up with Leon Russell.

Jett had found 'I Love Rock & Roll', a song performed by English New Wave band the Arrows.

The song lent itself to a big glam rock anthem, which was essentially an update of the Chinnichap sound as made famous by Suzi Quatro. Laguna and Cordell built a huge sound from handclaps and layered vocals that was big, dumb and fun. At a time when rock was suffering from pretentious art music, 'I Love Rock & Roll' was an irresistible return to core values. The song went to number one in early 1982 and has sold more than ten million copies.

"Well, it was an obvious way to do it," engineer Glen Kolotkin told Blair Jackson. "I knew it was going to be a hit and I wasn't going to let it slip away. We wanted the vocal overdubs to be almost like an audience.

"It took us almost no time to get a basic track on 'I Love Rock & Roll'. I thought it was a smash hit from the beginning. Then Laguna came in and Cordell came in and they were as knocked out as I was, and we finished the record up in one day. It just came together.

"We just kept building it up and up and up. I knew it was right when the hair stood up on the back of my neck."

Free Man in Paris Joni Mitchell

(Joni Mitchell) ✳ Asylum ✳ 1974 ✳ Appears on: *Court and Spark*

Joni Mitchell's 'Free Man in Paris' is a portrait of a showbusiness power broker. Mitchell captures the sense of the hurly-burly world of deals and personalities and juggling egos. She nails the personal side of the business – the endless negotiation of favours and the implicit hypocrisy of it. She also coins the phrase, "the star making machinery behind the popular song".

'Free Man in Paris' is specifically about David Geffen and it uses his own words in many of the dialogue sections. At the time Geffen managed Mitchell and most of the other singer/songwriters in California as well as owning the record company for which they recorded. Geffen was the classic achiever who appeared to get no personal nourishment from his success. But 'Free Man in Paris' applies to us all. Who amongst us doesn't at some point wish to just escape to a place where we can be "unfettered and alive"? Mitchell's genius was to find the universal in the particular.

The song is greatly aided by Tom Scott and the LA Express, a session band of jazz players whose light and breezy touch suited Mitchell's music at the time.

"I had no choice but to go with jazz musicians," she said. "I tried to play with all of the rock bands that were the usual sections for James Taylor when we made our transition from folk to folk-rock. They couldn't play my music, because it's so eccentric. They would try, but the straight-ahead two/four rock & roll running through would steamroller right over it."

David Geffen never did feel comfortable about the song, however.

"He didn't like it at the time," she said. "He begged me to take it off the record. I think he felt uncomfortable being shown in that light."

Summer in the City The Lovin' Spoonful

(John Sebastian/Mark Sebastian/Steve Boone) ✳ Kama Sutra ✳ 1966 ✳

Appears on: *The Hums of the Lovin' Spoonful*

The Spoonful took their name from a Willie Dixon song, and it's certain that whatever was on his spoon wasn't what the teenyboppers who followed this group had in mind.

John Sebastian was a folkie from the early Greenwich Village scene and his chosen metier was old-timey blues and jug band music. The Spoonful started out in that scene along with their friends who soon became the Byrds, the Mamas and the Papas and other big hit-makers. The Spoonful followed suit. They signed with Kama-Sutra, a label that specialised in pop, and churned out pleasant songs – 'Do You Believe in Magic', 'Did You Ever Have to Make Up Your Mind?', 'Rain on the Roof' and 'You Didn't Have to Be So Nice'. They

seemed like nice hippies whom you could take home to your mother. John Sebastian's songs – and he was the prime mover – were, however, extraordinary pop tunes, notably 'Darling Be Home Soon'. Then when Zal Yanovsky was busted for marijuana possession that image disappeared. When Zal cooperated with police they lost support from the counter culture.

'Summer in the City' was their high point. The pounding bass and drums with staccato organ jabs build an intense mood that's shattered by the sound effects of jackhammers and car horns. This really is the sound of the city and the promise of excitement and adventure to be had in the streets and nightclubs. The rhythmic motif runs through as if to suggest that the entire energy of Manhattan can be present in just the one kiss between a boy and a girl.

Interestingly, because studios were still primitive, the only way to get the sound effects onto the track was to have them dropped in – much as DJs would twenty-five years later – and this adds to the percussive effect.

Sebastian put the song together from a lyric his brother had written and a tune from bass player Steve Boone. It was the Lovin' Spoonful's biggest hit. As producer Erik Jacobsen said, "That record really nailed it."

X-Offender Blondie

(Debbie Harry/Gary Valentine) ✳ Private Stock/Chrysalis ✳ 1977 ✳ Appears on: *Blondie*

Of all the CBGB bands in the mid-'70s, Blondie was regarded as the least likely to be successful, let alone influential, yet they were to become one of the most influential '70s pop groups.

Blondie – singer Debbie Harry, guitarist Chris Stein, drummer Clem Burke and keyboard player Jimmy Destri – perhaps weren't the best musicians south of 14th Street, but they knew what they liked (early '60s girl groups, Black Sabbath, the British invasion, surf music). Clem Burke was their secret weapon. He understood pop right down to his Beatle boots. His dynamic style lifted Blondie's music to a level way above all the other power pop groups who came in the wake of punk rock. They had the trash aesthetic down pat and in Debbie Harry, one of the abiding sex symbols of the era.

When the New York labels started to come to the Bowery to hand out deals, no-one took Blondie seriously and they wound up on the small Private Stock. Richard Gottehrer, the writer and producer of '60s hits such as 'I Want Candy' and 'My Boyfriend's Back', was enlisted to co-produce with Craig Leon. It was an excellent choice.

"I remember going to a rehearsal and watching them play and grinning from ear to ear," said Gottehrer. "These were people that had great songs and were playing arrangements almost beyond their means. The execution wasn't perfect, but it had so much spirit. So that got me interested."

The first Blondie album referenced all the high points of sophisticated American pop and they added a twist. There's a homage to *West Side Story*, a surf tune and some early 'rriot grrl' proto punk. But the real focus of the record was Debbie Harry's ballads. She was somewhere between the innocence of the Shangri-Las and the smoky persona of Julie London. The love songs were all a little wounded and certainly way too knowing to be fully retro.

'X-Offender' was the first Blondie hit. Bassist Gary Valentine had a song, 'Sex Offender'. When he turned eighteen his fifteen-year-old girlfriend's parents had him arrested for carnal knowledge. Harry turned the lyric into a love song between a woman and a cop who arrested her.

The flip side, 'In the Flesh', gave them their first hit (number two in Australia, thanks to *Countdown*), which featured Brill Building queen Ellie Greenwich on backing vocals. But 'X-Offender' took off in Europe and suddenly Blondie were contenders.

"These were all people running around thinking they were French Symbolists," said Craig Leon. "And here comes Blondie, who are really like true punks and actually much more the mass-media future band than any of the others. In a way, some of those CBGBs bands might have been the dead end of progressive rock & roll. Not a lot of people really see that."

"Clem's influence was the perfect counter-punch to Chris' artier side, and that was really a driving force," said Destri. Blondie really understood pop. It was that openness to pop that meant in coming years they would break disco and rap into the mainstream rock audience.

"I always knew the songs were pretty well sussed," said Burke. "I didn't know too many people in my group of friends who really liked the Shangri-Las or the Velvet Underground. They were all in their bedrooms trying to be the next Jimmy Page. There was a specific vision we had that not many people had at the time."

The Ghetto   Donny Hathaway

(Donny Hathaway/Leroy Hutson) ✳ Atlantic ✳ 1970 ✳

Appears on: *Everything is Everything*

The sweet voice and smooth delivery of Donny Hathaway's songs belied a troubled man who threw himself out of his window at the age of thirty-three. However, in 1970, when he released his first album and first major single ('The Ghetto'), he had the world in his hands. He had been an arranger and a producer for Curtis Mayfield's label and also for the Chess label in his hometown of Chicago until saxophonist King Curtis brought him to Jerry Wexler at Atlantic. "He was the most brilliant musical theorist I ever encountered," Wexler said recently. He worked as a

producer, arranger, songwriter and session pianist/keyboardist for Aretha Franklin, Jerry Butler, Carla Thomas and the Staple Singers.

Hathaway was schooled in gospel and jazz as well as R&B and this broad palette served him very well. On 'The Ghetto' the message about racism and the streets is clear and strong. However, it's the context – powered by Hathaway's keys and an amazing, syncopated band including drummer Ric Powell and brilliant guitarist Phil Upchurch – that breathes the vibrant life of the ghetto and tells the real story here.

Hathaway became known for his soul ballads and his work with Roberta Flack, but it's here on his debut album that the legacy is most potent. You can hear Hathaway almost as much as Marvin and Mayfield in the subsequent R&B and soul music of the decade.

Ms Jackson OutKast

(Andre Benjamin/Antwan Andre Patton/David Sheats) ✳ La Face ✳ 2000 ✳
Appears on: *Stankonia*

OutKast may be remembered as hip-hop pioneers not for their outlandish clothes or for their hard beats or even their psychedelic jams, but for their humanism. "It's hard for humans to show emotion in this day and age," said Andre Benjamin around the time of the release of their fourth album, *Stankonia*. "That's why back in the '60s and '70s, music sounded so good, because nobody gave a fuck about showing emotion. Nowadays, everybody's got to be hard – hip-hop is all about 'keeping it real', so all your pictures got to be hard."

Dre certainly didn't dress hard. More like Prince or George Clinton – defying the image to contain him.

Stankonia contained the very vulnerable song 'Ms Jackson'. The song is addressed to the mother of his girlfriend Erykah Badu following the end of their relationship. The song mostly affirms that Benjamin and Badu will continue to be responsible for the happiness and security of their son, Seven Sirius.

"He wanted to give the world something to think about the baby's mama's mother and baby's daddy," said Badu. "My mom just laughs about 'Ms Jackson'. She and Dre are really pretty cool; they talk. He is a very humble, good brother. He is a really good person."

Moon River   Henry Mancini & His Orchestra

(Johnny Mercer/Henry Mancini) ❊ RCA ❊ 1961 ❊ Appears on: *Breakfast at Tiffany's*

Written for the film adaptation of Truman Capote's novella, *Breakfast at Tiffany's*, 'Moon River' combines Henry Mancini's Italianate romanticism with Johnny Mercer's southern idyllic reverie. The song is brief – a couple of verses, but it encapsulates a lifetime of experience.

In Blake Edwards' adaptation of Capote's book, Holly Golightly is a girl who has run away from the poverty and narrow horizons of her southern past for the glittering lights of a sophisticated New York. Johnny Mercer left his home in Savannah, Georgia, twenty years earlier. Broke and hoping to find work in New York as an actor, Mercer discovered his real talent was as a songwriter and by the time he teamed up with Mancini for 'Moon River' he was firmly established as one of the great American composers.

Nonetheless, in 'Moon River' you can hear nostalgia for Mercer's childhood on Burnside Island in the Back River, where he spent early summer afternoons picking wild huckleberries with his friends. The song neatly pivots on nostalgia for a lost youth and the romance of the future.

Mancini's music is even more powerful than the lyric. Mancini has said that the tune was inspired by the script and Audrey Hepburn. "I kind of knew what to write, at least what track I should I be on, by reading the script," he told Hepburn's biographer. "And Audrey's big eyes gave me the push to get a little more sentimental than I usually do. Those eyes of hers could carry it. I knew that. 'Moon River' was written for her. No-one else has ever understood it so completely."

Legend has it that a Paramount executive wanted the song taken out of the film and replaced by something more sprightly but Hepburn, in particular, insisted that the song stay. The liner notes to the soundtrack album quote a letter from the star to the composer: "Dear Henry, I have just seen our picture – *Breakfast at Tiffany's* – this time with your score. A movie without music is a little bit like an aeroplane without fuel. However beautifully the job is done, we are still on the ground and in a world of reality. Your music has lifted us all up and sent us soaring. Everything we cannot say with words or show with action you have expressed for us. You have done this with so much imagination, fun and beauty. You are the hippest of cats – and the most sensitive of composers! Thank you, dear Hank. Lots of love, Audrey."

'Moon River' has survived the film for which it was written. It has had thousands of cover versions of all kinds – notably by Frank Sinatra – and its melody has become a part of the fabric of our culture.

Papa's Got a Brand New Bag James Brown

(James Brown) ✳ King ✳ 1965 ✳ Appears on: *Papa's Got a Brand New Bag*

"Gospel always had the One," Brown told Barney Hoskyns, "but it became more dominant once I clarified it. You go to church now, you hear more James Brown than you do in the dance halls. Because it's a way of life. We put our foot down, we lead off with the left foot most times – that's what soldiers and everybody do – and go from left to right, left to right, and we try to put it down solid each time."

It was that simple lesson that created funk.

In February 1965 James Brown and the JBs cut this track, placing the emphasis on the first and the third beats. The JBs included Maceo Parker, Jimmy Nolan and Bernard Odum and the track jammed for seven minutes. The key was "the One". The players could do what they liked so long as they returned together to the first beat in the bar. This gave James Brown incredible propulsion, a shunting force supported by the horns and his own alchemical phrasing.

Few songs have changed music as much as the edited version of 'Papa's Got a Brand New Bag'. At this point soul music met funk and was changed forever.

Crazy Patsy Cline

(Willie Nelson) ✳ MCA ✳ 1961 ✳ Appears on: *The Patsy Cline Story*

Patsy Cline had bigger hits than 'Crazy'; however, the song has outlasted its time and place. Young songwriter Willie Nelson penned the tune in his first attempts to break into the Nashville scene. 'Crazy' bears the marks of Nelson's idiosyncratic personality – it's pop and jazz and western and not quite pure country.

Perhaps that's why Patsy Cline was reluctant to record the track when producer Owen Bradley introduced her to the song in August of 1961. At the time, Cline was walking with crutches after a car smash.

"Her ribs had been broken, and she couldn't hold the notes out," guitarist Harold Bradley told *Mix* magazine. "When we were doing this, there were no overdubs. She had to do it all live, and we all had to do it all live. By that time, we had progressed to three-track, but they wouldn't put anything in the middle. They put the band and the voice and spread everything left and right. But on this particular session, Patsy couldn't sing with the band."

Owen Bradley ran the sessions in his studio from behind a Hammond organ. The session players laid down the backing track two weeks later. There's an ephemeral quality to the lyric and the vocal line – it's got a pixie kind of feel, as though it may all just disappear in a plume of smoke. Cline came in to do the vocal and got it in one take.

"That was the magic session," said Harold Bradley. "It was the toughness of it – and the magic of it, too – that made it an incredible session. Neither one of them wanted to do anything else with it. They said, 'That's it.'"

El Paso Marty Robbins

(Marty Robbins) ❋ Columbia ❋ 1959 ❋ Appears on: *Gunfighter Ballads and Trail Songs*

Born and raised in Arizona, Robbins loved the cowboy genre. One of his first compositions and his signature tune, 'El Paso' is a tragic epic of lovers torn apart in a fatal eternal triangle. Robbins' spare use of language and his lilting melody transcend the melodrama.

Robbins penned the song while driving through El Paso, Texas. The song had an epic quality and an almost five-minute arrangement. Despite being two minutes longer than most singles of the day, radio stations programmed the track and it reached number one on both the pop and country charts. The song also won the first country music Grammy Award in 1960 and remains in the standard country and western repertoire.

Robbins recorded the track on 7 April 1959 at Bradley Studios, Nashville, Tennessee, in a twelve-song session that resulted in the *Gunfighter Ballads and Trail Songs* LP in September ('El Paso' was released as a single the following month). This album is possibly the best of its genre. It has certainly been the most influential western album of the period.

Let's Get It On Marvin Gaye

(Marvin Gaye/Ed Townsend) ✳ Motown ✳ 1973 ✳ Appears on: *Let's Get It On*

Like all of Marvin Gaye's transcendental work, 'Let's Get It On' is both seductive and a suggestion to himself to hold his life together.

The song was recorded at Motown's Hitsville West in March of 1973. Gaye used a group of musicians from the Motown house band (notably guitarist Melvin 'Wah Wah' Ragin) plus some of the era's best funk and jazz players, such as Joe Sample and Wilton Felder, as the basic tracks for the song were cut live.

Nine days later Gaye returned to the studio to put on his vocal. Writer Ben Edmonds noted that one of Gaye's acquaintances brought along sixteen-year-old Janis Hunter. For Gaye it was love at first sight. According to Edmonds, "The presence of this young girl compelled him to perform the song to her, and in so doing, it was transformed into the masterpiece of raw emotion we know so well."

Gaye and Hunter were married as soon as Gaye's divorce from his first wife was finalised. No doubt this new love brought a heightened focus to the album.

"I can't see anything wrong with sex between consenting anybodies," Gaye wrote in the liner notes to the *Let's Get It On* album. "I think we make far too much of it. After all, one's genitals are just one part of the magnificent human body ... I contend that SEX IS SEX and LOVE IS LOVE. When combined, they work well together, if two people are about the same mind ... Have your sex, it can be very exciting, if you're lucky."

Higher Ground Stevie Wonder

(Stevie Wonder) ✳ Motown ✳ 1973 ✳ Appears on: *Innervisions*

Stevie Wonder hit a creative peak on *Innervisions*. He unlocked new possibilities for the synthesiser and, particularly on 'Higher Ground', made the new electronics sound funky. The album and this song also expressed some of Wonder's spiritual beliefs perhaps better than he had done before. Wonder had taken to writing, playing and producing his albums all by himself, as was the case here. *Innervisions* was named after his creative process: "For the most part I've listened to just what's in my head," he said at the time. Nonetheless, the album also had some acute things to say about the state of the world on 'Living in the City'. 'Higher Ground' pulls these strands together.

On 6 August 1973, shortly after this album was completed, Wonder was in a car accident that put him in a coma. Malcolm Cecil, who was one of the synthesiser programmers on the *Innervisions* album, and tour manager Ira Tucker Jr visited Wonder in hospital and sang 'Higher Ground' to Stevie. At this point the singer moved a finger in time. That's truly the mark of an exceptional R&B groove.

Won't Get Fooled Again The Who

(Pete Townshend) ❋ Track ❋ 1971 ❋ Appears on: *Who's Next*

Townshend was a big believer in youth movements but his natural scepticism meant he kept his distance from the counterculture revolution in the '60s. When activist Abbie Hoffman, then one of the most famous men in the world, interrupted the Who's Woodstock set to make some political comment, Townshend famously hit him over the head with his guitar.

'Won't Get Fooled Again' was written for Townshend's Meher Baba project, *Lifehouse*, but it came to signify the end of the '60s movement.

"The people who were trying to harness rock in order to break down the right-wing British and US Establishments are now all dead or rich like Felix Dennis," Townshend said recently. "I am not a pacifist, but I felt my guitar sound, and the band's edge, came from and reflected its essentially working-class audience of non-intellectuals who knew they might have to fight and die like their fathers. They would not be fooled by university graduates telling them what to think. Even the ever-gorgeous Germaine Greer."

The song rides on the frenzied riffs of the ARP synthesiser. Townshend backs it up with fat chords from his acoustic guitar and a war whoop from Daltrey. "That big scream I did was totally instinctive, but it became a focal point of the song," said Daltrey.

Much of the album was recorded in the Rolling Stones' mobile studio parked at Mick Jagger's house, Stargroves. "What's great about *Who's Next* is that it was the only album where we played all those songs over and over again. They were our songs. They weren't just Pete's songs. That's the difference with *Who's Next*. We had that freedom to do that. We were never allowed that freedom after that."

In a Silent Way Miles Davis

(Joe Zawinul) ✲ Columbia ✲ 1969 ✲ Appears on: *In a Silent Way*

Although he was the emperor of jazz in 1968, Miles Davis also had an ear cocked to what was happening across town in R&B and rock. He was aware of James Brown and Jimi Hendrix and Sly Stone. He was intrigued by the possibilities of electronic instruments. On 18 February 1969 Miles Davis took his musicians – Chick Corea, Herbie Hancock, Dave Holland, John McLaughlin, Wayne Shorter, Tony Williams and Joe Zawinul – into the studio to rewrite jazz. One Zawinul piece in particular, 'In a Silent Way', stood out. Building on the fusion of previous years and his background in acoustic jazz, Miles just stretched out on this record.

There's a dreamlike quality to 'In a Silent Way' that comes from the three electric keyboards, all competing with one another, and the percussion. This is the kind of ethereal soundscape that Davis touched with *Kind of Blue* – a late-night meditation that glimpses the eternal.

Much credit for 'In a Silent Way' goes to Teo Macero who, with Davis, edited the improvisations into some kind of logic.

"You wouldn't know where the splices are," he said. "And those days we still were doing it with a razor blade. Joe Zawinul should give us half of his money for fixing it all up. Because, at the end, I didn't know, I thought it was all Miles' music. But apparently Joe Zawinul claimed it was his. So we paid him all the royalties.

"But I think *In a Silent Way* is really a remarkable record for what it is. I mean for a little bit of music it's turned into a classic. And we did that with a lot of other records of his where we would use bits and pieces of cassettes that he would send me and say, 'Put this in that new album we're working on.' I would really shudder. I'd say, 'Look, where the hell is it going to go? I don't know.' He says, 'Oh, you know.'"

She Set Fire to the House Stephen Cummings

(Stephen Cummings/Andrew Pendelbury) ✲ Liberation ✲ 2004 ✲ Appears on: *Close Ups*

Stephen Cummings is a very astute observer of the "murders that aren't murders" that we commit every day. This is a break-up song that is both simple in its small detail, and devastating. Cummings uses enough detail in the relationship between

Monica and the narrator so that you know it's drawn from life, and it's general enough that you can write yourself into the scene. We've all been there – passionate romance – she's beautiful, he's passive-aggressive – she puts up with it for seven years and finally leaves with a can of kerosene and a match made in hell.

'She Set Fire to the House', like a romance, starts well, but Cummings and Shane O'Mara build the tune with layers of guitar. O'Mara is one of the best producers of acoustic-based music this side of Daniel Lanois, and Cummings is his ideal foil. The song that had started out so definite and realistic becomes expressionistic and a little deranged by the end. The rhythm of the lyrics takes over and the narrator is lost in a pyre of regret and exhilaration at the prospect of freedom.

Wild Horses The Rolling Stones

(Mick Jagger/Keith Richards) ❋ Rolling Stones Records ❋ 1970 ❋
Appears on: *Sticky Fingers*

Keith Richards wrote the bulk of 'Wild Horses' as he was preparing for the Rolling Stones' 1969 American tour. His first son, Marlon, was born in August 1969, less than two months before the band was to leave for an extensive tour. The birth of Marlon was one of the most profound experiences of Richards' life. "You've never felt so loved in your life," he said. "And you realise, 'I've just been given the first two or three years of my life back.'" Jagger's verses for the tune were written about his break-up with Marianne Faithfull.

'Wild Horses' is one of the Rolling Stones' most vulnerable and gentle love songs and represents the beginning of a mature direction they would take in the future.

Richards' new best friend at the time was American country rocker Gram Parsons and it has been suggested that Parsons had something to do with the genesis of the song, but that's hard to demonstrate. Richards had the tune, the title and most of the lyrics worked out, and Jagger finished the song.

Recording of the song was mostly done at Muscle Shoals, Alabama, in early December 1969, three days before the tour finished at Altamont. The legendary producer Jim Dickerson played tack piano.

"When they cut at Muscle Shoals studio, where they did 'Brown Sugar' and 'Wild Horses', that was kinda my idea," Dickson recalled. "Stanley [Booth, journalist and friend to the Rolling Stones] called while they were on the road and asked if the Stones could record in Memphis. They had three days at the end of the '69 tour – 'cause they wanted to record when they were, hot from playing together. With [Musicians] Union regulations back then you could get either a touring or a recording permit but not both. They were in a position where they could tour but not record and had been prevented from recording in Los Angeles. So, they were looking for a place where nobody would care and I told 'em about Muscle Shoals.

"When the Stones got to Muscle Shoals I was the only outside person who was allowed to stay. On the third day, they recorded 'Wild Horses', which began with a minor chord, and Ian Stewart [Stones pianist and road manager] wouldn't play minor chords. Stew finally told me one day, at a hotel in New York, about his thing of not playing minor chords, and I thought 'thank god' man. But for that, I would have no claim to fame.

"That was a fantastic week," said Charlie Watts. "We cut some great tracks, which appeared on *Sticky Fingers* – 'You Gotta Move', 'Brown Sugar' and 'Wild Horses' . . . it's one of Keith's things to go in and record while you're in the middle of a tour and your playing is in good shape."

La Cienega Just Smiled Ryan Adams

(Ryan Adams) ❋ Lost Highway ❋ 2001 ❋ Appears on: *Gold*

Looking for role models, Ryan Adams fixated upon the troubled father of country rock, Gram Parsons. There was the very cool haircut, the friendship with Keith Richards, the reputation for a wild time and a romantic streak a mile wide. Somewhere in there too is a natural gift for songwriting.

Adams first recorded with his alternative country band Whiskeytown in the late '90s. Eventually he went solo with a strong collection of songs on the *Heartbreaker* album. Finally in 2001 he brought it all home with a very polished and sophisticated album, *Gold*.

Once again Adams was writing an album that charted the course of a doomed relationship. He loosely hung the narrative on the journey from New York to Los Angeles where he relocated to be with the object of his affections, actress Winona Ryder.

"Part of *Gold* is me taking my own defence," he said. "I knew I was sitting there involved with someone I shouldn't be involved with and enjoying every last miserable-ass moment of it. Because everybody does it, not just artists. Everybody loves a little bit of pain, 'cause it makes them feel real for a minute.

"See, my job is to talk about my fuckin' feelings or about what's on my mind as an artist. People don't fucking need clever anymore. If I hear one more clever record, I'm gonna throw up. What I wanna hear is the Band singing 'It makes no difference' and hearing Rick Danko nearly fucking break your fucking heart in absolute half when he hits the bridge.

"This journalist friend of mine said, 'Ryan, quit talking about your personal life in interviews.' And I went, 'That's the only reason anyone fuckin' likes my music!' I mean, I don't give myself totally away and dig all kindsa stuff. I don't know, am I being too outward, do you think, as an individual? Should I quit talking about my emotions?"

Beds are Burning Midnight Oil

(Garrett/Hirst/Moginie) ❉ Sony ❉ 1987 ❉ Appears on: *Diesel & Dust*

The rhythm of this track mimics a 4WD going flat-chat across the Western Desert with the corrugations syncopating the steady beat. Rising up out of bass is a massive horizon of guitars with a wide blue 360-degree vista and the acoustic guitar maintains time in a timeless landscape. 'Beds are Burning' would be remarkable even without a lyric that said everything that needs to be said about Aboriginal land rights.

In 1986 Midnight Oil toured the Aboriginal settlements of the Top End. In awe of the landscape and the people, Midnight Oil were equally horrified by the conditions that most of the Aboriginals suffered – chronic poverty, petrol-sniffing, inadequate medical care. The result was an album of songs, most of them touching on the desert experience.

"Musically I know it affected Rob and Jim and Martin in the way in which we started to put together the *Diesel* record," said singer Peter Garrett. "It became more rhythmic; it had more of an acoustic end to it. It also affected us because it made us understand that these people had been living in this place since time immemorial. They'd been telling their stories here for tens of thousands of years and they knew the land incredibly well and they could tell you a lot about it, they had a great knowledge. It gave us a sense that for these people it wasn't even an issue between competing rights and competing societies; it was actually an issue about their own profound being. Everything that they were was here because this was their home as well, and it really opened our eyes up to that."

The single 'Beds' was released six months before the 1988 Bicentennial – an event that highlighted the dispossession of Aboriginals by the Europeans. The congruence of the two events was not lost on Midnight Oil. The group had vowed to avoid being seen to support the Bicentennial celebrations and spent most of 1988 overseas where their extremely parochial song was an international hit.

Few protest songs have been so succinct and challenging and clear all at once and it remains one of the most powerful tracks ever to come out of Australia.

Land: Horses/Land of a Thousand Dances/ La Mer (de) Patti Smith

(Chris Kenner/Patti Smith) ❋ Arista ❋ 1975 ❋ Appears on: *Horses*

"It's time to figure out what happened in the '60s," Patti Smith said in 1976. Smith chose John Cale to be the producer of her first album. Cale had been a member of the Velvet Underground and had produced records for the Stooges and Nico. She could not have chosen a more sympathetic ear, but the collaboration was not a happy one.

According to Cale, the group's instruments were all warped and they had to get new instruments and then learn how to play them in tune. "As a producer," he wrote. "You've got to be a catalyst, an ally, a co-conspirator. Sometimes you have to introduce conflict in order to resolve it."

"All I was really looking for was a technical person," said Smith of Cale. "Instead, I got a total maniac artist. I went to pick out an expensive watercolour painting, and instead I got a mirror. It was really like 'A Season in Hell', for both of us. But inspiration doesn't always have to be someone sending me half a dozen American Beauty roses. There's a lotta inspiration going on between the murderer and the victim."

'Land' started out as a poem about the relationship between a murderer and victim. Its rambling epic journey touches on the power of '60s R&B with the soul anthem 'Land of a Thousand Dances.'

"At first it was just me and Lenny Kaye on electric guitar farting around at poetry readings," she said. "Then it started to gather force. We advertised for a piano player. And finally Richard Sohl came in wearing a sailor suit, and he was totally stoned and totally pompous. We said, 'This guy's fucked up.' Lenny gave him the big cosmic spiel and Sohl said, 'Look, buddy, just play.' So we just brought him in.

"And then we started looking for another guitarist. We'd make them do forty minutes of 'Gloria'. I'd go off on this long poem about a blue T-bird smashing into a wall of sound or some shit like that and Lenny would keep the same three chords going, louder and louder. And we'd see who dropped out first. If the guy auditioning dropped out first, that meant he wasn't any good. So finally Ivan Kral came in. This little Czechoslovakian would-be rock star. So we did 'Land of a Thousand Dances' and it went on so long I thought I was gonna puke. But Ivan was so nervous he wouldn't stop, and we figured that was really cool.

"Now it's at the point where I really love the group. I did a solo reading the other week in Philadelphia. I went great, but I was so lonely. I read 'Land Without Music', and right away I'm thinking, here's the part where Lenny always fucks up; here's where I'd look at Sohl and tell him to stop sleeping on the keyboard. I missed them so much I didn't want to ever again perform without them. They give me tremendous energy. I get like a little kid, and it's beautiful."

A Day in the Life The Beatles

(John Lennon/Paul McCartney) ✳ Parlophone ✳ 1967 ✳
Appears on: *Sgt. Pepper's Lonely Hearts Club Band*

This was one of the pivotal moments in 20th-century music. The Beatles incorporated bits of poetry and puerile lyrics with techniques of randomness, modern atonal orchestration, and then at the end of it all a death-like falling tone.

It's all there in a magnificent soundscape. The *Sgt. Pepper* album was a watershed in music when it was released, but it was this last track that was shocking. The Beatles had certainly used complex orchestration but never with such conceptual breadth and not usually with such a morbid theme. What could have sounded kitsch still sounds startling.

The song began with two fragments – one is Paul McCartney's story of an ordinary day, based he said on his schooldays. The other is Lennon's random collection of thoughts, mostly taken from newspaper stories, his recent film role in *How I Won the War*, and the death of a friend, Tara Browne. The Beatles and producer George Martin stuck these two unrelated ideas together. The song doesn't resemble any pop music, as it had been known, with its shifting tempos and moods and its gradual increase in intensity and momentum until the final release at the end of the piece.

The crucial element to the success of the whole venture is Martin's scoring.

In the initial recording the instrumental sections were left open to be recorded later. The end of one of these sections was marked with an alarm clock, the sound from which was eventually left in.

Eventually the orchestra was added, in costume as it happened.

"What I did there was to write, at the beginning of the twenty-four bars, the lowest possible note for each of the instruments in the orchestra," the producer said. "At the end of the twenty-four bars, I wrote the highest note each instrument could reach that was near a chord of E major. Then I put a squiggly line right through the twenty-four bars, with reference points to tell them roughly what note they should have reached during each bar ... Of course, they all looked at me as though I were completely mad.

"Come the night, I discovered that they'd also invited along all of their way-out friends, like Mick Jagger, Marianne Faithfull, and Simon and Marijke, the psychedelic artists who were running the Apple Shop in Baker Street. They were wandering in and out of the orchestra, passing out sparklers and joints and God knows what, and on top of that they had brought along a mass of party novelties. When I came back into the studio the sight was unbelievable. The orchestra leader, David McCallum, who used to be the leader of the Royal Philharmonic, was sitting there in a bright red false nose. He looked up at me through paper glasses!"

Lennon, McCartney, Starr, Martin and Mal Evans banging simultaneously on three pianos and holding the note for fifty-three seconds did the final piano chord.

Lennon's summation: "I thought it was a damn good piece of work."

Only the Lonely Roy Orbison

(Joe Melson/Roy Orbison) ✳ Monument ✳ 1961 ✳ Appears on: *Sings Lonely and Blue*

Roy Orbison said that he was tagged as "the lonely singer". His Texan, falsetto voice was steeped in country. With a slight quivering he could just embody heartbreak.

Having made his name as a rockabilly artist with Sun in Memphis, Orbison moved to Nashville where he worked with producer Fred Foster. After some success writing 'Claudette' for the Everly Brothers, Orbison was concentrating on perfecting his songwriting. Foster suggested that two half-good songs could be combined and 'Only the Lonely' was born. The Everly Brothers turned it down when first approached so Orbison took his version to number two on the national charts.

The song had the ethereal echo sound of his best work and that stoic vocal that seems to be holding back an ocean of heartbreak. Orbison's best work was filled with paranoia and fear.

"When I wrote, let's say, a sad song, a melancholy song, I was feeling good at the time," he said in his last interview. "I have to feel good and at peace with myself before I can think creatively. I've heard guys say, 'Well, I got my heart ripped out and got wasted for three weeks and wrote this song.' I couldn't do that. I'd be crying, I couldn't eat and all that. Of course, I knew what 'Only the Lonely' was about when I wrote that. I had been alone and lonely. I wasn't at the time, though."

Bring It on Home to Me Sam Cooke

(Sam Cooke) ✳ RCA ✳ 1962 ✳ Appears on: *The Best of Sam Cooke*

Although not much of a hit at the time, 'Bring It on Home to Me' is one of Sam Cooke's best-known and oft-covered songs. The key to the track is the simple but irresistible groove.

Cooke was one of the original soul stylists. He took the R&B of the '50s and brought a particular smoothness and sophistication to the grooves. Cooke was also a gospel singer, so there was that passion and sweetness together that made his solo records so distinctive.

'Bring It on Home to Me' was cut on 26 April 1962 as the B-side of his next single 'Havin' a Party'.

"Once we got our sounds, Sam pretty much produced himself," engineer Al Schmitt told *Mix* magazine. "He wrote most of the songs; he knew what he wanted. He had a vision in his head of the way these things should be, and that was pretty much it. He worked fast in the studio. We'd do three and sometimes even four songs in three hours, and then we'd usually choose the best take and that was the record.

"There was almost never any overdubbing with Sam, unless he was going to do his own backing vocal or something. And when I did 'Bring It on Home', that was Lou Rawls with Sam and that was live; they sang it together."

The song took off in England when the Animals had a hit with a cover version and it became almost a standard for groups of the era as well as for soul singers in the US.

"Sam was the best. He was the easiest person I ever worked with. Just a fabulous guy. We became really good friends. Everybody loved him. And he was a total professional, too."

St James Infirmary The Triffids

(traditional) ✳ Hot ✳ 1984 ✳ Appears on: *Raining Pleasure*

The 'St James Infirmary Blues' is over 200 years old. It is known variously as 'The Whores of the City', 'The Young Girl Cut Down in her Prime', 'The Streets of Laredo', 'Dying Crapshooter's Blues', 'Gambler's Blues' and 'The Dying Marine', amongst others. It has travelled from 18th-century Dublin to the Big Day Out. The song has been recorded by at least, and in no particular order, Cab Calloway, Louis Armstrong, Billie Holliday, Janis Joplin, the Doors, the Animals, the Triffids, the White Stripes and Van Morrison.

According to folklorist Kenneth S Goldstein, the ballad 'The Unfortunate Rake' was first notated in 1848 from a singer who claimed to have learnt it in 1790. Generally the early versions of the song centre on a lament for the death of either the narrator or his lover, generally from venereal disease. Obviously, the death of a lover from venereal disease can itself be a death sentence.

The St James Infirmary of the title is generally considered to be St James Hospital in London, founded in the 11th century for leprous women. The building was taken by Henry VIII and is now St James Palace. However, there have been numerous other sites suggested, generally the St James Hotel in New Orleans, which was used as a hospital in the Civil War, or the one in Cimarron, New Mexico, where Jesse James and his gang hung out.

'The Unfortunate Rake' made its way to America where it was known as 'Gambler's Blues', 'St James Infirmary' and, in buckskin, as 'The Streets of Laredo'. The song was passed from singer to singer, across racial and stylistic borders.

Once the song took hold in America as a blues it came to the attention of Louis Armstrong. He first recorded the song on 12 December 1928, crediting the lyric to Joe Primrose (aka Irving Mills). Two years later Mills, calling himself Sunny Smith, cut the track with the Harlem Hot Chocolates, who were Duke Ellington's band.

The song was also a favourite with the Singing Brakeman Jimmy Rodgers, who turned it into 'Those Gambler's Blues' and used lines in a number of his songs.

Blind Willie McTell took the song and made it into 'Dyin' Crapshooter Blues', which Bob Dylan then used as the basis for his song 'Blind Willie McTell'.

As the song made its way to the United States its location gravitated towards New Orleans where the St James Hotel was used as a hospital in the Civil War.

The real St James Infirmary is none of these places. It's the place where sinners go and are held accountable. Many things may change in 200 years, styles of music may come and go but one day we all meet in the St James Infirmary.

A century after it was first noted and half a world away, a Perth quintet recorded the song. In this tentative reading you can hear the song's hundred-year history. There's also the spectre of singer David McComb here writing his obituary, which would be read too soon.

Mama Tried Merle Haggard

(Merle Haggard) ❄ Capitol ❄ 1967 ❄ Appears on: *Mama Tried*

Merle Haggard was raised on the grapes of wrath. The Haggard family was part of the Okie diaspora who came to California in the Dust Bowl years. The family lived in a converted boxcar in Bakersfield, California. When Merle was nine his father died and the son went off the rails.

He told *Lost Highway* author Peter Guralnick: "I was a child that needed two parents and there was a period that came up that my mother just couldn't handle.

My dad wasn't there and my older brother tried to step in and of course I resented that. It just got all confused and messed up. Mama certainly did try."

Haggard's mama tried everything to control her wayward son, even committing him to a juvenile facility for a time. Throughout his teens he was involved in petty theft until at age twenty in 1957 he was sentenced to a maximum of fifteen years for attempted armed robbery. Possibly it was Johnny Cash's 1968 concert at San Quentin; possibly it was the memory of his father's fiddle playing. For whatever reason, when Haggard was released in 1960 he determined to make a go of it as a musician.

Haggard quickly became a key player in the Bakersfield country scene. His style was taken from a touch of western swing added to a honky tonk style. The influences of Jimmy Rodgers, Hank Williams and Lefty Frizzel were strong. His outlaw songs had the verisimilitude of a hard life to them, none better than 'Mama Tried'.

Strychnine The Sonics

(Gerry Roslie) ❋ Norton ❋ 1965 ❋ Appears on: *Here are the Sonics!!!*

"A lot of groups at that time were more into the love songs and pretty notes and we were more into the energy," said guitarist Larry Parypa. "If our records sound distorted, it's because they are," added bass player Andy Parypa. "My brother [Larry] was always fooling around with the amps. They were always overdriven. Or he was disconnecting the speakers and poking a hole in them with an ice pick. That's how we ended up sounding like a train wreck."

The rock scene around Seattle in the mid-'60s was very vibrant and arguably the Sonics ruled. Gerry Roslie's powerful expressive voice and the wild attitude of the band made them into a more viscious version of the Rolling Stones. They had a couple of Stones classics such as 'The Witch', 'Have Love Will Travel' and 'Strychnine'. The last track, recorded live in the studio, has the perfect balance between psychedelic guitar playing and the hard, driving Rolling Stones feel. 'Strychnine' also swings, and the lyric is agreeably tongue in cheek. "We were nasty," said Larry Parypa. "Everything you've heard people say about us is true."

Girl from the North Country Bob Dylan

(Bob Dylan) ❊ Columbia ❊ 1963 ❊ Appears on: *The Freewheelin' Bob Dylan*

The north country – the Minnesota of Dylan's childhood – has remained a constant theme in the almost half-century Dylan has been recording. This was his first explicit reference to it in song. Dylanologists generally believe that the girl in question was Bonnie Jean Beecher, Dylan's girlfriend during his short stint at the University of Minnesota in 1960. The song is a message back to a girl who was left behind as the singer began his travels around the world. He thinks of her as she was then and will be forever frozen in his memory as such. Not only is he saying goodbye to a lover, though, he's also farewelling his past self.

The tune is a rewrite of the traditional English ballad 'Scarborough Fair', which Dylan learned from British folkie Martin Carthy. That may explain the formal and certainly archaic lyric. It's very much in the tradition of the English ballad rather than the Americana of most of Dylan's songs from the period.

'Girl' was not initially planned for Dylan's second album, *The Freewheelin' Bob Dylan*; however, due to pressure from Columbia, Dylan dropped 'Talking John Birch Paranoid Blues' from the LP and used this opportunity to record new songs for the reshuffled album. 'Girl from the North Country' was among them.

Dylan recut the song, once again duetting with Johnny Cash, and that version appeared on *Nashville Skyline*. Perhaps the most powerful reading of this song, however, occurred at Dylan's 30th Anniversary Concert in 1992. At the end of many hours where the greatest artists in contemporary music had paid tribute to Dylan's work by singing one classic after another, Dylan appeared. Alone with his acoustic guitar he carried the immense weight of his body of work and the consequences of that – all the peace rallies, the newspaper stories, the triumphs and tragedies of a life lived hard. Then, of all the songs, he chose 'Girl from the North Country', which he sang in a voice now cracked by life. All of it came down to one dream, dreamed a long, long time ago.

You Really Got Me The Kinks

(Ray Davies) ✳ Pye ✳ 1964 ✳ Appears on: *The Kinks*

This track is considered to be, along with the Kingsmen's 'Louie Louie', a cornerstone of garage rock and punk, if not heavy metal. The Kinks certainly acknowledged the influence. But the Kinks' song transcended the garage; Ray Davies was too much the master of nuance to be held back. That said, there was no mistake in the carnal intent in 'You Really Got Me'. This was as raw as any Chicago bluesman, even if he had been brought up in the straitlaced north London suburb of Muswell Hill.

The Kinks started out as a blues band, one of the thousands populating Swinging London. They were signed to the famous impresario Larry Page and found themselves, like the Who and many other groups of the era, in the studio with American producer Shel Talmy. The first recordings were flops.

Davies wrote 'You Really Got Me' as a piano blues but then his brother Dave

added the guitar riff and took the tune to a different level. Then they cut a demo with Davies' dry vocal over a furiously distorted guitar sound from his brother. The sound had been achieved by slashing the guitar speakers with a razor blade. Davies got the idea from his home hi-fi, which was broken and made all music sound cracked and dirty.

Talmy recorded the song and cleaned it up, to the Kinks' horror. "As the band's manager," Page once said, "I asked him not to release it, but he wouldn't listen. So, as the band's publisher, I told him categorically that he couldn't release it, because the publisher controls the song." The song was re-cut as it was intended and not only went Top 10 globally but introduced the sound of distorted guitars into rock & roll.

It was also the song itself. Davies has attributed it to "an eclectic mixture of Gregorian Chant, musique concrete and the instrumental hit 'Tequila'". Mostly, though, it was the sheer minimalism of the refrain, chanted in such a lascivious manner over three chords with no romantic overtones whatsoever, that made the song so powerful. As Davies said, "G, F, B flat – those three chords were my life."

Promised You a Miracle Simple Minds

(Jim Kerr) ✳ Virgin ✳ 1982 ✳ Appears on: *New Gold Dream (81–82–83–84)*

"I think the music is searching and asking questions as opposed to trying to have answers lock, stock and barrel," said singer Jim Kerr. "It's instinct not logic. I'm attracted to that. I like actors who can never articulate but give off this heat, like De Niro. You mention Springsteen; it's true – you hear him speaking and he's bumbling away but he's got an instinct as opposed to an intellect."

Kerr and guitarist Charlie Burchill started Simple Minds in their hometown Glasgow as an arty punk group. Kerr's natural disposition, however, wasn't for the self-pitying navel gazing of Echo and the Bunnymen or the other post-punk groups. Kerr was a naturally optimistic man, excited and overawed by the possibilities of art and personal expression. Kerr was a true Romantic. In Burchill he had a foil that could provide vast musical soundscapes onto which Kerr could muse. The Minds embraced electronics – they embraced the sounds coming out of the clubs – and they turned them into pop. These were Scottish epics that, for a time, matched U2's Irish dreaming.

The Simple Minds sound came together on *New Gold Dream* – a work of grand possibilities, best expressed on the single 'Promised You a Miracle'. That title says it all.

"But is that it for us – rousing choruses and crashing drums?" mused Kerr. "There didn't seem any room for subtlety, and we always seem at our best when we're not trying to be powerful, but there's an underlying power coming through. That had been evident in some of the records from the past."

Diminuendo and Crescendo in Blue Duke Ellington

(Duke Ellington) ✳ Columbia ✳ 1956 ✳ Appears on: *Ellington at Newport 1956*

Duke Ellington, the finest bandleader and composer in American jazz, was in a slump in 1956 when he and his orchestra took to the stage for the final set at the Newport Jazz Festival.

Ellington's show had been a creditable statement on where he was at – some jazz standards among more ambitious compositions.

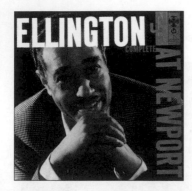

It's not certain that 'Diminuendo and Crescendo in Blue' was part of Ellington's original set list. In any case, as the set drew to an end he called for the song and instructed Paul Gonsalves to play the solo on his tenor saxophone.

According to legend, Ellington said to Gonsalves, "I'll bring you in and I'll take you out. That's all you have to do. Just get out there and blow your tail off. You've done it before." So Gonsalves did. For twenty-seven choruses over seven minutes. It was a historic moment that not only turned around the crowd that had been trickling out, but also Ellington's career.

Newport Festival impresario George Wein wrote in his memoir, "Most accounts have it that 'Diminuendo' was a surprise call by Duke. One story has Duke assembling the band backstage and suggesting the number, and the band looking around at each other in bewilderment. Then Paul Gonsalves asks, 'That's the one where I blow?' Duke answers, 'Yes, and don't stop until I tell you.'

"At the proper moment, Gonsalves dug in with his tenor and started blowing. Somewhere around the seventh chorus, it happened. A young blonde woman in a stylish black dress sprung up out of her box seat and began to dance. She had caught the spirit, and everyone took notice – Duke included.

"In a few moments, that exuberant feeling had spread throughout the crowd. People surged forward, leaving their seats and jitterbugging wildly in the aisles. Hundreds of them got up and stood on their chairs, others pressed forward toward the stage. Sam Woodyard and Jimmy Woode kept driving the beat mercilessly. The power of that beat, and the ferocity of Paul's solo, is what stirred the crowd to those heights. Duke himself was totally caught up in the moment. The audience was swelling up like a dangerous high tide.

"By the time Cat Anderson hit the final blast of 'Crescendo', the sea of bobbing heads had whipped itself into a squall. The tune ended and the applause and cheering was immense – stronger, louder, and more massive than anything ever heard at a jazz concert before."

A near riot ensued as Wein tried to close the evening down and Ellington came back for a number of songs. The legend of Gonsalves' heroic solo – where the discipline of a band like Ellington's is used to back a pure improvisation – spread far and wide. The album *Ellington at Newport* became the biggest selling of his career.

4'33" John Cage

(John Cage) ❋ Floating Earth ❋ 1991 ❋ Appears on: *4'33"*

On 29 August 1952 at the Maverick Concert Hall in Woodstock, New York pianist David Tudor sat at the piano and played nothing.

"People began whispering to one another, and some people began to walk out," said the composer John Cage. "They didn't laugh – they were just irritated when they realised nothing was going to happen, and they haven't forgotten it thirty years later: they're still angry."

For this performance Tudor had a score written with blank measures. The piece began with Tudor lifting the lid of the piano and reading the score while measuring the time with a stopwatch. At the end of the first movement he opened the lid. At the start of the second, he closed the lid again and followed the same procedure for the third movement.

4'33" is more than just a provocative art joke. Cage was a student of oriental philosophies, particularly Hinduism, Taoism and Zen Buddhism. From a Taoist or Zen perspective the distinctions between what is music and what is noise are arbitrary at best and probably non-existent. So for Cage, sitting in Maverick Hall, the first movement was dominated by the sound of the wind and the second by raindrops. In the third movement there was the sound of disgruntled music lovers.

Cage didn't believe in silence. He has recounted a visit to an anechoic chamber, that is, a chamber acoustically designed to be free of noise. While in there Cage heard the sound of his nervous system and the sound of his blood flowing.

"I literally expected to hear nothing," he said. "Try as we may to make a silence, we cannot. One need not fear for the future of music."

Another inspiration for the work was the white paintings that Cage's friend Robert Rauschenberg completed in 1951. "I responded immediately," he said, "not as objects, but as ways of seeing. I've said before that they were airports for shadows and for dust, but you could also say that they were mirrors of the air."

For Cage, *4'33"* was a way of hearing. He said in 1988, "No day goes by without my making use of that piece in my life and in my work. I listen to it every day . . . I don't sit down to do it. I turn my attention toward it. I realise that it's going on continuously. More than anything, it is the source of my enjoyment of life . . . Music is continuous. It is only we who turn away."

Has It Come to This? The Streets

(Mike Skinner) ✳ Locked On ✳ 2001 ✳ Appears on: *Original Pirate Material*

Mike Skinner, a twenty-four-year-old white boy from Birmingham, is Cliff Richard to Eminem's Elvis. He writes rap lyrics based on the experiences of a suburban English lad, drawing on the traditions of the Wu Tang Clan and Noel Coward.

"My songs are very simple," said Skinner. "In America, because I'm a white rapper, they always compare me to Eminem. The difference is when he's angry he writes music and when I'm angry I punch the wall. I aspire to be realistic, for people to hear the album and say, 'Yeah, this is us'. Rap gets people thinking about language who never would otherwise. Artists like Eminem, they have a great grasp of language and metre, maybe without even realising it."

'Has It Come to This?' was the Streets' first salvo: "a day in the life of a geezer". That pretty much revolves around the PlayStation, pot and some slap and tickle.

Skinner fits right in to the British kitchen sink tradition of Ray Davies, Billy Bragg and John Cooper Clarke, rather than strictly rapping. Nonetheless, the beats, most of which were written in his bedroom, are inventive and tough.

"My earliest memory is rap music," he told the *Los Angeles Times*. "Listening to my brothers' Beastie Boys and Run DMC albums and trying to make my own hip-hop tracks on a very cheap computer/tape recorder in my bedroom. The rhymes were like, 'I had a cat, it was fat, I wore a hat.' But I always knew I was going to be doing this."

West End Blues Louis Armstrong & His Hot Five

(King Oliver/Clarence Williams) ✳ OKeh ✳ 1928 ✳Appears on: *Ken Burns Jazz Volume 1*

'West End Blues' was first recorded by King Oliver and his Dixie Syncopaters. West End is a resort on Lake Pontchartrain outside New Orleans where people from the Crescent City would go to let their hair down.

Louis Armstrong's version of the song is generally considered to be the starting point of jazz. The session took place in Chicago on 28 June 1928. Armstrong takes this twelve-bar blues and stretches it with serendipities, technical mastery and completely idiosyncratic rhythms and melodies. He introduces the song with a complex, improvised trumpet solo, adds some scat singing and opens the space for Earl Hines to rip out a magnificent piano solo. Then Armstrong comes back for another elegant, magnificent solo.

Armstrong's insight for the capacities of the blues and his natural gifts as a musician and bandleader rewrote the book here.

Rhiannon Fleetwood Mac

(Stevie Nicks) ✳ Reprise ✳ 1975 ✳ Appears on: *Fleetwood Mac*

"'Rhiannon' was not written about the mythological mebanogian from Wales," Stevie Nicks told VH1. "She was written about a name that came up in a book that I read that somebody gave me. A little paperback novel. It was called *Triad* [by Mary Leader]. You can trace it down and find it. There were two women in it; they were named Rhiannon and Branwen.

"So, when everybody wants to say, 'Oh you write premonition, premonitions, you know you have premonitions', I don't think that I consciously have premonitions, but I do seem to have some sort of a psychic knowledge of what's gonna happen in the future. The whole thing about the birds and the sky and the, all this, this is all intricately woven through the myth. So I always think it's pretty interesting I play it that I had no idea about any of this when I wrote it. I just thought it was a beautiful name and I thought if I ever have a little girl maybe I'll name her Rhiannon, and that's really what I took to the piano to write the song.

"I also wrote this song in Aspen, same time I wrote 'Landslide'. There must have been a very creative force going on in Colorado at that moment that night."

Stevie Nicks will be forever identified with this song that is part New Age mysticism and part a song of great romance. Initially intended for her next album as part of Buckingham Nicks, she recorded the song with Fleetwood Mac and this song gave that group a new lease of life.

Instant Karma John Lennon & the Plastic Ono Band

(John Lennon) ❋ Apple ❋ 1970 ❋ Appears on: *Shaved Fish*

Lennon decided he wanted to make a single and have it out the next day. The song 'Instant Karma' was written and recorded in seven days but it took a further two weeks to have the song on the streets. He enlisted Beatle George Harrison and sideman Billy Preston for old times' sake.

With the Beatles over, Lennon was at a loose end. He had become close with Phil Spector and the two of them here make a massive, fat sound that is quite unlike anything else that had come before. It's like a dense fog of rock with chanting. In truth it's closest to T. Rex and to some extent the future sound of ELO. It's a record that has a spontaneity and lightness that's missing from most of Lennon's solo work.

My Way Frank Sinatra

(Paul Anka/Claude François/Jacques Revaux/Gilles Thibault) ❋ Reprise ❋ 1968 ❋ Appears on: *My Way*

Paul Anka was only fourteen when he cut his first single. A year later his parents gave him $1000 to go to New York to try his luck in showbusiness. He struck gold, getting a record deal and hit record, 'Diana', the following year. Anka had reasonable success as a teen heartthrob but he never lost sight of the big picture and that included songwriting. He placed songs with Buddy Holly (and narrowly missed catching the fateful flight on 3 February 1959).

By the time he was twenty, Anka was playing Vegas. He had 200 copyrights to his name and a million dollars in the bank. He wrote the theme song to Johnny Carson's *The Tonight Show*.

Anka was one of the first rock & roll stars to be big in France. In the early '60s he married a French model and in 1966 they were on holiday in France when Anka heard 'Comme d'Habitude' sung by Claude François.

The love gone wrong song appealed to Anka, who bought the copyright with the intention of writing English-language lyrics. In 1968 Sinatra was planning one of his many retirements. He approached Anka about writing him a swansong. 'My Way', based on the tune of 'Comme d'Habitude', was the result. Anka claimed that the lyric expressed the individualistic spirit of the late '60s as much as it did Sinatra's personality. The song suited Sinatra perfectly, however, and became one of his signature tunes.

"He always thought that song was self-serving and self-indulgent," the singer's daughter Tina told the BBC. "That song stuck and he couldn't get it off his shoe. He didn't love it."

Nothing Compares 2 U Sinéad O'Connor

(Prince) ✳ Ensign/Chrysalis ✳ 1990 ✳ Appears on: *I Do Not Want What I Haven't Got*

The Irish singer's first album, *The Lion and the Cobra*, was a cross between Celtic harmonies and post-punk folk rock. O'Connor had a difficult childhood – her alcoholic mother sexually abused her – and much of her work as a musician and her sometime erratic public statements can largely be attributed to this upbringing.

Perhaps as a result of that past, O'Connor is a powerful artist, not so much for her singing voice or for her lyrics, but her entire personality that she brings to a song.

Her second album featured a cover of a forgotten song that Prince had written for The Family, one of his protégé groups. O'Connor, in her version, strips the song back even further than Prince might have. She takes off the adornment and she inhabits the shell. This is a song of obsessive love and O'Connor finds its centre. She tries to do nothing but slowly lead herself through the modal arrangement. Mostly, though, it's just O'Connor. She holds her singing back as though there's a huge body of emotion behind her voice and she's just keeping it in check.

'Nothing Compares 2U' opened the way for the rest of the *I Do Not Want What I Haven't Got* album and even more candid songs about O'Connor's life.

"They said it was a piece of shit, like reading someone's diary," she said at the time when asked about her album. "They said it wouldn't sell and it would end up in the warehouse like, and I quote, 'Terence Trent D'Arby's second album.' I came up against that a lot. U2's the Edge said that the songs were too personal, but a guy who can't even call himself by his own name is obviously uncomfortable with his emotions."

All Tomorrow's Parties The Velvet Underground

(Lou Reed) ❋ Verve ❋ 1967 ❋ Appears on: *The Velvet Underground & Nico*

The Velvet Underground's only screen appearance was in the film *Midnight Cowboy* where they're seen playing at one of Andy Warhol's Happenings. Warhol's understanding of subculture recognised the genius in the Velvet Underground. He became their mentor and gave them the courage to pursue what was a decidedly uncommercial style of music.

Warhol's atelier was the Factory, a downtown New York warehouse where he made his films and artworks and where he encouraged a group of people who belonged nowhere else. Warhol called them superstars even though they hadn't the change for the subway. He glorified them and their lifestyles and he forever changed the way that people considered the concept of beauty.

It was a heady scene at the Factory and the Velvet Underground captured its quicksilver ambience of art and drugs and sex.

"I didn't appreciate what we were doing," said guitarist Sterling Morrison. "I never considered what it meant to be doing something with Andy Warhol and seeing all these weird people marching by and hanging around the loft. I just worried about little songs and how well they were played.

"We used to practise at the Factory and hang out there every day for a couple of years, from '66 to '68. We would arrive some time in the afternoon and every day would begin with the same question: 'What parties shall we go to tonight?' A thousand, thousand parties ... reflected on from a distance, they were almost unimaginable. Real high rolling affairs, with a lot of energetic depravity going on."

One of the flotsam starlets who drifted through the factory was Nico, a model and actress who had appeared in Fellini's *La Dolce Vita*. Despite the fact that she couldn't sing, Warhol suggested that the Velvets use her as vocalist.

"Andy suggested we use Nico," Morrison recalled. "She'd made a couple of singles with [Rolling Stones manager] Andrew Loog Oldham in London and one of them was not bad – sort of like early Marianne Faithfull. So we said fine, she looks great, and just gradually tried to work her in. There were problems from the very beginning because there were only so many songs that were appropriate for Nico and she wanted to sing them all – 'Waiting for the Man', 'Heroin', all of them. And she would try and do little sexual politics things in the band. Whoever seemed to be having undue influence on the course of events, you'd find Nico close by. So she went from Lou to Cale, but neither of those affairs lasted for very long."

She did a fine version of 'All Tomorrow's Parties', which has the perfect wistfulness to capture that innocent and decadent moment.

Do It Again   Queens of the Stone Age

(Homme/Oliveri) ❋ Interscope ❋ 2002 ❋ Appears on: *Songs for the Deaf*

The Queens rose from the ashes of Kyuss, a superstar stoner trio that formed in the Mojave Desert where they played all-night outdoor parties where the music could be turned beyond eleven. Guitarist Josh Homme and bass player Nick Oliveri from Kyuss are the core of the Queens. On this album they are joined by Mark Lanegan, singer from Seattle's Screaming Trees, and Dave Grohl of the Foo Fighters and Nirvana on drums. The album was pretty much the critics' unanimous pick as hard rock album of 2002.

The Queens were then charged with the responsibility of saving rock & roll. "I never noticed that rock was in a burning building and someone needed to rush in and grab it," said Homme. "I mean, if we saved rock from a burning building, what did the Strokes save it from? Drowning? Did the White Stripes rescue it after it broke its leg in a bizarre skiing accident? I'm sorry, I just don't perceive music that way."

On 'Do It Again' Queens of the Stone Age revisit the core values like a modern ZZ Top. The desert air once again fills with dust.

"However, it's impossible not to reflect the lights, the atmosphere, the space that the Mojave amplifies sound-wise," Homme told *Rock's Backpages* website. "If there is something that represents what surrounds us, it's the mastering of silence and the controlled explosions in our music.

"It's essential, and not just a minor detail or variety effect. Basically it is a representation of a driving experience from 29 Palms to Phoenix. When I drive, I tune in to all types of stations, weird broadcasts from religious to Mexican. It felt really fun to imagine those stations playing our music in their own context and style.

"In fact, we compose sounds to films that don't exist. Soundtracks without images. *Songs ...* is a record to be heard in a car. I do feel it is great road music, or at least was planned that way."

Oh, Pretty Woman   Roy Orbison

(Bill Dees/Roy Orbison) ❄ Monument ❄ 1964 ❄ Appears on: *Oh, Pretty Woman*

Even on this sunny return to his rockabilly roots, Roy Orbison sounds a little perverse. The song was written after admiring his wife Claudette and it is a kind of anthem for voyeurs.

No matter. Orbison rocks into this track with a perfect country rock boogie sound. His vocal is uncharacteristically exuberant – especially the little expletive "Mercy!" in the break.

Orbison was pigeonholed as a ballad singer but he had started out in Texas doing western swing country music and then rockabilly. Those influences come together perfectly on 'Oh, Pretty Woman.'

"Even in 'Pretty Woman', it goes through a lot of emotions," he said. "I didn't think of this as we were writing the song, but the guy's observing the girl, and he hits on her, real cool and macho, and then he gets worried and gets to pleading, and then he says, 'OK, forget it, I'm still cool', and then at the end she comes back to him, and he turns into the guy he really is. That range of emotion in a short piece of music I think is very important."

Lawyers, Guns and Money   Warren Zevon

(Warren Zevon) ❄ Asylum ❄ 1978 ❄ Appears on: *Excitable Boy*

Zevon's friend Jackson Browne described his work as "song noir". The outlaw character in the American drama endlessly fascinated Warren Zevon and he was frequently writing songs from the point of view of the morally bankrupt. Often times these songs rang more true of the American character than most others. So it is with 'Lawyers, Guns and Money', which has become something of an anarchist anthem.

The hero or anti-hero of the song is an adventurer, involved in so many of America's adventures battling the Soviet Union or stirring up trouble in South America and always relying on the three weapons of a rogue – lawyers, guns and money. In the '80s, the song wound up on the soundtrack of Lawrence Kasdan's film *Grand Canyon*, which Zevon scored.

"I went to a screening at 20th Century Fox, that was the first I'd heard of it," Zevon said. "It was too early in the morning for me. But I sat there and before I knew it Kevin Kline was singing along with the song. I thought: 'This is a good reason to get up early in the morning.' I'm a guy who likes anybody doing my songs. If I go down to the market and the guy making my sandwich is humming some song of mine, I'd be delighted. If Kevin Kline's singing it on a huge 70 mm screen, then I'm even more delighted. Delighted and compensated."

The Jackson Song   Patti Smith
(Fred 'Sonic' Smith/Patti Smith) ❋ Arista ❋ 1988 ❋ Appears on: *Dream of Life*

Patti Smith retired from public view in 1988 to live with her husband Fred Smith, guitarist in the MC5. Then suddenly she emerged with an album made in collaboration with her husband. She was a changed woman.

"I don't have a whole lot of time to think about myself ten years ago," she said. "That's not conscious, but nine years have gone by – or thirteen, because we made *Horses* in 1975. There have been many changes, a lot of learning. Being a mother, raising children, you develop a lot of new sensitivities – or ones that you already had are heightened. A few people have said, 'You mellowed out', and I hate that phrase – I don't think that developing in certain areas implies lost strength in others. One doesn't have to be shouting and kicking over amplifiers anymore. That doesn't mean I recant other ways of working. What I did fifteen years ago, I did with full heart; in that way Fred and I are no different."

All of that was true. 'The Jackson Song' is a gentle, beautiful ballad written about their son Jackson.

"Some people are embarrassed about liking it," she said. "They don't know what to think, and they get embarrassed to say they really like the 'Jackson Song'. One talks about intensity, but performing that song in the studio was at least as intense an experience as doing 'Rock & Roll Nigger' in the past. It's a relative thing. The older records have a lot of high adolescent energy. A lot of it was very sporadic, anarchistic, improvisational. To its credit, and to its vulnerableness, the old music was an expression of the type of people we were as a group. But I never subscribed to that idea of 'No future, no future'. That was never my credo."

Marcus Garvey Burning Spear

(Philip Fullwood/Winston Rodney) ✽ Mango ✽ 1975 ✽ Appears on: *Marcus Garvey*

Marcus Garvey was born in 1887 in St Ann's Bay, Jamaica. He became radicalised by the poverty and racism he encountered in his youth. To redress the balance, Garvey developed an ideology of economic independence for black people. In August 1914 he established the Universal Negro Improvement Association (UNIA) and African Community's League (ACL). In 1917 he relocated his organisation to a base in Harlem in New York where he found a receptive audience amongst the West Indian community and the African Americans. Garvey's organisational skills were not up to the resistance he encountered and his organisation faltered. Nonetheless, the ideology he promoted was an important part of black culture in Jamaica and the US.

Burning Spear vocalist Winston Rodney was also born in St Ann's Bay. Rodney was a strong supporter of Garvey's ideas. On this first track he attempts to put Garvey's message to a smouldering reggae beat. The song was originally recorded just for sound system play but was released as a single and quickly established Spear as one of the leading reggae acts of the mid-'70s.

Pony Blues Charley Patton

(Charley Patton/traditional) ✽ Paramount ✽ 1929 ✽
Appears on: *Martin Scorsese Presents the Blues: a Musical Journey*

The Will Dockery Plantation was a 40 square mile cotton farm outside Memphis in the Mississippi Delta. Such a large community bred its own culture and it was on Dockery's farm that Charley Patton, whose parents worked the plantation, learnt to play music. Patton picked up on the many and varied types of music from popular tunes of the day to the folk music of Africa and from other parts of the south, particularly the fife and string bands.

Charley Patton had a natural gift for the guitar, and for composition. His signature tune, 'Pony Blues', was propulsive and rhythmically strident and in its structure developed the template for the blues that came after it and then to rock & roll itself.

In June 1929 Patton cut fourteen songs for Paramount. He soon cut another thirty. However, Patton's influence is heard more in the fellows he came across in his travels. Patton played with or in front of most of the major artists to come out of the Mississippi Delta – Son House, Bukka White, John Lee Hooker and especially Robert Johnson. Howlin' Wolf knew Patton and his first recording session featured 'Saddle My Pony', a version of 'Pony Blues'.

The Delta blues has become institutionalised as folk music. In the '50s and '60s bourgeois intellectuals rediscovered this music. The original market – working-class and rural audiences, mostly black – moved on to jazz and R&B and now, of course, hip-hop and rap, and the music evolved. When Patton wrote his blues it was music for parties and juke joints. He was known for playing the guitar behind his neck and dropping to his knees for emphasis. The music still has that power, although you are unlikely to dance to it.

Patton was, if not the first, then the most important musician to meld together the rhythms of Africa, the work songs of the field and the popular music of his day.

On Dockery's plantation in the '20s Patton started something and from that has flowed the most dynamic musical tradition of the century.

Imagine John Lennon

(John Lennon) ✳ Apple ✳ 1971 ✳ Appears on: *Imagine*

John Lennon's musing here has become something more than a pop song. It has become an anthem that people sing when they need hope for mankind. It is unlikely that many of the song's fans have listened to the lyric. Lennon is advocating an atheistic, anarchist utopia. Lennon regarded the song as a sugar-coated version of the bilious 'Working Class Hero'.

"So you think 'Imagine' ain't political?" Lennon told the *Melody Maker*. "It's 'Working Class Hero' with sugar on it for conservatives."

Lennon wrote the song on the white piano at home at Ascot, his English estate. A strange place to be "imagining no possessions". The lyric, which was effectively written on the spot, was a fusion of Lennon's pacifism and his wife Yoko Ono's art statements from her book *Grapefruit*.

"The lyric, the concept, came from Yoko, but in those days I was more selfish, more macho, and omitted to mention her contribution," he said. "But it was right out of her *Grapefruit* book – there's a whole pile of pieces about imagine this and imagine that."

Lennon produced the track with Phil Spector, who was uncharacteristically restrained but lush enough to sugar-coat the minimal backing from Klaus Voorman on bass and Ringo Starr on drums.

Ultimately the word – imagine – wins out over everything. It's another word for hope.

Peter Gunn Henry Mancini

(Henry Mancini) ❋ RCA ❋ 1959 ❋ Appears on: *The Music from Peter Gunn*

In 1958, director/producer Blake Edwards needed a new spin on the detective drama for the NBC TV network. Edwards hit on a revolutionary idea. He made the private eye, Peter Gunn (as played by Craig Stevens), a hipster who dressed impeccably and spoke with a beatnik jargon while solving crimes. He was most likely to be found hanging out at Mother's, a Los Angeles jazz club. This was a particularly fertile period for West Coast jazz and Edwards picked up on the energy of that milieu.

Edwards' update of the noir detective lasted only 114 half-hour episodes but fundamentally changed the style of TV crime drama.

Edwards wanted to use jazz music not as a gimmick but as an important dramatic tool. He hired his friend Henry Mancini to score the show and its distinctive theme.

As Edwards wrote on the liner notes to *The Music from Peter Gunn*, "We already had many exciting components, but what was missing was some distinctive element to invest this series with something extra, something superlative. It hit me then – jazz. If we could use the music as an integral part of the dramatic action, fusing story line and score, we should have something very worthwhile.

"As creator of the show, I naturally insisted on using live music throughout. In this case aesthetic necessity was implemented by the fact that many of the nation's greatest jazz musicians are in the Hollywood area – an ideal opportunity to handpick the most creative jazzmen. To give us the musical background required, we also needed a composer with roots in the jazz idiom, one who could interpret dramatic action in the language of modern jazz. Henry Mancini is that composer."

Mancini was making a name for himself in Hollywood. 'The Peter Gunn Theme', however, was a major hit. The brash horn riffs were both cool and urgent. It had the feel of Hollywood noir, but updated for the faster times.

Mancini won a Grammy for 'Peter Gunn' at the first Grammy ceremony in 1959 and the tune has remained in circulation ever since. It was updated in the '80s for a Nintendo game and revised by the Art of Noise, and the original soundtracks have never been out of print.

White Flag Dido

(Dido Armstrong/Rollo Armstrong/Rick Nowels) ❊ Arista ❊ 2003 ❊
Appears on: *Life for Rent*

Dido Armstrong had a natural voice for the waiflike, obsessive love song, of which 'White Flag' was the best.

Armstrong had been making music for some time, mostly with her brother Rollo who had a dance-music outfit called Faithless. She had that nice bourgeois intelligentsia ambience in her work – her father is in book publishing and her mother a poet – so she was literate but streetwise. Emimem sampled her first album for his groundbreaking song 'Stan' at which point a great pressure descended on Dido.

"I'm not into the harder dance music," she told Q. "I like 130bpm, a nice melody, chuck your hands in the air. But my writing is traditional. Totally. Although I never realised it until I came here and saw that it fits in perfectly with the singer/ songwriter tradition."

'White Flag' is thoughtful, reflective, melancholy and even gut-wrenching in places.

"It's exactly what I wanted it to be, it makes me feel something still," she said. "The way I looked at it on the last record, if it makes me feel something, it goes on. But you don't know whether you're going to lose that perspective, 'cause of everything that's happened. But luckily I'm still really clear."

After the Goldrush Neil Young

(Neil Young) ✳ Reprise ✳ 1970 ✳ Appears on: *After the Goldrush*

"But, in all modesty, *After the Goldrush*, which was kind of the turning point, was a strong album," Neil Young told Cameron Crowe. "I really think it was. A lot of hard work went into it. Everything was there. The picture it painted was a strong one. *After the Goldrush* was the spirit of Topanga Canyon. It seemed like I realised that I'd gotten somewhere. I joined CSNY and was still working a lot with Crazy Horse . . . I was playing all the time. And having a great time. Right after that album, I left the house. It was a good coda."

The album, or at least the title track, was written as the theme for an independent film to be made by actor Dean Stockwell. The film, or at least what can be gleaned from interviews and the lyrics of this title song, involved the destruction of the planet and the human race's escape into space. The film was never made. This song remains as an exquisite ecology hymn. That the lyrics are somewhat obscure adds to the mystery. The accompaniment by Young and some horns is perfect and the tune is haunting. This is some of Young's best singing – before he became self-conscious about his voice – and he's really stretching out to the limits of it. *After the Goldrush* cemented Young's reputation before the next album, *Harvest*, made him a superstar and he had to commit thirty years of career suicide.

The Seed (2.0) The Roots

(Cody ChesnuTT/Tariq Trotter) ✳ MCA ✳ 2002 ✳ Appears on: *Phrenology*

The Roots demonstrated so decisively that hip-hop could come out of a live band that few have followed their lead out of fear of being shown up. Black Thought (Tariq Trotter) and drummer ?uestlove (Ahmir Khalib Thompson) started the Roots in 1987 at the Philadelphia High School for Creative Performing Arts. Bassist Hub (Leon Hubbard) and rapper Malik B finished up the core of the band.

Because of their versatility – they play hip-hop with a tough jazz flavour and the rhythm section of Hub and ?uestlove is one of the most dynamic powerhouses in the business – the Roots have frequently guested on other people's records. The favour was returned on 2002's *Phrenology*, notably with a version of Cody ChestnuTT's 'The Seed'. ?uestlove described the track as "Beck meets Tracy Chapman on acid."

Phenology is a hip-hop masterpiece where the songs ebb and flow around the mega-massive bass sound. Cody ChestnuTT is a songwriter/guitarist who adds his song, which is pretty much about love, action and the consequences. The Roots bring home the urgency and the physical action that is hinted at in the lyric. The Roots take the song and stretch it and then place it as the centrepiece of an eleven-minute medley.

"A lot of people think they've got us figured out, but it's important for us to establish that you can never take us for granted," ?uestlove told VH1. "Pretty much every Roots album has been a major departure. This is also the most leftfield album that we've ever done. The more to the right that we moved, we took it to farther extremes. We've never done an eleven-minute free jazz song like 'Water' before. The rock stuff, the punk interludes, the electronica experiments we did with Amiri Baraka – once we were into it we realised we're gonna move more to the left *and* to the right – which is something rare for a middle ground group to do."

Respect Yourself The Staple Singers

(Mack Rice/Luther Ingram) ❊ Stax ❊ 1971 ❊ Appears on: *The Best of the Staple Singers*

As a child in the Mississippi Delta in the '20s, Roebuck Pops Staples heard the original Delta blues legends. After moving to Chicago and embarking on his own career with his family – including his daughter Mavis – he took a more gospel bent with a large dose of R&B. They signed to Stax in the mid-'60s and recorded extensively with the strong and muscular Muscle Shoals rhythm section and other legendary Memphis session bands.

'Respect Yourself' was a perfect Staples Singers vehicle. The message of the song centres on non-violent black pride and it brings together the urgency of R&B with vocal arrangements evolved from gospel.

"Still, on this particular album, Al [producer Al Bell] and I talked a lot about all the different styles we wanted to incorporate," engineer Terry Manning told *Mix* magazine. "I was trying to bring in some rock elements – fuzz tone and various things. And Al was trying to bring in a Jamaican feel. He'd been on a trip to Montego Bay and he'd heard some of the early reggae and he brought that back with him: 'We need to get this feeling in with the R&B and the funk and the rock.' That may sound a bit grandiose because maybe you listen to that and think, 'It's just the Memphis sound, it's just R&B.' But it's not. It was a big thing to us at the time. I can hear Jamaican ska types of jumps that are on the drums, especially on 'I'll Take You There' – that off-beat, not all the way to reggae, mixed with R&B."

Manning had recently acquired a Moog synthesiser, then a new invention, and used it on the record as well – the first time a synthesiser appeared on an R&B record.

"At the time, they were just more sessions," Manning said. "I mean I always loved them, but we didn't know they were so great that we'd be hearing them still thirty years later."

Your Cheatin' Heart Hank Williams

(Hank Williams) ✳ MGM ✳ 1952 ✳ Appears on: *40 Greatest Hits*

"Hank and I became engaged in Nashville, Tennessee," said the songwriter's wife, Billie Jean Williams Horton. "This was early summer, 1952 . . . Hank started telling me about his problems with his ex-wife, Audrey. He said that one day her 'cheatin' heart' would pay. Then he said, 'Hey, that'd make a good song! Get out my tablet, baby; me and you are gonna write us a song!' Just about as fast as I could write, Hank quoted the words to me in a matter of minutes."

'Your Cheatin' Heart' became one of Williams' best known songs. It appeared shortly after his divorce from Audrey Mae Sheppard, although the song didn't appear on record until 1953 following Williams' death. Like many of his best songs, this came from his stormy first marriage, and it was Williams' ability to transform his personal storms to lyrics that distinguished his work.

The song gave the title to the biopic of Williams' life and is one of the cornerstones of country music. Tough and unsentimental, it prefigures the growth of country music in the postwar years. Although it touches on one of the constant themes of country music, Williams' writing is so poetic and direct here that it transcends any particular category.

Route 66 The Rolling Stones

(Bobby Troup) ✳ Decca ✳ 1964 ✳ Appears on: *The Rolling Stones*

The highway linking Chicago and Los Angeles was the road to fortune for jazz pianist Bobby Troup. In 1946 the aspiring songwriter was heading west, looking for opportunity, when he stopped for a bite.

"My wife and I were eating in a Howard Johnson's and looking at a road map," he said in an interview broadcast on NPR. "She said, 'Why don't you write about Route 40.' I said, 'That's silly because we're going to pick up Route 66 outside of Chicago and take it all the way to Los Angeles.' She said, 'Get your kicks on Route 66.' I said, 'God, that's a marvellous idea for a song.'" Troup finished the lyric in the car.

On arriving in Hollywood, Troup had an audition for Nat King Cole, who already had a reputation as a hot jazz pianist and singer with his King Cole Trio but was looking for something more pop. He jumped on 'Route 66' and made it a number one hit.

The charm of the song, which is essentially a litany of towns along the map, is that it captured the post-war optimism of America. It's as though the west had been opened a second time by the availability of the automobile. Americans became mobile in a way that no other people were. The freedom of the open road was a metaphor for the limitless possibilities offered by post-war prosperity. Few songs expressed that carefree time better than 'Route 66'.

The breezy, cool swing of Nat King Cole was given a makeover by the Stones, who added a bluesy raunchiness to the track very much in the style of Chuck Berry. Being English, 'Route 66' represented the dream of America – fast cars, big bustling towns like Chicago and Los Angeles. The mythology of the modern American west is all here, and the Stones expressed the urgency of kids the world over to get in on the action. In the hands of the Stones the hard rhythms created by the lyrics were that much more exciting. Ironically, the Stones learned the song from a Perry Como record. They used it to open their first album. It was the perfect blueprint for an extraordinary four decades.

Bobby Troup's song has entered the public consciousness so strongly that Route 66 has become a national monument, the most famous road in the world.

Can the Can Suzi Quatro

(Nicky Chinn/Mike Chapman) ❋ Rak ❋ 1973 ❋ Appears on: *Greatest Hits*

The 'Chinnichap' sound dominated the British and Australian pop charts in the early '70s. Simple songs with big, dumb choruses and fat bottom ends performed by artists with clearly identifiable images – these were the hallmarks of songwriter/ producers Nicky Chinn and Mike Chapman. They hit big with the Sweet, then Mud and later Smokie, but their star attraction was a young girl from Detroit whom über-producer Mickie Most moved to London.

Most saw her star potential but was unable to make hit records with her, so he enlisted Chinnichap.

"I was terrified to take over where Mickie couldn't succeed, but I told him that if he was prepared to take the risk, I was game," Chapman recalled. "Within a week or two, we had written 'Can the Can', and soon after that, it was number one. Mickie's problem with Suzi was that neither of them knew what her direction should be. The direction finally came from 'Can the Can' – when we had that song, Mickie had the image, the black leather and so on, and it thrilled Suzi to have that visual thing going. It was a classic example of a record creating an artist.

"Basically, once an artist had his or her direction, I could play something like the last record and let the next one develop from there.

"Somebody asked me what 'Can the Can' meant, so I made up a story. Then somebody else asked me, and I'd forgotten what I told the first person, so I ended up having four stories about this silly song 'Can the Can', which basically had no meaning at all – we were trying to write songs that had no meaning."

The meaning came when the song was married to the artist and the sound. Chinnichap had a retro sensibility – a '50s aesthetic of a simple time when girls and boys were 'good/bad but they ain't evil,' to paraphrase the Shangri-Las. Although Quatro arrived at concerts on the back of a motorcycle, escorted by local bikers, she was strangely unthreatening to teenagers. And the sheer simple thrust of the songs was irresistible.

Suzi Quatro fitted this image as tightly as she wore her leather cat suit. But Suzi was also emancipated in that she played the bass guitar, sang and clearly ran her band. Suzi was emancipated – sexually and economically.

"What I'm saying is, a lot of girls who are like me naturally, have been suppressed over the years," she said after the release of 'Can the Can'. "Now maybe they identify with me and feel they can say things, and I say, more power to them."

Suzi also announced that she was liberated from underwear. Just skin and leather and the bass guitar between her legs. "It was in Detroit," she reminisced. "I was playing really low and I felt this feeling come up and I had an orgasm right then and there."

In one of her more blunt but no less significant feminist statements, she said, "Just 'cause I've got a couple of buns in front don't mean I can't play rock & roll."

Israelites Desmond Dekker & the Aces

(Desmond Dekker/Leslie Kong) ☀ Trojan ☀ 1968 ☀ Appears on: *Tougher Than Tough*

Desmond Dekker's song of exodus was the first ska hit outside Jamaica. Leslie Kong was one of the seminal Jamaican producers. With Dekker he found his ideal foil – an expressive singer and a band, the Aces, that was punchy but had an easy, bouncy style. The bass line has the choppy ska feel but the drums ground it strongly in the melody.

Like many songs of the period, 'Israelites' is a song about release from oppression. In this case, and not for the first time in ska or reggae, Dekker draws a parallel between the Jews in bondage in Babylon and Egypt and the fate of the Jamaicans.

The ska sound was mostly adopted in Britain by right-wing skinheads – there's an irony there.

"I don't think British teenagers really understand the words to half the records because a lot are in Jamaican slang," said Dekker. "They just like the sound – it's easy for them to dance to, and that is all they want.

"I think the popularity of the music just had to come. As

soon as Bill Black Combo and Chubby Checker and then Johnny Nash started doing dance music records I knew the kids would want it."

After 'Israelites', ska and reggae were put on the pop music menu in the West and never looked back.

Jailhouse Rock Elvis Presley

(Jerry Leiber/Mike Stoller) ❋ RCA ❋ 1957 ❋ Appears on: *Elvis' Golden Records*

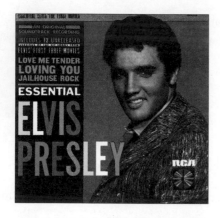

Jerry Leiber and Mike Stoller were the ideal team to write prison songs for Elvis Presley's third movie. One of the hottest writing teams in R&B, with a long string of hits mostly in the R&B charts, Leiber and Stoller also specialised in 'crime songs'. Another one of their biggest hits was the Coasters' 'Riot in Cell Block #91'.

"After Elvis covered 'Hound Dog', Colonel Parker and the Aberbach brothers, who had the publishing with Hill & Range, called us in and offered us a deal on writing songs specifically for pictures and recording sessions," said Leiber. The film *Jailhouse Rock* was their first gig. "We took the deal, and we wrote for about three years until it broke down. We did about four or five movies, and each one was sillier than the last. And we were getting cross-eyed from trying to keep our interest up. And then we ran into a problem with Colonel Parker, who was a colonel like I'm a ballet dancer."

Leiber and Stoller had been scuffling around the music business for many years. They were familiar with all the different styles of pop songs and pop stars and they could generally be counted on to come up with a solution on the spot.

'Jailhouse Rock' was a difficult task. Presley wisely chose to avoid the gay innuendo of the lyrics and just rocked right over the top, aided by an incredible take from his guitarist Scotty Moore.

"We'd never met him before we produced – uncredited – the songs in *Jailhouse Rock*," said Stoller. "He'd asked for us to be there. He was very energetic – I mean, he just kept going and going in the studio. He'd always be saying, 'Let's do another one'. He loved doing it, he had more fun in the studio than he did at home."

Into My Arms   Nick Cave & the Bad Seeds

(Nick Cave) ✳ Mute ✳ 1997 ✳ Appears on: *The Boatman's Call*

Perhaps it was encroaching middle age. Perhaps it was the end of his relationships with Vivien Carneiro and PJ Harvey. Perhaps it was just luck, but on *The Boatman's Call* Cave brings together his two great themes of love and God. The album opens with 'Into My Arms' – the only love song couched in a theological discussion about the nature of the Creator.

"This is my most personal album to date," he said at the time. "I kind of write what I'm given in a way, and I just felt at particular times, this year, very excited about writing about things that had happened to me, and that's simply the nature of doing what I do.

"I think that I've just been much more able to understand a lot of things that have gone on in my life whereas before I was more concerned with fictional writing, and it was far more exciting for me to write about other things that were outside of myself.

"To me this is the record I've always wanted to make. The record that took a reasonable amount of courage to actually do."

While writing this album Cave was completing his *Murder Ballads* album – a record of narratives about homicide. That siphoned off one strand of Cave's material and possibly as a result *The Boatman's Call* got an increase in the love songs.

Cave separated from Carneiro, the mother of his son and the longest nurturing relationship in his life thus far. He also had a passionate, intense relationship with songwriter Polly Harvey and possibly also with Tori Amos.

While his personal life may have been busy, Cave's career took off. The decade and half of work he had done had paid off and by 1996 he had a sizeable international following – so much so that Kylie Minogue agreed to a duet on one of the murder ballads and sent that record to the top of the charts.

'Into My Arms' is a vulnerable song. Cave is not only being candid about his feelings but matches the lyric with a tune worthy of their poetic qualities.

"So I didn't set out to write a personal record as such," he said. "I just found myself writing things in that way, and with quite a few of those it was significant for me at the time to articulate the events that had happened.

"I think there's some very bracing and sobering lessons that can be learnt from love. It doesn't really go the way it's supposed to go, or the way I've always believed that should be, which is the way we're constantly fed about the idea of love and particularly about committed relationships like marriage. That love, in terms of relationships, actually has little to do with things at all. It's about a commitment to a greater thing and that is the relationship and the relationship being the commitment of two people."

Rivers of Babylon The Melodians

(Brenton Dowe/Trevor McNaughton) ✳ Mango ✳ 1969 ✳
Appears on: *The Harder They Come*

The story of the Israelites taken in bondage from their homeland to toil in Babylon was a potent story for the descendants of Africans enslaved to work on the plantations in Jamaica. This track by the Melodians is one of the best songs of its type, certainly for western tastes. Producer Leslie Kong has crafted a masterful backing track that flows like a great river behind the vocal skills of the Melodians, rich with intertwined voices. The tempo of the track is stately like a hymn rather than a reggae hit. Nonetheless, the song was a success upon its release and after its inclusion on the soundtrack for *The Harder They Come* it became a classic. It even survived a Euro disco version by Boney M in the late '70s.

The lyric is a transcription of Psalm 137 from the Old Testament in which the Israelites bemoan their imprisonment and vow to keep alive the memory of Zion – the Promised Land.

Touch Me I'm Sick Mudhoney

(Mudhoney) ✳ Sub Pop ✳ 1988 ✳ Appears on: *Superfuzz Bigmuff Plus Early Single*

Mudhoney were just geeks playing obnoxious music in the late '80s. The group – guitarists Mark Arm and Steve Turner, bass player Matt Lukin and drummer Dan Peters – coagulated from seminal outfits like Green River and the Melvins who inhabited the Pacific Northwest around Seattle. Possessed of a fuzzbox and a crate of punk rock LPs, Mudhoney intended to have a good time. The first offering was 'Touch Me I'm Sick', which was funny, forceful, a little self-loathing and sometimes scary but mostly noisy.

The song was recorded quickly and two friends offered to start a label to release it as a 7-inch backed with 'Sweet Young Thing Ain't Sweet No More'. So began Sub Pop records and around Sub Pop in Seattle grew a music scene that was known as grunge. From here came Pearl Jam and Nirvana and Soundgarden and then a million groups in shorts and flannel shirts around the world. Few records that came after this founding release were as much fun.

"It's kind of surprising it took off as fast as it did," said drummer Dan Peters. "We didn't start off all that serious about it."

Maggot Brain Funkadelic

(George Clinton/Eddie Hazel) ❋ Westbound ❋ 1971 ❋ Appears on: *Maggot Brain*

The opening gambit on Funkadelic's breakthrough third album was a dark piece of acid-inspired protest at the war in Vietnam.

"That was originally a comment on the war in Vietnam, but it really took in the world at large," said Funkadelic commander George Clinton. "While I'm not trying to be goody goody, I'm saying we got to acknowledge the fact that we have a part in this shit just by the fact that we enjoy certain things without knowing the chain of events that leads to our comfort. Protest that and eat yourself fat, ain't you deep in your semi-first class seat. You can't take the bow without taking the blame. The whole point of Funkadelic was not to tell people what to think, just tell them they could think.

"There was a lot of black groups getting mad, because we had Vietnam hitting the black communities hard, and life in the ghettoes was meaner than a muthafucka. I could get mad enough at the world and how it was treating people to wait in an alley with a brick and kill some muthafucka and, like anybody else in the ghetto, if somebody made me mad I was ready to fight. But there ain't no winning in a situation like that, so once we got out of there I'd take acid to make sure I didn't get that mad no more. I'd start looking at, you know, alternative realities.

"There wasn't no other black groups taking acid at that time. At the time I didn't realise that we were doing what we were doing because we were doing so much acid, but I can see that now."

'Maggot Brain' is one of the finest pieces to come out of the Mothership – a catch-all that covered the work of Parliament, Funkadelic, Bootsy Collins and others. It confirmed George Clinton's place alongside Sly Stone and Jimi Hendrix as a R&B visionary.

The song is an extraordinary ten-minute jam that is part rock and part funk and part just out there. Recorded live in one take, there's an amazing guitar solo from Eddie Hazel. The guitarist was directed to "play like yo' mama just died". It worked. This is one of the saddest pieces of electric guitar of the era.

It's the End of the World as We Know It (and I Feel Fine) R.E.M.

(Michael Stipe/Peter Buck/Mike Mills/Bill Berry) ❋ IRS ❋ 1987 ❋ Appears on: *Document*

"These songs are like taking a picture of your bedroom," said guitarist Peter Buck of middle period R.E.M. "It may not make much sense to anyone else, but to you it's all the things in your life. We're certainly not setting out to be deliberately obscure, but you have to short-circuit the whole idea that literal language is what things are, because literal language is just codes for what happens. Without wanting to sound too arty about it, to bypass actions and go straight to the results is what we're trying to do, to make people feel moved by something without them even being sure of what we're writing about."

'It's the End of the World as We Know It (and I Feel Fine)' was one of the first R.E.M. songs to make sense or at least be decipherable. The group attacks the song at a breakneck pace as Michael Stipe sings out a litany of catastrophe and heroes, incidents and puns.

'It's the End of the World as We Know It (and I Feel Fine)' is an update of 'Too Much Monkey Business' and 'Subterranean Homesick Blues'. With the name checks for lost hipsters Lenny Bruce and Lester Bangs, 'End of the World' became a blueprint for alternative culture in the late '80s.

"We don't clarify things," said Buck. "When we first started, Michael and I used to say how much we hated most rock & roll lyrics. We had this idea that what we'd do is take clichés, sayings, lines from old songs, phrases you hear all the time, and skew them and twist them and meld them together so that you'd be getting these things that have always been evocative, but that were skewed just enough to throw you off and make you think in a different way. It seemed like a really pretentious thing to do, but that concept does work its way in."

Ring of Fire Johnny Cash

(June Carter Cash/Merle Kilgore) ✳ Columbia ✳ 1964 ✳

Appears on: *The Essential Johnny Cash*

Johnny Cash was so much the Man in Black that even when he fell in love he imagined it would be like hell. One of Johnny Cash's most endearing songs was written by his wife, June Carter Cash, and Merle Kilgore. With Cash's massive bass voice and his weary persona the 'Ring of Fire' of passion becomes the bittersweet fire of hell.

"I connected with June Carter the first time in 1956 backstage at the Grand Ole Opry, but it was about five years before I saw her again," Johnny Cash recalled of the woman who would be his love, saviour and muse for the rest of his life. "She was living in New York, going to dramatic school. But in late '61 we played the Big D in Dallas, Texas, and my manager at that time, Saul Holiff, said, 'We need a girl singer on the show tonight. They want more than just you and your band.' And I said, 'Well, get one.' He said, 'What do you think about June Carter?' and I said, 'I've always been a fan of hers.' So we booked June Carter on the Big D in Dallas and then that night she did such a great job, my manager asked if she would work the next tour with us.

"Merle Kilgore happened to be on that tour, and they were writing songs together and one of them was 'Love's Firey Ring'. And they worked it over until they changed it to 'Ring of Fire' and Anita Carter, June's sister, recorded it. And I said, 'Anita, I'll give you about five or six months, and if you don't hit with it, I'm gonna record it the way I feel it.' She said, 'OK.' Well, one night, not that I can claim any psychic powers or anything, I dreamed I heard 'Ring of Fire' with trumpets which was an outlandish kind of an innovation for country music. I called Don Law who was producing my records and I said, 'I want to record a song with trumpets with a Tex-Mex sound of trumpets.' And he said, 'Are you sure? Let's just bring in the

Tennessee Three', and I said, 'No, I want two trumpet players in Nashville for this session for one song and when you hear it, you'll know. I think you'll go along with it.' He didn't really, but he hired the trumpet players, and I went to Nashville and recorded 'Ring of Fire'."

Not only did it help the path of true love, 'Ring of Fire' put Johnny Cash back in the charts. Its adventurous production and forceful arrangement made the song a pop hit and revived his career for the '60s.

Down by the Water PJ Harvey

(PJ Harvey) ✳ Island ✳ 1995 ✳ Appears on: *To Bring You My Love*

PJ Harvey's progression from deranged West Country waif to pop star and sex symbol was only a matter of three or four years. A nervous breakdown followed the first album and subsequent depressive episodes informed her work. She was not a writer to gild the lily. By the time she came to record this third proper studio album she had moved a long way from the naïve, abrasive bluntness of her first two albums into a tougher but more welcoming collection of songs.

The blues was a big influence – the sexual urgency of Howlin' Wolf has been channelled here. There's also the influence of the white bluesmen – Nick Cave and Tom Waits and family friend Captain Beefheart – and the effects of therapy, which seem to have curbed those self-loathing moments that so dominated her early albums. She also dispensed with her road band in favour of a wider palette of sounds. She chose U2 producer Flood, who provided a sturdy and strong background without the violent arrangements of earlier records. Co-producer John Parrish was her boyfriend at the time.

'Down by the Water' is a brooding, sinister track that is not afraid of melody. The song touches on the southern Gothic, neo-religious imagery that was the stock in trade of Nick Cave and the Bad Seeds. Of course, the blues remains a significant theme here as well. Harvey was linked romantically to both Nick Cave and Bad Seed Mick Harvey and perhaps these relationships and her growing self-confidence helped her writing to open up.

Compared with the previous works, 'Down by the Water' is a velvet glove, but it still contains an iron fist.

Tear My Stillhouse Down Gillian Welch

(Gillian Welch) ✳ Almo Sounds ✳ 1996 ✳ Appears on: *Revival*

Some artists appear to be completely outside their own time. Gillian Welch, a Californian singer and songwriter, looks like she fled the Dust Bowl on the back of Tom Joad's wagon. Her songs sound like they come from at least that time. For all of that though, Welch is perfectly modern in her sensibility. The closest comparison would be the work of Robbie Robertson on the first Band LPs. These ancient songs are, in fact, timeless.

"This is just the kind of music that I am able to sing and play," she told *Austin City Limits.* "Believe it or not, this is what I've always sung and played since I was a little girl. I started, I had a music teacher when I was about five years old, in grade school, first grade, and she taught us Woodie Guthrie and Carter family songs because it was a proper hippie upbringing, you know, and I just immediately took to it. I can't even remember a time when I didn't like singing and that I didn't in particular like singing folk music. There's just something about it. There's something about the simplicity that isn't at all simple really, it's a very, very deep kind of music."

'Tear My Stillhouse Down' is a moonshiner's ballad, the song of a person contemplating death. Welch, backed by long-time accomplice David Rawlings and produced by T-Bone Burnett, sings the song with delicacy and an eerie understanding of the big-ticket issues.

"What we do isn't old time, and it isn't bluegrass, but it's got one foot over there," she said. "We're some strange modern cousin of all that stuff."

Seven Nation Army The White Stripes

(Jack White) ✳ V2 ✳ 2003 ✳ Appears on: *Elephant*

White Stripes songwriter Jack White told filmmaker Jim Jarmusch that 'Seven Nation Army' "is about this character who is involved in the realm of gossip with his friends and family and is so enraged by it that he wants to leave town."

With only a guitar and drums, the White Stripes peel off a blistering rock track as the opening to their third album. The album was recorded in London in a small studio on an eight-track machine. They used the same equipment and instrumentation that would have been available in 1963. The whole thing was done in ten days.

With mostly just drums and guitar, Jack and Meg White beat up a huge storm. They are channelling the blues of Hound Dog Taylor. However, the White Stripes are a product of their ironic education and self-consciously artistic inclinations. Which is fine. The mixture of the two plus a little bitterness is what makes 'Seven Nation Army' work.

"Vocals, guitars, drums; melody, storytelling and rhythm; red, white and black," Jack said to VH1 by way of explaining his aesthetic. White sees himself as an outsider. Which explains the force behind the call to arms of 'Seven Nation Army'. "The whole idea of the band is that it was all about what *not* to do. Why be repetitive? Why have two guitar players? Why have a bass player playing the same thing a guitar is playing? Let's break this down as much possible and have it still be rock & roll and show what two people can do."

Borderline Madonna

(Reggie Lucas/Madonna) ❊ Sire ❊ 1983 ❊ Appears on: *Madonna*

Madonna was a downtown dancer who couldn't sing very well when she signed to Sire. She was assigned producer Reggie Lucas, who had impeccable credits stretching back to his stint with Miles Davis and more recently with soulful R&B acts such as Mtume. Madonna was awed by Lucas' pedigree.

"Reggie, I thought, might be able to push me, having worked with Phyllis Hyman and Roberta Flack. The only problem was that he wanted to make me sound like them," Madonna told Barney Hoskyns. "I now know what I want on my next record. The production won't be so slick, because where Reggie and Mtume come from is a whole different school. I want a sound that's mine. There will be a more crossover approach to it this time. Maybe I should work with a British producer."

The best example of their working relationship is 'Borderline', which was a balance between the two creative impulses. Lucas pushes Madonna to find some emotional depth in the song and he provides a backing that is icy and contemporary but with a deep warm heart. 'Borderline' hinted at the range that Madonna's next twenty years would cover.

Helter Skelter The Beatles

(John Lennon/Paul McCartney) ✳ Apple ✳ 1968 ✳ Appears on: *The Beatles*

Paul McCartney supposedly heard that the Who had made the noisiest record ever and took that as a challenge, his response being this noise fest driven by his best Little Richard voice and a dive-bombing bass guitar.

This was one of the few songs at the time that was recorded by the Beatles as a band. Having stopped touring they beavered away in the recording studio, often individually, and their music tended towards the mid-tempo rather than the supercharged rock & roll of their early years.

A helter skelter is a child's playground slide built in a corkscrew shape and that's pretty much what the song is about – going up and down and turning around. The first take of the song lasted thirty minutes of intense jamming – Harrison's guitar matching the zooming bass from McCartney and Starr's amped-up Motown feel. The song's apparent dumbness added to the tornado effect. It rises and falls and then rises again until it comes to a stop and then goes straight back into it. The song captures that sense of being out of control.

Unfortunately 'Helter Skelter' will be forever associated with Charles Manson, who used the phrase in his crazed, homicidal spree in 1969. However, the memory of Manson fades and 'Helter Skelter' remains, as McCartney intended, to be one raucous piece of music.

Philadelphia Freedom Elton John

(Elton John/Bernie Taupin) ✳ Rocket ✳ 1975 ✳

Appears on: *Elton John's Greatest Hits Vol. 2*

Billie Jean King was a tennis champion in the '70s and a friend of Elton John's. When she presented him with a custom-made tracksuit he promised to give her a song. The track, dedicated to BJK and her team the Philadelphia Freedoms, was also a homage to the Philly soul sound of producers Gamble and Huff. The song heavily featured the lush string sections and punchy horns that were their signatures. 'Philadelphia Freedom' was an early attempt by a star of John's magnitude to pick up on the changing R&B sound that prefigured disco.

The name of the game here is dance music, a fact lyricist Bernie Taupin acknowledged at the time. "I'm quite honest about it," he said. "I'm sure fifty per cent of the people who liked it never even listened to the words. People don't buy a record because the words are good, or the words sound nice. They buy it for the old thing melody, or 'It's got a good beat, man. Yeah, I can dance to that one.' The words, at least in the beginning, are secondary.

"Later on they may play a part, because you have to have something to sing along to. But on 'Philadelphia Freedom', or any of the up-tempo things, the words just aren't that important. If they're palatable, and you can sing them, that's all that matters."

Nasty Janet Jackson

(James Harris/Janet Jackson/Terry Lewis) ❊ A&M ❊ 1986 ❊ Appears on: *Control*

Unlike other members of her famous family, Janet Jackson got funkier as she matured. 'Nasty' was a defiant statement from a woman who was no longer going to be a wallflower making wallpaper music.

Jackson enlisted the team of Jimmy Jam and Terry Lewis to work up their Minneapolis funk as the basis for her personal makeover. Jackson was leaving her husband and the domination of her notoriously patriarchal father and the comfort zone of the Jacksons. She also had to compete for attention with her brother, who at the time had the biggest selling albums in history.

Jam and Lewis spent a week talking with Jackson about the issues she wanted to address in her songs and on the basis of those conversations worked up 'Nasty' and the other tracks on the *Control* album – cutting the entire disc in three weeks. Not only did 'Nasty' give a new view of Janet, its polished sheen over a hard-edged beat told the emotional story and reinforced her stand as a woman taking charge. It was a style that was quickly adopted by other female vocalists. More than any other album, *Control* put Jam and Lewis on the map as producers du jour.

"We knew it would be a successful black album," Jimmy Jam said. "We tried to make the hardest, funkiest black album – almost a male singer's album. The edginess that's evident in the music on *Control* is her; that's our interpretation of Janet.

"Before *Control* it wasn't acceptable to have hard-edged black music on the radio. Now, it's the norm."

Nuthin' but a 'G' Thang   Dr Dre

(Dr Dre) ❋ Death Row ❋ 1992 ❋ Appears on: *The Chronic*

Coming out of the powerful NWA, Dre developed a sound that was so funky and fat that he quickly became one of the most inventive and powerful of rap producers. Part of his appeal came from his old school knowledge – he cleverly used Parliament/Funkadelic grooves, some funk guitar as well as the mega bass sound, and a clipped rhythm style.

'Nuthin' but a 'G' Thang' is a West Coast rap classic. As the title suggests, this is a song about gangsta life. However, while NWA were nominally political, 'G Thang' reduces life to chasing pussy. The song, on which Snoop Dogg does most of the rapping, is a piece of misogynistic nonsense.

It's a discussion of the possibilities of scoring some ass. The level of discourse is completely offensive to women and reads like the patter between two adolescent boys. Which is perhaps why gangsta rap essentially appealed to teenage males.

Yellow   Coldplay

(Guy Berryman/Jon Buckland/Will Champion/Chris Martin) ❋ Parlophone ❋ 2000 ❋ Appears on: *Parachutes*

"That song is about devotion," said Coldplay singer Chris Martin. "That's just about somebody throwing themselves in front of a car for somebody else. Yeah, it would be scary if you went up to someone you didn't know and said 'I'd bleed myself dry for you' – of course they're going to quake in their boots and run a mile. But if it was your wife or something, or your best mate ... I'd do anything for them and they'd do anything for me.

"I dunno. The lyrics just arrived. You've gotta have overstatement in your songs, haven't you? I'm sure Atomic Kitten don't really want you do it to them right now, but that's how it comes across."

Coldplay, the four geeks who met at college and went straight to the top of the charts with their first album, were the right group in the right place at the right time.

Chris Martin, who is the force driving the group, was nice in all the senses of that word. A good student at university, he had a fine grasp of modern rock. He translated Radiohead's paranoid soundscapes into something that was palatable to the mass audience. Coldplay became the Dire Straits of the new millennium. Which is not to say that the gorgeous, eerie tune 'Yellow' isn't a magnificent piece of pop music; it is more than a plastic imitation. It's a song of absolute love without a trace of irony in the chiming of its keyboard and guitar lines.

All the Tired Horses Bob Dylan

(Bob Dylan) ✳ Columbia ✳ 1970 ✳ Appears on: *Self Portrait*

The only lyric on the song is "All the tired horses in the sun/How'm I s'posed to get any riding done?," sung by the beautiful gospel voices of Hilda Harris, Albertine Robinson and Maeretha Stewart. This seems meagre from the pre-eminent lyricist of the day but it is as honest a lyric as Dylan has penned. He was in Woodstock with his new family. He was tired. He was happy. He was kicking back. Perhaps at that point Dylan didn't know if he would ever write again.

The voices and the string arrangement here, though, soar above the lethargy. It's a wonderful little tune that if nothing else highlights Dylan's facility with melody and one that may well be greater than his facility with lyric. It may not be as earth-changing as some of his songs but it as enjoyable as any.

Original Sufferhead Fela Kuti

(Fela Kuti) ✳ Shanachie ✳ 1984 ✳ Appears on: *Original Sufferhead*

Fela Anikulapo Kuti is Nigeria's superstar. A child of the Nigerian ruling classes, Kuti went to Britain in 1969 for his education and gave something back. Even then he was playing highlife, popular dance music from Africa to English audiences. In the west he discovered jazz, R&B and rock & roll – all influences he transformed into a sound he called Afrobeat. In the '60s he travelled to the US where he came in contact with the Black Power movement and was himself politicised.

"I did not know about African music," he said to Barney Hoskyns. "It was up to you to trace, to decipher what was happening, and how modern jazz came from Africa. After I went to America, I went home and decided to get deep, and thought maybe I'll start looking for the link. At that time I didn't even know that Africans had wind instruments, because at school they did not teach us these things."

Back in Nigeria his outspokenness caused trouble with the authorities. In November 1977 his house was attacked by the local military and sacked, resulting in multiple deaths including that of his mother. Kuti spent more than two years in jail. With over fifty albums to his name, he has remained steadfastly political and an outspoken critic of corruption and cronyism in Nigeria.

His music is heavily based around African highlife and the syncopated power of a large ensemble. Kuti, who sings and plays saxophone and trumpet, builds massive grooves that grow organically out of a theme, meander around and are finally resolved some twenty minutes later (as in the case of 'Original Sufferhead'). It's a worthwhile journey.

Ambulance Blues Neil Young

(Neil Young) ✳ Reprise ✳ 1974 ✳ Appears on: *On the Beach*

'Ambulance Blues' is Neil Young's sometimes rambling state of the nation address, touching on Nixon and Watergate, Patty Hearst and the SLA as well as his crumbling second marriage and the end of Crosby, Stills, Nash and Young. It sums up the themes that run through the album *On the Beach*, arguably the best album in his forty-year career.

Some of the songs were played to Crosby, Stills, Nash and Young, and the others, especially David Crosby, refused them on the basis that they were too controversial. As far as Young was concerned, Crosby, Stills, Nash and Young were suffocated by their own past and had lost whatever qualities they had begun with. The hippies and the whole Woodstock generation also disillusioned Young. He was uninterested in being a rock star. His son had recently been born with spina bifida. Young was not in a good way. The feeling on the album is of live recordings full of mistakes and sloppiness, but equally full of emotion.

'*On the Beach* is probably one of the most depressing records I've ever made. I don't want to get down to the point where I can't even get up. I mean there's something to going down there and looking around, but I don't know about sticking around."

Fuck and Run Liz Phair

(Liz Phair) ✳ Matador ✳ 1993 ✳ Appears on: *Exile in Guyville*

"They're totally how I talk, I have a potty mouth," said Liz Phair. "I know what I'm doing when I use the word fuck, but I think it's termed explicit because I'm a girl. The thrill of it is like, your little sister could be up there having these thoughts and you wouldn't know it. That's the titillation. It makes you look around at all the good girls and wonder what's going on in their heads." That was exactly the attraction of Liz Phair – she told the world what was really going on inside some women's heads.

She emerged in the wake of grunge as a straight-talking woman with a great feel for bare rock & roll. Her early tapes led to a recording deal and the sessions that resulted in her stone classic album *Exile in Guyville*.

Guyville was a song-to-song answer to the Stones' 1972 *Exile on Main Street*. "I started listening to *Exile on Main Street* over and over again and hearing what was underneath it," she said. "I kept thinking, I've got answers to this! But it wasn't like, 'You say this, I say that.' Sometimes it was like, 'I see it your way', or 'It's this way in my girly world'. I gave myself room, whether I was contradicting what they said, relearning it or using a parallel symbol. It was like answering a letter."

That would make 'Fuck and Run' the response to Keith Richard's 'Happy'. It's about a girl who's not happy. It's a clear and rather emotional response to a one-night stand. It captures the ambivalence and the emotional awkwardness that is stirred by random passion and the niggling longing for a love that will last.

"Liz is often imaged as a slut because she sings about blow jobs and sings the word fuck," said producer Brad Wood. "It's like they miss the whole point."

Stand By Your Man Tammy Wynette

(Billy Sherrill/Tammy Wynette) ✳ Epic ✳ 1968 ✳ Appears on: *Stand By Your Man*

Tammy Wynette was the first lady of country music, in large part because of this song. Her Nashville twang grows to epic proportions here. It's an iconic image of absolute love and devotion. It's also a sentiment that is deeply conservative – the comfort zone of the perfect union no matter how imperfect the participants.

Wynette was still new to the game when she cut the track. Coming from the poor white background that breeds so many country greats, Wynette was discovered in 1966 by producer Billy Sherrill who put her on the charts with 'Apartment #9'.

Sherrill had 'Stand By Your Man' for about a year before he recorded the track with Wynette.

"All that time, the world was barraged by ERA and Women's Lib so I decided that I wanted the song to be for all women everywhere who did not agree," he said. "I wanted it to be a tune for the truly liberated woman; it was for women who were secure enough in their own identity to enjoy it.

"Some people thought the song was about chauvinism, but that's their problem. They can like the song or lump it! It's just another way of saying I love you with no strings attached."

What'd I Say? Ray Charles

(Ray Charles) ✳ Atlantic ✳ 1959 ✳ Appears on: *The Ultimate Hits Collection*

"That was done early in the morning and we knew we had a tiger by the tail," said engineer Tom Dowd, who cut Ray Charles' legendary 'What'd I Say?' on 18 February 1959. "When it came to mixing the record down, I actually mixed three different versions because it was considered to be a promiscuous record. 'What'd I Say' had some lyrics on it . . . there was never any use of a poor word or bad words at all, but the connotation of some of the lyrics so offended some people. Because we knew it was going to be a hit record, no question."

Ray Charles was always a dynamic performer. One night when the crowd wouldn't let him off stage and all the songs were done he started improvising a riff on his electric piano. He made up lines and the Raelettes, his backing singers, just called them back – just like in church.

The lyrics weren't so sacred. "The people just went crazy, and they loved that little 'ummmmh, unnnnh'. But, hell, let's face it, everybody knows about the 'ummmmh, unnnnh'. That's how we all got here," Charles told *Rolling Stone* magazine in 1978.

Atlantic Records' founders Ahmet Ertegun and Jerry Wexler produced the session that kept all the lust and the passion of Charles' forthright performance for a record that went over two sides of a 45. Drummer Milt Turner is in the pocket with a syncopated beat to frame Charles' percussive roar on the piano.

"I realised that the best thing I could do with Ray was leave him alone," said Wexler. "He needed a producer like Ray Kroc needed a hamburger."

Under the Bridge The Red Hot Chili Peppers

(Flea/John Frusciante/Anthony Kiedis/Chad Smith) ❋ Warner Bros. ❋ 1991 ❋
Appears on: *BloodSugarSexMagik*

During the '80s California's funk rockers were more likely to wind up dead in the bath than to have a number one record. The group was legendary for its drug use – especially singer Anthony Kiedis – and they had already lost one guitarist to an overdose. For *BloodSugarSexMagik* the Chili Peppers enlisted producer Rick Rubin, who had a feel for both hard rock and funk. Then they holed up in a large house in Los Angeles and remade themselves.

BloodSugarSexMagik is one of the strongest albums of the '90s. Mostly it comes down to the strength of the songs – the pounding funky rock of 'Give It Away' and the heartbreaking melodies of 'Under the Bridge'. "The album title is an eloquent but abstract description of how we feel," said Kiedis. "We live in a world packed with desensitising forces, that strip the world of magic. And music can help restore a sense of magic. The world is full of negativity, but we fight back with positivity. We're inspired by oceans, forests, animals, Marx Brothers films. We can't help but project uplifting vibrations, because we love each other so much and get off on playing together."

'Under the Bridge' is a love song to Los Angeles, where Kiedis and bass player Flea grew up on the streets. The bridge in question was a shelter for the homeless and a place to score. For Kiedis' dysfunctional family life, the city was more a home to him than any house could be.

Guitarist John Frusciante, whose spidery guitar lines are elegant, shimmering and slightly tart – bittersweet, in fact – evocatively renders Kiedis' heartfelt tribute to Los Angeles.

"You know what LA is to me?" said Flea. "It's that bird that goes, ooooh-ah-oooh, ooh-ooh. The soul of this city is a huge part of who we are and I think the soul of this city is an old and beautiful thing."

You're Driving Me Insane   The Missing Links

(Baden Hutchens) ✳ Half A Cow ✳ 1965 ✳

Appears on: *Driving You Insane – The Complete Recordings*

The Missing Links were a watershed in the glorious history of psychedelic garage punk.

Richard Neville described the Missing Links as "wild, rebellious, accessible. That's how we felt on the inside, that's how they looked on the outside. Plus, their rock attitude was much more extreme than the mainstreamers. Johnny O'Keefe with his short hair and tight pants wasn't the Wild One any more – if he ever was. The Missing Links made all Oz 'legends' look so straight. After them, even the Beatles seemed dull; the Links' genre was much more the Stones and the Animals."

The Sydney-based band, then in their teens, didn't know there were rules to making rock & roll so they didn't follow them. The guitar playing on 'Some Kinda Fun' and 'Wild About You' is totally berserk and the rhythm section just won't quit. Those two tracks and the brilliant 'You're Driving Me Insane' would be enough to guarantee immortality, but the blues wailing 'Speak No Evil' and the later freak-out 'We 2 Should Live' are unspeakably great. The Links then go really way out on 'H'tuom Tuhs' with a Bo Diddley song played backwards. 'You're Driving Me Insane' is the masterpiece. Its psychedelic squalling and the relentless craziness deliver exactly on its title.

It's no surprise that the Saints included two Links songs in their repertoire as they took Australian punk to the gobbing multitudes back in 1977, or that the seminal Australian record store and label Missing Link was the original home of the Go-Betweens and the Birthday Party. The Missing Links were, for a brief moment while nobody was noticing, the best band Australia ever produced.

A Hard Rain's Gonna Fall   Bryan Ferry

(Bob Dylan) ✳ Virgin ✳ 1973 ✳ Appears on: *These Foolish Things*

Unlike most covers albums, it's not readily apparent whether Bryan Ferry likes or despises the thirteen tracks on *These Foolish Things*, his first solo album. The Roxy

Music singer teases them and buffs them and delivers the generally melodramatic lyrics with the devastating deadpan of a 3 a.m. drag queen. It's worth noting that this is the first rock album of its type to give a sleeve credit to the artist's tailor.

Ferry studied art under Richard Hamilton, Britain's most provocative pop artist (his most famous work, 'In Every Dream Home a Heartache', became the title of a Roxy Music song). There's more than a touch of pop art in these reworkings of pop music artefacts.

Ferry told the *Melody Maker*'s Caroline Coon, "I suppose I play around somewhere between pessimism and optimism. Cyril Connolly said an amazing thing about Scott Fitzgerald's work once – 'his message is despair'. I think that's terrific. Fitzgerald's one of my favourite writers. All his content, his message, is sad and moving, but the style by which it's conveyed has lightness, a charm and a delicacy about it. And I've always tried, I suppose, to do that myself."

Ferry brings a tailored despair to R&B standards 'Piece of My Heart', 'The Tracks of My Tears' and 'Loving You is Sweeter than Ever'. Then he adds dollops of irony to the sugary pop of 'It's My Party'. The Elvis track perhaps sums it up best: 'Baby I Don't Care.'

Having taken on pop, Ferry tackles the two heavy epics of the era, making a meagre joke out of the Stones' 'Sympathy for the Devil'. The most surprising cut on the album is Dylan's 'A Hard Rain's Gonna Fall' – already a song of despair. Ferry takes the lyrics at face value but adds a complete glam arrangement with solid vamping on the piano and prominent backing vocals from the Angelettes. It's pretty much impossible to determine whether he's serious or not. The record went to the top of the pop charts as the most unlikely hit single of 1973 – or any other year.

Caroline Coon observed in 1975, "Bryan does not consider himself so simple. He is not afraid to make a superhuman effort to turn fantasy into reality. But then, he can't escape the awkward feeling that at best he can only become a perfect copy of the real thing. Ultimately, therefore, he faces disappointment and ever more wistful fantasies."

Ferry is the real thing and his indulgence in wistful fantasies such as this reshaped the aesthetics of pop in the '70s and beyond.

You're No Good   Linda Ronstadt

(Clint Ballard Jr) ❋ Capitol ❋ 1974 ❋ Appears on: *Heart Like a Wheel*

Linda Ronstadt's voice became so ubiquitous in the '70s and '80s that we took it for granted, and then suddenly it was gone from the airwaves. Ronstadt, although she had her fair share of time in the tabloids (celebrity boyfriends, cocaine binges), never aimed to be that kind of a star. She was dedicated to the craft and little else. Her records in the late '70s were so associated with the slick, corporate California sound that it was easy to forget just how expressive a singer she was. In retrospect it appears that Ronstadt was, more than anyone, responsible for the careers of the Troubadour generation – the Eagles, Jackson Browne, Lowell George and the others who hung around that Los Angeles club. Ronstadt's 1974 album *Heart Like a Wheel* combined the Eagles and the Burrito Brothers in a kind of passing of the torch ceremony.

Heart Like a Wheel defined Ronstadt's platinum style. Peter Asher provided sympathetic, precise and unobtrusive backing to Ronstadt's reading of country, pop and rock songs. Her blend of these styles was so effortless that it's easy to forget how particular it is.

'You're No Good' was recorded by Betty Everett in 1963 but failed to make the Top 40. The following year she had her one hit with 'The Shoop Shoop Song'. Ronstadt took the R&B pop song and inflected it with a country twang without losing its visceral, soulful quality. Her singing is full of disdain and hurt, ameliorated by the magnificent backing vocals that act like a support group. Not surprisingly, the song shot straight to the top of the charts and accelerated the deluge coming down Laurel Canyon.

Ooby Dooby   Roy Orbison

(Wade Moore/Roy Orbison/Dick Penner) ❋ Sun ❋ 1956 ❋ Appears on: *At the Rockhouse*

Roy Orbison was pretty happy with country music until Elvis Presley and Jerry Lee Lewis visited East Texas. Orbison had himself a little band and a show on the local TV station in the town of Odessa.

"After Presley came through town for a show in late 1954 I began to notice the rhythm music," said Orbison. "I had heard groups like the Clovers and their hits like 'One Mint Julep', all based on seventh chords. I really didn't like them. But at a New Year's dance in 1954 we had to play through the actual time of midnight and when someone requested 'Shake, Rattle and Roll' we struck up on it, but we had nearly ten minutes to go to the hour so we kept playing the same song. By the time we were finished, I was fully converted. We just got ourselves a drummer."

Two Odessa local kids, Wade Moore and Dick Penner, knocked up a rockabilly track called 'Ooby Dooby', which they gave to Roy Orbison. He cut it at his first recording session in Clovis, New Mexico, and it was still in the set when Orbison made it to Memphis and Sun studios.

Sam Phillips, who ran Sun and currently had Carl Perkins and Johnny Cash in his care, liked the rockabilly edge in Roy Orbison's sound. In March 1956, Phillips recut Roy Orbison doing 'Ooby Dooby' and the song was a massive national hit.

"My aim at Sun Records was always to look for what was different in a singer or a player, and what I found in Roy Orbison was that he was a superlative and very stylised lead guitar player," said Phillips. "I felt that he had the potential to be one of the really great rockers. I really did. I thought that was his main instinct, even though he had a voice that was somewhat different and undoubtedly did also lend itself to the ballads that he later became famous for.

"I don't think people generally know how good a guitar player Roy was. He used a lot of the bass strings. He would do a lot of combination string stuff, but it was all pushing real good. It was strong. Also, Roy had probably the best ear for a beat of anybody I recorded outside of Jerry Lee Lewis. Roy would take his guitar by himself and if we had a session going he would come in early and pick an awful lot just warming up and getting his fingers working. His timing would amaze me, with him playing lead and filling in with some rhythm licks. I would kid him about it. I said 'Roy, what you're trying to do is to get rid of everybody else and do it all yourself.'"

The Outdoor Type Smudge

(Tom Morgan) ❋ Half a Cow ❋ 1997 ❋ Appears on: *Mo' Poontang*

This song, made famous by Evan Dando and the Lemonheads, was originally intended for songwriter Tom Morgan's trio, Smudge. Possibly the slackest band in the history of rock, Smudge had a certain magic. There is, in the unfinished quality of their records, room for the divine to shine. Smudge and the songs of Tom Morgan are one of Australia's best-kept secrets. For ten years Morgan has been popping out gems that are literate and funny and true – but also rarely heard.

'The Outdoor Type' was written by Morgan, who is decidedly the indoor type. On the one hand it's a funny story with nice asides about the virtues of first-run TV versus mountain biking. The song works, though, like the best of Cole Porter and the great Tin Pan Alley songsmiths, by having an emotional truth just under the surface. Here there is the eternal dilemma of honesty in a relationship, drawn neatly and with considerable wit.

Blister in the Sun Violent Femmes

(Gordon Gano) ❋ Slash ❋ 1983 ❋ Appears on: *Violent Femmes*

One of the great adolescent anthems is powered by one of the great bass riffs, which runs around the exploding, brushed drums and Gordon Gano's geeky whine about being on drugs and having sex. 'Blister in the Sun' has punk energy with a more direct rock edge. The group were discovered busking on the streets in Milwaukee by Pretenders' guitarist James Honeyman-Scott, who put them on the bill that same night.

A record deal with the hip Slash label followed swiftly and the Femmes were soon cutting their debut album with producer Mark Van Hecke. "He coaxed us into doing good live performances in the studio," said drummer Victor DeLorenzo. "Sometimes we'd end up doing a song about twenty times. If Brian [Ritchie] didn't feel particularly good about a bass part for some reason, we'd do the whole song over; we wouldn't overdub the bass part. It was a very meticulous production in that it succeeded in capturing our spontaneity. We left some mistakes on it – a track that's perfect can often be lifeless."

The Femmes with their acoustic bass and washtub drums were outside any particular genre but were eagerly adopted by American college radio. Their energetic live shows spread the word in Europe and Australia, where they were quickly one of the most popular live attractions of the era.

'Blister in the Sun' has become an adolescent anthem as perennial as 'My Generation' and is used in twenty-somethings' sitcoms and car advertisements. In 1994 'Blister in the Sun' was voted number one song of all time by listeners to KROQ in Los Angeles.

Tusk Fleetwood Mac

(Lindsey Buckingham) ❋ Reprise ❋ 1979 ❋ Appears on: *Tusk*

Fleetwood Mac was stunned by it all in 1978. They were the biggest group in the world. Rich beyond their dreams. On expensive drugs. Thinking, "what do you do now?" Lindsey Buckingham – songwriter, singer, guitarist and producer – was the craziest of them all. He wanted to turn into Brian Wilson. Fleetwood Mac would record their songs and Buckingham would take them away and do whatever was necessary to make them little symphonies.

"He was a maniac," said engineer Ken Caillat. "The first day, I set the studio up as usual. Then he said, 'Turn every knob 180 degrees from where it is now and see what happens.' He'd tape microphones to the studio floor and get into a sort of push-up position to sing. Early on, he came in and he'd freaked out in the shower and cut off all his hair with nail scissors. He was stressed. And into sound destruction."

"*Tusk*, from my point of view, was an attempt to derail the machine that kicked in after *Rumours*," said Buckingham. He was dealing with his inner turmoil; his pop obsessions and the New Wave and punk groups coming through threatened to make Fleetwood Mac artistically obsolete.

The *Tusk* album is a large sprawling pop edifice that has been appreciated more as time has caught up with it. The title track, a euphemism, was the album's crowning glory.

'Tusk' was a riff worked up by Mick Fleetwood and Buckingham at sound checks. Producer Richard Dashut turned it into a twenty-second tape loop as the basis of the song. The riff was then recorded with 112 members of the University of Southern California Marching Band in Dodger Stadium. With the rhythm as the core of the song it only remained to embellish the track with snatches of melody and vocal.

One of the great singles of the '70s, 'Tusk' did throw the Mac audience a curve ball and delight pop connoisseurs. It also probably saved Fleetwood Mac from irrelevance.

"My thought was, let's subvert the norm," said Buckingham.

Rikki Don't Lose That Number Steely Dan

(Walter Becker/Donald Fagen) ✳ ABC ✳ 1974 ✳ Appears on: *Pretzel Logic*

"By the time we were ready to start work on our third album, we were no longer the enthusiastic amateurs of the *Can't Buy a Thrill* period, champing at the bit to have our first real chance to get in the studio and record an album of our songs," wrote Steely Dan's Walter Becker and Donald Fagen. "Nor were we the shell-shocked road warriors of the *Countdown to Ecstasy* period, leading our little troop through the jazz-rock underbrush. Rather, we had settled into a comfortable writing and working groove, which was based on a calculated reversion to our pre-West Coast schizotypal tendencies and tastes. As it turned out, the sunny clime and prefab cookie-cutter robo-culture in which we now found ourselves only served to heighten our paranoia and alienation. We had our songs, some nice axes, good girlfriends, brand new drivers' licenses, lots of twenty-four-track studio time, and a warm place to compose."

Steely Dan occupies its own oddball corner of the pop world. They see themselves more in a jazz tradition than a pop one and their music is witty and antiseptic, intellectual rather than visceral.

Given all that, Steely Dan turned out hot singles through the '70s and none better than 'Rikki Don't Lose That Number'.

The bass line is taken from Horace Silver's 'Song For My Father' and drummer Jim Gordon powers the track along with a muscular but unobtrusive drum pattern. The melody is playful and joyous, perhaps despite Becker and Fagen's intentions.

The Rikki is a girl whom Fagen had an adolescent crush on while at college. The song is not about drugs or Eric Clapton or any number of pothead rumours that have circulated in the past thirty years.

This Guy's in Love with You Herb Alpert

(Burt Bacharach/Hal David) ✳ A&M ✳ 1968 ✳

Appears on: *The Look Of Love: The Burt Bacharach Collection*

Herb Alpert wasn't even a singer. Best known as the trumpet-playing leader of the Tijuana Brass and as half of A&M Records, Alpert picked this song as a piece for a TV special and suddenly the record was number one. Albert's warm – if limited – vocal is magnificently suited to the elegance of the tune. The song oozes charm and the sophistication of the songwriting team of Burt Bacharach and Hal David.

Their partnership was forged in the Brill Building in New York where they were staff writers for Famous Music. Bacharach and David maintained the Brill Building discipline even after the Beatles had swept that tradition away.

"We used to meet every day at Famous Music in New York," said Hal David, recalling the early days of their partnership. "I'd come in with some titles and some ideas for songs, lines. Burt would come in with opening strains of phrases or what might be part of a chorus section. It was like show and tell: I'd show him what I had thought of and he'd show me what he had thought of. And whatever seemed to spark the other would be the start of whatever song we started to write that day. I'd write four lines or sing lines of a lyric and he'd have a melody and, very often, we'd sit in the room and write the song together, sort of pound it out. I'd be writing lyrics and he'd be writing music and, all of a sudden, we'd have the structure of a song, which we'd keep working on. We didn't write songs so quickly that they were done overnight or that day. I'd take home his melody and he'd take home my lyrics and so, very often, we'd be working on three different songs at one time."

'This Guy's in Love with You' has been covered many times, notably by Dionne Warwick and interestingly by the Reels, whose electro pop version was way ahead of its time.

Once in a Lifetime Talking Heads

(David Byrne/Brian Eno/Chris Frantz/Jerry Harrison/Tina Weymouth) ✳ Sire ✳ 1980 ✳

Appears on: *Remain in Light*

Remain in Light was part of Talking Heads' African period. Head chief David Byrne and producer Brian Eno had already made an album of found sounds and African rhythms. The band's fourth album expanded on that, putting enormous weight on the polyrhythms while getting more esoteric in the lyric.

They were also listening to a lot of funk and to the just then breaking rap and hip-hop scene. Three years earlier they had been a preppy garage art rock band playing CBGB. By the time of *Remain in Light* they were ready to turn into a funk machine.

On 'Once in a Lifetime' Byrne piles on all his obsessions. The words were taken in part from an evangelist radio broadcast. The polyrhythms that underscored the track were based on African drumming and the character who sings the song is a white-bread suburban guy trapped in a metaphysical dream about his own life, as though he had been transported from Ghana to Connecticut.

"We weren't trying to do African music," said Byrne. "We were trying to use some of the things we thought we'd learn from that in making a newer version of our own music. I don't think it's like putting on a new set of clothes and 'here we are, it's all new'. It's saying, 'This might be a clearer version of what we've been trying to do anyway' – or a more refined version."

(Looking for) The Heart of Saturday Night Tom Waits

(Tom Waits) ❊ Asylum ❊ 1974 ❊ Appears on: *The Heart of Saturday Night*

The title track of Tom Waits' second album is a powerful piece of Americana. Waits wanted to be a beatnik. He had read up on the Beat Generation and his verse style was clearly based on that tradition – melancholy, nostalgic, working class, celebrating the essential virtues of American mass culture (e.g. the car).

Waits' blue-collar beatnik was out of step with most American singer/songwriters in 1973. Indeed, the only other practitioner of this kind of lyric was Bruce Springsteen. Waits' voice is appropriately described as having escaped from Alcatraz, and this song goes right to the heart of loneliness.

"It's a new song," he said by way of introducing the piece on a radio show back in 1973. "I'm anxious to play it. It's kind of about driving down Hollywood Boulevard on Saturday night. Bob Webb and I were kicking this around one afternoon, Saturday afternoon. It was, the idea of looking for the heart of Saturday night, hadn't really worked on any tune about it yet, we're both real Jack Kerouac fans and this is kind of a tribute to Kerouacians I guess".

The Last Time I Saw Richard Joni Mitchell

(Joni Mitchell) ✳ Reprise ✳ 1971 ✳ Appears on: *Blue*

The closing track of the harrowing journey that is the *Blue* album is kind of uplifting. 'The Last Time I Saw Richard' is a song about Chuck Mitchell, Joni's first husband. They were a folksinging duo who met in 1965 and married the following year. According to the *Detroit News*, which reported their union: "Chuck said, 'Joni and I have developed our act. We are not just folk singers now. We do comedy, sing some ragtime and do folk rock. We're ready for the big clubs.' Joni nodded her approval, as any dutiful wife would do."

By the following year they had split and Joni had moved to New York while Chuck remained singing folk and telling jokes in Detroit. Judging by Mitchell's note of their last meeting it seems that things hadn't worked out too well for her former partner. His love had turned to poison, his romance for life had turned to cynicism. He inhabited a dark bar drinking undistinguished cocktails while playing sappy love songs on the jukebox. Chuck had sold himself out for a dishwasher and a coffee percolator. He had run from love and life.

'The Last Time I Saw Richard' comes at the end of Mitchell's *Blue* journey and part of its power (and the album's) is that whatever she has been through, she's not prepared to stay in the dark café.

Mitchell has moved on from folk music too. The rhymes in the song are sprung brilliantly. The vocal melody dances around phrases like "he put a coin in the Wurlitzer/and the thing began to whirl". The backing is simple but the melody is delightful.

"My chords," she said. "Nobody in the coffeehouses ever played chords like those. And they're not jazz chords either. Harmonically speaking, I'm in my own kind of world."

Bo Mambo Yma Sumac

(Moises Vivanco) ✳ Capitol ✳ 1954 ✳ Appears on: *Mambo*

The '50s were a great time for exotica. The Third World held strange treasures and ancient wonders (and wasn't just a threat to tourism). Lobsang Rampa introduced Tibet to the west and at much the same time Yma Sumac brought the music of the

Andes. While there is some scepticism about her past, Yma Sumac claimed her full name to be Zoila Augusta Emperatriz Chavarri del Castillo, and to hail from Ichocán, Peru, a town high in the Andes. She claimed to be an Incan princess, directly descended from Atahualpa, the last Emperor of Peru. Sumac sang on Peruvian radio in the '40s and in 1950, accompanied by her husband and musical director Moises Vivanco, moved to New York.

Whatever her heritage, Sumac possessed a four-and-a-half octave range ("Her voice is that of birds and of the earthquake," as one writer put it). She and Vivanco picked up on the exotica craze that was sweeping America and made a number of records, many of which were related to the dance craze, the mambo. She was also associated with sun worship – a very sexy connotation in the early '50s – and with primitive folk music.

Yma was much in demand for TV appearances and concerts and she had a brief career in Hollywood. Her final appearance was on Hal Willner's Disney project *Stay Awake*.

Djed Tortoise

(Tortoise) ✳ Thrill Jockey ✳ 1996 ✳ Appears on: *Millions Now Living Will Never Die*

"Definitely when Tortoise started there were simple rules, like 'There's not going to be a guitarist'," said Dan Bitney of the Chicago ensemble. Although they came out of the alternative rock movement, Tortoise are a jazz band. "At that point grunge rock was being sold to everyone. Everybody in the group had always played in bands where the focus was on the guitarist. Tortoise was something different. There's no marketing plan. In punk rock there was a handful of innovators out of the whole thing who stole different styles from other people and cross-pollinated them. We're trying to do that too."

Tortoise is a noodling ambient trip – a combination of techno, beats-based musicianship, dub, dance hall reggae, Kraut rock and soundtrack-jazz, an instrumental genre that for better or worse attracted the name post-rock. Tortoise defined the genre and is its best exponent. Their epic 'Djed' clocks in at almost twenty-one minutes and exposes the full range of diversity from experimental electronica, touching on Jamaican dub and German Kraut rock and yet managing for all that to create a beautiful and haunting soundscape.

A Man Needs a Maid Neil Young

(Neil Young) ✳ Reprise ✳ 1972 ✳ Appears on: *Harvest*

'A Man Needs a Maid' is a spare acoustic ballad over which the London Symphony Orchestra is placed, with massive lush crescendos and soaring emotive riffs. Then there's the lyric – one of Young's more controversial at the time. It documents the break-up of his first marriage and the beginning of his second, to actress Carrie Snodgrass. She was then a rising star in independent films, including *Diary of a Mad Housewife*, which Young saw and as a consequence tracked her down. Eventually Snodgrass became his wife and mother to his children.

   In this song Young fantasises about a life as a bachelor whose need for female company could be satisfied by a maid who would cook and keep his house clean. Given that the women's movement had only recently started, this lyric was a red rag. On his anthology *Decade* he acknowledged that many people were upset about the song but noted that Bob Dylan had liked the lyrics and he said, "If it's good enough for Bob then it's good enough for me." Dylan was right.

Uptight (Everything's Alright) Stevie Wonder

(Henry Cosby/Sylvia Moy/Stevie Wonder) ✳ Motown ✳ 1965 ✳
Appears on: *Hitsville US*

At the tender age of fifteen it looked like Stevie Wonder was washed up. The child star's voice had broken and his recent records hadn't cracked the Top 20. It was time for Little Stevie Wonder to grow up. He came up with a hook and his producer Clarence Paul brought in Motown writers Sylvia Moy and Henry Cosby to write a song. Wonder earned his first songwriting credit on the track. His other input came from suggesting a more aggressive push in the rhythm department. He had been touring with the Rolling Stones and was impressed with the jazzy propulsion coming from Charlie Watts' drum kit. Consequently 'Uptight' positively bounces out of the blocks. It's way the most interesting thing that Wonder had done to this point and its tempo and changes were getting towards the blues – much tougher than the usual Motown sound. 'Uptight' put Stevie Wonder at the top of the R&B charts and assured his place in Hitsville.

Anarchy in the UK The Sex Pistols

(Steve Jones, Paul Cook, Johnny Rotten, Glen Matlock) ❋ EMI ❋ 1976 ❋

Appears on: *Never Mind the Bollocks*

Few records have had the impact of the Sex Pistols' debut 45. The London punk rock quartet signed to EMI records for a record advance of £40,000 on the basis of the buzz generated by the group's live shows and by the groundswell that was clearly building in the London music scene for snotty, amateurish rock bands.

With the encouragement of manager Malcolm McLaren, the musicians' natural bad behaviour was turned into a sociopathic political statement, best exemplified by their tune 'Anarchy in the UK'.

Image to the contrary, the Pistols were very serious about music. Guitarist Steve Jones rehearsed obsessively and bass player Glen Matlock, who wrote the bulk of the tunes, was also dedicated to his instrument.

"'Anarchy in the UK' was several of his tunes put together," Rotten told journalist Caroline Coon at the time. "I came in a bit late and they'd already put the basic melody and I just said 'I'll call it "Anarchy!'" The rest of the words came quite easily."

"We're more anti-social, than political," said Matlock.

The Sex Pistols' agenda was inchoate, to say the least. It was a general call to rebellion that falls apart at the slightest scrutiny. The real rebel yell came from Jones' guitars: a mass wall of sound based on the most simple, retro guitar riffs. Essentially, the Sex Pistols reinforced what the garage bands of the '60s had demonstrated – you don't need technique to make rock & roll. In a time when music had been increasingly complicated and defanged, the Sex Pistols' generational shift caused a real revolution.

The first attempt at recording had been poor. Then Chris Thomas was brought in as producer and he layered up the band's sound with take after take of the riff. The sheer size of the sound was breathtaking.

A month after release the record hit number twelve on the British charts. The group agreed to a TV interview, but somewhat drunk they were cajoled into swearing on TV and their performance caused an outrage. The Sex Pistols were front-page news. EMI workers refused to handle the stock and a month later EMI terminated their contract.

The bull was out of the gate, however. The Sex Pistols were no longer a band but a cultural phenomenon.

"If the single ['Anarchy in the UK'] gets into the charts then it will show that it's been worth it," Rotten told Caroline Coon. "That there are thousands of people who are pissed off with everything. And I really think they are. I can't see how they can put up with it. People say we're not the alternative. But we never said we were. We're just one alternative. There should be several."

Hey Bulldog The Beatles

(John Lennon/Paul McCartney) ✳ Apple ✳ 1969 ✳ Appears on: *Yellow Submarine*

Written and recorded in one day, 'Hey Bulldog' is an oft-neglected Beatle classic. The Beatles were short one of the four songs they were obliged to deliver to United Artists for the animated film *Yellow Submarine*. While filming a clip for 'Lady Madonna', McCartney suggested they cut a track and Lennon proffered this one. It's the group at their least self-conscious and Lennon at his least pretentious. The lyric, while not specific, is more acute than the word salads he came up with around this period. The performance, though, is top notch, including a rare lead solo from Lennon. There is no bulldog mentioned in the song. The title comes from impromptu barking by McCartney as the song fades.

Bust a Move Young MC

(Matt Dike/Michael Ross/Marvin Young) ✳ Delicious Vinyl ✳ 1989 ✳
Appears on: *Stone Cold Rhymin'*

Young MC (aka Marvin Young) was a promising hip-hop writer/performer who became known for this humorous, sexy invitation to shake one's booty. One of the great dance singles of the '80s, it may not have been heavy but it did spread the hip-hop gospel onto the pop charts.

Young was of Jamaican descent and had an eye on a straight career in business when he got sidetracked into performing and writing. "I listen to really deep, intense dancehall reggae, and I must admit that I get a lot of my style from it, 'cause

I like it. I was actually rapping very early, before I listened to reggae, but when I heard how fast and clear the toasters were toasting, I knew I had to emulate them, and start writing my lyrics that way."

Quincy Jones signed on to produce Young MC's debut album, which was a massive hit. Unfortunately his subsequent work failed to live up to the promise of the first light-hearted and funky joint.

"I'm starting a production company and a publishing company, and hopefully later a record company. My knowledge of data processing helps me with all the complicated instruments and studio equipment, and my knowledge of economics will help with the accounting," he said. But it didn't help his rhythm thing at all. It doesn't matter, 'Bust a Move' is still perfect.

Shivers The Boys Next Door

(Rowland Howard) ❋ White ❋ 1980 ❋ Appears on: *Door Door*

The Boys Next Door were pimply schoolboys high on art rock in the late '70s. With the nascent talents of Nick Cave and Mick Harvey still very wet behind the ears, it was apparent early on that something was happening here. Mostly it was Cave's ability to find the limit and push everything to it. As time went on the envelope just got bigger. The Boys Next Door were swept up in a quick frenzy by White Records and put into the studio with Greg Macainsh, who had been an enfant terrible only eight years before but was now a grumpy old man. With engineer Tony Cohen, the Boys Next Door and Greg Macainsh tried to find common ground. Halfway through the making of the record Rowland Howard, guitarist for the Young Charlatans, joined and brought some of his songs.

'Shivers' was a haunting ballad, a teenage mediation on narcissism, vanity, cruelty and beauty that was built around Howard's guitar figure – a style that had evolved from Robert Fripp.

'Shivers' was a powerful piece of songwriting. Majestic, sad pop music. Naturally and rightly, the Boys Next Door repudiated the song almost immediately and moved on to harsher ground. Despite their best endeavours to bury the track, it has become a classic.

What is Truth? Johnny Cash

(Johnny Cash) ❋ Columbia ❋ 1970 ❋ Appears on: *The Essential Johnny Cash 1955–1983*

The Vietnam War and permissive society polarised the United States. The Union was again divided across the Mason–Dixon line. By and large the country Establishment aligned itself with Richard Nixon and his Silent Majority. The rest of the music business challenged the values and the authority of the Establishment.

Johnny Cash was somewhere in between. His song 'What is Truth?' starts out wondering why the music is so different. Over subsequent verses Cash questions the war effort and the judicial system and the suspicion of the younger generation. It's an update and an improvement on his friend's 'The Times They Are A-Changin''.

Cash recalled that the song had its genesis backstage while watching Kenny Rogers and the First Edition.

"Merle [Haggard] made a – it wasn't a derogatory comment – he made a complimentary comment," Cash recalled. "He said, 'Boy, the young people are really coming up with some unusual chord changes in their songs these days.' He said, 'We didn't go from so and so to so and so back when I was learning to play the guitar.' He said, 'It was kinda hard to get used to.' And I said, 'They're terrific. I really like it.'

"So then about that same time, that same night, the producer of my show asked me if I would write a song especially for a campus special we were going to do, which I believe was one of my last network shows. It was near the last *Johnny Cash On Campus*. We had all the Vanderbilt University of Nashville in the Ryman Auditorium the night we taped, so I said, 'Well, I'll write a special song for the college' and so I wrote 'What is Truth?'. And I started off with Merle Travis' 'kids sure play funny music these days'."

Teenage Riot Sonic Youth

(Sonic Youth) ❋ Blast First/Enigma ❋ 1988 ❋ Appears on: *Daydream Nation*

Sonic Youth were the godparents of alternative rock. They started out in the No Wave New York scene of the early '80s playing art music with guitars. Guitarists Thurston Moore and Lee Ranaldo were members of Glenn Branca's guitar orchestra. By the time they began recording as Sonic Youth in 1982 their path was clear – they were deconstructing rock & roll and creating noise soundscapes while simultaneously loving classic rock & roll.

"We've always been called art-rock, in the most derogatory way, meaning dilettante, which was one reason we always toured, to show we were a real band," said bassist Kim Gordon. "That always guided us, trying to put weird music in a rock context, but I don't think we care any more, especially since we can see where the whole alternative scene is going, into the mainstream, which is really uninteresting. For us, it's more of a lifestyle thing, like a jazz or blues musician."

In 1988 Sonic Youth cut the double album *Daydream Nation*. On 'Teenage Riot' the massed guitars of Moore and Renaldo are yoked into a soundscape that bristles with hooks. The seven-minute epic was inspired as a tribute to Dinosaur Jr's J Mascis. The group stated on its website that the song had a working title of 'Rock & Roll for President', supposedly written about a fantasy world where J Mascis is president. Suddenly, though, the immense power of the underground sounded palpable. There was a sense that there was a new mood about to break. It was one of the true landmark songs of its era.

"We're the young white hope, or something, for young white urban/suburban/rural middle-class disaffected youth. Which is kind of funny," said Moore at the time. "They're promoting us as such. Like, for the entire fringe element of America, here's your band?"

Working Class Hero John Lennon

(John Lennon) ✲ Apple ✲ 1970 ✲ Appears on: *John Lennon/Plastic Ono Band*

John Lennon wasn't a working-class hero. He was a lower-middle-class hero but that doesn't have the same ring to it. This, one of the centrepieces of his first solo album, is a spare and dark and blunt song that attempts to erase his past.

Lennon's album was all about settling scores with himself.

He wanted to turn away from the super pop sound of the Beatles and find something more elemental. To this end, Lennon had only Klaus Voorman on bass, Ringo Starr on drums and Billy Preston on occasional keyboards through the whole album.

According to Voorman, "Just the fact that he asked Ringo and myself to play on the album meant to me that he wanted it to be a real close, intimate atmosphere. He did not say much about what we played.

"The playing itself, to him, was not important. It was more important to capture the feeling. We did mostly one or two takes. There's a lot of mistakes on there and timing changes, but it was exactly like a pulse, exactly what John wanted. He loved it."

'Working Class Hero' is both an attack on the class system in general and on capitalism. It's also a piece of self-loathing as Lennon vents his ambivalence at the experience of the Beatles.

"One has to completely humiliate oneself to be what the Beatles were," Lennon said at the time. "And I resent it."

Do You Know the Way to San Jose? Dionne Warwick

(Burt Bacharach/Hal David) ✳ Scepter ✳ 1968 ✳ Appears on: *Valley of the Dolls*

"When I was doing those songs with Dionne [Warwick], I was thinking in terms of miniature movies, you know?" said Burt Bacharach. "Three and a half minute movies with peak moments and not just one intensity level the whole way through. I never liked it where there's only one intensity from the singer, from the musical content, from the tracks and orchestration – it tends to beat you up."

Amongst Hal David's many gifts as a lyricist was his ability to tell a complete story. 'Do You Know the Way to San Jose?' is a precise, poignant story of a girl who is seduced by the bright lights of Hollywood. She finds that Hollywood Boulevard is crowded with girls just like her and that she will not be one of the chosen few. Armed with this self-knowledge she returns to her small-town life. It all happens in two verses.

"Sometimes I'd write against the mood," said David. "For instance, 'Do You Know the Way to San Jose?' is bright and rhythmic, and because of that you'd think it was instinctively happy. But it wasn't to me.

"I do labour over these things. I spend inordinate amounts of time deciding whether 'and' or 'but' is the right word. To a certain extent, lyrics flow easily, but no matter how much they flow at a given time, by the time you get it together, finished and refined to the best of your ability, it's a lot of work."

Go Your Own Way   Fleetwood Mac

(Lindsey Buckingham) ✳ Warner Bros. ✳ 1977 ✳ Appears on: *Rumours*

Much has been written about the circumstances of recording Fleetwood Mac's *Rumours* album. The relationships in the group were all irrevocably breaking down. They were taking too much cocaine. They were not talking. Yet at the end of the day they made a pop album that sold more than thirty million copies. At the end of the day, though, it wasn't the soap opera that made *Rumours* a masterpiece, it was guitarist Lindsey Buckingham's production.

"The only two instruments that were actually played together on that album was the guitar solo and drum track on 'The Chain'," said co-producer Richard Dashpot. "It wasn't necessary or even expedient for them all to be in the studio at once. Virtually every track is either an overdub, or lifted from a separate take of that particular song. What you hear is the best pieces assembled, a true aural collage. Lindsey and I did most of the production. That's not to take anything away from Ken or the others in the band – they were all involved. But Lindsey and myself really produced that record and he should've gotten the individual credit for it, instead of the whole band.

"I'd worked with Lindsey Buckingham and Stevie Nicks since their debut album, *Buckingham Nicks*. After they joined Fleetwood Mac, Lindsey invited me to do their live sound. They started recording *Rumours* in Sausalito, across the bay from San Francisco, with the Record Plant's engineer, but they fired him after four days for being too into astrology. I was really just around keeping Lindsey company, then Mick takes me into the parking lot, puts his arm around my shoulder and says, 'Guess what? You're producing the album.' The funny thing was, I never really wanted to be a producer. I brought in a friend from Wally Heider's studio in Los Angeles, Ken Caillat, to help me, and we started co-producing. Mick gave me and Ken an old Chinese I-Ching coin and said, 'Good luck'."

Best of all is Buckingham's farewell to Nicks: 'Go Your Own Way'. His vocal is impassioned and urgent and his wall of guitars is worthy of Brian Wilson. Mostly though, the song rests on Mick Fleetwood's drumming, which runs heavy on the tom toms with a galloping tempo that sparks the entire group while holding it together.

"'Go Your Own Way''s rhythm was a tom-tom structure that Lindsey demoed by hitting Kleenex boxes or something," Fleetwood said. "I never quite got to grips with what he wanted, so the end result was a mutated interpretation. It became a major part of the song, a completely back-to-front approach that came, I'm ashamed to say, from capitalising on my own ineptness."

I Am Trying to Break Your Heart Wilco

(Jeff Tweedy) ✳ Nonesuch ✳ 2002 ✳ Appears on: *Yankee Hotel Foxtrot*

The band Wilco is pretty much Jeff Tweedy, especially on this album. It was recorded amid internal conflicts and a hostile relationship with their label Reprise – resulting in the label refusing to release the album and it eventually finding a home at Nonesuch. Tweedy is a singer/songwriter who grew up steeped in Americana. He has taken the roots of American music – country and rock and blues – and fashioned something entirely his own. There's a freshness and ease to Wilco's music that works in contrast to Tweedy's often complex and allusive lyrics.

This album – produced by Jim O'Rourke – and its lead track have all those traditional elements but also a sense of wilfully being provocative with sounds and harmonies.

"I don't feel like I've ever really known exactly what a song was supposed to sound like," said Tweedy. "Originally, I really embraced that naïveté in a lot of ways ... not knowing anything about it technically and walking into the studio like I imagine Howling Wolf would and not having any fucking idea what it was going to be and being excited by what we sound like. At some point that stopped being as exciting, and it seemed like the only place to go to start being excited again was to experiment with a different type of performance. After that, the studio started to be looked at as a very different place to perform, with a lot of different equipment to use – and the easiest way to be excited again."

With 'I Am Trying to Break Your Heart' you have a place where singer/songwriter rock & roll starts to be exciting again.

All or Nothing at All Frank Sinatra

(Arthur Altman/Jack Lawrence) ❋ Columbia ❋ 1944 ❋
Appears on: *Sinatra in Hollywood 1940–1964*

This song had three covers in 1939, none of them a hit. The Harry James Orchestra cut a version that prominently featured their vocalist, Frank Sinatra. Even without a hit, Sinatra's career soon took off.

He signed to Columbia as a solo artist and in the '40s became a superstar, the most popular singer of his generation. Then in 1943, the American Federation of Musicians went on strike. Columbia, with no product, was desperate and they turned to this earlier recording which was effectively a Sinatra solo, and they re-pressed the disc substituting Frank Sinatra's name for the Harry James Orchestra.

According to lyricist Jack Lawrence, Sinatra told columnist Louella Parsons that it was this record that gave him his start.

"The manager out of the old Victor Hugo Café on the Sunset Strip in Hollywood came up and waved his hands for us to stop," said Sinatra of one of his original performances with the orchestra. "He said Harry's trumpet playing was too loud for the joint and my singing was just plain lousy. He said the two of us couldn't draw flies as an attraction – and I guess he was right. The room was as empty as a barn.

"It's a funny thing about that song. The recording we made of it five years ago is now in one of the top spots among the bestsellers. But it's the same old recording. It's also the song I used to audition for Tommy Dorsey, who signed me on the strength of it. And now it's my first big record."

The song has subsequently been recorded by Sarah Vaughan, Ella Fitzgerald, Perry Como, John Coltrane, George Shearing, Count Basie, Chet Baker, Diana Krall and Little Anthony and the Imperials.

Cry Baby Janis Joplin

(Jerry Ragavoy/Bert Berns) ❋ Columbia ❋ 1971 ❋ Appears on: *Pearl*

If Joplin's life was dogged by drugs and romantic disasters, her recording career was blighted by the wrong combinations of producers and musicians. Her third

attempt, the Full Tilt Boogie Band, was a combination of players professional enough to stay in tune and sensible enough to stay out of her way. Joplin was growing as well. The raw blues of her early hits was unsustainable over the long haul; also, public tastes changed and Joplin's recognition as an artist grew. In 1969 she reconnected with producer Paul Rothchild who was sympathetic to Joplin's needs in terms of recording and material.

The combination of Joplin, her new band and Rothchild worked on an album in Los Angeles – they were almost finished when she died from a heroin overdose in October 1970.

The album, which was posthumously released as *Pearl*, showed another, happier side to Joplin. It took some courage given that she feared, as she said to David Dalton, "Maybe my audience can enjoy my music more if they think I'm destroying myself."

With *Pearl*, she transcended that. *Pearl* is pure pop soul. Joplin sings 'Cry Baby' as a confident woman, no longer the victim of her demons. She is in control of her instrument – commanding the band and trusting in their support. 'Cry Baby' is the end of a long and difficult journey.

Waterloo Sunset The Kinks

(Ray Davies) ❊ Pye ❊ 1967 ❊ Appears on: *Something Else by the Kinks*

There is a transcendent quality to the Kinks single 'Waterloo Sunset'. The life of London, the taxis, the underground, people going places. Two lovers, Terry and Julie, are in the midst of them, in the great river of life, and it all means nothing and everything. 'Waterloo Sunset' is the best British pop single of the '60s. Right here you have the collision of the 'kitchen sink' drama that dominated British theatre, the folk and blues styling of Bob Dylan and Chuck Berry, and the dry, wry dispassion of Ray Davies himself.

"I never knowingly sat down and said I'm going to write kitchen-sink music," Davies said. "I just wrote about normal, everyday people, their hopes and fears."

The lovers of the song, he has said, were originally called Bernard and Dorothy, but were changed to Terry and Julie after Terence Stamp and Julie Christie who had recently starred in *Far from the Madding Crowd*. Davis has also said that the song was written about his nephew Terry who lived in Australia.

'Waterloo Sunset' shows a touch of British music hall in its lilting progress. The melody glistens with Davies' observations and it has a languid quality that also suits the lyric.

"When people go on about the song – I loved the song the first time I played it and finished it. But no-one else in the world knows that," Davies told *Uncut*. "I knew what I had. So I took my time doing it. If you isolate the elements, the voice is a bit edgy, there are a few rhymes that are on the verge of, dare I say it, naff. I guess it's the way you tell 'em. It exceeds the sum of its parts. And perhaps it's something else. It triggers people's imagination as well as what they're hearing from the gramophone or radio. It puts people into a world."

Davies achieved perfection in this song. Then he spent the next ten years trying to find it again with a series of rock operas and concept albums about Britishness and suburbia. They were destined to fail. 'Waterloo Sunset', 'Sunny Afternoon' and his other classics are miniatures; small, perfectly formed glimpses of the ineffable. They cannot be made larger.

Like Coleridge's 'Kubla Khan', 'Waterloo Sunset' has a dream-like quality. "It would make me proud to hear Frank Sinatra singing 'Waterloo Sunset'," said Davies. "That song came to me in a dream. I woke up singing it in my sleep."

Dazed and Confused Led Zeppelin

(Jimmy Page) ✳ Atlantic ✳ 1968 ✳ Appears on: *Led Zeppelin*

"Well, I tell you, I took quite a few of the ideas I developed in the Yardbirds with me," Jimmy Page recalled to *MOJO* magazine. "I remember playing the Fillmore with the Yardbirds and on 'Glimpses' I was doing the bowed guitar thing and had tapes panning across the stage on this high-fidelity stereo sampler, and it was quite avant-garde stuff for the time."

Page formed the New Yardbirds to fulfil European tour dates with session bass player John Paul Jones and a singer, Robert Plant, who had been recommended. Plant brought along a drummer, John Bonham. Led Zeppelin grew very quickly from that.

"I knew exactly the style I was after and the sort of musicians I wanted to play with, the sort of powerhouse sound I was really going for," said Page. "I guess it proves that the group was really meant to be, the way it all came together. And I was so lucky to find everybody so instantly, without making massive searches and doing numerous auditions that you hear about to fill the gaps."

Within a matter of weeks of that tour, Page had invested £1750 for thirty-seven hours of studio time and they had their first album in the can.

The upheavals of the '60s reached their zenith in 1968. This was to be felt in music. Page, who had seen the British pop explosion close-up as a session guitarist before his time in the Yardbirds, felt the winds of change. His new group would make albums and not release singles or market themselves as a pop group. This was not music for teens. It was experimental blues and folk music with a lot of volume.

"The first album was really our live act of the time," said John Paul Jones. "It was what we'd been doing on stage up to that point. It didn't take a lot of preparation. We had those Willie Dixon blues things, and 'How Many More Times' and 'Dazed and Confused' had arisen out of the Yardbirds' last days."

Ahmet Ertegun instantly saw the potential of Led Zeppelin, signed them for $200,000, and guaranteed Page complete control.

Page also understood that the underground music scene in America was way ahead of Britain and the group spent most of their time touring there. Right from the first tour supporting Vanilla Fudge, Led Zeppelin was a smash.

Led Zeppelin is widely regarded as the beginning of heavy metal but nothing could be further from the truth. It's a lot more Wagner that Ozzy. Within two years of its release, Zeppelin was arguably the biggest band in the world.

Tomorrow's Tears The Riptides

(Mark Callaghan) ✳ Able ✳ 1979 ✳ Appears on: *Tales of the Australian Underground*

The Riptides came out of the architecture faculty of Brisbane University on the back of the whole punk rock thing. Like the Go-Betweens, the Riptides played the same campus circuit and the soup kitchen café, struggling with the oppressive National Party regime and dreaming of escaping like the Saints.

'Tomorrow's Tears' was the second Riptides 45 and is one of the most accomplished power pop artefacts of the era. The addition of keyboard player and guitarist Andrew Leitch fleshed out the sound and it quite sparkles on this record. The tempo is breakneck and drummer Dennis Cantwell (who also played with the Go-Betweens) is spectacular. This is a track worthy of the best work from Blondie. Callaghan has brought in some ska to spice the power pop sound and the track snaps and crackles with pure enthusiasm.

Mainstream Thea Gilmore

(Thea Gilmore) ✳ Hungry Dog ✳ 2003 ✳ Appears on: *Avalanche*

"People like Kylie are part of the problem," said Thea Gilmore. The twenty-five-year-old is Britain's best new singer/songwriter. The problem she's referring to is the 21st-century emphasis on sexuality over substance in contemporary music. Gilmore is not unattractive, but her songs are things of beauty forever. Sometimes savage beauty.

Although she was born in 1979, the soundtrack to Gilmore's childhood was Bob Dylan, Joni Mitchell, the Beatles and the classic era of rock. At fifteen she was doing work experience at Fairport Convention's studio. It was there she met producer and later boyfriend Nigel Stonier and began writing songs.

At nineteen she had her first album, *Burning Dorothy*, on her own Shameless label. These were startling, bold songs that were embellished by her rich vocals and charged up with anger.

"But I don't write love songs," she told the *Guardian*. "Love is a problem most vicious. It's a dirty, filthy emotion with so much clouding of the issue. With men, love begins with sex and ends with a deep need for an emotional crutch."

Gilmore's songs then have that tough line on relationships, but she is also happy taking on the music business and politics. It all comes straight out her mouth, unfiltered – naïve and sometimes childlike. Gilmore has found her level in the folk community, but her records are far from folk. She has turned down the major labels on the grounds of creative control (i.e. she won't dress in gold hit pants) but has nevertheless built a strong cult following. Her independent stance stops her from reaching a mainstream audience.

Avalanche is her fifth album in four years. It's the most complete musically and has a particular self-assurance. Although she's ostensibly in the folk bin, her warm, deep sense of melody and arrangement owes a great deal to rock & roll and she's really uncategorisable. The lead track 'Mainstream' is like Elvis Costello meets Van Morrison only much, much better.

Biko Peter Gabriel

(Peter Gabriel) ✳ Charisma ✳ 1980 ✳ Appears on: *Peter Gabriel*

Steve Biko was a black South African who was tortured and killed for his anti-apartheid activism. His story provoked Peter Gabriel to pen a song that added to the international pressure on South Africa to end its apartheid policy.

"It's a white, middle-class, ex-public schoolboy, domesticated, English person observing his own reactions from afar," Gabriel said. "It seemed impossible to me that the South Africans had let him be killed when there had been so much international publicity about his imprisonment. He was very intelligent, well reasoned and not full of hate. His writings seemed very solid in a way that polarised politics often doesn't."

The simple potency of the track made it an international hit and helped make Biko a martyr of the anti-apartheid movement and to focus attention on the South African regime. This attention, ignited partly by Gabriel, ran through most of the rest of the decade – leading to films like *Cry Freedom* and *Biko* – until the final release of Nelson Mandela and the fall of the regime.

"I was quite uncertain about getting engaged in a political song," Gabriel said. "I'd never directly taken on an issue in that way. I just tried some ideas, and I felt the spine tingling. That to me is the musician's rubber stamp."

When Love Comes Back to Haunt You

Stephen Cummings

(Stephen Cummings/Colin Talbot) ❋ Truetone ❋ 1989 ❋ Appears on: *A New Kind of Blue*

Stephen Cummings is the maestro of the melancholy. He met his match with Melbourne journalist and novelist Colin Talbot. 'When Love Comes Back to Haunt You' was written for the soundtrack of Talbot's film *Sweethearts* – a tragic romance set by the shores of Port Phillip Bay.

Cummings was aided on this track by long-time collaborator Shane O'Mara, whose guitar work nicely embroiders Cummings' melody. The lyric is simple but set off against a lilting, modal tune. As with the best of Cummings' work, it's always 4 a.m. It's that time before dawn when one can't sleep and there's nothing on the TV. It's a time when regrets and mistakes and lost lovers choose to visit. It's a song that has that air of the perpetual insomniac but there are some truths here when you're too tired for denial.

Folsom Prison Blues   Johnny Cash

(Johnny Cash) ❋ Sun ❋ 1956 ❋ Appears on: *Johnny Cash with his Hot and Blue Guitar*

Few songs have had the impact of this one. Ostensibly a country song with a rockabilly accent, Johnny Cash's second single had the dispassionate emotion of Robert Johnson and the darkness of the Delta bluesmen. "I shot a man in Reno, just to watch him die," is a statement that is still chilling in its starkness. With that level of artistic bravery, Cash stretched himself beyond the bounds of any genre.

The inspiration for the song came while Cash was in the air force, stationed in Germany and watching a film called *The Walls of Folsom Prison*.

On his return to the US he wound up in Memphis, at Sun Studios.

He told Sylvia Simmons shortly before he died, "When Sam Phillips [Sun proprietor and producer] put me in front of that microphone at Sun Studios in 1955 for the first time he said, 'Let's hear what you've got', and I'd sing one or two and he'd say 'Sing another one, let's hear more.' On and on and I would sing for Sam Phillips until I had something he wanted to record – which was 'Folsom Prison

Blues', 'Cry, Cry, Cry' and 'Hey Porter'. Sam didn't boss me around. It was always, 'What do you want to sing now, Cash?'"

Cash brings a gravitas to the session and an unusually poetic eye. Calling on the detail from blues (the train whistle), he paints a clear portrait of a man doomed as a result of his crime. It's a song without self-pity but with the acceptance of his own evil and in that sense the song has touches of gospel and an uncanny sense of spirituality. It was above all a very modern song, prefiguring the rock and poetry explosion that would follow Bob Dylan some eight years hence.

Making Love to a Vampire with a Monkey on My Knee Captain Beefheart & the Magic Band

(Don Van Vliet) ❋ Virgin ❋ 1980 ❋ Appears on: *Doc at the Radar Station*

"God, please fuck my mind for good," sang Captain Beefheart in 'Making Love to a Vampire with a Monkey on My Knee'. Beefheart (aka Don Van Vliet) is a modernist abstract painter who loves the blues. His highly personal style has made him one of the most interesting and influential musicians of the past fifty years. Beefheart is a true primitive who has an exacting sense of what he wants. A rock & roll Thelonious Monk, he hears things that no-one else can and he rearranges things to an internal logic.

Beefheart started out playing straight R&B but gradually became increasingly lateral. He refined the notions of rhythm and melody and the instrumentation in popular song but somehow he retained a connection to the blues that grounded his wild flying ideas.

On *Doc at the Radar Station* he had a refreshed version of the Magic Band and a head full of steam.

According to Beefheart, *Doc* came about because "The people at Virgin Records told me ... that it wouldn't bother them at all if I just went all out and did some things like that, and I said, 'No problem.' Called up Jeff Tepper [guitars], Eric Drew Feldman [keyboards, bass], Bob Williams [drums], Bruce Fowler [trombone], and Drumbo [John French, drums, guitars, marimba, bass]. Gary Lucas showed up – didn't ask him, but he's a nice kid for a New Yorker – and he did a guitar solo and some French horn for free! I was in my Chinese gongs period at the time, and also did sax, harp, bass clarinet ... 'Sheriff of Hong Kong' was done on a grand piano. I played that damn thing exactly the way it is. I think guitar on one hand, bass on the thumb, and the other guitar on the other hand. Pianos are great to compose on, man. We got a-hold of a Mellotron too. Some damn band called the Gloomy Blues used to own it until they went techno! I heard that thing played so many horrible ways that I got interested in getting a-hold of one of them. The Mellotron's the only thing that can get that Merthiolate colour; you know what I mean? Really abused-throat."

The album was cut live in the studio. Beefheart jammed the blues out with 'Run Paint Run Run'. There are the usual spastic rhythms amongst glistening fractured melodic moments.

Beefheart's lyrics – what are they about? Don't know. Something about saving the planet and making sense of the crazy world. It doesn't matter in a literal sense but they do make their own sense.

"Don's music appears improvisatory to most people but, in fact, everything is meticulously worked out in advance," said guitarist Gary Lucas. "Everything is in perfect balance and it doesn't really lend itself to improvisation. It's like a mobile with all its elements spinning in space. The only spontaneous element is Don."

This was to be one of Beefheart's last albums before he retired to concentrate on painting. Punk rock suddenly made Beefheart look and sound not so far-out. If the rest of the world was catching up, Beefheart remained a sprightly step ahead, where he is still.

The Hissing of Summer Lawns Joni Mitchell

(Joni Mitchell) ✳ Asylum ✳ 1975 ✳ Appears on: *The Hissing of Summer Lawns*

Joni Mitchell's 1973 album *Court and Spark* was a massive hit and the singer/ songwriter was suddenly a superstar. She had also shaken off her folkie past and embraced a soft jazz style. With Tom Scott and the LA Express she found musicians who could give form to her melodic ideas. Mitchell went running into a jazz future but her folkie fans who just wanted sensitive lyrics were left somewhere behind.

"*The Hissing of Summer Lawns* is a suburban album," she said. The title refers to sprinklers and the implication is that this track and much of the album will be looking at what is happening behind the white picket fences.

"About the time that album came around I thought, 'I'm not going to be your sin eater any longer.' So I began to write social description as opposed to personal confession," she told Cameron Crowe. "I met with a tremendous amount of resentment. People thought suddenly that I was secure in my success, that I was being a snot and was attacking them. The basic theme of the album, which everybody thought was so abstract, was just any summer day in any neighbourhood when people turn their sprinklers on all up and down the block. It's just that hiss of suburbia.

"I had stopped being confessional. I think they were ready to nail me, anyway. They would have said, 'More morose, scathing introspection.' They were ready to get me; that's the way I figure it."

'The Hissing of Summer Lawns', however, is one of Mitchell's strongest pieces of work. The interplay between the jazz backing and her lyrics is completely unique in rock music. It's funny and carefully observed and complex. Mitchell drew some influence from African music, which was still novel in the west, and that further changed her sound. The tonal sophistication that Mitchell introduced on this record had a great influence, particularly in Los Angeles with artists like Steely Dan.

"There was a big stink about that. It was taboo," she said. "I don't think I realised how culturally isolated we were until the release of that record. In white culture it was problematic, but it got good reviews in the black magazines, where it was accidentally reviewed because there was an illustration of a black person on the cover. I thought it was adventuresome, but it was shocking how frightened people were of it. I think the record was inadvertently holding up a mirror to a change that people were on the brink of in this hemisphere, and people were disturbed by the teetering they were experiencing. The Third World was becoming more important and they were disoriented."

Ca Plane Pour Moi Plastic Bertrand

(Lou Deprijk/Lou Lacomblez) ✳ Vogue Belgium ✳ 1977 ✳ Appears on: *Ca Plane Pour Moi*

Plastic Bertrand was the first rock star I ever interviewed and he was perhaps the most revealing. In halting English he made no attempt to create a mystique around this hit punk rock song, and even less attempt to establish any punk credentials at all. It was, he announced, the work of a production company that churned out hits in many genres (including the Euro electronica of Telex) but mostly disco. 'Ca Plane Pour Moi' was a pastiche of the Sex Pistols sound (that being the most slick of punk recordings). Of course there is none of the angst, none of the anti-social themes of punk rock, but in its cheekiness and energy it made sense. Even better, of course, was the fact that they used the same backing track for another song, the English-language 'Jet Boy Jet Girl' by Elton Motello – its lyrics making no more sense than the French 'Ca Plane Pour Moi'.

According to the Clash's Joe Strummer in 1978, "By purist rules, it's not allowed to even mention Plastic Bertrand. Yet this record was probably a lot better than a lot of the so-called punk records."

Ballad of a Thin Man Bob Dylan

(Bob Dylan) ❋ Columbia ❋ 2001 ❋ Appears on: *Live 1966*

My brother used to tell me stories of seeing Bob Dylan at the Sydney Stadium in 1966, and how on that night the singer was so stoned that he had to be led to the microphone by a roadie. There, in a battered old boxing shed with a creaky revolving stage, Dylan played a set of songs accompanied only by his acoustic guitar. Then, after intermission, he resumed with his backing band. My cousin Robyn's memory of the night was that she slept through most of it and was rudely woken by the raucous noise of the backing band. Or perhaps it was the sound of the folkies jeering the electric music. Whatever, Dylan's 1965–66 tour was a pivotal moment in history: the point where the pop phenomenon of the Beatles met academic literary tradition and suddenly the beat had a meaning and vice versa.

This tour was the culmination of an eighteen-month burst of creativity in which Dylan recorded three albums, each a masterpiece and each a departure from the last. For those years he lived on cigarettes, coffee and amphetamines. Those albums notwithstanding, it was the live performances that defined the future sound of rock & roll.

When Dylan first went electric at the Newport Folk Festival and then shortly thereafter at a concert in New Jersey, it's said that there were howls of abuse. When plugging in his Fender Telecaster, Dylan drew a generational line in the sand. Any criticism from the guardians of good taste only encouraged him.

In a moment of pure serendipity, Dylan was introduced to a Canadian bar band, the Hawks, who had never heard of him. According to guitarist Robbie Robertson, "We met Bob and he said he was playing the Hollywood Bowl, would we like to play? And we said when and he said 'Saturday'".

The relationship continued, although without drummer Levon Helm who couldn't take the constant booing of the audiences and was replaced by session drummer Mickey Jones. Dylan's advice to the band when faced with boos from the audience was "play louder". He said he was looking for "that wild mercury sound". Robertson described the music as simply "violent".

The 1966 tour ended at London's Royal Albert Hall. A tape of a concert at Manchester's Free Trade Hall two nights previously was illegally pressed and distributed as 'Live at the Royal Albert Hall', one of the first rock bootlegs. Dylan has restored and remastered those tapes as the complete concert, dubbed simply *Live 1966*. Even better than the bootleg versions, *Live 1966* captures Dylan standing on the ledge of creative brilliance, the energy of his revolution pumping through his veins.

On the first, acoustic disc, there is so much clarity that you can hear his every breath. Dylan's singing has rarely sounded so strong. 'Fourth Time Around', 'Visions of Johanna', 'Just Like a Woman' and 'Mr Tambourine Man' roll around in his mouth like perfect luscious cherries. You can almost touch the fast ladies in the museum, feel the death squad's hand on the back of your neck or taste the contempt and sadness that Dylan felt as she broke just like a little girl. As the first disc closes Dylan plays his harmonica in an extended reverie as though he has really gone tripping to the skipping reels of time.

The second record in the set is rock & roll at its most raw. Robbie Roberston's guitar lines burst out like machine gun fire as he embellishes the lyric. Meanwhile the rhythm section and organ swirl around, sometimes elegiac and other times sleazy. Against the force of the music, Dylan sings the songs of a man out on the edge: "When your gravity fails and negativity won't pull you through/Don't put on any airs when you're down on Rue Morgue Avenue". He may well be on the brink of insanity, but the words just pour forth.

The songs themselves are full of spite toward ex-lovers or in the case of 'Like a

Rolling Stone', 'Ballad of a Thin Man' and 'Leopard Skin Pill Box Hat', toward a society just then emerging. The contempt in his lyric is softened in the studio but out in front of the raging band it's venomous. 'Ballad of a Thin Man', a diatribe against the media in particular, and an older generation that can't sense the changes in the world, is like a thunderstorm, a warning for the darkness that was to come in the latter half of the century.

A matter of days after this concert Dylan retreated from the world. Rumours of a motorcycle accident masked what was essentially rehab. His backing group became the Band and earned their own place in history and Dylan continued to make groundbreaking music. But no-one ever again tore the world of music apart.

More Than This Roxy Music

(Bryan Ferry) ✳ Island ✳ 1982 ✳ Appears on: *Avalon*

"The whole thing of trying to write something that is from the heart and is hopefully going to be popular and successful and all the rest of it is very stressful," Bryan Ferry said, giving a quick capsule of his recording career through the '70s and '80s. "And as the years go by it gets harder and harder – at least that's how it seems to me. Then I got sort of fed up with the group thing for a while and I thought I'd like to do some of my own songs under my own name. So I did a couple of albums like that – and then I missed the group thing again and went back to doing a couple of group albums. We did three – finished with *Avalon*. And then I got fed up with the constrictions of the group. Groups always end up bickering – because, if you think about it, it's unnatural to work with the same people forever."

Sessions for *Avalon*, the last studio effort from Roxy Music, took place over 1981 and early 1982. Produced by Chris Thomas, this was as slick and high-tech as was possible to get. Thomas encouraged the group to experiment with sounds and layering up sounds almost to the point of abstraction. And as guitarist Phil Manzenera noted, "for the last three albums, quite frankly, there were a lot more drugs around as well, which was good and bad. It created a lot of paranoia and a lot of spaced-out stuff."

As the album's title suggests, this was dreamscape, with a sense of myths and phantoms.

The record's lead track has an ethereal quality although it started out as a full-bodied pop song. "Halfway through, Bryan rebelled," Manzanera said. "It was all scrapped and simplified incredibly."

"I think Bryan decided he wanted a more adult type of lyric," said Manzanera. From the early days of Roxy Music, Bryan Ferry stated his intention to emulate American soul music and here in the last days he came closest.

Day Tripper The Beatles

(John Lennon/Paul McCartney) ❊ Parlophone ❊ 1965 ❊ Appears on: *The Beatles 1962–1966*

Those parents who were concerned about drugs and kids were put on notice by this single. The title was so thinly disguised that no matter what they said in interviews at the time, it was obvious that the Fab Four were no longer the boys next door. The song is powered by one of the Beatles' best riffs, which was taken almost perfectly from R&B guitarist Bobby Parker's 'Watch Your Step'. The song was cut practically live – three takes – with Lennon and McCartney trading vocals all the way as the song powered through its key changes.

"This was getting towards our psychedelic period when we were interested in winking to our friends and comrades-in-arms, putting in references that we knew our friends would get, but the great British public might not. So, 'She's a Big Teaser', was really 'She's a Prick Teaser'. The mums and dads didn't get it, but the kids did," said Paul McCartney.

Heroes David Bowie

(David Bowie/Brian Eno) ❊ RCA ❊ 1978 ❊ Appears on: *Heroes*

"I had no statement to make on *Low*," David Bowie said of his groundbreaking 1977 album. Bowie moved to Berlin with a bad drug habit, a chaotic home life and a need to get rid of the cobwebs of stardom. Collaborating with Brian Eno, he fashioned an entirely new type of rock & roll music, which bore fruit a year later with the *Heroes* album. "The strange thing that came out of *Low* is that in my meanderings in new processes and new methods of writing, when Eno and I listened back to it, we realised we had created new information without even realising it and that by not trying to write about anything we had written more about something or other that one couldn't quite put one's finger on than we could have had we actually gone out and said, 'let's do a concept album'.

"It was quite remarkable so we thought, great, fine, let's do that again, it's quite exciting, so we did that with *Heroes*. We used an immense amount of imagery and juxtaposed one against the other and used incredibly startling methods of writing, anything from random selections out of books. Musically as well – I mean, chord changes. We were quite arbitrary sometimes and the total effect astonished both of us when we sat back and listened to the finished thing."

It's surprising that Bowie and Eno had not worked together before. However, in Berlin they made up for lost time. Eno brought his ambient textures to the highly compressed sound. Guitarist Robert Fripp added an arty, angular counterpoint to the more soulful Carlos Alomar, while Tony Visconti played bass and mixed the project.

"We did *Low*," Tony Visconti recalled. "David wasn't too keen on recording any more if it would mean sustaining that Ziggy Stardust image, that monster he'd created, and he said he wanted to make an album of music which was very uncompromising and reflected the way he felt.

"Then we came to 'Heroes' – what we started to do on *Low*, we developed into a fine art on 'Heroes'. It was more expansive. We used a bigger studio, the Hansa Studio, which is just five hundred yards from the Wall, from East Berlin, and every afternoon, I'd sit down at the desk and see three Russian Red Guards looking at us with binoculars with their sten guns over their shoulders, and the barbed wire, and I knew there were mines buried in that wall – that atmosphere was so provocative and so stimulating and so frightening that the band played with an incredible amount of energy, because I think they wanted to go home, actually.

"The sound's so vast and so massive on that album, and a lot of the echo comes from that ambient sound; we didn't have to add much in the mix. By the time it got to 'Heroes', he had conquered the low period and he felt like a hero – every minute of the day he was in the studio, he'd get up to the microphone and sing at the top of his lungs. You can hear it on 'Heroes', his own particular style of yelling and screaming, which he calls 'Bowie histrionics'."

The title track saw Bowie at his unsentimental best yet somehow deeply emotional. It is the most ironic moment in this very ironic artist's repertoire.

The production of the album is ripe; saturated in ambient noise. Inside there are seductive riffs from Fripp breaking through the pea soup. Bowie's vocal is vulnerable and beseeching – yet it's hard to tell whether this is just a camp put-on. The lyrics too are some of the least oblique words Bowie has written.

Amidst the density of the track, Bowie sings of undying love in such a way that you believe him – and believe that he's putting you on.

Why Are We Sleeping Soft Machine

(Kevin Ayers/Mike Ratledge/Robert Wyatt) ✻ Probe ✻ 1968 ✻ Appears on: *Volume One*

"One record company bloke told us, 'I don't know whether you're our worst-selling rock group or our best-selling jazz group.'" That was drummer Robert Wyatt's tongue-in-cheek summation of Soft Machine's dilemma. They were neither, but they did spearhead fusion in the UK and were certainly the godfathers of progressive rock.

Soft Machine took their name from a William Burroughs novel when they were still gestating in Canterbury. The roots of the group were in avant-garde poetry and jazz with a slightly academic slant. The group started when second-generation bohemian teenager Robert Wyatt met Australian beatnik Daevid Allen. After some years of mucking about, a mixture of acid and the Yardbirds showed them a way into rock and prepared rock for the arrival of Soft Machine. Daevid Allen was deported from Britain, eventually moving to Germany where he assisted in the birth of Kraut rock. Soft Machine – guitarist Kevin Ayers, organist Mike Ratledge, bass player Hugh Hopper and Robert Wyatt – found an audience amongst the jazzers and the hippies.

'Why Are We Sleeping' on the first Soft Machine album is based on a poem by Allen as interpreted mostly by Ayres. The entire album was recorded in four days with Tom Wilson, producer of the Velvet Underground, the Mothers and Bob Dylan, helming the proceedings.

"We started out with some very good ideas," Ayers told *MOJO*, "but that album was amateurish, sloppy, badly produced – all he did was phone his girlfriends. I think he thought we were a bunch of little white shits playing this unfunky cerebral caterwauling."

Ayres' minimalist guitar noodlings and Ratledge's keyboard freak-outs made Soft Machine a little uncompromising but intriguing. Ayres and Wyatt were eventually fired. Both of them, especially Wyatt, were recognised as leading lights in left-field British music right up to the present, working with the likes of Eno and Costello.

The Harder They Come   Jimmy Cliff

(Jimmy Cliff) ✳ Mango ✳ 1972 ✳ Appears on: *The Harder They Come*

The film *The Harder They Come*, written and directed by Perry Henzell in 1971, captured the gangster life in the Trenchtown ghetto amongst the black youth of Jamaica. Jimmy Cliff, who had already had a hit in the UK, starred as Ivan – a country boy who comes to the city in search of fame as a singer. The film was the first real introduction to Rastafarianism and the thriving music culture of Jamaica.

"I went into that movie with a positive mind, not really having any idea of the impact that it would have, but I did have high hopes," said Cliff. "It seemed as though some of my subconscious dreams really did come true. But there was some dissatisfaction with it too. My character portrayed an innocent guy from the country that came into the city to experience the hard ways of the city. He found himself having to do things that were not really pretty. I wanted to show more of the positive stuff that goes on in the ghetto too. I wanted to be able to show that you can really survive in the ghetto without having to take up a gun or becoming violent."

'The Harder They Come', produced by Jimmy Cliff, is a song of defiance that became a rude boy anthem in Jamaica and a reggae standard elsewhere.

Stan   Eminem

(Dido Armstrong/P Herman/Marshall Mathers) ✳ Interscope ✳ 2000 ✳
Appears on: *The Marshall Mathers LP*

One of the most adventurous hip-hop records, 'Stan' unfolds like a mini drama. The lyric tells a story, as a duet, of a fan that tries to make a connection with his idol and when he doesn't get through and feels rejected he commits suicide. The bleak narrative is contrasted with a sample from Dido's haunting ballad 'I Thank You'. Not only does the song transcend the usual themes of rap but it also brings a unique narrative flow to the genre.

"Stan was just somebody completely made up, based on what could happen if you take my lyrics too seriously," Eminem told VH1. "I'm nice enough and courteous enough to tell the kids at the end of the day this is not how you want to be. You don't want to grow up to be just like me.

"Dido's words instantly put me there. Usually as I'm writing, the concept will form as I go along. But 'Stan' was one of the few songs that I actually sat down and had everything mapped out for. I knew what it was going to be about.

"Anybody who lives and breathes for an artist in music or movies is taking it too far."

Neat Neat Neat The Damned

(Brian James) ✳ Stiff ✳ 1977 ✳ Appears on: *Damned Damned Damned*

The Damned were the clown princes of punk rock. They were not spearheading any revolution. They didn't care about the monarchy or the oppression of the working classes; they were out to drink the old order into submission. They were anarchists because they weren't sober enough to subscribe to any other ideology.

The Damned were drawn into the punk movement then by default. Had punk not happened, the Damned – Brian James, Dave Vanian, Rat Scabies and Captain Sensible – would have been catcalled off the stage and returned to the dole queue.

Their garage-band virulence was recognised by Dave Robinson of Stiff and with Nick Lowe they quickly cut a single, 'New Rose', which became "the first punk single ever". It's one of the most pure and entertaining 45s of the era. With that in mind they recorded a debut album, *Damned Damned Damned*, in one day with Lowe again producing. He used Elvis Costello's demo tapes to record the album and it's claimed that there are still snatches of acoustic guitar to be heard faintly in the background.

"Compared with the Pistols album, which was very polished, ours was gnarled and beaten up. To me it was the punk rock sound," the Captain told *MOJO*.

The first single from the album was 'Neat Neat Neat', almost identical to 'New Rose'. The song is pumped up by Scabies' Spectoresque drumming. The lyrics are almost indecipherable and once deciphered are nonsensical, but it's all there in the mood, the almighty racket.

"It sounds like Eddie Cochran as played by a bunch of cider-fuelled crazies in a garage," Sensible said. "'Cause that's what it was."

Creep Radiohead

(Thom Yorke) ❋ Parlophone ❋ 1992 ❋ Appears on: *Pablo Honey*

"It's an on and off song," said Radiohead's vocalist Thom Yorke describing 'Creep'. "It's all about being drunk and following people around." The ironic self-loathing of the lyrics made 'Creep' a perfect gimmick song just as everything was going Generation X and grunge. Although Yorke acknowledged the humour in his unlikely hit, there was a truth at the heart of the tune. "Certain people self-destruct," he told *Juice* magazine. "Emotionally, it's a way of absorbing things that really hurt. What happens is that your lifestyle becomes twisted. Self-destruction is something I have to live with within myself. It comes and goes involuntarily, and I'm shocked to say it still does as well."

Radiohead were an unlikely act to rise to the top in a sea of alternative rock. Yorke's poetic lyrics were set against the elegiac playing of guitarists Jonny Greenwood and Ed O'Brien and the whole owed more to XTC and R.E.M. than grunge rock.

"I'm anti-rock & roll in the sense of long hair and blow jobs. Rock & roll to people back in the '60s was an attitude," Yorke said. "Rock & roll now is just the relics of that and it doesn't actually represent people, it's just something that they turn to as if it's still there, when it's not. They should be looking elsewhere.

"The only way that people seem to consume these things now is through pure hysteria. It's either hysteria or nostalgia. It's never their own genuine feelings. It's always something they're trying to borrow from other people all the time."

Radiohead transcended their gimmicky reputation and within a couple of years had become the saviours of rock & roll themselves.

Thank You (Falettinme be Mice Elf Agin)
Sly & the Family Stone

(Sylvester Stewart) ✳ Epic ✳ 1970 ✳ Appears on: *Greatest Hits*

Following a series of hit records and his appearance at Woodstock and the show-stopping segment in the film, Sly Stone was very, very hot in 1970. Perhaps it was the pressure of the drugs, but he delivered only two new tracks that were incorporated in the *Greatest Hits* album of that year. 'Thank You (Falettinme be Mice Elf Agin)' was an instant classic.

'Thank You' is one of Sly Stone's toughest grooves. Mostly it's notable for Larry Graham's slap and pop bass style. It was an innovation that greatly changed the sound of R&B and funk – which is the core of popular music after all. "I started to thump the strings with my thumb to make up for not having a drummer," said Graham. The bass figures here and the syncopated band arrangements set the course for funk in the '70s. Sly's production had lost the Vegas feel. It was more stripped back and direct.

It was a personal note from Sly Stone that he was withdrawing and, in fact, he was going into a very dark place from which he has yet to emerge.

Another Girl, Another Planet The Only Ones

(Peter Perrett) ✳ CBS ✳ 1978 ✳ Appears on: *The Only Ones*

A truly great piece of rock guitar, 'Another Girl, Another Planet' is one of the most dynamic rock songs of all time. It's a guitar duel between John Perry and singer/songwriter Peter Perrett that simply takes off into the stratosphere.

Perrett was a Dylan and Lou Reed devotee who formed the Only Ones in punk-dominated London. Their colleagues were the Pretenders and the Heartbreakers, with whom Perrett shared drug habits. Unlike most London bands of the period, the Only Ones were accomplished musicians who found that technique was no barrier to raw power when necessary. American guitarist John Perry had played with Robert Hunter and the Grateful Dead while drummer Mike Kellie was in the forgettable British '70s band Spooky Tooth. The combination of innocence and experience enlivened the Only Ones, especially on their early albums. Perrett's heroin addiction, however, drastically compromised his career. His world-weary vocals complemented his opiate verse and contrasted with the fire that came out of the guitar stacks.

'Another Girl', their second single, gets some of its excitement from being recorded live to tape. The long intro from the guitars is pushed along at punishing speed by the rhythm section, which steadily mounts the tension until Perry goes screaming up the guitar neck with a kind of banshee wail and then the song kicks into overdrive. The lyrics, more likely about heroin as a woman, are sly and witty and careless as only a Lou Reed fan could do.

Many groups have tried to replicate the messy brilliance of this track but none have. You had to be there.

Born to be Wild Steppenwolf

(Mars Bonfire) ✳ Dunhill ✳ 1968 ✳ Appears on: *Steppenwolf*

'Born to be Wild' is one of the great, greasy riffs in rock. It's ugly, dirty, sexy. With the chugging guitar and swirling organ on top of a funky rock beat, it has it all.

John Kay, guitarist and singer, was born in Germany and raised in Canada where his band Sparrow played the circuit before moving to Los Angeles. They met producer Gabriel Mekler, who named the group after the Herman Hesse novel and then gave them a sound that was darker and more sleazy than most of the rock bands of the period. When it was fashionable on the Sunset Strip to freak out, Steppenwolf had this churning, almost demonic funk happening. Their debut album featured a brilliant and scary version of Hoyt Axton's 'The Pusher' and the quirky 'Sookie Sookie'.

'Born to be Wild' was written by Sparrow Dennis Edmonton under the pseudonym Mars Bonfire. The lyrics included the famous line, "I like smokin' lightning, heavy metal thunder," which it was said named the genre. 'Born to be Wild' was not heavy metal – it was too fast and too complex for that.

The song was a hit in 1968. Dennis Hopper rightly picked the track for his film *Easy Rider* and used it to denote the spirit of rebelliousness and freedom that was at the core of the film. The combination of that riff and chopped Harley Davidson motorcycles was the iconic partnership of the era. Ever since then 'Born to be Wild'

has been associated with motorcycle clubs in particular and outlaw behaviour in general.

"'Born to be Wild' reached global anthem status," said singer John Kay. "It's one of those things that just outgrew its constraints and became its own animal."

People Get Ready The Impressions

(Curtis Mayfield) ❋ ABC ❋ 1965 ❋ Appears on: *People Get Ready*

The gospel style of this single seemed to be just the salvation ordered in 1965. The civil rights movement, the generation gap and the Vietnam War were starting to reach boiling point. Then this soul song with a big dose of gospel came along like a reality check. The deep soul groove of the song is played off against the gospel vocal parts and the meeting-the-maker tempo.

There is a calm directness in the vocal that is compassionate but doesn't avoid the dark realities – including death. This is basic redemptive preaching. Curtis Mayfield has said that the influence for the song came directly from the pulpit. The song was not a big hit at the time but it has become one of the longest-lasting soul singles of all time. Aretha Franklin's cover version on *Lady Soul* helped; the Vanilla Fudge's version gave it to a rock audience. The song has survived hundreds of readings. Its message has stayed fresh.

"As a youngster and a black, I was quite concerned with what was going on at the time. I wanted to bring a little gospel into the drive for reality with the song," Mayfield said. "And it also lent a pride to those who were oppressed and trying to define themselves on another level."

Caligari's Mirror Pere Ubu

(Tom Herman/Scott Krauss/Allen Ravenstine/David Thomas) ❋ Rough Trade ❋ 1978 ❋ Appears on: *Dub Housing*

Any outfit that takes its name from Alfred Jarry's absurdist play is not going to be easy listening. Ubu were Cleveland, Ohio's, answer to Kraut rock. They grasped recording technology by the neck and shook it like a chicken. Their arrangements were anarchic deconstructions of rock & roll songs whereby a heavy rhythm section was assaulted with noise, dissonance and melody while David Thomas contorted his vocal lines over the top. Cleveland was part of the new industrial north of the US and Thomas, who was effectively Ubu, drew inspiration from the cultural desolation that surrounded him. In relying heavily on Allen Ravenstine's synthesiser he recast the alienation of art rock into the modern world – like Woody Guthrie in the bones of a computer.

Cleveland in the mid-'70s was a hotbed of punk rock – notably the Dead Boys and nearby Devo – but Thomas' inspiration is decidedly more European. For instance, 'Caligari's Mirror' owes a debt to Brecht and Weill in its updating of an old sea shanty subjected to industrial pollution.

"Ubu was a grotesque synthesis of all that was ugly in human flesh," said Thompson to the *Melody Maker*. "Why the band is called Pere Ubu has to do with a number of things I can't easily explain, but on the simplest level it has to do with the thing that I am in a lot of ways: a grotesque character, and the band has a grotesque character.

"What we are not is pretty."

Oh Bondage, Up Yours X Ray Spex

(Poly Styrene) ✳ Virgin ✳ 1977 ✳ Appears on: *Germ Free Adolescents*

The London punk scene prided itself on female empowerment. Prior to punk rock, the role of rock star was an almost exclusively male preserve.

Marion Elliot was still a teenager when she saw the Sex Pistols and took up the microphone for herself as vocalist and songwriter Poly Styrene. The sheer force of her personality, her voice and the oddball quirkiness of X Ray Spex put a decidedly softer, but no less critical slant, on the punk movement.

Poly Styrene's songs just poured forth in the excitement of it all. Many of them dealt with issues of image and consumerism. She told *MOJO*, "I was trying to do a diary of 1977, to write about everyday experiences.

"One of the first songs we did was 'Oh Bondage, Up Yours'," she said at the time. "It was about being in bondage to the material life. A call for liberation. I was saying, 'Bondage? Forget it, I'm not going to be bound by the laws of consumerism.'"

Germ Free Adolescents was one of the better albums of the period, and of course the issues remain as relevant as ever.

The Tide is High Blondie

(John Holt) ✳ Chrysalis ✳ 1980 ✳ Appears on: *Autoamerican*

Originally recorded as a reggae ballad by the Paragons, Blondie added their own pop interpretation including a horn section and the superlative feel of drummer Clem Burke. Mike Chapman, who had produced the group's breakthrough, was again behind the board.

Guitarist Chris Stein recalls the sessions as intense, writing in the group's fan club newsletter, "Chapman hunches over the console into the wee hours. People are pressed flat against the back wall by his playback volume. Gallons of Jose Cuervo Gold are consumed ... Finally, the basic tracks wind down, and we move a block down the Strip to Studio B. The move marks the home stretch; the vocals, overdubs and finally the orchestral horns and what have you. Here is Mike Chapman's little magic room. In days gone by, these burlap walls saw the likes of the Righteous Brothers, Jan & Dean, the Beach Boys ... Now the control room is filled with a gigantic blue console that's hooked up to computers, satellites and atomic submarines off the coast of Maine. Here the songs get the 'chrome' put on."

'The Tide is High' retained its reggae groove, although with Deborah Harry singing, it had a kind of ironic distance. The *Autoamerican* album saw the group playing with roots styles – including 'Rapture', the first rap track recorded by a white band.

According to engineer Lenise Bent, "Magical things did happen; there was room for those spontaneous-combustion kinds of things."

Enter Sandman Metallica

(Kirk Hammett/James Hetfield/Lars Ulrich) ✳ Elektra ✳ 1991 ✳ Appears on: *Metallica*

The album's first track and the first hit single, 'Enter Sandman', was the key to Metallica's new direction – more personal, more simple and more radio friendly. The song was an instant smash that put the record in the charts at number one and eventually sold eight million copies.

"We went into the studio with the intent of making a real lively record that bounces off the walls," said Ulrich. "It should have gone quicker, in theory, than trying to get everything note perfect like we have before. But as usual with Metallica, all those theories and normalities go straight out the window." In fact, Ulrich confessed, "it took us twice as long to make a record that is twice as loose."

"We wanted to create a different record and offer something new to our audience," said Hammett. "I hate it when bands stop taking chances. A lot of bands put out the same record three or four times, and we didn't want to fall into that rut." Metallica turned the rut into the Grand Canyon.

"There are fewer key changes," guitarist Kirk Hammett said. "There aren't many flatted fourth progressions, or anything like that just straight-ahead major and minor keys. The most complex song is probably 'Anywhere I Roam', which suggests a Phrygian dominant scale."

1969 The Stooges

(Iggy Pop/Dave Alexander/Ron Asheton/Scott Asheton) ✳ Elektra ✳ 1969 ✳
Appears on: *The Stooges*

"Last year I was twenty-one/I didn't have a lot of fun/Now I'm gonna be twenty-two/I say 'Oh my and a boo-hoo'".

Like millions of other white, working-class kids in the suburbs, the '60s revolution passed the Stooges by.

The local kings, the MC5, however, looked like they were starting a Detroit movement and the Stooges were signed to Elektra on their coat-tails. John Cale, recently departed from the Velvet Underground, was assigned to produce them and what he captured was the inarticulate aggression of the band. The fact that all the songs were two-chord riffs made sense to him, although it wouldn't to the rest of the world for some time to come.

Guitarist Ron Asheton maintains that the group was heavily influenced by Ravi Shankar, Gregorian chants, John Coltrane and avant-gardist Harry Partch – but you wouldn't know it from hearing the record. The Stooges album is big and dumb.

As writer Lenny Kaye said at the time, "By any formal criteria, [the Stooges] are a retrogressive group, a pale copy of the early Rolling Stones. Their music revolves around one modified Bo Diddley chord progression, and neither the singing nor musicianship on their album attains any memorable level of competence ... The world of the Stooges, simply, revolves around boredom. Not only a mere lack of something to do, but rather a total negation of anything to do ... this is 1969 now, when the hope that came out of Haight Street is nearly dead, when the protest has been neatly swept up and glorified by the mass media. In consequence, the only stance that seems to be left is that of Iggy Stooge ... If 1967 was the year of the Beatles and 'Get Together', if 1968 was the year of the Band and *Beggar's Banquet*, then 1969 may well be the year of the Stooges. You might not like it, but you can't escape it."

In time, of course, the Stooges turned out to be more right than any number of protest singers.

(I'm) Stranded The Saints

(Ed Kuepper/Chris Bailey) ❊ Fatal ❊ 1976 ❊ Appears on: *(I'm) Stranded*

Modern Australian rock began here.

"I've got very kind of fond memories of my first ever recording session and it's stupid but I actually don't remember the recording too much," said Chris Bailey. "I remember going to it; I was wearing my girlfriend's coat and for the first time and probably the last time I actually felt like a pop star for the day. My other lingering

memory is when we got the record and I was playing it. I'd never been so happy, and I'm sure this is true for everyone but it was just fun to hold the thing."

The first recording, '(I'm) Stranded' (the flipside was 'No Time'), on the Fatal label, launched the Saints from the obscurity of the Brisbane backwaters into the international limelight. The Saints drew on a number of influences. The massive chording of Kuepper's guitars showed the influence of the Stooges and the Missing Links. The jazzy drum feel from Ivor Hay and Chris Bailey's sardonic bar room vocals was perfect punk even though it had been conceived and executed 15,000 km from Soho or

CBGB. The self-financed single was sent to the British music press who jumped on it: *Sounds* newspaper declared it single of the week. EMI London despatched orders to the colonies to find and track down the Saints – to make up for the ignominy of having fired the Sex Pistols.

"When you're sixteen or seventeen there's heaps of things that you get angry about – your parents, school, job if you've got it, police," said Bailey. "You're at an age where you want to be doing a whole range of things and you're restricted 'cause of the age that you are. Especially in Brisbane at the time there was active harassment from the police force. There was a political agenda at that stage too if you were in the least bit left-leaning and the Saints were quite blatantly left-leaning."

"One of the things I find that I'm drawn back to the most about Brisbane in the '70s is an overwhelming feeling of possibility," said Bailey. "For youngsters like me from the wrong side of the tracks coming into the city, you didn't need that much money to get mind-numbingly drunk, have fun, do lots of middle-class girls who seemed very keen on sexual exploration. [There were] massively fantastic parties and you could get away with feeling that you were a dyed-in-the-wool committed socialist while having this incredibly wonderful bourgeois life. That was Brisbane to me in the '70s."

The Saints, however, were determined to be original. The more resistance from the squares, the more they were reassured they were on the right path. Eschewing booking agencies or even the alternative radio station 4ZZZ, the Saints played mostly at parties at their house in Petrie Terrace, dubbed Club 76.

"I'm meant to be mocking and humble and I s'pose that's an alternative to lack of success and picking up sheilas but I won't be mockingly humble," said the singer. "Hindsight colours this. I think that we quite seriously thought that we were really quite good."

"Yeah, initially the reaction of the group of people who were supporting us in Brisbane was pretty positive," said Kuepper. "But that was only maybe a couple of dozen people. The response here was generally negative and in some cases violently so. Until the overseas response happened and that came in very quickly afterwards and then suddenly there was a shift in opinion. The early reviews in the pop press that we got here were abysmal . . . so abysmal that we used them in our own publicity."

Tom Traubert's Blues (Four Sheets to the Wind in Copenhagen) Tom Waits

(Tom Waits) ❋ Asylum ❋ 1976 ❋ Appears on: *Small Change*

Playing in Sydney in May 1979, Tom Waits introduced 'Tom Traubert's Blues' with this ambiguous patter: "This is a song where I kinda borrowed your unofficial national anthem on this whole thing ... I'll give it back when I'm done. Well I met this girl named Matilda. And eh, I had a little too much to drink that night. This is about throwing up in a foreign country." This is a song about heartbreak and love and alcohol and that moment when they all come together. The foreign country is specifically Denmark.

'Tom Traubert's Blues (Four Sheets to the Wind in Copenhagen)' includes a version of 'Waltzing Matilda', which was written by Banjo Patterson and Christina McPherson in the late 19th century. The tune was adapted from an old Scottish air, 'The Bonnie Wood of Craiglee' but all of this is somewhat irrelevant. The Matilda with whom Waits dances is Mathilde Bondo, a Danish violinist who entertained the American singer on a drunken Copenhagen evening in June 1976.

The following month he finished writing the songs for his *Small Change* album and no doubt Mathilde was somewhat on his mind as was Waits' itinerant lifestyle at the time: "A Matilda is a, eh, backpack. So 'Waltzing Matilda' just means, really just to take off, you know? Like blow town, you know? And eh, you know, that's what the song means, maybe ..."

According to producer Bones Howe, Waits was interested in drunkenness and investigating skid row. Howe recalled a phone conversation with Waits in the early hours on one morning: "He said the most wonderful thing about writing that song. He went down and hung around on skid row in Los Angeles because he wanted to get stimulated for writing this material. He called me up and said, 'I went down to skid row ... I bought a pint of rye. In a brown paper bag – hunkered down, drank the pint of rye, went home, threw up, and wrote 'Tom Traubert's Blues'. Every guy down there ... everyone I spoke to, a woman put him there.'"

As a writer Waits put together disparate ideas that all revolved around the journey from heartbreak to delirium. The song is rich with vignettes and character studies and the notion that really when you're drunk you're travelling in a foreign country where your bearings are lost and your language is useless.

The *Small Change* album was recorded in five days, from 15–20 July 1976, at the Wally Heider Studios in Hollywood and it was on the streets in September.

The elements of the song are identifiable; however, the piece has a mystery in it that's more than its component parts. As the songwriter himself said in 1990, "It's funny eh. This is one of those songs that I never quite figured it out. It's just one of those songs that puzzles me. And so I sing it and I get further puzzled. Eh, alcohol and, eh, writing don't mix. If they do it takes a long time to unravel them . . ."

1, 2, 3, Red Light 1910 Fruitgum Company

(B Trimachi/S Trimachi) ✳ Buddah ✳ 1968 ✳ Appears on: *1, 2, 3, Red Light*

"Well, we were the ones," Jeff Katz recalled in *Goldmine* magazine, "when we were talking about different things, we would gear 'em toward a certain audience, and we figured it was the teenagers, the young kids. And at the time we used to be chewing bubblegum and that, and my partner and I used to look at it and laugh and say, 'Ah, this is like bubblegum music.'

"Bubblegum music, in the real sense of sort of kiddie records, was around for quite a while, like various artists doing various songs. But there were very few that were doing it on some continuity where it was the same type of style or whatnot. We were gearing with all our writers for, as I said, a specific kids' [appeal]. We want hits, obviously; but we want these type of things, and we want our artists to be known for these type of things. And that's what we were knocking out."

Jerry Kasenetz and Jeff Katz met at the University of Arizona and had no interest in music. However, in 1966 the pair took on the Rare Breed and then had a number two hit with 'A Little Bit of Soul' by the Music Explosion – a bona fide garage rock classic. By 1967 they were working with Neil Bogart at Buddah Records. Katz's father came across a garage band then called Jeckyll and the Hydes in a New Jersey diner. Kasenetz and Katz renamed them the 1910 Fruitgum Company, gave them a song, 'Simon Says', and launched bubblegum music.

The Fruitgum Company was followed by the Ohio Express and others and a rush of imitators like the Archies.

It was a teen antidote to the pretensions that had swamped rock & roll in the late '60s, and to the political upheaval that engulfed America. Bubblegum had a slightly trippy tone to it and a deep suburban conservative take on the revolution that was happening in the streets.

Bubblegum was all about sex. Innuendo was never deep below the hook, especially in cases such as the '1, 2, 3, Red Light'. Male passion has rarely been better expressed in under two minutes.

The Fruitgum Company were at first a band but shortly devolved to singer Mark Gutkowski. Even he lost his berth if he wasn't at the Super K factory when the session commenced.

Despite the disparaging commentary Bubblegum received from the under-ground press, it has survived much better than progressive rock and its traditions have been upheld by no less than the Ramones and Kylie Minogue.

Start Me Up The Rolling Stones

(Mick Jagger/Keith Richards) ❋ Rolling Stones ❋ 1981 ❋ Appears on: *Tattoo You*

Mick Jagger and Keith Richards were no longer speaking in 1980, making recording a new album difficult. It fell to engineer Chris Kimsey to sort through ten years of out-takes to find the basis of the *Tattoo You* album. 'Start Me Up' was originally recorded at the *Some Girls* sessions on the same day as the disco hit 'Miss You', and promptly binned.

"'Miss You' took quite a time to come together," said Kimsey. "Bill [Wyman, bassist] needed to go to quite a few clubs before he got that bass line sorted out. But he did sort it out, and bless him, it made that song. Then, immediately after 'Miss You' was recorded, 'Start Me Up' got straightened out. They'd been throwing it around as a reggae song, but they rearranged it and, within twenty-four hours of 'Miss You', 'Start Me Up' was recorded.

"However, when I played it back, Keith said, 'Nah, it sounds like something I've heard on the radio. Wipe it.' Of course, I didn't, but he really didn't like it, and I'm not sure whether he likes it to this day. I don't think it's one of his favourite songs, although it's obviously everyone's favourite guitar riff; his guitar riff. Maybe because Keith loves reggae so much, he wanted it to be a reggae song.

"'Start Me Up' took about six hours to record. If they all played the right chords in the right time, went to the chorus at the right time and got to the middle eight together, that was a master. Don't forget, they would never sit down and work out a song. They would jam it and the song would evolve out of that. That's their magic."

Three years after the *Some Girls* sessions, Jagger returned to the track to put on vocals and a lyric, much of which was improvised with the music.

"He'd give it the full performance, moving all over the place," Kimsey told *Mix* magazine. "It was great to watch and equally great to record. He knows how to work a microphone. He might be at the back of the control room, just a bar before the verse, and all of a sudden he's in front of the mic. He backs off in the chorus when he's singing loud, he gets in close when he's singing soft, and he knows what to do. Keith, on the other hand, is the complete opposite. You need a shotgun to get him in front of the mic. He'll wander all over the place while singing, taking an attitude of 'You do your job, you record me.'"

Whatever Richards' reservations, if any, 'Start Me Up' made *Tattoo You* the Rolling Stones' most successful album and has been one of their signature tunes ever since.

A Very Cellular Song The Incredible String Band

(Mike Heron/Robin Williamson) ✳ Elektra ✳ 1968 ✳

Appears on: *The Hangman's Beautiful Daughter*

The cover says it all. This was the utopian dream of all hippies – great clothes, out in the woods with winsome girlfriends who had very long hair and names like Rosie and Liquorice. Can't beat that. The Incredibles were, for a while, the epitome of cool. Their number one fan was Robert Plant; Bob Dylan and Marianne Faithful sang their praises, and the Grateful Dead covered their songs.

The Incredibles – Mike Heron and Robin Williamson – were folk singers who jumped head-on into the counterculture. They took the roots of British folk, a touch of American music and dollops of what Robert Plant called Bulgarian scales and transformed them into something completely their own.

The music was eclectic enough. The lyrics touched on Celtic traditions and a smorgasbord of spirituality including, finally, Scientology.

The Hangman's Beautiful Daughter, produced by Joe Boyd, pulled everything together in the most concise way while still being right out there. There is some self-deprecating humour here, but most of the album is fey and ephemeral. Musically the Incredibles were on fire. Between the two of them they played organ, dulcimer, bass, guitar, harpsichord, horn, sitar, harmonica, mandolin, percussion, piano, violin, harp and oud. They also had a gimbri and they knew how to use it. The melodies and tempos flew off on tangents only to resolve themselves in unlikely ways.

The closing track of *Hangman's*, 'A Very Cellular Song', was their finest moment. "Part of 'Cellular Song' was written on acid actually," said Heron. "Most of it on one trip, kind of through the night, before the dawn. It wasn't personal though. I was writing a song for the world while on acid." The song is a suite built around an old hymn, which evolves into a chant that became a global incantation, the national anthem of communes: "May the long time sun shine upon you/All love surround you/And the pure light within you/Guide you all the way on."

Across the Universe The Beatles

(John Lennon/Paul McCartney) ✳ Apple ✳ 1970 ✳ Appears on: *Let It Be*

An often overlooked small masterstroke from John Lennon, 'Across the Universe' was written in 1967 and recorded in 1968 as a possible single (it lost out to 'Lady Madonna') and subsequently turned up on a charity record. Spike Milligan was in Abbey Road when the song was first recorded. He asked if he could have a song for a benefit album he was compiling for the World Wildlife Fund and the Beatles added some animal noises to this one and gave it away. Sixteen-year-old Brazilian Lizzie Bravo and seventeen-year-old Gayleen Pease, two Apple scruffs who camped on the steps of the Apple offices, supplied backing vocals. When working on *Let It Be*, Phil Spector took the original tapes and erased the sound effects and backing vocal and added strings.

There is a dreamlike quality to the song as it veers off into the cosmic. The Beatles at the time were studying with the Maharishi and the chorus name checks his guru, Dev.

Lennon was ultimately never satisfied with the Beatles' version of the song, telling a magazine in 1980, "The Beatles didn't make a good record of 'Across the Universe'. I thought Paul subconsciously tried to destroy my great songs. We would play experimental games with my great pieces, like 'Strawberry Fields', which I always felt was badly recorded. It worked, but it wasn't what it could have been. I allowed it, though. We would spend hours doing little, detailed cleaning up on Paul's songs, but when it came to mine – especially a great song like 'Strawberry Fields' or 'Across the Universe' – somehow an atmosphere of looseness and experimentation would come up.

"Paul will deny it, because he has a bland face and will say this doesn't exist. This is the kind of thing I'm talking about where I was always seeing what was going on and began to think, 'Well, maybe I'm paranoid.' But it is not paranoid. It is the absolute truth. The same thing happened to 'Across the Universe'. The song was never done properly. The words stand, luckily."

Lennon claimed the lyric came to him when he was trying to sleep and wouldn't go away until he had written it down.

"I was lying next to her in bed," he said. "And I was irritated. She must have been going on and on and on about something, and she'd gone to sleep and I kept on hearing these words over and over, flowing like an endless stream. I went downstairs and it turned into a sort of cosmic song rather than an irritated song. It drove me out of bed. I didn't want to write it, but I was slightly irritable and I went downstairs and I couldn't get to sleep until I put it down on paper, and then I went to sleep."

Glory Box Portishead

(Geoff Barrow/Henry Brooks/Beth Gibbons/Lalo Schifrin/Otis Turner/Adrian Utley) ✻ Go! Discs ✻ 1994 ✻ Appears on: *Dummy*

Seeping out of Bristol in the early '90s, Portishead turned trip hop into something. Geoff Barrow, a hip-hop producer, met singer Beth Gibbons at the dole office and began collaborating. The album *Dummy* was dark, mysterious, cinematic and enigmatic. The elegantly doomed break-beats were strangely popular, giving Portishead an instant mainstream audience.

Completed with guitarist Adrian Utley, *Dummy* was also a mixture of tenderness and dissonance, of torch songs and break-beats. There are starkly beautiful lines from the guitar and elegant moods from Barrow over gently pulsing beats, and then the deflowered, painfully dignified voice of Gibbons, which occasionally lets forth with rage. The overriding mood is dark and contemplative. "I can't stand the light stuff," said Barrow. "I'm not into it. All the hip-hop I liked was very, very dark hip-hop. And when I was sampling, I was always looking for something that had a strange emotional content to it, something that sparks some kind of emotion or theme or atmosphere. That's always my problem when we're working. I always think it's not enough. It's not dark enough. It's not emotionally hooked enough. But if I can get some emotion musically before Beth begins to write and sing over the tracks then there's something for her to hook into. A thread she can follow. We're looking for something that is quite emotionally powerful. And I don't want to take anyone down when they listen to our music, but I just don't think there's an awful lot of music out there that does it to people. And people can handle emotion."

Need You Tonight INXS

(Andrew Farriss/Michael Hutchence) ❊ Atlantic ❊ 1987 ❊ Appears on: *Kick*

Slinky, sparse and funky, 'Need You Tonight' was pretty much as sexy and funky as any white rock group has ever been. On their sixth album, INXS were forging a new direction. Producer Chris Thomas proved to be a hard taskmaster, forcing re-writes and re-takes but also allowing the group to stretch out.

The opening single on *Kick*, 'Need You Tonight' is not much in the lyrics. Michael Hutchence's delivery, however, says it all: he sings in a kittenish whisper, gently drawing back his breath, and makes his not-so-subtle declaration of intent. He sings this song with the inexorable lust of a tiger out hunting in the night – there's a carefully measured dance going on here. Restraint is everything, as though Hutchence knows that the prey will eventually come to him.

The vocals are aided by the crack rhythm section that is all about space. INXS in those days were like Curtis Mayfield-meets-AC/DC. Garry Beers' bass pads in between guitar and drums, dancing up the melody and mimicking the steady intent from the vocals.

The song was aided by a groundbreaking video by Richard Lowenstein and Lynne-Marie Milburn, but ultimately this was Michael Hutchence's moment. "I hate," he told me at the time, "more than anything else, sexless music."

Pick Up the Pieces   The Average White Band

(Roger Ball/Malcolm Duncan/Alan Gorie/Robbie McIntosh/Onnie McIntyre/Salazer/Hamish Stuart) ❄ Atlantic ❄ 1974 ❄ Appears on: *AWB*

"The name of the band started out as an 'in' saying among us, you know, we'd be listening to a track and say 'not bad for an average white band'. I guess it just stuck from there," said singer and bassist Alan Gorrie. "The slums of Dundee aren't pretty places to be either. They produce tough people who demand tough music. The same is true of the American ghettoes."

The Average White Band came out of Scotland to debut at Eric Clapton's Rainbow Concert in 1973 and surprised everyone who heard them with the authenticity of their soul/funk sound.

Guitarists Hamish Stuart and Onnie McIntyre aided Alan Gorrie with horn players Malcolm Duncan, Roger Ball and drummer Robbie McIntosh (who died soon after this breakthrough album).

The key was 'Pick Up the Pieces' – one of the most perfect soul/funk riffs, which was arranged and produced by Arif Mardin into a track that would become ubiquitous. The Average White Band had a musical dexterity to match the American masters. They brought a certain Scottish toughness, some jazz and rock feel to the party, and that gave them a distinction all their own.

"We're not out to be superstars, just to be a good, working band," said McIntosh. "In fact the biggest compliment you could pay us is to say that our sound is in the same bag as James Brown or the Temptations." They achieved those not so humble ambitions.

Cut Your Hair   Pavement

(Stephen Malkmus) ❄ Matador ❄ 1994 ❄ Appears on: *Crooked Rain Crooked Rain*

No genre in popular music had been so self-aware as indie rock. A side effect of mass media and post-modernism in the early '90s was the notion that each and every one owed their personality to marketing departments. The grunge revolution was not only televised but it was in re-runs and on talk shows rather than MTV. Pavement, the brainchild of Stephen Malkmus, fitted perfectly into the lo-fi movement – he cited influences as Black Sabbath and Rush – while having ambivalence to it.

The second Pavement album, *Crooked Rain Crooked Rain*, was their first masterpiece – flawless slacker rock music and witty, pertinent lyrics. Malkmus proved to be a gifted songwriter; playful and acute. 'Cut Your Hair' was an ode to grunge rock – the importance of style and appearance, the flood of groups who were largely interchangeable but all right-on:

Bands start up each and every day
I saw another one just the other day/A special new band
I remember lying/I don't remember a line
I don't remember a word/But I don't care, I care, I really don't care
Did you see the drummer's hair?

Malkmus was sufficiently confident of Pavement's abilities to satirise the scene. But what do you expect from Generation X?

While My Guitar Gently Weeps The Beatles

(George Harrison) ✳ Apple ✳ 1968 ✳ Appears on: *The Beatles*

This was where the quiet Beatle became less so. The Beatles (aka *White* album) was a confusing, unfocused sloppy mess. Only two tracks – 'Helter Skelter' and 'While My Guitar' – had the solidity and presence expected of the Beatles. Lennon's material was increasingly self-obsessed and McCartney's twee, but 'While My Guitar' couldn't be denied.

Harrison was never given his due by Lennon, McCartney or producer George Martin. When he presented this song to the others it received a lukewarm response.

After working on the track, Harrison was still dissatisfied. While giving Eric Clapton a lift he suggested that the Cream guitarist come in to do the electric guitar part. Clapton agreed and the song was cut with Harrison on organ (so it wasn't strictly his guitar that wept) and acoustic engineer Chris Thomas was enlisted to wobble an oscillator through Clapton's guitar part to give the track a sadder sound.

Good Vibrations The Beach Boys

(Brian Wilson/Mike Love) ❋ Capitol ❋ 1966 ❋ Appears on: *Smiley Smile*

Brain Wilson called it "a little pocket symphony". He toiled for nine months in five studios with a total budget of $60,000 to complete 'Good Vibrations'. Over that time it progressed from being a tough R&B track to an ethereal layering of harmony and melody quite unlike anything that preceded it.

A Wilson confidant, David Anderle, recalled, "Around the time of the fourth, final 'Good Vibrations', I heard it, and it knocked me out, and I said, uh oh, there's something happening here that is unbelievable. And then, the next time I came up, it was different. And then I came up one evening, and Brian said that he had decided to totally scrap 'Good Vibrations'. He was not going to put it out. The track was going to be sold to Warner Bros. to be put out as an R&B song, sung by a coloured group. It was a lot shorter, it was a lot simpler rhythmically, melodically it was a lot simpler than the final song. It was much more a commercial ditty, if that's possible. There were no lyrics at that time that he had recorded; he had just recorded tracks. Brian goes in and cuts all the tracks first. He is motivated by the music, generally; the music will then motivate the lyric, and a lot of times the lyric comes very late."

The song kept growing and changing. Wilson and his session players spent three months, from April to June 1966, recording the parts to the song. Over seventy hours of tape were collected and finally reassembled to make the single.

The mythology of Brian Wilson as fractured genius has swamped this song as much as it did the uncompleted (until 2004) *Smile* album. It's likely, however, that Wilson really didn't have a particular method but simply used the studio and musicians to make notes that were later edited into three minutes thirty-five.

"We would talk about this 'genius kid' on our other dates," session bass player Carol Kaye recalled. "Are you working a Beach Boys date tomorrow? Yeah, good. Are you? And so on. Happy to be part of this process of growth Brian was exhibiting."

If Phil Spector had been the first to use the recording studio as an instrument, Wilson took it all one step further with 'Good Vibrations'.

Compositionally, Wilson threw everything at the piece – jazz harmonies, R&B, the trademark Beach Boys harmonies and some neo-classical touches on the strings. On top of the constant bass figure, the record's themes drift and flow and burst into a supercharged reverie. Then there's the theremin – a primitive electronic instrument that Wilson added to give a particularly eerie feeling to the production.

As a final touch, Mike Love added a lyric that was vaguely in tune with the acid-soaked times and 'Good Vibrations' became one of the finest and most enduring pieces of pop, and pretty much Brian Wilson's artistic exit. He never matched that record again. But then, few even came close to reaching it.

"I could feel it when I dubbed it down, made the final mix from the sixteen-track down to mono," he said. "It was a feeling of power. It was a rush. A feeling of exultation. Artistic beauty. It was everything. I remember saying, 'Oh my God. Sit back and listen to this!'"

Freddie's Dead   Curtis Mayfield

(Curtis Mayfield) ✳ Curtom ✳ 1972 ✳ Appears on: *Superfly*

Gordon Parks' film *Superfly* was the first blaxploitation movie. Set in the ghetto world of pushers and pimps, Parks tried to tell it like it was and made his conflicted hero a drug pusher. Curtis Mayfield, one of the most versatile black singer/songwriters of the early '70s, was a perfect choice as the soundtrack's composer. Mayfield brought a tense, insistent funk to the film. His score influenced the way soundtracks were made from then on.

'Freddie's Dead' was already a hit when the film opened. Although only an instrumental section in the film, 'Freddie's Dead' covers the pathetic end of Freddie, a victim of the underworld and its charms.

"[The songs] were inspired by characters in the film script," said Mayfield. "If I brought them to life, maybe that's because I grew up poor in the ghetto streets, so I could identify and relate to a lot of things that people in this business are protected from. I'd seen the visual side of this low budget movie, and they were doing so much snorting, that it was important to me to show another side, or we'd just have one big cocaine commercial. Being 'fly' or 'superfly' was actually a reference to clothes, but it's easy to associate it with drugs.

"In all the films at that time, black people were portrayed as pimps and whores, who usually got ripped off at the end. Superfly had enough mind to get out of all that, and let the authorities know that he saw through their games. People concentrate on the hustlers, but there's never a complaint about the drug importers, 'cause they're hidden in their mansions, with their Rolls-Royces, legitimate businesses and donations to charities."

There's a dilemma for both the filmmakers and Mayfield in *Superfly* in that the drug business that is destroying the ghetto communities is also the main opportunity for black men to get out of their poverty. It's not a contradiction that Mayfield shirks.

"For me, when I first was reading it, it read very well. I mean all this was reality," said Mayfield. "We're not trying to sell it, but we're telling it to you like it is. But reading the script didn't tell you 'and then he took another hit of cocaine' and then about a minute later 'he took another hit.' So when I saw it visually, I thought 'this is a cocaine infomercial.' That's all it was.

"I made the commitment and of course I wasn't going to let go of my chance to do a movie. Yet I didn't want to be part of that infomercial. So it was important to me that I left the glitter and all the social stuff and tried to go straight in the lyrics. I tried to tell the stories of the people in depth and not insult the intelligence of those who were spending their money. That was an actual effort on my part.

"In that time and era, most times the black guys don't make it through the movie. For most black folks just making it was tough. So this guy did what he did and he was true to himself and he got out and kept his life. So that was noble to a lot of people that were going to see the movie anyway."

The low budget film had a low budget for the soundtrack. Mayfield brought the project in for $35,000 and was soon in demand for other scores.

"I was standing in Chicago right on State Street, the main street in the Chicago theatre district, right there in the loop. And I looked out and right there I could see the marquee for three of my movies at the same time, *Superfly*, *Let's Do It Again*, and I think it was *Claudine*. Right there in my hometown. So, you know, I felt like a big man."

Cross Road Blues Robert Johnson

(Robert Johnson) ❊ Columbia/Legacy ❊ 1966 ❊ Appears on: *King of the Delta Blues Singers*

The legend of Robert Johnson is one of the most enduring myths of popular music. Johnson was an itinerant blues singer and guitarist, born in 1911, who lived around Clarksdale and the other small towns of the Mississippi Delta. He was one of many performers, such as Charley Patton, Tommy Johnson, Son House and others, who travelled around playing in joints when not employed in the fields.

Legend has it that Johnson was not an exceptional musician, but that he met the Devil one night at a crossroads and made a Faustian pact. He returned to be the Delta's best guitarist. He applied a driving rhythm and a unique phrasing that was intense and emotional and, in its way, haunting.

Robert Palmer's book *Deep Blues* is an excellent guide to the background of Mississippi blues. As Palmer notes, only a generation separated the field workers of the Delta from Africa. African religious beliefs and the musical idioms were still in living memory.

Johnson still sang love and party songs but a large part of his repertoire was based around dealing with evil and the Devil. There was something in his existential struggle that would speak to white musicians such as Bob Dylan and Keith Richard thirty years after his death.

In November 1936 talent scout Ernie Oertle and Johnson went to San Antonio, Texas. In five days Johnson cut seventeen songs including 'Cross Road Blues'. Johnson's fame began to spread. He was booked for John Hammond's Carnegie Hall 'From Spirituals to Swing' concert in September 1938. That would have been the showcase to launch Johnson into the mainstream of American music. He never made the date.

In June 1937 he had another recording session, his last. On Saturday night, 13 August 1938, at a jook joint named Three Forks, Johnson played a gig. That night he died. Some say he was stabbed; others say he was poisoned and wound up crawling around on the floor howling like a dog.

Like the legend about Johnson himself, 'Cross Road Blues' is a song about making a pact at the cross roads. It's a song with roots that go back to African traditions and pay lip service to Christian ones. It's a song with a compelling melody that transcends its blues roots and was a harbinger for the music that came after.

Borrowed Tune   Neil Young

(Neil Young) ❋ Reprise ❋ 1975 ❋ Appears on: *Tonight's the Night*

"I would have to say that's the most liquid album I've ever made. You almost need a life preserver to get through that one," Young told Cameron Crowe. "We were all leaning on the ol' cactus ... and, again, I think that it's something people should hear. They should hear what the artist sounds like under all circumstances if they want to get a complete portrait. Everybody gets fucked up, man. Everybody gets fucked up sooner or later. You're just pretending if you don't let your music get just as liquid as you are when you're really high."

According to the lyrics, this song is written to a tune ('Lady Jane') borrowed from the Rolling Stones because Young was too wasted to write his own. There's a majestic degenerate air to this song. Yes, this is what being fucked up sounds like, but in a nice way.

Walk on By   Dionne Warwick

(Burt Bacharach/Hal David) ❋ Scepter ❋ 1964 ❋ Appears on: *Make Way For*

Burt Bacharach brought the lush romanticism of Debussy, Ellington and Gil Evans to R&B and created some of the most sophisticated pop music of the '60s. In Dionne Warwick, Bacharach and his partner Hal David found their muse. Warwick had a background in gospel that added to the richness of her voice. She had an enormous elegance and restraint. David was a writer of precise and acute lyrics whose often adventurous metre matched Bacharach's languid tempos. In the end, though, it all sounded effortless and in the case of 'Walk on By', heartbreaking.

Bacharach met Warwick in February 1961 on a session for the Drifters. "She had pigtails and dirty white sneakers," Bacharach recalled in 1970, "and she just shone. The group was dynamite but there was something about the way she carried herself that made me want to hear her sing by herself. After I did, she started to do all our demos."

"We've got a tremendous thing going between us," Bacharach said of his relationship with the singer. "There's a great kind of love transmitted, a happiness, she's the thing that makes everything lighter."

Prior to meeting Dionne Warwick, Bacharach and Davis were songwriters for hire – sometimes as a pair and sometimes with others. Together, though, there was a real chemistry that resulted in a series of sublime masterpieces from 1962 to 1973.

'Walk on By' was one of their first collaborations. Bacharach orchestrated the song with woodblock percussion and a halting tempo like the rhythm of deep sobbing, while the flugelhorn played its unearthly tune.

"We had done 'Walk on By' and 'Anyone Who had a Heart' at the same recording session," Davis recalled. "And we couldn't make up our minds which record to go with first. And we went back and forth and back and forth and finally elected to come out with 'Anyone Who had a Heart'". And so 'Walk on By' was always meant to be the next one."

"They're *songs*," Bacharach told Lillian Ross of the *New Yorker*. "The songs are basically sophisticated. I write the music the way I feel. Hal David, my lyricist, writes the words the way *he* feels. No matter how groovy the electronic devices are these days, there's got to be a song. Electronic devices are marvellous. But nobody's going to whistle electronic devices. You've got to have a song."

Went to See the Gypsy Bob Dylan

(Bob Dylan) ❋ Columbia ❋ 1970 ❋ Appears on: *New Morning*

As Dylan notes in his memoir, *Chronicles, Volume 1*, at the end of the '60s he was at a loose end. His fame had isolated him from the everyday world. He was lauded as the leader of a movement he didn't particularly understand and he didn't like what he saw. He had a young family but he was estranged from his manager, Albert Grossman. Everything was changing and the songs of a few years earlier weren't coming.

In spite of this, he was still recording. He was cutting country covers and some of his own new material with no clear direction. In 1970 he issued *Self Portrait* as an attempt to drive away his fans, he said. 'Went to See the Gypsy' was cut at around the same time.

The song is about a fan meeting a big star and seeing through the trappings that surround him. Dylan told guitarist Ron Cornelius that he wrote it after meeting Elvis Presley. There have been no reports of the two ever meeting, though, and

Dylan has never made any other mention of meeting Presley. It's more likely that the song is about Dylan meeting himself and about preferring to return to "that little Minnesota town" from which he came a decade earlier. The languid progression of the song and Dylan's enervated delivery suggests the ambivalence that he had then towards stardom. Nonetheless, the song is delightful and amusing and true.

Nothing Else Matters Metallica

(James Hetfield/Lars Ulrich) ❋ Elektra ❋ 1991 ❋ Appears on: *Metallica*

"We're just as pissed, but we're using the anger and hatred in a different way," said guitarist James Hetfield when discussing the remarkable about-face that was their fifth album, *Metallica*. "We're not battling it so much, we're more or less laughing at it. There's things every day that piss me off, but they don't affect me as much in the music. There's better things to think about than some old son of a bitch cutting me off in my car or some shit on the news. All that political stuff is shit that you can't change, which is not gonna matter in the long run anyway. I think instead of anger, boredom has become more of the theme in the last few albums. Life is about avoiding boredom, really. You gotta seize the day.

"It was never put on, so you can't just take it off. Life is much easier for us now than it was ten years ago, but god damn, there are still things in my past that really still piss me off. It's too personal to talk about, but I don't think those initial feelings will ever go away."

After the fast and furious and political stance of their first four albums, Metallica enlisted pop metal producer Bob Rock to spend a year making their fifth, complete with power ballads, orchestral arrangements and lush videos. Just weeks before the grunge revolution would overtake the young and the disaffected, Metallica moved themselves to the next level.

The most notable change was a departure from the quirky time changes and labyrinthine arrangements of the previous LP (*... And Justice For All*). The political bent that guided *Justice* was dumped for a more personal style based on Hetfield's bitter and perverse internal monologue. 'Nothing Else Matters' was a huge power ballad with lush orchestration.

April Sun in Cuba   Dragon

(Paul Hewson/Marc Hunter) ✳ CBS ✳ 1978 ✳ Appears on: *Running Free*

Dragon was one of the great pop bands of all time. Five New Zealanders with a background in progressive rock and fans of Lou Reed found themselves as teen sensations. This was largely due to the enormous charisma of singer Marc Hunter and the pop craftsmanship of pianist and writer Paul Hewson.

Their finest moment came in what is effectively a nonsense song with a massive hook and a stop-start, funky tempo.

Hewson was a chess fiend and idea for the lyric came from a story that chess champion Garry Kasparov, during a tournament in Cuba, claimed that the sun was putting him off his game.

"Paul had 'April Sun in Cuba' in the bag," said guitarist Robert Taylor. "It only took him about five minutes to write. We played it live once at the Rooty Hill RSL and the first time people heard it they went berserk so we knew people loved that riff. We recorded it in a couple of days."

The sessions were interrupted by a car accident that put Taylor out of action and the Divinyls' Mark McEntee plays the slide part while Dawkins added sound effects – to the band's ire. Nonetheless, the single went to number two and it remains an enigmatic classic.

"I think that annoying 'da da, da da' and the fact that it's 'April Sun in Cuba' just sounds like a happy pop song," said bass player Todd Hunter. "In 1957 Kasparov is complaining about the April sun in Cuba ruining his game and the whole missile crisis thing – it's all these layers underneath. So who knew? It's just this, you can just tell it's got that thing about it.

"Somebody said to us when we first came to Australia, 'OK you guys, in this country you've got to have fuck-you money or a fuck-you attitude.' It was obvious to us we were never going to get any fuck-you money so we just had the attitude."

All the Young Dudes   Mott the Hoople

(David Bowie) ✳ CBS ✳ 1973 ✳ Appears on: *All the Young Dudes*

As one onlooker tells it, "Dave was trembling when he knocked at Mott's dressing room door." It should have been the other way around. In 1972, when Bowie approached Mott the Hoople the group was about to disintegrate. They had been dropped from their label (Island) and three years of gigging had given them little more than the reputation as the best live band in Britain. They were beloved by rock critics and students who believed that Mott had achieved the perfect British rock sound. They were raw and sloppy and loud and quirky. David Bowie was an unabashed fan.

Mott was conceived and named in 1969 by record producer Guy Stevens to be a British synthesis of the Rolling Stones and Bob Dylan. In reality they would be neither but Ian Hunter was a charismatic enough singer and Mick Ralphs had the psychotic guitar-slinger pose down pat.

'All the Young Dudes' focused Mott's shambolic charm with Bowie's very determined production style. The song picked up on the British tradition of male bonding and identification in a '70s update of the Who's mod leanings. The song gave Mott a place to be in the rock scene rather than just another great live band with progressive rock overtones. Bowie's production especially brought Ian Hunter's vocals to the fore. The song was a hit in the UK and broke the group briefly in the US. However, subsequently left to its own devices, Mott slipped away to irrelevance.

"All we ever had," said Hunter, "at least in the beginning, was our ability to relate to audiences."

And When I Die Blood Sweat & Tears
(Laura Nyro) ❋ Columbia ❋ 1969 ❋ Appears on: Blood Sweat & Tears

"I'm most proud of our collective intent," said drummer Bobby Colomby. "We were trying to upgrade pop music by introducing a higher level of musicianship while combining different styles into one sound. There have been special moments over the years that still hold up, but I must say we have recorded some titles that wouldn't fall into the 'proud' category."

Blood Sweat & Tears were proud to wear the crown as fathers of jazz/rock and over time they, as much as anybody, were responsible for its parlous reputation.

Colomby's father and brother were involved in the New York jazz scene as managers for Thelonious Monk. When the Blues Project imploded, Colomby, organist Al Kooper and guitarist Steve Katz planned a new group that would incorporate jazz horns into a rock format. Part of the plan was a young horn player, Randy Brecker.

The first Blood Sweat & Tears album, *The Child is Father to the Man*, was an eclectic, ambitious failure after which Kooper left. "There was no way success could come to a band with that whining voice singing over a powerful rhythm section and four horns," said Colomby.

Canadian singer David Clayton-Thomas was brought into a less tempestuous band. James William Guercio was brought in to produce and the result was a hyped up version of soul jazz with a bit of rock. The song choices were impeccable: Laura Nyro's 'And When I Die', Billie Holiday's 'God Bless the Child', the Motown standard 'You've Made Me So Very Happy' and Clayton-Thomas' own hit 'Spinning Wheel'. As if to counter the pop smarts, Blood Sweat & Tears opened the album with Erik Satie's 'Variations on a Theme (First and Second Movements)', no doubt giving his estate their biggest ever royalty cheque.

Given their pedigree as musicians (and the reflected glory of Al Kooper) they had both hip credibility – headlining Woodstock and playing the Fillmore – and commercial success. For their second and subsequent albums they moved to the middle of the road and stayed there, watering down both jazz and rock. Their legacy, aside from the first two albums, was to be the even blander Chicago. However, on this album with Clayton-Thomas soaring over the horn and gliding across the jazzy feel, they have a taste of what might have been.

Time After Time Cyndi Lauper

(Cyndi Lauper) ✳ Portrait ✳ 1984 ✳ Appears on: *She's So Unusual*

Cyndi Lauper was a goddess to all those girls who didn't fit in. This was the era of the teen misfit (as portrayed so eloquently by John Hughes in the film *The Breakfast Club* or Francis Ford Coppola's *Rumble Fish*). Lauper was a perfect fit. She was also very televisual just as MTV kicked off and was looking for kooky, quirky and colourful.

It might have been a case of right time, right place, but Cyndi Lauper was also the right girl. She was a wonderful interpreter of songs, notably the chick-lib anthem 'Girls Just Want to Have Fun', Prince's 'When You Were Mine' and the Brains'

brilliant New Waver 'Money Changes Everything'. She can go from being Lucille Ball on one number to Judy Garland on another. Furthering the cause of women's emancipation is the first hit single about female masturbation – 'She Bop'. The real core of the album, however, is Lauper's own composition 'Time After Time' – a gorgeous stately ballad of heartbreak. The song was covered by Miles Davis and became his last hit.

Producer Rick Chertoff enlisted the appalling Philly rock band the Hooters to supply most of the backing on the album and it's a mark of Lauper's personality that she transcends their synthesiser sludge.

Lauper, who had already made an album with her band Blue Angel, put her heart and soul into *She's So Unusual* and it had a force that was simply undeniable. It was one of the few really great pop records to come out of the '80s and it happened because Lauper's Brooklyn whine and her personality cut through. And there was that haircut.

I Should Be So Lucky Kylie Minogue

(Matt Aitken/Pete Waterman) ✳ Mushroom ✳ 1988 ✳ Appears on: *Kylie*

"Kylie came to us via the BBC," recalls Mike Stock, the producing partner in the team Stock, Aitken and Waterman. "I remember the conversation: 'This girl is going to be big. We're going to run 'Neighbours' every evening at 5:30', or whatever the time was. So David Howells, our business affairs man, agreed with Pete Waterman that she should come into the studio in London. But nobody told me. As I'm the person that wrote the songs and made the records I was a bit in the dark on the day she turned up, having been sitting in her hotel for ten days waiting for me to call and me blissfully unaware that she was even in England.

"Anyway, finally I say hello to Kylie and I have to do a very quick analysis of what I'm dealing with here. I find out she's nineteen. I find out she's in this soap. She's very successful in her country, she's doing this, she's doing that and she sings and she's gorgeous looking and ... so I thought well she must have something wrong and I thought that maybe she wasn't going to be lucky in love.

"That started off the process of thinking about what we'll write with her. I told her to go and sit and have a coffee while Matt Aitken and I sat in the studio to toss the idea around, and 'I Should Be So Lucky' was the result.

"The bass on 'I Should Be So Lucky' is the same bass rhythm as in the verse of Madonna's 'Into the Groove'. It's pounding the eight rhythm against a four bass drum on the bass but there's a kick, it adds syncopation into it and that was inspired by Madonna's 'Into the Groove'. I thought that gave it a bit of a kick. Didn't make it sound too bland and in terms of the brashness of the instruments that sit on top of that, the drums are just giving us a straight four underneath so your syncopation plays off your straight four. Her voice cuts so you have to support it with some weight underneath and the high hat doesn't interfere in its frequencies with the vocals so you can hear every word she's saying. Somebody told me that we said, 'I should be so lucky' eighty-five times. Whatever. There was just enough repetition to fill the three minutes and not be too boring. It's simple songs sung in an honest way really.

"We wrote the song in about forty minutes and it took less to sing it because she's extremely quick. But you can't ignore the years of experience that went before that. You had to get to the point where you could do that and I drew on all my experience. I felt that I had to pull something out of the bag very quickly because she was going to get back on a plane and go home. Her ear is very tuned in so I sang her the tune and she sang it back to me, and at that point I put the tapes aside and went on to other things. That particular day I had Bananarama in the morning, she was in at lunchtime until mid-afternoon and then by the time I got rid of her Rick Astley came in. I was doing lots of different artists: working on their songs, finishing tracks off. I put the tape aside and it was only later on in the year that somebody dug the tape up and said, 'this is quite good'."

The rest is history.

To be Young, Gifted and Black Nina Simone

(Weldon Irvine/Nina Simone) ✳ RCA ✳ 1967 ✳ Appears on: *The Essential Nina Simone*

"To most white people, jazz means black and jazz means dirt and that's not what I play," said Nina Simone. "I play black classical music. That's why I don't like the term 'jazz', and Duke Ellington didn't either – it's a term that's simply used to identify black people.

"My original plan was to be the first black concert pianist – not a singer.

"Because I was hired to play the piano for forty-five minutes out of each hour for six hours a night, and since I hadn't played any popular music before, I had to incorporate jazz and classical motifs into what I was doing, and that developed into the difficult role I'm playing now. I didn't start singing until the manager of the bar told me that just playing wasn't good enough."

Nina Simone was not an easy person. A self-confessed diva, Simone's fractious temper and wildly inconsistent behaviour were tolerated for thirty-five years because she was one of the truly magnificent talents of the 20th century. Rightly dubbed the High Priestess of Soul, Simone was capable of pulling out breathtaking performances. A masterful reinterpreter of songwriters, Simone was also capable of classics herself.

In 1968, at the height of the civil rights movement, Simone and co-writer Weldon Irvine penned 'To be Young, Gifted and Black' in honour of her friend, playwright Lorraine Hansberry.

Released as a single in November 1969, it became her biggest RCA hit, reaching the Top 10 on the R&B charts and was covered by Aretha Franklin, Donny Hathaway and Dionne Warwick.

The song became an anthem for black America and the Congress of Racial Equality declared it to be the black national anthem.

"Yes," said Simone, "and then black America promptly refused it."

Sample and Hold Neil Young

(Neil Young) ❋ Geffen ❋ 1983 ❋ Appears on: *Trans*

The *Trans* album is about communication, specifically with Neil Young's son Ben, whose cerebral palsy makes speech nigh impossible. Technology was keeping his son alive and functioning, so Young thought that he might be able to embrace technology as a way of getting to his son. So the music was processed as much as possible and Young even passed his voice through a vococorder.

"We were involved in this program with my young son Ben for eighteen months, which consumed between fifteen and eighteen hours of every day we had," he told Nick Kent. "It was just all-encompassing and it had a direct effect on the music of *Re-ac-tor* and *Trans*. You see, my son is severely handicapped, and at that time was simply trying to find a way to talk, to communicate with other people. That's what

Trans is all about. And that's why, on that record, you know I'm saying something but you can't understand what it is. Well, that's the exact same feeling I was getting from my son."

The song 'Sample and Hold', which is eight minutes long, is typical of the perplexing nature of the album. Unsurprisingly the album didn't sell and Geffen Records took the unusual and unwise step of suing Young for not delivering 'Neil Young' records.

"Underrated! Well, let's say I don't underrate *Trans*," Young said. "I really like it, and think if anything is wrong, then it's down to the mixing. We had a lot of technical problems on that record, but the content of the record is great."

Beautiful Lie Love Me

(Tom Kristensen) ✳ Vitamin ✳ 2002 ✳ Appears on: *Greedy Hen*

This album is probably the first in the history of rock & roll to have been delayed a year while the bass player finished her PhD in mathematics. But then Love Me is not your average rock & roll band. Exquisite. Taciturn. Perverse. Lost. Unheralded. Haunting. Profound. Sublime. Love Me is all of these things, but never average.

The core of Love Me is the partnership between Tom Kristensen, Mandy Pearson and Madeleine King, augmented on this fourth album by guitarist Richard Boxhall. Hailing from Sydney's inner western suburbs, they have been playing around the traps for half a decade and the lucky few who have caught their shows have been converted as Saul was on the road to Damascus. There's Mandy playing a hat box instead of a drum kit and occasionally coming up front for a tap dance routine and otherwise whispering her vocal lines through a voice torn by a million cigarettes. Madeleine on bass has this kind of geeky friendliness that is quite the opposite of a pop princess and at the back Tom broods like Gram Parson's long lost nephew. Love Me don't wear shorts or have visible tattoos. They are not alienated. They are not chasing credibility or chart placing.

Kristensen's songs (and they are invariably his) touch on the eternal verities of country – love gone wrong, love gone right, disappointments and resignation. The instrumentation – spare drums and bass with twanging guitars – are country tropes but there's something drier and ironic, sarcastic and acerbic, which puts them closer to rock & roll. In the darkness of the night, in the early hours of the morning when the stars begin to fade, emotions come into high relief, the spaces are more profound, mingled with dreams and hallucinations. In those hours the sound of a guitar rings for miles. The harmonica sounds more lonesome. The sure foot becomes sloppy. As the bard said, between the thought and the expression.

Kristensen's love songs talk about romances and long-term, lifelong relationships where passion has moved on and something deeper has taken its place. He's not looking for the flash of romance but the long slow lingering kiss that lasts a decade.

Girlfriend's Boyfriend The Passengers

(Jeff Sullivan) ❋ Phantom ❋ 1979 ❋ Appears on: *It's Just That I Miss You*

'Girlfriend's Boyfriend' is the most perfect power pop record made in Australia. The Passengers lit up the Sydney rock scene for a nanosecond in 1978. The members of the five-piece band were mostly acolytes of Radio Birdman – singer Angie Pepper, guitarist Jeff Sullivan, drummer Alan Brown, keyboard player Steve Harris and bass player Jim Dickson.

The centrepiece of the Passengers' set was their version of the Shangri-Las 'Remember (Walkin' in the Sand)', which they delivered with all the fragile passion of the original but a strangely more dry and knowing modernity. Much of the credit goes to Pepper's arid, distant delivery that hit the emotional notes dead on.

'Girlfriend's Boyfriend' was the first song Sullivan wrote for this, his first band, and it's an absolutely perfect riff in a song about the perils of love, dressed up in the context of a '60s pop tune. Angie has an ocean of hurt and desire in her voice – tender and tough. The song just sparkles. It's the sound of love in first blush.

Mona Lisa The Neville Brothers

(N Jean) ❋ A&M ❋ 1981 ❋ Appears on: *Fiyo on the Bayou*

The Neville Brothers – Cyril, Art, Charles and Aaron – are one of those groups about whom musicians speak in awed tones and the public never quite gets. As members of the Meters and in their own right, Cyril (percussion) and Art (vocals – although they were all multi-instrumentalists), were right at the epicentre of New Orleans music for five decades. They worked with everyone from Allen Toussaint, Mac Rebbenack, Dr John and Fats Domino down. The Meters themselves were one of the most popular bands of the time; their Mardi Gras-inspired funk was the coolest R&B to be found in the early '70s. Just check out the propulsive percussion and depth on the killer 'Lady Marmalade'. Their 1973 album, *Fire on the Bayou*, was critically acclaimed but failed to cross over. Similarly, Aaron's solo career had never prospered, despite his extraordinary, angelic voice.

The Neville Brothers first recorded as such in 1978 with a disappointing album. Then, in 1981 they cut *Fiyo* with New York producer Joel Zorn. "It was one of the few times that I've made a record and was one hundred per cent satisfied when we finished. I felt *Fiyo on the Bayou* was the culmination of my career," he said.

The album was split between the funk ('Hey Pocky Way' and 'Sweet Honeydripper') and pop ('Sitting Here in Limbo'). The standouts, though, were where Aaron was allowed to soar, such as on 'Mona Lisa'. This reading of Nat King Cole's classic put the song into a whole new place and clearly announced Aaron Neville as one of the great interpretive singers. Although over the years, Neville's version has become almost ubiquitous, it failed to ignite interest in this album.

Fiyo remains a classic record in the New Orleans funk and R&B heritage and its essential qualities remain undiminished by the years.

Ever Fallen in Love The Buzzcocks

(Pete Shelley) ❋ United Artists ❋ 1979 ❋ Appears on: *Love Bites*

'Ever Fallen in Love' is the definitive love song of the punk era. "It's the whole reason I started writing intelligent love songs," said Pete Shelley. "I realised that most of the times I fell in love I'd end up being hurt and I'd hurt other people as well.

"If I'm a modern romantic, it's because I'm trying to find out what modern romance is. It's not that I'm a new version of the old kind of romantic – I'm trying to find something new.

"All the old kinds of romance are self-destructive because they don't take account of realities."

Lipstick X

(Steve Lucas/Ian Rilen) ❋ X Music ❋ 1979 ❋ Appears on: X-Aspirations

X is quintessence. Their debut album, *Aspirations*, was famously recorded in five hours. "We didn't care, we enjoyed not caring," said bass player Ian Rilen. "We went into Trafalgar studios to put a single down and we ended up putting down about twelve or fourteen songs in an afternoon."

Steve Lucas, Steve Caifero and Rilen set up, played the songs in a row with brief pauses for space between the tracks, then rewound the tapes and Lucas sang the album straight through from beginning to end. Any further effort would have ruined the whole thing. If ever a band in the '70s retained the spirit of Sun and Specialty and Chess, it was X.

'Lipstick' is X at their very best. Rilen carries the song with huge, fat, round bass notes that seem to drop out of the sky like a perfectly executed pattern bombing Lucas' bittersweet whine. It's a tale of dispassionate lust and the guitar notes fly up, piercing the melody line. The music is not so much minimal as economical, as though any effort would be too much.

"I'm not really one for sitting down with a pen and gazing out the window and trying to come up with a song," said Rilen. "I prefer to write live, get a sound, get a groove going with a microphone in front of you, and lyrics come in the disarray of whatever is going on."

Subterranean Homesick Blues Bob Dylan

(Bob Dylan) ❋ Columbia ❋ 1965 ❋ Appears on: Bringing it All Back Home

Dylan notes on the *Biograph* box set, "Probably 'Too Much Monkey Business' is in here somewhere. I don't even think we rehearsed it." It's a flat-out rock & roll song that neatly ties Chuck Berry's rant about the straight world into a new context of middle-class poetics and the hipster world of the mid-'60s.

The lyric was written in one burst in the apartment of his manager's friend shortly before the session in January 1965. Obviously cut live in one take, there is a beautiful, ramshackle energy to the track. Dylan's rhythmic singing seems to recall the chanting of jazz poetry rather than trying to follow the melody.

For Dylan's audience, this was a revolutionary act in itself. He was at the time the king of the protest singers and with this track he donned a leather jacket and joined the ranks of the rockers.

Apart from satirising the Establishment and the police, the theme here is paranoia, partly related to illegal drugs, but it also hints at the chasm that was about to broaden even further with the coming generation gap. As the '60s progressed and resistance to the Vietnam War increased, the level of fear about the authorities also increased.

While not a protest song in the manner of his acoustic ballads, this is a rebel song of which Woody Guthrie would have been proud. Dylan is rejecting the work-day world and suggesting that the worldview as presented by the mass media may in fact be completely crazy and he would have no part in it.

Some radicals took the song too far and named their militant organisation the Weathermen after a line in the song ("you don't need a weatherman to know which way the wind blows"). DA Pennebaker shot a short film of Dylan standing in an alley with flip cards of the lyrics (while poet Allen Ginsberg plays a vandal) which he added to his film *Don't Look Back,* and it's generally regarded as the first music video.

The song was Dylan's first hit single despite having no chorus or mention of the title in the words.

Pink Houses   John Cougar Mellencamp

(John Mellencamp) ❄ Riva ❄ 1983 ❄ Appears on: *Uh-Huh*

"I looked down and saw this old man early in the morning, sitting on the porch of his pink shack with a cat in his arms. He waved, and I waved back. That's how the song started." John Cougar Mellencamp is recalling 'Pink Houses', the song that gave him his real name back.

Johnny Cougar had tried to become a pop idol of sorts. Then in 1982 he went back to his Midwestern roots for the *American Fool* album and tapped into the perfect Reagan-era album. On its sequel, he found his voice as the poet of acceptance. Mellencamp made it all right to be comfortable with middle-class America. He was not complacent, however, and in songs like 'Authority Song' and 'Crumbling Down' he addressed the decline of traditional values. Mellencamp's genius was in the way he phrased his dissent – not as an intellectual leftist from Hollywood or New York but as a true-blue American who despised the big-city capitalists as much as the big government. Mellencamp touched a strong vein of rugged individualism and his personal narrative of trying to be a pop star in the big city and then rediscovering himself in the heartland reinforced the lyrics.

As befits the subject matter, the album was recorded on an Indiana farm over sixteen days. He warmed the studio up by producing an album for Mitch Ryder, a Detroit blue-eyed soul star from the '60s, and then ploughed right in.

Where is the Love? Black Eyed Peas

(Will Adams/Printz Board/Curtis/Michael Fratantuno/Jaime Gomez/George Pajon Jr/Allen Pineda/Justin Timberlake) ❋ A&M ❋ 2003 ❋ Appears on: *Elephunk*

Will.I.Am and Apl de Ap were part of Tribal Nation, a breakdancing crew who began making hip-hop that was closer to De La Soul than NWA – although they signed to Easy E's gangsta label Ruthless Records. With the arrival of MC Taboo, the Black Eyed Peas played around Los Angeles, combining their rap and their breaking skills, in the mid-'90s. By the time of the release of their debut LP *Behind the Front* in 1998, the Black Eyed Peas were already making their own flavour of hip-hop.

The third Black Eyed Peas LP, *Elephunk*, which featured new singer Fergie, was a real breakthrough. Part of the appeal of the album was the epic piece of conscious hip-hop 'Where is the Love', which featured Justin Timberlake. The piece, written in response to September 11, is a worthy successor to Marvin Gaye's or Curtis Mayfield's '70s classics.

"Conscience isn't a topic," said Will.I.Am on MTV. "It's what you have in your subconscious, the things you think about everyday. We ask questions like, 'Why did Kobe [Bryant] do what he did?' 'Why did she go up there in the first place?' 'Why did Mike [Tyson] bite that dude's ear off?' We view the world in strange ways and we put it in our music. I trust everybody. A lot of them really like jewellery, I know that's true. I like jewellery, too. But that's no reason not to trust them."

Werewolves of London Warren Zevon

(LeRoy Marinell/Waddy Wachtel/Warren Zevon) ✳ Asylum ✳ 1978 ✳

Appears on: *Excitable Boy*

It was an odd irony that many of the really exceptional lyricists of the '70s only ever touched the charts with novelty songs. It happened to Loudon Wainwright III with 'Dead Skunk' and to Randy Newman with 'Short People' and it happened to Warren Zevon with 'Werewolves of London'. Zevon's tune had some interesting cover versions from the Grateful Dead and the Flamin' Groovies and some notable appearances in films – not least of which was the film based on the song: *An American Werewolf in London*.

According to Zevon, the track was entirely Phil Everly's idea. Zevon had been part of the Everly Brothers' band. He and his wife were living with Everly, who suggested he write a dance song.

"So we were staying in Phil's guesthouse. And he said, 'I'm working on this solo album. Why don't you guys write a song for me? Write a dance song. Like, 'Werewolves of London''. That's exactly what he said. I just said, 'O-kaayy . . .'

"I was over at Roy Marinell's house, and Roy started playing the figure. And Waddy walked in and said, 'What are you guys doing?' And I said, 'We're doing the 'Werewolves of London''. And Waddy, without batting an eye, said, 'You mean, "Aah-Ooh! Werewolves of London"?' And we said, 'That's right.' And he sat down and we wrote it in twenty minutes. But it was entirely instigated by Philip.

"I think most of the first verse was entirely Waddy. I thought it was pretty remarkable that he spontaneously delivered himself of this sort of Paul Simon-esque verse. No sooner had we told him we were 'doing the Werewolves of London', than he said, 'I saw a werewolf with a Chinese menu in his hand/Walking through the streets of Soho in the rain'."

Guitarist Waddy Wachtel headed up an ensemble that recorded the song, including the Fleetwood Mac rhythm section of Mick Fleetwood and John McVie.

Zevon regarded the song as a tribute to one of his best friends. He describes it as, "one three-minute song that still seems funny, that was and is an homage to Hunter Thompson, I don't mind playing it. That's a fact that seems to elude most journalists because, I guess, it's so obvious. And it wouldn't occur to Hunter, because he's too much of a southern gentleman to consider the fact that he's been ripped off."

Piss Factory Patti Smith

(Patti Smith) ✳ Ork ✳ 1975 ✳ Appears on: *Land*

Patti Smith grew up listening to Bob Dylan and James Brown and reading the poetry of Arthur Rimbaud and William Blake. She gave herself an education in visionary artists. In the late '60s she moved from New Jersey to New York where she lived amongst the artists and hipsters, writing poetry and looking for her voice. A friendship with critic Lenny Kaye, who also played guitar, led to poetry readings on St Mark's Place in New York's East Village. One of these poems/songs was called 'Piss factory'. Clearly autobiographical, the song detailed her journey thus far and was also clearly a masterpiece of rock & roll. One of the patrons of the downtown scene, Terry Ork, recorded and released the song backed with a version of 'Hey Joe' and a star (or stars) was born.

"Repetition makes me carsick. I used to get carsick when I did piecework at the factory in south Jersey," she told Nick Tosches. "I'd have to inspect baby buggy bumper beepers – no shit – y'know, beep, beep, beep, and I'd wind up puking in the bathroom. I'd have to take those little yellow pills. I inspected beepers, steel sheets. It depended, it changed every week. I cut leather straps for baby carriages, made big cardboard boxes for baby mattresses. Toys, strollers, all that stuff.

"Some people told me that 'Piss Factory' was immoral, that it was base; it's not immoral, it's total truth. To me that little 'Piss Factory' thing is the most truthful thing I ever writ. It's autobiography. In fact, the truth was stronger than the poem. The stuff those women did to me at that factory was more horrible than I let on in the song. They did shit like gang up on me and stick my head in a toilet full of piss. People like beauty and purity. They pretend that's what it's all about. I don't like that. *That's* immoral."

Games Without Frontiers Peter Gabriel

(Peter Gabriel) ✳ Charisma ✳ 1980 ✳ Appears on: *Peter Gabriel (3)*

Peter Gabriel's third, eponymous solo album cemented his career as an artist of the first rank. The project was off to a difficult start, however, when Atlantic deemed the album uncommercial and dropped Gabriel. "I gather Ahmet Ertegun, the chairman, thought it was quite arty but the A&R department told him it was undesirable, too esoteric," he told Phil Sutcliff in 1980. "An Atlantic guy who came over to hear us in the studio asked me to make one song sound more like the Doobie Brothers."

Gabriel was not heading anywhere near Doobie Brothers territory. Certainly not with guest performers such as Paul Weller, Tony Levin, Robert Fripp and Kate Bush. These were the crème of British art rock and the album's strength is that tension between the outré and Gabriel's strong melodic and rhythmic instincts.

Gabriel has said that this was "the album on which I discovered a style." Certainly the single 'Jeux Sans Frontières' ('Games Without Frontiers') was the beginning of a new phase for Gabriel.

In My Life The Beatles

(John Lennon/Paul McCartney) ✳ Parlophone ✳ 1965 ✳ Appears on: *Rubber Soul*

The *Rubber Soul* album, which this closes, shows the influence that Bob Dylan was having on the Beatles. No longer were they churning out cute love songs. With this record they started writing songs that were clearly based on the experiences of their lives. 'In My Life' was Lennon's attempt to write a direct autobiography. "Before, we were just writing songs à la Everly Brothers, Buddy Holly – pop songs with no more thought to them than that," he said in 1980. The words were irrelevant. "'In My Life' started out as a bus journey from my house at 250 Menlove Avenue to town, mentioning all the places I could recall. I wrote it all down and it was boring. But then I laid back and these lyrics started coming to me about the places I remember . . . I'd struggled for days and hours trying to write clever lyrics. Then I gave up and 'In My life' came to me." The song is a very moving reverie on life and death, referring at one point to the fifth Beatle, Stu Sutcliffe.

McCartney came around and offered to help. Lennon claimed that the tune was almost completely his. Musicologists have trawled for clues but it's now generally accepted that the tune has the other Beatle's fingerprints all over it.

"He either forgot or didn't think I wrote the tune," said McCartney. "I remember he had the words, like a poem – sort of faces he remembered . . . and I recall going off for half-an-hour and sitting with the Mellotron he had, writing the tune, which was Miracles-inspired, as I remember."

The keyboard solo came from George Martin, while the Beatles were out of the room. "I thought it would be rather nice to have a harpsichord-like solo ... I did it with what I call a 'wound up' piano, which was at double speed – partly because you get a harpsichord sound by shortening the attack of everything, but also because I couldn't play it at real speed anyway," said Martin. "So I played it on piano at exactly half normal speed, and down an octave. And when you bring the tape back to normal speed again, it sounds pretty brilliant. It's a way of tricking everybody into thinking you can do something really well."

Billie Jean Michael Jackson

(Michael Jackson) ✳ Epic ✳ 1982 ✳ Appears on: *Thriller*

Michael Jackson's solo album *Thriller* had an air of unreality to it at the time. It was the apotheosis of pop music – the most popular album of all time with fifty million copies sold around the world. No other album (discounting greatest hits packages) has come close to its ubiquity. Yet in hindsight it has the hallmarks of a Greek tragedy. It made Michael Jackson the King of Pop but cost him his soul. Quincy Jones said, "It felt like entering hyperspace at one point. It almost scared me. I thought maybe this is going too far."

Produced at a cost of $750,000, producer Quincy Jones and Jackson laboured for a year over the album, sorting through 300 songs, casting the right cameos (Paul McCartney for a duet and Eddie Van Halen for a guitar solo). Then the marketing really took off with the videos. Jackson worked hard to make an album that would get played on MTV and rock radio – hence Van Halen – and he saw, before most, the possibility of MTV. None of that really explains why *Thriller* was so huge.

Much of the credit, of course, goes to Jackson. Although Quincy Jones is a producer of extraordinary vision dating back to his work with Miles Davis, it was Jackson's enigma that made *Thriller*. Things look different in retrospect, but listening to these songs now, there's a haunted, tortured quality – parodied perhaps in the title track but most present in the first single, 'Billie Jean'.

On the face of it, 'Billie Jean' is a song about a paternity suit. There's a funk bass line that dances around, pulsing the song forward with the seductive grip of the best R&B. On top of that is Jackson's almost sexless vocal – pleading innocence. Jackson makes this a song not about sex but identity. It's about the power of a rock star to break young girls' hearts. It's about conceiving a child without a relationship. It's about being hunted by the public. If the lyrics weren't enough, the 'Billie Jean' video reinforces all of the eerie qualities of this song. The fact that you can faintly hear Jackson dancing in the studio as he sang only adds a further ghostly layer to the track.

'Billie Jean' raises more questions than it answers. There's a suspicion here in the layers of vocal about the layers of Jackson's own personality and how they will come off. Listening to 'Billie Jean' is like hearing a train wreck in the middle of the night.

Over Stones for You Grant McLennan

(Grant McLennan) ✳ Beggars Banquet ✳ 1990 ✳ Appears on: *Watershed*

As you would be aware, in Queensland you can live for weeks and never touch the earth. The houses in the Far North are built off the ground to get above the thick air and the damp and the lazy taipans. The atmosphere itself is viscous with heat and moisture and the perfume of the bougainvillea, imported magnolia and the decadent fruit of the Moreton Bay figs. This is where Robert Forster and Grant McLennan grew up – a hothouse. In the late '70s the two friends learnt to play guitar and became the Byron and Shelley of punk rock. For more than a decade they persevered with their beautiful vision of a place where tropical dreams became night sweats and vice versa. Their quest took them around the world: to Scotland and London and New York and behind the Iron Curtain before it rusted. The Go-Betweens exploded in an emotional firestorm at the end of the '80s shortly after finishing the *16 Lovers Lane* record. That disc, their sixth, was practically perfect, the apotheosis of the Go-Betweens. It was matched by McLennan's first solo outing, *Watershed*. The key to the record, which is about love and the attempt to reconstruct a life and a reality in the face of love, is 'Over Stones for You'.

McLennan never had his feet on the ground. His otherworldliness, the refusal to acknowledge dull realities, probably also kept him from ever becoming, in the real world, the super pop star he saw in the mirror. On *Watershed*, Grant rewrote the soundtracks to *Don't Look Back*, *La Dolce Vita*, *Cocksucker Blues*, *Jules and Jim*, *Masculin Feminin* and *Vanishing Point*. In his head it was like the Chelsea Hotel circa 1967: Bob Dylan was in his room with typewriter and monkey on his back and

Janis Joplin had her limousine parked out in the street, Edie Sedgewick shot speed in her tiny ass and waited for Andy. Meanwhile on the second floor Warren Beatty, a well-thumbed copy of *Desolation Angels* in his hip pocket and Michael J Pollard at his side, arrives at Bob Altman's door looking to score pot. There's a party at Julie Christie's place.

Love Minus Zero/No Limit Bob Dylan

(Bob Dylan) ✻ Columbia ✻ 1965 ✻ Appears on: *Bringing it All Back Home*

Many people, including Joan Baez, have heard themselves in this beautiful Dylan song. It's one of his most complex melodies and like the rest of this album was recorded with little or no rehearsal.

However, the lyric would seem to sum up his attraction to Sara Lowndes, a romance that was just beginning and would become a marriage. As with many of the songs Dylan wrote about Sara, the woman described in this song is uninterested in the material world and distanced from the circus that Dylan's life was becoming. It's a song that draws on a Zen Buddhist acceptance of opposites – "she's true like ice like fire". It also has a Zen perspective on the impermanence and the illusion of the material world. While Dylan had written plenty of love songs before, 'Love Minus Zero' was the clearest indication of the new level Dylan's work had achieved.

American Girl Tom Petty & the Heartbreakers

(Tom Petty) ✻ Shelter ✻ 1976 ✻ Appears on: *Tom Petty & the Heartbreakers*

In 1976, Tom Petty single-handedly saved American rock & roll.

Born and raised in Florida, Petty moved to Los Angeles where he and the Heartbreakers worked as a bar band. It was good honest craft in an era of gigantism. Even Springsteen had ascended to Olympus, New Jersey. The singer/songwriters were, as Neil Young famously remarked, in the middle of the road. Heavy metal and radio rock was all puff and studio production. The more authentic groups were lost in endless jamming. Tom Petty was a dose of salts.

In New York there was a groundswell of new traditionalists at CBGB and Max's but that was way too arty to move beyond downtown. Petty, on the other hand, wasn't art school at all.

Tom Petty & the Heartbreakers were signed to Shelter Records, former home to Leon Russell. They were produced by Russell's former partner Denny Cordell, who understood how to get a tough, bright sound in just fifteen days. "That first album was a real oddity to everyone – I remember takin' it all around and people would just listen and say, 'How weird, what is it?'" he recalled. "At ABC [Shelter's distributor], it was 'We don't know what this is, I guess it's punk rock.' Which was because I happened to be wearing my leather jacket and the songs happened to be short. At that point the only 'rock bands' were playin' long guitar solos – heavy metal stuff."

Petty's short, sharp songs were as unsentimental as John Fogerty was and as rich texturally. Most distinctive was the use of twelve-string Rickenbacker guitars, a direct homage to the Byrds – this rooted Petty in the mainstream American tradition. As did the songs themselves.

The icing on the cake was Petty's gift as a lyricist. He could freshen a cliché – teen love, rock & roll. On tracks like 'Breakdown' he created an apparently effortless classic of chiming guitars and Stonesy feel. The best, however, came at the close with 'American Girl'. Here, over the sound of cascading, chiming guitars layered up into an epic, Petty puts the entire paradox of manifest destiny and the American Dream into the moment of a girl's life as she considers jumping to her death.

"The 'American Girl'," Petty told journalist Cynthia Rose, "is just one example of this character I write about a lot – the small-town kid who knows there's more out there for them but gets fucked up trying to find it. Like the song says, she was raised on promises. I've always felt sympathetic towards her."

At that point Petty reached out to the kids of America and led rock & roll back to the people.

Throw Your Arms Around Me Hunters & Collectors

(Hunters & Collectors) ✳ Mushroom ✳ 1985 ✳ Appears on: *Human Frailty*

Recorded live to a two-track machine, 'Throw Your Arms Around Me' became an anthem. A slight modal song, in its sparse lyric and melody is an ocean of romantic feeling. The song has been frequently covered, but never well. The Hunters recorded it four times, but never as well as the first. It's a song that has never been a hit single but is one of the most popular Australian ballads.

"When I came up with 'Throw Your Arms Around Me' the band and myself were pretty much entrenched in a different style of music," said lyricist Mark Seymour. "It was funk-orientated, heavy, very European sounding. And it wasn't driven by personal feelings. Whereas that song was very much my baby, I thought. I was writing about direct experience and I wanted to distil a very simple pure emotion.

"I was trying to make the song convey this idea of the inevitability of events: that when two people meet and they're passionate about each other, then things happen and there's nothing either of them can do to stop. There is an inevitability about love that fascinated me. I wanted to capture that idea that there was something happening that I couldn't stop, by setting the language in the future or the immediate future, like the next day or the next hour or the next minute.

"I wanted to capture that mood of being in a state of transition – like you've got your own abode in one part of the town and then she's at another end of the town and you have to keep travelling back and forth. And even though all the things around you are completely familiar your lifestyle has been thrown into upheaval and you're acutely aware of everything around you because of the fact that you're so deeply in love with this person.

"I keep getting asked to do it at weddings, like three or four times a year and sometimes I acquiesce and do it but most of the time I say no."

Orgasm Addict The Buzzcocks

(Pete Shelley/Howard Devoto) ❉ United Artists ❉ 1977 ❉

Appears on: *Singles Going Steady*

The Devoto-less Buzzcocks were quickly signed to United Artists on the basis of the *Spiral Scratch* EP and Pete Shelley began knocking out tunes about love ... sort of. Where other British punks had staked out their enemies – the ruling class, capitalism, older people – Shelley's was the world of romantic confusion. His songs reflected his recent adolescence and he wore his heart on his sleeve. In the context of the depressed British society at the time the songs just added to the sense that nothing was working in the UK for kids any more. As time went on, Shelley's opinions would become more acute, but 'Orgasm Addict' went straight for the big line.

There was plenty of anti-passion going on here, recorded brilliantly by Martin Rushent who was the Phil Spector of the industrial north. This song, with its ambivalence towards the climax, is both very funny and powered by a very powerful punk hook. It's yet another of the many pop singles on the subject of masturbation. "It was a song that everybody could relate to," said guitarist Steve Diggle.

A Whiter Shade of Pale Procol Harum

(Keith Reid/Gary Brooker) ✳ Regal Zonophone/Deram ✳ 1967 ✳ Appears on: *Procol Harum*

Keith Reid was a nerdy twenty-something in 1967 who, having studied English literature, fancied he'd like to write lyrics. Gary Brooker played journeyman piano in the R&B band the Paramounts. Hipster DJ and record producer Guy Stevens introduced them. Brooker added JS Bach's 'Suite no. 3 in D Major' to what were, in Reid's words, "a lot of abstract phrases," and together they wrote 'A Whiter Shade of Pale' – the perfect record for the summer of 1967. It sounded like a happening. It was mysterious – why were the sixteen vestal virgins leaving for the coast? What the hell is a vestal virgin anyway? It alluded to Chaucer and was therefore literary while sounding like what most people thought was going on at these LSD parties they were reading about in the Sunday papers. Even this group's name, Procol Harum, sounded groovy (it was borrowed from Stevens' cat).

The song went to number one around the world immediately.

Brooker called on former colleague Robin Trower and Matthew Fisher, who had played the haunting organ lines of 'Pale', to be the core of the band and they knocked out a debut album under the ear of producer/manager Denny Cordell.

While never coming close to the heights of that first magnificent single, Procol Harum continued to make interesting albums. Their third, *A Salty Dog* (1969), was possibly the best of them. The group also launched solo guitar virtuoso Robin Trower. However, they will always be remembered for those vestal virgins who launched progressive rock on an undeserving world.

Metal Machine Music, Part 1 Lou Reed

(Lou Reed) ❊ RCA ❊ 1976 ❊ Appears on: *Metal Machine Music*

Riding high on the back of the pop success of *Transformer* and *Rock & Roll Animal*, Lou Reed made the most unlistenable album of all time. Then he made it a double.

Metal Machine Music is exactly what it says – the sound of machines. While it may be uncomfortable and while not even Lou Reed can listen to it in its entirety, *Metal Machine Music* is one of the most important albums made during the rock era.

The late great critic Lester Bangs put it best when he wrote in *Creem* in 1976: "If you ever thought feedback was the best thing that ever happened to the guitar, well, Lou just got rid of the guitars. I realise that any idiot with the equipment could have made this album, including me, you or Lou. That's one of the main reasons I like it so much . . .

"In his excellent liner notes, Lou asserts that he and the other speed freaks did not start World Wars I, II, 'or the Bay of Pigs, for that matter'. And he's right. If everybody took amphetamines, all the time, everybody would understand each other. Either that or never listen or bother with the other son of a bitch, because they'd all be too busy spending three days drawing psychedelic lines around a piece of steno paper until it's totally black, writing eighty-page letters about meaningless occurrences to their mothers, or creating MMM. There would be no more wars, and peace and harmony would reign . . .

"I have heard this record characterised as 'anti-human' and 'anti-emotional'. That it is, in a sense, since it is music made more by tape recorders, amps, speakers, and microphones and ring modulators than any set of human hands and emotions. But so what? Almost all music today is anti-emotional and made by machines too. From Elton John to disco to *Sally Can't Dance* (which Lou doesn't realise is one of his best albums, precisely because it's so cold) it's computerised formula production line shit into which the human heart enters very rarely if at all. At least Lou is upfront about it, which makes him more human than the rest of those middle-of-the-road dick-noses. Besides which, any record that sends listeners fleeing the room screaming for surcease of aural flagellation or, alternately, getting physical and disturbing your medications to the point of breaking the damn thing, can hardly be accused, at least in results if not original creative man-hours, of lacking emotional content. Why do people go to see movies like *Jaws*, *The Exorcist*, or *Lisa, She Wolf of the SS*? So they can get beat over the head with baseball bats, have their nerves wrenched while electrodes are being stapled to their spines, and generally brutalised at least every once every fifteen minutes or so (the time between the face falling out of the bottom of the sunk boat and the guy's bit-off leg hitting the bottom of the ocean). This is what, today, is commonly understood as entertainment, as fun, as art even! So they've got a lot of nerve landing on Lou for *Metal Machine Music*. At least here there's no fifteen minutes of bullshit padding between brutalisation. Anybody who got off on *The Exorcist* should like this record. It's certainly far more moral a product.

"All landlords are mealy-mouthed bastards who would let the ruins of Pompeii fall on your four-poster before they'd lift a finger. They deserve whatever they get, and *Metal Machine Music* is the all-time guaranteed lease breaker. Every tenant in America should own a copy of this album. Forearmed!

"My pet land hermit crab, Spud, who sometimes goes for days at a time curled up inside his shell in a corner of the cage so you gotta check to see if he's dead, likes *Metal Machine Music* a lot. Every time I put it on, he comes out of his shell and starts crawling happily around the sand and climbing the bars. It is, in fact, the only time I ever see him get any exercise. Either that or he's dancing . . .

"I played it for President Idi 'Big Daddy' Amin of Uganda when he flew me and Lisa Robinson over there to interview him for upcoming cover articles in *Creem* and *Hit Parader*, and he absolutely loved it. I gave him a copy, and now by special edict he has it piped through the Muzak vents of every supermarket (all thirty-five of them) and doctor's waiting room (all eight) in his great nation, so that the citizens there may be inspired to ever fiercer heights of patriotism for his regime and all that it stands for. He wanted to declare it the Ugandan national anthem, but I told him that I would have to check with the American teenage shock vets first, and being a wise, fair, graciously diplomatic politician, he of course immediately assented, and then, genial host that he is, whisked us off to see a live multiple snuff film done sans cameras and celluloid. 'We can't afford them', he explained. 'And besides, the next time you have a dangling conversation with Paul Simon, you can inform him that the theatre is not really dead.'

"It is the greatest record ever made in the history of the human eardrum. Number two: *KISS Alive!*"

I Scare Myself Dan Hicks & His Hot Licks

(Dan Hicks) ✳ Epic ✳ 1969 ✳ Appears on: *Original Recordings*

As drummer in the Charlatans, Hicks was on the ground floor of the San Francisco sound. He took a curve just after the Summer of Love, abandoning acid R&B for his own eccentric brand of pop jazz. The Hot Licks owed a bit to swing and a bit to jug band blues and jazz but mostly they were on their own. The great John Mendelssohn described the sound as "a cocaine or some such vision of '40s romantic balladry – very spaced, and, yes, quite mellow. A psychedelic experience, no less." With two violins – one in the masterful hands of Sid Paige – two sexy girl singers and the swinging bass of Jaime Leopold, Hicks had a beautiful thing going. Always there was Hicks' sly wit, like a western Cole Porter on tracks like 'How Can I Miss You When You Won't Go Away?' The centrepiece here is his best tune: 'I Scare Myself'. This is five minutes of haunted music floating on Sid Paige's spectral violin. It's a rare track that goes beyond its conceit and looks into the deserted rooms of the heart.

Blank Generation Richard Hell & the Voidoids

(Richard Hell) ✳ Ork ✳ 1976 ✳ Appears on: *Blank Generation*

Richard Hell and school friend Tom Verlaine came to New York to be poets and rock stars. In the downtown scene of the mid-'70s they found themselves scuffling around trying to make music, first as the Neon Boys and later as Television. Hell, making the best of his poverty, restructured his T-shirts and jeans with safety pins and knocked out his versions of garage rock-via-symbolist poetry. London clothes designer Malcolm McLaren picked up on Hell's style and formed a band in his image. He called them the Sex Pistols.

Meanwhile Hell had been kicked out of Television and the Heartbreakers. Which was fortunate because he formed one of the best groups of the era – the Voidoids. Robert Quine's prickly, lyrical lines danced guitars with Ivan Julian and Mark Bell's heavy drums. Hell squirmed his way through vocals.

The lead track became a catchcry for the New York scene. Its title was a throwaway idea Hell had for a line in a poetry book.

"As for the song, I liked the idea of doing my versions of sorta genre songs, and a 'generation' song was one of them," Hell told Barney Hoskyns of Rocksbackpages.com. "I was way into the Who's first album [*The Who Sings My Generation*], and Tom had this funny, kitsch single by Rod McKuen called 'I Belong to the Beat Generation', so it just seemed like a perfect conjunction to use that classic 'Hit the Road Jack' chord sequence as the structure of that song.

"For me, it was an awareness of, like, Andy Warhol and Beckett and a whole bunch of people that I identified with but that were actually very different from each other. Samuel Beckett and Andy Warhol had very little in common, except that you could imagine applying the word 'blank' to them. But ultimately, when anything was discussed long enough, my conclusion was that I didn't care! It was kind of a defensive thing that kids that age will use. I think I felt just overwhelmed by input: the Vietnam war and the collapse of the '60s and the proliferation of media . . . it just felt like everything was too much to handle and you just tuned out. Blank seemed appropriate to me, because my own feeling was of sensory overload."

Blowin' in the Wind Peter, Paul & Mary

(Bob Dylan) ❋ Warner Bros. ❋ 1962 ❋ Appears on: *In the Wind*

Until around 1965 most people knew about Bob Dylan as a songwriter, chiefly for Peter, Paul & Mary. The folk trio was assembled by manager Albert Grossman as an act that could put folk music into the pop charts. And it worked. Peter Yarrow and Paul Stookey looked mildly bohemian but dressed in good suits; the collegiate friends to the lanky Mary Travers, her long blonde hair drifting breezily around her shoulders. Peter, Paul & Mary were vigorous, clean-cut and very good with their own songs and traditional love songs. There was also no danger that they would go all political like Pete Seeger and the Weavers had done.

Grossman, who was the king of the folk scene, took on management of Bob Dylan and so it was natural that he would offer Dylan's songs to Peter, Paul & Mary. He encouraged the trio to have a crack at the bitter love ballad 'Don't Think Twice It's All Right'. When they covered 'Blowin' in the Wind' instead they put protest music into every home in the western world.

"Instinctively, we knew the song carried the moment of its own time," said Yarrow.

According to his friends, Dylan realised early on that 'Blowin' in the Wind' was a powerful song. His friend David Blue claimed that the song was finished on 16 April 1962. He recalled that they had been drinking coffee at the Fat Black Pussycat. Dylan pulled out his guitar and went through the song, inspired by the traditional slave song 'Auction Block'. That evening, Dylan and Blue took the tune to the hoot night at Gerde's Folk City, where Gil Turner debuted the song to unanimous acclaim.

Dylan's fame went up a notch.

Two months later, at the Finjan Club, Montreal, Dylan introduced the song himself as: "Here's one that's called 'How Many Roads Must a Man Walk Down?' Here's a song that's in sort of a set . . . set pattern of songs that say . . . a little more than 'I love you, and you love me/An' . . . let's go over to the banks of Italy/And we'll raise a half a family/You for me, and me for me'."

For a time, Dylan blew apart the market for 'I Love You' folk songs. Once Peter, Paul & Mary topped the charts with 'Blowin' in the Wind' it became possible to have left-wing songs and hits at the same time. The impact was enormous.

"If you could imagine the March on Washington with Martin Luther King, and singing that song in front of a quarter of a million people, black and white, who believed they could make America more generous and compassionate in a nonviolent way, you begin to know how incredible that belief was," said Travers. "And still is. To sing the line, 'How many years can some people exist before they're allowed to be free?' in front of some crummy little building that refuses to admit Jews in 1983, the song elicits the same response now as it did then. It addresses the same questions. 'How many deaths will it take till they know that too many people have died?' Sing that line in a prison yard where political prisoners from El Salvador are being kept. Or sing it with Bishop Tutu. Same response. Same questions."

Shot by Both Sides Magazine

(Pete Shelley/Howard Devoto) ❋ Virgin ❋ 1977 ❋ Appears on: *Real Life*

Having recorded the *Spiral Scratch* EP with the Buzzcocks, Howard Devoto swiftly turned his back on punk rock, and for a time, on his musical career. It didn't take long to cobble together Magazine with the talented if sometimes obtuse guitarist

John McGeogh. Devoto said that his singular reason for Magazine was to record this song, but a burst of creativity helped by an advance from Virgin prompted him to take a step further.

Devoto, unlike most punk rockers, came from a literary background. Magazine's cover versions included works by John Barry, Captain Beefheart and Sly Stone. Their influences included Frank Zappa, progressive rockers Soft Machine and King Crimson, and contemporary acts like the Residents. This diverse stew and Devoto's credentials made 'Shot by Both Sides' the first volley in the post-punk revolution. All manner of pompous ink was spilled in their name. The *NME* declared Devoto "the most important man alive".

He wasn't that, but this hymn to ambivalence and paranoia packs an iron/velvet punch.

Theme from Shaft Isaac Hayes

(Isaac Hayes) ✳ Enterprise ✳ 1971 ✳ Appears on: *Shaft*

Isaac Hayes was an integral part of Stax/Volt records and the Memphis scene in the '60s. He was one of the best keyboard players and arrangers at Stax even before he started writing in partnership with lyricist David Porter. Their hits included Carla Thomas' 'B-A-B-Y' and Sam and Dave's 'Soul Man', 'Hold On, I'm Comin'', and 'When Something is Wrong with My Baby', among others.

Shaft was an early blaxploitation film for which Hayes was employed to write the score. Hayes sets the film up with one of the most dramatic pieces of film music. The track starts out on the high hat and then in comes a scratchy Curtis Mayfield-style guitar with a scratch wah wah theme drenched in reverb and the groove just doesn't quit. Hayes eventually comes in crooning praise for Shaft in his rumbling bass voice: "the private dick who's a sex machine to all the chicks".

The theme from *Shaft* increased the seismic shift in R&B towards funk and towards a jazzier, blacker sound. The song embodies this new idea of the African-American as a cool guy, brimming with machismo – proud and lethal and righteous.

'Theme from Shaft' won an Academy Award and the score won Hayes an Oscar as well – the first black composer to take the statue.

Stolen Car   Bruce Springsteen & the E Street Band

(Bruce Springsteen) ❋ Columbia ❋ 1980 ❋ Appears on: *The River*

Cars had been a sustaining metaphor for Bruce Springsteen since the early days. By 1980, all the cars on *The River* were either wrecked or stolen; their only destination was to take the singer back to see his faded dreams.

In 'Stolen Car' the character rides the streets at night in a stolen car in the hope, which is never satisfied, of being arrested in order to prove that he exists. It's perhaps the most existential piece of writing in rock. If Kafka had been a hot rod enthusiast, this is what *The Castle* would have been.

According to Springsteen, "'Stolen Car' was the predecessor for a good deal of the music I'd be writing in the future. It was inner-directed, psychological; this was the character whose progress I'd soon be following on *Tunnel of Love*. He was the archetype for the male role in my later songs about men and women."

The music here is so quiet. It's minimal and held back like the early hours in which the car drives. The keyboards are like a fog on the road and the voice is just drifting in the murk, barely alive.

Holiday   Madonna

(Madonna) ❋ Sire ❋ 1983 ❋ Appears on: *Madonna*

"For me, it was superstardom from the word go, and I thought, what is this shit? It's just a home away from home. So I left and came back to New York, and it was ... hell. New York is good to me now, but it was a really horrible in the beginning," Madonna told Barney Hoskyns back in 1983 when she was just another downtown girl with black roots in her hair and an overload of cheap jewellery.

Madonna would be the first to admit that she's no great singer but she knows two things. First of all, she knows what's going to happen next in music. Second, she knows that nothing so insignificant as a meagre vocal range is going to stop her.

In the early '80s, Madonna was a girl from the suburbs who wanted to make it in the downtown New York scene. She danced, she modelled, she acted and she sang. She met all the right people, including Sire Records' president Seymour Stein, who, legend has it, signed her contract while laid up in a hospital bed.

Stein put Madonna with Roberta Flack's producer Reggie Lucas, who described the sessions as "very informal and casual. It was my first pop project, and she was just a new artist. I had no idea it would be the biggest thing since sliced bread."

The record initially had a lukewarm reaction.

It was the single 'Holiday', a much more club-oriented track produced by Madonna's boyfriend and DJ Jellybean Benitez, that became a breakout hit. Suddenly Madonna was on her way, and she never lost control again.

"I think it stands up well," she said of her debut album. "It just took a long time for people to pay attention to me – and I thank God they did."

Love Rain (Suite) Jill Scott

(Vidal Davis/Jill Scott) ❋ Hidden Beach/Sony ❋ 2001 ❋
Appears on: *Experience: Jill Scott 826+*

Jill Scott is the latest in a line of soulful divas (Macy Gray, Erykah Badu, Alicia Keys, Kelis) but the funk and soul on her second LP, *Experience: Jill Scott 826+*, is explicitly '70s down to its syncopated bootstraps. Nowhere is she more potent than on this epic.

Scott was discovered by rap group the Roots, which led to an affiliation with DJ Jazzy Jeff and his sidekick Will Smith as a writer and performer. On her own with the 2000 debut, *Who is Jill Scott?*, she answers the question by eschewing the taut metre of rap, going for the more risky but exotic rhythm of her own poetry. Likewise she opted for a live rhythm section and strings rather than samples, beats and keyboards and, what the hell, it came out sounding like something from the mid-'70s.

Scott has the verse stylings of a latter-day Gil Scott-Heron with the high-octane sensuality of Marvin Gaye. Most of all she has the delivery. Full, soulful, honeyed vocals that can slide around a melody. The nostalgic tip of Scott's music comes from its fusion of soul and jazz, which was so popular before the disco era. In some respects this works against the artist's ability to establish herself as a voice for the future.

Experience is a double; the first disc recorded live with material from the first album while the second is new material. The concert, taped in Washington DC in 2004, does capture the dynamics of Scott's performance and the versatility that a funk band can bring to material. Rather than being just a revision of the previous record, these tunes benefit from the excitement that clearly ripples through the crowd. The slow fire quickly becomes a furnace.

Get Back The Beatles

(John Lennon/Paul McCartney) ✳ Apple ✳ 1970 ✳ Appears on: *Let It Be*

Paul McCartney borrowed the line "Get back to where you once belonged," from George's song 'Sour Milk Sea' as sung by Apple recording artist Jackie Lomax. An early version of the song contained a quote from Conservative politician Enoch Powell, who ran a virulent racist line against Pakistani immigration. McCartney wisely dropped the reference. Lennon, however, thought it to be an attack on Yoko. He told a magazine shortly before his death, "I've always thought there was this underlying thing in Paul's 'Get Back'. When we were in the studio recording it, every time he sang the line 'Get back to where you once belonged', he'd look at Yoko."

Initially it was to be the title of the album but by the time that record was finished, so were the Beatles, and McCartney's wishful thinking was less appropriate as a title than the requiem *Let It Be*.

There are two main versions of the song – a studio version, which was a hit single, and the album version, which closes *Let It Be* and which was recorded on the roof of the Apple office.

The rooftop version has a certain sloppiness and warmth and finishes with the faint voice of a policeman saying, "I'm afraid it's just too long." Then Lennon chimes in with the greatest understatement of the century, "I'd like to say thank you on behalf of the group and ourselves, and I hope we passed the audition."

Body and Soul Billie Holiday

(Johnny Green/Eddie Heyman/Robert Sour/Frank Eyton) ✳ Verve ✳ 1946 ✳
Appears on: *All or Nothing at All*

To please his father, Johnny Green went to Wall Street to become a banker. However, by the time of the Great Crash he was already writing hit songs. His best-known song was written in 1930 for English singer Gertrude Lawrence when Green was in his early twenties. Then it came back across the Atlantic for the Broadway musical *Three's a Crowd* where it was sung by Libby Holman.

'Body and Soul' was the most covered, most performed work of the 20th century. Its interpreters included Louis Armstrong, Django Reinhardt, John Coltrane, Thelonious Monk, Sonny Rollins, Frank Sinatra, Betty Carter and Archie Shepp. The tune's harmonic versatility lends itself to improvisation but the melody is sufficient to withstand even the most determined stylist.

Charlie Parker made his recording debut with this song. Critic Gary Giddins described Coleman Hawkins' version as "One of the most celebrated improvisations in music, and a gauntlet tossed at every other saxophonist in jazz. There is nothing to compare with Coleman Hawkins . . . Hawkins' variations became as much a part of jazz as the original melody."

Billie Holiday, too, made it her own. She brought the Lady Day sadness to a song that was ethereal to start with. Her take on the melody sounds as eternal as night-time.

When asked for an explanation of the success of his songs, Green said, "What we write is inventive but it's also in good taste. It's natural, it's musical. Or as we used to say, you don't go from New York to Boston by way of Philadelphia. That's the way my harmonies go."

Boobs a Lot The Fugs

(Steve Weber) ✳ Broadside ✳ 1965 ✳ Appears on: *The Fugs First Album*

Ed Sanders and Tuli Kupferberg were Beatnik poets in New York in the mid-'60s when they turned their minds to music and were joined by Ken Weaver and Holy Modal Rounders' Steve Weber and Peter Stampfel. The Fugs' material ranged from setting William Blake to jug band music to their own barbed and inventive lyrics. Musical prowess was not high on the agenda. It's appropriate that Harry Smith (of the legendary Anthology) supervised the recording of this first album.

"Our goal was to make the revolution," Kupferberg told *Perfect Sound Forever*. "We would go to a place called the Dom on St Marks. We would go there and try to dance, listening to the Beatles and the Stones. We decided that we could do something like that. So we decided to enter the field and we were sort of an instant hit. We had a wide range – Ed was a wild, crazy, Midwestern young man and I was a

New York radical Jew. So together we had everything or, as some people would say, nothing."

Simeon, of avant-garde act Silver Apples, recalls playing the Fillmore with the Fugs: "The bass player had apparently been taking huge quantities of acid and had, in his own tripped-out mind, assumed the identity of Paul McCartney. He had crawled under the piano, wedged himself in, in such a way that nobody could get him out. And he was playing, note for note, the bass line for every Beatles song from 'I Want to Hold Your Hand' on up. Fortunately, somewhere around 'Lovely Rita' he passed out."

As was appropriate, the Fugs' songs dealt with sex, drugs, the war in Vietnam, the soulless nature of suburbia and religion. They were frequently very funny and often offensive. 'Boobs a Lot' was a tasteless but exhuberant contribution to the women's liberation debate delivered with the Fugs' bohemian amateurism.

"I was sort of opposed to the idea of perfecting our music," said Kupferberg. "I felt that it would interfere with our message: love, sex, dope."

All Right Now Free

(Andy Fraser/Paul Rodgers) ✳ Island ✳ 1970 ✳ Appears on: *Fire & Water*

The first concert I ever saw was the beginning of the end for Free. It was on 9 May 1971 at Randwick Racecourse for $3 with Manfred Mann's Earth Band opening and Deep Purple closing. Free took the day with their unassuming, workmanlike rock. This working-class quartet was never going to achieve the grand heights of Zeppelin or the Rolling Stones. Their virtue was their ordinariness.

Paul Rodgers had an impressive high register that brought Robert Plant to mind and Paul Kossoff had an interesting if limited blues style, but mostly it was their modesty that was Free's charm. For a while it seemed as though they would adopt the mantle of the next big British band, but they never lived up to it.

Free had their admirers, not least of whom became Prime Minister. "Paul Rodgers was the man whose voice I most wanted to emulate," Tony Blair told the BBC. "If I could have sung like that I would probably have stuck with being a rock musician."

Bassist Andy Fraser had the distinction of having briefly played with John Mayall when he met Simon Kirke and the other members of the band. They were a traditional British blues-rock band at that time until venereal disease laid up the singer and he and Fraser began writing songs. Their best work betrayed their teenage years with its simplistic lyrics while the lugubrious tempos and simple if soulful bottom end went perfectly with cheap wine and Mandrax.

They hit their stride with the third album, *Fire & Water*, which contained the anthems 'Mr Big', 'Fire & Water' and their signature tune 'All Right Now'. This was a big dumb album with massive choruses. Rodgers described the writing of 'All Right Now' to Mat Snow as, "I just put myself in the position of your average bloke chatting up your average chick and that's timeless."

Love Will Tear Us Apart Joy Division

(Ian Curtis/Peter Hook/Stephen Morris/Bernard Sumner) ✳ Factory ✳ 1981 ✳
Appears on: *Substance*

Inevitably and forever this song will live in the shadow of Ian Curtis' suicide. Shortly after its recording the singer and principal lyricist, father of a one-year-old daughter, hung himself in the kitchen at home near Manchester in the early hours of 18 May 1980. In March, the group had spent two weeks in London's Britannia Row Studios, recording what would become their second LP, *Closer*. Although it's likely that Joy Division would have forever broken out of their Mancunian provincialism anyway, Curtis' death just added to the story. These weren't just English boys moaning in their bedsits.

Joy Division began in June 1976 when the Sex Pistols played Manchester and bassist Peter Hook and guitarist Bernard Sumner resolved to form a band. They asked an acquaintance, Ian Curtis, to be the singer.

"Ian brought a direction," Sumner told Jon Savage. "He was into the extremities of life. He wanted to make extreme music: he wanted to be totally extreme on stage, no half measures. Ian's influence seemed to be madness and insanity.

"Everyone says Joy Division's music is gloomy and heavy; I often get asked why this is so. I can only guess why it was heavy for Ian, but for me it was because the whole neighbourhood that I'd grown up in was completely decimated in the mid-'60s. At the end of our street was a huge chemical factory: where I used to live is just oil drums filled with chemicals.

"When I left school and got a job, I was chained in this horrible office: every day, every week, every year, with maybe three weeks' holiday a year. The horror enveloped me. So the music of Joy Division was about the death of optimism, of youth."

The first album, *Unknown Pleasures*, was described by Jon Savage as "a definitive northern Gothic statement: guilt-ridden, romantic, and claustrophobic." Great wads of keyboard and guitar surrounded Hook's melodic bass lines and Curtis' strangled voice.

Closer was the next step for the group. A substantial leap.

Curtis had severe epilepsy that he was medicating with Benzedrine. He was chronically depressed and had been threatening suicide since his teens and tried three times before finally succeeding. Added to all this, his marriage was failing, he was in a relationship with another woman and there was a new child. The world was closing in on Curtis.

"The mood he was in when he wrote that stuff is a very big question," Factory boss Tony Wilson told Savage. "It's almost as if writing that album contributed to his state: he immersed himself in it, rather than just expressing it."

According to his wife, Deborah Curtis, "I think he [Ian] enjoyed being unhappy, that he wallowed in it. When we were kids, lots of people were miserable; they grew out of it. I thought Ian would."

One of the last things recorded before Curtis' death was the single, 'Love Will Tear Us Apart', which became one of the great love ballads of the decade. The album *Closer*, however, was the epitaph for Joy Division and set the tone for serious young bands for the future.

Man Overboard Do Re Mi

(Dorland Bray/Do Re Mi) ❋ Virgin ❋ 1985 ❋ Appears on: *Domestic Harmony*

With Stephen Philip's prickly guitar lines jabbing at Helen Carter's melody on the bass and Deborah Conway's epic voice accusing her lover of "penis envy," 'Man Overboard' was an unlikely hit single. Do Re Mi had recorded the song on an EP some years previously but in the interim and with English producer Gavin McKillop they evolved their post-punk perversity into a mature sound.

"People used to make a fuss that it had penis envy, pubic hair and anal humour in the lyric, but actually the most scandalous thing about it was that it didn't actually have a chorus," said Deborah Conway of the song that made her an overnight feminist icon.

Probably the fact that it did have slightly risqué lyrics was something that propelled it towards the top of the charts. This was ironic considering that the lyric was largely penned by male drummer Dorland Bray. It's a reverie about infidelity and about loathing and is one of the most caustic little vignettes of the gap between the sexes.

"I suppose 'Man Overboard' was considered a bit of a feminist anthem in a way," Conway said. "It's just a groove. The lyric is chanted over the top. There was something inherent in the song that was very gripping for people."

Louie Louie The Kingsmen

(Richard Berry) ❊ Jerdon ❊ 1963 ❊

Appears on: *The Kingsmen in Person Featuring Louie Louie*

'Louie Louie' became more than a song. It is an anthem that symbolises the phenomenon of garage rock. In the forty years since the Kingsmen's version broke out of the Pacific Northwest to hit number one on the Cashbox charts the song has been covered more than 1500 times, been the subject of a thirty-one-month investigation by the FBI, and inspired millions of would-be rock stars.

The song was written by Richard Berry as an R&B/calypso tune. The lyric was a tale told by a homesick and lovesick sailor to his barman. As such it was a minor West Coast hit in 1959. Oregon band the Wailers adapted it and it became a regional standard in the early '60s. As such it entered the repertoire of Oregon bands such as Paul Revere and the Raiders and the Kingsmen – Jack Ely (guitar and vocals), Mike Mitchell (guitar), Dan Gallucci (piano), Bob Norby (bass) and Lynn Earton (drums). The Kingsmen cut their version as a demo to secure a job working a cruise ship bound for Australia.

The session cost $36 and took less than an hour at Northwest Recorders in Portland, Oregon. The band ran the song down live in the studio with one microphone. This guttural pumping, full of amateurish enthusiasm and little technique, is simply perfect. Even better is that the muddy sound drowns out Jack Ely's vocal, making the lyrics, as the FBI discovered, unintelligible.

Local impresario Jerry Dennon pressed a few hundred copies on his regional label, Jerdon. The disc became a cult favourite in Boston and was re-released by

Wand and worked into a minor hit in several cities. Then suddenly rumours began to spread about the real subject of the lyrics – it was believed that hidden meanings could be determined when the 45 was played at 33⅓. Parents were outraged to the extent that the state of Indiana banned the song. The FBI began an investigation (some of the files are now available at www.thesmokinggun.com). The controversy sent the single to the top of the charts.

'Louie Louie' symbolised the subversive nature of rock & roll to the straight world. At the same time its ham-fisted arrangement of the classic one-four-five chord structure was an inspiration to millions of kids. The song could be played just as well after drinking gallons of beer. The combination of stupidity and illicit sex made the song a classic amongst college students. The Kingsmen, too, were famous for a year or so – even appearing in the beach party movie *How to Stuff a Wild Bikini*. But talent will out.

The song has a mojo all its own. Amongst its many permutations, Toots and the Maytals turned it into reggae and the Stooges performed an epic three-minute vamping of the song as Iggy Pop is beaten by Hell's Angels.

As Dave Marsh wrote in his book on the song, "Embrace 'Louie Louie' tightly enough and you may come to know more about yourself than it's easy to contemplate, let alone tolerate."

Death Defying   Hoodoo Gurus

(Dave Faulkner) ✳ Big Time ✳ 1983 ✳ Appears on: *Mars Needs Guitars*

Dave Faulkner was once asked whether the Hoodoo Gurus, the band he sings and plays guitar for, had left an influence. "I know we have," he replied. "I see it in lots of things going on, but whether it's our influence or people that we were influenced by, who can tell? I see our way of thinking, which is something that when we started I didn't see as much of."

Sixties garage rock, the music that was the original punk rock, wasn't about tattoos and Mohawks. It was garage bands – young bands trying to work out what this new music called rock & roll was all about. Typically the best of them made one single or one album and then disappeared, only to be reborn on the Nuggets compilation – an absolutely essential album. In Australia, combos like the Throb, the Missing Links, the Easybeats and later the Masters Apprentices all made great rock & roll. It was devil-may-care music, garage punk sounds as if the Beatles tried to cover *The Rolling Stones Now!* album.

The Gurus' first masterpiece was *Mars Needs Guitars*. Less self-consciously pop culture than their debut, the album had killer songs, the best of which was the ballad 'Death Defying'. As powerful a lyric as you're likely to hear, it was matched by a melody. Dave Faulkner once told me that one of his heroes was Cole Porter. It sounded incongruous coming from the leader of a garage band, but then a track like this makes him a contender in that league.

Sex & Drugs & Rock & Roll Ian Dury & the Blockheads

(Ian Dury/Chaz Jankel) ❋ Stiff ❋ 1977 ❋ Appears on: *New Boots and Panties*

This phrase is now part of everyday speech. Ian Dury was a painter by trade, a bit of a poet and bit of a jazz buff, when he fell into rock & roll. He was a mature-age rocker, forming the Blockheads in the mid-'70s at the age of thirty-five. Prior to that he had scuffled around with music and began writing his often amusing lyrics with a Cockney slant. The Blockheads, who revolved around keyboardist Chaz Jankel, were a versatile bunch with a taste for classic R&B and jazz rather than rock. They were, unlike most other bands of that period, funky. The Blockheads' feel and Dury's Cockney spoken rhyming basically laid the way for British hip-hop – especially acid jazz, which was for the most part a poor imitation of what the Blockheads were doing in 1977.

"The first thing we recorded was 'Sex & Drugs & Rock & Roll'," Dury told Chris Welch before his death in 2000. "It had a sound and a simplicity, because it's basically just three people, with Chaz on guitars and pianos, Charlie [Charles] and Norman [Watt-Roy] on drums and bass. It was long before the age of click tracks. We just played and if it sped up a bit, so what.

"'Sex & Drugs' started as a mild admonishment and ended as a lovely anthem. When me and Jankel wrote this song we stole the riff from a Charlie Haden bass solo on a 1960 Ornette Coleman album called *Change of the Century*. I met Charlie Haden later and he told me that he'd nicked the riff too, from a Cajun folk tune. It was banned by the BBC when we released it as a single but it sold about 18,000 copies.

"With this song I was trying to suggest there was more to life than either of those three – sex, drugs and rock & roll, or pulling a lever all day in a factory.

"I was saying, 'If all you think about is sex and drugs and rock & roll, there is something wrong.' The title was used in headlines all over the world. I wish I'd got a quid every time that title has been used."

Brilliant Disguise   Bruce Springsteen

(Bruce Springsteen) ❋ Columbia ❋ 1987 ❋ Appears on: *Tunnel of Love*

For a man who just got married, *Tunnel of Love* is a decidedly bleak album. In his book of lyrics, prosaically titled *Songs*, Springsteen wrote, "For twenty years I'd written about the man on the road. On *Tunnel of Love* that changed, and my music turned to the hopes and fears of the man in the house."

On the cover he is dressed in the wedding suit, leaning on the convertible, but you get the impression that he's in half a mind to jump right in. Springsteen's marriage to actress Julianne Phillips was a troubled affair that didn't last much beyond the release of this album. Beyond the pros and cons of his romantic life though, this was an album by a man searching for identity.

"The centre of *Tunnel of Love* is 'Brilliant Disguise'," Springsteen wrote. "Trust is a fragile thing; it requires allowing others to see as much of ourselves as we have the courage to reveal. But you drop one mask and find another behind it, until you begin to doubt your own feelings about who you are. It's the twin issues of love and identity that form the core of *Tunnel of Love*."

Recorded mostly at home by himself with some input from the E-Street Band, these songs are intimate and dark, but their moods stay with you.

"My characters were no longer kids," he wrote.

I Say a Little Prayer   Aretha Franklin

(Burt Bacharach/Hal David) ❋ Atlantic ❋ 1968 ❋ Appears on: *Aretha Now*

Written for Dionne Warwick, Jerry Wexler produced Aretha Franklin's version and substantially changed the song – altering the tempo and pumping up the gospel flavour. Where Warwick had been wistful, Aretha just let it all hang out. This was the only time that Burt Bacharach felt a cover version had improved on his original arrangement.

"We'd sit in a room," said lyricist Hal David, "and start with maybe a line that I had, or four bars of Burt's music, and we'd build a song sort of like we were building a house. Very often we were writing three songs at a time.

"There are a lot of songs where the music is fine and the lyric is fine, yet they seem to come in, get in front of you and just fly away. They don't hold on. What I try to do is to find something that's a little rougher, something that's not so smooth that it evaporates. Often, in searching for that feeling, you go almost against the grain.

"In 'I Say a Little Prayer' where the chorus is 'forever forever', that's where the title would ordinarily be, and yet the song for me took place in the verses, so that's where I put the title."

Franklin, whose father was a minister and who sang in church before she could talk, brought her enormous power to this song. Bacharach's tunes tended to be based around tonal colour, where Franklin just "took it back to church".

Rabbit in Your Headlights Unkle

(J Davis/Thom Yorke) ❋ MoWax ❋ 1998 ❋ Appears on: *Psyence Fiction*

For the purposes of this masterwork James Lavelle joined US hip-hop producer DJ Shadow. Two years of recording, sampling and mixing went into the final product. "Josh [DJ Shadow] likes to compare it with *Titanic*," said Lavelle, who preferred the analogy of *Hearts of Darkness*, the documentary about the making of *Apocalypse Now!* "Both were projects that everyone assumed were going to be disasters and turned out to be triumphs. It went on for so long, there were so many things they couldn't control fucking with them, so many relationships disintegrating, that in the end I couldn't avoid the parallels between that and my album, even though my troubles were on a much smaller scale. I can't say what Coppola went through to make that film, but I do know that we went through a lot of shit to make this record. And in our own way, we did indeed go slowly mad."

The relationships he mentions include Beastie Boy Mike D, Thom Yorke, Badly Drawn Boy and Richard Ashcroft. Shadow's comfort zone was trip-hop and electronica and on this album he is obliged to deal with vocalists who have a wide range of skills and strengths. This is definitely one of the most ambitious electronic projects of its era. The album reaches its full fruition on the penultimate track where Thom Yorke is his usual ethereal, existential self and brings it all home – joy and paranoia at once.

"This was always an ambitious project, so I wanted the very best people in their respective areas of music to be involved, and by bringing in Shadow I knew that the focus and the right emotion was going to be there," Lavelle explained. "The main thing though is that Shadow knows me very well, knows how to interpret what I'm hearing in my head. We have a lot of very similar reference points – musically, film-wise – and it just seemed to click."

California Dreamin' The Mamas & the Papas

(John Phillips) ❋ Dunhill ❋ 1966 ❋ Appears on: *If You Can Believe Your Eyes and Ears*

Hal Blaine, who had drummed for every major group in the Los Angeles area in the '60s, described a session with the Mamas & the Papas as like "a visit from the angels". No doubt he was referring to their voices – their personal lives were quite the opposite. Journalist Lillian Roxon wrote in her famous *Encyclopedia*, "The Mamas and the Papas were the royal family of American rock . . . because they were the first, with the Spoonful, of the big American groups, the first, that is, since the Beatles."

The Mamas & the Papas were folkies from the early-'60s coffeehouse circuit. Their friends included Roger McGuinn (the Byrds), Barry McGuire, John Sebastian and Zal Yanovsky (the Lovin' Spoonful). Of the four, Cass Elliott and Denny Doherty had the voices, John Phillips wrote the songs and his wife Michelle Phillips looked beautiful.

While scuffling around in the New York winter of 1963, Phillips wrote a song about wishing he were in warmer California. In any event, they took off for the Virgin Islands where they stayed until the credit card was maxed and they wound up in Los Angeles in the office of Lou Adler, who cut the song for Barry McGuire and offered the Mamas & the Papas a deal. "What we really want is a steady flow of money from your office to our house," said Phillips. They then re-did the vocals on McGuire's record with Doherty singing lead. The song was an instant classic.

Season of the Witch Donovan

(Donovan Leitch) ❊ Epic ❊ 1966 ❊ Appears on: *Sunshine Superman*

DA Pennebaker's film *Don't Look Back* captures the meeting between Bob Dylan and Donovan Leitch, whom Dylan reputedly feared to be his English competition. Within a few minutes of first contact, Dylan vanquishes the Brit folkie who never knew quite what hit him. A handy tunesmith with a sweet voice, Donovan was never other than a pop performer.

His early folk pop on *Pye* has some real gems: 'Catch the Wind', 'Colours', 'To Sing for You' and, notably, 'Hey Gyp (Dig the Slowness)', which has been covered formidably by Ed Kuepper, the Animals and others. However, Donovan found his best voice with Mickey Most, England's super-pop producer.

Sunshine Superman was the beginning of the new Donovan and his most consistent album. There's still a strong pulse of British blues in tracks such as 'The Fat Angel' (key line: "Fly Jefferson Airplane, get you there on time"), 'Ferris Wheel' and 'Bert's Blues'. On songs like the title track and the self-explanatory 'The Trip', Donovan brought the Haight Ashbury experience right into your suburban living room. The centrepiece of the album is the spiky, psychedelic 'Season of the Witch', which is both fey and threatening in its ambiguity.

Produced by Mickie Most, the track features future Led Zeppelin bass player John Paul Jones and guitarist Jimmy Page working up a psychedelic storm. It's unclear what the "season of the witch" will bring other than rabbits running in a ditch, but mostly it doesn't sound too good. The song is a vision of the darkness that came with the summer of love – madness, death and degradation – though few saw it at the time.

She Cries Your Name Beth Orton

(Beth Orton) ❊ Heavenly ❊ 1997 ❊ Appears on: *Trailer Park*

According to Chemical Brother Ed Simmons, Beth Orton is "A London girl at large, not some soppy girl with Laura Ashley dresses who reached grade seven on the violin. She drives a big old BMW and lives in Hackney." Orton had one of the most mysterious voices of the late '90s – dry and ethereal and haunting for all that. Her songs matched. Perhaps most unusual was that she came to public attention via working with producer William Orbit and electronica artists the Chemical Brothers on *Exit Planet Dust* and then with 'Where Do I Begin' on *Dig Your Own Hole*. Her second album, *Trailer Park*, of which this is the lead track, brought it all home. It's a masterful and unique mixture of winsome British folk rock set against subdued beats. "I've got no snobbery about any sort of music," she said. "When I worked with William Orbit, I'd come home and listen to Neil Young and Rickie Lee Jones ... for this I wanted pure emotion, because that's what I listen to as well as dance."

Your Song Elton John

(Elton John/Bernie Taupin) ❋ DJM ❋ 1970 ❋ Appears on: *Elton John*

Elton John was the singer that Britain just had to have. His piano playing was so intimate and his singing so intense that one couldn't help but think that the lyrics, sent in the post by Bernie Taupin, must mean something at least as profound as those of the American singer/songwriters who were all over the charts. John was different from the other singer/songwriters inasmuch as not only did he not write the lyrics but he paid no attention to their meaning – a good thing since mostly they were oddball fantasies and often a little puerile. Elton has a knack for being able to find a tune on the spot for any string of words. This instant response gave immediacy to his delivery, which was often captivating.

The former Reg Dwight had an exceptional gift for a tune. His trade had been learnt the hard way, touring with third-division blues bands and pounding out covers for supermarket albums. A first album died. Then came the eponymous second LP.

'Your Song' is the track that put Elton John on the map. Much of the credit for this breakthrough goes to producer Gus Dudgeon and string arranger Paul Buckmeister, who wrapped Elton with a lush soundscape that was neither saccharine middle-of-the-road nor too avant-garde. They were helped, too, by an unusually direct lyric from Taupin. The mood of the song was quite ethereal as befitting this romantic tale. The details were odd but potent. According to the producer, "No-one else had ever attempted to fuse a rock rhythm section with an orchestra on the scale and standard of sophistication of arrangement that we were attempting."

They Dance Alone Sting

(Sting) ✳ A&M ✳ 1987 ✳ Appears on: ... *Nothing Like the Sun*

Even when he was pretending to be a punk rocker with the Police, Sting always seemed like he was slumming. In fact the Police were way too literate for a genuine rock band, with their quirky rhythms and sophisticated chord shadings. Once he embarked on a solo career, all trappings fell away and out came the jazzers.

This second album is Sting's most coherent and interesting statement. Like his contemporaries Peter Gabriel and David Byrne, Sting turned to ethnic rhythms – reggae, Latin, Brazilian, jazz. Lyrically it was as free-ranging, with topics as diverse as the "disappeared" in Chile and the legendary dilettante author Quentin Crisp. The former track, 'They Dance Alone', was one of the highpoints of Sting's career.

The album was written in 1987 during a five-month stay in New York. "I had this kind of monkish life," he said. "I lived on my own. I cooked my own food. I went to the gym every day. I took piano lessons. The phone was off the hook. I worked usually from twelve midday to very late at night."

The double album features Mark Knopfler, Ruben Blades and Eric Clapton as well as Branford Marsalis, who was so influential to Sting's jazz period.

"I don't give a fuck about rock music," Sting declared in 1987. Unfortunately he was never going to escape its pull, but this champing at the bit was a worthy attempt.

Two Sevens Clash Culture

(Roy S Dayes/R Gordon/Joseph Hill/Delroy Thompson/Albert Walker) ✳ Mango ✳ 1976 ✳
Appears on: *Tougher Than Tough*

Marcus Garvey was an intellectual who, in the early part of the 20th century, promoted the idea of Africa as a utopian vision for the African diaspora created by slavery. Garvey was a principal architect of Rastafarianism and the belief that Ethiopia was the promised land. Culture singer Joseph Hill developed the idea that the apocalypse would start and Jah would return when the two sevens clash – the 7th day of the 7th month of the 77th year. The song combines Garvey's prophecies with some extemporising by Hill.

In 1976, when Culture penned the tune, the nation was in complete turmoil as a consequence of endemic poverty and lawlessness. According to legend, Hill's claim of Garvey's prophecy was sufficiently potent that on the appointed day the army was put on alert and businesses closed.

The song is one of the classics of the golden age of reggae and is uplifting rather than doom-laden. Joseph Hill's energised vocals are ably supported by Ralph Walker and Kenneth Dayes' harmonies.

Not only was the track a hit in Jamaica but it gave bassist Paul Simenon the name of his band – the Clash.

Luka   Suzanne Vega

(Suzanne Vega) ✳ A&M ✳ 1985 ✳ Appears on: *Suzanne Vega*

Vega almost single-handedly started her own female folk boom. The breakthrough of this album was soon matched by a flood of girl singers. However, few (the exception being Michelle Shocked) had the musicality and the vocabulary to match Vega. Vega, almost acoustically (with help from producer Lenny Kaye), made an album of modern folk music within the context of the modern world. It had the sensibilities of folk music with its intimacy and unsparing eye. In other words, Vega sounded fresh.

'Luka' was the key track, with its story of a youth trying to find a path in the modern jungle and surviving abuse. Her song rang true as a narrative and with an emotional heft.

Other tracks like 'Small Blue Thing' and the hit single 'Marlene on the Wall' perfectly capture that Sylvia Plath/bluestocking girl reading. It was out of step with the gargantuan sound of the mid-'80s, when everything was larger and bigger.

Vega said, "The structures behind folk music and folk songs are very elemental, sort of like water. You go through your fads with wine and soft drinks and everything else, but water is the basic thing you always go back to."

From this auspicious start, Vega has continued to make interesting records, many of which have embraced moods and sounds much more sophisticated. This debut remains as elegant and as elemental as ever.

She Loves You   The Beatles

(John Lennon/Paul McCartney) ❋ Parlophone ❋ 1963 ❋ Appears on: *With the Beatles*

Lennon and McCartney wrote 'She Loves You' on 26 June 1963 after the initial success of 'Love Me Do'. The pair were still finding their feet as songwriters. The biggest selling British single of the '60s, 'She Loves You' was a watershed for the Beatles. The chorus with its "yeah, yeah, yeah" refrain sounded very working class and modern to British and some American ears. There was nothing polite about it. The words weren't tightened up from the street vernacular and it grated against the Establishment. Not only were these boys not cutting their hair, they seemed indifferent to polite society. Even McCartney's father was reputedly not happy with the lyric.

That lyric, combined with an impossibly catchy hook in the melody and the Beatles' exuberance, then became a catchphrase. Of course nonsense and gimmicky hooks had been common in rock & roll for some time, but not in white British music and there was an immediate social divide between the kids and the Establishment who thought the whole thing lowbrow and working class. The track also moves. The energy level of the Beatles' recordings and the simplicity of this lyric provided the template for the garage bands that would follow in their wave for the next ten years, at least until the Ramones.

Heart Like a Wheel   Kate & Anna McGarrigle

(Anna McGarrigle) ❋ Warner Bros. ❋ 1976 ❋ Appears on: *Kate & Anna McGarrigle*

Maria Muldaur brought a demo of 'The Work Song' to the sessions for her first album. Producer Joe Boyd and executive producer Lenny Waronker were so intrigued by the voices on the tape that the McGarrigles soon found themselves flown out from Los Angeles and shortly after, working on their first, self-titled album.

Kate & Anna McGarrigle owes much of its allure to the unique combination of the sisters' voices. They grew up in French Canada in a musical house. "My parents came from a generation where people didn't play records," said Anna. "They got up and sang songs. It was Gershwin, songs from the First World War." There were

French and Latin influences there as well. During the early-'60s folk boom, the sisters could be found doing the coffeehouses around Montreal.

Their songwriting was coming into its own by the early '70s (at which time Kate had married songwriter Loudon Wainwright III and borne son Rufus). Linda Ronstadt covered Anna's 'Heart Like a Wheel' (her first composition as it happens) on her breakthrough album of the same name. The McGarrigle sisters on their own had a drier approach to love and romance. Neither cynical nor sappy, the McGarrigles were eloquent and luscious in their folk-infected tales. Perhaps the least ambitious act in show business, they had the courage to hang back and let the songs go where they may. This is one of the last great albums of the singer/songwriter era.

Drive On Johnny Cash

(Johnny Cash) ❋ American ❋ 1994 ❋ Appears on: *American Recordings*

Johnny Cash, after forty years, doesn't have to prove a thing. The man in black defined the ultimate hipster ethos with his dark, amphetamine country rockabilly in the '50s. His star had grown encrusted with schmaltz over the years until producer Rick Rubin put a new spin on Cash with this elemental collection of songs.

Accompanied only by acoustic guitar, Cash touches on gospel, country, blues and folk tunes from an eclectic range of sources. His best songs, as always, are those of men in search of redemption. Cash conjures the spirits of the Old Testament with the authority of a true southerner. His voice, cracked by life, gives the lyric the ring of truth. When he talks of life's travails and temptations in Tom Waits' 'Down There by the Train' you know that he bought a ticket.

'Drive On' is a chilling song about a Vietnam survivor. There's history written between the lines – all the stories that can never be told. It's a song that acknowledges that life has moved on, that his children will never understand what has happened. Do they still make Americans as stoic as Johnny Cash any more? Do they make songwriters who can tell such truths with such a cold, hard eye?

If the evidence of a life lived hard is in Cash's throat, at times he falls back on his charisma to carry a tune where his voice will no longer go. However, this is a minor quibble. *American Recordings* lives up to its title as an album of true stories sung by an American icon.

It's Like That Run-DMC

(Darryl 'DMC' McDaniels/Joe 'Run' Simmons/Larry Smith) ❋ Profile ❋ 1984 ❋
Appears on: *Run-DMC*

The marriage of metal and rap has been a longstanding affair, which began here. The trio from Queens, New York, were the first hardcore rappers, whose tough lyrics over tougher, spare beats set the template for the rap explosion that was to come. They took the rhyming that had been going on with Bronx parties and gave it a new form, especially with integration of metal guitar riffs over their beats. With this album they showed how rap could translate to an LP form rather than 12-inch singles and live performances.

Run (Joseph Simmons) and DMC (Darryl McDaniels) had a unique style of rapping over each other, finishing the other's sentences and using their dual syntax as syncopation with the beats from DJ Jam Master Jay. Their first single, 'It's Like That', was an R&B hit.

Where other rappers were there to toast the party or brag, Run-DMC had a confrontational approach to urban tales of life as it is on the streets. According to Run, "It's good to be raw."

Producer, manager and elder brother Russel Simmons brought freshness to the rap sounds on the album and put it into the R&B charts. The addition of some guitar made 'It's Like That' acceptable for MTV. According to Run, "I was trying to get a record that was positive because I knew that radio didn't want to play anything negative."

Genius of Love Tom Tom Club

(Tom Tom Club) ❋ Sire ❋ 1981 ❋ Appears on: *Tom Tom Club*

"We had just finished the big *Remain in Light* tour with Talking Heads, and David had announced that he was going to do a solo project and Jerry [Harrison] had announced he was going to do one, and I thought, 'Well, what do we do?' So we decided to do a record, and Chris Blackwell of Island, whom we had met while working with the Talking Heads down in Nassau, said, 'Why don't you come down to my studio ...'" That's how Chris Franz, Talking Heads' drummer, explained the genesis of the Tom Tom Club, a side project that threatened to eclipse the mother ship.

Franz and his wife, Talking Heads' bassist Tina Weymouth, set up some grooves with a Caribbean flavour – some reggae, a hint of calypso and some hip-hop – and then added vocals from Weymouth and her sisters.

The first single, 'Wordy Rappinghood', was heavily influenced by the early Bronx rap (which had yet to move out of Manhattan) but with a childlike quality. Not only was it endearing but it was a hit.

The Tom Tom Club brought their arty friends (including guitarist Adrian Belew) and their own art school backgrounds to bear.

Their funky version of 'Under the Boardwalk' was a beautiful culture clash for pop R&B. The other lead track, 'Genius of Love', was even better and remains much sampled today. The funkiness of the band, with cheesy keyboards and breezy vocals, was a pure delight and a precursor to hip-hop from the likes of De La Soul and Deee-Lite. The Tom Tom Club was essential club music in the early '80s.

As Weymouth said at the time: "It's pushing it to the extreme, because we're extremely light with Tom Tom Club. If Talking Heads wasn't so extremely serious on the other side, I don't think we ever could have come up with such light music."

Poison Arrow ABC

(Martin Fry/Mark Lickley/Steve Singleton/Mark White) ❋ Mercury ❋ 1982 ❋

Appears on: *The Lexicon of Love*

Like Bryan Ferry, ABC singer Martin Fry was a working-class lad from the north who looked good in a suit and had a wistful croon. ABC updated Roxy Music and Bowie for the New Romantic era. Initially a post-punk electronic outfit in the style of early Human League, Fry refashioned the group.

"It was a really revolutionary time," he told BBC News Online. "The technology changed almost overnight and it was the start of deconstructing pop groups – the drums, bass and guitar of the Beatles was over. An affordable synthesiser meant you could make music a lot more easily than learning to play the guitar.

"Our music was definitely escapism, not just a generation sipping cocktails in a newly opened wine bar and voting for Thatcher – it was the opposite," Fry said.

"There was a generation that had seen the Sex Pistols and the Clash and wanted to create something very different for themselves.

"We were definitely a product of the times – and I guess our music had a romantic edge, but I wasn't up there in a Pierrot outfit."

Fry was fortunate to come across producer Trevor Horn, one of the genuine visionary producers. *The Lexicon of Love* was the first major project for Horn and his team (Gary Langan, Anne Dudley) who would be later known as the Art of Noise.

'Poison Arrow' is crammed with massive layers of cinematic strings and widescreen synthesisers over which the gold laméd Fry could declare the perfectly '80s phrase, he was "looking for the girl who meets supply with demand."

Light Flight   Pentangle

(Terry Cox/Bert Jansch/Jacqui McShee/John Renbourn/Danny Thompson) ✳
Transatlantic/Reprise ✳ 1969 ✳ Appears on: *Basket of Light*

Pentangle were described as "Britain's first electric folk-rock supergroup" – as though that were a good thing. The "super" came from the two virtuoso guitarists Bert Jansch and John Renbourn, arguably the best in Britain in the mid-'60s. The former had a lot of blues in his folk style and was much lauded by Donovan who named a song after him and Jimmy Page who stole a song off him. Renbourn was more traditionally English. "Right from school I started taking an interest in Elizabethan music," he said at the time. With the addition of the much-in-demand bassist Danny Thompson and drummer Terry Cox plus plaintive vocalist Jacqui McShee, Pentangle were an instant cult hit. 'Light Flight' was their one real mainstream bona fide hit.

Producer Shel Talmy told journalist Richie Unterberger, "Certainly it was probably the most rewarding stuff I ever did, because we did everything from medieval chants to modern jazz, and all the stages in between. And that was just great. Every session was a new session.

"The best parts probably were the fact that they were as good as they were. They were the best, I thought, of their representative fields. They were all intelligent, which always made me happy. It made it a lot more fun. And they were all just super-duper musicians, and I mean really, I guess, it was really the superstar group of that time for the type of music they were doing.

"Actually, I listen to them every now and then just for the pleasure of listening to them, quite frankly, which I don't do with most of the stuff I've done."

Renbourn and Jansch had their own careers and it's likely that Pentangle had run its course within a few years of this release. Elizabethan fusion was never the same after this.

I'm Not in Love 10CC

(Eric Stewart/Graham Gouldman) ✳ Mercury ✳ 1975 ✳

Appears on: *The Original Soundtrack*

"We dream in clichés, we dream in parodies," said popmeister Graham Gouldman in a 1975 interview. 10CC were the masters of immoderate studio production – as were so many others who tried to outdo George Martin and the Beatles' arrangements. However, 10CC had a vicious sense of irony that gave a bite to the otherwise soppy strings.

Essentially a studio conceit from the start, Eric Stewart, a refugee from Merseybeat, had a studio in Manchester where with Kevin Godley and Lol Crème he had a 1970 novelty hit, 'Neanderthal Man', as Hotlegs.

By 1972, with the addition of Graham Gouldman who wrote many of the biggest hits of the '60s for the Yardbirds, the Hollies, Herman's Hermits and others, they became 10CC. A first album full of satiric pastiches was an instant hit. By 1975, when they released this, their third album, they were busting with ideas. The best of them was the track 'I'm Not in Love', notable for its 256 vocal parts.

Stewart explained the genesis of the song in *MOJO* magazine: "It was a silly phase I was going through with my wife, about not wanting to say 'I love you' every day because it lost its meaning. I mentioned this to Graham, because we were going to write a love song, and we came up with the idea of saying, I'm not in love – but here are all the reasons why I am. That's basically the start of the song. We wrote it in about three hours.

"We actually recorded thirteen notes of a chromatic scale onto a sixteen-track machine and fed them through the control desk with the four of us – myself, Graham, Kevin and Lol – all working the faders like a keyboard down onto a stereo pair."

In an age of overdubbing excess, 10CC's dry wit under pop craftsmanship gave their discs a rare longevity. There was one more album (*How Dare You*) and Godley and Crème left to pursue concept albums and, ultimately, pop videos. Gouldman and Stewart continued 10CC and racked up even bigger hits but never matched the understated glory of 'I'm Not in Love' or the opening track, 'Une Nuit à Paris: One Night in Paris, pt. 1/The Same Night in Paris, pt. 2'.

The esteemed critic Ken Barnes noted that "10CC's *Original Soundtrack* is a fascinating record. Musically there's more going on than in ten Yes albums . . ." This was the triumph of British art rock.

Strawberry Fields Forever The Beatles

(John Lennon/Paul McCartney) ✳ Parlophone ✳ 1967 ✳
Appears on: *The Beatles 1967–1970*

The real Strawberry Field was a Salvation Army orphanage near Lennon's childhood home in Menlove Avenue, Liverpool. As a child he played in the extensive grounds of the large Victorian building. Its almost Gothic design and large grounds were otherworldly for an imaginative child like Lennon.

While in Spain filming *How I Won the War*, Lennon started a song reminiscing about his childhood and innocence. He was now one of the most famous people on the planet and perhaps he missed those innocent days. The song started out as melancholy blues but was gradually transformed into the most complex pop song of its time.

The first few run-throughs, featuring extensive use of the Mellotron, failed to yield the song that Lennon heard in his head. It's worth noting that he was using a lot of drugs at this point, especially hallucinogens.

According to George Martin, "Before the very first recording of 'Strawberry Fields Forever' John stood opposite me in the studio and played me the song on his acoustic guitar and it was absolutely wonderful. Then when we actually taped it with the usual instruments it started to get a bit heavy. John didn't say anything but

I knew it wasn't what he had originally wanted. So I wasn't totally surprised when he came back to me a week or so later and suggested we have another go at recording it, perhaps even bringing in some outside musicians. Together we worked out that I should score the song for trumpets and cellos."

The Beatles kept at the song, keeping versions as they went.

In early December they were back in the studio with only engineer Dave Harries on deck. "We recorded Ringo's cymbals, played them backwards. Paul and George were on timpani and bongos, Mal Evans played tambourine, and we overdubbed the guitars."

According to Mark Lewishon's book on the Beatles' sessions, George Martin and engineer Geoff Emerick returned later that night and edited together the first three-quarters of take fifteen with the last quarter of take twenty-four and mixed it to become take twenty-five.

In 1966 recording studios only had four tracks on which to record so parts were progressively mixed or bounced down to one track to leave space for further overdubs.

Percussion, including backward cymbals and an Indian instrument called a swordmandel, cellos and trumpets were added. The song was now a cacophony of edgy strings and winds with a thick, heavy percussion on the bottom end and a tense, speedy feel.

Lennon then added his lyrics. What was a reverie about innocence had become a questioning of existence and reality. If that wasn't enough, he added random phrases like "cranberry sauce," which was misheard as "I buried Paul".

After a month of recording, Lennon was still not happy. "John told me he liked both versions of 'Strawberry Fields Forever', the original, lighter version and the more intense, scored version," Martin recalled. "He said to me, 'Why don't you join the beginning of the first one to the end of the second one?' I told him that there were two problems. One was that they were both in completely different keys and two was that they were both running at different tempos. He said, 'Well you can fix it.'"

Martin sped up the first section and slowed down the second to compensate for the difference in keys and then decreased the pitch of the first version at the join, sixty seconds into the song.

'Strawberry Fields' was released as a single with McCartney's ode to his Liverpool childhood, 'Penny Lane', on the other A-side. The disc demonstrated the divergence that was happening in the Beatles. Lennon's track is still a benchmark in pop history.

Moonlight on Vermont   Captain Beefheart & the Magic Band

(Don Van Vliet) ❋ Straight/Reprise ❋ 1969 ❋ Appears on: *Trout Mask Replica*

Matt Groening, the creator of Bart Simpson and 'Life in Hell' and one of the most perspicacious commentators on modern music, wrote: "The first time I heard *Trout Mask Replica*, when I was fifteen years old, I thought it was the worst thing I'd ever heard. I said to myself, they're not even trying! It was just a sloppy cacophony … About the third time, I realised they were doing it on purpose: they meant it to sound exactly this way. About the sixth or seventh time, it clicked in, and I thought it was the greatest album I'd ever heard.

"I played *Trout Mask Replica* for my blues-loving friends, who all went through all the same reaction I had, and we'd sit around saying, 'Wow, if this is how great pop music is in 1969, just think what it'll be like in 1984!' Of course we didn't realise this was the best album of 1984 … and it remains the best album I've ever heard."

Trout Mask Replica is generally thought of as one of the great albums of the 20th century. Its conception and execution pushed the boundaries of popular music in ways that no other artist, before or since, has. Don Van Vliet's (aka Captain Beefheart's) starting point is, as ever, the Delta blues and jazz. A song that starts out as a blues can wind up in waltz time. However, he stretches those idioms in ways that are so boldly idiosyncratic that it becomes something else again. It's only Van Vliet's sheer genius that holds this disparate collection of noise together.

Van Vliet spent a year rehearsing the Magic Band, carefully scripting the intricate rhythm patterns and the flights of underground fancy in the woodwinds and the guitars.

Some tracks, such as this, were put down at the beginning of the process but the bulk of the record was cut in one take over a four-hour session, with Van Vliet singing live in the studio and only the faint sound of the band tracks coming through the walls.

The vocals stretch Van Vliet's enormous range from the blues growl worthy of Howlin' Wolf through to almost pop and jazz phrasing. The songs generally address ecology and the relationship of man and nature. There is a story that Beefheart was concerned about two eucalypts outside the house where the band were rehearsing and put tree surgeons on the recording budget, causing a fallout between the Captain and his teenage buddy Frank Zappa, whose Bizarre label financed the album.

Whatever the cost, it was worth it.

"I just told the group to let out who they are," Van Vliet said. "What would you call it, middle-class apple turnovers. We just got together and stirred up a sensation."

There was method to the madness. Beefheart was channelling, especially on this track. Here you have a title based on a Sinatra song ('Moonlight in Vermont') used on a track that is a lot closer to Howlin' Wolf.

Presence of the Lord   Blind Faith

(Eric Clapton) ✻ Polydor ✻ 1969 ✻ Appears on: *Blind Faith*

Never before has an album with so much riding on it been so rushed and half-baked. Blind Faith was the first supergroup. It combined Ginger Baker and Eric Clapton from Cream with Steve Winwood from Traffic and the little known Rick Gretch. Clapton's friend David Litvanoff had played the guitarist a bootleg copy of *The Basement Tapes* and Clapton immediately disbanded Cream in search of something more pastoral and song-based.

Baker invited himself along and Clapton, in fear of the drummer, allowed him to stay and psychologically left the room himself. The first album was assembled hastily. Six songs running a total of less than three-quarters of an hour (and one-third of that being a drum solo) is the sum total of *Blind Faith*. But Clapton was right – the combination of his melancholic persona and guitar style with Steve Winwood's keening bittersweet voice and beautiful, delicate melodies was extraordinary.

The songs expressed the sense of being wasted. There's an eerie sense of a search for meaning – almost all the tracks are mid-tempo ballads.

Clapton's contribution, 'Presence of the Lord', was in tune with the new Christianity that was overtaking the charts at the time. He said he unfolded two posters of Humphrey Bogart and James Cagney and a picture of Jesus dropped out. A moment later two Christians appeared at Clapton's hotel room door. He told

Uncut recently, "I remember playing it one night with Blind Faith. The audience turned into devils or angels according to what I played." One suspects the 'Clapton is God' graffiti had gone to his head and perhaps drugs played a part too.

Do the Strand Roxy Music

(Bryan Ferry) ❉ Island ❉ 1973 ❉ Appears on: *For Your Pleasure*

"It's the most complete. The one that captured what I wanted to do most clearly," is how Bryan Ferry summed up *For Your Pleasure* for *MOJO* magazine.

Roxy Music's second album is built on the creative tension between Ferry and Brian Eno: the former a traditionalist and the latter at the absolute edge of pop music. This would be their best work but at the end of it, Eno was out of the group.

"I saw Bryan's songs in the context of pop art," said Eno. "That was the period when pop music became self-conscious, in the sense that it started to look at its own history as material that could be used. We wanted to say, 'We know we're working in pop music, we know there's a history to it and we know it's a showbiz game.' And knowing all that, we're still going to try to do something new."

A retro futurism infected Roxy Music and the group revelled in the stupidity of the paradox. On the one hand they co-opted titles from serious British artists ('Every Dream Home a Heartache') and on the other made up silly dance songs ('Do the Strand').

In 1973 Roxy Music were out on their own limb, conceptually miles ahead of every would-be art band. Then with 'Do the Strand' they reached out and touched a Top 40 audience. A significant amount of credit must go to producer Chris Thomas who, with an innate sense of song craft, has a capacity to make pop out of any cloth.

"We had so many ideas that it was like, 'Christ! Let's get them all down before they go away'," Ferry said in 1997. "Later you start to compromise, for fear of your music going over people's heads. On Roxy Music it was like, 'Let's do this thing right next to that, edit straight in from this to that . . .' and so you never got bored with it. I mean, there are many flaws on that first album – the singing is terrible, and the recording isn't very good – but it's also incredibly exciting. I think we enjoyed making *For Your Pleasure* more, because we felt a little more in control. We still had a producer, but I think Brian had a lot more to do with the sound. And I think I underestimated what a help Brian was to me when we split up."

There is No Time Lou Reed

(Lou Reed) ✳ Sire ✳ 1989 ✳ Appears on: *New York*

This opens with one of the angriest pieces of noise in the history of rock. The guitar positively rips into the riff like a starving junkyard dog that's just scored itself a rat. The merciless vitriol from Reed and co-guitarist Mike Rathke is pissed off and frightened. Over the course of forty years, Lou Reed has frequently been revolutionary but only on the *New York* album political. Reed looked around the streets of his hometown and saw apocalypse: the homeless, the parade of AIDS casualties, crack addicts, the poor, the downtrodden, the pollution – even the death of the whale. He saw intolerance – even his own. Hatred, anger, exploitation and even moments of love.

It's not in Reed's nature to preach or sermonise and on this track he doesn't. He just warns of the fire and the brimstone: "This is no time to swallow anger/This is no time to ignore hate/This is no time to be acting frivolous/Because the time is getting late/This is no time for private vendettas/This is no time to not know who you are/Self knowledge is a dangerous thing/The freedom of who you are".

The urgency of the lyrics is magnified by the ferocity with which the musicians attack the track. These sessions were mostly recorded live, cutting a song a day with Reed's toughest band since *Rock & Roll Animal*. The post-punk prodigy Fred Maher on drums complements Rob Wasserman's jazz stylings on bass and the hard-edged Mike Rathke on guitar. On this track the musicians feed off each other and the chanting vocals, building the rage in the song until it's white-hot.

The strength of this album is its specificity. If you want to hear what the desperate ruin of the Reagan era was like, it's here. It's unfortunate that the song still sounds fresh and appropriate.

Crimson and Clover Tommy James & the Shondells

(Tommy James) ✳ Rhino ✳ 1968 ✳ Appears on: *Anthology*

Tommy Jackson (aka James) cut one of the great singles of all time when he was just thirteen and working in a record shop. It wasn't until three years later in 1966 that 'Hanky Panky' became a national number one. The song has that classic 'Louie Louie' progression behind James' twangy voice. James teamed up with producer/writers Bo Gentry and Richie Cordell for a string of exquisite pop songs including 'I Think We're Alone Now' and 'Mony Mony'. James' sweet and sexy material had him tagged as a bubblegum artist.

Then, in 1968, he released his first self-produced single, 'Crimson and Clover'. Pure psychedelic pop with groundbreaking production, the 45 sold five million copies and the album had liner notes from Vice President Hubert Humphrey. "I never set out to make a so-called psychedelic record," James said. "I was just having fun with the new technology. I wanted to make sounds swim, make 'em wiggle a little bit." The trippy vocal sound came from James singing through his guitar amp with the tremolo turned up. Add layers of guitar and echo and in one session the classic was recorded and mixed.

The album also featured the equally trippy 'Crystal Blue Persuasion'. By 1970, James had cut nine albums in three years and collapsed on stage in Montgomery, Alabama. He recuperated enough to have another hit with 'Draggin' the Line' in 1972. While his legend has not lived large, the songs have – each one has been a hit for at least one other artist. The originals remain works of staggering pop beauty.

Bangkok   Alex Chilton

(Alex Chilton) ❋ Ork ❋ 1978 ❋ Appears on: *19 Years: A Collection*

Alex Chilton is the patron saint of alternative rock songwriters. His knack for sweet '60s pop is tempered with demons. He is forever seeking unfulfilled promise.

Chilton started out fast. In Memphis his teenage band became the Box Tops and under the dictatorship of Dan Penn defined late-'60s blue-eyed soul with hits such as 'The Letter', 'Cry Like a Baby', 'Neon Rainbow' and 'Soul Deep'. Classics all, Chilton nonetheless quit and in Neil Young's phrase "headed for the ditch". He moved to New York chasing the Velvet Underground. He soon returned to Memphis and within two years had put Big Star together; the prototype post-grunge pop band.

"He was kind of an art brat," is how producer and Memphis legend Jim Dickinson described Chilton to *MOJO*'s Barney Hoskyns. "The first time I saw Alex, he couldn't have been more than ten or eleven. William Eggleston [the photographer whose famous light bulb shot graces the cover of *Radio City*] had given him peyote, and his eyes were like that scene in *The Wind in the Willows* where Mr Toad's eyes distended."

Big Star made three albums over which rock critics drooled and which the public disdained. By 1977 Chilton was in New York where the CBGB crowd hailed him as a hero. Chilton by this time was deeply fucked up. He was addicted to drugs and liquor. At the urging of downtown musicians like Chris Stamey and Peter Holsapple (later the dBs) Chilton made sporadic recordings and live performances.

There's a voyeuristic quality to Chilton's work. It's like watching a slow motion car crash.

"Songs like 'Bangkok' were not romantic," said Chris Stamey, who played guitar. "There was a famous quote: 'tuning is such a European concept'".

Got to Get You Into My Life The Beatles

(John Lennon/Paul McCartney) ✳ Parlophone ✳ 1966 ✳ Appears on: *Revolver*

The Beatles' studio innovations weren't always about acid rock gimmicks. As the group were getting more spacey, McCartney pulled out this gem – a homage to soul music that was every bit as powerful as anything coming out of Detroit, the home of Motown, at the time.

According to engineer Geoff Emerick, "I was getting frustrated listening to American records like the Motown stuff because the bass content was a lot stronger than we were putting on our records. We were governed by certain rules and regulations at Abbey Road, so I could never get the sound I really wanted. So in desperation one day I figured that we could use a loudspeaker as a microphone – it works the same way in reverse, so it's effectively the same thing. That way the speaker could take the weight of the air vibrations from a bass. There was also a woollen sweater with four necks that they had received from a fan – they wore it on one of their Christmas shows. It was around the studio, so I stuffed it into the bass drum to deaden the sound. And I moved the bass drum microphone very close to the drum itself, which wasn't really considered the thing to do at that time."

McCartney allegedly claimed that the song was inspired by marijuana and referred to it as "an ode to pot, like someone else might write an ode to chocolate or a good claret".

The main thing here is the sheer size of the song. "You listen to early Beatles mixes and the bass and bass drum aren't there at all," said McCartney. "We were starting to take over ourselves and bass was coming to the fore in many ways ... I was listening to a lot of Motown, Marvin Gaye and Stax stuff, who were putting some nice little bass lines in."

Death Cab for Cutie The Bonzo Dog Doo-Dah Band

(Viv Stanshall) ❊ Liberty ❊ 1967 ❊ Appears on: *Gorilla*

"I take a hell of a lot of drugs," Vivian Stanshall once said when asked where his inspiration came from. Stanshall was being disingenuous. He didn't need drugs; whimsical absurdism came to him naturally. Primarily a visual artist, Stanshall was entranced by Dadaism and found himself in a band with Neil Innes and 'Legs' Larry Smith that played jazz and vaudeville numbers with a twist.

Then the Beatles cast the Bonzos in their film *Magical Mystery Tour*, where they played 'Death Cab for Cutie' and were thrust into the centre of psychedelic London. The missing link between the Goons and Monty Python, the Bonzos had an enormous impact on rock music and the counterculture.

The Bonzo Dog Doo-Dah Band took the tradition of whimsical English eccentricity to a new level. Then, when Paul McCartney produced their single 'I'm the Urban Spaceman', they suddenly had a hit. The TV program *Do Not Adjust Your Set* made them stars and introduced them to Eric Idle, Terry Jones, Michael Palin and Terry Gilliam. The Monty Python team owes a great deal to Stanshall and the Bonzos. Neil Innes eventually became a de facto Python.

Innes will be best remembered for *The Rutles* – a film partly financed by George Harrison, which parodied the story of the Beatles and gave us such classics as 'All You Need is Cash'.

The Bonzos were deeply appreciated by the Beatles and other English superstars – 'Legs' Larry Smith worked with Elton John, John Cale and George Harrison.

Stanshall became a national institution with his radio and theatrical performances. His character 'Sir Henry of Rawlinson End' was the subject of albums and short films. Stanshall appeared as the narrator of Mike Oldfield's *Tubular Bells* and was much beloved by the British rock superstars. He worked with Steve

Winwood, who also produced his 1974 solo album *Men Opening Umbrellas Ahead*.

Stanshall was plagued with depression and its consequent side effects of alcohol and drug problems. Nevertheless, he maintained a substantial output until his death in a house fire in 1995.

Gorilla was the Bonzos' debut and was uncluttered by expectation. Rougher and more frivolous, it is a most accurate and witty representation of the time. Dedicated to King Kong, the album features 'The Equestrian Statue', 'Jazz, Delicious Hot, Disgusting Cold!', 'Death Cab for Cutie', 'The Intro and the Outro', 'Big Shot' and 'Piggy Bank Love'.

By 1970 the group was over, but the legacy was everywhere – American critic Ira Robbins named his exceptional music magazine *Trouser Press* after one of their songs. Their hits and misses are collected on the anthology *The History of the Bonzos* but for the best single statement, *Gorilla* is the beast.

Cattle and Cane The Go-Betweens

(Grant McLennan) ❄ Stunn ❄ 1983 ❄ Appears on: *Before Hollywood*

Precious fans of Bob Dylan and the Gang of Four, the Go-Betweens were ostensibly a semi-acoustic punk band with two naturally gifted songwriters in Forster and McLennan. A first album of dysrhythmic New Wave saw the group floundering. On the second album they returned to their strengths as folk rockers. But it all fell into place with 'Cattle and Cane' with its gorgeous melody on the bass guitar.

"We had all the tracks for the album," McLennan recalled. "But I was at a party where Nick Cave and Tracey Pew were living in London. Nick had brought this acoustic guitar and at that stage he couldn't play guitar very well. Neither could I but I picked it up and weird chords came to me and the phrase, 'The railroad takes him home', came straight away. So I worked on it and it became 'Cattle and Cane'. I knew that I wanted three verses and I wanted a different point of view to come in at the end of the song so I asked Robert to contribute an overview character. We nailed that song. I still get such a rush when I hear it because it's such a different sounding song and you don't write many songs like that."

With the addition of Lindy Morrison's rolling, militant drum pattern, the song was full of hooks and wistfulness and a young man's sense of purpose.

According to McLennan, "'Cattle and Cane' was a reaction to where I'd grown up in north Queensland, near the coast surrounded by sugar cane farms and then moving out to a cattle station and being surrounded by Hereford cattle and dirt roads and then finding yourself in London at twenty, twenty-one, playing music, such personal music."

Come Together The Beatles

(John Lennon/Paul McCartney) ✳ Apple ✳ 1969 ✳ Appears on: *Abbey Road*

One of the darkest and most funky of Beatles' songs, 'Come Together' rides on Paul McCartney's dirty bass parts that slide into the song and make it swing. The treated percussion sounds and details bejewel this track. The groove here comes from Chuck Berry's 'You Can't Catch Me' – undeniably a lift for which Lennon confessed. The lyrics for the chorus come from acid guru Timothy Leary, who used the slogan 'Come Together' in a Californian gubernatorial race and for whom Lennon whipped out a campaign song along those lines.

'Come Together' is much, more than just a rehash of Chuck Berry. The sounds here are layered and the studio effects are carefully manipulated for a Beatles sound unlike any other. The sheer fatness over the top of a boogie beat here prefigures the glam rock that was only two years away.

The lyrics are a typical Lennon word salad, fitting in with the swamp groove of the track without meaning anything in particular. Whatever the case, it's perhaps the funkiest they ever got.

Whole Wide World Wreckless Eric

(Eric Goulden) ✳ Stiff ✳ 1977 ✳ Appears on: *A Bunch of Stiffs*

Eric Goulden was an aspiring pop singer working in a lemonade factory when he sent a demo tape of songs to the just-starting Stiff. Perhaps it was the fact that he taped over an old Eric Clapton cassette that appealed to the Stiff sense of humour, or perhaps it was just the pure pop perfection of this tale of lost love that appealed to them. In any case Nick Lowe put Eric in the studio and bashed out this 45. It is a gem. Apparently taken from real life – Eric was dumped by a girl from Sheffield, not the South Pacific – the song has a particular veracity that just can't be manufactured. But it can never be surpassed either.

Eric never quite made it again. Success, it seems, went to his head.

"I used to get drunk a lot," he wrote recently in the *Sunday Times*. "'Whole Wide World' came out as a single and got to number one in the alternative charts. We were the new big thing. I split up with my girlfriend – I think I got famous and completely confused."

Fortunate Son   Creedence Clearwater Revival

(John Fogerty) ✳ Fantasy ✳ 1969 ✳ Appears on: *Willie and the Poor Boys*

Even the critic paid to write the sleeve notes on their first album damned Creedence Clearwater Revival with faint praise. The quartet from the suburbs never fitted into the hip San Francisco scene. Their ability to knock out astounding, powerful 45s rather than unfocused and rambling jams had them consigned to the Top 40 bin. Nonetheless, Creedence is one of the few San Francisco groups of the period whose records now sound as vital as when they were cut.

John Fogerty, who wrote, produced, sang and played most of the instruments, is a formidable writer. Coming from a dysfunctional working-class family, there's a lot of anger in his tracks. He's one of the few American rock writers to raise the issue of class. 'Fortunate Son' then, isn't just another hippie anti-war song, but a critique on the American aristocracy sending the poor to fight and die "in a war no-one even pretends to believe in".

"I see things through lower-class eyes," said Fogerty. "If you sit around and think about all that money, you can never write a song about where you came from."

The song took twenty minutes to write. Recording took a couple of hours and the entire *Willie and the Poor Boys* LP was done in less than ten days.

The venom of the lyrics is matched by stinging guitar lines from Fogerty and the rhythm section of Doug Clifford (drums), Stu Cook (bass) and Tom Fogerty (rhythm guitar) going hell for leather. While many of Creedence's songs to this point had been southern boogie music and good-time rock & roll, there was no ambiguity about the meaning of 'Fortunate Son'.

Creedence didn't appeal to the cognoscenti; their audience was precisely the kind of white kids who were in the Vietnam jungles. As Fogerty said, referring to the children of the Republican Party's aristocracy, "Julie Nixon was hanging around with David Eisenhower, and you just had the feeling that none of these people were going to be too involved with the war."

Light My Fire The Doors

(Robbie Krieger/Jim Morrison/Ray Manzarek/John Densmore) ❋ Elektra ❋ 1967 ❋
Appears on: *The Doors*

In 1967 few people took the Doors seriously. They were regulars at the Whiskey Au Go Go nightclub where their bluesy, psychedelic Oedipal epic 'The End' got them a bit of a reputation. Then there was Jim Morrison – stunningly handsome and fucked-up on drugs – always an attractive combination. Behind Morrison the band struggled to develop a version of jazz rock. Although all the compositions were jointly credited, the bulk of the songwriting was split between Krieger, whose tastes veered towards pop music, and Morrison, whose lyrics were mostly inane babblings.

Jac Holzman signed the group to Elektra and assigned producer Paul Rothchild who cut their eponymous debut in ten days. The album was split between Morrison's dark poetic musings and Krieger's powerful pop tunes. The former gave them some credibility but it was the latter that turned the group into a chart success and made them more than a footnote in an anthology of cult acts. Morrison and the Doors needed each other. Without him they were a bunch of fairly bloodless would-be jazz players. The combination, however, was very potent.

'Light My Fire' was a perfect synthesis of all that was best about the Doors – a swinging drum part and deliciously melodic work from Krieger and organ player Ray Manzarek. On top of that the lyrics that Morrison delivered positively dripped with sexual desire.

It was a brilliant debut for Krieger, who had never attempted writing before. "Jim had been writing all the songs and one day he said, 'We don't have enough tunes. Why don't you guys try to write some?' That night I wrote my first song ever, 'Light My Fire'. I brought it into rehearsal the next day and everyone liked it. Ray wrote the intro keyboard part in just a few minutes.

"And working with Jim made me write a certain way because I had to compete with his songs, which were pretty heavy. He was really cool about it, too."

An edited version of the seven-minute track was a major hit single and put the Doors on the national map. Which was just as well because they had been banned from the Whisky Au Go Go.

Now on the world stage, Morrison could come up with his statement to Michael Lydon, "Maybe you could call us erotic politicians. We're a rock & roll band, a blues band, just a band, but that's not all. A Doors concert is a public meeting called by us for a special kind of dramatic discussion and entertainment. When we perform, we're participating in the creation of a world, and we celebrate that creation with the audience. It becomes the sculpture of bodies in action.

"That's politics, but our power is sexual. We make concerts sexual politics. The sex starts out with just me, then moves out to include the charmed circle of musicians on stage. The music we make goes out to the audience and interacts with them, they go home and interact with the rest of reality, then I get it back by interacting with that reality, so the whole sex thing works out to be one big ball of fire."

Fair enough, but it was the sultry pop of 'Light My Fire' that made it possible.

Sheela-Na-Gig PJ Harvey

(PJ Harvey) ✳ Too Pure ✳ 1992 ✳ Appears on: *Dry*

PJ Harvey's first album was a startling debut. The songs were raw and hard, the tunes carved from ancient stone. And that was just the music. The lyrics addressed male and female relations with a bare-knuckle honesty that bordered on the violent. This is not what people speak of when they talk of love but rather what they think in the dark recesses of their mind, things they would not dare speak when they lay themselves bare in lust or desire or the quest for love.

Harvey grew up in Dorset in England's west country, the child of two hippies. Her father was the best friend of Rolling Stone pianist Ian Stewart, her mother an artist and sculptor.

Harvey's first single was based on a sculpture, but it was more closely tied to bad sex: the imperious male demands and female self-loathing. The music ranges from careful whispers to full-throttle angst – the full gamut of fury undercut with a snatch of lyric from Rogers and Hammerstein's *South Pacific*.

"A sheela-na-gig is a stone carving found on the side of the churches, like a gargoyle," Harvey said. "There's a lot of them in Ireland and a few in England. It's usually of a woman crouching down, pulling her vagina open with her hands and grinning and looking mad at the same time.

"People used to touch them if they were infertile. They were thought to be able to ward off demons, too. There are several different translations – 'holy woman of god', 'Sheila on her hunkers' and 'the idle hole'. I liked the image – the combination of pulling yourself apart and laughing at the same time – I wanted that sense of humour in the song."

Cry for a Shadow The Beatles

(George Harrison/John Lennon) ✳ Polydor ✳ 1962 ✳ Appears on: *Anthology 1*

The first recorded Beatle song was not credited to John Lennon/Paul McCartney. George Harrison, age eighteen, had written an instrumental spoof based on the sound of the Shadows, then Britain's leading hit-makers. While the Silver Beatles were in Hamburg playing dive bars with third-division British singers like Tony Sheridan, they came to the attention of Bert Kaempfert, a South African bandleader known for cheesy instrumentals.

Kaempfert put Sheridan in the studio with the Beatles to cut 'My Bonnie' and 'When the Saints Go Marchin' In' and he passed over the group's other originals, preferring this Harrison tune for the B-side.

'Cry for a Shadow' shows Harrison's already inventive guitar work – especially in reaction to John Lennon's driving rhythm guitar. The influence of the Sun players is there and also a possibly grudging nod to the Shadows' Hank Marvin who was the closest thing Britain had to a guitar hero until Eric Clapton came along.

According to drummer Pete Best, "'Cry for a Shadow' was born during our first Hamburg tour, the result of trying to take the mickey out of Rory Storm. It was put together by George in a few minutes after Rory had called in on us during a rehearsal at the Kaiserkeller. He was telling us how much he liked the Shadows' song 'Frightened City'. 'Can you play it?', he asked. 'It goes like this', he added, starting to sing the opening bars. George intentionally began to play around with the Shadows' melody in a sort of counterpart – without Rory having the slightest suspicion that he was being sent up. John joined in and I picked up the beat. What emerged was a catchy little number in unmistakable Shadows' style, which we liked well enough to include in our repertoire."

While this song shows the wit and spirit of the Beatles, it was a request for the vastly less interesting 'My Bonnie' at the record bar in Brian Epstein's store that sent the young furniture salesman down to the Cavern Club and he resolved to make them Fab.

Roadrunner The Modern Lovers

(Jonathan Richman) ※ Berserkeley ※ 1976 ※ Appears on: *The Modern Lovers*

"By the time I was fifteen years old I was pretty lonely," Jonathan Richman wrote in the early '70s. "High school and I didn't understand each other well at all. So I heard the Velvet Underground, got inspired, took up guitar and drove into Boston from my suburb of Nantick to terrorise Boston audiences with my four-and-a-third-note vocal range and crude guitar playing.

"Well, I got lonely doing that, so I put a band together when I was nineteen and called it the Modern Lovers. I've been changing and growing ever since".

Richman's first Modern Lovers (Ernie Brooks, bass; David Robinson, drums; Jerry Harrison, keyboards) was perfect. The songs were prosaic in the best Lou Reed style but instead of writing about junkies in New York he wrote about the world in which he lived – suburbia. It was a neat inversion of the Velvets delivered in monochromatic style.

'Roadrunner' is Richman's classic. It's a driving song in the rock & roll tradition, but rather than having a flash car, the singer is on a bicycle. He records, not the glamorous Route 66, but rather, the stores on Route 128.

The song is a one-chord riff that hits a perfect groove and floats Richman's vocal on top of Harrison's cheesy organ line and the unbeatable enthusiasm when Richman shouts out "Radio on!" Its honesty and its innocence are impossible to beat.

John Cale recorded the Lovers' debut album in 1973 for Warner Bros., who could make neither head nor tail of it and it was shelved until Berserkeley Records bought the tapes back and the album became a cult hit. By then the band was disbanded and Richman off on his idiot savant trip. But 'Roadrunner' is the real deal.

Bodysnatcher Magic Dirt

(Magic Dirt) ❊ Au Go Go ❊ 1996 ❊ Appears on: *Friends in Danger*

Magic Dirt have a deft touch with squalling guitars – feedback, over-powered pedal effects and murky production all add up to the sound of a nervous breakdown. In the midst of this tempest, Magic Dirt sashay along with Zen-like serenity. The Dirt (vocalist/guitarist Adalita Srsen, guitarist Dave Thomas, bassist Dean Turner and drummer Adam Robertson) carried their laid-back provincial Australianness as far as it could go. That tension between emotional passion and nonchalant delivery was the single most enticing thing about the Dirt, at least in this early phase. What Sonic Youth achieved through intellectual rigour, Magic Dirt just conjured out of the backyards of their minds. They are also a band with a genuine knack for pop music, so their noise storms always throw around hooks with the debris.

'Bodysnatcher' is a Homeric tale of child abuse. It grounded their first full-length LP. The Dirt mirror this story of seduction and violence with the dynamics of the band. Srsen whispers the frightening lyrics before exploding into fury and scorn, which is taken up by the guitars. There's a constant push and pull between abstraction and bluntness that is almost exhausting.

Better Get a Lawyer The Cruel Sea

(James Cruickshank/Jim Elliott/Ken Gormly/Stephen Perkins/Danny Rumour/Wayne) ❊ Red Eye ❊ 1995 ❊ Appears on: *Three Legged Dog*

It was the combination of soulful and sinful that crossed the Cruel Sea from the alternative market to the mainstream. For this album they chose to heap on the voodoo. *Three Legged Dog* reversed the platinum formula of past releases, which is just as well. The Cruel Sea was in danger of becoming muzak for the politically correct.

The Cruel Sea swings. Jim Elliott is a drummer of exceptional versatility. With the bass of Ken Gormly to anchor the rhythms and provide nicely sprung melodies, the Cruel Sea packs a funk. The guitars of James Cruickshank and Danny Rumour are very erudite. They continue on this album to play with different forms of roots music, from the Caribbean to the African coast. Unlike previous albums, however, they are drawing more on blues and R&B.

The combo started as an instrumental outfit augmented by occasional vocals by Tex Perkins who was, it appeared, on loan from the Beasts of Bourbon. If the Cruel Sea was ironic and wistful, the Beasts was a roaring, blues-wailing monster and it was common for pundits to wonder whether Perkins could reconcile these two sides of his muse. Perkins' worldview is generally confrontational. Tales like 'Better Get a Lawyer', 'Too Fast for Me' or 'Brain Wash' are told from a point of view of action first, regrets later. His romances are part passion and mostly confusion. They are rarely happy affairs, sometimes comic and often just hard. The quizzical funk of most of this album gives an appropriate ambiguity to Tex's tall stories.

Where the previous Cruel Sea albums have covered psychedelic surf music and afro-reggae pub rock, this album sticks close to the "down home". 'This Is What It Is' features an organ riff that could have come straight off Booker T That's about all that's straight. If there are influences or echoes in these tracks there is more than a touch of Captain Beefheart, some bone-crackling riffs that recall the team of Taylor and Richards keeping the riffs dirty and the slide guitar slippery. But these are just like spectres in the crypt. Ultimately, and as on their previous turf, the Cruel Sea has created a roiling storm all their own. This record shines like vinyl: black and sexy.

Gallows Pole Led Zeppelin

(Jimmy Page/Robert Plant) ❋ Atlantic ❋ 1970 ❋ Appears on: *Led Zeppelin III*

Robert Plant has described the third Zeppelin album as their single most important statement. In the previous two years, Zeppelin had revolutionised rock music and given new meaning to the word "heavy".

"The idea of using acoustic guitars and developing much more of a textural thing came about because if we weren't careful we were going to end up part of a whole Grand Funk Railroad, James Gang thing that was sort of two-dimensional," added Plant. "By the time 'Whole Lotta Love' had been such a statement, it was definitely time to veer over to the left and see how far we could take it in another direction."

Page had long admired the British folk tradition – Bert Jansch and John Renbourn of Pentangle, Roy Harper, John Martyn, Davey Graham and Fairport Convention. Plant shared his enthusiasm and also loved the weirdly fey Incredible String Band.

In the bucolic hills around the Bron-Yr-Aur farm they started re-writing Led Zeppelin.

"So we went to Wales and lived on the side of a hill and wrote those songs and walked and talked and thought and went off to the Abbey where they hid the Grail," said Plant. "No matter how cute and comical it might be now to look back at that, it gave us so much energy, because we were really close to something. We believed. It was absolutely wonderful, and my heart was so light and happy. At that time, at that age, 1970 was like the biggest blue sky I ever saw."

The rhythm section was equally ready to head off into the open fields. The album was cut relatively quickly at another rural estate, Hedley Grange.

The acoustic tracks had the intensity of old, largely through the dynamic production by Page. 'Gallows Pole' is a reworking of a Leadbelly song that blends the British folk traditions with American blues in an entirely new way.

The album was finished in America where it was mastered by Terry Manning, who had the wizard Alister Crowley's mottos: 'Do What Thou Wilt' on side one, and on side two, 'So Mote it Be'.

Zeppelin's acoustic turn shocked the music public, but within weeks most heavy bands were bringing stools and acoustic guitars on stage for a bracket of "wooden music". *Led Zeppelin III* added another texture to the rock palette of the new decade.

Porpoise Song The Monkees

(Gerry Goffin/Carole King) ❊ Colgems ❊ 1969 ❊ Appears on: *Head*

The film *Head* was an incredible flop that encompassed both the failure of bubblegum pop and psychedelic within the one film and soundtrack.

Assembled by pop-meister Don Kirshner to turn the Beatles into a sitcom, the *Monkees* were an instant hit. Almost as soon as they became teen sensations they were vilified for a lack of credibility. This was the first time the concept of "credibility" was used in pop or rock music.

The psychedelic times even crept into the sitcom. The humour drifted into absurdism. The fourth wall came down and was never repaired. Watching the second year of the *Monkees* was like watching an acid trip in suburbia.

So it was that they made a movie.

Bob Rafelson, who had helped devise the series, set up the film as his first shot at directing with his pal Jack Nicholson as the writer. "We didn't shoot the movie on acid," Rafelson said, "but Jack did structure the movie in his mind on an acid trip."

The film is a psychedelic deconstruction of Hollywood, the *Monkees*, the music business, America, Vietnam and mysticism. The plot doesn't unfold, it explodes.

This is what the Monkees and their critics had been asking for – if you deconstruct pop what you get is glorious nonsense, non sequitur and beautiful images that make no sense.

Within the chaos there are some flashes of genius, not the least of which is Peter Tork's 'Long Title: Do I Have To Do This All over Again', Mike Nesmith's best song, 'Circle Sky', and the Goffin–King psychedelic epic 'Porpoise Song'.

No Woman, No Cry Bob Marley & the Wailers

(Vincent Ford/Bob Marley) ❋ Tuff Gong ❋ 1975 ❋ Appears on: *Live!*

Bob Marley & the Wailers had taken their rebel music to the verge of superstardom. Reggae, which had been bubbling out of Jamaica through white rock & roll for three years or so, was no longer completely exotic. However, the real reggae experience of a large and soulful band grooving on their version of R&B was an experience that was confined to the Jamaican diaspora and a few white fans. 'No Woman, No Cry' appeared on 1974's *Natty Dread*, credited to Vincent Ford, a Jamacian cook, who had fed Marley when he was impoverished. The song is a tribute to solidarity and generosity.

Partly it was the politics and the Rastafarianism that put the public off reggae music at first. Marley was a committed Rasta but he also understood R&B music. What he delivered on the live version of 'No Woman, No Cry' was the Rosetta Stone of reggae. It was a love song with a romantic flavour that transcended all cultural boundaries.

Bob Marley & the Wailers' two-night stand at the Lyceum in London on 18 and 19 July 1975 was a turning point in the history of music.

"The first night at the Lyceum, the intensity and the vibe were just nuts," Steve Smith, who co-produced the live recording with Chris Blackwell, told *MOJO*. "They opened up the roof because it was so hot. After the gig, Chris asked if I wanted to record the following night's show. I said, 'Get the Rolling Stones' Mobile and I'll do it.' The recording would never have been as good as it was if it hadn't been for Dave Harper, who mixed the live sound out front. So much of the mix is to do with those live hall mikes, and you can hear that in 'No Woman, No Cry', the ultimate sing-along.

"And it was bizarre. Blackwell took the tapes back to Basing Street, and Phill Brown mixed it as a live performance. Phill set up all the EQs, and he and Chris did a performance, in the same way the band had walked onstage, plugged in, and played to the end of the set. It was pretty fucking brave. After that, the Tim Clarks and Brian Blevins took over, and they just beat up on Blackwell to put out a single. About six weeks later he reluctantly agreed, and released 'No Woman, No Cry'. The damn thing just jumped off the radio. Someone said there were only ever three great live albums: Ray Charles at Newport in 1958, James Brown at the Apollo in 1962, and Bob Marley at the Lyceum in 1975. I tend to agree."

Maggie May Rod Stewart

(Rod Stewart/Martin Quittenton) ❋ Mercury ❋ 1971 ❋

Appears on: *Every Picture Tells a Story*

Let's face it, if 'Maggie May' was released in our current century, the singer would be hounded to death by tabloid headlines declaring "Rod Stewart: the victim of child sexual abuse!" It's the story of a teenager seduced and abandoned by an older woman, his innocence lost forever and a deep scar left on his soul. Times have changed. In the context of *Every Picture Tells a Story*, this was just another adventure for a young man in search of a good time.

Stewart was a lad before the word became a demographic: liked his soccer, liked a pint and a dolly bird, liked music. Stewart the songwriter wore his heart on his sleeve, not in the manner of American lyricists who aspired to be literary, but because he couldn't be bothered making stuff up.

Everything came together on *Every Picture* – American folk music, full tilt R&B, straight rock and pastoral English folk. The sheer size and expansiveness of the album comes from Stewart's synthesis of diverse styles. Although many of the songs were American and others used American motifs, there was something quintessentially English about Rod Stewart. 'Maggie May' itself was based on an old Liverpudlian folk song and given an R&B feel.

Every Picture says it all in the first seconds of the LP. A reflective, melancholy guitar theme opens the title track and then as the last note hangs suspended, gently fading, Mickey Waller's drums thump it down like a thousand-pound hammer. Then Stewart comes in with the lyric, "Spent some time feeling inferior/Standing in front of my mirror/Combed my hair in a thousand ways/Came out looking just the same". On this note of self-discovery, the singer embarks on his world tour; the odyssey of this album.

The key to Stewart's classic period was his sidemen. The importance of Ronnie Wood can't be overestimated. Wood was a versatile musician whose guitar and bass parts complemented Stewart in a way that no other collaborator has. Mostly it's Wood's style – loose and funky one minute, driving hard the next and then soft and reflective. He wove the melodies around Stewart's humour – relaxing him and stopping him from taking himself too seriously. The moment that partnership ended, so did Stewart's golden age.

With Wood playing the Sundance Kid the rest of the hole-in-the-wall gang represented the best aspects of British rock from the late '60s: acoustic guitarist Martin Quittenton; drummer Mickey Waller, whose rambunctious style matched Wood; Pete Sears on piano. If all else failed there was the Faces.

Every Picture is not just the high point of Rod Stewart's career but the foundation of British rock as something more than just a regurgitated version of American music. Having achieved that, within a couple of years Stewart made his Atlantic crossing and never looked back. He would have bigger hits but, like Maggie's schoolboy, he lost his innocence.

I Want to Hold Your Hand The Beatles

(John Lennon/Paul McCartney) ❊ Parlophone ❊ 1963 ❊
Appears on: *The Beatles 1962–1966*

Beatlemania had already started in the UK in 1963 but it wasn't until this single appeared in early 1964 in the US that things went over the top. This was the first British rock hit in the US and it opened up that country to a new style of music. The fact that the Beatles had borrowed most of the tropes from the Americans wasn't an issue. They reinterpreted it – they had their own dynamics of light and shade; loud and soft sections; they had their screams; and they had tense licks from Harrison to complement McCartney's agile bass playing.

The song was begun in the basement of Jane and Peter Asher's parents. Jane Asher was McCartney's girlfriend. Peter Asher was a singer who later became a record producer, first for Apple and then for everybody. McCartney was at the piano and Lennon on the pump organ when the song began and when McCartney hit a discord by mistake, Lennon suggested that was the beginning of the song. The record is deceptively simple. It's the details like the ascending choruses and the syncopated melody that really lift the song out of itself.

The lyrics are typical of the period – all euphemism and innuendo. They're carried by the sheer energy of the Beatles. The key to the Beatles, unlike so many of the bands of the time, was that they had spent many hard years playing live in clubs under often hostile conditions and their sessions have that energy still. The combination of their performances and the fact that they were such great singers and were also writing reasonable material had an enormous impact.

Bob Dylan recalled his reaction to hearing this record as: "They were doing things nobody was doing. Their chords were outrageous, just outrageous, and their harmonies made it all valid."

Fountain of Sorrow Jackson Browne

(Jackson Browne) ✳ Asylum ✳ 1974 ✳ Appears on: *Late for the Sky*

Even before Jackson Browne had made his first album, David Crosby described him to *Rolling Stone* as, "one of the probably ten best songwriters around ... he's got songs that'll make your hair stand on end; he's incredible". The most hair-raising of Browne's album was his third, a picture of apocalypse.

Browne's first two albums put him into the first rank of confessional singer/songwriters. His work had already been recorded by the Eagles, Gregg Allman, the Jackson 5 and Nico. Browne, with his high mellifluous voice and waifish, sensitive features could easily have become a major heartthrob. However, *Late for the Sky* was a complex series of songs about death and loss, with jazz inflections coming into his idiosyncratic pop tunes, and it was clear that the Eagles would have the country-pop-rock field all to themselves.

Browne's arty piano tunes dominate the tracks, aided by David Lindley on guitar, violin and slide, and organist Jai Winding, and David Crosby adding his incomparable harmony vocals. Bud Scoppa called it "the first genuine innovation in what has become known as the LA Sound since the Byrds recorded 'Mr Tambourine Man'."

'Fountain of Sorrow' is a masterpiece of Browne's lyric writing, playing around with images of death and loss and love and pain with a literary touch far more sophisticated than any of his contemporaries. 'Fountain of Sorrow', like most of the rest of this LP, is disquieting. The mixture of hyper-charged romanticism with particular, prosaic details has rarely been handled so well.

"I certainly don't cultivate disappointment in order to write," he said shortly after 'Fountain of Sorrow' was released. "I even had a song at one point in which my accountant comes up to me and slaps me round the face and says 'This is no time to get happy. You're making too much by being sad and serious.' That actually occurred to me. It's in my notes somewhere but I think it'd be a little too indulgent writing about that kind of thing. The audience wouldn't really relate to it. Most of them don't have accountants!"

Who Do You Love? Quicksilver Messenger Service

(Ellas McDaniel) ❋ Capitol ❋ 1969 ❋ Appears On: *Happy Trails*

Quicksilver was, along with Jefferson Airplane, the Grateful Dead and Big Brother & the Holding Company, one of the legendary San Francisco bands of the Haight Ashbury era (1966–69). Like the Dead, they were known for long improvisations and guitar pyrotechnics, mostly from lead guitarist John Cipollina. His style was quite angular and his lines were suited to extended jamming. Thus Quicksilver's second album is mostly made up of a live version of Bo Diddley's 'Who Do You Love?' that twists and turns its way around the beat. As with the other bands from the San Francisco ballroom scene, there was a fine line between freedom of expression and self-indulgence. On this track, Quicksilver shows mostly the former.

The version of the song was assembled as the band was falling apart with the departure of singer Dino Valente and guitarist Greg Duncan. Drugs played a significant part in the lifestyle of the Quicksilver musicians and that influenced the way this album was put together from performances at the Fillmore East and West.

"We had to edit a little bit out of 'Who Do You Love?' because ... I think it was like thirty-five minutes long," recalled bass player David Freiberg. "We used the centre part from a San Francisco gig and the rest was from a New York gig. So the weird part in the middle was when everybody was stoned on acid ... and the audience was just as much a part of it with the clapping.

"I guess we stretched anything whenever we felt like it. An instrumental would last us 'til we could figure out a way to get out of it.

"I don't know . . . the audience would go for anything . . . John's guitar would never be in tune. We'd be standing there five, ten minutes. Waiting for him to get in tune. I used to worry about it . . . One time I was at the Avalon, really stoned and watching. I looked at the audience and they were enthralled watching John trying to tune his guitar, completely entertained. So I realised . . . 'Oh, we can do anything we want. Why worry about it?' So it's the same kind of attitude, that if you felt like taking a chance . . . Why not do it?"

Marquee Moon Television

(Tom Verlaine) ✻ Elektra ✻ 1977 ✻ Appears on: *Marquee Moon*

Patti Smith accurately described Tom Verlaine's guitar playing as "a thousand bluebirds screaming". This song features the best piece of electric guitar since Jimi Hendrix. Verlaine's long, snaky and abstract lines create their own logic and resolve the melodies in all kinds of obtuse but exciting ways. This is like rock & roll reinvented, but the achievement was so singular that it has never been copied.

Tom Miller took the name of French Symbolist poet Paul Verlaine when he came to New York to be a rock star in the early '70s. He scuffled through the downtown music scene for five years, gradually assembling Television and building a stage at a Bowery bar – CBGB – that would later attract the New York punk crowd.

Verlaine's milieu was the bohemian downtown scene. His musical influences included Dylan and the Rolling Stones, the psychedelic sounds of the Nuggets era bands and especially the 13th Floor Elevators, plus he liked a lot of jazz. Verlaine had a jazz approach to making rock & roll – a rhythm section that could swing behind two guitar players improvising off each other. Television played long songs but the ingenuity of Verlaine and second guitarist Richard Lloyd was the main attraction. Verlaine's songs had a dry romanticism about them – more florid and abstract than Lou Reed but something of that order.

A first single, 'Little Johnny Jewel', attracted attention with its jagged guitar attack against a jazzy, spastic drum pattern. For their major-label debut, Television settled on producer Andy Johns, fresh from working with the Stones. Johns set up a commercial rock sound for Television and Verlaine told him to dismantle it.

The centrepiece of it all was 'Marquee Moon', the strange story of a night on the town. The narrative is elusive and dreamlike to match the music. It's a song of the city – all hard pavements and neon lights and bright spots polka-dotting the night air. The song flows along, pushed by the loping and lazy beat of Billy Ficca's drums and Fred Smith's shy bass playing. The narrative is in the guitar lines – sometimes percussive jabs and at other times languid meditations on the state of the night. There's a conversation going on between Verlaine and Lloyd here unlike anything else before or since.

The take of 'Marquee Moon' on the first album was recorded in the first run down of the song – Ficca thought it was a rehearsal. Johns wanted to have another crack at the song but Verlaine announced that he was done. And he's right.

"I generally end up following something in a dreamlike sort of way," said Verlaine of his method. "It's like watching pictures unfold. I don't really have any ideas, not even about the guitar. A lot of it has to do with developing what the physical sound of that guitar is, coming off the amp. Time and time again the music is about returning to the physicality of the sound, and maybe that in itself generates ideas."

Midnight at the Oasis Maria Muldaur

(David Nichtern) ✳ Warner Bros. ✳ 1973 ✳ Appears on: *Maria Muldaur*

Growing up in New York in the late '50s, Muldaur was exposed to the first folk boom and learnt her trade at the knee of the Rev Gary Davis, Mississippi John Hurt, Skip James and Bukka White. She travelled to Appalachia to meet Doc Watson and in the early '60s joined the Even Dozen Jug Band with John Sebastian, Stefan Grossman and David Grisman. After a more successful time in the Jim Kweskin Jug Band, she struck out on her own in the early '70s.

Lenny Waronker, probably the most important and creative American record producer, who was then creating what became the West Coast sound, produced her debut album. A bit jazzy and a bit bluesy, Maria Muldaur made classy, good-time music, but the players on this album – including Ry Cooder, Dr John, Amos Garrett, David Grisman and Clarence White among others – represented a whole new approach.

Nichtern's 'Midnight at the Oasis' was an instant hit. It was backed by songs from new writers such as the McGarrigle sisters, Dolly Parton and Wendy Waldman. The playing is tasteful and understated, and reveals Muldaur's depth of feeling for the blues.

Song Index